Programming
Windows® 95
with MFC

D1545053

Jeff Prosise

PUBLISHED BY
Microsoft Press
A Division of Microsoft Corporation
One Microsoft Way
Redmond, Washington 98052-6399

Library of Congress Cataloging-in-Publication Data
Prosise, Jeff.
    Programming Windows 95 with MFC : create programs for Windows
  quickly with the Microsoft Foundation Class library / Jeff Prosise.
       p.   cm.
  Includes index.
  ISBN 1-55615-902-1
    1. Microsoft Windows (Computer file)   2. Operating systems
  (Computers)   3. Microsoft foundation class library.   I. Title.
  QA76.76.O63P79   1996
  005.265--dc20   96-1170
                                                  CIP

Printed and bound in the United States of America.

1 2 3 4 5 6 7 8 9 Rand-T 1 0 9 8 7 6

Distributed to the book trade in Canada by Macmillan of Canada, a division of Canada Publishing Corporation.

A CIP catalogue record for this book is available from the British Library.

Microsoft Press books are available through booksellers and distributors worldwide. For further information about international editions, contact your local Microsoft Corporation office. Or contact Microsoft Press International directly at fax (206) 936-7329.

Apple, Macintosh, and TrueType are registered trademarks of Apple Computer, Inc. Lucida is a registered trademark of Bigelow and Holmes. Turbo Pascal is a registered trademark of Borland International, Inc. CompuServe is a registered trademark of CompuServe, Inc. Pentium is a registered trademark of Intel Corporation. MCI Mail is a registered trademark of MCI Communications Corporation. Microsoft, the Microsoft logo, Microsoft Press, MS, MS-DOS, PowerPoint, Visual Basic, Visual C++, Win32, Windows, Windows NT, and the Windows operating system logo are registered trademarks of Microsoft Corporation.

Acquisitions Editor: Eric Stroo
Project Editor: Erin O'Connor
Technical Editor: Jim Fuchs

To Amy

Contents at a Glance

Contents

Part II
The Document/View Architecture

Part III
Advanced Topics

Acknowledgments

Let me take a moment to say thanks to the cast of people who labored behind the scenes to bring this book to life.

First and foremost, a heartfelt thanks to all the folks at Microsoft Press who were involved in various aspects of the book's design, editing, and production. I'm especially grateful to Eric Stroo, Erin O'Connor, and Jim Fuchs, all of whom were involved with the book from day one and treated it as if it were their own. I'm also indebted to Shawn Peck, the book's principal proofreader and copy editor, and to all those who assisted him—Richard Carey, Ron Drummond, Patrick Forgette, Stephanie Marr, Patricia Masserman, Devon Musgrave, Lisa Theobald, and Paula Thurman. Peggy Herman and Sandra Haynes transformed raw Word for Windows files into the polished product you hold in your hands. Kim Eggleston, Michael Victor, Gregory J. Erickson, and Glenn Mitsui are responsible for the book's overall design and the beautiful artwork inside and out. Julie Kawabata did a masterful job creating the book's index. To her and to all the others at Microsoft Press, I say thanks for a job well done.

You can't read the acknowledgments page of an MFC or a Visual C++ book without seeing Dean McCrory mentioned somewhere. Dean has spent a good part of his career at Microsoft as the MFC development lead, and he knows more about MFC than anyone else on this planet. He was also gracious enough to take time out of a hectic schedule to review the chapter manuscripts and answer an endless stream of questions. Francis Hogle of Microsoft's Windows User Interface Group reviewed every chapter from a non-MFC angle, corrected numerous errors in my understanding of how Windows operates, and spent copious amounts of time educating me about Windows 95 internals. Microsoft is full of smart people, and Dean and Francis are two of the smartest. They're also two of the nicest, and it was truly a pleasure to work with them.

I would be remiss if I didn't express my gratitude to the two people who, more than anyone else, are responsible for this book's existence. Claudette Moore urged me to write the book and worked with Dean Holmes at Microsoft Press to make sure there was a match between author, book, and publisher. Claudette was the one who talked me into writing computer books in the first place, and without her encouragement, I'd probably still be working a day job and writing magazine articles by night. Dean had the faith to sign me on to the project even though I still had much to learn about MFC. Soon after bringing me on board, Dean dropped out of the rat race to pursue other ambitions. Claudette, if I haven't said it before, let me say it now: Thanks. Dean, I owe you a round of golf. But first give me some time to practice up.

Let me also say thanks to my editors at *PC Magazine* and *Microsoft Systems Journal,* who have been understanding beyond reason in the past year and have bent over backwards to accommodate my writing schedule. Some authors find book writing relatively easy; for me, it's a 9- to 12-month period of tribulation that alternates between exhilaration and despair. I couldn't do it without the encouragement of my friends and the support of my editors. Very often my friends and editors are one and the same. For that I feel exceedingly fortunate.

Finally, thanks to my wife, Lori. If there's anyone in the world who understands the toll a book like this one takes on its author, it's the author's spouse. Lori is now a veteran of five computer books, and I'm not being fanciful when I say that I couldn't do it without her. Thanks, Kiddo. Thanks for sticking by me and reminding me that there's a light at the end of the tunnel. Thanks for putting up with all those nights and weekends at the keyboard. And thanks for being a wonderful wife and mother.

Introduction

In December of 1993, my life as a Windows programmer underwent a profound and monumental change. While attending a Win32 developer's conference put on by Microsoft in Anaheim, California, I sat in on a session about porting 16-bit Windows apps to the 32-bit world of Windows NT. Like many other Windows developers at that time, I was just beginning to make the transition from 16-bit to 32-bit programming, so I was intensely interested in any tips that might save me some time down the road. The presenter that day went through a long list of "gotchas" to watch out for when porting 16-bit code to the Win32 platform, but what struck me most was that the discussion of almost every item on the agenda closed with the comment, "Of course, if your 16-bit code was written with MFC, all you have to do is recompile. MFC will do the rest."

I confess that I had paid little attention to MFC up until that moment and that even for some months afterward I failed to understand the extent to which MFC would one day change the face of Windows programming. What finally convinced me was the extensive OLE 2 support featured in MFC 2.5. Writing an OLE container or server is a C programmer's worst nightmare, and containers and servers are just one tiny corner of the OLE universe. OLE and other components of the Windows API are evolving so quickly that it's nearly impossible to stay on top of all the latest developments. That's why it's helpful to have a class library put an insulating layer between you and the API. It's also why, in the future, programmers who write to the Windows API could be looked upon the way assembly language programmers are today.

Once it became clear to me that MFC had compelling benefits to offer next-generation Windows programmers, I headed for the bookstore. Like countless other Windows programmers, I had learned Windows programming from Charles Petzold's *Programming Windows,* and I hoped to find a similarly helpful book on MFC programming. Unfortunately, there was no such book, so I had to learn MFC programming the hard way: by writing code and making mistakes (lots of mistakes) and going back later to fix what I did wrong the first time. It was this experience that made me decide to write a book that would give MFC the same thorough, detailed, and comprehensive treatment that *Programming Windows* gives the Windows API. The result is the book you hold in your hands. It's the book I'd like to have had when I was learning MFC. And it's designed to prevent you from repeating many of the missteps I made on the road to becoming an MFC programmer.

WHO SHOULD READ THIS BOOK

I wrote *Programming Windows 95 with MFC* with two kinds of people in mind:

■ Windows API programmers who are ready to make the move to C++ and MFC

■ C++ programmers who have never before programmed Windows— let alone Windows 95

I can't emphasize enough that this is an MFC book, not a Visual C++ book. It won't teach you what buttons to click in AppWizard or how to set up a message handler with ClassWizard. What it *will* teach you is how to use MFC to write 32-bit applications for Windows 95 and how to understand the code that AppWizard, ClassWizard, and other code generators produce. It will also help you see what goes on under the hood in MFC—and how you can leverage that knowledge to write better Windows applications.

Programming Windows 95 with MFC assumes that you have at least a rudimentary knowledge of C++ programming up front. Fortunately, MFC uses what its architects call a "sane subset" of C++, so you don't have to be an expert in the language to become a proficient MFC programmer. If you know how to derive a class and you understand what a virtual function is, you know most of what you need to know to read this book. The rest you can pick up as you go along.

THE ROAD TO MFC

Have you ever looked at AppWizard-generated code and wondered why there are so many files and where the code for the Open and Save commands in the File menu is hidden? AppWizard code is liable to be puzzling the first time you see it because it's structured according to MFC's document/view architecture. Document/view applications can do incredibly powerful things with precious little code because they lean heavily on code in the class library. But beginning your career as an MFC programmer by rushing headlong into documents and views is a little like trying to design a computer when you don't know what an integrated circuit is. I believe taking on documents and views before mastering the more fundamental aspects of MFC is putting the cart before the horse. I think that's why sometimes even experienced Windows programmers flip open the pages of a Visual C++ book and find themselves feeling more than a little bewildered after the first chapter or two.

The good news is that you don't *have* to use documents and views to write Windows programs with MFC. And that's what enables *Programming Windows 95 with MFC* to take a unique approach to teaching MFC. For the first seven chapters, the document/view architecture is mentioned only in passing while you learn about the Windows event-driven programming model and get acquainted with basic MFC classes such as *CWnd* and *CListBox*. By the time we take up documents and views in Chapter 8, the document/view architecture will be little more than an extension of what you've already learned. I think you'll find that this makes MFC as a whole more approachable and that it does a better job of building the foundation that makes a good Windows programmer.

This book contains 14 chapters organized into three sections. The seven chapters in Part I cover the ABCs of Windows 95 and MFC programming, beginning with a simple "Hello, MFC" application and one by one introducing menus, controls, dialog boxes, and other building blocks common to most Windows applications. Part II builds on the concepts introduced in Part I with a detailed look at the document/view architecture. In particular, Chapters 8 and 9 reveal much of the "magic" behind documents and views and explain not only how to write basic document/view applications but also how to implement some not-so-basic features such as split window views of a document. Part III goes beyond documents and views to some of the more advanced programming features of Windows 95 and MFC—features such as color palettes, bitmap handling, and multiple threads of execution. By the time you're finished with Chapter 14, you'll be well versed in the art of 32-bit Windows programming using MFC. And you'll have prodigious amounts of sample code to draw from when it's time to strike out on your own and write your first great Windows 95 application.

WHAT'S NOT COVERED—AND WHY

Windows programming has become such a vast subject that it's impossible to cover all aspects of it in a book such as this one without sacrificing a tremendous amount of detail. Early on, I made a conscious decision to be thorough in covering the topics I presented even if that meant excluding other topics. That's why I haven't written about memory-mapped files, Windows 95 shell extensions, or asynchronous file I/O, among other things. Fortunately, these and other aspects of Win32 programming are covered quite well in other Microsoft Press books such as Jeffrey Richter's *Advanced Windows*.

The most difficult decision was what to do about OLE. Up until almost the very end, I intended to include a chapter on OLE containers and servers that would demonstrate how to write an app that meets the requirements of the Windows 95 logo program. MFC makes writing embedded object containers and servers, which are based on a protocol known as OLE Documents, significantly less work than does the SDK, but writing a commercial-quality application that's fully OLE-enabled still requires a few thousand lines of code. Don't be fooled by the simple OLE code skeletons that AppWizard generates for you; they're great for getting started, but the applications they create are barely functional as containers and servers. You have to do a lot of rewiring to convert them into "real" OLE applications. Even with MFC's OLE classes providing a buffer between you and the raw OLE API, doing OLE and doing it properly requires months of study and commitment.

Realizing that OLE Documents would be a book unto itself, I ultimately decided that if I couldn't give it the treatment it needed, I wouldn't treat it at all—at least for now. I do intend to update this book periodically, and I will look again at OLE Documents when the time comes to plan the second edition. Certain parts of OLE are very promising and will in all likelihood play a huge role in the future of Windows programming, but I personally find the OLE Documents protocol overly difficult to implement (even with MFC's help) and of limited value in the real world. The notion of embedding an Excel spreadsheet in a Word document and being able to edit it in place sounds appealing, but the price such a capability exacts in performance—and the trouble it can cause—is more than a user should have to bear. Let me know what you think; you'll find instructions for contacting me below.

The OLE Documents protocol is just one of OLE's many facets. The other major components include OLE Automation, OLE controls (recently renamed ActiveX Controls), structured storage, and OLE data transfers. It's very likely that the next edition of this book will include a chapter on OLE's Uniform Data Transfer (UDT) model, which in plain English means richer clipboard data transfers and OLE drag and drop. But what I cover in the next edition depends partially on what I hear from you. For now, if you're eager to dive into OLE, I'd recommend reading two other Microsoft Press books: Adam Denning's *OLE Controls Inside Out* and David Kruglinski's *Inside Visual C++*. Adam's book is the definitive work on OLE controls, and David's includes a wealth of information regarding the practical side of OLE programming.

WHAT'S ON THE CD

The CD in the back of the book contains source code and executables for all of the book's sample programs. You can copy the contents of the CD (about 2 MB's worth of files) to a local hard disk by running the Setup.exe program in the CD's root directory and following the instructions on the screen, or you can access the files directly from the CD. The root directory contains a subdirectory for each chapter of the book, and inside are additional subdirectories holding the programs themselves. To run Chapter 13's Wanderer application from the CD, for example, you would type

```
d:\chap13\wanderer\wanderer
```

at a command prompt or in the Open field of the Start Menu's Run dialog. (This assumes, of course, that your CD-ROM drive is the D: drive.)

Each set of source code files on the CD is accompanied by a Visual C++ 4 make (.mak) file and a 0-length project workspace (.mdp) file. You can open a project in Visual C++ by opening the corresponding project workspace file. If you're going to modify the source code and rebuild the applications, copy the files to your hard disk first.

When you build a project with Visual C++, you have the option of linking with the MFC library statically or dynamically. Dynamic linking produces a smaller .exe file, but static linking creates a stand-alone .exe file that runs without the aid of the MFC DLLs. The sample programs on the CD were designed for dynamic linking in order to keep the source code as simple as possible. If you want to build a statically linked .exe from one of the sample programs, you should add the statements

```
#include <afxres.rc>
#include <afxprint.h>
#include <afxolecl.rc>
```

to the program's .rc file. Afxres.rc, Afxprint.rc, and Afxolecl.rc contain string resources that are part of the application framework. Dynamically linked applications obtain these strings from the MFC DLLs, but statically linked applications can access them only if the strings are compiled along with the projects' conventional resources. A statically linked application will build without the *#include* statements, but unless it's a very simple program that makes minimal use of the class library, it won't work as you expect it to.

There are other .rc files containing additional MFC string resources, but the three shown above are sufficient for all of the sample programs in this book. If you use AppWizard to generate an MFC project, AppWizard will add the necessary *#include* statements for you based on the options you enter in response to its queries.

FEEDBACK

Are there other topics you'd like me to have explored in this book or topics you think should be covered differently? If there are, drop me a line. From the Internet, you can reach me by sending e-mail to 72241.44@compuserve.com. From CompuServe, send mail to 72241,44. If MCI Mail is your preferred mode of communication, address your envelopes to 312-3074. I may or may not have the time to answer specific questions, but rest assured that I'll read every piece of e-mail that comes my way and take your considerations into account in planning future editions of the book.

Enjoy!

—Jeff Prosise

Part I

MFC Basics

Chapter 1

Hello, MFC

A few short years ago, the person learning to program Windows for the first time had a limited number of programming tools to choose from. C was the language spoken by the Windows Software Development Kit (SDK), and alternative Windows programming environments such as Visual Basic and Turbo Pascal for Windows hadn't arrived on the scene. Most Windows applications were written in C, and the fledgling Windows programmer faced the daunting task not only of learning the ins and outs of a new operating system but also of getting acquainted with the hundreds of different application programming interface (API) functions that Windows supports.

Today most Windows programs are still written in C. But that's changing, and fast. The variety of Windows programming environments becoming available means that commercial-quality Windows programs can be written in C, C++, Pascal, BASIC, and a number of other languages. Moreover, C++ is rapidly replacing C as the professional Windows programmer's language of choice because the sheer complexity of Windows, coupled with the wide-ranging scope of the Windows API, cries out for an object-oriented programming language. Many Windows programmers are finding that C++ offers a compelling alternative to C that, combined with a class library that abstracts the API and encapsulates the basic behavior of windows and other objects in reusable classes, makes Windows programming simpler. And an overwhelming majority of C++ programmers have settled on the Microsoft Foundation Class library, better known by the acronym MFC, as their class library of choice. There are other Windows class libraries available, but only MFC was written by the company that writes the operating system. MFC is continually updated to incorporate the latest changes to Windows itself, and it provides a comprehensive set of classes representing everything from rectangles to windows to OLE containers and servers in order to make the job of writing Windows applications easier.

If you're coming to MFC from a traditional Windows programming environment such as C and the Windows SDK, you're already familiar with many of the concepts you need to know to understand Windows programming with MFC. But if you're coming from a character-oriented environment such as MS-DOS or Unix, you'll find that Windows programming is fundamentally different from anything you've done before. This chapter begins with an overview of the Windows programming model and a peek under the hood at how Windows applications work. It continues with a brief overview of MFC and of the classes MFC puts at your disposal. After the introductions are out of the way, you'll develop your very first Windows application—one that uses MFC to create a resizeable window in which the message "Hello, MFC" is displayed.

THE WINDOWS PROGRAMMING MODEL

Programs written for traditional operating environments use a procedural programming model in which programs execute from top to bottom in an orderly fashion. The path taken from start to finish may vary with each invocation of the program depending on the input it receives or the conditions under which it is run, but the path remains fairly predictable. In a C program, execution begins with the first line in the function named *main* and ends when *main* returns. In between, *main* might call other functions and these functions might call even more functions, but ultimately it is the program—not the operating system—that determines what gets called and when.

Windows programs operate differently. Windows employs the event-driven programming model illustrated in Figure 1-1. Applications respond to "events" by processing messages sent by the operating system. An event could be a keystroke, a mouse click, a command for a window to redraw itself, or something else entirely such as a notification that Windows is shutting down. The entry point for a Windows program is a function named *WinMain*, but most of the action takes place in another function known as the *window procedure*. The window procedure processes messages sent to the application's window. *WinMain* creates that window and then enters a loop, retrieving messages and dispatching them to the window procedure. Messages wait in a message queue until they are retrieved. A typical Windows application performs the bulk of its processing in response to the messages it receives, and in between messages, it does little except wait for the next message to arrive.

In 16-bit Windows, the act of checking the message queue for pending messages implicitly yielded the CPU to other active applications if the message queue was empty. Thus, it was incumbent upon Windows applications to check their message queues early and often, and to process messages as expediently as possible in order to prevent other applications from being starved for processor time. Windows 95

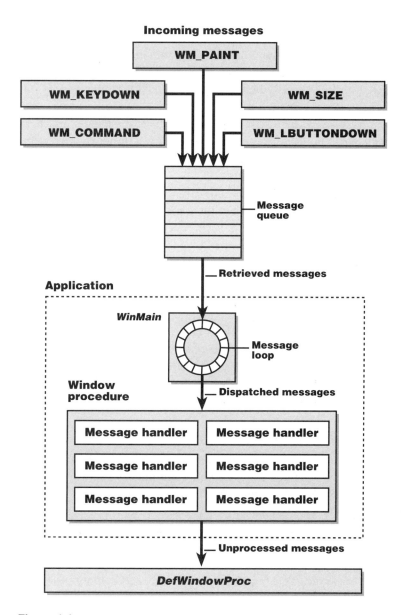

Figure 1-1. *The Windows programming model.*

decouples the message loop from multitasking performance by employing a pre-emptive multitasking model, but it is still important to respond to messages as quickly as possible so that applications won't seem "jerky" and unresponsive.

Figure 1-1 illustrates the Windows programming model schematically. The message loop inside *WinMain* spins in a continuous cycle, retrieving and dispatching messages. The loop ends when the special WM_QUIT message is retrieved from the message queue, signaling that it's time for the application to end. This message usually appears because the user selected Exit from the File menu, clicked the close button (the small button with an X in the window's upper right corner), or selected Close from the window's system menu. When the message loop ends, *WinMain* returns and the application terminates.

The window procedure typically calls on other functions to help process the messages it receives. It can call other functions local to the application, and it can call API functions in the Windows kernel. API functions are contained in special modules known as *dynamic link libraries,* or DLLs, and Windows uses a technique known as *dynamic linking* to direct the API calls that an application makes to the appropriate addresses in memory. Windows 95 supports hundreds of API functions that an application can call to perform various tasks such as creating a window, drawing on the screen, and performing file input and output. In C, the window procedure is typically implemented as a monolithic function containing a large *switch* statement with cases for individual messages. The code associated with a *case* statement is known as a *message handler.* Messages that an application doesn't care to process are passed on to an API function named *DefWindowProc*, which provides default responses to unprocessed messages.

More About Messages

Just where do messages come from, and what kinds of information do they convey? In all, Windows 95 defines about 200 different message types. Each message has a name that begins with the letters "WM" and an underscore, as in WM_CREATE and WM_PAINT. There are various ways to classify these messages, but for the moment classification is not nearly as important as realizing the critical role messages play in the operation of Windows. The table on the facing page shows ten of the most common messages an application receives and what they signify. A program receives a WM_PAINT message, for example, when it needs to repaint the interior of its window. One way to characterize a Windows program is to think of it as a large collection of event handlers that respond to messages directed to the window procedure. To a large extent, it is a program's unique way of responding to these messages that gives it its personality.

COMMON WINDOWS MESSAGES

Message	*Sent When*
WM_CHAR	A character is input from the keyboard.
WM_COMMAND	The user selects an item from a menu, or a child window has a notification to send to its parent.
WM_CREATE	A window is created.
WM_DESTROY	A window is destroyed.
WM_LBUTTONDOWN	The left mouse button is pressed.
WM_LBUTTONUP	The left mouse button is released.
WM_MOUSEMOVE	The mouse pointer is moved within the window's client area.
WM_PAINT	A window needs repainting.
WM_QUIT	The application is about to terminate.
WM_SIZE	A window is resized.

As you've already learned, a message manifests itself in the form of a call to the window procedure. That call contains four input parameters: the handle of the window to which the message is directed, a message ID, and two 32-bit parameters known as *wParam* and *lParam*. (The "w" in *wParam* stands for WORD; the "l" in *lParam* stands for LONG.) The window handle is a unique value that identifies a window. Internally, the value references a data structure in which Windows stores relevant information about the window such as its size, style, and position on the screen. The message ID is a numeric value that identifies the message type: WM_CREATE, WM_PAINT, and so on. *wParam* and *lParam* contain information specific to the message type. When a WM_LBUTTONDOWN message arrives, for example, *wParam* holds a series of bit flags identifying the state of the Ctrl and Shift keys and the mouse buttons. *lParam* holds two 16-bit values identifying the location of the mouse pointer when the button was pressed. Together, these parameters provide the window procedure with all the information it needs to process the WM_LBUTTONDOWN message.

From a historical perspective, it's interesting to note that in Windows 95, messages generated by mouse and keyboard input are temporarily buffered in a system-wide hardware input queue and then transferred to the appropriate thread message queue. In previous versions of Windows, mouse and keyboard messages were dispatched directly from an input queue shared by all active applications. This design had an inherent flaw in that if one application stopped responding to messages (or simply went for too long without checking its message queue), other applications couldn't retrieve input messages, either. That Windows 95 directs incoming mouse and keyboard messages to individual thread message queues, coupled with the fact that it uses preemptive scheduling to distribute processor time among active processes rather than link processor allocation to the message retrieval mechanism, means it can also provide a better environment in which to run application programs.

Windows Programming, SDK-Style

If you haven't programmed Windows in C before, it's instructive to see what the source code for a simple program looks like. Figure 1-2 contains the skeleton of a program that creates a window and responds to WM_PAINT and WM_DESTROY messages. This code is similar to the source code you'll find in books such as Charles Petzold's *Programming Windows 95* (Microsoft Press, 1996) and other books that teach Windows programming in C.

```
#include <windows.h>

LONG WINAPI WndProc (HWND, UINT, WPARAM, LPARAM);

int WINAPI WinMain (HINSTANCE hInstance, HINSTANCE hPrevInstance,
                    LPSTR lpszCmdLine, int nCmdShow)
{
    static char szAppName[] = "MyApp";
    WNDCLASS wc;
    HWND hwnd;
    MSG msg;

    wc.style = 0;                                   // Class style
    wc.lpfnWndProc = (WNDPROC) WndProc;             // Window procedure address
    wc.cbClsExtra = 0;                              // Class extra bytes
    wc.cbWndExtra = 0;                              // Window extra bytes
    wc.hInstance = hInstance;                       // Instance handle
    wc.hIcon = LoadIcon (NULL, IDI_APPLICATION);    // Icon handle
    wc.hCursor = LoadCursor (NULL, IDC_ARROW);      // Cursor handle
    wc.hbrBackground = COLOR_WINDOW + 1;            // Background color
    wc.lpszMenuName = NULL;                         // Menu name
    wc.lpszClassName = szAppName;                   // WNDCLASS name

    RegisterClass (&wc);

    hwnd = CreateWindow (
        szAppName,                  // WNDCLASS name
        szAppName,                  // Window title
        WS_OVERLAPPEDWINDOW,        // Window style
        CW_USEDEFAULT,              // Horizontal position
        CW_USEDEFAULT,              // Vertical position
```

Figure 1-2. *C source code for a simple Windows program.*

```
            CW_USEDEFAULT                // Initial width
            CW_USEDEFAULT                // Initial height
            HWND_DESKTOP,                // Handle of parent window
            NULL,                        // Menu handle
            hInstance,                   // Application's instance handle
            NULL                         // Window-creation data
    );

    ShowWindow (hwnd, nCmdShow);
    UpdateWindow (hwnd);

    while (GetMessage (&msg, NULL, 0, 0)) {
        TranslateMessage (&msg);
        DispatchMessage (&msg);
    }
    return msg.wParam;
}

LRESULT CALLBACK WndProc (HWND hwnd, UINT message,
                          WPARAM wParam, LPARAM lParam)
{
    PAINTSTRUCT ps;
    HDC hdc;

    switch (message) {

    case WM_PAINT:
        hdc = BeginPaint (hwnd, &ps);
        //
        // *** Insert statements to draw in the window ***
        //
        EndPaint (hwnd, &ps);
        return 0;

    case WM_DESTROY:
        PostQuitMessage (0);
        return 0;
    }
    return DefWindowProc (hwnd, message, wParam, lParam);
}
```

WinMain starts off by calling the API function *RegisterClass* to register a window class. The window class defines important characteristics of a window such as its window procedure address, its default background color, and its icon. These and other properties are defined by filling in the fields of a WNDCLASS structure, whose address is subsequently passed to *RegisterClass*. An application must specify a window class when it creates a window, and a class must be registered before it can be used. That's why *RegisterClass* is called at the outset of the program. It's important to note that a WNDCLASS-type window class is not the same as a C++ window class. To avoid confusion, I'll use the term WNDCLASS throughout this book to refer to the types of classes created by *RegisterClass*. The term "window class" will refer to C++ classes derived from MFC's *CWnd* class.

Once the WNDCLASS is registered, *WinMain* calls the all-important *CreateWindow* function to create the application's window. The first parameter to *CreateWindow* specifies the name of the WNDCLASS from which the window will be created. The second parameter specifies the text that will appear in the window's title bar. The third specifies the window style. WS_OVERLAPPEDWINDOW is a commonly used style that creates a top-level window with a resizing border, a title bar, a system menu, and buttons for minimizing, maximizing, and closing the window. The next four parameters specify the window's initial position and size: the *x* and *y* screen coordinates of the window's upper left corner and the window's width and height in pixels. CW_USEDEFAULT tells Windows to use default values for these four parameters. The final four parameters specify, in order, the handle of the window's parent window; the handle of the menu associated with the window, if any; the application's instance handle (a value that uniquely identifies each instance of a program that is executed); and a pointer to application-specific window-creation data. We could easily devote a section of this book to *CreateWindow* and its parameters, but as you'll see later, MFC hides much of this knotty detail inside the class library. A typical MFC application doesn't have a *WinMain* function (at least not one you can see), and it doesn't call *RegisterClass* or *CreateWindow*.

The window that *CreateWindow* creates is not initially visible on the screen because it was not created with the WS_VISIBLE style. (Had it been used, WS_VISIBLE would have been combined with WS_OVERLAPPEDWINDOW in the call to *CreateWindow*.) Therefore, *WinMain* follows *CreateWindow* with calls to *ShowWindow* and *UpdateWindow*, which make the window visible and make sure that a WM_PAINT message, which is normally given a low priority among messages waiting in a message queue, is sent immediately so that the window will paint itself. Then comes the message loop. In order to retrieve and dispatch messages, *WinMain* executes a simple *while* loop that calls the *GetMessage*, *TranslateMessage*, and *DispatchMessage* API functions repeatedly:

```
while (GetMessage (&msg, NULL, 0, 0)) {
    TranslateMessage (&msg);
    DispatchMessage (&msg);
}
```

GetMessage checks the message queue. If a message is available, it is removed from the queue and copied to *msg*; otherwise, *GetMessage* blocks on the empty message queue and doesn't return until a message is available. *msg* is an instance of the structure MSG, whose fields contain pertinent message parameters such as the message ID and the time at which the message was placed in the queue. *TranslateMessage* converts a keyboard message denoting a character key to an easier-to-understand WM_CHAR message, and *DispatchMessage* dispatches a message to the window procedure. The message loop continues to execute until *GetMessage* returns 0, which happens only when a WM_QUIT message is retrieved from the queue. When this occurs, execution falls through to the *return* statement that ends *WinMain* and the program terminates.

Messages dispatched with *DispatchMessage* generate calls to the program's window procedure *WndProc*. The sample program in Figure 1-2 processes just two message types, WM_PAINT and WM_DESTROY; all other message types are passed to *DefWindowProc* for default processing. A *switch-case* structure inspects the message ID passed in the *message* parameter and activates the appropriate message handler. The WM_PAINT handler calls the *BeginPaint* API function to obtain a device context handle—the "magic cookie" that permits the application to draw on the screen—and calls the *EndPaint* API function when painting is finished. *EndPaint* releases the device context handle and signals Windows that WM_PAINT processing is complete. The WM_DESTROY handler calls the *PostQuitMessage* API function to post a WM_QUIT message to the application's message queue and ultimately cause the program to terminate. The WM_DESTROY message is sent to a window just before it is destroyed. A top-level window must call *PostQuitMessage* when a WM_DESTROY message arrives, or else the message loop will not fall through and the program will never end.

This is a lot to digest if you've never programmed Windows before, but it brings to light a few very important concepts. First, Windows is an event-driven, message-based operating system. Messages are the key to everything that goes on in the system, and for an application, very few things happen that are not the direct result of receiving a message. Second, there are many different API functions and many different message types, which complicates application development and makes it hard to predict all of the scenarios an application might encounter. Third, seeing how Windows programming is done the hard way provides a baseline for evaluating MFC and other class libraries. MFC is not the panacea some of its proponents would have you believe, but it undeniably makes certain aspects of Windows programming easier. And the higher order it lends to Windows programs frees programmers to spend more time developing the structural components of a program and less time worrying about the style bits passed to *CreateWindow* and other nuances of the API. If you haven't given MFC a look, now is the time to consider it. Windows programming isn't getting any easier, and MFC lets you benefit from tens of thousands of lines of code already written and tested.

INTRODUCING MFC

MFC is the C++ class library Microsoft provides to place an object-oriented wrapper around the Windows API. Version 4 contains nearly 200 classes, some of which you'll use directly and others of which will serve primarily as base classes for classes of your own. Some of the classes are exceedingly simple, such as the *CPoint* class that encapsulates a point object (a location characterized by *x* and *y* coordinates). Others are complex, such as the *CWnd* class that encapsulates the functionality of a window. In an MFC program, you rarely need to call the Windows API directly. Instead, you create objects from MFC classes and call member functions belonging to those objects. Many of the hundreds of member functions defined in the class library are thin wrappers around the Windows API and even have the same names as the corresponding API functions. An obvious benefit of this naming convention is that it speeds the transition for C programmers making the move to MFC. Want to move a window? A C programmer would probably call the *SetWindowPos* API function. Look up *SetWindowPos* in an MFC reference, and you'll find that MFC supports *SetWindowPos*, too. It's a member of the *CWnd* class, which makes sense when you think of a window as an object and *SetWindowPos* as an operation you might want to perform on that object.

MFC is also an *application framework*. More than merely a collection of classes, MFC helps define the structure of an application and handles many routine chores on the application's behalf. Starting with *CWinApp*, the class that represents the application itself, MFC encapsulates virtually every aspect of a program's operation. The framework supplies the *WinMain* function, and *WinMain* in turn calls the application object's member functions to make the program go. One of the *CWinApp* member functions called by *WinMain—Run—*encapsulates the message loop and literally runs the program. The framework also provides abstractions that go above and beyond what the Windows API has to offer. For example, MFC's document/view architecture builds a powerful infrastructure on top of the API that separates a program's data from graphical representations, or views, of that data. Such abstractions are totally foreign to the API and don't exist outside the framework of MFC or a similar class library.

The Benefits of Using C++ and MFC

The fact that you're reading this book means you've probably already heard the traditional arguments in favor of using an object-oriented design methodology: reusability, tighter binding of code and data, and so on. And you should already be familiar with common object-oriented programming (OOP) terms such as *object, inheritance,* and *encapsulation,* particularly as they pertain to the C++ language. But without a good class library to serve as a starting point, OOP does little to reduce the amount of code you write.

That's where MFC comes in. Want to add a toolbar to your application—one that can be docked to different sides of a window or floated in a window of its own? No problem; MFC provides a *CToolBar* class that does 99 percent of the work for you. Want to implement a dynamic data exchange (DDE) connection that enables a running instance of your application to open a document whose icon is double-clicked in the operating system shell? That's easy, too: MFC's *CFrameWnd* class has all the intelligence built in. Buttons with pictures on them are also a snap, thanks to MFC's *CBitmapButton* class. And don't forget about OLE. Few among us have the desire or the know-how to write the code for an OLE container or server from scratch. But MFC simplifies the development of OLE-enabled applications by providing the bulk of the code you need in classes such as *COleDocument*.

Another advantage to using MFC is that the framework uses a lot of tricks to make Windows objects such as windows, dialog boxes, and controls behave like C++ objects. Suppose you want to write a reusable list box class that displays a navigable list of drives and directories on the host PC. Unless you create a custom control to do the job, you can't implement such a list box in C because clicking an item in the list box sends a notification to the list box's parent (the window or the dialog box in which the list box appears), and it's up to the parent to process that notification. In other words, the list box control doesn't control its own destiny; it's the parent's job to update the list box's contents when a drive or a directory is changed. Not so with MFC. In an MFC application, windows and dialogs reflect unprocessed notifications back to the controls that sent them. You can create a self-contained and highly reusable list box class that responds to its own click notifications by deriving a class from *CListBox* and overriding the list box's virtual *OnChildNotify* function. Inside *OnChildNotify*, you provide handlers for different list box events. The resulting list box class implements its own behavior and can be ported to another application with little more than an *#include* statement in a source code file. That's what OOP reusability is all about.

The MFC Design Philosophy

When the programmers at Microsoft set out to create MFC, they had a vision of the future that included a pair of key design goals:

- MFC should provide an object-oriented interface to the Windows operating system that supports reusability, self-containment, and other tenets of OOP.

- It should do so without imposing undue overhead on the system or unnecessarily adding to an application's memory requirements.

The first goal was accomplished with some clever programming using virtual functions such as *CWnd::OnChildNotify*. The second required MFC's architects to make some choices early on about how windows, menus, and other objects would be wrapped by MFC classes such as *CWnd* and *CMenu*. Efficient use of memory was important then and it's important today, because nobody likes a class library that produces bloated code.

One of the ways in which MFC's designers sought to minimize the overhead added by the class library is manifested in the relationship between MFC objects and Windows objects. In Windows, information regarding the characteristics and current state of a window is stored in data structures allocated in memory owned by the operating system. This information is hidden from applications, which deal exclusively with window handles, or "HWNDs." Rather than duplicate all the information associated with an HWND in the data members of the *CWnd* class, MFC wraps a window in a *CWnd* by storing the HWND in a public *CWnd* data member named *m_hWnd*. This method of encapsulating Window properties conserves memory by avoiding redundant data storage, and it means that given a *CWnd* object or a pointer to a *CWnd* object, you can easily convert it to a window handle by retrieving the value of *m_hWnd*, as shown here:

```
HWND hWnd = pWnd->m_hWnd;
```

This is a good thing to know if you want to call an API function that requires a window handle but you have a *CWnd* instead of an HWND. The same holds true for menus and other objects native to the operating system. As a rule, if Windows exposes an object through a handle of some type, the corresponding MFC class will contain a data member for that handle.

When you buy Visual C++ or a third-party MFC compiler, you get the source code for MFC, too. Browse through the source code, and you'll see evidence of another element of the MFC design philosophy: defensive programming. The code for MFC is laced with ASSERT and ASSERT_VALID macros verifying that the class library is getting the results it expects. If an assertion fails, a message box pops up to inform you where the error occurred. Better still, the macros compile only in debug builds, so they add no overhead to the retail code that goes out the door. If you'd like, you can do as MFC does and sprinkle ASSERT and ASSERT_VALID macros throughout your code as a first line of defense against bugs. ASSERT fails if the expression between parentheses evaluates to FALSE. The following statement will trigger an assertion error if the value assigned to *m_nCount* is less than 1 or greater than MAXCOUNT:

```
ASSERT (m_nCount >= 1 && m_nCount <= MAXCOUNT);
```

ASSERT_VALID instructs an object to perform an internal validity check on itself, and it fails if the validity check fails. The following statement triggers an assertion error if the object referenced by the pointer *pObject* has been corrupted or perhaps wasn't initialized properly:

```
ASSERT_VALID (pObject);
```

ASSERT_VALID works only for objects of classes derived from *CObject* because internally it calls the *AssertValid* function that a *CObject*-derived class inherits from *CObject*. You'll learn more about *CObject::AssertValid* and other members of *CObject* in just a few moments.

Another aspect of MFC's source code that deserves mentioning is the variable naming convention it uses. MFC follows the tradition established by SDK programmers and uses Hungarian notation, in which each variable name begins with one or more lowercase characters identifying the variable's data type: *h* for handle, *wnd* for window (as in *CWnd*), and so on. The table below lists some of the Hungarian prefixes commonly used by MFC programmers. Prefixes are often combined to form other prefixes, as in *psz* for "pointer to zero-delimited string" and *lp* for "long pointer." You'll undoubtedly encounter other prefixes that don't appear in the table below, but their meanings will probably be clear to you. MFC also adds *m_* prefixes to its classes' data members so that it's obvious which are member variables and which are not. A temporary *CString* variable created on the stack might have the name *strWndClass*, but if it's a class member it will be called *m_strWndClass*. You don't have to abide by any of these rules yourself, of course, but observing established naming conventions might make your code more readable to other MFC programmers who do.

COMMON HUNGARIAN NOTATION PREFIXES

Prefix	Data Type
b	BOOL
c	char
cx, cy	distance in horizontal or vertical direction
dw	DWORD
h	handle
l	LONG
n	int
p	pointer
pt	*CPoint* or POINT
rc	*CRect* or RECT
str	*CString*
sz	zero-delimited string
w	WORD
wnd	*CWnd*

The Document/View Architecture

The cornerstone of MFC's application framework is the document/view architecture, which defines a program structure that relies on document objects to hold an application's data and view objects to present views of that data. MFC provides the infrastructure for documents and views in the classes *CDocument* and *CView*. *CWinApp*, *CFrameWnd*, *CDocTemplate*, and other classes work in conjunction with *CDocument* and *CView* to ensure that all the pieces fit together. It's a little early to discuss the details of the document/view architecture, but you should be at least familiar with the term document/view because it will inevitably come up in any discussion of MFC.

The reason documents and views are so important is that document/view applications derive the greatest benefit from the application framework. You can write MFC programs that don't use documents and views (and we'll do a lot of that in this book, especially in Chapters 1 through 7), but to get the most out of the framework and take advantage of some of MFC's most advanced features, you must use the document/view architecture. That's not as restricting as it sounds because almost any program that relies on documents of some type can be cast in the document/view mold. Don't let the term "document" mislead you into thinking that the document/view architecture is useful only for writing word processors and spreadsheet programs. A document is simply an abstract representation of a program's data. A document could just as easily be a byte array that stores board positions in a computerized game of chess as it could be a spreadsheet.

What kinds of support does MFC provide to document/view applications? Here are just a few examples:

■   MFC provides much of the logic for saving documents to disk and loading them back into memory.

■   MFC recognizes when an application is about to terminate and provides the user with a chance to save his or her changes if a document contains unsaved data.

■   MFC vastly simplifies printing and print previewing.

■   MFC provides the means to convert ordinary documents into OLE containers and to convert applications that produce documents into OLE servers.

You'll learn all about the document/view architecture in Part II of this book, but only after you've done some programming without documents and views so that you can get acquainted with MFC without having too much heaped on your plate at once.

The MFC Class Hierarchy

MFC provides a variety of classes designed to serve a wide range of needs. You'll find a handy diagram of the MFC class hierarchy inside the front cover of this book. The first step on the road to becoming an MFC programmer is becoming familiar with the classes. The following overview, while by no means exhaustive, should give you an idea of the kind of infrastructure MFC provides.

CObject, the Mother of All Classes

Look at the hierarchy chart inside the front cover of the book, and you'll see that the majority of MFC classes are derived, either directly or indirectly, from *CObject.* You'll sometimes use *CObject* as the base class for classes of your own, but more often you'll take advantage of the features it contributes to the built-in MFC classes. *CObject* provides three basic services to classes that inherit from it:

- Serialization support

- Run-time class information support

- Diagnostic and debugging support

Serialization is the process by which objects archive themselves to and from a storage object such as a file on a disk. *CObject* includes two member functions that play a role in serialization: *IsSerializable* and *Serialize.* The *IsSerializable* function returns TRUE if an object supports serialization, and FALSE if it does not. (Serialization support is an option, not a requirement.) *Serialize* serializes the object's data members to a storage medium represented by a *CArchive* object. One of the steps involved in building a class that supports serialization is overriding the *Serialize* function inherited from *CObject* and providing class-specific code for serializing the class's data members. MFC provides overloaded insertion and extraction operators for common data types that make writing a *Serialize* function easy. The *Serialize* function for a *CBirthday* class derived from *CObject* might look like this:

```
void CBirthday::Serialize (CArchive& ar)
{
    CObject::Serialize (ar);
    if (ar.IsStoring)
        ar << m_day << m_month << m_year;
    else
        ar >> m_day >> m_month >> m_year;
}
```

CBirthday::Serialize first calls the *CObject* base class's *Serialize* function so that the base class can archive its own data members. Then *CBirthday::Serialize* calls the *CArchive* object's *IsStoring* function to determine whether data is being streamed in or out, and uses the << and >> operators to archive its own data members accordingly. *CArchive* performs the physical disk I/O through a *CFile* object; it also buffers data going in and out to optimize performance. In a document/view application, the framework even provides the *CArchive* object for you. Storing the data for the applications you write in *CObject*s and providing the kind of serialization support shown here vastly simplify the logic for loading and saving document files.

Another feature *CObject*-derived classes inherit from *CObject* is support for runtime class information. Given a pointer to an object of a class derived from *CObject*, a program can retrieve the object's class name as well as other information about the object, and test the object's relationship to a specified class. *CObject* provides two member functions to help out: *IsKindOf* and *GetRuntimeClass*. The latter returns a pointer to a *CRuntimeClass* structure containing, among other things, a pointer to the class name and a pointer to a *CRuntimeClass* structure describing the base class. *IsKindOf* accepts a *CRuntimeClass* pointer specifying a class and returns TRUE or FALSE indicating whether the object was created from that class or one of its derivatives. For example, the statement

```
ASSERT (pObject->IsKindOf (RUNTIME_CLASS (CWnd)));
```

causes an assertion error if the object to which *pObject* refers is not a *CWnd* or derivative. MFC's RUNTIME_CLASS macro returns a *CRuntimeClass* pointer for the class name in parentheses. One use for *IsKindOf* is to validate the parameters passed to functions that accept pointers to classes. Note that *CObject*'s support for run-time class information is implemented independently of C++'s run-time type identification (RTTI) mechanism because MFC predated RTTI by several years.

A third feature that *CObject* provides to its derived classes is diagnostic support. The virtual member function *AssertValid* instructs an object to perform a validity check on itself using a series of assertions. The virtual member function *Dump* performs a diagnostic dump of the object's data members, which is helpful for debugging a program and the objects it uses. *CObject*-derived classes often override these functions and provide class-specific code to perform meaningful validity checks and diagnostic dumps. A *CBirthday* class might implement *AssertValid* and *Dump* as follows:

```
#ifdef _DEBUG
void CBirthday::AssertValid () const
{
    CObject::AssertValid ();
    ASSERT (m_day > 0);
    ASSERT (m_month > 0);
    ASSERT (m_year > 0);
    ASSERT (m_day <= 31);
    ASSERT (m_month <= 12);
}
#endif
```

```
#ifdef _DEBUG
void CBirthday::Dump (CDumpContext& dc) const
{
    CObject::Dump (dc);
    dc << "Birthday = " << m_month << "-" << m_day <<
        "-" << m_year";
}
#endif
```

dc normally refers to a predefined *CDumpContext* object named *afxDump*, which dumps output to a debugging terminal using Windows' *OutputDebugString* function. Note the use of *#ifdef* and *#endif* to ensure that *AssertValid* and *Dump* are implemented only in debug builds of your application. These functions are not declared in retail builds, so they shouldn't be implemented if the _DEBUG symbol is not defined.

CObject provides other benefits to its derived classes as well. For example, it overloads the *new* and *delete* operators to provide protection against memory leaks. If you allocate a *CObject* in your application and fail to delete it before the application terminates, MFC will warn you by displaying a debugger message. The overarching importance of this most basic of MFC classes will become increasingly clear as you grow more familiar with MFC.

Application Architecture Classes

The application architecture classes represent the basic architectural elements of a program and include *CWinApp*, which represents the application itself. Just about all MFC applications derive a class from *CWinApp* and instantiate the derived class to create an application object. *CWinApp* includes a number of useful public data members such as *m_szExeName*, which holds the application's executable file name. It also includes helpful member functions such as *ProcessShellCommand*, which processes command-line arguments, and *OnFileOpen*, which contains the code that implements the File menu's Open command. And *CWinApp* contains key virtual functions such as *InitInstance*, which can be overridden to perform routine startup chores such as creating a window. *CWinApp* inherits some of its functionality from *CWinThread*, which represents a thread of execution.

The application architecture group also includes the *CDocument* class, which defines the basic characteristics of the document objects used to store data in document/view applications. As mentioned earlier, a document in MFC is an abstract representation of a program's data. The data itself is typically stored in data members declared in the document class and accessed with public member functions. *CDocument* provides some important member functions of its own, including *IsModified* for determining whether a document has been modified since it was last saved, and *UpdateAllViews* for updating the views of a document when the document's data changes. *CDocument* overridables such as *DeleteContents* and *OnNewDocument* enable a derived document class to be customized to work in cooperation with the framework. Another of *CDocument*'s new features is the *OnFileSendMail* function, which sends a mail message with the document attached to it. This function makes it easy to add a Send Mail command to the File menu of a document/view application.

CWinApp, *CDocument*, and other application architecture classes are derived from *CCmdTarget*, which contributes function and data members that transform a class into a "command target" capable of receiving and processing messages. As you'll see later in this chapter, MFC applications use message maps to correlate incoming messages with class member functions. To use a message map, a class must be derived from *CCmdTarget*. In addition to providing message map support, *CCmdTarget* also lays the groundwork for a sophisticated command-routing system that enables messages generated by menu selections and other user interface events to be handled in the document class, the application class, and elsewhere. Without the support provided by *CCmdTarget*, these messages could be processed only in the window class in which they are actually received.

Window Classes

MFC's *CWnd* class encapsulates the properties of a window. It provides default handlers for many messages, and it includes dozens of member functions that can be called to perform operations on a window or overridden to change the way a window behaves. *CWnd* is never used directly; instead, it's used as the base class for other classes. MFC includes several *CWnd*-derived classes of its own, including *CFrameWnd* and *CMDIFrameWnd*, which model the behavior of top-level windows containing menus, toolbars, and other objects; *CView*, which forms the foundation for views in document/view applications; *CDialog*, which encapsulates dialog boxes; and the MFC control classes corresponding to push buttons, list boxes, and other objects. Beginning in MFC 4, the control classes also include wrappers for the new control types provided in the Windows 95 common controls library.

GDI Classes

GDI stands for Graphics Device Interface and is the component of Windows responsible for output to screens, printers, and other devices. MFC's *CDC* class encapsulates the functionality of the Windows device context, which links an application to a screen, printer, or other output device and allows GDI output functions to be executed. MFC applications write their output using *CDC* member functions such as *DrawText* and *LineTo*, and control the attributes of a device context with member functions such as *SetTextColor* and *SetMapMode*. *CDC* derivatives such as *CPaintDC*, *CWindowDC*, and *CClientDC* are special cases of the more generic *CDC* class. *CPaintDC*, for example, automatically calls the *BeginPaint* and *EndPaint* API functions from its constructor and destructor, simplifying the processing of WM_PAINT messages. The *CMetaFileDC* class, meanwhile, provides a wrapper for GDI metafiles—files in which drawing commands are "recorded" and later played back to do the actual drawing.

When Windows applications draw to an output device, they use pens, brushes, and other GDI objects. *CGdiObject* is the base class for MFC's representation of these objects, with *CGdiObject*-derived classes such as *CPen* and *CBrush* representing the objects themselves. In MFC, creating a GDI pen involves instantiating an object from the *CPen* class and initializing the object to define line characteristics such as width and color. Once selected into a device context with the *CDC* class's *SelectObject* function, the pen may be used to draw lines. This model—create an object, select it into a device context, and draw with it—closely mimics the GDI drawing model that Windows SDK programmers are familiar with. Other classes derived from *CGdiObject* include *CBitmap*, which represents bitmaps; *CPalette*, which represents color palettes; and *CRgn*, which encapsulates GDI objects known as *regions*—areas of the screen defined by combining rectangles, polygons, ellipses, and other shapes.

File Classes

MFC's *CFile* class provides an object-oriented interface to files by taking standard file I/O functions such as *Read* and *Write* and implementing them in the context of file objects. Static member functions such as *Rename* and *Remove* are provided for performing simple file management operations. *CFile* also serves as the base class for other classes, including *CMemFile*, which represents files that are stored in memory rather than on disk; *COleStreamFile*, which maps *CFile* functions to functions in the OLE *IStream* interface; *CSocketFile*, which can be combined with a *CArchive* object to serialize objects over networks using Windows sockets; and *CStdioFile*, which supports buffered file I/O in text and binary modes.

Exception Classes

CException is an abstract base class from which an assortment of MFC exception classes designed for use with C++'s *try/throw/catch* exception handling mechanism are derived. One of the derived classes, *CFileException*, describes exceptions generated by file operations. Public *CFileException* data members contain error codes revealing the exact nature of the error that caused the exception. Other exception classes include *CMemoryException* for out-of-memory errors, *CArchiveException* for archive errors, *COleException* for OLE errors, and *CResourceException* for errors loading and creating Windows resources. MFC throws exceptions of various types from its own code so that applications can use *catch* blocks to detect errors and act accordingly. MFC also provides global functions such as *AfxThrowFileException* and *AfxThrowMemoryException* to aid applications in throwing exceptions.

OLE Classes

One of the greatest benefits of using MFC is that it simplifies the chore of adding OLE support to your applications. OLE is a complicated protocol that defines standard interfaces enabling objects and users of those objects to communicate with each other.

On a more practical level, OLE is the basis for such features as in-place activation (also known as *visual editing*), drag-and-drop data transfers, OLE controls, and more. The name OLE is somewhat outdated: originally conceived to allow documents created by one application to be linked to or embedded in documents created by another, OLE has since been expanded to address a wide range of issues that are central to Windows' evolution into an object-oriented, document-centric operating system. OLE is also something that programmers can no longer afford to ignore. Most applications that work with documents must include OLE support to qualify for the Windows 95 logo. Furthermore, OLE is gradually being woven into the fabric of Windows itself. If you don't believe that, check out the OLE interfaces that the Windows 95 shell uses to communicate with shell extension DLLs, file viewers, and other add-on user interface components.

MFC provides an assortment of OLE classes to aid in the chore of grafting OLE support onto the framework of an application program. Comprising more than 20,000 lines of prewritten code, these classes can reduce the time required to write and debug the OLE part of a program by an order of magnitude or more. Simply put, it makes little sense to write OLE applications outside MFC. Windows programmers used to despair over the complexity of writing DDE code. And compared to OLE, DDE is child's play. Why reinvent the wheel when Microsoft will lend you one that has already been designed, manufactured, and tested?

OLE classes aren't isolated in any one part of the class hierarchy but are sprinkled throughout the hierarchy. Base classes such as *COleDocument* and *CDocItem* provide basic container and server support and serve as base classes for other, more specialized, OLE classes. The *COleDropSource*, *COleDropTarget*, *COleDataSource*, and *COleDataObject* classes encapsulate the interfaces used to perform OLE data transfers. OLE dialog classes derived from *COleDialog* provide object-oriented wrappers around OLE dialog boxes. Finally, miscellaneous OLE classes such as *CRectTracker*, which creates a border around an item inserted in a compound document so that the item can be moved and resized, round out MFC's support for OLE by filling in some of the cracks between the other classes.

Database Classes

MFC generalizes the interface to database management systems fitted with Open Database Connectivity (ODBC) drivers through the *CDatabase* and *CRecordset* classes. *CDatabase* represents an ODBC connection to a data source, and *CRecordset* represents a set of records in that data source. Together, these classes abstract the ODBC API and let information in a database be treated as an object that is queried, modified, and operated on in other ways with member functions of *CRecordset*. The *CRecordView* class further simplifies database operations by connecting a recordset object to a dialog-like form view that displays the values of the fields in the current record. The helper class *CLongBinary* provides an abstract representation of large binary objects such as bitmaps. When it encounters a *CLongBinary* object implemented as a data member in a recordset object, MFC's record field exchange (RFX) mechanism allocates memory to store the object and loads it from the database. This prevents the programmer from having to supply special logic to read and write database fields that don't fit neatly into a predefined data type.

MFC 4 extends the framework's database support with Data Access Object (DAO) classes encapsulating the OLE interface to the Microsoft Jet database engine that serves Microsoft Access. *CDaoDatabase* represents an open DAO database, and *CDaoWorkspace* represents a "workspace" containing a collection of *CDaoDatabase* objects. Other DAO classes place object-oriented wrappers around tables, fields, and records. Jet databases can also be accessed through MFC's ODBC classes, but the DAO classes offer richer interfaces than their ODBC counterparts and may deliver superior performance, too, because calls to DAO member functions travel through fewer layers before reaching the underlying database engine. In general, the DAO classes are ideal for accessing small, locally stored Microsoft Access databases, while the ODBC classes are useful for accessing any database served by an ODBC driver.

Threading Classes

MFC 3 introduced the *CWinThread* class, which encapsulates threads of execution and the API functions used to manipulate them. MFC 4 complements *CWinThread* with a collection of classes derived from *CSyncObject* that aid in synchronizing concurrently executing threads. *CCriticalSection*, *CMutex*, *CEvent*, and *CSemaphore* are wrappers around the similarly named thread synchronization objects implemented in the Windows kernel. A pair of helper classes, *CMultiLock* and *CSingleLock*, work hand in hand with the synchronization classes to provide thread-safe access to variables and other resources. You'll learn more about MFC's threading classes and about programming issues related to multithreaded applications in Chapter 14.

Collection Classes and Templates

A group of classes known as the MFC *collection classes* provides class library support for common data structures such as arrays and linked lists. *CByteArray*, *CPtrArray*, *CStringArray*, and other array classes implement arrays that can be sized dynamically. Array classes are ideal for storing document data. An entire word processing file, for example, might be implemented as a *CByteArray* object that grows as the user types text into the document (or that shrinks as text is deleted). List classes such as *CStringList* and *CObList* implement the MFC versions of the doubly linked list, whose members contain pointers to the next and previous elements in the list. Map classes support tables of data types keyed ("mapped") by other data types. The *CMapWordToPtr* class, for example, keys each pointer variable in the table with a 16-bit word value supplied by the caller. A pointer added to the table can be retrieved by passing its key to the *CMapWordToPtr::LookUp* function. MFC also provides generic versions of the collection classes in the form of C++ templates.

What's most remarkable about these classes is that because they support serialization, an entire array, list, or table can be archived to disk with a single line of code. You'll use these classes time and time again as you develop MFC applications.

General-Purpose Classes

MFC includes a number of general-purpose classes to represent simple data types such as points and rectangles and more complex data types such as strings. The extraordinarily useful *CString* class implements a BASIC-like string data type complete with standard operators such as =, +=, <, and >. Other general-purpose classes include *CPoint*, *CSize*, *CRect*, *CTime*, and *CTimeSpan*. The *CPoint* and *CRect* classes are particularly useful in the Windows environment because points and rectangles are frequently passed as parameters to MFC member functions. *CTime* represents absolute times and dates and includes a useful static function named *GetCurrentTime* that returns a *CTime* object initialized with the current date and time. *CTime* also overloads +, −, +=, −=, and other operators so that times and dates can be manipulated with the ease of simple integers.

The *Afx* Functions

Not all of the functions that MFC offers are members of classes. MFC provides an API of sorts all its own in the form of global functions whose names begin with *Afx*. Class member functions can be called only in the context of the objects to which they belong, but *Afx* functions are available to everyone.

The table on the facing page lists some of the more commonly used *Afx* functions and the duties they perform. *AfxBeginThread* and *AfxEndThread* simplify the process of creating and terminating secondary threads of execution. *AfxMessageBox* is the global equivalent of the Windows *MessageBox* function and, unlike *CWnd::MessageBox*, can be called just as easily from a document class as from a window class. *AfxFormatString1* is often used in conjunction with *AfxMessageBox* to perform *printf*-like string formatting, substituting one string for a "%1" placeholder in another and copying the result to a *CString* object. A similar function named *AfxFormatString2* accepts two strings and two placeholders ("%1" and "%2"). *AfxGetApp* and *AfxGetMainWnd* return pointers to the application object and the application's main window and are useful when you want to access a function or data member of those objects but don't have a pointer readily available. *AfxGetInstanceHandle* is handy when you need an instance handle to pass to a Windows API function. (Even MFC programs call API functions every now and then!) Finally, *AfxRegisterWndClass* is indispensable when the default WNDCLASS that MFC registers for your application's window won't do and you want to register a WNDCLASS of your own.

Afx FUNCTION SAMPLER

Function Name	Description
AfxAbort	Unconditionally terminates an application. Usually called when an unrecoverable error occurs.
AfxBeginThread	Creates a new thread and begins executing it.
AfxEndThread	Terminates the thread that is currently executing.
AfxFormatString1	Substitutes a specified string for instances of "%1" in a string resource and copies the resultant string to a *CString* object.
AfxMessageBox	Displays a Windows message box.
AfxGetApp	Returns a pointer to the application object.
AfxGetAppName	Returns the name of the application.
AfxGetMainWnd	Returns a pointer to the application's main window.
AfxGetInstanceHandle	Returns a handle identifying the current application instance.
AfxRegisterWndClass	Registers a custom WNDCLASS for an MFC application.

YOUR FIRST MFC APPLICATION

Because theory and background information can take you only so far, it's time to build your first MFC application. And what better place to start than with one that displays the message "Hello, MFC" in a window? Based on the classic "Hello, world" program immortalized in Kernighan and Ritchie's *The C Programming Language,* this very minimal program, which I'll call Hello, demonstrates some of the fundamental principles involved in using MFC to write a Windows application. You'll get a close-up look at the *CWinApp* and *CFrameWnd* classes and see firsthand how classes are derived from them and plugged into the application. You'll also learn about the important *CPaintDC* class, which serves as the conduit through which text and graphics are drawn in a window in response to WM_PAINT messages. Finally, you'll be introduced to *message mapping,* the mechanism MFC uses to correlate the messages your application receives with member functions in your classes.

Figure 1-3 lists the source code files for Hello. The Hello.h file contains the declarations for two derived classes, and Hello.cpp contains the implementations of those classes. Among C++ programmers, it's traditional to put class definitions in .h files and source code in .cpp files. We'll honor that tradition here and throughout the rest of this book. For large applications containing tens or perhaps hundreds of classes, it's also beneficial to put class declarations and implementations in separate source code files. That's overkill for the programs in the first few chapters of this book, but later on, when we begin working with documents and views, we'll do as Visual C++ does and give each class its own .h and .cpp files. On the CD in the back of the book, in the subdirectory named Chap01, you'll find a copy of the compiled executable Hello.exe as well as copies of Hello.h and Hello.cpp.

Hello.h

```
//*********************************************************************
//
//  Hello.h
//
//*********************************************************************

class CMyApp : public CWinApp
{
public:
    virtual BOOL InitInstance ();
};

class CMainWindow : public CFrameWnd
{
public:
    CMainWindow ();

protected:
    afx_msg void OnPaint ();
    DECLARE_MESSAGE_MAP ()
};
```

Hello.cpp

```
//*********************************************************************
//
//  Hello.cpp
//
//*********************************************************************

#include <afxwin.h>
#include "Hello.h"

CMyApp myApp;


/////////////////////////////////////////////////////////////////////
// CMyApp member functions
```

Figure 1-3. *The Hello.h and Hello.cpp source code files.*

```
BOOL CMyApp::InitInstance ()
{
    m_pMainWnd = new CMainWindow;
    m_pMainWnd->ShowWindow (m_nCmdShow);
    m_pMainWnd->UpdateWindow ();
    return TRUE;
}

////////////////////////////////////////////////////////////////////////////
// CMainWindow message map and member functions

BEGIN_MESSAGE_MAP (CMainWindow, CFrameWnd)
    ON_WM_PAINT ()
END_MESSAGE_MAP ()

CMainWindow::CMainWindow ()
{
    Create (NULL, "The Hello Application");
}

void CMainWindow::OnPaint ()
{
    CPaintDC dc (this);

    CRect rect;
    GetClientRect (&rect);

    dc.DrawText ("Hello, MFC", -1, &rect,
        DT_SINGLELINE | DT_CENTER | DT_VCENTER);
}
```

Figure 1-4 on the next page shows the output from Hello. When you run Hello, notice that the window is entirely functional; you can move it, resize it, minimize it, maximize it, and close it. And when the window is resized, "Hello, MFC" is redrawn in the center of the window.

Most of Hello's functionality comes from Windows. Windows, for example, draws the exterior, or *nonclient area,* of the window: the title bar, the buttons on the title bar, and the window frame. When the user grabs the window border and drags it with the left mouse button held down, Windows animates the resizing operation. And when the mouse button is released, Windows sends the program a WM_SIZE message followed by a WM_PAINT message saying, "Repaint your client area." All we're responsible for is creating the window and processing WM_PAINT messages to paint the interior, or *client area,* of the window. Let's look at the source code more closely to see how Hello works.

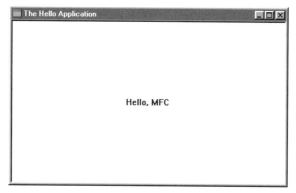

Figure 1-4. *The Hello window.*

The Application Object

The heart of an MFC application is the application object based on the *CWinApp* class. *CWinApp* lies at the end of an inheritance chain that begins with *CObject* and includes both *CCmdTarget* and *CWinThread*. It includes member functions for initializing the application and performing common operations such as saving program settings to disk. *CWinApp* also includes functions that can be overridden to customize the application's behavior, including a *Run* function that encapsulates the message loop. An MFC application can have one—and only one—application object, and that object must be declared with global scope so that it will be instantiated in memory at the very outset of the program.

Hello's application class is called *CMyApp* and is instantiated in Hello.cpp with the global declaration

```
CMyApp myApp;
```

The declaration for *CMyApp* appears in Hello.h:

```
class CMyApp : public CWinApp
{
public:
    virtual BOOL InitInstance ();
};
```

CMyApp declares no data members and overrides just one function inherited from *CWinApp*. The *InitInstance* function is called early in the application's lifetime, right after the application starts but before the window is created. In fact, unless *InitInstance* creates a window, the application doesn't *have* a window. That's why even a minimal MFC application must derive a class from *CWinApp* and override *CWinApp::Init-Instance*.

The *InitInstance* Function

CWinApp::InitInstance is a virtual function whose default implementation contains just one statement:

```
return TRUE;
```

The purpose of *InitInstance* is to provide the application with the opportunity to initialize itself. The value returned by *InitInstance* determines what the framework does next. Returning FALSE from *InitInstance* shuts down the application. If initialization goes as planned, *InitInstance* should return TRUE in order to allow the program to proceed. *InitInstance* is the perfect place in which to perform initializations that need to be done each time the program starts. At the very least, this means creating the window that will represent the application on the screen.

CMyApp's implementation of *InitInstance*, which appears in Hello.cpp, creates the Hello window by instantiating an object from the Hello class *CMainWindow*. The statement

```
m_pMainWnd = new CMainWindow;
```

instantiates the window object and copies its address to the application object's *m_pMainWnd* data member. After the window is created, *InitInstance* displays it— remember, a window is not initially visible unless it is created with a WS_VISIBLE attribute—by calling *ShowWindow* and *UpdateWindow* through the *CMainWindow* pointer:

```
m_pMainWnd->ShowWindow (m_nCmdShow);
m_pMainWnd->UpdateWindow ();
```

ShowWindow and *UpdateWindow* are *CWnd* members common to all window objects, including objects of the *CFrameWnd* class from which the Hello program derives *CMainWindow*. These functions are little more than wrappers around the API functions of the same name. To call a regular Windows API function from an MFC program, make it a practice to preface the function name with the global scope resolution operator ::, as in

```
::UpdateWindow (hwnd);
```

This notation will ensure that the API function is called even if the object that makes the call has a member function with the same name. In the remainder of this book, Windows API functions will be prefaced with :: to distinguish them from MFC member functions.

ShowWindow accepts just one parameter: an integer that specifies whether the window should initially be shown minimized, maximized, or neither minimized nor maximized. In accordance with Windows programming protocol, Hello passes *Show-Window* the value stored in the application object's *m_nCmdShow* variable, which holds the *nCmdShow* parameter passed to *WinMain*. The *m_nCmdShow* value is usually SW_SHOWNORMAL, indicating that the window should be displayed in its normal, unmaximized and unminimized, state. However, depending on how the user starts an application, Windows will occasionally slip in a value such as SW_SHOW-MAXIMIZED or SW_SHOWMINIMIZED. Unless there is a specific reason for it to do otherwise, *InitInstance* should always pass the *m_nCmdShow* variable instead of a hardcoded SW_ value to *ShowWindow*.

UpdateWindow completes the job that *ShowWindow* started by forcing an immediate repaint. Its work done, *InitInstance* returns TRUE to allow the application to proceed.

Other *CWinApp* Overridables

InitInstance is just one of several virtual *CWinApp* member functions you can override to customize the behavior of the application object. Look up the *CWinApp* overridables in your MFC documentation, and you'll see a list of more than a dozen others with names such as *WinHelp* and *ProcessWndProcException*. Most of these functions are seldom overridden, but a few are extremely useful and are overridden almost as often as *InitInstance*. In particular, *ExitInstance* is useful for cleaning up before an application terminates. If you use *InitInstance* to allocate memory or other resources, *ExitInstance* is the perfect place to deallocate those resources. The default implementation of *ExitInstance* saves certain program settings in document/view applications and performs some routine cleanup chores required by the framework, so you should be sure to call the base class version if you've overridden *ExitInstance*. Ultimately, the value returned by *ExitInstance* is the exit code returned by *WinMain*.

Other interesting *CWinApp* overridables include *OnIdle*, *Run*, and *PreTranslateMessage*. *OnIdle* is handy for performing background processing chores such as spooling a document to a printer or performing garbage collection on in-memory data structures. Because *OnIdle* is called when an application is "idle"—that is, when there are no messages waiting—it provides an excellent mechanism for performing low-priority background tasks without spawning a separate thread of execution. *OnIdle* is discussed in detail in Chapter 7. *Run* can be overridden to customize the message loop by replacing it with a message loop of your own. If you just want to perform some specialized preprocessing on certain messages before they are dispatched to the program, you can override *PreTranslateMessage* and save yourself the trouble of writing a whole new message loop.

How MFC Uses the Application Object

To someone who has never seen an MFC application's source code before, one of the more remarkable aspects of Hello will be that it contains no executable code outside the classes it defines. There is no *main* or *WinMain* function, for example; the only statement in the entire program that has global scope is the statement that instantiates the application object. So what is it that actually starts the program running, and when does the application object come into the picture?

The best way to understand what goes on underneath the hood of MFC is to look at the framework's source code. One of the source code files provided with MFC—Winmain.cpp—contains a *WinMain* function that MFC links into your application. This version of *WinMain* makes extensive use of the application object, which is one reason the application object must be declared globally. Global variables and objects are created before any code is executed, and the application object must be extant in memory before *WinMain* starts.

Right after starting, the MFC-supplied *WinMain* calls *AfxGetApp* to get a pointer to the application object. It then calls a function named *AfxWinInit* to initialize the framework and copy *hInstance*, *nCmdShow*, and other *WinMain* function parameters to data members of the application object. Next it calls the application object's virtual *InitApplication* and *InitInstance* functions. In 16-bit versions of MFC, *InitApplication* is called only if the *hPrevInstance* parameter passed to *WinMain* is NULL, indicating that this is the only instance of the application currently running. In the Win32 environment, *hPrevInstance* is always NULL, so the framework doesn't bother to check it. A 32-bit application could just as easily use *InitApplication* to initialize itself as use *InitInstance*, but *InitApplication* is provided for compatibility with previous versions of MFC and should not be used in 32-bit Windows applications. If the *AfxWinInit*, *InitApplication*, or *InitInstance* function returns 0, *WinMain* terminates instead of proceeding further and the application is shut down.

Only if all of the aforementioned functions return nonzero values does *WinMain* perform the next critical step. The statement

```
pApp->Run();
```

calls the application object's *Run* function, which executes the message loop and begins pumping messages to the application's window. The message loop repeats until a WM_QUIT message is retrieved from the message queue, at which point *Run* breaks out of the loop, calls *ExitInstance*, and returns to *WinMain*. *WinMain* finishes up by calling *AfxWinTerm* to clean up after the application and finally executes a *return* to end the application.

The Window Object

MFC uses *CWnd* and classes derived from *CWnd* to provide object-oriented interfaces to the window or windows an application creates. MFC's *CFrameWnd* class models the behavior of "frame windows" like the one Hello uses. For now, you can think of a frame window as a top-level window that serves as an application's primary interface to the outside world. In the greater context of the document/view architecture, frame windows play a larger role by serving as intelligent containers for the view objects that provide visual representations of an application's data.

Creating a Window

An MFC application creates a window by instantiating a window class and calling the resulting object's *Create* or *CreateEx* function. Hello derives a frame window class named *CMainWindow* from *CFrameWnd* and instantiates it in *CMyApp::InitInstance*. The derivation for *CMainWindow* in Hello.h looks like this:

```
class CMainWindow : public CFrameWnd
{
public:
    CMainWindow ();

protected:
    afx_msg void OnPaint ();
    DECLARE_MESSAGE_MAP ()
};
```

When *CMyApp* creates an instance of *CMainWindow* with *new*, *CMainWindow*'s constructor calls *CFrameWnd::Create* to create the window you see on the screen:

```
Create (NULL, "The Hello Application");
```

Create is one of approximately 20 member functions that *CFrameWnd* defines in addition to the functions it inherits from *CWnd*. *CFrameWnd::Create* is prototyped as follows:

```
BOOL Create (LPCTSTR lpszClassName,
    LPCTSTR lpszWindowName,
    DWORD dwStyle = WS_OVERLAPPEDWINDOW,
    const RECT& rect = rectDefault,
    CWnd* pParentWnd = NULL,
    LPCTSTR lpszMenuName = NULL,
    DWORD dwExStyle = 0,
    CCreateContext* pContext = NULL)
```

As you can see, default values are defined for six of the eight parameters *Create* accepts. Hello does the minimum amount of work required, specifying values for the function's first two parameters and accepting the defaults for the remaining six. The first parameter to *Create*—*lpszClassName*—specifies the name of the WNDCLASS that the window is based on. Specifying NULL for this parameter creates a default frame window based on a WNDCLASS registered by the framework. The *lpszWindowName* parameter specifies the title that will appear at the top of the window. The title is usually the name of the application but frequently includes a document name as well.

The *dwStyle* parameter specifies the window style. The default is WS_OVER-LAPPEDWINDOW. You can change the window style by specifying an alternative style or combination of styles in the call to *Create*. You'll find a complete list of window styles in the documentation for *CFrameWnd::Create*. Two of the styles frequently used with frame windows are WS_HSCROLL and WS_VSCROLL, which add horizontal and vertical scroll bars to the bottom and right edges of the window's client area. The statement

```
Create (NULL, "Hello", WS_OVERLAPPEDWINDOW | WS_VSCROLL);
```

creates an overlapped window that contains a vertical scroll bar. As this example shows, multiple styles may be combined using the C++ | operator. WS_OVERLAPPEDWINDOW combines the WS_OVERLAPPED, WS_CAPTION, WS_SYSMENU, WS_MINIMIZEBOX, WS_MAXIMIZEBOX, and WS_THICKFRAME styles, so if you'd like to create a window that looks just like a WS_OVERLAPPEDWINDOW window but lacks the maximize button in the title bar, you could say

```
Create (NULL, "Hello", WS_OVERLAPPED | WS_CAPTION |
    WS_SYSMENU | WS_MINIMIZEBOX | WS_THICKFRAME);
```

An alternative way to specify a window style is to override the virtual *PreCreateWindow* function that a window inherits from *CWnd* and modify the *style* field of the CREATE-STRUCT structure passed to *PreCreateWindow*. This is a handy capability to have when the framework creates your application's main window for you, as is frequently the case in document/view applications, but it's not necessary when your code calls *Create* directly and therefore controls the parameters passed to it. Later in this book, you'll see examples demonstrating when and how *PreCreateWindow* is used.

Additional window styles known as *extended styles* can be specified in *CFrameWnd::Create*'s *dwExStyle* parameter. Window styles are divided into standard and extended styles for a historical reason: Windows 3.1 added support for additional window styles by introducing the *::CreateWindowEx* API function. *::CreateWindowEx* is similar to *::CreateWindow*, but its argument list includes an additional parameter specifying the window's extended style. Windows 3.1 supported just five extended styles. Windows 95 offers a much greater selection that includes the WS_EX_WINDOWEDGE and WS_EX_CLIENTEDGE styles, which give window borders a more pronounced 3D look. The framework automatically adds these styles to frame windows for you, so it's rarely necessary for you to specify them yourself. Other useful extended styles include WS_EX_TOPMOST, which creates a "topmost" window that remains on top of other windows even when it's behind them in the z-order—the front-to-back ordering of windows that determines which windows are obscured behind others. Another is WS_EX_ACCEPTFILES, which enables a window to accept files dragged and dropped from other windows.

After the *dwStyle* parameter comes *rect*, which is a C++ reference to a *CRect* object or a C-style RECT structure specifying the window's initial screen position and size. The default is *rectDefault*, which is a static member of the *CFrameWnd* class that simply tells Windows to choose the window's default initial position and size. If you want to, you can specify the initial position and size by initializing a *CRect* object with coordinates describing a rectangle on the screen and passing it to *Create*. The following statement creates a standard overlapped window whose upper left corner is located 32 pixels to the right of and 64 pixels down from the upper left corner of the screen and whose initial width and height are 320 and 240 pixels, respectively:

```
Create (NULL, "Hello", WS_OVERLAPPEDWINDOW,
    CRect (32, 64, 352, 304));
```

Note that the window's width and height are determined by the *difference* between the first and third parameters and the second and fourth parameters rather than by the absolute values of the third and fourth parameters. In other words, the *CRect* object specifies the rectangular region of the screen that the window will occupy. The four parameters passed to *CRect*'s constructor specify, in order, the rectangle's left, top, right, and bottom screen coordinates.

The *pParentWnd* parameter to *Create* identifies the window's parent window. This parameter should be NULL for top-level windows because top-level windows have no parents. (Actually, specifying NULL for *pParentWnd* makes the desktop window—the window that forms the backdrop for the screen—the window's parent. But that's an implementation detail that matters only to Windows.) In Chapter 5, you'll learn about child-window controls such as push buttons and list boxes and what it means to make one window the parent of another. When you create a child-window control, *pParentWnd* identifies the window in which the control appears.

Create's *lpszMenuName* parameter identifies the menu associated with the window. NULL indicates that the window has no menu. We'll begin using non-NULL values for this parameter in Chapter 4, when we take up the subject of menus and menu resources.

The final parameter to *CFrameWnd::Create*, *pContext*, contains a pointer to a *CCreateContext* structure that is used by the framework when it initializes frame windows in document/view applications. Outside the document/view architecture, this parameter is meaningless and should be set to NULL.

Create offers a tremendous variety of options to the programmer. The number of choices might seem a bit overwhelming at this early stage, especially if you haven't programmed for Windows before, but experience will teach you how and when to exercise the options available to you. Meanwhile, the class library's use of default function arguments hides much of the complexity when a standard *CFrameWnd*-type window is all you need. This is one example of the ways in which MFC makes Windows programming just a little bit easier.

Painting the Window's Client Area

Hello doesn't draw to the screen just whenever it wants to. Instead, it draws in response to WM_PAINT messages from Windows signaling that it's time to update the window. WM_PAINT messages can be generated for a variety of reasons. The default WNDCLASS that MFC registers for frame windows includes CS_HREDRAW and

CS_VREDRAW style attributes (see the documentation for WNDCLASS for a complete list of WNDCLASS styles), so the entire client area is repainted whenever the window is resized horizontally or vertically. A WM_PAINT message might also be sent because another window was moved and a part of Hello's window previously obscured by that window is now visible. Whatever the stimulus that prompted the event, it is the application's responsibility to paint the client area of its window in response to WM_PAINT messages. Windows draws the nonclient area so that all applications will have a consistent look, but if the application doesn't implement its own drawing routines for the client area, the interior of the window will be blank.

In Hello, WM_PAINT messages are processed by *CMainWindow::OnPaint*, which is activated anytime a WM_PAINT message arrives. *OnPaint*'s job is to draw "Hello, MFC" in the center of the window's client area. It begins by constructing a *CPaintDC* object named *dc*:

```
CPaintDC dc (this);
```

MFC's *CPaintDC* class is derived from MFC's more generic *CDC* class, which encapsulates a Windows device context and includes dozens of member functions for drawing on screens, printers, and other output devices. In Windows, all graphical output is performed through device context objects that abstract the interfaces to output devices and contain relevant state information. *CPaintDC* is a special case of *CDC* that is used only in WM_PAINT message handlers. Before drawing in a window in response to a WM_PAINT message, an application must call the Windows *::BeginPaint* API function to obtain a device context and prepare the device context for painting. When it's finished painting, the application must call *::EndPaint* to release the device context and inform Windows that painting is complete. If an application fails to call *::BeginPaint* and *::EndPaint* when it processes a WM_PAINT message, the message will not be removed from the message queue and the program will get stuck in an endless loop. Not surprisingly, *CPaintDC* calls *::BeginPaint* from its constructor and *::EndPaint* from its destructor to ensure that this doesn't happen.

In MFC, you'll always draw to the screen with a *CDC* object of some type, but you must use a *CPaintDC* object only inside *OnPaint* handlers. Furthermore, it's important to create *CPaintDC* objects on the stack so that their destructors will be called when *OnPaint* ends. You can instantiate a *CPaintDC* object with the *new* operator if you want to, but then it becomes critically important to delete that object before *OnPaint* ends. Otherwise, *::EndPaint* won't be called and your application won't redraw itself properly.

Before doing any drawing, *OnPaint* constructs a *CRect* object representing a rectangle and uses *CWnd::GetClientRect* to initialize the rectangle with the coordinates of the window's client area:

```
CRect rect;
GetClientRect (&rect);
```

OnPaint then uses a *CDC* output function to display "Hello, MFC" in the window's client area:

```
dc.DrawText ("Hello, MFC", -1, &rect,
    DT_SINGLELINE | DT_CENTER | DT_VCENTER);
```

CDC::DrawText is a powerful general-purpose function for outputting text. It accepts four parameters: a pointer to the string to display, the number of characters in the string or −1 if the string is terminated with a NULL character, the address of a RECT structure or of a *CRect* object specifying the formatting rectangle (the rectangle in which the string is displayed), and flags specifying the output format. In Hello, *CMain-Window::OnPaint* combines the DT_SINGLELINE, DT_CENTER, and DT_VCENTER flags to display a single line of text that is centered both horizontally and vertically in the formatting rectangle. *rect* describes the window's client area, so the resulting output is perfectly centered in the window's interior.

Conspicuously missing from *DrawText*'s argument list are parameters specifying output characteristics such as font and text color. These and other text characteristics are attributes of the device context and are controlled with *CDC* member functions such as *SelectObject* and *SetTextColor*. The *DrawText* function and other text output functions use the font that is currently "selected into" the device context. Since Hello doesn't select a font into the device context, the device context's default font is used. Had we wanted to spruce up the window by displaying "Hello, MFC" in, say, a 72-point Arial font, we would have first created a *CFont* object for that font and then selected it into the device context with a statement like this one:

```
dc.SelectObject (&font);
```

Similarly, *DrawText* draws text in the device context's current text color, and it fills in the remainder of the formatting rectangle with the current background color. A device context's current text and background colors, which default to black and white, respectively, can be changed to red and green with the following statements:

```
dc.SetTextColor (RGB (255, 0, 0));
dc.SetBkColor (RGB (0, 255, 0));
```

The parameters passed to the Windows RGB macro specify red, green, and blue color components, in that order. Valid values range from 0 through 255, with higher numbers representing higher intensities.

The Message Map

Just how is it that a WM_PAINT message from Windows turns into a call to *CMain-Window::OnPaint*? The answer lies in the message map. A message map is a table that correlates messages with the member functions an application provides to handle those messages. The message map is MFC's way of avoiding the lengthy vtables that would be required if every class had a virtual function for every possible message it might receive. Any class derived from *CCmdTarget* can contain a message map. What MFC does internally to implement message maps is hidden behind some rather complex macros, but *using* a message map is exceedingly simple. Here's all you have to do to add a message map to a class:

1. Declare the message map by adding a DECLARE_MESSAGE_MAP statement to the class declaration.

2. In the class implementation, create and initialize the message map by placing macros identifying the messages that the class will handle between calls to BEGIN_MESSAGE_MAP and END_MESSAGE_MAP.

3. Add member functions to handle the messages.

Hello's *CMainWindow* class handles just one message type, WM_PAINT, so its message map is implemented as follows:

```
BEGIN_MESSAGE_MAP (CMainWindow, CFrameWnd)
    ON_WM_PAINT ()
END_MESSAGE_MAP ()
```

BEGIN_MESSAGE_MAP begins the message map and identifies both the class to which the message map belongs and the base class. (Message maps are passed by inheritance just as other class members are, and the base class name is required so that the framework can identify the message map associated with the base class.) END_MESSAGE_MAP ends the message map. In between BEGIN_MESSAGE_MAP and END_MESSAGE_MAP are macros identifying message map entries. ON_WM_PAINT is a macro defined in the MFC header file Afxmsg_.h, which adds an entry for WM_PAINT messages to the message map. The macro accepts no parameters because it is hardcoded to link WM_PAINT messages to the class member function named *OnPaint*. MFC provides macros for more than 100 Windows messages ranging from WM_ACTIVATE to WM_WININICHANGE. You can get the name of the message handler that corresponds to a given ON_WM macro from the MFC documentation, but it's fairly easy to deduce the name yourself by replacing WM_ with *On* and converting all the remaining letters except those at the beginning of the word to lowercase. Thus, WM_PAINT becomes *OnPaint*, and WM_LBUTTONDOWN becomes *OnLButtonDown*. You'll have to consult the MFC documentation to determine what kinds of arguments the message handler receives and what type of value it returns. *OnPaint* takes no arguments and returns no value, but *OnLButtonDown* is prototyped like this:

```
afx_msg void OnLButtonDown (UINT nFlags, CPoint point)
```

nFlags contains bit flags specifying the states of the mouse buttons as well as the states of the Ctrl and Shift keys, and *point* identifies the location at which the click occurred. The arguments passed to a message handler come from the *wParam* and *lParam* parameters that accompanied the message. But whereas *wParam* and *lParam* are of necessity generic, the parameters passed to an MFC message handler are both specific and type-safe.

What happens if you want to process a message for which MFC does not provide a message-map macro? You create an entry for the message using the ON_MESSAGE macro, which accepts two parameters: the message ID and the address of the corresponding class member function. The following statement maps WM_SETTEXT messages to a member function named *OnSetText*:

```
ON_MESSAGE (WM_SETTEXT, OnSetText)
```

Other special-purpose message-map macros provided by MFC include ON_COMMAND, which maps menu selections and other user-interface (UI) events to class member functions, and ON_UPDATE_COMMAND_UI, which correlates menu items and toolbar buttons with special "update handlers" that keep UI objects in sync with other elements of the application. You'll be introduced to these and other message-map macros in the chapters that follow.

Getting back to Hello for a moment: *CMainWindow*'s *OnPaint* function and message map are declared with the following statements in Hello.h:

```
afx_msg void OnPaint ();
DECLARE_MESSAGE_MAP ()
```

afx_msg is a visual reminder that *OnPaint* is a message handler. You can omit it if you'd like because it reduces to whitespace when it's compiled. The term "afx_msg" is meant to connote a function that behaves as a virtual function does but without requiring a vtable entry. DECLARE_MESSAGE_MAP is usually the final statement in the class declaration because it uses C++ access specifiers to specify the visibility of its members. You can follow DECLARE_MESSAGE_MAP with member declarations of your own, but if you do, you should also lead off with a *public*, *protected*, or *private* keyword to ensure the visibility you want for those members.

Under the Hood: How Message Maps Work

You can find out how message maps work by examining the DECLARE_MESSAGE-_MAP, BEGIN_MESSAGE_MAP, and END_MESSAGE_MAP macros in Afxwin.h and the code for *CWnd::WindowProc* in Wincore.cpp. Here's a synopsis of what goes on under the hood when you use message-mapping macros in your code, and of how the framework uses the code and data generated by the macros to convert messages into calls to corresponding class member functions.

To begin with, MFC's DECLARE_MESSAGE_MAP macro adds three members to the class declaration: a private array of AFX_MSGMAP_ENTRY structures named *_messageEntries* that contains information correlating messages and message handlers; a static AFX_MSGMAP structure named *messageMap* that contains a pointer to the class's *_messageEntries* array and a pointer to the base class's *messageMap* structure;

and a virtual function named *GetMessageMap* that returns *messageMap*'s address. (The macro implementation is slightly different for an MFC application that's dynamically rather than statically linked, but the principle is the same.) BEGIN_MESSAGE_MAP contains the implementation for the *GetMessageMap* function and code to initialize the *messageMap* structure. The macros that appear between BEGIN_MESSAGE_MAP and END_MESSAGE_MAP fill in the _*messageEntries* array, and END_MESSAGE_MAP marks the end of the array with a NULL entry. For the statements

```
// In the class declaration
DECLARE_MESSAGE_MAP ()

// In the class implementation
BEGIN_MESSAGE_MAP (CMainWindow, CFrameWnd)
    ON_WM_PAINT ()
END_MESSAGE_MAP ()
```

the compiler's preprocessor generates this:

```
// In the class declaration
private:
    static const AFX_MSGMAP_ENTRY _messageEntries[];
protected:
    static const AFX_MSGMAP messageMap;
    virtual const AFX_MSGMAP* GetMessageMap() const;

// In the class implementation
const AFX_MSGMAP* CMainWindow::GetMessageMap() const
    { return &CMainWindow::messageMap; }

const AFX_MSGMAP CMainWindow::messageMap = {
    &CFrameWnd::messageMap,
    &CMainWindow::_messageEntries[0]
};

const AFX_MSGMAP_ENTRY CMainWindow::_messageEntries[] = {
    { WM_PAINT, 0, 0, 0, AfxSig_vv,
        (AFX_PMSG)(AFX_PMSGW)(void (CWnd::*)(void))OnPaint },
    {0, 0, 0, 0, AfxSig_end, (AFX_PMSG)0 }
};
```

With this infrastructure in place, the framework can call *GetMessageMap* to get a pointer to *CMainWindow*'s *messageMap* structure. It can then scan the _*messageEntries* array to see if *CMainWindow* has a handler for the message, and if necessary it can grab a pointer to *CFrameWnd*'s *messageMap* structure and scan the base class's message map, too.

That's a pretty good description of what happens when a message for *CMain-Window* arrives. To dispatch the message, the framework calls the virtual *WindowProc* function that *CMainWindow* inherits from *CWnd*. *WindowProc* calls *OnWndMsg*, which in turn calls *GetMessageMap* to get a pointer to *CMainWindow::messageMap* and searches *CMainWindow::_messageEntries* for an entry whose message ID matches the ID of the message that is currently awaiting processing. If the entry is found, the corresponding *CMainWindow* function (whose address is stored in the *_messageEntries* array along with the message ID) is called. Otherwise, *OnWndMsg* consults *CMain-Window::messageMap* for a pointer to *CFrameWnd::messageMap* and repeats the process for the base class. If the base class doesn't have a handler for the message, the framework ascends another level and consults the base class's base class, systematically working its way up the inheritance chain until it finds a message handler or passes the message to Windows for default processing. Figure 1-5 illustrates *CMain-Window*'s message map schematically and shows the route that the framework travels as it searches for a handler to match a given message ID, beginning with the message map entries for *CMainWindow*.

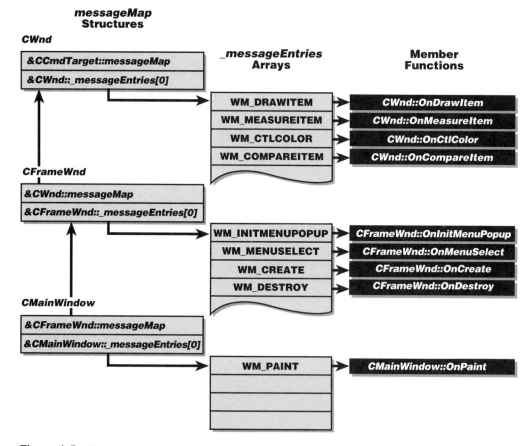

Figure 1-5. *Message map processing.*

What MFC's message mapping mechanism amounts to is a very efficient way of connecting messages to message handlers without using virtual functions. Virtual functions are not space-efficient because they require vtables, and vtables consume memory even if the functions in them are not overridden. The amount of memory used by a message map, in contrast, is proportional to the number of message entries it contains. Since it's extremely rare for a programmer to implement a window class that includes handlers for all of the different message types, message mapping conserves a few hundred bytes of memory just about every time a *CWnd* is wrapped around an HWND.

The Big Picture

Before we move on, let's pause for a moment and review some of the important concepts you've learned from Hello. The very first thing that happens in Hello is that a globally declared application object is instantiated from a class derived from *CWinApp*. A hidden *WinMain* function then starts the program, calling the application object's *InitInstance* function to initialize the application and *Run* to start the message loop. The application object's *InitInstance* function constructs a window object, and that object's constructor uses *CFrameWnd::Create* to create the window that eventually appears on the screen. After the window is created, *InitInstance* calls the window's *ShowWindow* function to make it visible and *UpdateWindow* to send it its very first WM_PAINT message. WM_PAINT messages are converted by MFC's message mapping mechanism into calls to *CMainWindow::OnPaint*, and *OnPaint* draws the text "Hello, MFC" in the window's client area by creating a *CPaintDC* object and calling *CPaintDC::DrawText*.

If you're coming to MFC straight from a background of programming for Windows in C, this probably seems a like a pretty strange way to do business. Two-step window creation? Application objects? No more *WinMain*? It's definitely different from the way Windows *used* to be programmed. But compare Hello's source code to the C program listing back in Figure 1-2, and you'll find that MFC undeniably simplifies things. MFC doesn't necessarily make the source code easier to understand—after all, Windows programming is still Windows programming—but by moving a lot of the boilerplate stuff out of the source code and into the class library, MFC reduces the amount of code you have to write. That, combined with the fact that you can modify the behavior of any MFC class by deriving from it a class of your own, makes MFC a pretty effective tool for programming Windows. The benefits will really become apparent when you begin tapping into some of the more sophisticated features of Windows such as OLE. With MFC, you can get an OLE application up and running in nothing flat. With C—well, good luck.

Hello lacks many of the elements that characterize a full-blown Windows program, but it's still a good first step on the road to becoming an MFC Windows programmer. In subsequent chapters, we'll build on the foundation we've laid here by introducing additional user interface elements such as menus, dialog boxes, and controls into our programs. We'll also see how Windows programs read input from the mouse and keyboard and learn more about the Windows GDI. Chapter 2 leads off by introducing some additional *CDC* drawing functions and demonstrating how to add scroll bars to a frame window so that we can view a workspace larger than the window's client area. In other words, we're just getting started. Roll up your sleeves and be prepared to get dirty, because there's still plenty of code left to write.

Drawing in
a Window

If you've been around PCs for a while, you probably remember what graphics programming was like before Windows came along. If you were lucky, you had a decent graphics library with routines like *DrawLine* and *DrawCircle* to draw graphics primitives for you. If you weren't so lucky, you probably spent a lot of time writing your own output routines and tweaking them to shave a few microseconds here and there. And whether it was your code or someone else's doing the drawing, you knew that when a new graphics standard emerged—in those days, that meant whenever IBM introduced a new graphics adapter like the EGA or VGA—you'd be scrambling to support the latest hardware. That invariably meant buying an updated version of the graphics library, adding new code to your own routines, or writing a driver for the new video card. For the graphics programmer, the platform was a moving target that never seemed to stand still for very long. And even if you did manage to draw a bead on the video hardware, there was still plenty of work to be done adapting your code so that it would work with printers and other output devices.

Windows changed all that by bringing to the PC platform something it sorely needed: a device-independent graphics output model. In Windows, the graphics code you write will work on any video adapter for which a Windows driver is available. These days, that's just about every adapter on the planet. And to a very large extent, the same code that sends output to the screen will work with printers and other hardcopy devices, too. This one-size-fits-all approach to graphics programming has a number of advantages, chief among them the fact that programmers can now spend their time developing code for their applications rather than code for the hardware their applications will run on. Moreover, you no longer need third-party graphics libraries to do your work because Windows provides a wide-ranging assortment of graphics API functions that do everything from drawing lines to creating complex clipping regions that serve as stencils for other output routines.

The part of Windows responsible for graphics output is the Graphics Device Interface, or GDI. GDI services are provided by the dynamic link libraries Gdi.exe and Gdi32.dll, which contain the 16- and 32-bit halves of the GDI, respectively. Like other core components of Windows 95, the GDI was split into two parts so that it could lend equal support to 16- and 32-bit applications. As a programmer, you don't need to be concerned about the 16- /32-bit code dichotomy. You simply call a GDI service (or its MFC equivalent), and Windows makes sure your call gets routed to the appropriate library. GDI provides a number of different services an application can call. Together, these services constitute a powerful and robust graphics programming language whose richness rivals that of some third-party graphics libraries. MFC works on top of the graphics API and codifies the interface with C++ classes representing the various components of the Windows GDI.

Now that you know how to create a window, it's time to do something with that window. In Chapter 1, you saw how *CDC::DrawText* is used to output text to a window. *DrawText* is just one of many member functions the *CDC* class provides for text and graphics output. This chapter looks at the *CDC* class and its derivative classes in more detail, and introduces two of the most commonly used GDI graphics objects—pens and brushes. We'll develop three sample programs: one that demonstrates how to draw simple figures in a window; a second that adds a scroll bar to the window so that we can see everything we've drawn, and a third that lets the class library do the scrolling. Though the part of the GDI that it examines is just the tip of the iceberg, this chapter will help acquaint you with the GDI and with the MFC classes that encapsulate it.

DRAWING WITH THE GDI

In a single-tasking environment such as MS-DOS, the name of the game when it comes to screen output is "anything goes." A running application is free to do just about whatever it wants whenever it wants, whether that involves drawing a line on the screen, reprogramming the adapter's color palette, or switching to another video mode. In a windowed, multitasking environment such as Windows, programs can't be afforded such freedom because the output from program A must be protected from the output of program B. First and foremost, this means that each program's output must be restricted to its own window. The GDI uses a simple mechanism to make sure every program that draws in a window plays by the rules. That mechanism is the device context.

When a Windows program draws to a screen, a printer, or another output device, it doesn't communicate directly with the device as an MS-DOS program is apt to do. Rather, the Windows program draws to a logical "display surface" represented by a device context (DC). Deep inside Windows, a device context is a data structure containing fields that describe everything the GDI needs to know about the display surface and the context in which it is being used. Before it draws anything on the screen, a Windows program acquires a device context handle from the GDI. It then passes that handle back to the GDI each time it calls a GDI screen output function. Without a valid device context handle, the GDI won't draw the first pixel. And through the device context, the GDI can make sure that everything the program draws is clipped to a particular area of the screen. Device contexts play a huge role in making the GDI device-independent because, given a handle to a device context, the same GDI functions can be used to draw to a diverse assortment of output devices.

When you program Windows with MFC, the device context has an even greater significance. In addition to serving as the key that unlocks the door to the display surface, a device context object encapsulates the GDI functions a program calls to change drawing attributes and produce output. In MFC, you don't grab a handle to a device context and call GDI output functions, at least not directly; instead, you use a device context object and its member functions to do your drawing. MFC's *CDC* class wraps a Windows device context and the GDI functions that require a device context handle into one convenient package, and *CDC*-derived classes such as *CPaintDC* and *CClientDC* represent the different types of device contexts that Windows applications use.

The MFC Device Context Classes

One way to get a device context in an MFC application is to call *CWnd::GetDC*, which returns a pointer to a *CDC* object encapsulating a Windows device context. A device context pointer acquired with *CWnd::GetDC* must be released with *CWnd::ReleaseDC* when drawing is completed to prevent memory leaks. The following code gets a *CDC* pointer from *GetDC*, does some drawing, and calls *ReleaseDC* to release the device context:

```
CDC* pDC = GetDC ();
// Do some drawing
ReleaseDC (pDC);
```

If the same code were to appear in an *OnPaint* handler, *CWnd::BeginPaint* and *CWnd::EndPaint* would be used in place of *GetDC* and *ReleaseDC* to ensure proper handling of the WM_PAINT message:

```
PAINTSTRUCT ps;
CDC* pDC = BeginPaint (&ps);
// Do some drawing
EndPaint (&ps);
```

The GDI also supports the concept of *metafiles,* which store sequences of GDI commands that can be "played back" to produce physical output. To acquire a device context for a metafile's output, you would use yet another set of functions to obtain and release the *CDC* pointer. And to acquire a *CDC* pointer for a device context that permits drawing anywhere in the window (as opposed to one that permits drawing only in the window's client area), you would call *CWnd::GetWindowDC* rather than *GetDC* or *BeginPaint* and release the device context with *ReleaseDC.*

To save you the trouble of having to remember which functions to call to acquire and release a device context (and to help ensure that a device context is released when the message handler that uses the device context ends), MFC provides the *CDC*-derived classes *CPaintDC, CClientDC, CWindowDC,* and *CMetafileDC* representing paint device contexts, client-area device contexts, full-window device contexts, and metafile device contexts. Unlike *CDC,* these classes are designed to be instantiated directly. Each class's constructor and destructor call the appropriate functions to get and release the device context so that using a device context is no more complicated than this:

```
CPaintDC dc (this);
// Do some drawing
```

The pointer passed to the class constructor identifies the window the device context pertains to. When a device context object is constructed on the stack, its destructor is called automatically when the object goes out of scope. And when the destructor is called, the device context is released back to Windows. The only time you need to be concerned about releasing one of these device contexts yourself is when (and if) you create a device context object on the heap with *new*, as shown here:

```
CPaintDC* pDC = new CPaintDC (this);
```

In this case, it's important to execute a

```
delete pDC;
```

statement before the function that created the device context ends so that the object's destructor will be called and the device context will be released. There are occasions when it's useful to create a device context on the heap rather than on the stack, but generally you're a lot better off creating device context objects on the stack and letting the compiler do the deleting for you.

The *CPaintDC* Class

MFC's *CPaintDC* class represents a paint device context and should be used only in *OnPaint* handlers. As you learned in Chapter 1, a window processes WM_PAINT messages with an *OnPaint* handler connected to the messaging system through the message map. WM_PAINT messages are different from all other Windows messages in one very important respect: If the handler fails to call the Windows *::BeginPaint* and *::EndPaint* functions (or the MFC equivalents—*CWnd::BeginPaint* and *CWnd-::EndPaint*), the WM_PAINT message will not be removed from the message queue no matter how much drawing your program does. As a result, the program will get stuck in a loop processing the same WM_PAINT message over and over. *CPaintDC* virtually ensures that this won't happen by calling *::BeginPaint* and *::EndPaint* from its constructor and destructor, respectively.

The receipt of a WM_PAINT message doesn't necessarily mean that the entire window needs repainting. If a WM_PAINT message is generated because one corner of a window that was previously hidden behind another window is exposed, only that corner needs to be updated. Windows keeps track of a window's "invalid" areas and combines them to form an *update region*. The update region could be a simple rectangle, or it could be a complex outline formed from the union of several rectangles. Multiple rectangles sometimes find their way into the update region because WM_PAINT messages are given low priority relative to other messages and are retrieved only when the message queue is empty.

When an application constructs a *CPaintDC* object, *::BeginPaint* fills in the *rcPaint* field of the PAINTSTRUCT structure represented by the public data member *CPaintDC::m_ps* with the coordinates of a bounding box that encloses the update region. Because output to areas outside the update region is clipped, it's sometimes expeditious to optimize WM_PAINT processing by restricting a program's output to the bounding box and avoiding unnecessary GDI calls. *rcPaint* is a RECT structure, which is defined as follows in Winuser.h:

```
struct tagRECT {
    int left;
    int top;
    int right;
    int bottom;
} RECT;
```

rcPaint.left and *rcPaint.right* hold the x coordinates of the bounding rectangle's left and right borders, and *rcPaint.top* and *rcPaint.bottom* hold the y coordinates of the top and bottom borders. The unit of measurement is the pixel. The pixel in the upper left corner of the client area is (0,0), and values of x and y increase as you move right and down, respectively. If a window's client area measures 200 by 200 pixels and the update region is wholly contained in the right lower one-fourth of the window, *rcPaint* will describe a rectangle whose upper left corner is (100,100) and whose lower right corner is (199,199).

The following *OnPaint* function copies the coordinates of the bounding rectangle to a *CRect* object and then uses the *CDC::Rectangle* function to highlight the rectangle. *CRect* is the class MFC provides to represent rectangles. A *CRect* object is similar to a RECT structure, but it includes member functions and operators you can use to manipulate a rectangle and obtain widths, heights, and other information. Note the use of *CRect*'s = operator to initialize a *CRect* object with the coordinates stored in a RECT structure:

```
void CMainWindow::OnPaint ()
{
    CPaintDC dc (this);
    CRect rect = dc.m_ps.rcPaint;
    dc.Rectangle (rect);
}
```

This is a rather trivial use of the information in PAINTSTRUCT's *rcPaint* field, but it's illustrative nonetheless because it demonstrates how you can determine what part of a window needs updating and be selective about where you paint.

The *CClientDC* and *CWindowDC* Classes

Windows programs don't always do their painting by means of *OnPaint*. Suppose you're writing a program that draws a circle on the screen wherever the left mouse button is clicked. One approach to processing button-click messages is to call *CWnd-::Invalidate* or *CWnd::InvalidateRect* to invalidate all or part of the window's client area and let *OnPaint* do the drawing. Unfortunately, this method is inefficient because it might force other circles to be redrawn, too. A better approach is to let the *OnL-ButtonDown* handler that gets called when the left mouse button is pressed down draw the new circle. The resultant program is more responsive because each button click draws just one circle and there's no delay waiting for WM_PAINT messages.

That's what MFC's *CClientDC* class is for. *CClientDC* creates a client-area device context that can be used outside *OnPaint*. The following message handler uses *CClientDC* and two of its member functions to draw an X connecting the corners of the window's client area when the left mouse button is clicked:

```
void CMainWindow::OnLButtonDown (UINT nFlags, CPoint point)
{
    CRect rect;
    GetClientRect (&rect);

    CClientDC dc (this);
    dc.MoveTo (rect.left, rect.top);
    dc.LineTo (rect.right, rect.bottom);
    dc.MoveTo (rect.right, rect.top);
    dc.LineTo (rect.left, rect.bottom);
}
```

MoveTo and *LineTo* are line-drawing functions that *CClientDC* inherits from the *CDC* class. You'll learn more about these two functions in a moment.

For the rare occasions on which you'd like to paint not only the window's client area but the nonclient area, too (the title bar, the window border, and so on), MFC provides the *CWindowDC* class. *CWindowDC* works just as *CClientDC* does, but the device context it represents encompasses everything within the window's borders. Programmers sometimes use *CWindowDC* for unusual effects such as custom-drawn title bars and windows with rounded corners. In general, *CWindowDC* isn't something you'll need very often. If you do want to do your own painting in a window's nonclient area, you can trap WM_NCPAINT messages with an *OnNcPaint* handler to determine when the nonclient area needs to be painted. Unlike *OnPaint*, an *OnNcPaint* handler need not (and should not) call *BeginPaint* and *EndPaint*.

For the even rarer occasions in which a program requires access to the entire screen, you can construct a *CClientDC* or *CWindowDC* object and pass its constructor a NULL pointer instead of a pointer to a window object. The statements

```
CRect rect;
GetClientRect (&rect);

CClientDC dc (NULL);
dc.MoveTo (rect.left, rect.top);
dc.LineTo (rect.right, rect.bottom);
dc.MoveTo (rect.right, rect.top);
dc.LineTo (rect.left, rect.bottom);
```

draw an X that crisscrosses the entire screen. Screen capture programs frequently use full-screen DCs to access the whole screen. Needless to say, drawing outside your own window is a very unfriendly thing to do unless you have a specific reason for doing so.

Drawing with Device Contexts

Once you have a device context in hand, you're ready to start drawing. You've already seen two of the more commonly used *CDC* functions that MFC applications use for screen output. *MoveTo* sets the "current position," an imaginary pointer that specifies a particular point on the display surface. *LineTo* draws a line from the current position to the position specified in the call and automatically updates the current position so that the next line will be drawn from the end of the previous one. The statements

```
dc.MoveTo (100, 100);
dc.LineTo (200, 100);
dc.LineTo (200, 200);
dc.LineTo (100, 200);
dc.LineTo (100, 100);
```

draw a square whose upper left corner is positioned at (100,100) and whose lower right corner lies at (200,200). As this example demonstrates, there's no need to preface every call to *LineTo* with *MoveTo* if the current position is already where you want it. Alternative forms of the *MoveTo* and *LineTo* functions accept POINT structures and *CPoint* objects rather than integers specifying x and y coordinates. If the coordinates of the square's four corners were stored in an array of POINTs or *CPoint*s named *point*, the same square could be drawn like this:

```
dc.MoveTo (point[0]);
dc.LineTo (point[1]);
dc.LineTo (point[2]);
dc.LineTo (point[3]);
dc.LineTo (point[0]);
```

MFC overloads the *MoveTo* and *LineTo* functions so that the compiler will accept parameters of either type.

One peculiarity of the *CDC::LineTo* function is that it draws the pixel at the beginning of the line but doesn't draw the pixel at the end. In other words, if you draw a line from (0,0) to (100,100) with the statements

```
dc.MoveTo (0, 0);
dc.LineTo (100, 100);
```

the pixel at (0,0) will be set to the line color, as will the pixels at (1,1), (2,2), and so on up to and including (99,99). But the pixel at (100,100) will still be the color it was before. If you want the line's final pixel to be set just like the rest of the line, you must set it yourself. One way to do that is to use the *CDC::SetPixel* function, which sets a single pixel to the color you specify.

The *CDC* class also provides functions for drawing simple geometric objects such as circles, ellipses, rectangles, wedges, and splines. These functions are merely thin wrappers around the GDI functions of the same names. Here's a brief list of functions that might be useful to you.

CDC DRAWING FUNCTION SAMPLER

Function	*Description*
Rectangle	Draws a rectangle with square corners.
RoundRect	Draws a rectangle with round (or elliptical) corners.
Ellipse	Draws a circle or an ellipse.
Pie	Draws a pie-shaped wedge.
Polygon	Draws a polygon by connecting an array of points.
PolyBezier	Draws a Bézier spline from an array of points.

Many of these functions take as a parameter the coordinates of a *bounding rectangle* that circumscribes the figure being drawn. When you draw a circle with *CDC::Ellipse*, for example, you don't specify a center point and a radius; instead, you specify the circle's bounding box. The coordinates can be passed explicitly, like this:

```
dc.Ellipse (0, 0, 100, 100);
```

50

or they can be passed in a RECT structure or a *CRect* object, like this:

```
CRect rect (0, 0, 100, 100);
dc.Ellipse (rect);
```

When this circle is drawn, it will touch the $x=0$ line at the left of the bounding box and the $y=0$ line at the top, but it will fall one pixel short of the $x=100$ line at the right and one pixel short of the $y=100$ line at the bottom. In other words, figures are drawn from the left and upper limits of the bounding box up to (but not including) the right and lower limits. If you call the *CDC::Rectangle* function like this:

```
dc.Rectangle (0, 0, 8, 4);
```

you'll get the output shown in Figure 2-1. Observe that the right and lower limits of the rectangle fall at $x=7$ and $y=3$, not $x=8$ and $y=4$.

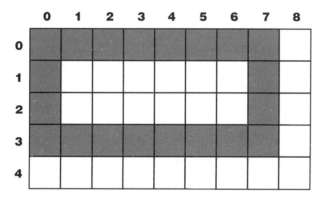

Figure 2-1. *Rectangle drawn with the statement* dc.Rectangle (0, 0, 8, 4).

In all, MFC's *CDC* class provides more than 100 functions to help you draw on a display surface represented by a device context, query the GDI for information about the device context, and change the attributes of your output. If you haven't already, open your MFC reference and browse through the long list of *CDC* member functions. This simple exercise will give you an idea of the breadth of the functions the GDI provides.

Setting the Attributes of a Device Context

When you draw a line, a rectangle, a text string, or another object using *CDC* member functions, certain characteristics of the output aren't specified in the function call but are obtained from the device context itself. When you call *CDC::DrawText*, for example, you specify the text string and the location on the screen at which it will appear. But you don't specify the text color or the font because both are attributes of the device context. If you want to change the font or the text color, you call *CDC* member functions to change the device context's attributes before you call *DrawText*.

The following table lists some of the device context attributes that come into play most often, their default values, and the functions used to access them.

KEY DEVICE CONTEXT ATTRIBUTES

Attribute	Default	Set With	Get With
Text color	Black	*CDC::SetTextColor*	*CDC::GetTextColor*
Background color	White	*CDC::SetBkColor*	*CDC::GetBkColor*
Background mode	OPAQUE	*CDC::SetBkMode*	*CDC::GetBkMode*
Mapping mode	MM_TEXT	*CDC::SetMapMode*	*CDC::GetMapMode*
Drawing mode	R2_COPYPEN	*CDC::SetROP2*	*CDC::GetROP2*
Pen position	(0, 0)	*CDC::MoveTo*	*CDC::GetCurrentPosition*
Pen	BLACK_PEN	*CDC::SelectObject*	*CDC::SelectObject*
Brush	WHITE_BRUSH	*CDC::SelectObject*	*CDC::SelectObject*
Font	SYSTEM_FONT	*CDC::SelectObject*	*CDC::SelectObject*

Some attributes of a device context are specified directly, such as the text color (*CDC::SetTextColor*) and the pen position (*CDC::MoveTo*). Others you specify indirectly by selecting an object into the device context. When you draw a line with *LineTo*, for example, the GDI uses the current pen to determine the line's color, width, and style (solid, dotted, dashed, and so on). Similarly, when you draw a rectangle with the *Rectangle* function, the GDI borders the rectangle with the current pen and fills the rectangle with the current brush. Pens and brushes are GDI objects represented in MFC by the classes *CPen* and *CBrush*. The *CDC::SelectObject* function selects a pen or a brush into a device context. Unless you call *SelectObject* to change the current pen or current brush, GDI uses the device context's default pen and brush. The default pen draws solid black lines 1 pixel wide. The default brush paints solid white. You can create pens and brushes of your own and select them into a device context to change the attributes of the output. If you wanted to draw a solid red circle with a 10-pixel-wide black border, for example, you could create a black pen 10 pixels wide and a red brush and select them into the device context with *SelectObject* before calling *Ellipse*. Assuming that *pPen* is a pointer to the pen object, that *pBrush* is a pointer to the brush object, and that *dc* represents the device context, the code might look like this:

```
dc.SelectObject (pPen);
dc.SelectObject (pBrush);
Ellipse (0, 0, 100, 100);
```

SelectObject is overloaded to accept pointers to objects of various types. Its return value is a pointer to the object of the same type that was previously selected into the device context.

Each time you get a device context from Windows, its attributes are reset to the defaults. Consequently, if you want to use a red pen and a blue brush to paint your window in response to WM_PAINT messages, you must select the pen and brush into the device context each time *OnPaint* is called and a new *CPaintDC* object is created. Otherwise, the default 1-pixel-wide black pen and white brush will be used. If you don't want to have to reinitialize a device context every time you use it, you can save its current state with the *CDC::SaveDC* function and restore it to the same state the next time around with *CDC::RestoreDC*. Another option is to register a custom WNDCLASS that includes the CS_OWNDC style, which causes Windows to allocate each instance of your application its own private device context that retains its settings. (A related but seldom used WNDCLASS style, CS_CLASSDC, allocates all windows created from the same WNDCLASS a private device context that is shared by all.) If you select a red pen and a blue brush into a private device context, those objects remain selected until another pen or brush is selected in.

CS_OWNDC can deliver performance gains if you do your painting in lots of tiny chunks because it eliminates the overhead of repeatedly preparing the DC for painting. But it also increases a program's working set size, so the increase in performance must be balanced against the resultant increase in the application's memory requirements.

Logical vs. Device Coordinates

When an application draws a line from point A to point B, the coordinates passed to *MoveTo* and *LineTo* don't specify physical locations on the screen. Instead, they specify coordinates within a logical coordinate system whose properties are defined by the device context. The GDI translates *logical coordinates* into physical locations on the screen, or *device coordinates,* using equations that factor in the current mapping mode as well as other attributes of the device context. In the device coordinate system, the point (0,0) corresponds to the upper left corner of the device context's display surface, values of x and y increase as you move right and down, and one device unit equals one pixel. In a logical coordinate system, the point (0,0) defaults to the upper left corner of the display surface but can be moved, and the orientation of the x and y axes and the physical distance that corresponds to one unit in the x or y direction are governed by the mapping mode. You can change the mapping mode with the *CDC::SetMapMode* function, and you can move the origin of a logical coordinate system with the *CDC::SetViewportOrg* and *CDC::SetWindowOrg* functions. It's not important to know everything there is to know about mapping modes at this early stage, but developing a fundamental understanding of the relationship between logical and device coordinates early on will save you worlds of time and trouble down the road when you begin to use some of the GDI's more advanced features.

Windows supports eight different mapping modes. Their properties are summarized in the following table.

GDI MAPPING MODES

Mapping Mode	Distance Corresponding to One Logical Unit	Orientation of the x and y Axes
MM_TEXT	1 pixel	→+x ↓+y
MM_LOMETRIC	0.1 mm	→+x ↓-y
MM_HIMETRIC	0.01 mm	→+x ↓-y
MM_LOENGLISH	0.01 in.	→+x ↓-y
MM_HIENGLISH	0.001 in.	→+x ↓-y
MM_TWIPS	$1/1440$ in. (0.0007 in.)	→+x ↓-y
MM_ISOTROPIC	User-defined (x and y scale identically)	User-defined
MM_ANISOTROPIC	User-defined (x and y scale independently)	User-defined

The default MM_TEXT mapping mode is the easiest of all the mapping modes to understand because in that mode, logical coordinates translate directly to device coordinates: one logical unit in the x or y direction equals one pixel on the screen, and values of x and y increase as you move right and down. In MM_TEXT, as in all of the other mapping modes, the origin of the logical coordinate system coincides with the origin of the device coordinate system unless it is moved with *CDC::SetWindowOrg* or *CDC::SetViewportOrg*. For a client-area device context, this means that the pixel in the upper left corner of the window's client area initially has the logical coordinates (0, 0), which produces the coordinate system shown in Figure 2-2.

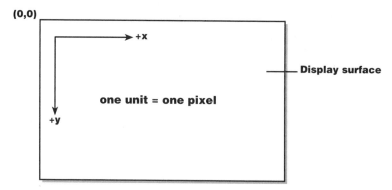

Figure 2-2. *The default MM_TEXT coordinate system.*

If you'd prefer that the origin of the coordinate system be in the center of the display surface rather than in the upper left corner, you can move it with *CDC::Set-WindowOrg* or *CDC::SetViewportOrg*. This option applies to all mapping modes, not just MM_TEXT. If you use *CWnd::GetClientRect* to initialize a *CRect* object named *rect* with the device coordinates of a window's client area and *dc* represents a client-area device context, the statement

```
dc.SetViewportOrg (rect.Width () / 2, rect.Height () / 2);
```

moves the origin of the coordinate system to the center of the client area. If the mapping mode is MM_TEXT, the statement

```
dc.SetWindowOrg (-rect.Width () / 2, -rect.Height () / 2);
```

has the same effect. It's easy to get *SetViewportOrg* and *SetWindowOrg* confused, but the distinction between them is actually quite clear. Changing the "viewport" origin to (x, y) with *SetViewportOrg* tells the GDI to map the logical point (0,0) to the device point (x, y), where x and y specify a pixel distance from the upper left corner of the display surface. Changing the "window" origin to (x, y) by means of *SetWindowOrg* does the reverse, telling the GDI to map the logical point (x, y) to the upper left corner of the display surface (the device point (0,0)). In the MM_TEXT mapping mode, the only real difference between the two functions is the signs of x and y. In other mapping modes, there's a little more to it than that because *SetViewportOrg* deals in device coordinates and *SetWindowOrg* deals in logical coordinates. You'll see examples of how both functions are used later in this book. One of those examples will come up later in this chapter, when we use *SetWindowOrg* to move the origin of the coordinate system in preparation for drawing in a window containing a scroll bar.

The other mapping modes use other means of translating logical coordinates into device coordinates and orient the axes differently. In the MM_LOMETRIC mapping mode, for example, one logical unit corresponds to a distance of 0.1 millimeter on the display surface, and values of x and y increase as you move right and up. MM_LOMETRIC, MM_HIMETRIC, MM_LOENGLISH, MM_HIENGLISH, and MM_TWIPS work with physical distances rather than pixel counts to make a program's output independent of the display resolution. A 100-unit line drawn in one of these mapping modes will be roughly the same length on any screen, but a 100-unit line drawn on a 640-by-480 display in the MM_TEXT mapping mode will be about half as long as the same line drawn on a 1,280-by-1,024 display.

MM_ISOTROPIC and MM_ANISOTROPIC are do-it-yourself mapping modes that give you the freedom to define not only the origin of the coordinate system, but also the orientation of its axes and the scaling factors used to translate logical units to device units. The only difference between the two is that the scaling factors for the x and y directions are always the same in the MM_ISOTROPIC mapping mode but can differ in the MM_ANISOTROPIC mapping mode. There's much more that could be said about mapping modes that I'll leave unsaid for now to avoid getting bogged down in the details. We'll discuss mapping modes again in Chapter 7, and in one of that chapter's sample applications we'll use the MM_ISOTROPIC mapping mode to create a custom coordinate system that scales dynamically to match the size of the client area.

GDI Pens and the *CPen* Class

The GDI provides a number of API functions an application can call to create custom pens and brushes, including *::CreatePen*, *::CreateSolidBrush*, *::CreateHatchBrush*, and *::CreatePatternBrush*. MFC wraps these functions in the *CPen* and *CBrush* classes so pens and brushes can be dealt with as objects rather than through the raw handles the GDI provides.

MFC represents pens with objects of the class *CPen*. The simplest way to create a GDI pen is to construct a *CPen* object and pass it the parameters defining the pen:

```
CPen pen (PS_SOLID, 1, RGB (255, 0, 0));
```

A second way to create a GDI pen is to construct an uninitialized *CPen* object and call *CPen::CreatePen*.

```
CPen pen;
pen.CreatePen (PS_SOLID, 1, RGB (255, 0, 0));
```

Yet a third method is to construct an uninitialized *CPen* object, fill in a LOGPEN structure describing the pen, and then call *CPen::CreatePenIndirect* to create the pen:

```
CPen pen;
LOGPEN lp;
lp.lopnStyle = PS_SOLID;
lp.lopnWidth = 1;
lp.lopnColor = RGB (255, 0, 0);
pen.CreatePenIndirect (&lp);
```

CreatePen and *CreatePenIndirect* return TRUE if a pen is successfully created, FALSE if it is not. If you allow the object's constructor to create the pen, an exception of type *CResourceException* is thrown if the pen can't be created. This should happen only if the system is critically low on memory.

A pen has three defining characteristics: style, width, and color. All three of these examples create a pen whose style is PS_SOLID, whose width is 1 logical unit, and whose color is bright red. The first of the three parameters passed to the *CPen* constructor, *CreatePen*, or *CreatePenIndirect* specifies the pen style, which defines the type of line the pen will draw. PS_SOLID creates a pen that draws solid, unbroken lines. The other pen styles, which are illustrated in Figure 2-3, include PS_DASH, which draws dashed lines; PS_DOT, which draws dotted lines; PS_DASHDOT, which draws lines composed of alternating dashes and dots; PS_DASHDOTDOT, which draws lines with alternating dashes and double dots; and PS_NULL, which creates a NULL pen

PS_SOLID ─────────────────────

PS_DASH ─ ─ ─ ─ ─ ─ ─ ─ ─

PS_DOT - - - - - - - - - - - - -

PS_DASHDOT ─·──·──·──·──·

PS_DASHDOTDOT ─··──··──··──··

PS_NULL

PS_INSIDEFRAME ─────────────────

Figure 2-3. *The pen styles.*

that draws nothing. The special PS_INSIDEFRAME style draws solid lines that stay within the bounding rectangle, or "inside the frame," of the figure being drawn. Draw a circle whose diameter is 100 units with a PS_SOLID pen that is 20 units wide with any of the other pen styles, for example, and the actual diameter of the circle, measured from any point on the circle's outside edge to the point diametrically opposed to it on the other side, will be 120 units, as shown in Figure 2-4. Why? Because the border drawn by the pen will extend 10 units outward on either side of the theoretical circle. Draw the same circle with a PS_INSIDEFRAME pen, and the diameter will be exactly 100 units. The PS_INSIDEFRAME style does not affect lines drawn with *LineTo* and other functions that don't use a bounding rectangle.

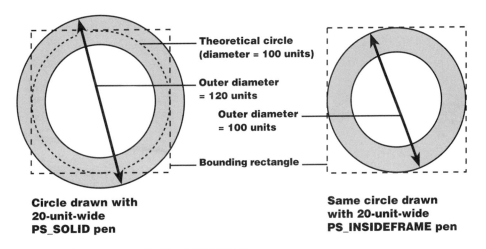

Circle drawn with 20-unit-wide PS_SOLID pen

Theoretical circle (diameter = 100 units)

Outer diameter = 120 units

Outer diameter = 100 units

Bounding rectangle

Same circle drawn with 20-unit-wide PS_INSIDEFRAME pen

Figure 2-4. *Drawing with PS_INSIDEFRAME.*

Why would you ever want to create a NULL pen? Believe it or not, there are times when a NULL pen comes in handy. Suppose, for example, that you want to draw a solid red circle with no border. If you draw the circle with MFC's *CDC::Ellipse* function, Windows will automatically border the circle with the pen currently selected into the device context. You can't tell the *Ellipse* function you don't want a border, but you *can* select a NULL pen into the device context so that the circle will have no visible border. NULL brushes are used in a similar way. If you wanted the circle to have a border but wanted the interior of the circle to be transparent, you could select a NULL brush into the device context before doing your drawing.

The second parameter passed to *CPen*'s pen-create functions specifies the pen width—the width of the lines the pen will draw. Pen widths are specified in logical units whose physical meanings depend on the mapping mode. You can create PS_SOLID, PS_NULL, and PS_INSIDEFRAME pens of any logical width, but PS_DASH, PS_DOT, PS_DASHDOT, and PS_DASHDOTDOT pens must be one logical unit in width. Specifying a pen width of 0 in any style creates a pen that is 1 pixel wide, no matter what the mapping mode.

The third and final parameter specified when a pen is created is the pen's color. Windows uses a 24-bit RGB color model in which each possible color is defined by red, green, and blue color values from 0 through 255. The higher the value, the brighter the corresponding color component. The RGB macro combines values specifying the three independent color components into one COLORREF value that can be passed to the GDI. The statement

```
CPen pen (PS_SOLID, 1, RGB (255, 0, 0));
```

creates a bright red pen (red=255, green=0, and blue=0), while the statement

```
CPen pen (PS_SOLID, 1, RGB (255, 255, 0));
```

creates a bright yellow pen by combining red and green. If the display adapter doesn't support 24-bit color, Windows compensates by dithering colors it can't display directly. Only PS_INSIDEFRAME pens greater than one logical unit in width can use dithered colors. For the other pen styles, Windows maps the color of the pen to the nearest solid color that can be displayed. You can be reasonably certain of getting the exact color you want on all adapters by sticking to "primary" color combinations—combinations of red, green, and blue values equal to 0, 128, or 255. These primary colors are part of the basic palette Windows programs into the color registers of every video adapter in the interest of making sure that a common subset of colors is available to any program running on any kind of hardware.

Windows predefines three special solid, 1-pixel-wide pens you can use without explicitly creating a pen object. Called *stock pens,* these pens belong to a group of GDI objects known as *stock objects* and are "created" with the *CreateStockObject* function a pen object inherits from *CGdiObject*. Stock pens are identified by the constants

WHITE_PEN, BLACK_PEN, and NULL_PEN. WHITE_PEN is a solid white pen, BLACK-_PEN is a solid black pen, and NULL_PEN is a NULL pen. The statements

```
CPen pen;
pen.CreateStockObject (WHITE_PEN);
```

create a white pen. Lines drawn by this pen are identical to lines drawn with the following pen:

```
CPen pen;
pen.CreatePen (PS_SOLID, 0, RGB (255, 255, 255));
```

BLACK_PEN is the default pen initially selected into every device context. That's why functions such as *CDC::LineTo* draw black lines 1 pixel wide if a pen isn't selected first. Stock pens may be selected directly into a device context, without being created first, by a call to *CDC::SelectStockObject*. The statement

```
dc.SelectStockObject (WHITE_PEN);
```

selects WHITE_PEN directly into the device context.

In case none of the basic pen styles fits your needs, the *CPen* class provides a separate constructor for "cosmetic" and "geometric" pens that support a wider variety of styling options. You can create a geometric pen, for example, that draws a pattern described by a bitmap image, and you can exercise precise control over endpoints and joins by specifying the end cap style (flat, round, or square) and join style (beveled, mitered, or rounded). The following code creates a geometric pen 16 units wide and draws solid green lines with flat ends. Where two lines meet, the adjoining ends are rounded to form a smooth intersection:

```
LOGBRUSH lb;
lb.lbStyle = BS_SOLID;
lb.lbColor = RGB (0, 255, 0);
CPen pen (PS_GEOMETRIC | PS_SOLID | PS_ENDCAP_FLAT |
    PS_JOIN_ROUND, 16, &lb);
```

Windows 95 places several restrictions on the use of cosmetic and geometric pens, not the least of which is that for the endpoint and join styles to work, figures must first be drawn as "paths" and then rendered with *CDC::StrokePath* or a related function. You define a path by enclosing drawing commands between calls to *CDC::Begin-Path* and *CDC::EndPath*, as shown here:

```
dc.BeginPath ();      // Begin the path definition
dc.MoveTo (0, 0);     // "Draw" a rectangle
dc.LineTo (100, 0);
dc.LineTo (100, 100);
dc.LineTo (0, 100);
dc.CloseFigure ();
dc.EndPath ();        // End the path definition
dc.StrokePath ();     // Draw the path using the current pen
```

Paths are a powerful feature of the GDI that can be used for all sorts of interesting effects. We'll look at paths more closely—and at the *CDC* functions that use them—in Chapter 12.

GDI Brushes and the *CBrush* Class

MFC's *CBrush* class encapsulates GDI brushes. Brushes come in three basic varieties: solid brushes, hatch brushes, and pattern brushes. Solid brushes paint with solid colors. If your display hardware won't allow a particular solid brush color to be displayed directly, Windows simulates the color by dithering colors that *can* be displayed. A hatch brush paints with one of six predefined hatch styles modeled after hatching patterns used in engineering and architectural drawings. A pattern brush paints with a bitmap. The *CBrush* class provides a constructor for each different brush style.

You can create a solid brush in one step by passing a COLORREF value to the *CBrush* constructor:

```
CBrush brush (RGB (255, 0, 0));
```

Or you can create a solid brush in two steps by creating an uninitialized *CBrush* object and calling *CBrush::CreateSolidBrush*:

```
CBrush brush;
brush.CreateSolidBrush (RGB (255, 0, 0));
```

Both examples create a solid brush that paints bright red. You can also create a brush by initializing a LOGBRUSH structure and calling *CBrush::CreateBrushIndirect*. As with *CPen* constructors, all *CBrush* constructors that create a brush for you throw a resource exception if the GDI is critically low on memory and a brush can't be created.

Hatch brushes are created by passing *CBrush*'s constructor both a hatch index and a COLORREF value, or by calling *CBrush::CreateHatchBrush*. The statement

```
CBrush brush (HS_DIAGCROSS, RGB (255, 0, 0));
```

creates a hatch brush that paints perpendicular crosshatch lines oriented at 45 degree angles, as do the statements

```
CBrush brush;
brush.CreateHatchBrush (HS_DIAGCROSS, RGB (255, 0, 0));
```

HS_DIAGCROSS is one of six hatch styles you can choose from (see Figure 2-5). When painting with a hatch brush, Windows fills the space between hatch lines with the default background color (white) unless you change the device context's current background color with *CDC::SetBkColor* or turn off background fills by changing the background mode from OPAQUE to TRANSPARENT with *CDC::SetBkMode*. The statements

```
CBrush brush (HS_DIAGCROSS, RGB (255, 255, 255));
dc.SelectObject (&brush);
dc.SetBkColor (RGB (192, 192, 192));
dc.Rectangle (0, 0, 100, 100);
```

draw a rectangle 100 units square and fill it with white crosshatch lines drawn against a light gray background. The statements

```
CBrush brush (HS_DIAGCROSS, RGB (0, 0, 0));
dc.SelectObject (&brush);
dc.SetBkMode (TRANSPARENT);
dc.Rectangle (0, 0, 100, 100);
```

draw a black crosshatched rectangle against the existing background. The background color and background mode also determine how Windows fills the gaps in lines drawn with stylized pens (pens that aren't solid, such as PS_DASH) and fills behind the characters in text strings.

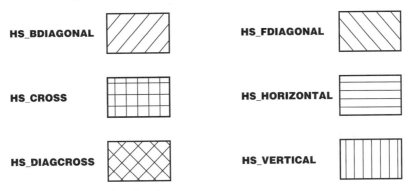

Figure 2-5. *Hatch brush styles.*

Windows makes seven stock brushes available: BLACK_BRUSH, DKGRAY-_BRUSH, GRAY_BRUSH, LTGRAY_BRUSH, HOLLOW_BRUSH, NULL_BRUSH, and WHITE_BRUSH. All are solid brushes, and in each case the identifier is an accurate indicator of the brush's color. HOLLOW_BRUSH and NULL_BRUSH are two different ways of referring to the same thing: a brush that paints nothing. WHITE_BRUSH is a device context's default brush. Like stock pens, stock brushes can be "created" with *CGdiObject::CreateStockObject* or selected into a device context directly with *CDC::SelectStockObject*.

The Brush Origin

One attribute of a device context you should be aware of when using dithered brush colors or hatch brushes is the brush origin. When Windows fills an area with a hatched or dithered brush pattern, it tiles an 8-by-8 pattern of pixels horizontally and vertically within the affected area. By default, the origin for this pattern, better known as the *brush origin,* is the device point (0,0)—the screen pixel that corresponds to the upper left corner of the device context. This means that a pattern drawn in a rectangle that begins, say, 100 pixels to the right of and below the origin will be aligned somewhat differently with respect to the rectangle's border than a pattern drawn in a rectangle positioned a few pixels to the left or right, as shown in Figure 2-6. In many applications, it doesn't matter; the user isn't likely to notice minute differences in brush alignment. However, in some instances it matters a great deal. Suppose you're using a hatch brush to fill a rectangle and you're animating the motion of that rectangle by repeatedly erasing it and redrawing it one pixel to the right or left. If you don't reset the brush origin to a point that stays in the same position relative to the rectangle before each redraw, the hatch pattern will "walk" inside the rectangle.

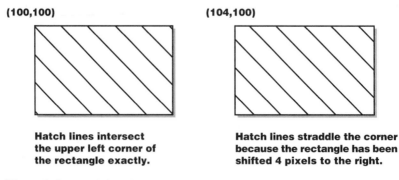

(100,100)   **(104,100)**

Hatch lines intersect   **Hatch lines straddle the corner**
the upper left corner of   **because the rectangle has been**
the rectangle exactly.   **shifted 4 pixels to the right.**

Figure 2-6. *Hatch brush alignment.*

The solution? Before selecting the brush into the device context and drawing the rectangle, call *CDC::SetBrushOrg* to set the brush origin to the rectangle's upper left corner, as shown here:

```
CPoint point (x1, y1);
dc.LPtoDP (&point);
point.x %= 8;
point.y %= 8;
dc.SetBrushOrg (point);
dc.SelectObject (brush);
dc.Rectangle (x1, y1, x2, y2);
```

point is a *CPoint* object that holds the logical coordinates of the rectangle's upper left corner. *LPtoDP* is called to convert logical coordinates into device coordinates (brush origins are always specified in device coordinates), and a modulo-8 operation is performed on the resulting x and y coordinates because values passed to *SetBrushOrg* must be from 0 through 7. After *SetBrushOrg* is called to set the new brush origin, the hatch pattern will be aligned consistently no matter where in the window the rectangle is drawn.

Deleting Pens and Brushes

Pens and brushes are GDI resources that consume space in memory, so it's important to delete them when you're finished with them. If you create a *CPen* or a *CBrush* on the stack frame, the associated GDI object is automatically deleted by the class destructor when the *CPen* or *CBrush* object goes out of scope. If you create a pen or a brush with C++'s *new* operator, be sure to delete the object at some point so that its destructor will be called. The GDI pen or brush associated with a *CPen* or *CBrush* object can also be deleted by calling *CGdiObject::DeleteObject*. Stock pens and brushes don't need to be deleted, even if they are "created" with *CreateStockObject*.

In previous versions of Windows, pens and brushes were frequent contributors to the problem of resource leakage, in which the Free System Resources figure reported by Program Manager gradually decreased as applications were started and terminated because some programs failed to delete the GDI objects they created. Windows 95 alleviates the problem by tracking the resources a program allocates and deleting them when the program ends. However, it's *still* important to delete GDI objects when they're no longer needed so that the GDI doesn't run out of resource space before a program terminates. Imagine an *OnPaint* handler that creates four pens and brushes every time it's called but neglects to delete them. By the time the program has redrawn its window a few hundred times, *OnPaint* will have created several hundred GDI objects occupying space in system memory owned by the GDI. Pretty soon the application's *OnPaint* handler will stop working because the GDI will run out of space, and calls to create pens and brushes will mysteriously fail. Get rid of pens and brushes as soon as you can, and you'll avoid this problem. If your application uses the same pens and brushes over and over, you can improve its painting performance just a bit by creating the pens and brushes early in the program's lifetime and deleting them just before the program ends. Create them in the window's class constructor or in its *OnCreate* handler, and destroy them in the class destructor or in its *OnDestroy* handler. The only drawback to this approach is that it limits the GDI resources available to other programs. That shouldn't be a factor unless Windows grows critically short of memory.

If you're developing an MFC application with Visual C++, there's an easy way to tell whether you're failing to delete pens, brushes, or other resources: Simply run a debug build of your application in debugging mode. When the application terminates, resources that weren't freed will be listed in the debugging window. MFC tracks memory allocations for *CPen*, *CBrush*, and other *CObject*-derived classes so that it can notify you when an object hasn't been deleted. If you have difficulty ascertaining from the debug messages which objects weren't deleted, add the statement

```
#define new DEBUG_NEW
```

to your application's source code files after the *#include <afxwin.b>* statement that loads the main MFC header file. Debug messages for unfreed objects will then include line numbers and file names to help you pinpoint the sources of leaks. Make it a practice to check for resource leaks at various stages during the development of an application, and you can be reasonably certain that the code you ship out the door cleans up after itself properly.

As you write code that draws with GDI pens and brushes, keep in mind the cardinal rule of GDI programming: *never delete a GDI object that is selected into a device context*. Many Windows programmers make it a practice to save the pointer returned by *SelectObject* and use that pointer to reselect the original object before allowing the object that was selected into the device context to be deleted. An alternative approach is to select a stock pen or stock brush into the device context before deleting the pens and brushes you created. The first of these two methods is illustrated by the following code:

```
CPen* pMyPen = new CPen (PS_SOLID, 1, RGB (255, 0, 0));
CPen* pOldPen = dc.SelectObject (pMyPen);
// Draw with the pen
dc.SelectObject (pOldPen);
delete pMyPen;
```

The second method works like this:

```
CPen* pMyPen = new CPen (PS_SOLID, 1, RGB (255, 0, 0));
dc.SelectObject (pMyPen);
// Draw with the pen
dc.SelectStockObject (BLACK_PEN);
delete pMyPen;
```

Which of the two methods you choose is up to you. The second might be preferable if you're selecting several pens or brushes into the device context and the structure of your code makes it difficult to determine which one will be selected first. If you select a stock object into the device context, it won't matter what was selected in the device context originally.

Since the *SelectObject* function returns a pointer to the object selected out of the device context, it might be tempting to try to select an object out and delete it in one step, like this:

```
delete dc.SelectObject (pOldPen);
```

But don't do it. It works fine with pens, but it might not work with brushes. Why? Because if you create two identical *CBrush*es, Windows 95 conserves memory by creating just one GDI brush and you'll wind up with two *CBrush* pointers referencing the same HBRUSH. (An HBRUSH is a handle that uniquely identifies a GDI brush, just as an HWND identifies a window and an HDC identifies a device context. A *CBrush* wraps an HBRUSH and stores the HBRUSH handle in its *m_hObject* data member.) Because *CDC::SelectObject* uses an internal table maintained by the framework to convert the HBRUSH handle returned by *::SelectObject* to a *CBrush* pointer, and because that table assumes a 1-to-1 mapping between HBRUSHes and *CBrush*es, the *CBrush* pointer you get back may not match the *CBrush* pointer returned by *new*. Be sure you pass *delete* the pointer returned by *new*. Then both the GDI object and the C++ object will be properly destroyed.

The GdiDemo1 Application

The best way to learn about the GDI and about the MFC classes that encapsulate its services is to write code. Let's start with a very simple application. Figure 2-7 contains the source code for GdiDemo1, which draws lines and rectangles with pens and brushes of various types. The output is organized into three sections: Pen Styles, Pen Widths, and Brush Styles. Under Pen Styles, you'll find lines drawn with 1-pixel-wide pens of assorted styles. The Pen Widths section depicts varying pen widths, ranging from a low of 2 pixels through a high of 24. Finally, the Brush Styles section contains filled rectangles illustrating the six hatch patterns that *CBrush* supports as well as a solid-colored brush. Though GdiDemo1 makes only the simplest use of pens and brushes, it very clearly demonstrates the steps one goes through to create a GDI object, select it into a device context, and draw with it. It also paints a meaningful picture of the numerous pen and brush styles that Windows puts at your disposal.

GdiDemo1.rc

```
//*************************************************************************
//
//  GdiDemo1.rc
//
//*************************************************************************

#include <afxres.h>

AFX_IDI_STD_FRAME ICON GdiDemo.ico
```

GdiDemo1.h

```
//*************************************************************************
//
//  GdiDemo1.h
//
//*************************************************************************

class CMyApp : public CWinApp
{
public:
    virtual BOOL InitInstance ();
};

class CMainWindow : public CFrameWnd
{
private:
```

Figure 2-7. *The GdiDemo1 source code.*

(continued)

GdiDemo1.h *continued*

```
    int m_cxChar;
    int m_cyChar;

    void ShowPenStyles (CDC*, int, int);
    void ShowPenWidths (CDC*, int, int);
    void ShowBrushStyles (CDC*, int, int);

public:
    CMainWindow ();

protected:
    afx_msg int OnCreate (LPCREATESTRUCT);
    afx_msg void OnPaint ();

    DECLARE_MESSAGE_MAP ()
};

struct STYLES {
    int nStyle;
    char szStyleName[16];
};
```

GdiDemo1.cpp

```
//*********************************************************************
//
//  GdiDemo1.cpp
//
//*********************************************************************

#include <afxwin.h>
#include "GdiDemo1.h"

CMyApp myApp;

/////////////////////////////////////////////////////////////////////
// CMyApp member functions

BOOL CMyApp::InitInstance ()
{
    m_pMainWnd = new CMainWindow;
    m_pMainWnd->ShowWindow (m_nCmdShow);
    m_pMainWnd->UpdateWindow ();
    return TRUE;
}
```

```
///////////////////////////////////////////////////////////////////////
// CMainWindow message map and member functions

BEGIN_MESSAGE_MAP (CMainWindow, CFrameWnd)
    ON_WM_CREATE ()
    ON_WM_PAINT ()
END_MESSAGE_MAP ()

CMainWindow::CMainWindow ()
{
    Create (NULL, "GdiDemo1");
}

int CMainWindow::OnCreate (LPCREATESTRUCT lpcs)
{
    if (CFrameWnd::OnCreate (lpcs) == -1)
        return -1;

    TEXTMETRIC tm;
    CClientDC dc (this);
    dc.GetTextMetrics (&tm);
    m_cxChar = tm.tmAveCharWidth;
    m_cyChar = tm.tmHeight;
    return 0;
}

void CMainWindow::OnPaint ()
{
    CPaintDC dc (this);

    ShowPenStyles (&dc, m_cxChar * 2, m_cyChar);
    ShowPenWidths (&dc, m_cxChar * 2, m_cyChar * 15);
    ShowBrushStyles (&dc, m_cxChar * 2, m_cyChar * 27);
}

void CMainWindow::ShowPenStyles (CDC* pDC, int x, int y)
{
    static struct STYLES styles[] = {
        PS_SOLID,       "PS_SOLID",
        PS_DASH,        "PS_DASH",
        PS_DOT,         "PS_DOT",
        PS_DASHDOT,     "PS_DASHDOT",
        PS_DASHDOTDOT,  "PS_DASHDOTDOT",
        PS_NULL,        "PS_NULL",
        PS_INSIDEFRAME, "PS_INSIDEFRAME"
    };
```

(continued)

GdiDemo1.cpp *continued*

```cpp
    pDC->SetTextColor (RGB (0, 0, 0));
    pDC->TextOut (x, y, "Pen Styles");

    int dy = (m_cyChar * 3) / 2;
    int x1 = x + (m_cxChar * 2);
    int x2 = x + (m_cxChar * 22);
    int x3 = x + (m_cxChar * 46);

    CPen* pOldPen;
    pDC->SetTextColor (RGB (255, 0, 0));

    for (int i=0; i<7; i++) {
        y += dy;
        pDC->TextOut (x1, y, styles[i].szStyleName);

        CPen pen (styles[i].nStyle, 1, RGB (255, 0, 0));
        pOldPen = pDC->SelectObject (&pen);

        pDC->MoveTo (x2, y + (m_cyChar / 2));
        pDC->LineTo (x3, y + (m_cyChar / 2));

        pDC->SelectObject (pOldPen);
    }
}

void CMainWindow::ShowPenWidths (CDC* pDC, int x, int y)
{
    static int nPenWidths[] = { 2, 8, 16, 24 };

    pDC->SetTextColor (RGB (0, 0, 0));
    pDC->TextOut (x, y, "Pen Widths");

    int dy = m_cyChar * 2;
    int x1 = x + (m_cxChar * 2);
    int x2 = x + (m_cxChar * 22);
    int x3 = x + (m_cxChar * 46);

    CPen* pOldPen;
    CString strDescription;
    pDC->SetTextColor (RGB (0, 0, 255));

    for (int i=0; i<4; i++) {
        y += dy;
        strDescription.Format ("%d Pixels", nPenWidths[i]);
        pDC->TextOut (x1, y, strDescription);
```

```
        CPen pen (PS_SOLID, nPenWidths[i], RGB (0, 0, 255));
        pOldPen = pDC->SelectObject (&pen);

        pDC->MoveTo (x2, y + (m_cyChar / 2));
        pDC->LineTo (x3, y + (m_cyChar / 2));

        pDC->SelectObject (pOldPen);
    }
}

void CMainWindow::ShowBrushStyles (CDC* pDC, int x, int y)
{
    static struct STYLES styles[] = {
        HS_BDIAGONAL,   "HS_BDIAGONAL",
        HS_CROSS,       "HS_CROSS",
        HS_DIAGCROSS,   "HS_DIAGCROSS",
        HS_FDIAGONAL,   "HS_FDIAGONAL",
        HS_HORIZONTAL,  "HS_HORIZONTAL",
        HS_VERTICAL,    "HS_VERTICAL"
    };

    pDC->SetTextColor (RGB (0, 0, 0));
    pDC->TextOut (x, y, "Brush Styles");

    int dy = m_cyChar * 3;
    int x1 = x + (m_cxChar * 2);
    int x2 = x + (m_cxChar * 22);
    int x3 = x + (m_cxChar * 46);

    CBrush* pOldBrush;

    for (int i=0; i<6; i++) {
        y += dy;
        pDC->TextOut (x1, y, styles[i].szStyleName);

        CRect rect (x2, y - m_cyChar, x3, y + m_cyChar);
        CBrush brush (styles[i].nStyle, RGB (0, 255, 0));

        CPoint point (rect.left, rect.top);
        pDC->LPtoDP (&point);
        point.x %= 8;
        point.y %= 8;
        pDC->SetBrushOrg (point);
```

(continued)

GdiDemo1.cpp *continued*

```
        pOldBrush = pDC->SelectObject (&brush);
        pDC->Rectangle (rect);

        pDC->SelectObject (pOldBrush);
    }


    y += dy;
    pDC->TextOut (x1, y, "Solid");

    CBrush brush (RGB (0, 255, 0));
    pOldBrush = pDC->SelectObject (&brush);
    pDC->Rectangle (x2, y - m_cyChar, x3, y + m_cyChar);
    pDC->SelectObject (pOldBrush);
}
```

The structure of GdiDemo1 is similar to that of the Hello application presented in Chapter 1. The *CMyApp* class represents the application itself. *CMyApp::InitInstance* creates a frame window by constructing a *CMainWindow* object, and *CMainWindow*'s constructor calls *CFrameWnd::Create* to create the window you see on the screen. *CMainWindow::OnPaint* handles all the drawing by calling the private member functions *ShowPenStyles*, *ShowPenWidths*, and *ShowBrushStyles*. Each of these functions accepts a pointer to a device context object *pDC* and the *x* and *y* coordinates where drawing will begin. *OnPaint* creates a paint device context object named *dc* by instantiating the *CPaintDC* class and then passes the object's address to *ShowPenStyles*, *ShowPenWidths*, and *ShowBrushStyles*, along with *x* and *y* coordinates specifying pixel positions in the window's client area. The resulting output is shown in Figure 2-8.

The *OnCreate* Function

Shortly after a window is created but before it is actually displayed, it receives a WM_CREATE message. In an MFC application, the WM_CREATE message is mapped to a member function named *OnCreate* with an ON_WM_CREATE message map entry. *OnCreate* receives one argument: a pointer to a CREATESTRUCT structure containing information about the window that was just created, including its initial screen position and size. *OnCreate* is where most Windows applications place the bulk of their initialization code. If an initialization fails that would prevent the application from running properly, *OnCreate* can return −1 to shut the application down. A 0 return allows the application to proceed. When you override *CFrameWnd::OnCreate*, you should make it a practice to call the base class's *OnCreate* handler before executing any code of your own and returning −1 if *CFrameWnd::OnCreate* returns −1. This is especially important in document/view applications, where *CFrameWnd::OnCreate* is charged with such critical tasks as creating the view that appears inside a frame window.

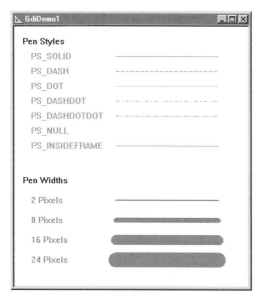

Figure 2-8. *The GdiDemo1 window.*

An *OnCreate* handler is an excellent place for an application to perform initializations that depend on the existence of a window. After calling *CFrameWnd-::OnCreate* and checking the return value, *CMainWindow::OnCreate* initializes a pair of private data members named *m_cxChar* and *m_cyChar* with the width and height of a character in the device context's default font:

```
TEXTMETRIC tm;
CClientDC dc (this);
dc.GetTextMetrics (&tm);
m_cxChar = tm.tmAveCharWidth;
m_cyChar = tm.tmHeight;
```

CDC::GetTextMetrics initializes a TEXTMETRIC structure with information about the font that is selected into the device context. The TEXTMETRIC structure contains a number of fields, but the two we're interested in are *tmAveCharWidth* and *tmHeight*, which define the average width of a character—a device context's default font is proportionally spaced, so individual character widths differ—and the height of the cell in which each character is drawn. These are the fields whose values are copied to *m_cxChar* and *m_cyChar*. If you browse through the source code for *CMainWindow*, you'll see that *m_cxChar* and *m_cyChar* are referenced repeatedly. The former is used as a reference distance for spacing GdiDemo1's output in the horizontal direction, and the latter as a reference distance for spacing the output vertically. Since the font's pixel dimensions may vary from one video driver to the next, using font dimensions rather than hardcoded pixel counts ensures that GdiDemo1's output will be reasonably uniform on every PC it is run on.

Could *CMainWindow* be rewritten so that it initializes *m_cxChar* and *m_cyChar* in its constructor rather than in *OnCreate*? It could, but if you choose to go that route there's a common trap you should avoid that ensnares many beginning MFC programmers. Suppose the constructor were rewritten to read

```
TEXTMETRIC tm;
CClientDC dc (this);
dc.GetTextMetrics (&tm);
m_cxChar = tm.tmAveCharWidth;
m_cyChar = tm.tmHeight;
Create (NULL, "GdiDemo1");
```

Can you spot what's wrong with this code? Because the window doesn't exist before the call to *Create* is placed, the *m_hWnd* data member of the window class won't hold a valid window handle and *CClientDC* won't be properly initialized. In a debug build of your code, you'll get an assertion error from MFC alerting you to that fact. In a retail build, the application will work, but only by coincidence. *CClientDC*'s constructor will end up passing a NULL window handle to *::GetDC*, and *::GetDC*, which is one of only a handful of Windows API functions that will accept a NULL window handle, will return a handle to a full-screen device context rather than to a client-area device context. Here's the proper way to write a constructor that initializes *m_cxChar* and *m_cyChar*:

```
Create (NULL, "GdiDemo1");
TEXTMETRIC tm;
CClientDC dc (this);
dc.GetTextMetrics (&tm);
m_cxChar = tm.tmAveCharWidth;
m_cyChar = tm.tmHeight;
```

Now *CClientDC* will be initialized properly, and so, too, will *m_cxChar* and *m_cyChar*.

The *ShowPenStyles* Function

GdiDemo1 performs all of its screen output in response to WM_PAINT messages. The first of the three *CMainWindow* member functions that *OnPaint* calls to do the drawing is *ShowPenStyles*, which creates seven pens of the various styles and uses each to draw a horizontal line 1 pixel wide. The bulk of the drawing is done in a *for* loop that retrieves pen styles (and text strings describing those styles) from the statically declared *styles* array:

```
for (int i=0; i<7; i++) {
    y += dy;
    pDC->TextOut (x1, y, styles[i].szStyleName);

    CPen pen (styles[i].nStyle, 1, RGB (255, 0, 0));
    pOldPen = pDC->SelectObject (&pen);

    pDC->MoveTo (x2, y + (m_cyChar / 2));
```

```
    pDC->LineTo (x3, y + (m_cyChar / 2));

    pDC->SelectObject (pOldPen);
}
```

Each pass through the loop, *ShowPenStyles* increments the value of *y* by *dy* (which equals *m_cyChar* * 3 / 2) to achieve interline spacing. It then displays the next style name in the *styles* array, creates a pen, selects the pen into the device context, and draws a line. Afterward, it selects the default pen, whose address was copied to *pOldPen*, back into the device context. Because it was created on the stack, the pen used to draw the line is automatically deleted before the next iteration begins.

ShowPenStyles introduces another *CDC* member function an application can use for text output. *CDC::TextOut* is similar to but more rudimentary than *CDC::DrawText*, and it's perfect for drawing single lines of text in a window when no special formatting is required. By default, the coordinates passed to *TextOut* specify the position of the upper left corner of the string's leftmost character cell. However, the relationship between the coordinates passed to *TextOut* and the characters in the output string, a property known as the *text alignment*, is an attribute of the device context and can be changed with *CDC::SetTextAlign*. For example, after a

```
    pDC->SetTextAlign (TA_RIGHT);
```

statement is executed, the *x* coordinate passed to *TextOut* specifies the rightmost position in the character cell—perfect for drawing right-aligned text.

SetTextAlign can also be called with a TA_UPDATECP flag to instruct *TextOut* to ignore the *x* and *y* arguments passed to it and use the current pen position instead. When the text alignment includes TA_UPDATECP, *TextOut* updates the *x* component of the pen position each time a string is output. One use for this feature is to achieve proper spacing between two or more character strings output on the same line.

The *ShowPenWidths* Function

ShowPenWidths is similar to *ShowPenStyles* except that it varies the widths of the pens it draws with rather than the styles. One of the interesting aspects of *ShowPenWidths* is the way it formulates the text string it displays at the beginning of each line. Rather than hardcode strings in an array as *ShowPenStyles* does, *ShowPenWidths* builds the strings on the fly using *CString*'s handy *Format* function:

```
    strDescription.Format ("%d Pixels", nPenWidths[i]);
```

CString::Format works like C's *printf* function, converting numeric variables to text and substituting them for placeholders in a formatting string. Windows programmers who do their work in C frequently use the *::wsprintf* API function for text formatting. *Format* does the same thing for *CString* objects without requiring an external function call. And unlike *::wsprintf*, *Format* supports the full range of *printf* formatting codes, including codes for floating-point and string variable types.

The *ShowBrushStyles* Function

The third of the three output routines called by GdiDemo1's *OnPaint* handler draws a series of rectangles bordered with 1-pixel-wide black lines and filled with brushes of various styles. Six of the seven rectangles are filled with hatch brushes and are drawn in a *for* loop that retrieves hatch styles from an array. The final rectangle is filled with a solid green brush.

Before drawing a rectangle that's filled with a hatch brush, *ShowBrushStyles* sets the brush origin to the upper left corner of the rectangle to ensure consistent brush alignment. Setting the brush origin isn't strictly necessary in GdiDemo1 because the rectangles are always drawn in the same position relative to the upper left corner of the window's client area. But later, when scrolling capabilities are added, proper brush alignment will become a critical factor in the quality of the program's output.

The Application Icon

One feature found in almost every Windows application is an application icon. An icon is a small image the operating system uses to represent an application, a document, or other object on the screen. The best way to create an icon is to draw it with a resource editor, save it as an .ico file, and include the .ico file in your application's .rc file with an ICON statement as shown here:

```
IDI_MYICON ICON MyIcon.rc
```

The icon stored in MyIcon.rc then becomes an icon resource your application can load with a simple function call:

```
HICON hIcon = AfxGetApp ()->LoadIcon (IDI_MYICON);
```

LoadIcon is a *CWinApp* member function that loads an icon resource. The HICON value returned by *LoadIcon* is a handle that uniquely identifies the icon. Given that handle, the application can do useful things with the icon such as display it on the screen or use it to create a custom mouse cursor.

Let's spend a little more time on the subject of resources, because it's one that will come up repeatedly in your career as a Windows programmer. A *resource* is a data object added to your application by a program known as a *resource compiler*. Windows supports several types of resources, including icons, menus, bitmaps, strings, and dialog box templates. Resources are defined in your application's .rc file with statements such as ICON, BITMAP, and DIALOG. The resource compiler, which is provided with the Windows SDK and is also built into Visual C++ and other Windows development environments, compiles the statements in the .rc file into binary resources and links them into the application's .exe file. Every resource is identified by a string or an integer ID such as "MyIcon" (string) or IDI_MYICON (integer). By convention, integer resource IDs are given human-readable names such as IDI_MYICON by means of #*define* statements in a header file. Each resource of a given type must be assigned a unique ID, but resources of different types can share IDs. You wouldn't want to assign two icon resources the same ID value, for example, but it's perfectly acceptable to use the same ID value for an icon and a bitmap. Windows can distinguish between the two because the resource types are different.

A single .ico file, and therefore a single icon resource, can include several icon images. An application icon is an icon that represents the application itself. *The Windows Interface Guidelines for Software Design* (Microsoft Press, 1995) recommends that a Windows 95 application supply at least three different icon images for an application icon:

- A 16-color icon that measures 16 by 16 pixels
- A 16-color icon that measures 32 by 32 pixels
- A 256-color icon that measures 48 by 48 pixels

Windows refers to 16-by-16 icons as "small icons" and 32-by-32 and 48-by-48 icons as "large icons." Windows 95 uses small icons in title bars, in the taskbar, and when small-icon, list, or detail view is selected in an Explorer window. It uses 32-by-32 icons on the desktop and when large-icon view is selected in an Explorer window, and it uses 48-by-48 icons in place of 32-by-32 icons if Microsoft Plus! is installed and "Use large icons" is checked in the Plus! page of the system's Display Properties property sheet. (In the future, the "Use large icons" option will probably be built into the base operating system and won't require an add-on software package.) You can supply only a 32-by-32 icon if you wish, and Windows will generate the 16-by-16 and 48-by-48 versions for you by scaling the 32-by-32 image. However, scaling frequently exaggerates pixelation effects and rarely produces a result as pleasing to the eye as the original icon image.

There are several ways to assign an application an icon. The sections that follow discuss the three most common methods, including the method used by GdiDemo1.

Assigning an Application Icon: Method 1

The technique used to assign GdiDemo1 an application icon works for any MFC application whose window is a *CFrameWnd* or *CMDIFrameWnd*. It's easy. Here are the steps involved:

1. Use the Visual C++ icon editor or a similar icon editing tool to draw the icon images, and save them in an .ico file.

2. If your application's window class is derived from *CFrameWnd*, add an .rc file to your project and include the statements

    ```
    #include <afxres.h>
    AFX_IDI_STDFRAME ICON filename
    ```

75

where *filename* is the name of the .ico file. For a window class derived from *CMDIFrameWnd*, substitute AFX_IDI_STD_MDIFRAME for AFX_IDI_STD_FRAME.

In GdiDemo1, the file GdiDemo.ico contains the icon images, and GdiDemo1.rc contains the following statement referencing that file:

```
AFX_IDI_STD_FRAME ICON GdiDemo.ico
```

When the application is compiled, it magically uses the icons stored in GdiDemo.ico. AFX_IDI_STD_FRAME and AFX_IDI_STD_MDIFRAME are special IDs recognized by MFC as icon resources for frame windows. The simple act of assigning an icon resource one of these IDs makes it the application icon, provided the window class is derived from either *CFrameWnd* or *CMDIFrameWnd*. The code that makes it happen is buried deep down in the MFC framework, but basically what happens is that the framework registers a unique WNDCLASS for each frame window and specifies AFX_IDI_STD_FRAME or AFX_IDI_STD_MDIFRAME as the class icon. If there is no icon resource with the magic ID, the system icon IDI_APPLICATION is used instead. The core code in MFC looks like this:

```
if ((pWndCls->hIcon = ::LoadIcon (hInst,
    MAKEINTRESOURCE (nIDIcon))) == NULL)
{
    // Use default icon
    pWndCls->hIcon = ::LoadIcon (NULL, IDI_APPLICATION);
}
```

You can see it for yourself by looking up the *RegisterWithIcon* function in MFC's Wincore.cpp source code file.

Assigning an Application Icon: Method 2

An alternative method for assigning an application an icon—one that works with frame windows and nonframe windows alike—is to do as the MFC framework does and register your own WNDCLASS. This method is particularly appropriate when you derive a window class directly from *CWnd* because *CWnd::CreateEx* (the function used to create top-level *CWnd*-type windows) won't accept a NULL WNDCLASS name the way *CFrameWnd::Create* will. MFC's *AfxRegisterWndClass* function makes it easy to register a custom WNDCLASS, and one of the parameters the function accepts is an icon handle. Here's what the constructor for a *CWnd*-derived window class named *CMainWindow* might look like if it were to register a WNDCLASS with a custom icon:

```
CString strWndClass = AfxRegisterWndClass (
    0,
    AfxGetApp ()->LoadStandCursor (IDC_ARROW),
    (HBRUSH) (COLOR_WINDOW + 1),
    AfxGetApp ()->LoadIcon (IDI_MYICON)
```

```
    );

    CreateEx (0, strWndClass, "My Application",
        WS_OVERLAPPEDWINDOW, CW_USEDEFAULT, CW_USEDEFAULT, CW_USEDEFAULT,
        CW_USEDEFAULT, NULL, NULL);
```

It's really just two function calls, but admittedly those function calls take a lot of parameters. We'll look at *AfxRegisterWndClass* and *CWnd::CreateEx* in more detail in the next chapter.

Assigning an Application Icon: Method 3

A third method for assigning an application an icon is Windows 95's new WM_SET-ICON message, which MFC wraps with *CWnd::SetIcon*. The statements

```
    HICON hIcon = AfxGetApp ()->LoadIcon (IDI_MYICON);
    SetIcon (hIcon, TRUE);
```

make IDI_MYICON the application icon. Passing TRUE as the second parameter tells Windows that *hIcon* is a large icon. If the icon resource contains a small icon as well as a large icon, *SetIcon* should be called a second time—this time with the second parameter equal to FALSE—to assign the small icon. A good place to call *SetIcon* is in the window's constructor or its *OnCreate* handler.

When WM_SETICON really comes in handy is when you write an application that changes its icon on the fly to reflect different program states. For example, if you wrote a wastebasket utility that worked like the Windows 95 Recycle Bin but could be toggled between "delete" mode and "shredder" mode, you could use a different icon for each mode. Then there would be no guessing about the fate of a file dropped into the wastebasket.

SEEING WHAT YOU'VE DRAWN

Unfortunately, there is one small problem with GdiDemo1's output: Unless you're running the program on a very high resolution video adapter, you can't see everything it draws. Even on a 1,024-by-768 screen, the window can't be stretched tall enough to make all the output visible. And what doesn't fit inside the window's client area is clipped by the GDI. We could go back and modify the sample program to be more efficient with the real estate it uses and pack its output a little more tightly, but that still wouldn't do much for someone running Windows on a 640-by-480 screen. No, there's a better solution, one that's entirely independent of the screen resolution. That solution is a scroll bar.

Adding a Scroll Bar to a Window

A scroll bar is a special type of window with an arrow at each end and a traveling "thumb" in between that can be dragged with the mouse. Scroll bars can be oriented horizontally or vertically, but never at an angle. When the user clicks one of the scroll bar arrows, moves the thumb, or clicks the scroll bar shaft, the scroll bar lets the window it's attached to know by sending it a message. It's up to the window to decide what, if anything, to do with that message because a scroll bar does very little on its own. It doesn't, for example, magically scroll the window's contents. What it does do is provide a very intuitive and nearly universally recognized mechanism for scrolling backward and forward over a virtual landscape too large to fit within the physical confines of a window.

Adding a scroll bar to a window is among the easiest things you'll ever do in a Windows program. To add a vertical scroll bar, simply create the window with a WS_VSCROLL style attribute. To add a horizontal scroll bar, use WS_HSCROLL instead. Recall that the third parameter passed to *CFrameWnd::Create* specifies the window style, and that the style defaults to WS_OVERLAPPEDWINDOW. An application that creates a conventional frame window with the statement

```
Create (NULL, "MyApp");
```

can create a frame window containing a vertical scroll bar with the statement

```
Create (NULL, "MyApp", WS_OVERLAPPEDWINDOW | WS_VSCROLL);
```

Accordingly, Windows will provide a scroll bar that extends the height of the client area of the window from top to bottom on the right side. Windows 95 also supports a new window style named WS_EX_LEFTSCROLLBAR that places a vertical scroll bar on the left side of a window. For a frame window, this style can be specified in the *dwExStyle* parameter passed to *CFrameWnd::Create*.

Setting a Scroll Bar's Range, Position, and Page Size

After a scroll bar is created, it must be initialized with a range, position, and page size. The range is a pair of integers defining the upper and lower limits of the scroll bar's travel. The position is an integer value specifying the current location within that range and is reflected in the position of the scroll bar thumb. The page size, which is a new feature of Windows 95, sets the size of the thumb to provide a visual representation of the relationship between the size of the window and the size of the scrollable view. You don't have to set the page size (Windows will pick a default size for you), but setting the page size yourself makes your application a better citizen in the Windows 95 environment.

One way to set a scroll bar's range and position is with the *CWnd::SetScrollRange* and *CWnd::SetScrollPos* functions. The statement

```
SetScrollRange (SB_VERT, 0, 99, TRUE);
```

sets a vertical scroll bar's range to 0 through 99, while the statement

```
SetScrollPos (SB_VERT, 50, TRUE);
```

sets the current position to 50 and consequently moves the thumb to the middle of the scroll bar. (For horizontal scroll bars, use SB_HORZ instead of SB_VERT.) A scroll bar maintains a record of its current range and position internally, and you can query the scroll bar for those values at any time with *CWnd*'s *GetScrollRange* and *GetScrollPos* functions.

The TRUE parameter passed to *SetScrollRange* and *SetScrollPos* specifies that the scroll bar should be redrawn to reflect the change that was just made to it. You can prevent redraws by specifying FALSE. If you specify neither TRUE nor FALSE, both *SetScrollRange* and *SetScrollPos* default to TRUE. You generally want a scroll bar to redraw itself after one of these functions is called, but not if both are called in quick succession. Allowing a scroll bar to redraw itself twice in a very short period of time produces an undesirable flashing effect. If you're setting both the range and the position in a single step, do it like this:

```
SetScrollRange (SB_VERT, 0, 99, FALSE);
SetScrollPos (SB_VERT, 50, TRUE);
```

It doesn't matter which of the two functions you call first as long as the second one does the redrawing. But remember that if you call *SetScrollPos* first, the call won't work as expected if the new scroll bar position is outside the current range.

In Windows 95, the preferred way to set a scroll bar's range and position is with the *CWnd::SetScrollInfo* function. In addition to allowing the range and position to be set with a single function call, *SetScrollInfo* also provides a means—the *only* means, as it turns out—for setting the page size. *SetScrollInfo* accepts three parameters: an SB_VERT or SB_HORZ parameter specifying whether the scroll bar is vertical or horizontal (or SB_BOTH if you want to initialize two scroll bars at once), a pointer to a SCROLLINFO structure, and a Boolean value (TRUE or FALSE) specifying whether the scroll bar should be redrawn. SCROLLINFO is defined as follows in Winuser.h:

```
typedef struct tagSCROLLINFO
{
    UINT    cbSize;
    UINT    fMask;
    int     nMin;
    int     nMax;
    UINT    nPage;
    int     nPos;
    int     nTrackPos;
} SCROLLINFO, FAR *LPSCROLLINFO;
```

cbSize specifies the size of the structure, *nMin* and *nMax* specify the scroll bar range, *nPage* specifies the page size, and *nPos* specifies the position. *nTrackPos* is not used in calls to *SetScrollInfo*, but it contains the scroll bar's current thumb position when the complementary *GetScrollInfo* function is called to retrieve information about the scroll bar while the thumb is being dragged. The *fMask* field holds a combination of one or more of the following bit flags: SIF_DISABLENOSCROLL, which disables the scroll bar; SIF_PAGE, which indicates that *nPage* holds the page size; SIF_POS, which indicates that *nPos* holds the scroll bar position; SIF_RANGE, which indicates that *nMin* and *nMax* hold the scroll bar range; and SIF_ALL, which is equivalent to SIF_PAGE ! SIF_POS ! SIF_RANGE. *SetScrollInfo* ignores fields for which bit flags are not specified. The statements

```
SCROLLINFO si;
si.fMask = SIF_POS;
si.nPos = 50;
SetScrollInfo (SB_VERT, &si, TRUE);
```

set the position while leaving the range and page size unaffected, and

```
SCROLLINFO si;
si.fMask = SIF_RANGE ! SIF_POS ! SIF_PAGE;   // Or SIF_ALL
si.nMin = 0;
si.nMax = 99;
si.nPage = 25;
si.nPos = 50;
SetScrollInfo (SB_VERT, &si, TRUE);
```

sets the range, page size, and position in one fell swoop. You don't need to initialize *cbSize* before calling *SetScrollInfo* or *GetScrollInfo* because the framework will initialize it for you.

You can make a scroll bar disappear by setting the upper limit of its range equal to the lower limit. The scroll bar doesn't go away entirely; it's still there, even though you can't see it, and—more important—you can bring it back by making the range upper and lower limits different again. This turns out to be quite a useful trick if you want to hide the scroll bar because the window has been enlarged to the point that a scroll bar is no longer required. *SetScrollInfo*'s SIF_DISABLENOSCROLL flag prevents a scroll bar from accepting further input, but it doesn't make the scroll bar disappear. Having a disabled scroll bar visible inside a window can be confusing to users, who are apt to wonder why the scroll bar is there if it can't be used.

When you're setting a scroll bar's range, page size, and position, it's important to conform to the model Windows uses for scroll bars, in which the page size and the proportionally sized scroll bar thumb represent the size of your window, the range represents the size of the workspace, and the position represents the window's current position in the workspace. Suppose your window's client area is 100 units high and the workspace you want to cover with a vertical scroll bar is 400 units high, as shown in Figure 2-9. The easiest way to configure the scroll bar is to set the range to 0 through 399 and the page size to 100. Accordingly, Windows will draw the scroll bar thumb so that it is one-fourth the height of the scroll bar. When the scroll bar position is 0, the thumb will be positioned at the top of the scroll bar. As the thumb is scrolled down, you scroll the contents of your window up an amount proportional to the distance the thumb was moved. And if you limit the scroll bar's maximum position to 300 (the difference between the magnitude of the scroll bar range and the page size), the bottom of the thumb will reach the bottom of the scroll bar at the same time that the bottom of the workspace scrolls into view at the bottom of the window's client area.

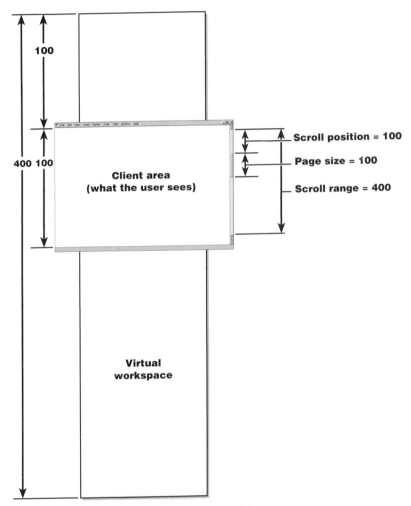

Figure 2-9. *The Windows 95 scroll bar model.*

Processing Scroll Bar Messages

A scroll bar notifies the window it is attached to of scroll bar events by sending messages. A vertical scroll bar sends WM_VSCROLL messages, and a horizontal scroll bar sends WM_HSCROLL messages. In MFC, WM_VSCROLL messages are directed to a window's *OnVScroll* function through the message map. *OnVScroll* is prototyped like this:

```
afx_msg void OnVScroll (UINT nCode, UINT nPos, CScrollBar* pScrollBar)
```

nCode identifies the type of event that precipitated the message; *nPos* contains the latest thumb position if the thumb is being dragged or was just dragged and released; and, for a scroll bar that was created by adding a WS_VSCROLL style bit to a window, *pScrollBar* is NULL.

There are seven different event notifications your program might receive in *OnVScroll*'s *nCode* parameter:

Event Code	*Sent When*
SB_LINEUP	The arrow at the top of the scroll bar is clicked.
SB_LINEDOWN	The arrow at the bottom of the scroll bar is clicked.
SB_PAGEUP	The scroll bar shaft is clicked between the up-arrow and the thumb.
SB_PAGEDOWN	The scroll bar shaft is clicked between the thumb and the down-arrow.
SB_ENDSCROLL	The mouse button is released, and no more SB_LINEUP, SB_LINEDOWN, SB_PAGEUP, or SB_PAGEDOWN notifications are forthcoming.
SB_THUMBTRACK	The scroll bar thumb is dragged.
SB_THUMBPOSITION	The thumb is released after being dragged to a new location.

Horizontal scroll bars send the same notifications as vertical scroll bars, but the notifications have slightly different meanings. For a horizontal scroll bar, SB_LINEUP signifies that the left-arrow was clicked, SB_LINEDOWN means that the right-arrow was clicked, SB_PAGEUP means that the scroll bar was clicked between the left-arrow and the thumb, and SB_PAGEDOWN means that the scroll bar was clicked between the thumb and the right-arrow. For convenience, Windows 95 defines four new identifiers for horizontal scroll bars—SB_LINELEFT, SB_LINERIGHT, SB_PAGELEFT, and SB_PAGERIGHT—that may be used in lieu of SB_LINEUP, SB_LINEDOWN, SB_PAGEUP, and SB_PAGEDOWN. The discussions in the remainder of this chapter deal exclusively with vertical scroll bars, but keep in mind that anything said about vertical scroll bars applies to horizontal scroll bars, too.

If the user clicks a scroll bar or scroll bar arrow and leaves the mouse button depressed, your program will receive a series of SB_LINEUP, SB_LINEDOWN, SB_PAGEUP, or SB_PAGEDOWN messages in rapid succession, similar to the stream of typematic key codes generated when a key is held down. SB_ENDSCROLL terminates a stream of UP or DOWN messages and notifies you that the mouse button has been released. Even a single click of a scroll bar or scroll bar arrow generates an UP or a DOWN message followed by an SB_ENDSCROLL message. Similarly, a window is bombarded with SB_THUMBTRACK messages reporting new thumb positions as a scroll bar thumb is dragged, and it receives one final SB_THUMBPOSITION message when the thumb is released. When an SB_THUMBTRACK or SB_THUMBPOSITION message arrives, *OnVScroll*'s *nPos* parameter holds the latest thumb position. For other event codes, the value of *nPos* is undefined.

How your program responds to scroll bar event messages is up to you. Most programs that use scroll bars disregard SB_ENDSCROLL messages and respond to SB_LINEUP, SB_LINEDOWN, SB_PAGEUP, and SB_PAGEDOWN messages instead. A typical response to SB_LINEUP and SB_LINEDOWN messages is to scroll the contents of the window down or up one line and call *SetScrollPos* or *SetScrollInfo* to set the new scroll bar position and update the thumb location. "Line" might mean one pixel, or it might mean the height of one line of text. Similarly, the usual response to SB_PAGEUP and SB_PAGEDOWN messages is to scroll down or up a distance equal to or slightly less than one "page," which is typically defined to mean the height of the window's client area or something slightly less, and call *SetScrollInfo* to set the new scroll position. In any event, it's your responsibility to update the scroll bar position; the scroll bar doesn't do that by itself. Another, though less common, approach to processing UP and DOWN messages is to continually move the scroll bar thumb by calling *SetScrollPos* or *SetScrollInfo* but to defer scrolling the window until an SB-_ENDSCROLL notification arrives. I once used this technique in a multimedia application that was relatively slow to respond to positional changes so that the latency of commands sent to a CD-ROM drive wouldn't impede the smooth movement of the scroll bar thumb.

SB_THUMBTRACK and SB_THUMBPOSITION messages are handled a little differently. Since SB_THUMBTRACK messages are liable to come fast and furious when the thumb is dragged, many Windows applications ignore SB_THUMBTRACK messages and respond only to SB_THUMBPOSITION messages. Therefore, the window doesn't scroll until the thumb is released. If you can scroll the contents of your window quickly enough to keep up with SB_THUMBTRACK messages, you can make your program more responsive to user input by scrolling interactively as the thumb is dragged. As when you're processing UP and DOWN messages from a scroll bar control, it's still up to you to update the scroll bar position each time you scroll the information in a window. Windows animates the movement of the scroll bar thumb as it's dragged up and down, but if you fail to call *SetScrollPos* or *SetScrollInfo* in response to SB_THUMBTRACK or SB_THUMBPOSITION messages, the thumb will snap back to its original position the moment it's released.

Scrolling the Contents of a Window

Now that you have a feel for how a scroll bar works, it's time to think about how to scroll the contents of a window in response to scroll bar messages. Here's the simplistic approach.

1. Write your *OnPaint* handler so that it uses the scroll position to determine what should appear in the window's first line. If a window displays 400 lines of text, for example, and the current scroll position is 100, have *OnPaint* ignore the first 100 lines and begin drawing with the 101st line.

2. Each time a scroll bar message arrives, update the scroll bar position and use *CWnd::Invalidate* to invalidate the window's client area to force a redraw. This will activate the *OnPaint* handler and redraw the window's contents using the new scroll position.

The problem with this technique is that it is slow—*very* slow, for that matter. If the user clicks the up-arrow to scroll the window contents up one line, it's wasteful to redraw the entire window because most of the information you want to display is already there, albeit in the wrong location. A more efficient approach to processing SB_LINEUP messages would be to copy everything currently displayed in the window down one line using a fast block copy and then to draw just the new top line. That's exactly what *CWnd::ScrollWindow* is designed to help you do.

ScrollWindow scrolls the contents of a window's client area—in whole or in part—up or down, left or right, by one or more pixels using a fast block pixel transfer. Moreover, it invalidates only the part of the window contents that is "uncovered" by the scrolling operation so that the next WM_PAINT message doesn't have to repaint the contents of the entire client area. If called to scroll the contents of a window downward by 10 pixels, *ScrollWindow* performs the scroll by doing a block copy. Then it invalidates the rectangle encompassing the window's top ten rows. This activates *OnPaint* and causes just the top ten rows to be redrawn. Even if *OnPaint* tries to redraw the contents of the entire client area, performance will be improved because most of the output will be clipped. A really smart *OnPaint* handler could boost performance even further by restricting the calls it makes to those that affect pixels in the bounding box surrounding the window's update region. This complicates the program logic, however, so it is typically done only when scrolling performance is unsatisfactory otherwise.

ScrollWindow accepts four parameters. Two are required and two are optional. *ScrollWindow* is prototyped as follows:

```
void ScrollWindow (int xAmount, int yAmount,
    LPCRECT lpRect = NULL, LPCRECT lpClipRect = NULL)
```

The *xAmount* and *yAmount* parameters are signed integers specifying the number of pixels to scroll horizontally and vertically. Negative values scroll left and up, while positive values scroll right and down. *lpRect* points to a *CRect* object or a RECT structure specifying the part of the client area to scroll, and *lpClipRect* points to a *CRect* object or a RECT structure specifying a clipping rectangle. Specifying NULL for *lpRect* and *lpClipRect* scrolls the contents of the entire client area. The statement

```
ScrollWindow (0, 10);
```

scrolls everything in a window's client area downward by 10 pixels and prompts a redraw of the first ten rows.

You can use *ScrollWindow* whether your application displays text, graphics, or both. Remember that in Windows, all things are graphical images, including lines of text. Therefore, *ScrollWindow* is equally as useful for scrolling tables of text as it is for scrolling large bitmaps.

The GdiDemo2 Application

Let's put this newfound knowledge to work by adding scrolling capabilities to our application. GdiDemo2, whose source code appears in Figure 2-10, is functionally identical to GdiDemo1 in all but one respect: it features a vertical scroll bar enabling the user to scroll through the virtual workspace and view all of the program's output, as seen in Figure 2-11 on page 92. In addition to providing a hands-on demonstration of the principles discussed in the preceding sections, GdiDemo2 also brings to light a few practical considerations such as how to reprogram the scroll bar to change the page size when the frame window is resized. The bulk of the code added to support the vertical scroll bar is found in the *CMainWindow::OnSize* and *CMainWindow::OnVScroll* functions. The remaining code should look familiar to you from GdiDemo1.

GdiDemo2.rc

```
//*************************************************************************
//
//  GdiDemo2.rc
//
//*************************************************************************

#include <afxres.h>

AFX_IDI_STD_FRAME ICON GdiDemo.ico
```

GdiDemo2.h

```
//*************************************************************************
//
//  GdiDemo2.h
//
//*************************************************************************
```

Figure 2-10. *The GdiDemo2 source code.* *(continued)*

GdiDemo2.h *continued*

```
class CMyApp : public CWinApp
{
public:
    virtual BOOL InitInstance ();
};

class CMainWindow : public CFrameWnd
{
private:
    int m_cxChar;
    int m_cyChar;
    int m_nPageSize;
    int m_nScrollPos;

    void ShowPenStyles (CDC*, int, int);
    void ShowPenWidths (CDC*, int, int);
    void ShowBrushStyles (CDC*, int, int);

public:
    CMainWindow ();

protected:
    afx_msg int OnCreate (LPCREATESTRUCT);
    afx_msg void OnPaint ();
    afx_msg void OnSize (UINT, int, int);
    afx_msg void OnVScroll (UINT, UINT, CScrollBar*);

    DECLARE_MESSAGE_MAP ()
};

struct STYLES {
    int nStyle;
    char szStyleName[16];
};
```

GdiDemo2.cpp

```
//****************************************************************************
//
//  GdiDemo2.cpp
//
//****************************************************************************

#include <afxwin.h>
```

```
#include "GdiDemo2.h"

#define VHEIGHT (m_cyChar * 50)

CMyApp myApp;

/////////////////////////////////////////////////////////////////////////
// CMyApp member functions

BOOL CMyApp::InitInstance ()
{
    m_pMainWnd = new CMainWindow;
    m_pMainWnd->ShowWindow (m_nCmdShow);
    m_pMainWnd->UpdateWindow ();
    return TRUE;
}


/////////////////////////////////////////////////////////////////////////
// CMainWindow message map and member functions

BEGIN_MESSAGE_MAP (CMainWindow, CFrameWnd)
    ON_WM_CREATE ()
    ON_WM_PAINT ()
    ON_WM_SIZE ()
    ON_WM_VSCROLL ()
END_MESSAGE_MAP ()

CMainWindow::CMainWindow ()
{
    m_nScrollPos = 0;
    Create (NULL, "GdiDemo2", WS_OVERLAPPEDWINDOW | WS_VSCROLL);
}

int CMainWindow::OnCreate (LPCREATESTRUCT lpcs)
{
    if (CFrameWnd::OnCreate (lpcs) == -1)
        return -1;

    TEXTMETRIC tm;
    CClientDC dc (this);
    dc.GetTextMetrics (&tm);
    m_cxChar = tm.tmAveCharWidth;
    m_cyChar = tm.tmHeight;
    return 0;
}
```

(continued)

GdiDemo2.cpp *continued*

```
void CMainWindow::OnPaint ()
{
    CPaintDC dc (this);

    dc.SetWindowOrg (0, m_nScrollPos);
    ShowPenStyles (&dc, m_cxChar * 2, m_cyChar);
    ShowPenWidths (&dc, m_cxChar * 2, m_cyChar * 15);
    ShowBrushStyles (&dc, m_cxChar * 2, m_cyChar * 27);
}

void CMainWindow::OnSize (UINT nType, int cx, int cy)
{
    CFrameWnd::OnSize (nType, cx, cy);

    int nScrollMax;
    if (cy < VHEIGHT) {
        nScrollMax = VHEIGHT;
        m_nPageSize = cy;
        m_nScrollPos = min (m_nScrollPos, VHEIGHT - m_nPageSize);
    }
    else
        nScrollMax = m_nScrollPos = m_nPageSize = 0;

    SCROLLINFO si;
    si.fMask = SIF_PAGE | SIF_RANGE | SIF_POS;
    si.nMin = 0;
    si.nMax = nScrollMax;
    si.nPos = m_nScrollPos;
    si.nPage = m_nPageSize;

    SetScrollInfo (SB_VERT, &si, TRUE);
}

void CMainWindow::OnVScroll (UINT nCode, UINT nPos, CScrollBar* pScrollBar)
{
    int nDelta;
    int nMaxPos = VHEIGHT - m_nPageSize;

    switch (nCode) {

    case SB_LINEUP:
        if (m_nScrollPos <= 0)
            return;
        nDelta = -(min (m_cyChar, m_nScrollPos));
        break;
```

```
        case SB_PAGEUP:
            if (m_nScrollPos <= 0)
                return;
            nDelta = -(min (m_nPageSize, m_nScrollPos));
            break;

        case SB_THUMBPOSITION:
            nDelta = (int) nPos - m_nScrollPos;
            break;

        case SB_PAGEDOWN:
            if (m_nScrollPos >= nMaxPos)
                return;
            nDelta = min (m_nPageSize, nMaxPos - m_nScrollPos);
            break;

        case SB_LINEDOWN:
            if (m_nScrollPos >= nMaxPos)
                return;
            nDelta = min (m_cyChar, nMaxPos - m_nScrollPos);
            break;

        default: // Ignore other scroll bar messages
            return;
    }

    m_nScrollPos += nDelta;
    SetScrollPos (SB_VERT, m_nScrollPos, TRUE);
    ScrollWindow (0, -nDelta);
}

void CMainWindow::ShowPenStyles (CDC* pDC, int x, int y)
{
    static struct STYLES styles[] = {
        PS_SOLID,        "PS_SOLID",
        PS_DASH,         "PS_DASH",
        PS_DOT,          "PS_DOT",
        PS_DASHDOT,      "PS_DASHDOT",
        PS_DASHDOTDOT,   "PS_DASHDOTDOT",
        PS_NULL,         "PS_NULL",
        PS_INSIDEFRAME,  "PS_INSIDEFRAME"
    };

    pDC->SetTextColor (RGB (0, 0, 0));
    pDC->TextOut (x, y, "Pen Styles");
```

(continued)

GdiDemo2.cpp *continued*

```cpp
        int dy = (m_cyChar * 3) / 2;
        int x1 = x + (m_cxChar * 2);
        int x2 = x + (m_cxChar * 22);
        int x3 = x + (m_cxChar * 46);

        CPen* pOldPen;
        pDC->SetTextColor (RGB (255, 0, 0));

        for (int i=0; i<7; i++) {
            y += dy;
            pDC->TextOut (x1, y, styles[i].szStyleName);

            CPen pen (styles[i].nStyle, 1, RGB (255, 0, 0));
            pOldPen = pDC->SelectObject (&pen);

            pDC->MoveTo (x2, y + (m_cyChar / 2));
            pDC->LineTo (x3, y + (m_cyChar / 2));

            pDC->SelectObject (pOldPen);
        }
    }

    void CMainWindow::ShowPenWidths (CDC* pDC, int x, int y)
    {
        static int nPenWidths[] = { 2, 8, 16, 24 };

        pDC->SetTextColor (RGB (0, 0, 0));
        pDC->TextOut (x, y, "Pen Widths");

        int dy = m_cyChar * 2;
        int x1 = x + (m_cxChar * 2);
        int x2 = x + (m_cxChar * 22);
        int x3 = x + (m_cxChar * 46);

        CPen* pOldPen;
        CString strDescription;
        pDC->SetTextColor (RGB (0, 0, 255));

        for (int i=0; i<4; i++) {
            y += dy;
            strDescription.Format ("%d Pixels", nPenWidths[i]);
            pDC->TextOut (x1, y, strDescription);

            CPen pen (PS_SOLID, nPenWidths[i], RGB (0, 0, 255));
            pOldPen = pDC->SelectObject (&pen);
```

```
        pDC->MoveTo (x2, y + (m_cyChar / 2));
        pDC->LineTo (x3, y + (m_cyChar / 2));

        pDC->SelectObject (pOldPen);
    }
}

void CMainWindow::ShowBrushStyles (CDC* pDC, int x, int y)
{
    static struct STYLES styles[] = {
        HS_BDIAGONAL,   "HS_BDIAGONAL",
        HS_CROSS,       "HS_CROSS",
        HS_DIAGCROSS,   "HS_DIAGCROSS",
        HS_FDIAGONAL,   "HS_FDIAGONAL",
        HS_HORIZONTAL,  "HS_HORIZONTAL",
        HS_VERTICAL,    "HS_VERTICAL"
    };

    pDC->SetTextColor (RGB (0, 0, 0));
    pDC->TextOut (x, y, "Brush Styles");

    int dy = m_cyChar * 3;
    int x1 = x + (m_cxChar * 2);
    int x2 = x + (m_cxChar * 22);
    int x3 = x + (m_cxChar * 46);

    CBrush* pOldBrush;

    for (int i=0; i<6; i++) {
        y += dy;
        pDC->TextOut (x1, y, styles[i].szStyleName);

        CRect rect (x2, y - m_cyChar, x3, y + m_cyChar);
        CBrush brush (styles[i].nStyle, RGB (0, 255, 0));

        CPoint point (rect.left, rect.top);
        pDC->LPtoDP (&point);
        point.x %= 8;
        point.y %= 8;
        pDC->SetBrushOrg (point);

        pOldBrush = pDC->SelectObject (&brush);
        pDC->Rectangle (rect);
```

(continued)

GdiDemo2.cpp *continued*

```
        pDC->SelectObject (pOldBrush);
    }


    y += dy;
    pDC->TextOut (x1, y, "Solid");

    CBrush brush (RGB (0, 255, 0));
    pOldBrush = pDC->SelectObject (&brush);
    pDC->Rectangle (x2, y - m_cyChar, x3, y + m_cyChar);
    pDC->SelectObject (pOldBrush);
}
```

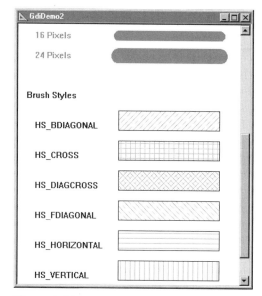

Figure 2-11. *The GdiDemo2 window.*

GdiDemo2's *CMainWindow* class contains two private data members that Gdi-Demo1's *CMainWindow* class does not. *m_nScrollPos* holds the current scroll position. It is initialized to 0 by the class constructor and updated in response to scroll bar messages. *m_nPageSize* represents the page size. It is initialized to the height of the window's client area and updated by the window's *OnSize* handler anytime the window size changes. *OnSize* is one of three *CMainWindow* member functions that play key roles in the scroll bar's operation. Let's look at each one of them to see what it takes to make a scroll bar work.

The *OnSize* Handler

When a window is resized, it receives a WM_SIZE message informing it of the change and reporting the new size of its client area. The first WM_SIZE message arrives when a window is created, soon after the WM_CREATE message. Subsequent WM_SIZE messages are generated when anything happens that changes the size of the window or its client area. The *OnSize* handler that processes WM.SIZE messages is prototyped as follows:

```
afx_msg void OnSize (UINT nType, int cx, int cy)
```

The *nType* parameter informs the window whether it has been minimized, maximized, or resized but neither minimized nor maximized using the code SIZE_MINIMIZED, SIZE_MAXIMIZED, or SIZE_RESTORED. (WM_SIZE messages are also sent with *nType* values equal to SIZE_MAXHIDE or SIZE_MAXSHOW when a window belonging to another application is maximized or restored.) *cx* and *cy* specify the client area's new dimensions in pixels. When you override a frame window's *OnSize* handler, it's a good idea to call the base class's *OnSize* handler, too.

CMainWindow's *OnSize* handler initializes the scroll bar when the program is started and reinitializes it when the window size changes. It begins by calling *CFrameWnd::OnSize*. It then computes new values for *m_nPageSize*, *m_nScrollPos*, and a local variable named *nScrollMax*:

```
if (cy < VHEIGHT) {
    nScrollMax = VHEIGHT;
    m_nPageSize = cy;
    m_nScrollPos = min (m_nScrollPos, VHEIGHT - m_nPageSize);
}
else
    nScrollMax = m_nScrollPos = m_nPageSize = 0;
```

cy is the same *cy* parameter passed to *OnSize*, which specifies the height of the window's client area. If *cy* is less than VHEIGHT, which is the height of the window's virtual workspace (*m_cyChar* * 50), then a scroll bar is needed because the window doesn't cover the full height of the workspace. Accordingly, *nScrollMax* is set to VHEIGHT, *m_nPageSize* is initialized to the client-area height, and *m_nScroll-Pos* is set to the lesser of its current value and the difference between the virtual height and *m_nPageSize*. Using the lesser of the values ensures that if the window is lengthened downward when it is already at the bottom of the scroll range, the scroll position will be adjusted upward so that the output will fill the window. (If you have trouble visualizing what this means, comment out the line that recomputes *m_nScrollPos*, recompile the program, scroll to the bottom of the workspace, and pull down the bottom of the window to make it larger. You'll see exactly what I mean.) If, on the other hand, *cy* is greater than or equal to VHEIGHT, then no scroll bar is needed and all three variables are set to 0.

After initializing a SCROLLINFO structure with the values just calculated, the *OnSize* handler calls *SetScrollInfo* to reconfigure the scroll bar:

```
si.fMask = SIF_PAGE | SIF_RANGE | SIF_POS;
si.nMin = 0;
si.nMax = nScrollMax;
si.nPos = m_nScrollPos;
si.nPage = m_nPageSize;

SetScrollInfo (SB_VERT, &si, TRUE);
```

If the height of the window's client area is less than the height of the workspace (cy < VHEIGHT), the scroll bar is initialized with a scroll range that equals the virtual workspace height and a page size that equals the height of the client area. But if the window is large enough to show all the program's output, the scroll range is set to 0 and the scroll bar consequently disappears from view. Moreover, since all this happens in the *OnSize* handler, the scroll bar is configured once when the program first starts up and again anytime the window size changes. The scroll bar comes and goes as needed, and the scroll bar's thumb is always sized in proportion to the ratio of the window size to the workspace size. If your video hardware is capable of running Windows at a resolution of 1,280 by 1,024, you can see for yourself that the scroll bar disappears and reappears: simply enlarge the window so that it spans almost the full height of the screen, and then shrink it back down again.

The *OnVScroll* Handler

The logic that makes the scroll bar work is provided by *CMainWindow::OnVScroll*. A *switch-case* structure converts the notification code passed in *nCode* into a signed *nDelta* value that represents the number of pixels the window should be scrolled up or down. Nominally, SB_LINEUP and SB_LINEDOWN notifications set *nDelta* to −*m_cyChar* and *m_cyChar*, respectively, while SB_PAGEUP and SB_PAGEDOWN notifications set it to −*m_nPageSize* and *m_nPageSize*. In each case, the value of *nDelta* is adjusted if necessary to ensure that *m_nScrollPos* won't go negative or exceed the maximum permitted scroll position, which equals the workspace height minus the page height. The SB_THUMBPOSITION handler simply sets *nDelta* to the difference between the current scroll position and the position reported in *nPos*. Once *nDelta* is initialized, the scroll position is adjusted by *nDelta* pixels and the window scrolled a corresponding amount with the statements

```
m_nScrollPos += nDelta;
SetScrollPos (SB_VERT, m_nScrollPos, TRUE);
ScrollWindow (0, -nDelta);
```

GdiDemo2 does not process SB_THUMBTRACK messages, although it wouldn't be difficult to add an SB_THUMBTRACK case to *OnVScroll* to scroll the window interactively as the scroll bar thumb is dragged. That's an exercise you might want to try yourself to test your understanding of the application's scrolling logic.

The *OnPaint* Handler

The final piece of the puzzle is *CMainWindow::OnPaint*, which does the drawing when *OnVScroll* calls *ScrollWindow* and consequently invalidates all or part of the window's client area. The handler is just five lines long:

```
CPaintDC dc (this);

dc.SetWindowOrg (0, m_nScrollPos);
ShowPenStyles (&dc, m_cxChar * 2, m_cyChar);
ShowPenWidths (&dc, m_cxChar * 2, m_cyChar * 15);
ShowBrushStyles (&dc, m_cxChar * 2, m_cyChar * 27);
```

The first line, of course, creates the device context object we need in order to draw in the window. The final three lines call the private *CMainWindow* member functions that produce the program's output, exactly as they did in GdiDemo1. The only thing that's new is the statement

```
dc.SetWindowOrg (0, m_nScrollPos);
```

which repositions the window origin in preparation for drawing. It is this statement that factors the current scroll position into the output. Recall that *CDC::SetWindowOrg* tells Windows to map the logical point (*x*, *y*) to the device point (0,0), which, for a client-area device context, corresponds to the upper left corner of the window's client area. The statement shown above effectively moves the origin of the coordinate system in which *OnPaint* draws upward by *m_nScrollPos* pixels. If *OnPaint* or one of its helper routines subsequently tries to paint the pixel at (0,0), the coordinate pair is transparently transformed by the GDI into (0,–*m_nScrollPos*). If the current scroll position is 100, the first 100 rows will be clipped from the program's output and the *real* output—the output the user can see—will begin with the 101st row. Repositioning the origin in this way is a simple and effective way to move a window over a virtual display surface.

And with that, all the pieces are in place. The user clicks the scroll bar or drags the scroll bar thumb; *OnVScroll* receives the message and responds by updating the scroll position and scrolling the window; and *OnPaint* redraws the invalid part of the window, using *SetWindowOrg* to move the drawing origin an amount that equals the current scroll position. The program's entire workspace is now accessible, despite the physical limitations the window size imposes on the output. And all for about 50 additional lines of code. How could it be any easier?

Funny you should ask. Because that's exactly what the remainder of this chapter is all about.

Scrolling Made Easy

GdiDemo2 is definitely a better application than GdiDemo1 because, no matter how large or small a window you run it in, you can see everything it draws. The only problem with GdiDemo2 is that we're the ones doing all the work. Windows takes some of the responsibility for managing the scroll bar, but it's our job to provide the scrolling logic, make sure the scroll bar thumb has the right proportions, make the scroll bar go away if the window grows large enough, and so on. All things considered, supporting a scroll bar is a highly manual process—just the sort of thing you'd hope a class library would help out with. After all, isn't MFC supposed to make Windows programming easier? What we did to add scrolling capabilities to GdiDemo2 wasn't all that different from what a C programmer would do. And it was certainly no less work.

GdiDemo2 is the perfect starting point for an example of how MFC *can* make Windows programming easier. MFC provides a special class called *CScrollView* that encapsulates the functionality of a window with a scroll bar. An application that uses *CScrollView* doesn't need an *OnVScroll* handler because the class library provides the handler and all the logic to go with it. Take away the *OnVScroll* code, and GdiDemo2 wouldn't be much more complicated than GdiDemo1. The only catch is that MFC's *CScrollView* is a view class designed to be used in document/view applications. To use it outside the document/view architecture, we'll have to bend the rules a bit and "get unconventional." But it turns out that that's a pretty easy thing to do. And as you'll see, the reward is well worth the effort.

The *CScrollView* Class

CScrollView is a view class derived from *CView*. In MFC, a view is a special type of window designed to display a view of the data stored in a document. A given document can have any number of views associated with it, each providing a different pictorial representation of the document's data. Though the true nature of a view is often obscured by the application framework, a view is really just a window and is not all that different from other windows you see on the screen. You probably didn't realize it, but when you look at the interior of a frame window in a document/view application, what you see isn't the client area of the frame window but a view window laid over the top of it. The view is created by the framework in the process of creating the frame window. Significantly, there's nothing preventing an application from creating a view and attaching it to a frame window on its own, without the framework's intervention.

Once created, a *CScrollView*-type view automatically processes WM_VSCROLL (and, if desired, WM_HSCROLL) messages on behalf of the application. The view also provides several useful member functions the application can call to initialize and manipulate the view. Chief among these functions is *CScrollView::SetScrollSizes*, which is somewhat similar to *CWnd:SetScrollInfo*. *SetScrollSizes* is prototyped as follows:

```
void SetScrollSizes (int nMapMode, SIZE sizeTotal,
    const SIZE& sizePage = sizeDefault,
    const SIZE& sizeLine = sizeDefault)
```

The *nMapMode* parameter is the GDI mapping mode the view will use, which for us will be MM_TEXT. *sizeTotal* is a SIZE structure or *CSize* object that specifies the size of the scrollable view (the size of the virtual workspace) in the x and y directions. *sizePage* defines the page size, or the distance that the view will scroll in response to SB_PAGEUP, SB_PAGEDOWN, SB_PAGELEFT, and SB_PAGERIGHT messages. Finally, *sizeLine* is the distance that the view will be scrolled in response to SB_LINEUP, SB_LINEDOWN, SB_LINELEFT, and SB_LINERIGHT messages. The default values for *sizePage* and *sizeLine* are $1/10$ of *sizeTotal* and $1/10$ of *sizePage*, respectively. The statement

```
SetScrollSizes (MM_TEXT, CSize (400, 400),
    CSize (100, 100), CSize (20, 5));
```

initializes a scroll view that encompasses a workspace measuring 400 by 400 pixels that scrolls 100 pixels up, down, left, or right when a scroll bar is clicked, and that scrolls 20 pixels horizontally and 5 pixels vertically when a scroll bar arrow is clicked. Normally, you'll find it advantageous to set *sizePage* to the window's client-area height and width (or values slightly less) to correlate the window size to the sizes of the vertical and horizontal scroll bar thumbs. If you'd like the view to support vertical scrolling only, you can set the x members of the *CSize* objects to 0 and the horizontal scroll bar will be removed from the window. Similarly, setting the y members to 0 disables vertical scrolling.

How do you create a scroll view and attach it to a frame window? It's easy: just derive a view class from *CScrollView* and instantiate it in the frame window's *OnCreate* handler. Then call the view's *Create* function like this:

```
pMyView->Create (NULL, NULL, WS_CHILD ¦ WS_VISIBLE,
    CRect (0, 0, 0, 0), this, AFX_IDW_PANE_FIRST, NULL);
```

The combination of the WS_CHILD style attribute and the *this* pointer identifying the frame window as the parent makes the view a child of the frame window. AFX_IDW_PANE_FIRST cements the relationship by assigning the view window the special ID value MFC uses for a view attached to a frame window. And the WS_VISIBLE attribute ensures that the view window will be visible so that we don't have to call *ShowWindow* for it as we do for a frame window. The window size passed in the *CRect* object is irrelevant because a view window is automatically sized to match the client area of its parent. Once a view window is created in this way, it becomes, for all intents and purposes, the client area of the application's window. If you want to, you can move member variables that were formerly part of the main window class to the view class and also direct messages to the view class. That's how seasoned MFC programmers do it when they develop document/view applications.

That's basically all there is to it; the rest is detail. Now that the introductions are out of the way, let's get down to business and modify our sample application one last time to take advantage of the scrolling logic built into MFC.

The GdiDemo3 Application

The output from this chapter's final sample program, GdiDemo3, is identical to the output from GdiDemo2. Put the two windows side by side and you'll be hard pressed to tell them apart save for the window titles. But inside, the programs are very different. Whereas GdiDemo2 contained lots of extra code to handle scrolling, GdiDemo3 contains no *OnVScroll* handler and overall resembles GdiDemo1 more than it resembles GdiDemo2.

The source code is shown in Figure 2-12. The first and most obvious difference between GdiDemo3 and its predecessors is that in addition to the derived *CMainWindow* class, the header file contains a derivation for a view class named *CMyView*. *CMyView* comes from *CScrollView* and includes the private member variables *m_cxChar* and *m_cyChar* as well as the private member functions *ShowPenStyles*, *ShowPenWidths*, and *ShowBrushStyles*, all of which should be familiar to you by now. *CMyView* also contains a message map directing WM_CREATE and WM_SIZE messages to its own *OnCreate* and *OnSize* member functions. Curiously, neither *CMyView* nor *CMainWindow* contains an *OnPaint* function, although *CMyView* includes a member function named *OnDraw* that looks suspiciously like an *OnPaint* handler and even receives a *CDC* pointer through its parameter list. What's going on here?

GdiDemo3.rc

```
//********************************************************************
//
//  GdiDemo3.rc
//
//********************************************************************

#include <afxres.h>

AFX_IDI_STD_FRAME ICON GdiDemo.ico
```

Figure 2-12. *The GdiDemo3 source code.*

GdiDemo3.h

```
//**************************************************************************
//
//  GdiDemo3.h
//
//**************************************************************************

class CMyApp : public CWinApp
{
public:
    virtual BOOL InitInstance ();
};

class CMyView : public CScrollView
{
private:
    int m_cxChar;
    int m_cyChar;

    void ShowPenStyles (CDC*, int, int);
    void ShowPenWidths (CDC*, int, int);
    void ShowBrushStyles (CDC*, int, int);

protected:
    virtual void OnDraw (CDC*);

    afx_msg int OnCreate (LPCREATESTRUCT);
    afx_msg void OnSize (UINT, int, int);

    DECLARE_MESSAGE_MAP ()
};

class CMainWindow : public CFrameWnd
{
public:
    CMainWindow ();

protected:
    afx_msg int OnCreate (LPCREATESTRUCT);
    DECLARE_MESSAGE_MAP ()
};

struct STYLES {
    int nStyle;
    char szStyleName[16];
};
```

GdiDemo3.cpp

```cpp
//****************************************************************************
//
//  GdiDemo3.cpp
//
//****************************************************************************

#include <afxwin.h>
#include "GdiDemo3.h"

#define VHEIGHT (m_cyChar * 50)

CMyApp myApp;

///////////////////////////////////////////////////////////////////////////
// CMyApp member functions

BOOL CMyApp::InitInstance ()
{
    m_pMainWnd = new CMainWindow;
    m_pMainWnd->ShowWindow (m_nCmdShow);
    m_pMainWnd->UpdateWindow ();
    return TRUE;
}


///////////////////////////////////////////////////////////////////////////
// CMainWindow message map and member functions

BEGIN_MESSAGE_MAP (CMainWindow, CFrameWnd)
    ON_WM_CREATE ()
END_MESSAGE_MAP ()

CMainWindow::CMainWindow ()
{
    Create (NULL, "GdiDemo3");
}

int CMainWindow::OnCreate (LPCREATESTRUCT lpcs)
{
    if (CFrameWnd::OnCreate (lpcs) == -1)
        return -1;

    CMyView* pMyView = new CMyView;
    pMyView->Create (NULL, NULL, WS_CHILD | WS_VISIBLE,
            CRect (0, 0, 0, 0), this, AFX_IDW_PANE_FIRST, NULL);
    return 0;
}
```

```
/////////////////////////////////////////////////////////////////////
// CMyView message map and member functions

BEGIN_MESSAGE_MAP (CMyView, CScrollView)
    ON_WM_CREATE ()
    ON_WM_SIZE ()
END_MESSAGE_MAP ()

int CMyView::OnCreate (LPCREATESTRUCT lpcs)
{
    if (CScrollView::OnCreate (lpcs) == -1)
        return -1;

    TEXTMETRIC tm;
    CClientDC dc (this);
    dc.GetTextMetrics (&tm);
    m_cxChar = tm.tmAveCharWidth;
    m_cyChar = tm.tmHeight;
    return 0;
}

void CMyView::OnSize (UINT nType, int cx, int cy)
{
    SetScrollSizes (MM_TEXT, CSize (0, VHEIGHT), CSize (0, cy),
        CSize (0, m_cyChar));
}

void CMyView::OnDraw (CDC* pDC)
{
    CPaintDC dc (this);

    ShowPenStyles (pDC, m_cxChar * 2, m_cyChar);
    ShowPenWidths (pDC, m_cxChar * 2, m_cyChar * 15);
    ShowBrushStyles (pDC, m_cxChar * 2, m_cyChar * 27);
}

void CMyView::ShowPenStyles (CDC* pDC, int x, int y)
{
    static struct STYLES styles[] = {
        PS_SOLID,       "PS_SOLID",
        PS_DASH,        "PS_DASH",
        PS_DOT,         "PS_DOT",
        PS_DASHDOT,     "PS_DASHDOT",
        PS_DASHDOTDOT,  "PS_DASHDOTDOT",
        PS_NULL,        "PS_NULL",
```

(continued)

```
        PS_INSIDEFRAME, "PS_INSIDEFRAME"
    };

    pDC->SetTextColor (RGB (0, 0, 0));
    pDC->TextOut (x, y, "Pen Styles");

    int dy = (m_cyChar * 3) / 2;
    int x1 = x + (m_cxChar * 2);
    int x2 = x + (m_cxChar * 22);
    int x3 = x + (m_cxChar * 46);

    CPen* pOldPen;
    pDC->SetTextColor (RGB (255, 0, 0));

    for (int i=0; i<7; i++) {
        y += dy;
        pDC->TextOut (x1, y, styles[i].szStyleName);

        CPen pen (styles[i].nStyle, 1, RGB (255, 0, 0));
        pOldPen = pDC->SelectObject (&pen);

        pDC->MoveTo (x2, y + (m_cyChar / 2));
        pDC->LineTo (x3, y + (m_cyChar / 2));

        pDC->SelectObject (pOldPen);
    }
}

void CMyView::ShowPenWidths (CDC* pDC, int x, int y)
{
    static int nPenWidths[] = { 2, 8, 16, 24 };

    pDC->SetTextColor_(RGB (0, 0, 0));
    pDC->TextOut (x, y, "Pen Widths");

    int dy = m_cyChar * 2;
    int x1 = x + (m_cxChar * 2);
    int x2 = x + (m_cxChar * 22);
    int x3 = x + (m_cxChar * 46);

    CPen* pOldPen;
    CString strDescription;
    pDC->SetTextColor (RGB (0, 0, 255));

    for (int i=0; i<4; i++) {
        y += dy;
```

```
            strDescription.Format ("%d Pixels", nPenWidths[i]);
            pDC->TextOut (x1, y, strDescription);

            CPen pen (PS_SOLID, nPenWidths[i], RGB (0, 0, 255));
            pOldPen = pDC->SelectObject (&pen);

            pDC->MoveTo (x2, y + (m_cyChar / 2));
            pDC->LineTo (x3, y + (m_cyChar / 2));

            pDC->SelectObject (pOldPen);
        }
    }

    void CMyView::ShowBrushStyles (CDC* pDC, int x, int y)
    {
        static struct STYLES styles[] = {
            HS_BDIAGONAL,    "HS_BDIAGONAL",
            HS_CROSS,        "HS_CROSS",
            HS_DIAGCROSS,    "HS_DIAGCROSS",
            HS_FDIAGONAL,    "HS_FDIAGONAL",
            HS_HORIZONTAL,   "HS_HORIZONTAL",
            HS_VERTICAL,     "HS_VERTICAL"
        };

        pDC->SetTextColor (RGB (0, 0, 0));
        pDC->TextOut (x, y, "Brush Styles");

        int dy = m_cyChar * 3;
        int x1 = x + (m_cxChar * 2);
        int x2 = x + (m_cxChar * 22);
        int x3 = x + (m_cxChar * 46);

        CBrush* pOldBrush;

        for (int i=0; i<6; i++) {
            y += dy;
            pDC->TextOut (x1, y, styles[i].szStyleName);

            CRect rect (x2, y - m_cyChar, x3, y + m_cyChar);
            CBrush brush (styles[i].nStyle, RGB (0, 255, 0));

            CPoint point (rect.left, rect.top);
            pDC->LPtoDP (&point);
            point.x %= 8;
            point.y %= 8;
            pDC->SetBrushOrg (point);
```

(continued)

GdiDemo3.cpp *continued*

```
        pOldBrush = pDC->SelectObject (&brush);
        pDC->Rectangle (rect);

        pDC->SelectObject (pOldBrush);
    }

    y += dy;
    pDC->TextOut (x1, y, "Solid");

    CBrush brush (RGB (0, 255, 0));
    pOldBrush = pDC->SelectObject (&brush);
    pDC->Rectangle (x2, y - m_cyChar, x3, y + m_cyChar);
    pDC->SelectObject (pOldBrush);
}
```

It's simple, really. One of the benefits of MFC's document/view architecture is the abstraction of WM_PAINT messages. A view class's default *OnPaint* handler creates a *CPaintDC* device context object and then calls the virtual *OnDraw* function with a pointer to that object. All you have to do to make a view draw itself is override *OnDraw* and provide the necessary drawing logic; even the device context is provided for you. You don't have to call *CDC::SetWindowOrg* to move the origin of the coordinate system because *CScrollView* does it for you in its override of a virtual function named *CView::OnPrepareDC* that gets called before *OnDraw*. The use of *OnDraw* instead of *OnPaint* might not seem like that big a deal at the moment, but in the larger context of the document/view architecture, it makes plenty of sense because it allows the framework to call the same code to do drawing, printing, and print previewing. You'll learn more about this rather unique—and very handy—feature of MFC in Chapter 10.

The view is instantiated and the view window created by the frame window with the following statements in *CMainWindow::OnCreate*:

```
CMyView* pMyView = new CMyView;
pMyView->Create (NULL, NULL, WS_CHILD | WS_VISIBLE,
    CRect (0, 0, 0, 0), this, AFX_IDW_PANE_FIRST, NULL);
```

pMyView stores the pointer to the view object. The call to *Create* is identical to the one shown in the previous section, complete with the AFX_IDW_PANE_FIRST value that connects the view to the frame window. Since the view is itself a window, it too receives a WM_CREATE message, and the code that initializes *m_cxChar* and *m_cyChar*—code that was part of *CMainWindow::OnCreate* in GdiDemo1 and GdiDemo2—is now located in *CMyView::OnCreate*.

Just as GdiDemo2's *OnSize* handler called *SetScrollInfo* to reconfigure the scroll bar in response to WM_SIZE messages, GdiDemo3's *OnSize* handler calls the scroll view's *SetScrollSizes* function. *CMyView::OnSize* is much simpler than GdiDemo2's *CMainWindow::OnSize* function, containing just one line of code:

```
SetScrollSizes (MM_TEXT, CSize (0, VHEIGHT), CSize (0, cy),
    CSize (0, m_cyChar));
```

It's no longer necessary to set the scroll range to 0 if the window is large enough to show the entire workspace, because the view does that automatically. Our responsibility for maintaining the scroll bar begins and ends with this simple statement in *OnSize*, and even that wouldn't be necessary if we were content to leave the page size constant rather than keying it to the window size. We would still need to call *SetScrollSizes* one time to initialize the view, but that could be done in *CMyView::OnCreate* or in *CMyView*'s constructor. Fortunately, supplying a one-line *OnSize* function and one additional message map entry is a small price to pay for having the scroll bar automatically adapt to changes in window size.

Allowing *CScrollView* to provide the scrolling logic does more than simplify the source code; it also adds one very nice feature to the program. Drag GdiDemo3's scroll bar thumb up and down, and you'll find that the window scrolls interactively. Unlike the *OnVScroll* code we added to GdiDemo2, *CScrollView*'s built-in *OnVScroll* handler responds to SB_THUMBTRACK messages. So by deriving a view class from *CScrollView* and letting it do the scrolling, you get thumb tracking for free. Not bad!

Lest you be misled into thinking that *CScrollView* is a cure-all and that you'll never have to write source code for scroll bars again, you should be aware of a couple of issues. The first is that *CScrollView* is great for this particular application—one in which a frame window is used to provide a view into a virtual workspace—but there are other uses for scroll bars that don't map so easily to the capabilities of a *CScrollView*. Remember that multimedia application I mentioned earlier? I used a scroll bar to allow the user to move forward and backward in audio tracks playing in a CD-ROM drive. A *CScrollView* object wasn't much help in that situation because there was really nothing to view.

The other issue is speed. *CScrollView* works pretty well for GdiDemo3 because the virtual workspace isn't that much larger than the window. But what if the virtual workspace were 30,000 pixels tall and the window were only 100? *CScrollView* would still work, but it would be painfully slow because the *OnDraw* handler would try to draw all 30,000 lines of output each time a scroll event occurred. To compensate, you'd need to modify the *OnDraw* code to get the scroll position by calling *CScrollView::GetScrollPosition* and localize drawing to the workspace's visible area. Of course, that means writing additional code to make the *OnDraw* handler more intelligent. So while *CScrollView* is definitely a useful class to have around, rest assured that the time we spent with GdiDemo2 won't be wasted.

Loose Ends

Before we finish up with GdiDemo3 and close out the chapter, there is one loose end that needs to be tied up. Shortly after the program starts, *CMainWindow::OnCreate* creates a view object with the following statement:

```
CMyView* pMyView = new CMyView;
```

Since the object is instantiated with *new*, it remains in memory after *OnCreate* terminates and in fact will not go away until it is deleted with a *delete* statement. Yet nowhere in GdiDemo3's source code will you find such a statement. For that matter, the frame window object isn't visibly deleted anywhere in the code, either; there is no *delete m_pMainWnd* statement to counter the statement

```
m_pMainWnd = new CMainWindow;
```

in *CMyApp::InitInstance*. On the surface, this would seem to be a problem. After all, every C++ programmer knows that every *new* must be countered with a *delete* or objects will be left behind in memory. So what gives?

As you probably suspected, the class library deletes these objects for you. To be more precise, the objects delete themselves. The key to this little trick is that the very last message a window receives before it goes away for good is WM_NCDESTROY. If you look at the source code for *CWnd::OnNcDestroy*, you'll see that it calls a virtual function named *PostNcDestroy*. Both *CFrameWnd* and *CView* override *PostNcDestroy* and execute a

```
delete this;
```

statement to delete themselves. Therefore, when a frame window or a view is destroyed, the object associated with that window is automatically deleted, too. GdiDemo3's frame window is destroyed when the user clicks the close button on the title bar or selects Close from the system menu. And when any window is destroyed, its children are automatically destroyed, too—Windows sees to that. Thus, closing down GdiDemo3 initiates a chain of events that ultimately destroys the frame window and the view window *and* the C++ objects associated with those windows. It's worth noting as an aside that *CWnd*'s own implementation of *PostNcDestroy* does not delete the associated window object. Therefore, should you derive your own window class directly from *CWnd*, you'll also need to override *PostNcDestroy* in the derived class and execute a *delete this* statement. Otherwise, the *CWnd* object will not be properly deleted. You'll see what I mean in the next chapter.

Chapter 3

The Mouse and the Keyboard

If life were like the movies, traditional input devices would have given way long ago to speech-recognition units, 3D headsets, and other human-machine interface gadgets. At present, however, the two most common input devices remain the mouse and keyboard. Microsoft Windows handles some mouse and keyboard input itself, automatically dropping down a menu, for example, when the user clicks an item in the menu bar, and sending the application a WM_COMMAND message when an item is selected from the menu. It's entirely possible to write a full-featured Windows program that processes no mouse or keyboard input directly, but as an application developer, you'll eventually discover the need to read input from the mouse and keyboard directly. And when you do, you'll need to know about the mouse and keyboard interfaces that Windows provides.

Not surprisingly, mouse and keyboard input comes in the form of messages. Device drivers process mouse and keyboard interrupts signaling input events and put the resultant event notifications in a systemwide queue known as the *raw input queue*. The entries in the raw input queue have WM_ message identifiers just as conventional messages do, but the data in them is "raw" and requires further processing before it is meaningful to an application. A dedicated thread owned by the operating system monitors the raw input queue and transfers each message that shows up there to the appropriate application-owned message queue. The "cooking" of the message data is performed later, in the context of the receiving application, and the message is ultimately retrieved and dispatched just as any other message is.

This input model differs from that of Windows 3.1, which stored mouse and keyboard messages in a single systemwide input queue until they were retrieved by an application. This arrangement proved to be an Achilles' heel of sorts because it meant that one application that failed to dispose of input messages in a timely way could prevent other applications from doing the same. Windows 95's asynchronous input model solves this problem by using the raw input queue as a temporary holding buffer and moving input messages to thread message queues at the earliest opportune moment. The impact of this architecture is difficult to appreciate unless you've experienced ill-behaved Win16 applications that slowed the rest of the system to a crawl by taking too much time to process messages, but rest assured that the asynchronous input model is superior and that its benefits are very real. A 32-bit application that goes too long between calls to *::GetMessage* will respond sluggishly to user input, but it won't affect the responsiveness of other processes running on the system.

Learning to respond to mouse and keyboard input in a Windows application is largely a matter of learning about which messages to process. This chapter introduces mouse and keyboard messages and the various functions, both in MFC and the API, that are useful for processing them. We'll take the concepts presented here from the blackboard to the real world by developing four sample applications:

- TicTac, a tic-tac-toe game that demonstrates how to respond to mouse clicks

- MouseCap, a simple drawing program that demonstrates how mouse capturing works and how nonclient-area mouse messages are processed

- GdiDemo4, an improved version of Chapter 2's GdiDemo3 program that adds a keyboard interface to the *CScrollView* window

- VisualKB, a typing program that brings mouse and keyboard handlers together under one roof and lists the keyboard messages it receives

There's a lot of ground to cover, so let's get started.

GETTING INPUT FROM THE MOUSE

Windows uses a number of different messages—more than 20 in all—to report input events involving the mouse. These messages fall into two rather broad categories: client-area mouse messages, which report events that occur in a window's client area, and nonclient-area mouse messages, which pertain to events in a window's nonclient area. An "event" can mean

- The press or release of a mouse button

- The double-click of a mouse button

- The movement of the mouse

You'll typically ignore events in the nonclient area of your window and allow Windows to handle them instead. If your program processes mouse input, it's client-area mouse messages you'll probably be concerned with.

Client-Area Mouse Messages

Windows reports mouse events in a window's client area with the client-area mouse messages shown below:

CLIENT-AREA MOUSE MESSAGES

Message	*Handler*	*Sent When*
WM_LBUTTONDOWN	*OnLButtonDown*	The left mouse button is pressed.
WM_LBUTTONUP	*OnLButtonUp*	The left mouse button is released.
WM_LBUTTONDBLCLK	*OnLButtonDblClk*	The left mouse button is double-clicked.
WM_MBUTTONDOWN	*OnMButtonDown*	The middle mouse button is pressed.
WM_MBUTTONUP	*OnMButtonUp*	The middle mouse button is released.
WM_MBUTTONDBLCLK	*OnMButtonDblClk*	The middle mouse button is double-clicked.
WM_RBUTTONDOWN	*OnRButtonDown*	The right mouse button is pressed.
WM_RBUTTONUP	*OnRButtonUp*	The right mouse button is released.
WM_RBUTTONDBLCLK	*OnRButtonDblClk*	The right mouse button is double-clicked.
WM_MOUSEMOVE	*OnMouseMove*	The mouse is moved over the window's client area.

Messages that begin with WM_LBUTTON pertain to the left mouse button, WM_MBUTTON messages to the middle mouse button, and WM_RBUTTON messages to the right mouse button. If the user's mouse has only two buttons, your application won't receive WM_MBUTTON messages. It won't receive WM_RBUTTON messages if the mouse has just one button. The vast majority of PCs running Windows have two-button mice, so it's reasonably safe to assume that the right mouse button exists. However, if you'd like to be certain (or if you'd like to determine whether there is a third button, too), you can call the Windows *::GetSystemMetrics* API function as follows:

```
::GetSystemMetrics (SM_CMOUSEBUTTONS);
```

The return value is the number of mouse buttons, or 0 in the unlikely event that a mouse is not installed.

WM_*x*BUTTONDOWN and WM_*x*BUTTONUP messages report button presses and releases. A WM_LBUTTONDOWN message is normally followed by a WM_LBUTTONUP message, but don't count on it. Mouse messages go to the window underneath the cursor (the Windows term for the mouse pointer), so if the user clicks the left mouse button over a window's client area and then moves the cursor outside the window before releasing the button, the window will receive a WM_LBUTTONDOWN message but not a WM_LBUTTONUP message. Many programs react only to button-down messages and ignore button-up messages, in which case the pairing of the two isn't important. If pairing is essential, a program can "capture" the mouse on receipt of a button-down message and release it when a button-up message arrives. In between, all mouse messages, even those pertaining to events outside the window, are directed to the window that performed the capture. This ensures that a button-up message will be received no matter where the cursor is when the button is released. We'll look more closely at mouse capturing shortly.

When two clicks of the same button occur within a very short period of time, the second button-down message is replaced by a WM_*x*BUTTONDBLCLK message. Significantly, this happens only if the window's WNDCLASS includes the class style CS_DBLCLKS. The default WNDCLASS that MFC registers for frame windows has the CS_DBLCLKS style, so frame windows receive double-click messages by default. For a CS_DBLCLKS-style window, two rapid clicks of the left mouse button over the window's client area produce the following sequence of messages:

```
WM_LBUTTONDOWN
WM_LBUTTONUP
WM_LBUTTONDBLCLK
WM_LBUTTONUP
```

However, the same two button clicks produce the following sequence of messages if the window is not registered to be notified of double-clicks:

```
WM_LBUTTONDOWN
WM_LBUTTONUP
WM_LBUTTONDOWN
WM_LBUTTONUP
```

How your application responds to these messages—or whether it responds to them at all—is up to you. Something you'll probably want to steer away from, though, is having clicks and double clicks of the same mouse button on the same object (or in the same area of the window) carry out two unrelated tasks. A double-click message will always be preceded by a single-click message, so the actions that generate the two messages are not easily divorced. The usual solution is to have the first click select an object, and the second click take some action upon it. When you double-click a folder in the right pane of the Windows 95 Explorer, for example, the first click selects the folder, and the second click—if it comes—opens the folder and displays its contents.

WM_MOUSEMOVE messages signify that the cursor has moved within the window's client area. As the mouse is moved, the window underneath the cursor receives a flurry of WM_MOUSEMOVE messages reporting the latest cursor position. Windows has an interesting way of delivering WM_MOUSEMOVE messages that prevents slow applications from being overwhelmed by messages reporting every position in the cursor's travel. Rather than stuff a WM_MOUSEMOVE message into an application's message queue each time the mouse is moved, Windows simply sets a flag in the message queue. The next time the application retrieves a message, Windows, seeing that the flag is set, manufactures a WM_MOUSEMOVE message with the current cursor coordinates. Therefore, an application receives WM_MOUSEMOVE messages only as often as it can handle them. If the cursor is moved very slowly, every point in its journey will be reported unless the application is busy doing other things. But if the cursor is whisked very rapidly across the screen, most applications will receive only a handful of WM_MOUSEMOVE messages.

In an MFC program, an ON_WM_LBUTTONDOWN entry in the message map routes WM_LBUTTONDOWN messages to the class's *OnLButtonDown* member function, an ON_WM_LBUTTONUP entry sends WM_LBUTTONUP messages to *OnLButtonUp*, and so on. All client-area mouse message handlers are prototyped as follows:

```
afx_msg void OnMsgName (UINT nFlags, CPoint point)
```

nFlags contains a series of bit flags identifying the state of the mouse buttons and of the Shift and Ctrl keys at the time the event occurred, and *point* identifies the location of the cursor. For WM_*x*BUTTONDOWN and WM_*x*BUTTONDBLCLK messages, *point* specifies the location of the cursor when the button was clicked. For WM_*x*BUTTONUP messages, *point* specifies the cursor location at which the button was released. And for WM_MOUSEMOVE messages, *point* specifies the cursor's latest position. In all cases, positions are reported in device coordinates relative to the upper left corner of the window's client area. A WM_LBUTTONDOWN message with *point.x* equal to 32 and *point.y* equal to 64 means the left mouse button was clicked 32 pixels to the right of and 64 pixels below the client area's upper left corner. If necessary, these coordinates can be converted to logical coordinates using MFC's *CDC::DPtoLP* function.

The *nFlags* parameter specifies the state of the mouse buttons and of the Shift and Ctrl keys at the time the message was generated. You can find out from this parameter whether a particular button or key is up or down by means of the bit masks shown in the table on the next page.

Mask	Meaning If Set
MK_LBUTTON	The left mouse button is depressed.
MK_MBUTTON	The middle mouse button is depressed.
MK_RBUTTON	The right mouse button is depressed.
MK_CONTROL	The Ctrl key is depressed.
MK_SHIFT	The Shift key is depressed.

The statement

```
nFlags & MK_LBUTTON
```

is nonzero if and only if the left mouse button is depressed, while

```
nFlags & MK_CONTROL
```

is nonzero if the Ctrl key was held down when the event occurred. Some programs respond differently to mouse events if the Shift or Ctrl key is held down. For example, a drawing program might constrain the user to drawing only horizontal or only vertical lines if the Ctrl key is depressed as the mouse is moved by checking the MK_CONTROL bit in the *nFlags* parameter accompanying WM_MOUSEMOVE messages.

The TicTac Application

To see how easy it is to process mouse messages, let's build a sample application that takes input from the mouse. TicTac, whose output is shown in Figure 3-1, is a tic-tac-toe program that responds to three types of client-area mouse events: left button clicks, right button clicks, and left button double-clicks. Clicking the left mouse button over an empty square places an X in that square. Clicking the right mouse button places an O in an empty square. (The program prohibits cheating by making sure that Xs and Os are alternated.) Double-clicking the left mouse button over the thick black lines that separate the squares clears the playing grid and starts a new game. After each X or O is placed, the program checks to see if there's a winner or if the game has been played to a draw. A draw is declared when all nine squares are filled and neither player has managed to claim three squares in a row horizontally, vertically, or diagonally. In addition to providing a hands-on demonstration of mouse-message processing, TicTac also introduces some handy new MFC functions such as *CWnd::MessageBox*, which displays a message box window, and *CRect::PtInRect*, which quickly tells your application whether a given point lies inside a rectangle represented by a *CRect* object. TicTac's source code appears in Figure 3-2.

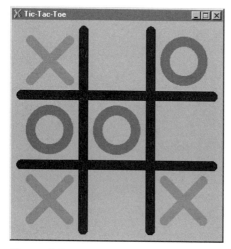

Figure 3-1. *The TicTac window.*

Resource.h

```
//****************************************************************************
//
//   Resource.h
//
//****************************************************************************

#define IDI_APPICON 100
```

TicTac.rc

```
//****************************************************************************
//
//   TicTac.rc
//
//****************************************************************************

#include "Resource.h"

IDI_APPICON ICON TicTac.ico
```

Figure 3-2. *The TicTac program.*

TicTac.h

```
//******************************************************************************
//
//  TicTac.h
//
//******************************************************************************

class CMyApp : public CWinApp
{
public:
    virtual BOOL InitInstance ();
};

class CMainWindow : public CWnd
{
private:
    static const CRect m_rcSquares[9];
    int m_nGameGrid[9];
    int m_nNextChar;

    int GetRectID (CPoint);
    void DrawBoard (CDC*);
    void DrawX (CDC*, int);
    void DrawO (CDC*, int);
    void ResetGame ();
    void CheckForGameOver ();
    int IsWinner ();
    BOOL IsDraw ();

public:
    CMainWindow ();

protected:
    virtual void PostNcDestroy ();

    afx_msg void OnPaint ();
    afx_msg void OnLButtonDown (UINT, CPoint);
    afx_msg void OnLButtonDblClk (UINT, CPoint);
    afx_msg void OnRButtonDown (UINT, CPoint);

    DECLARE_MESSAGE_MAP ()
};
```

TicTac.cpp

```
//***************************************************************************
//
// TicTac.cpp
//
//***************************************************************************

#include <afxwin.h>
#include "Resource.h"
#include "TicTac.h"

#define EX 1
#define OH 2

CMyApp myApp;

///////////////////////////////////////////////////////////////////////////
// CMyApp member functions

BOOL CMyApp::InitInstance ()
{
    m_pMainWnd = new CMainWindow;
    m_pMainWnd->ShowWindow (m_nCmdShow);
    m_pMainWnd->UpdateWindow ();
    return TRUE;
}

///////////////////////////////////////////////////////////////////////////
// CMainWindow message map and member functions

BEGIN_MESSAGE_MAP (CMainWindow, CWnd)
    ON_WM_PAINT ()
    ON_WM_LBUTTONDOWN ()
    ON_WM_LBUTTONDBLCLK ()
    ON_WM_RBUTTONDOWN ()
END_MESSAGE_MAP ()

const CRect CMainWindow::m_rcSquares[9] = {
    CRect ( 16,  16, 112, 112),
    CRect (128,  16, 224, 112),
    CRect (240,  16, 336, 112),
    CRect ( 16, 128, 112, 224),
    CRect (128, 128, 224, 224),
    CRect (240, 128, 336, 224),
```

(continued)

TicTac.cpp *continued*

```
    CRect ( 16, 240, 112, 336),
    CRect (128, 240, 224, 336),
    CRect (240, 240, 336, 336)
};

CMainWindow::CMainWindow ()
{
    m_nNextChar = EX;
    ::ZeroMemory (m_nGameGrid, 9 * sizeof (int));

    CString strWndClass = AfxRegisterWndClass (
        CS_DBLCLKS,                             // Class style
        myApp.LoadStandardCursor (IDC_ARROW),   // Class cursor
        (HBRUSH) (COLOR_3DFACE + 1),            // Class background brush
        myApp.LoadIcon (IDI_APPICON)            // Class icon
    );

    CreateEx (0, strWndClass, "Tic-Tac-Toe",
        WS_OVERLAPPED | WS_SYSMENU | WS_CAPTION | WS_MINIMIZEBOX,
        CW_USEDEFAULT, CW_USEDEFAULT, CW_USEDEFAULT, CW_USEDEFAULT,
        NULL, NULL);

    CRect rect (0, 0, 352, 352);
    CalcWindowRect (&rect);

    SetWindowPos (NULL, 0, 0, rect.Width (), rect.Height (),
        SWP_NOZORDER | SWP_NOMOVE | SWP_NOREDRAW);
}

void CMainWindow::PostNcDestroy ()
{
    delete this;
}

void CMainWindow::OnPaint ()
{
    CPaintDC dc (this);
    DrawBoard (&dc);
}

void CMainWindow::OnLButtonDown (UINT nFlags, CPoint point)
{
    if (m_nNextChar != EX)
        return;
```

```
    int nPos = GetRectID (point);
    if (nPos == -1)
        return;

    if (m_nGameGrid[nPos] != 0)
        return;

    m_nNextChar = OH;
    m_nGameGrid[nPos] = EX;

    CClientDC dc (this);
    DrawX (&dc, nPos);

    CheckForGameOver ();
}

void CMainWindow::OnRButtonDown (UINT nFlags, CPoint point)
{
    if (m_nNextChar != OH)
        return;

    int nPos = GetRectID (point);
    if (nPos == -1)
        return;

    if (m_nGameGrid[nPos] != 0)
        return;

    m_nNextChar = EX;
    m_nGameGrid[nPos] = OH;

    CClientDC dc (this);
    DrawO (&dc, nPos);

    CheckForGameOver ();
}

void CMainWindow::OnLButtonDblClk (UINT nFlags, CPoint point)
{
    CClientDC dc (this);
    if (dc.GetPixel (point) == RGB (0, 0, 0))
        ResetGame ();
}

int CMainWindow::GetRectID (CPoint point)
```

(continued)

TicTac.cpp *continued*

```
{
    for (int i=0; i<9; i++) {
        if (m_rcSquares[i].PtInRect (point))
            return i;
    }
    return -1;
}

void CMainWindow::DrawBoard (CDC* pDC)
{
    CPen pen (PS_SOLID, 16, RGB (0, 0, 0));
    CPen* pOldPen = pDC->SelectObject (&pen);

    pDC->MoveTo (120, 16);
    pDC->LineTo (120, 336);

    pDC->MoveTo (232, 16);
    pDC->LineTo (232, 336);

    pDC->MoveTo (16, 120);
    pDC->LineTo (336, 120);

    pDC->MoveTo (16, 232);
    pDC->LineTo (336, 232);

    for (int i=0; i<9; i++) {
        if (m_nGameGrid[i] == EX)
            DrawX (pDC, i);
        else if (m_nGameGrid[i] == OH)
            DrawO (pDC, i);
    }
    pDC->SelectObject (pOldPen);
}

void CMainWindow::DrawX (CDC* pDC, int nPos)
{
    CPen pen (PS_SOLID, 16, RGB (255, 0, 0));
    CPen* pOldPen = pDC->SelectObject (&pen);

    pDC->MoveTo (m_rcSquares[nPos].left + 16,
        m_rcSquares[nPos].top + 16);
    pDC->LineTo (m_rcSquares[nPos].right - 16,
        m_rcSquares[nPos].bottom - 16);

    pDC->MoveTo (m_rcSquares[nPos].left + 16,
```

```
            m_rcSquares[nPos].bottom - 16);
    pDC->LineTo (m_rcSquares[nPos].right - 16,
        m_rcSquares[nPos].top + 16);

    pDC->SelectObject (pOldPen);
}

void CMainWindow::DrawO (CDC* pDC, int nPos)
{
    CPen pen (PS_SOLID, 16, RGB (0, 0, 255));
    CPen* pOldPen = pDC->SelectObject (&pen);
    pDC->SelectStockObject (NULL_BRUSH);

    CRect rect = m_rcSquares[nPos];
    rect.DeflateRect (16, 16);
    pDC->Ellipse (rect);

    pDC->SelectObject (pOldPen);
}

void CMainWindow::CheckForGameOver ()
{
    int nWinner;

    if (nWinner = IsWinner ()) {
        CString string = (nWinner == EX) ?
            "The X's win!" : "The O's win!";
        MessageBox (string, "Game Over", MB_ICONEXCLAMATION | MB_OK);
        ResetGame ();
    }
    else if (IsDraw ()) {
        MessageBox ("It's a draw!", "Game Over",
            MB_ICONEXCLAMATION | MB_OK);
        ResetGame ();
    }
}

int CMainWindow::IsWinner ()
{
    static int nPattern[8][3] = {
        0, 1, 2,
        3, 4, 5,
        6, 7, 8,
        0, 3, 6,
        1, 4, 7,
```

(continued)

TicTac.cpp *continued*

```
        2, 5, 8,
        0, 4, 8,
        2, 4, 6
    };

    for (int i=0; i<8; i++) {
        if ((m_nGameGrid[nPattern[i][0]] == EX) &&
            (m_nGameGrid[nPattern[i][1]] == EX) &&
            (m_nGameGrid[nPattern[i][2]] == EX))
            return EX;

        if ((m_nGameGrid[nPattern[i][0]] == OH) &&
            (m_nGameGrid[nPattern[i][1]] == OH) &&
            (m_nGameGrid[nPattern[i][2]] == OH))
            return OH;
    }
    return 0;
}

BOOL CMainWindow::IsDraw ()
{
    for (int i=0; i<9; i++) {
        if (m_nGameGrid[i] == 0)
            return FALSE;
    }
    return TRUE;
}

void CMainWindow::ResetGame ()
{
    m_nNextChar = EX;
    ::ZeroMemory (m_nGameGrid, 9 * sizeof (int));
    Invalidate ();
}
```

Processing Mouse Messages

The first step in processing mouse input is adding the entries for the messages you want your window to handle to the message map. The *CMainWindow* message map in TicTac.cpp contains the following mouse-message entries:

```
ON_WM_LBUTTONDOWN ()
ON_WM_LBUTTONDBLCLK ()
ON_WM_RBUTTONDOWN ()
```

These three statements correlate WM_LBUTTONDOWN, WM_LBUTTONDBLCLK, and WM_RBUTTONDOWN messages to the *CMainWindow* member functions *OnLButton-*

Down, OnLButtonDblClk, and *OnRButtonDown.* And when the messages start arriving, the fun begins.

The *OnLButtonDown* handler processes clicks of the left mouse button in *CMainWindow*'s client area. After checking *m_nNextChar* to verify that it's X's turn and not O's (and returning without doing anything if it's not), *OnLButtonDown* calls the private member function *GetRectID* to determine whether the click occurred in one of the nine rectangles corresponding to squares in the tic-tac-toe grid. The rectangle's coordinates are stored in the static *CMainWindow::m_rcSquares* array, which is actually an array of *CRect* objects. *GetRectID* uses a *for* loop to determine whether the cursor location passed to it by the message handler lies within any of the squares:

```
for (int i=0; i<9; i++) {
    if (m_rcSquares[i].PtInRect (point))
        return i;
}
return -1;
```

CRect::PtInRect returns TRUE if the point passed to it lies within the rectangle represented by the *CRect* object, or FALSE if it does not. If *PtInRect* returns TRUE for any of the rectangles in the *m_rect* array, *GetRectID* returns the rectangle ID. The ID is an integer from 0 through 8, with 0 representing the square in the upper left corner of the grid, 1 the square to its right, 2 the square in the upper right corner, 3 the leftmost square in the second row, and so on. Each square has a corresponding element in the *m_nGameGrid* array, which initially holds all zeros representing empty squares. If none of the calls to *PtInRect* returns TRUE, *GetRectID* returns −1 to indicate that the click occurred outside the squares and *OnLButtonDown* ignores the mouse click. If, however, *GetRectID* returns a valid ID and the corresponding square is empty, *OnLButtonDown* records the X in the *m_nGameGrid* array and then calls *CMainWindow::DrawX* to draw an X in the square. *DrawX* creates a red pen 16 pixels wide and draws two intersecting lines aligned at 45-degree angles.

OnRButtonDown works in much the same way as *OnLButtonDown* except that it draws an O in an empty square instead of an X. The routine that does the drawing is *CMainWindow::DrawO.* Before it draws an O with the *CDC::Ellipse* function, *DrawO* selects a NULL brush into the device context:

```
pDC->SelectStockObject (NULL_BRUSH);
```

This prevents the interior of the O from being filled with the device context's default white brush. (As an alternative, we could have created a brush whose color matched the window's background color and selected it into the device context, but drawing with a NULL brush is slightly faster because it produces no physical screen output.) The O is then drawn with the statements

```
CRect rect = m_rcSquares[nPos];
```

```
rect.DeflateRect (16, 16);
pDC->Ellipse (rect);
```

The first statement copies the rectangle representing the grid square to a local *CRect* object named *rect*; the second uses *CRect::DeflateRect* to "deflate" the rectangle by 16 pixels in each direction and form the circle's bounding box; and the third draws the circle. The result is a nicely formed O centered in the square in which it is drawn.

Double-clicking the grid lines separating the squares clears the Xs and Os and begins a new game. While this is admittedly a poor way to design a user interface, it does give us an excuse to write a double-click handler. (A better solution would be a push button control with the words "New Game" stamped on it or a "New Game" menu item, but since we haven't covered menus and controls yet, the perfect user interface will just have to wait.) Left mouse button double-clicks are processed by *CMainWindow::OnLButtonDblClk*, which contains these simple statements:

```
CClientDC dc (this);
if (dc.GetPixel (point) == RGB (0, 0, 0))
    ResetGame ();
```

To determine whether the double-click occurred over the thick black strokes separating the squares in the playing grid, *OnLButtonDblClk* calls *CDC::GetPixel* to get the color of the pixel under the cursor and compares it to black (RGB (0, 0, 0)). If there's a match, *ResetGame* is called to reset the game. Otherwise, *OnLButtonDblClk* returns and the double-click is ignored. Testing the color of the pixel underneath the cursor is an effective technique for hit-testing irregularly shaped areas, but be wary of using nonprimary colors that a display driver is likely to dither. Pure black (RGB (0, 0, 0)) and pure white (RGB (255, 255, 255)) are supported on every PC that Windows runs on, so you can safely assume that neither of these colors will be dithered.

To be consistent with Windows 95 user interface guidelines, applications should not use the right mouse button to carry out application-specific tasks as TicTac does. Instead, Windows applications should respond to right mouse clicks by popping up context menus like those displayed by the Windows 95 shell. When a WM_RBUT-TONUP message is passed to the system for default processing, Windows 95 puts a WM_CONTEXTMENU message in the message queue. We'll explore this new feature of Windows 95 more fully in the next chapter.

Message Boxes

Before returning, *OnLButtonDown* and *OnRButtonDown* call *CMainWindow::Check-ForGameOver* to find out if the game is over and, if necessary, reset the playing grid. If a player has managed to align three Xs or Os in a row or if no empty squares remain, *CheckForGameOver* calls the window class's *MessageBox* function to pop up a message box announcing a win or a draw as shown in Figure 3-3. *CWnd::MessageBox* is an extraordinarily useful tool to have at your disposal because it provides a one-step means for displaying a message on the screen and optionally obtaining a response.

Figure 3-3. *A Windows message box.*

CWnd::MessageBox is prototyped as follows:

```
int MessageBox (LPCTSTR lpszText, LPCTSTR lpszCaption = NULL,
    UINT nType = MB_OK)
```

lpszText specifies the text that will appear in the body of the message box, *lpszCaption* specifies the caption in the message box's title bar, and *nType* contains one or more bit flags defining the message box's style. The return value identifies the button that was clicked to dismiss the message box. *lpszText* and *lpszCaption* can be *CString* objects or pointers to conventional text strings. (Because the *CString* class overloads the LPCTSTR operator, you can always pass a *CString* object to a function that accepts an LPCTSTR data type.) A NULL *lpszCaption* value displays the caption "Error" in the title bar.

The simplest use for *MessageBox* is to display a message and pause until the user clicks the OK button:

```
// Do something
MessageBox ("Click OK to continue", "My Application");
// Continue what you were doing
```

Accepting the default value for *nType* (MB_OK) means the message box will have an OK button but no other buttons. Consequently, the only possible return value is IDOK. But suppose you wanted to use a message box to ask the user whether to save a file before exiting the application. For this, you could use the MB_YESNOCANCEL style:

```
MessageBox ("Your document contains unsaved data. Save it?",
    "My Application", MB_YESNOCANCEL);
```

Now the message box will contain three buttons—Yes, No, and Cancel—and the value returned from the *MessageBox* function will be IDYES, IDNO, or IDCANCEL. The program could then test the return value and save the data before closing (IDYES), close without saving (IDNO), or return to the application without shutting down (IDCANCEL). The table on the next page lists the six message box types and the corresponding return values, with the default push button—the one that's "clicked" if the user presses the Enter key—highlighted in boldface type.

MESSAGE BOX TYPES

Type	Buttons	Possible Return Codes
MB_ABORTRETRYIGNORE	**Abort**, Retry, Ignore	IDABORT, IDRETRY, IDIGNORE
MB_OK	**OK**	IDOK
MB_OKCANCEL	**OK**, Cancel	IDOK, IDCANCEL
MB_RETRYCANCEL	**Retry**, Cancel	IDRETRY, IDCANCEL
MB_YESNO	**Yes**, No	IDYES, IDNO
MB_YESNOCANCEL	**Yes**, No, Cancel	IDYES, IDNO, IDCANCEL

In message boxes with multiple buttons, the first (leftmost) button is normally the default push button. You can make the second or third button the default by ORing MB_DEFBUTTON2 or MB_DEFBUTTON3 into the value specifying the message box type. The statement

```
MessageBox ("Your document contains unsaved data. Save it?",
    "My Application", MB_YESNOCANCEL | MB_DEFBUTTON3);
```

displays the same message box as before but makes Cancel the default action.

By default, message boxes are application-modal, meaning the application that called the *MessageBox* function is disabled until the message box is dismissed. If you'd like, you can add MB_SYSTEMMODAL to the *nType* parameter and make the message box system-modal. In 16-bit Windows, system-modal means that input to *all* applications is suspended until the message box is dismissed. In the Win32 environment, Windows makes the message box a topmost window that stays on top of other windows, but the user is still free to switch to other applications. System-modal message boxes should be used only when a serious error demands immediate attention.

You can add an artistic touch to your message boxes by using MB_ICON identifiers. MB_ICONINFORMATION displays a small text balloon with an "i" for "information" in it in the upper left corner of the message box. The "i" is generally used when information is being provided to the user but no questions are being asked, as in

```
MessageBox ("No errors found. Click OK to continue",
    "My Application", MB_ICONINFORMATION | MB_OK);
```

MB_ICONQUESTION displays a question mark instead of an "i" and is normally used for queries such as "Save before closing?" MB_ICONSTOP displays a red circle with an X and usually indicates that an unrecoverable error has occurred—for example, that an out of memory error is forcing the program to terminate prematurely. Finally, MB_ICONEXCLAMATION displays a yellow triangle with an exclamation mark punctuating the message. Figure 3-3 back on the previous page shows an example of a message box that uses the MB_ICONEXCLAMATION style.

MFC provides an alternative to *CWnd::MessageBox* in the form of the global *AfxMessageBox*. The two are very similar, but *AfxMessageBox* can be called from application classes, document classes, and other non-*CWnd* classes. One situation in which *AfxMessageBox* is irreplaceable is when a severe error occurs in the application object's *InitInstance* function and you want to report that error to the user. *MessageBox* requires a valid *CWnd* pointer and therefore can't be called until after a window is created. *AfxMessageBox*, on the other hand, can be called at any time.

What? No Frame Window?

TicTac is different from the sample programs in Chapters 1 and 2 in one important respect. Rather than use a frame window for its main window, it derives its own window class from *CWnd*. It's not that a *CFrameWnd* wouldn't have worked; it's that *CWnd* has everything TicTac needs and more. Depending on what kinds of applications you write, deriving from *CWnd* is something you might need to do often, or it could be something you'll never find the need to do. Still, it's something every MFC programmer should know *how* to do, and deriving your own window class from *CWnd* also serves to underscore the point that MFC programs don't have to use frame windows.

Creating your own *CWnd*-derived window class is simple. For starters, derive the window class from *CWnd* instead of from *CFrameWnd*, as shown in TicTac.h. In the BEGIN_MESSAGE_MAP macro, be sure to specify *CWnd*, not *CFrameWnd*, as the base class. Then, in the window's constructor, use *AfxRegisterWndClass* to register a WNDCLASS with the desired attributes, and call *CWnd::CreateEx* to create the window. Remember the beginning of Chapter 1, where we looked at the C source code for an SDK-style Windows application? Before creating a window, *WinMain* initialized a WNDCLASS structure with values describing the window's class attributes and then called *::RegisterClass* to register the WNDCLASS. Normally you don't have to register a WNDCLASS in an MFC program because MFC registers one for you. Specifying NULL in the first parameter to *CFrameWnd::Create* accepts the default WNDCLASS. When you derive from *CWnd*, however, you must register your own WNDCLASS because *CWnd::CreateEx* will not accept a NULL WNDCLASS name.

The *AfxRegisterWndClass* Function

MFC makes WNDCLASS registration easy with its global *AfxRegisterWndClass* function. If you use *::RegisterClass* or MFC's *AfxRegisterClass* to register a WNDCLASS, you're obliged to initialize every field in the WNDCLASS structure. But *AfxRegisterWndClass* fills in most of the fields for you, leaving you to specify values for just the four that MFC applications are typically concerned with. *AfxRegisterWndClass* is prototyped as follows:

```
LPCTSTR AfxRegisterWndClass (UINT nClassStyle, HCURSOR hCursor = 0,
    HBRUSH hbrBackground = 0, HICON hIcon = 0)
```

The value returned by *AfxRegisterWndClass* is a null-terminated string containing the WNDCLASS name. Before seeing how TicTac uses *AfxRegisterWndClass*, let's take a closer look at the function itself and the parameters it accepts.

nClassStyle specifies the class style, which defines certain specialized behavioral characteristics of a window. *nClassStyle* is a combination of zero or more of the following bit flags:

Class Style	Description
CS_BYTEALIGNCLIENT	Ensures that a window's client area is always aligned on a byte boundary in the video buffer to speed drawing operations.
CS_BYTEALIGNWINDOW	Ensures that the window itself is always aligned on a byte boundary in the video buffer to speed moving and resizing operations.
CS_CLASSDC	Specifies that the window should share a device context with other windows created from the same WNDCLASS.
CS_DBLCLKS	Specifies that the window should be notified of double-clicks with WM_*x*BUTTONDBLCLK messages.
CS_GLOBALCLASS	Registers the WNDCLASS globally so that all applications can use it. (By default, only the application that registers a WNDCLASS can create windows from it.) Used primarily for child window controls.
CS_HREDRAW	Specifies that the client area should be invalidated when the window is resized horizontally.
CS_NOCLOSE	Disables the Close command on the system menu and the close button on the title bar.
CS_OWNDC	Specifies that each window created from this WNDCLASS should have its own device context. Helpful when optimizing repaint performance because an application doesn't have to reinitialize a private device context each time the device context is acquired.
CS_PARENTDC	Specifies that a child window should inherit the device context of its parent.
CS_SAVEBITS	Specifies that areas of the screen covered by windows created from this WNDCLASS should be saved in bitmap form for quick repainting. Used primarily for menus and other windows with short life spans.
CS_VREDRAW	Specifies that the client area should be invalidated when the window is resized vertically.

The CS_BYTEALIGNCLIENT and CS_BYTEALIGNWINDOW styles were useful back in the days of dumb frame buffers and monochrome video systems, but they are largely obsolete today. CS_CLASSDC, CS_OWNDC, and CS_PARENTDC are used to implement special handling of device contexts. You'll probably use CS_GLOBALCLASS only if you write custom controls to complement list boxes, push buttons, and other built-in control types. The CS_HREDRAW and CS_VREDRAW styles are useful for creating resizeable windows whose content scales with the window size.

hCursor identifies the default mouse pointer for windows created from this WNDCLASS. When the cursor moves over a window's client area, Windows retrieves the handle of the class cursor from the window's WNDCLASS and uses it to draw the cursor image. You can create custom cursors that are stored as resources in your application's .exe file and load them with *CWinApp::LoadCursor* or *::LoadCursor*. The following statement loads a custom cursor resource whose ID is IDC_MYCURSOR:

```
AfxGetApp ()->LoadCursor (IDC_MYCURSOR);
```

Resources can optionally be assigned string IDs instead of integer IDs. If the custom cursor were assigned the string ID "MyCursor", it would be loaded like this:

```
AfxGetApp ()->LoadCursor ("MyCursor");
```

Windows also provides the predefined cursors shown in Figure 3-4 on the next page that an application can use without defining a custom cursor resource. Predefined cursors are loaded with *CWinApp::LoadStandardCursor* or *::LoadCursor*. The statement

```
AfxGetApp ()->LoadStandardCursor (IDC_ARROW);
```

returns the handle of the arrow cursor most Windows applications use, as does the statement

```
::LoadCursor (NULL, IDC_ARROW);
```

Generally speaking, only the IDC_ARROW, IDC_IBEAM, and IDC_CROSS cursors are useful as class cursors.

The *hbrBackground* parameter passed to *AfxRegisterWndClass* specifies the class background brush, which in turn defines the window's default background color. Specifically, *hbrBackground* identifies the GDI brush used to erase the window's interior in response to the WM_ERASEBKGND messages generated when a WM_PAINT handler calls *::BeginPaint*. (Windows' default response to WM_ERASEBKGND messages is to retrieve the class background brush from the WNDCLASS structure and fill the window's client area with that brush. You can display custom window backgrounds—for example, backgrounds formed from bitmap images—by processing WM_ERASEBKGND messages yourself and returning a nonzero value to prevent Windows from erasing the background.) You can either provide a brush handle for *hbrBackground* or specify one of the Windows system colors such as COLOR_WINDOW or COLOR_APPWORKSPACE with the value 1 added to it, as in COLOR_WINDOW + 1. See the documentation for the *::GetSysColor* API function for a complete list of system colors.

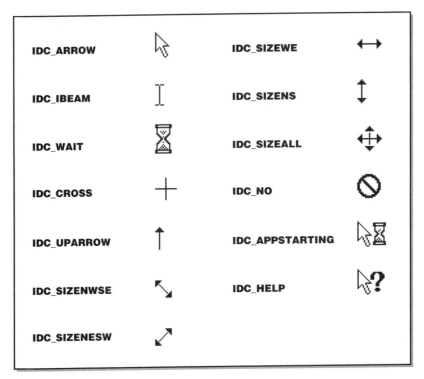

Figure 3-4. *The predefined cursor types.*

The final *AfxRegisterWndClass* parameter, *hIcon*, specifies the handle of the icon that Windows will use to represent the application on the desktop, in the taskbar, and elsewhere. You can create a custom icon resource for your application and load it with *CWinApp::LoadIcon*, or you can load one of the Windows predefined icons with *CWinApp::LoadStandardIcon*. You can even load icons from other executable files using the *::ExtractIcon* API function.

Here's what the code to register a custom WNDCLASS looks like in TicTac.cpp:

```
CString strWndClass = AfxRegisterWndClass (
    CS_DBLCLKS,
    myApp.LoadStandardCursor (IDC_ARROW),
    (HBRUSH) (COLOR_3DFACE + 1),
    myApp.LoadIcon (IDI_APPICON)
);
```

The class style CS_DBLCLKS registers the TicTac window to receive double-click messages. IDC_ARROW tells Windows to display the standard arrow when the cursor is over the TicTac window, and IDI_APPICON is the ID of the application icon (a custom icon resource defined in TicTac.rc). The value COLOR_3DFACE + 1 specified for the background brush assigns the TicTac window the same background color as push buttons, window frames, dialog boxes, and other 3D display elements. COLOR_3DFACE defaults to light gray but can be changed through the system's Display Properties property sheet. Using COLOR_3DFACE for the background color gives your window the same 3D look as a Windows 95 dialog box or message box and enables it to automatically adapt to changes in the Windows color scheme.

The *AfxRegisterWndClass* function isn't only for applications that derive their own window classes from *CWnd*; it's also used to register custom WNDCLASSes for frame windows. The default WNDCLASS that MFC registers for frame windows has the following attributes:

- *nClassStyle* = CS_DBLCLKS | CS_HREDRAW | CS_VREDRAW

- *hCursor* = the handle of the predefined cursor IDC_ARROW

- *hbrBackground* = COLOR_WINDOW + 1

- *hIcon* = the handle of the icon whose ID is AFX_IDI_STD_FRAME or AFX_IDI_STD_MDIFRAME, or the predefined IDI_APPLICATION icon if no such resource is defined

Suppose you want to create a *CFrameWnd* frame window that doesn't have the CS_DBLCLKS style, that uses its own application icon (ID=IDI_MYICON), and that uses COLOR_APPWORKSPACE as its default background color. Here's how you'd create a frame window that meets these qualifications:

```
CString strWndClass = AfxRegisterWndClass (
    CS_HREDRAW | CS_VREDRAW,
    myApp.LoadStandardCursor (IDC_ARROW),
    (HBRUSH) (COLOR_APPWORKSPACE + 1),
    myApp.LoadIcon (IDI_MYICON)
);

Create (strWndClass, WS_OVERLAPPEDWINDOW);
```

The statements above would replace the

```
Create (NULL, WS_OVERLAPPEDWINDOW);
```

statement that normally appears in a frame window's constructor.

Creating and Initializing the TicTac Window

After registering a WNDCLASS for its main window, TicTac creates the window with a call to *CWnd::CreateEx*:

```
CreateEx (0, strWndClass, "Tic-Tac-Toe",
    WS_OVERLAPPED | WS_SYSMENU | WS_CAPTION | WS_MINIMIZEBOX,
    CW_USEDEFAULT, CW_USEDEFAULT, CW_USEDEFAULT, CW_USEDEFAULT,
    NULL, NULL);
```

The first parameter specifies the extended window style and is a combination of zero or more of the WS_EX flags documented in the SDK. TicTac requires no extended window styles, so this parameter is 0. The second parameter is the WNDCLASS name returned by *AfxRegisterWndClass*, and the third is the window title. The fourth specifies the window style. The combination of WS_OVERLAPPED, WS_SYSMENU, WS_CAPTION, and WS_MINIMIZEBOX creates a window similar to a window with the style WS_OVERLAPPEDWINDOW but lacking a maximize button and the ability to be resized. What is it about the window that makes it nonresizeable? Look up the definition of WS_OVERLAPPEDWINDOW in Winuser.h, and you'll see something like this:

```
#define WS_OVERLAPPEDWINDOW (WS_OVERLAPPED ¦ WS_CAPTION ¦ \
    WS_SYSMENU ¦ WS_THICKFRAME ¦ WS_MINIMIZE ¦ WS_MAXIMIZE)
```

The WS_THICKFRAME style adds a resizing border whose edges and corners can be grabbed and dragged with the mouse. TicTac's window lacks this style, so it can't be resized by the user.

The next four parameters passed to *CWnd::CreateEx* specify the window's initial position and size. TicTac uses CW_USEDEFAULT for all four so that Windows will pick the initial position and size. Yet clearly the TicTac window is not arbitrarily sized; it is sized to match the playing grid. But how? The statements following the call to *CreateEx* hold the answer:

```
CRect rect (0, 0, 352, 352);
CalcWindowRect (&rect);

SetWindowPos (NULL, 0, 0, rect.Width (), rect.Height (),
    SWP_NOZORDER ¦ SWP_NOMOVE ¦ SWP_NOREDRAW);
```

The first of these statements creates a *CRect* object that holds the desired size of the window's client area—352 by 352 pixels. It wouldn't do to pass these values directly to *CreateEx* because *CreateEx*'s sizing parameters specify the size of the entire window, not just its client area. Since the sizes of the various elements in the window's nonclient area (for example, the height of the title bar) vary with different video drivers and display resolutions, we must calculate the size of the window rectangle from the client rectangle and then size the window to fit. MFC's *CWnd::CalcWindowRect* is the perfect tool for the job. Given a pointer to a *CRect* object representing a window's client area, *CalcWindowRect* calculates the corresponding window rectangle. The width and height of that rectangle can then be passed to *CWnd::SetWindowPos* to effect the proper window size. The only catch is that *CalcWindowRect* must be called *after* the window is created so that it can factor in the dimensions of the window's nonclient area.

The *PostNcDestroy* Function

A final consideration involved in using a window class derived directly from *CWnd* is that once created, the window object must somehow be deleted. As described in Chapter 2, the very last message a window receives before it is destroyed is WM_NC-DESTROY. *CWnd* provides a default *OnNcDestroy* handler that performs some routine cleanup chores and then, as its very last act, calls a virtual function named *PostNcDestroy*. *CFrameWnd* objects delete themselves when the windows they are attached to are destroyed by overriding *PostNcDestroy* and executing a *delete this* statement. *CWnd::PostNcDestroy* does not perform a *delete this*, so a class derived from *CWnd* should provide its own version of *PostNcDestroy* that does. TicTac includes a trivial *PostNcDestroy* function that destroys the *CMainWindow* object just before the program terminates:

```
void CMainWindow::PostNcDestroy ()
{
    delete this;
}
```

The question "who deletes it" is something you should always think about when you derive a window class from *CWnd*.

Nonclient-Area Mouse Messages

When the mouse is clicked inside or moved over a window's nonclient area, Windows sends the window a nonclient-area mouse message. The first table on the next page shows the nonclient-area mouse messages an application may receive. Note the parallelism between the client-area mouse messages shown in the table on page 109 and the nonclient-area mouse messages; the only difference is the letters NC in the message identifier. Unlike double-click messages in a window's client area, WM_NC*x*-BUTTONDBLCLK messages are transmitted regardless of whether the window was registered with the CS_DBLCLKS style.

Message handlers for nonclient-area mouse messages are prototyped this way:

```
afx_msg void OnMsgName (UINT nHitTest, CPoint point)
```

As in client-area mouse messages, the *point* parameter specifies the location in the window at which the event occurred. But for nonclient-area mouse messages, *point.x* and *point.y* contain screen coordinates rather than client coordinates. In screen coordinates, (0, 0) corresponds to the upper left corner of the screen, and as in the client area, one unit in any direction equals one pixel. Screen coordinates are easily converted to client coordinates with *CWnd::ScreenToClient*. The *nHitTest* parameter contains a hit-test code identifying where in the window's nonclient area the event occurred. Some of the most interesting hit-test codes are shown in the table at the bottom of the next page.

NONCLIENT-AREA MOUSE MESSAGES

Message	Handler	Sent When
WM_NCLBUTTONDOWN	*OnNcLButtonDown*	The left mouse button is pressed.
WM_NCLBUTTONUP	*OnNcLButtonUp*	The left mouse button is released.
WM_NCLBUTTONDBLCLK	*OnNcLButtonDblClk*	The left mouse button is double-clicked.
WM_NCMBUTTONDOWN	*OnNcMButtonDown*	The middle mouse button is pressed.
WM_NCMBUTTONUP	*OnNcMButtonUp*	The middle mouse button is released.
WM_NCMBUTTONDBLCLK	*OnNcMButtonDblClk*	The middle mouse button is double-clicked.
WM_NCRBUTTONDOWN	*OnNcRButtonDown*	The right mouse button is pressed.
WM_NCRBUTTONUP	*OnNcRButtonUp*	The right mouse button is released.
WM_NCRBUTTONDBLCLK	*OnNcRButtonDblClk*	The right mouse button is double-clicked.
WM_NCMOUSEMOVE	*OnNcMouseMove*	The mouse is moved over the window's nonclient area.

KEY HIT-TEST CODES

Value	Corresponding Location
HTCAPTION	The title bar
HTCLOSE	The close button
HTGROWBOX	The restore button (same as HTSIZE)
HTHSCROLL	The window's horizontal scroll bar
HTMENU	The menu bar
HTREDUCE	The minimize button
HTSIZE	The restore button (same as HTGROWBOX)
HTSYSMENU	The system menu box
HTVSCROLL	The window's vertical scroll bar
HTZOOM	The maximize button

You can find a complete list of hit-test codes in the documentation for WM_NCHITTEST or *CWnd::OnNcHitTest*.

Programs don't usually process nonclient-area mouse messages but allow Windows to process them instead. Windows provides appropriate default responses that frequently result in still more messages being sent to the window. For example, when Windows processes a WM_NCLBUTTONDBLCLK message with a hit-test value equal to HTSYSMENU, it sends the window a WM_SYSCOMMAND message with *wParam* equal to SC_CLOSE, which in turn initiates a series of actions that closes the window. If you wanted to prevent double clicks of the system menu box from shutting down your application, you could do so with the following message handler:

```
void CMainWindow::OnNcLButtonDblClk (UINT nHitTest, CPoint point)
{
    if (nHitTest != HTSYSMENU)
        CWnd::OnNcLButtonDblClk (nHitTest, point);
}
```

Calling the base class's *OnNcLButtonDblClk* handler passes the message to Windows and allows default processing to take place. Returning without calling the base class prevents Windows from knowing that the double-click occurred. You can use other hit-test values to customize the window's response to other nonclient-area mouse events.

The WM_NCHITTEST Message

Before a window receives a client-area or nonclient-area mouse message, it receives a WM_NCHITTEST message with a *CPoint* object containing the screen coordinates of the cursor. If the message is passed on for default processing, Windows examines the *x* and *y* values contained in the *CPoint* object and uses the information to generate a subsequent client-area or nonclient-area mouse message. One clever use for an *OnNcHitTest* handler is to substitute the HTCAPTION hit-test code for HTCLIENT, which creates a window that can be dragged by its client area:

```
UINT CMainWindow::OnNcHitTest (CPoint point)
{
    UINT nHitTest = CFrameWnd::OnNcHitTest (point);
    if (nHitTest == HTCLIENT)
        nHitTest = HTCAPTION;
    return nHitTest;
}
```

Each WM_NCHITTEST that you don't process should be forwarded to the base class so that other aspects of the program's operation will be unaffected.

Capturing the Mouse

One problem that frequently crops up in programs that process mouse messages is that the receipt of a button-down message doesn't necessarily mean a button-up message will follow. Suppose you've written a drawing program that saves the *point* parameter passed to *OnLButtonDown* and uses it as an anchor point to draw a line whose other endpoint follows the cursor, an action known as "rubber-banding" a line.

When a WM_LBUTTONUP message arrives, the application erases the rubber-band line and draws a real line in its place. But what happens if the user moves the mouse outside the window's client area before releasing the mouse button? The application will never get that WM_LBUTTONUP message. Consequently, the rubber-band line will be left hanging in limbo and the real line won't be drawn.

Windows provides an elegant solution to this problem by allowing an application to "capture" the mouse upon receipt of a button-down message and to continue to receive mouse messages no matter where the cursor goes on the screen until the button is released or capture is canceled. (In the Win32 environment, the system stops sending mouse messages to a window that owns the capture if the button is released to prevent applications from monopolizing the mouse.) The mouse is captured with *CWnd::SetCapture* and released with *CWnd::ReleaseCapture*. Calls to these functions are normally paired in button-down and button-up handlers, as shown here:

```
void CMainWindow::OnLButtonDown (UINT nFlags, CPoint point)
{
    SetCapture ();
}

void CMainWindow::OnLButtonUp (UINT nFlags, CPoint point)
{
    ReleaseCapture ();
}
```

In between, *CMainWindow* receives WM_MOUSEMOVE messages reporting the cursor position even if the cursor leaves it. Client-area mouse messages continue to report cursor positions in client coordinates, but coordinates can now go negative and can also exceed the dimensions of the window's client area.

A related function, *CWnd::GetCapture*, returns a *CWnd* pointer to the window that owns the capture. In the Win32 environment, *GetCapture* returns NULL if the mouse is not captured or if it's captured by a window belonging to another thread. The most common use for *GetCapture* is to determine whether your own window has captured the mouse by executing an

```
if (GetCapture () == this)
```

statement.

How would an application's capturing the mouse solve the problem with the rubber-banded line? By capturing the mouse in response to a WM_LBUTTONDOWN message and releasing it when a WM_LBUTTONUP message arrives, the application is guaranteed to get the WM_LBUTTONUP message when the mouse button is released. Therefore, the application is assured of the opportunity to erase the rubber-band line and draw a real line in its place. The practical effect of such a capture is illustrated by the sample program in the next section.

Mouse Capturing in Action

Figure 3-5's MouseCap application is a rudimentary paint program that enables the user to draw lines with the mouse. To draw a line, the user presses the left mouse button anywhere in the window's client area and drags the cursor with the button held down. As the mouse is moved, a thin line is rubber-banded between the starting point (the point at which the mouse button was pressed) and the current position of the cursor. When the user lets go of the mouse button, the rubber-band line is erased and a red line 16 pixels wide is drawn in its place. Because of the special mouse-capturing logic built into the program, it continues to respond to mouse events during rubber-banding even if the mouse is moved outside the client area. And no matter where the cursor is when the mouse button is released, a red line is drawn between the anchor point and the endpoint. The visible portion of the line never extends outside the window's client area, of course. If the mouse button is released outside the client area, the line is drawn up to the border of the client area in the direction of the point at which the release occurred.

MouseCap.h

```
//********************************************************************
//
//  MouseCap.h
//
//********************************************************************

class CMyApp : public CWinApp
{
public:
    virtual BOOL InitInstance ();
};

class CMainWindow : public CFrameWnd
{
private:
    CPoint m_ptFrom;
    CPoint m_ptTo;
    BOOL m_bTracking;
    BOOL m_bCaptureEnabled;

    void InvertLine (CDC*, CPoint, CPoint);

public:
    CMainWindow ();
```

Figure 3-5. *The MouseCap program.*

(continued)

MouseCap.h *continued*

```
protected:
    afx_msg void OnLButtonDown (UINT, CPoint);
    afx_msg void OnLButtonUp (UINT, CPoint);
    afx_msg void OnMouseMove (UINT, CPoint);
    afx_msg void OnNcLButtonDown (UINT, CPoint);

    DECLARE_MESSAGE_MAP ()
};
```

MouseCap.cpp

```
//*****************************************************************
//
//  MouseCap.cpp
//
//*****************************************************************

#include <afxwin.h>
#include "MouseCap.h"

CMyApp myApp;

/////////////////////////////////////////////////////////////////
// CMyApp member functions

BOOL CMyApp::InitInstance ()
{
    m_pMainWnd = new CMainWindow;
    m_pMainWnd->ShowWindow (m_nCmdShow);
    m_pMainWnd->UpdateWindow ();
    return TRUE;
}

/////////////////////////////////////////////////////////////////
// CMainWindow message map and member functions

BEGIN_MESSAGE_MAP (CMainWindow, CFrameWnd)
    ON_WM_LBUTTONDOWN ()
    ON_WM_LBUTTONUP ()
    ON_WM_MOUSEMOVE ()
    ON_WM_NCLBUTTONDOWN ()
END_MESSAGE_MAP ()
```

```
CMainWindow::CMainWindow ()
{
    m_bTracking = FALSE;
    m_bCaptureEnabled = TRUE;

    CString strWndClass = AfxRegisterWndClass (
        0,
        myApp.LoadStandardCursor (IDC_CROSS),
        (HBRUSH) (COLOR_WINDOW + 1),
        myApp.LoadStandardIcon (IDI_APPLICATION)
    );

    Create (strWndClass, "Mouse Capture Demo (Capture Enabled)");
}

void CMainWindow::OnLButtonDown (UINT nFlags, CPoint point)
{
    m_ptFrom = point;
    m_ptTo = point;
    m_bTracking = TRUE;

    if (m_bCaptureEnabled)
        SetCapture ();
}

void CMainWindow::OnMouseMove (UINT nFlags, CPoint point)
{
    if (m_bTracking) {
        CClientDC dc (this);
        InvertLine (&dc, m_ptFrom, m_ptTo);
        InvertLine (&dc, m_ptFrom, point);
        m_ptTo = point;
    }
}

void CMainWindow::OnLButtonUp (UINT nFlags, CPoint point)
{
    if (m_bTracking) {
        m_bTracking = FALSE;
        if (GetCapture () == this)
            ReleaseCapture ();

        CClientDC dc (this);
        InvertLine (&dc, m_ptFrom, m_ptTo);

        CPen pen (PS_SOLID, 16, RGB (255, 0, 0));
```

(continued)

MouseCap.cpp *continued*

```
        dc.SelectObject (&pen);

        dc.MoveTo (m_ptFrom);
        dc.LineTo (point);
    }
}

void CMainWindow::OnNcLButtonDown (UINT nHitTest, CPoint point)
{
    if (nHitTest == HTCAPTION) {
        m_bCaptureEnabled = m_bCaptureEnabled ? FALSE : TRUE;

        SetWindowText (m_bCaptureEnabled ?
            "Mouse Capture Demo (Capture Enabled)" :
            "Mouse Capture Demo (Capture Disabled)");
    }
    CFrameWnd::OnNcLButtonDown (nHitTest, point);
}

void CMainWindow::InvertLine (CDC* pDC, CPoint ptFrom, CPoint ptTo)
{
    int nOldMode = pDC->SetROP2 (R2_NOT);

    pDC->MoveTo (ptFrom);
    pDC->LineTo (ptTo);

    pDC->SetROP2 (nOldMode);
}
```

Most of the action takes place in MouseCap's *OnLButtonDown*, *OnMouseMove*, and *OnLButtonUp* handlers. *OnLButtonDown* starts the drawing process by initializing a trio of variables that are members of the *CMainWindow* class:

```
m_ptFrom = point;
m_ptTo = point;
m_bTracking = TRUE;
```

m_ptFrom and *m_ptTo* are the starting and ending points for the rubber-band line. The *m_ptTo* variable is continually updated by the *OnMouseMove* handler as the mouse is moved. *m_bTracking*, which is TRUE when the left button is down and FALSE when it is not, is a flag that lets the *OnMouseMove* and *OnLButtonUp* handlers know whether a line is being rubber-banded. *OnLButtonDown*'s only other action is to capture the mouse if *m_bCaptureEnabled* is TRUE:

```
if (m_bCaptureEnabled)
    SetCapture ();
```

m_bCaptureEnabled is initialized to TRUE by *CMainWindow*'s constructor. It is toggled by the window's *OnNcLButtonDown* handler so that you can turn mouse capturing on and off and see the effect mouse capturing has on the operation of the program. (More on this in a moment.)

OnMouseMove's job is to move the rubber-band line and update *m_ptTo* with the new cursor position whenever the mouse is moved. The statement

```
InvertLine (&dc, m_ptFrom, m_ptTo);
```

erases the previously drawn rubber-band line, and

```
InvertLine (&dc, m_ptFrom, point);
```

draws a new one. *InvertLine* is a member of *CMainWindow*. It draws a line not by setting each pixel to a certain color but by flipping the existing color bits using a Boolean NOT operation. This ensures that the line can be seen no matter what background it is drawn against and that drawing the line again in the same location will erase it by restoring the original screen colors. The statement

```
int nOldMode = pDC->SetROP2 (R2_NOT);
```

sets the device context's drawing mode—the attribute that determines how the color of the current pen or brush is blended with pixels on the screen—to R2_NOT, which inverts pixel colors at the destination regardless of the color of the pen or brush selected into the device context. The GDI supports 256 different drawing modes, 16 of which are used frequently enough that they're assigned identifiers such as R2_NOT. The default drawing mode is R2_COPYPEN, which copies pen and brush colors directly to the display surface.

When the left mouse button is released, *CMainWindow::OnLButtonUp* is called. After setting *m_bTracking* to FALSE and releasing the mouse, it erases the rubber-band line drawn by the last call to *OnMouseMove*:

```
CClientDC dc (this);
InvertLine (&dc, m_ptFrom, m_ptTo);
```

OnLButtonUp then creates a solid red pen 16 pixels wide, selects it into the device context, and draws a thick red line:

```
CPen pen (PS_SOLID, 16, RGB (255, 0, 0));
dc.SelectObject (&pen);

dc.MoveTo (m_ptFrom);
dc.LineTo (point);
```

Its work done, *OnLButtonUp* returns, and the drawing operation is complete. Figure 3-6 on the next page shows what the MouseCap window looks like after a few lines have been drawn and as a new line is rubber-banded.

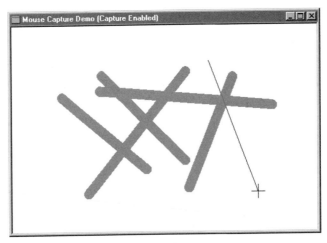

Figure 3-6. *The MouseCap window.*

After you've played around with the program a bit, click the title bar to activate the *OnNcLButtonDown* handler and toggle the *m_bCaptureEnabled* flag from TRUE to FALSE. The window title should change from "Mouse Capture Demo (Capture Enabled)" to "Mouse Capture Demo (Capture Disabled)." *OnNcLButtonDown* traps left button clicks in the window's nonclient area and uses *CWnd::SetWindowText* to change the window title if the hit-test code in *nHitTest* is equal to HTCAPTION, indicating that the click occurred in the title bar. Now draw a few lines with mouse capturing disabled. Observe that if you move the mouse outside the window while rubber-banding a line, the line freezes until the mouse reenters the client area. And if you release the mouse button outside the window, the program gets out of sync. The rubber-band line follows the mouse when you move it back to the interior of the window (even though the mouse button is no longer depressed), and it is never erased. Click the title bar once again to reenable mouse capturing, and the program will revert to its normal self.

MouseCap graphically illustrates the importance of capturing the mouse when tracking mouse movements in an application that counts on receiving a button-up message for each button-down message. Still, the program suffers from one rather serious flaw. Because the coordinates of the lines the user draws are not saved anywhere, there is no *OnPaint* handler to repaint the window when all or part of the client area is invalidated. We'll correct that deficiency in Chapter 4, when we develop a more robust paint program that uses a *CLine* class to represent lines drawn on the screen and MFC's *CObArray* class to manage an array of *CLine* objects.

The Cursor

One aspect of mouse handling we've yet to address is how to change the appearance of the cursor. Rather than the arrow-shaped cursor you see in most Windows applications, MouseCap uses a crosshair cursor typical of painting and drawing programs. These are but two of several predefined cursor types Windows places at your disposal, and if none of the predefined cursors fits the bill, you can always create your own. As usual, Windows provides programmers a great deal of latitude in this area.

First, a bit of background on how cursors work. As you're already aware, every window on the screen has a corresponding WNDCLASS whose characteristics are defined in a WNDCLASS structure. One of the fields of the WNDCLASS structure is *hCursor*, which holds the handle of the class cursor—the image displayed when the cursor is over a window's client area. When the mouse is moved, Windows erases the cursor from its old location by redrawing the background behind it and sends the window under the cursor a WM_SETCURSOR message containing a hit-test code. Windows' default response to this message is to call *::SetCursor* to display the class cursor if the hit-test code is HTCLIENT, or to display an arrow if the hit-test code indicates the cursor is outside the client area. As a result, the cursor is automatically updated as it is moved about the screen. When you move the cursor into an edit control, for example, it changes to a vertical bar, or "I-beam." This happens because Windows registers a global class named "EDIT" for edit controls and specifies the I-beam cursor as the class cursor.

It follows that one way to change the cursor's appearance is to register a custom WNDCLASS and specify the desired cursor type as the class cursor. In MouseCap, *CMainWindow*'s constructor registers a WNDCLASS whose class cursor is IDC_CROSS and passes the WNDCLASS name to *CFrameWnd::Create*:

```
CString strWndClass = AfxRegisterWndClass (
    0,
    myApp.LoadStandardCursor (IDC_CROSS),
    (HBRUSH) (COLOR_WINDOW + 1),
    myApp.LoadStandardIcon (IDI_APPLICATION)
);

Create (strWndClass, "Mouse Capture Demo (Capture Enabled)");
```

Thus, by default, Windows displays a crosshair cursor anytime the mouse pointer is positioned in *CMainWindow*'s client area. MouseCap references the application object *myApp* directly because *myApp* is declared in the same source code file that registers the window class. Had *myApp* been located in a separate file, the application object could have been accessed using *AfxGetApp*. The class registration code would then have looked like this:

```
CString strWndClass = AfxRegisterWndClass (
    0,
    AfxGetApp ()->LoadStandardCursor (IDC_CROSS),
    (HBRUSH) (COLOR_WINDOW + 1),
    AfxGetApp ()->LoadStandardIcon (IDI_APPLICATION)
);
```

AfxGetApp will come in handy time and time again when you write large MFC programs with classes implemented in separate .cpp files. Note that MouseCap uses the standard Windows application icon IDI_APPLICATION to keep the source code simple. In a real application, you should give the application a unique icon of its own.

A second way to customize the cursor is to call the API function *::SetCursor* in response to WM_SETCURSOR messages. The following *OnSetCursor* function displays the cursor whose handle is stored in *CMainWindow::m_hCursor* when the cursor is over *CMainWindow*'s client area:

```
BOOL CMainWindow::OnSetCursor (CWnd* pWnd, UINT nHitTest,
    UINT message)
{
    if (nHitHitTest == HTCLIENT) {
        ::SetCursor (m_hCursor);
        return TRUE;
    }
    return CFrameWnd::OnSetCursor (pWnd, nHitTest, message);
}
```

Returning TRUE after calling *::SetCursor* tells Windows that the cursor has been set. WM_SETCURSOR messages generated outside the window's client area are passed to the base class so that the default cursor will be displayed. The class cursor is ignored because *OnSetCursor* never gives Windows the opportunity to display it.

Why would you ever want to use *OnSetCursor* rather than just registering *m_hCursor* as the class cursor? Suppose you want to display an arrow cursor when the cursor is in the top half of the window and an I-beam cursor when the cursor is in the bottom half. A class cursor won't suffice in this case, but *OnSetCursor* will do the job quite nicely. The following *OnSetCursor* handler sets the cursor to either *m_hCursorArrow* or *m_hCursorIBeam* when the cursor is in *CMainWindow*'s client area:

```
BOOL CMainWindow::OnSetCursor (CWnd* pWnd, UINT nHitTest,
    UINT message)
{
    if (nHitTest == HTCLIENT) {
        DWORD dwPos = ::GetMessagePos ();
        CPoint point (LOWORD (dwPos), HIWORD (dwPos));
        ScreenToClient (&point);
        CRect rect;
        GetClientRect (&rect);
        ::SetCursor ((point.y < rect.Height () / 2) ?
            m_hCursorArrow : m_hCursorIBeam);
        return TRUE;
    }
    return CFrameWnd::OnSetCursor (pWnd, nHitTest, message);
}
```

::GetMessagePos returns a DWORD value containing the cursor's *x* and *y* screen coordinates at the moment the WM_SETCURSOR message was retrieved. *CWnd::Screen-ToClient* converts screen coordinates to client coordinates. If the converted point's *y* coordinate is less than half the height of the window's client area, the cursor is set to *m_hCursorArrow*. But if *y* is greater than or equal to half the client area height, the cursor is set to *m_hCursorIBeam* instead. The VisualKB application presented later in this chapter uses a similar technique to change the cursor to an I-beam when it enters a rectangle surrounding a text-entry field.

Should the need ever arise, you can make the cursor go away entirely with the statement

```
::ShowCursor (FALSE);
```

and restore it again with

```
::ShowCursor (TRUE);
```

Internally, Windows maintains a display count that's incremented each time *::Show-Cursor* (TRUE) is called and decremented by each call to *::ShowCursor* (FALSE). The count is initially set to 0 if a mouse is installed and −1 if no mouse is present, and the cursor is displayed whenever the count is greater than or equal to 0. Thus, if you call *::ShowCursor* (FALSE) twice to hide the cursor, you must call *::ShowCursor* (TRUE) twice to display it again.

The Hourglass Cursor

When an application responds to a message by undertaking a lengthy processing task during which no other messages will be processed, it's customary to change the cursor to an hourglass to remind the user that the application is "busy." Windows provides the cursor for you, and its identifier is IDC_WAIT. MFC's *CCmdTarget* class provides handy member functions named *BeginWaitCursor* for changing the cursor to an hourglass and *EndWaitCursor* for changing it back again. Assuming the *this* pointer refers to a *CCmdTarget*-derived object (which includes all window objects since *CCmdTarget* is the base class for *CWnd*), the statement

```
BeginWaitCursor ();
```

changes the cursor to an hourglass, and

```
EndWaitCursor ();
```

restores the cursor to its previous form. Each call to *BeginWaitCursor* increments an internal reference count, and the hourglass cursor is displayed as long as the count is greater than 0. If you call *BeginWaitCursor* twice, you must call *EndWaitCursor* twice to restore the normal cursor. As an alternative, you can call *CCmdTarget::Restore-WaitCursor* once to undo nested calls to *BeginWaitCursor* and redisplay the original cursor. These functions should always be called within the scope of the same message handler to prevent Windows from repainting the class cursor in response to a WM_SET-CURSOR message.

An easier way to display an hourglass cursor is to declare a variable of type *CWait-Cursor* on the stack, like this:

```
CWaitCursor wait;
```

CWaitCursor's constructor displays an hourglass cursor, and its destructor restores the original cursor. If you'd like to restore the cursor before the variable goes out of scope, simply call *CWaitCursor::Restore*:

```
wait.Restore ();
```

You should call *Restore* before taking any action that would allow a WM_SETCURSOR message to seep through and destroy the hourglass—for example, before displaying a message box or dialog box. You can change the cursor displayed by *CWaitCursor-::CWaitCursor* and *BeginWaitCursor* by overriding *CWinApp*'s virtual *DoWaitCursor* function. Use the default implementation of *CWinApp::DoWaitCursor* found in MFC's Appui.cpp source code file as a model for your own implementations.

In Windows 95 and other Win32 environments, you can often avoid having to use hourglass cursors by performing lengthy tasks in secondary threads of execution and allowing the thread that processes messages to proceed. If it's not feasible to perform a task in another thread and waiting is unavoidable, be sure to display an hourglass cursor to make it clear that further input is temporarily suspended.

Mouse Miscellanea

As mentioned earlier, calling the Windows *::GetSystemMetrics* API function with an SM_CMOUSEBUTTONS argument queries the system for the number of mouse buttons. (There is no MFC equivalent to *::GetSystemMetrics*, so you must call it directly.) The usual return value is 1, 2, or 3, but a 0 return means no mouse is attached. You can also find out whether a mouse is present by calling *::GetSystemMetrics* this way:

```
::GetSystemMetrics (SM_MOUSEPRESENT);
```

The return value is nonzero if there is a mouse attached, 0 if there is not. In the early days of Windows, programmers had to consider the possibility that someone might be using Windows without a mouse. Today that's rarely a concern, and a program that queries the system to determine whether a mouse is present is a rare program indeed.

Other mouse-related *::GetSystemMetrics* parameters include SM_CXDOUBLE-CLK and SM_CYDOUBLECLK, which specify the maximum horizontal and vertical distances (in pixels) that can separate the two halves of a double-click, and SM_SWAP-BUTTON, which returns a nonzero value if the user has swapped the left and right mouse buttons using Control Panel. When the mouse buttons are swapped, the left mouse button generates WM_RBUTTON messages and the right mouse button generates WM_LBUTTON messages. Generally you don't need to be concerned about this, but if for some reason your application wants to be sure that the left mouse button *really* means the left mouse button, it can use *::GetSystemMetrics* to determine whether the buttons have been swapped.

The API functions *::SetDoubleClickTime* and *::GetDoubleClickTime* enable an application program to set and retrieve the mouse double-click time—the maximum amount of time permitted between clicks when a mouse button is double-clicked. The statement

```
::GetDoubleClickTime ();
```

returns the double-click time in milliseconds, while

```
::SetDoubleClickTime (250);
```

sets the double-click time to 250 milliseconds, or one quarter of a second. When the same mouse button is clicked twice in succession, Windows uses both the double-click time and the SM_CXDOUBLECLK and SM_CYDOUBLECLK values returned by *::GetSystemMetrics* to determine whether to report the second of the two clicks as a double-click.

A function that processes mouse messages can determine which, if any, mouse buttons are depressed by checking the *nFlags* parameter passed to the message handler. It's also possible to query the state of a mouse button outside a mouse message handler by calling *::GetKeyState* or *::GetAsyncKeyState* with a VK_LBUTTON, VK_MBUTTON, or VK_RBUTTON parameter. *::GetKeyState* should be called only from a keyboard message handler because it returns the state of the specified mouse button at the time the keyboard message was generated. *::GetAsyncKeyState* can be called from anywhere. It works in real time, returning the state of the button at the moment the function is called. A negative return value from

```
::GetKeyState (VK_LBUTTON);
```

or

```
::GetAsyncKeyState (VK_LBUTTON);
```

indicates that the left mouse button is depressed. Swapping the mouse buttons does not affect *::GetAsyncKeyState*, so if you use this function, you should also use *::GetSystemMetrics* to determine whether the buttons have been swapped. The statement

```
::GetAsyncKeyState (::GetSystemMetrics (SM_SWAPBUTTON) ?
    VK_RBUTTON : VK_LBUTTON);
```

checks the state of the left mouse button asynchronously and automatically queries the right mouse button instead if the buttons have been swapped.

Windows provides a pair of API functions named *::GetCursorPos* and *::SetCursorPos* for getting and setting the cursor position manually. *::GetCursorPos* is similar to *::GetMessagePos*, but it retrieves the cursor position asynchronously just as *::GetAsyncKeyState* retrieves keyboard information asynchronously. Windows also provides a function named *::ClipCursor* that restricts the cursor to a particular area of the screen. *::ClipCursor* accepts a pointer to a RECT structure describing, in screen coordinates, the clipping rectangle. Client-area coordinates local to a window can be converted to screen coordinates with *CWnd::ClientToScreen*. Since the cursor is a global resource shared by all applications, an application that uses *::ClipCursor* must free the cursor by calling

```
::ClipCursor (NULL);
```

before terminating, or else the cursor will remain locked into the clipping rectangle indefinitely.

GETTING INPUT FROM THE KEYBOARD

A Windows application learns of keyboard events the same way it learns about mouse events: through messages. A program receives a message whenever a key is pressed or released. If you want to know when the Page Up or Page Down key is pressed so that your application can react accordingly, you can process WM_KEYDOWN messages and check for key codes identifying the Page Up or Page Down key. If you'd rather know when a key is released, you can process WM_KEYUP messages instead. For keys that produce printable characters, you can ignore key-down and key-up messages and process WM_CHAR messages denoting characters typed at the keyboard. Relying on WM_CHAR messages instead of WM_KEYUP/DOWN messages simplifies processing by enabling Windows to factor in events and circumstances surrounding the keystroke, such as whether the Shift key is depressed, whether Caps Lock is on or off, and differences in keyboard layouts.

Like the mouse, the keyboard is a global hardware resource shared by all applications. Windows decides which window to send mouse messages to by getting the handle of the window under the cursor. Keyboard messages are targeted differently. Windows directs keyboard messages to the window with the "input focus." Often the window with the input focus is the main window of the active application. However, the input focus might belong to a child of the main window, or to a control in a dialog box. Regardless, Windows *always* sends keyboard messages to the window that owns the focus. If your application uses no child windows, keyboard processing is relatively straightforward: When your application is active, its main window receives keyboard messages. If the focus shifts to a child window, keyboard messages go to the child window instead and the flow of messages to the main window ceases.

Windows notifies an application program that it is about to receive or lose the input focus with WM_SETFOCUS and WM_KILLFOCUS messages, which MFC programs process with *OnSetFocus* and *OnKillFocus* handlers. An application can shift the input focus to another window with *CWnd::SetFocus*:

```
pWnd->SetFocus ();
```

The input focus can also be assigned with the *::SetFocus* API function, which takes the handle of the window that will receive the input focus as a parameter:

```
::SetFocus (hwnd);
```

The *::GetFocus* API function and its MFC equivalent, *CWnd::GetFocus*, identify the window with the input focus. In the Win32 environment, both functions return NULL if the window that owns the focus was not created by the calling thread.

Keystroke Messages

Windows reports key presses and releases by sending WM_KEYDOWN and WM_KEYUP messages to the window with the input focus. These messages are commonly referred to as *keystroke messages*. When a key is pressed, the window with the focus receives a WM_KEYDOWN message with a virtual key code identifying the key. When the key is released, the window receives a WM_KEYUP message. If other keys are pressed and released while the key is held down, the resultant WM_KEYDOWN and WM_KEYUP messages separate the WM_KEYDOWN and WM_KEYUP messages generated by the key that's held down. Windows reports keyboard events as they happen in the order in which they happen, so by examining the stream of keystroke messages coming into your application, you can tell exactly what the user typed and when the user typed it.

Every key but two generates WM_KEYDOWN and WM_KEYUP messages. The two exceptions are Alt and F10, which are "system" keys that have a special meaning to Windows. When either of these keys is pressed and released, a window receives a WM_SYSKEYDOWN message followed by a WM_SYSKEYUP message. If other keys are pressed while the Alt key is held down, they, too, generate WM_SYSKEYDOWN and WM_SYSKEYUP messages instead of WM_KEYDOWN and WM_KEYUP messages.

An application processes keystroke messages by providing message map entries and handling functions for the messages it is interested in. WM_KEYDOWN, WM_KEYUP, WM_SYSKEYDOWN, and WM_SYSKEYUP messages are processed by a class's *OnKeyDown*, *OnKeyUp*, *OnSysKeyDown*, and *OnSysKeyUp* member functions, respectively. When activated, these handlers are provided a wealth of information about the keystroke, including a code identifying the key that was pressed or released. The message handlers are prototyped as follows:

```
afx_msg void OnMsgName (UINT nChar, UINT nRepCnt, UINT nFlags)
```

nChar is the virtual key code of the key that was pressed or released. *nRepCnt* is the repeat count: the number of keystrokes encoded in the message. *nRepCnt* is usually equal to 1 for WM_KEYDOWN or WM_SYSKEYDOWN messages and is always 1 for WM_KEYUP or WM_SYSKEYUP messages. If key-down messages arrive so fast that your application can't keep up, Windows will combine two or more WM_KEYDOWN or WM_SYSKEYDOWN messages into one and increase the repeat count accordingly. Most programs ignore the repeat count and treat combinatorial key-down messages (messages in which *nRepCnt* is greater than 1) as a single keystroke to prevent over-runs—situations in which a program continues to scroll or otherwise respond to key-stroke messages after the user's finger has left the key. In contrast to the PC's keyboard BIOS, which buffers incoming keystrokes and reports each one individually, Windows' method of reporting consecutive presses of the same key to your application provides a built-in hedge against keyboard overruns.

The *nFlags* parameter contains the key's scan code and zero or more of the bit flags described in the following table:

Bit(s)	Meaning	Description
0–7	OEM scan code	8-bit OEM scan code
8	Extended key flag	1 if the key is an extended key, 0 if it is not
9–12	Reserved	N/A
13	Context code	1 if the Alt key is held down, 0 if it is not
14	Previous key state	1 if the key was previously down, 0 if it was up
15	Transition state	0 if the key is being pressed, 1 if it is being released

The extended key flag allows an application to differentiate between the duplicate keys that appear on many keyboards. On the 101- and 102-key keyboards used with the majority of IBM-compatible PCs, the extended key flag is set for the Ctrl and Alt keys on the right side of the keyboard, the Home, End, Insert, Delete, Page Up, Page Down, and arrow keys that are clustered between the main part of the keyboard and the numeric keypad, and the keypad's Enter and forward-slash (/) keys. For all other keys, the extended key flag is 0. The OEM scan code is an 8-bit value that identifies the key to the keyboard BIOS. Most Windows applications ignore this field because it is inherently hardware-dependent. (If the application calls for it, scan codes can be translated into hardware-independent virtual key codes with the *::MapVirtualKey* API function.) The transition state, previous key state, and context code are generally disregarded, too, but are useful on occasion. A previous key state value equal to 1 identifies typematic keystrokes—keystrokes generated when a key is pressed and held down for some length of time. Holding down the Shift key for a second or so, for instance, generates the following sequence of messages:

Message	*Virtual Key Code*	*Previous Key State*
WM_KEYDOWN	VK_SHIFT	0
WM_KEYDOWN	VK_SHIFT	1
WM_KEYDOWN	VK_SHIFT	1
WM_KEYDOWN	VK_SHIFT	1
WM_KEYDOWN	VK_SHIFT	1
WM_KEYDOWN	VK_SHIFT	1
WM_KEYDOWN	VK_SHIFT	1
WM_KEYDOWN	VK_SHIFT	1
WM_KEYDOWN	VK_SHIFT	1
WM_KEYUP	VK_SHIFT	1

If you want your application to disregard keystrokes generated as a result of typematic action, simply have it ignore WM_KEYDOWN messages with previous key state values equal to 1. The transition state value is 0 for WM_KEYDOWN and WM_SYSKEYDOWN messages and 1 for WM_KEYUP and WM_SYSKEYUP messages. Finally, the context code indicates whether the Alt key was depressed when the message was generated. With certain (usually unimportant) exceptions, the code is 1 for WM_SYSKEYDOWN and WM_SYSKEYUP messages and 0 for WM_KEYDOWN and WM_KEYUP messages.

In general, applications shouldn't process WM_SYSKEYDOWN and WM_SYSKEYUP messages but should allow Windows to process them instead. If these messages don't eventually find their way to *::DefWindowProc*, system keyboard commands such as Alt-Tab and Alt-Esc will stop working. Windows puts a tremendous amount of power in your hands by routing all mouse and keyboard messages through your application first, even though many of these messages are meaningful first and foremost to the operating system. As with nonclient-area mouse messages, the improper handling of system keystroke messages—in particular, the failure to pass these messages on to the operating system—can result in all sorts of quirky behavior.

Virtual Key Codes

The most important value by far that gets passed to a keystroke message handler is the *nChar* value identifying the key that was pressed or released. So that applications won't have to rely on hardcoded values or OEM scan codes that may differ from keyboard to keyboard, Windows identifies keys with the virtual key codes shown in the table on the next page.

VIRTUAL KEY CODES

Virtual Key Code(s)	Corresponding Key(s)
VK_F1–VK_F12	Function keys F1–F12
VK_NUMPAD0–VK_NUMPAD9	Numeric keypad 0–9 with Num Lock on
VK_CANCEL	Ctrl-Break
VK_RETURN	Enter
VK_BACK	Backspace
VK_TAB	Tab
VK_CLEAR	Numeric keypad 5 with Num Lock off
VK_SHIFT	Shift
VK_CONTROL	Ctrl
VK_MENU	Alt
VK_PAUSE	Pause
VK_ESCAPE	Esc
VK_SPACE	Spacebar
VK_PRIOR	Page Up and PgUp
VK_NEXT	Page Down and PgDn
VK_END	End
VK_HOME	Home
VK_LEFT	Left arrow
VK_UP	Up arrow
VK_RIGHT	Right arrow
VK_DOWN	Down arrow
VK_SNAPSHOT	Print Screen
VK_INSERT	Insert and Ins
VK_DELETE	Delete and Del
VK_MULTIPLY	Numeric keypad *
VK_ADD	Numeric keypad +
VK_SUBTRACT	Numeric keypad −
VK_DECIMAL	Numeric keypad .
VK_DIVIDE	Numeric keypad /
VK_CAPITAL	Caps Lock
VK_NUMLOCK	Num Lock
VK_SCROLL	Scroll Lock

Conspicuously missing from this table are virtual key codes for the letters A through Z and a through z and the numerals 0 through 9. The virtual key codes for these keys are the same as the corresponding characters' ASCII codes: 0x41 through 0x5A for A through Z, 0x61 through 0x7A for a through z, and 0x30 through 0x39 for 0 through 9.

If you look inside Winuser.h, where the virtual key codes are defined, you'll find a few key codes that aren't listed above, including VK_SELECT, VK_PRINT, VK_EXECUTE, and VK_F13 through VK_F24. These codes are provided for use on other platforms and can't be generated on conventional IBM keyboards. Nonletter and nonnumeric keys for which Windows does not provide virtual key codes—for example, the semicolon (;) and square bracket ([ ]) keys—are best avoided when processing key-down and key-up messages because their IDs may vary on international keyboards. This doesn't mean that your program can't process punctuation symbols and other characters for which no VK_ identifiers exist; it simply means that there's a better way to do it than relying on key-up and key-down messages. That "better way" is WM_CHAR messages, which we'll take a look at in a moment.

Shift States and Toggles

When you write a message handler for WM_KEYDOWN, WM_KEYUP, WM_SYSKEY-DOWN, or WM_SYSKEYUP messages, your program may need to know whether the Shift, Ctrl, or Alt key is held down before deciding how to respond. Shift-state information regarding the Shift and Ctrl keys is not encoded in keyboard messages as it is in mouse messages, so Windows provides the *::GetKeyState* function. Given a virtual key code, *::GetKeyState* reports whether the key in question is held down. The statement

```
::GetKeyState (VK_SHIFT)
```

returns a negative value if the Shift key is held down, or a nonnegative value if it is not. Similarly, the statement

```
::GetKeyState (VK_CONTROL)
```

returns a negative value if the Ctrl key is held down. Thus, the bracketed statements in the following code fragment taken from an *OnKeyDown* handler will be executed only when Ctrl-Left (the left arrow key in combination with the Ctrl key) is pressed:

```
if ((nChar == VK_LEFT) && (::GetKeyState (VK_CONTROL) < 0)) {
    .
    .
    .
}
```

To inquire about the Alt key, you can call *::GetKeyState* with a VK_MENU parameter or simply check the context code bit in the *nFlags* parameter. Usually even that amount of effort isn't necessary because, if the Alt key is depressed, your window will receive a WM_SYSKEYDOWN or WM_SYSKEYUP message instead of a WM__KEYDOWN or WM_KEYUP message. In other words, the *context* of the message generally tells you all you need to know about the Alt key. As a bonus, you can use the identifiers VK_LBUTTON, VK_MBUTTON, and VK_RBUTTON in conjunction with *::GetKeyState* to determine if any of the mouse buttons is held down.

An application can also use *::GetKeyState* to determine whether Num Lock, Caps Lock, and Scroll Lock are on or off. Whereas the high bit of the return code indicates whether a key is currently depressed (yielding a negative number when the high bit is 1), the low bit—bit 0—indicates the state of the toggle. The statement

```
::GetKeyState (VK_NUMLOCK) & 0x01
```

returns nonzero if Num Lock is on and 0 if it is not. The same technique works for the VK_CAPITAL (Caps Lock) and VK_SCROLL (Scroll Lock) keys, too. It's important to mask off all but the lowest bit of the return code before testing because the high bit still indicates whether the key itself is up or down.

In all cases, *::GetKeyState* reports the state of the key or the mouse button *at the time the keyboard message was generated,* and not at the precise moment in which the function is called. This is a feature, not a bug, because it means you don't have to worry about a shift key being released before your message handler gets around to inquiring about the key state. The *::GetKeyState* function should never be called outside a keyboard message handler because the information it returns is valid only after a keyboard message has been retrieved from the message queue. If you really need to know the current state of a key or a mouse button, or if you want to check a key or a mouse button outside a keyboard message handler, use *::GetAsyncKeyState* instead.

Adding a Keyboard Interface to GdiDemo3

As a first cut at processing keyboard messages, let's enhance Chapter 2's GdiDemo3 program by adding a keyboard interface. We'll modify the program so that pressing the up or down arrow key scrolls the contents of the window by one line and pressing Page Up or Page Down scrolls the contents of the window by one full page. In the resulting application, GdiDemo4, the user will have the option of scrolling with the mouse or the keyboard. And because the scrolling logic is already there, adding a keyboard interface requires only a few additional lines of code.

The source code for GdiDemo4 appears in Figure 3-7. The primary difference between GdiDemo3 and GdiDemo4 is the latter's inclusion of a *CMyView::OnKeyDown* function that processes WM_KEYDOWN messages corresponding to the up arrow, down arrow, Page Up, and Page Down keys. *OnKeyDown* uses a *switch-case* structure to branch to the appropriate handling routine based on the virtual key code in *nChar*. Each handling routine executes a single statement: a *SendMessage* call that simulates a scroll bar event by sending a WM_VSCROLL message to the view window with *wParam* holding the appropriate notification code. When the user presses the up arrow key, for example, *OnKeyDown* sends a WM_VSCROLL message with *wParam* equal to SB_LINEUP:

```
case VK_UP:
    SendMessage (WM_VSCROLL, SB_LINEUP, 0);
    break;
```

This is almost exactly the same thing that happens when the user clicks a scroll bar up-arrow, but here it's our program that generates the message rather than the scroll bar. It's all the same to the scroll view. It neither knows nor cares who sent the message; it simply responds to the message and scrolls the contents of the window down one line. We could have done the same thing with more code by querying the view for the current scroll position with *CScrollView::GetScrollPosition*, calculating a new scroll position, and scrolling to the new position with *CScrollView::ScrollToPosition*, but the *SendMessage* method is simpler and more efficient.

GdiDemo4.rc

```
//*****************************************************************
//
//  GdiDemo4.rc
//
//*****************************************************************

#include <afxres.h>

AFX_IDI_STD_FRAME ICON GdiDemo.ico
```

GdiDemo4.h

```
//*****************************************************************
//
//  GdiDemo4.h
//
//*****************************************************************

class CMyApp : public CWinApp
{
public:
    virtual BOOL InitInstance ();
};

class CMyView : public CScrollView
{
private:
    int m_cxChar;
    int m_cyChar;

    void ShowPenStyles (CDC*, int, int);
    void ShowPenWidths (CDC*, int, int);
```

Figure 3-7. *The GdiDemo4 program.*

(continued)

GdiDemo4.h *continued*

```cpp
    void ShowBrushStyles (CDC*, int, int);

protected:
    virtual void OnDraw (CDC*);

    afx_msg int OnCreate (LPCREATESTRUCT);
    afx_msg void OnSize (UINT, int, int);
    afx_msg void OnKeyDown (UINT, UINT, UINT);

    DECLARE_MESSAGE_MAP ()
};

class CMainWindow : public CFrameWnd
{
private:
    CMyView* m_pMyView;

public:
    CMainWindow ();

protected:
    afx_msg int OnCreate (LPCREATESTRUCT);
    afx_msg void OnSetFocus (CWnd*);

    DECLARE_MESSAGE_MAP ()
};

struct STYLES {
    int nStyle;
    char szStyleName[16];
};
```

GdiDemo4.cpp

```cpp
//*****************************************************************
//
// GdiDemo4.cpp
//
//*****************************************************************

#include <afxwin.h>
#include "GdiDemo4.h"

#define VHEIGHT (m_cyChar * 50)
```

```
CMyApp myApp;

/////////////////////////////////////////////////////////////////////
// CMyApp member functions

BOOL CMyApp::InitInstance ()
{
    m_pMainWnd = new CMainWindow;
    m_pMainWnd->ShowWindow (m_nCmdShow);
    m_pMainWnd->UpdateWindow ();
    return TRUE;
}


/////////////////////////////////////////////////////////////////////
// CMainWindow message map and member functions

BEGIN_MESSAGE_MAP (CMainWindow, CFrameWnd)
    ON_WM_CREATE ()
    ON_WM_SETFOCUS ()
END_MESSAGE_MAP ()

CMainWindow::CMainWindow ()
{
    m_pMyView = NULL;
    Create (NULL, "GdiDemo4");
}

int CMainWindow::OnCreate (LPCREATESTRUCT lpcs)
{
    if (CFrameWnd::OnCreate (lpcs) == -1)
        return -1;

    m_pMyView = new CMyView;
    m_pMyView->Create (NULL, NULL, WS_CHILD | WS_VISIBLE,
        CRect (0, 0, 0, 0), this, AFX_IDW_PANE_FIRST, NULL);
    return 0;
}

void CMainWindow::OnSetFocus (CWnd* pWnd)
{
    if (m_pMyView != NULL)
        m_pMyView->SetFocus ();
}
```

(continued)

GdiDemo4.cpp *continued*

```
///////////////////////////////////////////////////////////////////////
// CMyView message map and member functions

BEGIN_MESSAGE_MAP (CMyView, CScrollView)
    ON_WM_CREATE ()
    ON_WM_SIZE ()
    ON_WM_KEYDOWN ()
END_MESSAGE_MAP ()

int CMyView::OnCreate (LPCREATESTRUCT lpcs)
{
    if (CScrollView::OnCreate (lpcs) == -1)
        return -1;

    TEXTMETRIC tm;
    CClientDC dc (this);
    dc.GetTextMetrics (&tm);
    m_cxChar = tm.tmAveCharWidth;
    m_cyChar = tm.tmHeight;
    return 0;
}

void CMyView::OnSize (UINT nType, int cx, int cy)
{
    SetScrollSizes (MM_TEXT, CSize (0, VHEIGHT), CSize (0, cy),
        CSize (0, m_cyChar));
}

void CMyView::OnDraw (CDC* pDC)
{
    CPaintDC dc (this);

    ShowPenStyles (pDC, m_cxChar * 2, m_cyChar);
    ShowPenWidths (pDC, m_cxChar * 2, m_cyChar * 15);
    ShowBrushStyles (pDC, m_cxChar * 2, m_cyChar * 27);
}

void CMyView::OnKeyDown (UINT nChar, UINT nRepCnt, UINT nFlags)
{
    switch (nChar) {

    case VK_UP:
        SendMessage (WM_VSCROLL, SB_LINEUP, 0);
        break;
```

```
        case VK_PRIOR:
            SendMessage (WM_VSCROLL, SB_PAGEUP, 0);
            break;

        case VK_NEXT:
            SendMessage (WM_VSCROLL, SB_PAGEDOWN, 0);
            break;

        case VK_DOWN:
            SendMessage (WM_VSCROLL, SB_LINEDOWN, 0);
            break;
    }
}

void CMyView::ShowPenStyles (CDC* pDC, int x, int y)
{
    static struct STYLES styles[] = {
        PS_SOLID,        "PS_SOLID",
        PS_DASH,         "PS_DASH",
        PS_DOT,          "PS_DOT",
        PS_DASHDOT,      "PS_DASHDOT",
        PS_DASHDOTDOT,   "PS_DASHDOTDOT",
        PS_NULL,         "PS_NULL",
        PS_INSIDEFRAME,  "PS_INSIDEFRAME"
    };

    pDC->SetTextColor (RGB (0, 0, 0));
    pDC->TextOut (x, y, "Pen Styles");

    int dy = (m_cyChar * 3) / 2;
    int x1 = x + (m_cxChar * 2);
    int x2 = x + (m_cxChar * 22);
    int x3 = x + (m_cxChar * 46);

    CPen* pOldPen;
    pDC->SetTextColor (RGB (255, 0, 0));

    for (int i=0; i<7; i++) {
        y += dy;
        pDC->TextOut (x1, y, styles[i].szStyleName);

        CPen pen (styles[i].nStyle, 1, RGB (255, 0, 0));
        pOldPen = pDC->SelectObject (&pen);

        pDC->MoveTo (x2, y + (m_cyChar / 2));
```

(continued)

GdiDemo4.cpp *continued*

```
            pDC->LineTo (x3, y + (m_cyChar / 2));

            pDC->SelectObject (pOldPen);
        }
}

void CMyView::ShowPenWidths (CDC* pDC, int x, int y)
{
    static int nPenWidths[] = { 2, 8, 16, 24 };

    pDC->SetTextColor (RGB (0, 0, 0));
    pDC->TextOut (x, y, "Pen Widths");

    int dy = m_cyChar * 2;
    int x1 = x + (m_cxChar * 2);
    int x2 = x + (m_cxChar * 22);
    int x3 = x + (m_cxChar * 46);

    CPen* pOldPen;
    CString strDescription;
    pDC->SetTextColor (RGB (0, 0, 255));

    for (int i=0; i<4; i++) {
        y += dy;
        strDescription.Format ("%d Pixels", nPenWidths[i]);
        pDC->TextOut (x1, y, strDescription);

        CPen pen (PS_SOLID, nPenWidths[i], RGB (0, 0, 255));
        pOldPen = pDC->SelectObject (&pen);

        pDC->MoveTo (x2, y + (m_cyChar / 2));
        pDC->LineTo (x3, y + (m_cyChar / 2));

        pDC->SelectObject (pOldPen);
    }
}

void CMyView::ShowBrushStyles (CDC* pDC, int x, int y)
{
    static struct STYLES styles[] = {
        HS_BDIAGONAL,    "HS_BDIAGONAL",
        HS_CROSS,        "HS_CROSS",
        HS_DIAGCROSS,    "HS_DIAGCROSS",
        HS_FDIAGONAL,    "HS_FDIAGONAL",
        HS_HORIZONTAL,   "HS_HORIZONTAL",
```

```
        HS_VERTICAL,      "HS_VERTICAL"
};

pDC->SetTextColor (RGB (0, 0, 0));
pDC->TextOut (x, y, "Brush Styles");

int dy = m_cyChar * 3;
int x1 = x + (m_cxChar * 2);
int x2 = x + (m_cxChar * 22);
int x3 = x + (m_cxChar * 46);


CBrush* pOldBrush;

for (int i=0; i<6; i++) {
    y += dy;
    pDC->TextOut (x1, y, styles[i].szStyleName);

    CRect rect (x2, y - m_cyChar, x3, y + m_cyChar);
    CBrush brush (styles[i].nStyle, RGB (0, 255, 0));

    CPoint point (rect.left, rect.top);
    pDC->LPtoDP (&point);
    point.x %= 8;
    point.y %= 8;
    pDC->SetBrushOrg (point);

    pOldBrush = pDC->SelectObject (&brush);
    pDC->Rectangle (rect);

    pDC->SelectObject (pOldBrush);
}

y += dy;
pDC->TextOut (x1, y, "Solid");

CBrush brush (RGB (0, 255, 0));
pOldBrush = pDC->SelectObject (&brush);
pDC->Rectangle (x2, y - m_cyChar, x3, y + m_cyChar);
pDC->SelectObject (pOldBrush);
}
```

The only other difference between GdiDemo3 and GdiDemo4 is the latter's *CMainWindow::OnSetFocus* message handler, which contains just two lines of code:

```
if (m_pMyView != NULL)
    m_pMyView->SetFocus ();
```

When *CMainWindow::OnCreate* creates the scroll-view window, it saves the pointer in *m_ pMyView*. And whenever *CMainWindow* receives the input focus, it uses that pointer to pass the input focus to the view window. Why? Remember that keyboard messages are directed to the window that owns the input focus, which in this case could be either the frame window or the scroll-view window. For *CMyView::OnKey-Down* to be alerted to key presses, the scroll view must have the input focus. Therefore, if the frame window gains the input focus for any reason, it immediately passes the input focus to the view so that the up and down arrow and Page Up and Page Down keys won't suddenly become dysfunctional. You can see for yourself why this is necessary by commenting out the call to *SetFocus* and recompiling the program. When the program is first started, the keys won't work because the main window has the input focus. But click the interior of the window once to manually shift the input focus to the view, and the keyboard interface will work just fine. The *OnSetFocus* handler makes this automatic by ensuring that the view window has the input focus whenever the program is active.

Character Messages

One of the problems you'll encounter if you rely exclusively on key-up and key-down messages for keyboard input is exemplified in the following scenario. Suppose you're writing a text-entry application that turns messages signifying presses of character keys into characters on the screen. The A key is pressed, and a WM_KEYDOWN message arrives with a virtual key code equal to 0x41. Before you put an A on the screen, you call *::GetKeyState* to determine whether the Shift key is held down. If it is, you output an uppercase "A"; otherwise, you output a lowercase "a." So far, so good. But what if Caps Lock is enabled too? Caps Lock undoes the effect of the Shift key, converting "A" to "a" and "a" to "A." Now there are four different permutations of the letter A that you must consider:

Virtual Key Code	VK_SHIFT	Caps Lock	Result
0x41	No	Off	a
0x41	Yes	Off	A
0x41	No	On	A
0x41	Yes	On	a

While you might reasonably expect to overcome this problem by writing code to sense all the possible shift and toggle states, your work is complicated by the fact that the user might have the Ctrl key held down, too. And the problem is only compounded when your application is run outside the United States, where keyboard layouts typically differ from the US keyboard layout. An American user presses Shift-0 to enter a right parenthesis symbol. But Shift-0 produces an equal sign symbol on most international keyboards and an apostrophe on Dutch keyboards. Users aren't going to appreciate it very much if the characters your program displays don't match the characters they type.

That's why Windows provides the *::TranslateMessage* API function. So that character input can be performed independent of keyboard type, the *::TranslateMessage* function translates WM_KEYDOWN/WM_KEYUP and WM_SYSKEYDOWN/WM_SYS-KEYUP messages involving character keys into WM_CHAR and WM_SYSCHAR messages. The default message loop provided by the framework calls *::TranslateMessage* for you, so in an MFC application you don't have to do anything special to translate keystroke messages into WM_CHAR messages. And when you rely on WM_CHAR to input characters from the keyboard, you don't have to worry about virtual key codes and shift states because each WM_CHAR message includes an ANSI character code that maps directly to a symbol in the ANSI character set. (See Figure 3-8 on the next page.) Assuming Caps Lock is not turned on, the user's pressing Shift-A produces the following sequence of messages:

Message	Virtual Key Code	ANSI Code
WM_KEYDOWN	VK_SHIFT	
WM_KEYDOWN	0x41	
WM_CHAR		0x41 ("A")
WM_KEYUP	0x41	
WM_KEYUP	VK_SHIFT	

Now you can safely ignore key-up and key-down messages because everything you need to know about the keystroke is encoded in the WM_CHAR message. Had the Alt key been held down, your application would have received a WM_SYSCHAR message instead:

Message	Virtual Key Code	ANSI Code
WM_SYSKEYDOWN	VK_SHIFT	
WM_SYSKEYDOWN	0x41	
WM_SYSCHAR		0x41 ("A")
WM_SYSKEYUP	0x41	
WM_SYSKEYUP	VK_SHIFT	

Since Alt-key combinations are generally used for special purposes, most applications ignore WM_SYSCHAR messages and process WM_CHAR messages instead.

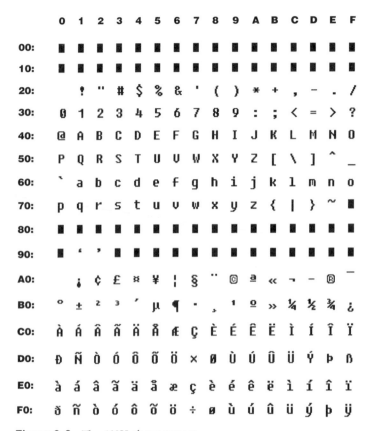

Figure 3-8. *The ANSI character set.*

In an MFC application, WM_CHAR messages are routed through a class's message map to the member function *OnChar*, which is prototyped as follows:

```
afx_msg void OnChar (UINT nChar, UINT nRepCnt, UINT nFlags)
```

nRepCnt and *nFlags* have the same meanings they do in keystroke messages. *nChar* holds an ANSI character code. You need to be careful when you display characters received through WM_CHAR (or WM_SYSCHAR) messages that the font you're using is an ANSI font and not an OEM font. The OEM character set is the one built into the character-generator ROM of most video adapters; you see it when you switch an MS-DOS application to full-screen mode or boot your PC with MS-DOS. For character codes 32 through 127, the characters in ANSI and OEM fonts are identical. Outside this range, however, the ANSI and OEM characters differ. If a user with a German keyboard types a capital O with an umlaut (Ö), your application will receive a WM-_CHAR message with *nChar* equal to 214. If you display this character using an ANSI font, it will be displayed correctly. Display it in an OEM font, however, and Windows will display an odd-looking graphic character. Fortunately, the default system font Windows selects into its device contexts is an ANSI font, as are most of the other Windows fonts you'll ever come across. One exception is OEM_FIXED_FONT, which is one of the stock fonts you can select with *CDC::SelectStockObject*.

In the event you should ever need to convert a string of character codes from OEM to ANSI format or vice versa, Windows provides a pair of API functions named *::OemToAnsi* and *::AnsiToOem* for that purpose. MFC's *CString* class provides equivalent functions named *OemToAnsi* and *AnsiToOem*. One use for *OemToAnsi* is translating text files created with MS-DOS applications into ANSI format for display in a Windows application. Bear in mind that the translation may be less than perfect, however. If a character in the string being translated doesn't exist in the other character set, Windows will do its best to find a reasonable facsimile using a translation table supplied by the keyboard driver. But the resulting output probably won't look as good as the original.

The Caret

The flashing vertical bar word processors and other Windows applications use to mark the point where the next character will be inserted is called the *caret*. The caret serves the same purpose in a Windows application that the blinking underscore cursor does in a character-mode application. MFC's *CWnd* class provides the seven caret handling functions shown below. The one essential function missing from this table, *::DestroyCaret*, must be called directly from the Windows API because there is no MFC equivalent.

CWnd CARET HANDLING FUNCTIONS

Function	*Description*
CreateCaret	Creates a caret from a bitmap.
CreateSolidCaret	Creates a solid line or block caret.
CreateGrayCaret	Creates a gray line or block caret.
GetCaretPos	Retrieves the current caret position.
SetCaretPos	Sets the caret position.
ShowCaret	Displays the caret.
HideCaret	Hides the caret.

The caret, like the mouse cursor, is a global resource shared by everyone. There is only one caret, and only one program can own it at a time. Therefore, a program can't use the caret just any way it wants to; it must be mindful of the needs of other programs. The rules for using the caret are shown on the next page.

- A window that uses the caret should "create" a caret when it receives the input focus and "destroy" the caret when it loses the input focus. A caret is created with *CreateCaret*, *CreateSolidCaret*, or *CreateGrayCaret* and is destroyed with *::DestroyCaret*.

- Once a caret is created, it isn't visible until *ShowCaret* is called to make it visible. The caret can be hidden again by a call to *HideCaret*. If calls to *HideCaret* are nested—that is, if *HideCaret* is called twice or more in succession—*ShowCaret* must be called an equal number of times to make the caret visible again.

- When your program draws in the area of a window that contains the caret outside an *OnPaint* handler, it should hide the caret to avoid corrupting the display. Your program can redisplay the caret after drawing is complete. You don't need to hide and redisplay the caret in an *OnPaint* handler because *::BeginPaint* and *::EndPaint* do that for you.

- A program moves the caret by calling *SetCaretPos*. Windows doesn't move the caret for you; it's your program's job to process incoming keyboard messages (and perhaps mouse messages) and manipulate the caret accordingly. *GetCaretPos* can be called to retrieve the caret's current position.

As noted earlier, a window receives a WM_SETFOCUS message when it receives the input focus and a WM_KILLFOCUS message when it loses the focus. The following message handler creates a caret, positions it, and displays it when a window gains the input focus:

```
void CMainWindow::OnSetFocus (CWnd* pWnd)
{
    CreateSolidCaret (2, m_cyChar);
    SetCaretPos (m_ptCaretPos);
    ShowCaret ();
}
```

And this message handler saves the caret position and hides and destroys the caret when the input focus is lost:

```
void CMainWindow::OnKillFocus (CWnd* pWnd)
{
    HideCaret ();
    m_ptCaretPos = GetCaretPos ();
    ::DestroyCaret ();
}
```

In these examples, *m_cyChar* holds the caret height and *m_ptCaretPos* holds the caret position, which is saved when the focus is lost and restored when the focus is regained. Since only one window can have the input focus at a time and keyboard messages are directed to the window with the input focus, this approach to caret handling ensures that the window that "owns" the keyboard will also own the caret. If all programs behave this way, there will never be a problem with two programs vying for the caret at the same time.

The caret-create functions serve a dual purpose: to define the look of the caret and to claim ownership of the caret from Windows. The caret is actually a bitmap, so you can customize its appearance by supplying a bitmap to *CWnd::CreateCaret*. But more often than not you'll find that the easier-to-use *CreateSolidCaret* function ("easier to use" because it doesn't require a bitmap) does the job nicely. *CreateSolidCaret* creates a solid block caret that, depending on how you shape it, can look like a rectangle, a horizontal or vertical line, or something in between. In the *OnSetFocus* example above, the statement

```
CreateSolidCaret (2, m_cyChar);
```

creates a vertical-line caret 2 pixels wide whose height equals the character height of the current font (*m_cyChar*). This is the traditional way of creating a caret for use with a proportional font, although some programs key the width of a vertical-line caret to a system variable such as the SM_CXBORDER value obtainable with *::GetSystemMetrics*. For fixed-pitch fonts, you may prefer to use a block caret whose width and height equal the width and height of one character, as in

```
CreateSolidCaret (m_cxChar, m_cyChar);
```

A block caret wouldn't make sense for a proportionally spaced font because of the varying character widths. *CWnd*'s *CreateGrayCaret* function works just as *CreateSolidCaret* does except that it creates a gray caret rather than a solid black caret. Caret dimensions are expressed in logical units, so if you change the mapping mode before calling a caret-create function, the dimensions you specify will be transformed accordingly.

As mentioned above, it's your job—not Windows'—to move the caret. *CWnd::SetCaretPos* repositions the caret, accepting a *CPoint* object that encapsulates the *x* and *y* client-area coordinates of the new cursor position. Positioning the caret in a string of text is fairly straightforward if you're using a fixed-pitch font because you can calculate a new *x* offset into the string by multiplying the character position by the character width. If the font is proportionally spaced, you'll have to do a little more work. MFC's *CDC::GetTextExtent* and *CDC::GetTabbedTextExtent* functions enable an application to determine the width, in logical units, of a string of characters rendered in a proportional font. (Use *GetTabbedTextExtent* if the string contains tab characters.) Given a character position, a program can determine the corresponding caret position by calling *GetTextExtent* or *GetTabbedTextExtent* to find the cumulative width of the characters up to the character position. If the string "Hello, world" is displayed at the position specified by *point*, the following statements on the next page position the caret after the "w" (the eighth character).

```
CSize size = dc.GetTextExtent ("Hello, w", 8);
SetCaretPos (CPoint (point.x + size.cx, point.y));
```

GetTextExtent returns a *CSize* object whose *cx* and *cy* members reflect the string's width and height. Positioning the caret *cx* units to the right of the point at which the string begins after making this call places the caret between the "w" and the "o" in the word "world."

Caret positioning gets slightly more complicated if you're using a proportional font and don't have a character offset to work with, which is exactly the situation you'll find yourself in when you write an *OnLButtonDown* handler that repositions the caret when the left mouse button is clicked. Suppose your application maintains a variable named *m_nCurrentPos* that denotes the current character position—the position within a string at which the next typed character will be inserted. It's easy to calculate the new caret position when the left or right arrow key is pressed: just decrement or increment *m_nCurrentPos*, and call *GetTextExtent* or *GetTabbedTextExtent* with the new character position to compute a new offset. But what if the left mouse button is clicked at some arbitrary location in the string? There is no relationship between the point at which the mouse click occurred and *m_nCurrentPos*, so you must use the horizontal difference between the cursor position and the beginning of the string to work backward to a character position, and *then* calculate the final caret position. This inevitably involves some iteration since there is neither a Windows API function nor an MFC class member function that accepts a string and a pixel offset and returns the character at that offset. Fortunately, it's not terribly difficult to write that function yourself. You'll see how it's done in the next section.

THE VISUALKB APPLICATION

Let's put together everything we've learned in this chapter by developing a sample application that accepts text input from the keyboard, displays the text in a window, and enables the user to perform simple text-editing functions that include moving the caret with the arrow keys and the mouse. For educational purposes, let's add a scrolling display of the various keyboard messages the program receives and the parameters bundled with those messages, similar to the KEYLOOK program featured in Chapter 5 of Charles Petzold's *Programming Windows 95*. In addition to providing a hands-on lesson in mouse and keyboard handling, the program, which I've called VisualKB, demonstrates some techniques for handling proportionally spaced text. VisualKB also provides a handy tool for examining the stream of messages coming from the keyboard and experimenting to see what messages result from specific keystrokes and key combinations.

Figure 3-9 shows what the VisualKB window looks like right after the program is started and the letters "MFC" are typed. The typed characters appear in the text-entry rectangle at the top of the window, and the corresponding keyboard messages are displayed in the rectangle below. The first and final messages were generated when the Shift key was pressed and released. In between, you see the WM_KEYDOWN, WM_CHAR, and WM_KEYUP messages generated by the M, F, and C keystrokes. To the right of each message name, VisualKB displays the message parameters. "Char" is the virtual key code or character code passed to the message handler in *nChar*. "Rep" is the repeat count in *nRepCnt*. "Scan" is the OEM scan code stored in bits 0 through 7 of the *nFlags* parameter, and "Ext," "Con," "Prv," and "Tran" represent the extended key flag, context code, previous key state, and transition state values. VisualKB also displays WM_SYSKEYDOWN, WM_SYSCHAR, and WM_SYSKEYUP messages, which you can verify by pressing an Alt key combination such as Alt-S.

Message	Char	Rep	Scan	Ext	Con	Prv	Tran
WM_KEYDOWN	16	1	42	0	0	0	0
WM_KEYDOWN	77	1	50	0	0	0	0
WM_CHAR	77	1	50	0	0	0	0
WM_KEYUP	77	1	50	0	0	1	1
WM_KEYDOWN	70	1	33	0	0	0	0
WM_CHAR	70	1	33	0	0	0	0
WM_KEYUP	70	1	33	0	0	1	1
WM_KEYDOWN	67	1	46	0	0	0	0
WM_CHAR	67	1	46	0	0	0	0
WM_KEYUP	67	1	46	0	0	1	1
WM_KEYUP	16	1	42	0	0	1	1

Figure 3-9. *The VisualKB window after the letters "MFC" have been typed.*

Take a moment or two to play with VisualKB and see what happens when you press various keys and combinations of keys. In addition to typing in text, you can use the following editing keys:

■ The left and right arrow keys move the caret one character to the left and right. Home and End move the caret to the beginning and end of the line. The caret can also be moved with mouse clicks.

■ The Backspace key deletes the character to the left of the caret and moves the caret one position to the left.

■ The Esc and Enter keys clear the text and reset the caret to the beginning of the line.

Typed characters are entered in overstrike mode, so if the caret isn't at the end of the line, the next character you type will replace the character to the right. If you type beyond the end of the line (about one character position to the left of the far right end of the text-entry rectangle), the text is automatically cleared. I resisted the urge to add features such as horizontal scrolling and insert mode to keep the program from becoming unnecessarily complicated. Besides, in the real world you can avoid writing a lot of the code for a program like this one by using an edit control, which provides similar text-entry capabilities and includes support for cutting and pasting, scrolling, and much more. Unless you're writing the world's next great word processor, an edit control probably has everything you need. Still, it's useful to see how text entry is done the hard way, not only because it's instructive but also because you'll have a better feel for what's happening inside Windows when we start using edit controls in Chapter 5.

There is much to be learned from VisualKB's source code, which appears in Figure 3-10. The sections that follow point out a few of the highlights.

Resource.h

```
//*******************************************************************
//
//  Resource.h
//
//*******************************************************************

#define IDI_APPICON 100
```

VisualKB.rc

```
//*******************************************************************
//
//  VisualKB.rc
//
//*******************************************************************

#include "Resource.h"

IDI_APPICON ICON VisualKB.ico
```

VisualKB.h

```
//*******************************************************************
//
//  VisualKB.h
//
//*******************************************************************
```

Figure 3-10. *The VisualKB program.*

```
#define MAX_STRINGS 12

class CMyApp : public CWinApp
{
public:
    virtual BOOL InitInstance ();
};

class CMainWindow : public CWnd
{
private:
    int m_cxChar;
    int m_cyChar;
    int m_cyLine;
    int m_nTextPos;
    int m_nTabStops[7];
    int m_nTextLimit;
    int m_nMsgPos;

    HCURSOR m_hCursorArrow;
    HCURSOR m_hCursorIBeam;

    CPoint m_ptTextOrigin;
    CPoint m_ptHeaderOrigin;
    CPoint m_ptUpperMsgOrigin;
    CPoint m_ptLowerMsgOrigin;
    CPoint m_ptCaretPos;

    CRect m_rcTextBox;
    CRect m_rcTextBoxBorder;
    CRect m_rcMsgBoxBorder;
    CRect m_rcScroll;

    CString m_strInputText;
    CString m_strMessages[MAX_STRINGS];

    int GetNearestPos (CPoint);
    void PositionCaret (CDC* = NULL);
    void DrawInputText (CDC*);
    void ShowMessage (LPCTSTR, UINT, UINT, UINT);
    void DrawMessageHeader (CDC*);
    void DrawMessages (CDC*);

public:
    CMainWindow ();
```

(continued)

VisualKB.h *continued*

```
protected:
    virtual void PostNcDestroy ();

    afx_msg int OnCreate (LPCREATESTRUCT);
    afx_msg void OnPaint ();
    afx_msg void OnSetFocus (CWnd*);
    afx_msg void OnKillFocus (CWnd*);
    afx_msg BOOL OnSetCursor (CWnd*, UINT, UINT);
    afx_msg void OnLButtonDown (UINT, CPoint);
    afx_msg void OnKeyDown (UINT, UINT, UINT);
    afx_msg void OnKeyUp (UINT, UINT, UINT);
    afx_msg void OnSysKeyDown (UINT, UINT, UINT);
    afx_msg void OnSysKeyUp (UINT, UINT, UINT);
    afx_msg void OnChar (UINT, UINT, UINT);
    afx_msg void OnSysChar (UINT, UINT, UINT);

    DECLARE_MESSAGE_MAP ()
};
```

VisualKB.cpp

```
//*************************************************************************
//
//  VisualKB.cpp
//
//*************************************************************************

#include <afxwin.h>
#include "Resource.h"
#include "VisualKB.h"

CMyApp myApp;

///////////////////////////////////////////////////////////////////////////
// CMyApp member functions

BOOL CMyApp::InitInstance ()
{
    m_pMainWnd = new CMainWindow;
    m_pMainWnd->ShowWindow (m_nCmdShow);
    m_pMainWnd->UpdateWindow ();
    return TRUE;
}
```

```
///////////////////////////////////////////////////////////////////////////
// CMainWindow message map and member functions

BEGIN_MESSAGE_MAP (CMainWindow, CWnd)
    ON_WM_CREATE ()
    ON_WM_PAINT ()
    ON_WM_SETFOCUS ()
    ON_WM_KILLFOCUS ()
    ON_WM_SETCURSOR ()
    ON_WM_LBUTTONDOWN ()
    ON_WM_KEYDOWN ()
    ON_WM_KEYUP ()
    ON_WM_SYSKEYDOWN ()
    ON_WM_SYSKEYUP ()
    ON_WM_CHAR ()
    ON_WM_SYSCHAR ()
END_MESSAGE_MAP ()

CMainWindow::CMainWindow ()
{
    m_nTextPos = 0;
    m_nMsgPos = 0;

    m_hCursorArrow = myApp.LoadStandardCursor (IDC_ARROW);
    m_hCursorIBeam = myApp.LoadStandardCursor (IDC_IBEAM);

    CString strWndClass = AfxRegisterWndClass (
        0,
        NULL,
        (HBRUSH) (COLOR_3DFACE + 1),
        myApp.LoadIcon (IDI_APPICON)
    );

    CreateEx (0, strWndClass, "Visual Keyboard",
        WS_OVERLAPPED | WS_SYSMENU | WS_CAPTION | WS_MINIMIZEBOX,
        CW_USEDEFAULT, CW_USEDEFAULT, CW_USEDEFAULT, CW_USEDEFAULT,
        NULL, NULL);
}

int CMainWindow::OnCreate (LPCREATESTRUCT lpcs)
{
    if (CWnd::OnCreate (lpcs) == -1)
        return -1;

    CClientDC dc (this);
```

(continued)

VisualKB.cpp *continued*

```
TEXTMETRIC tm;
dc.GetTextMetrics (&tm);
m_cxChar = tm.tmAveCharWidth;
m_cyChar = tm.tmHeight;
m_cyLine = tm.tmHeight + tm.tmExternalLeading;

m_rcTextBoxBorder.SetRect (16, 16, (m_cxChar * 64) + 16,
    ((m_cyChar * 3) / 2) + 16);

m_rcTextBox = m_rcTextBoxBorder;
m_rcTextBox.InflateRect (-2, -2);

m_rcMsgBoxBorder.SetRect (16, (m_cyChar * 4) + 16,
    (m_cxChar * 64) + 16, (m_cyLine * MAX_STRINGS) +
    (m_cyChar * 6) + 16);

m_rcScroll.SetRect (m_cxChar + 16, (m_cyChar * 6) + 16,
    (m_cxChar * 63) + 16, (m_cyLine * MAX_STRINGS) +
    (m_cyChar * 5) + 16);

m_ptTextOrigin.x = m_cxChar + 16;
m_ptTextOrigin.y = (m_cyChar / 4) + 16;
m_ptCaretPos = m_ptTextOrigin;
m_nTextLimit = (m_cxChar * 63) + 16;

m_ptHeaderOrigin.x = m_cxChar + 16;
m_ptHeaderOrigin.y = (m_cyChar * 3) + 16;

m_ptUpperMsgOrigin.x = m_cxChar + 16;
m_ptUpperMsgOrigin.y = (m_cyChar * 5) + 16;

m_ptLowerMsgOrigin.x = m_cxChar + 16;
m_ptLowerMsgOrigin.y = (m_cyChar * 5) +
    (m_cyLine * (MAX_STRINGS - 1)) + 16;

m_nTabStops[0] = (m_cxChar * 24) + 16;
m_nTabStops[1] = (m_cxChar * 30) + 16;
m_nTabStops[2] = (m_cxChar * 36) + 16;
m_nTabStops[3] = (m_cxChar * 42) + 16;
m_nTabStops[4] = (m_cxChar * 46) + 16;
m_nTabStops[5] = (m_cxChar * 50) + 16;
m_nTabStops[6] = (m_cxChar * 54) + 16;

CRect rect (0, 0, m_rcMsgBoxBorder.right + 16,
    m_rcMsgBoxBorder.bottom + 16);
```

```
    CalcWindowRect (&rect);

    SetWindowPos (NULL, 0, 0, rect.Width (), rect.Height (),
        SWP_NOZORDER : SWP_NOMOVE : SWP_NOREDRAW);
    return 0;
}

void CMainWindow::PostNcDestroy ()
{
    delete this;
}

void CMainWindow::OnPaint ()
{
    CPaintDC dc (this);

    dc.DrawEdge (m_rcTextBoxBorder, EDGE_SUNKEN, BF_RECT);
    dc.DrawEdge (m_rcMsgBoxBorder, EDGE_SUNKEN, BF_RECT);

    DrawInputText (&dc);
    DrawMessageHeader (&dc);
    DrawMessages (&dc);
}

void CMainWindow::OnSetFocus (CWnd* pWnd)
{
    CreateSolidCaret (max (2, ::GetSystemMetrics (SM_CXBORDER)),
        m_cyChar);
    SetCaretPos (m_ptCaretPos);
    ShowCaret ();
}

void CMainWindow::OnKillFocus (CWnd* pWnd)
{
    HideCaret ();
    m_ptCaretPos = GetCaretPos ();
    ::DestroyCaret ();
}

BOOL CMainWindow::OnSetCursor (CWnd* pWnd, UINT nHitTest, UINT message)
{
    if (nHitTest == HTCLIENT) {
        DWORD dwPos = ::GetMessagePos ();
        CPoint point (LOWORD (dwPos), HIWORD (dwPos));
        ScreenToClient (&point);
        ::SetCursor (m_rcTextBox.PtInRect (point) ?
```

(continued)

VisualKB.cpp *continued*

```
                m_hCursorIBeam : m_hCursorArrow);
        return TRUE;
    }
    return CWnd::OnSetCursor (pWnd, nHitTest, message);
}

void CMainWindow::OnLButtonDown (UINT nFlags, CPoint point)
{
    if (m_rcTextBox.PtInRect (point)) {
        m_nTextPos = GetNearestPos (point);
        PositionCaret ();
    }
}

void CMainWindow::OnKeyDown (UINT nChar, UINT nRepCnt, UINT nFlags)
{
    ShowMessage ("WM_KEYDOWN", nChar, nRepCnt, nFlags);

    switch (nChar) {

    case VK_LEFT:
        if (m_nTextPos != 0) {
            m_nTextPos--;
            PositionCaret ();
        }
        break;

    case VK_RIGHT:
        if (m_nTextPos != m_strInputText.GetLength ()) {
            m_nTextPos++;
            PositionCaret ();
        }
        break;

    case VK_HOME:
        m_nTextPos = 0;
        PositionCaret ();
        break;

    case VK_END:
        m_nTextPos = m_strInputText.GetLength ();
        PositionCaret ();
        break;
    }
}
```

```
void CMainWindow::OnChar (UINT nChar, UINT nRepCnt, UINT nFlags)
{
    ShowMessage ("WM_CHAR", nChar, nRepCnt, nFlags);

    CClientDC dc (this);

    switch (nChar) {

    case VK_ESCAPE:
    case VK_RETURN:
        m_strInputText.Empty ();
        m_nTextPos = 0;
        break;

    case VK_BACK:
        if (m_nTextPos != 0) {
            m_strInputText = m_strInputText.Left (m_nTextPos - 1) +
                m_strInputText.Right (m_strInputText.GetLength () -
                m_nTextPos);
            m_nTextPos--;
        }
        break;

    default:
        if ((nChar >= 0) && (nChar <= 31))
            return;

        if (m_nTextPos == m_strInputText.GetLength ()) {
            m_strInputText += nChar;
            m_nTextPos++;
        }
        else
            m_strInputText.SetAt (m_nTextPos++, nChar);

        CSize size = dc.GetTextExtent (m_strInputText,
            m_strInputText.GetLength ());

        if ((m_ptTextOrigin.x + size.cx) > m_nTextLimit) {
            m_strInputText = nChar;
            m_nTextPos = 1;
        }
        break;
    }

    HideCaret ();
    DrawInputText (&dc);
```

(continued)

VisualKB.cpp *continued*

```
    PositionCaret (&dc);
    ShowCaret ();
}

void CMainWindow::OnKeyUp (UINT nChar, UINT nRepCnt, UINT nFlags)
{
    ShowMessage ("WM_KEYUP", nChar, nRepCnt, nFlags);
    CWnd::OnKeyUp (nChar, nRepCnt, nFlags);
}

void CMainWindow::OnSysKeyDown (UINT nChar, UINT nRepCnt, UINT nFlags)
{
    ShowMessage ("WM_SYSKEYDOWN", nChar, nRepCnt, nFlags);
    CWnd::OnSysKeyDown (nChar, nRepCnt, nFlags);
}

void CMainWindow::OnSysChar (UINT nChar, UINT nRepCnt, UINT nFlags)
{
    ShowMessage ("WM_SYSCHAR", nChar, nRepCnt, nFlags);
    CWnd::OnSysChar (nChar, nRepCnt, nFlags);
}

void CMainWindow::OnSysKeyUp (UINT nChar, UINT nRepCnt, UINT nFlags)
{
    ShowMessage ("WM_SYSKEYUP", nChar, nRepCnt, nFlags);
    CWnd::OnSysKeyUp (nChar, nRepCnt, nFlags);
}

void CMainWindow::PositionCaret (CDC* pDC)
{
    BOOL bRelease = FALSE;

    if (pDC == NULL) {
        pDC = GetDC ();
        bRelease = TRUE;
    }

    CPoint point = m_ptTextOrigin;
    CString string = m_strInputText.Left (m_nTextPos);
    point.x += (pDC->GetTextExtent (string, string.GetLength ())).cx;
    SetCaretPos (point);

    if (bRelease)
        ReleaseDC (pDC);
}
```

```
int CMainWindow::GetNearestPos (CPoint point)
{
    if (point.x <= m_ptTextOrigin.x)
        return 0;

    CClientDC dc (this);
    int nLen = m_strInputText.GetLength ();
    if (point.x >= (m_ptTextOrigin.x +
        (dc.GetTextExtent (m_strInputText, nLen)).cx))
        return nLen;

    int i = 0;
    int nPrevChar = m_ptTextOrigin.x;
    int nNextChar = m_ptTextOrigin.x;

    while (nNextChar < point.x) {
        i++;
        nPrevChar = nNextChar;
        nNextChar = m_ptTextOrigin.x +
            (dc.GetTextExtent (m_strInputText.Left (i), i)).cx;
    }
    return ((point.x - nPrevChar) < (nNextChar - point.x)) ? i - 1: i;
}

void CMainWindow::DrawInputText (CDC* pDC)
{
    pDC->ExtTextOut (m_ptTextOrigin.x, m_ptTextOrigin.y,
        ETO_OPAQUE, m_rcTextBox, m_strInputText, NULL);
}

void CMainWindow::ShowMessage (LPCTSTR pszMessage, UINT nChar,
    UINT nRepCnt, UINT nFlags)
{
    CString string;
    string.Format ("%s\t %u\t  %u\t  %u\t  %u\t  %u\t   %u",
        pszMessage, nChar, nRepCnt, nFlags & 0xFF,
        (nFlags >> 8) & 0x01,
        (nFlags >> 13) & 0x01,
        (nFlags >> 14) & 0x01,
        (nFlags >> 15) & 0x01);

    ScrollWindow (0, -m_cyLine, &m_rcScroll);
    ValidateRect (m_rcScroll);

    CClientDC dc (this);
    dc.SetBkColor ((COLORREF) ::GetSysColor (COLOR_3DFACE));
```

(continued)

VisualKB.cpp *continued*

```
        m_strMessages[m_nMsgPos] = string;
        dc.TabbedTextOut (m_ptLowerMsgOrigin.x, m_ptLowerMsgOrigin.y,
            m_strMessages[m_nMsgPos], m_strMessages[m_nMsgPos].GetLength (),
            sizeof (m_nTabStops), m_nTabStops, m_ptLowerMsgOrigin.x);

    if (++m_nMsgPos == MAX_STRINGS)
        m_nMsgPos = 0;
}

void CMainWindow::DrawMessageHeader (CDC* pDC)
{
    static CString string =
        "Message\tChar\tRep\tScan\tExt\tCon\tPrv\tTran";

    pDC->SetBkColor ((COLORREF) ::GetSysColor (COLOR_3DFACE));
    pDC->TabbedTextOut (m_ptHeaderOrigin.x, m_ptHeaderOrigin.y,
        string, string.GetLength (), sizeof (m_nTabStops), m_nTabStops,
        m_ptHeaderOrigin.x);
}

void CMainWindow::DrawMessages (CDC* pDC)
{
    int nPos = m_nMsgPos;
    pDC->SetBkColor ((COLORREF) ::GetSysColor (COLOR_3DFACE));

    for (int i=0; i<MAX_STRINGS; i++) {
        pDC->TabbedTextOut (m_ptUpperMsgOrigin.x,
            m_ptUpperMsgOrigin.y + (m_cyLine * i),
            m_strMessages[nPos], m_strMessages[nPos].GetLength (),
            sizeof (m_nTabStops), m_nTabStops, m_ptUpperMsgOrigin.x);

        if (++nPos == MAX_STRINGS)
            nPos = 0;
    }
}
```

Handling the Caret

CMainWindow's *OnSetFocus* and *OnKillFocus* handlers create a caret when the VisualKB window receives the input focus and destroy the caret when the input focus goes away. *OnSetFocus* sets the caret width to the maximum of 2 or to the SM_CX-BORDER value returned by *::GetSystemMetrics* so that the caret will be visible even on very high resolution displays:

```
void CMainWindow::OnSetFocus (CWnd* pWnd)
{
    CreateSolidCaret (max (2, ::GetSystemMetrics (SM_CXBORDER)),
        m_cyChar);
    SetCaretPos (m_ptCaretPos);
    ShowCaret ();
}
```

OnKillFocus hides the caret, saves the current caret position so that it can be restored the next time *OnSetFocus* is called, and then destroys the caret:

```
void CMainWindow::OnKillFocus (CWnd* pWnd)
{
    HideCaret ();
    m_ptCaretPos = GetCaretPos ();
    ::DestroyCaret ();
}
```

m_ptCaretPos is initialized with the coordinates of the leftmost character cell in VisualKB's text-entry field in *CMainWindow::OnCreate*. It is reinitialized with the current caret position whenever the window loses the input focus. Therefore, the call to *SetCaretPos* in *OnSetFocus* sets the caret to the beginning of the text-entry field when the program is first activated and restores the caret to the position it previously occupied in subsequent invocations.

The *OnKeyDown* handler moves the caret when the left arrow, right arrow, Home, or End key is pressed. None of these keys generates WM_CHAR messages, so we must sense them with WM_KEYDOWN messages instead. A *switch-case* structure executes the appropriate handling routine based on the virtual key code passed in *nChar*. The handler for the left arrow key (whose virtual key code is VK_LEFT) consists of the following statements:

```
case VK_LEFT:
    if (m_nTextPos != 0) {
        m_nTextPos--;
        PositionCaret ();
    }
    break;
```

m_nTextPos is the position at which the next character will be inserted into the text string. The text string itself is stored in the *CString* object *m_tstrInputText*. *PositionCaret* is a private *CMainWindow* member function that uses *GetTextExtent* to find the pixel position in the text string that corresponds to the character position stored in *m_nTextPos* and then moves the caret to that position with *SetCaretPos*. After checking *m_nTextPos* to make sure it hasn't run out of room to move the caret further left, the VK_LEFT handler decrements *m_nTextPos* and calls *PositionCaret* to move the caret. If *m_nTextPos* is 0, which indicates that the caret is already positioned at the

left end of the entry field, the keystroke is ignored. The other VK_ handlers are similarly straightforward. The VK_END handler, for example, moves the caret to the end
of the text string with the statements

```
m_nTextPos = m_strInputText.GetLength ();
PositionCaret ();
```

GetLength is a *CString* member function that returns the number of characters in the
string. The use of a *CString* object to hold the text entered into VisualKB makes text
handling much simpler than it would be if strings were handled simply as arrays of
characters. For example, all the *OnChar* handler has to do to add a new character to
the end of the string is

```
m_strInputText += nChar;
```

When it comes to string handling, it doesn't get much easier than that. Browse through
VisualKB.cpp, and you'll see several *CString* member functions and operators in use,
including *CString::Left*, which returns a *CString* object containing the string's left *n*
characters; *CString::Right*, which returns the rightmost *n* characters; and *CString::For-
mat*, which performs *printf*-like string formatting.

It seemed a shame not to have VisualKB do anything with the mouse when half
of this chapter is devoted to mouse input, so I added an *OnLButtonDown* handler
enabling the caret to be moved by clicking the left mouse button in the entry field. In
addition to adding a nice feature to the program, the *OnLButtonDown* handler also
gives us the opportunity to examine a function that takes the point at which a mouse
click occurred and returns the corresponding character position within a text string.
The button handler itself is exceedingly simple:

```
void CMainWindow::OnLButtonDown (UINT nFlags, CPoint point)
{
    if (m_rcTextBox.PtInRect (point)) {
        m_nTextPos = GetNearestPos (point);
        PositionCaret ();
    }
}
```

m_rcTextBox is the rectangle that bounds the text-entry field. After calling *CRect-
::PtInRect* to determine whether the click occurred inside the rectangle (and returning without doing anything if it didn't), *OnLButtonDown* computes a new value for
m_nTextPos with *CMainWindow::GetNearestPos* and calls our old friend *PositionCaret*
to reposition the caret accordingly. *GetNearestPos* first checks to see if the mouse was
clicked to the left of the character string and returns 0 for the new character position
if it was:

```
if (point.x <= m_ptTextOrigin.x)
    return 0;
```

m_ptTextOrigin holds the coordinates of the character string's upper left corner. *GetNearestPos* next returns an integer value that equals the string length if the mouse was clicked beyond the string's rightmost extent:

```
CClientDC dc (this);
int nLen = m_strInputText.GetLength ();
if (point.x >= (m_ptTextOrigin.x +
    (dc.GetTextExtent (m_strInputText, nLen)).cx))
    return nLen;
```

The result? If the mouse was clicked inside the text rectangle but to the right of the rightmost character, the caret is moved to the end of the string.

If *GetNearestPos* makes it beyond the *return nLen* statement, we can conclude that the cursor was clicked inside the text-entry field somewhere between the character string's left and right extents. *GetNearestPos* next initializes three variables and executes a *while* loop that calls *GetTextExtent* repeatedly until *nPrevChar* and *nNextChar* hold values that bracket the *x* coordinate of the point at which the click occurred:

```
while (nNextChar < point.x) {
    i++;
    nPrevChar = nNextChar;
    nNextChar = m_ptTextOrigin.x +
        (dc.GetTextExtent (m_strInputText.Left (i), i)).cx;
}
```

When the loop falls through, *i* holds the number of the character position to the right of where the click occurred, and *i*−1 identifies the character position to the left. Now finding the character position is a simple matter of finding out whether *point.x* is closer to *nNextChar* or *nPrevChar* and returning *i* or *i*−1. This is accomplished with the following one-liner:

```
return ((point.x - nPrevChar) < (nNextChar - point.x)) ? i - 1: i;
```

That's it; given an arbitrary point in the window's client area, *GetNearestPos* returns a matching character position in the string *m_strInputText*. There is a small amount of inefficiency built into this process because the farther to the right the point lies, the greater the number of times *GetTextExtent* is called. (The *while* loop starts with the leftmost character in the string and moves right one character at a time until it finds the character that lies just to the right of the point at which the click occurred.) A really smart implementation of *GetNearestPos* could do better by using a binary-halving approach, starting in the middle of the character string and iterating to the left or right by a number of characters equal to half the area that hasn't already been covered until it zeroes in on the characters to the left and right of the point at which the click occurred. A character position in a string 128 characters long could then be located with no more than 8 calls to *GetTextExtent*. The brute force technique employed by *GetNearestPos* could require as many as 127 calls.

Entering and Editing Text

All of the code for entering and editing the string displayed in the text-entry field is found in *CMainWindow::OnChar. OnChar*'s processing strategy can be summarized this way:

1.   Echo the message to the screen.

2.   Modify the text string using the character code in *nChar*.

3.   Draw the modified text string on the screen.

4.   Reposition the caret.

Step 1 is accomplished by calling *CMainWindow::ShowMessage*, which we'll examine more closely in a moment. How the text string is modified in step 2 depends on what the character code in *nChar* is. If the character is an escape or a return (VK_ESCAPE or VK_RETURN), *m_strInputText* is cleared by a call to *CString::Empty* (another handy member of the *CString* class) and *m_nTextPos* is set to 0. If the character is a backspace (VK_BACK) and *m_nTextPos* isn't 0, the character at *m_nTextPos*–1 is deleted and *m_nTextPos* is decremented. If the character is any other value between 0 and 31, inclusive, it is ignored. If *nChar* represents any other character, it is added to *m_strInputText* at the current character position and *m_nTextPos* is incremented accordingly.

With the character that was just entered now added to *m_strInputText, OnChar* hides the caret and proceeds to step 3, in which the modified string is drawn on the screen. This is accomplished by calling *CMainWindow::DrawInputText*, which in turn relies on *CDC::ExtTextOut* for text output. *ExtTextOut* is similar to *TextOut*, but it offers a few options that *TextOut* doesn't. One of those options is an ETO_OPAQUE flag that fills a rectangle surrounding the text with the device context's current background color. Repainting the entire rectangle erases artifacts left over from the previous text-output operation if the string's new width is less than its previous width. The border around the text-entry field (and the border around the panel in which keyboard messages are displayed) is drawn with the *CDC::DrawEdge* function, which calls through to the new *::DrawEdge* API function introduced in Windows 95. *DrawEdge* is the easy way to draw 3D borders that conform to the specifications prescribed in *The Windows Interface Guidelines for Software Design* and that automatically adapt to changes in the system colors used for highlights and shadows. A related *CDC* function, *Draw3dRect*, can be used to draw simple 3D rectangles in your choice of colors.

OnChar finishes up by calling *PositionCaret* to reposition the caret using the value in *m_nTextPos* and then *ShowCaret* to redisplay the caret. As an experiment, comment out *OnChar*'s calls to *HideCaret* and *ShowCaret*, recompile the program, and type a few characters into the text-entry field. This simple exercise will make plainly clear why it's important to hide the caret before painting the corresponding region of the window.

Other Points of Interest

As you move the mouse cursor around inside the VisualKB window, notice that it changes from an arrow when it's outside the text-entry field to an I-beam when it's inside. *CMainWindow*'s constructor registers a WNDCLASS with a NULL class cursor and stores the handles for arrow and I-beam cursors in *m_hCursorArrow* and *m_hCursorIBeam*. Each time *CMainWindow* receives a WM_SETCURSOR message, its *OnSetCursor* handler checks the current cursor location and calls *::SetCursor* to display the appropriate cursor.

VisualKB echoes keyboard messages to the screen by calling *CMainWindow::ShowMessage* each time a message is received. *ShowMessage* formulates a new output string with help from *CString::Format*, copies the result to the least recently used entry in the *m_strMessages* array, scrolls the current message display up one line, and calls *CDC::TabbedTextOut* to display the new message string on the bottom line. *TabbedTextOut* is used in lieu of *TextOut* so that columns will be properly aligned in the output. (Without tab characters, it's virtually impossible to get characters in a proportionally spaced font to line up in columns.) The tab stop settings are initialized in *OnCreate* using values based on the average character width and stored in the *m_nTabStops* array. Message strings are saved in the *m_strMessages* array so that the *OnPaint* handler can repaint the message display when necessary. The *CMainWindow* data member *m_nMsgPos* marks the current position in the array—the index of the array element that the next string will be copied to. *m_nMsgPos* is incremented each time *ShowMessage* is called and wrapped around to 0 when it reaches the array limit so that *m_strMessages* can maintain a record of the last 12 keyboard messages received.

Visual KB's *CMainWindow* class includes *OnKeyUp*, *OnSysKeyDown*, *OnSysKeyUp*, and *OnSysChar* handlers whose only purpose is to echo keyboard messages to the screen. Each message handler is careful to call the corresponding message handler in the base class before returning, as shown here:

```
void CMainWindow::OnSysKeyDown (UINT nChar, UINT nRepCnt, UINT nFlags)
{
    :
    :

    CWnd::OnSysKeyDown (nChar, nRepCnt, nFlags);
}
```

Nonclient-area mouse messages and system keyboard messages are frequently catalysts for other messages, so it's important to forward them to the base class so default processing can take place.

INTERNATIONAL KEYBOARD PROCESSING CONSIDERATIONS

There are two keyboard messages we didn't discuss because they are rarely used by application programs. Many international keyboard drivers allow users to enter a character accented with a diacritic by typing a "dead key" representing the diacritic followed by typing the character itself. The Windows *::TranslateMessage* function translates WM_KEYUP messages corresponding to dead keys into WM_DEADCHAR messages and WM_SYSKEYUP messages generated by dead keys into WM_SYS-DEADCHAR messages. Windows provides the logic that combines these messages with character messages to produce accented characters, so dead-key messages are usually passed on for default processing. Some applications go the extra mile by intercepting dead-key messages and displaying the corresponding diacritics. The keystroke following the dead key then replaces the diacritic with an accented character. This provides visual feedback to the user and prevents dead keys from having to be typed "blind."

Programmers accustomed to using the ASCII character set frequently use C's *toupper* and *tolower* functions to convert characters to upper or lower case. They sometimes even use the old trick of setting or clearing bit 5 of the 8-bit character code, as in

```
ch &= 0xDF;    // Convert ch to upper case
ch |= 0x20;    // Convert ch to lower case
```

Neither of these methods should be used with characters typed into a Windows program. They work fine with conventional characters, but they don't work with the accented characters an international user is likely to enter. To perform case conversions on character strings, use the Windows *::CharUpper* and *::CharLower* functions or *CString*'s *MakeLower* and *MakeUpper* functions. Using either of these sets of functions will prevent case conversions from failing when your application is used in an international setting.

::CharLower and *::CharUpper* belong to a family of Win32 API functions that allow input from the keyboard to be processed consistently regardless of the character set being used. Other useful members of the family include *::IsCharAlpha, ::IsCharAlphaNumeric, ::IsCharLower,* and *::IsCharUpper*, which return nonzero values if the specified character is a letter of the alphabet, a letter of the alphabet or numeral, lowercase, or uppercase, respectively. To parse the characters in an input string, use *::CharPrev* and *::CharNext* to retrieve individual characters rather than assume that each character is only one byte in length. Some international character sets use two bytes for certain characters, and the Unicode character set used by Windows NT uses two bytes for *all* characters. Using Win32 character-handling functions in your code now will not only make it more friendly to international users but will ease the chore of porting it to other Win32 platforms later on.

Chapter 4

Menus

Up to now, the programs we've developed have lacked an important feature found in nearly every Windows application: a menu. It's time to remedy that omission by learning how to incorporate menus into our code.

Drop-down menus may be the most widely recognized user interface element in the world. Nearly everyone who sits down in front of a computer and sees a menu knows that clicking an item in the menu bar displays a drop-down list of commands. Even novices who have never used a computer before quickly adapt once they see the use of menus demonstrated a time or two. Many computer users remember what it was like to use a new MS-DOS application—learning unintuitive key combinations and memorizing obscure commands to carry out basic tasks. Menus, which sprang out of research at Xerox's famed Palo Alto Research Center (PARC) in the 1970s and were popularized by the Apple Macintosh in the 1980s, make computers vastly more approachable by making concise lists of commands readily available and allowing those commands to be selected through the simple act of pointing and clicking. Menus aren't required in Windows programs, but they generally make an application easier to use. The more complicated the program and its command structure, the more likely it is to benefit from a menu-based user interface.

Because menus are such an important part of the user interface, Windows provides a great deal of support to applications that use them. The operating system does the bulk of the work involved in menu handling, including displaying the menu bar, displaying a drop-down menu when an item on the menu bar is clicked, and notifying the application when a menu item is selected. MFC further enhances the menu processing model by routing menu item commands to designated class member functions, providing an update mechanism for keeping menu items in sync with the state of the application, and more.

We'll begin in this chapter by looking at menu fundamentals and building a rudimentary paint program that features an overhead menu. Then we'll move on to more advanced topics and enhance our code sample to produce a functional paint program that demonstrates firsthand a variety of practical menu handling techniques.

MENU BASICS

Let's begin by defining a few terms. The menu bar that appears at the top of a window is an application's *top-level menu,* and the commands in it are called *top-level menu items* or *menu titles.* The menu that appears when a top-level menu item is clicked is a *drop-down menu,* and items in that menu are referred to as *menu items.* Windows also supports *popup menus* that look like drop-down menus but can be popped up anywhere on the screen. The context menu that appears when you right-click an object in the Windows 95 shell is an example of a popup menu. Drop-down menus are actually popup menus that are attached to a top-level menu as "submenus."

Most frame windows and other primary windows encapsulating views of an application's data also feature a *system menu* containing commands for restoring, moving, sizing, minimizing, maximizing, and closing the window. This menu is provided by Windows and is displayed by clicking the left mouse button on the small icon in the window's title bar, by clicking the right mouse button in the body of the title bar, or by pressing Alt-Spacebar. The system menu is a special case of what *The Windows User Interface Guidelines for Software Design* refers to as a "window popup menu," which is simply a popup menu that appears when a window is clicked with the right mouse button.

MFC encapsulates menus and the actions that can be performed on them in the *CMenu* class. *CMenu* contains one public data member—an HMENU named *m_hMenu* that holds the handle of the corresponding menu—and several member functions that provide object-oriented wrappers around menu-handling functions in the Windows API. *CMenu::TrackPopupMenu,* for example, displays a popup menu at a specified location on the screen, and *CMenu::EnableMenuItem* enables or disables a menu item. *CMenu* also contains a pair of virtual functions named *DrawItem* and *MeasureItem* that can be overridden to create stylized menu items containing bitmaps and other graphical user interface elements.

There are three ways to create a menu with MFC. You can create the menu from scratch, piecing it together programmatically using *CreateMenu, InsertMenu,* and other *CMenu* functions; you can fill in a series of data structures defining the menu's contents and create it with *CMenu::LoadMenuIndirect;* or you can include a menu template in your application's .rc file and load the resulting menu resource by either calling *CMenu::LoadMenu* or specifying the resource ID when you create your application's window. The third of these three methods is far and away the most common because it allows a menu to be defined offline with a resource editor or other visual construction tool. The first and second methods are the most useful when you're dealing with menus whose contents can't be determined until run-time.

Creating a Menu

The easiest way to define a menu is to add a menu template to your application's .rc file. Once compiled, the template becomes a binary resource that is linked into the application's .exe file along with icons and other resources.

When you create the skeleton of an application with the Visual C++ AppWizard, the compiler creates a menu template similar to the one shown in Figure 4-1. This template defines a single menu resource consisting of a top-level menu and several drop-down submenus. IDR_MAINFRAME is the menu's integer resource ID, which is typically defined along with other resource IDs in a header file named Resource.h. As with other resources, you can specify any string or integer resource ID you like. PRELOAD and DISCARDABLE are resource attributes. PRELOAD indicates that the menu resource should be loaded into memory when the application is started. The

```
IDR_MAINFRAME MENU PRELOAD DISCARDABLE BEGIN
    POPUP "&File"
    BEGIN
        MENUITEM "&New\tCtrl+N",          ID_FILE_NEW
        MENUITEM "&Open...\tCtrl+O",       ID_FILE_OPEN
        MENUITEM "&Save\tCtrl+S",          ID_FILE_SAVE
        MENUITEM "Save &As...",            ID_FILE_SAVE_AS
        MENUITEM SEPARATOR
        MENUITEM "Recent File",            ID_FILE_MRU_FILE1,GRAYED
        MENUITEM SEPARATOR
        MENUITEM "E&xit",                  ID_APP_EXIT
    END
    POPUP "&Edit"
    BEGIN
        MENUITEM "&Undo\tCtrl+Z",          ID_EDIT_UNDO
        MENUITEM SEPARATOR
        MENUITEM "Cu&t\tCtrl+X",           ID_EDIT_CUT
        MENUITEM "&Copy\tCtrl+C",          ID_EDIT_COPY
        MENUITEM "&Paste\tCtrl+V",         ID_EDIT_PASTE
    END
    POPUP "&View"
    BEGIN
        MENUITEM "&Toolbar",               ID_VIEW_TOOLBAR
        MENUITEM "&Status Bar",            ID_VIEW_STATUS_BAR
    END
    POPUP "&Help"
    BEGIN
        MENUITEM "&About MyApp...",        ID_APP_ABOUT
    END
END
```

Figure 4-1. *A menu template generated by the Visual C++ resource editor.*

alternative is LOADONCALL, which tells Windows to defer bringing a menu resource into memory until the first time it is used. Both PRELOAD and LOADONCALL are artifacts of 16-bit Windows and are ignored in 32-bit applications. DISCARDABLE allows Windows to discard the resource from memory if the memory is needed for other uses. If a discarded resource is needed again, Windows reloads it from the application's .exe file. All resources are discardable in the Win32 environment, so DISCARDABLE and related keywords, such as FIXED and MOVEABLE, have no effect on an application's behavior; they, too, are relics of days gone by.

The statements between the opening and closing BEGIN and END statements define the top-level menu, with POPUP statements defining top-level menu items and associated submenus. The BEGIN and END statements following POPUP statements bracket MENUITEM statements defining the items in the submenus. The special MENUITEM SEPARATOR statement adds a thin horizontal line and provides visual separation between groups of menu items. The ampersands in the submenu names identify shortcut keys the user can press in combination with the Alt key to display a submenu without using the mouse. Ampersands in MENUITEM text identify shortcut keys that can be used to make a selection once the menu is displayed. In this example, the File-New command can be selected by pressing Alt-F and then N. Windows underlines the F in "File" and the N in "New" so that they're easily identifiable as shortcut keys. If two or more items in the same menu are assigned the same shortcut key, the shortcut cycles among the menu items and no selection is made until the Enter key is pressed.

The ellipsis (...) in some of the menu items identifies commands that require further input from the user. If the user selects Save, the document is saved immediately. But if the user selects Save As, a dialog box is displayed instead. To be consistent with other Windows applications, use an ellipsis for any menu item whose action is deferred until subsequent input is received from the user. If an item in the top-level menu executes a command instead of displaying a submenu, the text of the item should be followed with an exclamation mark, as in

```
IDR_MAINFRAME MENU PRELOAD DISCARDABLE
BEGIN
    POPUP "&File"
        [...]
    POPUP "&Edit"
        [...]
    POPUP "&View"
        [...]
    POPUP "&Help"
        [...]
    MENUITEM "E&xit!",        ID_APP_EXIT
END
```

It's legal to include MENUITEM statements in top-level menus this way, but these days it's considered bad form. And it's likely to surprise your users, most of whom are accustomed to seeing top-level menu items display submenus rather than take direct action themselves.

The ID_ values following the menu item names in the MENUITEM statements are integer IDs identifying the menu items. Every menu item should be assigned a unique ID because it is this value that identifies the menu item to your application when the user makes a selection. By convention, IDs are defined with #*define* statements in Resource.h and each is given the name ID_ or IDM_ followed by an item name spelled in capitals. MFC's Afxres.h header file defines ID_ values for commonly used commands such as File-New and Edit-Paste. When you write document/view applications, using the predefined IDs automatically connects certain menu items to handling functions provided by the framework. In non-document/view applications, use of the predefined IDs is optional. MFC Technical Note #20 recommends that you use the prefix ID_ for menu items "using the MFC command architecture" and IDM_ for those that do not, which basically means using ID_ for document/view applications and IDM_ for other kinds of applications. There are practical reasons for heeding this advice, so it's a convention we'll adopt for naming menu items in this chapter and throughout the rest of the book.

Valid values for menu item IDs range from 1 through 0xEFFF, but MFC Technical Note #20 further recommends restricting the range to 0x8000 through 0xDFFF. IDs equal to 0xF000 and higher are reserved for Windows—specifically, for items in the system menu. The range 0xE000 to 0xEFFF is reserved for MFC. In practice, it's perfectly safe to use values lower than 0x8000, and in fact there's a very good reason to ignore the documentation's advice and stick to menu item IDs equal to 0x7FFF or less in Windows 95 applications. If you assign an owner-drawn menu item (a menu item drawn by your application rather than by Windows) an ID equal to 0x8000 or higher, Windows 95 will unwittingly sign-extend the value when passing the value between the 16- and 32-bit halves of USER. The result? The menu item ID 0x8000 becomes 0xFFFF8000, 0x8001 becomes 0xFFFF8001, and so on, and your owner-drawn code will no longer work unless it masks off the upper 16 bits of the ID values passed in WM_MEASUREITEM and WM_DRAWITEM messages. Using ID values lower than 0x8000 fixes this problem by eliminating the 1 in the upper bit.

Menu items for which accelerators are provided normally include text identifying the accelerators. An *accelerator* is a key or combination of keys that, when pressed, has the same effect as selecting a menu item. Commonly used accelerators include Ctrl-X for Edit-Cut, Ctrl-C for Edit-Copy, and Ctrl-V for Edit-Paste. Menu item text and accelerator text should be separated by one or more \t characters representing tabs so that text denoting accelerator keys will be aligned in a straight line vertically. The default font that Windows uses for menus is proportionally spaced, so it's futile to try to align menu text with spaces. Programmers sometimes use \a instead of \t to right-justify text specifying accelerator keys, but *The Windows User Interface Guidelines for Software Design* discourages this practice.

When you define a menu item with a MENUITEM statement, you also have the option of specifying the item's initial state. The GRAYED keyword accompanying the File-Recent File menu item in Figure 4-1 disables the menu item so that it can't be selected and "grays it out" as a visual reminder that the item is disabled. Grayed menu text is displayed in the system color COLOR_GRAYTEXT, which defaults to gray, with a thin border added to create a 3D "chiseled" effect. Another commonly used keyword is CHECKED, which puts a check mark beside a menu item, indicating that the item is selected. INACTIVE disables a menu item without graying it. The little-used MENUBREAK and MENUBARBREAK keywords can be used for special effects such as multicolumn drop-down menus and multiline menu bars. While common in Windows applications written in C using the SDK, menu item state specifiers are often omitted in MFC applications because the framework provides a mechanism for updating menu item states programmatically. You'll learn more about this feature of the framework in a moment.

Displaying the Menu

A top-level menu created from a template is displayed when it is loaded and attached to a window. The following statement creates a frame window with *CFrameWnd::Create* and attaches the menu whose resource ID is IDR_MAINFRAME:

```
Create (NULL, "My Application", WS_OVERLAPPEDWINDOW,
    rectDefault, NULL, MAKEINTRESOURCE (IDR_MAINFRAME));
```

The sixth argument to *Create* identifies the menu resource. The MAKEINTRESOURCE macro converts an integer resource ID to an LPTSTR data type ID compatible with functions that expect string-based resource IDs. When the window appears on the screen, the menu will be visible just below the title bar.

An alternative method for loading a top-level menu and attaching it to a window is to construct a *CMenu* object, call *CMenu::LoadMenu* to load the menu resource, and call *CWnd::SetMenu*, like this:

```
CMenu menu;
menu.LoadMenu (IDR_MAINFRAME);
SetMenu (&menu);
menu.Detach ();
```

MAKEINTRESOURCE isn't required in this example because MFC overloads *CMenu::LoadMenu* to accept both integer and string data types. *CMenu::Detach* is called to detach the menu from the *CMenu* object so that the menu won't be destroyed prematurely when *menu* goes out of scope. The *CMenu* class helps guard against resource leaks by calling *CMenu::DestroyMenu* from its destructor. As a rule, a menu loaded with *LoadMenu* should be destroyed with *DestroyMenu* before the application that loaded the menu terminates. However, a menu attached to a window is automatically destroyed when the window is destroyed, so detaching a menu from a *CMenu* object after attaching it to a window won't cause a resource leak unless the menu is later detached from the window without a subsequent call to *DestroyMenu*.

The *LoadMenu-SetMenu* technique offers no advantage over simply passing the menu name to *Create* when a program contains just one menu, but it's very useful in programs that contain two or more menus. Suppose you write an application that allows the user to choose short or long menus and contains menu resources for both. At startup, the menus are loaded into *CMenu* objects named *m_menuLong* and *m_menu-Short* that are members of the window class. The appropriate menu is then chosen based on the value of another data member named *m_bShortMenu*, which is TRUE if short menus were last selected and FALSE if they were not. Here's what the window's constructor might look like:

```
Create (NULL, "My Application");
m_menuLong.LoadMenu (IDR_LONGMENU);
m_menuShort.LoadMenu (IDR_SHORTMENU);
SetMenu (m_bShortMenu ? &m_menuShort : &m_menuLong);
```

In response to a command from the user, the following code would switch from long menus to short menus:

```
m_bShortMenu = TRUE;
SetMenu (&m_menuShort);
DrawMenuBar ();
```

And these statements would switch back to long menus again:

```
m_bShortMenu = FALSE;
SetMenu (&m_menuLong);
DrawMenuBar ();
```

CWnd::DrawMenuBar redraws the menu bar to reflect the change. You should always follow calls to *SetMenu* with calls to *DrawMenuBar*, particularly if the window is visible on the screen.

What about code to delete the menus, since only one will be attached to a window when the application ends? Since *m_menuLong* and *m_menuShort* are data members of the window class, their destructors will be called when *CMainWindow* is deleted and the menus associated with them will be destroyed. Therefore, explicit calls to *DestroyMenu* are not required.

Responding to Menu Commands

When the user drops down a menu, the window that the menu is attached to receives a series of messages. One of the first to arrive is a WM_INITMENU message notifying the window that a top-level menu item was selected. Before a submenu is displayed, the window receives a WM_INITMENUPOPUP message. Windows programs written in C sometimes take this opportunity to update the submenu's menu items—for example, putting a check mark next to the Toolbar item in the View menu if the application's toolbar is displayed, or unchecking the menu item if the toolbar is currently hidden. As the highlight bar travels up and down the menu, the window receives WM_MENUSELECT messages reporting the highlight's latest position in the menu. In SDK-style programs, WM_MENUSELECT messages are sometimes used to display context-sensitive menu help in a status bar.

The most important message of all is the WM_COMMAND message sent when the user selects an item from the menu. The low word of the message's *wParam* parameter holds the menu item ID. SDK programmers often use a *switch-case* structure to examine the menu item ID and activate the appropriate handling routine, but in MFC, there's a better way. MFC's ON_COMMAND macro creates a message map entry linking WM_COMMAND messages referencing a particular menu item to the class member function, or *command handler,* of your choice. If you want *CMainWindow::OnFileSave* to be activated when the user selects Save from the File menu and the menu item ID is IDM_FILE_SAVE, simply add the statement

```
ON_COMMAND (IDM_FILE_SAVE, OnFileSave)
```

to *CMainWindow*'s message map. Other items in the File menu might be mapped like this:

```
ON_COMMAND (IDM_FILE_NEW, OnFileNew)
ON_COMMAND (IDM_FILE_OPEN, OnFileOpen)
ON_COMMAND (IDM_FILE_SAVE, OnFileSave)
ON_COMMAND (IDM_FILE_SAVE_AS, OnFileSaveAs)
ON_COMMAND (IDM_FILE_EXIT, OnFileExit)
```

Now *OnFileNew* will be activated when File-New is selected, *OnFileOpen* will be called when File-Open is selected, and so on.

Command handlers take no arguments and return no values. The *OnFileExit* function, for example, is typically implemented like this:

```
void CMainWindow::OnFileExit ()
{
    SendMessage (WM_CLOSE, 0, 0);
}
```

This command handler terminates the application by sending *CMainWindow* a WM_CLOSE message using *CWnd::SendMessage*. This ultimately ends the application by placing a WM_QUIT message in its message queue. An *OnFileExit* handler should not execute any more code after sending a WM_CLOSE message because after *SendMessage* returns, the application is in the final stages of shutting down. However, it's safe to do more in *OnFileExit* if the message is posted to the message queue with

PostMessage rather than sent with *SendMessage*. A *sent* message is processed immediately, but a *posted* message isn't processed until after the current message handler returns and another message is retrieved from the message queue.

Command handlers can be named whatever you like. There are no naming criteria as there are for conventional WM_ message handlers. The handlers for WM_PAINT and WM_CREATE must be named *OnPaint* and *OnCreate* unless you'd care to rewrite MFC's ON_WM_PAINT and ON_WM_CREATE message-map macros. But the message-map handler entries for our File menu above could just as well have been written

```
ON_COMMAND (IDM_FILE_NEW, CreateMeAFile)
ON_COMMAND (IDM_FILE_OPEN, OpenMeAFile)
ON_COMMAND (IDM_FILE_SAVE, SaveThisFile)
ON_COMMAND (IDM_FILE_SAVE_AS, SaveThisFileUnderAnotherName)
ON_COMMAND (IDM_FILE_EXIT, KillThisAppAndDoItNow)
```

provided the member functions were named accordingly.

In non-document/view MFC applications, menu commands are usually mapped to member functions of the window that owns the menu, but they can also be handled in the application class. In document/view applications, menu commands can be handled just about anywhere—in the view class, the frame class, the application class, or even the document class. The framework adds another dimension to WM_COMMAND processing by implementing a sophisticated command-routing system that gives each of the program's major architectural components a chance at processing each menu command. You'll learn more about command routing and see it in action in Chapter 8, when we begin writing applications that take advantage of the document/view architecture.

Defining Command Ranges

Sometimes it's more efficient to process an entire range of menu item IDs with a single command handler than to provide a separate member function for each ID. Consider a drawing application that contains a Color menu from which the user may choose red, green, or blue. Selecting a color from the menu sets a member variable named *m_nCurrentColor* to the ID of the selected item and subsequently changes the color of what the user draws on the screen. The message-map entries and command handlers for these menu items might be implemented as follows:

```
// In the message map
ON_COMMAND (IDM_COLOR_RED, OnColorRed)
ON_COMMAND (IDM_COLOR_GREEN, OnColorGreen)
ON_COMMAND (IDM_COLOR_BLUE, OnColorBlue)
    .
    .
    .
void CMainWindow::OnColorRed ()
```

(continued)

```
    {
        m_nCurrentColor = IDM_COLOR_RED;
    }

    void CMainWindow::OnColorGreen ()
    {
        m_nCurrentColor = IDM_COLOR_GREEN;
    }

    void CMainWindow::OnColorBlue ()
    {
        m_nCurrentColor = IDM_COLOR_BLUE;
    }
```

This isn't a terribly efficient way to process messages from the Color menu because each message handler does essentially the same thing. And the inefficiency would be compounded if there were 10 or 20 colors to choose from rather than just 3.

One way to reduce the redundancy in this program's menu handling logic is to map all three menu items to the same *CMainWindow* member function and retrieve the menu item ID with *CWnd::GetCurrentMessage*, like this:

```
    // In the message map
    ON_COMMAND (IDM_COLOR_RED, OnColor)
    ON_COMMAND (IDM_COLOR_GREEN, OnColor)
    ON_COMMAND (IDM_COLOR_BLUE, OnColor)
        .
        .
        .
    void CMainWindow::OnColor ()
    {
        UINT nID = (UINT) LOWORD (GetCurrentMessage ()->wParam);
        m_nCurrentColor = nID;
    }
```

This works, but it's an imperfect solution because it relies on the value of *wParam*. If the meaning of the *wParam* parameter accompanying WM_COMMAND messages changes in a future release of Windows (as it did between Windows 3.1 and Windows 95), this code may have to be modified to work properly. And even though we've reduced the number of command handlers from three to one, we're still adding three separate entries to the class's message map at a cost of 24 bytes each.

A better solution is MFC's ON_COMMAND_RANGE macro, which maps a range of IDs to a common member function and supplies the ID of the item that prompted the message to the command handler. Now, assuming that IDM_COLOR_RED, IDM_COLOR_GREEN, and IDM_COLOR_BLUE contain consecutive values and that IDM_COLOR_RED and IDM_COLOR_BLUE represent the low and high ends of the range (for example, IDM_COLOR_RED=100, IDM_COLOR_GREEN=101, and IDM_COLOR_BLUE=102), we can rewrite the code for the Color menu like this:

```
// In the message map
ON_COMMAND_RANGE (IDM_COLOR_RED, IDM_COLOR_BLUE, OnColor)
  :
  :

void CMainWindow::OnColor (UINT nID)
{
    m_nCurrentColor = nID;
}
```

When *CMainWindow::OnColor* is called because the user chose an item from the Color menu, *nID* will contain IDM_COLOR_RED, IDM_COLOR_GREEN, or IDM_COLOR_-_BLUE. And one simple statement will set *m_nCurrentColor* to the proper value, no matter which menu item was selected.

Keeping Menu Items in Sync with Your Application

In many applications, menu items must be constantly updated to reflect internal states of the application or its data. When a color is selected from the previous section's Color menu, for example, the corresponding menu item should be checked to indicate the current color. If your application features an Edit menu with Cut, Copy, and Paste commands, it should disable the Cut and Copy menu items when no data is selected and disable the Paste menu item when the clipboard is empty. Menus are more than just lists of commands. Deployed properly, they provide visual feedback to the user regarding the current state of the application and make plainly evident what commands are (and are not) available at any given moment.

Windows programmers have traditionally taken one of two approaches to keeping menu items up-to-date. The first is illustrated by the following code sample, which is a modified version of the *OnColor* function presented in the previous section:

```
void CMainWindow::OnColor (UINT nID)
{
    CMenu* pMenu = GetMenu ();
    pMenu->CheckMenuItem (m_nCurrentColor, MF_UNCHECKED);
    pMenu->CheckMenuItem (nID, MF_CHECKED);
    m_nCurrentColor = nID;
}
```

In this example, the Color menu is updated the moment an item is selected. First *CMenu::CheckMenuItem* is called with an MF_UNCHECKED flag to uncheck the item that's currently checked. Then *CheckMenuItem* is called with an MF_CHECKED flag to place a check mark by the item that was just selected. The next time the Color menu is pulled down, the check mark will identify the current color.

That's one approach. Another is to move the code that updates the menu to an *OnInitMenuPopup* handler that's activated in response to WM_INITMENUPOPUP messages so that the check mark will be placed just before the Color menu is displayed. *OnInitMenuPopup* receives three parameters: a *CMenu* pointer referencing the submenu that's about to pop up, a UINT value holding the submenu's 0-based index in the top-level menu, and a BOOL value that's nonzero if the message pertains to the system menu and not a submenu. Here's what an *OnInitMenuPopup* handler for the Color menu might look like. COLOR_MENU_INDEX is an index specifying the Color menu's position in the top-level menu:

```
// In the message map
ON_WM_INITMENUPOPUP ()
    .
    .
    .

CMainWindow::OnInitMenuPopup (CMenu* pPopupMenu, UINT nIndex,
    BOOL bSysMenu)
{
    if (!bSysMenu && (nIndex == COLOR_MENU_INDEX)) {
        pPopupMenu->CheckMenuItem (IDM_COLOR_RED, MF_UNCHECKED);
        pPopupMenu->CheckMenuItem (IDM_COLOR_GREEN, MF_UNCHECKED);
        pPopupMenu->CheckMenuItem (IDM_COLOR_BLUE, MF_UNCHECKED);
        pPopupMenu->CheckMenuItem (m_nCurrentColor, MF_CHECKED);
    }
}
```

This method is more robust than the first because it decouples the code that processes commands from the code that updates the menu. Now any function anywhere in the application can change the drawing color, and the menu will be updated automatically.

The MFC application framework provides an even easier mechanism for keeping menu items up-to-date. Through the use of ON_UPDATE_COMMAND_UI macros in your message map, you can assign member functions to serve as "update handlers" for individual menu items. When the user pulls down a menu, the framework traps the ensuing WM_INITMENUPOPUP message and calls the update handlers for all the items in the menu. Each update handler is passed a pointer to a *CCmdUI* object whose member functions may be used to change the menu item's appearance. And because the *CCmdUI* class isn't specific to any particular type of user interface (UI) element, the same update handler can be used for menus, toolbars, and other UI objects. Abstracting user interface updates in this way simplifies the program logic and helps make an application independent of the operating system it's written for.

Here's one way the code for the Color menu could be rewritten to take advantage of update handlers:

```
// In the message map
ON_COMMAND_RANGE (IDM_COLOR_RED, IDM_COLOR_BLUE, OnColor)
ON_UPDATE_COMMAND_UI (IDM_COLOR_RED, OnUpdateColorRedUI)
ON_UPDATE_COMMAND_UI (IDM_COLOR_GREEN, OnUpdateColorGreenUI)
ON_UPDATE_COMMAND_UI (IDM_COLOR_BLUE, OnUpdateColorBlueUI)
    .
    .
    .
```

```
CMainWindow::OnColor (UINT nID)
{
    m_nCurrentColor = nID;
}


CMainWindow::OnUpdateColorRedUI (CCmdUI* pCmdUI)
{
    pCmdUI->SetCheck (m_nCurrentColor == IDM_COLOR_RED ? 1 : 0);
}


CMainWindow::OnUpdateColorGreenUI (CCmdUI* pCmdUI)
{
    pCmdUI->SetCheck (m_nCurrentColor == IDM_COLOR_GREEN ? 1 : 0);
}


CMainWindow::OnUpdateColorBlueUI (CCmdUI* pCmdUI)
{
    pCmdUI->SetCheck (m_nCurrentColor == IDM_COLOR_BLUE ? 1 : 0);
}
```

ON_UPDATE_COMMAND_UI connects commands and update handlers just as ON-
_COMMAND connects commands and command handlers. Now selecting a color from
the Color menu will activate *CMainWindow::OnColor*, and before that—before the
Color menu is displayed—each item's update handler will be called. The handlers
shown here do their updating by calling *CCmdUI::SetCheck* with a 1 or a 0 to check
or uncheck the corresponding menu item.

   SetCheck is just one of the methods the *CCmdUI* class provides for changing
the appearance of menu items and other interface elements. The table below shows
a complete list, along with a description of each function's effect on a menu item:

Function	*Description*
CCmdUI::Enable	Enables or disables a menu item.
CCmdUI::SetCheck	Checks or unchecks a menu item.
CCmdUI::SetRadio	Bullets or unbullets a menu item.
CCmdUI::SetText	Changes the text of a menu item.

SetRadio works like *SetCheck* but adds or removes a bullet instead of a check mark.
This is one of those MFC functions for which there is no direct counterpart in the
Windows API; the framework does some work behind the scenes to allow menu items
to be bulleted rather than checked. Ideally, you'd use a bullet to indicate which item
in a group of mutually exclusive menu items is currently selected and a check mark
to indicate whether a feature is on or off. (In practice, check marks are frequently
used for both, so it's your choice.) *Enable* enables or disables a menu item. A menu

item disabled with *CCmdUI::Enable* cannot be selected and is grayed out like a menu item initialized with GRAYED in a menu template.

For updating groups of menu items with a single update handler, MFC provides the ON_UPDATE_COMMAND_UI_RANGE macro, which is to ON_COMMAND_RANGE as ON_UPDATE_COMMAND_UI is to ON_COMMAND. To understand how ON_UP-DATE_COMMAND_UI_RANGE is used, let's take the Color menu one step further and assume that it contains eight color choices: black, blue, green, cyan, red, magenta, yellow, and white, in that order. The corresponding menu item IDs are IDM_COLOR-_BLACK through IDM_COLOR_WHITE. Let's also suppose that we want to put a bullet by the current color. Here's the most concise way to do it:

```
// In the message map
ON_COMMAND_RANGE (IDM_COLOR_BLACK, IDM_COLOR_WHITE, OnColor)
ON_UPDATE_COMMAND_UI_RANGE (IDM_COLOR_BLACK, IDM_COLOR_WHITE,
    OnUpdateColorUI)
    :
    :

void CMainWindow::OnColor (UINT nID)
{
    m_nCurrentColor = nID;
}

void CMainWindow::OnUpdateColorUI (CCmdUI* pCmdUI)
{
    pCmdUI->SetRadio (pCmdUI->m_nID == m_nCurrentColor);
}
```

m_nID is a public data member of *CCmdUI* that holds the ID of the menu item for which the update handler was called. By comparing *m_nID* to *m_nCurrentColor* and passing the result to *SetRadio*, you can ensure that only the current color is bulleted.

Just how useful is MFC's command-update mechanism? Later in this chapter, we'll develop a sample program that uses two identical Color menus—one that's invoked from a top-level menu and another that's invoked from a right-click context menu. The same command and update handler will serve both menus, and no matter how a color is selected, both menus will be updated to match—with *one line of code,* no less. It's hard to imagine how it could be any easier.

Keyboard Accelerators

As you design your application's menus, you have the option of using keyboard accelerators to assign shortcut keys to any or all of the menu items. An accelerator produces a WM_COMMAND message just as making a menu selection does. Adding keyboard accelerators to your application is simplicity itself. You create an accelerator table resource—a special resource that correlates menu item IDs to keys or key combinations—and load the resource into your program with a function call. If the application's main window is a frame window, Windows and the framework do the rest, automatically trapping presses of accelerator keys and notifying your application with WM_COMMAND messages.

An accelerator table resource is defined by including an ACCELERATORS block in your application's .rc file. The general format is

```
ResourceID ACCELERATORS
BEGIN
    ⋮
END
```

ResourceID is the accelerator table's resource ID. The statements between BEGIN and END identify the accelerator keys and the corresponding menu item IDs. The Visual C++ AppWizard generates accelerator tables using the following format:

```
IDR_MAINFRAME ACCELERATORS PRELOAD MOVEABLE
BEGIN
    "N",           ID_FILE_NEW,           VIRTKEY,CONTROL
    "O",           ID_FILE_OPEN,          VIRTKEY,CONTROL
    "S",           ID_FILE_SAVE,          VIRTKEY,CONTROL
    "Z",           ID_EDIT_UNDO,          VIRTKEY,CONTROL
    "X",           ID_EDIT_CUT,           VIRTKEY,CONTROL
    "C",           ID_EDIT_COPY,          VIRTKEY,CONTROL
    "V",           ID_EDIT_PASTE,         VIRTKEY,CONTROL
    VK_BACK,       ID_EDIT_UNDO,          VIRTKEY,ALT
    VK_DELETE,     ID_EDIT_CUT,           VIRTKEY,SHIFT
    VK_INSERT,     ID_EDIT_COPY,          VIRTKEY,CONTROL
    VK_INSERT,     ID_EDIT_PASTE,         VIRTKEY,SHIFT
END
```

In this example, IDR_MAINFRAME is the accelerator table's resource ID. PRELOAD and MOVEABLE are load options that, like the equivalent keywords in MENU statements, have no effect in the Win32 environment. Each line in the table defines one accelerator. The first entry in each line defines the accelerator key, and the second identifies the corresponding menu item. The VIRTKEY keyword tells the resource compiler that the first entry is a virtual key code, and the keyword following it—CONTROL, ALT, or SHIFT—identifies an optional modifier key. In this example, Ctrl-N is an accelerator for File-New, Ctrl-O is an accelerator for File-Open, and so on. The Edit menu's Undo, Cut, Copy, and Paste functions have two accelerators each defined: Ctrl-Z and Alt-Backspace for Undo, Ctrl-X and Shift-Del for Cut, Ctrl-C and Ctrl-Ins for Copy, and Ctrl-V and Shift-Ins for Paste.

You can combine ALT, SHIFT, and CONTROL modifiers to create accelerators that use multiple modifiers. For example, the statement

```
VK_F9, ID_FILE_PRINT, VIRTKEY, CONTROL, ALT
```

creates a Ctrl-Alt-F9 accelerator for the ID_FILE_PRINT command.

Occasionally it's useful to create accelerators from ordinary character keys, like this:

```
"X", ID_FILE_EXIT, VIRTKEY
```

The resulting accelerator executes an ID_FILE_EXIT command whenever the X key is pressed. For the even rarer occasions when a character-key accelerator should be sensitive to case, omit the VIRTKEY keyword or replace it with an ASCII keyword as shown here:

```
"X", ID_FILE_EXIT, ASCII
```

This accelerator generates a WM_COMMAND message only when an uppercase X is entered. Note that the ALT, SHIFT, and CONTROL keywords can't be used without VIRTKEY.

The next step in adding a keyboard accelerator to your application is to load the accelerator table resource. For a frame window, simply call *CFrameWnd::LoadAccelTable* with the accelerator table's resource ID. The statement

```
LoadAccelTable (MAKEINTRESOURCE (IDR_MAINFRAME));
```

loads the accelerator table whose ID is IDR_MAINFRAME. In SDK programs, accelerators don't become "active" until the message loop is modified to preprocess messages with *::TranslateAccelerator*, as shown here:

```
while (GetMessage (&msg, NULL, 0, 0)) {
    if (!TranslateAccelerator (hwnd, hAccel, &msg)) {
        TranslateMessage (&msg);
        DispatchMessage (&msg);
    }
}
```

A nonzero return from *::TranslateAccelerator* means that a WM_KEYDOWN or WM_SYSKEYDOWN message was translated into a WM_COMMAND or WM_SYSCOMMAND message and dispatched, so *::TranslateMessage* and *::DispatchMessage* need not be called. In MFC, the *CFrameWnd* class overrides the virtual *CWnd::PreTranslateMessage* function and calls *::TranslateAccelerator* for you if an accelerator table has been loaded—that is, if the frame window's *m_hAccelTable* data member contains a non-NULL accelerator table handle. Not surprisingly, *LoadAccelTable* not only loads an accelerator resource but copies the handle to *m_hAccelTable*, too.

Accelerator tables are handled differently when loaded for non-frame windows that lack the accelerator support provided by *CFrameWnd*. Suppose you derived a custom window class from *CWnd* and wanted to load an accelerator table, too. Here's how you'd go about it:

1.   Add an *m_hAccelTable* data member (type HACCEL) to the window class.

2. Early in your application's lifetime, use the API function *::LoadAccelerators* to load the accelerator table. Copy the handle returned by *::LoadAccelerators* to *m_hAccelTable*.

3. In the window class, override *PreTranslateMessage* and call *::TranslateAccelerator* with the handle stored in *m_hAccelTable*. Use the value returned by *::TranslateAccelerator* as the return value for *PreTranslateMessage* so that the message won't be translated and dispatched if *::TranslateAccelerator* has dispatched it already.

Here's how it looks in code:

```
// In CMainWindow's constructor
m_hAccelTable = ::LoadAccelerators (AfxGetInstanceHandle (),
    MAKEINTRESOURCE (IDR_MAINFRAME));

// PreTranslateMessage override
BOOL CMainWindow::PreTranslateMessage (MSG* pMsg)
{
    if (CWnd::PreTranslateMessage (pMsg))
        return TRUE;
    return ((m_hAccelTable != NULL) &&
        ::TranslateAccelerator (m_hWnd, m_hAccelTable, pMsg));
}
```

With this framework in place, a *CWnd*-type window will use accelerators just as a frame window does. Note that accelerators loaded with *::LoadAccelerators* (or *LoadAccelTable*) don't need to be deleted before termination because Windows deletes them automatically.

There are two reasons why using accelerators to provide keyboard equivalents for commonly used menu options is preferable to processing keystroke messages manually. The first is that accelerators simplify the programming logic. Why write WM_KEYDOWN and WM_CHAR handlers if you don't have to? The second is that if your application's window contains child windows and a child window has the input focus, keyboard messages will be directed to the child window instead of the main window. As you learned in Chapter 3, keyboard messages always go to the window with the input focus. But when an accelerator is pressed, Windows makes sure the resulting WM_COMMAND message goes to the main window even if one of its children has the input focus.

Accelerators are so useful for trapping keystrokes that they're sometimes used apart from menus. If your application wanted to be notified any time the Ctrl-Shift-F12 combination was pressed, for example, it could include a

```
VK_F12, ID_CTRL_SHIFT_F12, VIRTKEY, CONTROL, SHIFT
```

statement in the accelerator table and map the accelerator to a class member function by adding an

```
ON_COMMAND (IDM_CTRL_SHIFT_F12, OnCtrlShiftF12)
```

entry to the message map. Presses of Ctrl-Shift-F12 would thereafter activate *OnCtrl-ShiftF12*, even if there was no menu item assigned the ID value ID_CTRL_SHIFT_F12.

Deciding What Key Combinations to Use (and Avoid)

Windows gives the programmer a great deal of latitude when it comes to picking the keys to serve as keyboard accelerators, but you shouldn't make the mistake of choosing accelerator keys arbitrarily. Alt key combinations are generally best avoided because Alt and letter keys marked with ampersands in menu templates already function as shortcuts of sorts, and Alt is used with other keys (such as the spacebar) to invoke system actions. The safest and most common choices for accelerators include character keys shifted with the Ctrl key (for example, Ctrl-F for Find) and the function keys, either alone or in conjunction with Shift or Ctrl.

To promote a consistent user interface, Table B.2 in *The Windows Interface Guidelines for Software Design* lists common menu items such as Cut, Copy, and Paste and the accelerators that should be assigned to them. It also lists keys that shouldn't be used as accelerators because they're reserved for other uses. F1, for example, should invoke an application's help facility. Alt-F4 closes an application by invoking the Close command in the system menu. Using either of these keys as an accelerator would make your application nonstandard in the sense that it wouldn't respond to established keyboard shortcuts the way other applications do.

The Paint1 Application

Let's put what we've learned so far to work by building an application that uses menus and accelerators and also uses MFC's UI update mechanism to keep menu items in sync with data members that specify global application states. Paint1 lets the user draw multicolored lines of various widths on the screen. Like the previous chapter's MouseCap application, Paint1 captures the mouse when the left mouse button is pushed down, rubber-bands a line as the mouse is moved, and draws a colored line when the mouse button is released. Line widths and colors are selected from menus, as shown in Figure 4-2. The Width menu lists line widths (very thin, thin, medium, thick, and very thick), and the Color menu lists eight colors the user may choose from. The current width and color are checked. The File menu contains two options: New to clear the window's drawing area, and Exit to exit the application. The New menu item is disabled when the drawing area is empty and enabled when it isn't.

Before we analyze the program, take a moment to play with it and familiarize yourself with how it works. To draw a line, press and hold the left mouse button and drag the rubber-band line until the line is positioned where you want it. Release the

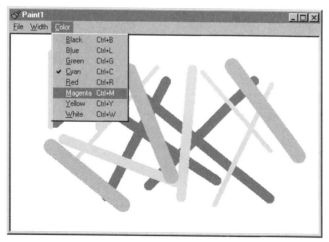

Figure 4-2. *The Paint1 window.*

mouse button, and a thick red line will appear. To change the width or the color of the next line you draw, select a new width or color from the Width or Color menu or press the corresponding accelerator. Observe that Paint1, unlike MouseCap, repaints itself properly when any part of its client area is invalidated. That's because it keeps a record of the lines you draw in an array of *CLine* objects and includes an *OnPaint* handler that iterates through the array and redraws the lines. To clear the drawing area and start over, select New from the File menu. To exit the program, pull down the File menu and select Exit.

Paint1's source code consists of four files: Resource.h, which contains IDs for the program's resources and menu items; Paint1.rc, which contains the menu template and accelerator table; Paint1.h, which contains class declarations, including the declaration for the *CLine* class; and Paint1.cpp, which contains the class implementations. The contents of these files are reproduced in Figure 4-3. Note that Paint1.rc substitutes { and } for some of the BEGIN and END keywords seen in the menu template in Figure 4-1. For example, the File menu is defined like this:

```
POPUP "&File" {
    MENUITEM "&New\tCtrl+N",          IDM_FILE_NEW
    MENUITEM SEPARATOR
    MENUITEM "E&xit",                 IDM_FILE_EXIT
}
```

rather than like this:

```
POPUP "&File"
BEGIN
    MENUITEM "&New\tCtrl+N",          IDM_FILE_NEW
    MENUITEM SEPARATOR
    MENUITEM "E&xit",                 IDM_FILE_EXIT
END
```

I find menu templates to be more readable when popup menu entries are bracketed with { and } characters, but which method you choose is purely a matter of personal style.

Resource.h

```
//**********************************************************************
//
// Resource.h
//
//**********************************************************************

#define IDR_MAINFRAME            100

#define IDM_FILE_NEW             110
#define IDM_FILE_EXIT            111

#define IDM_WIDTH_VTHIN          120
#define IDM_WIDTH_THIN           121
#define IDM_WIDTH_MEDIUM         122
#define IDM_WIDTH_THICK          123
#define IDM_WIDTH_VTHICK         124

#define IDM_COLOR_BLACK          130
#define IDM_COLOR_BLUE           131
#define IDM_COLOR_GREEN          132
#define IDM_COLOR_CYAN           133
#define IDM_COLOR_RED            134
#define IDM_COLOR_MAGENTA        135
#define IDM_COLOR_YELLOW         136
#define IDM_COLOR_WHITE          137
```

Paint1.rc

```
//**********************************************************************
//
// Paint1.rc
//
//**********************************************************************

#include <afxres.h>
#include "Resource.h"

IDR_MAINFRAME ICON Paint.ico
```

Figure 4-3. *Paint1.*

```
IDR_MAINFRAME MENU
BEGIN
    POPUP "&File" {
        MENUITEM "&New\tCtrl+N",           IDM_FILE_NEW
        MENUITEM SEPARATOR
        MENUITEM "E&xit",                  IDM_FILE_EXIT
    }
    POPUP "&Width" {
        MENUITEM "&Very Thin\tF5",         IDM_WIDTH_VTHIN
        MENUITEM "&Thin\tF6",              IDM_WIDTH_THIN
        MENUITEM "&Medium\tF7",            IDM_WIDTH_MEDIUM
        MENUITEM "Thi&ck\tF8",             IDM_WIDTH_THICK
        MENUITEM "Very Thic&k\tF9",        IDM_WIDTH_VTHICK
    }
    POPUP "&Color" {
        MENUITEM "&Black\tCtrl+B",         IDM_COLOR_BLACK
        MENUITEM "B&lue\tCtrl+L",          IDM_COLOR_BLUE
        MENUITEM "&Green\tCtrl+G",         IDM_COLOR_GREEN
        MENUITEM "&Cyan\tCtrl+C",          IDM_COLOR_CYAN
        MENUITEM "&Red\tCtrl+R",           IDM_COLOR_RED
        MENUITEM "&Magenta\tCtrl+M",       IDM_COLOR_MAGENTA
        MENUITEM "&Yellow\tCtrl+Y",        IDM_COLOR_YELLOW
        MENUITEM "&White\tCtrl+W",         IDM_COLOR_WHITE
    }
END

IDR_MAINFRAME ACCELERATORS
BEGIN
    "N",      IDM_FILE_NEW,          VIRTKEY,    CONTROL

    VK_F5,    IDM_WIDTH_VTHIN,       VIRTKEY
    VK_F6,    IDM_WIDTH_THIN,        VIRTKEY
    VK_F7,    IDM_WIDTH_MEDIUM,      VIRTKEY
    VK_F8,    IDM_WIDTH_THICK,       VIRTKEY
    VK_F9,    IDM_WIDTH_VTHICK,      VIRTKEY

    "B",      IDM_COLOR_BLACK,       VIRTKEY,    CONTROL
    "L",      IDM_COLOR_BLUE,        VIRTKEY,    CONTROL
    "G",      IDM_COLOR_GREEN,       VIRTKEY,    CONTROL
    "C",      IDM_COLOR_CYAN,        VIRTKEY,    CONTROL
    "R",      IDM_COLOR_RED,         VIRTKEY,    CONTROL
    "M",      IDM_COLOR_MAGENTA,     VIRTKEY,    CONTROL
    "Y",      IDM_COLOR_YELLOW,      VIRTKEY,    CONTROL
    "W",      IDM_COLOR_WHITE,       VIRTKEY,    CONTROL
END
```

Paint1.h

```
//*********************************************************************
//
//  Paint1.h
//
//*********************************************************************

class CLine : public CObject
{
private:
    CPoint m_ptFrom;
    CPoint m_ptTo;
    UINT m_nWidth;
    COLORREF m_crColor;

public:
    CLine (CPoint, CPoint, UINT, COLORREF);
    virtual void Draw (CDC*);
};

class CMyApp : public CWinApp
{
public:
    virtual BOOL InitInstance ();
};

class CMainWindow : public CFrameWnd
{
private:
    UINT m_nColor;
    UINT m_nWidth;
    CPoint m_ptFrom;
    CPoint m_ptTo;
    CObArray m_lineArray;

    void InvertLine (CDC*, CPoint, CPoint);
    void DeleteAllLines ();

public:
    CMainWindow ();
    ~CMainWindow ();

protected:
    afx_msg void OnPaint ();
    afx_msg void OnFileNew ();
    afx_msg void OnUpdateFileNewUI (CCmdUI*);
```

```
    afx_msg void OnFileExit ();
    afx_msg void OnWidth (UINT);
    afx_msg void OnUpdateWidthUI (CCmdUI*);
    afx_msg void OnColor (UINT);
    afx_msg void OnUpdateColorUI (CCmdUI*);
    afx_msg void OnLButtonDown (UINT, CPoint);
    afx_msg void OnMouseMove (UINT, CPoint);
    afx_msg void OnLButtonUp (UINT, CPoint);

    DECLARE_MESSAGE_MAP ()
};
```

Paint1.cpp

```
//*********************************************************************
//
//  Paint1.cpp
//
//*********************************************************************

#include <afxwin.h>
#include "Resource.h"
#include "Paint1.h"

CMyApp myApp;

/////////////////////////////////////////////////////////////////////
// CMyApp member functions

BOOL CMyApp::InitInstance ()
{
    m_pMainWnd = new CMainWindow;
    m_pMainWnd->ShowWindow (m_nCmdShow);
    m_pMainWnd->UpdateWindow ();
    return TRUE;
}

/////////////////////////////////////////////////////////////////////
// CMainWindow message map and member functions

BEGIN_MESSAGE_MAP (CMainWindow, CFrameWnd)
    ON_WM_PAINT ()
    ON_COMMAND (IDM_FILE_NEW, OnFileNew)
    ON_COMMAND (IDM_FILE_EXIT, OnFileExit)
```

(continued)

Paint1.cpp *continued*

```
    ON_COMMAND_RANGE (IDM_WIDTH_VTHIN, IDM_WIDTH_VTHICK, OnWidth)
    ON_COMMAND_RANGE (IDM_COLOR_BLACK, IDM_COLOR_WHITE, OnColor)
    ON_UPDATE_COMMAND_UI (IDM_FILE_NEW, OnUpdateFileNewUI)
    ON_UPDATE_COMMAND_UI_RANGE (IDM_WIDTH_VTHIN, IDM_WIDTH_VTHICK,
        OnUpdateWidthUI)
    ON_UPDATE_COMMAND_UI_RANGE (IDM_COLOR_BLACK, IDM_COLOR_WHITE,
        OnUpdateColorUI)
    ON_WM_LBUTTONDOWN ()
    ON_WM_MOUSEMOVE ()
    ON_WM_LBUTTONUP ()
END_MESSAGE_MAP ()

CMainWindow::CMainWindow ()
{
    m_nColor = IDM_COLOR_RED;
    m_nWidth = IDM_WIDTH_MEDIUM;
    m_lineArray.SetSize (0, 64);

    CString strWndClass = AfxRegisterWndClass (
        0,
        myApp.LoadStandardCursor (IDC_CROSS),
        (HBRUSH) (COLOR_WINDOW + 1),
        myApp.LoadIcon (IDR_MAINFRAME)
    );

    Create (strWndClass, "Paint1", WS_OVERLAPPEDWINDOW,
        rectDefault, NULL, MAKEINTRESOURCE (IDR_MAINFRAME));

    LoadAccelTable (MAKEINTRESOURCE (IDR_MAINFRAME));
}

CMainWindow::~CMainWindow ()
{
    DeleteAllLines ();
}

void CMainWindow::OnPaint ()
{
    CPaintDC dc (this);
    int nCount = m_lineArray.GetSize ();

    if (nCount) {
        for (int i=0; i<nCount; i++)
            ((CLine*) m_lineArray[i])->Draw (&dc);
    }
}
```

```
void CMainWindow::OnFileNew ()
{
    DeleteAllLines ();
    Invalidate ();
}

void CMainWindow::OnUpdateFileNewUI (CCmdUI* pCmdUI)
{
    pCmdUI->Enable (m_lineArray.GetSize ());
}

void CMainWindow::OnFileExit ()
{
    SendMessage (WM_CLOSE, 0, 0);
}

void CMainWindow::OnWidth (UINT nID)
{
    m_nWidth = nID;
}

void CMainWindow::OnColor (UINT nID)
{
    m_nColor = nID;
}

void CMainWindow::OnUpdateWidthUI (CCmdUI* pCmdUI)
{
    pCmdUI->SetCheck (pCmdUI->m_nID == m_nWidth);
}

void CMainWindow::OnUpdateColorUI (CCmdUI* pCmdUI)
{
    pCmdUI->SetCheck (pCmdUI->m_nID == m_nColor);
}

void CMainWindow::OnLButtonDown (UINT nFlags, CPoint point)
{
    m_ptFrom = point;
    m_ptTo = point;
    SetCapture ();
}

void CMainWindow::OnMouseMove (UINT nFlags, CPoint point)
```

(continued)

Paint1.cpp *continued*

```
{
    if (GetCapture () == this) {
        CClientDC dc (this);
        InvertLine (&dc, m_ptFrom, m_ptTo);
        InvertLine (&dc, m_ptFrom, point);
        m_ptTo = point;
    }
}

void CMainWindow::OnLButtonUp (UINT nFlags, CPoint point)
{
    static COLORREF crColors[8] = {
        RGB (  0,   0,   0),    // Black
        RGB (  0,   0, 255),    // Blue
        RGB (  0, 255,   0),    // Green
        RGB (  0, 255, 255),    // Cyan
        RGB (255,   0,   0),    // Red
        RGB (255,   0, 255),    // Magenta
        RGB (255, 255,   0),    // Yellow
        RGB (255, 255, 255)     // White
    };

    static UINT nWidths[5] = { 1, 8, 16, 24, 32 };

    if (GetCapture () == this) {
        ReleaseCapture ();

        CClientDC dc (this);
        InvertLine (&dc, m_ptFrom, m_ptTo);
        CLine* pLine = NULL;

        try {
            pLine = new CLine (m_ptFrom, m_ptTo,
                nWidths[m_nWidth - IDM_WIDTH_VTHIN],
                crColors[m_nColor - IDM_COLOR_BLACK]);

            m_lineArray.Add (pLine);
            pLine->Draw (&dc);
        }
        catch (CMemoryException* e) {
            MessageBox ("Out of memory. You must clear the " \
                "drawing area before adding more lines.", "Error",
                MB_ICONEXCLAMATION | MB_OK);

            if (pLine != NULL)
                delete pLine;
```

```
                    e->Delete ();
            }
        }
}


void CMainWindow::InvertLine (CDC* pDC, CPoint ptFrom, CPoint ptTo)
{
    int nOldMode = pDC->SetROP2 (R2_NOT);

    pDC->MoveTo (ptFrom);
    pDC->LineTo (ptTo);

    pDC->SetROP2 (nOldMode);
}

void CMainWindow::DeleteAllLines ()
{
    int nCount = m_lineArray.GetSize ();

    for (int i=0; i<nCount; i++)
        delete m_lineArray[i];

    m_lineArray.RemoveAll ();
}

//////////////////////////////////////////////////////////////////////////
// CLine member functions

CLine::CLine (CPoint ptFrom, CPoint ptTo, UINT nWidth, COLORREF crColor)
{
    m_ptFrom = ptFrom;
    m_ptTo = ptTo;
    m_nWidth = nWidth;
    m_crColor = crColor;
}

void CLine::Draw (CDC* pDC)
{
    CPen pen (PS_SOLID, m_nWidth, m_crColor);

    CPen* pOldPen = pDC->SelectObject (&pen);
    pDC->MoveTo (m_ptFrom);
    pDC->LineTo (m_ptTo);

    pDC->SelectObject (pOldPen);
}
```

Before we look at the code for Paint1's menus and accelerators, let's first look at how Paint1 stores its data. Once you understand what the *CLine* class does and how MFC's *CObArray* class is used to manage an array of *CLine* objects, you'll have an easy time understanding the rest of the program as well.

The *CLine* and *CObArray* Classes

As mentioned, Paint1 stores information about the lines you draw in an array of *CLine* objects. The *CLine* class is publicly derived from *CObject* in Paint1.h. Paint1 doesn't explicitly use any of the features *CLine* inherits from *CObject*, but as we'll see in Chapter 6, the fact that *CLine* is derived from *CObject* will make it easy for us to add serialization support to the *CLine* class so that entire drawings can be saved and restored with just a few lines of code.

CLine encapsulates all the information needed to describe a line drawn in Paint1's client area—endpoint coordinates, width, and color. Its constructor initializes a *CLine* object with a pair of endpoints, a width, and a color, and its virtual *Draw* function draws the line on the screen. When Paint1's *OnPaint* function redraws the window's client area, it doesn't do any drawing on its own; rather, it invokes each *CLine* object's *Draw* function, commanding the line to draw itself. *OnPaint*'s contribution to the process is a pointer to a device context object that *CLine::Draw* uses to do its drawing. This more object-oriented approach to storing (and displaying) an application's data leads to a more robust program design. It's also a preview of things to come in later chapters, where we'll learn to write document/view applications that store their data in document objects built from MFC's *CDocument* class.

The *CLine* class is declared as follows:

```
class CLine : public CObject
{
private:
    CPoint m_ptFrom;
    CPoint m_ptTo;
    UINT m_nWidth;
    COLORREF m_crColor;

public:
    CLine (CPoint, CPoint, UINT, COLORREF);
    virtual void Draw (CDC*);
};
```

m_ptFrom and *m_ptTo* are *CPoint* objects containing the coordinates of the line's endpoints. *m_nWidth* holds the line's width in pixels. *m_crColor* is a COLORREF value that describes the color of the line. *CLine::Draw* uses *m_crColor* and *m_nWidth* to create a GDI pen matching the line's characteristics. Then it selects the pen into the device context and draws a line from *m_ptFrom* to *m_ptTo*.

CLine objects—or rather, pointers to *CLine* objects—are stored in *m_lineArray*, which is declared with the following statement in the *CMainWindow* class declaration:

```
CObArray m_lineArray;
```

MFC's *CObArray* class is an array class that holds pointers to *CObject*-derived objects. It's one of several array classes MFC provides for managing collections of data. The primary reason for using a *CObArray* to store *CLine* objects is so that the array can grow dynamically as lines are added. *CObArray* handles memory allocation on its own, and it provides a number of useful tools for manipulating an array and acquiring information about it. Adding a pointer to a *CLine* object to the array is a simple matter of calling *CObArray::Add*, like this:

```
m_lineArray.Add (pLine);
```

Add returns the pointer's 0-based index in the array. If necessary, the array will automatically allocate the additional memory needed to store the object pointer (or throw an exception of type *CMemoryException* if it can't). Should you want to draw the line later, and if *i* holds the line's array index, the following statement will draw the line in the window associated with *dc*:

```
((Cline*) m_lineArray[i])->Draw (&dc);
```

Other useful *CObArray* functions include *GetSize*, which returns the number of elements in the array, and *RemoveAll*, which empties the array. *RemoveAll* does not delete the objects referenced in the array; it only removes the pointers. That's why *CMainWindow::OnFileNew* and *CMainWindow::~CMainWindow* call *CMainWindow::DeleteAllLines*, which loops through the array executing

```
delete m_lineArray[i];
```

statements before calling *RemoveAll*. If this were not done, no *CLine* objects would be deleted until the program terminated.

To give you an idea of the kinds of capabilities the *CObArray* class provides, the table on the next page summarizes its function members.

Before a *CObArray* object is used for the first time, you should call *SetSize* to set the number of elements to 0 and specify the array's "grow size"—the number of additional elements that memory will be allocated for when a size increase is necessary to accommodate a new element. Paint1 sets the grow size to 64 in *CMainWindow's* constructor so that additional memory allocations will be necessary only every 64th time *Add* is called:

```
m_lineArray.SetSize (0, 64);
```

Small grow sizes impede performance by requiring frequent memory allocations and by often forcing the array's contents to be copied from one memory block to another. (*CObArrays* are always stored in contiguous memory, so if the memory allocated to a *CObArray* can't be grown contiguously when additional memory is required, the object must be moved to a new location that can accommodate its increased size.) Large grow sizes improve performance but result in slightly less efficient memory usage. An array that contains one element and has a grow size of 64 will occupy as much memory as an array with 64 elements. Fortunately, this doesn't waste an inordinate amount of memory because *CObArrays* store 32-bit object pointers and not the objects themselves.

CObArray FUNCTIONS AND OPERATORS

Function/Operator	Description
Add	Adds a new element to the end of the array.
ElementAt	Returns a reference to the *CObject* pointer stored at the specified position in the array.
FreeExtra	Frees any unused memory at the end of the array.
GetAt	Returns the element at the specified position in the array.
GetSize	Returns the number of elements in the array.
GetUpperBound	Returns the array's upper bound (the number of elements for which memory is currently allocated). This value may be greater than the size returned by *GetSize*.
InsertAt	Inserts a new element or a range of elements at a specified position in the array. Elements above the inserted element(s) are shifted up.
RemoveAll	Empties the array by setting the element count to 0. This function does not delete the objects referenced in the array.
RemoveAt	Removes one or more elements from a specified position in the array.
SetAt	Copies a *CObject* pointer to the specified position in the array. Unlike *SetAtGrow* (below), this function does not automatically allocate additional memory for the array if additional memory is required.
SetAtGrow	Copies a *CObject* pointer to the specified position in the array and allocates additional memory if necessary.
SetSize	Sets the number of elements in the array and the number of elements by which the array will grow when additional memory allocations are necessary.
operator []	Equivalent to *GetAt* or *SetAt*.

With the *CLine* and *CObArray* infrastructure in place, the logic for storing the lines that the user draws is straightforward. When the left mouse button is released after the user rubber-bands a line, the *OnLButtonUp* handler releases the mouse, constructs a *CClientDC* object, and erases the rubber-band line. Then it creates a new *CLine* object, adds it to *m_lineArray*, and draws the line. The core code looks like this:

```
pLine = new CLine (m_ptFrom, m_ptTo,
    nWidths[m_nWidth - IDM_WIDTH_VTHIN],
    crColors[m_nColor - IDM_COLOR_BLACK]);

m_lineArray.Add (pLine);
pLine->Draw (&dc);
```

Redrawing the lines stored in *m_lineArray* in response to WM_PAINT messages is a simple matter of querying *m_lineArray* for the number of lines represented in the array and executing a *for* loop that calls each line's *Draw* method:

```
CPaintDC dc (this);
int nCount = m_lineArray.GetSize ();

if (nCount) {
    for (int i=0; i<nCount; i++)
        ((CLine*) m_lineArray[i])->Draw (&dc);
}
```

CObArray's [] operator returns a generic *CObject* pointer, so the return value must be cast to a *CLine* pointer in order for *CLine*'s *Draw* function to be called.

The *OnLButtonUp* code that creates a new *CLine* and adds it to *m_lineArray* is enclosed in a *try* block to catch memory exceptions. The framework throws an exception of type *CMemoryException* if either *new* or *CObArray::Add* fails for lack of memory. *CMemoryException* is one of several exception classes provided by MFC to represent common error conditions. *OnLButtonUp* handles memory exceptions locally with the following *catch* block:

```
catch (CMemoryException* e) {
    MessageBox ("Out of memory. You must clear the " \
        "drawing area before adding more lines.", "Error",
        MB_ICONEXCLAMATION | MB_OK);

    if (pLine != NULL)
        delete pLine;
    e->Delete ();
}
```

After displaying a message box warning the user of the error, the exception handler checks *pLine* and deletes the *CLine* it points to if *pLine* isn't NULL. This ensures that a *CLine* won't be left behind in memory if it was *CObArray::Add* and not *new* that failed. The handler then deletes the *CMemoryException* object by calling that object's *Delete* function. You should make it a practice to call *CException::Delete* on exception objects unless your code rethrows the exception to pass it up the ladder to another exception handler.

One of the greatest benefits of using *CObArray* is that it simplifies the program logic by letting the class library do the memory management. Writing the code for a resizeable storage array in C is no fun, so programmers frequently take the easy way out by allocating much more memory than is needed or placing artificial restrictions on the number of elements that can be added. This is less a concern when you program with MFC, because *CObArray* and other MFC collection classes are always available to lend a hand. More important, if the collection classes lack certain features you need, you can modify them by deriving from them new classes of your own.

The Paint1 Menus and Accelerators

The New and Exit commands in Paint1's File menu are handled by *CMainWindow*'s *OnFileNew* and *OnFileExit* member functions, respectively. File-New is also linked to the update handler *OnUpdateFileNewUI*, which contains a single statement:

```
pCmdUI->Enable (m_lineArray.GetSize ());
```

m_lineArray.GetSize returns the number of *CLine* objects in *m_lineArray*. If the array is empty, *GetSize* returns 0 and *pCmdUI->Enable* disables the menu item. If *GetSize* returns a nonzero value, the menu item is enabled so that the window can be cleared. Selecting New from the File menu activates *OnFileNew*, which in turn calls *CMainWindow::DeleteAllLines* to delete the *CLine* objects referenced in *m_lineArray* and invalidates the window's client area so that it will be repainted without any lines.

Two command handlers process all the commands in the Width and Color menus. The message map entries

```
ON_COMMAND_RANGE (IDM_WIDTH_VTHIN, IDM_WIDTH_VTHICK, OnWidth)
ON_COMMAND_RANGE (IDM_COLOR_BLACK, IDM_COLOR_WHITE, OnColor)
```

correlate items in the Width menu with *CMainWindow::OnWidth* and items in the Color menu with *CMainWindow::OnColor*. *OnWidth* sets *CMainWindow::m_nWidth*, which denotes the current line width, equal to the ID of the menu item that was selected. *OnColor* does the same for *CMainWindow::m_nColor*:

```
void CMainWindow::OnWidth (UINT nID)
{
    m_nWidth = nID;
}

void CMainWindow::OnColor (UINT nID)
{
    m_nColor = nID;
}
```

The check marks in the Width and Color menus are placed there by the update handlers *OnUpdateWidthUI* and *OnUpdateColorUI*. Update events involving items in the Width and Color menus are linked to the update handlers via these ON_UPDATE-_COMMAND_UI_RANGE macros:

```
ON_UPDATE_COMMAND_UI_RANGE (IDM_WIDTH_VTHIN, IDM_WIDTH_VTHICK,
    OnUpdateWidthUI)

ON_UPDATE_COMMAND_UI_RANGE (IDM_COLOR_BLACK, IDM_COLOR_WHITE,
    OnUpdateColorUI)
```

The update handlers use *CCmdUI::SetCheck* to put a check mark by the menu item if (and only if) the item's ID, which is contained in *pCmdUI->m_nID*, equals the current width or color stored in *m_nWidth* or *m_nColor*:

```
void CMainWindow::OnUpdateWidthUI (CCmdUI* pCmdUI)
{
    pCmdUI->SetCheck (pCmdUI->m_nID == m_nWidth);
}

void CMainWindow::OnUpdateColorUI (CCmdUI* pCmdUI)
{
    pCmdUI->SetCheck (pCmdUI->m_nID == m_nColor);
}
```

Using command ranges for the Width and Color menus simplifies the code by condensing what would have been 26 separate functions—five command handlers and five update handlers for the Width menu, plus eight command handlers and eight update handlers for the Color menu—into four very simple functions.

Accelerators are included for all menu items except File-Exit. The accelerator table is defined in Paint1.rc and given the same resource ID—IDR_MAINFRAME—as the application's menu. (The IDs don't have to be the same, but menus and accelerators are often given the same resource IDs so it's obvious that they go together.) The accelerators are loaded in *CMainWindow::CMainWindow* with the statement

```
LoadAccelTable (MAKEINTRESOURCE (IDR_MAINFRAME));
```

Accelerators consume very little memory and next to no processor time, so you lose nothing by including them, even if they don't get used. More than likely, though, people who use your application regularly will appreciate being able to enter frequently used menu commands from the keyboard, too.

MENU MAGIC

The first half of this chapter probably covered 80 percent of everything you'll ever need to know about menus. Occasionally, however, you'll need to go beyond the basics and do something extra. The "something extras" discussed in the second half of the chapter include

■   Techniques for creating and modifying menus on the fly

■   Menus that display graphics instead of text

■   Cascading menus

■   Right-click context menus

We'll also look at the system menu and at methods you can use to customize it.

Creating and Modifying Menus Programmatically

Loading a menu resource from your application's .exe file isn't the only way to create a menu. You can also do it programmatically using functions provided by MFC's *CMenu* class. We've yet to explore *CMenu* in any detail because basic menu support doesn't require a *CMenu*. *CMenu* comes in handy when you want to create a menu on the fly, perhaps from information that isn't available until run-time, or when you want to modify an existing menu. In situations such as these, *CMenu* will be your best friend.

Menus are created programmatically using a combination of *CMenu::Create-Menu*, *CMenu::CreatePopupMenu*, and *CMenu::AppendMenu*. A top-level menu and its submenus are built by creating a menu with *CreateMenu*, creating the submenus with *CreatePopupMenu*, and attaching the submenus to the top-level menu with *AppendMenu*. The following program listing creates a menu identical to the menu featured in Paint1 and attaches it to the frame window. The only difference is that this menu is created by the application, not by the resource editor.

```
CMenu menuMain;
menuMain.CreateMenu ();

CMenu menuPopup;
menuPopup.CreatePopupMenu ();
menuPopup.AppendMenu (MF_STRING, IDM_FILE_NEW, "&New\tCtrl+N");
menuPopup.AppendMenu (MF_SEPARATOR);
menuPopup.AppendMenu (MF_STRING, IDM_FILE_EXIT, "E&xit");
menuMain.AppendMenu (MF_POPUP, (UINT) menuPopup.Detach (), "&File");

menuPopup.CreatePopupMenu ();
menuPopup.AppendMenu (MF_STRING, IDM_WIDTH_VTHIN, "&Very Thin\tF5");
menuPopup.AppendMenu (MF_STRING, IDM_WIDTH_THIN, "&Thin\tF6");
```

```
menuPopup.AppendMenu (MF_STRING, IDM_WIDTH_MEDIUM, "&Medium\tF7");
menuPopup.AppendMenu (MF_STRING, IDM_WIDTH_THICK, "Thi&ck\tF8");
menuPopup.AppendMenu (MF_STRING, IDM_WIDTH_VTHICK, "Very
    Thic&k\tF9");
menuMain.AppendMenu (MF_POPUP, (UINT) menuPopup.Detach (), "&Width");

menuPopup.CreatePopupMenu ();
menuPopup.AppendMenu (MF_STRING, IDM_COLOR_BLACK, "&Black\tCtrl+B");
menuPopup.AppendMenu (MF_STRING, IDM_COLOR_BLUE, "B&lue\tCtrl+L");
menuPopup.AppendMenu (MF_STRING, IDM_COLOR_GREEN, "&Green\tCtrl+G");
menuPopup.AppendMenu (MF_STRING, IDM_COLOR_CYAN, "&Cyan\tCtrl+C");
menuPopup.AppendMenu (MF_STRING, IDM_COLOR_RED, "&Red\tCtrl+R");
menuPopup.AppendMenu (MF_STRING, IDM_COLOR_MAGENTA,
    "&Magenta\tCtrl+M");
menuPopup.AppendMenu (MF_STRING, IDM_COLOR_YELLOW,
    "&Yellow\tCtrl+Y");
menuPopup.AppendMenu (MF_STRING, IDM_COLOR_WHITE, "&White\tCtrl+W");
menuMain.AppendMenu (MF_POPUP, (UINT) menuPopup.Detach (), "&Color");

SetMenu (&menuMain);
menuMain.Detach ();
```

The first two statements create a *CMenu* object named *menuMain* that represents an empty top-level menu. The next block of statements creates a popup menu named *menuPopup* and adds three items to it—New, a separator bar, and Exit—using *AppendMenu*. The final statement in that block adds the popup menu to the top-level menu. The MF_POPUP parameter passed to *AppendMenu* tells Windows that the second parameter is a popup menu handle, not a menu item ID, and *Detach* both detaches the menu from the *menuPopup* object and retrieves the menu handle. It's important to detach the menu from the C++ object encapsulating it so that the menu won't be destroyed when the object goes out of scope. The third and fourth statement blocks create the Width and Color popup menus and add them to the top-level menu. Finally, the call to *SetMenu* attaches the newly-formed menu to the frame window, and *Detach* disassociates the top-level menu and *menuMain* so the former won't be destroyed as soon as the function ends. (If the window is already visible on the screen when *SetMenu* is called, you should also call *DrawMenuBar* to make the menu visible.)

In addition to creating menus dynamically, you can also modify existing menus by adding, changing, or removing menu items. Items are added with *CMenu::AppendMenu* and *CMenu::InsertMenu*, changed with *CMenu::ModifyMenu*, and removed with *CMenu::RemoveMenu* and *CMenu::DeleteMenu*. The difference between *RemoveMenu* and *DeleteMenu* is that if the item being removed has an associated popup menu, *DeleteMenu* removes the item and destroys the popup menu, too. *RemoveMenu* removes the item but leaves the popup menu extant in memory.

DeleteMenu is the one you'll usually want to use, but *RemoveMenu* is useful if you want to preserve the popup menu for reuse later.

If *menuPopup* refers to the Color menu in the previous example, the statements

```
menuPopup.ModifyMenu (IDM_COLOR_CYAN, MF_STRING | MF_BYCOMMAND,
    IDM_COLOR_CYAN, "Blue-Gree&n");

menuPopup.ModifyMenu (5, MF_STRING | MF_BYPOSITION,
    IDM_COLOR_MAGENTA, "Re&d-Blue");
```

modify the Cyan and Magenta menu items to read "Blue-Green" and "Red-Blue." The first statement identifies the menu item by its menu item ID (IDM_COLOR_CYAN); the second identifies it by its 0-based position in the menu (5). The MF_BYCOMMAND and MF_BYPOSITION flags tell Windows which method of identification you're using. If you specify neither flag, the default is MF_BYCOMMAND. The third parameter passed to the *ModifyMenu* function is the menu item's new ID. We have no desire to change the IDs, so we specify IDM_COLOR_CYAN and IDM_COLOR_MAGENTA again. If the menu item you're changing is a popup menu rather than an ordinary menu item, the third parameter holds the handle of the popup menu instead of a menu item ID. Given a *CMenu* pointer to a popup menu, you can always get the menu handle from the object's *m_hMenu* data member.

Before you can modify a menu by adding, changing, or deleting menu items, you need a *CMenu* pointer. MFC's *CWnd::GetMenu* function returns a *CMenu* pointer for a window's top-level menu, or NULL if the window doesn't have a top-level menu. Let's say you've loaded Paint1's IDR_MAINFRAME menu and attached it to your application's main window, and later on you want to delete the Color menu. Here's how you would do it:

```
CMenu* pMenu = GetMenu ();
pMenu->DeleteMenu (2, MF_BYPOSITION);
```

The 2 passed as *DeleteMenu*'s first parameter is the Color menu's 0-based index. The File menu occupies position 0, the Width menu position 1, and the Color menu position 2. MF_BYPOSITION tells *DeleteMenu* that the first parameter is a positional index and not a menu item ID. In this case, your only choice is to identify the menu item by position because Color is a popup menu that has no menu item ID. And because you used *DeleteMenu* instead of *RemoveMenu*, the popup menu is automatically deleted, too.

To apply *ModifyMenu*, *DeleteMenu*, and other *CMenu* functions to items in a submenu, you need either a pointer to the main menu or a pointer to the submenu. *CMenu::GetSubMenu* returns a pointer to a submenu. The following code fragment uses *GetMenu* to get a pointer to the main menu and *GetSubMenu* to get a pointer to the Color menu. It then deletes the Cyan and Magenta menu items with a pair of calls to *DeleteMenu*:

```
CMenu* pMenu = GetMenu ()->GetSubMenu (2);
pMenu->DeleteMenu (IDM_COLOR_CYAN, MF_BYCOMMAND);
pMenu->DeleteMenu (5, MF_BYPOSITION);
```

The lone parameter passed to *GetSubMenu* is the 0-based index of the submenu. Since you identified the Cyan menu item by ID and not by position, you could also delete it by calling *DeleteMenu* through the pointer to the main menu, like this:

```
CMenu* pMenu = GetMenu ();
pMenu->DeleteMenu (IDM_COLOR_CYAN, MF_BYCOMMAND);
```

As long as a menu item is identified by ID, you can access it through a pointer to the menu in which it appears or a pointer to any higher-level menu. Don't try to use MF_BYPOSITION to delete an item in a submenu with the pointer returned by *GetMenu*—you might delete a popup menu by mistake.

Once you have a *CMenu* pointer in hand, there are plenty of other things you can do to the menu, too. Here's a short list of other *CMenu* functions you might find useful:

CMenu FUNCTION SAMPLER

Function	*Description*
CheckMenuItem	Checks or unchecks a menu item.
EnableMenuItem	Enables or disables a menu item.
GetMenuItemCount	Returns the number of items in a menu.
GetMenuItemID	Returns the ID of a menu item given its position in the menu.
GetMenuState	Returns a series of bit flags identifying a menu item's current state (checked, unchecked, enabled, disabled, and so on).
GetMenuString	Returns the text assigned to a menu item.
SetMenuItemBitmaps	Specifies the bitmaps Windows displays next to checked and unchecked menu items.

As you can see, MFC's *CMenu* class provides just about everything you could ever need for manipulating menus. The only menu-related API function that isn't wrapped in an MFC class is *::GetMenuCheckMarkDimensions*, which returns the height and width of the bitmap Windows uses to draw check marks in popup menus. Applications can substitute their own bitmaps for the check mark by calling *SetMenuItemBitmaps*. When they do, they typically call *::GetMenuCheckMarkDimensions* first to determine the bitmap's proper size. In Windows 95, applications should abstain from calling *::GetMenuCheckMarkDimensions* and instead size check mark bitmaps using the CXMENUCHECK and CYMENUCHECK values returned by *::GetSystemMetrics*.

Owner-Drawn Menus

Menus that display strings of text are fine for most applications, but some menus cry out for pictures instead of text. One example is the Color menu featured in Paint1. Many users won't know that cyan is a fifty-fifty mix of blue and green, or that magenta is a mix of equal parts red and blue. But if the menu contained color swatches instead of words such as "Cyan" and "Magenta," the meanings of the menu items would be crystal clear. Graphical menus are a little more work to put together than text menus, but the reward is often worth the effort.

The easiest way to do graphical menus is to create bitmaps depicting the menu items and use them in calls to *CMenu::AppendMenu*. MFC represents bitmapped images with the class *CBitmap*, and one form of *AppendMenu* accepts a pointer to a *CBitmap* object whose image then becomes the menu item. Once a *CBitmap* object is appended to the menu, Windows displays the bitmap when the menu is displayed. The drawback to using bitmaps is that they're fixed in size and not easily adapted to changes in screen metrics.

A more flexible way to replace text with graphics in a menu is to use *owner-drawn* menu items. When a menu containing an owner-drawn menu item is displayed, Windows sends the menu's owner (the window to which the menu is attached) a WM_DRAWITEM message saying, "It's time to draw the menu item, and here's where I want you to draw it." Windows even supplies a device context in which to do the drawing. The WM_DRAWITEM handler might display a bitmap, or it could use GDI functions to literally draw the menu item at the specified location. Before a menu containing an owner-drawn menu item is displayed for the first time, Windows sends the menu's owner a WM_MEASUREITEM message to inquire about the menu item's dimensions. If a submenu contains, say, five owner-drawn menu items, the window that the menu is attached to will receive five WM_MEASUREITEM messages the first time the submenu is displayed and five WM_DRAWITEM messages. Each time the submenu is displayed thereafter, the window will receive five WM_DRAWITEM messages but no further WM_MEASUREITEM messages.

The very first step in implementing an owner-drawn menu is to stamp all the owner-drawn menu items with the label MF_OWNERDRAW. Unfortunately, MF_OWNERDRAW can't be specified in a MENU template as other attributes such as MF_CHECKED and MF_DISABLED can be. Instead, you must either create MF_OWNERDRAW menu items programmatically and add them to your menu with *AppendMenu* or *InsertMenu*, or use *ModifyMenu* to add the MF_OWNERDRAW attribute to existing menu items.

The second step is adding an *OnMeasureItem* handler and associated message-map entry so that your application can respond to WM_MEASUREITEM messages. *OnMeasureItem* is prototyped as follows:

```
afx_msg void OnMeasureItem (int nIDCtl, LPMEASUREITEMSTRUCT lpmis)
```

nIDCtl contains a control ID identifying the control to which the message pertains and is meaningless for owner-drawn menus. (WM_MEASUREITEM messages are used for owner-drawn list boxes and combo boxes as well as owner-drawn menus. When *OnMeasureItem* is called for a list box or combo box control, *nIDCtl* identifies the control.) *lpmis* points to a structure of type MEASUREITEMSTRUCT, which has the following form:

```
typedef struct tagMEASUREITEMSTRUCT {
    UINT    CtlType;
    UINT    CtlID;
    UINT    itemID;
    UINT    itemWidth;
    UINT    itemHeight;
    DWORD   itemData;
} MEASUREITEMSTRUCT;
```

OnMeasureItem's job is to fill in the *itemWidth* and *itemHeight* fields, informing Windows of the menu item's horizontal and vertical dimensions, in pixels. An *OnMeasure-Item* handler can be as simple as this:

```
lpmis->itemWidth = 64;
lpmis->itemHeight = 16;
```

To compensate for differing video resolutions, however, a better approach is to base the width and height of items in an owner-drawn menu on some standard such as the SM_CYMENU value returned by *::GetSystemMetrics*:

```
lpmis->itemWidth = ::GetSystemMetrics (SM_CYMENU) * 4;
lpmis->itemHeight = ::GetSystemMetrics (SM_CYMENU);
```

SM_CYMENU is the height of the menu bars the system draws for top-level menus. By basing the height of owner-drawn menu items on this value and scaling the width accordingly, you can ensure that owner-drawn menu items will have roughly the same proportions as menu items drawn by Windows.

The *CtlType* field of the MEASUREITEMSTRUCT structure is set to ODT_MENU if the message pertains to an owner-drawn menu, and is used to differentiate between owner-drawn user interface elements if a window contains owner-drawn list boxes or combo boxes in addition to owner-drawn menu items. *CtlID* and *itemData* are not used for menus, but *itemID* contains the menu item ID. If the owner-drawn menu items your application creates are of different heights and widths, you can use this field to determine which menu item *OnMeasureItem* was called for.

The third and final step in implementing owner-drawn menu items is to provide an *OnDrawItem* handler and message-map entry for WM_DRAWITEM messages. Inside *OnDrawItem* is where the actual drawing is done. The function is prototyped as follows:

```
afx_msg void OnDrawItem (int nIDCtl, LPDRAWITEMSTRUCT lpdis)
```

Once again, *nIDCtl* is undefined for owner-drawn menu items. *lpdis* points to a DRAW-ITEMSTRUCT structure, which contains the following members:

```
typedef struct tagDRAWITEMSTRUCT {
    UINT    CtlType;
    UINT    CtlID;
    UINT    itemID;
    UINT    itemAction;
    UINT    itemState;
    HWND    hwndItem;
    HDC     hDC;
    RECT    rcItem;
    DWORD   itemData;
} DRAWITEMSTRUCT;
```

As in MEASUREITEMSTRUCT, *CtlType* is set to ODT_MENU if the message pertains to an owner-drawn menu item, *itemID* holds the menu item ID, and *CtlID* and *itemData* are unused. *hDC* holds the handle of the device context in which the menu item is drawn, and *rcItem* is a RECT structure containing the coordinates of the rectangle in which the item appears. The size of the rectangle described by *rcItem* is based on the dimensions you provided to Windows in response to the WM_MEASUREITEM message for this particular menu item. Windows does not clip what you draw to the rectangle but instead relies on your code to be "well-behaved" and stay within the bounds described by *rcItem*. *hwndItem* holds the handle of the menu to which the menu item belongs. This value isn't often used because the other fields provide most or all of the information that's needed.

DRAWITEMSTRUCT's *itemAction* and *itemState* fields describe the drawing action required and the current state of the menu item—checked or unchecked, enabled or disabled, and so on. For an owner-drawn menu item, *itemAction* contains one of two values: ODA_DRAWENTIRE means that the entire item should be drawn, while ODA_SELECT means that you can optionally redraw just the part of the item that changes when the item is highlighted or unhighlighted. When the highlight bar is moved from one owner-drawn menu item to another, the menu's owner application receives a WM_DRAWITEM message for the item that's losing the highlight without the ODA_SELECT flag, and another WM_DRAWITEM message for the item that's becoming highlighted with an ODA_SELECT flag. Programs that use owner-drawn menus often ignore the value in *itemAction* and redraw the menu item in its entirety no matter what the value of *itemAction*, using *itemState* to decide whether the item should be drawn with or without highlighting.

itemState contains zero or more of the bit flags shown in the table on the next page to specify the menu item's current state.

Value	Meaning
ODS_CHECKED	The menu item is currently checked.
ODS_DISABLED	The menu item is currently disabled.
ODS_GRAYED	The menu item is currently grayed.
ODS_SELECTED	The menu item is currently selected.

This state information is important because it tells you how the menu item should be drawn. Which of the bit flags you examine depends on which states you allow the menu item to assume. You should always check the ODS_SELECTED flag and highlight the menu item if the flag is set. If your application includes code to check and uncheck owner-drawn menu items, you should check ODS_CHECKED and draw a check mark next to the menu item if the flag is set. Similarly, if you allow the item to be enabled and disabled and grayed and ungrayed, you should check for ODS-_DISABLED and ODS_GRAYED flags and draw accordingly. By default, the framework automatically disables a menu item if you provide neither an ON_COMMAND handler nor an ON_UPDATE_COMMAND_UI handler for it, so it's sometimes possible for menu items to become disabled even though your application didn't explicitly disable them. You can disable this feature of MFC for frame windows by setting *CFrameWnd::m_bAutoMenuEnable* to FALSE. Or you can make sure a command or update handler is present to prevent the framework from disabling a menu item.

An alternative method for implementing owner-drawn menus is to attach the menu to a *CMenu* object and override *CMenu*'s virtual *MeasureItem* and *DrawItem* functions to do the drawing. This technique is useful for creating self-contained menu objects that do their own drawing rather than rely on the parent frame to do the drawing. In cases in which a menu is loaded from a resource and attached to a window without using a *CMenu* object as an intermediary, however, it's just as easy to let the window that processes menu commands draw the menu items as well. That's the approach we'll use when we modify Paint1 a little later on to see a hands-on demonstration of owner-drawn menus.

OnMenuChar Processing

One drawback to using owner-drawn menus is that Windows doesn't provide keyboard shortcuts such as Alt-C-M for Color-Magenta. Even if you define the menu item text as "&Magenta" before using *ModifyMenu* to change the menu item to MF_OWN-ERDRAW, Alt-C-M will no longer work. Alt-C will still pull down the Color menu, but the M key will do nothing.

Windows provides a solution to this problem in the form of WM_MENUCHAR messages. A window receives a WM_MENUCHAR message when a menu is displayed and a key that doesn't correspond to a menu item is pressed. By processing

WM_MENUCHAR messages, you can add keyboard shortcuts to owner-drawn menu items. MFC's *CWnd::OnMenuChar* function is prototyped as follows:

```
afx_msg LRESULT OnMenuChar (UINT nChar, UINT nFlags, CMenu* pMenu)
```

When *OnMenuChar* is called, *nChar* contains the ASCII code of the key that was pressed, *nFlags* contains an MF_POPUP flag if the menu to which the message pertains is a popup menu, and *pMenu* identifies the menu itself. The pointer stored in *pMenu* may be a temporary one created by the framework and should not be saved for later use.

The value returned by *OnMenuChar* tells Windows how to respond to the keystroke. The high word of the return value should be set to one of the following values:

- 0 if Windows should ignore the keystroke

- 1 if Windows should close the menu

- 2 if Windows should select one of the items displayed in the menu

If the high word of the return value is 2, the low word should hold the ID of the corresponding menu item. Windows provides a MAKELRESULT macro for setting the high and low words of an LRESULT value. The following statement sets the high word of an LRESULT value to 2 and the low word to IDM_COLOR_MAGENTA:

```
LRESULT lResult = MAKELRESULT (IDM_COLOR_MAGENTA, 2);
```

Of course, you can always rely on keyboard accelerators instead. They work just fine with owner-drawn menu items. But, thanks to WM_MENUCHAR messages, you have the option of providing conventional keyboard shortcuts as well.

Cascading Menus

When you click the Start button in the Windows 95 taskbar, a popup menu appears listing the various options for starting applications, opening documents, changing system settings, and so on. Some of the menu items have little arrows next to them indicating that clicking invokes another popup menu. And in some cases, popup menus are nested several levels deep. Click Start-Programs-Accessories-Games, for example, and the Games menu is the fourth in a series of menus cascaded across the screen. This multitiered menu structure permits items in the Start menu to be organized like entries in a hierarchical database and prevents individual menus from being so cluttered that they become practically useless.

Cascading menus aren't something only the operating system can use; application programs can take advantage of them, too. Creating a cascading menu is as simple as inserting a popup menu into another menu as if it were a menu item. Windows sweats the details, which include drawing the arrow next to the item name and displaying the cascaded menu without a button click if the cursor pauses over the item for a second or so. Here's how Paint1's main menu would be defined if we were to remove the Width and Color menu items from the top-level menu, add an Options popup menu, and insert what used to be the Width and Color menus into the Options menu as cascaded menus:

```
IDR_MAINFRAME MENU
BEGIN
    POPUP "&File" {
        MENUITEM "&New\tCtrl+N",          IDM_FILE_NEW
        MENUITEM SEPARATOR
        MENUITEM "E&xit",                 IDM_FILE_EXIT
    }
    POPUP "&Options" {
        POPUP "&Width" {
            MENUITEM "&Very Thin\tF5",     IDM_WIDTH_VTHIN
            MENUITEM "&Thin\tF6",          IDM_WIDTH_THIN
            MENUITEM "&Medium\tF7",        IDM_WIDTH_MEDIUM
            MENUITEM "Thi&ck\tF8",         IDM_WIDTH_THICK
            MENUITEM "Very Thic&k\tF9",    IDM_WIDTH_VTHICK
        }
        POPUP "&Color" {
            MENUITEM "&Black\tCtrl+B",     IDM_COLOR_BLACK
            MENUITEM "B&lue\tCtrl+L",      IDM_COLOR_BLUE
            MENUITEM "&Green\tCtrl+G",     IDM_COLOR_GREEN
            MENUITEM "&Cyan\tCtrl+C",      IDM_COLOR_CYAN
            MENUITEM "&Red\tCtrl+R",       IDM_COLOR_RED
            MENUITEM "&Magenta\tCtrl+M",   IDM_COLOR_MAGENTA
            MENUITEM "&Yellow\tCtrl+Y",    IDM_COLOR_YELLOW
            MENUITEM "&White\tCtrl+W",     IDM_COLOR_WHITE
        }
    }
END
```

Figure 4-4 on the next page shows what the resulting menu would look like. Clicking Width or Color in the Options menu displays a cascading menu from which line widths or colors may be selected. Moreover, the remainder of the program works as it did before, so the command and update handlers associated with the Width and Color menus don't need to be changed.

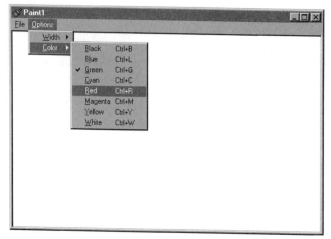

Figure 4-4. *Cascading menus.*

It's a bit more work to get a *CMenu* pointer to a cascaded menu than to a popup menu that's attached to the top-level menu, but it's still not difficult to do. Just as the statement

```
CMenu* pMenu = GetMenu ()->GetSubMenu (1);
```

initializes *pMenu* with a pointer to the Options menu in the top-level menu above, the statement

```
CMenu* pMenu = GetMenu ()->GetSubMenu (1)->GetSubMenu (0);
```

initializes *pMenu* with a pointer to the Width menu. With this pointer in hand, you can manipulate the Width menu just as you can any other menu. You can add items, delete items, modify items, or do anything else that *CMenu*'s member functions allow. You can even make items in a cascaded menu owner-drawn, as this chapter's next sample program will demonstrate. Of course, if you're manipulating menu items by ID and not position, you don't have to have a pointer to the submenu; a top-level *GetMenu* pointer will do just fine.

Context Menus

The Windows 95 shell uses right-click context menus extensively to make objects displayed by the shell easier to manipulate. Right-click the My Computer icon on the desktop, for example, and you get a context menu displaying a concise list of actions that can be performed on My Computer: Explore, Rename, Map Network Drive, and so on. Right-click the desktop itself, and you get a completely different context menu, one whose options reflect actions you might want to perform on the desktop. Developers are encouraged to include context menus in their applications to be consistent with the shell and to reinforce the object-oriented user interface paradigm. Windows makes that easy by sending your application a WM_CONTEXTMENU message when the right mouse button is clicked in a window's client area or title bar.

A context menu is nothing more than a popup menu that isn't attached to a top-level menu. MFC's *CMenu::TrackPopupMenu* function displays a popup menu on the screen at the location you specify. *TrackPopupMenu* is prototyped as follows:

```
BOOL TrackPopupMenu (UINT nFlags, int x, int y, CWnd* pWnd,
    LPCRECT lpRect = 0)
```

x and *y* identify the location on the screen (in screen coordinates) at which the popup menu will appear. *nFlags* contains bit flags specifying the menu's horizontal alignment relative to *x* and which mouse button (or buttons) may be used to select items from the menu. The alignment flags TPM_LEFTALIGN, TPM_CENTERALIGN, and TPM_RIGHTALIGN tell Windows that *x* specifies the location of the menu's left edge, center, or right edge, while the TPM_LEFTBUTTON and TPM_RIGHTBUTTON flags specify whether menu selections will be made with the left or the right mouse button. Only one of the alignment flags may be specified, but either or both of the button flags may be used. *pWnd* identifies the window that owns the popup menu (which is also the window that will receive messages from it), and *lpRect* points to a *CRect* object or RECT structure containing the screen coordinates of the rectangle within which the user can click without dismissing the menu. If *lpRect* is 0, clicking anywhere outside the menu automatically dismisses it. Assuming *pMenu* points to a popup menu and *this* refers to the application's main window, the statement

```
pMenu->TrackPopupMenu (TPM_LEFTALIGN | TPM_LEFTBUTTON |
    TPM_RIGHTBUTTON, 32, 64, this);
```

displays a popup menu whose upper left corner is positioned 32 pixels right and 64 pixels down from the upper left corner of the screen. The user can make selections from the menu with either the left or the right mouse button. While the menu is displayed, the window referenced by the *this* pointer will receive menu messages pertaining to the popup menu just as if the popup menu were attached to a top-level menu. Once the menu is dismissed, the messages will cease until the menu is displayed again.

MFC's ON_WM_CONTEXTMENU macro maps WM_CONTEXTMENU messages to a window's *OnContextMenu* handler. *OnContextMenu* receives two parameters: a *CWnd* pointer identifying the window in which the click occurred and a *CPoint* containing the mouse's screen coordinates:

```
afx_msg void OnContextMenu (CWnd* pWnd, CPoint point)
```

If necessary, you can translate the screen coordinates passed in *point* into coordinates local to *pWnd* or local to your application's main window with *ScreenToClient*. The *pWnd* parameter might point to the main window, or it might point to a child window. When a WM_CONTEXTMENU message is passed to *::DefWindowProc* and *pWnd* pertains to a child window, the message is passed to the child's parent so that it can have the first crack at processing the message. In addition, *::DefWindowProc* processes WM_CONTEXTMENU messages resulting from clicks in a window's title bar by displaying the system menu. Therefore, if an *OnContextMenu* handler looks at *pWnd* or *point* and decides not to display a context menu, it should pass the message to the base class. The following *OnContextMenu* handler for a frame window displays the context menu referenced by *pContextMenu* if the button click occurred in the client area and passes it to the base class if the click occurred elsewhere:

```
void CMainWindow::OnContextMenu (CWnd* pWnd, CPoint point)
{
    CRect rect;
    GetClientRect (&rect);
    ClientToScreen (&rect);

    if (rect.PtInRect (point)) {
        pContextMenu->TrackPopupMenu (TPM_LEFTALIGN |
            TPM_LEFTBUTTON | TPM_RIGHTBUTTON, point.x, point.y, this);
        return;
    }
    CFrameWnd::OnContextMenu (pWnd, point);
}
```

Such hit-testing is often unnecessary in document/view applications because you can put the *OnContextMenu* handler in the view class. It's a little early to be discussing that just yet, so for the moment simply remember that if you provide an *OnContextMenu* handler for a frame window or other top-level window, it's up to you to determine whether the click occurred in the window's client or nonclient area and respond accordingly.

How do you get a pointer to a context menu in order to display it? One method is to construct a *CMenu* object and build the menu with *CMenu* member functions. Another is to load the menu from a resource in the same way that a top-level menu is loaded. The following menu template defines a menu resource that contains one popup menu:

```
IDR_CONTEXTMENU MENU
BEGIN
    POPUP "" {
        MENUITEM "&Copy",        IDM_CONTEXT_COPY
        MENUITEM "&Rename",      IDM_CONTEXT_RENAME
        MENUITEM "&Delete",      IDM_CONTEXT_DELETE
    }
END
```

And the following *OnContextMenu* handler displays the popup menu as a context menu when the right mouse button is clicked in the frame window's client area:

```
void CMainWindow::OnContextMenu (CWnd* pWnd, CPoint point)
{
    CRect rect;
    GetClientRect (&rect);
    ClientToScreen (&rect);

    if (rect.PtInRect (point)) {
        CMenu menu;
        menu.LoadMenu (IDR_CONTEXTMENU);
        CMenu* pContextMenu = menu.GetSubMenu (0);
        pContextMenu->TrackPopupMenu (TPM_LEFTALIGN |
            TPM_LEFTBUTTON | TPM_RIGHTBUTTON, point.x, point.y, this);
        return;
    }
    CFrameWnd::OnContextMenu (pWnd, point);
}
```

LoadMenu loads the menu and attaches it to *menu*. *GetSubMenu* returns a *CMenu* pointer to the popup menu whose index is 0, and *TrackPopupMenu* displays the popup menu. If your application uses several context menus, you could define each context menu as a separate submenu of IDR_CONTEXTMENU. Or you could define each one as a separate menu resource. In any event, attaching the context menu to a *CMenu* object that resides on the stack ensures that the menu will be destroyed when the object goes out of scope. The menu is no longer needed after *TrackPopupMenu* returns, so deleting it frees up memory that can be put to other uses.

The Paint2 Application

Paint2 is an improved version of Paint1 that features an owner-drawn Color menu and a context menu. The owner-drawn items in the Color menu replace words such as "Blue" and "Red" with real color samples, as seen in Figure 4-5 on the next page. The context menu, which is shown in Figure 4-6, contains three items: New, Width, and Color. New performs the same function as the New command in the File menu. Clicking Width or Color displays a cascading Width or Color menu. Because all of the items in the context menu are duplicates of items in the overhead menu and use the same menu item IDs, no additional code is needed to process selections and updates. Clicking New in the context menu, for example, activates the same *OnFileNew* handler that is activated when File-New is selected, and the same update handler—*OnUpdateFileNewUI*—works with the New items in both menus.

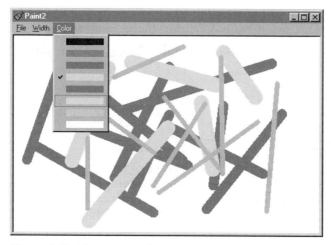

Figure 4-5. *The Paint2 Color menu.*

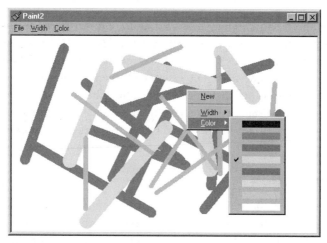

Figure 4-6. *Paint2's context menu with the cascading Color menu displayed.*

Paint2's source code appears in Figure 4-7. Paint2 is identical to Paint1 except for the code added to support the owner-drawn menu items and the context menu. Let's look at the new code more closely, starting with that which implements the owner-drawn menu items.

Resource.h

```
//*********************************************************************
//
//  Resource.h
//
//*********************************************************************

#define IDR_MAINFRAME           100
#define IDR_CONTEXTMENU         101

#define IDM_FILE_NEW            110
#define IDM_FILE_EXIT           111

#define IDM_WIDTH_VTHIN         120
#define IDM_WIDTH_THIN          121
#define IDM_WIDTH_MEDIUM        122
#define IDM_WIDTH_THICK         123
#define IDM_WIDTH_VTHICK        124

#define IDM_COLOR_BLACK         130
#define IDM_COLOR_BLUE          131
#define IDM_COLOR_GREEN         132
#define IDM_COLOR_CYAN          133
#define IDM_COLOR_RED           134
#define IDM_COLOR_MAGENTA       135
#define IDM_COLOR_YELLOW        136
#define IDM_COLOR_WHITE         137
```

Paint2.rc

```
//*********************************************************************
//
//  Paint2.rc
//
//*********************************************************************

#include <afxres.h>
#include "Resource.h"

IDR_MAINFRAME ICON Paint.ico

IDR_MAINFRAME MENU
BEGIN
    POPUP "&File" {
```

Figure 4-7. *Paint2.*   *(continued)*

Paint2.rc *continued*

```
        MENUITEM "&New\tCtrl+N",          IDM_FILE_NEW
        MENUITEM SEPARATOR
        MENUITEM "E&xit",                 IDM_FILE_EXIT
    }
    POPUP "&Width" {
        MENUITEM "&Very Thin\tF5",        IDM_WIDTH_VTHIN
        MENUITEM "&Thin\tF6",             IDM_WIDTH_THIN
        MENUITEM "&Medium\tF7",           IDM_WIDTH_MEDIUM
        MENUITEM "Thi&ck\tF8",            IDM_WIDTH_THICK
        MENUITEM "Very Thic&k\tF9",       IDM_WIDTH_VTHICK
    }
    POPUP "&Color" {
        MENUITEM "",                      IDM_COLOR_BLACK
        MENUITEM "",                      IDM_COLOR_BLUE
        MENUITEM "",                      IDM_COLOR_GREEN
        MENUITEM "",                      IDM_COLOR_CYAN
        MENUITEM "",                      IDM_COLOR_RED
        MENUITEM "",                      IDM_COLOR_MAGENTA
        MENUITEM "",                      IDM_COLOR_YELLOW
        MENUITEM "",                      IDM_COLOR_WHITE
    }
END


IDR_MAINFRAME ACCELERATORS
BEGIN
    "N",    IDM_FILE_NEW,         VIRTKEY,    CONTROL

    VK_F5,  IDM_WIDTH_VTHIN,      VIRTKEY
    VK_F6,  IDM_WIDTH_THIN,       VIRTKEY
    VK_F7,  IDM_WIDTH_MEDIUM,     VIRTKEY
    VK_F8,  IDM_WIDTH_THICK,      VIRTKEY
    VK_F9,  IDM_WIDTH_VTHICK,     VIRTKEY

    "B",    IDM_COLOR_BLACK,      VIRTKEY,    CONTROL
    "L",    IDM_COLOR_BLUE,       VIRTKEY,    CONTROL
    "G",    IDM_COLOR_GREEN,      VIRTKEY,    CONTROL
    "C",    IDM_COLOR_CYAN,       VIRTKEY,    CONTROL
    "R",    IDM_COLOR_RED,        VIRTKEY,    CONTROL
    "M",    IDM_COLOR_MAGENTA,    VIRTKEY,    CONTROL
    "Y",    IDM_COLOR_YELLOW,     VIRTKEY,    CONTROL
    "W",    IDM_COLOR_WHITE,      VIRTKEY,    CONTROL
END


IDR_CONTEXTMENU MENU
BEGIN
    POPUP "" {
```

```
        MENUITEM "&New",                IDM_FILE_NEW
        MENUITEM SEPARATOR
        POPUP "&Width" {
            MENUITEM "&Very Thin",      IDM_WIDTH_VTHIN
            MENUITEM "&Thin",           IDM_WIDTH_THIN
            MENUITEM "&Medium",         IDM_WIDTH_MEDIUM
            MENUITEM "Thi&ck",          IDM_WIDTH_THICK
            MENUITEM "Very Thic&k",     IDM_WIDTH_VTHICK
        }
        POPUP "&Color" {
            MENUITEM "",                IDM_COLOR_BLACK
            MENUITEM "",                IDM_COLOR_BLUE
            MENUITEM "",                IDM_COLOR_GREEN
            MENUITEM "",                IDM_COLOR_CYAN
            MENUITEM "",                IDM_COLOR_RED
            MENUITEM "",                IDM_COLOR_MAGENTA
            MENUITEM "",                IDM_COLOR_YELLOW
            MENUITEM "",                IDM_COLOR_WHITE
        }
    }
END
```

Paint2.h

```
//*********************************************************************
//
// Paint2.h
//
//*********************************************************************

class CLine : public CObject
{
private:
    CPoint m_ptFrom;
    CPoint m_ptTo;
    UINT m_nWidth;
    COLORREF m_crColor;

public:
    CLine (CPoint, CPoint, UINT, COLORREF);
    virtual void Draw (CDC*);
};

class CMyApp : public CWinApp
{
```

(continued)

Paint2.h *continued*

```
public:
    virtual BOOL InitInstance ();
};

class CMainWindow : public CFrameWnd
{
private:
    UINT m_nColor;
    UINT m_nWidth;
    CPoint m_ptFrom;
    CPoint m_ptTo;
    CObArray m_lineArray;

    static const COLORREF crColors[8];

    void InvertLine (CDC*, CPoint, CPoint);
    void DeleteAllLines ();

public:
    CMainWindow ();
    ~CMainWindow ();

protected:
    afx_msg void OnPaint ();
    afx_msg void OnFileNew ();
    afx_msg void OnUpdateFileNewUI (CCmdUI*);
    afx_msg void OnFileExit ();
    afx_msg void OnWidth (UINT);
    afx_msg void OnUpdateWidthUI (CCmdUI*);
    afx_msg void OnColor (UINT);
    afx_msg void OnUpdateColorUI (CCmdUI*);
    afx_msg void OnLButtonDown (UINT, CPoint);
    afx_msg void OnMouseMove (UINT, CPoint);
    afx_msg void OnLButtonUp (UINT, CPoint);
    afx_msg void OnContextMenu (CWnd*, CPoint);
    afx_msg void OnMeasureItem (int, LPMEASUREITEMSTRUCT);
    afx_msg void OnDrawItem (int, LPDRAWITEMSTRUCT);

    DECLARE_MESSAGE_MAP ()
};
```

Paint2.cpp

```
//**********************************************************************
//
//  Paint2.cpp
//
//**********************************************************************

#define OEMRESOURCE

#include <afxwin.h>
#include "Resource.h"
#include "Paint2.h"

CMyApp myApp;

///////////////////////////////////////////////////////////////////////
// CMyApp member functions

BOOL CMyApp::InitInstance ()
{
    m_pMainWnd = new CMainWindow;
    m_pMainWnd->ShowWindow (m_nCmdShow);
    m_pMainWnd->UpdateWindow ();
    return TRUE;
}

///////////////////////////////////////////////////////////////////////
// CMainWindow message map and member functions

BEGIN_MESSAGE_MAP (CMainWindow, CFrameWnd)
    ON_WM_PAINT ()
    ON_COMMAND (IDM_FILE_NEW, OnFileNew)
    ON_COMMAND (IDM_FILE_EXIT, OnFileExit)
    ON_COMMAND_RANGE (IDM_WIDTH_VTHIN, IDM_WIDTH_VTHICK, OnWidth)
    ON_COMMAND_RANGE (IDM_COLOR_BLACK, IDM_COLOR_WHITE, OnColor)
    ON_UPDATE_COMMAND_UI (IDM_FILE_NEW, OnUpdateFileNewUI)
    ON_UPDATE_COMMAND_UI_RANGE (IDM_WIDTH_VTHIN, IDM_WIDTH_VTHICK,
        OnUpdateWidthUI)
    ON_UPDATE_COMMAND_UI_RANGE (IDM_COLOR_BLACK, IDM_COLOR_WHITE,
        OnUpdateColorUI)
    ON_WM_LBUTTONDOWN ()
    ON_WM_MOUSEMOVE ()
    ON_WM_LBUTTONUP ()
    ON_WM_CONTEXTMENU ()
    ON_WM_MEASUREITEM ()
    ON_WM_DRAWITEM ()
END_MESSAGE_MAP ()
```

(continued)

Paint2.cpp *continued*

```
const COLORREF CMainWindow::crColors[8] = {
    RGB (  0,   0,   0),    // Black
    RGB (  0,   0, 255),    // Blue
    RGB (  0, 255,   0),    // Green
    RGB (  0, 255, 255),    // Cyan
    RGB (255,   0,   0),    // Red
    RGB (255,   0, 255),    // Magenta
    RGB (255, 255,   0),    // Yellow
    RGB (255, 255, 255)     // White
};

CMainWindow::CMainWindow ()
{
    m_nColor = IDM_COLOR_RED;
    m_nWidth = IDM_WIDTH_MEDIUM;
    m_lineArray.SetSize (0, 64);

    CString strWndClass = AfxRegisterWndClass (
        0,
        myApp.LoadStandardCursor (IDC_CROSS),
        (HBRUSH) (COLOR_WINDOW + 1),
        myApp.LoadIcon (IDR_MAINFRAME)
    );

    Create (strWndClass, "Paint2", WS_OVERLAPPEDWINDOW,
        rectDefault, NULL, MAKEINTRESOURCE (IDR_MAINFRAME));

    LoadAccelTable (MAKEINTRESOURCE (IDR_MAINFRAME));

    CMenu* pMenu = GetMenu ();
    for (int i=0; i<8; i++)
        pMenu->ModifyMenu (IDM_COLOR_BLACK + i, MF_BYCOMMAND |
            MF_OWNERDRAW, IDM_COLOR_BLACK + i);
}

CMainWindow::~CMainWindow ()
{
    DeleteAllLines ();
}

void CMainWindow::OnPaint ()
{
    CPaintDC dc (this);
    int nCount = m_lineArray.GetSize ();
```

```
    if (nCount) {
        for (int i=0; i<nCount; i++)
            ((CLine*) m_lineArray[i])->Draw (&dc);
    }
}

void CMainWindow::OnFileNew ()
{
    DeleteAllLines ();
    Invalidate ();
}

void CMainWindow::OnUpdateFileNewUI (CCmdUI* pCmdUI)
{
    pCmdUI->Enable (m_lineArray.GetSize ());
}

void CMainWindow::OnFileExit ()
{
    SendMessage (WM_CLOSE, 0, 0);
}

void CMainWindow::OnWidth (UINT nID)
{
    m_nWidth = nID;
}

void CMainWindow::OnColor (UINT nID)
{
    m_nColor = nID;
}

void CMainWindow::OnUpdateWidthUI (CCmdUI* pCmdUI)
{
    pCmdUI->SetCheck (pCmdUI->m_nID == m_nWidth);
}

void CMainWindow::OnUpdateColorUI (CCmdUI* pCmdUI)
{
    pCmdUI->SetCheck (pCmdUI->m_nID == m_nColor);
}

void CMainWindow::OnLButtonDown (UINT nFlags, CPoint point)
{
    m_ptFrom = point;
    m_ptTo = point;
```

(continued)

Paint2.cpp *continued*

```
    SetCapture ();
}

void CMainWindow::OnMouseMove (UINT nFlags, CPoint point)
{
    if (GetCapture () == this) {
        CClientDC dc (this);
        InvertLine (&dc, m_ptFrom, m_ptTo);
        InvertLine (&dc, m_ptFrom, point);
        m_ptTo = point;
    }
}

void CMainWindow::OnLButtonUp (UINT nFlags, CPoint point)
{
    static UINT nWidths[5] = { 1, 8, 16, 24, 32 };

    if (GetCapture () == this) {
        ReleaseCapture ();

        CClientDC dc (this);
        InvertLine (&dc, m_ptFrom, m_ptTo);
        CLine* pLine = NULL;

        try {
            pLine = new CLine (m_ptFrom, m_ptTo,
                nWidths[m_nWidth - IDM_WIDTH_VTHIN],
                crColors[m_nColor - IDM_COLOR_BLACK]);

            m_lineArray.Add (pLine);
            pLine->Draw (&dc);
        }
        catch (CMemoryException* e) {
            MessageBox ("Out of memory. You must clear the " \
                "drawing area before adding more lines.", "Error",
                MB_ICONEXCLAMATION | MB_OK);

            if (pLine != NULL)
                delete pLine;
            e->Delete ();
        }
    }
}

void CMainWindow::OnContextMenu (CWnd* pWnd, CPoint point)
{
```

```
    CRect rect;
    GetClientRect (&rect);
    ClientToScreen (&rect);

    if (rect.PtInRect (point)) {
        CMenu menu;
        menu.LoadMenu (IDR_CONTEXTMENU);
        CMenu* pContextMenu = menu.GetSubMenu (0);

        for (int i=0; i<8; i++)
            pContextMenu->ModifyMenu (IDM_COLOR_BLACK + i,
                MF_BYCOMMAND | MF_OWNERDRAW, IDM_COLOR_BLACK + i);

        pContextMenu->TrackPopupMenu (TPM_LEFTALIGN | TPM_LEFTBUTTON |
            TPM_RIGHTBUTTON, point.x, point.y, this);
        return;
    }
    CFrameWnd::OnContextMenu (pWnd, point);
}

void CMainWindow::OnMeasureItem (int nIDCtl, LPMEASUREITEMSTRUCT lpmis)
{
    lpmis->itemWidth = ::GetSystemMetrics (SM_CYMENU) * 4;
    lpmis->itemHeight = ::GetSystemMetrics (SM_CYMENU);
}

void CMainWindow::OnDrawItem (int nIDCtl, LPDRAWITEMSTRUCT lpdis)
{
    BITMAP bm;
    CBitmap bitmap;
    bitmap.LoadOEMBitmap (OBM_CHECK);
    bitmap.GetObject (sizeof (bm), &bm);

    CDC dc;
    dc.Attach (lpdis->hDC);

    CBrush* pBrush = new CBrush (::GetSysColor ((lpdis->itemState &
        ODS_SELECTED) ? COLOR_HIGHLIGHT : COLOR_MENU));
    dc.FrameRect (&(lpdis->rcItem), pBrush);
    delete pBrush;

    if (lpdis->itemState & ODS_CHECKED) {
        CDC dcMem;
        dcMem.CreateCompatibleDC (&dc);
        CBitmap* pOldBitmap = dcMem.SelectObject (&bitmap);
```

(continued)

Paint2.cpp *continued*

```
            dc.BitBlt (lpdis->rcItem.left + 4, lpdis->rcItem.top +
                (((lpdis->rcItem.bottom - lpdis->rcItem.top) -
                bm.bmHeight) / 2), bm.bmWidth, bm.bmHeight, &dcMem,
                0, 0, SRCCOPY);

            dcMem.SelectObject (pOldBitmap);
        }

        pBrush = new CBrush (crColors[lpdis->itemID - IDM_COLOR_BLACK]);
        CRect rect = lpdis->rcItem;
        rect.DeflateRect (6, 4);
        rect.left += bm.bmWidth;
        dc.FillRect (rect, pBrush);
        delete pBrush;

        dc.Detach ();
    }

    void CMainWindow::InvertLine (CDC* pDC, CPoint ptFrom, CPoint ptTo)
    {
        int nOldMode = pDC->SetROP2 (R2_NOT);

        pDC->MoveTo (ptFrom);
        pDC->LineTo (ptTo);

        pDC->SetROP2 (nOldMode);
    }

    void CMainWindow::DeleteAllLines ()
    {
        int nCount = m_lineArray.GetSize ();

        for (int i=0; i<nCount; i++)
            delete m_lineArray[i];

        m_lineArray.RemoveAll ();
    }

    //////////////////////////////////////////////////////////////////////////
    // CLine member functions

    CLine::CLine (CPoint ptFrom, CPoint ptTo, UINT nWidth, COLORREF crColor)
    {
        m_ptFrom = ptFrom;
        m_ptTo = ptTo;
        m_nWidth = nWidth;
```

```
    m_crColor = crColor;
}

void CLine::Draw (CDC* pDC)
{
    CPen pen (PS_SOLID, m_nWidth, m_crColor);

    CPen* pOldPen = pDC->SelectObject (&pen);
    pDC->MoveTo (m_ptFrom);
    pDC->LineTo (m_ptTo);

    pDC->SelectObject (pOldPen);
}
```

The New and Improved Color Menu

Right after the code that creates the application's main window in *CMainWindow*
::CMainWindow, you'll find the code that converts the items in the Color menu into
owner-drawn menu items by adding MF_OWNERDRAW attributes:

```
CMenu* pMenu = GetMenu ();
for (int i=0; i<8; i++)
    pMenu->ModifyMenu (IDM_COLOR_BLACK + i, MF_BYCOMMAND |
        MF_OWNERDRAW, IDM_COLOR_BLACK + i);
```

The first statement initializes *pMenu* with a pointer to a *CMenu* object representing
the main menu. *ModifyMenu* is then called eight times in succession to change the
items in the Color menu to MF_OWNERDRAW. After the *for* loop has run its course,
any text associated with the Color menu menu items will no longer be displayed. For
this reason, the MENUITEM statements pertaining to the Color menu in Paint2.rc specify
empty strings ("") for the menu item text.

CMainWindow::OnMeasureItem and *CMainWindow::OnDrawItem* contain the
code that draws the menu items. *OnMeasureItem* contains just two statements: one
specifying the height of each menu item (the SM_CYMENU value returned by *::Get*
SystemMetrics), and the other specifying the width (SM_CYMENU * 4). *OnDrawItem*
is a bit more complicated because it's responsible for doing the actual drawing. After
doing some preliminary work involving a *CBitmap* object we'll focus on in a moment,
OnDrawItem constructs an empty *CDC* object and attaches to it the device context
handle provided in the DRAWITEMSTRUCT structure using *CDC::Attach*:

```
CDC dc;
dc.Attach (lpdis->hDC);
```

This converts *dc* into a valid device context object whose member functions may be
used to draw in the menu. This device context should be returned to Windows in the
same state in which it was received. Objects selected into the device context should

be selected back out, and any changes made to the state of the device context (for example, to the background mode or the text color) should be undone before *OnDrawItem* ends.

Next, *OnDrawItem* creates a brush object whose color is either COLOR_MENU or COLOR_HIGHLIGHT, depending on whether the ODS_SELECTED bit in the *item-State* field is set, and then outlines the menu item by calling *CDC::FrameRect* with a pointer to the brush:

```
CBrush* pBrush = new CBrush (::GetSysColor ((lpdis->itemState &
    ODS_SELECTED) ? COLOR_HIGHLIGHT : COLOR_MENU));
dc.FrameRect (&(lpdis->rcItem), pBrush);
delete pBrush;
```

COLOR_MENU and COLOR_HIGHLIGHT are system colors whose values are obtained with *::GetSysColor*. COLOR_MENU is the default menu background color, while COLOR_HIGHLIGHT is the color of a menu's highlight bar. *CDC::FrameRect* uses the specified brush to draw a rectangle with lines 1 pixel wide. The code above draws a rectangle around the menu item in the background color if the item is not selected, or in the highlight color if it is. This is the rectangle you see when you pull down the Color menu and move the mouse up and down—the rectangle that identifies the currently selected menu item. Drawing the rectangle using the menu background color if the ODS_SELECTED bit is not set erases the selection rectangle when a menu item generates a WM_DRAWITEM message because the highlight just passed from that item to another menu item.

OnDrawItem's next task is to draw a check mark next to the menu item if the ODS_CHECKED bit is set. Unfortunately, drawing check marks is a detail you have to take care of yourself when you use owner-drawn menus. More unfortunate still, there is no *DrawCheckMark* function in either MFC or the Windows API to make drawing a check mark easy. The only alternative is to do it the hard way. That means creating a bitmap object depicting the check mark and using *CDC::BitBlt* to "blit" the check mark to the screen. We'll look into bitmaps and *CDC::BitBlt* in more detail in Chapter 12, but even without that background preparation, the *OnDrawItem* code that draws a check mark if ODS_CHECKED is set is relatively easy to understand:

```
CDC dcMem;
dcMem.CreateCompatibleDC (&dc);
CBitmap* pOldBitmap = dcMem.SelectObject (&bitmap);

dc.BitBlt (lpdis->rcItem.left + 4, lpdis->rcItem.top +
    (((lpdis->rcItem.bottom - lpdis->rcItem.top) -
    bm.bmHeight) / 2), bm.bmWidth, bm.bmHeight, &dcMem,
    0, 0, SRCCOPY);

dcMem.SelectObject (pOldBitmap);
```

dcMem represents a memory device context—a virtual display surface in memory that can be drawn to as if it were a screen or other output device. *CreateCompatibleDC* creates a memory device context. The Windows GDI doesn't let you blit bitmaps directly to a display surface, so instead you must select the bitmap into a memory DC and blit from the memory DC to the screen DC. Once the code in *OnDrawItem* has created the memory DC, it calls the memory DC's *SelectObject* function to select the bitmap object named *bitmap*. The screen DC's *BitBlt* function is then called to copy the bitmap from the memory DC to a location near the left end of the rectangle described by *lpdis->rcItem* in the screen DC. When *BitBlt* returns, the bitmap that was selected out of the memory DC when the new bitmap was selected in is reselected in preparation for the memory DC to be destroyed when *dcMem* goes out of scope.

How is it that this code draws a check mark next to the menu item? The first four statements in *OnDrawItem* create an empty *CBitmap* object, initialize it with the bitmap that Windows uses to draw check marks in menus, and copies information regarding the bitmap (including its width and height) to a structure of type BITMAP:

```
BITMAP bm;
CBitmap bitmap;
bitmap.LoadOEMBitmap (OBM_CHECK);
bitmap.GetObject (sizeof (bm), &bm);
```

OBM_CHECK is the bitmap ID; *CBitmap::LoadOEMBitmap* copies the bitmap to a *CBitmap* object. *CBitmap::GetObject* copies information about the bitmap to a BITMAP structure, and the width and height values stored in the structure's *bmWidth* and *bmHeight* fields are used in the call to *BitBlt*. *bmWidth* is used again toward the end of *OnDrawItem* to indent the left end of each color sample by an amount that equals the width of the check mark. Note that in order for OBM_CHECK to be recognized, your .cpp file must contain the statement

```
#define OEMRESOURCE
```

before the statement that includes Afxwin.h.

After the selection rectangle is drawn or erased and the check mark is drawn if the ODS_SELECTED bit is set, *OnDrawItem* draws the colored rectangle representing the menu item itself. To do so, it creates a solid brush, creates a *CRect* object from the *rcItem* structure passed in DRAWITEMSTRUCT, shrinks the rectangle a few pixels, and paints the rectangle using *CDC::FillRect*:

```
pBrush = new CBrush (crColors[lpdis->itemID - IDM_COLOR_BLACK]);
CRect rect = lpdis->rcItem;
rect.DeflateRect (6, 4);
rect.left += bm.bmWidth;
dc.FillRect (rect, pBrush);
delete pBrush;
```

CDC::FillRect is yet another *CDC* rectangle function. It fills the interior of the rectangle with a specified brush rather than with the brush selected into the device context, and it does not outline the rectangle with the current pen. Using *FillRect* rather than *Rectangle* prevents us from having to select a pen and a brush into the device context and select them back out again when we're done. The color of the brush passed to *FillRect* is determined by subtracting IDM_COLOR_BLACK from the menu item ID supplied in *lpdis->itemID* and using the result as an index into the *crColors* array of COLORREF values.

OnDrawItem's final act before returning is to detach *dc* from the device context handle obtained from DRAWITEMSTRUCT. This final step is important because it prevents *dc*'s destructor from deleting the device context when *OnDrawItem* ends. Normally you *want* a device context to be deleted when a message handler returns, but this device context was borrowed from Windows and therefore should be deleted only by Windows. *CDC::Detach* disassociates a *CDC* object and its device context so that the object can safely go out of scope.

The Context Menu

Paint2's context menu is a popup menu that's part of a menu resource whose ID is IDR_CONTEXTMENU. The menu resource is defined as follows in Paint2.rc:

```
IDR_CONTEXTMENU MENU
BEGIN
    POPUP "" {
        MENUITEM "&New",            IDM_FILE_NEW
        MENUITEM SEPARATOR
        POPUP "&Width" {
            MENUITEM "&Very Thin",      IDM_WIDTH_VTHIN
            MENUITEM "&Thin",           IDM_WIDTH_THIN
            MENUITEM "&Medium",         IDM_WIDTH_MEDIUM
            MENUITEM "Thi&ck",          IDM_WIDTH_THICK
            MENUITEM "Very Thic&k",     IDM_WIDTH_VTHICK
        }
        POPUP "&Color" {
            MENUITEM "",                IDM_COLOR_BLACK
            MENUITEM "",                IDM_COLOR_BLUE
            MENUITEM "",                IDM_COLOR_GREEN
            MENUITEM "",                IDM_COLOR_CYAN
            MENUITEM "",                IDM_COLOR_RED
            MENUITEM "",                IDM_COLOR_MAGENTA
            MENUITEM "",                IDM_COLOR_YELLOW
            MENUITEM "",                IDM_COLOR_WHITE
        }
    }
END
```

When the right mouse button is clicked in *CMainWindow*'s client area, the context menu is loaded and displayed with these statements in *CMainWindow::OnContextMenu*:

```
CMenu menu;
menu.LoadMenu (IDR_CONTEXTMENU);
CMenu* pContextMenu = menu.GetSubMenu (0);

for (int i=0; i<8; i++)
    pContextMenu->ModifyMenu (IDM_COLOR_BLACK + i,
        MF_BYCOMMAND | MF_OWNERDRAW, IDM_COLOR_BLACK + i);

pContextMenu->TrackPopupMenu (TPM_LEFTALIGN | TPM_LEFTBUTTON |
    TPM_RIGHTBUTTON, point.x, point.y, this);
```

The *ModifyMenu* loop tags the items in the Color menu with MF_OWNERDRAW attributes so that they, like the items in the main menu's Color menu, can be filled with colored rectangles. The conversion must be performed each time the menu is loaded because when *menu* goes out of scope, the menu is destroyed and the modifications made to it are lost.

Paint2's context menu handling logic is very simple because the same context menu is displayed no matter where in the window's client area the right mouse button is clicked. When you implement context menus in your own applications, you may want to do some hit-testing on the coordinates passed in *OnContextMenu*'s *point* parameter or the *CWnd* pointer passed in *pWnd* so that commands in the context menu can target specific objects or groups of objects. It might even be appropriate to customize the context menu individually for each *type* of object that's clicked. Right-clicking a line of text in Microsoft Word 7.0, for example, pops up a context menu featuring formatting commands and commands for cutting, copying, and pasting. Right-clicking an embedded bitmap displays a different context menu, one that includes an Edit Picture command for editing the image. Context menus are an important element of the Windows 95 user interface and should be supported whenever possible.

The System Menu

Let's close out this part of the chapter by taking a look at the system menu. Just as an application can call *CWnd::GetMenu* to obtain a *CMenu* pointer to its top-level menu, it can call *CWnd::GetSystemMenu* to obtain a pointer to its system menu. Most applications are content to let Windows manage the system menu, but every now and then the need to do something special arises, such as adding a menu item of your own to the system menu or changing the behavior of an existing menu item. When you're faced with such a requirement, *GetSystemMenu* is your ticket to paradise.

Suppose you want to add an About MyApp menu item to your application's system menu. When selected, About MyApp displays a dialog box with your name, the application's version number, and other information about the application. About menu items are normally put in the Help menu, but maybe your application doesn't have a Help menu. Or maybe your application is a small utility program that doesn't have any menus at all, in which case adding About MyApp to the system menu will be more efficient than loading an entire menu for the benefit of just one menu item.

The first step is to get a pointer to the system menu, like this:

```
CMenu* pSystemMenu = GetSystemMenu (FALSE);
```

The FALSE parameter tells *GetSystemMenu* that you want a pointer to a copy of the system menu that you can modify. (TRUE resets the system menu to its default state.) The second step is to add the About MyApp menu item to the system menu:

```
pSystemMenu->AppendMenu (MF_SEPARATOR);
pSystemMenu->AppendMenu (MF_STRING, IDM_SYSMENU_ABOUT,
    "&About MyApp");
```

The first call to *AppendMenu* adds a menu item separator to set your menu item apart from the default system menu items; the second adds the About MyApp menu item, whose ID is IDM_SYSMENU_ABOUT, to the system menu. A good place to put this code is in the main window's *OnCreate* handler or constructor. Items added to the system menu should be assigned IDs that are multiples of 16 (16, 32, 48, and so on). Windows uses the lower four bits of a system menu ID internally, so if you use any of those bits, you could receive some unexpected results.

If you compile and run your program right now, the new item will show up in the system menu but it won't do anything. When the user picks an item from the system menu, the window receives a WM_SYSCOMMAND message with *wParam* equal to the menu item ID. The following frame window *OnSysCommand* handler inspects the menu item ID and displays a dialog box if the ID equals IDM_SYSMENU_ABOUT:

```
// In the message map
ON_WM_SYSCOMMAND ()
    :
    :
void CMainWindow::OnSysCommand (UINT nID, LPARAM lParam)
{
    if (nID & 0xFFF0) == IDM_SYSMENU_ABOUT) {
        // Display the dialog box
        return;
    }
    CFrameWnd::OnSysCommand (nID, lParam);
}
```

An *nID* value equal to IDM_SYSMENU_ABOUT means that About MyApp was selected. If *nID* equals anything else, you must call the base class's *OnSysCommand* handler, or else the system menu (and other parts of the program, too) will cease to function. Before you test the *nID* value passed to *OnSysCommand*, you should AND it with 0xFFF0 to strip off any bits Windows may have added to it.

You can also use *OnSysCommand* to modify the behavior of items Windows places in the system menu. For example, you could disable the Close command that appears in the system menu of a frame window with this message handler:

```
void CMainWindow::OnSysCommand (UINT nID, LPARAM lParam)
{
    if ((nID & 0xFFF0) != SC_CLOSE)
        CFrameWnd::OnSysCommand (nID, lParam);
}
```

This version of *OnSysCommand* tests *nID* and passes the message to *CFrameWnd* only if *nID* represents an item other than Close. Alternatives to disabling Close with an *OnSysCommand* handler include disabling the menu item with *CMenu::Enable-MenuItem* or deleting it altogether with *CMenu::DeleteMenu*, as shown here:

```
CMenu* pSystemMenu = GetSystemMenu (FALSE);
pSystemMenu->EnableMenuItem (SC_CLOSE,              // Disable it
    MF_BYCOMMAND | MF_DISABLED);
```

or

```
CMenu* pSystemMenu = GetSystemMenu (FALSE);
pSystemMenu->DeleteMenu (SC_CLOSE, MF_BYCOMMAND);   // Delete it
```

The IDs for Close and other preexisting system menu items are listed in the documentation for *OnSysCommand*.

TOOLBARS AND STATUS BARS

A chapter on menus is the perfect place to talk about toolbars and status bars, too. With its *CToolbar* and *CStatusBar* classes, MFC makes it easy to give your application toolbars with buttons that provide one-click access to frequently used menu commands and status bars that provide context-sensitive help for items in a menu. To see for yourself how easy it is, try this simple exercise:

1. Add a *CStatusBar* data member named *m_wndStatusBar* to the *CMain-Window* class in Paint2.h.

2. Add the following *CMainWindow::OnCreate* handler to Paint2.cpp to create a status bar from *m_wndStatusBar*. (Don't forget to add the function declaration to the class declaration in Paint2.h, too.)

```
int CMainWindow::OnCreate (LPCREATESTRUCT lpcs)
{
    if (CFrameWnd::OnCreate (lpcs) == -1)
        return -1;

    m_wndStatusBar.Create (this);
    UINT nIndicator = ID_SEPARATOR;
    m_wndStatusBar.SetIndicators (&nIndicator, 1);
}
```

3.   Add the following statements to Paint2.rc to create a string table resource containing help text for the items in the menu:

```
STRINGTABLE
BEGIN
    AFX_IDS_IDLEMESSAGE      "Ready"
    IDM_FILE_NEW             "Clear the drawing area"
    IDM_FILE_EXIT            "Exit the application"
    IDM_WIDTH_VTHIN          "Set the pen width to 1 pixel"
    IDM_WIDTH_THIN           "Set the pen width to 8 pixels"
    IDM_WIDTH_MEDIUM         "Set the pen width to 16 pixels"
    IDM_WIDTH_THICK          "Set the pen width to 24 pixels"
    IDM_WIDTH_VTHICK         "Set the pen width to 32 pixels"
    IDM_COLOR_BLACK          "Set the drawing color to black"
    IDM_COLOR_BLUE           "Set the drawing color to blue"
    IDM_COLOR_GREEN          "Set the drawing color to green"
    IDM_COLOR_CYAN           "Set the drawing color to cyan"
    IDM_COLOR_RED            "Set the drawing color to red"
    IDM_COLOR_MAGENTA        "Set the drawing color to magenta"
    IDM_COLOR_YELLOW         "Set the drawing color to yellow"
    IDM_COLOR_WHITE          "Set the drawing color to white"
END
```

Now rebuild the application and run it to see what happens. The bottom of the window will now contain a status bar that displays context-sensitive help for menu commands. To see the status bar in action, pull down the Width or Color menu and drag the highlight up and down; the text in the status bar will change each time the highlight moves to a new item. To change the text for a given menu item, simply edit the corresponding string (the one assigned the same ID as the menu item) in the string table and recompile. Notice that the status bar provides help for items in the system menu, too: "Change the window size" for Size, "Reduce the window to an icon" for Minimize, and so on. These strings are supplied by the framework when you include Afxres.h in your application's .rc file.

But dig a little deeper, and you'll discover that the implementation is flawed. For example, drawing a line that extends beyond the window's lower border draws over the top of the status bar. You can easily fix that by adding the style WS_CLIP-CHILDREN to the window, but there are other problems, too. For one, calculating the client area of the window is no longer a simple matter of calling *CWnd::Get-ClientRect*; to compute the effective client area (the client area minus the space occupied by the status bar), you must subtract the height of the status bar from the coordinates returned by *GetClientRect*. That's not terribly difficult either, but if your application included a toolbar as well as a status bar, and if you enabled *CToolbar*'s docking support so that the toolbar could be detached and docked to another side of the window, calculating the window's effective client area would suddenly become very complicated. Another problem is that the status bar doesn't blend with the window border as status bars do in document/view applications created by AppWizard. You could fix that by overriding *CFrameWnd::PreCreateWindow* and removing the WS_EX_CLIENTEDGE style that the framework adds automatically to frame windows, but then the interior of the window would look flat rather than indented. That, too, could be fixed by slapping a *CView* window over the window's client area and assigning it the style WS_EX_CLIENTEDGE, but then...well, you get the picture.

The point is that *CToolbar* objects and *CStatusBar* objects work best in document/view applications. Making them work properly in non-document/view applications requires you to write a lot of code that the framework provides for you when you use documents and views. Therefore, I'll put off further discussion of toolbars and status bars until Chapter 11. In the meantime, there's still plenty of ground left to cover. Next on the agenda are controls—push buttons, list boxes, and other user interface gadgets that Windows puts at your disposal, along with the MFC classes that wrap them.

Chapter 5

Controls

In Chapters 3 and 4, you learned about two of the most common forms of input a Windows program receives. First came input from the mouse and the keyboard. When the user hits a key, moves the mouse, or clicks a mouse button, Windows translates the action into an input message and sends it to the window that was the target of the event. For mouse input, the "target" is the window underneath the cursor; for keyboard input, it's the window with the input focus. Next came input from menu selections. When the user selects an item from a menu or presses an accelerator, the menu's owner receives a WM_COMMAND message identifying the item that was selected. The MFC application framework simplifies the handling of input messages by calling the appropriate class member functions based on information supplied in message maps.

Another common form of input is input from controls—push buttons, list boxes, and other user interface gadgets. Controls reduce the tedium of Windows programming and help promote a consistent user interface by providing canned implementations of common user interface objects. A control is actually a window, complete with its own window procedure. A Windows application that uses a push button control doesn't have to draw the push button on the screen and process mouse messages to know when the button is clicked. Instead, it creates the push button with a simple function call and receives WM_COMMAND messages when the push button is clicked. The control's own WM_PAINT handler paints the button on the screen, and other message handlers inside the control translate the user's mouse and keyboard input into notifications for the control's parent.

Controls are sometimes referred to as *child window* controls because of their special relationship to other windows. An MFC function that creates a window accepts a *CWnd* pointer identifying the window's parent. If the pointer is non-NULL and the window is created with the style WS_CHILD, that window becomes a child of the specified window. Child windows are clipped to their parents, move when their parents move, and are automatically destroyed when their parents are destroyed. Child window controls also send notification messages to their parents. Much of what you'll learn in this chapter revolves around the various types of notifications that controls send and the MFC functions that wrap messages that parents send to their children.

Windows 95 comes with more than 20 prepackaged control types. Six of the control types have been supported since the very first version of Windows and are implemented in User.exe. The others, which the Win32 documentation refers to as the *common controls*, are new to Windows 95 and are implemented in Comctl32.dll. This chapter introduces the six basic control types and the MFC classes that encapsulate them. (We'll get to the common controls in Chapter 13.) Among the many benefits of programming controls the MFC way is the ease with which you can modify a control's default behavior by deriving new control classes from the MFC-provided control classes. MFC also makes it possible to build reusable, self-contained control classes that respond to their own notification messages and that port easily to other applications.

We'll get the fundamentals out of the way first by learning about the basic control types and their interfaces. Then we'll move on to more advanced topics such as owner-drawn controls, derived control classes, and techniques for writing reusable control classes. By the end of the chapter, you'll have a firm grasp of the Windows control architecture and the object-oriented approach to control programming made possible by MFC.

THE MFC CONTROL CLASSES

Windows makes the controls found in User.exe available to application programs by registering six predefined WNDCLASSes—one for each control type. The control types, their WNDCLASSes, and their corresponding MFC control classes are shown in the table below.

THE SIX BASIC CONTROL TYPES

Control Type	WNDCLASS	MFC Class
Buttons	"BUTTON"	CButton
List boxes	"LISTBOX"	CListBox
Edit controls	"EDIT"	CEdit
Combo boxes	"COMBOBOX"	CComboBox
Scroll bars	"SCROLLBAR"	CScrollBar
Static controls	"STATIC"	CStatic

If a control appears in a dialog box, you don't have to create it explicitly; you can define it in a dialog box resource, and Windows will create it for you when the dialog box is created. For the moment, we'll ignore this aspect of control creation and restrict our consideration of controls to the ones we create ourselves. We'll take up dialog boxes and methods for interacting with dialog box controls in Chapter 6. For now, and for the rest of this chapter, it's up to us to create the controls we want to use.

MFC provides means for both creating child window controls and communicating with them once they're created. A control is created by constructing an object from a control class and calling that object's *Create* function. All of the MFC control classes override the *Create* function inherited from *CWnd* to simplify control creation. Assuming *m_ctlPushButton* is an object of type *CButton*, the statement

```
m_ctlPushButton.Create ("Start", WS_CHILD | WS_VISIBLE |
    BS_PUSHBUTTON, rect, this, IDC_BUTTON);
```

creates a push button control and attaches it to *m_ctlPushButton*. The first parameter is the text that will appear on the face of the button. The second is the button style. The combination of WS_CHILD, WS_VISIBLE, and BS_PUSHBUTTON creates a push button control that is a child of the window identified in the fourth parameter and that is initially visible. *rect* is a RECT structure or a *CRect* object specifying the control's location and size with respect to the upper left corner of the parent window. *this* identifies the parent window, and IDC_BUTTON is an integer value that identifies the control. This value is also known as the *child window ID*. It's important to assign a unique child window ID to each control you create so that you can map events involving the control to member functions via message maps.

Once the control is created, it notifies its parent window of input events via WM_COMMAND messages. Information encoded in *wParam* and *lParam* identifies the control and the type of event that prompted the notification. Rather than process raw WM_COMMAND messages, MFC applications use message maps to link specific controls and events to class member functions. The following message map entry maps clicks of the push button IDC_BUTTON to the member function *OnButtonClicked*:

```
ON_BN_CLICKED (IDC_BUTTON, OnButtonClicked);
```

Now *OnButtonClicked* will be activated whenever the button is clicked. ON_BN_CLICKED is one of several message map macros MFC provides for mapping control notifications to class member functions. In addition to ON_BN macros for button controls, there are also ON_LBN macros for list boxes, ON_CBN macros for combo boxes, ON_EN macros for edit controls, and ON_STN macros for static controls. The generic ON_CONTROL macro maps notifications without regard for control type, and ON_CONTROL_RANGE maps groups of controls to a single notification handler. There are no control-specific message map macros for scroll bar controls because scroll bars send

WM_VSCROLL and WM_HSCROLL messages instead of WM_COMMAND messages.

Member functions that process control notifications accept no parameters and return no values. An *OnButtonClicked* handler for *CMainWindow* would be implemented as follows:

```
void CMainWindow::OnButtonClicked ()
{
    // Process the button click
}
```

You don't have to process every notification message from every control. As with other Windows messages, you can ignore those you're not interested in and Windows will provide default processing for you. An edit control sends out several kinds of notifications, but to get a string of input text from the user, you can just create the control and call its *GetWindowText* function when you're ready to retrieve the text. On the other hand, it wouldn't make much sense *not* to process button-click notifications from push button controls because sensing button clicks is generally the reason for creating a push button in the first place.

In addition to the member functions it inherits from *CWnd*, each MFC control class supports several member functions specific to the control type it represents. A good example is the *CButton::SetCheck* function, which checks a check box or a radio button control. If *m_ctlCheckBox* is a *CButton* object representing a check box, the statement

```
m_ctlCheckBox.SetCheck (BST_CHECKED);
```

puts a check mark in the check box. In C, a check box is checked by sending it a BM_SETCHECK message as shown here:

```
SendMessage (hwndButton, BM_SETCHECK, BST_CHECKED, 0);
```

It should come as no surprise to you that *CButton::SetCheck* is merely a wrapper around a call to *::SendMessage*. MFC provides an object-oriented view of a button control. The check box is an object, and *SetCheck* is an operation you can perform on it.

Because a control is a window, many of the member functions a control inherits from *CWnd* are useful in the context of control programming as well. For example, *CWnd::SetWindowText* changes the text displayed on the face of a push button, and *CWnd::GetWindowText* retrieves text from an edit control. *CWnd::EnableWindow* enables and disables a control, and *CWnd::SetFont* changes a control's font. If you want to do something to a control and can't find an appropriate member function in the control class, check *CWnd*'s function members. You'll probably find the one you're looking for.

One of the peculiarities of control usage in Windows 95 is that certain controls default to the "flat" Windows 3.*x* look outside a dialog box. Create a list box or an edit control in a dialog box, and the control will have a 3D border that appears to be sculpted into the surface of the dialog. But create the same control in a frame window, and Windows will border the list box or the edit control with ordinary lines. If you prefer the 3D look, create the control with the style WS_EX_CLIENTEDGE. Unfortunately, that rules out using the control's *Create* function because WS_EX_CLIENT-EDGE is an extended style and none of the controls' *Create* functions accepts extended styles. The solution? Use *CreateEx* instead. Rather than create a list box like this

```
m_ctlListBox.Create (WS_CHILD | WS_VISIBLE | LBS_STANDARD,
    rect, this, IDC_LISTBOX);
```

create it like this:

```
m_ctlListBox.CreateEx (WS_EX_CLIENTEDGE, "LISTBOX", NULL,
    WS_CHILD | WS_VISIBLE | LBS_STANDARD, x, y, cx, cy,
    m_hWnd, (HMENU) IDC_LISTBOX);
```

The second parameter to *CreateEx* specifies the name of the WNDCLASS the control is created from. "LISTBOX" is the predefined WNDCLASS that corresponds to list boxes.

A slightly more elegant solution is to derive your own control class from *CListBox* or *CEdit* and override the *Create* or *PreCreateWindow* function with a version of your own. For a *CListBox* derivative named *C3dListBox*, *Create* might be defined as follows:

```
BOOL C3dListBox::Create (DWORD dwStyle, const RECT& rect,
    CWnd* pParentWnd, UINT nID)
{
    return CreateEx (WS_EX_CLIENTEDGE, "LISTBOX", NULL, dwStyle,
        rect.left, rect.top, rect.right - rect.left, rect.bottom -
        rect.top, pParentWnd->m_hWnd, (HMENU) nID);
}
```

Now *Create* will produce a list box with 3D borders no matter who the list box's parent is. But because *Create* is not a virtual function, a better approach is to override *PreCreateWindow* and OR the WS_EX_CLIENTEDGE flag into the *dwExStyle* member of the CREATESTRUCT structure referenced in *PreCreateWindow*'s argument list:

```
BOOL C3dListBox::PreCreateWindow (CREATESTRUCT& cs)
{
    if (!CListBox::PreCreateWindow (cs))
        return FALSE;

    cs.dwExStyle |= WS_EX_CLIENTEDGE;
    return TRUE;
}
```

PreCreateWindow is a virtual *CWnd* function that a derived window class can override to implement its own window-creation settings independent of the settings specified in the call to *Create* or *CreateEx*. *PreCreateWindow* is extremely useful in document/view applications when you want a frame or a view to have a certain property but can't specify that property in a call to *Create* or *CreateEx* because it's the framework, not your application, that creates the window. A 0 return from *PreCreateWindow* stops the window-creation process, and a nonzero return allows it to proceed.

The *CButton* Class

CButton represents button controls based on the "BUTTON" WNDCLASS. Button controls come in four flavors: push buttons, check boxes, radio buttons, and group boxes. Push buttons are 3D rectangles that appear to go up and down when clicked, as if they were push buttons on a control panel. A click on a push button control usually initiates an immediate action, such as printing a document or dismissing a dialog box. Check boxes are small squares in which check marks can be toggled on and off. Radio buttons are small circles that are checked with a solid dot, or bullet, when clicked. Because radio buttons are normally used to present lists of mutually exclusive options to the user, checking one radio button typically unchecks the others in the group. Finally, group boxes are rectangles used for visual effect.

A button can be "clicked" with the left mouse button or the spacebar, but the spacebar works only if the button has the input focus. A button indicates that it has the input focus by displaying a thin dotted rectangle known as a *focus rectangle*. Group boxes never receive the input focus and don't respond to clicks of any type.

A button control is created with *CButton::Create*, which is defined as follows:

```
BOOL Create (LPCTSTR lpszCaption, DWORD dwStyle,
      const RECT& rect, CWnd* pParentWnd, UINT nID)
```

lpszCaption specifies the button text; *dwStyle* is the button style; *rect* is a rectangle that defines the button's position relative to the upper left corner of its parent, in pixels, and its size, also in pixels; *pParentWnd* identifies the button's parent; and *nID* specifies the button's child window ID. *dwStyle* defines not only the type of button that is being created—push button, check box, radio button, or group box—but also the button's properties. The *dwStyle* parameter is usually a combination of the WS_CHILD and WS_VISIBLE styles and one of the button styles shown in the table on the facing page.

Windows 95 supports a number of other button styles that can be ORed with the styles above to control text alignment. BS_LEFTTEXT (or BS_RIGHTBUTTON) moves the text assigned to a radio button or a check box from the button's right (the default) to its left. The new BS_LEFT, BS_CENTER, and BS_RIGHT styles left-justify, center, and right-justify text in the control rectangle, while BS_TOP, BS_VCENTER, and BS_BOTTOM position text vertically. BS_MULTILINE allows text too long to fit on one line to be broken into two or more lines.

BUTTON STYLES

Style	*Description*
BS_PUSHBUTTON	A standard push button control.
BS_DEFPUSHBUTTON	A push button control with a thick border. Used in dialog boxes to identify the default push button.
BS_CHECKBOX	A check box control.
BS_AUTOCHECKBOX	A check box control that checks and unchecks itself when clicked.
BS_3STATE	A 3-state check box control.
BS_AUTO3STATE	A 3-state check box control that cycles through three states—checked, unchecked, and indeterminate—when clicked.
BS_RADIOBUTTON	A radio button control.
BS_AUTORADIOBUTTON	A radio button control that, when clicked, checks itself and automatically unchecks other radio buttons in the same group.
BS_GROUPBOX	A group box control.
BS_OWNERDRAW	An owner-drawn button. Most often used in conjunction with MFC's *CBitmapButton* class to create owner-drawn push buttons.

In Windows 95, the new BS_NOTIFY button style creates a button that sends BN_DOUBLECLICKED, BN_KILLFOCUS, and BN_SETFOCUS messages to its parent. OR it with the other button styles to create a push button, a check box, or a radio button that notifies its parent when it's double-clicked or when it gains or loses the input focus.

Push Buttons

You create a push button control by specifying the style BS_PUSHBUTTON or BS_DEFPUSHBUTTON in the call to *CButton::Create*. BS_DEFPUSHBUTTON creates a default push button. This style is normally reserved for buttons used in dialog boxes, where the default push button is the one that's clicked if the Enter key is pressed while another control has the input focus. Default push buttons are emphasized with thick borders to distinguish them from nondefault push buttons. You'll learn more about default push buttons in Chapter 6.

When clicked, a push button control notifies its parent by sending it a WM_COMMAND message with the low word of *wParam* holding the button ID, *lParam* holding the button's window handle, and the high word of *wParam* holding a notification code. For a button that wasn't created with the style BS_NOTIFY, the only possible notification is BN_CLICKED, indicating that the button was clicked. In an MFC program, button-click notifications are linked to class member functions with ON-_BN_CLICKED macros. The message map entry

```
ON_BN_CLICKED (IDC_BUTTON, OnButtonClicked)
```

links *OnButtonClicked* to clicks of the button whose child window ID is IDC_BUTTON. A trivial implementation of *OnButtonClicked* looks like this:

```
void CMainWindow::OnButtonClicked ()
{
    MessageBox ("I've been clicked!");
}
```

If you'd like to create a push button that displays a graphical image instead of text, you can create an owner-drawn push button by replacing BS_PUSHBUTTON with the style BS_OWNERDRAW. MFC simplifies owner-drawn push buttons with its *CBitmapButton* class, which we'll look at later in this chapter. Windows 95 offers alternatives to owner-drawn buttons with its new BS_BITMAP and BS_ICON styles, which create buttons that display bitmaps or icons instead of text. They, too, will be discussed later in this chapter.

Check Boxes

Check boxes are buttons created with the style BS_CHECKBOX or BS_AUTO-CHECKBOX (or BS_3STATE or BS_AUTO3STATE). When clicked, a BS_AUTOCHECK-BOX-style check box toggles the check mark on or off itself. A BS_CHECKBOX-style check box must be checked and unchecked manually with *CButton::SetCheck*. For a check box object named *m_ctlCheckBox*, the statement

```
m_ctlCheckBox.SetCheck (BST_CHECKED);
```

turns the check mark on, and

```
m_ctlCheckBox.SetCheck (BST_UNCHECKED);
```

turns it off.

Like a push button control, a check box control sends a BN_CLICKED notification to its parent window when clicked. You can designate a button-click handler by adding an ON_BN_CLICKED entry to the message map of the check box's parent. A BN_CLICKED handler is optional for BS_AUTOCHECKBOX check boxes, but a standard check box won't toggle when clicked unless there's a BN_CLICKED handler to do the toggling. The following BN_CLICKED handler toggles the check mark on and off in response to button clicks:

```
void CMainWindow::OnCheckBoxClicked ()
{
    m_ctlCheckBox.SetCheck (m_ctlCheckBox.GetCheck () ?
        BST_UNCHECKED : BST_CHECKED);
}
```

CButton::GetCheck returns BST_CHECKED if the control is currently checked and BST_UNCHECKED if it is not.

The special BS_3STATE and BS_AUTO3STATE check box styles create a check box that can assume a third state in addition to the normal checked and unchecked states. The third state is called the *indeterminate* state and is entered when the user clicks a BS_AUTO3STATE check box that is currently checked or when *SetCheck* is called with a BST_INDETERMINATE parameter:

```
m_ctlCheckBox.SetCheck (BST_INDETERMINATE);
```

An indeterminate check box contains a grayed check mark. The indeterminate state is used to indicate that something is neither wholly on nor wholly off. An example would be a text editor that provides a check box for selecting and deselecting bold-face type. As the caret moves through the document, the check box is continually updated to reflect the state of the character at the caret. If the user highlights a selection that includes both normal and boldface type, the check box can be put in the indeterminate state to indicate that neither normal nor boldface applies wholly to the selection.

Radio Buttons

You create a radio button by calling *CButton::Create* with the style BS_RADIOBUTTON or the style BS_AUTORADIOBUTTON. Radio buttons normally come in groups, with each button denoting one in a list of mutually exclusive options. When clicked, a BS_AUTORADIOBUTTON-style radio button checks itself *and* unchecks any other radio buttons in the same group. If you use BS_RADIOBUTTON buttons instead, it's up to you to supply a BN_CLICKED handler for each button, one that checks the corresponding button and unchecks the others. *CButton::SetCheck* and *CButton::GetCheck* work the same for radio buttons as they do for check boxes.

Radio buttons send BN_CLICKED notifications to their parents as push buttons and check boxes do. The following BN_CLICKED handler checks the radio button represented by *m_ctlRadioButton1* when the button is clicked and unchecks three other radio buttons in the same group:

```
void CMainWindow::OnRadioButton1Clicked ()
{
    m_ctlRadioButton1.SetCheck (BST_CHECKED);
    m_ctlRadioButton2.SetCheck (BST_UNCHECKED);
    m_ctlRadioButton3.SetCheck (BST_UNCHECKED);
    m_ctlRadioButton4.SetCheck (BST_UNCHECKED);
}
```

It's important to uncheck the other radio buttons to maintain the exclusivity of the selection. If one option is selected, the others must be unselected so that two options can't be selected at once. A BN_CLICKED handler is not necessary if you use

BS_AUTORADIOBUTTON, though you may still provide one if you want to respond to changes in a radio button's state at the instant the button is clicked.

For BS_AUTORADIOBUTTON radio buttons to properly deselect the other buttons in the group, you must group the buttons so that Windows knows which buttons belong to the group. Grouping is performed through strategic placement of the window style WS_GROUP. To create a group of BS_AUTORADIOBUTTON radio buttons, follow this procedure:

1.   In your application's code, create the buttons in sequence, one after another; don't create any other controls in between.

2.   To mark the beginning of the group, assign the style WS_GROUP to the first radio button you create.

3.   If other controls are created after the radio buttons are created, assign the WS_GROUP style to the first one. This implicitly marks the previous control (the last radio button) as the final one in its group. If there are no other controls after the radio buttons but there are other controls in the window, mark the first control with WS_GROUP so that the end of the radio button group won't wrap around.

The following code fragment illustrates how you'd create four BS_AUTO-RADIOBUTTON radio buttons belonging to one group and three belonging to another group, with a check box control in between:

```
m_ctlRadioButton1.Create ("COM1", WS_CHILD ¦ WS_VISIBLE ¦
    WS_GROUP ¦ BS_AUTORADIOBUTTON, rect1, this, IDC_COM1);
m_ctlRadioButton2.Create ("COM2", WS_CHILD ¦ WS_VISIBLE ¦
    BS_AUTORADIOBUTTON, rect2, this, IDC_COM2);
m_ctlRadioButton3.Create ("COM3", WS_CHILD ¦ WS_VISIBLE ¦
    BS_AUTORADIOBUTTON, rect3, this, IDC_COM3);
m_ctlRadioButton4.Create ("COM4", WS_CHILD ¦ WS_VISIBLE ¦
    BS_AUTORADIOBUTTON, rect4, this, IDC_COM4);
m_ctlRadioButton1.SetCheck (BST_CHECKED);

m_ctlCheckBox.Create ("Save settings on exit",
    WS_CHILD ¦ WS_VISIBLE ¦ WS_GROUP ¦ BS_AUTOCHECKBOX,
    rectCheckBox, this, IDC_SAVESETTINGS);

m_ctlRadioButton5.Create ("9600", WS_CHILD ¦ WS_VISIBLE ¦
    WS_GROUP ¦ BS_AUTORADIOBUTTON, rect5, this, IDC_9600);
m_ctlRadioButton6.Create ("14400", WS_CHILD ¦ WS_VISIBLE ¦
    BS_AUTORADIOBUTTON, rect6, this, IDC_14400);
m_ctlRadioButton7.Create ("28800", WS_CHILD ¦ WS_VISIBLE ¦
    BS_AUTORADIOBUTTON, rect7, this, IDC_28800);
m_ctlRadioButton5.SetCheck (BST_CHECKED);
```

Because of the BS_AUTORADIOBUTTON styles and the logical grouping provided by the WS_GROUP styles, checking any of the first four radio buttons will automatically uncheck the other three in the group, and checking a radio button in the second group will automatically uncheck the other two.

For good form, the code above calls *SetCheck* to check a button in each group. One of the buttons in a group of radio buttons should always be checked, even if the user has yet to provide any input. Radio buttons are never checked by default, so it's your responsibility to do the initial checking.

Group Boxes

A group box is a button control created with the style BS_GROUPBOX. It is unlike other button controls in that it sends no notification messages to its parent.

Group boxes are most often used to visually delineate control groups. Enclosing groups of radio buttons (and sometimes other controls) with group boxes makes it apparent to the user which controls go together. In addition, you can use the text associated with a group box to label the control group. Group boxes have nothing to do with the *logical* grouping of controls, so don't expect a series of radio buttons to function as a group simply because there's a group box around them.

The *CListBox* Class

MFC's *CListBox* class encapsulates Windows list box controls—windows created from the predefined "LISTBOX" WNDCLASS that display lists of text strings called *items*. An item is anything you can describe with a string: a file name, for example, or a name, address, and phone number. You can have a list box optionally sort the strings added to it, and scrolling capabilities are built in so that the list box's contents won't be limited by the physical dimensions of the list box window. A list box is extremely useful for presenting a list of information and enabling the user to select items from that list. When an item is clicked (or double-clicked), a list box notifies its parent with a WM_COMMAND message. MFC simplifies the processing of these messages by providing ON_LBN message map macros to route list box notifications to the appropriate handling functions in your application.

A standard list box displays text strings in a vertical column and allows only one item to be selected at a time. The currently selected item in a list box is highlighted with the system color COLOR_HIGHLIGHT. Windows supports a number of variations on the standard list box, including multiple-selection list boxes, multicolumn list boxes, and owner-drawn list boxes that display images instead of text.

Creating a List Box

You create a list box by constructing a *CListBox* object and calling *CListBox::Create*. The following statement creates a *CListBox* object and attaches it to *m_ctlListBox*:

```
m_ctlListBox.Create (WS_CHILD | WS_VISIBLE | LBS_STANDARD,
    rect, this, IDC_LISTBOX);
```

where *rect* is a RECT structure or *CRect* object specifying the list box rectangle, *this* specifies the list box's parent window, and IDC_LISTBOX is the list box ID. The first parameter specifies the list box's style. LBS_STANDARD combines the styles WS-_BORDER, WS_VSCROLL, LBS_NOTIFY, and LBS_SORT to create a list box that has a border and a vertical scroll bar, that notifies its parent window when an item is clicked or double-clicked, and that alphabetically sorts strings that are added to it. By default, the scroll bar is visible only when the number of items in the list box exceeds the number that can be displayed within the physical dimensions of the list box. If you'd like the scroll bar to be visible at all times, include the style LBS_DISABLENOSCROLL. A list box does not have a vertical scroll bar at all unless it is created with the style WS_VSCROLL or LBS_STANDARD. Similarly, it doesn't have a border unless it is created with the style WS_BORDER or LBS_STANDARD. You might want to omit the border if you create a list box that encompasses the entire client area of its parent. These are but a few of the many styles you can use to customize a list box's appearance and behavior. The full range of list box styles is summarized in the table on the next page.

List boxes have keyboard interfaces built in. When a single-selection list box has the input focus, the up arrow, down arrow, Page Up, Page Down, Home, and End keys move the highlighted bar identifying the current selection. In addition, pressing a character key moves the selection to the next item beginning with that character. Keyboard input works in multiple-selection list boxes, too, but it's the position of a dotted focus rectangle, and not the selection, that changes. Pressing the spacebar toggles the selection state of the item with the focus in a multiple-selection list box. You can customize a list box's keyboard interface by creating the list box with the LBS-_WANTKEYBOARDINPUT style and processing WM_VKEYTOITEM and WM_CHAR-TOITEM messages. An MFC application can map these messages to *OnVKeyToItem* and *OnCharToItem* handlers using the ON_WM_VKEYTOITEM and ON_WM_CHAR-TOITEM message map macros. A derived list box class can handle these messages itself by overriding the virtual *CListBox::VKeyToItem* and *CListBox::CharToItem* functions. One use for this capability is to create a self-contained list box class that responds to presses of Ctrl-D by deleting the item that is currently selected.

Because the default font that Windows uses for list boxes is proportionally spaced, it is virtually impossible to line up columns of information in a list box by separating them with space characters. One solution is to use a list box's *SetFont* function to change the list box font to a fixed-pitch font. A better way to create columnar list box displays is to assign the list box the style LBS_USETABSTOPS and separate columns of information with tab characters. An LBS_USETABSTOPS list box treats tab characters the way a word processor does, advancing to the next tab stop when a tab character is encountered. By default, tab stops are evenly spaced about eight character widths apart. You can change the default tab stop settings with the *CListBox::SetTabStops* function.

LIST BOX STYLES

Style	Description
LBS_STANDARD	A "standard" list box that has a border and a vertical scroll bar, notifies its parent window when the selection changes or an item is double-clicked, and sorts items alphabetically. Equivalent to WS_BORDER ¦ WS_VSCROLL ¦ LBS_NOTIFY ¦ LBS_SORT.
LBS_SORT	A list box that sorts items alphabetically. Without this style, items appear in the order in which they were added to the list box.
LBS_NOSEL	A list box whose items can be viewed but not selected.
LBS_NOTIFY	A list box that notifies its parent when the selection changes or an item is double-clicked.
LBS_DISABLENOSCROLL	A list box whose vertical scroll bar is displayed, but in a disabled state, when the list box does not contain enough items for scrolling to be enabled. By default, the scroll bar is hidden when it isn't needed.
LBS_MULTIPLESEL	A multiple-selection list box.
LBS_EXTENDEDSEL	A multiple-selection list box with extended selection capabilities. Used in conjunction with LBS_MULTIPLESEL.
LBS_MULTICOLUMN	A multicolumn list box. Column widths may be set with *CListBox::SetColumnWidth*.
LBS_OWNERDRAW	An owner-drawn list box whose items can vary in height.
LBS_OWNERDRAWFIXED	An owner-drawn list box whose items are the same height.
LBS_USETABSTOPS	A list box that expands tab characters in item text. Default tab stop settings can be changed with *CListBox::SetTabStops*.
LBS_NOREDRAW	A list box that does not automatically redraw itself when an item is added or removed. Redraws can be selectively enabled and disabled programmatically using WM_SETREDRAW messages.
LBS_HASSTRINGS	A list box that "remembers" the strings added to it. Conventional list boxes have this style by default; owner-drawn list boxes don't.
LBS_WANTKEYBOARDINPUT	A list box that sends its parent a WM_VKEYTOITEM or WM_CHARTOITEM message when a key is pressed and the list box has the input focus. Used to customize the list box's response to keyboard input.
LBS_NOINTEGRALHEIGHT	A list box whose height does not have to be an exact multiple of the item height. By default, Windows adjusts a list box's height to prevent the final item from being partially clipped. An LBS_NOINTEGRALHEIGHT list box will be the exact size you specify.

By default, Windows adjusts the height of a list box so that the final item isn't partially clipped. You might specify a height of 110 pixels when creating the list box, but if each item is 14 pixels high, the list box's actual height will be 98 pixels (7 times 14) plus the height of the top and bottom borders. The adjusted height is called the *integral height* because it allows the list box to display an integral number of items. If you want the list box to be exactly the height you specify, specify the style LBS_NOINTEGRALHEIGHT in the call to *Create.*

A list box repaints itself anytime an item is added or removed. Usually that's just what you want, but if you're adding hundreds or perhaps thousands of items in a short period of time, the repeated repaints will produce a flashing effect and slow down the insertion process. You can create a list box that doesn't automatically repaint itself with the LBS_NOREDRAW style. Such a list box will be repainted only when its client area is invalidated. An alternative to using LBS_NOREDRAW is to create a normal list box and temporarily disable automatic redraws before initiating a lengthy insertion process. Redraws are selectively enabled and disabled by sending WM_SET-REDRAW messages to the list box, as shown here:

```
m_ctlListBox.SendMessage (WM_SETREDRAW, FALSE, 0);
// Add code to insert items into the list box
m_ctlListBox.SendMessage (WM_SETREDRAW, TRUE, 0);
```

A list box is automatically invalidated when redraws are enabled with a WM_SET-REDRAW message, so it's not necessary to call *Invalidate* on the list box yourself.

Unless a list box is created with the style LBS_MULTIPLESEL, only one item may be selected at a time. In a single-selection list box, clicking an unselected item both selects that item and deselects the one that was formerly selected. In a multiple-selection list box, however, any number of items can be selected. Most multiple-selection list boxes are also created with the style LBS_EXTENDEDSEL, which enables a feature known as "extended selections." In an extended-selection list box, the user selects the first item by clicking it and selects subsequent items by clicking with the Ctrl key depressed. In addition, the user can select entire ranges of contiguous items by clicking the first item in the range and then clicking the last item in the range with the Shift key held down. Use of the Ctrl and Shift keys can be combined to select multiple items and ranges, the net result being a handy interface for selecting arbitrary combinations of items.

The LBS_MULTICOLUMN style creates a multicolumn list box. Multicolumn list boxes are usually created with the WS_HSCROLL style so that their contents can be scrolled horizontally if all of the items can't be displayed at once. (Multicolumn list boxes can't be scrolled vertically.) You can adjust the column width with the *CListBox-::SetColumnWidth* function, which specifies the new column width in pixels. Normally, the column width should be based on the average width of a character in the system font, or, if the list box font has been changed, the average width of a character in the list box font. The default column width is enough to display about 16 characters, so if you'll be inserting strings longer than that, you should expand the column width to prevent columns from overlapping.

Adding and Removing List Box Items

A list box is empty until items are added to it. Items are added with *CListBox::AddString* and *CListBox::InsertString*. The statement

```
m_ctlListBox.AddString (string);
```

adds the *CString* object named *string* to the list box. If the list box was created with the style LBS_SORT, the string is positioned according to its lexical value; otherwise, it is added to the end of the list. *InsertString* adds an item to the list box at a location specified by a 0-based index. The statement

```
m_ctlListBox.InsertString (3, string);
```

inserts *string* into the list box and makes it the fourth item. The list box style LBS_SORT has no effect on strings added with *InsertString*. When successful, both *AddString* and *InsertString* return a 0-based index specifying the string's position in the list box. If either function fails, it returns LB_ERRSPACE to indicate that the list box is full or LB_ERR to indicate that the string could not be added for some other reason. You shouldn't see the LB_ERRSPACE return value very often because in Windows 95 the capacity of a list box was expanded from 8,192 items and 64K of text to 32,768 items and as much text as available memory permits. *CListBox::GetCount* returns the total number of items in a list box.

Strings are removed from a list box with *CListBox::DeleteString*. *DeleteString* takes a single parameter: the index of the item to be removed. It returns the number of items remaining in the list box. To remove all the strings from a list box at once, use *CListBox::ResetContent*.

If you want to, you can associate a 32-bit pointer or a DWORD value with each item added to a list box by means of the *CListBox::SetItemDataPtr* and *CListBox::SetItemData* functions. Item data is retrieved with *CListBox::GetItemDataPtr* and *CListBox::GetItemData*. Here's one example of how you might use these functions. Suppose you write an application that uses *CWnd::GetNextWindow* to enumerate all the top-level windows in the system and display the window titles in a list box. (*GetNextWindow* returns a *CWnd* pointer, and the window title can be retrieved by calling *GetWindowText* through that pointer.) Double-clicking a window title pops up a dialog box with further information about the corresponding window, such as its WNDCLASS attributes and window style. Rather than piece the information together anew each time an item is double-clicked, you could build a data structure for each item when the list box is initialized and use *SetItemDataPtr* to associate the structure's address with the list box item. Then, when an item is double-clicked, you could call *GetItemDataPtr* to retrieve the structure's address and enjoy nearly instantaneous access to the information you need. Note that *GetItemDataPtr* returns a pointer to a void data type, so you'll need to cast before using the pointer.

Another technique programmers often use to associate data with a list box item—particularly if the data is text-based—is to create the list box with the LBS_USE-TABSTOPS style, set the first tab stop beyond the right margin of the list box, and append the extra data to the text of the list box item with a tab character separating the strings. The extra data will be invisible since the list box isn't wide enough to display it, but *CListBox::GetText* will return the full text of the list box item—additional text included.

Other List Box Operations

The *CListBox* class includes a number of member functions for manipulating the current selection and querying a list box for information. *CListBox::GetCurSel* returns the 0-based index of the item that is currently selected in a single-selection list box. A return value equal to LB_ERR means that nothing is selected. *GetCurSel* is often called to get an item number following a click or double-click notification. A program can set the current selection itself with the *SetCurSel* function. Passing *SetCurSel* the value −1 deselects all items, causing the bar highlighting the current selection to disappear from the list box. If you want to find out whether a particular item is selected, use *CListBox::GetSel*.

SetCurSel identifies an item by its index, but items can also be selected by content. *CListBox::SelectString* searches a single-selection list box for an item that begins with a specified text string and selects the item if a match is found. The statement

```
m_listbox.SelectString (-1, "Times");
```

starts the search with the first item in the list box and highlights the first item that begins with "Times"—for example, "Times New Roman" or "Times Roman." The search is not case-sensitive, so "times" is treated the same as "Times." The first parameter to *SelectString* specifies the index of the item before the one at which the search begins; −1 instructs the list box to start with item 0. If the search is begun anywhere else, the search routine will wrap around to the first item if necessary so that all list box items are searched.

To search a list box for a particular string without selecting an item, use *CListBox-::FindString* or *CListBox::FindStringExact*. *FindString* performs a string search on a list box's contents and returns the index of the first item whose text matches or begins with a specified string. A return value equal to LB_ERR means that no match was found. *FindStringExact* does the same but reports a match only if the item text matches the search text exactly. Once you have an item's index in hand, you can retrieve the text of the item with *CListBox::GetText*. The following statements query the list box for the currently selected item and copy the text of that item to a *CString* named *string*:

```
int nIndex = m_ctlListBox.GetCurSel ();
if (nIndex != LB_ERR)
    m_ctlListBox.GetText (nIndex, string);
```

The length of the text associated with an item can be retrieved with *CListBox-::GetTextLength*. This usually isn't necessary when you use *CString* objects for text retrieval, but it could be handy if you're using *GetText* to copy item text to a buffer and need to know how much memory to allocate.

Selections in multiple-selection list boxes are handled differently than selections in single-selection list boxes. In particular, the *GetCurSel*, *SetCurSel*, and *SelectString* functions don't work with multiple-selection list boxes. Instead, items are selected (and deselected) with the *SetSel* and *SelItemRange* functions. The following statements select items 0, 5, 6, 7, 8, and 9 and deselect item 3:

```
m_ctlListBox.SetSel (0);
m_ctlListBox.SelItemRange (TRUE, 5, 9);
m_ctlListBox.SetSel (3, FALSE);
```

CListBox also provides the *GetSelCount* function for getting a count of selected items and the *GetSelItems* function for retrieving the indexes of all selected items. In a multiple-selection list box, the dotted rectangle representing the item with the focus can be moved without changing the current selection. The focus rectangle can be moved and queried with *SetCaretIndex* and *GetCaretIndex*. Most other list box functions, including *GetText*, *GetTextLength*, *FindString*, and *FindStringExact*, work the same for multiple-selection list boxes as they do for the single-selection variety.

One of *CListBox*'s most powerful functions is *Dir*, which fills a list box with a specified combination of file names, directory names, and drive letters. The statement

```
m_ctlListBox.Dir (0x10, "*.*");
```

fills a list box with the names of all the files and directories in the current directory. In the old days, this feature was widely used to create lists of files, directories, and drives in file-open and file-save dialog boxes. Today *Dir* is all but obsolete because Windows provides default implementations of these and other dialog boxes in the common dialog library.

List Box Notifications

A list box sends notifications to its parent window through WM_COMMAND messages. In an MFC application, list box notifications are mapped to handling functions with ON_LBN message map entries. The table on the next page briefly describes the six notification types and identifies the corresponding ON_LBN macros. LBN_DBLCLK, LBN_SELCHANGE, and LBN_SELCANCEL notifications are sent only if the list box was created with the style LBS_NOTIFY or LBS_STANDARD. The three others are sent regardless of the list box style.

LIST BOX NOTIFICATIONS

Notification	Sent When	Message Map Macro	LBS_NOTIFY Required?
LBN_SETFOCUS	The list box gains the input focus.	ON_LBN_SETFOCUS	No
LBN_KILLFOCUS	The list box loses the input focus.	ON_LBN_KILLFOCUS	No
LBN_ERRSPACE	A list box operation failed because of insufficient memory.	ON_LBN_ERRSPACE	No
LBN_DBLCLK	An item is double-clicked.	ON_LBN_DBLCLK	Yes
LBN_SELCHANGE	The list box selection changes.	ON_LBN_SELCHANGE	Yes
LBN_SELCANCEL	The list box selection is canceled.	ON_LBN_SELCANCEL	Yes

The two list box notifications that programmers rely on most are LBN_DBLCLK and LBN_SELCHANGE. The former is sent when a list box item is double-clicked. To determine the index of the item that was double-clicked in a single-selection list box, use the list box's *GetCurSel* function as shown here:

```
// In the message map
ON_LBN_DBLCLK (IDC_LISTBOX, OnItemDoubleClicked)
    :
    :
void CMainWindow::OnItemDoubleClicked ()
{
    nIndex = m_ctlListBox.GetCurSel ();
    // Do something with the item
}
```

For a multiple-selection list box, use *GetCaretIndex* instead of *GetCurSel*, or use *GetSelItems* to enumerate all the currently selected items. There is no keyboard equivalent of an item double-click unless you supply one yourself.

An LBN_SELCHANGE notification is sent when the user changes the selection but not when the selection is changed programmatically. The single-selection list box parent receives LBN_SELCHANGE notifications when an item is clicked and when the selection is changed from the keyboard. The parent of a multiple-selection list box receives LBN_SELCHANGE notifications when an item is clicked, when an item's selection state is toggled with the spacebar, and when the focus rectangle is moved.

The *CStatic* Class

CStatic, which represents controls created from Windows' "STATIC" WNDCLASS, is the simplest of the MFC control classes. At least it *used* to be—Windows 95 adds so many new features and options to static controls that *CStatic* now rivals *CButton* and some of the other control classes for complexity.

Static controls come in three flavors: text strings, rectangles, and images. The following statement creates a static text control that displays the string "Name:"

```
m_ctlStatic.Create ("Name", WS_CHILD | WS_VISIBLE | SS_LEFT,
    rect, this, IDC_STATIC);
```

The style SS_LEFT creates a static text control whose text is left-aligned in the rectangle denoted by *rect*. If the text is too long to fit on one line and the control rectangle is large enough to display two or more lines of text, the text is automatically wrapped. The SS_LEFTNOWORDWRAP style creates an SS_LEFT-like control that clips everything that won't fit on one line. Text can be centered horizontally or right-aligned in the control rectangle by specifying SS_CENTER or SS_RIGHT instead of SS_LEFT or SS_LEFTNOWORDWRAP. Another alternative is the little-used SS_SIMPLE style, which is similar to SS_LEFT but creates a control whose text can't be altered with *CWnd::SetWindowText*. By default, the text assigned to a static text control is aligned along the upper edge of the control rectangle. To center text vertically in the control rectangle, OR the style SS_CENTERIMAGE into the other style or styles you specify.

By default, an ampersand in control text is not displayed. Instead, it's interpreted as a command to underline the following character in the text string. If a control's text includes ampersands and you want ampersands to be displayed, include the SS_NOPREFIX style as shown here:

```
m_ctlStatic.Create ("&A&B&C&D", WS_CHILD | WS_VISIBLE |
    SS_LEFT | SS_NOPREFIX, rect, this, IDC_STATIC);
```

You can also draw a sunken border around a static control by including the style SS_SUNKEN.

A second use for static controls is to draw rectangles. The control style specifies the type of rectangle that is drawn. You can choose from the styles shown in the table on the next page. The statement

```
m_ctlStatic.Create ("", WS_CHILD | WS_VISIBLE | SS_ETCHEDFRAME,
    rect, this, IDC_STATIC);
```

creates a static control that draws an "etched" rectangle whose appearance is similar to the appearance of a group box. For best results, etched rectangles should be drawn on surfaces whose color is the same as the default dialog box color (the system color COLOR_3DFACE). A static rectangle control does not display text, even if you specify a nonnull text string in the call to *Create*.

STATIC RECTANGLE CONTROL STYLES

Style	Description
SS_BLACKFRAME	A hollow rectangle in the system color COLOR_WINDOWFRAME (default = black)
SS_BLACKRECT	A solid rectangle in the system color COLOR_WINDOWFRAME (default = black)
SS_ETCHEDFRAME	A hollow rectangle with etched borders
SS_ETCHEDHORZ	A hollow rectangle with etched top and bottom borders
SS_ETCHEDVERT	A hollow rectangle with etched left and right borders
SS_GRAYFRAME	A hollow rectangle in the system color COLOR_BACKGROUND (default = gray)
SS_GRAYRECT	A solid rectangle in the system color COLOR_BACKGROUND (default = gray)
SS_WHITEFRAME	A hollow rectangle in the system color COLOR_WINDOW (default = white)
SS_WHITERECT	A solid rectangle in the system color COLOR_WINDOW (default = white)

A third use for static controls is to display images formed from bitmaps, icons, cursors, or metafiles. A static image control must have one of the styles shown in the table below.

STATIC IMAGE CONTROL STYLES

Style	Description
SS_BITMAP	A static control that displays a bitmap
SS_ENHMETAFILE	A static control that displays a metafile
SS_ICON	A static control that displays an icon or a cursor

After the control is created, a bitmap, a metafile, an icon, or a cursor is associated with it by a call to the *CStatic* function *SetBitmap*, *SetEnhMetaFile*, *SetIcon*, or *SetCursor*. Conversely, the bitmap, metafile, icon, or cursor associated with a control can be retrieved with *GetBitmap*, *GetEnhMetaFile*, *GetIcon*, or *GetCursor*. The statements

```
m_ctlStatic.Create ("", WS_CHILD | WS_VISIBLE | SS_ICON,
    rect, this, IDC_STATIC);
m_ctlStatic.SetIcon (hIcon);
```

create a static control that displays an icon and assign it the icon whose handle is *hIcon*. By default, the icon image is positioned in the upper left corner of the control, and if the image is larger than the control rectangle, the rectangle is automatically expanded so that the image won't be clipped. To prevent resizing and enable clipping, include the SS_REALSIZEIMAGE style in the statement that creates the control. You can use the SS_CENTERIMAGE style to center the image in the control rectangle. A side effect of using SS_CENTERIMAGE is that it prevents the control from being resized to match the image just as SS_REALSIZEIMAGE does. You don't have to be concerned about clipping and resizing for SS_ENHMETAFILE controls because the metafile image is scaled to match the control size. For a neat special effect, create a sunken border around a static image control with the SS_SUNKEN style as shown here:

```
m_ctlStatic.Create ("", WS_CHILD | WS_VISIBLE |
    SS_BITMAP | SS_SUNKEN, rect, this, IDC_STATIC);
m_ctlStatic.SetBitmap (hBitmap);
```

In this example, the control will be resized so that the bitmap exactly fills its interior, and the bitmap will be outlined with a thin border that makes it appear to be sunken slightly below the level of the surface on which it is drawn.

By default, a static control sends no notifications to its parent. But if you create a static control with the SS_NOTIFY style, it can send the four types of notifications shown below.

STATIC CONTROL NOTIFICATIONS

Notification	*Sent When*	*Message Map Macro*
STN_CLICKED	The control is clicked.	ON_STN_CLICKED
STN_DBLCLK	The control is double-clicked.	ON_STN_DBLCLK
STN_DISABLE	The control is disabled.	ON_STN_DISABLE
STN_ENABLE	The control is enabled.	ON_STN_ENABLE

The STN_CLICKED and STN_DBLCLK notifications are useful for creating static controls that do something when they're clicked. In previous versions of Windows, none of which supported the SS_NOTIFY style, sensing static control clicks required window subclassing or other such measures. In Windows 95, the statements

```
// In the message map
ON_STN_CLICKED (IDC_STATIC, OnClicked)
    :
    :
// In CMainWindow::OnCreate
m_ctlStatic.Create ("Click me", WS_CHILD | WS_VISIBLE |
    SS_CENTER | SS_CENTERIMAGE | SS_NOTIFY | SS_SUNKEN, rect,
    this, IDC_STATIC);
    :
    :
void CMainWindow::OnClicked ()
{
    m_ctlStatic.PostMessage (WM_CLOSE, 0, 0);
}
```

create a static text control that displays "Click me" in the center of a sunken rectangle and that disappears from the screen when it's clicked. If a static control does not have the SS_NOTIFY style, mouse messages go through to the underlying window because the control's window procedure returns HTTRANSPARENT in response to WM_NCHIT-TEST messages.

The FontView Application

Let's pause for a moment and put what we've learned so far about buttons, list boxes, and static controls to use in an application. Rather than contrive a program that creates every possible variety of *CButton*, *CListBox*, and *CStatic* control but serves no other useful purpose, I decided to create a sample application that really *does* something.

The FontView application shown in Figure 5-1 lists the names of all the fonts installed on the host PC in a list box. When a font name is selected, a sample is drawn in a group box at the bottom of the window. The sample text is really a static text control, so all FontView has to do when a font is selected is call *SetFont* to assign the font to the control. If the check box labeled "Show TrueType fonts only" is checked, non-TrueType fonts are excluded from the list. In addition to showing how push button, check box, list box, group box, and static text controls are put to use in a real application, FontView also demonstrates a very important MFC programming technique—the use of C++ member functions as Windows callback functions. The term "callback function" may not mean much to you at the moment, but you'll learn all about it shortly.

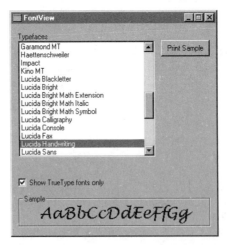

Figure 5-1. *The FontView window.*

FontView's source code appears in Figure 5-2. The six control objects FontView uses are private members of the *CMainWindow* class:

- *m_ctlLBTitle*, which corresponds to the static text control labeled "Typefaces"

- *m_ctlListBox*, which corresponds to the list box

- *m_ctlCheckBox*, which corresponds to the "Show TrueType fonts only" check box

- *m_ctlGroupBox*, which corresponds to the "Sample" group box

- *m_ctlSampleText*, which corresponds to the static text control that displays font samples

- *m_ctlPushButton*, which corresponds to the "Print Sample" push button

The controls are created one by one in *CMainWindow::OnCreate*. Their sizes and positions are based on *CMainWindow::m_cxChar* and *CMainWindow::m_cyChar*, which represent the average width and height of a character in the control font. Note the use of *CreateEx* to create the list box control so it will have a 3D border. Also notice that the style parameter for the Print Sample push button includes the specifier WS_DISABLED, which means that the button is initially disabled. It is enabled when an LBN_SELCHANGE notification arrives, indicating that the user has selected a font.

FontView.h

```
//*********************************************************************
//
//  FontView.h
//
//*********************************************************************

class CMyApp : public CWinApp
{
public:
    virtual BOOL InitInstance ();
};

class CMainWindow : public CWnd
{
private:
    int m_cxChar;
    int m_cyChar;

    CFont m_fontMain;
    CFont m_fontSample;
```

Figure 5-2. *The FontView source code.*   *(continued)*

FontView.h *continued*

```
    CStatic m_ctlLBTitle;
    CListBox m_ctlListBox;
    CButton m_ctlCheckBox;
    CButton m_ctlGroupBox;
    CStatic m_ctlSampleText;
    CButton m_ctlPushButton;

    void FillListBox ();

public:
    CMainWindow ();

    static int CALLBACK EnumFontFamProc (ENUMLOGFONT*,
        NEWTEXTMETRIC*, int, LPARAM);

protected:
    virtual void PostNcDestroy ();

    afx_msg int OnCreate (LPCREATESTRUCT);
    afx_msg void OnPushButtonClicked ();
    afx_msg void OnCheckBoxClicked ();
    afx_msg void OnSelChange ();

    DECLARE_MESSAGE_MAP ()
};
```

FontView.cpp

```
//*********************************************************************
//
//  FontView.cpp
//
//*********************************************************************

#include <afxwin.h>
#include "FontView.h"

#define IDC_PRINT       100
#define IDC_CHECKBOX    101
#define IDC_LISTBOX     102
#define IDC_SAMPLE      103

CMyApp myApp;
```

```
/////////////////////////////////////////////////////////////////////////
// CMyApp member functions

BOOL CMyApp::InitInstance ()
{
    m_pMainWnd = new CMainWindow;
    m_pMainWnd->ShowWindow (m_nCmdShow);
    m_pMainWnd->UpdateWindow ();
    return TRUE;
}

/////////////////////////////////////////////////////////////////////////
// CMainWindow message map and member functions

BEGIN_MESSAGE_MAP (CMainWindow, CWnd)
    ON_WM_CREATE ()
    ON_BN_CLICKED (IDC_PRINT, OnPushButtonClicked)
    ON_BN_CLICKED (IDC_CHECKBOX, OnCheckBoxClicked)
    ON_LBN_SELCHANGE (IDC_LISTBOX, OnSelChange)
END_MESSAGE_MAP ()

CMainWindow::CMainWindow ()
{
    CString strWndClass = AfxRegisterWndClass (
        0,
        myApp.LoadStandardCursor (IDC_ARROW),
        (HBRUSH) (COLOR_3DFACE + 1),
        myApp.LoadStandardIcon (IDI_APPLICATION)
    );

    CreateEx (0, strWndClass, "FontView",
        WS_OVERLAPPED | WS_SYSMENU | WS_CAPTION | WS_MINIMIZEBOX,
        CW_USEDEFAULT, CW_USEDEFAULT, CW_USEDEFAULT, CW_USEDEFAULT,
        NULL, NULL, NULL);

    CRect rect (0, 0, m_cxChar * 68, m_cyChar * 26);
    CalcWindowRect (&rect);

    SetWindowPos (NULL, 0, 0, rect.Width (), rect.Height (),
        SWP_NOZORDER | SWP_NOMOVE | SWP_NOREDRAW);
}

int CMainWindow::OnCreate (LPCREATESTRUCT lpcs)
{
    if (CWnd::OnCreate (lpcs) == -1)
        return -1;
```

(continued)

FontView.cpp *continued*

```
CClientDC dc (this);
int nHeight = -((dc.GetDeviceCaps (LOGPIXELSY) * 8) / 72);

m_fontMain.CreateFont (nHeight, 0, 0, 0, FW_NORMAL, 0, 0, 0,
    DEFAULT_CHARSET, OUT_CHARACTER_PRECIS, CLIP_CHARACTER_PRECIS,
    DEFAULT_QUALITY, DEFAULT_PITCH | FF_DONTCARE, "MS Sans Serif");

CFont* pOldFont = dc.SelectObject (&m_fontMain);
TEXTMETRIC tm;
dc.GetTextMetrics (&tm);
m_cxChar = tm.tmAveCharWidth;
m_cyChar = tm.tmHeight + tm.tmExternalLeading;
dc.SelectObject (pOldFont);

CRect rect (m_cxChar * 2, m_cyChar, m_cxChar * 48, m_cyChar * 2);
m_ctlLBTitle.Create ("Typefaces", WS_CHILD | WS_VISIBLE | SS_LEFT,
    rect, this);

rect.SetRect (m_cxChar * 2, m_cyChar * 2, m_cxChar * 48,
    m_cyChar * 18);
m_ctlListBox.CreateEx (WS_EX_CLIENTEDGE, "listbox", NULL,
    WS_CHILD | WS_VISIBLE | LBS_STANDARD, rect.left, rect.top,
    rect.Width (), rect.Height (), m_hWnd, (HMENU) IDC_LISTBOX,
    NULL);

rect.SetRect (m_cxChar * 2, m_cyChar * 19, m_cxChar * 48,
    m_cyChar * 20);
m_ctlCheckBox.Create ("Show TrueType fonts only", WS_CHILD |
    WS_VISIBLE | BS_AUTOCHECKBOX, rect, this, IDC_CHECKBOX);

rect.SetRect (m_cxChar * 2, m_cyChar * 21, m_cxChar * 66,
    m_cyChar * 25);
m_ctlGroupBox.Create ("Sample", WS_CHILD | WS_VISIBLE | BS_GROUPBOX,
    rect, this, (UINT) -1);

rect.SetRect (m_cxChar * 4, m_cyChar * 22, m_cxChar * 64,
    (m_cyChar * 99) / 4);
m_ctlSampleText.Create ("", WS_CHILD | WS_VISIBLE | SS_CENTER, rect,
    this, IDC_SAMPLE);

rect.SetRect (m_cxChar * 50, m_cyChar * 2, m_cxChar * 66,
    m_cyChar * 4);
m_ctlPushButton.Create ("Print Sample", WS_CHILD | WS_VISIBLE |
    WS_DISABLED | BS_PUSHBUTTON, rect, this, IDC_PRINT);
```

```
    m_ctlLBTitle.SetFont (&m_fontMain, FALSE);
    m_ctlListBox.SetFont (&m_fontMain, FALSE);
    m_ctlCheckBox.SetFont (&m_fontMain, FALSE);
    m_ctlGroupBox.SetFont (&m_fontMain, FALSE);
    m_ctlPushButton.SetFont (&m_fontMain, FALSE);

    FillListBox ();
    return 0;
}

void CMainWindow::PostNcDestroy ()
{
    delete this;
}

void CMainWindow::OnPushButtonClicked ()
{
    MessageBox ("This feature is currently unimplemented. Sorry!",
        "Error", MB_ICONINFORMATION | MB_OK);
}

void CMainWindow::OnCheckBoxClicked ()
{
    FillListBox ();
    OnSelChange ();
}

void CMainWindow::OnSelChange ()
{
    int nIndex = m_ctlListBox.GetCurSel ();

    if (nIndex == LB_ERR) {
        m_ctlPushButton.EnableWindow (FALSE);
        m_ctlSampleText.SetWindowText ("");
    }
    else {
        m_ctlPushButton.EnableWindow (TRUE);
        if ((HFONT) m_fontSample != NULL)
            m_fontSample.DeleteObject ();

        CString strFaceName;
        m_ctlListBox.GetText (nIndex, strFaceName);
```

(continued)

FontView.cpp *continued*

```
        m_fontSample.CreateFont (-m_cyChar * 2, 0, 0, 0, FW_NORMAL,
            0, 0, 0, DEFAULT_CHARSET, OUT_CHARACTER_PRECIS,
            CLIP_CHARACTER_PRECIS, DEFAULT_QUALITY, DEFAULT_PITCH |
            FF_DONTCARE, strFaceName);

        m_ctlSampleText.SetFont (&m_fontSample);
        m_ctlSampleText.SetWindowText ("AaBbCcDdEeFfGg");
    }
}

void CMainWindow::FillListBox ()
{
    m_ctlListBox.ResetContent ();

    CClientDC dc (this);
    ::EnumFontFamilies ((HDC) dc, NULL, (FONTENUMPROC) EnumFontFamProc,
        (LPARAM) this);
}

int CALLBACK CMainWindow::EnumFontFamProc (ENUMLOGFONT* lpelf,
    NEWTEXTMETRIC* lpntm, int nFontType, LPARAM lParam)
{
    CMainWindow* pWnd = (CMainWindow*) lParam;

    if ((pWnd->m_ctlCheckBox.GetCheck () == BST_UNCHECKED) ||
        (nFontType & TRUETYPE_FONTTYPE))
        pWnd->m_ctlListBox.AddString (lpelf->elfLogFont.lfFaceName);

    return 1;
}
```

FontView processes three types of control notifications: BN_CLICKED notifications from the push button and check box controls and LBN_SELCHANGE notifications from the list box. The corresponding message map entries look like this:

```
ON_BN_CLICKED (IDC_PRINT, OnPushButtonClicked)
ON_BN_CLICKED (IDC_CHECKBOX, OnCheckBoxClicked)
ON_LBN_SELCHANGE (IDC_LISTBOX, OnSelChange)
```

CMainWindow::OnPushButtonClicked is activated when the Print Sample button is clicked. Printing is a complex undertaking in a Windows application, so *OnPushButton-Clicked* simply pops up a message box informing the user that this feature is not implemented. *CMainWindow::OnCheckBoxClicked* handles BN_CLICKED notifications from the check box. Since the check box was created with the style BS_AUTOCHECK-BOX, the check mark turns on and off automatically when the control is clicked. The purpose of the *OnCheckBoxClicked* handler is to refresh the font list in the list box when the check mark is toggled. To do that, it calls *CMainWindow::FillListBox* to reinitialize the list box, followed by *CMainWindow::OnSelChange* to update the sample text.

OnSelChange is also called when the list box selection changes. It begins by calling *GetCurSel* to get the index of the currently selected item. If *GetCurSel* returns LB_ERR indicating that nothing is selected, the handler disables the push button and erases the sample text. Otherwise, it enables the button, retrieves the text of the selected item with *CListBox::GetText*, and creates a font using the string returned by *GetText* as the typeface name. It then calls *m_ctlSampleText*'s *SetFont* function to change the font assigned to the static text control, followed by *SetWindowText* to set the control text to "AaBbCcDdEeFfGg."

The lone parameter passed to *SetFont* is a pointer to a *CFont* object representing a GDI font. FontView uses two font objects: *m_fontSample* for the sample text and *m_fontMain* for all the other controls. *m_fontSample* is initialized anew each time the list box selection changes. *m_fontMain* is created once, at the outset of the program. The font it represents is 8-point MS Sans Serif, which is used throughout Windows 95 for child window controls. After creating the controls, *OnCreate* assigns *m_fontMain* to all of them except *m_ctlSampleText*:

```
m_ctlLBTitle.SetFont (&m_fontMain, FALSE);
m_ctlListBox.SetFont (&m_fontMain, FALSE);
m_ctlCheckBox.SetFont (&m_fontMain, FALSE);
m_ctlGroupBox.SetFont (&m_fontMain, FALSE);
m_ctlPushButton.SetFont (&m_fontMain, FALSE);
```

After creating *m_fontMain*, *OnCreate* selects it into a device context so that *CDC::GetTextMetrics* will return font metrics for 8-point MS Sans Serif rather than the default system font. These font metrics are then used to initialize *m_cxChar* and *m_cyChar*, which in turn are used to size and position the controls.

Fonts and the *CFont* Class

m_fontMain and *m_fontSample* are objects of type *CFont*. *CFont* is the class MFC uses to represent fonts—groups of characters of a particular size (height) and typeface. Font sizes are measured in units called *points,* and there are 72 points to an inch. Each character in a 12-point font is nominally ⅙ inch tall, but the actual height will vary somewhat depending on the physical characteristics of the output device. The term *typeface* describes a font's basic style. Times New Roman is one example of a typeface; Courier New is another.

In MFC, fonts are represented by the *CFont* class. Once a *CFont* object is constructed, a font is created by calling the object's *CreateFont* or *CreateFontIndirect* function. A font is a GDI object, just as a pen or a brush is. Constructing a *CFont* object and calling *CreateFont* is analogous to creating an empty *CPen* object and calling

CreatePen. FontView's *OnCreate* function creates an 8-point MS Sans Serif font and attaches it to *m_fontMain* like this:

```
m_fontMain.CreateFont (nHeight, 0, 0, 0, FW_NORMAL, 0, 0, 0,
    DEFAULT_CHARSET, OUT_CHARACTER_PRECIS, CLIP_CHARACTER_PRECIS,
    DEFAULT_QUALITY, DEFAULT_PITCH | FF_DONTCARE, "MS Sans Serif");
```

Of the many parameters passed to *CreateFont*, three are critically important: the font height (parameter 1), the font weight (parameter 5), and the typeface name (parameter 14). In this example, the font height is *nHeight*, the weight is FW_NORMAL, and the typeface is "MS Sans Serif." FW_NORMAL specifies a "normal," or nonbold, font. Had we wanted a bold font instead, we could have specified FW_BOLD. *nHeight* specifies the font height in pixels and is computed by multiplying the point size (8) by the number of pixels per inch in the vertical direction on the output device and then dividing by the number of points per inch (72). In code, it looks like this:

```
int nHeight = -((dc.GetDeviceCaps (LOGPIXELSY) * 8) / 72);
```

Called with a LOGPIXELSY parameter, *CDC::GetDeviceCaps* returns the logical display resolution (in the *y* direction) of the specified device. The result is converted to a negative number because *CreateFont* interprets the font height differently depending on the sign of the value. A negative value means that the height parameter specifies the font's character height; a positive value means that it specifies the *cell* height—the character height plus internal leading (space reserved above each character for diacritics and other accent marks). You'll normally use the character height when you're creating a font based on a desired point size. You can also specify 0 for the font height, in which case Windows will pick a default size for you.

After creating a font, an application can select it into a device context and draw with it using *DrawText*, *TextOut*, and other *CDC* functions, or it can use *SetFont* to assign the font to a control. A font assigned to a control should not be deleted unless the control is deleted, too. FontView's *OnSelChange* handler deletes the font assigned to *m_ctlSampleText*, but it immediately—and in the context of the same message handler—calls *SetFont* to assign the control a new font.

Enumerating Fonts

The job of filling the list box with font names falls to *CMainWindow::FillListBox*. *FillListBox* is called by *OnCreate* to initialize the list box when the program is started. It is also called by *OnCheckBoxClicked* to reinitialize the list box when the "Show TrueType fonts only" check box is clicked. *FillListBox* first clears the list box by calling *CListBox::ResetContent*. It then enumerates all the fonts installed in the system and adds the corresponding typeface names to the list box.

The enumeration process is begun by constructing a device context object named *dc* and using the *CDC* class's HDC operator to extract a device context handle and pass it as an argument to Windows' *::EnumFontFamilies* function:

```
CClientDC dc (this);
::EnumFontFamilies ((HDC) dc, NULL, (FONTENUMPROC) EnumFontFamProc,
    (LPARAM) this);
```

The NULL second parameter tells *::EnumFontFamilies* that we want information about all currently installed fonts. The next parameter is the address of a *callback function*. A callback function is a function in your application that Windows *calls back* with information you requested. For each font enumerated with *::EnumFontFamilies*, Windows calls *CMainWindow::EnumFontFamProc*, which is defined as follows:

```
int CALLBACK CMainWindow::EnumFontFamProc (ENUMLOGFONT FAR* lpelf,
    NEWTEXTMETRIC FAR* lpntm, int nFontType, LPARAM lParam)
```

lpelf is a pointer to an ENUMLOGFONT structure, which contains a wealth of information about the font, including its typeface name. *lpntm* is a pointer to a structure of type NEWTEXTMETRIC, which contains font metrics—height, width, internal leading, and so on. *nFontType* specifies the font type. TrueType fonts can be identified by logically ANDing *nFontType* with the value TRUETYPE_FONTTYPE; if the result is nonzero, then the font is a TrueType font. The fourth and final parameter, *lParam*, is an optional 32-bit LPARAM value passed to *::EnumFontFamilies*. *FillListBox* passes the *this* pointer referring to the current instance of *CMainWindow*, for reasons I'll explain in a moment.

It's actually the callback function, not *FillListBox*, that adds the typeface names to the list box. Each time *EnumFontFamProc* is called, it casts the *lParam* value passed to it from *FillListBox* into a *CMainWindow* pointer:

```
CMainWindow* pWnd = (CMainWindow*) lParam;
```

It then uses the pointer to add the typeface name to the list box, but only if the "Show TrueType fonts only" check box is unchecked or the font is a TrueType font:

```
if ((pWnd->m_ctlCheckBox.GetCheck () == BST_UNCHECKED) ||
    (nFontType & TRUETYPE_FONTTYPE))
    pWnd->m_ctlListBox.AddString (lpelf->elfLogFont.lfFaceName);

return 1;
```

The nonzero return value tells Windows to continue the enumeration process. (The callback function can halt the process at any time by returning 0, a handy option to have if you've allocated a fixed amount of memory to store font information and the memory fills up.) After Windows has called *EnumFontFamProc* for the last time, the call that *FillListBox* placed to *::EnumFontFamilies* returns and the enumeration process is complete.

You're probably already wondering: why does *FillListBox* pass a *this* pointer to the callback function, and why does *EnumFontFamProc* go to the trouble of casting the pointer to a *CMainWindow* pointer when it, too, is a member of *CMainWindow*?

Look closely at the declaration for *CMainWindow* in FontView.h, and you'll see that *EnumFontFamProc* is declared with the *static* keyword. A static member function doesn't receive a *this* pointer, so it can't access nonstatic members of its own class. In order to call *m_ctlCheckBox*'s *GetCheck* function and *m_ctlListBox*'s *AddString*, *EnumFontFamProc* needs pointers to *m_ctlCheckBox* and *m_ctlListBox* or a pointer to the *CMainWindow* object to which those objects belong. By casting the *lParam* value received from *FillListBox* to a *CMainWindow* pointer, *EnumFontFamProc* is able to access nonstatic members of the *CMainWindow* class just as a nonstatic member function can.

EnumFontFamProc was declared static in the first place because callbacks require special handling in C++ applications. Windows rigidly defines a callback function's interface—the parameters passed to it through its argument list. When a member function of a C++ class is declared, the compiler silently tacks on an extra argument to hold the *this* pointer. Unfortunately, the added parameter means that the callback function's argument list doesn't match the argument list Windows expects, and all sorts of bad things can happen as a result, including GPFs, the nemeses of all Windows programmers. There are a number of solutions to this problem, but declaring the callback to be a static member function is among the simplest and most direct. In C++, a static member function isn't passed a *this* pointer, so its argument list is unaltered.

Callback functions are common in Windows, so the technique demonstrated here is useful for more than just enumerating fonts. Many Windows API functions that rely on callbacks support an application-defined *lParam* value, which is perfect for passing *this* pointers to statically declared callback functions. Should you use an enumeration function that doesn't support an application-defined *lParam*, you'll have to resort to other means to make a pointer available. One alternative is to make the *this* pointer visible to the callback function by copying it to a global variable just before the enumeration process begins.

The *CEdit* Class

MFC's *CEdit* class encapsulates the functionality of Windows edit controls created from the predefined WNDCLASS named "EDIT." Edit controls are used for text entry and editing. They offer a number of useful features, including built-in support for cut/copy/paste operations and an undo function. Edit controls come in two varieties: single-line and multiline. Single-line edit controls are perfect for soliciting one-line text strings such as names, passwords, and product IDs. To see what a multiline edit control looks like, check out the Windows 95 Notepad applet. The client area of the Notepad window is really a multiline edit control.

The only blemish on *CEdit*'s record is that even in Windows 95 it's limited to about 60K of text. That's not much of a restriction for single-line edit controls, but for a multiline edit control it can be severely limiting. If you need the capability to handle large amounts of text, use Windows 95's rich text edit control instead—a greatly enhanced version of the standard edit control that is part of the common controls library. Though designed to handle richly formatted text of the type seen in word processors, rich text edit controls are quite capable of handling ordinary text, too, and can even be used to convert RTF (rich text format) files into plain text. The Windows 95 WordPad applet uses a rich text edit control for text entry, so without writing a line of code you can see for yourself the kinds of features rich text edit controls have to offer.

Creating an Edit Control

Once a *CEdit* object is constructed, an edit control is created and attached with *CEdit::Create*. If *m_ctlEdit* is a *CEdit* object, the statement

```
m_ctlEdit.Create (WS_CHILD | WS_VISIBLE | WS_BORDER |
    ES_AUTOHSCROLL, rect, this, IDC_EDIT);
```

creates a single-line edit control that automatically scrolls horizontally when the caret moves beyond the control's border. WS_BORDER draws a border around the control; without this style, the border is invisible. Like list box controls, Windows 95 edit controls are drawn with flat borders if they are created outside a dialog box unless they are created with the style WS_EX_CLIENTEDGE. Therefore, if you want to create a single-line edit control with a 3D border in a top-level window, do it this way:

```
m_ctlEdit.CreateEx (WS_EX_CLIENTEDGE, "EDIT", NULL,
    WS_CHILD | WS_VISIBLE | WS_BORDER | ES_AUTOHSCROLL,
    x, y, cx, cy, m_hWnd, (HMENU) IDC_EDIT);
```

m_hWnd is the window handle of the window referenced by the *this* pointer. *x* and *y* are the coordinates (relative to the upper left corner of the parent's client area) of the control's upper left corner, and *cx* and *cy* are the control's width and height in pixels. A single-line edit control generally looks best when the height of the control rectangle is $1\frac{3}{4}$ to 2 times the height of a character in the current control font.

A multiline edit control is created by specifying the style ES_MULTILINE, as in

```
m_edit.Create (WS_CHILD | WS_VISIBLE | WS_BORDER |
    WS_HSCROLL | WS_VSCROLL | ES_AUTOHSCROLL | ES_AUTOVSCROLL,
    rect, this, IDC_EDIT);
```

The WS_HSCROLL and WS_VSCROLL styles add horizontal and vertical scroll bars to the control, while ES_AUTOHSCROLL and ES_AUTOVSCROLL add horizontal and vertical scrolling capabilities. If you omit ES_AUTOVSCROLL, the user will be limited to entering the number of lines the height of the control allows. Omit ES_AUTOHSCROLL, and line lengths will be limited by the width of the control. You can use *CEdit::SetRect* or *CEdit::SetRectNP* to specify a formatting rectangle that defines the boundaries of text entry independent of the control's boundaries. One use for these functions is to define a "page size" that remains constant even if the control is resized. You can also use *CEdit::SetMargins* (new in Windows 95) to specify left and right margin widths in pixels. The default margin widths are 0. The table below shows the styles that apply to edit controls. ES_LEFT, ES_CENTER, and ES_RIGHT specify the text alignment. The default is ES_LEFT. The alignment style applies to *all* the text in the edit control; you can't vary the alignment of individual lines or paragraphs in a multiline edit control as you can in a rich text edit control. ES_UPPERCASE and ES_LOWERCASE force all text entered in an edit control to upper and lower case, respectively. ES_PASSWORD creates a password-style edit control that displays asterisks rather than the characters that are typed. If you want to, you can replace the asterisks with the character of your choice with *CEdit::SetPasswordChar*. ES_READONLY creates a read-only edit control in which text can be displayed but not edited. Once the control is created, you can turn the read-only flag on and off with the *CEdit::SetReadOnly* function.

EDIT CONTROL STYLES

Style	*Description*
ES_LEFT	An edit control with left-aligned text.
ES_CENTER	An edit control with centered text.
ES_RIGHT	An edit control with right-aligned text.
ES_AUTOHSCROLL	An edit control that scrolls horizontally. To add a horizontal scroll bar, include the style WS_HSCROLL when you create the control.
ES_AUTOVSCROLL	An edit control that scrolls vertically. To add a vertical scroll bar, include the style WS_VSCROLL when you create the control.
ES_MULTILINE	A multiline edit control.
ES_LOWERCASE	An edit control that displays all characters in lowercase.
ES_UPPERCASE	An edit control that displays all characters in uppercase.
ES_PASSWORD	A password-style edit control that displays asterisks instead of typed characters.
ES_READONLY	A read-only edit control whose text cannot be edited.
ES_NOHIDESEL	An edit control that doesn't hide text selections when it loses the input focus.
ES_OEMCONVERT	An edit control that performs an ANSI-to-OEM-to-ANSI conversion on all characters so that the application won't get unexpected results if it performs an ANSI-to-OEM conversion of its own. Normally used for single-line edit controls that accept file names.
ES_WANTRETURN	A multiline edit control in a dialog box in which the Enter key breaks lines instead of invoking the dialog box's default push button.

By default, an edit control with a highlighted text selection temporarily deselects the text, or "hides" the selection, when it loses the input focus, and it restores the selection when it regains the input focus. If you want text selections to be displayed at all times, even when the control doesn't own the input focus, use the style ES_NOHIDESEL. ES_OEMCONVERT is handy for single-line edit controls that accept file names. It creates a control that converts each character entered into it from the ANSI character set to the OEM character set and back to ANSI again, which ensures that the application won't get unexpected results if it performs an ANSI-to-OEM conversion of its own. ES_WANTRETURN specifies that presses of the Enter key should break lines in multiline edit controls used in dialog boxes. If this style is omitted, the Enter key will invoke the dialog box's default push button rather than break a line when the control has the input focus.

When an edit control is first created, the limit on the number of characters it will accept is about 30,000. You can set the limit higher or lower with *CEdit::LimitText* or the new Win32-specific *CEdit::SetLimitText*. The following statement sets the maximum number of characters that an edit control will accept to 32:

```
m_ctlEdit.SetLimitText (32);
```

When used with a multiline edit control, *SetLimitText* limits the total amount of text entered into the control, not the length of each line. There is no built-in way to limit the number of characters per line in a multiline edit control, but there are ways you can do it yourself. One approach is to use *SetFont* to switch the edit control font to a fixed-pitch font and *CEdit::SetRect* to specify a formatting rectangle whose width is slightly greater than the width of a character times the desired number of characters per line.

Another function sometimes used to initialize a freshly created edit control is *CEdit::SetTabStops*, which sets the spacing between tab stops. Default tab stops are set about eight character widths apart. You can change the tab stop setting to anything you like and even vary the spacing between tab stops. Like *CListBox::SetTabStops*, *CEdit::SetTabStops* measures distances in *dialog units*. One dialog unit is approximately equal to one-fourth the average width of a character in the system font. The statement

```
m_ctlEdit.SetTabStops (64);
```

expands the space between tab stops from 32 (the default) to 64 dialog units, while

```
int nTabStops[] = { 32, 48, 64, 128 };
m_ctlEdit.SetTabStops (4, nTabStops);
```

sets variable tab stops at 32, 48, 64, and 128 dialog units.

Inserting and Retrieving Text

The text of an edit control is set and retrieved with the *SetWindowText* and *GetWindowText* functions the control inherits from *CWnd*. The statement

```
m_ctlEdit.SetWindowText ("Hello, MFC");
```

inserts the text string "Hello, MFC" into the edit control associated with *m_ctlEdit*, while

```
m_ctlEdit.GetWindowText (string);
```

retrieves the text into a *CString* object named *string*. *GetWindowText* and *SetWindowText* work with both single-line and multiline edit controls. Text inserted with *SetWindowText* replaces any text already present in the control, and *GetWindowText* returns all the text in the edit control, even if the text spans multiple lines. To erase all the text in an edit control, call *SetWindowText* with a null string:

```
m_ctlEdit.SetWindowText ("");
```

You can insert text into an edit control without erasing what's already there with *CEdit::ReplaceSel*. If one or more characters are selected when *ReplaceSel* is called, the inserted text replaces the selected text; otherwise, the new text is inserted at the current caret position.

A multiline edit control automatically breaks a line before a word that would extend beyond the right border of the current formatting rectangle. If you'd like to know where the line breaks are in text retrieved from a multiline edit control with *GetWindowText*, call *CEdit::FmtLines* as shown here:

```
m_ctlEdit.FmtLines (TRUE);
```

When the line formatting feature is on, lines are delimited with soft line breaks—two carriage returns (ASCII 13) followed by a line feed character (ASCII 10). To disable soft line breaks, call *FmtLines* with a FALSE parameter:

```
m_ctlEdit.FmtLines (FALSE);
```

Now word wrap line breaks won't be denoted in any special way. Hard returns—line breaks inserted manually when the user presses the Enter key—are signified by single carriage return/line feed pairs regardless of the *FmtLines* setting. *FmtLines* doesn't affect the appearance of the text in a multiline edit control. It affects only the way in which the control stores text internally and the format of text retrieved with *GetWindowText*.

To read just one line of text from a multiline edit control, use *CEdit::GetLine*. *GetLine* copies the contents of a line to a buffer whose address you provide. The line is identified with a 0-based index. The statement

```
m_ctlEdit.GetLine (0, pBuffer, sizeof (pBuffer));
```

copies the first line of text in a multiline edit control to the buffer pointed to by *pBuffer*. The third parameter is the maximum number of bytes to be copied. *GetLine* returns the number of characters copied to the buffer. The return value is important because the text copied to the buffer is not delimited with a 0 as a conventional C/C++ string is. Without the return value, you wouldn't know where the string ends. You can determine how much buffer space you need before retrieving a line with *CEdit::Line-Length*. And you can find out how many lines of text a multiline edit control contains by calling *CEdit::GetLineCount*. Note that *GetLineCount* never returns 0; the return value is 1 even if no text has been entered.

Clear, Cut, Copy, Paste, and Undo

CEdit provides easy-to-use member functions that perform the programmatic equivalents of the Clear, Cut, Copy, Paste, and Undo items in an application's Edit menu. The statement

```
m_ctlEdit.Clear ();
```

removes the selected text without affecting what's in the clipboard. The statement

```
m_ctlEdit.Cut ();
```

removes the selected text and copies it to the clipboard. And the statement

```
m_ctlEdit.Copy ();
```

copies the selected text to the clipboard without altering the contents of the edit control. You can query the control for the current selection by calling *CEdit::GetSel*, which returns a DWORD value with two packed 16-bit integers specifying the indexes of the beginning and ending characters in the selection. An alternate form of *GetSel* copies the indexes to a pair of integers whose addresses are passed by reference. If the indexes are equal, then no text is currently selected. The following *IsTextSelected* function, which you might add to a custom edit control derived from *CEdit*, returns a nonzero value if a selection exists and 0 if it does not:

```
BOOL CMyEdit::IsTextSelected ()
{
    int nStart, nEnd;
    GetSel (nStart, nEnd);
    return (nStart != nEnd);
}
```

CEdit::Cut and *CEdit::Copy* do nothing if no text is selected.

Text can be selected programmatically with *CEdit::SetSel*. The statement

```
m_ctlEdit.SetSel (100, 149);
```

selects 50 characters beginning with the 101st (the character whose 0-based index is 100) and scrolls the selection into view if it isn't visible already. To prevent scrolling, include a third parameter and set it equal to TRUE. When you're selecting text in a multiline edit control, it is often necessary to convert a line number and possibly an offset within that line into an index that can be passed to *SetSel*. *CEdit::LineIndex* accepts a 0-based line number and returns the index of the first character in that line. The code fragment at the top of the next page uses *LineIndex* to determine the index of the first character in the eighth line of a multiline edit control, *LineLength* to retrieve the line's length, and *SetSel* to select everything on that line:

```
int nStart = m_ctlEdit.LineIndex (7);
int nLength = m_ctlEdit.LineLength (7);
m_ctlEdit.SetSel (nStart, nStart + nLength - 1);
```

CEdit also provides a function named *LineFromChar* for computing a line number from a character index.

Text is pasted into an edit control with *CEdit::Paste*. The following statement pastes the text currently in the Windows clipboard into an edit control named *m_ctlEdit*:

```
m_ctlEdit.Paste ();
```

If the clipboard contains no text, *CEdit::Paste* does nothing. If no text is selected when *Paste* is called, the clipboard text is inserted at the current caret position. If a selection exists, the text retrieved from the clipboard replaces the text selected in the control. You can determine ahead of time whether the clipboard contains any text (and therefore whether the *Paste* function will actually do anything) by calling *::IsClipboardFormatAvailable* from the Windows API. The statement

```
BOOL bCanPaste = ::IsClipboardFormatAvailable (CF_TEXT);
```

sets *bCanPaste* to TRUE if text is available in the clipboard, and FALSE if it is not.

Edit controls also feature a built-in undo capability that "rolls back" the previous editing operation. The statement

```
m_ctlEdit.Undo ();
```

undoes the last operation, provided that operation can be undone. You can determine ahead of time whether calling *Undo* will accomplish anything with *CEdit::CanUndo*. A related function, *CEdit::EmptyUndoBuffer*, manually resets the undo flag so that subsequent calls to *Undo* will do nothing (and calls to *CanUndo* will return FALSE) until after another editing operation has been performed.

Edit Control Notifications

Edit controls send notifications to their parents to report various events. In MFC applications, these notifications are mapped to handling functions with ON_EN message map macros. Edit control notifications and the corresponding message map macros are summarized in the table on the facing page.

One common use for the EN_CHANGE notification is to update the states of other controls to keep them in sync with the state of an edit control. Suppose, for example, that you create an electronic order form in which the user enters a name, an address, a phone number, and other information in fields formed from single-line edit controls. Once the information is filled in, the user clicks a push button to place the order. You can do without the name and address if you have to, but it's essential that the phone

EDIT CONTROL NOTIFICATIONS

Notification	Sent When	Message Map Macro
EN_UPDATE	The text inside an edit control is about to change.	ON_EN_UPDATE
EN_CHANGE	The text inside an edit control has changed.	ON_EN_CHANGE
EN_KILLFOCUS	The edit control loses the input focus.	ON_EN_KILLFOCUS
EN_SETFOCUS	The edit control receives the input focus.	ON_EN_SETFOCUS
EN_HSCROLL	The edit control is scrolled horizontally using a scroll bar.	ON_EN_HSCROLL
EN_VSCROLL	The edit control is scrolled vertically using a scroll bar.	ON_EN_VSCROLL
EN_MAXTEXT	A character can't be entered because the edit control already contains the number of characters specified with *CEdit::LimitText* or *CEdit::SetLimitText*. Also sent if a character can't be entered because the caret is at the right or bottom edge of the control's formatting rectangle and the control lacks the style ES_AUTOHSCROLL or ES_AUTOVSCROLL.	ON_EN_MAXTEXT
EN_ERRSPACE	A text insertion or other editing operation has failed because of insufficient memory.	ON_EN_ERRSPACE

number field not be left blank. You could check the phone number field when the push button is clicked and display an error message if the field is empty. A better solution, however, is to provide interactive feedback by selectively enabling and disabling the push button control depending on the contents of the phone number edit control. If the edit control holding the phone number is empty, the push button is disabled. But if the edit control contains text, the push button is enabled. This way, the order can't be placed until a phone number is filled in.

Assuming that the push button is *m_ctlPushButton*, that the edit control is *m_ctlPhoneNumber*, that the edit control's ID is IDC_PHONE, and that the parent of both controls is *CMainWindow*, the following code dynamically enables and disables the push button as characters are added to and removed from the phone number:

```
// In the message map
ON_EN_CHANGE (IDC_PHONE, OnUpdateButton)
    .
    .
    .
void CMainWindow::OnUpdateButton ()
{
    m_ctlPushButton.EnableWindow (m_ctlPhoneNumber.LineLength ());
}
```

291

When the text in the edit control changes, *OnUpdateButton* uses *CEdit::LineLength* to obtain a character count. The push button is enabled if the count is nonzero or disabled if *LineLength* returns 0. From the user's perspective, the push button lights up when a character is entered in the phone number field and grays out again if the phone number is subsequently erased. You could key the state of the push button to multiple edit controls by supplying an ON_EN_CHANGE message map entry for each one and writing *OnUpdateButton* so that it checks all the edit controls.

Presto! Instant Notepad

The CtlDemo1 application listed in Figure 5-3 uses a multiline edit control to create a near clone of the Windows 95 Notepad. As you can see from the source code, the edit control does the bulk of the work. *CEdit* functions such as *Undo* and *Cut* implement the commands in the application's Edit menu, while *CMainWindow::IsText-Selected* provides the logic for updating the Cut, Copy, and Delete items in the Edit menu depending on the current selection state. The value returned by the Windows API function *::IsClipboardFormatAvailable* is used to update the Paste item depending on whether either Cut or Copy has been selected. CtlDemo1 also uses *CEdit-::SetMargins* to create 8-pixel-wide margins between the text displayed by the control and the control's left and right borders.

Note the use of an *OnSize* handler to key the size of the edit control to the size of the frame window. The edit control's height and width are initially set to 0, but when the first WM_SIZE message arrives (and each time a WM_SIZE message is received thereafter), the control is resized to fill the client area of its parent. A one-line *OnSetFocus* handler shifts the input focus to the edit control anytime the focus goes to *CMainWindow*.

Resource.h

```
//*********************************************************************
//
//  Resource.h
//
//*********************************************************************

#define IDR_MAINFRAME          100

#define IDM_FILE_NEW           110
#define IDM_FILE_EXIT          111
```

Figure 5-3. *The CtlDemo1 source code.*

```
#define IDM_EDIT_UNDO           120
#define IDM_EDIT_CUT            121
#define IDM_EDIT_COPY           122
#define IDM_EDIT_PASTE          123
#define IDM_EDIT_DELETE         124


#define IDC_EDIT                130
```

CtlDemo1.rc

```
//******************************************************************************
//
//  CtlDemo1.rc
//
//******************************************************************************

#include <afxres.h>
#include "Resource.h"

IDR_MAINFRAME MENU
BEGIN
    POPUP "&File" {
        MENUITEM "&New\tCtrl+N",        IDM_FILE_NEW
        MENUITEM SEPARATOR
        MENUITEM "E&xit",               IDM_FILE_EXIT
    }
    POPUP "&Edit" {
        MENUITEM "&Undo\tCtrl+Z",       IDM_EDIT_UNDO
        MENUITEM SEPARATOR
        MENUITEM "Cu&t\tCtrl+X",        IDM_EDIT_CUT
        MENUITEM "&Copy\tCtrl+C",       IDM_EDIT_COPY
        MENUITEM "&Paste\tCtrl+V",      IDM_EDIT_PASTE
        MENUITEM "&Delete\tDel",        IDM_EDIT_DELETE
    }
END

IDR_MAINFRAME ACCELERATORS
BEGIN
    "N",    IDM_FILE_NEW,       VIRTKEY,    CONTROL
END
```

(continued)

CtlDemo1.h

```
//***********************************************************************
//
// CtlDemo1.h
//
//***********************************************************************

class CMyApp : public CWinApp
{
public:
    virtual BOOL InitInstance ();
};

class CMainWindow : public CFrameWnd
{
private:
    CEdit m_ctlEdit;

    BOOL IsTextSelected ();

public:
    CMainWindow ();

protected:
    afx_msg int OnCreate (LPCREATESTRUCT);
    afx_msg void OnSize (UINT, int, int);
    afx_msg void OnSetFocus (CWnd*);
    afx_msg void OnFileNew ();
    afx_msg void OnFileExit ();
    afx_msg void OnEditUndo ();
    afx_msg void OnEditCut ();
    afx_msg void OnEditCopy ();
    afx_msg void OnEditPaste ();
    afx_msg void OnEditDelete ();
    afx_msg void OnUpdateEditUndoUI (CCmdUI*);
    afx_msg void OnUpdateEditCutUI (CCmdUI*);
    afx_msg void OnUpdateEditCopyUI (CCmdUI*);
    afx_msg void OnUpdateEditPasteUI (CCmdUI*);
    afx_msg void OnUpdateEditDeleteUI (CCmdUI*);

    DECLARE_MESSAGE_MAP ()
};
```

CtlDemo1.cpp

```cpp
//****************************************************************
//
//  CtlDemo1.cpp
//
//****************************************************************

#include <afxwin.h>
#include "Resource.h"
#include "CtlDemo1.h"

CMyApp myApp;

///////////////////////////////////////////////////////////////
// CMyApp member functions

BOOL CMyApp::InitInstance ()
{
    m_pMainWnd = new CMainWindow;
    m_pMainWnd->ShowWindow (m_nCmdShow);
    m_pMainWnd->UpdateWindow ();
    return TRUE;
}

///////////////////////////////////////////////////////////////
// CMainWindow message map and member functions

BEGIN_MESSAGE_MAP (CMainWindow, CFrameWnd)
    ON_WM_CREATE ()
    ON_WM_SIZE ()
    ON_WM_SETFOCUS ()
    ON_COMMAND (IDM_FILE_NEW, OnFileNew)
    ON_COMMAND (IDM_FILE_EXIT, OnFileExit)
    ON_COMMAND (IDM_EDIT_UNDO, OnEditUndo)
    ON_COMMAND (IDM_EDIT_CUT, OnEditCut)
    ON_COMMAND (IDM_EDIT_COPY, OnEditCopy)
    ON_COMMAND (IDM_EDIT_PASTE, OnEditPaste)
    ON_COMMAND (IDM_EDIT_DELETE, OnEditDelete)
    ON_UPDATE_COMMAND_UI (IDM_EDIT_UNDO, OnUpdateEditUndoUI)
    ON_UPDATE_COMMAND_UI (IDM_EDIT_CUT, OnUpdateEditCutUI)
    ON_UPDATE_COMMAND_UI (IDM_EDIT_COPY, OnUpdateEditCopyUI)
    ON_UPDATE_COMMAND_UI (IDM_EDIT_PASTE, OnUpdateEditPasteUI)
    ON_UPDATE_COMMAND_UI (IDM_EDIT_DELETE, OnUpdateEditDeleteUI)
END_MESSAGE_MAP ()
```

(continued)

CtlDemo1.cpp *continued*

```cpp
CMainWindow::CMainWindow ()
{
    Create (NULL, "CtlDemo1", WS_OVERLAPPEDWINDOW,
        rectDefault, NULL, MAKEINTRESOURCE (IDR_MAINFRAME));

    LoadAccelTable (MAKEINTRESOURCE (IDR_MAINFRAME));
}

int CMainWindow::OnCreate (LPCREATESTRUCT lpcs)
{
    if (CFrameWnd::OnCreate (lpcs) == -1)
        return -1;

    m_ctlEdit.Create (WS_CHILD | WS_VISIBLE | WS_VSCROLL | ES_MULTILINE |
        ES_AUTOVSCROLL, CRect (0, 0, 0, 0), this, IDC_EDIT);

    m_ctlEdit.SetMargins (8, 8);
    return 0;
}

void CMainWindow::OnSize (UINT nType, int cx, int cy)
{
    CFrameWnd::OnSize (nType, cx, cy);
    m_ctlEdit.MoveWindow (0, 0, cx, cy);
}

void CMainWindow::OnSetFocus (CWnd* pOldWnd)
{
    m_ctlEdit.SetFocus ();
}

void CMainWindow::OnFileNew ()
{
    m_ctlEdit.SetWindowText ("");
}

void CMainWindow::OnFileExit ()
{
    SendMessage (WM_CLOSE, 0, 0);
}

void CMainWindow::OnEditUndo ()
{
    m_ctlEdit.Undo ();
}
```

```
void CMainWindow::OnEditCut ()
{
    m_ctlEdit.Cut ();
}

void CMainWindow::OnEditCopy ()
{
    m_ctlEdit.Copy ();
}

void CMainWindow::OnEditPaste ()
{
    m_ctlEdit.Paste ();
}

void CMainWindow::OnEditDelete ()
{
    m_ctlEdit.Clear ();
}

void CMainWindow::OnUpdateEditUndoUI (CCmdUI* pCmdUI)
{
    pCmdUI->Enable (m_ctlEdit.CanUndo ());
}

void CMainWindow::OnUpdateEditCutUI (CCmdUI* pCmdUI)
{
    pCmdUI->Enable (IsTextSelected ());
}

void CMainWindow::OnUpdateEditCopyUI (CCmdUI* pCmdUI)
{
    pCmdUI->Enable (IsTextSelected ());
}

void CMainWindow::OnUpdateEditPasteUI (CCmdUI* pCmdUI)
{
    pCmdUI->Enable (::IsClipboardFormatAvailable (CF_TEXT));
}

void CMainWindow::OnUpdateEditDeleteUI (CCmdUI* pCmdUI)
{
    pCmdUI->Enable (IsTextSelected ());
}
```

(continued)

CtlDemo1.cpp *continued*

```
BOOL CMainWindow::IsTextSelected ()
{
    int nStart, nEnd;
    m_ctlEdit.GetSel (nStart, nEnd);
    return (nStart != nEnd);
}
```

The *CComboBox* Class

The combo box control combines a single-line edit control and a list box into one convenient package. Combo boxes are created from the Windows predefined "COMBO-BOX" class. In MFC, of course, you can construct a *CComboBox* object and create a combo box control to go with it by means of *CComboBox::Create.*

A combo box is basically an edit control sitting on top of a list box. Combo boxes come in three varieties: simple, drop-down, and drop-down list, corresponding to the styles CBS_SIMPLE, CBS_DROPDOWN, and CBS_DROPDOWNLIST. In a simple combo box, the list box is permanently displayed. When the user selects an item from the list box, the item is automatically copied to the edit control. Text may also be typed into a simple combo box's edit control. If the text entered by the user matches an item in the list box, the item is automatically highlighted and scrolled into view. A drop-down combo box is similar to a simple combo box, but the list box is displayed only when the user clicks the downward-pointing arrow to the right of the edit control or presses the equivalent key or key combination while the combo box has the input focus. A drop-down list combo box works the same way but doesn't allow text to be typed into the edit control. This effectively restricts the user's selection to items appearing in the list box.

The full range of combo box control styles is shown in the table on the facing page. Many of these styles will look familiar because they're patterned after list box and edit control styles. CBS_AUTOHSCROLL, for example, does the same thing for the edit control attached to a combo box control that ES_AUTOHSCROLL does for an independent edit control: it enables horizontal scrolling so that text entered into the control isn't limited by the boundaries of the control itself. When you create a combo box control, don't forget to include the style WS_VSCROLL if you want the list box to have a vertical scroll bar, and WS_BORDER if you want the control to have a visible border. The statement

```
    m_ctlComboBox.Create (WS_CHILD | WS_VISIBLE | WS_BORDER |
        WS_VSCROLL | CBS_DROPDOWNLIST | CBS_SORT, rect, this,
        IDC_COMBOBOX);
```

creates a drop-down list combo box whose list box contains a vertical scroll bar when the number of items in the list box exceeds the number of items that can be displayed, and that automatically sorts the items added to it. The control rectangle you specify in the call to *CComboBox::Create* should be large enough to encompass the list box part of the control as well as the edit box.

COMBO BOX STYLES

Style	Description
CBS_AUTOHSCROLL	A combo box whose edit control scrolls horizontally.
CBS_DISABLENOSCROLL	A combo box whose scroll bar is displayed in a disabled state when the list box doesn't contain enough items for scrolling to be enabled. By default, the scroll bar is hidden when it isn't needed.
CBS_DROPDOWN	A drop-down combo box.
CBS_DROPDOWNLIST	A drop-down list combo box.
CBS_HASSTRINGS	A combo box that "remembers" the strings added to it. Conventional combo boxes have this style by default; owner-drawn combo boxes do not.
CBS_LOWERCASE	A combo box that displays only lowercase text.
CBS_NOINTEGRALHEIGHT	A combo box whose list box height doesn't have to be an exact multiple of the item height.
CBS_OEMCONVERT	A combo box whose edit control performs an ANSI-to-OEM-to-ANSI conversion on all characters so that the application won't get unexpected results if it performs an ANSI-to-OEM conversion of its own. Normally used for file names.
CBS_OWNERDRAWFIXED	An owner-drawn combo box whose items are all the same height.
CBS_OWNERDRAWVARIABLE	An owner-drawn combo box whose items vary in height.
CBS_SIMPLE	A simple combo box.
CBS_SORT	A combo box whose list box items are sorted as they are added.
CBS_UPPERCASE	A combo box that displays only uppercase text.

Combo Box Operations

Not surprisingly, the list of *CComboBox* member functions reads a lot like the function lists for *CEdit* and *CListBox*. Strings are added to a combo box's list box, for example, with *CComboBox::AddString* and *CComboBox::InsertString*, and the maximum character count for a combo box's edit control is set with *CComboBox::LimitText*. The

GetWindowText and *SetWindowText* functions inherited from *CWnd* get and set the text in the edit control, as you might expect. Functions unique to combo boxes include *GetLBText*, which retrieves the text of an item identified by a 0-based index; *GetLBTextLen*, which returns the length of an item; *ShowDropDown*, which hides or displays the list box for a drop-down list box or a drop-down list combo box; and *GetDroppedState*, which returns a value indicating whether the list box is currently dropped down. The special *SetExtendedUI* function enables and disables a drop-down list box's or a drop-down list combo box's extended user interface. The extended user interface differs from the "default" user interface in the following respects:

- Normally, clicking a combo box displays the drop-down list box. When the extended user interface is in effect, however, clicking displays the drop-down list box for CBS_DROPDOWNLIST-style combo boxes only.

- By default, pressing F4 or Alt and the down arrow key when the combo box has the input focus displays the drop-down list, and pressing the down arrow key by itself "scrolls" through the items in the list box, displaying them one after another in the edit box. When the extended user interface is active, F4 is disabled and the down arrow key drops down the list box.

Normally, you should use the extended UI unless there is a specific reason not to. You can determine which user interface is in effect at any time with *CComboBox-::GetExtendedUI*.

Combo Box Notifications

Combo boxes send notifications to their parents much as edit controls and list boxes do. The table on the facing page lists the notifications the parent can expect, the corresponding MFC message map macros, and the types of combo boxes the notifications apply to.

Not all notifications apply to all combo box types. CBN_DROPDOWN and CBN_CLOSEUP notifications, for example, are not sent to CBS_SIMPLE combo boxes because the list box attached to a simple combo box doesn't drop down or close up. By the same token, CBS_DROPDOWN and CBS_DROPDOWNLIST-style combo boxes don't receive CBN_DBLCLK notifications because items appearing in a drop-down list can't be double-clicked. (Why? Because the list box closes after the first click.) CBN_EDITUPDATE and CBN_EDITCHANGE notifications are equivalent to EN_UPDATE and EN_CHANGE notifications sent by edit controls, and CBN_SELCHANGE is to combo boxes as LBN_SELCHANGE is to list boxes.

One nuance you should be aware of when processing CBN_SELCHANGE notifications is that when a notification arrives, the edit control has not been updated to match the list box selection. Therefore, you should use *GetLBText* to retrieve the newly selected text instead of *GetWindowText*. You can get the index of the selected item with *CComboBox::GetCurSel*.

COMBO BOX NOTIFICATIONS

Notification	Message Map Macro	Simple	Drop-Down	Drop-Down List
CBN_DROPDOWN Sent when a combo box's drop-down list box is displayed.	ON_CBN_DROPDOWN		■	■
CBN_CLOSEUP Sent when a combo box's drop-down list box is closed.	ON_CBN_CLOSEUP		■	■
CBN_DBLCLK Sent when an item in the list box is double-clicked.	ON_CBN_DBLCLK	■		
CBN_SELCHANGE Sent when the list box selection changes.	ON_CBN_SELCHANGE	■	■	■
CBN_SELENDOK Sent when a selection is made.	ON_CBN_SELENDOK	■	■	■
CBN_SELENDCANCEL Sent when a selection is canceled.	ON_CBN_SELENDCANCEL		■	■
CBN_EDITUPDATE Sent when the text in the edit control is about to change.	ON_CBN_EDITUPDATE	■	■	
CBN_EDITCHANGE Sent when the text in the edit control has changed.	ON_CBN_EDITCHANGE	■	■	
CBN_KILLFOCUS Sent when the combo box loses the input focus.	ON_CBN_KILLFOCUS	■	■	■
CBN_SETFOCUS Sent when the combo box receives the input focus.	ON_CBN_SETFOCUS	■	■	■
CBN_ERRSPACE Sent when a combo box operation has failed because of insufficient memory.	ON_CBN_ERRSPACE	■	■	■

The *CScrollBar* Class

MFC's *CScrollBar* class encapsulates scroll bar controls created from the Windows predefined "SCROLLBAR" WNDCLASS. Scroll bar controls are identical in most respects to the "window" scroll bar used in Chapter 2's GdiDemo2 application. But whereas window scroll bars are created for you, scroll bar controls are created explicitly with *CScrollBar::Create*. And while a window scroll bar runs the full length of the window's client area and is inherently glued to the window border, scroll bar controls can be placed anywhere on the window and come in all heights and widths.

Vertical scroll bars are created by specifying the style SBS_VERT, and horizontal scroll bars by specifying SBS_HORZ. The statements

```
m_ctlVScrollBar.Create (WS_CHILD | WS_VISIBLE | WS_BORDER |
    SBS_VERT, rectVert, this, IDC_VSCROLLBAR);
m_ctlHScrollBar.Create (WS_CHILD | WS_VISIBLE | WS_BORDER |
    SBS_HORZ, rectHorz, this, IDC_HSCROLLBAR);
```

create a pair of scroll bar controls, one vertical and the other horizontal. You can query Windows for the standard width of a vertical scroll bar or the standard height of a horizontal scroll bar with the *::GetSystemMetrics* API function. The following code fragment sets *nWidth* and *nHeight* to the system's standard scroll bar width and height:

```
int nWidth = ::GetSystemMetrics (SM_CXVSCROLL);
int nHeight = ::GetSystemMetrics (SM_CYHSCROLL);
```

An alternative way to create a scroll bar with a standard height or width is to specify the style SBS_TOPALIGN, SBS_BOTTOMALIGN, SBS_LEFTALIGN, or SBS_RIGHT-ALIGN when creating it. SBS_LEFTALIGN and SBS_RIGHTALIGN align a vertical scroll bar control along the left or right border of the rectangle specified in the call to *Create* and assign it a standard width. SBS_TOPALIGN and SBS_BOTTOMALIGN align a horizontal scroll bar control along the top or bottom border of the rectangle and assign it a standard height.

Unlike other controls, scroll bar controls don't communicate with their parents with WM_COMMAND messages. Instead, they send WM_VSCROLL and WM_HSCROLL messages just as window scroll bars do. As described in Chapter 2, MFC applications process these messages with *OnVScroll* and *OnHScroll* handlers. When called, these handlers receive three input parameters: a notification code specifiying the event that prompted the message, an integer specifying the new thumb position if the thumb was moved (SB_THUMBTRACK and SB_THUMBPOSITION notifications only), and a pointer to the scroll bar object that sent the message. Two notification codes were not mentioned in Chapter 2 because they apply only to scroll bar controls, and then only to scroll bar controls created with the style WS_TABSTOP. SB_TOP means that the user pressed the Home key while the scroll bar had the input focus, and

SB_BOTTOM means that the user pressed End. A scroll bar control can receive the input focus only if it is created with the style WS_TABSTOP.

CScrollBar provides a handful of member functions for manipulating scroll bars, most of which you're already familiar with because they work just as the *CWnd* functions with the same names do. *CScrollBar::GetScrollPos* and *CScrollBar::SetScrollPos* get and set the scroll bar's thumb position, while *CScrollBar::GetScrollRange* and *CScrollBar::SetScrollRange* get and set the scroll bar range. In Windows 95, use *CScrollBar::SetScrollInfo* to set the range, position, and thumb size in one step. For details, refer to the discussion of *CWnd::SetScrollInfo* in Chapter 2.

ADVANCED CONTROL PROGRAMMING

Now that you're acquainted with the MFC control classes and the controls they represent, it's time to learn about some of the tricks and techniques MFC programmers use to make the controls do their bidding. The topics we'll cover in the remainder of this chapter include:

- An easy way to add a dialog-like keyboard interface to windows containing child window controls

- Modifying a control's behavior by deriving a new control class from the corresponding MFC control class

- Owner-drawn list boxes

- Push buttons that display pictures instead of text

- Techniques for changing a control's colors

- Message reflection

One of the highlights that awaits you is an owner-drawn list box class derived from *CListBox* that displays icons rather than text strings. We'll implement the control in a window that accepts drag and drop file names and that displays icons extracted from files dropped onto the list box. You can use the icon list box class as is in other applications, or as a model for derived control classes of your own. Either way, you'll appreciate how easy it is to shape the controls and make them work the way *you* want them to work by combining the best features of C++ and MFC.

Adding a Keyboard Interface

As you experimented with the FontView application presented earlier in this chapter, you may have noticed that to move the input focus from one control to another you had to click the control with the mouse. In a dialog box, the Tab key cycles the input focus from control to control, and most controls are assigned shortcut keys consisting of Alt and a letter key. This interface is provided automatically for dialog boxes, but top-level windows don't have a built-in mechanism for moving the input focus between controls.

There are a number of ways to add a dialog-like keyboard interface to top-level windows containing child window controls. One solution is to use a dialog box as a main window, a technique you'll see demonstrated in Chapter 6. One huge advantage to using a dialog box as a main window is that the application doesn't have to create the controls itself; instead, the controls are defined in a dialog box template and Windows creates them from the resultant dialog box resource. Another solution is a technique known as *window subclassing,* in which the parent window intercepts messages intended for the controls and responds to keyboard messages signifying that the Tab key or a shortcut key was pressed by calling *SetFocus* to move the input focus from one control to the next. *CWnd*'s *GetNextDlgTabItem* function is useful in this context because it returns a pointer to the next (or previous) control in the tab order. Subclassing is performed by replacing a control's window procedure with a proxy window procedure that filters incoming messages. The new window procedure processes certain messages itself (for example, WM_CHAR messages signifying presses of the Tab key) while passing others on to the window procedure it replaced. A subclassed control therefore continues to work as normal in most respects.

Fortunately, there is an easier way—*much* easier, in fact. Simply calling *::IsDialogMessage* from the message loop before calling *TranslateMessage* and *DispatchMessage* adds the keyboard processing logic that a top-level window needs in order to behave like a dialog box. An MFC program's message loop is hidden away in the application object, but you can insert your own window-specific message processing code into the message loop just before *::TranslateMessage* and *::DispatchMessage* are called by overriding the window's *PreTranslateMessage* function as shown here:

```
BOOL CMainWindow::PreTranslateMessage (MSG* pMsg)
{
    return ::IsDialogMessage (m_hWnd, pMsg);
}
```

::IsDialogMessage accepts two parameters: the handle of the window to which the message pertains and a pointer to the MSG structure containing the message. The window handle is obtained from the *m_hWnd* data member of the window object; the MSG pointer is obtained from *PreTranslateMessage*'s argument list. *PreTranslateMessage* returns a Boolean value telling the framework whether the message was processed. A nonzero return indicates that the message has been processed, which causes the framework to skip calls to *::TranslateMessage* and *::DispatchMessage*. If *PreTranslateMessage* returns 0, then the framework translates and dispatches the

message in the normal way. It just so happens that *::IsDialogMessage* returns a non-zero value if it processed the message and 0 if it didn't, so you can use the value returned by *::IsDialogMessage* as the return value for *PreTranslateMessage*.

Adding *::IsDialogMessage* to the message loop is simple enough, but there's one other thing you must do to make the keyboard interface work. A control can't be tabbed to if it wasn't created with the style WS_TABSTOP, so you must add WS-_TABSTOP to all the controls you want to include in the tab order. The order in which the input focus is passed between WS_TABSTOP controls is identical to the order in which the controls were created. Static controls and group boxes don't receive the input focus, so don't use WS_TABSTOP with these types of controls. If your top-level window includes radio button controls, use the WS_GROUP style to group them as described earlier, and with *::IsDialogMessage* in the message loop, the up and down arrow keys will move the selection within the group when one of the radio buttons has the input focus.

::IsDialogMessage also makes it possible to assign shortcut keys to individual controls. Creating a shortcut key is a simple operation. For *CButton* controls, identify the shortcut key by putting an ampersand in front of a character in the control's text. The user's typing that character at the keyboard with the Alt key held down will then "click" the button. The statement

```
m_ctlPushButton.Create ("&Print", WS_CHILD | WS_VISIBLE |
    WS_TABSTOP | BS_PUSHBUTTON, rect, this, IDC_PRINT);
```

creates a push button control labeled "Print" that responds to presses of Alt-P. Windows underlines the P on the face of the button to identify it as a shortcut. The WS_TABSTOP style enables the button to be tabbed to with the Tab key as well. For non-*CButton* controls, you can't specify a shortcut key directly because the *Create* function doesn't accept any control text. But you can create a shortcut key indirectly by labeling the control with a static control and including an ampersand in the static control's text. The statements

```
m_ctlLabel.Create ("&Name", WS_CHILD | WS_VISIBLE | SS_LEFT,
    rectStatic, this);

m_edit.Create (WS_CHILD | WS_VISIBLE | WS_BORDER | WS_TABSTOP |
    ES_AUTOHSCROLL, rectEdit, this, IDC_NAME);
```

create an edit control that receives the input focus when Alt-N is pressed. When *::IsDialogMessage* sees that Alt-N has been pressed and determines that the shortcut key belongs to a static control, it passes the input focus to the next WS_TABSTOP-style control. Therefore, the edit control must be created immediately after the static control in order for the shortcut to work.

Modifying Control Behavior

One advantage to using MFC's control classes (besides their provision of an object-oriented interface to the controls) is that you can use the control classes as base classes and derive control classes of your own. By adding new member functions to a derived class or overriding member functions inherited from the base class, you can modify the control's behavior while leaving other aspects of its operation fundamentally unchanged.

A perfect example of a derived control class is a phone number edit control. An edit control normally accepts a wide range of characters, including letters of the alphabet and punctuation symbols, but a phone number contains numbers, hyphens, and parentheses. Ideally, a phone number edit control should reject invalid characters and accept only those that might reasonably make sense in a phone number.

Creating a phone number edit control is no big deal in an MFC application since the basic features of an edit control are defined in *CEdit*. Thanks to the class inheritance features of C++ and the message mapping ability of MFC, we can freely derive a control class from *CEdit* and supply custom message handlers to change the way an edit control responds to input. The following *CNumEdit* class creates an edit control that accepts numbers, hyphens, spaces, and parentheses but rejects any other characters.

```
class CNumEdit : public CEdit
{
protected:
    afx_msg void OnChar (UINT, UINT, UINT);
    DECLARE_MESSAGE_MAP ()
};

BEGIN_MESSAGE_MAP (CNumEdit, CEdit)
    ON_WM_CHAR ()
END_MESSAGE_MAP ()

void CNumEdit::OnChar (UINT nChar, UINT nRepCnt, UINT nFlags)
{
    if (((nChar >= '0') && (nChar <= '9')) ||
        (nChar == VK_BACK) || (nChar == '(') || (nChar == ')') ||
        (nChar == '-') || (nChar == ' '))

        CEdit::OnChar (nChar, nRepCnt, nFlags);
}
```

How does *CNumEdit* work? When an edit control has the input focus and a character key is pressed, the control's window procedure receives a WM_CHAR message. By deriving a new class from *CEdit*, mapping WM_CHAR messages to our own *OnChar* handler, and designing *OnChar* so that it passes WM_CHAR messages to the base class only if the character encoded in the message is one the modified control will accept, we can create an edit control that rejects invalid characters. Note that VK_BACK is included in the list of character codes that *OnChar* passes to the base class so that the Backspace key won't cease to function. It's not necessary to test for other editing keys such as Home and Del because they, unlike the Backspace key, don't generate WM_CHAR messages.

The CtlDemo2 application in Figure 5-4 creates two single-line edit controls: one a *CEdit* and the other a *CNumEdit*. You can type anything you like into the *CEdit* control, but the *CNumEdit* control accepts only numbers, spaces, hyphens, and parentheses. CtlDemo2's *CMainWindow* class also overrides *PreTranslateMessage* and uses *::IsDialogMessage* to implement a dialog-like keyboard interface. You can tab between the edit controls by pressing the Tab key or Shift-Tab. Because of the shortcut characters defined in the static controls that serve as labels for the edit controls, you can also move the input focus with Alt-S (Standard) and Alt-N (Numeric). Both edit controls are assigned the style WS_EX_CLIENTEDGE so that they'll have sunken rather than flat borders. And both are assigned the font 8-point MS Sans Serif so that they'll look like other Windows 95 edit controls.

CtlDemo2.h

```
//*************************************************************************
//
//  CtlDemo2.h
//
//*************************************************************************

class CNumEdit : public CEdit
{
protected:
    afx_msg void OnChar (UINT, UINT, UINT);
    DECLARE_MESSAGE_MAP ()
};

class CMyApp : public CWinApp
{
public:
    virtual BOOL InitInstance ();
};

class CMainWindow : public CFrameWnd
{
private:
    int m_cxChar;
    int m_cyChar;
    CFont m_font;
```

Figure 5-4. *The CtlDemo2 source code.* *(continued)*

CtlDemo2.h *continued*

```
    CStatic m_ctlLabel1;
    CStatic m_ctlLabel2;
    CEdit m_ctlStdEdit;
    CNumEdit m_ctlNumEdit;

public:
    CMainWindow ();

    virtual BOOL PreTranslateMessage (MSG*);

protected:
    afx_msg int OnCreate (LPCREATESTRUCT);
    DECLARE_MESSAGE_MAP ()
};
```

CtlDemo2.cpp

```
//*********************************************************************
//
// CtlDemo2.cpp
//
//*********************************************************************

#include <afxwin.h>
#include "CtlDemo2.h"

#define IDC_STDEDIT 100
#define IDC_NUMEDIT 101

CMyApp myApp;

/////////////////////////////////////////////////////////////////////
// CMyApp member functions

BOOL CMyApp::InitInstance ()
{
    m_pMainWnd = new CMainWindow;
    m_pMainWnd->ShowWindow (m_nCmdShow);
    m_pMainWnd->UpdateWindow ();
    return TRUE;
}
```

```
///////////////////////////////////////////////////////////////////////
// CMainWindow message map and member functions

BEGIN_MESSAGE_MAP (CMainWindow, CFrameWnd)
    ON_WM_CREATE ()
END_MESSAGE_MAP ()

CMainWindow::CMainWindow ()
{
    CString strWndClass = AfxRegisterWndClass (
        0,
        myApp.LoadStandardCursor (IDC_ARROW),
        (HBRUSH) (COLOR_3DFACE + 1),
        myApp.LoadStandardIcon (IDI_APPLICATION)
    );

    Create (strWndClass, "CtlDemo2");
}

int CMainWindow::OnCreate (LPCREATESTRUCT lpcs)
{
    if (CFrameWnd::OnCreate (lpcs) == -1)
        return -1;

    CClientDC dc (this);
    int nHeight = -((dc.GetDeviceCaps (LOGPIXELSY) * 8) / 72);

    m_font.CreateFont (nHeight, 0, 0, 0, FW_NORMAL, 0, 0, 0,
        DEFAULT_CHARSET, OUT_CHARACTER_PRECIS, CLIP_CHARACTER_PRECIS,
        DEFAULT_QUALITY, DEFAULT_PITCH | FF_DONTCARE, "MS Sans Serif");

    CFont* pOldFont = dc.SelectObject (&m_font);
    TEXTMETRIC tm;
    dc.GetTextMetrics (&tm);
    m_cxChar = tm.tmAveCharWidth;
    m_cyChar = tm.tmHeight + tm.tmExternalLeading;
    dc.SelectObject (pOldFont);

    int x1 = m_cxChar * 2;
    int x2 = m_cxChar * 24;
    int x3 = m_cxChar * 25;
    int x4 = m_cxChar * 50;

    int y1 = m_cyChar;
    int y2 = (m_cyChar * 11) / 4;
```

(continued)

309

CtlDemo2.cpp *continued*

```
    int y3 = m_cyChar * 4;
    int y4 = (m_cyChar * 23) / 4;
    int dy = m_cyChar / 2;

    m_ctlLabel1.Create ("&Standard edit control", WS_CHILD | WS_VISIBLE |
        SS_LEFT, CRect (x1, y1 + dy, x2, y2), this);

    m_ctlStdEdit.CreateEx (WS_EX_CLIENTEDGE, "edit", NULL,
        WS_CHILD | WS_VISIBLE | WS_BORDER | WS_TABSTOP | ES_AUTOHSCROLL,
        x3, y1, x4 - x3, y2 - y1, m_hWnd, (HMENU) IDC_STDEDIT, NULL);

    m_ctlLabel2.Create ("&Numeric edit control", WS_CHILD | WS_VISIBLE |
        SS_LEFT, CRect (x1, y3 + dy, x2, y4), this);

    m_ctlNumEdit.CreateEx (WS_EX_CLIENTEDGE, "edit", NULL,
        WS_CHILD | WS_VISIBLE | WS_BORDER | WS_TABSTOP | ES_AUTOHSCROLL,
        x3, y3, x4 - x3, y4 - y3, m_hWnd, (HMENU) IDC_NUMEDIT, NULL);

    m_ctlLabel1.SetFont (&m_font, FALSE);
    m_ctlLabel2.SetFont (&m_font, FALSE);
    m_ctlStdEdit.SetFont (&m_font, FALSE);
    m_ctlNumEdit.SetFont (&m_font, FALSE);
    return 0;
}

BOOL CMainWindow::PreTranslateMessage (MSG* pMsg)
{
    return ::IsDialogMessage (m_hWnd, pMsg);
}


///////////////////////////////////////////////////////////////////////////
// CNumEdit message map and member functions

BEGIN_MESSAGE_MAP (CNumEdit, CEdit)
    ON_WM_CHAR ()
END_MESSAGE_MAP ()

void CNumEdit::OnChar (UINT nChar, UINT nRepCnt, UINT nFlags)
{
    if ((((nChar >= '0') && (nChar <= '9')) ||
        (nChar == VK_BACK) || (nChar == '(') || (nChar == ')') ||
        (nChar == '-') || (nChar == ' '))

        CEdit::OnChar (nChar, nRepCnt, nFlags);
}
```

CNumEdit could be improved in a number of ways. For example, you could add an *IsValid* function that performs a validity check on the phone number and returns FALSE if the number contains fewer than 7 digits. You could also add a *SetNumber* function to initialize the control with a number and ensure that no invalid input slips by, and a *GetNumber* function to retrieve a number. You could even have the *OnChar* handler convert letters of the alphabet into the equivalent numbers on the telephone dial so that A, B, or C becomes 2; D, E, or F becomes 3; and so on. Before long, you'd have a robust numeric control class perfectly suited for reuse in other Windows applications.

CNumEdit is just one example of how a control can be customized by deriving a class from an MFC control class. Let's look at another example—a self-contained and highly reusable list box class that displays icons instead of text.

Owner-Drawn List Boxes

By default, items in a list box consist of strings of text. Should you need a list box that displays graphical images instead of text, you can create an owner-drawn list box— one whose contents are drawn by your application, not by Windows—by following these simple steps:

1. Derive a new list box class from *CListBox*, and override *CListBox::MeasureItem* and *CListBox::DrawItem* with versions of your own. Also override *PreCreateWindow*, and make sure that either LBS_OWNERDRAW-FIXED or LBS_OWNERDRAWVARIABLE is included in the list box style.

2. Construct an object from the derived class, and call *Create* or *CreateEx* to create the list box.

Operationally, owner-drawn list boxes are similar to owner-drawn menus. When an item in an owner-drawn list box needs to be drawn (or redrawn), Windows sends the list box's parent a WM_DRAWITEM message with a pointer to a DRAWITEMSTRUCT structure containing all the information required to do the drawing, including a device context handle and a 0-based index identifying the item to be drawn. Before the first WM_DRAWITEM message arrives, the list box's parent receives one or more WM_MEASUREITEM messages requesting the height of the items in the list box. If the list box style is LBS_OWNERDRAWFIXED, WM_MEASUREITEM is sent just one time. For LBS_OWNERDRAWVARIABLE list boxes, a WM_MEASUREITEM message is sent for each item. In MFC, the application framework calls the list box object's virtual *DrawItem* function when the parent receives a WM_DRAWITEM message and *MeasureItem* when it receives a WM_MEASUREITEM message. Therefore, you don't have to modify the parent window class or worry about message maps and message handlers; just override *DrawItem* and *MeasureItem* in the list box class, and your list box can do its own drawing without any help from its parent.

CListBox supports two other owner-draw overridables in addition to *DrawItem* and *MeasureItem*. If an owner-drawn list box is created with the style LBS_SORT and items are added to it with *AddString*, *CListBox::CompareItem* must be overridden with a version that compares the two items specified in a COMPAREITEMSTRUCT structure and returns −1 if item 1 comes before item 2, 0 if they are lexically equal, and 1 if item 1 comes after item 2. Owner-drawn list boxes are seldom created with the style LBS_SORT because sorting is a concept that rarely applies to nontextual data, so it's usually not necessary to write a *CompareItem* function. If you don't implement *CompareItem* in a derived owner-drawn list box class, you should override *PreCreateWindow* and make sure the list box style doesn't include the LBS_SORT bit.

If you'd like to know when an item is deleted from an owner-drawn list box, override the *CListBox::DeleteItem* function. *DeleteItem* is called when an item is deleted with *DeleteString*, when the list box's contents are erased with *ResetContent*, and when the list box is destroyed if there are items in it at the time. *DeleteItem* is called once per item being deleted, and it receives a pointer to a structure of type DELETEITEMSTRUCT with details about the item. If a list box uses per-item resources (for example, bitmaps) that should be freed when an item is deleted or the list box is destroyed, *DeleteItem* is the perfect place to free those resources.

The following *COwnerDrawnListBox* class is a nearly complete C++ implementation of an LBS_OWNERDRAWFIXED owner-drawn list box:

```
class COwnerDrawnListBox : public CListBox
{
public:
    virtual BOOL PreCreateWindow (CREATESTRUCT&);
    virtual void MeasureItem (LPMEASUREITEMSTRUCT);
    virtual void DrawItem (LPDRAWITEMSTRUCT);
};

BOOL COwnerDrawnListBox::PreCreateWindow (CREATESTRUCT& cs)
{
    if (!CListBox::PreCreateWindow (cs))
        return FALSE;

    cs.style &= ~(LBS_OWNERDRAWVARIABLE | LBS_SORT);
    cs.style |= LBS_OWNERDRAWFIXED;
    return TRUE;
}

void COwnerDrawnListBox::MeasureItem (LPMEASUREITEMSTRUCT lpmis)
{
    lpmis->itemHeight = 32;    // Item height in pixels
}

void COwnerDrawnListBox::DrawItem (LPDRAWITEMSTRUCT lpdis)
```

```
{
    CDC dc;
    dc.Attach (lpdis->hDC);
    CRect rect = lpdis->rcItem;
    UINT nIndex = lpdis->itemID;

    CBrush* pBrush = new CBrush (::GetSysColor ((lpdis->itemState &
        ODS_SELECTED) ? COLOR_HIGHLIGHT : COLOR_WINDOW));
    dc.FillRect (rect, pBrush);
    delete pBrush;

    if (lpdis->itemState & ODS_FOCUS)
        dc.DrawFocusRect (rect);

    if (nIndex != (UINT) -1) {
        // Draw the item
    }
    dc.Detach ();
}
```

To customize *COwnerDrawnListBox* and create an owner-drawn list box class of your own, just change the 32 in *COwnerDrawnListBox::MeasureItem* to the item height in pixels and replace the comment "Draw the item" in *COwnerDrawnList-Box::DrawItem* with code to draw the item whose list box index is *nIndex*. Use the *dc* device context object to do the drawing and restrict your output to the rectangle specified by *rect*, and the list box should function superbly. (Be sure to preserve the state of the device context so that it's the same going out as it was coming in.) The code in *COwnerDrawnListBox::DrawItem* paints the item's background with the system color COLOR_HIGHLIGHT if the item is selected (if the *lpdis->itemState*'s ODS_SELECTED bit is set), or COLOR_WINDOW if it is not, and draws a focus rectangle if the item has the input focus (if the *lpdis->itemState*'s ODS_FOCUS bit is set). All you have to do is draw the item itself. The *PreCreateWindow* override ensures that LBS_OWNERDRAWFIXED is set and that LBS_OWNERDRAWVARIABLE is not. It also clears the LBS_SORT bit to prevent calls to *CompareItem*.

One other thing you must do to transform *COwnerDrawnListBox* into a complete class is implement an *AddItem* function so that items can be added to the list box. If the list box accepts bitmap handles (HBITMAPs), for example, *AddItem* might look like this:

```
COwnerDrawnListBox::AddItem (HBITMAP hBitmap)
{
    int nIndex = AddString ("");
    if ((nIndex != LB_ERR) && (nIndex != LB_ERRSPACE))
        SetItemData (nIndex, (DWORD) hBitmap);
    return nIndex;
}
```

In this example, *SetItemData* associates the bitmap handle with a list box index so that, given an index, *GetItemData* can retrieve the corresponding bitmap handle. Bitmaps are resources that must be deleted when they're no longer needed. You could either leave it to the list box's parent to delete the bitmaps or override *CListBox::DeleteItem* and let the list box delete the bitmaps itself.

The IconView Application

The IconView application, listed in Figure 5-5, uses *COwnerDrawnListBox* as the model for an owner-drawn list box class named *CIconListBox* that displays icons. *CIconListBox* overrides the *PreCreateWindow*, *MeasureItem*, and *DrawItem* functions it inherits from *CListBox* and adds two functions of its own: *AddIcon* adds an icon to the list box, and *ProjectImage* "projects" the currently selected icon onto a display surface. The image can be blown up (or shrunk) to any size. The caller specifies the rectangle the projected image will fill, and *ProjectImage* adapts its output accordingly.

IconView.h

```
//**************************************************************************
//
//  IconView.h
//
//**************************************************************************

class CMyApp : public CWinApp
{
public:
    virtual BOOL InitInstance ();
};

class CIconListBox : public CListBox
{
public:
    virtual BOOL PreCreateWindow (CREATESTRUCT&);
    virtual void MeasureItem (LPMEASUREITEMSTRUCT);
    virtual void DrawItem (LPDRAWITEMSTRUCT);
    int AddIcon (HICON);
    void ProjectImage (CDC*, LPRECT, COLORREF);
};

class CMainWindow : public CWnd
{
private:
    int m_cxChar;
    int m_cyChar;
```

Figure 5-5. *The IconView source code.*

```
    CFont m_font;
    CRect m_rcImage;

    CButton m_ctlGroupBox;
    CIconListBox m_ctlIconListBox;
    CStatic m_ctlLabel;

public:
    CMainWindow ();

protected:
    virtual void PostNcDestroy ();

    afx_msg int OnCreate (LPCREATESTRUCT);
    afx_msg void OnPaint ();
    afx_msg void OnSetFocus (CWnd*);
    afx_msg void OnDropFiles (HDROP);
    afx_msg void OnSelChange ();

    DECLARE_MESSAGE_MAP ()
};
```

IconView.cpp

```
//*********************************************************************
//
//  IconView.cpp
//
//*********************************************************************

#include <afxwin.h>
#include "IconView.h"

#define IDC_LISTBOX 100

CMyApp myApp;

///////////////////////////////////////////////////////////////////////
// CMyApp member functions

BOOL CMyApp::InitInstance ()
{
    m_pMainWnd = new CMainWindow;
    m_pMainWnd->ShowWindow (m_nCmdShow);
```

(continued)

IconView.cpp *continued*

```
    m_pMainWnd->UpdateWindow ();
    return TRUE;
}

//////////////////////////////////////////////////////////////////////////
// CMainWindow message map and member functions

BEGIN_MESSAGE_MAP (CMainWindow, CWnd)
    ON_WM_CREATE ()
    ON_WM_PAINT ()
    ON_WM_SETFOCUS ()
    ON_WM_DROPFILES ()
    ON_LBN_SELCHANGE (IDC_LISTBOX, OnSelChange)
END_MESSAGE_MAP ()

CMainWindow::CMainWindow ()
{
    CString strWndClass = AfxRegisterWndClass (
        0,
        myApp.LoadStandardCursor (IDC_ARROW),
        (HBRUSH) (COLOR_3DFACE + 1),
        myApp.LoadStandardIcon (IDI_APPLICATION));

    CreateEx (0, strWndClass, "IconView",
        WS_OVERLAPPED ! WS_SYSMENU ! WS_CAPTION ! WS_MINIMIZEBOX,
        CW_USEDEFAULT, CW_USEDEFAULT, CW_USEDEFAULT, CW_USEDEFAULT,
        NULL, NULL, NULL);

    CRect rect (0, 0, m_cxChar * 84, m_cyChar * 21);
    CalcWindowRect (&rect);

    SetWindowPos (NULL, 0, 0, rect.Width (), rect.Height (),
        SWP_NOZORDER ! SWP_NOMOVE ! SWP_NOREDRAW);
}

int CMainWindow::OnCreate (LPCREATESTRUCT lpcs)
{
    if (CWnd::OnCreate (lpcs) == -1)
        return -1;

    CClientDC dc (this);
    int nHeight = -((dc.GetDeviceCaps (LOGPIXELSY) * 8) / 72);

    m_font.CreateFont (nHeight, 0, 0, 0, FW_NORMAL, 0, 0, 0,
```

```
        DEFAULT_CHARSET, OUT_CHARACTER_PRECIS, CLIP_CHARACTER_PRECIS,
        DEFAULT_QUALITY, DEFAULT_PITCH | FF_DONTCARE, "MS Sans Serif");

    CFont* pOldFont = dc.SelectObject (&m_font);
    TEXTMETRIC tm;
    dc.GetTextMetrics (&tm);
    m_cxChar = tm.tmAveCharWidth;
    m_cyChar = tm.tmHeight + tm.tmExternalLeading;
    dc.SelectObject (pOldFont);

    m_rcImage.SetRect (m_cxChar * 4, m_cyChar * 3, m_cxChar * 46,
        m_cyChar * 19);

    m_ctlGroupBox.Create ("Detail", WS_CHILD | WS_VISIBLE | BS_GROUPBOX,
        CRect (m_cxChar * 2, m_cyChar, m_cxChar * 48, m_cyChar * 20),
        this, (UINT) -1);

    m_ctlLabel.Create ("Icons", WS_CHILD | WS_VISIBLE | SS_LEFT,
        CRect (m_cxChar * 50, m_cyChar, m_cxChar * 82, m_cyChar * 2),
        this);

    m_ctlIconListBox.Create (WS_CHILD | WS_VISIBLE | WS_VSCROLL |
        WS_BORDER | LBS_NOTIFY | LBS_NOINTEGRALHEIGHT,
        CRect (m_cxChar * 50, m_cyChar * 2, m_cxChar * 82, m_cyChar * 20),
        this, IDC_LISTBOX);

    m_ctlGroupBox.SetFont (&m_font);
    m_ctlLabel.SetFont (&m_font);

    DragAcceptFiles ();
    return 0;
}

void CMainWindow::PostNcDestroy ()
{
    delete this;
}

void CMainWindow::OnPaint ()
{
    CPaintDC dc (this);
    m_ctlIconListBox.ProjectImage (&dc, m_rcImage,
        ::GetSysColor (COLOR_3DFACE));
}
```

(continued)

IconView.cpp *continued*

```cpp
void CMainWindow::OnSetFocus (CWnd* pWnd)
{
    m_ctlIconListBox.SetFocus ();
}

void CMainWindow::OnDropFiles (HDROP hDropInfo)
{
    int nCount = ::DragQueryFile (hDropInfo, (UINT) -1, NULL, 0);

    if (nCount == 1) { // One file at a time, please
        m_ctlIconListBox.ResetContent ();

        char szFile[MAX_PATH];
        ::DragQueryFile (hDropInfo, 0, szFile, sizeof (szFile));
        int nIcons = (int) ::ExtractIcon (NULL, szFile, (UINT) -1);

        if (nIcons) {
            HICON hIcon;
            for (int i=0; i<nIcons; i++) {
                hIcon = ::ExtractIcon (AfxGetInstanceHandle (),
                    szFile, i);
                m_ctlIconListBox.AddIcon (hIcon);
            }
        }

        CString strWndTitle = szFile;
        strWndTitle += " - IconView";
        SetWindowText (strWndTitle);

        CClientDC dc (this);
        m_ctlIconListBox.SetCurSel (0);
        m_ctlIconListBox.ProjectImage (&dc, m_rcImage,
            ::GetSysColor (COLOR_3DFACE));
    }
    ::DragFinish (hDropInfo);
}

void CMainWindow::OnSelChange ()
{
    CClientDC dc (this);
    m_ctlIconListBox.ProjectImage (&dc, m_rcImage,
        ::GetSysColor (COLOR_3DFACE));
}
```

```
//////////////////////////////////////////////////////////////////////////
// CIconListBox member functions

BOOL CIconListBox::PreCreateWindow (CREATESTRUCT& cs)
{
    if (!CListBox::PreCreateWindow (cs))
        return FALSE;

    cs.dwExStyle |= WS_EX_CLIENTEDGE;
    cs.style &= ~(LBS_OWNERDRAWVARIABLE | LBS_SORT);
    cs.style |= LBS_OWNERDRAWFIXED;
    return TRUE;
}

void CIconListBox::MeasureItem (LPMEASUREITEMSTRUCT lpmis)
{
    lpmis->itemHeight = 36;
}

void CIconListBox::DrawItem (LPDRAWITEMSTRUCT lpdis)
{
    CDC dc;
    dc.Attach (lpdis->hDC);
    CRect rect = lpdis->rcItem;
    int nIndex = lpdis->itemID;

    CBrush* pBrush = new CBrush (::GetSysColor ((lpdis->itemState &
        ODS_SELECTED) ? COLOR_HIGHLIGHT : COLOR_WINDOW));
    dc.FillRect (rect, pBrush);
    delete pBrush;

    if (lpdis->itemState & ODS_FOCUS)
        dc.DrawFocusRect (rect);

    if (nIndex != (UINT) -1)
        dc.DrawIcon (rect.left + 4, rect.top + 2,
            (HICON) GetItemData (nIndex));

    dc.Detach ();
}

int CIconListBox::AddIcon (HICON hIcon)
{
    int nIndex = AddString ("");
    if ((nIndex != LB_ERR) && (nIndex != LB_ERRSPACE))
        SetItemData (nIndex, (DWORD) hIcon);
```

(continued)

IconView.cpp *continued*

```
        return nIndex;
}

void CIconListBox::ProjectImage (CDC* pDC, LPRECT pRect,
    COLORREF crBkColor)
{
    CDC dcMem;
    dcMem.CreateCompatibleDC (pDC);

    CBitmap bitmap;
    bitmap.CreateCompatibleBitmap (pDC, 32, 32);
    CBitmap* pOldBitmap = dcMem.SelectObject (&bitmap);

    CBrush* pBrush = new CBrush (crBkColor);
    dcMem.FillRect (CRect (0, 0, 32, 32), pBrush);
    delete pBrush;

    int nIndex = GetCurSel ();
    if (nIndex != LB_ERR)
        dcMem.DrawIcon (0, 0, (HICON) GetItemData (nIndex));

    pDC->StretchBlt (pRect->left, pRect->top, pRect->right - pRect->left,
        pRect->bottom - pRect->top, &dcMem, 0, 0, 32, 32, SRCCOPY);

    dcMem.SelectObject (pOldBitmap);
}
```

Figure 5-6 on the next page shows what the IconView window looks like with a collection of icons displayed. The icons were extracted from Pifmgr.dll, one of the DLLs supplied with Windows 95. The only form of user input IconView accepts is drag and drop. To try it out, open My Computer or an Explorer window, grab an .exe, a .dll, or an .ico file with the left mouse button, drag it to the IconView window, and release the mouse button to execute a drop. If the file contains one or more icons, the icons will be displayed in the list box and a blown-up version of the first icon will be displayed in the Detail window. To get a close-up view of any of the other icons in the file, just click the icon or cursor through the list with the up and down arrow keys.

CMainWindow::OnDropFiles extracts the icons from files dropped over the IconView window and adds them to the list box. When a drop occurs, *OnDropFiles* clears the list box with *CListBox::ResetContent* and calls *::ExtractIcon* to determine how many icons the file contains. Then it calls *::ExtractIcon* once per icon to extract the icons and add them to the list box with *CIconListBox::AddIcon*:

```
int nIcons = (int) ::ExtractIcon (NULL, szFile, (UINT) -1);

if (nIcons) {
    HICON hIcon;
    for (int i=0; i<nIcons; i++) {
        hIcon = ::ExtractIcon (AfxGetInstanceHandle (),
            szFile, i);
        m_ctlIconListBox.AddIcon (hIcon);
    }
}
```

The first statement sets *nIcons* equal to the number of icons in the file. The *for* loop performs the extractions and insertions. *CIconListBox::AddIcon* is almost identical to the *AddItem* function we looked at in the previous section. It adds a null string to the list box and then uses *SetItemData* to associate the icon handle *bIcon* with the newly added item. After the *for* loop finishes, *OnDropFiles* adds the name of the file that was dropped to the title bar, calls the list box's *SetCurSel* function to select the first item in the list box, and calls *ProjectImage* to draw an enlarged view of that icon.

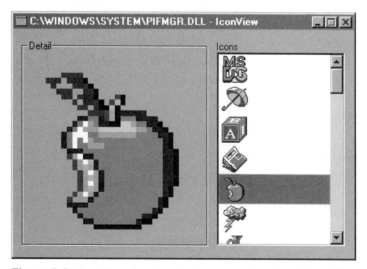

Figure 5-6. *IconView showing the icons contained in Pifmgr.dll.*

The job of drawing the icons in the list box falls to *CIconListBox::DrawItem*. After painting the item's background and possibly outlining the item with a focus rectangle, *DrawItem* calls *CDC*'s handy *DrawIcon* function to draw the icon itself:

```
dc.DrawIcon (rect.left + 4, rect.top + 2,
    (HICON) GetItemData (nIndex));
```

CDC::DrawIcon accepts three parameters: the *x* and *y* coordinates of the icon's upper left corner and the handle of the icon to be drawn. The icon handle is obtained with *GetItemData*. The call to *DrawIcon* is skipped if *nIndex*—the index of the currently selected list box item—is −1. That's important because *DrawItem* is called with a list box index of −1 when an empty list box receives the input focus, so that a focus rectangle will be drawn around the nonexistent item 0. You should not assume that *DrawItem* will always be called with a valid item index.

    CMainWindow's *OnPaint* handler does nothing more than construct a paint DC and call the list box's *ProjectImage* function to draw a blown-up version of the currently selected icon in the window's client area. *ProjectImage* accepts three parameters: a pointer to a *CDC* object representing the output surface, a RECT pointer or a *CRect* object specifying the output location and size, and a COLORREF value identifying the color used to fill in the background behind the icon. The technique used to draw the image is rather interesting. *ProjectImage* first calls *CDC::CreateCompatibleDC* to create a memory device context compatible with the device context supplied by the caller. It then calls *CBitmap::CreateCompatibleBitmap* to create a temporary bitmap 32 pixels wide and 32 pixels tall, selects the bitmap into the memory DC, and uses *CDC::FillRect* to initialize the bitmap to the background color specified by the caller. The fill takes place on the virtual display surface represented by the memory DC, so the user sees nothing—yet.

    Next the currently selected icon is drawn to the memory DC with *CDC::DrawIcon* and blitted to the caller's DC with *CDC::StretchBlt*. It is only after *StretchBlt* is called that the icon image is actually displayed in the window. This somewhat protracted process, culminating in the call to *StretchBlt*, is necessary because *CDC::DrawIcon* draws icons only in their actual sizes and the Win32 *::DrawIconEx* function (which *will* stretch an icon image) doesn't work with icons loaded by *::ExtractIcon*.

Responding to Drop Events

IconView uses the simple drag and drop mechanism first introduced in Windows 3.1 to respond to drop events over its window. The statement

```
DragAcceptFiles ();
```

in *CMainWindow::OnCreate* registers *CMainWindow* as a drop target for file objects. As such, it receives a WM_DROPFILES message whenever a file is dropped on top of it. The message, in turn, activates *CMainWindow::OnDropFiles*, which receives an HDROP object containing the name of the file or files that were dropped. (HDROP is actually a handle to a global memory block containing the names of the files involved in the drag and drop operation and other information such as the coordinates of the drop point.) File names are extracted from the memory block with the Windows *::DragQueryFile* function, which accepts four parameters: the HDROP object, the 0-based index of the file whose name you want to retrieve, the address of the buffer that will receive the file name, and the buffer size, in that order. Specifying −1 for the second parameter returns the number of files involved in the transfer.

OnDropFiles calls *::DragQueryFile* once to determine the file count:

```
int nCount = ::DragQueryFile (hDropInfo, (UINT) -1, NULL, 0);
```

If *nCount* is 1, *OnDropFiles* calls *::DragQueryFile* again to get the name of the file that was dropped:

```
char szFile[MAX_PATH];
::DragQueryFile (hDropInfo, 0, szFile, sizeof (szFile));
```

MAX_PATH is defined in Windef.h and represents the maximum number of characters a Win32 path name can contain (260). Before returning, *OnDropFiles* calls *::Drag-Finish* to notify Windows that the drag and drop operation is complete and the HDROP object is no longer needed. Windows responds by freeing the memory associated with the HDROP object.

Bitmap Buttons

MFC provides three derived control classes of its own: *CCheckListBox*, *CDragListBox*, and *CBitmapButton*. *CCheckListBox* turns a normal list box into a "check" list box—a list box with a check box by each item and added functions such as *GetCheck* and *SetCheck* for getting and setting check box states. *CDragListBox* creates a list box whose items can be dragged and dropped. *CBitmapButton* encapsulates owner-drawn push buttons that display pictures instead of text. It supplies its own *DrawItem* handler that draws a push button in response to WM_DRAWITEM messages. All you have to do is create the button and supply bitmap images representing the button in various states.

Windows 95 provides alternatives to MFC's *CBitmapButton* class with two new button styles: BS_BITMAP and BS_ICON. The former creates a push button that displays a bitmap. The latter creates a push button that displays an icon. We'll discuss all three button types and then develop a sample application that demonstrates how they work.

The *CBitmapButton* Class

Creating a *CBitmapButton* is simple. The first step is to use a bitmap editor such as the SDK's Image Editor or the Visual C++ resource editor to create the button's bitmaps. *CBitmapButton* can use as many as four bitmapped images: one depicting the button in its normal, undepressed, state; a second depicting the button when it is depressed; a third depicting the button when it is undepressed and has the input focus; and a fourth depicting the button when it is disabled. At a minimum, you should supply "up" and "down" bitmaps showing the button in its normal and depressed states. When the button is clicked, the framework redraws the button using the down bitmap so that the button appears to recede into the screen. When the button is released, it is redrawn with the up bitmap. The "focus" and "disabled" bitmaps are optional. You'll probably want to supply a focus bitmap if the button will be part of the tab order in a dialog box or top-level window. You'll need to supply a disabled bitmap only if you'll allow the button to become disabled.

After you create the button bitmaps and save them as .bmp files, the next step is to convert them into bitmap resources by adding them to your program's .rc file. The following resource statements create four bitmap resources for use with a *CBitmapButton*:

```
CheckU BITMAP Checku.bmp
CheckD BITMAP Checkd.bmp
CheckF BITMAP Checkf.bmp
CheckX BITMAP Checkx.bmp
```

Note the resource names: CheckU is the up bitmap, CheckD is the down bitmap, CheckF is the focus bitmap, and CheckX is the disabled bitmap. The part of the resource name preceding these letters should match the text assigned to the button when the button is created. This naming convention isn't strictly necessary when you create a *CBitmapButton* in a top-level window (indeed, the button doesn't even have to be assigned any text), but it's very important for *CBitmapButton*s that appear in dialog boxes. You'll see why in the next chapter.

The third and final step is to create the bitmap button and load the button bitmaps. This is usually done in the parent window's *OnCreate* handler. The statements

```
m_ctlBitmapButton.Create ("Check", WS_CHILD | WS_VISIBLE |
    BS_OWNERDRAW, rect, this, IDC_BUTTON);
m_ctlBitmapButton.LoadBitmaps ("CheckU", "CheckD", "CheckF",
    "CheckX");
```

create the button and assign it four bitmap resources. Note the BS_OWNERDRAW style, which *must* be included so that the button will be owner-drawn. The button width and height specified in *rect* should match the pixel dimensions of the button bitmaps. The parameters passed to *CBitmapButton::LoadBitmaps* specify, in order, the up bitmap, the down bitmap, the focus bitmap, and the disabled bitmap. For any of these bitmaps you choose not to supply, specify a NULL parameter instead of a resource name. After the bitmaps are loaded, the framework does the rest, automatically drawing the appropriate bitmap on the screen in response to WM_DRAWITEM messages indicating that the button needs to be repainted.

When drawing the bitmaps for a *CBitmapButton*-style button, follow a few simple rules to make the button's appearance consistent with that of other buttons. Figure 5-7 shows close-up views of four button bitmaps. Each bitmap is 72 pixels wide and 40 pixels tall. You can size the bitmaps any way you want, but it's important that all four be the same size. For best results, the button's face and edges should be drawn with the colors shown on the diagram. Start with the up bitmap, and then create the down bitmap by reversing the borders and moving the image on the face of the button right and down one pixel. This gives the illusion that the button goes down when it's clicked. Because clicking the button gives it the input focus, the down bitmap should also include a dotted focus rectangle if you supply a focus bitmap, too. Create the focus bitmap by duplicating the up bitmap and adding a dotted focus rectangle. Finally, create the disabled bitmap from the up bitmap by outlining the image on the button face in dark gray and shadowing the outline with white pixels. Shadowing is done by drawing a white pixel one pixel to the right of and below each dark gray pixel. This gives the image on the button's face an "etched" look that makes it obvious the button is disabled but still communicates the button's purpose. Of course, there's no hard-and-fast rule saying the button bitmaps *have* to be styled this way. You can be as creative as you want, but users will generally judge your application more favorably if the appearance and behavior of its controls are consistent with the appearance and behavior of other Windows applications.

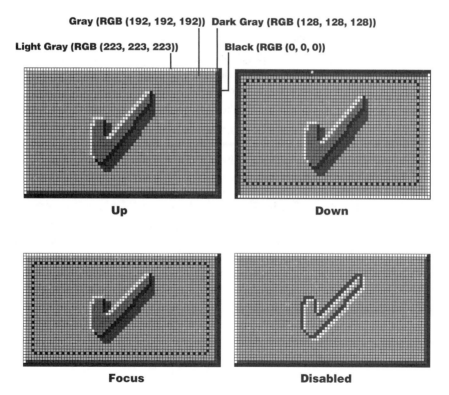

Figure 5-7. CBitmapButton *bitmaps.*

The BS_BITMAP Style

If your application is targeted for Windows 95 and compatibility with previous versions of Windows isn't a concern, an even easier way to create a bitmap button is to use the style BS_BITMAP and assign a bitmap to the button with *CButton::SetBitmap*. These statements load a bitmap resource named "Check," create a BS_BITMAP button from a *CButton* named *m_ctlBitmapButton*, and assign the bitmap to the button:

```
m_hBitmap = ::LoadBitmap (AfxGetInstanceHandle (), "Check");
m_ctlBitmapButton.Create ("", WS_CHILD | WS_VISIBLE | BS_BITMAP,
    rect, this, IDC_BUTTON);
m_ctlBitmapButton.SetBitmap (m_hBitmap);
```

Later, after the button is destroyed or just before the application terminates, the bitmap should be destroyed to prevent resource leaks:

```
::DeleteObject (m_hBitmap);
```

CBitmapButton destroys the bitmaps for you. A BS_BITMAP button, however, does not the destroy the bitmap on its own.

The bitmap assigned to a BS_BITMAP button depicts just what's on the face of the button; it doesn't include the button's edges as *CBitmapButton* bitmaps do. Figure 5-8 shows what a typical button bitmap looks like. Windows centers the bitmap on the face of the button unless you specify otherwise by including one or more of the button styles shown in the following table.

BUTTON BITMAP ALIGNMENT STYLES

Button Style	Description
BS_LEFT	Aligns the bitmap with the left edge of the button face.
BS_RIGHT	Aligns the bitmap with the right edge of the button face.
BS_TOP	Aligns the bitmap with the top edge of the button face.
BS_BOTTOM	Aligns the bitmap with the bottom edge of the button face.
BS_CENTER	Centers the bitmap horizontally.
BS_VCENTER	Centers the bitmap vertically.

BS_BITMAP-style buttons offer three advantages over buttons created from MFC's *CBitmapButton* class:

■ You have to supply only one bitmap. Windows takes responsibility for drawing the button in the up, down, focus, and disabled states.

■ Windows draws the button's edges for you. If button-edge styles change in a future version of Windows, as they did in Windows 95, *CBitmapButton* bitmaps must be redrawn to implement the new styles. A BS_BITMAP button, on the other hand, receives the new edge styles automatically.

■ The button's size is independent of the bitmap size. A *CBitmapButton* must be sized to the bitmap, or else the control rectangle won't match the button image. An image that's larger than the control rectangle will be clipped. If the image is smaller than the control rectangle, mouse clicks outside the button's borders could inadvertently click the button.

Given the constraints placed on *CBitmapButtons* and the popularity of bitmap buttons in general, it's easy to see why BS_BITMAP is a welcome addition to the operating system in Windows 95.

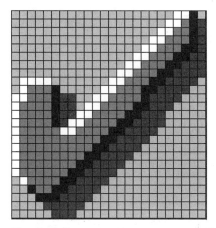

Figure 5-8. *Bitmap for a BS_BITMAP button.*

The BS_ICON Style

The BS_ICON button style is similar to BS_BITMAP. The only difference is that a BS-_ICON button uses an icon rather than a bitmap for the button image. The following statements create a BS_ICON button and assign it an icon resource:

```
m_ctlIconButton.Create ("", WS_CHILD | WS_VISIBLE | BS_ICON,
    rect, this, IDC_BUTTON);
m_ctlIconButton.SetIcon (AfxGetApp ()->LoadIcon ("Check"));
```

The icon is drawn in the center of the button unless you alter its alignment with one or more of the button styles in the table in the previous section. Unlike a bitmap loaded with *::LoadBitmap*, an icon loaded with *CWinApp::LoadIcon* doesn't need to be destroyed to prevent resource leaks.

The disadvantage in using BS_ICON is that the size of the image is restricted to the maximum size of an icon—48 by 48 pixels. But BS_ICON buttons have one neat feature that BS_BITMAP buttons don't have: because icons can be drawn with "transparent" pixels (pixels that assume the screen color underneath them), icon buttons can automatically adapt to changes in the system color that defines the color of push buttons. The default color for button faces is light gray, but the user can easily change the default. You'll see what kind of trouble this can cause for *CBitmapButton*s and BS_BITMAP buttons in the next section.

Putting It All Together: The CtlDemo3 Application

As shown in Figure 5-9, the CtlDemo3 application creates three bitmap buttons in a frame window: a *CBitmapButton*, a BS_BITMAP button, and a BS_ICON button. The face of each button is emblazoned with a green check mark. The buttons don't actually do anything because there are no ON_BN_CLICKED handlers for them. But you can click the buttons to see what they look like in the down and focus states. The *CBitmapButton* uses the bitmaps shown in Figure 5-7 on page 325. The BS_BITMAP button uses the bitmap shown in Figure 5-8 on page 327. The BS_ICON button uses an icon identical to the BS_BITMAP bitmap, but the icon contains transparent pixels everywhere the bitmap contains light gray pixels.

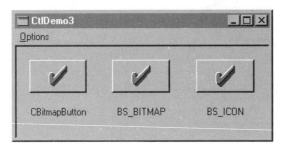

Figure 5-9. *The three types of bitmap buttons.*

To see why *CBitmapButton*s are still sometimes preferable to BS_BITMAP and BS_ICON buttons, select Disable Buttons from CtlDemo3's Options menu to disable the push buttons. The results, shown in Figure 5-10, probably aren't quite what you expected. The disabled *CBitmapButton* looks fine since it uses a bitmap we supplied. But the disabled BS_BITMAP and BS_ICON buttons, whose images were generated by Windows, leave a little to be desired. It's nearly impossible to create a BS_BITMAP bitmap that looks as good disabled as it does enabled. BS_ICON buttons adapt reasonably well to being disabled if you keep the images simple (see the toolbar buttons in Visual C++ and Word 7.0 for examples), but even so, you should test a BS_ICON button in its disabled state before shipping it in an application.

Figure 5-10. *Disabled bitmap buttons.*

You can use CtlDemo3, listed in Figure 5-11, as a test bed by substituting the name of your .ico file for Check.ico in CtlDemo3.rc and recompiling.

Resource.h

```
//***********************************************************************
//
//   Resource.h
//
//***********************************************************************

#define IDR_MAINFRAME              100

#define IDM_OPTIONS_DISABLE        110
#define IDM_OPTIONS_EXIT           111

#define IDC_BUTTON1                120
#define IDC_BUTTON2                121
#define IDC_BUTTON3                122
```

CtlDemo3.rc

```
//***********************************************************************
//
//   CtlDemo3.rc
//
//***********************************************************************

#include <afxres.h>
#include "Resource.h"

CheckU  BITMAP  Checku.bmp
CheckD  BITMAP  Checkd.bmp
CheckF  BITMAP  Checkf.bmp
CheckX  BITMAP  Checkx.bmp

Check   BITMAP  Check.bmp
Check   ICON    Check.ico

IDR_MAINFRAME MENU
BEGIN
    POPUP "&Options" {
        MENUITEM "&Disable Buttons",    IDM_OPTIONS_DISABLE
        MENUITEM SEPARATOR
        MENUITEM "E&xit",               IDM_OPTIONS_EXIT
    }
END
```

Figure 5-11. *The CtlDemo3 source code.*

CtlDemo3.h

```
//*********************************************************************
//
//  CtlDemo3.h
//
//*********************************************************************

class CMyApp : public CWinApp
{
public:
    virtual BOOL InitInstance ();
};

class CMainWindow : public CFrameWnd
{
private:
    CFont m_font;
    HBITMAP m_hBitmap;

    CBitmapButton m_ctlButton1;
    CButton m_ctlButton2;
    CButton m_ctlButton3;

    CStatic m_ctlLabel1;
    CStatic m_ctlLabel2;
    CStatic m_ctlLabel3;

public:
    CMainWindow ();

protected:
    afx_msg int OnCreate (LPCREATESTRUCT);
    afx_msg void OnDestroy ();
    afx_msg void OnOptionsDisable ();
    afx_msg void OnOptionsExit ();
    afx_msg void OnUpdateOptionsDisableUI (CCmdUI*);

    DECLARE_MESSAGE_MAP ()
};
```

CtlDemo3.cpp

```
//*********************************************************************
//
// CtlDemo3.cpp
//
//*********************************************************************

#include <afxwin.h>
#include <afxext.h>
#include "Resource.h"
#include "CtlDemo3.h"

CMyApp myApp;

///////////////////////////////////////////////////////////////////////
// CMyApp member functions

BOOL CMyApp::InitInstance ()
{
    m_pMainWnd = new CMainWindow;
    m_pMainWnd->ShowWindow (m_nCmdShow);
    m_pMainWnd->UpdateWindow ();
    return TRUE;
}


///////////////////////////////////////////////////////////////////////
// CMainWindow message map and member functions

BEGIN_MESSAGE_MAP (CMainWindow, CFrameWnd)
    ON_WM_CREATE ()
    ON_WM_DESTROY ()
    ON_COMMAND (IDM_OPTIONS_DISABLE, OnOptionsDisable)
    ON_COMMAND (IDM_OPTIONS_EXIT, OnOptionsExit)
    ON_UPDATE_COMMAND_UI (IDM_OPTIONS_DISABLE, OnUpdateOptionsDisableUI)
END_MESSAGE_MAP ()

CMainWindow::CMainWindow ()
{
    CString strWndClass = AfxRegisterWndClass (
        0,
        myApp.LoadStandardCursor (IDC_ARROW),
```

(continued)

CtlDemo3.cpp *continued*

```
        (HBRUSH) (COLOR_3DFACE + 1),
        myApp.LoadStandardIcon (IDI_APPLICATION)
    );

    Create (strWndClass, "CtlDemo3", WS_OVERLAPPEDWINDOW,
        rectDefault, NULL, MAKEINTRESOURCE (IDR_MAINFRAME));
}

int CMainWindow::OnCreate (LPCREATESTRUCT lpcs)
{
    if (CFrameWnd::OnCreate (lpcs) == -1)
        return -1;

    m_ctlButton1.Create ("Check", WS_CHILD | WS_VISIBLE | BS_OWNERDRAW,
        CRect (16, 16, 88, 56), this, IDC_BUTTON1);
    m_ctlButton1.LoadBitmaps ("CheckU", "CheckD", "CheckF", "CheckX");

    m_hBitmap = ::LoadBitmap (AfxGetInstanceHandle (), "Check");
    m_ctlButton2.Create ("", WS_CHILD | WS_VISIBLE | BS_BITMAP,
        CRect (120, 16, 192, 56), this, IDC_BUTTON2);
    m_ctlButton2.SetBitmap (m_hBitmap);

    m_ctlButton3.Create ("", WS_CHILD | WS_VISIBLE | BS_ICON,
        CRect (224, 16, 296, 56), this, IDC_BUTTON3);
    m_ctlButton3.SetIcon (myApp.LoadIcon ("Check"));

    m_ctlLabel1.Create ("CBitmapButton", WS_CHILD | WS_VISIBLE |
        SS_CENTER, CRect (8, 72, 96, 100), this);

    m_ctlLabel2.Create ("BS_BITMAP", WS_CHILD | WS_VISIBLE | SS_CENTER,
        CRect (112, 72, 200, 100), this);

    m_ctlLabel3.Create ("BS_ICON", WS_CHILD | WS_VISIBLE | SS_CENTER,
        CRect (216, 72, 304, 100), this);

    CClientDC dc (this);
    int nHeight = -((dc.GetDeviceCaps (LOGPIXELSY) * 8) / 72);

    m_font.CreateFont (nHeight, 0, 0, 0, FW_NORMAL, 0, 0, 0,
        DEFAULT_CHARSET, OUT_CHARACTER_PRECIS, CLIP_CHARACTER_PRECIS,
        DEFAULT_QUALITY, DEFAULT_PITCH | FF_DONTCARE, "MS Sans Serif");

    m_ctlLabel1.SetFont (&m_font, FALSE);
    m_ctlLabel2.SetFont (&m_font, FALSE);
```

```
    m_ctlLabel3.SetFont (&m_font, FALSE);
    return 0;
}

void CMainWindow::OnDestroy ()
{
    ::DeleteObject (m_hBitmap);
}

void CMainWindow::OnOptionsExit ()
{
    SendMessage (WM_CLOSE, 0, 0);
}

void CMainWindow::OnOptionsDisable ()
{
    if (m_ctlButton1.IsWindowEnabled ()) {
        m_ctlButton1.EnableWindow (FALSE);
        m_ctlButton2.EnableWindow (FALSE);
        m_ctlButton3.EnableWindow (FALSE);
    }
    else {
        m_ctlButton1.EnableWindow (TRUE);
        m_ctlButton2.EnableWindow (TRUE);
        m_ctlButton3.EnableWindow (TRUE);
    }
}

void CMainWindow::OnUpdateOptionsDisableUI (CCmdUI* pCmdUI)
{
    pCmdUI->SetText (m_ctlButton1.IsWindowEnabled () ?
        "&Disable Buttons" : "&Enable Buttons");
}
```

You can demonstrate one other shortcoming of bitmap buttons by using Control Panel to change the 3D Objects screen color to something other than light gray. Because the pixels surrounding the check mark in the check mark icon were set to the screen color, the BS_ICON button will change with the screen. But the *CBitmapButton* won't change at all, and in the BS_BITMAP button, only the part of the button that surrounds the bitmap image will change. In previous versions of Windows, there wasn't an easy solution to this problem. But Windows 95 offers a new API function named *::LoadImage* that will load a bitmap and in the process transform the colors in the bitmap image into their system-color equivalents, as shown in the table on the next page.

Color	Transformed Into
Dark gray (RGB (128, 128, 128))	COLOR_3DSHADOW
Gray (RGB (192, 192, 192))	COLOR_3DFACE
Light gray (RGB (223, 223, 223))	COLOR_3DLIGHT

With *::LoadImage* to lend a hand, it's easy to modify CtlDemo3 so that the BS-_BITMAP adapts to changes in system colors. In *CMainWindow::OnCreate*, replace the statement that loads the "Check" bitmap with

```
m_hBitmap = (HBITMAP) ::LoadImage (AfxGetInstanceHandle (),
    "Check", IMAGE_BITMAP, 0, 0, LR_LOADMAP3DCOLORS);
```

This simple change ensures that the button will assume the system colors when it is created. Now, to update the button dynamically if the system colors change after the button is created, add the following message map entry and message handler to the *CMainWindow* class:

```
// In the message map
ON_WM_SYSCOLORCHANGE ()
    .
    .
    .
void CMainWindow::OnSysColorChange ()
{
    HBITMAP hBitmap = (HBITMAP) ::LoadImage (AfxGetInstanceHandle (),
        "Check", IMAGE_BITMAP, 0, 0, LR_LOADMAP3DCOLORS);
    ::DeleteObject (m_ctlButton2.SetBitmap (hBitmap));
    m_hBitmap = hBitmap;
}
```

Windows sends a WM_SYSCOLORCHANGE message to all top-level windows when a system color changes. The *OnSysColorChange* handler shown above responds by reloading (and re-color mapping) the button bitmap, calling *SetBitmap* to assign the new bitmap to the button, and deleting the old bitmap. You could also update the BS_ICON button's colors by calling *::LoadImage* with an IMAGE_ICON flag. Then, if the dark gray color the system defaults to for 3D shadows changes, the shadow behind the check mark in the icon image will be updated, too.

Color changes aren't incorporated as easily in a *CBitmapButton* because *CBitmapButton::LoadBitmaps* loads the button bitmaps with *CBitmap::LoadBitmap*, which in turn calls *::LoadBitmap* rather than *::LoadImage*. One way to create a *CBitmapButton* control that responds to color changes is to derive a class from *CBitmapButton* and replace *LoadBitmaps* with a version that uses *::LoadImage*.

What about buttons that contain text as well as bitmaps? Neither MFC nor Windows offers a built-in way to create buttons with both text and images, so the usual solution is to make the text part of the bitmap. You'll see an example of how this is done in the next chapter.

Changing a Control's Colors

Perhaps the most glaring deficiency of buttons, static text controls, and other built-in control types is that there's no obvious way to change their colors. You can change a control's font with *SetFont*, but there's no *SetColor* function or equivalent. Button controls and static controls look fine as long as they're displayed against a COLOR-_3DFACE background because they paint their own backgrounds with COLOR_3D-FACE. But display them on any other background, and they'll stick out like sore thumbs.

In MFC, there are two ways to change the colors a control uses. Both hinge on the fact that before a control paints itself it sends its parent a message with the handle of the device context that will be used to do the painting. The control's parent can change the control's color by using *CDC::SetTextColor* and *CDC::SetBkColor* to alter the attributes of the device context. In addition, the value returned by the message handler is a brush handle (HBRUSH) the control will use to paint its background. A static text control, for example, sends its parent a WM_CTLCOLORSTATIC message just before painting itself. The message's *wParam* holds the device context handle, and *lParam* contains the control's window handle. If the parent supplies a message handler that sets the text color to red and the background color to white and returns an HBRUSH value for a blue brush, the control's text will be drawn in red, the gaps in and between characters will be colored white, and the background—everything inside the control's borders not covered by text—will be blue.

One way, then, to change a control's colors is to add a color message handler to the parent window class. In MFC, the ON_WM_CTLCOLOR message map macro directs WM_CTLCOLORSTATIC and other WM_CTLCOLOR messages to a handler named *OnCtlColor*. *OnCtlColor* is prototyped as follows:

```
afx_msg HBRUSH OnCtlColor (CDC* pDC, CWnd* pWnd, UINT nCtlColor)
```

pDC is a pointer to the control's device context, *pWnd* points to the control object itself, and *nCtlColor* identifies the type of WM_CTLCOLOR message that prompted the call—one of the seven values shown in the table on the next page. Five pertain to child window controls, and two (CTLCOLOR_DLG and CTLCOLOR_MSGBOX) apply to dialog boxes and message boxes. Notice that static text controls aren't the only controls that send WM_CTLCOLORSTATIC messages. In Windows 95, any control that paints text against a "default" COLOR_3DFACE background sends a WM_CTLCOLOR-STATIC message to its parent prior to painting.

nCtlColor VALUES PASSED TO *OnCtlColor*

nCtlColor	Control Type
CTLCOLOR_BTN	Push button. Processing this message has no effect on a button's appearance in Windows 95.
CTLCOLOR_DLG	Dialog box.
CTLCOLOR_EDIT	Edit control and the edit control part of a combo box.
CTLCOLOR_LISTBOX	List box and the list box part of a combo box.
CTLCOLOR_MSGBOX	Message box.
CTLCOLOR_SCROLLBAR	Scroll bar.
CTLCOLOR_STATIC	Static text control, check box, radio button, group box, read-only or disabled edit control, and the edit control in a disabled combo box.

The following *OnCtlColor* handler changes the color of a static text control named *m_ctlText* to white-on-red in a frame window:

```
HBRUSH CMainWindow::OnCtlColor (CDC* pDC, CWnd* pWnd,
    UINT nCtlColor)
{
    if (m_ctlText.m_hWnd == pWnd->m_hWnd) {
        pDC->SetTextColor (RGB (255, 255, 255));
        pdc->SetBkColor (RGB (255, 0, 0));
        return (HBRUSH) m_brRedBrush;
    }
    CFrameWnd::OnCtlColor (pDC, pWnd, nCtlColor);
}
```

m_brRedBrush is a *CBrush* data member of the *CMainWindow* class. It is initialized as follows in *CMainWindow::CMainWindow* or in *CMainWindow::OnCreate*:

```
m_brRedBrush.CreateSolidBrush (RGB (255, 0, 0));
```

Casting a *CBrush* to an HBRUSH works in MFC because the *CBrush* class provides an HBRUSH operator that returns the brush handle stored in *m_hObject*.

That's one way to change a control's color. The problem with this technique is that it's up to the parent to do the changing. A derived control class can set its own colors by using the ON_WM_CTLCOLOR_REFLECT macro to pass those WM_CTL-COLOR messages that aren't handled by the control's parent back to the control. Here's the code for a *CStatic*-like class whose controls paint themselves white-on-red:

```
class CColorStatic : public CStatic
{
public:
    CColorStatic ();

protected:
    CBrush m_brRedBrush;
    afx_msg HBRUSH CtlColor (CDC*, UINT);
    DECLARE_MESSAGE_MAP ()
};

BEGIN_MESSAGE_MAP (CColorStatic, CStatic)
    ON_WM_CTLCOLOR_REFLECT ()
END_MESSAGE_MAP ()

CColorStatic::CColorStatic ()
{
    m_brRedBrush.CreateSolidBrush (RGB (255, 0, 0));
}

HBRUSH CColorStatic::OnCtlColor (CDC* pDC, UINT nCtlColor)
{
    pDC->SetTextColor (RGB (255, 255, 255));
    pDC->SetBkColor (RGB (255, 0, 0));
    return (HBRUSH) m_brRedBrush;
}
```

CtlColor is similar to *OnCtlColor*, but it doesn't receive the *pWnd* parameter that *OnCtlColor* does. It doesn't need to because the control to which the message applies is implicit in the call.

Figures 5-12 and 5-13 contain the source code for a pair of programs named CtlDemo4 and CtlDemo5 that demonstrate both methods for changing the color of static text controls. Each program creates a static text control that reads, "Click a button to change my color." Adjacent to the static control are three radio buttons labeled Red, Green, and Blue. In CtlDemo4, the control's parent (*CMainWindow*) sets the control's color. The *OnCtlColor* handler looks like this:

```
HBRUSH CMainWindow::OnCtlColor (CDC* pDC, CWnd* pWnd,
    UINT nCtlColor)
{
    if (pWnd->m_hWnd == m_ctlText.m_hWnd) {
        COLORREF crColor;
        if (m_ctlRadioButtonRed.GetCheck ())
            crColor = RGB (255, 0, 0);
        else if (m_ctlRadioButtonGreen.GetCheck ())
            crColor = RGB (0, 255, 0);
```

(continued)

```
            else
                crColor = RGB (0, 0, 255);

            pDC->SetTextColor (crColor);
            pDC->SetBkColor (::GetSysColor (COLOR_3DFACE));
            return ::GetSysColorBrush (COLOR_3DFACE);
        }
        return CFrameWnd::OnCtlColor (pDC, pWnd, nCtlColor);
    }
```

Clicking a radio button invalidates the control to force a repaint and thus a call to *OnCtlColor*:

```
    // In the message map
    ON_BN_CLICKED (IDC_RED, OnButtonClicked)
    ON_BN_CLICKED (IDC_GREEN, OnButtonClicked)
    ON_BN_CLICKED (IDC_BLUE, OnButtonClicked)
        .
        .
        .
    void CMainWindow::OnButtonClicked ()
    {
        m_ctlText.Invalidate ();
    }
```

CtlDemo4.h

```
//******************************************************************
//
// CtlDemo4.h
//
//******************************************************************

class CMyApp : public CWinApp
{
public:
    virtual BOOL InitInstance ();
};

class CMainWindow : public CFrameWnd
{
private:
    int m_cxChar;
    int m_cyChar;
    CFont m_font;
```

Figure 5-12. *The CtlDemo4 source code.*

```
    CStatic m_ctlText;
    CButton m_ctlRadioButtonRed;
    CButton m_ctlRadioButtonGreen;
    CButton m_ctlRadioButtonBlue;
    CButton m_ctlGroupBox1;
    CButton m_ctlGroupBox2;

public:
    CMainWindow ();

protected:
    afx_msg int OnCreate (LPCREATESTRUCT);
    afx_msg HBRUSH OnCtlColor (CDC*, CWnd*, UINT);
    afx_msg void OnButtonClicked ();

    DECLARE_MESSAGE_MAP ()
};
```

CtlDemo4.cpp

```
//****************************************************************************
//
// CtlDemo4.cpp
//
//****************************************************************************

#include <afxwin.h>
#include "CtlDemo4.h"

#define IDC_RED      100
#define IDC_GREEN    101
#define IDC_BLUE     102

CMyApp myApp;

///////////////////////////////////////////////////////////////////////////
// CMyApp member functions

BOOL CMyApp::InitInstance ()
{
    m_pMainWnd = new CMainWindow;
    m_pMainWnd->ShowWindow (m_nCmdShow);
    m_pMainWnd->UpdateWindow ();
    return TRUE;
}
```

(continued)

CtlDemo4.cpp *continued*

```
//////////////////////////////////////////////////////////////////////////
// CMainWindow message map and member functions

BEGIN_MESSAGE_MAP (CMainWindow, CFrameWnd)
    ON_WM_CREATE ()
    ON_WM_CTLCOLOR ()
    ON_BN_CLICKED (IDC_RED, OnButtonClicked)
    ON_BN_CLICKED (IDC_GREEN, OnButtonClicked)
    ON_BN_CLICKED (IDC_BLUE, OnButtonClicked)
END_MESSAGE_MAP ()

CMainWindow::CMainWindow ()
{
    CString strWndClass = AfxRegisterWndClass (
        0,
        myApp.LoadStandardCursor (IDC_ARROW),
        (HBRUSH) (COLOR_3DFACE + 1),
        myApp.LoadStandardIcon (IDI_APPLICATION)
    );

    Create (strWndClass, "CtlDemo4");
}

int CMainWindow::OnCreate (LPCREATESTRUCT lpcs)
{
    if (CFrameWnd::OnCreate (lpcs) == -1)
        return -1;

    CClientDC dc (this);
    int nHeight = -((dc.GetDeviceCaps (LOGPIXELSY) * 8) / 72);

    m_font.CreateFont (nHeight, 0, 0, 0, FW_NORMAL, 0, 0, 0,
        DEFAULT_CHARSET, OUT_CHARACTER_PRECIS, CLIP_CHARACTER_PRECIS,
        DEFAULT_QUALITY, DEFAULT_PITCH | FF_DONTCARE, "MS Sans Serif");

    CFont* pOldFont = dc.SelectObject (&m_font);
    TEXTMETRIC tm;
    dc.GetTextMetrics (&tm);
    m_cxChar = tm.tmAveCharWidth;
    m_cyChar = tm.tmHeight + tm.tmExternalLeading;
    dc.SelectObject (pOldFont);

    m_ctlGroupBox1.Create ("Sample text", WS_CHILD | WS_VISIBLE |
        BS_GROUPBOX, CRect (m_cxChar * 2, m_cyChar, m_cxChar * 62,
        m_cyChar * 8), this, UINT (-1));
```

```
    m_ctlText.Create ("Click a button to change my color",
        WS_CHILD | WS_VISIBLE | SS_CENTER, CRect (m_cxChar * 4,
        m_cyChar * 4, m_cxChar * 60, m_cyChar * 6), this);

    m_ctlGroupBox2.Create ("Color", WS_CHILD | WS_VISIBLE |
        BS_GROUPBOX, CRect (m_cxChar * 64, m_cyChar, m_cxChar * 80,
        m_cyChar * 8), this, UINT (-1));

    m_ctlRadioButtonRed.Create ("Red", WS_CHILD | WS_VISIBLE | WS_GROUP |
        BS_AUTORADIOBUTTON, CRect (m_cxChar * 66, m_cyChar * 3,
        m_cxChar * 78, m_cyChar * 4), this, IDC_RED);

    m_ctlRadioButtonGreen.Create ("Green", WS_CHILD | WS_VISIBLE |
        BS_AUTORADIOBUTTON, CRect (m_cxChar * 66, (m_cyChar * 9) / 2,
        m_cxChar * 78, (m_cyChar * 11) / 2), this, IDC_GREEN);

    m_ctlRadioButtonBlue.Create ("Blue", WS_CHILD | WS_VISIBLE |
        BS_AUTORADIOBUTTON, CRect (m_cxChar * 66, m_cyChar * 6,
        m_cxChar * 78, m_cyChar * 7), this, IDC_BLUE);

    m_ctlRadioButtonRed.SetCheck (1);

    m_ctlGroupBox1.SetFont (&m_font, FALSE);
    m_ctlGroupBox2.SetFont (&m_font, FALSE);
    m_ctlRadioButtonRed.SetFont (&m_font, FALSE);
    m_ctlRadioButtonGreen.SetFont (&m_font, FALSE);
    m_ctlRadioButtonBlue.SetFont (&m_font, FALSE);
    return 0;
}

HBRUSH CMainWindow::OnCtlColor (CDC* pDC, CWnd* pWnd, UINT nCtlColor)
{
    if (pWnd->m_hWnd == m_ctlText.m_hWnd) {
        COLORREF crColor;
        if (m_ctlRadioButtonRed.GetCheck ())
            crColor = RGB (255, 0, 0);
        else if (m_ctlRadioButtonGreen.GetCheck ())
            crColor = RGB (0, 255, 0);
        else
            crColor = RGB (0, 0, 255);

        pDC->SetTextColor (crColor);
        pDC->SetBkColor (::GetSysColor (COLOR_3DFACE));
        return ::GetSysColorBrush (COLOR_3DFACE);
    }
```

(continued)

CtlDemo4.cpp *continued*

```
    return CFrameWnd::OnCtlColor (pDC, pWnd, nCtlColor);
}


void CMainWindow::OnButtonClicked ()
{
    m_ctlText.Invalidate ();
}
```

CtlDemo5 works differently. The static text control is created from a derived class named *CColorStatic* that is similar to the control class in CtlDemo4. But this time the class's colors are not hardcoded; *CColorStatic* defaults to black on COLOR_3DFACE, but it also provides public function members named *SetTextColor* and *SetBkColor* that anyone can call to change its colors. Clicking a radio button, for instance, now calls the control's *SetTextColor* function with the appropriate RGB color value:

```
ON_BN_CLICKED (IDC_RED, OnRedButtonClicked)
ON_BN_CLICKED (IDC_GREEN, OnGreenButtonClicked)
ON_BN_CLICKED (IDC_BLUE, OnBlueButtonClicked)
    .
    .
    .

void CMainWindow::OnRedButtonClicked ()
{
    m_ctlText.SetTextColor (RGB (255, 0, 0));
}

void CMainWindow::OnGreenButtonClicked ()
{
    m_ctlText.SetTextColor (RGB (0, 255, 0));
}

void CMainWindow::OnBlueButtonClicked ()
{
    m_ctlText.SetTextColor (RGB (0, 0, 255));
}
```

That's how controls are *supposed* to work. And yet, before MFC 4 rolled around, it was virtually impossible to write a self-contained control class that set its own colors because there was no built-in mechanism for reflecting WM_CTLCOLOR messages back to the controls that sent them as there was for WM_DRAWITEM messages and other selected message types.

CtlDemo5.h

```
//****************************************************************
//
//  CtlDemo5.h
//
//****************************************************************

class CColorStatic : public CStatic
{
protected:
    COLORREF m_crTextColor;
    COLORREF m_crBkColor;
    CBrush m_brBkgnd;

public:
    CColorStatic ();
    void SetTextColor (COLORREF);
    void SetBkColor (COLORREF);

protected:
    afx_msg HBRUSH CtlColor (CDC*, UINT);
    DECLARE_MESSAGE_MAP ()
};

class CMyApp : public CWinApp
{
public:
    virtual BOOL InitInstance ();
};

class CMainWindow : public CFrameWnd
{
private:
    int m_cxChar;
    int m_cyChar;
    CFont m_font;

    CColorStatic m_ctlText;
    CButton m_ctlRadioButtonRed;
    CButton m_ctlRadioButtonGreen;
    CButton m_ctlRadioButtonBlue;
    CButton m_ctlGroupBox1;
    CButton m_ctlGroupBox2;

public:
    CMainWindow ();
```

Figure 5-13. *The CtlDemo5 source code.* *(continued)*

343

CtlDemo5.h *continued*

```
protected:
    afx_msg int OnCreate (LPCREATESTRUCT);
    afx_msg void OnRedButtonClicked ();
    afx_msg void OnGreenButtonClicked ();
    afx_msg void OnBlueButtonClicked ();

    DECLARE_MESSAGE_MAP ()
};
```

CtlDemo5.cpp

```
//*****************************************************************************
//
//  CtlDemo5.cpp
//
//*****************************************************************************

#include <afxwin.h>
#include "Resource.h"
#include "CtlDemo5.h"

#define IDC_RED     100
#define IDC_GREEN   101
#define IDC_BLUE    102

CMyApp myApp;

///////////////////////////////////////////////////////////////////////////
// CMyApp member functions

BOOL CMyApp::InitInstance ()
{
    m_pMainWnd = new CMainWindow;
    m_pMainWnd->ShowWindow (m_nCmdShow);
    m_pMainWnd->UpdateWindow ();
    return TRUE;
}

///////////////////////////////////////////////////////////////////////////
// CMainWindow message map and member functions

BEGIN_MESSAGE_MAP (CMainWindow, CFrameWnd)
    ON_WM_CREATE ()
    ON_BN_CLICKED (IDC_RED, OnRedButtonClicked)
```

```
    ON_BN_CLICKED (IDC_GREEN, OnGreenButtonClicked)
    ON_BN_CLICKED (IDC_BLUE, OnBlueButtonClicked)
END_MESSAGE_MAP ()

CMainWindow::CMainWindow ()
{
    CString strWndClass = AfxRegisterWndClass (
        0,
        myApp.LoadStandardCursor (IDC_ARROW),
        (HBRUSH) (COLOR_3DFACE + 1),
        myApp.LoadStandardIcon (IDI_APPLICATION)
    );

    Create (strWndClass, "CtlDemo5");
}

int CMainWindow::OnCreate (LPCREATESTRUCT lpcs)
{
    if (CFrameWnd::OnCreate (lpcs) == -1)
        return -1;

    CClientDC dc (this);
    int nHeight = -((dc.GetDeviceCaps (LOGPIXELSY) * 8) / 72);

    m_font.CreateFont (nHeight, 0, 0, 0, FW_NORMAL, 0, 0, 0,
        DEFAULT_CHARSET, OUT_CHARACTER_PRECIS, CLIP_CHARACTER_PRECIS,
        DEFAULT_QUALITY, DEFAULT_PITCH | FF_DONTCARE, "MS Sans Serif");

    CFont* pOldFont = dc.SelectObject (&m_font);
    TEXTMETRIC tm;
    dc.GetTextMetrics (&tm);
    m_cxChar = tm.tmAveCharWidth;
    m_cyChar = tm.tmHeight + tm.tmExternalLeading;
    dc.SelectObject (pOldFont);

    m_ctlGroupBox1.Create ("Sample text", WS_CHILD | WS_VISIBLE |
        BS_GROUPBOX, CRect (m_cxChar * 2, m_cyChar, m_cxChar * 62,
        m_cyChar * 8), this, UINT (-1));

    m_ctlText.Create ("Click a button to change my color",
        WS_CHILD | WS_VISIBLE | SS_CENTER, CRect (m_cxChar * 4,
        m_cyChar * 4, m_cxChar * 60, m_cyChar * 6), this);

    m_ctlGroupBox2.Create ("Color", WS_CHILD | WS_VISIBLE |
        BS_GROUPBOX, CRect (m_cxChar * 64, m_cyChar, m_cxChar * 80,
        m_cyChar * 8), this, UINT (-1));
```

(continued)

CtlDemo5.cpp *continued*

```
    m_ctlRadioButtonRed.Create ("Red", WS_CHILD | WS_VISIBLE | WS_GROUP |
        BS_AUTORADIOBUTTON, CRect (m_cxChar * 66, m_cyChar * 3,
        m_cxChar * 78, m_cyChar * 4), this, IDC_RED);

    m_ctlRadioButtonGreen.Create ("Green", WS_CHILD | WS_VISIBLE |
        BS_AUTORADIOBUTTON, CRect (m_cxChar * 66, (m_cyChar * 9) / 2,
        m_cxChar * 78, (m_cyChar * 11) / 2), this, IDC_GREEN);

    m_ctlRadioButtonBlue.Create ("Blue", WS_CHILD | WS_VISIBLE |
        BS_AUTORADIOBUTTON, CRect (m_cxChar * 66, m_cyChar * 6,
        m_cxChar * 78, m_cyChar * 7), this, IDC_BLUE);

    m_ctlRadioButtonRed.SetCheck (1);
    m_ctlText.SetTextColor (RGB (255, 0, 0));

    m_ctlGroupBox1.SetFont (&m_font, FALSE);
    m_ctlGroupBox2.SetFont (&m_font, FALSE);
    m_ctlRadioButtonRed.SetFont (&m_font, FALSE);
    m_ctlRadioButtonGreen.SetFont (&m_font, FALSE);
    m_ctlRadioButtonBlue.SetFont (&m_font, FALSE);
    return 0;
}

void CMainWindow::OnRedButtonClicked ()
{
    m_ctlText.SetTextColor (RGB (255, 0, 0));
}

void CMainWindow::OnGreenButtonClicked ()
{
    m_ctlText.SetTextColor (RGB (0, 255, 0));
}

void CMainWindow::OnBlueButtonClicked ()
{
    m_ctlText.SetTextColor (RGB (0, 0, 255));
}


//////////////////////////////////////////////////////////////////////
// CColorStatic message map and member functions

BEGIN_MESSAGE_MAP (CColorStatic, CStatic)
    ON_WM_CTLCOLOR_REFLECT ()
END_MESSAGE_MAP ()
```

```
CColorStatic::CColorStatic ()
{
    m_crTextColor = RGB (0, 0, 0);
    m_crBkColor = ::GetSysColor (COLOR_3DFACE);
    m_brBkgnd.CreateSolidBrush (m_crBkColor);
}

void CColorStatic::SetTextColor (COLORREF crColor)
{
    m_crTextColor = crColor;
    Invalidate ();
}

void CColorStatic::SetBkColor (COLORREF crColor)
{
    m_crBkColor = crColor;
    m_brBkgnd.DeleteObject ();
    m_brBkgnd.CreateSolidBrush (crColor);
    Invalidate ();
}

HBRUSH CColorStatic::CtlColor (CDC* pDC, UINT nCtlColor)
{
    pDC->SetTextColor (m_crTextColor);
    pDC->SetBkColor (m_crBkColor);
    return (HBRUSH) m_brBkgnd;
}
```

Different controls respond to *OnCtlColor/CtlColor* handlers in different ways. You've already seen how static controls and other controls that display text respond to *SetTextColor*, *SetBkColor*, and brush handles. For a scroll bar control, *SetTextColor* and *SetBkColor* do nothing, but the brush handle returned by the message handler sets the color of the scroll bar's shaft. For a list box, *SetTextColor* and *SetBkColor* affect unhighlighted list box items but have no effect on highlighted items, and the background brush determines the color of the list box's background—anything on an empty or unhighlighted line that is not painted over with text. For a push button, *OnCtlColor* and *CtlColor* have no effect whatsoever because Windows 95 uses system colors to draw push button controls. If *nCtlType* contains the code CTLCOLOR-_BTN, you might as well pass it on to the base class because nothing you do to the DC will affect how the control is drawn.

Message Reflection

ON_WM_CTLCOLOR_REFLECT is one of several new message map macros featured in MFC 4 that permit messages from controls to be reflected back to the controls that sent them. Message reflection is a powerful tool for building reusable control classes because it allows the classes you derive from MFC control classes to be self-contained. Previous versions of MFC reflected certain messages back to the controls that sent them and used a virtual *CWnd* function named *OnChildNotify* to allow controls to process their own notifications relayed in the form of WM_COMMAND and WM_NOTIFY messages. MFC 4, however, genericizes the concept of message reflection so that a control can map *any* message sent to its parent to a member function in the control class. You saw an example of how it works in the previous section when we derived a new class from *CStatic* and allowed it to handle its own WM_CTLCOLOR messages.

Here's a list of the message reflection macros MFC provides and short descriptions of what they do.

MFC MESSAGE REFLECTION MACROS

Macro	*Description*
ON_CONTROL_REFLECT	Reflects notifications relayed through WM_COMMAND messages.
ON_NOTIFY_REFLECT	Reflects notifications relayed through WM_NOTIFY messages.
ON_UPDATE_COMMAND_UI_REFLECT	Reflects update notifications to toolbars, status bars, and other UI objects.
ON_WM_CTLCOLOR_REFLECT	Reflects WM_CTLCOLOR messages.
ON_WM_DRAWITEM_REFLECT	Reflects WM_DRAWITEM messages sent by owner-drawn controls.
ON_WM_MEASUREITEM_REFLECT	Reflects WM_MEASUREITEM messages sent by owner-drawn controls.
ON_WM_COMPAREITEM_REFLECT	Reflects WM_COMPAREITEM messages sent by owner-drawn controls.
ON_WM_DELETEITEM_REFLECT	Reflects WM_DELETEITEM messages sent by owner-drawn controls.
ON_WM_CHARTOITEM_REFLECT	Reflects WM_CHARTOITEM messages sent by list boxes.
ON_WM_VKEYTOITEM_REFLECT	Reflects WM_VKEYTOITEM messages sent by list boxes.
ON_WM_HSCROLL_REFLECT	Reflects WM_HSCROLL messages sent by scroll bars.
ON_WM_VSCROLL_REFLECT	Reflects WM_VSCROLL messages sent by scroll bars.
ON_WM_PARENTNOTIFY_REFLECT	Reflects WM_PARENTNOTIFY messages.

One use for these reflection macros is to develop a self-contained list box class that pops up a dialog box allowing the text of an item to be edited when that item is double-clicked. In an SDK-style application, the list box's parent would have to pop up the dialog box. In an MFC application, the list box can handle the LBN_DBLCLK notification and display the dialog box itself. Here's what the derived list box class might look like:

```
class CEditListBox : public CListBox
{
protected:
    afx_msg void OnEditItem ();
    DECLARE_MESSAGE_MAP ()
};

BEGIN_MESSAGE_MAP (CEditListBox, CListBox)
    ON_CONTROL_REFLECT (LBN_DBLCLK, OnEditItem)
END_MESSAGE_MAP ()

void CEditListBox::OnEditItem ()
{
    CString strItemText;
    int nIndex = GetCurSel ();
    GetText (nIndex, strItemText);
    // Display the dialog, and allow strItemText to be edited...
    DeleteString (nIndex);
    if (GetStyle () & LBS_SORT)
        AddString (strItemText);
    else
        InsertString (nIndex, strItemText);
}
```

The ON_CONTROL_REFLECT entry in the list box's message map causes the framework to call *CEditListBox::OnEditItem* anytime the list box sends an LBN_DBLCLK notification to its parent—in other words, anytime its parent receives a WM_COMMAND message with the high word of *wParam* equal to LBN_DBLCLK. We'll use a list box class very similar to this one in the next chapter.

Chapter 6

Dialog Boxes and Property Sheets

In the real world, most controls appear not in top-level windows but in dialog boxes. A *dialog box,* also known as a "dialog," is a special window designed to solicit input from the user. Dialogs simplify the use of push buttons, list boxes, and other controls because the controls in a dialog don't have to be created manually with *Create* and *CreateEx*. Instead, these controls are sized and positioned in *dialog templates* defined offline with a resource editor and linked into your application along with menus, icons, bitmaps, and other resources. Given a dialog template's resource ID, one simple state- ment creates a dialog box and its controls.

Dialog boxes come in two basic varieties: *modal* and *modeless*. A modal dialog disables its application owner until the dialog is dismissed. It's an application's way of saying, "I can't do anything else until you supply me with the input I need." The Open dialog displayed when you select Open from an application's File menu is one example of a modal dialog. Modeless dialogs behave more like ordinary windows. When a modeless dialog is displayed, the user is free to reactivate the main window and leave the dialog floating in the background. The Find dialog in the Windows 95 WordPad applet is an example of a modeless dialog.

MFC encapsulates the functionality of both modal and modeless dialog boxes in the class *CDialog*. Dialog box handling is relatively easy when you program in C using the Windows SDK, but it's even easier with the support MFC provides. *CDialog*, for example, provides default handlers for the OK and Cancel buttons found in most dialogs, and MFC provides a mechanism for transferring data between a dialog's controls and data members of the dialog class. Even complex dialog boxes containing dozens of controls can often be built from just a few lines of code, speeding program development and reducing the likelihood of errors. MFC also provides convenient C++ implementations of the Windows 95 *common dialogs*—Open dialogs, Print dialogs, and other dialogs commonly found in Windows applications—implementations that move much of the boilerplate code found in C programs out of your code and into the class library where it belongs.

Of course, you can't talk about dialog boxes without discussing property sheets, too. A *property sheet* is a special type of dialog box featuring tabbed pages. Property sheets are great for lending a higher level of organization to the controls in a dialog. They're also space-efficient (allowing more controls to fit in a finite amount of space), and they're fast becoming commonplace in Windows applications. MFC makes property sheet handling simple with its *CPropertySheet* and *CPropertyPage* classes. And when MFC creates a property sheet in Windows 95, it uses the operating system's native property sheet implementation in lieu of its own implementation. Take it from someone who's been there: if you've programmed property sheets in C, you'll appreciate the work the framework does on your behalf to make dealing with property sheets fundamentally no different from—and no more difficult than—dealing with ordinary dialog boxes.

MODAL DIALOG BOXES AND THE *CDIALOG* CLASS

Creating a modal dialog box is a three-step process: create a dialog template, construct a *CDialog* object, and call *CDialog::DoModal* to display the dialog. For very simple modal dialogs, you can sometimes instantiate *CDialog* directly. More often, however, you'll need to derive a dialog class of your own so that you can override key virtual functions that govern a dialog's behavior. Let's begin by examining the three-step creation process in more detail and follow up with a series of sample programs demonstrating common dialog box programming techniques. After that, we'll apply what we've learned to modeless dialogs and property sheets, too.

The Dialog Template

The first step in creating a dialog box is creating a dialog template. The template defines the fundamental properties of the dialog box, from the types of controls it contains to the caption in its title bar. There are two ways to create a dialog template: programmatically or from resource statements in an application's .rc file. The programmatic method, which involves initializing a DLGTEMPLATE structure with data describing the dialog box and DLGITEMTEMPLATE structures describing the dialog's controls, is by far the more difficult (and less common) of the two and is normally used only for dialogs that are built on the fly from information gathered at run-time.

The easy way to create a dialog template is to use the Visual C++ resource editor, the SDK's Dialog Editor, or a similar editing tool to design the dialog box and save it as a series of resource statements in your application's .rc file. The dialog template resource can then be compiled, bound to the application's .exe file, and referenced by name or ID number in the source code.

The following resource statements create a dialog template whose resource ID is IDD_MYDIALOG. The dialog box the template describes contains four controls: a single-line edit control for entering text, a static text control that serves as a label for the edit control, an OK button, and a Cancel button:

```
IDD_MYDIALOG DIALOG 0, 0, 160, 68
STYLE DS_MODALFRAME | WS_POPUP | WS_VISIBLE | WS_CAPTION | WS_SYSMENU
CAPTION "Enter Your Name"
FONT 8, "MS Sans Serif"
BEGIN
    LTEXT           "&Name", -1, 8, 14, 24, 8
    EDITTEXT        IDC_NAME, 34, 12, 118, 12, ES_AUTOHSCROLL
    DEFPUSHBUTTON   "OK", IDOK, 60, 34, 40, 14, WS_GROUP
    PUSHBUTTON      "Cancel", IDCANCEL, 112, 34, 40, 14, WS_GROUP
END
```

The numbers on the first line specify the location of the dialog's upper left corner and its dimensions. (0, 0) means that the dialog will initially be positioned in the upper left corner of its parent, while (160, 68) specifies the dialog width and height. All measurements are in dialog box units. Horizontally, one dialog box unit is approximately equal to one-fourth the average width of a character in the default dialog font, which for Windows 95 is 8-point MS Sans Serif. Vertically, one dialog box unit equals one-eighth the character height. Because characters are generally about twice as tall as they are wide, the distance represented by one horizontal dialog box unit is roughly equal to that of one vertical dialog box unit. A width and height equal to (160, 68) means that the dialog will be about 40 characters wide and 8½ characters high. Measuring distances in dialog box units rather than pixels allows a dialog's relative proportions to be defined independent of the screen resolution.

The STYLE statement in the dialog template specifies the dialog's window style. The styles that begin with WS_ are the same ones you pass to *Create* or *CreateEx* when you create a conventional window. WS_POPUP should always be specified since a dialog box is a popup window, and WS_VISIBLE is almost universally included so that *ShowWindow* doesn't have to be called to make the dialog visible on the screen. WS_CAPTION gives the dialog a title bar, and WS_SYSMENU adds a close button to the title bar. Styles prefixed with DS_ are specific to dialog boxes. By convention, modal dialog boxes are assigned the style DS_MODALFRAME. In previous versions of Windows, designating this style placed a thick border around the dialog window that was a visual reminder of the dialog's modal nature. In Windows 95, DS_MODALFRAME has subtle effects on a dialog's behavior but does nothing to change the dialog window's looks because all dialog borders are drawn in the same style. Other interesting dialog styles include DS_CENTER, which centers a dialog box on the screen, and DS_CONTEXTHELP, which adds a question mark button to the dialog's title bar so that the user can get context-sensitive help regarding the dialog's controls.

You can create a "system-modal" dialog box by including DS_SYSMODAL in the STYLE statement. In 16-bit Windows, a system-modal dialog box disables all others windows in the system until it is dismissed and is typically used to report critical errors that must be attended to before any further processing is performed. In 32-bit Windows, where processes are physically isolated from one another by the operating system, the DS_SYSMODAL style simply makes the dialog box a topmost window. The dialog is visible above all other windows, but the user is free to switch to other applications while the dialog is displayed.

The CAPTION statement specifies the dialog's title. The title can also be set programmatically with the *SetWindowText* function a *CDialog* object inherits from *CWnd*. FONT specifies the dialog box font, which is automatically assigned to all the controls in the dialog. The statement

```
FONT 8, "MS Sans Serif"
```

is somewhat redundant in Windows 95 because 8-point MS Sans Serif is now the default dialog font. If your dialogs will also be used in other versions of Windows, include this statement to be certain that the dialog will use 8-point MS Sans Serif. You can change the fonts assigned to individual controls in a dialog box using *CWnd::SetFont*.

The statements between BEGIN and END define the dialog box controls. Each statement corresponds to one control, specifying its type (push button, check box, list box, and so on), its child window ID, its location relative to the upper left corner of the dialog, its width and height (in dialog box units), and its style. For static and button controls, the control text can be specified, too. In the example on the previous page, LTEXT creates a static text control labeled "&Name" whose ID is −1, whose text is left-aligned in the control rectangle, whose upper left corner lies 8 horizontal dialog box units to the right of and 14 vertical dialog box units below the dialog box's upper left corner, and whose width and height are 24 horizontal dialog box units and 8 vertical dialog box units, respectively. The ampersand in the control text makes N (or Alt-N) a shortcut for the edit control that is created in the EDITTEXT line.

LTEXT is just one of several resource statements you can use to define dialog box controls and their properties; a complete list appears in the table on the facing page. In essence, these statements are shorthand ways of creating the same kinds of controls we created in Chapter 5 by constructing a control object and calling that

RESOURCE STATEMENTS FOR CREATING DIALOG BOX CONTROLS

Keyword	Control Type	Default Styles
LTEXT	Static text control with left-aligned text	SS_LEFT ¦ WS_GROUP
CTEXT	Static text control with centered text	SS_CENTER ¦ WS_GROUP
RTEXT	Static text control with right-aligned text	SS_RIGHT ¦ WS_GROUP
PUSHBUTTON	Push button	BS_PUSHBUTTON ¦ WS_TABSTOP
DEFPUSHBUTTON	Default push button	BS_DEFPUSHBUTTON ¦ WS_TABSTOP
EDITTEXT	Edit control	ES_LEFT ¦ WS_BORDER ¦ WS_TABSTOP
CHECKBOX	Check box	BS_CHECKBOX ¦ WS_TABSTOP
AUTOCHECKBOX	Automatic check box	BS_AUTOCHECKBOX ¦ WS_TABSTOP
STATE3	3-state check box	BS_3STATE ¦ WS_TABSTOP
AUTO3STATE	Automatic 3-state check box	BS_AUTO3STATE ¦ WS_TABSTOP
RADIOBUTTON	Radio button	BS_RADIOBUTTON ¦ WS_TABSTOP
AUTORADIOBUTTON	Automatic radio button	BS_AUTORADIOBUTTON ¦ WS_TABSTOP
GROUPBOX	Group box	BS_GROUPBOX
LISTBOX	List box	LBS_NOTIFY ¦ WS_BORDER
COMBOBOX	Combo box	CBS_SIMPLE ¦ WS_TABSTOP
SCROLLBAR	Scroll bar	SBS_HORZ
ICON	Static icon control	SS_ICON

object's *Create* or *CreateEx* function. Because they are defined in a dialog template, these controls are created by Windows. Each keyword has certain default styles associated with it, and note that all build in the styles WS_CHILD and WS_VISIBLE. Buttons, edit controls, and combo boxes include the style WS_TABSTOP. But since LISTBOX does not, you must specify the WS_TABSTOP style explicitly if you want a list box to be included in the tab order.

You can remove an implicit style with the NOT operator. The following resource statement creates a combo box control without the default WS_TABSTOP style:

```
COMBOBOX IDC_COMBOBOX, 32, 16, 48, 12, NOT WS_TABSTOP
```

In previous versions of Windows, the NOT operator was sometimes used to create automatic check box and radio button controls. For example, the statement

```
RADIOBUTTON IDC_RADIOBUTTON, 32, 16, 48, 12,
    NOT BS_RADIOBUTTON ¦ BS_AUTORADIOBUTTON
```

created an automatic radio button control. The AUTOCHECKBOX, STATE3, AUTO3-STATE, and AUTORADIOBUTTON keywords were added to the Windows 95 resource compiler so that nondefault check boxes and radio buttons could be created more easily than in earlier versions.

If you specify a style that conflicts with one of the implicit styles, your style will generally take precedence. For example, SCROLLBAR builds in the style SBS_HORZ so that a horizontal scroll bar will be created if you specify neither SBS_HORZ nor SBS_VERT. But the statement

```
SCROLLBAR IDC_SCROLLBAR, 8, 8, 16, 64, SBS_VERT
```

creates a vertical scroll bar. Similarly, you can create a non-CBS_SIMPLE-style combo box by specifying CBS_DROPDOWN or CBS_DROPDOWNLIST in a COMBOBOX statement.

You can also define dialog box controls with the more generic CONTROL command. Sometimes you'll see a dialog box defined this way:

```
IDD_MYDIALOG DIALOG 0, 0, 160, 68
STYLE DS_MODALFRAME ¦ WS_POPUP ¦ WS_VISIBLE ¦ WS_CAPTION ¦ WS_SYSMENU
CAPTION "Enter Your Name"
BEGIN
    CONTROL     "&Name", -1, "STATIC", SS_LEFT, 8, 14, 24, 8
    CONTROL     "", IDC_NAME, "EDIT", WS_BORDER ¦ ES_AUTOHSCROLL ¦
                ES_LEFT ¦ WS_TABSTOP, 34, 12, 118, 12
    CONTROL     "OK", IDOK, "BUTTON", BS_DEFPUSHBUTTON ¦
                WS_TABSTOP ¦, WS_GROUP, 60, 34, 40, 14
    CONTROL     "Cancel", IDCANCEL, "BUTTON", BS_PUSHBUTTON ¦
                WS_TABSTOP ¦ WS_GROUP, 112, 34, 40, 14
END
```

This dialog template is equivalent to the one on page 353. The CONTROL statement builds in the styles WS_CHILD and WS_VISIBLE, but all other styles must be specified explicitly. The third parameter in a CONTROL statement specifies the WNDCLASS the control is based on—"BUTTON" for push buttons, radio buttons, check boxes, and group boxes; "EDIT" for edit controls; and so on. Because the WNDCLASS is specified explicitly in a CONTROL statement, you can use CONTROL to create controls from custom control classes registered with *::RegisterClass*. It's with CONTROL statements, in fact, that you add progress bars, spin buttons, and other common controls to a dialog box—something we'll explore more fully in Chapter 13.

The Dialog Box Keyboard Interface

When you create a modal dialog box, Windows supplies a keyboard interface that allows the user to tab among the controls, move the input focus within groups of controls with the arrow keys, go directly to designated controls by pressing shortcut keys, and more. When you define a dialog template, you define the dialog box's keyboard interface, too. The elements of the dialog template that affect the keyboard interface include

- The order in which the controls are defined

- The use of ampersands in control text to designate shortcut keys

- The use of the WS_GROUP style to group controls

- The use of DEFPUSHBUTTON to designate a default push button

The ordering of the controls in the dialog template determines the *tab order*— the order in which the input focus is passed around when Tab or Shift-Tab is pressed. Since the keyboard processing logic is provided for you, all you have to do is make sure the controls are defined in the order in which you want the input focus to move. Most dialog editors enable you to specify the tab order visually. Under the hood, they simply reorder the resource statements to match the tab order you've specified. Don't forget that a control can't be tabbed to unless it has been assigned the style WS_TAB-STOP. That's why so many of the resource statements discussed in the previous section include WS_TABSTOP by default.

To create a shortcut key for a push button, a radio button, or a check box control, precede the shortcut letter in the control text with an ampersand, as in

```
PUSHBUTTON "&Reset", IDC_RESET, 112, 34, 40, 24, WS_GROUP
```

Now presses of Alt-R (or simply R if the input focus rests on another button control) will select the Reset button unless another control has been assigned the same mnemonic, in which case repeated presses of the shortcut key will cycle the input focus between the two controls. For list boxes, edit controls, and other nonbutton controls, you create a shortcut by immediately preceding the resource statement that creates the control with a statement that creates a static text control and including an ampersand in the static control's text. For example, the statements

```
LTEXT       "&Name", -1, 8, 14, 24, 8
EDITTEXT    IDC_NAME, 34, 12, 118, 12, ES_AUTOHSCROLL
```

create a static LTEXT control labeled "Name" and a single-line edit control to the right of it. Pressing Alt-N moves the input focus to the edit control.

Another element of the keyboard interface you need to consider when you're creating a dialog template, especially if the dialog includes radio buttons, is the grouping of the controls. Recall from Chapter 5 that BS_AUTORADIOBUTTON-style radio buttons must be grouped if all the other buttons in the group are to be unchecked when one of the buttons in the group is clicked. In addition, Windows uses radio button control groupings to determine how to cycle the input focus among radio buttons when the arrow keys are pressed. To define a group of radio buttons, assign the style WS_GROUP to the first radio button in the group and to the first control following the final radio button in the group. Windows programmers often assign WS_GROUP to push buttons and check boxes, too, so that the arrow keys won't move the input focus away from non-radio-button controls.

A final consideration to keep in mind as you design your dialog box's keyboard interface is which push button should serve as the default. In most dialog boxes, you designate one push button (typically the OK button) as the default by creating it with a DEFPUSHBUTTON statement or assigning it the BS_DEFPUSHBUTTON style. When the Enter key is pressed, Windows simulates a click of the default push button in the dialog box. If the input focus is on a non-push-button control, the default push button is the one you designated as the default in the dialog template. As the input focus is cycled among push buttons, however, the "defaultness" moves with it. You can always tell which push button is the default by the thick border Windows draws around it.

The Dialog Class

For all but the most trivial of modal dialog boxes, the next step after creating the dialog template is to derive a class from *CDialog* that defines the dialog box's behavior. *CDialog* provides three key functions you can override to initialize the dialog box controls and respond to clicks of the OK and Cancel buttons: *OnInitDialog*, *OnOK*, and *OnCancel*. Although each of these functions corresponds to a dialog box message, you don't need a message map to process them because *CDialog* defines them as virtual. *CDialog* also provides default implementations of all three, so you can often get away without overriding any of them.

When a dialog box is first created, it receives a WM_CREATE message just as any other window does. But when the WM_CREATE message arrives, the controls defined in the dialog template have yet to be created and therefore can't be initialized by the application. The dialog box is, in effect, empty. The internal window procedure that Windows uses to process dialog box messages responds to WM_CREATE messages by creating the controls defined in the associated dialog template. Windows then sends the dialog box a WM_INITDIALOG message providing it the opportunity to perform any necessary initializations, including those involving the controls. In a *CDialog*-derived class, the WM_INITDIALOG message activates the dialog box's *OnInitDialog* handler, which is prototyped as follows:

```
virtual BOOL OnInitDialog ()
```

OnInitDialog is where you do anything you need to do to get the dialog box ready for action—click a radio button, add text to an edit control, and so on. At the moment *OnInitDialog* is called, the dialog box is extant in memory but not yet visible on the screen. The user won't see what you do in *OnInitDialog*, but he or she *will* see the results. MFC programmers often have *OnInitDialog* call the *CenterWindow* function that a dialog box inherits from *CWnd* to center the dialog box relative to its parent window, as shown here:

```
BOOL CMyDialog::OnInitDialog ()
{
    CDialog::OnInitDialog ();
    CenterWindow ();
    return TRUE;
}
```

CenterWindow overrides the dialog box coordinates entered in the dialog template. If you'd prefer that the dialog box be centered on the screen, forget *CenterWindow* and include a DS_CENTER specifier in the dialog template's STYLE statement instead.

The value returned from *OnInitDialog* tells Windows what to do with the input focus. If *OnInitDialog* returns TRUE, Windows assigns the input focus to the first control in the tab order. To assign the input focus to a control other than the first one, call that control's *SetFocus* function from *OnInitDialog* and return FALSE to prevent Windows from setting the input focus itself. When you override *OnInitDialog*, make it a habit to call the base class's *OnInitDialog* handler, too. Why this is important will become apparent later on, when we discuss MFC's built-in data exchange and validation mechanism.

When the user clicks the dialog box's OK button, the dialog box receives a WM_COMMAND message reporting the button click, and MFC in turn calls the dialog's virtual *OnOK* handler. For this mechanism to work properly, you must assign the OK button the special ID value IDOK as demonstrated in the following resource statement:

```
DEFPUSHBUTTON "OK", IDOK, 60, 34, 40, 24, WS_GROUP
```

You can override *OnOK* to perform specialized processing before the dialog box is dismissed, which might include extracting data from the controls in the dialog box and possibly validating the data (for example, making sure that a numeric value entered in an edit control falls within an allowable range). If you do provide your own implementation of *OnOK*, be sure to close it out by calling *EndDialog* to dismiss the dialog box or by calling the base class's *OnOK* handler to dismiss it for you. Otherwise, the dialog box won't disappear when OK is clicked. The integer value passed to *EndDialog* is returned through the *DoModal* function that created the dialog box. By convention, *EndDialog* is passed the value IDOK when it's called from an *OnOK* handler and IDCANCEL when it's called from *OnCancel*.

A Cancel button must be assigned the predefined ID IDCANCEL for *OnCancel* to be called when the button is clicked. But be aware that even if your dialog box doesn't include a Cancel button, *OnCancel* will still be called if the Esc key is pressed or the close button in the dialog box's title bar is clicked. *OnCancel* is not usually overridden because data doesn't usually need to be read from the dialog box controls if changes are being canceled. The default implementation of *OnCancel* calls *EndDialog* with an IDCANCEL parameter to dismiss the dialog box and inform the caller that changes in the dialog box controls should be ignored.

With the exception of the WM_INITDIALOG message, which is unique to dialog boxes, dialog boxes receive the same messages that conventional windows do. You can map any of these messages to member functions with a message map, including WM_COMMAND messages generated by the controls. If your dialog box includes a Reset button whose ID is IDC_RESET and you want your dialog class's *OnReset* function to be activated when the button is clicked, use the following message map entry to connect the two:

```
ON_BN_CLICKED (IDC_RESET, OnReset)
```

Dialog boxes can even handle WM_PAINT messages—somewhat unusual but doable nonetheless. Most dialog boxes neither need nor use *OnPaint* handlers because the controls repaint themselves when the area of the dialog box window they occupy is invalidated.

Dialog Box Data and Type-Safe Access to the Controls

One advantage of programming dialog boxes in C++ and deriving your own dialog class from *CDialog* is that data associated with the dialog box and its controls can be declared as data members of the dialog class. Suppose your dialog box contains two single-line edit controls in which the user enters a name and a phone number. Since these data items are intrinsically tied to the dialog box itself, you simply implement them as *CString* objects and declare them to be members of your *CDialog*-derived class. The class declaration might look like this:

```
class CMyDialog : public CDialog
{
public:
    CString m_name;
    CString m_phone;

protected:
    virtual void OnOK ();
};
```

Now *m_name* and *m_phone* will store the text strings retrieved from the edit controls. And since the *CString* objects are public data members of the dialog box class, they provide a convenient means for getting data in and out of the dialog box.

In this example, the job of retrieving text from the edit controls when the OK button is clicked falls to the dialog box's *OnOK* handler. (Similarly, strings could be stuffed into the edit controls in *OnInitDialog*.) One way to implement *CMyDialog-::OnOK* is like this:

```
void CMyDialog::OnOK ()
{
    GetDlgItemText (IDC_NAME, m_name);
    GetDlgItemText (IDC_PHONE, m_phone);
    CDialog::OnOK ();
}
```

Given a control ID and a *CString* reference, *CWnd::GetDlgItemText* copies the text entered into an edit control into the *CString*. However, a better way to write *CMyDialog::OnOK* is like this:

```
void CMyDialog::OnOK ()
{
    CEdit* pName = (CEdit*) GetDlgItem (IDC_NAME);
    pName->GetWindowText (m_name);
    CEdit* pPhone = (CEdit*) GetDlgItem (IDC_PHONE);
    pPhone->GetWindowText (m_phone);
    CDialog::OnOK ();
}
```

Using *GetDlgItem* to get *CEdit* pointers to the controls and *CEdit* member functions to read the text permits the controls to be accessed in a type-safe way. MFC programmers often include private member functions in their dialog box classes to simplify control access. For example, if the *CMyDialog* class were rewritten to include the following inline member functions,

```
CEdit& name () { return *(CEdit*) GetDlgItem (IDC_NAME); }
CEdit& phone () { return *(CEdit*) GetDlgItem (IDC_PHONE); }
```

CMyDialog::OnOK could be rewritten like this:

```
void CMyDialog::OnOK ()
{
    name ().GetWindowText (m_name);
    phone ().GetWindowText (m_phone);
    CDialog::OnOK ();
}
```

This technique provides a convenient solution to the problem that because the controls in a dialog box are created by Windows, you don't get control objects with which to access them unless you create them yourself. For truly seamless access to the controls, you could declare a private data member for each control and attach the control objects to the control window in *OnInitDialog* using *CWnd::Attach*. The lengths you go to to make the controls in a dialog box accessible in an object-oriented way are up to you.

Overriding *OnInitDialog* and *OnOK* and calling the control's member functions is one way to get data in and out of the controls. It's instructive to see it done this way because it's the way Windows programmers have traditionally done it, and it's the way we'd all be doing it still if it weren't for MFC. But there's a better way, one that's handled entirely by the framework. We're not ready to go into it just yet, but the time will come—soon.

Creating a Modal Dialog Box

Once the dialog box template is defined and the dialog class is declared, creating a modal dialog box is a simple matter of constructing an object from your *CDialog*-derived class and calling that object's *DoModal* function. *DoModal* doesn't return until after the dialog box is dismissed. When it does return, its return value is the value that was passed to *EndDialog*. Applications typically test the *DoModal* return value and take action only if the return value is IDOK, indicating that the dialog box was dismissed with the OK button. If the return value is anything else (most likely ID-CANCEL), then the information entered into the dialog box is ignored.

CDialog defines two constructors: one that accepts the name of a dialog template resource and a pointer to the parent window, and another that accepts an integer dialog template resource ID and a pointer to the parent window. The *CWnd* pointer identifying the dialog box's parent can be omitted, in which case the dialog box is automatically parented to the application's main window. If the dialog template's resource ID is IDD_MYDIALOG and the dialog class is *CMyDialog*, then the dialog box is created as follows:

```
CMyDialog dlg (IDD_MYDIALOG, this);
dlg.DoModal ();
```

When the user dismisses the dialog by clicking OK or Cancel, *DoModal* returns and the function that called *DoModal* continues.

To make derived dialog classes more object-like and more self-contained, MFC programmers often provide their own dialog class constructors that build in references to the dialog templates. A simple inline constructor for *CMyDialog* could be written like this:

```
CMyDialog::CMyDialog (CWnd* pParentWnd = NULL) :
    CDialog (IDD_MYDIALOG, pParentWnd) {}
```

This constructor simplifies the code that creates the dialog box and eliminates the possibility of inadvertently passing the constructor the wrong resource identifier:

```
CMyDialog dlg (this);
dlg.DoModal ();
```

If the action taken following the call to *DoModal* depends on whether the data entered in the dialog box was okayed or canceled (and it almost inevitably will), the return value can be tested, like this:

```
CMyDialog dlg (this);
if (dlg.DoModal () == IDOK) {
    // The user clicked OK; do something!
}
```

By default, the only values *DoModal* will return are IDOK and IDCANCEL. However, you can write your dialog class to return other values by calling *EndDialog* with a value other than IDOK or IDCANCEL. You could, for example, include an End This Application button in a dialog box and wire it into the program as follows:

```
// In the dialog class
BEGIN_MESSAGE_MAP (CMyDialog, CDialog)
    ON_BN_CLICKED (IDC_ENDAPP, OnEndThisApplication)
END_MESSAGE_MAP ()
    :
    :

void CMyDialog::OnEndThisApplication ()
{
    EndDialog (IDC_ENDAPP);
}

// In the main window class
CMyDialog dlg (this);
int nReturn = dlg.DoModal ();
if (nReturn == IDOK) {
    // The user clicked OK; do something!
}
else if (nReturn == IDC_ENDAPP)
    PostMessage (WM_CLOSE, 0, 0);
```

When the user clicks End This Application in the dialog box, the return value IDC-_ENDAPP alerts the caller that the user wants to terminate the application. Consequently, a WM_CLOSE message is posted to the message queue to initiate a shutdown. (Posting rather than sending the WM_CLOSE message gives the message handler that displayed the dialog box time to perform additional processing if necessary before the application shuts down.) IDC_ENDAPP should be assigned an ID value equal to 2 or higher to avoid conflicting with the predefined IDOK and IDCANCEL button IDs.

Creating a Simple About Box

Let's see how the preceding discussion translates into code by creating a modal About box that displays the title of the application and a brief copyright notice. The DlgDemo1 application, listed in Figure 6-1 on the next page, does the bare minimum amount of work necessary to get a dialog box up on the screen. To display the About dialog box, the user selects About DlgDemo1 from the program's Options menu. The dialog template, whose resource ID is IDD_ABOUTDLG, is located in DlgDemo1.rc, and the dialog box itself is created in *CMainWindow::OnOptionsAbout* with the following statements:

```
CDialog dlg (IDD_ABOUTDLG, this);
dlg.DoModal ();
```

In this example, it isn't necessary to derive a dialog class from *CDialog*. The dialog box is so simple that *CDialog* provides all the functionality we need. When the OK button is clicked, the dialog box is dismissed by *CDialog*'s *OnOK* handler. If the user presses Esc or clicks the close box, the dialog is dismissed by *CDialog*'s *OnCancel* handler.

Resource.h

```
//*****************************************************************
//
//  Resource.h
//
//*****************************************************************

#define IDR_MAINFRAME       100

#define IDM_OPTIONS_EXIT    110
#define IDM_OPTIONS_ABOUT   111

#define IDD_ABOUTDLG        120
```

DlgDemo1.rc

```
//*****************************************************************
//
//  DlgDdemo1.rc
//
//*****************************************************************

#include "afxres.h"
#include "Resource.h"

AFX_IDI_STD_FRAME ICON DlgDemo.ico

IDR_MAINFRAME MENU
```

Figure 6-1. *The DlgDemo1 program.*

```
BEGIN
    POPUP "&Options" {
        MENUITEM "E&xit",                IDM_OPTIONS_EXIT
        MENUITEM SEPARATOR
        MENUITEM "&About DlgDemo1...",  IDM_OPTIONS_ABOUT
    }
END

IDD_ABOUTDLG DIALOG 32, 32, 186, 98
STYLE DS_MODALFRAME ¦ WS_POPUP ¦ WS_VISIBLE ¦ WS_CAPTION ¦ WS_SYSMENU
CAPTION "About DlgDemo1"
FONT 8, "MS Sans Serif"
BEGIN
    CTEXT           "Dialog Demo 1", -1, 12, 28, 162, 10
    CTEXT           "Copyright © 1996 by Jeff Prosise", -1,
                    12, 40, 162, 10
    DEFPUSHBUTTON   "OK", IDOK, 68, 72, 50, 14
END
```

DlgDemo1.h

```
//*****************************************************************************
//
//  DlgDemo1.h
//
//*****************************************************************************

class CMyApp : public CWinApp
{
public:
    virtual BOOL InitInstance ();
};

class CMainWindow : public CFrameWnd
{
private:
    void DoGradientFill (CDC*, CRect*);
    void DoDrawText (CDC*, CRect*);

public:
    CMainWindow ();

protected:
    afx_msg BOOL OnEraseBkgnd (CDC*);
    afx_msg void OnPaint ();
```

(continued)

```
    afx_msg void OnOptionsExit ();
    afx_msg void OnOptionsAbout ();

    DECLARE_MESSAGE_MAP ()
};
```

DlgDemo1.cpp

```
//*************************************************************************
//
//  DlgDemo1.cpp
//
//*************************************************************************

#include <afxwin.h>
#include "Resource.h"
#include "DlgDemo1.h"

#define FONTHEIGHT 72

CMyApp myApp;

/////////////////////////////////////////////////////////////////////////
// CMyApp member functions

BOOL CMyApp::InitInstance ()
{
    m_pMainWnd = new CMainWindow;
    m_pMainWnd->ShowWindow (m_nCmdShow);
    m_pMainWnd->UpdateWindow ();
    return TRUE;
}

/////////////////////////////////////////////////////////////////////////
// CMainWindow message map and member functions

BEGIN_MESSAGE_MAP (CMainWindow, CFrameWnd)
    ON_WM_ERASEBKGND ()
    ON_WM_PAINT ()
    ON_COMMAND (IDM_OPTIONS_EXIT, OnOptionsExit)
    ON_COMMAND (IDM_OPTIONS_ABOUT, OnOptionsAbout)
END_MESSAGE_MAP ()
```

```
CMainWindow::CMainWindow ()
{
    Create (NULL, "DlgDemo1", WS_OVERLAPPEDWINDOW, rectDefault, NULL,
        MAKEINTRESOURCE (IDR_MAINFRAME));
}

BOOL CMainWindow::OnEraseBkgnd (CDC* pDC)
{
    CRect rect;
    GetClientRect (&rect);
    DoGradientFill (pDC, &rect);
    return TRUE;
}

void CMainWindow::OnPaint ()
{
    CRect rect;
    GetClientRect (&rect);

    CPaintDC dc (this);
    DoDrawText (&dc, &rect);
}

void CMainWindow::OnOptionsExit ()
{
    SendMessage (WM_CLOSE, 0, 0);
}

void CMainWindow::OnOptionsAbout ()
{
    CDialog dlg (IDD_ABOUTDLG, this);
    dlg.DoModal ();
}

void CMainWindow::DoGradientFill (CDC* pDC, CRect* pRect)
{
    CPen* pPen[64];
    for (int i=0; i<64; i++)
        pPen[i] = new CPen (PS_SOLID, 1, RGB (0, 0, 255 - (i * 4)));

    int nWidth = pRect->Width ();
    int nHeight = pRect->Height ();

    for (i=0; i<nHeight; i++) {
        pDC->SelectObject (pPen[(i * 63) / nHeight]);
        pDC->MoveTo (0, i);
```

(continued)

DlgDemo1.cpp *continued*

```
        pDC->LineTo (nWidth, i);
    }

    pDC->SelectStockObject (BLACK_PEN);
    for (i=0; i<64; i++)
        delete pPen[i];
}

void CMainWindow::DoDrawText (CDC* pDC, CRect* pRect)
{
    CFont font;
    int nHeight = -((pDC->GetDeviceCaps (LOGPIXELSY) * FONTHEIGHT) / 72);

    font.CreateFont (nHeight, 0, 0, 0, FW_BOLD, TRUE, 0, 0,
        DEFAULT_CHARSET, OUT_CHARACTER_PRECIS, CLIP_CHARACTER_PRECIS,
        DEFAULT_QUALITY, DEFAULT_PITCH | FF_DONTCARE, "Times New Roman");

    pDC->SetBkMode (TRANSPARENT);
    pDC->SetTextColor (RGB (255, 255, 255));

    CFont* pOldFont = pDC->SelectObject (&font);
    pDC->DrawText ("Hello, MFC", -1, pRect, DT_SINGLELINE | DT_CENTER |
        DT_VCENTER);

    pDC->SelectObject (pOldFont);
}
```

DlgDemo1 is shown in Figure 6-2 with its About dialog box displayed. The dialog contains three controls: two CTEXT controls containing text, and an OK button. The window background is painted with a color gradient that fades from bright blue to black. Painting is done in response to WM_ERASEBKGND messages, which are generated when a window's background needs repainting before *OnPaint* paints the foreground. An *OnEraseBkgnd* handler that paints a custom window background should return a nonzero value to notify Windows that the background has been "erased." (For a cool effect, try using an *OnEraseBkgnd* handler that does nothing but return TRUE. What do you get? A see-through window!) *CMainWindow::OnErase-Bkgnd* calls *CMainWindow::DoGradientFill*, which creates 64 1-pixel-wide *CPen* objects representing various shades of blue and executes a *for* loop that traverses the window from top to bottom, one scan line at a time. At each pass through the loop, a shade of blue is computed from the current row number and the corresponding pen is used to draw a horizontal line. The higher the row number, the lower the color component and the darker the shade of blue. By the time the final row is reached, blue has dropped to near 0, producing a beautiful gradient fill not unlike the ones seen in Microsoft PowerPoint and other presentation packages.

Figure 6-2. *The DlgDemo1 window and About dialog box.*

If you run DlgDemo1 on a display adapter that supports either 16- or 24-bit color, the window will look like the picture in Figure 6-2. But run it on 16- or 256-color video hardware, and it will look more like the one in Figure 6-3 on the next page. Obviously, there's a problem: instead of a smooth gradient fill, the window contains just three different colors. What happened? In Chapter 2, I mentioned that 1-pixel-wide pens are not dithered but are mapped by Windows to the nearest solid color. Pens with blue values ranging from 192 through 255 get mapped to RGB (0, 0, 255), pens with blue values from 64 through 191 get mapped to RGB (0, 0, 128), and pens with blue values from 0 through 63 get mapped to RGB (0, 0, 0). Never mind that a 256-color device can support a wide range of blues; unless you take special steps to make the extra shades of blue available, Windows treats a 256-color display as if it were a standard 16-color VGA device.

There are two solutions to the problem of limited color availability. One is to create a GDI palette containing 64 different shades of blue and paint with the colors in the palette. This solution would produce a smooth gradient fill on 256-color display adapters but would have no effect on 16-color devices. (Palettes will be discussed in detail in Chapter 12.) The other solution is to draw with brushes instead of pens because Windows will willingly dither brush colors to simulate a richer selection of colors. This technique has two advantages: it's simple to implement in code, and it works as well on 16-color devices as it does on 256-color devices. Furthermore, if you use the brush method on video hardware capable of displaying thousands or

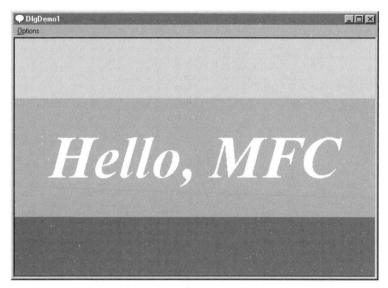

Figure 6-3. *The DlgDemo1 window on 16- or 256-color video hardware.*

perhaps millions of colors, you'll get that perfect gradient fill you wanted. Let's see for ourselves by modifying DlgDemo1 to draw 1-pixel-wide lines with brushes instead of pens. While we're at it, we'll soup up the About dialog box so that it's more representative of the About boxes featured in commercial Windows applications.

Building a Better About Box

The About dialog box featured in DlgDemo1 is okay for a start, but no self-respecting Windows programmer would want to stop there. An About box is, after all, an expression of your inner self, a chance to display your wares in ways that aren't confined by the needs of the application itself. Some About boxes are mini-apps in disguise, playing music and displaying animated credit screens when prompted by some magic (and usually undocumented) sequence of mouse and keyboard events. That may be more trouble than you're willing to go to, but there's still a lot you can do to improve DlgDemo1's About box without writing a lot of code.

Figure 6-4 contains the source code for DlgDemo2. The header file declares a dialog class named *CAboutDialog* whose constructor calls *CDialog*'s constructor with the resource ID IDD_ABOUTDLG. Accordingly, the .rc file includes an IDD_ABOUT-DLG dialog template containing a series of LTEXT-type static text controls as well as a default OK button for dismissing the dialog. The first LTEXT control—the one whose ID is IDC_ICONRECT—is actually a dummy control that's deleted before the dialog box is displayed. The following statements in *CAboutDialog::OnInitDialog* perform the deletion:

```
CStatic* pStatic = (CStatic*) GetDlgItem (IDC_ICONRECT);
pStatic->GetWindowRect (&m_rect);
pStatic->DestroyWindow ();
```

Right after the control is deleted, the control rectangle that's copied to *m_rect* by *GetWindowRect* is converted from screen coordinates to client coordinates with *ScreenToClient*:

```
ScreenToClient (&m_rect);
```

m_rect now describes a rectangle encompassing roughly the left third of the dialog box window.

Resource.h

```
//*********************************************************************
//
//  Resource.h
//
//*********************************************************************

#define IDR_MAINFRAME        100

#define IDM_OPTIONS_EXIT     110
#define IDM_OPTIONS_ABOUT    111

#define IDD_ABOUTDLG         120
#define IDC_ICONRECT         121
```

DlgDemo2.rc

```
//*********************************************************************
//
//  DlgDemo2.rc
//
//*********************************************************************

#include "afxres.h"
#include "Resource.h"

AFX_IDI_STD_FRAME ICON DlgDemo.ico

IDR_MAINFRAME MENU
BEGIN
    POPUP "&Options" {
        MENUITEM "E&xit",                  IDM_OPTIONS_EXIT
```

Figure 6-4. *The DlgDemo2 program.*   *(continued)*

DlgDemo2.rc *continued*

```
        MENUITEM SEPARATOR
        MENUITEM "&About DlgDemo2...",  IDM_OPTIONS_ABOUT
    }
END


IDD_ABOUTDLG DIALOG 0, 0, 256, 98
STYLE DS_MODALFRAME | DS_CENTER | WS_POPUP | WS_VISIBLE |
    WS_CAPTION | WS_SYSMENU
CAPTION "About DlgDemo2"
FONT 8, "MS Sans Serif"
BEGIN
    LTEXT            "", IDC_ICONRECT, 14, 12, 80, 74
    LTEXT            "Dialog Demo 2", -1, 108, 12, 136, 8
    LTEXT            "From the book", -1, 108, 32, 136, 8
    LTEXT            """Programming Windows 95 with MFC""", -1,
                     108, 42, 136, 8
    LTEXT            "Copyright © 1996 by Jeff Prosise", -1,
                     108, 52, 136, 8
    DEFPUSHBUTTON    "OK", IDOK, 108, 72, 50, 14
END
```

DlgDemo2.h

```
//****************************************************************************
//
//  DlgDemo2.h
//
//****************************************************************************

class CMyApp : public CWinApp
{
public:
    virtual BOOL InitInstance ();
};

class CMainWindow : public CFrameWnd
{
private:
    void DoGradientFill (CDC*, CRect*);
    void DoDrawText (CDC*, CRect*);

public:
    CMainWindow ();

protected:
    afx_msg BOOL OnEraseBkgnd (CDC*);
```

```
    afx_msg void OnPaint ();
    afx_msg void OnOptionsExit ();
    afx_msg void OnOptionsAbout ();

    DECLARE_MESSAGE_MAP ()
};

class CAboutDialog : public CDialog
{
private:
    CRect m_rect;

public:
    CAboutDialog (CWnd* pParentWnd = NULL) :
        CDialog (IDD_ABOUTDLG, pParentWnd) {}

    virtual BOOL OnInitDialog ();

protected:
    afx_msg void OnPaint ();
    DECLARE_MESSAGE_MAP ()
};
```

DlgDemo2.cpp

```
//*********************************************************************
//
//  DlgDemo2.cpp
//
//*********************************************************************

#include <afxwin.h>
#include "Resource.h"
#include "DlgDemo2.h"

#define FONTHEIGHT 72

CMyApp myApp;

///////////////////////////////////////////////////////////////////////
// CMyApp member functions

BOOL CMyApp::InitInstance ()
{
    m_pMainWnd = new CMainWindow;
    m_pMainWnd->ShowWindow (m_nCmdShow);
```

(continued)

DlgDemo2.cpp *continued*

```
    m_pMainWnd->UpdateWindow ();
    return TRUE;
}


///////////////////////////////////////////////////////////////////////////
// CMainWindow message map and member functions

BEGIN_MESSAGE_MAP (CMainWindow, CFrameWnd)
    ON_WM_ERASEBKGND ()
    ON_WM_PAINT ()
    ON_COMMAND (IDM_OPTIONS_EXIT, OnOptionsExit)
    ON_COMMAND (IDM_OPTIONS_ABOUT, OnOptionsAbout)
END_MESSAGE_MAP ()

CMainWindow::CMainWindow ()
{
    Create (NULL, "DlgDemo2", WS_OVERLAPPEDWINDOW, rectDefault, NULL,
        MAKEINTRESOURCE (IDR_MAINFRAME));
}

BOOL CMainWindow::OnEraseBkgnd (CDC* pDC)
{
    CRect rect;
    GetClientRect (&rect);
    DoGradientFill (pDC, &rect);
    return TRUE;
}

void CMainWindow::OnPaint ()
{
    CRect rect;
    GetClientRect (&rect);

    CPaintDC dc (this);
    DoDrawText (&dc, &rect);
}

void CMainWindow::OnOptionsExit ()
{
    SendMessage (WM_CLOSE, 0, 0);
}

void CMainWindow::OnOptionsAbout ()
{
    CAboutDialog dlg (this);
    dlg.DoModal ();
}
```

```
void CMainWindow::DoGradientFill (CDC* pDC, CRect* pRect)
{
    CBrush* pBrush[64];
    for (int i=0; i<64; i++)
        pBrush[i] = new CBrush (RGB (0, 0, 255 - (i * 4)));

    int nWidth = pRect->Width ();
    int nHeight = pRect->Height ();
    CRect rect;

    for (i=0; i<nHeight; i++) {
        rect.SetRect (0, i, nWidth, i + 1);
        pDC->FillRect (&rect, pBrush[(i * 63) / nHeight]);
    }

    for (i=0; i<64; i++)
        delete pBrush[i];
}

void CMainWindow::DoDrawText (CDC* pDC, CRect* pRect)
{
    CFont font;
    int nHeight = -((pDC->GetDeviceCaps (LOGPIXELSY) * FONTHEIGHT) / 72);

    font.CreateFont (nHeight, 0, 0, 0, FW_BOLD, TRUE, 0, 0,
        DEFAULT_CHARSET, OUT_CHARACTER_PRECIS, CLIP_CHARACTER_PRECIS,
        DEFAULT_QUALITY, DEFAULT_PITCH | FF_DONTCARE, "Times New Roman");

    pDC->SetBkMode (TRANSPARENT);
    pDC->SetTextColor (RGB (255, 255, 255));

    CFont* pOldFont = pDC->SelectObject (&font);
    pDC->DrawText ("Hello, MFC", -1, pRect, DT_SINGLELINE | DT_CENTER |
        DT_VCENTER);

    pDC->SelectObject (pOldFont);
}

/////////////////////////////////////////////////////////////////////
// CAboutDialog message map and member functions

BEGIN_MESSAGE_MAP (CAboutDialog, CDialog)
    ON_WM_PAINT ()
END_MESSAGE_MAP ()
```

(continued)

DlgDemo2.cpp *continued*

```
BOOL CAboutDialog::OnInitDialog ()
{
    CDialog::OnInitDialog ();

    CStatic* pStatic = (CStatic*) GetDlgItem (IDC_ICONRECT);
    pStatic->GetWindowRect (&m_rect);
    pStatic->DestroyWindow ();
    ScreenToClient (&m_rect);

    return TRUE;
}

void CAboutDialog::OnPaint ()
{
    CPaintDC dc (this);
    HICON hIcon = (HICON) ::GetClassLong (AfxGetMainWnd ()->m_hWnd,
        GCL_HICON);

    if (hIcon != NULL) {
        CDC dcMem;
        dcMem.CreateCompatibleDC (&dc);

        CBitmap bitmap;
        bitmap.CreateCompatibleBitmap (&dc, 32, 32);
        CBitmap* pOldBitmap = dcMem.SelectObject (&bitmap);

        CBrush brush (::GetSysColor (COLOR_3DFACE));
        dcMem.FillRect (CRect (0, 0, 32, 32), &brush);
        dcMem.DrawIcon (0, 0, hIcon);

        dc.StretchBlt (m_rect.left, m_rect.top, m_rect.Width(),
            m_rect.Height (), &dcMem, 0, 0, 32, 32, SRCCOPY);

        dcMem.SelectObject (pOldBitmap);
    }
}
```

The stored rectangle coordinates are used by *CAboutDialog*'s *OnPaint* handler. You can paint in a dialog box using the same procedure you would use in a conventional window. Windows prevents you from painting over the top of the dialog box's controls, so you don't need to be overly concerned about painting in the wrong places. (If you *want* to paint over a control, you can call *UpdateWindow* to validate the control rectangle before painting.) *CAboutDialog*'s *OnPaint* handler does something rather interesting: it uses *::GetClassLong* and *AfxGetMainWnd* to obtain an HICON handle for the icon associated with the application's main window and then paints an enlarged image of the icon in the rectangle described by *m_rect*. The procedure used to paint the image, which involves using *CDC::DrawIcon* to draw the icon into a memory DC and *CDC::StretchBlt* to blit the image from the memory DC to the paint DC, is similar to the one used by the *CIconListBox::ProjectImage* function in Chapter 5's IconView program. The resulting dialog box is shown in Figure 6-5. Because the icon handle is obtained at run-time rather than hardcoded into the dialog box, *CAboutDialog* can be used as is in other applications and the image in the dialog box will be updated accordingly.

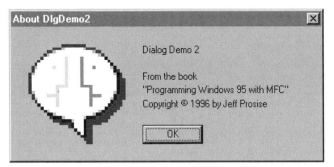

Figure 6-5. *The new and improved DlgDemo2 About dialog box.*

If you want to display an icon in a dialog box in its normal size, you don't have to trap WM_PAINT messages and paint the icon yourself. Instead, you can embed the icon directly in your dialog template. Rewritten to display the icon directly rather than to draw the icon image with *StretchBlt*, DlgDemo2's About dialog box template would look like this:

```
IDD_ABOUTDLG DIALOG 0, 0, 256, 98
STYLE DS_MODALFRAME ¦ DS_CENTER ¦ WS_POPUP ¦ WS_VISIBLE ¦
    WS_CAPTION ¦ WS_SYSMENU
CAPTION "About DlgDemo2"
FONT 8, "MS Sans Serif"
BEGIN
    ICON            AFX_IDI_STD_FRAME, -1, 14, 12, 0, 0
    LTEXT           "Dialog Demo 2", -1, 108, 12, 136, 8
    LTEXT           "From the book", -1, 108, 32, 136, 8
    LTEXT           """Programming Windows 95 with MFC""", -1,
                    108, 42, 136, 8
    LTEXT           "Copyright © 1996 by Jeff Prosise", -1,
                    108, 52, 136, 8
    DEFPUSHBUTTON   "OK", IDOK, 108, 72, 50, 14
END
```

An icon drawn with an ICON statement is drawn in the standard icon size—32 by 32 pixels—no matter what width and height you specify in the template.

As Figure 6-6 illustrates, DlgDemo2 does a much better job drawing a gradient fill on 16- and 256-color displays than DlgDemo1 did. That's because the *DoGradientFill* function now uses brushes rather than pens to draw lines. Here's how DlgDemo2 paints the window's client area with 1-pixel-wide lines:

```
for (i=0; i<nHeight; i++) {
    rect.SetRect (0, i, nWidth, i + 1);
    pDC->FillRect (&rect, pBrush[(i * 63) / nHeight]);
}
```

The call to *SetRect* initializes *rect* so that it describes a rectangle whose width equals the width of the window's client area and whose height is just two pixels, including the top and bottom borders. Since rectangles drawn with *CDC::FillRect* and other rectangle functions extend up to but don't include the bottom border, each rectangle output to the screen is just one pixel high.

Figure 6-6. *The DlgDemo2 window displayed on 16-color video hardware.*

A More Complex Dialog Box

Now let's add a more complex dialog box to our dialog demo application—one designed to get information in as well as give information out. Figure 6-7 contains the source code for DlgDemo3, which adds a Settings command to the Options menu featured in DlgDemo1 and DlgDemo2.

Resource.h

```
//*********************************************************************
//
// Resource.h
//
//*********************************************************************

#define IDR_MAINFRAME           100

#define IDM_OPTIONS_SETTINGS    110
#define IDM_OPTIONS_EXIT        111
#define IDM_OPTIONS_ABOUT       112

#define IDD_ABOUTDLG            120
#define IDC_ICONRECT            121

#define IDD_SETTINGSDLG         130
#define IDC_SOLID               131
#define IDC_GRADIENT            132
#define IDC_RED                 133
#define IDC_GREEN               134
#define IDC_BLUE                135
#define IDC_MAGENTA             136
#define IDC_CYAN                137
#define IDC_TEXT                138
#define IDC_HEIGHT              139
#define IDC_BOLD                140
#define IDC_ITALIC              141
#define IDC_DEFAULTS            142
```

DlgDemo3.rc

```
//*********************************************************************
//
// DlgDemo3.rc
//
//*********************************************************************

#include "afxres.h"
#include "Resource.h"

AFX_IDI_STD_FRAME ICON DlgDemo.ico
```

Figure 6-7. *The DlgDemo3 program.*   *(continued)*

DlgDemo3.rc *continued*

```
IDR_MAINFRAME MENU
BEGIN
    POPUP "&Options" {
        MENUITEM "&Settings...",        IDM_OPTIONS_SETTINGS
        MENUITEM "E&xit",               IDM_OPTIONS_EXIT
        MENUITEM SEPARATOR
        MENUITEM "&About DlgDemo3...",  IDM_OPTIONS_ABOUT
    }
END

IDD_SETTINGSDLG DIALOG 0, 0, 224, 149
STYLE DS_MODALFRAME ¦ DS_CENTER ¦ WS_POPUP ¦ WS_VISIBLE ¦
    WS_CAPTION ¦ WS_SYSMENU
CAPTION "Settings"
FONT 8, "MS Sans Serif"
BEGIN
    GROUPBOX       "Fill Type", -1, 12, 8, 80, 40
    AUTORADIOBUTTON "&Solid Fill", IDC_SOLID, 20, 20, 64, 10,
                   WS_TABSTOP ¦ WS_GROUP
    AUTORADIOBUTTON "Gr&adient Fill", IDC_GRADIENT, 20, 32, 64, 10,
                   WS_TABSTOP
    GROUPBOX       "Fill Color", -1, 12, 60, 80, 76, WS_GROUP
    AUTORADIOBUTTON "&Red", IDC_RED, 20, 72, 64, 10, WS_TABSTOP ¦ WS_GROUP
    AUTORADIOBUTTON "&Green", IDC_GREEN, 20, 84, 64, 10, WS_TABSTOP
    AUTORADIOBUTTON "&Blue", IDC_BLUE, 20, 96, 64, 10, WS_TABSTOP
    AUTORADIOBUTTON "&Magenta", IDC_MAGENTA, 20, 108, 64, 10, WS_TABSTOP
    AUTORADIOBUTTON "&Cyan", IDC_CYAN, 20, 120, 64, 10, WS_TABSTOP
    LTEXT          "&Text", -1, 104, 16, 20, 8
    EDITTEXT       IDC_TEXT, 128, 12, 84, 12, ES_AUTOHSCROLL ¦ WS_GROUP
    LTEXT          "Text &Height (in points)", -1, 104, 36, 76, 8
    EDITTEXT       IDC_HEIGHT, 184, 32, 28, 12, ES_AUTOHSCROLL ¦ WS_GROUP
    AUTOCHECKBOX   "Bo&ld",IDC_BOLD, 104, 56, 40, 10,
                   WS_TABSTOP ¦ WS_GROUP
    AUTOCHECKBOX   "&Italic", IDC_ITALIC, 152, 56, 40, 10,
                   WS_TABSTOP ¦ WS_GROUP
    DEFPUSHBUTTON  "OK", IDOK, 164, 84, 50, 14, WS_GROUP
    PUSHBUTTON     "Cancel", IDCANCEL, 164, 104, 50, 14, WS_GROUP
    PUSHBUTTON     "&Defaults", IDC_DEFAULTS, 164, 124, 49, 14, WS_GROUP
END

IDD_ABOUTDLG DIALOG 0, 0, 256, 98
STYLE DS_MODALFRAME ¦ DS_CENTER ¦ WS_POPUP ¦ WS_VISIBLE ¦
    WS_CAPTION ¦ WS_SYSMENU
CAPTION "About DlgDemo3"
FONT 8, "MS Sans Serif"
```

```
BEGIN
    LTEXT           "", IDC_ICONRECT, 14, 12, 80, 74
    LTEXT           "Dialog Demo 3", -1, 108, 12, 136, 8
    LTEXT           "From the book", -1, 108, 32, 136, 8
    LTEXT           """Programming Windows 95 with MFC""", -1,
                    108, 42, 136, 8
    LTEXT           "Copyright © 1996 by Jeff Prosise", -1,
                    108, 52, 136, 8
    DEFPUSHBUTTON   "OK", IDOK, 108, 72, 50, 14
END
```

DlgDemo3.h

```
//***********************************************************************
//
//  DlgDemo3.h
//
//***********************************************************************

class CMyApp : public CWinApp
{
public:
    virtual BOOL InitInstance ();
};

class CMainWindow : public CFrameWnd
{
private:
    int m_nFillType;
    int m_nFillColor;
    CString m_text;
    int m_nHeight;
    BOOL m_bBold;
    BOOL m_bItalic;

    void DoSolidFill (CDC*, CRect*);
    void DoGradientFill (CDC*, CRect*);
    void DoDrawText (CDC*, CRect*);

public:
    CMainWindow ();

protected:
    afx_msg BOOL OnEraseBkgnd (CDC*);
    afx_msg void OnPaint ();
    afx_msg void OnOptionsSettings ();
```

(continued)

DlgDemo3.h *continued*

```
    afx_msg void OnOptionsExit ();
    afx_msg void OnOptionsAbout ();

    DECLARE_MESSAGE_MAP ()
};

class CSettingsDialog : public CDialog
{
private:
    CEdit& ctlText () { return *(CEdit*) GetDlgItem (IDC_TEXT); }
    CEdit& ctlHeight () { return *(CEdit*) GetDlgItem (IDC_HEIGHT); }
    CButton& ctlBold () { return *(CButton*) GetDlgItem (IDC_BOLD); }
    CButton& ctlItalic () { return *(CButton*) GetDlgItem (IDC_ITALIC); }
    int GetCheckedRadioButton (int, int);

public:
    int m_nFillType;
    int m_nFillColor;
    CString m_text;
    int m_nHeight;
    BOOL m_bBold;
    BOOL m_bItalic;

    CSettingsDialog (CWnd* pParentWnd = NULL) :
        CDialog (IDD_SETTINGSDLG, pParentWnd) {}

    virtual BOOL OnInitDialog ();

protected:
    virtual void OnOK ();

    afx_msg void OnDefaults ();
    DECLARE_MESSAGE_MAP ()
};

class CAboutDialog : public CDialog
{
private:
    CRect m_rect;

public:
    CAboutDialog (CWnd* pParentWnd = NULL) :
        CDialog (IDD_ABOUTDLG, pParentWnd) {}

    virtual BOOL OnInitDialog ();
```

```
protected:
    afx_msg void OnPaint ();
    DECLARE_MESSAGE_MAP ()
};
```

DlgDemo3.cpp

```
//*****************************************************************************
//
//  DlgDemo3.cpp
//
//*****************************************************************************

#include <afxwin.h>
#include <stdlib.h>
#include "Resource.h"
#include "DlgDemo3.h"

CMyApp myApp;

///////////////////////////////////////////////////////////////////////////
// CMyApp member functions

BOOL CMyApp::InitInstance ()
{
    m_pMainWnd = new CMainWindow;
    m_pMainWnd->ShowWindow (m_nCmdShow);
    m_pMainWnd->UpdateWindow ();
    return TRUE;
}

///////////////////////////////////////////////////////////////////////////
// CMainWindow message map and member functions

BEGIN_MESSAGE_MAP (CMainWindow, CFrameWnd)
    ON_WM_ERASEBKGND ()
    ON_WM_PAINT ()
    ON_COMMAND (IDM_OPTIONS_SETTINGS, OnOptionsSettings)
    ON_COMMAND (IDM_OPTIONS_EXIT, OnOptionsExit)
    ON_COMMAND (IDM_OPTIONS_ABOUT, OnOptionsAbout)
END_MESSAGE_MAP ()

CMainWindow::CMainWindow ()
{
    m_nFillType = 1;
    m_nFillColor = 2;
```

(continued)

DlgDemo3.cpp *continued*

```
    m_text = "Hello, MFC";
    m_nHeight = 72;
    m_bBold = TRUE;
    m_bItalic = TRUE;

    Create (NULL, "DlgDemo3", WS_OVERLAPPEDWINDOW, rectDefault, NULL,
        MAKEINTRESOURCE (IDR_MAINFRAME));
}

BOOL CMainWindow::OnEraseBkgnd (CDC* pDC)
{
    CRect rect;
    GetClientRect (&rect);

    m_nFillType == 1 ? DoGradientFill (pDC, &rect) :
        DoSolidFill (pDC, &rect);
    return TRUE;
}

void CMainWindow::OnPaint ()
{
    CRect rect;
    GetClientRect (&rect);

    CPaintDC dc (this);
    DoDrawText (&dc, &rect);
}

void CMainWindow::OnOptionsSettings ()
{
    CSettingsDialog dlg (this);

    dlg.m_nFillType = m_nFillType;
    dlg.m_nFillColor = m_nFillColor;
    dlg.m_text = m_text;
    dlg.m_nHeight = m_nHeight;
    dlg.m_bBold = m_bBold;
    dlg.m_bItalic = m_bItalic;

    if (dlg.DoModal () == IDOK) {
        m_nFillType = dlg.m_nFillType;
        m_nFillColor = dlg.m_nFillColor;
        m_text = dlg.m_text;
        m_nHeight = dlg.m_nHeight;
        m_bBold = dlg.m_bBold;
        m_bItalic = dlg.m_bItalic;
```

```
        Invalidate ();
    }
}

void CMainWindow::OnOptionsExit ()
{
    SendMessage (WM_CLOSE, 0, 0);
}

void CMainWindow::OnOptionsAbout ()
{
    CAboutDialog dlg (this);
    dlg.DoModal ();
}

void CMainWindow::DoSolidFill (CDC* pDC, CRect* pRect)
{
    static COLORREF crColor[5] = {
        RGB (255,   0,   0),
        RGB (  0, 255,   0),
        RGB (  0,   0, 255),
        RGB (255,   0, 255),
        RGB (  0, 255, 255),
    };

    CBrush brush (crColor[m_nFillColor]);
    pDC->FillRect (pRect, &brush);
}

void CMainWindow::DoGradientFill (CDC* pDC, CRect* pRect)
{
    CBrush* pBrush[64];
    for (int i=0; i<64; i++) {
        switch (m_nFillColor) {

        case 0:
            pBrush[i] = new CBrush (RGB (255 - (i * 4), 0, 0));
            break;

        case 1:
            pBrush[i] = new CBrush (RGB (0, 255 - (i * 4), 0));
            break;

        case 2:
            pBrush[i] = new CBrush (RGB (0, 0, 255 - (i * 4)));
            break;
```

(continued)

DlgDemo3.cpp *continued*

```
        case 3:
            pBrush[i] = new CBrush (RGB (255 - (i * 4), 0,
                255 - (i * 4)));
            break;

        case 4:
            pBrush[i] = new CBrush (RGB (0, 255 - (i * 4),
                255 - (i * 4)));
            break;
        }
    }

    int nWidth = pRect->Width ();
    int nHeight = pRect->Height ();
    CRect rect;

    for (i=0; i<nHeight; i++) {
        rect.SetRect (0, i, nWidth, i + 1);
        pDC->FillRect (&rect, pBrush[(i * 63) / nHeight]);
    }

    for (i=0; i<64; i++)
        delete pBrush[i];
}

void CMainWindow::DoDrawText (CDC* pDC, CRect* pRect)
{
    CFont font;
    int nHeight = -((pDC->GetDeviceCaps (LOGPIXELSY) * m_nHeight) / 72);

    font.CreateFont (nHeight, 0, 0, 0, m_bBold ? FW_BOLD : FW_NORMAL,
        m_bItalic, 0, 0, DEFAULT_CHARSET, OUT_CHARACTER_PRECIS,
        CLIP_CHARACTER_PRECIS, DEFAULT_QUALITY, DEFAULT_PITCH |
        FF_DONTCARE, "Times New Roman");

    pDC->SetBkMode (TRANSPARENT);
    pDC->SetTextColor (RGB (255, 255, 255));

    CFont* pOldFont = pDC->SelectObject (&font);
    pDC->DrawText (m_text, -1, pRect, DT_SINGLELINE | DT_CENTER |
        DT_VCENTER);

    pDC->SelectObject (pOldFont);
}
```

```
/////////////////////////////////////////////////////////////////////////
// CSettingsDialog message map and member functions

BEGIN_MESSAGE_MAP (CSettingsDialog, CDialog)
    ON_BN_CLICKED (IDC_DEFAULTS, OnDefaults)
END_MESSAGE_MAP ()

BOOL CSettingsDialog::OnInitDialog ()
{
    CDialog::OnInitDialog ();

    CheckRadioButton (IDC_SOLID, IDC_GRADIENT, IDC_SOLID + m_nFillType);
    CheckRadioButton (IDC_RED, IDC_CYAN, IDC_RED + m_nFillColor);

    ctlText ().SetWindowText (m_text);
    ctlText ().LimitText (32);

    char szHeight[4];
    _itoa (m_nHeight, szHeight, 10);
    ctlHeight ().SetWindowText (szHeight);
    ctlHeight ().LimitText (3);

    ctlBold ().SetCheck (m_bBold ? BST_CHECKED : BST_UNCHECKED);
    ctlItalic ().SetCheck (m_bItalic ? BST_CHECKED : BST_UNCHECKED);
    return TRUE;
}

void CSettingsDialog::OnOK ()
{
    m_nFillType = GetCheckedRadioButton (IDC_SOLID, IDC_GRADIENT);
    m_nFillColor = GetCheckedRadioButton (IDC_RED, IDC_CYAN);

    ctlText ().GetWindowText (m_text);

    char szHeight[4];
    ctlHeight ().GetWindowText (szHeight, 4);
    m_nHeight = atoi (szHeight);

    if ((m_nHeight < 8) || (m_nHeight > 144)) {
        MessageBox ("Text height must be an integer from 8 through 144");
        ctlHeight ().SetFocus ();
        ctlHeight ().SetSel (0, -1);
        return;
    }
```

(continued)

DlgDemo3.cpp *continued*

```
    m_bBold = (ctlBold ().GetCheck () == BST_CHECKED) ? TRUE : FALSE;
    m_bItalic = (ctlItalic ().GetCheck () == BST_CHECKED) ? TRUE : FALSE;

    CDialog::OnOK ();
}

void CSettingsDialog::OnDefaults ()
{
    CheckRadioButton (IDC_SOLID, IDC_GRADIENT, IDC_GRADIENT);
    CheckRadioButton (IDC_RED, IDC_CYAN, IDC_BLUE);

    ctlText ().SetWindowText ("Hello, MFC");
    ctlHeight ().SetWindowText ("72");

    ctlBold ().SetCheck (BST_CHECKED);
    ctlItalic ().SetCheck (BST_CHECKED);
}

int CSettingsDialog::GetCheckedRadioButton (int nFirst, int nLast)
{
    int nCount = nLast - nFirst + 1;

    for (int i=0; i<nCount; i++)
        if (IsDlgButtonChecked (nFirst + i))
            return i;

    return -1;
}

////////////////////////////////////////////////////////////////////////
// CAboutDialog message map and member functions

BEGIN_MESSAGE_MAP (CAboutDialog, CDialog)
    ON_WM_PAINT ()
END_MESSAGE_MAP ()

BOOL CAboutDialog::OnInitDialog ()
{
    CDialog::OnInitDialog ();

    CStatic* pStatic = (CStatic*) GetDlgItem (IDC_ICONRECT);
    pStatic->GetWindowRect (&m_rect);
    pStatic->DestroyWindow ();
    ScreenToClient (&m_rect);

    return TRUE;
}
```

```
void CAboutDialog::OnPaint ()
{
    CPaintDC dc (this);
    HICON hIcon = (HICON) ::GetClassLong (AfxGetMainWnd ()->m_hWnd,
        GCL_HICON);

    if (hIcon != NULL) {
        CDC dcMem;
        dcMem.CreateCompatibleDC (&dc);

        CBitmap bitmap;
        bitmap.CreateCompatibleBitmap (&dc, 32, 32);
        CBitmap* pOldBitmap = dcMem.SelectObject (&bitmap);

        CBrush brush (::GetSysColor (COLOR_3DFACE));
        dcMem.FillRect (CRect (0, 0, 32, 32), &brush);
        dcMem.DrawIcon (0, 0, hIcon);

        dc.StretchBlt (m_rect.left, m_rect.top, m_rect.Width(),
            m_rect.Height (), &dcMem, 0, 0, 32, 32, SRCCOPY);

        dcMem.SelectObject (pOldBitmap);
    }
}
```

The new menu item in the Options menu invokes the Settings dialog box shown in Figure 6-8. Through the dialog, the user can change the color of the window's background, choose between a solid fill and a gradient fill, and modify the text displayed in the foreground.

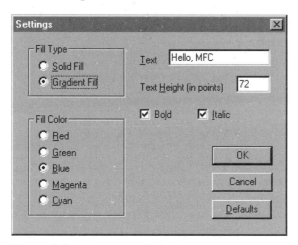

Figure 6-8. *The Settings dialog box.*

The *CSettingsDialog* class from which the Settings dialog box is created matches each control or in the case of radio buttons, each *group* of controls with a data member—*m_nFillType* for the Fill Type radio buttons, *m_nFillColor* for the Fill Color radio buttons, *m_text* for the edit control, and so on. The *CMainWindow* class contains identically named data members whose values determine how the main window will be painted. The following *CMainWindow::OnOptionsSettings* code creates the dialog box, initializes the dialog box's data members with the corresponding values from *CMainWindow*, and if the dialog box is dismissed with the OK button, copies the modified dialog box data members back to *CMainWindow* and updates the window by forcing a repaint:

```
CSettingsDialog dlg (this);

dlg.m_nFillType = m_nFillType;
dlg.m_nFillColor = m_nFillColor;
dlg.m_text = m_text;
dlg.m_nHeight = m_nHeight;
dlg.m_bBold = m_bBold;
dlg.m_bItalic = m_bItalic;

if (dlg.DoModal () == IDOK) {
    m_nFillType = dlg.m_nFillType;
    m_nFillColor = dlg.m_nFillColor;
    m_text = dlg.m_text;
    m_nHeight = dlg.m_nHeight;
    m_bBold = dlg.m_bBold;
    m_bItalic = dlg.m_bItalic;

    Invalidate ();
}
```

For this to work, the *CSettingsDialog* data members must be declared public so that they can be accessed outside the dialog class. This is the technique used by the majority of MFC programmers to get data in and out of dialog boxes. Other options include declaring settings variables globally so that both *CMainWindow* and *CSettingsDialog* can access them and making *CSettingsDialog*'s data members private but providing public member functions for accessing them. The latter technique provides a stricter encapsulation of the dialog box's data members, but declaring the data members public is both simpler and more direct.

CSettingsDialog::OnInitDialog uses the values copied to the dialog's data members in *CMainWindow::OnOptionsSettings* to initialize the controls. The radio button groups are initialized with the *CheckRadioButton* function that a dialog box inherits from *CWnd*. Given a range of radio button IDs and the ID of one of the buttons, *CheckRadioButton* checks the specified radio button and unchecks the others. The remaining dialog box controls are accessed in a type-safe way by means of inline member functions. For example, the statement

```
ctlText ().SetWindowText (m_text);
```

copies the text string in *m_text* to the edit control labeled "Text." When *OnInitDialog* returns, each dialog box control has been initialized to match the value of the corresponding dialog data member. Thus, if the user changes the background color to red and then displays the Settings dialog again, the Red radio button will be checked to reflect the current program settings. The value stored in *m_nFillColor* is a 0-based integer index identifying the currently selected radio button: 0 for Red, 1 for Green, 2 for Blue, and so on.

Values are read back from the controls in *CSettingsDialog::OnOK*. New values for *m_nFillType* and *m_nFillColor* are determined by calling *CSettingsDialog-::GetCheckedRadioButton*, which, given a range of radio button IDs, returns the 0-based index of the first (and presumably only) radio button that is checked. The other controls are read using *CEdit* and *CButton* member functions. *CEdit* and *CButton* pointers are obtained by means of the same type-safe member functions employed in *OnInitDialog*. Before dismissing the dialog box by calling the base class's *OnOK* function, *CSettingsDialog::OnOK* verifies that the user entered a legitimate value for the text height by converting the text in the Text Height edit control to an integer value and checking that it falls in the range 8 through 144:

```
char szHeight[4];
ctlHeight ().GetWindowText (szHeight, 4);
m_nHeight = atoi (szHeight);

if ((m_nHeight < 8) || (m_nHeight > 144)) {
    MessageBox ("Text height must be an integer from 8 through 144");
    ctlHeight ().SetFocus ();
    ctlHeight ().SetSel (0, -1);
    return;
}
```

If the integer is out of range, a warning is displayed in a message box and *OnOK* returns without calling the base class's *OnOK* function and thus without dismissing the dialog box. Before returning, the validation routine sets the input focus back to the edit control and selects the text in it so that where the error lies is obvious.

The Settings dialog's Defaults button, which resets all the controls to their default values, demonstrates how buttons other than OK and Cancel are handled in a dialog box. An ON_BN_CLICKED entry in the dialog class's message map links clicks of the Defaults button to the *CSettingsDialog* member function *OnDefaults*. *OnDefaults* doesn't modify the dialog's data members; instead, it writes new values to each of the controls. It isn't necessary to modify the data members because that will be done by the *OnOK* handler if and when the OK button is clicked.

DlgDemo3 is a complete, working example of an application that uses a dialog box to retrieve input from the user. Most of the code in the *CSettingsDialog* class is for transferring data between the dialog data members and the dialog box controls. Imagine how trivial the implementation of *CSettingsDialog* would be if we didn't have to initialize the controls in *OnInitDialog* and read them back in *OnOK*—that is, if we could provide a "data map" of sorts correlating controls in the dialog box to data members of the dialog class and let the framework perform the data transfers for us. Sound farfetched? In fact, that's exactly what the MFC framework does for us when we take advantage of its Dialog Data Exchange and Dialog Data Validation mechanism, better known by the acronym DDX/DDV. The mechanism is simple to use, and it vastly simplifies the code for MFC dialog classes. Many times, it obviates the need to supply custom *OnInitDialog* and *OnOK* handlers altogether, even if your dialog box contains dozens of controls. Let's take a look at DDX/DDV and see what it can do to simplify the Settings dialog box.

Dialog Data Exchange and Validation

If you're a Visual C++ programmer and you use ClassWizard to conjure up your dialog classes, you're probably aware that you can use ClassWizard to create dialog data members and associate them with controls in a dialog box. It's easy: select a control ID from a list box, click the Add Variable button, and fill in the variable's name and properties. When the dialog box is created, the controls are magically initialized to match the values assigned to the corresponding member variables. And when the dialog box is dismissed by clicking OK, the data entered into the controls magically finds its way back to the member variables. Even a limited amount of data validation is performed. If an integer value the user enters into an edit control falls outside a range you specify, for example, a message box pops up notifying the user of the error. When the user dismisses the message box, the dialog box remains on the screen and the input focus is assigned to the offending control, with a flashing caret prompting the user to enter a valid value.

The secret to ClassWizard's ability to link the controls in a dialog box to data members of the dialog class is the MFC framework's DDX/DDV mechanism. Here's what happens behind the scenes to make it work. For its part, ClassWizard adds a member function named *DoDataExchange* containing one or more calls to DDX/DDV functions associating controls and data members to your dialog class. For a simple dialog box containing but one DDX/DDV connection—an edit control in which a user enters an integer data value—*DoDataExchange* might look like this:

```
void CMyDialog::DoDataExchange (CDataExchange* pDX)
{
    DDX_Text (pDX, IDC_EDIT, m_nIntVal);
    DDV_MinMaxInt (pDX, m_nIntVal, 0, 100);
}
```

In this simple example, IDC_EDIT is the control ID and *m_nIntVal* is the associated member variable. The *pDX* parameter passed to *DoDataExchange* is a pointer to a *CDataExchange* object supplied by the framework. Among other things, the *CData-Exchange* object tells *DDX_Text* and *DDV_MinMaxInt* in which direction the information is flowing—whether data is being transferred from the data members to the controls or from the controls to the data members. MFC programmers often refer to the statements in *DoDataExchange* as a *data map* because these statements correlate dialog box controls to dialog data members just as message maps correlate messages to class member functions.

ClassWizard creates the data map, but MFC makes it work. When the dialog box is created, *CDialog::OnInitDialog* calls the *UpdateData* function a dialog object inherits from *CWnd* with a FALSE parameter to initialize the dialog box controls. *Update-Data*, in turn, creates a *CDataExchange* object and calls the dialog's *DoDataExchange* function, passing it a pointer to the *CDataExchange* object. Each DDX function called by *DoDataExchange* initializes a control using the value of a member variable. In the preceding example, *m_nIntVal* is converted from integer to text form and copied to the edit control by the *DDX_Text* function. Later, when the user clicks OK, *CDialog-::OnOK* calls *UpdateData* with a TRUE parameter causing *DDX_Text* to do just the opposite of what it did earlier: read a text string from the edit control, convert it into an integer value, and store the result in *m_nIntVal*. In addition, MFC's *DDV_MinMaxInt* function verifies that *m_nIntVal* falls in the range 0 through 100. If the integer value checks out, *DoDataExchange* returns and the dialog box is dismissed. Otherwise, the *CDataExchange* object's *Fail* function is called, which causes a warning message to be displayed and the dialog box to remain on the screen with the input focus on the edit control.

DDX_Text and *DDV_MinMaxInt* are just two of several DDX/DDV functions MFC provides; complete lists are shown in the tables on the next page. The relationship between a control and the associated dialog data member depends on the DDV function connecting the two. For example, an int variable linked to a group of radio buttons with *DDX_Radio* is a 0-based index identifying one member of the group. If the int's value is 2 when the dialog is created, *DDX_Radio* checks the third button in the group. When the OK button is clicked, *DDX_Radio* copies the index of the currently selected button to the member variable. An int variable connected to a scroll bar with *DDX_Scroll* specifies the position of the scroll bar thumb, and an int variable associated with a check box by means of *DDX_Check* specifies the check box's state—BST_CHECKED, BST_UNCHECKED, or BST_INDETETERMINATE. The indeterminate state applies to 3-state check boxes only.

DIALOG DATA EXCHANGE (DDX) FUNCTIONS

DDX Function	*Description*
DDX_Text	Associates a BYTE, an int, a short, a UINT, a long, a DWORD, a *CString*, a float, or a double variable with an edit control.
DDX_Check	Associates an int variable with a check box control.
DDX_Radio	Associates an int variable with a group of radio buttons.
DDX_LBIndex	Associates an int variable with a list box.
DDX_LBString	Associates a *CString* variable with a list box.
DDX_LBStringExact	Associates a *CString* variable with a list box.
DDX_CBIndex	Associates an int variable with a combo box.
DDX_CBString	Associates a *CString* variable with a combo box.
DDX_CBStringExact	Associates a *CString* variable with a combo box.
DDX_Scroll	Associates an int variable with a scroll bar.

DDV routines fall into two categories: those that validate numeric variables to ensure that they fall within specified limits, and one that validates a *CString* variable to verify that its length doesn't exceed a certain value. The DDV range-validation routines are not overloaded to accept multiple data types, so if you write a data map yourself, you must be careful to match the function to the data type. A DDV routine should be called immediately after the DDX routine for the same data member to ensure that the framework can set the input focus to the proper control if the validation procedure fails. A word of advice: In most instances, you're better off using *CEdit::LimitText* or *CEdit::SetLimitText* to limit the number of characters that can be entered into an edit control than you are using *DDV_MaxChars* to check the number of characters that have been entered when the user clicks OK. Most users would rather see errors be prevented up front than reported after the fact.

DIALOG DATA VALIDATION (DDV) FUNCTIONS

Function	*Description*
DDV_MinMaxByte	Verifies that a BYTE value falls within specified limits.
DDV_MinMaxInt	Verifies that an int value falls within specified limits.
DDV_MinMaxLong	Verifies that a long value falls within specified limits.
DDV_MinMaxUInt	Verifies that a UINT value falls within specified limits.
DDV_MinMaxDWord	Verifies that a DWORD value falls within specified limits.
DDV_MinMaxFloat	Verifies that a float value falls within specified limits.
DDV_MinMaxDouble	Verifies that a double value falls within specified limits.
DDV_MaxChars	Verifies that a *CString* variable contains no more than a specified number of characters.

What DDX/DDV amounts to is a painless way to get data in and out of dialog box controls and perform simple validation procedures on the data. In practice, DDX/DDV prevents you from having to write code like the DlgDemo3 *CSettingsDialog-::OnInitDialog* and *CSettingsDialog::OnOK* functions. The DlgDemo4 application, listed in Figure 6-9, relies on DDX to transfer data between *CSettingsDialog* member variables and DDV to validate the text height. The *OnOK* and *OnInitDialog* handlers are gone completely, their work now done by DDX and DDV. Earlier I mentioned that it's important to call the base class versions of *OnOK* and *OnInitDialog* if you override them in a derived class. Now you know why. If you fail to call the base class implementations of these functions, the framework won't get the opportunity to call *UpdateData* and your DDX/DDV routines won't work.

Resource.h

```
//****************************************************************
//
//  Resource.h
//
//****************************************************************

#define IDR_MAINFRAME           100

#define IDM_OPTIONS_SETTINGS    110
#define IDM_OPTIONS_EXIT        111
#define IDM_OPTIONS_ABOUT       112

#define IDD_ABOUTDLG            120
#define IDC_ICONRECT            121

#define IDD_SETTINGSDLG         130
#define IDC_SOLID               131
#define IDC_GRADIENT            132
#define IDC_RED                 133
#define IDC_GREEN               134
#define IDC_BLUE                135
#define IDC_MAGENTA             136
#define IDC_CYAN                137
#define IDC_TEXT                138
#define IDC_HEIGHT              139
#define IDC_BOLD                140
#define IDC_ITALIC              141
#define IDC_DEFAULTS            142
```

Figure 6-9. *The DlgDemo4 program.*

DlgDemo4.rc

```
//****************************************************************
//
// DlgDemo4.rc
//
//****************************************************************

#include "afxres.h"
#include "Resource.h"

AFX_IDI_STD_FRAME ICON DlgDemo.ico

IDR_MAINFRAME MENU
BEGIN
    POPUP "&Options" {
        MENUITEM "&Settings...",        IDM_OPTIONS_SETTINGS
        MENUITEM "E&xit",               IDM_OPTIONS_EXIT
        MENUITEM SEPARATOR
        MENUITEM "&About DlgDemo4...",  IDM_OPTIONS_ABOUT
    }
END

IDD_SETTINGSDLG DIALOG 0, 0, 224, 149
STYLE DS_MODALFRAME | DS_CENTER | WS_POPUP | WS_VISIBLE |
    WS_CAPTION | WS_SYSMENU
CAPTION "Settings"
FONT 8, "MS Sans Serif"
BEGIN
    GROUPBOX        "Fill Type", -1, 12, 8, 80, 40
    AUTORADIOBUTTON "&Solid Fill", IDC_SOLID, 20, 20, 64, 10,
                    WS_TABSTOP | WS_GROUP
    AUTORADIOBUTTON "Gr&adient Fill", IDC_GRADIENT, 20, 32, 64, 10,
                    WS_TABSTOP
    GROUPBOX        "Fill Color", -1, 12, 60, 80, 76, WS_GROUP
    AUTORADIOBUTTON "&Red", IDC_RED, 20, 72, 64, 10, WS_TABSTOP | WS_GROUP
    AUTORADIOBUTTON "&Green", IDC_GREEN, 20, 84, 64, 10, WS_TABSTOP
    AUTORADIOBUTTON "&Blue", IDC_BLUE, 20, 96, 64, 10, WS_TABSTOP
    AUTORADIOBUTTON "&Magenta", IDC_MAGENTA, 20, 108, 64, 10, WS_TABSTOP
    AUTORADIOBUTTON "&Cyan", IDC_CYAN, 20, 120, 64, 10, WS_TABSTOP
    LTEXT           "&Text", -1, 104, 16, 20, 8
    EDITTEXT        IDC_TEXT, 128, 12, 84, 12, ES_AUTOHSCROLL | WS_GROUP
    LTEXT           "Text &Height (in points)", -1, 104, 36, 76, 8
    EDITTEXT        IDC_HEIGHT, 184, 32, 28, 12, ES_AUTOHSCROLL | WS_GROUP
    AUTOCHECKBOX    "Bo&ld",IDC_BOLD, 104, 56, 40, 10,
                    WS_TABSTOP | WS_GROUP
    AUTOCHECKBOX    "&Italic", IDC_ITALIC, 152, 56, 40, 10,
                    WS_TABSTOP | WS_GROUP
```

```
    DEFPUSHBUTTON      "OK", IDOK, 164, 84, 50, 14, WS_GROUP
    PUSHBUTTON         "Cancel", IDCANCEL, 164, 104, 50, 14, WS_GROUP
    PUSHBUTTON         "&Defaults", IDC_DEFAULTS, 164, 124, 49, 14, WS_GROUP
END


IDD_ABOUTDLG DIALOG 0, 0, 256, 98
STYLE DS_MODALFRAME ¦ DS_CENTER ¦ WS_POPUP ¦ WS_VISIBLE ¦
    WS_CAPTION ¦ WS_SYSMENU
CAPTION "About DlgDemo4"
FONT 8, "MS Sans Serif"
BEGIN
    LTEXT            "", IDC_ICONRECT, 14, 12, 80, 74
    LTEXT            "Dialog Demo 4", -1, 108, 12, 136, 8
    LTEXT            "From the book", -1, 108, 32, 136, 8
    LTEXT            """Programming Windows 95 with MFC""", -1,
                     108, 42, 136, 8
    LTEXT            "Copyright © 1996 by Jeff Prosise", -1,
                     108, 52, 136, 8
    DEFPUSHBUTTON    "OK", IDOK, 108, 72, 50, 14
END
```

DlgDemo4.h

```
//*********************************************************************
//
// DlgDemo4.h
//
//*********************************************************************

class CMyApp : public CWinApp
{
public:
    virtual BOOL InitInstance ();
};

class CMainWindow : public CFrameWnd
{
private:
    int m_nFillType;
    int m_nFillColor;
    CString m_text;
    int m_nHeight;
    BOOL m_bBold;
    BOOL m_bItalic;
```

(continued)

DlgDemo4.h *continued*

```
    void DoSolidFill (CDC*, CRect*);
    void DoGradientFill (CDC*, CRect*);
    void DoDrawText (CDC*, CRect*);

public:
    CMainWindow ();

protected:
    afx_msg BOOL OnEraseBkgnd (CDC*);
    afx_msg void OnPaint ();
    afx_msg void OnOptionsSettings ();
    afx_msg void OnOptionsExit ();
    afx_msg void OnOptionsAbout ();

    DECLARE_MESSAGE_MAP ()
};

class CSettingsDialog : public CDialog
{
public:
    int m_nFillType;
    int m_nFillColor;
    CString m_text;
    int m_nHeight;
    BOOL m_bBold;
    BOOL m_bItalic;

    CSettingsDialog (CWnd* pParentWnd = NULL) :
        CDialog (IDD_SETTINGSDLG, pParentWnd) {}

protected:
    virtual void DoDataExchange (CDataExchange*);

    afx_msg void OnDefaults ();
    DECLARE_MESSAGE_MAP ()
};

class CAboutDialog : public CDialog
{
private:
    CRect m_rect;

public:
    CAboutDialog (CWnd* pParentWnd = NULL) :
        CDialog (IDD_ABOUTDLG, pParentWnd) {}

    virtual BOOL OnInitDialog ();
```

```
protected:
    afx_msg void OnPaint ();
    DECLARE_MESSAGE_MAP ()
};
```

DlgDemo4.cpp

```
//***********************************************************************
//
//  DlgDemo4.cpp
//
//***********************************************************************

#include <afxwin.h>
#include "Resource.h"
#include "DlgDemo4.h"

CMyApp myApp;

//////////////////////////////////////////////////////////////////////
// CMyApp member functions

BOOL CMyApp::InitInstance ()
{
    m_pMainWnd = new CMainWindow;
    m_pMainWnd->ShowWindow (m_nCmdShow);
    m_pMainWnd->UpdateWindow ();
    return TRUE;
}

//////////////////////////////////////////////////////////////////////
// CMainWindow message map and member functions

BEGIN_MESSAGE_MAP (CMainWindow, CFrameWnd)
    ON_WM_ERASEBKGND ()
    ON_WM_PAINT ()
    ON_COMMAND (IDM_OPTIONS_SETTINGS, OnOptionsSettings)
    ON_COMMAND (IDM_OPTIONS_EXIT, OnOptionsExit)
    ON_COMMAND (IDM_OPTIONS_ABOUT, OnOptionsAbout)
END_MESSAGE_MAP ()

CMainWindow::CMainWindow ()
{
    m_nFillType = 1;
    m_nFillColor = 2;
```

(continued)

DlgDemo4.cpp *continued*

```
    m_text = "Hello, MFC";
    m_nHeight = 72;
    m_bBold = TRUE;
    m_bItalic = TRUE;

    Create (NULL, "DlgDemo4", WS_OVERLAPPEDWINDOW, rectDefault, NULL,
        MAKEINTRESOURCE (IDR_MAINFRAME));
}

BOOL CMainWindow::OnEraseBkgnd (CDC* pDC)
{
    CRect rect;
    GetClientRect (&rect);

    m_nFillType == 1 ? DoGradientFill (pDC, &rect) :
        DoSolidFill (pDC, &rect);
    return TRUE;
}

void CMainWindow::OnPaint ()
{
    CRect rect;
    GetClientRect (&rect);

    CPaintDC dc (this);
    DoDrawText (&dc, &rect);
}

void CMainWindow::OnOptionsSettings ()
{
    CSettingsDialog dlg (this);

    dlg.m_nFillType = m_nFillType;
    dlg.m_nFillColor = m_nFillColor;
    dlg.m_text = m_text;
    dlg.m_nHeight = m_nHeight;
    dlg.m_bBold = m_bBold;
    dlg.m_bItalic = m_bItalic;

    if (dlg.DoModal () == IDOK) {
        m_nFillType = dlg.m_nFillType;
        m_nFillColor = dlg.m_nFillColor;
        m_text = dlg.m_text;
        m_nHeight = dlg.m_nHeight;
        m_bBold = dlg.m_bBold;
        m_bItalic = dlg.m_bItalic;
```

```
        Invalidate ();
    }
}

void CMainWindow::OnOptionsExit ()
{
    SendMessage (WM_CLOSE, 0, 0);
}

void CMainWindow::OnOptionsAbout ()
{
    CAboutDialog dlg (this);
    dlg.DoModal ();
}

void CMainWindow::DoSolidFill (CDC* pDC, CRect* pRect)
{
    static COLORREF crColor[5] = {
        RGB (255,   0,   0),
        RGB (  0, 255,   0),
        RGB (  0,   0, 255),
        RGB (255,   0, 255),
        RGB (  0, 255, 255),
    };

    CBrush brush (crColor[m_nFillColor]);
    pDC->FillRect (pRect, &brush);
}

void CMainWindow::DoGradientFill (CDC* pDC, CRect* pRect)
{
    CBrush* pBrush[64];
    for (int i=0; i<64; i++) {
        switch (m_nFillColor) {

        case 0:
            pBrush[i] = new CBrush (RGB (255 - (i * 4), 0, 0));
            break;

        case 1:
            pBrush[i] = new CBrush (RGB (0, 255 - (i * 4), 0));
            break;

        case 2:
            pBrush[i] = new CBrush (RGB (0, 0, 255 - (i * 4)));
            break;
```

(continued)

DlgDemo4.cpp *continued*

```
        case 3:
            pBrush[i] = new CBrush (RGB (255 - (i * 4), 0,
                255 - (i * 4)));
            break;

        case 4:
            pBrush[i] = new CBrush (RGB (0, 255 - (i * 4),
                255 - (i * 4)));
            break;
        }
    }

    int nWidth = pRect->Width ();
    int nHeight = pRect->Height ();
    CRect rect;

    for (i=0; i<nHeight; i++) {
        rect.SetRect (0, i, nWidth, i + 1);
        pDC->FillRect (&rect, pBrush[(i * 63) / nHeight]);
    }

    for (i=0; i<64; i++)
        delete pBrush[i];
}

void CMainWindow::DoDrawText (CDC* pDC, CRect* pRect)
{
    CFont font;
    int nHeight = -((pDC->GetDeviceCaps (LOGPIXELSY) * m_nHeight) / 72);

    font.CreateFont (nHeight, 0, 0, 0, m_bBold ? FW_BOLD : FW_NORMAL,
        m_bItalic, 0, 0, DEFAULT_CHARSET, OUT_CHARACTER_PRECIS,
        CLIP_CHARACTER_PRECIS, DEFAULT_QUALITY, DEFAULT_PITCH |
        FF_DONTCARE, "Times New Roman");

    pDC->SetBkMode (TRANSPARENT);
    pDC->SetTextColor (RGB (255, 255, 255));

    CFont* pOldFont = pDC->SelectObject (&font);
    pDC->DrawText (m_text, -1, pRect, DT_SINGLELINE | DT_CENTER |
        DT_VCENTER);

    pDC->SelectObject (pOldFont);
}
```

```
//////////////////////////////////////////////////////////////////////////
// CSettingsDialog message map and member functions

BEGIN_MESSAGE_MAP (CSettingsDialog, CDialog)
    ON_BN_CLICKED (IDC_DEFAULTS, OnDefaults)
END_MESSAGE_MAP ()

void CSettingsDialog::OnDefaults ()
{
    m_nFillType = 1;
    m_nFillColor = 2;
    m_text = "Hello, MFC";
    m_nHeight = 72;
    m_bBold = TRUE;
    m_bItalic = TRUE;

    UpdateData (FALSE);
}

void CSettingsDialog::DoDataExchange (CDataExchange* pDX)
{
    CDialog::DoDataExchange (pDX);

    DDX_Radio (pDX, IDC_SOLID, m_nFillType);
    DDX_Radio (pDX, IDC_RED, m_nFillColor);
    DDX_Text (pDX, IDC_TEXT, m_text);
    DDX_Text (pDX, IDC_HEIGHT, m_nHeight);
    DDV_MinMaxInt (pDX, m_nHeight, 8, 144);
    DDX_Check (pDX, IDC_BOLD, m_bBold);
    DDX_Check (pDX, IDC_ITALIC, m_bItalic);
}

//////////////////////////////////////////////////////////////////////////
// CAboutDialog message map and member functions

BEGIN_MESSAGE_MAP (CAboutDialog, CDialog)
    ON_WM_PAINT ()
END_MESSAGE_MAP ()

BOOL CAboutDialog::OnInitDialog ()
{
    CDialog::OnInitDialog ();

    CStatic* pStatic = (CStatic*) GetDlgItem (IDC_ICONRECT);
    pStatic->GetWindowRect (&m_rect);
    pStatic->DestroyWindow ();
    ScreenToClient (&m_rect);
```

(continued)

DlgDemo4.cpp *continued*

```
        return TRUE;
    }


void CAboutDialog::OnPaint ()
{
    CPaintDC dc (this);
    HICON hIcon = (HICON) ::GetClassLong (AfxGetMainWnd ()->m_hWnd,
        GCL_HICON);

    if (hIcon != NULL) {
        CDC dcMem;
        dcMem.CreateCompatibleDC (&dc);

        CBitmap bitmap;
        bitmap.CreateCompatibleBitmap (&dc, 32, 32);
        CBitmap* pOldBitmap = dcMem.SelectObject (&bitmap);

        CBrush brush (::GetSysColor (COLOR_3DFACE));
        dcMem.FillRect (CRect (0, 0, 32, 32), &brush);
        dcMem.DrawIcon (0, 0, hIcon);

        dc.StretchBlt (m_rect.left, m_rect.top, m_rect.Width(),
            m_rect.Height (), &dcMem, 0, 0, 32, 32, SRCCOPY);

        dcMem.SelectObject (pOldBitmap);
    }
}
```

One item you should note in DlgDemo4 is the way in which *CSettingsDialog-::OnDefaults* is implemented. It's perfectly legal to call *UpdateData* yourself to synchronize member variables and controls, and in this case, *UpdateData* is called with a FALSE parameter when the Defaults button is clicked. This sets the controls to the values of the member variables. To read data out of the controls and into the member variables, pass *UpdateData* a TRUE parameter.

Don't misconstrue the presence of DDX and DDV to mean that you'll never again have to write code to interface with dialog controls. There are certain things that DDX/DDV won't do, such as limit the number of characters that can be typed into an edit control. For that, you'll still have to use *CEdit::LimitText* or *CEdit::SetLimitText*. The alternative is to write your own DDX/DDV routines. If you're interested, refer to *MFC Tech Note #26* in the online help for a discussion of custom DDX/DDV functions and how they can be integrated into ClassWizard and to the MFC source code files Dlgdata.cpp and Dlgfloat.cpp to see how MFC's DDX/DDV functions are implemented.

Another situation that requires direct interaction with a control occurs when a dialog box contains a list box that lists the names of all the fonts installed in the system. If the list box is of the *CListBox* variety, you'll need to override *OnInitDialog* and initialize the list box with font names. However, you can still use *DDX_LBIndex*, *DDX_LBString*, or *DDX_LBStringExact* to get and set the list box selection. A more elegant solution is to write your own *CFontListBox* class that initializes itself with font names when the list box is created. Then the *OnInitDialog* override will no longer be needed, and the list box can be handled exclusively with DDX/DDV.

Using Derived Control Classes in Dialog Boxes

As Chapter 5 demonstrated, one of the advantages of programming controls with MFC is that you can customize a control's behavior by deriving a new control class from an MFC control class. Objects of derived control classes require special handling in dialog boxes because of the manner in which they are created. Take Chapter 5's *CNumEdit* class, for example. To create a *CNumEdit* control in a top-level window, you'd create an object of that class and call its *Create* or *CreateEx* function. But in a dialog box, the edit control wrapped by a *CNumEdit* object is created for you from an EDITTEXT statement in the dialog template. Unfortunately, there's no way to specify in the dialog template that it's a *CNumEdit* control you want and not a standard *CEdit*-type control, so you have to make a choice: either omit the control from the template and create it manually in *OnInitDialog* or somehow convert an edit control into a *CNumEdit* after the dialog is created. Simply casting a *CEdit* pointer to a *CNumEdit* pointer won't work because casting won't force messages sent to the control to pass through *CNumEdit*'s message map. And without the message map, *CNumEdit* is no different than *CEdit*.

The key to converting a *CEdit* control into a *CNumEdit* control in a dialog box is MFC's *CWnd::SubclassDlgItem* function. *SubclassDlgItem* dynamically subclasses a dialog box control, attaching it to a C++ object and subclassing the control's window procedure so that messages pass through the object's message map. Here's a simple three-step procedure for incorporating a derived control class in a dialog box:

1. Include the control in your dialog box template with a resource statement corresponding to the base control type: PUSHBUTTON, EDITTEXT, and so on.

2. In your dialog class, declare an object of the derived class. Because it is a member of the dialog class, the object will be constructed automatically when the dialog is constructed.

3. Override *CDialog::OnInitDialog*, and call the object's *SubclassDlgItem* function to attach it to a dialog box control.

The following statements convert an edit control created with an EDITTEXT statement in a dialog template into a *CNumEdit* control. The derived control's ID is IDC_NUMEDIT:

```
// In the declaration for the dialog class
CNumEdit m_ctlNumEdit;
    .
    .
    .
// In the OnInitDialog override
m_ctlNumEdit.SubclassDlgItem (IDC_NUMEDIT, this);
```

The first parameter to *SubclassDlgItem* identifies the control that's being subclassed. The second identifies the control's parent.

MFC's *CBitmapButton* is a derived control class, but it's a special case in that you don't have to call *SubclassDlgItem* to associate a *CBitmapButton* object with a push button in a dialog. Instead, you call *CBitmapButton::AutoLoad*, which calls *CBitmapButton::LoadBitmaps* to load the bitmaps depicting the push button in its various states and *SubclassDlgItem* to subclass the push button control. Unlike *LoadBitmaps*, which accepts up to four text strings or integer IDs identifying bitmap resources, *AutoLoad* generates the resource names on the fly using the text assigned to the push button as a base. If the button text is "OK," then the up bitmap depicting the button in its undepressed state must be stored in a resource named "OKU." Similarly, the down, focus, and disabled bitmaps must be stored in resources named "OKD," "OKF," and "OKX," respectively. For a Cancel button, the corresponding resource names would be "CancelU," "CancelD," "CancelF," and "CancelX." As in *LoadBitmaps*, you don't have to provide all four bitmaps in *AutoLoad*. But in a dialog box, you should make it a practice to include a focus bitmap so that it will be obvious when an owner-drawn push button has the input focus.

The FoneList application, listed in Figure 6-10, features a dialog box with a *CNumEdit* control and a pair of *CBitmapButton* controls. FoneList displays a simple list of names and phone numbers in a list box sized to fill the interior of a frame window. To add an entry to the list, the user selects New from the Options menu and enters the information in the ensuing dialog box, as shown in Figure 6-11 on page 414. If the user clicks OK, the new entry will appear in the main window. To edit an entry, the user double-clicks it with the left mouse button. The Add/Edit Entry dialog box will appear again, this time with the Name and Phone fields initialized with the information from the list box item. The *CFoneListBox* class the list box is created from is a self-contained list box class that uses message reflection to process its own LBN_DBLCLK notifications so that it can display the dialog box itself rather than pass the job off to its parent.

Resource.h

```
//*********************************************************************
//
//  Resource.h
//
//*********************************************************************

#define IDR_MAINFRAME        100

#define IDM_OPTIONS_NEW      110
#define IDM_OPTIONS_EXIT     111

#define IDD_EDITDLG          120
#define IDC_NAME             121
#define IDC_PHONE            122

#define IDC_LISTBOX          130
```

FoneList.rc

```
//*********************************************************************
//
//  FoneList.rc
//
//*********************************************************************

#include <afxres.h>
#include "Resource.h"

OKU      BITMAP OKU.bmp
OKD      BITMAP OKD.bmp
OKF      BITMAP OKF.bmp
OKX      BITMAP OKX.bmp

CancelU BITMAP CancelU.bmp
CancelD BITMAP CancelD.bmp
CancelF BITMAP CancelF.bmp

IDR_MAINFRAME MENU
BEGIN
    POPUP "&Options" {
        MENUITEM "&New...",      IDM_OPTIONS_NEW
        MENUITEM SEPARATOR
```

Figure 6-10. *The FoneList program.*

(continued)

FoneList.rc *continued*

```
        MENUITEM "E&xit",          IDM_OPTIONS_EXIT
    }
END


IDD_EDITDLG DIALOG 0, 0, 160, 88
STYLE DS_MODALFRAME | DS_CENTER | WS_POPUP | WS_VISIBLE |
    WS_CAPTION | WS_SYSMENU
CAPTION "Add/Edit Entry"
FONT 8, "MS Sans Serif"
BEGIN
    LTEXT           "&Name", -1, 8, 14, 24, 8
    EDITTEXT        IDC_NAME, 34, 12, 118, 12, ES_AUTOHSCROLL
    LTEXT           "&Phone", -1, 8, 34, 24, 8
    EDITTEXT        IDC_PHONE, 34, 32, 118, 12, ES_AUTOHSCROLL
    DEFPUSHBUTTON   "OK", IDOK, 50, 54, 40, 24, BS_OWNERDRAW | WS_GROUP
    PUSHBUTTON      "Cancel", IDCANCEL, 104, 54, 40, 24, BS_OWNERDRAW |
                    WS_GROUP
END
```

FoneList.h

```
//****************************************************************
//
// FoneList.h
//
//****************************************************************

class CNumEdit : public CEdit
{
protected:
    afx_msg void OnChar (UINT, UINT, UINT);
    DECLARE_MESSAGE_MAP ()
};

class CFoneListBox : public CListBox
{
private:
    CFont m_font;

public:
    virtual BOOL PreCreateWindow (CREATESTRUCT&);
    void PromptForNewEntry ();

protected:
    afx_msg int OnCreate (LPCREATESTRUCT);
    afx_msg void OnEditItem ();
```

```
    DECLARE_MESSAGE_MAP ()
};

class CMyApp : public CWinApp
{
public:
    virtual BOOL InitInstance ();
};

class CMainWindow : public CFrameWnd
{
private:
    CFoneListBox m_ctlListBox;

public:
    CMainWindow ();

protected:
    afx_msg int OnCreate (LPCREATESTRUCT);
    afx_msg void OnSize (UINT, int, int);
    afx_msg void OnOptionsNew ();
    afx_msg void OnOptionsExit ();

    DECLARE_MESSAGE_MAP ()
};

class CEditDialog : public CDialog
{
public:
    CString m_strName;
    CString m_strPhone;

    CBitmapButton m_ctlOKButton;
    CBitmapButton m_ctlCancelButton;
    CNumEdit m_ctlPhone;

    CEditDialog (CWnd* pParentWnd = NULL) :
        CDialog (IDD_EDITDLG, pParentWnd) {}

    virtual BOOL OnInitDialog ();

protected:
    virtual void DoDataExchange (CDataExchange*);
    afx_msg void OnUpdateOKButton ();

    DECLARE_MESSAGE_MAP ()
};
```

FoneList.cpp

```cpp
//*************************************************************************
//
//   FoneList.cpp
//
//*************************************************************************

#include <afxwin.h>
#include <afxext.h>
#include "Resource.h"
#include "FoneList.h"

CMyApp myApp;

///////////////////////////////////////////////////////////////////////////
// CMyApp member functions

BOOL CMyApp::InitInstance ()
{
    m_pMainWnd = new CMainWindow;
    m_pMainWnd->ShowWindow (m_nCmdShow);
    m_pMainWnd->UpdateWindow ();
    return TRUE;
}


///////////////////////////////////////////////////////////////////////////
// CMainWindow message map and member functions

BEGIN_MESSAGE_MAP (CMainWindow, CFrameWnd)
    ON_WM_CREATE ()
    ON_WM_SIZE ()
    ON_COMMAND (IDM_OPTIONS_NEW, OnOptionsNew)
    ON_COMMAND (IDM_OPTIONS_EXIT, OnOptionsExit)
END_MESSAGE_MAP ()

CMainWindow::CMainWindow ()
{
    Create (NULL, "Names and Phones", WS_OVERLAPPEDWINDOW, rectDefault,
        NULL, MAKEINTRESOURCE (IDR_MAINFRAME));
}

int CMainWindow::OnCreate (LPCREATESTRUCT lpcs)
{
    if (CFrameWnd::OnCreate (lpcs) == -1)
        return -1;
```

```
    m_ctlListBox.Create (WS_CHILD | WS_VISIBLE, CRect (0, 0, 0, 0),
        this, IDC_LISTBOX);
    return 0;
}

void CMainWindow::OnSize (UINT nType, int cx, int cy)
{
    m_ctlListBox.SetWindowPos (NULL, 0, 0, cx, cy,
        SWP_NOMOVE | SWP_NOZORDER);
}

void CMainWindow::OnOptionsNew ()
{
    m_ctlListBox.PromptForNewEntry ();
}

void CMainWindow::OnOptionsExit ()
{
    SendMessage (WM_CLOSE, 0, 0);
}

/////////////////////////////////////////////////////////////////////////
// CEditDialog message map and member functions

BEGIN_MESSAGE_MAP (CEditDialog, CDialog)
    ON_EN_CHANGE (IDC_NAME, OnUpdateOKButton)
END_MESSAGE_MAP ()

BOOL CEditDialog::OnInitDialog ()
{
    CDialog::OnInitDialog ();

    m_ctlOKButton.AutoLoad (IDOK, this);
    m_ctlCancelButton.AutoLoad (IDCANCEL, this);
    m_ctlPhone.SubclassDlgItem (IDC_PHONE, this);

    OnUpdateOKButton ();
    return TRUE;
}

void CEditDialog::OnUpdateOKButton ()
{
    CEdit* pCtlName = (CEdit*) GetDlgItem (IDC_NAME);
    m_ctlOKButton.EnableWindow (pCtlName->LineLength ());
}
```

(continued)

FoneList.cpp *continued*

```cpp
void CEditDialog::DoDataExchange (CDataExchange* pDX)
{
    CDialog::DoDataExchange (pDX);

    DDX_Text (pDX, IDC_NAME, m_strName);
    DDV_MaxChars (pDX, m_strName, 32);
    DDX_Text (pDX, IDC_PHONE, m_strPhone);
    DDV_MaxChars (pDX, m_strPhone, 32);
}


/////////////////////////////////////////////////////////////////////////////
// CFoneListBox message map and member functions

BEGIN_MESSAGE_MAP (CFoneListBox, CListBox)
    ON_WM_CREATE ()
    ON_CONTROL_REFLECT (LBN_DBLCLK, OnEditItem)
END_MESSAGE_MAP ()

BOOL CFoneListBox::PreCreateWindow (CREATESTRUCT& cs)
{
    if (!CListBox::PreCreateWindow (cs))
        return FALSE;

    cs.style |= LBS_SORT | LBS_USETABSTOPS | LBS_NOTIFY |
        LBS_NOINTEGRALHEIGHT;
    return TRUE;
}

int CFoneListBox::OnCreate (LPCREATESTRUCT lpcs)
{
    if (CListBox::OnCreate (lpcs) == -1)
        return -1;

    CClientDC dc (this);
    int nHeight = -((dc.GetDeviceCaps (LOGPIXELSY) * 8) / 72);

    m_font.CreateFont (nHeight, 0, 0, 0, FW_NORMAL, 0, 0, 0,
        DEFAULT_CHARSET, OUT_CHARACTER_PRECIS, CLIP_CHARACTER_PRECIS,
        DEFAULT_QUALITY, DEFAULT_PITCH | FF_DONTCARE, "MS Sans Serif");
    SetFont (&m_font, FALSE);

    SetTabStops (128);
    return 0;
}
```

```
void CFoneListBox::OnEditItem ()
{
    CEditDialog dlg;

    CString strItem;
    int nIndex = GetCurSel ();
    GetText (nIndex, strItem);
    int nPos = strItem.Find ('\t');

    dlg.m_strName = strItem.Left (nPos);
    dlg.m_strPhone = strItem.Right (strItem.GetLength () - nPos - 1);

    if (dlg.DoModal () == IDOK) {
        strItem = dlg.m_strName + "\t" + dlg.m_strPhone;
        DeleteString (nIndex);
        AddString (strItem);
    }
    SetFocus ();
}

void CFoneListBox::PromptForNewEntry ()
{
    CEditDialog dlg;
    if (dlg.DoModal () == IDOK) {
        CString strItem = dlg.m_strName + "\t" + dlg.m_strPhone;
        AddString (strItem);
    }
    SetFocus ();
}

///////////////////////////////////////////////////////////////////////
// CNumEdit message map and member functions

BEGIN_MESSAGE_MAP (CNumEdit, CEdit)
    ON_WM_CHAR ()
END_MESSAGE_MAP ()

void CNumEdit::OnChar (UINT nChar, UINT nRepCnt, UINT nFlags)
{
    if (((nChar >= '0') && (nChar <= '9')) ||
        (nChar == VK_BACK) || (nChar == '(') || (nChar == ')') ||
        (nChar == '-') || (nChar == ' '))

        CEdit::OnChar (nChar, nRepCnt, nFlags);
}
```

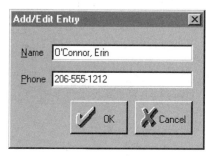

Figure 6-11. *The Add/Edit Entry dialog box for the FoneList application.*

Of the four controls in the Add/Edit Entry dialog box, three are wrapped by derived control classes. The Phone edit control comes from *CNumEdit*, and the OK and Cancel buttons from *CBitmapButton*. The Name edit control is a standard *CEdit* control. You can verify that the Phone edit control works as a *CNumEdit* control by trying to type nonnumeric characters into it. Only characters that might reasonably appear in a phone number are accepted. *CEditDialog* declares the following control data members:

```
CBitmapButton m_ctlOKButton;      // OK button
CBitmapButton m_ctlCancelButton;  // Cancel button
CNumEdit m_ctlPhone;              // Phone number edit control
```

In *CEditDialog::OnInitDialog*, *m_ctlPhone* is connected to the edit control with the following statement:

```
m_ctlPhone.SubclassDlgItem (IDC_PHONE, this);
```

Similarly, *m_ctlOKButton* and *m_ctlCancelButton* are associated with the OK and Cancel buttons using *CBitmapButton::AutoLoad*:

```
m_ctlOKButton.AutoLoad (IDOK, this);
m_ctlCancelButton.AutoLoad (IDCANCEL, this);
```

The bitmaps implicitly referenced in the calls to *AutoLoad* are declared with BITMAP statements in FoneList.rc. Again, note that it isn't necessary to call *SubclassDlgItem* for the push buttons because *AutoLoad* calls it for you. Calling *SubclassDlgItem* after *AutoLoad* in a debug build of your application will prompt an assertion error from MFC.

SubclassDlgItem is a powerful function whose simplicity belies the complexity within. Internally, subclassing is accomplished by using *::SetWindowLong* to replace the control's window procedure address with the address of a window procedure supplied by the framework. Messages handled by the derived class never make it past the new window procedure. Messages passed on to the base class are sent to the old window procedure for default processing. C programmers sometimes use window subclassing to modify control behavior, but the process is eminently cleaner in MFC because there's no API equivalent of *SubclassDlgItem* that would make window subclassing a one-step procedure. Nor do non-MFC programs have any concept of message maps, which further simplify control subclassing by allowing the message handling logic to be localized inside the control class and eliminating the need to write special callback procedures to process subclassed messages.

MODELESS DIALOG BOXES

Once you've mastered modal dialog boxes, you'll find that modeless dialog boxes are just a variation on what you've already learned. Modal and modeless dialogs are more alike than they are different. The key differences between the implementations of modal and modeless dialog boxes are as follows:

■ Whereas a modal dialog box is displayed by calling *CDialog::DoModal*, modeless dialogs are displayed with *CDialog::Create*. Unlike *DoModal*, which doesn't return until the dialog box is dismissed, *Create* returns as soon as the dialog box is created. Consequently, the dialog box is still displayed when *Create* returns.

■ Modeless dialogs are dismissed by calling *DestroyWindow*, not *EndDialog*. You mustn't allow *CDialog::OnOK* or *CDialog::OnCancel* to be called, because both call *EndDialog*.

■ Since *OnCancel* (and usually *OnOK*) must be overridden to prevent *EndDialog* from being called, you'll never create a modeless dialog directly from *CDialog*; you must derive your own class. Always override *OnCancel* in the derived class. Override *OnOK*, too, if the dialog box has an OK button or any other push button assigned the ID value IDOK.

■ Modal dialogs are usually created on the stack frame so that destruction is automatic. Modeless dialogs are normally created with *new* so that the dialog object won't be destroyed prematurely. To ensure that the modeless dialog object will be deleted when the dialog box is destroyed, override *CDialog::PostNcDestroy* in the derived dialog class and execute a *delete this* statement.

Other differences between modal and modeless dialog boxes are hidden behind the framework. For example, messages destined for a modeless dialog box are retrieved and dispatched by the main window's message loop, whereas modal dialog boxes are serviced by a message loop located inside Windows itself. An SDK application that uses a modeless dialog has to insert calls to *::IsDialogMessage* into the message loop to forward messages to the dialog box. But in an MFC application that uses a modeless dialog box, messages are forwarded automatically because *CDialog* overrides *CWnd::PreTranslateMessage* and calls *::IsDialogMessage* for you. (MFC 4 implements modal dialog boxes not by calling the underlying *::DialogBox*

API function as previous versions did but by creating a modeless dialog box and manually disabling the dialog's parent. The result? You can now override *CDialog-::PreTranslateMessage* for modal dialogs and perform specialized message processing of your own. In the past, *PreTranslateMessage* had no effect on modal dialogs because the application's message loop was bypassed by the call to *::DialogBox.*)

In general, MFC genericizes the interface for modeless dialogs so that using them is little different from using modal dialogs. Let's demonstrate to ourselves that this is so by modifying this chapter's dialog demo application one more time and converting DlgDemo4's Settings dialog into a modeless dialog box.

The DlgDemo5 Application

Figure 6-12's DlgDemo5 application is functionally identical to DlgDemo4 in all respects but one: the Settings dialog box is modeless rather than modal. Following an interface convention designed to clarify the controls' intent, the OK and Cancel buttons are now labeled Apply and Close. The Apply button applies the settings entered in the dialog box to the DlgDemo5 window but does not dismiss the dialog. The Close button removes the dialog box from the screen and discards any changes, just as the Cancel button in DlgDemo4 does. Despite the name change, the button IDs are still IDOK and IDCANCEL. This means that *OnOK* and *OnCancel* can still be used to process button clicks and that Enter and Esc still serve as the buttons' keyboard equivalents.

Resource.h

```
//*********************************************************************
//
//  Resource.h
//
//*********************************************************************

#define IDR_MAINFRAME           100

#define IDM_OPTIONS_SETTINGS    110
#define IDM_OPTIONS_EXIT        111
#define IDM_OPTIONS_ABOUT       112

#define IDD_ABOUTDLG            120
#define IDC_ICONRECT            121

#define IDD_SETTINGSDLG         130
#define IDC_SOLID               131
#define IDC_GRADIENT            132
```

Figure 6-12. *The DlgDemo5 program.*

```
#define IDC_RED              133
#define IDC_GREEN            134
#define IDC_BLUE             135
#define IDC_MAGENTA          136
#define IDC_CYAN             137
#define IDC_TEXT             138
#define IDC_HEIGHT           139
#define IDC_BOLD             140
#define IDC_ITALIC           141
#define IDC_DEFAULTS         142
```

DlgDemo5.rc

```
//***********************************************************************
//
//  DlgDemo5.rc
//
//***********************************************************************

#include "afxres.h"
#include "Resource.h"

AFX_IDI_STD_FRAME ICON DlgDemo.ico

IDR_MAINFRAME MENU
BEGIN
    POPUP "&Options" {
        MENUITEM "&Settings...",        IDM_OPTIONS_SETTINGS
        MENUITEM "E&xit",               IDM_OPTIONS_EXIT
        MENUITEM SEPARATOR
        MENUITEM "&About DlgDemo5...",  IDM_OPTIONS_ABOUT
    }
END

IDD_SETTINGSDLG DIALOG 0, 0, 224, 149
STYLE DS_CENTER | WS_POPUP | WS_VISIBLE | WS_CAPTION | WS_SYSMENU
CAPTION "Settings"
FONT 8, "MS Sans Serif"
BEGIN
    GROUPBOX        "Fill Type", -1, 12, 8, 80, 40
    AUTORADIOBUTTON "&Solid Fill", IDC_SOLID, 20, 20, 64, 10,
                    WS_TABSTOP | WS_GROUP
    AUTORADIOBUTTON "Gr&adient Fill", IDC_GRADIENT, 20, 32, 64, 10,
                    WS_TABSTOP
    GROUPBOX        "Fill Color", -1, 12, 60, 80, 76, WS_GROUP
    AUTORADIOBUTTON "&Red", IDC_RED, 20, 72, 64, 10, WS_TABSTOP | WS_GROUP
```

(continued)

DlgDemo5.rc *continued*

```
        AUTORADIOBUTTON "&Green", IDC_GREEN, 20, 84, 64, 10, WS_TABSTOP
        AUTORADIOBUTTON "&Blue", IDC_BLUE, 20, 96, 64, 10, WS_TABSTOP
        AUTORADIOBUTTON "&Magenta", IDC_MAGENTA, 20, 108, 64, 10, WS_TABSTOP
        AUTORADIOBUTTON "&Cyan", IDC_CYAN, 20, 120, 64, 10, WS_TABSTOP
        LTEXT           "&Text", -1, 104, 16, 20, 8
        EDITTEXT        IDC_TEXT, 128, 12, 84, 12, ES_AUTOHSCROLL | WS_GROUP
        LTEXT           "Text &Height (in points)", -1, 104, 36, 76, 8
        EDITTEXT        IDC_HEIGHT, 184, 32, 28, 12, ES_AUTOHSCROLL | WS_GROUP
        AUTOCHECKBOX    "Bo&ld",IDC_BOLD, 104, 56, 40, 10,
                        WS_TABSTOP | WS_GROUP
        AUTOCHECKBOX    "&Italic", IDC_ITALIC, 152, 56, 40, 10,
                        WS_TABSTOP | WS_GROUP
        DEFPUSHBUTTON   "Apply", IDOK, 164, 84, 50, 14, WS_GROUP
        PUSHBUTTON      "Close", IDCANCEL, 164, 104, 50, 14, WS_GROUP
        PUSHBUTTON      "&Defaults", IDC_DEFAULTS, 164, 124, 49, 14, WS_GROUP
END

IDD_ABOUTDLG DIALOG 0, 0, 256, 98
STYLE DS_MODALFRAME | DS_CENTER | WS_POPUP | WS_VISIBLE |
    WS_CAPTION | WS_SYSMENU
CAPTION "About DlgDemo5"
FONT 8, "MS Sans Serif"
BEGIN
        LTEXT           "", IDC_ICONRECT, 14, 12, 80, 74
        LTEXT           "Dialog Demo 5", -1, 108, 12, 136, 8
        LTEXT           "From the book", -1, 108, 32, 136, 8
        LTEXT           """Programming Windows 95 with MFC""", -1,
                        108, 42, 136, 8
        LTEXT           "Copyright © 1996 by Jeff Prosise", -1,
                        108, 52, 136, 8
        DEFPUSHBUTTON   "OK", IDOK, 108, 72, 50, 14
END
```

DlgDemo5.h

```
//*********************************************************************
//
// DlgDemo5.h
//
//*********************************************************************

typedef struct tagPROPERTIES
{
    int nFillType;
    int nFillColor;
```

```
    CString text;
    int nHeight;
    BOOL bBold;
    BOOL bItalic;
} PROPERTIES, * PPROPERTIES;

class CMyApp : public CWinApp
{
public:
    virtual BOOL InitInstance ();
};

class CSettingsDialog : public CDialog
{
public:
    int m_nFillType;
    int m_nFillColor;
    CString m_text;
    int m_nHeight;
    BOOL m_bBold;
    BOOL m_bItalic;

protected:
    virtual void OnOK ();
    virtual void OnCancel ();
    virtual void DoDataExchange (CDataExchange*);
    virtual void PostNcDestroy ();

    afx_msg void OnDefaults ();
    DECLARE_MESSAGE_MAP ()
};

class CMainWindow : public CFrameWnd
{
    friend void CSettingsDialog::PostNcDestroy ();

private:
    int m_nFillType;
    int m_nFillColor;
    CString m_text;
    int m_nHeight;
    BOOL m_bBold;
    BOOL m_bItalic;

    CSettingsDialog* m_pDlg;
```

(continued)

DlgDemo5.h *continued*

```
        void DoSolidFill (CDC*, CRect*);
        void DoGradientFill (CDC*, CRect*);
        void DoDrawText (CDC*, CRect*);

public:
        CMainWindow ();

protected:
        afx_msg BOOL OnEraseBkgnd (CDC*);
        afx_msg void OnPaint ();
        afx_msg void OnOptionsSettings ();
        afx_msg void OnOptionsExit ();
        afx_msg void OnOptionsAbout ();
        afx_msg LONG OnApplySettings (UINT, LONG);

        DECLARE_MESSAGE_MAP ()
};

class CAboutDialog : public CDialog
{
private:
        CRect m_rect;

public:
        CAboutDialog (CWnd* pParentWnd = NULL) :
            CDialog (IDD_ABOUTDLG, pParentWnd) {}

        virtual BOOL OnInitDialog ();

protected:
        afx_msg void OnPaint ();
        DECLARE_MESSAGE_MAP ()
};
```

DlgDemo5.cpp

```
//*********************************************************************
//
//  DlgDemo5.cpp
//
//*********************************************************************

#include <afxwin.h>
#include "Resource.h"
#include "DlgDemo5.h"
```

```
CMyApp myApp;

///////////////////////////////////////////////////////////////////////////
// CMyApp member functions

BOOL CMyApp::InitInstance ()
{
    m_pMainWnd = new CMainWindow;
    m_pMainWnd->ShowWindow (m_nCmdShow);
    m_pMainWnd->UpdateWindow ();
    return TRUE;
}


///////////////////////////////////////////////////////////////////////////
// CMainWindow message map and member functions

BEGIN_MESSAGE_MAP (CMainWindow, CFrameWnd)
    ON_WM_ERASEBKGND ()
    ON_WM_PAINT ()
    ON_COMMAND (IDM_OPTIONS_SETTINGS, OnOptionsSettings)
    ON_COMMAND (IDM_OPTIONS_EXIT, OnOptionsExit)
    ON_COMMAND (IDM_OPTIONS_ABOUT, OnOptionsAbout)
    ON_MESSAGE (WM_USER, OnApplySettings)
END_MESSAGE_MAP ()

CMainWindow::CMainWindow ()
{
    m_pDlg = NULL;

    m_nFillType = 1;
    m_nFillColor = 2;
    m_text = "Hello, MFC";
    m_nHeight = 72;
    m_bBold = TRUE;
    m_bItalic = TRUE;

    Create (NULL, "DlgDemo5", WS_OVERLAPPEDWINDOW, rectDefault, NULL,
        MAKEINTRESOURCE (IDR_MAINFRAME));
}

BOOL CMainWindow::OnEraseBkgnd (CDC* pDC)
{
    CRect rect;
    GetClientRect (&rect);

    m_nFillType == 1 ? DoGradientFill (pDC, &rect) :
        DoSolidFill (pDC, &rect);
```

(continued)

DlgDemo5.cpp *continued*

```
        return TRUE;
    }

    void CMainWindow::OnPaint ()
    {
        CRect rect;
        GetClientRect (&rect);

        CPaintDC dc (this);
        DoDrawText (&dc, &rect);
    }

    void CMainWindow::OnOptionsSettings ()
    {
        if (m_pDlg != NULL) {
            m_pDlg->SetFocus ();
            return;
        }

        m_pDlg = new CSettingsDialog;

        m_pDlg->m_nFillType = m_nFillType;
        m_pDlg->m_nFillColor = m_nFillColor;
        m_pDlg->m_text = m_text;
        m_pDlg->m_nHeight = m_nHeight;
        m_pDlg->m_bBold = m_bBold;
        m_pDlg->m_bItalic = m_bItalic;

        m_pDlg->Create (IDD_SETTINGSDLG, this);
    }

    void CMainWindow::OnOptionsExit ()
    {
        SendMessage (WM_CLOSE, 0, 0);
    }

    void CMainWindow::OnOptionsAbout ()
    {
        CAboutDialog dlg (this);
        dlg.DoModal ();
    }

    LONG CMainWindow::OnApplySettings (UINT wParam, LONG lParam)
    {
        PPROPERTIES pProp = (PPROPERTIES) lParam;
```

```
    m_nFillType = pProp->nFillType;
    m_nFillColor = pProp->nFillColor;
    m_text = pProp->text;
    m_nHeight = pProp->nHeight;
    m_bBold = pProp->bBold;
    m_bItalic = pProp->bItalic;

    Invalidate ();
    return 0;
}

void CMainWindow::DoSolidFill (CDC* pDC, CRect* pRect)
{
    static COLORREF crColor[5] = {
        RGB (255,   0,   0),
        RGB (  0, 255,   0),
        RGB (  0,   0, 255),
        RGB (255,   0, 255),
        RGB (  0, 255, 255),
    };

    CBrush brush (crColor[m_nFillColor]);
    pDC->FillRect (pRect, &brush);
}

void CMainWindow::DoGradientFill (CDC* pDC, CRect* pRect)
{
    CBrush* pBrush[64];
    for (int i=0; i<64; i++) {
        switch (m_nFillColor) {

        case 0:
            pBrush[i] = new CBrush (RGB (255 - (i * 4), 0, 0));
            break;

        case 1:
            pBrush[i] = new CBrush (RGB (0, 255 - (i * 4), 0));
            break;

        case 2:
            pBrush[i] = new CBrush (RGB (0, 0, 255 - (i * 4)));
            break;

        case 3:
            pBrush[i] = new CBrush (RGB (255 - (i * 4), 0,
                255 - (i * 4)));
            break;
```

(continued)

DlgDemo5.cpp *continued*

```
        case 4:
            pBrush[i] = new CBrush (RGB (0, 255 - (i * 4),
                255 - (i * 4)));
            break;
        }
    }

    int nWidth = pRect->Width ();
    int nHeight = pRect->Height ();
    CRect rect;

    for (i=0; i<nHeight; i++) {
        rect.SetRect (0, i, nWidth, i + 1);
        pDC->FillRect (&rect, pBrush[(i * 63) / nHeight]);
    }

    for (i=0; i<64; i++)
        delete pBrush[i];
}

void CMainWindow::DoDrawText (CDC* pDC, CRect* pRect)
{
    CFont font;
    int nHeight = -((pDC->GetDeviceCaps (LOGPIXELSY) * m_nHeight) / 72);

    font.CreateFont (nHeight, 0, 0, 0, m_bBold ? FW_BOLD : FW_NORMAL,
        m_bItalic, 0, 0, DEFAULT_CHARSET, OUT_CHARACTER_PRECIS,
        CLIP_CHARACTER_PRECIS, DEFAULT_QUALITY, DEFAULT_PITCH |
        FF_DONTCARE, "Times New Roman");

    pDC->SetBkMode (TRANSPARENT);
    pDC->SetTextColor (RGB (255, 255, 255));

    CFont* pOldFont = pDC->SelectObject (&font);
    pDC->DrawText (m_text, -1, pRect, DT_SINGLELINE | DT_CENTER |
        DT_VCENTER);

    pDC->SelectObject (pOldFont);
}

///////////////////////////////////////////////////////////////////////
// CSettingsDialog message map and member functions

BEGIN_MESSAGE_MAP (CSettingsDialog, CDialog)
    ON_BN_CLICKED (IDC_DEFAULTS, OnDefaults)
END_MESSAGE_MAP ()
```

```
void CSettingsDialog::OnOK ()
{
    UpdateData (TRUE);

    PROPERTIES prop;
    prop.nFillType = m_nFillType;
    prop.nFillColor = m_nFillColor;
    prop.text = m_text;
    prop.nHeight = m_nHeight;
    prop.bBold = m_bBold;
    prop.bItalic = m_bItalic;

    AfxGetMainWnd ()->SendMessage (WM_USER, 0, (LPARAM) &prop);
}

void CSettingsDialog::OnCancel ()
{
    DestroyWindow ();
}

void CSettingsDialog::PostNcDestroy ()
{
    ((CMainWindow*) AfxGetMainWnd ())->m_pDlg = NULL;
    delete this;
}

void CSettingsDialog::OnDefaults ()
{
    m_nFillType = 1;
    m_nFillColor = 2;
    m_text = "Hello, MFC";
    m_nHeight = 72;
    m_bBold = TRUE;
    m_bItalic = TRUE;

    UpdateData (FALSE);
}

void CSettingsDialog::DoDataExchange (CDataExchange* pDX)
{
    CDialog::DoDataExchange (pDX);

    DDX_Radio (pDX, IDC_SOLID, m_nFillType);
    DDX_Radio (pDX, IDC_RED, m_nFillColor);
    DDX_Text (pDX, IDC_TEXT, m_text);
    DDX_Text (pDX, IDC_HEIGHT, m_nHeight);
```

(continued)

```
    DDV_MinMaxInt (pDX, m_nHeight, 8, 144);
    DDX_Check (pDX, IDC_BOLD, m_bBold);
    DDX_Check (pDX, IDC_ITALIC, m_bItalic);
}

/////////////////////////////////////////////////////////////////////////
// CAboutDialog message map and member functions

BEGIN_MESSAGE_MAP (CAboutDialog, CDialog)
    ON_WM_PAINT ()
END_MESSAGE_MAP ()

BOOL CAboutDialog::OnInitDialog ()
{
    CDialog::OnInitDialog ();

    CStatic* pStatic = (CStatic*) GetDlgItem (IDC_ICONRECT);
    pStatic->GetWindowRect (&m_rect);
    pStatic->DestroyWindow ();
    ScreenToClient (&m_rect);

    return TRUE;
}

void CAboutDialog::OnPaint ()
{
    CPaintDC dc (this);
    HICON hIcon = (HICON) ::GetClassLong (AfxGetMainWnd ()->m_hWnd,
        GCL_HICON);

    if (hIcon != NULL) {
        CDC dcMem;
        dcMem.CreateCompatibleDC (&dc);

        CBitmap bitmap;
        bitmap.CreateCompatibleBitmap (&dc, 32, 32);
        CBitmap* pOldBitmap = dcMem.SelectObject (&bitmap);

        CBrush brush (::GetSysColor (COLOR_3DFACE));
        dcMem.FillRect (CRect (0, 0, 32, 32), &brush);
        dcMem.DrawIcon (0, 0, hIcon);

        dc.StretchBlt (m_rect.left, m_rect.top, m_rect.Width(),
            m_rect.Height (), &dcMem, 0, 0, 32, 32, SRCCOPY);

        dcMem.SelectObject (pOldBitmap);
    }
}
```

As before, the Settings dialog is invoked by selecting Settings from the Options menu. *CMainWindow::OnOptionsSettings* constructs the dialog object, initializes the dialog's data members, and creates a modeless dialog box in this way:

```
m_pDlg = new CSettingsDialog;

m_pDlg->m_nFillType = m_nFillType;
m_pDlg->m_nFillColor = m_nFillColor;
m_pDlg->m_text = m_text;
m_pDlg->m_nHeight = m_nHeight;
m_pDlg->m_bBold = m_bBold;
m_pDlg->m_bItalic = m_bItalic;

m_pDlg->Create (IDD_SETTINGSDLG, this);
```

To avoid automatic destruction, the dialog object is created with *new* rather than constructed on the stack frame. The dialog pointer is saved in *CMainWindow::m_pDlg*, which is initialized to NULL by *CMainWindow*'s constructor and reset to NULL when the dialog box is destroyed. Any member function of *CMainWindow* can determine whether the dialog box is currently displayed by checking *m_pDlg* for a non-NULL value. This turns out to be quite useful because, before creating the Settings dialog box, *OnOptionsSettings* checks *m_pDlg* to see if the dialog box is already displayed. If the answer is yes, *OnOptionsSettings* uses the *m_pDlg* pointer to set the focus to the existing dialog box rather than to create a new one:

```
if (m_pDlg != NULL) {
    m_pDlg->SetFocus ();
    return;
}
```

Without this precaution, every invocation of Options-Settings would create a new instance of the dialog, even if other instances already existed. There's normally no reason to have two or more copies of the same dialog box on the screen at the same time, so you shouldn't allow the user to open multiple instances of a modeless dialog unless some circumstance would clearly warrant it.

Processing Messages from the Apply and Close Buttons

One fundamental difference between modal and modeless dialog classes is in how they handle *OnOK* and *OnCancel* notifications. A modal dialog class rarely overrides *OnCancel* because the default implementation in *CDialog* calls *EndDialog* to close the dialog box and return IDCANCEL to *DoModal*. Even *OnOK* rarely needs to be overridden because the *CDialog* implementation of *OnOK* calls *UpdateData* to update the dialog's data members before dismissing the dialog box. If the dialog box's controls and data members are linked by a data map, the default action provided by *CDialog::OnOK* is usually sufficient.

But a modeless dialog just about always overrides both *OnOK* and *OnCancel*. As mentioned earlier, it's important to prevent *CDialog::OnOK* and *CDialog::OnCancel* from being called in a modeless dialog box because modeless dialogs are dismissed with *DestroyWindow*, not *EndDialog*. (If *EndDialog* were called, the dialog box would appear to go away but in reality would remain behind in memory.) *OnOK* needs to be overridden if any one of the buttons in the dialog box has the ID value IDOK. *OnCancel* should always be overridden because an IDCANCEL notification is sent when the user presses the Esc key or clicks the dialog box's Close button regardless of whether the dialog contains a Cancel button.

In DlgDemo5, the Apply and Close buttons generate calls to *OnOK* and *OnCancel*, so *CSettingsDialog* overrides both. *CSettingsDialog::OnOK* contains the following statements:

```
UpdateData (TRUE);

PROPERTIES prop;
prop.nFillType = m_nFillType;
prop.nFillColor = m_nFillColor;
prop.text = m_text;
prop.nHeight = m_nHeight;
prop.bBold = m_bBold;
prop.bItalic = m_bItalic;

AfxGetMainWnd ()->SendMessage (WM_USER, 0, (LPARAM) &prop);
```

The first statement updates the dialog's member variables to match the current state of the controls. A modeless dialog box that relies on DDX and DDV must call *UpdateData* from the *OnOK* handler itself because calling *CDialog::OnOK* and letting it call *UpdateData* isn't an option. The next block of statements instantiates the PROPERTIES structure declared in DlgDemo5.h and copies the dialog's data members into the fields of the data structure. The final statement sends a WM_USER message to the application's window telling it to apply the settings contained in the PROPERTIES structure to the dialog box. WM_USER, which is defined as 0x400 in the header file Winuser.h, specifies the low end of a range of message IDs an application can use without conflicting with the message IDs of standard Windows messages such as WM_CREATE and WM_PAINT. An application is free to use message IDs from WM_USER's 0x400 through 0x7FFF for its own purposes. Messages in this range are referred to as *user-defined messages*.

A message transmitted with *SendMessage* includes two parameters the sender can use to pass data to the receiver: a 32-bit value of type WPARAM and another 32-bit value whose type is LPARAM. When *CSettingsDialog::OnOK* sends a message to the main window, it sends along a pointer to a PROPERTIES structure containing the settings retrieved from the dialog box. The main window processes the message with

CMainWindow::OnApplySettings, which is referenced in the message map with the following message map entry:

```
ON_MESSAGE (WM_USER, OnApplySettings);
```

The ON_MESSAGE macro maps user-defined messages to their corresponding handling functions. When activated, *OnApplySettings* copies the settings out of the data structure and into its own data members. It then invalidates its window to force a repaint incorporating the new settings:

```
LONG CMainWindow::OnApplySettings (UINT wParam, LONG lParam)
{
    PPROPERTIES pProp = (PPROPERTIES) lParam;

    m_nFillType = pProp->nFillType;
    m_nFillColor = pProp->nFillColor;
    m_text = pProp->text;
    m_nHeight = pProp->nHeight;
    m_bBold = pProp->bBold;
    m_bItalic = pProp->bItalic;

    Invalidate ();
    return 0;
}
```

The value returned by a handler for a user-defined message is returned to the caller through *SendMessage*. *CSettingsDialog::OnOK* attaches no meaning to the return value, so *OnApplySettings* simply returns 0.

SendMessage isn't the only mechanism a modeless dialog box can use to communicate with its parent. MFC programmers sometimes find it more expedient to grab a pointer to the main window and use that pointer to call a public member function of the main window. The PropDemo application, which we'll look at later in this chapter, uses this technique to communicate changes entered into a property sheet.

CSettingsDialog::OnCancel doesn't use *SendMessage*. It contains just one statement: a call to *DestroyWindow* to destroy the dialog box. Ultimately, this action activates *CSettingsDialog::PostNcDestroy*, which is defined as follows:

```
void CSettingsDialog::PostNcDestroy ()
{
    ((CMainWindow*) AfxGetMainWnd ())->m_pDlg = NULL;
    delete this;
}
```

The first statement sets *CMainWindow*'s *m_pDlg* pointer to NULL so that the main window will know that the dialog box has been destroyed. Rather than declare *m_pDlg* public and risk the chance that it might be corrupted by a non-*CSettingsDialog* object or even by other member functions of *CSettingsDialog*, *CMainWindow* declares *CSettingsDialog::PostNcDestroy* to be a friend of *CMainWindow* in DlgDemo5.h so that the function can access *CMainWindow*'s private data members. Are there other ways to reset the dialog pointer? You bet. The dialog box could, for example, send a user-defined message to the main window saying, "I'm about to close, so reset your *m_pDlg* pointer to NULL." Or it could call a public *CMainWindow* member function to reset *m_pDlg*. Whichever route you choose, don't forget to finish up with a *delete this* statement to delete the dialog object.

You might be tempted to skip overriding *PostNcDestroy* in a modeless dialog box and shift the responsibility for deleting the dialog object to the window that created the dialog box. But be very careful if you do this because pitfalls await the unwary programmer who doesn't consider all the implications. Suppose *CMainWindow* had a public member function named *DeleteMe* that the dialog could call through *AfxGetMainWnd* to delete itself. The function might look like this:

```
void CMainWindow::DeleteMe ();
{
    m_pDlg->DestroyWindow ();
    delete m_pDlg;
    m_pDlg = NULL;
}
```

One problem with this approach is that when *DeleteMe* returns, the dialog box has been destroyed and the dialog object deleted. Needless to say, letting a function call return to an object that no longer exists invites disaster. Using *SendMessage* instead of calling a member function to avoid overriding *PostNcDestroy* is no better because *SendMessage* doesn't return until after the message is processed. You could use *PostMessage* instead of *SendMessage*, but you would still need to override *PostNcDestroy* and delete the dialog object in case the application is closed while the dialog box is displayed. In the end, it's easier to do as DlgDemo5 does and let *PostNcDestroy* reset the dialog pointer as well as delete the dialog object.

Using a Modeless Dialog Box as a Main Window

If you write an application whose primary user interface is a dialog-like collection of controls—the Windows 95 Phone Dialer is one example that comes to mind—you should consider using a modeless dialog box as a main window. Charles Petzold immortalized this technique with the HexCalc program featured in his book *Programming Windows*. Scores of developers have adopted similar techniques for creating small, utility-type application programs whose main windows are more easily defined in dialog templates than within the programmatic confines of *OnCreate* handlers. In this section, we'll see how it's done with the calculator applet named DlgCalc listed in Figure 6-13. DlgCalc's window, shown in Figure 6-14 on page 445, is a modeless dialog box. DlgCalc differs from the calculator applet supplied with Windows in one important respect: it uses the postfix, or reverse Polish, notation (RPN) form of data entry familiar to users of Hewlett-Packard calculators.

Resource.h

```
//*********************************************************************
//
//  Resource.h
//
//*********************************************************************

#define IDI_CALCDLG          100
#define IDR_CALCDLG          101

#define IDD_CALCDLG          110
#define IDD_ABOUTDLG         111

#define IDC_0                120
#define IDC_1                121
#define IDC_2                122
#define IDC_3                123
#define IDC_4                124
#define IDC_5                125
#define IDC_6                126
#define IDC_7                127
#define IDC_8                128
#define IDC_9                129

#define IDC_CHGSIGN          130
#define IDC_EXP              131
#define IDC_STO              132
#define IDC_RCL              133
#define IDC_ENTER            134
#define IDC_FIX              135
#define IDC_CLX              136
#define IDC_SUBTRACT         137
#define IDC_ADD              138
#define IDC_MULTIPLY         139
#define IDC_DIVIDE           140
#define IDC_DECIMAL          141
#define IDC_DEL              142

#define IDC_DISPLAYRECT      150
#define IDC_ICONRECT         151

#define IDM_SYSMENU_ABOUT    256
```

Figure 6-13. *The DlgCalc program.*

DlgCalc.rc

```
//*********************************************************************
//
// DlgCalc.rc
//
//*********************************************************************

#include "afxres.h"
#include "Resource.h"

IDI_CALCDLG ICON DlgCalc.ico

IDD_CALCDLG DIALOG 0, 0, 108, 132
STYLE WS_POPUP | WS_CAPTION | WS_SYSMENU | WS_MINIMIZEBOX
CAPTION "DlgCalc"
FONT 8, "MS Sans Serif"
BEGIN
    LTEXT       "", IDC_DISPLAYRECT, 4, 12, 100, 12
    PUSHBUTTON  "±", IDC_CHGSIGN, 4, 36, 16, 12
    PUSHBUTTON  "Exp", IDC_EXP, 24, 36, 24, 12
    PUSHBUTTON  "Sto", IDC_STO, 52, 36, 24, 12
    PUSHBUTTON  "Rcl", IDC_RCL, 80, 36, 24, 12
    PUSHBUTTON  "Enter", IDC_ENTER, 4, 52, 44, 12
    PUSHBUTTON  "Fix", IDC_FIX, 52, 52, 24, 12
    PUSHBUTTON  "Clx", IDC_CLX, 80, 52, 24, 12
    PUSHBUTTON  "-", IDC_SUBTRACT, 4, 68, 16, 12
    PUSHBUTTON  "7", IDC_7, 24, 68, 24, 12
    PUSHBUTTON  "8", IDC_8, 52, 68, 24, 12
    PUSHBUTTON  "9", IDC_9, 80, 68, 24, 12
    PUSHBUTTON  "+", IDC_ADD, 4, 84, 16, 12
    PUSHBUTTON  "4", IDC_4, 24, 84, 24, 12
    PUSHBUTTON  "5", IDC_5, 52, 84, 24, 12
    PUSHBUTTON  "6", IDC_6, 80, 84, 24, 12
    PUSHBUTTON  "x", IDC_MULTIPLY, 4, 100, 16, 12
    PUSHBUTTON  "1", IDC_1, 24, 100, 24, 12
    PUSHBUTTON  "2", IDC_2, 52, 100, 24, 12
    PUSHBUTTON  "3", IDC_3, 80, 100, 24, 12
    PUSHBUTTON  "÷", IDC_DIVIDE, 4, 116, 16, 12
    PUSHBUTTON  "0", IDC_0, 24, 116, 24, 12
    PUSHBUTTON  ".", IDC_DECIMAL, 52, 116, 24, 12
    PUSHBUTTON  "Del", IDC_DEL, 80, 116, 24, 12
END

IDR_CALCDLG ACCELERATORS
BEGIN
    "0",        IDC_0
```

```
        "1",        IDC_1
        "2",        IDC_2
        "3",        IDC_3
        "4",        IDC_4
        "5",        IDC_5
        "6",        IDC_6
        "7",        IDC_7
        "8",        IDC_8
        "9",        IDC_9
        "+",        IDC_ADD
        "-",        IDC_SUBTRACT
        "*",        IDC_MULTIPLY
        "/",        IDC_DIVIDE
        ".",        IDC_DECIMAL
        "S",        IDC_STO,        VIRTKEY
        "R",        IDC_RCL,        VIRTKEY
        "F",        IDC_FIX,        VIRTKEY
        "C",        IDC_CLX,        VIRTKEY
        "P",        IDC_CHGSIGN,    VIRTKEY
        "E",        IDC_EXP,        VIRTKEY
        VK_RETURN,  IDC_ENTER,      VIRTKEY
        VK_DELETE,  IDC_DEL,        VIRTKEY
        VK_BACK,    IDC_DEL,        VIRTKEY
END


IDD_ABOUTDLG DIALOG 0, 0, 256, 98
STYLE DS_MODALFRAME | DS_CENTER | WS_POPUP | WS_VISIBLE |
    WS_CAPTION | WS_SYSMENU
CAPTION "About DlgCalc"
FONT 8, "MS Sans Serif"
BEGIN
    LTEXT           "", IDC_ICONRECT, 14, 12, 80, 74
    LTEXT           "DlgCalc Version 1.0", -1, 108, 12, 136, 8
    LTEXT           "From the book", -1, 108, 32, 136, 8
    LTEXT           """Programming Windows 95 with MFC""", -1,
                    108, 42, 136, 8
    LTEXT           "Copyright © 1996 by Jeff Prosise", -1,
                    108, 52, 136, 8
    DEFPUSHBUTTON   "OK", IDOK, 108, 72, 50, 14
END
```

DlgCalc.h

```
//*********************************************************************
//
//  DlgCalc.h
//
//*********************************************************************

class CMyApp : public CWinApp
{
public:
    virtual BOOL InitInstance ();
};

class CCalcDialog : public CDialog
{
private:
    HACCEL m_hAccel;
    double m_dbStack[4];
    double m_dbMemory;
    CString m_strDisplay;
    CString m_strFormat;
    CRect m_rect;
    int m_cxChar;
    int m_cyChar;

    BOOL m_bFixPending;
    BOOL m_bErrorFlag;
    BOOL m_bDecimalInString;
    BOOL m_bStackLiftEnabled;
    BOOL m_bNewX;

    void LiftStack ();
    void DropStack ();
    void DisplayXRegister ();
    void UpdateDisplay (CString&);

public:
    CCalcDialog ();
    virtual BOOL OnInitDialog ();
    virtual BOOL PreTranslateMessage (MSG*);

protected:
    virtual BOOL OnCommand (WPARAM, LPARAM);
    virtual void OnCancel ();
    virtual void PostNcDestroy ();
```

```
    afx_msg void OnPaint ();
    afx_msg void OnSysCommand (UINT, LPARAM);
    afx_msg void OnDigit (UINT);
    afx_msg void OnAdd ();
    afx_msg void OnSubtract ();
    afx_msg void OnMultiply ();
    afx_msg void OnDivide ();
    afx_msg void OnEnter ();
    afx_msg void OnChangeSign ();
    afx_msg void OnExponent ();
    afx_msg void OnStore ();
    afx_msg void OnRecall ();
    afx_msg void OnFix ();
    afx_msg void OnClear ();
    afx_msg void OnDecimal ();
    afx_msg void OnDelete ();

    DECLARE_MESSAGE_MAP ()
};

class CAboutDialog : public CDialog
{
private:
    CRect m_rect;

public:
    CAboutDialog (CWnd* pParentWnd = NULL) :
        CDialog (IDD_ABOUTDLG, pParentWnd) {}

    virtual BOOL OnInitDialog ();

protected:
    afx_msg void OnPaint ();
    DECLARE_MESSAGE_MAP ()
};
```

DlgCalc.cpp

```
//****************************************************************
//
//  DlgCalc.cpp
//
//****************************************************************

#include <afxwin.h>
#include <math.h>
```

(continued)

DlgCalc.cpp *continued*

```cpp
#include "Resource.h"
#include "DlgCalc.h"

#define MAXCHARS 22

CMyApp myApp;

/////////////////////////////////////////////////////////////////////////
// CMyApp member functions

BOOL CMyApp::InitInstance ()
{
    m_pMainWnd = new CCalcDialog;
    m_pMainWnd->ShowWindow (m_nCmdShow);
    m_pMainWnd->UpdateWindow ();
    return TRUE;
}

/////////////////////////////////////////////////////////////////////////
// CCalcDialog message map and member functions

BEGIN_MESSAGE_MAP (CCalcDialog, CDialog)
    ON_WM_PAINT ()
    ON_WM_SYSCOMMAND ()
    ON_CONTROL_RANGE (BN_CLICKED, IDC_0, IDC_9, OnDigit)
    ON_BN_CLICKED (IDC_ADD, OnAdd)
    ON_BN_CLICKED (IDC_SUBTRACT, OnSubtract)
    ON_BN_CLICKED (IDC_MULTIPLY, OnMultiply)
    ON_BN_CLICKED (IDC_DIVIDE, OnDivide)
    ON_BN_CLICKED (IDC_ENTER, OnEnter)
    ON_BN_CLICKED (IDC_CHGSIGN, OnChangeSign)
    ON_BN_CLICKED (IDC_EXP, OnExponent)
    ON_BN_CLICKED (IDC_STO, OnStore)
    ON_BN_CLICKED (IDC_RCL, OnRecall)
    ON_BN_CLICKED (IDC_FIX, OnFix)
    ON_BN_CLICKED (IDC_CLX, OnClear)
    ON_BN_CLICKED (IDC_DECIMAL, OnDecimal)
    ON_BN_CLICKED (IDC_DEL, OnDelete)
END_MESSAGE_MAP ()

CCalcDialog::CCalcDialog ()
{
    for (int i=0; i<4; i++)
        m_dbStack[i] = 0.0;

    m_dbMemory = 0.0;
    m_strFormat = "%0.2f";
```

```
    m_bFixPending = FALSE;
    m_bErrorFlag = FALSE;
    m_bDecimalInString = FALSE;
    m_bStackLiftEnabled = FALSE;
    m_bNewX = TRUE;

    Create (IDD_CALCDLG);
    m_hAccel = ::LoadAccelerators (AfxGetInstanceHandle (),
        MAKEINTRESOURCE (IDR_CALCDLG));

    SetIcon (myApp.LoadIcon (IDI_CALCDLG), TRUE);
}

void CCalcDialog::OnCancel ()
{
    DestroyWindow ();
}

void CCalcDialog::PostNcDestroy ()
{
    delete this;
}

BOOL CCalcDialog::PreTranslateMessage (MSG* pMsg)
{
    if (m_hAccel != NULL)
        if (::TranslateAccelerator (m_hWnd, m_hAccel, pMsg))
            return TRUE;

    return CDialog::PreTranslateMessage (pMsg);
}

BOOL CCalcDialog::OnInitDialog ()
{
    CDialog::OnInitDialog ();

    CMenu* pMenu = GetSystemMenu (FALSE);
    pMenu->DeleteMenu (SC_SIZE, MF_BYCOMMAND);
    pMenu->DeleteMenu (SC_MAXIMIZE, MF_BYCOMMAND);
    pMenu->AppendMenu (MF_SEPARATOR);
    pMenu->AppendMenu (MF_STRING, IDM_SYSMENU_ABOUT,
        "&About DlgCalc...");

    CStatic* pRect = (CStatic*) GetDlgItem (IDC_DISPLAYRECT);
    pRect->GetWindowRect (&m_rect);
    pRect->DestroyWindow ();
    ScreenToClient (&m_rect);
```

(continued)

DlgCalc.cpp *continued*

```
    TEXTMETRIC tm;
    CClientDC dc (this);
    dc.GetTextMetrics (&tm);
    m_cxChar = tm.tmAveCharWidth;
    m_cyChar = tm.tmHeight - tm.tmDescent;

    DisplayXRegister ();
    return TRUE;
}

void CCalcDialog::OnSysCommand (UINT nID, LPARAM lParam)
{
    if ((nID & 0xFFF0) == IDM_SYSMENU_ABOUT) {
        CAboutDialog dlg (this);
        dlg.DoModal ();
        return;
    }
    CDialog::OnSysCommand (nID, lParam);
}

void CCalcDialog::OnPaint ()
{
    CPaintDC dc (this);
    dc.DrawEdge (m_rect, EDGE_SUNKEN, BF_RECT);
    UpdateDisplay (m_strDisplay);
}

BOOL CCalcDialog::OnCommand (WPARAM wParam, LPARAM lParam)
{
    int nID = (int) LOWORD (wParam);

    if (m_bErrorFlag && (nID != IDC_CLX)) {
        ::MessageBeep (MB_ICONASTERISK);
        return TRUE;
    }

    if (m_bFixPending &&
        ((nID < IDC_0) || (nID > IDC_9)) &&
        (nID != IDC_CLX)) {
        ::MessageBeep (MB_ICONASTERISK);
        return TRUE;
    }
    return CDialog::OnCommand (wParam, lParam);
}
```

```
void CCalcDialog::OnDigit (UINT nID)
{
    char cDigit = (char) nID;

    if (m_bFixPending) {
        m_strFormat.SetAt (3, cDigit - IDC_0 + 0x30);
        DisplayXRegister ();
        m_bFixPending = FALSE;
        m_bStackLiftEnabled = TRUE;
        m_bNewX = TRUE;
        return;
    }

    if (m_bNewX) {
        m_bNewX = FALSE;
        if (m_bStackLiftEnabled) {
            m_bStackLiftEnabled = FALSE;
            LiftStack ();
        }
        m_bDecimalInString = FALSE;
        m_strDisplay.Empty ();
    }

    int nLength = m_strDisplay.GetLength ();
    if ((nLength == MAXCHARS) ||
        ((nLength == (MAXCHARS - 10)) && !m_bDecimalInString))
        ::MessageBeep (MB_ICONASTERISK);
    else {
        m_strDisplay += (cDigit - IDC_0 + 0x30);
        UpdateDisplay (m_strDisplay);
        m_dbStack[0] = strtod (m_strDisplay.GetBuffer (0), NULL);
    }
}

void CCalcDialog::OnAdd ()
{
    m_dbStack[0] += m_dbStack[1];
    DisplayXRegister ();
    DropStack ();
    m_bStackLiftEnabled = TRUE;
    m_bNewX = TRUE;
}

void CCalcDialog::OnSubtract ()
{
    m_dbStack[0] = m_dbStack[1] - m_dbStack[0];
```

(continued)

DlgCalc.cpp *continued*

```cpp
        DisplayXRegister ();
        DropStack ();
        m_bStackLiftEnabled = TRUE;
        m_bNewX = TRUE;
    }

    void CCalcDialog::OnMultiply ()
    {
        m_dbStack[0] *= m_dbStack[1];
        DisplayXRegister ();
        DropStack ();
        m_bStackLiftEnabled = TRUE;
        m_bNewX = TRUE;
    }

    void CCalcDialog::OnDivide ()
    {
        if (m_dbStack[0] == 0.0) {
            m_bErrorFlag = TRUE;
            ::MessageBeep (MB_ICONASTERISK);
            UpdateDisplay (CString ("Divide by zero error"));
        }
        else {
            m_dbStack[0] = m_dbStack[1] / m_dbStack[0];
            DisplayXRegister ();
            DropStack ();
            m_bStackLiftEnabled = TRUE;
            m_bNewX = TRUE;
        }
    }

    void CCalcDialog::OnEnter ()
    {
        LiftStack ();
        DisplayXRegister ();
        m_bStackLiftEnabled = FALSE;
        m_bNewX = TRUE;
    }

    void CCalcDialog::OnChangeSign ()
    {
        if (m_dbStack[0] != 0.0) {
            m_dbStack[0] = -m_dbStack[0];
            if (m_strDisplay[0] == '-') {
                int nLength = m_strDisplay.GetLength ();
```

```
                m_strDisplay = m_strDisplay.Right (nLength - 1);
        }
        else
            m_strDisplay = "-" + m_strDisplay;
        UpdateDisplay (m_strDisplay);
    }
}

void CCalcDialog::OnExponent ()
{
    if (((m_dbStack[1] == 0.0) && (m_dbStack[0] < 0.0)) ||
        ((m_dbStack[1] == 0.0) && (m_dbStack[0] == 0.0)) ||
        ((m_dbStack[1] < 0.0) &&
        (floor (m_dbStack[0]) != m_dbStack[0]))) {
        m_bErrorFlag = TRUE;
        ::MessageBeep (MB_ICONASTERISK);
        UpdateDisplay (CString ("Invalid operation error"));
    }
    else {
        m_dbStack[0] = pow (m_dbStack[1], m_dbStack[0]);
        DisplayXRegister ();
        DropStack ();
        m_bStackLiftEnabled = TRUE;
        m_bNewX = TRUE;
    }
}

void CCalcDialog::OnStore ()
{
    DisplayXRegister ();
    m_dbMemory = m_dbStack[0];
    m_bStackLiftEnabled = TRUE;
    m_bNewX = TRUE;
}

void CCalcDialog::OnRecall ()
{
    LiftStack ();
    m_dbStack[0] = m_dbMemory;
    DisplayXRegister ();
    m_bStackLiftEnabled = TRUE;
    m_bNewX = TRUE;
}

void CCalcDialog::OnFix ()
```

(continued)

DlgCalc.cpp *continued*

```
{
    m_bFixPending = TRUE;
}

void CCalcDialog::OnClear ()
{
    if (m_bFixPending) {
        m_bFixPending = FALSE;
        return;
    }

    m_bErrorFlag = FALSE;
    m_dbStack[0] = 0.0;
    DisplayXRegister ();
    m_bStackLiftEnabled = FALSE;
    m_bNewX = TRUE;
}

void CCalcDialog::OnDecimal ()
{
    if (m_bNewX) {
        m_bNewX = FALSE;
        if (m_bStackLiftEnabled) {
            m_bStackLiftEnabled = FALSE;
            LiftStack ();
        }
        m_bDecimalInString = FALSE;
        m_strDisplay.Empty ();
    }

    int nLength = m_strDisplay.GetLength ();
    if ((nLength == MAXCHARS) || (m_bDecimalInString))
        ::MessageBeep (MB_ICONASTERISK);
    else {
        m_bDecimalInString = TRUE;
        m_strDisplay += (char) 0x2E;
        UpdateDisplay (m_strDisplay);
        m_dbStack[0] = strtod (m_strDisplay.GetBuffer (0), NULL);
    }
}

void CCalcDialog::OnDelete ()
{
    int nLength = m_strDisplay.GetLength ();
```

```
    if (!m_bNewX && (nLength != 0)) {
        if (m_strDisplay[nLength - 1] == '.')
            m_bDecimalInString = FALSE;
        m_strDisplay = m_strDisplay.Left (nLength - 1);
        UpdateDisplay (m_strDisplay);
        m_dbStack[0] = strtod (m_strDisplay.GetBuffer (0), NULL);
    }
}

void CCalcDialog::LiftStack ()
{
    for (int i=3; i>0; i--)
        m_dbStack[i] = m_dbStack[i-1];
}

void CCalcDialog::DropStack ()
{
    for (int i=1; i<3; i++)
        m_dbStack[i] = m_dbStack[i+1];
}

void CCalcDialog::DisplayXRegister ()
{
    double dbVal = m_dbStack[0];

    if ((dbVal >= 1000000000000.0) || (dbVal <= -1000000000000.0)) {
        UpdateDisplay (CString ("Overflow error"));
        m_bErrorFlag = TRUE;
        MessageBeep (MB_ICONASTERISK);
    }
    else {
        m_strDisplay.Format (m_strFormat, dbVal);
        UpdateDisplay (m_strDisplay);
    }
}

void CCalcDialog::UpdateDisplay (CString& string)
{
    CClientDC dc (this);
    CFont* pOldFont = dc.SelectObject (GetFont ());
    CSize size = dc.GetTextExtent (string);

    CRect rect = m_rect;
    rect.InflateRect (-2, -2);
    int x = rect.right - size.cx - m_cxChar;
    int y = rect.top + ((rect.Height () - m_cyChar) / 2);
```

(continued)

DlgCalc.cpp *continued*

```
    dc.ExtTextOut (x, y, ETO_OPAQUE, rect, string, NULL);
    dc.SelectObject (pOldFont);
}


/////////////////////////////////////////////////////////////////////////
// CAboutDialog message map and member functions

BEGIN_MESSAGE_MAP (CAboutDialog, CDialog)
    ON_WM_PAINT ()
END_MESSAGE_MAP ()

BOOL CAboutDialog::OnInitDialog ()
{
    CDialog::OnInitDialog ();

    CStatic* pStatic = (CStatic*) GetDlgItem (IDC_ICONRECT);
    pStatic->GetWindowRect (&m_rect);
    pStatic->DestroyWindow ();
    ScreenToClient (&m_rect);

    return TRUE;
}

void CAboutDialog::OnPaint ()
{
    CPaintDC dc (this);
    HICON hIcon = AfxGetMainWnd ()->GetIcon (TRUE);

    if (hIcon != NULL) {
        CDC dcMem;
        dcMem.CreateCompatibleDC (&dc);

        CBitmap bitmap;
        bitmap.CreateCompatibleBitmap (&dc, 32, 32);
        CBitmap* pOldBitmap = dcMem.SelectObject (&bitmap);

        CBrush brush (::GetSysColor (COLOR_3DFACE));
        dcMem.FillRect (CRect (0, 0, 32, 32), &brush);
        dcMem.DrawIcon (0, 0, hIcon);

        dc.StretchBlt (m_rect.left, m_rect.top, m_rect.Width(),
            m_rect.Height (), &dcMem, 0, 0, 32, 32, SRCCOPY);

        dcMem.SelectObject (pOldBitmap);
    }
}
```

Figure 6-14. *The DlgCalc window.*

DlgCalc's main window is created in *CMyApp::InitInstance*, which constructs a *CCalcDialog* object, copies the object's address to *CMyApp::m_pMainWnd*, and calls *ShowWindow* and *UpdateWindow* to display the window—the same techniques used to create frame windows in conventional MFC applications:

```
m_pMainWnd = new CCalcDialog;
m_pMainWnd->ShowWindow (m_nCmdShow);
m_pMainWnd->UpdateWindow ();
```

What's different about DlgCalc is that the *CCalcDialog* class is derived from *CDialog*, not from *CFrameWnd*. *CCalcDialog*'s constructor initializes the dialog object's data members and calls *Create* to create a modeless dialog box window:

```
Create (IDD_CALCDLG);
```

This statement creates a modeless dialog box from the dialog template IDD_CALCDLG. The resulting window looks like a dialog box, and it *is* a dialog box as far as Windows is concerned. But it doubles as a main window since it has no parent and its address is tucked away in the application object's *m_pMainWnd* data member.

The bulk of the code in DlgCalc.cpp is provided to process clicks of the calculator buttons. I won't go into all the details behind the logic because understanding the logic requires some familiarity with the internal operation of an RPN calculator. Suffice it to say that DlgCalc works very much as a genuine RPN calculator does, both inside and out. To add 2 and 2, the user would enter

2 <Enter> 2 +

To multiply 3.46 by 9, add 13, divide by 10, and raise the result to a power of 2.5, the user would enter

3.46 <Enter> 9 * 13 + 10 / 2.5 <Exp>

445

The Sto key copies the number in the calculator display to memory (stores it), and Rcl recalls it. Clx clears the calculator display (the "x" in "Clx" is a reference to the calculator's X register, whose contents are always shown in the calculator display), and the ± button changes the sign of the number that's currently displayed. Fix sets the number of digits displayed to the right of the decimal point. To change from two decimal places to four, the user would click Fix and then the 4 button. The Del button deletes the rightmost character in the numeric display. For each button on the face of the calculator, there is an equivalent key on the keyboard, as shown in the table below. The P key assigned to the ± button is a crude mnemonic for "plus or minus." Most users find it slow going to click calculator buttons with the mouse, so the keyboard shortcuts are an important part of this application's user interface.

KEYBOARD EQUIVALENTS FOR DLGCALC'S CALCULATOR BUTTONS

Button(s)	*Key(s)*	*Button(s)*	*Key(s)*
±	P	0–9	0–9
Exp	E	–	–
Sto	S	+	+
Rcl	R	x	×
Enter	Enter	÷	/
Fix	F	.	.
Clx	C	Del	Del, Backspace

Adding the DlgCalc Keyboard Interface

Because it's unusual for a dialog box to implement its own keyboard interface on top of the one that Windows provides, DlgCalc's keyboard processing logic deserves a closer look. One difficulty in processing keyboard input in a dialog box is that WM-_CHAR messages are processed by *::IsDialogMessage*. You can add an *OnChar* handler to a dialog class, but it will never get called because *::IsDialogMessage* sees messages before *::TranslateMessage* does. Another problem is that once a control gets the input focus, subsequent keyboard messages go to the control instead of to the dialog window.

Some clever coding can take care of both of these problems, but DlgCalc takes a more simpleminded approach that's equally effective. Rather than process keyboard messages itself, DlgCalc lets an accelerator table do the work. Right after the dialog box is created, the *CCalcDialog* constructor loads the accelerator table with the following statement:

```
m_hAccel = ::LoadAccelerators (AfxGetInstanceHandle (),
    MAKEINTRESOURCE (IDR_CALCDLG));
```

When we used accelerators in Chapter 4, we didn't have to call *::TranslateAccelerator* because the framework made the call for us. Now, however, the onus is on us to ensure that *::TranslateAccelerator* is a part of the message retrieval and dispatch loop because *CDialog* doesn't build in calls to *::TranslateAccelerator* as *CFrameWnd* does. The following *PreTranslateMessage* override translates accelerator keys into WM_COMMAND messages by invoking *::TranslateAccelerator* before each pass through the message loop:

```
BOOL CCalcDialog::PreTranslateMessage (MSG* pMsg)
{
    if (m_hAccel != NULL)
        if (::TranslateAccelerator (m_hWnd, m_hAccel, pMsg))
            return TRUE;

    return CDialog::PreTranslateMessage (pMsg);
}
```

Since the accelerator keys are assigned the same command IDs as the calculator's push buttons, the same ON_BN_CLICKED handlers can process both button clicks *and* keypresses.

Assigning the Application Icon

When you build an application around a frame window, you can create an application icon by assigning an icon resource the ID value AFX_IDI_STD_FRAME or AFX_IDI_STD_MDIFRAME. There is no magic icon ID for an application that uses a dialog box as a main window, so unless you call the dialog's *SetIcon* function to explicitly assign it an icon, it won't have an icon. *SetIcon* is a new *CWnd* function that sends a window a WM_SETICON message. In *CCalcDialog::CCalcDialog*, the statement

```
SetIcon (myApp.LoadIcon (IDI_CALCDLG), TRUE);
```

loads the icon resource whose ID is IDI_CALCDLG and assigns it to the dialog window. Accordingly, the statement in *CAboutDialog::OnPaint* that retrieves the application icon has been changed so that it calls *GetIcon* instead of *::GetClassLong*:

```
HICON hIcon = AfxGetMainWnd ()->GetIcon (TRUE);
```

You can verify that the *OnPaint* statement works by bringing up DlgCalc's About box. An enlarged icon image will appear in the left half of the About dialog window.

Which brings up another question: how do you display the About box when the application has no menu? Click the calculator icon in DlgCalc's title bar to display the system menu and you'll find an About DlgCalc item at the bottom of the menu. (The system menu is a great place to stash menu commands in an application that has no menu of its own.) The menu item is added to the system menu by the following statements in *CCalcDialog::OnInitDialog* on the next page.

```
CMenu* pMenu = GetSystemMenu (FALSE);
    .
    .
    .
pMenu->AppendMenu (MF_SEPARATOR);
pMenu->AppendMenu (MF_STRING, IDM_SYSMENU_ABOUT,
    "&About DlgCalc...");
```

For purely esthetic reasons, *OnInitDialog* also removes the Size and Maximize items from the system menu. The calculator window can't be resized or maximized, so the Size and Maximize commands that appear in the system menu by default serve no useful purpose in this application.

Preprocessing WM_COMMAND messages

Before a WM_COMMAND message emanating from a control is routed through a class's message map, the framework calls the parent's virtual *OnCommand* function. The default implementation of *OnCommand* is the starting point for a command routing system put in place to ensure that all relevant objects associated with a running application program, including the document, view, and application objects used in document/view applications, see the message and get a crack at it. If you want it to, an application can preprocess WM_COMMAND messages by overriding *OnCommand* and providing its own private implementation. When preprocessing is complete, the application can call the base class's *OnCommand* function to pass the message on for normal processing, or it can "eat" the message by returning without calling the base class. An *OnCommand* handler that doesn't call the base class's *OnCommand* handler should return TRUE to inform Windows that message processing is complete.

DlgCalc does something else that is relatively unusual for an MFC application: it overrides *OnCommand* and filters out selected WM_COMMAND messages if either *CCalcDialog::m_bErrorFlag* or *CCalcDialog::m_bFixPending* is TRUE. *CCalcDialog::OnCommand* begins by obtaining the ID of the control that generated the message from the low word of the *wParam* value passed to it by the framework:

```
int nID = (int) LOWORD (wParam);
```

It then examines *m_bErrorFlag*, which, if TRUE, indicates that a divide-by-zero or other error has occurred and that the calculator display currently contains an error message. The user must click Clx to clear the display after an error occurs, so *OnCommand* rejects all buttons but Clx if *m_bErrorFlag* is TRUE:

```
if (m_bErrorFlag && (nID != IDC_CLX)) {
    ::MessageBeep (MB_ICONASTERISK);
    return TRUE;
}
```

Similarly, if the *m_bFixPending* flag is set indicating that the calculator is awaiting a press of a numeric key following a press of the Fix key, all buttons other than 0 through 9 and the Clx key, which cancels a pending fix operation, are rejected:

```
if (m_bFixPending &&
    ((nID < IDC_0) || (nID > IDC_9)) &&
    (nID != IDC_CLX)) {
    ::MessageBeep (MB_ICONASTERISK);
    return TRUE;
}
```

In both cases, the *::MessageBeep* API function is called to produce an audible tone signifying an invalid button press. The base class's *OnCommand* handler is called only if *m_bErrorFlag* and *m_bFixPending* are both FALSE. Putting the code that tests these flags in the *OnCommand* handler prevents the code from having to be duplicated in every ON_BN_CLICKED handler.

Another item of interest related to WM_COMMAND messages is the fact that DlgCalc processes clicks of the 0 through 9 buttons with a common handler. An ON_CONTROL_RANGE statement in the message map directs BN_CLICKED notifications from each of the ten buttons to *CCalcDialog::OnDigit*:

```
ON_CONTROL_RANGE (BN_CLICKED, IDC_0, IDC_9, OnDigit)
```

An ON_CONTROL_RANGE handler receives a UINT parameter identifying the control that sent the notification, and it returns void. In DlgCalc's case, the alternative to ON_CONTROL_RANGE would have been ten separate ON_BN_CLICKED macros and a handler that called *CWnd::GetCurrentMessage* to retrieve the control ID from the message's *wParam*. One message map entry is obviously more memory-efficient than ten, and the job of extracting control IDs from message parameters is best left to the framework when possible to ensure compatibility with future versions of Windows.

PROPERTY SHEETS

One exciting new feature of Windows 95 that programmers of every stripe will appreciate is property sheets—tabbed dialog boxes containing pages of controls the user can switch among with mouse clicks. Property sheets live in the common controls library provided with every copy of Windows 95. They're something of a chore to program in C and the SDK and the API, but they're relatively easy to implement in C++ and MFC thanks to the support provided by the framework. In fact, adding a property sheet to an MFC application isn't all that different from adding a dialog box. An MFC application that uses property sheets and runs on Windows 95 or Windows NT 3.51 or later automatically uses the operating system's native property sheet implementation. On other platforms, MFC's private implementation is used instead.

The functionality of property sheets is neatly encapsulated in a pair of MFC classes named *CPropertySheet* and *CPropertyPage*. *CPropertySheet* represents the property sheet itself and is derived from *CWnd*. *CPropertyPage* represents the property sheet's pages and is derived from *CDialog*. Both are defined in the header file Afxdlgs.h. Like dialog boxes, property sheets can be modal or modeless. *CPropertySheet::DoModal* creates a modal property sheet, and *CPropertySheet::Create* creates a modeless property sheet.

The general procedure for creating a modal property sheet using classes based on *CPropertySheet* and *CPropertyPage* goes like this:

1. For each page in the property sheet, add a dialog template to your application's .rc file defining the page's contents and characteristics. In the dialog template's STYLE statement, specify the styles WS_CHILD, WS_BORDER, WS_CAPTION, and WS_DISABLED. Use a CAPTION statement to specify the title that will appear on the tab at the top of the page. As an alternative, you may omit the CAPTION statement and specify the page title when you construct the page.

2. For each page in the property sheet, derive a dialog-like class from *CPropertyPage* with data members for the page's controls. As you normally do when you derive a dialog class, make the data members public so that they can be accessed from the outside. Write a data map (a *DoDataExchange* function) to transfer data between the member variables and the controls and optionally to validate the user's input.

3. Construct a property sheet object from *CPropertySheet* or a class derived from *CPropertySheet* and construct property sheet page objects from the *CPropertyPage* classes you derived in step 2. Use *CPropertySheet::AddPage* to add the pages to the property sheet in the order in which you want them to appear.

4. Initialize the pages' data members, and call the property sheet's *DoModal* function to display it on the screen. If the property sheet is dismissed with the OK button, *DoModal* will return IDOK. Otherwise, it will return IDCANCEL—just as a dialog box does.

To simplify property sheet creation, most MFC programmers derive their own property sheet classes from *CPropertySheet* and include data members for the property sheet pages so that the pages will be constructed automatically. Accordingly, each property sheet page class is provided with a default constructor that calls the base class constructor with the ID of the associated dialog template. The property sheet's constructor calls *AddPage* to add the property sheet pages one by one. The class declarations for a property sheet and its pages might look like this:

```
class CFirstPage : public CPropertyPage
{
public:
    // Declare CFirstPage's data members here
    CFirstPage () : CPropertyPage (IDD_FIRSTPAGE);
```

```
protected:
    virtual void DoDataExchange (CDataExchange*);
};

class CSecondPage : public CPropertyPage
{
public:
    // Declare CSecondPage's data members here
    CSecondPage () : CPropertyPage (IDD_SECONDPAGE);

protected:
    virtual void DoDataExchange (CDataExchange*);
};

class CMyPropertySheet : public CPropertySheet
{
public:
    CFirstPage m_firstPage;         // First page
    CSecondPage m_secondPage;       // Second page

    // Constructor adds the pages automatically
    CMyPropertySheet (CWnd* pParentWnd = NULL) :
        CPropertySheet (IDD_PROPERTIES, pParentWnd)
    {
        AddPage (&m_firstPage);
        AddPage (&m_secondPage);
    }
};
```

In this example, *CFirstPage* represents the first page in the property sheet and *CSecondPage* represents the second. The associated dialog resources, which are referenced in the pages' class constructors, are IDD_FIRSTPAGE and IDD_SECONDPAGE. With this infrastructure in place, a modal property sheet can be constructed and displayed with two simple statements:

```
CMyPropertySheet ps (this);
ps.DoModal ();
```

Like *CDialog::DoModal, CPropertySheet::DoModal* returns IDOK if the property sheet was dismissed with the OK button, or IDCANCEL otherwise.

The dialog templates for property sheet pages should not include OK and Cancel buttons as conventional dialog templates do because the property sheet provides these buttons on its own. A property sheet also includes an Apply button and an optional Help button. The Apply button is disabled when the property sheet first appears and is enabled when a property sheet page calls the *SetModified* function it inherits from *CPropertyPage*. *SetModified* should be called anytime the settings embodied in the property sheet are changed—for example, whenever the text of an edit control is modified or a radio button is clicked. An ON_BN_CLICKED handler in the property sheet class traps clicks of the Apply button, whose ID is IS_APPLY_NOW. The click handler should call *UpdateData* with a TRUE parameter to update the active page's member variables and apply the changes to the property sheet's parent, sending it a message or calling a public member function. Afterward, the click handler should disable the Apply button by calling *SetModified* with a FALSE parameter for each of the property sheet pages.

Note that the Apply button's ON_BN_CLICKED handler calls *UpdateData* for only the *active property sheet page*—the one that's currently displayed. That's important because property sheet pages are not physically created until they are activated by the person using the property sheet. Calling *UpdateData* for a property sheet page whose tab hasn't been clicked produces an assertion error from MFC. The framework calls *UpdateData* for the active page when the user clicks a tab to switch to another page, so when the user clicks the Apply button, the only page whose data members need to be updated is the page that's currently active. You can get a pointer to the active page with *CPropertySheet::GetActivePage*. The ON_BN_CLICKED handler for an Apply button might look like this:

```
// In the message map
ON_BN_CLICKED (ID_APPLY_NOW, OnApplyNow)

// In the class implementation
void CMyPropertySheet::OnApplyNow ()
{
    GetActivePage ()->UpdateData (TRUE);
    GetParent ()->SendMessage (WM_USER_APPLY_NOW, 0, 0);
    m_firstPage.SetModified (FALSE);
    m_secondPage.SetModified (FALSE);
}
```

Assuming that the main window knows how to handle the user-defined message WM_USER_APPLY_NOW sent by the property sheet, this handler will apply any and all changes entered into the property sheet's pages and disable the Apply button until further changes are made.

Using DDX and DDV to transfer data between controls and data members in property sheet pages and to validate data extracted from the controls is more than a matter of convenience; it allows the framework to do much of the dirty work involved in property sheet handling. The first time a property sheet page is displayed, for example, the page's *OnInitDialog* function is called. The default implementation of *OnInitDialog* calls *UpdateData* to initialize the page's controls. If the user then clicks a tab to activate another page, the current page's *OnKillActive* function is called and the framework calls *UpdateData* to retrieve and validate the controls' data. Shortly thereafter, the newly activated page receives an *OnSetActive* notification and possibly an *OnInitDialog* notification, too. If the user then goes on to click the property sheet's OK button, the current page's *OnOK* handler is called and the framework calls *UpdateData* to retrieve and validate that page's data.

The point is that a property sheet works the way it does because the framework provides default implementations of key virtual functions that govern the property sheet's behavior. You can customize a property sheet's operation by overriding the pages' *OnInitDialog, OnSetActive, OnKillActive, OnOK*, and *OnCancel* functions and performing specialized processing of your own; but if you do, be sure to call the equivalent functions in the base class so that the framework can do its part. And if you don't use DDX and DDV, you need to override *all* of these functions for every page in the property sheet to ensure that each page's data is handled properly. DDX and DDV simplify property sheet usage by letting the framework do the bulk of the work.

A final consideration to be aware of when you're coding a property sheet is that if the user enters a change you can't reverse, you should call *CPropertyPage::Cancel-ToClose* to change the property sheet's Cancel button into a Close button. This simple measure, which is part of property sheet protocol, will prevent the user from mistakenly thinking that changes made up to this point can be canceled with a button click.

The PropDemo Application

The PropDemo application, listed in Figure 6-15, is almost identical to DlgDemo4 and DlgDemo5, but it uses a property sheet instead of a dialog box to expose configuration settings to the user. The property sheet is shown in Figure 6-16 on page 465. The Background page contains radio buttons for selecting the fill type and color. The Text page contains controls for modifying the text displayed in the frame window. The property sheet is modal, so the main window can't be reactivated while the property sheet is displayed.

Resource.h

```
//**************************************************************************
//
//  Resource.h
//
//**************************************************************************

#define IDR_MAINFRAME            100

#define IDM_OPTIONS_PROPERTIES   110
#define IDM_OPTIONS_EXIT         111
#define IDM_OPTIONS_ABOUT        112
```

Figure 6-15. *The PropDemo program.* *(continued)*

Resource.h *continued*

```
#define IDD_ABOUTDLG            120
#define IDC_ICONRECT            121

#define IDD_BKGNDPAGE           130
#define IDC_SOLID               131
#define IDC_GRADIENT            132
#define IDC_RED                 133
#define IDC_GREEN               134
#define IDC_BLUE                135
#define IDC_MAGENTA             136
#define IDC_CYAN                137

#define IDD_TEXTPAGE            140
#define IDC_TEXT                141
#define IDC_HEIGHT              142
#define IDC_BOLD                143
#define IDC_ITALIC              144
```

PropDemo.rc

```
//******************************************************************
//
//  PropDemo.rc
//
//******************************************************************

#include "afxres.h"
#include "Resource.h"

AFX_IDI_STD_FRAME ICON PropDemo.ico

IDR_MAINFRAME MENU
BEGIN
    POPUP "&Options" {
        MENUITEM "&Properties...",       IDM_OPTIONS_PROPERTIES
        MENUITEM "E&xit",                IDM_OPTIONS_EXIT
        MENUITEM SEPARATOR
        MENUITEM "&About PropDemo...",   IDM_OPTIONS_ABOUT
    }
END

IDD_BKGNDPAGE DIALOG 0, 0, 132, 144
STYLE WS_CHILD | WS_CAPTION | WS_BORDER | WS_DISABLED
CAPTION "Background"
FONT 8, "MS Sans Serif"
```

```
BEGIN
    GROUPBOX        "Fill Type", -1, 12, 8, 80, 40
    AUTORADIOBUTTON "&Solid Fill", IDC_SOLID, 20, 20, 64, 10,
                    WS_TABSTOP | WS_GROUP
    AUTORADIOBUTTON "Gr&adient Fill", IDC_GRADIENT, 20, 32, 64, 10,
                    WS_TABSTOP
    GROUPBOX        "Fill Color", -1, 12, 60, 80, 76, WS_GROUP
    AUTORADIOBUTTON "&Red", IDC_RED, 20, 72, 64, 10, WS_TABSTOP | WS_GROUP
    AUTORADIOBUTTON "&Green", IDC_GREEN, 20, 84, 64, 10, WS_TABSTOP
    AUTORADIOBUTTON "&Blue", IDC_BLUE, 20, 96, 64, 10, WS_TABSTOP
    AUTORADIOBUTTON "&Magenta", IDC_MAGENTA, 20, 108, 64, 10, WS_TABSTOP
    AUTORADIOBUTTON "&Cyan", IDC_CYAN, 20, 120, 64, 10, WS_TABSTOP
END


IDD_TEXTPAGE DIALOG 0, 0, 132, 144
STYLE WS_CHILD | WS_CAPTION | WS_BORDER | WS_DISABLED
CAPTION "Text"
FONT 8, "MS Sans Serif"
BEGIN
    LTEXT           "&Text", -1, 12, 16, 20, 8
    EDITTEXT        IDC_TEXT, 36, 12, 84, 12, ES_AUTOHSCROLL | WS_GROUP
    LTEXT           "Text &Height (in points)", -1, 12, 36, 76, 8
    EDITTEXT        IDC_HEIGHT, 92, 32, 28, 12, ES_AUTOHSCROLL | WS_GROUP
    AUTOCHECKBOX    "&Bold",IDC_BOLD, 12, 56, 40, 10,
                    WS_TABSTOP | WS_GROUP
    AUTOCHECKBOX    "&Italic", IDC_ITALIC, 60, 56, 40, 10,
                    WS_TABSTOP | WS_GROUP
END


IDD_ABOUTDLG DIALOG 0, 0, 256, 98
STYLE DS_MODALFRAME | DS_CENTER | WS_POPUP | WS_VISIBLE |
    WS_CAPTION | WS_SYSMENU
CAPTION "About PropDemo"
FONT 8, "MS Sans Serif"
BEGIN
    LTEXT           "", IDC_ICONRECT, 14, 12, 80, 74
    LTEXT           "Property Sheet Demo", -1, 108, 12, 136, 8
    LTEXT           "From the book", -1, 108, 32, 136, 8
    LTEXT           """Programming Windows 95 with MFC""", -1,
                    108, 42, 136, 8
    LTEXT           "Copyright © 1996 by Jeff Prosise", -1,
                    108, 52, 136, 8
    DEFPUSHBUTTON   "OK", IDOK, 108, 72, 50, 14
END
```

PropDemo.h

```
//****************************************************************************
//
//  PropDemo.h
//
//****************************************************************************

class CMyApp : public CWinApp
{
public:
    virtual BOOL InitInstance ();
};

class CBkgndPage : public CPropertyPage
{
public:
    int m_nFillType;
    int m_nFillColor;

    CBkgndPage () : CPropertyPage (IDD_BKGNDPAGE) {}

protected:
    virtual void DoDataExchange (CDataExchange*);

    afx_msg void OnChange (UINT);
    DECLARE_MESSAGE_MAP ()
};

class CTextPage : public CPropertyPage
{
public:
    CString m_text;
    int m_nHeight;
    BOOL m_bBold;
    BOOL m_bItalic;

    CTextPage () : CPropertyPage (IDD_TEXTPAGE) {}

protected:
    virtual void DoDataExchange (CDataExchange*);

    afx_msg void OnChange ();
    DECLARE_MESSAGE_MAP ()
};

class CMyPropertySheet : public CPropertySheet
{
```

```
public:
    CBkgndPage m_bkgndPage;
    CTextPage m_textPage;

    CMyPropertySheet (CWnd* = NULL);

protected:
    afx_msg void OnApplyNow ();
    DECLARE_MESSAGE_MAP ()
};

class CMainWindow : public CFrameWnd
{
private:
    int m_nFillType;
    int m_nFillColor;
    CString m_text;
    int m_nHeight;
    BOOL m_bBold;
    BOOL m_bItalic;

    void DoSolidFill (CDC*, CRect*);
    void DoGradientFill (CDC*, CRect*);
    void DoDrawText (CDC*, CRect*);

public:
    CMainWindow ();
    void ApplyNow (CMyPropertySheet*);

protected:
    afx_msg BOOL OnEraseBkgnd (CDC*);
    afx_msg void OnPaint ();
    afx_msg void OnOptionsProperties ();
    afx_msg void OnOptionsExit ();
    afx_msg void OnOptionsAbout ();

    DECLARE_MESSAGE_MAP ()
};

class CAboutDialog : public CDialog
{
private:
    CRect m_rect;

public:
    CAboutDialog (CWnd* pParentWnd = NULL) :
```

(continued)

```
        CDialog (IDD_ABOUTDLG, pParentWnd) {}

    virtual BOOL OnInitDialog ();

protected:
    afx_msg void OnPaint ();
    DECLARE_MESSAGE_MAP ()
};
```

PropDemo.cpp

```
//*********************************************************************
//
//  PropDemo.cpp
//
//*********************************************************************

#include <afxwin.h>
#include <afxdlgs.h>
#include "Resource.h"
#include "PropDemo.h"

CMyApp myApp;

///////////////////////////////////////////////////////////////////
// CMyApp member functions

BOOL CMyApp::InitInstance ()
{
    m_pMainWnd = new CMainWindow;
    m_pMainWnd->ShowWindow (m_nCmdShow);
    m_pMainWnd->UpdateWindow ();
    return TRUE;
}

///////////////////////////////////////////////////////////////////
// CMainWindow message map and member functions

BEGIN_MESSAGE_MAP (CMainWindow, CFrameWnd)
    ON_WM_ERASEBKGND ()
    ON_WM_PAINT ()
    ON_COMMAND (IDM_OPTIONS_PROPERTIES, OnOptionsProperties)
    ON_COMMAND (IDM_OPTIONS_EXIT, OnOptionsExit)
    ON_COMMAND (IDM_OPTIONS_ABOUT, OnOptionsAbout)
END_MESSAGE_MAP ()
```

```
CMainWindow::CMainWindow ()
{
    m_nFillType = 1;
    m_nFillColor = 2;
    m_text = "Hello, MFC";
    m_nHeight = 72;
    m_bBold = TRUE;
    m_bItalic = TRUE;

    Create (NULL, "PropDemo", WS_OVERLAPPEDWINDOW, rectDefault, NULL,
        MAKEINTRESOURCE (IDR_MAINFRAME));
}

BOOL CMainWindow::OnEraseBkgnd (CDC* pDC)
{
    CRect rect;
    GetClientRect (&rect);

    m_nFillType == 1 ? DoGradientFill (pDC, &rect) :
        DoSolidFill (pDC, &rect);
    return TRUE;
}

void CMainWindow::OnPaint ()
{
    CRect rect;
    GetClientRect (&rect);

    CPaintDC dc (this);
    DoDrawText (&dc, &rect);
}

void CMainWindow::OnOptionsProperties ()
{
    CMyPropertySheet ps (this);

    ps.m_bkgndPage.m_nFillType = m_nFillType;
    ps.m_bkgndPage.m_nFillColor = m_nFillColor;
    ps.m_textPage.m_text = m_text;
    ps.m_textPage.m_nHeight = m_nHeight;
    ps.m_textPage.m_bBold = m_bBold;
    ps.m_textPage.m_bItalic = m_bItalic;

    if (ps.DoModal () == IDOK) {
        m_nFillType = ps.m_bkgndPage.m_nFillType;
        m_nFillColor = ps.m_bkgndPage.m_nFillColor;
```

(continued)

PropDemo.cpp *continued*

```cpp
        m_text = ps.m_textPage.m_text;
        m_nHeight = ps.m_textPage.m_nHeight;
        m_bBold = ps.m_textPage.m_bBold;
        m_bItalic = ps.m_textPage.m_bItalic;

        Invalidate ();
    }
}

void CMainWindow::OnOptionsExit ()
{
    SendMessage (WM_CLOSE, 0, 0);
}

void CMainWindow::OnOptionsAbout ()
{
    CAboutDialog dlg (this);
    dlg.DoModal ();
}

void CMainWindow::ApplyNow (CMyPropertySheet* pPs)
{
    m_nFillType = pPs->m_bkgndPage.m_nFillType;
    m_nFillColor = pPs->m_bkgndPage.m_nFillColor;
    m_text = pPs->m_textPage.m_text;
    m_nHeight = pPs->m_textPage.m_nHeight;
    m_bBold = pPs->m_textPage.m_bBold;
    m_bItalic = pPs->m_textPage.m_bItalic;

    Invalidate ();
}

void CMainWindow::DoSolidFill (CDC* pDC, CRect* pRect)
{
    static COLORREF crColor[5] = {
        RGB (255,   0,   0),
        RGB (  0, 255,   0),
        RGB (  0,   0, 255),
        RGB (255,   0, 255),
        RGB (  0, 255, 255),
    };

    CBrush brush (crColor[m_nFillColor]);
    pDC->FillRect (pRect, &brush);
}
```

```
void CMainWindow::DoGradientFill (CDC* pDC, CRect* pRect)
{
    CBrush* pBrush[64];
    for (int i=0; i<64; i++) {
        switch (m_nFillColor) {

        case 0:
            pBrush[i] = new CBrush (RGB (255 - (i * 4), 0, 0));
            break;

        case 1:
            pBrush[i] = new CBrush (RGB (0, 255 - (i * 4), 0));
            break;

        case 2:
            pBrush[i] = new CBrush (RGB (0, 0, 255 - (i * 4)));
            break;

        case 3:
            pBrush[i] = new CBrush (RGB (255 - (i * 4), 0,
                255 - (i * 4)));
            break;

        case 4:
            pBrush[i] = new CBrush (RGB (0, 255 - (i * 4),
                255 - (i * 4)));
            break;
        }
    }

    int nWidth = pRect->Width ();
    int nHeight = pRect->Height ();
    CRect rect;

    for (i=0; i<nHeight; i++) {
        rect.SetRect (0, i, nWidth, i + 1);
        pDC->FillRect (&rect, pBrush[(i * 63) / nHeight]);
    }

    for (i=0; i<64; i++)
        delete pBrush[i];
}

void CMainWindow::DoDrawText (CDC* pDC, CRect* pRect)
{
    CFont font;
    int nHeight = -((pDC->GetDeviceCaps (LOGPIXELSY) * m_nHeight) / 72);
```

(continued)

PropDemo.cpp *continued*

```
    font.CreateFont (nHeight, 0, 0, 0, m_bBold ? FW_BOLD : FW_NORMAL,
        m_bItalic, 0, 0, DEFAULT_CHARSET, OUT_CHARACTER_PRECIS,
        CLIP_CHARACTER_PRECIS, DEFAULT_QUALITY, DEFAULT_PITCH |
        FF_DONTCARE, "Times New Roman");

    pDC->SetBkMode (TRANSPARENT);
    pDC->SetTextColor (RGB (255, 255, 255));

    CFont* pOldFont = pDC->SelectObject (&font);
    pDC->DrawText (m_text, -1, pRect, DT_SINGLELINE | DT_CENTER |
        DT_VCENTER);

    pDC->SelectObject (pOldFont);
}

/////////////////////////////////////////////////////////////////////////
// CMyPropertySheet message map and member functions

BEGIN_MESSAGE_MAP (CMyPropertySheet, CPropertySheet)
    ON_BN_CLICKED (ID_APPLY_NOW, OnApplyNow)
END_MESSAGE_MAP ()

CMyPropertySheet::CMyPropertySheet (CWnd* pParentWnd) :
    CPropertySheet ("Properties", pParentWnd)
{
    AddPage (&m_bkgndPage);
    AddPage (&m_textPage);
}

void CMyPropertySheet::OnApplyNow ()
{
    GetActivePage ()->UpdateData (TRUE);
    ((CMainWindow*) AfxGetMainWnd ())->ApplyNow (this);

    m_bkgndPage.SetModified (FALSE);
    m_textPage.SetModified (FALSE);
}

/////////////////////////////////////////////////////////////////////////
// CBkgndPage message map and member functions

BEGIN_MESSAGE_MAP (CBkgndPage, CPropertyPage)
    ON_CONTROL_RANGE (BN_CLICKED, IDC_SOLID, IDC_CYAN, OnChange)
END_MESSAGE_MAP ()
```

```
void CBkgndPage::OnChange (UINT nID)
{
    SetModified (TRUE);
}

void CBkgndPage::DoDataExchange (CDataExchange* pDX)
{
    CPropertyPage::DoDataExchange (pDX);

    DDX_Radio (pDX, IDC_SOLID, m_nFillType);
    DDX_Radio (pDX, IDC_RED, m_nFillColor);
}

///////////////////////////////////////////////////////////////////////////
// CTextPage message map and member functions

BEGIN_MESSAGE_MAP (CTextPage, CPropertyPage)
    ON_EN_CHANGE (IDC_TEXT, OnChange)
    ON_EN_CHANGE (IDC_HEIGHT, OnChange)
    ON_BN_CLICKED (IDC_BOLD, OnChange)
    ON_BN_CLICKED (IDC_ITALIC, OnChange)
END_MESSAGE_MAP ()

void CTextPage::OnChange ()
{
    SetModified (TRUE);
}

void CTextPage::DoDataExchange (CDataExchange* pDX)
{
    CPropertyPage::DoDataExchange (pDX);

    DDX_Text (pDX, IDC_TEXT, m_text);
    DDX_Text (pDX, IDC_HEIGHT, m_nHeight);
    DDV_MinMaxInt (pDX, m_nHeight, 8, 144);
    DDX_Check (pDX, IDC_BOLD, m_bBold);
    DDX_Check (pDX, IDC_ITALIC, m_bItalic);
}

///////////////////////////////////////////////////////////////////////////
// CAboutDialog message map and member functions

BEGIN_MESSAGE_MAP (CAboutDialog, CDialog)
    ON_WM_PAINT ()
END_MESSAGE_MAP ()
```

(continued)

PropDemo.cpp *continued*

```cpp
BOOL CAboutDialog::OnInitDialog ()
{
    CDialog::OnInitDialog ();

    CStatic* pStatic = (CStatic*) GetDlgItem (IDC_ICONRECT);
    pStatic->GetWindowRect (&m_rect);
    pStatic->DestroyWindow ();
    ScreenToClient (&m_rect);

    return TRUE;
}

void CAboutDialog::OnPaint ()
{
    CPaintDC dc (this);
    HICON hIcon = (HICON) ::GetClassLong (AfxGetMainWnd ()->m_hWnd,
        GCL_HICON);

    if (hIcon != NULL) {
        CDC dcMem;
        dcMem.CreateCompatibleDC (&dc);

        CBitmap bitmap;
        bitmap.CreateCompatibleBitmap (&dc, 32, 32);
        CBitmap* pOldBitmap = dcMem.SelectObject (&bitmap);

        CBrush brush (::GetSysColor (COLOR_3DFACE));
        dcMem.FillRect (CRect (0, 0, 32, 32), &brush);
        dcMem.DrawIcon (0, 0, hIcon);

        dc.StretchBlt (m_rect.left, m_rect.top, m_rect.Width(),
            m_rect.Height (), &dcMem, 0, 0, 32, 32, SRCCOPY);

        dcMem.SelectObject (pOldBitmap);
    }
}
```

The property sheet, which is represented by a *CMyPropertySheet* object, is created when the user selects Properties from the PropDemo Options menu. After an object of the *CMyPropertySheet* class is constructed on the stack frame but before *DoModal* is called, the *CMainWindow* member variables whose values define the current application settings are copied to the corresponding member variables of the property sheet pages so that the property sheet's controls will be initialized accordingly.

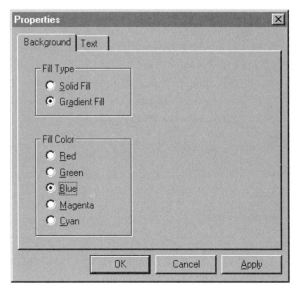

Figure 6-16. *The PropDemo property sheet.*

```
CMyPropertySheet ps (this);

ps.m_bkgndPage.m_nFillType = m_nFillType;
ps.m_bkgndPage.m_nFillColor = m_nFillColor;
ps.m_textPage.m_text = m_text;
ps.m_textPage.m_nHeight = m_nHeight;
ps.m_textPage.m_bBold = m_bBold;
ps.m_textPage.m_bItalic = m_bItalic;

if (ps.DoModal () == IDOK) {
    m_nFillType = ps.m_bkgndPage.m_nFillType;
    m_nFillColor = ps.m_bkgndPage.m_nFillColor;
    m_text = ps.m_textPage.m_text;
    m_nHeight = ps.m_textPage.m_nHeight;
    m_bBold = ps.m_textPage.m_bBold;
    m_bItalic = ps.m_textPage.m_bItalic;

    Invalidate ();
}
```

If the property sheet is dismissed with the OK button, the settings are copied back from the property sheet pages and *Invalidate* is called to repaint the window and apply the changes.

PropDemo's property sheet pages are represented by the classes *CBkgndPage* and *CTextPage*. Instances of both classes are declared in *CMyPropertySheet* so that the pages will be constructed automatically when the property sheet is constructed. The *CBgndPage* and *CTextPage* classes map ON_BN_CLICKED notifications (*CText-Page* also maps ON_EN_CHANGE notifications) from their controls to member functions named *OnChange*. *OnChange* contains but one statement: a call to *SetModified* to enable the property sheet's Apply button. *CBkgndPage*'s *OnChange* handler and message map looks like this:

```
BEGIN_MESSAGE_MAP (CBkgndPage, CPropertyPage)
    ON_CONTROL_RANGE (BN_CLICKED, IDC_SOLID, IDC_CYAN, OnChange)
END_MESSAGE_MAP ()

void CBkgndPage::OnChange (UINT nID)
{
    SetModified (TRUE);
}
```

And *CTextPage*'s *OnChange* handler and message map look like this:

```
BEGIN_MESSAGE_MAP (CTextPage, CPropertyPage)
    ON_EN_CHANGE (IDC_TEXT, OnChange)
    ON_EN_CHANGE (IDC_HEIGHT, OnChange)
    ON_BN_CLICKED (IDC_BOLD, OnChange)
    ON_BN_CLICKED (IDC_ITALIC, OnChange)
END_MESSAGE_MAP ()

void CTextPage::OnChange ()
{
    SetModified (TRUE);
}
```

Now any button click in a property sheet page, or any change to the text of an edit control, will automatically enable the Apply button if it isn't already enabled.

When the Apply button is clicked, *CMyPropertySheet*'s *OnApplyNow* function takes over and executes the following routine to update the data members associated with the active property sheet page, apply the changes to the main window, and disable the Apply button:

```
GetActivePage ()->UpdateData (TRUE);
((CMainWindow*) AfxGetMainWnd ())->ApplyNow (this);

m_bkgndPage.SetModified (FALSE);
m_textPage.SetModified (FALSE);
```

Unlike DlgDemo5, which used *SendMessage* to communicate the new settings to the main window, PropDemo casts the pointer returned by *AfxGetMainWnd* to a *CMain-Window* pointer and calls a public *CMainWindow* member function named *ApplyNow*.

The single parameter supplied to *ApplyNow* is a pointer to the property sheet object, which is used to access the property sheet's pages and through them the pages' data members.

```
void CMainWindow::ApplyNow (CMyPropertySheet* pPs)
{
    m_nFillType = pPs->m_bkgndPage.m_nFillType;
    m_nFillColor = pPs->m_bkgndPage.m_nFillColor;
    m_text = pPs->m_textPage.m_text;
    m_nHeight = pPs->m_textPage.m_nHeight;
    m_bBold = pPs->m_textPage.m_bBold;
    m_bItalic = pPs->m_textPage.m_bItalic;

    Invalidate ();
}
```

The call to *Invalidate* after the variable values are transferred from the property sheet to the main window forces a repaint using the new settings.

THE COMMON DIALOGS

Some dialog boxes appear so frequently in application programs that they have rightfully taken their places as components of the operating system. Before Windows 3.1, programmers had to write their own Open and Save As dialog boxes to get a file name from the user before opening or saving a file. Because both the design and the implementation of these dialog boxes were left up to the programmer, every Open and Save As dialog was different and some were far inferior to others. Windows 3.1 fixed this long-standing problem by providing standard implementations of commonly used dialog boxes in a DLL known as the *common dialog library*. Windows 95 enhances the library with improved versions of the Windows 3.1 common dialogs and a new Page Setup dialog for entering page layouts.

MFC provides C++ interfaces to the common dialogs with the classes shown in the table below.

THE COMMON DIALOG CLASSES

Class	Dialog Type(s)
CFileDialog	Open and Save As dialog boxes
CPrintDialog	Print and Print Setup dialog boxes
CPageSetupDialog	Page Setup dialog boxes
CFindReplaceDialog	Find and Replace dialog boxes
CColorDialog	Color dialog boxes
CFontDialog	Font dialog boxes

In C, a common dialog is invoked by filling in the fields of a data structure and calling an API function such as *::GetOpenFileName*. When the function returns, certain fields of the data structure contain values input by the user. MFC simplifies the interface by providing default input values for most fields and member functions for retrieving dialog box data. In an MFC application, getting a file name from the user before opening a file is normally no more complicated than this:

```
char szFilters[] =
    "Text files (*.txt)¦*.txt¦All files (*.*)¦*.*¦¦";

CFileDialog dlg (TRUE, "txt", "*.txt",
    OFN_FILEMUSTEXIST ¦ OFN_HIDEREADONLY, szFilters, this);

if (dlg.DoModal () == IDOK) {
    filename = dlg.GetPathName ();
    // Open the file and read it
}
```

The TRUE parameter passed to *CFileDialog*'s constructor tells MFC that we want an Open dialog rather than a Save As dialog. The "txt" and "*.txt" parameters specify the default file name extension that is appended to the file name if the user doesn't enter an extension and the text that initially appears in the file name box. The OFN values are bit flags that specify the dialog's properties: OFN_FILEMUSTEXIST tells the dialog to test the file name the user enters and reject it if the file doesn't exist, and OFN_HIDEREADONLY hides the read-only check box that appears in the dialog box by default. *szFilters* points to a string specifying the file types the user can select from. *this* identifies the dialog box's parent. When *DoModal* returns, the file name that the user entered, complete with path name, can be retrieved with *CFileDialog::GetPath-Name*. Other useful *CFileDialog* functions include *GetFileName*, which retrieves a file name without the path, and *GetFileTitle*, which retrieves a file name with neither path nor extension.

Generally, you'll find that MFC's common dialog classes are exceptionally easy to use, in part because you can often instantiate a common dialog class directly and avoid deriving classes of your own. Let's resurrect the Paint2 application we developed in Chapter 4 and modify it so that the user can save drawings to disk and read them back again. We'll need an Open dialog box so that the user can enter a file name before a file is loaded, and we'll need a Save As dialog so that the user can enter a file name before saving a file. Of course, we'll use *CFileDialog* for both dialogs.

But first we need to consider file input and output. MFC encapsulates traditional file I/O methods in the handy *CFile* class, but it also supports a more powerful (and object-based) method of file I/O known as *serialization*. Now's as good a time as any to start learning about serialization and what it means to serialize a document to or from disk—something you'll become intimately familiar with when we shift gears in Chapter 8 and begin using MFC's document/view architecture. Serialization is so powerful that many MFC applications use it for all of their file I/O and never read or write disk data directly. Because a drawing in Paint3 is nothing more than an array of *CLine* objects and because *CLine* inherits serialization support from *CObject*, a Paint3 drawing is a perfect candidate for serialization. Serialization starts with a *CFile* object, so we'll begin with a brief tour through MFC's *CFile* class. After that, we'll examine the steps required to create a serializable class. Then we'll finish up by applying what we've learned to a real application program.

File Input and Output and the *CFile* Class

File I/O services are a staple of any operating system. The Win32 API provides a number of functions for opening and closing files, reading and writing file data, seeking to a specified location in a file, and performing other file-oriented disk operations. MFC casts these functions in an object-oriented mold with its *CFile* class, which allows disk files to be treated as abstract objects that are operated upon with member functions such as *CFile::Read* and *CFile::Write*. In addition, *CFile* derivatives such as *CMemFile* provide file-like access to alternative storage mediums such as clipboard memory.

The following code fragment demonstrates how a *CFile* object might be used to read part of a file into memory. The statements open a disk file named MyFile.doc and read as much as 32K of the file into the buffer pointed to by *pBuffer*:

```
CFile file ("MyFile.doc", CFile::modeRead);
UINT nBytesRead = file.Read (pBuffer, 0x8000);
```

A *CFile* object constructed this way automatically opens MyFile.doc using the file-open flags specified in the second parameter. *CFile::modeRead* is an enumerated constant defined in Afx.h that translates into a GENERIC_READ access specifier when MFC calls the Win32 *::CreateFile* function to open the file. Other commonly used flags include *modeWrite* for write access, *modeReadWrite* for read/write access, and *modeCreate* for creating a new file even if a file with the same name already exists. Constants for specifying the sharing mode are also provided. *CFile::shareExclusive*, for example, claims exclusive access to a file. The *CFile::Read* function reads the specified number of bytes from the file. The return value is the number of bytes actually read, which may be less than the number requested if the end of the file is encountered. Since the *file* object in this example is constructed on the stack frame, MyFile.doc is closed automatically when *file* goes out of scope and its destructor is called. Alternatively, you can close a file before the associated file object is destroyed by calling *CFile::Close*.

The following routine uses a wider range of *CFile* functions to convert all of the uppercase characters in a file to lowercase:

```
char* pBuffer = new char[0x1000];
CFile file (szFileName, CFile::modeReadWrite);
DWORD dwBytesRemaining = file.GetLength ();
```

(continued)

```
UINT nBytesRead;
DWORD dwPosition;

while (dwBytesRemaining) {
    dwPosition = file.GetPosition ();
    nBytesRead = file.Read (pBuffer, 0x1000);
    ::CharLowerBuff (pBuffer, nBytesRead);
    file.Seek ((LONG) dwPosition, CFile::begin);
    file.Write (pBuffer, nBytesRead);
    dwBytesRemaining -= nBytesRead;
}
delete[] pBuffer;
```

After a file I/O buffer is allocated with *new*, the file is opened for reading and writing and *dwBytesRemaining* is initialized to equal the file's length, in bytes. Data is then read from the file in 4K blocks, converted to lowercase by means of *::CharLower-Buff*, and written back out by means of *CFile::Write*. Before each read, the current offset from the beginning of the file is retrieved with *CFile::GetPosition* and saved in *dwPosition*. So that the new data will overwrite the old, the file pointer is moved to the offset stored in *dwPosition* before each write. The *while* loop that does the reading and writing ends when *dwBytesRemaining* reaches 0, and the buffer is deallocated to free the memory allocated for it earlier.

File Exceptions and the *CFileException* Class

On the surface, the use of *CFile* and its member functions seems to be pretty straightforward. If you've written file I/O code for any operating system before, the basics of using *CFile* will come to you pretty quickly because each operation *CFile* supports through its member functions has an analogue in traditional file I/O systems. *CFile* makes things a little easier by opening and closing files automatically, but there's something else about *CFile* you should be aware of before you structure your application's file handling code around it.

Traditional file I/O functions indicate success or failure by returning special codes that reveal the outcome of the operation. *CFile* functions, on the other hand, respond to error conditions by throwing exceptions with pointers to *CFileException* objects. That's good in the sense that it saves you from having to test every return value from every file I/O function and include redundant error handling code, but any C++ programmer who has dealt with exception handlers knows the mishaps that await the unsuspecting programmer when unanticipated exceptions are thrown. It's easy, for example, to get memory leaks from objects that were allocated on the heap with *new* when an exception occurs and calls to *delete* are bypassed as the call tree is "unwound." When you use *CFile* objects, remember that just about any function you call can generate an exception. For example, *CFile::Read* throws an exception if an error occurs during a read. *CFile::Write* throws an exception if the disk fills up. Even *CFile's* constructor throws an exception if it's passed a file name and the file doesn't exist or can't be opened for some reason.

You can avoid generating exceptions when opening files by using the default *CFile* constructor to create an empty *CFile* object and calling *CFile::Open* to open the file. *Open* returns a nonzero value if the file was successfully opened (or 0 if it wasn't) and optionally initializes an existing *CFileException* object with information detailing the results of the operation, but it never throws an exception. Here's how MyFile.doc could be opened for reading without risk of a file exception:

```
CFile file;
if (file.Open ("MyFile.doc", CFile::modeRead)) {
    // Read the file
}
else // Open failed
    MessageBox ("Unable to open MyFile.doc");
```

If you'd like to know more about why the operation failed in the event that a failure does occur, you can construct a *CFileException* object and pass its address to *CFile::Open*. If *CFile::Open* returns 0, the *CFileException* object's *m_cause* data member (which is public) will contain an error code such as *CFileException::fileNotFound* indicating that the file could not be found or *CFileException::tooManyOpenFiles* indicating that no more file handles are available. The following code tries to open MyFile.doc and reports any such failures:

```
CFile file;
CFileException e;

if (file.Open ("MyFile.doc", CFile::modeRead, &e)) {
    // Read the file
}
else { // Open failed
    if (e.m_cause == CFileException::fileNotFound)
        MessageBox ("File not found");
    else if (e.m_cause == CFileException::tooManyOpenFiles)
        MessageBox ("No more file handles available");
    else // Open failed for some other reason.
        MessageBox ("Open failed");
}
```

The final *else* statement is a catchall that reports errors for which specific tests aren't provided.

You can avoid exceptions when opening files, but you can't avoid them when performing reads, writes, and other file operations. Unhandled exceptions aren't necessarily bad because MFC provides a default exception handler that reports errors in a message box. But they are bad if they result in memory leaks or cause normally recoverable errors to be fatal. Unfortunately, by the time an unhandled exception finds its way up the ladder to MFC's default handler, a lot of code has probably been bypassed. You'll often find when you're dealing with *CFile* objects that it's better to write an exception handler to assure proper cleanup when exceptions occur and provide descriptive error messages identifying the exact nature of the error. Let's take the file conversion routine presented in the previous section as an example. If a file exception is thrown by one of the *CFile* functions called by the routine, the statement

```
delete[] pBuffer;
```

will be skipped and the 4K buffer will be orphaned. It's simple enough to fix this problem by providing an exception handler to process file exceptions locally:

```
char* pBuffer = new char[0x1000];
try {
    CFile file (szFileName, CFile::modeReadWrite);
    DWORD dwBytesRemaining = file.GetLength ();

    UINT nBytesRead;
    DWORD dwPosition;

    while (dwBytesRemaining) {
        dwPosition = file.GetPosition ();
        nBytesRead = file.Read (pBuffer, 0x1000);
        ::CharLowerBuff (pBuffer, nBytesRead);
        file.Seek ((LONG) dwPosition, CFile::begin);
        file.Write (pBuffer, nBytesRead);
        dwBytesRemaining -= nBytesRead;
    }
}
catch (CFileException* e) {
    if (e->m_cause == CFileException::fileNotFound)
        MessageBox ("File not found");
    else if (e->m_cause == CFileException::tooManyOpenFiles)
        MessageBox ("No more file handles available");
    else if (e->m_cause == CFileException::hardIO)
        MessageBox ("Hardware error");
    else
        MessageBox ("Unknown file error");
    e->Delete ();
}
delete[] pBuffer;
```

Of course, you could flesh out the *catch* handler by adding more *if* clauses corresponding to other types of file exceptions. The more thorough you are in anticipating errors and reporting them, the better. Don't forget that when you use the C++ exception handling keywords rather than the equivalent MFC macros (TRY, CATCH, and so on), it's your responsibility to delete the exception objects MFC throws to you by calling the objects' *Delete* functions.

CFileException is just one of several exception classes MFC provides. Others include *CMemoryException* for out-of-memory exceptions, *CResourceException* for resource exceptions (*CPen*'s inability to create a GDI pen because of resource constraints, for example), and *CArchiveException* for errors that occur during serialization, to name but a few. MFC also provides an assortment of *AfxThrow* functions you can use to throw exceptions from your own code. The statement

```
AfxThrowFileException (cause);
```

throws a file exception with *CFileException::m_cause* equal to *cause*. One use for this function is to transfer control to an exception handler if you call a Win32 file I/O function from your code and the requested operation fails.

Serialization and the *CArchive* Class

You can largely avoid direct use of *CFile* functions but still endow an application with open and save capabilities by building the application's data from objects that serialize themselves to and from disk. *Serialization* is a process by which an object writes a record of itself to a persistent storage medium such as a disk file and reloads itself by reading the record back. Serialization is an important concept in MFC programming because it is the basis for the framework's ability to open and save documents in document/view applications.

Writing a Serializable Class

For an object to support serialization, it must be created from a serializable class. You can make a class serializable by following these five steps:

1. Derive the class from *CObject* (or from a *CObject*-derived class) so that it will inherit *CObject*'s support for serialization, dynamic creation, and runtime type identification.

2. In the class declaration, call MFC's DECLARE_SERIAL macro. DECLARE_SERIAL accepts just one parameter: the name of the class for which it is being called.

3. Override the base class's *Serialize* function with one that serializes the derived class's data members.

4. If the derived class doesn't have a default constructor (one that takes no arguments), add one. This step is necessary because as an object is serialized from disk, MFC creates it on the fly using the default class constructor and initializes the object's data members with values retrieved from storage.

5. In the class implementation, call MFC's IMPLEMENT_SERIAL macro. The IMPLEMENT_SERIAL macro takes three parameters: the class name, the name of the base class, and a schema number. The *schema number* is an integer value that tags a serializable class with a version number. When it reads an object into memory, MFC throws a *CArchiveException* exception if the schema number of the object on the disk doesn't match the schema number of the object in memory. You should increment the schema number any time you modify the class's storage format. We'll look at serialization routines that support multiple schemas in Chapter 11.

Suppose you've written a simple date class named *CDate* that has data members for the month, day, and year as well as member functions for accessing those values and you'd like to add serialization support. Originally, the class declaration looks like this:

```
class CDate
{
private:
    int m_month, m_day, m_year;

public:
    CDate (int month, int day, int year);
    int GetMonth ();
    int GetDay ();
    int GetYear ();
    void SetMonth (int);
    void SetDay (int);
    void SetYear (int);
};
```

It's easy to make this class serializable. Here's how it looks after you've added serialization support:

```
class CDate : public CObject
{
    DECLARE_SERIAL (CDate)

private:
    int m_month, m_day, m_year;

public:
    CDate () {}
    CDate (int month, int day, int year);
    void Serialize (CArchive&);
    int GetMonth ();
    int GetDay ();
    int GetYear ();
```

```
        void SetMonth (int);
        void SetDay (int);
        void SetYear (int);
};
```

The class's *Serialize* function would be written like this:

```
void CDate::Serialize (CArchive& ar)
{
    CObject::Serialize (ar);
    if (ar.IsStoring ())
        ar << m_month << m_day << m_year;
    else // Loading, not storing
        ar >> m_month >> m_day >> m_year;
}
```

And somewhere in the class's implementation file you would add the statement

```
IMPLEMENT_SERIAL (CDate, CObject, 1)
```

Once you've made these modifications, the class is fully serializable. The schema number is 1, so if you later add a fourth data member to *CDate* specifying whether the year is A.D. or B.C., you should bump the schema number up to 2 so that the framework can distinguish between *CDate* objects serialized to disk by different versions of your program.

Let's pause for a moment to examine *CDate::Serialize* more closely. The *CDate* class has three private data members that are written to or read from disk when a *CDate* object is serialized. Before the class archives its own data members, it calls *CObject::Serialize* to serialize the data members belonging to the base class. *CObject::Serialize* doesn't actually do anything, but had *CDate* been derived from a *CObject*-derivative, it's entirely possible that the base class would have contained data members that also needed to be serialized. Therefore, you should make it a practice to call the base class version of *Serialize* to ensure that all of an object's components are archived.

After *CObject::Serialize* returns, *CDate::Serialize* determines the direction of the data flow by calling *CArchive::IsStoring*. *IsStoring* returns a nonzero value if objects are being written to disk and 0 if they are being read into memory. MFC's *CArchive* class abstracts the interface to a *CFile* object and buffers data going in and out to increase performance. If *IsStoring* indicates that objects are being written to disk, *CDate* writes *m_month*, *m_day*, and *m_year* to disk using the << operator. If *IsStoring* returns FALSE, the data members are read back into memory by means of the >> operator. *CArchive* overloads the << and >> operators to work with *CObject* pointers and primitive data types such as int, BYTE, WORD, and DWORD. The << and >> operators also work with *CPoint*, *CRect*, and other classes for which MFC provides overloaded insertion and extraction operators.

Serializing an Object

Now that the *CDate* class is serializable, how do you go about serializing a *CDate* object? Serializing an object outside the document/view architecture is a three-step process:

1. Construct a *CFile* object, and open the file the serializable object will be read from or written to. If the object is being read from the archive, open the file with the flag *CFile::modeRead*. If the object is being written to the archive, use *CFile::modeCreate* and *CFile::modeWrite*.

2. Create a *CArchive* object, passing its constructor a pointer to the *CFile* object initialized in step 1 and a *CArchive::load* parameter if data is being read or a *CArchive::store* if data is being written.

3. Call the object's *Serialize* function, and pass it a reference to the *CArchive* object.

It's as simple as it sounds—maybe simpler. The following program statements open MyFile.doc for reading and serialize a *CDate* object named *date* from the file:

```
CFile file;
if (file.Open ("MyFile.doc", CFile::modeRead)) {
    CArchive ar (&file, CArchive::load);
    date.Serialize (ar);
}
```

Serializing the object to disk is equally simple:

```
CFile file;
if (file.Open ("MyFile.doc", CFile::modeCreate | CFile::modeWrite)) {
    CArchive ar (&file, CArchive::store);
    date.Serialize (ar);
}
```

Once serialization is complete, you can close the archive and the file by calling *CArchive::Close* and *CFile::Close*. Or you can allow the *CArchive* and *CFile* destructors to close the archive and the file for you when the objects go out of scope.

Despite its outward simplicity, serialization is a complex process involving equally complex issues. The *CDate* object in the previous paragraph was serialized by a direct call to its *Serialize* function because *CArchive* overloads the << and >> operators for *CObject* pointers but it doesn't overload << and >> for *CObject*s. In other words, the following statement won't work:

```
ar << date;
```

You could work around this by rewriting the statement to read

```
ar << &date;
```

but then you'd end up doing some really messy stuff to deserialize the object back out of the archive. There's nothing wrong with calling an object's *Serialize* function directly, but because *Serialize* reads and writes raw data, the version checking involving schema numbers is bypassed when the object is deserialized. For reasons I'll explain in Chapter 11, version checking is performed only when the << and >> operators are used.

Serialization really comes in handy when you write document/view applications because the framework does much of the work for you when it comes to serializing documents to and from disk. You supply the document's *Serialize* function, and the framework supplies the *CFile* and *CArchive* objects. The framework even displays the Open or Save As dialog to solicit a file name from the user. We'll have to handle these details ourselves for the moment, but it won't be long before we start writing document/view applications that tap into the full power of the framework.

The Paint3 Application

Paint3 is an improved version of Chapter 4's Paint2 application that you can use to create and store simple line drawings. Line colors and widths can be chosen from the overhead menu or from the context menu displayed when the right mouse button is clicked in the window's client area. Unlike Paint2, Paint3 includes Open, Save, and Save As items in its File menu for saving and restoring drawings. Paint3's source code, which is listed in Figure 6-17, provides a working example of how a program's data, which in this case is an array of *CLine* objects representing lines drawn on the screen, is serialized to and from disk. Paint3's code also shows firsthand how MFC's *CFileDialog* class is used to present Open and Save As dialog boxes to the user.

Resource.h

```
//*********************************************************************
//
//  Resource.h
//
//*********************************************************************

#define IDR_MAINFRAME          100
#define IDR_CONTEXTMENU        101

#define IDM_FILE_NEW           110
#define IDM_FILE_OPEN          111
#define IDM_FILE_SAVE          112
```

Figure 6-17. *The Paint3 program.*

(continued)

Resource.h *continued*

```
#define IDM_FILE_SAVE_AS         113
#define IDM_FILE_EXIT            114

#define IDM_WIDTH_VTHIN          120
#define IDM_WIDTH_THIN           121
#define IDM_WIDTH_MEDIUM         122
#define IDM_WIDTH_THICK          123
#define IDM_WIDTH_VTHICK         124

#define IDM_COLOR_BLACK          130
#define IDM_COLOR_BLUE           131
#define IDM_COLOR_GREEN          132
#define IDM_COLOR_CYAN           133
#define IDM_COLOR_RED            134
#define IDM_COLOR_MAGENTA        135
#define IDM_COLOR_YELLOW         136
#define IDM_COLOR_WHITE          137
```

Paint3.rc

```
//*******************************************************************
//
//  Paint3.rc
//
//*******************************************************************

#include <afxres.h>
#include "Resource.h"

IDR_MAINFRAME ICON Paint.ico

IDR_MAINFRAME MENU
BEGIN
    POPUP "&File" {
        MENUITEM "&New\tCtrl+N",          IDM_FILE_NEW
        MENUITEM "&Open...\tCtrl+O",       IDM_FILE_OPEN
        MENUITEM "&Save\tCtrl+S",          IDM_FILE_SAVE
        MENUITEM "Save &As...\tCtrl+A",    IDM_FILE_SAVE_AS
        MENUITEM SEPARATOR
        MENUITEM "E&xit",                  IDM_FILE_EXIT
    }
    POPUP "&Width" {
        MENUITEM "&Very Thin\tF5",         IDM_WIDTH_VTHIN
        MENUITEM "&Thin\tF6",              IDM_WIDTH_THIN
```

```
            MENUITEM "&Medium\tF7",           IDM_WIDTH_MEDIUM
            MENUITEM "Thi&ck\tF8",            IDM_WIDTH_THICK
            MENUITEM "Very Thic&k\tF9",       IDM_WIDTH_VTHICK
        }
        POPUP "&Color" {
            MENUITEM "",                      IDM_COLOR_BLACK
            MENUITEM "",                      IDM_COLOR_BLUE
            MENUITEM "",                      IDM_COLOR_GREEN
            MENUITEM "",                      IDM_COLOR_CYAN
            MENUITEM "",                      IDM_COLOR_RED
            MENUITEM "",                      IDM_COLOR_MAGENTA
            MENUITEM "",                      IDM_COLOR_YELLOW
            MENUITEM "",                      IDM_COLOR_WHITE
        }
END


IDR_MAINFRAME ACCELERATORS
BEGIN
    "N",      IDM_FILE_NEW,         VIRTKEY,      CONTROL
    "O",      IDM_FILE_OPEN,        VIRTKEY,      CONTROL
    "S",      IDM_FILE_SAVE,        VIRTKEY,      CONTROL
    "A",      IDM_FILE_SAVE_AS,     VIRTKEY,      CONTROL

    VK_F5,    IDM_WIDTH_VTHIN,      VIRTKEY
    VK_F6,    IDM_WIDTH_THIN,       VIRTKEY
    VK_F7,    IDM_WIDTH_MEDIUM,     VIRTKEY
    VK_F8,    IDM_WIDTH_THICK,      VIRTKEY
    VK_F9,    IDM_WIDTH_VTHICK,     VIRTKEY

    "B",      IDM_COLOR_BLACK,      VIRTKEY,      CONTROL
    "L",      IDM_COLOR_BLUE,       VIRTKEY,      CONTROL
    "G",      IDM_COLOR_GREEN,      VIRTKEY,      CONTROL
    "C",      IDM_COLOR_CYAN,       VIRTKEY,      CONTROL
    "R",      IDM_COLOR_RED,        VIRTKEY,      CONTROL
    "M",      IDM_COLOR_MAGENTA,    VIRTKEY,      CONTROL
    "Y",      IDM_COLOR_YELLOW,     VIRTKEY,      CONTROL
    "W",      IDM_COLOR_WHITE,      VIRTKEY,      CONTROL
END


IDR_CONTEXTMENU MENU
BEGIN
    POPUP "" {
        POPUP "&Width" {
            MENUITEM "&Very Thin",            IDM_WIDTH_VTHIN
            MENUITEM "&Thin",                 IDM_WIDTH_THIN
            MENUITEM "&Medium",               IDM_WIDTH_MEDIUM
```

(continued)

Paint3.rc *continued*

```
            MENUITEM "Thi&ck",             IDM_WIDTH_THICK
            MENUITEM "Very Thic&k",        IDM_WIDTH_VTHICK
        }
        POPUP "&Color" {
            MENUITEM "",                   IDM_COLOR_BLACK
            MENUITEM "",                   IDM_COLOR_BLUE
            MENUITEM "",                   IDM_COLOR_GREEN
            MENUITEM "",                   IDM_COLOR_CYAN
            MENUITEM "",                   IDM_COLOR_RED
            MENUITEM "",                   IDM_COLOR_MAGENTA
            MENUITEM "",                   IDM_COLOR_YELLOW
            MENUITEM "",                   IDM_COLOR_WHITE
        }
    }
END
```

Paint3.h

```
//****************************************************************************
//
//  Paint3.h
//
//****************************************************************************

class CLine : public CObject
{
    DECLARE_SERIAL (CLine)

private:
    CPoint m_ptFrom;
    CPoint m_ptTo;
    UINT m_nWidth;
    COLORREF m_crColor;

public:
    CLine () {}
    CLine (CPoint, CPoint, UINT, COLORREF);
    virtual void Serialize (CArchive&);
    virtual void Draw (CDC*);
};

class CMyApp : public CWinApp
{
public:
    virtual BOOL InitInstance ();
};
```

```
class CMainWindow : public CFrameWnd
{
private:
    UINT m_nColor;
    UINT m_nWidth;
    CPoint m_ptFrom;
    CPoint m_ptTo;
    CObArray m_lineArray;
    CString m_strFileName;
    CString m_strPathName;

    static const COLORREF crColors[8];
    static const char szFilters[];

    BOOL LoadFile (LPCSTR);
    BOOL SaveFile (LPCSTR);
    void UpdateWindowTitle ();
    void InvertLine (CDC*, CPoint, CPoint);
    void DeleteAllLines ();

public:
    CMainWindow ();
    ~CMainWindow ();

protected:
    afx_msg void OnPaint ();
    afx_msg void OnFileNew ();
    afx_msg void OnFileOpen ();
    afx_msg void OnFileSave ();
    afx_msg void OnFileSaveAs ();
    afx_msg void OnFileExit ();
    afx_msg void OnUpdateFileUI (CCmdUI*);
    afx_msg void OnWidth (UINT);
    afx_msg void OnUpdateWidthUI (CCmdUI*);
    afx_msg void OnColor (UINT);
    afx_msg void OnUpdateColorUI (CCmdUI*);
    afx_msg void OnLButtonDown (UINT, CPoint);
    afx_msg void OnMouseMove (UINT, CPoint);
    afx_msg void OnLButtonUp (UINT, CPoint);
    afx_msg void OnContextMenu (CWnd*, CPoint);
    afx_msg void OnMeasureItem (int, LPMEASUREITEMSTRUCT);
    afx_msg void OnDrawItem (int, LPDRAWITEMSTRUCT);

    DECLARE_MESSAGE_MAP ()
};
```

Paint3.cpp

```
//****************************************************************************
//
//  Paint3.cpp
//
//****************************************************************************

#define OEMRESOURCE

#include <afxwin.h>
#include <afxdlgs.h>
#include "Resource.h"
#include "Paint3.h"

CMyApp myApp;

///////////////////////////////////////////////////////////////////////////
// CMyApp member functions

BOOL CMyApp::InitInstance ()
{
    m_pMainWnd = new CMainWindow;
    m_pMainWnd->ShowWindow (m_nCmdShow);
    m_pMainWnd->UpdateWindow ();
    return TRUE;
}

///////////////////////////////////////////////////////////////////////////
// CMainWindow message map and member functions

BEGIN_MESSAGE_MAP (CMainWindow, CFrameWnd)
    ON_WM_PAINT ()
    ON_COMMAND (IDM_FILE_NEW, OnFileNew)
    ON_COMMAND (IDM_FILE_OPEN, OnFileOpen)
    ON_COMMAND (IDM_FILE_SAVE, OnFileSave)
    ON_COMMAND (IDM_FILE_SAVE_AS, OnFileSaveAs)
    ON_COMMAND (IDM_FILE_EXIT, OnFileExit)
    ON_COMMAND_RANGE (IDM_WIDTH_VTHIN, IDM_WIDTH_VTHICK, OnWidth)
    ON_COMMAND_RANGE (IDM_COLOR_BLACK, IDM_COLOR_WHITE, OnColor)
    ON_UPDATE_COMMAND_UI (IDM_FILE_NEW, OnUpdateFileUI)
    ON_UPDATE_COMMAND_UI (IDM_FILE_SAVE, OnUpdateFileUI)
    ON_UPDATE_COMMAND_UI (IDM_FILE_SAVE_AS, OnUpdateFileUI)
    ON_UPDATE_COMMAND_UI_RANGE (IDM_WIDTH_VTHIN, IDM_WIDTH_VTHICK,
        OnUpdateWidthUI)
    ON_UPDATE_COMMAND_UI_RANGE (IDM_COLOR_BLACK, IDM_COLOR_WHITE,
        OnUpdateColorUI)
```

```
    ON_WM_LBUTTONDOWN ()
    ON_WM_MOUSEMOVE ()
    ON_WM_LBUTTONUP ()
    ON_WM_CONTEXTMENU ()
    ON_WM_MEASUREITEM ()
    ON_WM_DRAWITEM ()
END_MESSAGE_MAP ()

const COLORREF CMainWindow::crColors[8] = {
    RGB (  0,   0,   0),    // Black
    RGB (  0,   0, 255),    // Blue
    RGB (  0, 255,   0),    // Green
    RGB (  0, 255, 255),    // Cyan
    RGB (255,   0,   0),    // Red
    RGB (255,   0, 255),    // Magenta
    RGB (255, 255,   0),    // Yellow
    RGB (255, 255, 255)     // White
};

const char CMainWindow::szFilters[] =
    "Paint Files (*.pnt)|*.pnt|All Files (*.*)|*.*||";

CMainWindow::CMainWindow ()
{
    m_nColor = IDM_COLOR_RED;
    m_nWidth = IDM_WIDTH_MEDIUM;
    m_lineArray.SetSize (0, 64);

    CString strWndClass = AfxRegisterWndClass (
        0,
        myApp.LoadStandardCursor (IDC_CROSS),
        (HBRUSH) (COLOR_WINDOW + 1),
        myApp.LoadIcon (IDR_MAINFRAME)
    );

    Create (strWndClass, "Paint3", WS_OVERLAPPEDWINDOW,
        rectDefault, NULL, MAKEINTRESOURCE (IDR_MAINFRAME));

    LoadAccelTable (MAKEINTRESOURCE (IDR_MAINFRAME));

    CMenu* pMenu = GetMenu ();
    for (int i=0; i<8; i++)
        pMenu->ModifyMenu (IDM_COLOR_BLACK + i, MF_BYCOMMAND |
            MF_OWNERDRAW, IDM_COLOR_BLACK + i);
}
```

(continued)

Paint3.cpp *continued*

```cpp
CMainWindow::~CMainWindow ()
{
    DeleteAllLines ();
}

void CMainWindow::OnPaint ()
{
    CPaintDC dc (this);
    int nCount = m_lineArray.GetSize ();

    if (nCount) {
        for (int i=0; i<nCount; i++)
            ((CLine*) m_lineArray[i])->Draw (&dc);
    }
}

void CMainWindow::OnFileNew ()
{
    m_strFileName.Empty ();
    m_strPathName.Empty ();
    UpdateWindowTitle ();

    DeleteAllLines ();
    Invalidate ();
}

void CMainWindow::OnFileOpen ()
{
    CFileDialog dlg (TRUE, "pnt", "*.pnt",
        OFN_FILEMUSTEXIST | OFN_HIDEREADONLY, szFilters, this);

    if (dlg.DoModal () == IDOK) {
        if (LoadFile (dlg.GetPathName ())) {
            m_strFileName = dlg.GetFileTitle ();
            m_strPathName = dlg.GetPathName ();
            UpdateWindowTitle ();
        }
    }
}

void CMainWindow::OnFileSave ()
{
    if (!m_strFileName.IsEmpty ())
        SaveFile (m_strPathName);
    else // Need a file name first
        OnFileSaveAs ();
}
```

```
void CMainWindow::OnFileSaveAs ()
{
    CFileDialog dlg (FALSE, "pnt", m_strPathName,
        OFN_OVERWRITEPROMPT | OFN_PATHMUSTEXIST | OFN_HIDEREADONLY,
        szFilters, this);

    if (dlg.DoModal () == IDOK) {
        if (SaveFile (dlg.GetPathName ())) {
            m_strFileName = dlg.GetFileTitle ();
            m_strPathName = dlg.GetPathName ();
            UpdateWindowTitle ();
        }
    }
}

void CMainWindow::OnUpdateFileUI (CCmdUI* pCmdUI)
{
    pCmdUI->Enable (m_lineArray.GetSize ());
}

void CMainWindow::OnFileExit ()
{
    SendMessage (WM_CLOSE, 0, 0);
}

void CMainWindow::OnWidth (UINT nID)
{
    m_nWidth = nID;
}

void CMainWindow::OnColor (UINT nID)
{
    m_nColor = nID;
}

void CMainWindow::OnUpdateWidthUI (CCmdUI* pCmdUI)
{
    pCmdUI->SetCheck (pCmdUI->m_nID == m_nWidth);
}

void CMainWindow::OnUpdateColorUI (CCmdUI* pCmdUI)
{
    pCmdUI->SetCheck (pCmdUI->m_nID == m_nColor);
}
```

(continued)

Paint3.cpp *continued*

```cpp
void CMainWindow::OnLButtonDown (UINT nFlags, CPoint point)
{
    m_ptFrom = point;
    m_ptTo = point;
    SetCapture ();
}

void CMainWindow::OnMouseMove (UINT nFlags, CPoint point)
{
    if (GetCapture () == this) {
        CClientDC dc (this);
        InvertLine (&dc, m_ptFrom, m_ptTo);
        InvertLine (&dc, m_ptFrom, point);
        m_ptTo = point;
    }
}

void CMainWindow::OnLButtonUp (UINT nFlags, CPoint point)
{
    static UINT nWidths[5] = { 1, 8, 16, 24, 32 };

    if (GetCapture () == this) {
        ReleaseCapture ();

        CClientDC dc (this);
        InvertLine (&dc, m_ptFrom, m_ptTo);
        CLine* pLine = NULL;

        try {
            pLine = new CLine (m_ptFrom, m_ptTo,
                nWidths[m_nWidth - IDM_WIDTH_VTHIN],
                crColors[m_nColor - IDM_COLOR_BLACK]);

            m_lineArray.Add (pLine);
            pLine->Draw (&dc);
        }
        catch (CMemoryException* e) {
            MessageBox ("Out of memory. You must clear the " \
                "drawing area before adding more lines.", "Error",
                MB_ICONEXCLAMATION | MB_OK);

            if (pLine != NULL)
                delete pLine;
            e->Delete ();
        }
    }
}
```

```
void CMainWindow::OnContextMenu (CWnd* pWnd, CPoint point)
{
    CRect rect;
    GetClientRect (&rect);
    ClientToScreen (&rect);

    if (rect.PtInRect (point)) {
        CMenu menu;
        menu.LoadMenu (IDR_CONTEXTMENU);
        CMenu* pContextMenu = menu.GetSubMenu (0);

        for (int i=0; i<8; i++)
            pContextMenu->ModifyMenu (IDM_COLOR_BLACK + i,
                MF_BYCOMMAND | MF_OWNERDRAW, IDM_COLOR_BLACK + i);

        pContextMenu->TrackPopupMenu (TPM_LEFTALIGN | TPM_LEFTBUTTON |
            TPM_RIGHTBUTTON, point.x, point.y, this);
        return;
    }
    CFrameWnd::OnContextMenu (pWnd, point);
}

void CMainWindow::OnMeasureItem (int nIDCtl, LPMEASUREITEMSTRUCT lpmis)
{
    lpmis->itemWidth = ::GetSystemMetrics (SM_CYMENU) * 4;
    lpmis->itemHeight = ::GetSystemMetrics (SM_CYMENU);
}

void CMainWindow::OnDrawItem (int nIDCtl, LPDRAWITEMSTRUCT lpdis)
{
    BITMAP bm;
    CBitmap bitmap;
    bitmap.LoadOEMBitmap (OBM_CHECK);
    bitmap.GetObject (sizeof (bm), &bm);

    CDC dc;
    dc.Attach (lpdis->hDC);

    CBrush* pBrush = new CBrush (::GetSysColor ((lpdis->itemState &
        ODS_SELECTED) ? COLOR_HIGHLIGHT : COLOR_MENU));
    dc.FrameRect (&(lpdis->rcItem), pBrush);
    delete pBrush;

    if (lpdis->itemState & ODS_CHECKED) {
        CDC dcMem;
        dcMem.CreateCompatibleDC (&dc);
```

(continued)

Paint3.cpp *continued*

```cpp
        CBitmap* pOldBitmap = dcMem.SelectObject (&bitmap);

        dc.BitBlt (lpdis->rcItem.left + 4, lpdis->rcItem.top +
            (((lpdis->rcItem.bottom - lpdis->rcItem.top) -
            bm.bmHeight) / 2), bm.bmWidth, bm.bmHeight, &dcMem,
            0, 0, SRCCOPY);

        dcMem.SelectObject (pOldBitmap);
    }

    pBrush = new CBrush (crColors[lpdis->itemID - IDM_COLOR_BLACK]);
    CRect rect = lpdis->rcItem;
    rect.DeflateRect (6, 4);
    rect.left += bm.bmWidth;
    dc.FillRect (rect, pBrush);
    delete pBrush;

    dc.Detach ();
}

void CMainWindow::InvertLine (CDC* pDC, CPoint ptFrom, CPoint ptTo)
{
    int nOldMode = pDC->SetROP2 (R2_NOT);

    pDC->MoveTo (ptFrom);
    pDC->LineTo (ptTo);

    pDC->SetROP2 (nOldMode);
}

void CMainWindow::DeleteAllLines ()
{
    int nCount = m_lineArray.GetSize ();

    for (int i=0; i<nCount; i++)
        delete m_lineArray[i];

    m_lineArray.RemoveAll ();
}

BOOL CMainWindow::LoadFile (LPCSTR lpszFileName)
{
    CFile file;
    BOOL bResult = TRUE;
```

```
    if (file.Open (lpszFileName, CFile::modeRead)) {
        CWaitCursor wait;
        DeleteAllLines ();
        CArchive ar (&file, CArchive::load);
        m_lineArray.Serialize (ar);
        Invalidate ();
    }
    else {
        CString string;
        string.Format ("Unable to open %s", lpszFileName);
        MessageBox (string, "Error", MB_ICONEXCLAMATION | MB_OK);
        bResult = FALSE;
    }
    return bResult;
}

BOOL CMainWindow::SaveFile (LPCSTR lpszFileName)
{
    CFile file;
    BOOL bResult = TRUE;

    if (file.Open (lpszFileName, CFile::modeCreate | CFile::modeWrite)) {
        CWaitCursor wait;
        CArchive ar (&file, CArchive::store);
        m_lineArray.Serialize (ar);
    }
    else {
        CString string;
        string.Format ("Unable to create %s", lpszFileName);
        MessageBox (string, "Error", MB_ICONEXCLAMATION | MB_OK);
        bResult = FALSE;
    }
    return bResult;
}

void CMainWindow::UpdateWindowTitle ()
{
    CString strTitle;

    if (m_strFileName.IsEmpty ())
        strTitle = "Paint3";
    else
        strTitle = m_strFileName + " - Paint3";

    SetWindowText (strTitle);
}
```

(continued)

Paint3.cpp *continued*

```
/////////////////////////////////////////////////////////////////////////
// CLine member functions

IMPLEMENT_SERIAL (CLine, CObject, 1)

CLine::CLine (CPoint ptFrom, CPoint ptTo, UINT nWidth, COLORREF crColor)
{
    m_ptFrom = ptFrom;
    m_ptTo = ptTo;
    m_nWidth = nWidth;
    m_crColor = crColor;
}

void CLine::Serialize (CArchive& ar)
{
    CObject::Serialize (ar);

    if (ar.IsStoring ())
        ar << m_ptFrom << m_ptTo << m_nWidth << (DWORD) m_crColor;
    else
        ar >> m_ptFrom >> m_ptTo >> m_nWidth >> (DWORD) m_crColor;
}

void CLine::Draw (CDC* pDC)
{
    CPen pen (PS_SOLID, m_nWidth, m_crColor);

    CPen* pOldPen = pDC->SelectObject (&pen);
    pDC->MoveTo (m_ptFrom);
    pDC->LineTo (m_ptTo);

    pDC->SelectObject (pOldPen);
}
```

CMainWindow::OnFileOpen handles the File menu's Open command. *OnFile-Open* starts out by constructing an Open dialog and displaying it with *CFileDialog-::DoModal*:

```
CFileDialog dlg (TRUE, "pnt", "*.pnt",
    OFN_FILEMUSTEXIST | OFN_HIDEREADONLY, szFilters, this);

    if (dlg.DoModal () == IDOK) {
     .
     .
    }
```

szFilters is a text string that includes two file name filters: "*.pnt" for "Paint Files" and
"*.*" for "All Files":

```
const char CMainWindow::szFilters[] =
    "Paint Files (*.pnt)|*.pnt|All Files (*.*)|*.*||";
```

If *DoModal* returns IDOK indicating that the user clicked OK, *OnFileOpen* retrieves
the file name from the dialog and passes it to *CMainWindow::LoadFile*. *LoadFile*, in
turn, opens the file, initializes a *CArchive* object, and calls *m_lineArray*'s *Serialize*
function to serialize the objects stored in the file to *m_lineArray*. *m_lineArray* is a
CObArray object that stores pointers to *CLine* objects. The file name that the user
entered in the dialog box should be valid because *CFileDialog*'s constructor was called
with the flag OFN_FILEMUSTEXIST, but just to be safe, the file is opened with *CFile-
::Open* rather than with *CFile*'s constructor:

```
CFile file;
    .
    .
    .
if (file.Open (lpszFileName, CFile::modeRead)) {
    CWaitCursor wait;
    DeleteAllLines ();
    CArchive ar (&file, CArchive::load);
    m_lineArray.Serialize (ar);
    Invalidate ();
}
```

The instantiation of *CWaitCursor* changes the cursor to an hourglass while the drawing is loaded. The cursor is automatically restored to its previous form when *wait* goes
out of scope. The call to *CMainWindow::DeleteAllLines* deletes any existing *CLine*
objects. The call to *Invalidate* after *Serialize* returns invalidates *CMainWindow*'s client area and displays the *CLine* objects read from the archive. Recall from Chapter 4
that the *CLine* class includes a virtual member function named *Draw* that draws a line
represented by a *CLine* object. *Invalidate* forces a call to *CMainWindow::OnPaint*,
which calls *CObArray::GetSize* to retrieve the number of objects in the array and iterates through the array elements calling each object's *Draw* function.

An important point that's easy to miss here is that *LoadFile* does not have to
serialize *CLine* objects individually. Because *CLine* objects are stored in an array of
type *CObArray*, and because *CObArray* is derived from *CObject* and is itself a serializable
object, one call to *m_lineArray*'s *Serialize* function loads all the *CLine* objects stored
in the archive. When *CObArray::Serialize* is called, it creates a *CLine* object for each
object recorded in the archive and calls *CLine::Serialize* to fill in the object's data
members. A *CLine* object is serialized as follows:

```
void CLine::Serialize (CArchive& ar)
{
    CObject::Serialize (ar);

    if (ar.IsStoring ())
        ar << m_ptFrom << m_ptTo << m_nWidth << (DWORD) m_crColor;
    else
        ar >> m_ptFrom >> m_ptTo >> m_nWidth >> (DWORD) m_crColor;
}
```

In Paint3, a line is characterized by four properties: the coordinates of its two end-points, its width, and its color. *CLine::Serialize* archives a *CLine* object by reading or writing the four corresponding member variables. The COLORREF value *m_crColor* is cast to a DWORD during the serialization process because the << and >> operators aren't explicitly overloaded for the COLORREF data type.

If *CFile::Open* returns 0 indicating that the file could not be opened, *LoadFile* displays a message box with the text "Unable to open *filename*." Again, this shouldn't happen because *CFileDialog* is invoked with an OFN_FILEMUSTEXIST flag, which results in an error notification from the dialog box if the user enters the name of a nonexistent file. But in a multitasking environment, you can't count on the file name's validity because there's always the chance that a background process will delete the file in the brief interval between the time the dialog box is closed and *CFile::Open* is called. Checking the value returned by *CFile::Open* ensures that an obscure error won't bring the program crashing to the ground. And opening the file manually rather than allowing *CFile*'s constructor to do the opening means that a file exception won't be thrown if the file-open operation fails.

When the user selects File-Save As, *CMainWindow::OnFileSaveAs* displays a Save As dialog and passes the file name to *CMainWindow::SaveFile*, which serializes *m_line-Array* to disk:

```
CFileDialog dlg (FALSE, "pnt", m_strpathName,
    OFN_OVERWRITEPROMPT | OFN_PATHMUSTEXIST | OFN_HIDEREADONLY,
    szFilters, this);

if (dlg.DoModal () == IDOK) {
    if (SaveFile (dlg.GetPathName ())) {
        :
        :
    }
}
```

Specifying FALSE in the first parameter to the *CFileDialog* constructor invokes a Save As dialog rather than an Open dialog, and including the OFN_OVERWRITEPROMPT flag tells *CFileDialog* to ask the user to verify his or her selection if the name of an existing file is entered. If *DoModal* returns IDOK, it's safe to assume that the file name is the one the user wants us to use even if it means that a file of the same name will be overwritten. Similarly, OFN_PATHMUSTEXIST tells the dialog box to verify that a valid path name was entered. For its part, *CMainWindow::SaveFile* archives the current drawing to disk by creating a new file with write access, creating a *CArchive::store CArchive* object to go with it, and passing the archive object to *m_lineArray*'s *Serialize* function:

```
CFile file;
   .
   .
   .
if (file.Open (lpszFileName, CFile::modeCreate | CFile::modeWrite)) {
    CWaitCursor wait;
    CArchive ar (&file, CArchive::store);
    m_lineArray.Serialize (ar);
}
```

If *CFile::Open* returns 0, an error message is displayed indicating that the file could not be created.

Paint3 does a commendable job of demonstrating how MFC's *CFileDialog* class is used and how to write a serializable class whose objects archive themselves to and from disk. What it doesn't do very well is handle errors and safeguard the user's data. If a disk full error occurs as *m_lineArray* is being archived, the framework catches the file exception and displays a helpful error message. But Paint3 does nothing to prevent memory leaks from occurring in the wake of the exception. Worse, if a drawing contains unsaved data when a new drawing is started, an existing drawing is loaded, or the application is shut down, Paint3 fails to provide the user with a chance to save the changes. Needless to say, that's not how a real application should behave. But don't worry: document handling is infinitely cleaner when performed in the context of the document/view architecture, and soon, in Chapter 8, we'll transform Paint3 into a document/view application. Then the framework will make sure that exceptions are handled cleanly and that the user gets the opportunity to save changes made to a drawing. If you've never written a document/view application before, you'll be pleasantly surprised at the level of support the framework provides.

Modifying the Common Dialogs

There are a number of ways to modify the behavior of *CFileDialog* and other common dialog classes. One method involves nothing more than changing the parameters passed to the dialog's constructor. For example, *CFileDialog::CFileDialog*'s third parameter accepts about two dozen different bit flags affecting the dialog's appearance and behavior. One use for these flags is to create an Open dialog that features a multiple-selection list box that allows the user to select several files instead of just one. Rather than construct the dialog like this,

```
CFileDialog dlg (TRUE, "pnt", "*.pnt",
    OFN_FILEMUSTEXIST | OFN_HIDEREADONLY, szFilters, this);
```

you would do it like this:

```
CFileDialog dlg (TRUE, "pnt", "*.pnt",
    OFN_FILEMUSTEXIST | OFN_HIDEREADONLY | OFN_ALLOWMULTISELECT,
    szFilters, this);
```

After *DoModal* returns, a list of file names is stored in the buffer referenced by the dialog object's *m_ofn.lpstrFile* data member. The file names are easily retrieved from the buffer with *CFileDialog*'s *GetStartPosition* and *GetNextPathName* functions.

When you construct a dialog box from *CFileDialog*, the class constructor fills in the fields of an OPENFILENAME structure with values defining the title for the dialog window, the initial directory, and other parameters. The structure's address is subsequently passed to *::GetOpenFileName* or *::GetSaveFileName*. Some of the values used to initialize the structure are taken from *CFileDialog*'s constructor parameter list, but other parameters are filled with default values appropriate for the majority of applications. Another way to customize an Open or Save As dialog is to modify the fields of the OPENFILENAME structure after constructing the dialog object but before calling *DoModal*. The OPENFILENAME structure is accessible through the public data member *m_ofn*.

Suppose you'd like to change the title of a multiple-selection file dialog to "Select File(s)" instead of "Open." In addition, you'd like the file name filter that was selected when the dialog box was closed to be selected again the next time the dialog box is displayed. Here's how you could make these changes:

```
CFileDialog dlg (TRUE, "pnt", NULL,
    OFN_FILEMUSTEXIST | OFN_ALLOWMULTISELECT,
    szFilters, this);

dlg.m_ofn.nFilterIndex = m_nFilterIndex;
static char szTitle[] = "Select File(s)";
dlg.m_ofn.lpstrTitle = szTitle;

if (dlg.DoModal == IDOK) {
    m_nFilterIndex = dlg.m_ofn.nFilterIndex;
        :
        :
}
```

When the program is started, *m_nFilterIndex* should be set to 1. The first time the dialog box is created, the first file filter will be selected by default. When the user dismisses the dialog box with the OK button, the index of the currently selected filter is copied out of the OPENFILENAME structure and saved in *m_nFilterIndex*. The next time the dialog box is invoked, the same filter will be selected automatically. In other words, the dialog box will "remember" the user's filter selection. For a more thorough encapsulation, you could make *m_nFilterIndex* a part of the dialog box rather than a member of an external class by deriving your own dialog class from *CFileDialog*, declaring *m_nFilterIndex* to be a static member variable of that class, and initializing it to 1 before constructing a *CMyFileDialog* object for the first time.

You can implement more extensive changes by deriving your own dialog class from *CFileDialog* and overriding key virtual functions. In addition to *OnOK* and *OnCancel*, the virtual functions *OnFileNameOK*, *OnLBSelChangeNotify*, and *OnShare-Violation* can be overridden to customize the way the dialog box validates file names, responds to changes in file name selections, and handles sharing violations. *OnInit-Dialog* can be overridden to perform all sorts of stunts such as increasing the size of the dialog box and adding or deleting controls. (If you override *CFileDialog::OnInit-Dialog*, be sure to call the base class version from your own implementation.) You could, for example, stretch the dialog box horizontally and create a preview area that displays a thumbnail sketch of the contents of the currently selected file. By overriding *OnLBSelChangeNotify*, you could update the preview window when the selection changes.

The ultimate in modifying *CFileDialog* comes when you replace the default dialog template in Commdlg.dll with a template of your own. You accomplish this by specifying the new template's name or resource ID in the OPENFILENAME structure's *lpTemplateName* field, copying the application's instance handle (obtainable with *AfxGetInstanceHandle* or *AfxGetResourceHandle*) to the *bInstance* field, and inserting an OFN_ENABLETEMPLATE flag into the *Flags* field. This is a complicated undertaking I won't go into here—I'll prevent an already long chapter from growing even longer—but realize that the capability is there should you need it. Among other things, you must take care to duplicate the controls and control IDs in the default dialog template, or the dialog box won't work properly. If you add controls of your own to the template, use a message map in the derived dialog class to trap corresponding event notifications.

Chapter 7

Timers and Idle Processing

Not all processing is performed in response to user input. Some processing is inherently time-based—the actions performed by an autosave routine that saves open documents at 5- or 10-minute intervals, for instance. Windows helps out by providing *timers* that can be programmed to notify an application at regular intervals. Another useful form of time-based processing is *idle processing*—work performed during "idle" periods, when there are no messages waiting to be processed. MFC provides a framework for idle-time processing by calling an application's virtual *OnIdle* function each time the "message pump" in *CWinThread* finds the message queue empty.

In the first half of this chapter, we'll look at timers, which can be programmed for intervals as low as 55 milliseconds. Here are just a few of the ways in which timers can be put to use:

■ In applications that simulate a wall clock or display the current time in a status bar. Most such applications set a timer to fire at intervals ranging from a half second to as many as 60 seconds. When a timer notification arrives, the display is updated to reflect the current time.

■ In unattended backup programs, disk defragmenters, and other applications that sit dormant until a specified time and then spring into action.

■ In resource monitors, free-memory gauges, and other applications that monitor the state of the system.

In the second half of the chapter, we'll leave timers behind and move on to idle processing. A few of the many uses for the framework's *OnIdle* mechanism include background print spooling and garbage collection. Some chores that were ideal candidates for idle processing in 16-bit Windows are better done in background threads in Windows 95, but *OnIdle* still has its uses. We'll look at one example of how idle calls can be put to work in a 32-bit application in the second of this chapter's two sample programs.

TIMERS

There are only two functions you need to know about to use timers. *CWnd::SetTimer* programs a timer to fire at specified intervals, and *CWnd::KillTimer* stops a running timer. Depending on the parameters passed to *SetTimer*, a timer notifies an application that a time interval has elapsed in one of two ways:

■   By sending a WM_TIMER message

■   By calling an application-defined callback function

The WM_TIMER method is the simpler of the two, but the callback method is sometimes preferable when multiple timers are used. Both types of timer notifications receive low priority when they are sent to an application. They're processed only when the message queue is devoid of other messages.

Timer notifications are never allowed to stack up in the message queue. If you've set a timer to fire every 100 milliseconds and a full second goes by while your application is busy processing other messages, it won't suddenly receive ten rapid-fire timer notifications when the message queue empties. Instead, it will receive just one. You don't need to worry that you'll take so much time to process a timer notification that another will arrive before you're finished with the first one and start a race condition. Still, a Windows application should never spend an excessive amount of time processing a message unless processing has been delegated to a secondary thread because responsiveness will suffer if the primary thread goes too long without checking the message queue.

Setting a Timer: Method 1

The easiest way to set a timer is to call *SetTimer* with nothing more than a timer ID and a time-out value and then map WM_TIMER messages to an *OnTimer* function in your application's window class. A timer ID is a nonzero value that identifies the timer. When *OnTimer* is activated in response to a WM_TIMER message, the timer ID is passed as an argument. If you use only one timer, the ID value probably won't interest you because all WM_TIMER messages will come from the same timer. An application that uses two or more timers can use the timer ID to determine which timer a message has come from.

The time-out value passed to *SetTimer* specifies the interval between WM_TIMER messages in thousandths of a second. Valid values range from 1 through the highest number a 32-bit integer will hold: $2^{32} - 1$ milliseconds, which equals slightly more than $49\frac{1}{2}$ days. The statement

```
SetTimer (1, 500, NULL);
```

allocates a timer, assigns it the ID 1, and programs it to send the window whose *SetTimer* function was called a WM_TIMER message every 500 milliseconds. The NULL third parameter configures the timer to send WM_TIMER messages rather than use a callback function. Although the programmed interval is 500 milliseconds, the window will actually receive a WM_TIMER message about once every 550 milliseconds because the hardware timer upon which timers are based ticks once every 54.9 milliseconds, give or take a few microseconds. In effect, Windows rounds the value you pass to *SetTimer* up to the next multiple of 55 milliseconds. Thus, the statement

```
SetTimer (1, 1, NULL);
```

programs a timer to send a WM_TIMER message roughly every 55 milliseconds, as does the statement

```
SetTimer (1, 50, NULL);
```

But change the timer interval to 60, as in

```
SetTimer (1, 60, NULL);
```

and WM_TIMER messages will arrive, on average, every 110 milliseconds.

How regular is the spacing between WM_TIMER messages once a timer is set? The following list of elapsed times between timer messages was taken from a 32-bit Windows application that programmed a timer for 500-millisecond intervals:

Notification No.	Interval	Notification No.	Interval
1	0.542 second	11	0.604 second
2	0.557 second	12	0.550 second
3	0.541 second	13	0.549 second
4	0.503 second	14	0.549 second
5	0.549 second	15	0.550 second
6	0.549 second	16	0.508 second
7	1.936 second	17	0.550 second
8	0.261 second	18	0.549 second
9	0.550 second	19	0.549 second
10	0.549 second	20	0.550 second

As you can see, the average elapsed time is very close to 550 milliseconds, and most of the individual elapsed times are very close to 550 milliseconds with a few exceptions such as 261, 503, 508, and 604 milliseconds. The only significant perturbation, the elapsed time of 1.936 seconds between the sixth and seventh WM_TIMER messages, occurred as the window was dragged across the screen. It's obvious from this list that Windows does not allow timer messages to accumulate in the message queue. If it did, the window would have received three or four timer messages in quick succession following the 1.936-second delay.

The lesson to be learned from this analysis is that timers can't be relied upon for stopwatch-like accuracy. If you write a clock application that programs a timer for 1,000-millisecond intervals and updates the display each time a WM_TIMER message arrives, you shouldn't assume that 60 WM_TIMER messages means that one minute has passed. Instead, you should check the current time whenever a message arrives and update the clock accordingly. Then, if the flow of timer messages is interrupted, the clock's accuracy will be maintained.

If you write an application that demands precision timing, you can use Windows multimedia timers in lieu of conventional timers and program them for intervals of 1 millisecond or less. Multimedia timers offer superior precision and are ideal for specialized applications such as MIDI sequencers, but they also incur more overhead and can adversely impact other processes running in the system.

The value returned by *SetTimer* is the timer ID if the function succeeded or 0 if it failed. In previous versions of Windows, timers were a shared global resource of which a limited number were available. In Windows 95, the number of timers the system can dole out is limited only by available memory. Failures should be rare, but it's still prudent to check the return value just in case the system is critically low on resources. (Don't forget, too, that a little discretion goes a long way because an application that sets too many timers can drag down the performance of the entire system.) The timer ID returned by *SetTimer* will equal the timer ID you specified in the function's first parameter unless you specify 0, in which case *SetTimer* will return a timer ID of 1. *SetTimer* won't fail if you assign two or more timers the same ID. Rather, it will assign duplicate IDs as requested.

SetTimer can also be used to change a previously assigned time-out value. If timer 1 already exists, the statement

```
SetTimer (1, 1000, NULL);
```

reprograms it for intervals of 1,000 milliseconds. Reprogramming a timer also resets its internal clock so that the next notification won't arrive until the specified time period has elapsed.

Responding to WM_TIMER Messages

MFC's ON_WM_TIMER message map macro directs WM_TIMER messages to a class member function named *OnTimer*. *OnTimer* is prototyped as follows:

```
afx_msg void OnTimer (UINT nTimerID)
```

nTimerID is the ID of the timer that generated the message. You can do anything in *OnTimer* that you can do in other message processing functions, including grabbing a DC and painting in a window. The following program fragment uses an *OnTimer* handler to draw ellipses of random sizes and colors in a frame window's client area. The timer is programmed for 100-millisecond intervals in the window's *OnCreate* handler:

```
BEGIN_MESSAGE_MAP (CMainWindow, CFrameWindow)
    ON_WM_CREATE ()
    ON_WM_TIMER ()
END_MESSAGE_MAP ()

int CMainWindow::OnCreate (LPCREATESTRUCT lpcs)
{
    if (CFrameWnd::OnCreate (lpcs) == -1)
        return -1;

    if (!SetTimer (ID_TIMER_ELLIPSE, 100, NULL)) {
        MessageBox ("Error: SetTimer failed");
        return -1;
    }
    return 0;
}

void CMainWindow::OnTimer (UINT nTimerID)
{
    CRect rect;
    GetClientRect (&rect);

    int x1 = rand () % rect.right;
    int x2 = rand () % rect.right;
    int y1 = rand () % rect.bottom;
    int y2 = rand () % rect.bottom;

    CClientDC dc (this);
    CBrush brush (RGB (rand () % 255, rand () % 255,
        rand () % 255));
    CBrush* pOldBrush = dc.SelectObject (&brush);
    dc.Ellipse (min (x1, x2), min (y1, y2), max (x1, x2),
        max (y1, y2));
    dc.SelectObject (pOldBrush);
}
```

Here's how the same code fragment would look if the application were modified to use two timers—one for drawing ellipses and another for drawing rectangles:

```
BEGIN_MESSAGE_MAP (CMainWindow, CFrameWindow)
    ON_WM_CREATE ()
    ON_WM_TIMER ()
END_MESSAGE_MAP ()

int CMainWindow::OnCreate (LPCREATESTRUCT lpcs)
{
    if (CFrameWnd::OnCreate (lpcs) == -1)
        return -1;

    if (!SetTimer (ID_TIMER_ELLIPSE, 100, NULL) ||
        !SetTimer (ID_TIMER_RECTANGLE, 100, NULL)) {
        MessageBox ("Error: SetTimer failed");
        return -1;
    }
    return 0;
}

void CMainWindow::OnTimer (UINT nTimerID)
{
    CRect rect;
    GetClientRect (&rect);

    int x1 = rand () % rect.right;
    int x2 = rand () % rect.right;
    int y1 = rand () % rect.bottom;
    int y2 = rand () % rect.bottom;

    CClientDC dc (this);
    CBrush brush (RGB (rand () % 255, rand () % 255, rand () % 255));
    CBrush* pOldBrush = dc.SelectObject (&brush);
    if (nTimerID == ID_TIMER_ELLIPSE)
        dc.Ellipse (min (x1, x2), min (y1, y2), max (x1, x2),
            max (y1, y2));
    else // nTimerID == ID_TIMER_RECTANGLE
        dc.Rectangle (min (x1, x2), min (y1, y2), max (x1, x2),
            max (y1, y2));
    dc.SelectObject (pOldBrush);
}
```

As you can see, *OnTimer* inspects the *nTimerID* value passed through the parameter list to decide whether to draw an ellipse or a rectangle.

You might not write too many applications that draw ellipses and rectangles endlessly, but using timer messages to execute a certain task or sequence of tasks repeatedly provides an easy solution to a common problem encountered in Windows programming. Suppose you write an application with two push button controls labeled "Start" and "Stop" and that clicking the Start button starts a drawing loop that looks like this:

```
m_bContinue = TRUE;
while (m_bContinue)
    DrawRandomEllipse ();
```

The loop draws ellipses over and over until the Stop button is clicked, which sets *m_bContinue* to FALSE so that the *while* loop will fall through. It looks reasonable, but try it and you'll find that it doesn't work. Once the Start button is clicked, the *while* loop will continue running until the Windows session is terminated or until the application is manually aborted with Ctrl-Alt-Del. Why? Because the statement that sets *m_bContinue* to FALSE gets executed only if the WM_COMMAND message generated by the Stop button is retrieved and then dispatched and routed through the message map to the corresponding ON_COMMAND handler. But as long as the *while* loop is spinning in a continuous cycle without checking for messages, the WM_COMMAND message will sit idle in the message queue, waiting to be retrieved. *m_bContinue* will never change from TRUE to FALSE, and the program will be stuck in an infinite loop.

There are a number of solutions to this problem. One is to do the drawing in a secondary thread so that the primary thread can continue to process messages and the Stop button's WM_COMMAND message can get through. Another is to add a message pump to the *while* loop so that the program periodically checks the message queue while drawing ellipses. A third solution is to draw ellipses in response to WM_TIMER messages. In between WM_TIMER messages, other messages will continue to be processed normally. The only drawback to this solution is that drawing ellipses at a rate of more than about 18 per second requires multiple timers, whereas a thread that starts drawing the next ellipse as soon as the previous one is finished might draw dozens or perhaps hundreds of ellipses per second, depending on the speed of the video hardware and the sizes of the ellipses.

An important point to take home here is that WM_TIMER messages are not processed asynchronously with respect to other messages. That is, one WM_TIMER message will never interrupt another WM_TIMER message in the same thread, nor will it interrupt a nontimer message, for that matter. WM_TIMER messages wait their turn in the message queue just as other messages do and are not processed until they are retrieved and dispatched by the message loop. If a regular message handling function and *OnTimer* modify the same member variable, you can safely assume that access to that variable will be serialized so that *OnTimer* won't modify the variable's value while another message is being processed. Of course, this rule doesn't hold true if the two timers were created by two separate threads. We'll examine techniques for coordinating concurrently running threads in Chapter 14.

Setting a Timer: Method 2

Timers don't have to generate WM_TIMER messages. If you prefer, you can configure a timer to call a callback function inside your application rather than post a WM_TIMER message to the message queue. This method is often used in applications that use multiple timers so that each timer can be handled independently.

A common misconception among Windows programmers is that timer callbacks are processed more expediently than timer messages because callbacks are sent directly to the application's window procedure whereas WM_TIMER messages are posted to the message queue. In reality, callbacks and messages are handled identically up to the point at which *::DispatchMessage* is called. When a timer fires, Windows sets a flag in the message queue to indicate that a timer message or callback is awaiting processing. (The on/off nature of the flag explains why timer notifications don't stack up in the message queue. The flag is not incremented when a timer interval elapses, but is merely set to "on.") If *::GetMessage* finds that the message queue is empty and no windows need repainting, it checks the timer flag. If the flag is set, *::GetMessage* builds a WM_TIMER message that is subsequently dispatched by *::DispatchMessage*. If the timer that generated the message is of the WM_TIMER variety, the message is dispatched to the window procedure. But if a callback function is registered instead, *::DispatchMessage* calls the callback function. Therefore, callback timers enjoy virtually no performance advantage over message timers. Slightly less overhead is involved when a timer callback is invoked because no sorting of message IDs has to be done in the message map or the window procedure, but the difference is all but immeasurable. In practice, you'll find that WM_TIMER-type timers and callback timers work with the same regularity (or irregularity, depending on how you look at it).

To set a timer that uses a callback, specify the name of the callback function in the third parameter to *SetTimer*, like this:

```
SetTimer (ID_TIMER, 100, TimerProc);
```

The callback procedure, which is named *TimerProc* in this example, is prototyped as follows:

```
void CALLBACK TimerProc (HWND hWnd, UINT nMsg,
    UINT nTimerID, DWORD dwTime)
```

The *hWnd* parameter to *TimerProc* contains the window handle, *nMsg* contains the message ID WM_TIMER, *nTimerID* holds the timer ID, and *dwTime* specifies the number of milliseconds that have elapsed since Windows was started. (The Win32 documentation for *TimerProc* says *dwTime* "specifies the system time in Coordinated Universal Time format." This is a bug in the documentation.) The callback function should be declared a static member function of the window class, or other measures should be taken to prevent a *this* pointer from being passed on the stack. For more information on static callback functions and the problems that nonstatic member functions pose for C++ applications, refer to Chapter 5.

One obstacle you'll run into when you're using a static member function as a timer callback is that the timer procedure doesn't receive a user-defined *lParam* value as some Windows callback functions do. When we used a static member function to field callbacks from the *::EnumFontFamilies* function in Chapter 5, we passed an object pointer through the 32-bit *lParam* so that the callback function could access nonstatic member variables of the window class. In a timer procedure, you have to manufacture that window pointer yourself if you want to access nonstatic function and data members. Fortunately, you can get a pointer to your application's main window with MFC's *AfxGetMainWnd* function:

```
CMainWindow* pMainWnd = (CMainWindow*) AfxGetMainWnd ();
```

Casting the return value to a *CMainWindow* pointer is necessary if you want to access *CMainWindow* function and data members because the pointer returned by *AfxGetMainWnd* is a generic *CWnd* pointer. Once *pMainWnd* is initialized in this way, a *TimerProc* function that is also a member of *CMainWindow* can access nonstatic *CMainWindow* function and data members as if it, too, were a nonstatic member function.

Stopping a Timer

The counterpart of *CWnd::SetTimer* is *CWnd::KillTimer*, which stops a timer and stops the flow of WM_TIMER messages or callbacks. The following statement releases the timer whose ID is 1:

```
KillTimer (1);
```

A good place to kill a timer created in *OnCreate* is in the window's *OnClose* or *OnDestroy* handler. If an application fails to free a timer before it terminates, Windows 95 will clean up after it when the process ends. Still, good form dictates that every call to *SetTimer* should be paired with a call to *KillTimer* to ensure that timer resources are properly deallocated.

The Clock Application

The Clock application, listed in Figure 7-1 on the next page, uses a timer set to fire at 1-second intervals to periodically redraw its client area, which contains a graphical depiction of an analog clock that includes an hour hand, a minute hand, and a second hand, as shown in Figure 7-2 on page 519. Clock also includes a number of interesting features that have nothing to do with timers, including

■ A system menu command for removing the window's title bar

■ A system menu command for making the window a topmost window—one that's drawn on top of other windows even when it's running in the background

■   A persistent frame window that remembers its size and position

■   A frame window that can be dragged by its client area

Clock also introduces some useful new programming tools, including MFC's *CTime* class, which puts an object-oriented wrapper around dates and times; the WM_MINMAXINFO message, which controls minimum and maximum window sizes; and the MM_ISOTROPIC mapping mode, which allows images drawn in a window to be scaled to match the window size.

Resource.h

```
//*******************************************************************
//
//   Resource.h
//
//*******************************************************************

#define IDI_APPICON                  100

#define IDM_SYSMENU_FULL_WINDOW       16
#define IDM_SYSMENU_STAY_ON_TOP       32
#define IDM_SYSMENU_ABOUT             48

#define IDD_ABOUTDLG                 200
#define IDC_ICONRECT                 201

#define ID_TIMER_CLOCK                 1
```

Clock.rc

```
//*******************************************************************
//
//   Clock.rc
//
//*******************************************************************

#include <afxres.h>
#include "Resource.h"

IDI_APPICON ICON Clock.ico

IDD_ABOUTDLG DIALOG 0, 0, 256, 98
```

Figure 7-1. *The Clock program.*

```
STYLE DS_MODALFRAME | DS_CENTER | WS_POPUP | WS_VISIBLE | WS_CAPTION |
    WS_SYSMENU
CAPTION "About Clock"
FONT 8, "MS Sans Serif"
BEGIN
    LTEXT           "", IDC_ICONRECT, 14, 12, 80, 74
    LTEXT           "Clock Version 1.0", -1, 108, 12, 136, 8
    LTEXT           "From the book", -1, 108, 32, 136, 8
    LTEXT           """Programming Windows 95 with MFC""", -1,
                    108, 42, 136, 8
    LTEXT           "Copyright © 1996 by Jeff Prosise", -1,
                    108, 52, 136, 8
    DEFPUSHBUTTON   "OK", IDOK, 108, 72, 50, 14
END
```

Clock.h

```
//*********************************************************************
//
// Clock.h
//
//*********************************************************************

class CMyApp : public CWinApp
{
public:
    virtual BOOL InitInstance ();
};

class CMainWindow : public CFrameWnd
{
private:
    BOOL m_bFullWindow;
    BOOL m_bStayOnTop;

    int m_nPrevSecond;
    int m_nPrevMinute;
    int m_nPrevHour;

    void DrawClockFace (CDC*);
    void DrawSecondHand (CDC*, int, int, int, COLORREF);
    void DrawHand (CDC*, int, int, int, COLORREF);

    void SetTitleBarState ();
    void SetTopMostState ();
```

(continued)

Clock.h *continued*

```
    void SaveWindowState ();
    void UpdateSystemMenu (CMenu*);

public:
    CMainWindow ();
    virtual BOOL PreCreateWindow (CREATESTRUCT&);
    BOOL RestoreWindowState ();

protected:
    afx_msg int OnCreate (LPCREATESTRUCT);
    afx_msg void OnGetMinMaxInfo (MINMAXINFO*);
    afx_msg void OnTimer (UINT);
    afx_msg void OnPaint ();
    afx_msg UINT OnNcHitTest (CPoint);
    afx_msg void OnSysCommand (UINT, LPARAM);
    afx_msg void OnContextMenu (CWnd*, CPoint);
    afx_msg void OnEndSession (BOOL);
    afx_msg void OnClose ();

    DECLARE_MESSAGE_MAP ()
};

class CAboutDialog : public CDialog
{
private:
    CRect m_rect;

public:
    CAboutDialog (CWnd* pParentWnd) :
        CDialog (IDD_ABOUTDLG, pParentWnd) {}

    virtual BOOL OnInitDialog ();

protected:
    afx_msg void OnPaint ();
    DECLARE_MESSAGE_MAP ()
};
```

Clock.cpp

```
//*********************************************************************
//
// Clock.cpp
//
//*********************************************************************
```

```
#include <afxwin.h>
#include <math.h>
#include "Resource.h"
#include "Clock.h"

#define SQUARESIZE 20

CMyApp myApp;

//////////////////////////////////////////////////////////////////////
// CMyApp member functions

BOOL CMyApp::InitInstance ()
{
    SetRegistryKey ("Programming Windows 95 with MFC");

    m_pMainWnd = new CMainWindow;

    if (!((CMainWindow*) m_pMainWnd)->RestoreWindowState ())
        m_pMainWnd->ShowWindow (m_nCmdShow);

    m_pMainWnd->UpdateWindow ();
    return TRUE;
}

//////////////////////////////////////////////////////////////////////
// CMainWindow message map and member functions

BEGIN_MESSAGE_MAP (CMainWindow, CFrameWnd)
    ON_WM_CREATE ()
    ON_WM_PAINT ()
    ON_WM_TIMER ()
    ON_WM_GETMINMAXINFO ()
    ON_WM_NCHITTEST ()
    ON_WM_SYSCOMMAND ()
    ON_WM_CONTEXTMENU ()
    ON_WM_ENDSESSION ()
    ON_WM_CLOSE ()
END_MESSAGE_MAP ()

CMainWindow::CMainWindow ()
{
    m_bAutoMenuEnable = FALSE;

    CTime time = CTime::GetCurrentTime ();
```

(continued)

Clock.cpp *continued*

```
    m_nPrevSecond = time.GetSecond ();
    m_nPrevMinute = time.GetMinute ();
    m_nPrevHour = time.GetHour () % 12;

    CString strWndClass = AfxRegisterWndClass (
        CS_HREDRAW | CS_VREDRAW,
        myApp.LoadStandardCursor (IDC_ARROW),
        (HBRUSH) (COLOR_3DFACE + 1),
        myApp.LoadIcon (IDI_APPICON)
    );

    Create (strWndClass, "Clock");
}

BOOL CMainWindow::PreCreateWindow (CREATESTRUCT& cs)
{
    if (!CFrameWnd::PreCreateWindow (cs))
        return FALSE;

    cs.dwExStyle &= ~WS_EX_CLIENTEDGE;
    return TRUE;
}

int CMainWindow::OnCreate (LPCREATESTRUCT lpcs)
{
    if (CFrameWnd::OnCreate (lpcs) == -1)
        return -1;

    if (!SetTimer (ID_TIMER_CLOCK, 1000, NULL)) {
        MessageBox ("SetTimer failed", "Error", MB_ICONSTOP | MB_OK);
        return -1;
    }

    CMenu* pMenu = GetSystemMenu (FALSE);
    pMenu->AppendMenu (MF_SEPARATOR);
    pMenu->AppendMenu (MF_STRING, IDM_SYSMENU_FULL_WINDOW,
        "Remove &Title");
    pMenu->AppendMenu (MF_STRING, IDM_SYSMENU_STAY_ON_TOP,
        "Stay on To&p");
    pMenu->AppendMenu (MF_SEPARATOR);
    pMenu->AppendMenu (MF_STRING, IDM_SYSMENU_ABOUT,
        "&About Clock...");
    return 0;
}

void CMainWindow::OnClose ()
```

```
{
    SaveWindowState ();
    KillTimer (ID_TIMER_CLOCK);
    CFrameWnd::OnClose ();
}

void CMainWindow::OnEndSession (BOOL bEnding)
{
    if (bEnding)
        SaveWindowState ();
    CFrameWnd::OnEndSession (bEnding);
}

void CMainWindow::OnGetMinMaxInfo (MINMAXINFO* pMMI)
{
    pMMI->ptMinTrackSize.x = 120;
    pMMI->ptMinTrackSize.y = 120;
}

UINT CMainWindow::OnNcHitTest (CPoint point)
{
    UINT nHitTest = CFrameWnd::OnNcHitTest (point);
    if ((nHitTest == HTCLIENT) && (::GetAsyncKeyState (MK_LBUTTON) < 0))
        nHitTest = HTCAPTION;
    return nHitTest;
}

void CMainWindow::OnSysCommand (UINT nID, LPARAM lParam)
{
    UINT nMaskedID = nID & 0xFFF0;

    if (nMaskedID == IDM_SYSMENU_FULL_WINDOW) {
        m_bFullWindow = m_bFullWindow ? 0 : 1;
        SetTitleBarState ();
        return;
    }
    else if (nMaskedID == IDM_SYSMENU_STAY_ON_TOP) {
        m_bStayOnTop = m_bStayOnTop ? 0 : 1;
        SetTopMostState ();
        return;
    }
    else if (nMaskedID == IDM_SYSMENU_ABOUT) {
        CAboutDialog dlg (this);
        dlg.DoModal ();
        return;
    }
    CFrameWnd::OnSysCommand (nID, lParam);
```

(continued)

Clock.cpp *continued*

```
}

void CMainWindow::OnContextMenu (CWnd* pWnd, CPoint point)
{
    CRect rect;
    GetClientRect (&rect);
    ClientToScreen (&rect);

    if (rect.PtInRect (point)) {
        CMenu* pMenu = GetSystemMenu (FALSE);
        UpdateSystemMenu (pMenu);

        int nID = (int) pMenu->TrackPopupMenu (TPM_LEFTALIGN |
            TPM_LEFTBUTTON | TPM_RIGHTBUTTON | TPM_RETURNCMD, point.x,
            point.y, this);

        if (nID > 0)
            SendMessage (WM_SYSCOMMAND, nID, 0);

        return;
    }
    CFrameWnd::OnContextMenu (pWnd, point);
}

void CMainWindow::OnTimer (UINT nTimerID)
{
    if (IsIconic ()) // Don't paint while window is minimized!
        return;

    CTime time = CTime::GetCurrentTime ();
    int nSecond = time.GetSecond ();
    int nMinute = time.GetMinute ();
    int nHour = time.GetHour () % 12;

    if ((nSecond == m_nPrevSecond) &&
        (nMinute == m_nPrevMinute) &&
        (nHour == m_nPrevHour))
        return;

    CRect rect;
    GetClientRect (&rect);

    CClientDC dc (this);
    dc.SetMapMode (MM_ISOTROPIC);
    dc.SetWindowExt (1000, 1000);
    dc.SetViewportExt (rect.Width (), -rect.Height ());
    dc.SetViewportOrg (rect.Width () / 2, rect.Height () / 2);
```

```
        COLORREF crColor = (COLORREF) GetSysColor (COLOR_3DFACE);

    if (nMinute != m_nPrevMinute) {
        DrawHand (&dc, 200, 4, (m_nPrevHour * 30) + (m_nPrevMinute / 2),
            crColor);
        DrawHand (&dc, 400, 8, m_nPrevMinute * 6, crColor);
        m_nPrevMinute = nMinute;
        m_nPrevHour = nHour;
    }

    if (nSecond != m_nPrevSecond) {
        DrawSecondHand (&dc, 400, 8, m_nPrevSecond * 6, crColor);
        DrawSecondHand (&dc, 400, 8, nSecond * 6, RGB (0, 0, 0));
        DrawHand (&dc, 200, 4, (nHour * 30) + (nMinute / 2),
            RGB (0, 0, 0));
        DrawHand (&dc, 400, 8, nMinute * 6, RGB (0, 0, 0));
        m_nPrevSecond = nSecond;
    }
}

void CMainWindow::OnPaint ()
{
    CRect rect;
    GetClientRect (&rect);

    CPaintDC dc (this);
    dc.SetMapMode (MM_ISOTROPIC);
    dc.SetWindowExt (1000, 1000);
    dc.SetViewportExt (rect.Width (), -rect.Height ());
    dc.SetViewportOrg (rect.Width () / 2, rect.Height () / 2);

    DrawClockFace (&dc);
    DrawHand (&dc, 200, 4, (m_nPrevHour * 30) +
        (m_nPrevMinute / 2), RGB (0, 0, 0));
    DrawHand (&dc, 400, 8, m_nPrevMinute * 6, RGB (0, 0, 0));
    DrawSecondHand (&dc, 400, 8, m_nPrevSecond * 6, RGB (0, 0, 0));
}

void CMainWindow::DrawClockFace (CDC* pDC)
{
    static CPoint point[12] = {
        CPoint (  0,  450),    // 12 o'clock
        CPoint ( 225,  390),   //  1 o'clock
        CPoint ( 390,  225),   //  2 o'clock
        CPoint ( 450,    0),   //  3 o'clock
        CPoint ( 390, -225),   //  4 o'clock
```

(continued)

Clock.cpp *continued*

```
            CPoint ( 225, -390),    //  5 o'clock
            CPoint (   0, -450),    //  6 o'clock
            CPoint (-225, -390),    //  7 o'clock
            CPoint (-390, -225),    //  8 o'clock
            CPoint (-450,    0),    //  9 o'clock
            CPoint (-390,  225),    // 10 o'clock
            CPoint (-225,  390),    // 11 o'clock
    };

    pDC->SelectStockObject (NULL_BRUSH);

    for (int i=0; i<12; i++)
        pDC->Rectangle (point[i].x - SQUARESIZE,
            point[i].y + SQUARESIZE, point[i].x + SQUARESIZE,
            point[i].y - SQUARESIZE);
}

void CMainWindow::DrawHand (CDC* pDC, int nLength, int nScale,
    int nDegrees, COLORREF crColor)
{
    CPoint point[4];
    double nRadians = (double) nDegrees * 0.017453292;

    point[0].x = (int) (nLength * sin (nRadians));
    point[0].y = (int) (nLength * cos (nRadians));

    point[2].x = -point[0].x / nScale;
    point[2].y = -point[0].y / nScale;

    point[1].x = -point[2].y;
    point[1].y = point[2].x;

    point[3].x = -point[1].x;
    point[3].y = -point[1].y;

    CPen pen (PS_SOLID, 0, crColor);
    CPen* pOldPen = pDC->SelectObject (&pen);

    pDC->MoveTo (point[0]);
    pDC->LineTo (point[1]);
    pDC->LineTo (point[2]);
    pDC->LineTo (point[3]);
    pDC->LineTo (point[0]);

    pDC->SelectObject (pOldPen);
}
```

```
void CMainWindow::DrawSecondHand (CDC* pDC, int nLength, int nScale,
    int nDegrees, COLORREF crColor)
{
    CPoint point[2];
    double nRadians = (double) nDegrees * 0.017453292;

    point[0].x = (int) (nLength * sin (nRadians));
    point[0].y = (int) (nLength * cos (nRadians));

    point[1].x = -point[0].x / nScale;
    point[1].y = -point[0].y / nScale;

    CPen pen (PS_SOLID, 0, crColor);
    CPen* pOldPen = pDC->SelectObject (&pen);

    pDC->MoveTo (point[0]);
    pDC->LineTo (point[1]);

    pDC->SelectObject (pOldPen);
}

void CMainWindow::SetTitleBarState ()
{
    CMenu* pMenu = GetSystemMenu (FALSE);

    if (m_bFullWindow ) {
        ModifyStyle (WS_CAPTION, 0);
        pMenu->ModifyMenu (IDM_SYSMENU_FULL_WINDOW, MF_STRING,
            IDM_SYSMENU_FULL_WINDOW, "Restore &Title");
    }
    else {
        ModifyStyle (0, WS_CAPTION);
        pMenu->ModifyMenu (IDM_SYSMENU_FULL_WINDOW, MF_STRING,
            IDM_SYSMENU_FULL_WINDOW, "Remove &Title");
    }

    SetWindowPos (NULL, 0, 0, 0, 0, SWP_NOMOVE | SWP_NOSIZE |
        SWP_NOZORDER | SWP_DRAWFRAME);
}

void CMainWindow::SetTopMostState ()
{
    CMenu* pMenu = GetSystemMenu (FALSE);

    if (m_bStayOnTop) {
        SetWindowPos (&wndTopMost, 0, 0, 0, 0, SWP_NOMOVE | SWP_NOSIZE);
        pMenu->CheckMenuItem (IDM_SYSMENU_STAY_ON_TOP, MF_CHECKED);
    }
```

(continued)

Clock.cpp *continued*

```cpp
    else {
        SetWindowPos (&wndNoTopMost, 0, 0, 0, 0, SWP_NOMOVE | SWP_NOSIZE);
        pMenu->CheckMenuItem (IDM_SYSMENU_STAY_ON_TOP, MF_UNCHECKED);
    }
}

BOOL CMainWindow::RestoreWindowState ()
{
    CString version = "Version 1.0";

    m_bFullWindow = myApp.GetProfileInt (version, "FullWindow", 0);
    SetTitleBarState ();

    m_bStayOnTop = myApp.GetProfileInt (version, "StayOnTop", 0);
    SetTopMostState ();

    WINDOWPLACEMENT wp;
    wp.length = sizeof (WINDOWPLACEMENT);
    GetWindowPlacement (&wp);

    if (((wp.flags =
            myApp.GetProfileInt (version, "flags", -1)) != -1) &&
        ((wp.showCmd =
            myApp.GetProfileInt (version, "showCmd", -1)) != -1) &&
        ((wp.rcNormalPosition.left =
            myApp.GetProfileInt (version, "x1", -1)) != -1) &&
        ((wp.rcNormalPosition.top =
            myApp.GetProfileInt (version, "y1", -1)) != -1) &&
        ((wp.rcNormalPosition.right =
            myApp.GetProfileInt (version, "x2", -1)) != -1) &&
        ((wp.rcNormalPosition.bottom =
            myApp.GetProfileInt (version, "y2", -1)) != -1)) {

        wp.rcNormalPosition.left = min (wp.rcNormalPosition.left,
            ::GetSystemMetrics (SM_CXSCREEN) -
            ::GetSystemMetrics (SM_CXICON));
        wp.rcNormalPosition.top = min (wp.rcNormalPosition.top,
            ::GetSystemMetrics (SM_CYSCREEN) -
            ::GetSystemMetrics (SM_CYICON));

        SetWindowPlacement (&wp);
        return TRUE;
    }
    return FALSE;
}

void CMainWindow::SaveWindowState ()
```

```
{
    CString version = "Version 1.0";

    myApp.WriteProfileInt (version, "FullWindow", m_bFullWindow);
    myApp.WriteProfileInt (version, "StayOnTop", m_bStayOnTop);

    WINDOWPLACEMENT wp;
    wp.length = sizeof (WINDOWPLACEMENT);
    GetWindowPlacement (&wp);

    myApp.WriteProfileInt (version, "flags", wp.flags);
    myApp.WriteProfileInt (version, "showCmd", wp.showCmd);
    myApp.WriteProfileInt (version, "x1", wp.rcNormalPosition.left);
    myApp.WriteProfileInt (version, "y1", wp.rcNormalPosition.top);
    myApp.WriteProfileInt (version, "x2", wp.rcNormalPosition.right);
    myApp.WriteProfileInt (version, "y2", wp.rcNormalPosition.bottom);
}

void CMainWindow::UpdateSystemMenu (CMenu* pMenu)
{
    static UINT nState[2][5] = {
        { MFS_GRAYED,  MFS_ENABLED, MFS_ENABLED,
          MFS_ENABLED, MFS_DEFAULT },
        { MFS_DEFAULT, MFS_GRAYED,  MFS_GRAYED,
          MFS_ENABLED, MFS_GRAYED  }
    };

    if (IsIconic ()) // Shouldn't happen, but let's be safe
        return;

    int i = 0;
    if (IsZoomed ())
        i = 1;

    CString strMenuText;
    pMenu->GetMenuString (SC_RESTORE, strMenuText, MF_BYCOMMAND);
    pMenu->ModifyMenu (SC_RESTORE, MF_STRING | nState[i][0], SC_RESTORE,
        strMenuText);

    pMenu->GetMenuString (SC_MOVE, strMenuText, MF_BYCOMMAND);
    pMenu->ModifyMenu (SC_MOVE, MF_STRING | nState[i][1], SC_MOVE,
        strMenuText);

    pMenu->GetMenuString (SC_SIZE, strMenuText, MF_BYCOMMAND);
    pMenu->ModifyMenu (SC_SIZE, MF_STRING | nState[i][2], SC_SIZE,
        strMenuText);
```

(continued)

Clock.cpp *continued*

```cpp
    pMenu->GetMenuString (SC_MINIMIZE, strMenuText, MF_BYCOMMAND);
    pMenu->ModifyMenu (SC_MINIMIZE, MF_STRING | nState[i][3], SC_MINIMIZE,
        strMenuText);

    pMenu->GetMenuString (SC_MAXIMIZE, strMenuText, MF_BYCOMMAND);
    pMenu->ModifyMenu (SC_MAXIMIZE, MF_STRING | nState[i][4], SC_MAXIMIZE,
        strMenuText);

    SetMenuDefaultItem (pMenu->m_hMenu, i ? SC_RESTORE :
        SC_MAXIMIZE, FALSE);
}

///////////////////////////////////////////////////////////////////////////
// CAboutDialog message map and member functions

BEGIN_MESSAGE_MAP (CAboutDialog, CDialog)
    ON_WM_PAINT ()
END_MESSAGE_MAP ()

BOOL CAboutDialog::OnInitDialog ()
{
    CDialog::OnInitDialog ();

    CStatic* pStatic = (CStatic*) GetDlgItem (IDC_ICONRECT);
    pStatic->GetWindowRect (&m_rect);
    pStatic->DestroyWindow ();
    ScreenToClient (&m_rect);

    return TRUE;
}

void CAboutDialog::OnPaint ()
{
    CPaintDC dc (this);
    HICON hIcon = (HICON) ::GetClassLong (AfxGetMainWnd ()->m_hWnd,
        GCL_HICON);

    if (hIcon != NULL) {
        CDC dcMem;
        dcMem.CreateCompatibleDC (&dc);

        CBitmap bitmap;
        bitmap.CreateCompatibleBitmap (&dc, 32, 32);
        CBitmap* pOldBitmap = dcMem.SelectObject (&bitmap);

        CBrush brush (::GetSysColor (COLOR_3DFACE));
        dcMem.FillRect (CRect (0, 0, 32, 32), &brush);
```

```
        dcMem.DrawIcon (0, 0, hIcon);

        dc.StretchBlt (m_rect.left, m_rect.top, m_rect.Width(),
            m_rect.Height (), &dcMem, 0, 0, 32, 32, SRCCOPY);

        dcMem.SelectObject (pOldBitmap);
    }
}
```

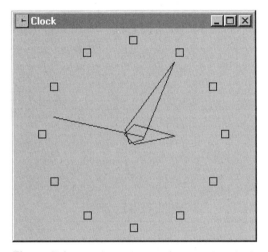

Figure 7-2. *Clock rendition of an analog clock.*

Processing Timer Messages

Clock uses *SetTimer* to program a timer in *OnCreate*. The timer is released in *OnClose* with *KillTimer*. When a WM_TIMER message arrives, *CMainWindow::OnTimer* gets the current time and compares the hour, minute, and second to the hour, minute, and second previously recorded in the private member variables *m_nPrevHour*, *m_nPrevMinute*, and *m_nPrevSecond*. If the current hour, minute, and second equal the hour, minute, and second recorded earlier, *OnTimer* returns without doing anything. Otherwise, it updates *m_nPrevHour* and *m_nPrevMinute* with the current hour and minute and moves the hour and minute hands to their new positions if the number of minutes past the hour has changed, and it updates *m_nPrevSecond* and moves the second hand to its new position if the number of seconds has changed. *CMainWindow::DrawHand* draws the hour and minute hands, and *DrawSecondHand* draws the second hand. A hand is moved by two calls to the corresponding drawing function: one to erase the hand from its old position by drawing over it with the window background color (COLOR_3DFACE) and one to draw the hand—in black—in its new position.

With this mechanism in place, the clock's second hand is moved roughly once per second and the hour and minute hands are moved whenever the current number of minutes past the hour no longer equals the previously recorded minutes-past-the-hour value. Because the hands are drawn to reflect the current time and not some assumed time based on the number of WM_TIMER messages received, it doesn't matter if WM_TIMER messages are skipped as the window is dragged or resized. If you watch closely, you'll occasionally see the second hand advance by two seconds rather than one. That's because every now and then a WM_TIMER message arrives just before the number of seconds is incremented and the next WM_TIMER message arrives a split second after the number of seconds is incremented again. You could prevent this from happening by lowering the timer interval to, say, 0.5 second. The cost would be a little more overhead to the system, but that additional overhead would be minimal because the *OnTimer* function is structured so that it redraws only the clock hands (by far the most labor-intensive part of the process) if the time has changed since the last timer message.

Before doing anything else, *OnTimer* calls the main window's *IsIconic* function to determine whether the window is currently minimized. *IsIconic* returns TRUE for a minimized window and FALSE for an unminimized window. (A complementary function, *CWnd::IsZoomed*, returns TRUE if a window is maximized and FALSE if it is not.) If *IsIconic* returns TRUE, *OnTimer* exits immediately to prevent the clock display from being updated when the window isn't displayed. When a minimized window calls *GetClientRect* in Windows 95, the returned rectangle is a NULL rectangle —one whose coordinates equal 0. The application can try to paint in this rectangle, but the GDI will clip the output. Checking for a minimized window on each timer tick and bypassing Clock's output routines if *IsIconic* returns TRUE reduces the load on the CPU by eliminating unnecessary drawing.

If you'd rather that Clock not sit idle while its window is minimized, try rewriting the beginning of the *OnTimer* function so that it looks like this:

```
CTime time = CTime::GetCurrentTime ();
int nSecond = time.GetSecond ();
int nMinute = time.GetMinute ();
int nHour = time.GetHour () % 12;

if (IsIconic ()) {
    CString strTime;
    strTime.Format ("%0.2d:%0.2d:%0.2d", nHour, nMinute, nSecond);
    SetWindowText (strTime);
    return;
}

SetWindowText ("Clock");
  .
  .
  .
```

An application can change the text displayed next to its icon in the taskbar by changing the window title with *CWnd::SetWindowTitle*. If modified as shown above, Clock will tick off the seconds in the taskbar while running minimized.

Getting the Current Time: The *CTime* Class

To query the system for the current time, Clock uses an object constructed from MFC's *CTime* class. *CTime* represents absolute times and dates. It includes convenient member functions for getting the current time, the day of the week (Sunday, Monday, Tuesday, and so on), and other time and date information. Overloaded operators such as +, −, <, and > allow times and dates to be manipulated with the ease of simple integers.

The *CTime* member functions that interest us are *GetCurrentTime*, which is a static function that returns a *CTime* object initialized to the current date and time; *GetHour*, which returns the hour (0 through 23); *GetMinute*, which returns the number of minutes past the hour (0 through 59); and *GetSecond*, which returns the number of seconds (0 through 59). *OnTimer* uses the following statements to get the current hour, minute, and second in preparation for determining whether the clock display needs to be updated:

```
CTime time = CTime::GetCurrentTime ();
int nSecond = time.GetSecond ();
int nMinute = time.GetMinute ();
int nHour = time.GetHour () % 12;
```

The modulo-12 operation applied to the value returned by *GetHour* converts the hour to an integer from 0 through 11. Similar code is executed by *CMainWindow*'s constructor to initialize *m_nPrevHour*, *m_nPrevMinute*, and *m_nPrevSecond* with values reflecting the current time. Once the current hour, minute, and second are known, it's a simple matter for Clock to determine whether the display should be updated by comparing the latest time-of-day values to the ones recorded earlier.

The MM_ISOTROPIC Mapping Mode

Up to now, all the applications we've developed have used the default MM_TEXT mapping mode. The mapping mode governs how Windows converts the logical units passed to *CDC* drawing functions into device units (pixels) on the display. In the MM_TEXT mapping mode, logical units and device units are one and the same, so if an application draws a line from (0,0) to (50,100), the line is drawn from the pixel in the upper left corner of the display surface represented by the device context (normally the window's client area) to the pixel that lies 50 pixels to the right of and 100 pixels down from the upper left corner. This assumes, of course, that the drawing origin hasn't been moved from its default location in the upper left corner of the display surface.

MM_TEXT is fine for most applications, but there are other GDI mapping modes you can use to lessen an application's dependency on the physical characteristics of the display. (For a review of GDI mapping modes, refer back to Chapter 2.) In the MM_LOENGLISH mapping mode, for example, one logical unit is equal to 1/100th of an inch, so if you want to draw a line exactly 1 inch long, you can set its length to 100 logical units and Windows will factor in the number of pixels per inch when it scan-converts the line into pixels on the screen. To do so, it uses the LOGPIXELSX and LOGPIXELSY values obtainable from *::GetDeviceCaps* (short for "Get Device Capabilities"), which represent the number of pixels per inch in the horizontal and vertical directions on the designated output device. The conversion may not be perfect for screen DCs because Windows uses assumed pixel-per-inch values for screens that aren't based on the physical screen size, but Windows at least makes the output consistent by measuring all distances against a standard yardstick. LOGPIXELSX and LOGPIXELSY *do* hold physically correct values for printers and other hardcopy devices, so by using MM_LOENGLISH for printer output, you really can draw a line 1 inch long.

Clock uses the MM_ISOTROPIC mapping mode. The word "isotropic" means "equal in all directions." In the MM_ISOTROPIC mapping mode, logical units measured along the x axis have the same physical dimensions as logical units measured along the y axis. This is the perfect mapping mode for drawing round circles and square squares because ellipses with equal heights and widths come out round and rectangles with equal heights and widths come out square. This characteristic of the MM_ISOTROPIC mapping mode meshes well with the needs of our application, in which the circle described by the squares representing numeric positions on the clock face should approximate a true circle as closely as possible.

MM_ISOTROPIC is also one of only two mapping modes—the other mapping mode is MM_ANISOTROPIC—that support user-defined scaling parameters. After setting the mapping mode with *CDC::SetMapMode*, you can specify the window's logical height and width (the "window extents") with *CDC::SetWindowExt* and its physical height and width (the "viewport extents") with *CDC::SetViewportExt*. The GDI then uses the relative sizes of those extents to convert logical coordinates to device coordinates when you draw in the window. If you set the window extents to 10 units wide and 10 units high and the viewport extents to the window's width and height in pixels and then draw a circle 8 units wide and 8 units tall, the GDI will scale the circle so that its height and width equal 80 percent of the window's height or width, whichever is shorter.

Before drawing the clock's face and hands in response to a WM_TIMER or WM_PAINT message, Clock first measures the window's client area with *GetClientRect* and obtains a DC for it. Then it sets the mapping mode to MM_ISOTROPIC, moves the origin of the coordinate system so that the logical point (0,0) lies at the center of the window's client area, and sets the window extents so that the window's client area measures 1,000 logical units in each direction. Here's how it looks in code:

```
CRect rect;
GetClientRect (&rect);

CClientDC dc (this); // In OnPaint, use CPaintDC instead
dc.SetMapMode (MM_ISOTROPIC);
dc.SetWindowExt (1000, 1000);
dc.SetViewportExt (rect.Width (), -rect.Height ());
dc.SetViewportOrg (rect.Width () / 2, rect.Height () / 2);
```

The negative value passed to *SetViewportExt* specifying the viewport's physical height orients the coordinate system such that values of *y* increase in the upward direction. If the negative sign were omitted, increasing values of *y* would move down the screen rather than up because Windows numbers pixels at the bottom of the screen higher than it does pixels at the top. Figure 7-3 shows what the coordinate system looks like after it is transformed. The coordinate system is centered in the window's client area, and values of *x* and *y* increase as you move to the right and up. The result is a four-quadrant Cartesian coordinate system that happens to be a very convenient model for drawing an analog clock face.

Once you've configured the coordinate system this way, you can write the output routines that draw the clock's face and hands without regard for the physical dimensions of the window. When *DrawHand* is called to draw a clock hand, the length value passed in the second parameter is either 200 or 400 depending on whether an hour hand or a minute hand is being drawn. Similarly, *DrawSecondHand* is passed a length of 400 for the second hand. Since it's 500 logical units from the origin of the coordinate system to the edge of the window, the minute and second hands will extend

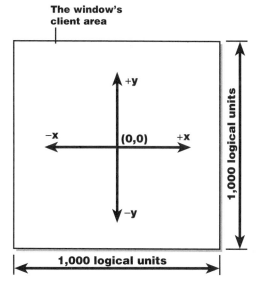

Figure 7-3. *The coordinate system in which the clock face is drawn.*

outward 80 percent of the distance to the nearest window edge and the hour hand will span 40 percent of the distance. If you were using the MM_TEXT mapping mode instead, you'd have to scale every coordinate and every distance manually before passing it to the GDI.

One drawback to letting Windows do the scaling manifests itself when the Clock window is very small: the squares lining the perimeter of the clock face sometimes differ in size by a pixel or two. The difference isn't noticeable if the squares are relatively large, but it's very noticeable when the squares' heights and widths measure only a few pixels. The problem is a round-off error incurred when large logical units are converted into small device units. The error is never more than one pixel, but when the objects you're drawing are only a few pixels wide or tall, the error is magnified because one pixel is a larger percentage of the whole. One solution to the problem of minute scaling errors in the sizes of the rectangles is to compute the rectangles' locations (in device coordinates) while in MM_ISOTROPIC mode but to switch back to MM_TEXT mode before drawing the rectangles.

Adding and Removing the Title Bar

Clock's system menu contains three extra commands: Remove Title, Stay On Top, and About Clock. Remove Title removes the window's title bar so that the clock face fills the entire window. You can restore the title bar by displaying the system menu again and selecting Restore Title, which appears where Remove Title used to be. The magic underlying this transformation is simple, yet adding or removing a title bar on the fly is enough to make even seasoned Windows programmers scratch their heads the first time they try to do it without someone else's source code to serve as a guide.

The secret to making it work is found in *CMainWindow::SetTitleBarState*. The attribute that determines whether a window has a title bar is the WS_CAPTION style bit, which is built into the WS_OVERLAPPEDWINDOW style used for most frame windows. Creating a window without a title bar is as simple as specifying a window style that lacks a WS_CAPTION style bit. It follows that a title bar can be removed after a window is created by resetting the WS_CAPTION bit to 0. MFC's *CWnd::ModifyStyle* function changes a window's style with one simple function call. When Remove/Restore Title is selected from Clock's system menu, *CMainWindow::OnSysCommand* toggles the value stored in *CMainWindow::m_bFullWindow* from 0 to 1 or 1 to 0 and then calls *CMainWindow::SetTitleBarState*, which adds or removes the WS_CAPTION style based on the current value of *m_bFullWindow*:

```
if (m_bFullWindow ) {
    ModifyStyle (WS_CAPTION, 0);
    pMenu->ModifyMenu (IDM_SYSMENU_FULL_WINDOW, MF_STRING,
        IDM_SYSMENU_FULL_WINDOW, "Restore &Title");
}
else {
```

```
    ModifyStyle (0, WS_CAPTION);
    pMenu->ModifyMenu (IDM_SYSMENU_FULL_WINDOW, MF_STRING,
        IDM_SYSMENU_FULL_WINDOW, "Remove &Title");
}
```

The first parameter passed to *ModifyStyle* specifies the style or styles to remove, and the second parameter specifies the style or styles to add. *SetTitleBarState* also sets the menu item text to match the state of the style bit: "Remove Title" if the title bar is displayed and "Restore Title" if it is not.

The trick is getting the window to repaint itself with or without the title bar after the WS_CAPTION bit is toggled. *CWnd::Invalidate* won't do it, but calling *Set-WindowPos* with a SWP_DRAWFRAME parameter will:

```
SetWindowPos (NULL, 0, 0, 0, 0, SWP_NOMOVE ! SWP_NOSIZE !
    SWP_NOZORDER ! SWP_DRAWFRAME);
```

The combination of *SetWindowPos* and SWP_DRAWFRAME causes the entire window, including the frame that surrounds it and the frame's title bar, to be redrawn. The other SWP flags passed to *SetWindowPos* preserve the window's position, size, and position in the z-order—the front-to-back ordering of windows that determines which windows are painted on top of others.

Implementing Client-Area Drag

One problem with a window without a title bar is that the window can't be repositioned with the mouse. Windows are dragged by their title bars, and if the title bar is hidden, there's nothing for the user to grab onto. Clock solves this little dilemma by playing a trick with the window's WM_NCHITTEST handler so that the window can be dragged by its client area, a feature Windows programmers call *client-area drag*.

In Windows, every mouse message a window receives is preceded by a WM_NCHITTEST message with screen coordinates identifying the cursor location. The message is normally handled by *::DefWindowProc*, which returns a code that tells Windows what part of the window the cursor is over. Windows uses the return value to decide what type of mouse message to send. For example, if the left mouse button is clicked over the window's title bar, *::DefWindowProc*'s WM_NCHITTEST handler returns HTCAPTION and Windows sends the window a WM_NCLBUTTONDOWN message. If *::DefWindowProc* returns HTCLIENT instead, Windows converts the cursor coordinates from screen coordinates to client coordinates and passes them to the window in a WM_LBUTTONDOWN message.

The fact that an application sees mouse messages in raw form before Windows does makes for some interesting possibilities. The frame window *OnNcHitTest* handler on the next page implements client-area drag by fooling Windows into thinking that the mouse is over the title bar when in fact it's over the window's client area.

```
UINT CMainWindow::OnNcHitTest (CPoint point)
{
    UINT nHitTest = CFrameWnd::OnNcHitTest (point);
    if (nHitTest == HTCLIENT)
        nHitTest = HTCAPTION;
    return nHitTest;
}
```

With this *OnNcHitTest* handler in place, a window is as easily dragged by its client area as by its title bar. And it works even if the window doesn't *have* a title bar. Try it: click the left mouse button in Clock's client area, and move the mouse with the button held down. The window will move wherever the mouse goes.

Clock uses an *OnNcHitTest* handler similar to the one shown above. The only difference is that Clock checks to see that the left mouse button is held down before replacing an HTCLIENT return code with HTCAPTION so that other mouse messages —particularly right-button mouse messages that precede WM_CONTEXTMENU messages—will get through unscathed:

```
UINT CMainWindow::OnNcHitTest (CPoint point)
{
    UINT nHitTest = CFrameWnd::OnNcHitTest (point);
    if ((nHitTest == HTCLIENT) &&
        (::GetAsyncKeyState (MK_LBUTTON) < 0))
        nHitTest = HTCAPTION;
    return nHitTest;
}
```

The call to *::GetAsyncKeyState* checks the left mouse button in real time (hence the "Async") and returns a negative value if the button is currently down.

The System Menu as a Context Menu

Removing the title bar has other implications for a window's operation. Without a title bar, there's nothing for the user to click on to display the system menu so that the title bar can be restored. Clock's solution is an *OnContextMenu* handler that displays the system menu as a context menu when the right mouse button is clicked in the window's client area. Popping up a system menu at an arbitrary location is easier said than done because there's no convenient API function for displaying a system menu programmatically. Clock.cpp shows one technique you can use to do it yourself.

When the right mouse button is clicked in Clock's client area, *CMainWindow*'s *OnContextMenu* handler retrieves a *CMenu* pointer to the system menu with *GetSystemMenu* and displays the menu with *CMenu::TrackPopupMenu*:

```
CMenu* pMenu = GetSystemMenu (FALSE);
    :
    :

int nID = (int) pMenu->TrackPopupMenu (TPM_LEFTALIGN |
    TPM_LEFTBUTTON | TPM_RIGHTBUTTON | TPM_RETURNCMD, point.x,
    point.y, this);
```

One problem with this solution is that commands selected from the menu produce WM_COMMAND messages instead of WM_SYSCOMMAND messages. To compensate, Clock passes *TrackPopupMenu* a TPM_RETURNCMD flag instructing it to return the ID of the selected menu item. (Don't look for a description of TPM_RETURNCMD in the Windows 95 documentation set; it was inadvertently omitted.) If *TrackPopupMenu* returns a positive, nonzero value indicating that an item was selected, the application sends itself a WM_SYSCOMMAND message with *wParam* equal to the menu item ID:

```
if (nID > 0)
    SendMessage (WM_SYSCOMMAND, nID, 0);
```

As a result, *OnSysCommand* gets called to process selections from the pseudo–system menu just as it does for selections from the real system menu. To prevent the framework from disabling the items *OnCreate* added to the system menu because of the lack of ON_COMMAND handlers, *CMainWindow*'s constructor sets *m_bAutoMenu-Enable* to FALSE. Normally, the framework's automatic enabling and disabling of menu items doesn't affect items added to the system menu, but Clock's system menu is an exception because it's treated as a conventional menu when it's displayed with *Track-PopupMenu*.

So far, so good. There's just one problem remaining. Windows interactively enables and disables certain commands in the system menu so that the selection of commands available is consistent with the window state. For example, the Move, Size, and Maximize commands are grayed in a maximized window's system menu but the Restore and Minimize commands are not. If the same window is restored to its un-maximized size, Restore is grayed out but all other commands are enabled. Unfortunately, when you get a menu pointer with *GetSystemMenu*, the menu items haven't been updated yet. Therefore, *OnContextMenu* calls a *CMainWindow* function named *UpdateSystemMenu* to manually update the menu item states based on the current state of the window. After *UpdateSystemMenu* updates the system menu by placing a series of calls to *CMenu::GetMenuString* and *CMenu::ModifyMenu*, it uses the new *::SetMenuDefaultItem* API function to set the default menu item (the one displayed in boldface type) to either Restore or Maximize, depending on whether the window is maximized. The default menu item is the one that's invoked when the left mouse button is double-clicked. *UpdateSystemMenu* is hardly an ideal solution, but it works, and to date I haven't found a better way to keep the items in a programmatically displayed system menu in sync with the window the menu belongs to.

Topmost Windows

One innovation introduced in Windows 3.1 was the notion of a *topmost window*—a window whose position in the z-order is implicitly higher than those of conventional, or nontopmost, windows. Normally, the window at the top of the z-order is painted on top of other windows, the window that's second in the z-order is painted on top of windows other than the first, and so on. A topmost window, however, receives priority over other windows so that it's not obscured even if it's at the bottom of the z-order. It's always visible, even while it's running in the background.

To see an example of a topmost window, you need look no further than the Windows 95 taskbar. By default, the taskbar is designated a topmost window so that it will be drawn on top of other windows. If two (or more) topmost windows are displayed at the same time, the normal rules of z-ordering determine the visibility of each one relative to the other. Topmost windows should be used sparingly because if all windows were topmost windows, a topmost window would no longer be accorded priority among its peers.

The difference between a topmost window and a nontopmost window is an extended window style bit. WS_EX_TOPMOST makes a window a topmost window. A topmost frame window can be created by including a WS_EX_TOPMOST flag in the call to *Create*, like this:

```
Create (NULL, "MyWindow", WS_OVERLAPPEDWINDOW, rectDefault,
    NULL, NULL, WS_EX_TOPMOST);
```

The alternative is to add the style bit after the window is created by calling *SetWindowPos* with a *&wndTopMost* parameter, as shown here:

```
SetWindowPos (&wndTopMost, 0, 0, 0, 0, SWP_NOMOVE : SWP_NOSIZE);
```

A topmost window can be converted into a nontopmost window by calling *SetWindowPos* with the first parameter equal to *&wndNoTopMost* rather than *&wndTopMost*.

Clock uses *SetWindowPos* to make its window a topmost window when Stay On Top is checked in the system menu and a nontopmost window when Stay On Top is unchecked. The work is done by *CMainWindow::SetTopmostState*, which is called by *OnSysCommand* when Stay On Top is selected from the menu. When Stay On Top is checked, Clock is visible on the screen at all times, even if it's running in the background and it overlaps the application running in the foreground.

Persistent Configuration Settings

Clock is our first sample program thus far that makes program settings persistent by recording them on disk. The word "persistent" comes up a lot in discussions of Windows programming. Saying that a piece of information is persistent means that it's preserved across sessions. If you like Clock to run in a tiny window in the lower right corner of your screen, you can size it and position it once and it will automatically come back up in the same size and position the next time it's started. To users who like to arrange their desktops a certain way, it's little touches like this one that make the difference between a good application and a great one. Other Clock configuration settings are preserved, too, including the title bar and stay-on-top states.

The key to preserving configuration information across sessions is to store it on the hard disk so that it can be read back again the next time the application is started. In 16-bit Windows, it's common for applications to use *::WriteProfileString, ::ReadProfileString*, and other API functions to store configuration settings in Win.ini or private .ini files. In Windows 95, .ini files are still supported for backward compatibility, but programmers are discouraged from using them. 32-bit applications should store configuration settings in the registry instead.

The registry is a binary database that serves as a central data depository for the operating system and the applications it hosts. Information in the registry is stored under keys and subkeys, which are analogous to directories and subdirectories on a hard disk. Keys contain named data entries analogous to files, and individual entries can be assigned text or binary values. The uppermost level in the registry's hierarchy is a set of six root keys named HKEY_CLASSES_ROOT, HKEY_USERS, HKEY_CURRENT_USER, HKEY_LOCAL_MACHINE, HKEY_CURRENT_CONFIG, and HKEY_DYN_DATA. Per Microsoft's recommendations, Windows 95 applications should store private configuration settings under the key

```
HKEY_CURRENT_USER\Software\CompanyName\ProductName\Version
```

where *CompanyName* is the company name, *ProductName* is the product name, and *Version* is the product's version number. A registry entry that recorded the user-selectable window background color for version 2.0 of a product named WidgetMaster from WinWidgets, Inc., might look like this:

```
HKEY_CURRENT_USER\Software\WinWidgets, Inc.\WidgetMaster\Version 2.0\BkgndColor=4
```

Because the information is stored under HKEY_CURRENT_USER, it is maintained on a per-user basis. That is, if another user logs in and runs the same application but selects a different background color, a separate *BkgndColor* value will be recorded for that user.

The Win32 API includes an assortment of functions for reading and writing to the registry, but MFC provides a layer on top of the API that makes reading and writing application-specific registry values no different from using ordinary .ini files. A call to *CWinApp::SetRegistryKey* with the name of a registry key directs the framework to use the registry instead of an .ini file. The key name passed to *SetRegistryKey* corresponds to the company name—for example, our "WinWidgets, Inc." in the registry entry shown above. String and numeric data are written to the registry with *CWinApp*'s *WriteProfileString* and *WriteProfileInt* functions and read back with *GetProfileString* and *GetProfileInt*. In an application named MyWord.exe, the statements

```
SetRegistryKey ("WordSmith");
WriteProfileInt ("Version 1.0", "MRULength", 8);
```

create the following numeric registry entry:

```
HKEY_CURRENT_USER\Software\WordSmith\MYWORD\Version 1.0\MRULength=8
```

The statement

```
m_nMRULength = GetProfileInt ("Version 1.0", "MRULength", 4);
```

reads it back and returns 4 if the entry doesn't exist. Note that MFC generates the product name for you by stripping the .exe extension from the executable file name.

Before it terminates, Clock records the following configuration settings in the registry:

- The value of *CMainWindow::m_bFullWindow*, which indicates whether the title bar is displayed.

- The value of *CMainWindow::m_bStayOnTop*, which indicates whether Stay On Top is selected.

- The size and position of the frame window.

When the application starts up, the settings are read back. The full complement of entries that Clock writes to the registry is shown in Figure 7-4. Entries are written and read with the *CMainWindow* functions *SaveWindowState* and *RestoreWindowState*. *SaveWindowState* is called from the window's *OnClose* and *OnEndSession* handlers, which are called just before the application closes and just before Windows shuts down, respectively. If Windows is shut down, a running application doesn't receive a WM_CLOSE message, but it does receive a WM_ENDSESSION message. If you want your application to know if Windows is preparing to shut down, simply add an ON_WM_ENDSESSION entry to the main window's message map and include an *OnEndSession* handler to go with it. The *bEnding* parameter passed to *OnEndSession* indicates whether Windows is in fact shutting down. A nonzero value means it is; 0 means Windows was about to shut down but another application vetoed the operation. A WM_ENDSESSION message is preceded by a WM_QUERYENDSESSION message, in which each application is given a chance to say yes or no to an impending shutdown.

Clock's title bar and stay-on-top settings are saved to the HKEY_CURRENT_USER-\Software\Programming Windows 95 with MFC\CLOCK\Version 1.0 branch of the registry with these statements in *SaveWindowState*:

```
CString version = "Version 1.0";

myApp.WriteProfileInt (version, "FullWindow", m_bFullWindow);
myApp.WriteProfileInt (version, "StayOnTop", m_bStayOnTop);
```

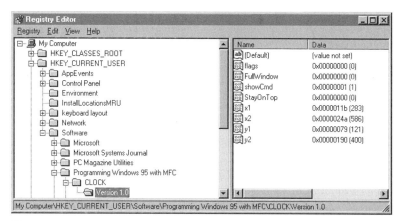

Figure 7-4. *A view of Clock's registry entries through Windows 95's RegEdit utility.*

The same settings are read back and applied to the window in *RestoreWindowState*:

```
CString version = "Version 1.0";

m_bFullWindow = myApp.GetProfileInt (version, "FullWindow", 0);
SetTitleBarState ();

m_bStayOnTop = myApp.GetProfileInt (version, "StayOnTop", 0);
SetTopMostState ();
```

RestoreWindowState is called by *CMyApp::InitInstance* right after the window is created but before it is displayed.

Saving and restoring the window's size and position is a little tricker. If you've never written an application with a window that remembers its size and position, you might think it would be a simple matter of saving the coordinates returned by *CWnd::GetWindowRect* so that they can be passed to *Create* or *CreateEx*. But there's more to it than that. If you fail to take into account the window's current state (minimized, maximized, or neither minimized nor maximized), all kinds of things can happen. For example, if you pass the coordinates of a maximized window to *Create* or *CreateEx*, the resultant window will occupy the full extents of the screen but its title bar will have a maximize box instead of a restore box. A persistent window that's closed while it's minimized or maximized should come back up in the minimized or maximized state, and it should also remember its normal size so that restoring it will restore its former size.

The key to preserving a window's size and position and taking relevant state information into account lies in a pair of *CWnd* functions named *GetWindowPlacement* and *SetWindowPlacement*. Each accepts the address of a WINDOWPLACEMENT structure, which is defined as follows in Winuser.h:

```
typedef struct tagWINDOWPLACEMENT {
    UINT  length;
    UINT  flags;
    UINT  showCmd;
    POINT ptMinPosition;
    POINT ptMaxPosition;
    RECT  rcNormalPosition;
} WINDOWPLACEMENT;
```

WINDOWPLACEMENT brings together in one place everything Windows needs to know to characterize a window's screen state. The *length* member specifies the size of the WINDOWPLACEMENT structure. Both *CWnd::GetWindowPlacement* and *CWnd::SetWindowPlacement* fill in the field for you. *flags* contains zero or more bit flags specifying information about minimized windows. The WPF_RESTORETO-MAXIMIZED flag indicates that a minimized window will be maximized when it is restored. *showCmd* specifies the window's current display state. It is set to SW_SHOW-MINIMIZED if the window is minimized, SW_SHOWMAXIMIZED if the window is maximized, or SW_SHOWNORMAL if the window is neither minimized nor maximized. *ptMinPosition* and *ptMaxPosition* hold the screen coordinates of the window's upper left corner when it is minimized and maximized, respectively. (Don't rely on the coordinate values of *ptMinPosition* to tell you anything; in Windows 95, *ptMinPosition* is set to (3000,3000) when a window is minimized.) *rcNormalPosition* contains the screen coordinates of the window's "normal," or unminimized and unmaximized, screen position. When a window is minimized or maximized, *rcNormalPosition* specifies the position and size the window will be restored to when the restore box in its title bar is clicked or when Restore is selected from the system menu—provided, of course, that the WPF_RESTORETOMAXIMIZED flag isn't set to force a restored window to full screen.

A window's screen state can be preserved across sessions by saving the *flags*, *showCmd*, and *rcNormalPosition* values in the window's WINDOWPLACEMENT structure and restoring these values when the window is re-created. *ptMinPosition* and *ptMaxPosition* don't need to be saved because their values are filled in by Windows when the window is minimized or maximized. Clock's *SaveWindowState* function initializes a WINDOWPLACEMENT structure by calling *GetWindowPlacement* and then writes the pertinent members of that structure to the registry. The window state is restored when *CMyApp::InitInstance* calls *CMainWindow::RestoreWindowState*, which in turn calls *GetWindowPlacement* to fill in a WINDOWPLACEMENT structure, reads the *flags*, *showCmd*, and *rcNormalPosition* values from the registry and copies them to the structure, and calls *SetWindowPlacement*. The SW_SHOWMINIMIZED, SW-_SHOWMAXIMIZED, or SW_SHOWNORMAL parameter passed to *SetWindowPlacement* in *showCmd* makes the window visible, so there's no need to call *ShowWindow* if *RestoreWindowState* returns TRUE indicating that the window state was successfully restored. In fact, the usual call placed to *ShowWindow* from *InitInstance* should be skipped if *RestoreWindowState* returns TRUE since the application object's *m_n-CmdShow* parameter may alter the window's state. Clock's *InitInstance* function looks like this:

```
BOOL CMyApp::InitInstance ()
{
    SetRegistryKey ("Programming Windows 95 with MFC");

    m_pMainWnd = new CMainWindow;

    if (!((CMainWindow*) m_pMainWnd)->RestoreWindowState ())
        m_pMainWnd->ShowWindow (m_nCmdShow);

    m_pMainWnd->UpdateWindow ();
    return TRUE;
}
```

The first time Clock is executed, *ShowWindow* is called in the normal way because *RestoreWindowState* returns FALSE. In subsequent invocations, the window's size, position, and visibility state are set by *RestoreWindowState,* and *ShowWindow* is skipped.

Before calling *SetWindowPlacement* to effect the state values retrieved from the registry, *RestoreWindowState* ensures that a window positioned near the edge of a 1,024-by-768 screen won't disappear if Windows is restarted in 640-by-480 or 800-by-600 mode by comparing the window's normal position with the screen extents:

```
wp.rcNormalPosition.left = min (wp.rcNormalPosition.left,
    ::GetSystemMetrics (SM_CXSCREEN) -
    ::GetSystemMetrics (SM_CXICON));
wp.rcNormalPosition.top = min (wp.rcNormalPosition.top,
    ::GetSystemMetrics (SM_CYSCREEN) -
    ::GetSystemMetrics (SM_CYICON));
```

Called with SM_CXSCREEN and SM_CYSCREEN parameters, *::GetSystemMetrics* returns the screen's width and height, respectively, in pixels. If the window coordinates retrieved from the registry are 700 and 600 and Windows is running at a resolution of 640 by 480, this simple procedure will transform the 700 and 600 into 640 and 480 minus the width and height of an icon. Rather than appear out of sight off the screen and probably leave the user wondering why the application didn't start up, the window will appear just inside the lower right corner of the screen.

A good way to test a program that preserves a window's position and size is to resize the window to some arbitrary size, maximize it, minimize it, and then close the application with the window minimized. When the program is restarted, the window should come up minimized, and clicking the minimized window's icon in the taskbar should remaximize it. Clicking the restore button should then restore the window's original size and position. Try this procedure with Clock, and you'll find that it passes the test with flying colors.

Controlling the Window Size: The WM_GETMINMAXINFO Message

A final aspect of Clock that deserves scrutiny is its *OnGetMinMaxInfo* handler. When the user grabs the border of a resizeable window and moves the mouse to resize the window, the window receives a series of WM_GETMINMAXINFO messages with *lParam* pointing to a MINMAXINFO structure containing information about the window's minimum and maximum "tracking" sizes. You can limit the minimum and maximum sizes of a window by processing WM_GETMINMAXINFO messages and copying the minimum width and height to the *x* and *y* members of the structure's *ptMinTrackSize* field and the maximum width and height to the *x* and *y* members of the *ptMaxTrackSize* field. Clock prevents its window from being reduced to less than 120 pixels horizontally and vertically with the following *OnGetMinMaxInfo* handler:

```
void CMainWindow::OnGetMinMaxInfo (MINMAXINFO* pMMI)
{
    pMMI->ptMinTrackSize.x = 120;
    pMMI->ptMinTrackSize.y = 120;
}
```

The tracking dimensions copied to MINMAXINFO are measured in device units, or pixels. In this example, the window's maximum size is unconstrained because *pMMI->ptMaxTrackSize* is left unchanged. If you wanted to limit the maximum window size to one-half the screen size, you could do so with the version of *OnGetMinMaxInfo* shown here:

```
void CMainWindow::OnGetMinMaxInfo (MINMAXINFO* pMMI)
{
    pMMI->ptMinTrackSize.x = 120;
    pMMI->ptMinTrackSize.y = 120;
    pMMI->ptMaxTrackSize.x = ::GetSystemMetrics (SM_CXSCREEN) / 2;
    pMMI->ptMaxTrackSize.y = ::GetSystemMetrics (SM_CYSCREEN) / 2;
}
```

IDLE PROCESSING

Since MFC's application class, *CWinApp*, provides the message loop that retrieves and dispatches messages, it's a simple matter for *CWinApp* to call a function in your application when there are no messages to be processed. If you look at the source code for the *CWinThread::Run* function that gets called by *WinMain* to start the application running, you'll see something that looks like this:

```
BOOL bIdle = TRUE;
LONG lIdleCount = 0;

for (;;)
{
```

```
while (bIdle &&
    !::PeekMessage(&m_msgCur, NULL, NULL, NULL, PM_NOREMOVE))
{
    if (!OnIdle(lIdleCount++))
        bIdle = FALSE; // Assume "no idle" state.
}

do
{
    if (!PumpMessage())
        return ExitInstance();

    if (IsIdleMessage(&m_msgCur))
    {
        bIdle = TRUE;
        lIdleCount = 0;
    }

} while (::PeekMessage(&m_msgCur, NULL, NULL, NULL, PM_NOREMOVE));
}
```

Before it calls *PumpMessage* to retrieve and dispatch a message, *Run* first calls *::Peek-Message* with a PM_NOREMOVE flag to check the message queue. If a message is waiting to be retrieved, *::PeekMessage* copies it to an MSG structure and returns TRUE but doesn't remove the message from the queue. If no messages are waiting, *::Peek-Message* returns FALSE. Unlike *::GetMessage*, *::PeekMessage* doesn't wait for a message to appear in the message queue before returning; it returns immediately. If *::PeekMessage* returns TRUE, indicating that there are messages waiting to be processed, *CWinThread::Run* enters a *do-while* loop that calls *CWinThread::PumpMessage* repeatedly to retrieve and dispatch the messages. But if *::PeekMessage* returns FALSE and the *bIdle* flag is set, *CWinThread::Run* calls a member function named *OnIdle* to give the application an opportunity to perform idle processing. Because *OnIdle* is a virtual function and because *CWinApp* is derived from *CWinThread*, a derived application class can hook into the idle loop by overriding *CWinApp::OnIdle* with an *OnIdle* function of its own.

Back in the days of Windows 3.*x*, when applications were inherently single-threaded, an *OnIdle* call was the perfect time to perform background processing tasks such as spooling a document to a printer or doing garbage collection on in-memory data structures. In Windows 95, *CWinApp::OnIdle*'s usefulness is diminished because low-priority tasks can be performed more efficiently in secondary threads of execution. There are still legitimate uses for *OnIdle*, however. MFC's application framework uses idle time to update interface objects such as toolbar buttons and status bar panes by calling those objects' WM_UPDATE_COMMAND_UI handlers. The framework also takes advantage of times when the application isn't busy processing messages by deleting temporary objects created by functions such as *CWnd::FromHandle* and *CWnd::GetMenu.*

When you call *FromHandle* to get a *CWnd* pointer to a window identified by a window handle, the framework first searches an internal table that correlates *CWnd* objects with window handles and if a match is found, returns a pointer to the corresponding *CWnd* object. If, however, a *CWnd* doesn't exist for that window, *FromHandle* creates a temporary *CWnd* object and returns its address to the caller. The next time *OnIdle* is called (which won't occur until after the message handler that called *FromHandle* returns), the framework cleans up after itself by deleting the temporary *CWnd* object. That's why the documentation for some MFC functions warns that returned pointers may be temporary and "should not be stored for later use." What that really means is that an object referenced by one of these temporary pointers isn't guaranteed to exist outside the scope of the current message handler because, once that handler returns, *OnIdle* is liable to be called—and the object deleted—at any moment.

Overriding *CWinApp::OnIdle*

As mentioned earlier, an application can perform idle processing of its own by overriding the application object's virtual *OnIdle* function. *OnIdle* is prototyped as follows:

```
virtual BOOL OnIdle (LONG lCount)
```

lCount is a 32-bit value that specifies the number of times *OnIdle* has been called since the last message was processed. The count continually increases until the message loop in *CWinThread::Run* calls *PumpMessage* to retrieve and dispatch another message. The count is then reset to 0 and starts again. Mouse messages, WM_PAINT messages, and WM_SYSTIMER messages don't cause *lCount* to be reset. (WM_SYSTIMER is an undocumented message used internally by Windows.) *lCount* can be used as a rough measure of the time elapsed since the last message, or of the length of time the application has been idle. If you have two background tasks you'd like to perform during idle time, one that's high priority and another that's low, you can use *lCount* to determine when to execute each task. For example, the high-priority task might be executed when *lCount* reaches 10, and the low-priority task might be deferred until *lCount* is 100 or even 1,000.

If you could log the calls to an application's *OnIdle* function without slowing it down, you'd find that 1,000 is not all that high a number. Typically, *OnIdle* is called 100 or more times per second when the message queue is empty, so a low-priority background task that kicks off when *lCount* reaches 1,000 would be executed when the user stopped typing or moving the mouse for a few seconds. A high-priority task that begins when *lCount* reaches 10 would be executed much more often because the count frequently reaches or exceeds 10 even when the message loop is relatively busy. Idle processing should be carried out as quickly as possible because message traffic is blocked until the *OnIdle* function returns.

The value returned by *OnIdle* determines whether *OnIdle* will be called again. If *OnIdle* returns a nonzero value, it is called again if the message queue is still empty. If *OnIdle* returns 0, however, further calls to *OnIdle* are suspended until another message finds its way into the message queue, and the idle state is reentered after the message is dispatched. The mechanism that makes this work is the *bIdle* flag in *CWinThread::Run*, which is initially set to TRUE but is set to FALSE if *OnIdle* returns FALSE. The *while* loop that calls *OnIdle* tests the value of *bIdle* at the beginning of each iteration and falls through if *bIdle* is FALSE. *bIdle* is set to TRUE again when a message shows up in the message queue and *PumpMessage* is called to retrieve and dispatch it. From a practical standpoint, you can save a few CPU cycles by returning FALSE from your *OnIdle* override if background processing is complete for the moment and you don't want *OnIdle* to be called again until the flow of messages resumes. Be careful, however, not to return FALSE before the framework has finished its most recent spate of idle processing chores and thus deprive it of the idle time that it needs. There's an easy way to avoid this trap that we'll see in just a moment.

The cardinal rule in using *OnIdle* is to call the base class version of *OnIdle* from the overridden version. The following *OnIdle* override demonstrates the proper technique. The base class's *OnIdle* function is called first, and after the call returns, the application performs its own idle processing:

```
BOOL CMyApp::OnIdle (LONG lCount)
{
    CWinApp::OnIdle (lCount);
    DoIdleWork (); // Do custom idle processing
    return TRUE;
}
```

An even better approach is to accord higher priority to the framework's *OnIdle* handler by delaying the start of your own idle processing until *lCount* reaches a value of 2 or higher:

```
BOOL CMyApp::OnIdle (LONG lCount)
{
    CWinApp::OnIdle (lCount);
    if (lCount >= 2)
        DoIdleWork (); // Do custom idle processing
    return TRUE;
}
```

The framework does its processing when *lCount* is 0 and 1. You can find out exactly what's done and when by looking at the source code for *CWinThread::OnIdle* in Thrdcore.cpp and *CWinApp::OnIdle* in Appcore.cpp.

Because the version of *OnIdle* shown on the preceding page always returns TRUE, an application will continue receiving *OnIdle* calls even if both it and the framework are finished doing idle chores for the time being. The following *OnIdle* override minimizes wasted clock cycles by returning FALSE when the application's own idle processing is complete:

```
BOOL CMyApp::OnIdle (LONG lCount)
{
    CWinApp::OnIdle (lCount);
    BOOL bContinue = TRUE;
    if (lCount == 2) {
        DoIdleWork (); // Do custom idle processing
        bContinue = FALSE;
    }
    return bContinue;
}
```

The fact that application-specific idle processing isn't started until *lCount* equals 2 means that the framework won't be deprived of the idle time it needs if the application's *OnIdle* function returns FALSE.

It's important to do idle processing as quickly as possible to avoid reducing the application's responsiveness. If necessary, break up large *OnIdle* tasks into smaller, more manageable, pieces and process one piece at a time in successive calls to *OnIdle*. The following *OnIdle* function begins its work when *lCount* reaches 2 and continues responding to *OnIdle* calls until *DoIdleWork* returns FALSE, indicating that no further idle time is required:

```
BOOL CMyApp::OnIdle (LONG lCount)
{
    CWinApp::OnIdle (lCount);
    BOOL bContinue = TRUE;
    if (lCount >= 2)
        bContinue = DoIdleWork (); // Do custom idle processing
    return bContinue;
}
```

The IdleDemo Application

The IdleDemo application, listed in Figure 7-5, demonstrates one very practical use for a custom *OnIdle* handler. Suppose you've written a paint program with a status bar that contains an *x* and *y* cursor-coordinate readout. To update the readout whenever the mouse is moved, you include an *OnMouseMove* handler that displays the latest *x* and *y* cursor coordinates. But then you notice a problem. When the cursor leaves the window's client area, WM_MOUSEMOVE messages cease and the readout freezes with the coordinates of the last cursor position. That's hardly a fatal flaw, but a well-designed application should blank out the coordinate display when the cursor leaves the window. The question is, How? A window doesn't receive a message informing it that the cursor has left it. Some programmers have tried to solve this problem by blanking the coordinate display in response to WM_NCMOUSEMOVE messages, only to find that if the mouse is moved rapidly enough, the final mouse message the window receives is a WM_MOUSEMOVE message.

Resource.h

```
//****************************************************************************
//
//  Resource.h
//
//****************************************************************************

#define IDR_MAINFRAME   100
#define IDM_EXIT        101
```

IdleDemo.rc

```
//****************************************************************************
//
//  IdleDemo.rc
//
//****************************************************************************

#include <afxres.h>
#include "Resource.h"

IDR_MAINFRAME MENU
BEGIN
    POPUP "&Options" {
        MENUITEM "E&xit",    IDM_EXIT
    }
END
```

IdleDemo.h

```
//****************************************************************************
//
//  IdleDemo.h
//
//****************************************************************************
```

Figure 7-5. *The IdleDemo program.* *(continued)*

IdleDemo.h *continued*

```
class CMyApp : public CWinApp
{
public:
    virtual BOOL InitInstance ();
    virtual BOOL OnIdle (LONG);
};

class CMainWindow : public CFrameWnd
{
public:
    CMainWindow ();
    BOOL CursorInClient ();
    void UpdateReadout (CDC* = NULL);

protected:
    afx_msg void OnPaint ();
    afx_msg void OnMouseMove (UINT, CPoint);
    afx_msg void OnExit ();

    DECLARE_MESSAGE_MAP ()
};
```

IdleDemo.cpp

```
//****************************************************************************
//
//  IdleDemo.cpp
//
//****************************************************************************

#include <afxwin.h>
#include "Resource.h"
#include "IdleDemo.h"

CMyApp myApp;

///////////////////////////////////////////////////////////////////////////
// CMyApp member functions

BOOL CMyApp::InitInstance ()
{
    m_pMainWnd = new CMainWindow;
    m_pMainWnd->ShowWindow (m_nCmdShow);
    m_pMainWnd->UpdateWindow ();
    return TRUE;
}
```

```
}

BOOL CMyApp::OnIdle (LONG lCount)
{
    CWinApp::OnIdle (lCount);

    BOOL bReturn = TRUE;
    if (lCount >= 2) {
        CMainWindow* pWnd = (CMainWindow*) m_pMainWnd;
        if (!pWnd->CursorInClient ()) {
            pWnd->UpdateReadout ();
            bReturn = FALSE;
        }
    }
    return bReturn;
}


/////////////////////////////////////////////////////////////////////////
// CMainWindow message map and member functions

BEGIN_MESSAGE_MAP (CMainWindow, CFrameWnd)
    ON_WM_PAINT ()
    ON_WM_MOUSEMOVE ()
    ON_COMMAND (IDM_EXIT, OnExit)
END_MESSAGE_MAP ()

CMainWindow::CMainWindow ()
{
    Create (NULL, "IdleDemo", WS_OVERLAPPEDWINDOW, rectDefault,
        NULL, MAKEINTRESOURCE (IDR_MAINFRAME));
}

void CMainWindow::OnPaint ()
{
    CPaintDC dc (this);
    UpdateReadout (&dc);
}

void CMainWindow::OnMouseMove (UINT nFlags, CPoint point)
{
    UpdateReadout ();
}

void CMainWindow::OnExit ()
{
    SendMessage (WM_CLOSE, 0, 0);
}
```

(continued)

IdleDemo.cpp *continued*

```
BOOL CMainWindow::CursorInClient ()
{
    CRect rect;
    GetClientRect (&rect);
    ClientToScreen (&rect);

    POINT point;
    ::GetCursorPos (&point);

    BOOL bReturn = FALSE;
    if (rect.PtInRect (point) && (WindowFromPoint (point) == this))
        bReturn = TRUE;

    return bReturn;
}

void CMainWindow::UpdateReadout (CDC* pDC)
{
    BOOL bDeleteDC = FALSE;
    if (pDC == NULL) {
        pDC = new CClientDC (this);
        bDeleteDC = TRUE;
    }

    CRect rect;
    GetClientRect (&rect);
    int nWidth = rect.Width ();
    int nHeight = rect.Height ();

    TEXTMETRIC tm;
    pDC->GetTextMetrics (&tm);
    int cx = tm.tmAveCharWidth;
    int cy = tm.tmHeight;

    rect.left = (nWidth - (cx * 16)) / 2;
    rect.right = rect.left + (cx * 16);
    rect.top = (nHeight - (cy * 2)) / 2;
    rect.bottom = rect.top + (cy * 2);
    pDC->Rectangle (rect);

    if (CursorInClient ()) {
        POINT point;
        ::GetCursorPos (&point);
        ScreenToClient (&point);
```

```
    CString strReadout;
    strReadout.Format ("%d,%d", point.x, point.y);

    pDC->DrawText (strReadout, &rect, DT_CENTER | DT_VCENTER |
        DT_SINGLELINE);
}


if (bDeleteDC)
    delete pDC;
}
```

IdleDemo's solution is to hook the *OnIdle* function and use it to erase the readout when the cursor leaves the window. The IdleDemo application displays an *x* and *y* cursor-coordinate readout in its client area, as Figure 7-6 illustrates. (We won't get to status bars until Chapter 11, so it's a little early to use a real status bar.) IdleDemo updates the readout when the mouse moves or the window needs repainting by calling *CMainWindow::UpdateReadout*. It also includes an *OnIdle* function that erases the cursor-coordinate numbers when the mouse leaves the client area. When called with an *lCount* value greater than or equal to 2, *CMyApp::OnIdle* calls *CMainWindow::CursorInClient* to determine where the cursor is located. If the return value is non-zero, which means that the cursor is inside the client area, *OnIdle* returns TRUE so that the framework will call it again later. But if *CursorInClient* returns FALSE, *OnIdle* calls *UpdateReadout* to blank the cursor coordinates now that the cursor is no longer in the window. *OnIdle* then returns FALSE so that it won't be called again until the application exits and reenters the idle state.

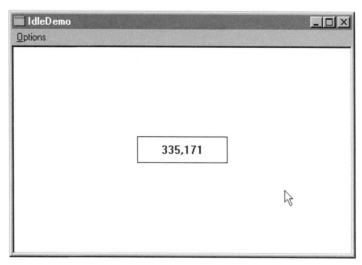

Figure 7-6. *The IdleDemo window.*

Note that IdleDemo's *OnIdle* function tests the cursor position not when *lCount* equals 2, but when *lCount* equals 2 *or higher*. WM_MOUSEMOVE is one of the few messages that doesn't reset *lCount* to 0, so if the line that tests *lCount* were written like this

```
if (lCount == 2)
```

instead of like this

```
if (lCount >= 2)
```

OnIdle would sometimes fail to reset the coordinate display.

When called upon to determine whether the cursor is in the window's client area, *CMainWindow::CursorInClient* performs a pair of tests. First it initializes a *CRect* object with a rectangle describing the client area, converts the rectangle from client coordinates to screen coordinates, gets the current cursor position (in screen coordinates) with *::GetCursorPos*, and uses *CRect::PtInRect* to see if the point is inside the rectangle. If the window were guaranteed to be running in the foreground, no further testing would be required. But since *OnIdle* might be called while IdleDemo is running in the background, *CursorInClient* must also make sure that if *PtInRect* answers in the affirmative, the point in the client area that corresponds to the cursor position isn't obscured by another window. Therefore, it calls *CWnd::Window-FromPoint* to get a *CWnd* pointer identifying the window under the cursor and compares the pointer to the *this* pointer representing its own window. Both tests are performed in a single *if* statement:

```
if (rect.PtInRect (point) && (WindowFromPoint (point) == this))
    // It's a match!
```

Only if both tests prove positive is it safe to conclude that the cursor is in the window's client area. The use of *WindowFromPoint* prevents *CursorInClient* from being fooled if the cursor is moved from the IdleDemo window to an overlapping window belonging to another application.

In Chapter 14, we'll learn about another way to perform low-priority background tasks that involves secondary threads of execution. Threads aren't the perfect solution to every multiprocessing woe because they're not supported in 16-bit Windows and multithreaded apps are notoriously difficult to write and debug. Besides the relative simplicity of its implementation, one of the primary advantages of using MFC's *OnIdle* mechanism is that if your application is targeted for both 16- and 32-bit Windows, the same code will work on both platforms.

Part II

The Document/ View Architecture

Chapter 8

Documents, Views, and the Single Document Interface

In the early days of MFC, applications were architected in very much the same style as the sample programs in Part I of this book. In MFC 1.0, an application had two principal components: an application object representing the application itself and a window object representing the application's window. The application object's primary duty was to create a window, and the window in turn processed messages. Other than the fact that it provided general-purpose classes such as *CString* and *CTime* to represent objects unrelated to Windows, MFC was little more than a thin wrapper around the Windows API that grafted an object-oriented interface onto windows, dialog boxes, device contexts, and other objects already present in Windows in one form or another.

MFC 2.0 changed the way Windows applications are written by introducing the document/view architecture. In a document/view application, the application's data is represented by a document object and views of that data are represented by one or more view objects. The document and view objects work together to process the user's input and draw textual and graphical representations of the resulting data. MFC's *CDocument* class is the base class for document objects, and the *CView* class and its derivatives are base classes for view objects. The application's main window, whose behavior is modeled in MFC's *CFrameWnd* and *CMDIFrameWnd* classes, is no longer the focal point for message processing but serves primarily as a container for views, toolbars, status bars, and other objects.

A programming model that separates documents from their views provides many benefits, not the least of which is that it more clearly defines the division of labor among software components and results in a higher degree of object modularity. But the more compelling reason to take advantage of MFC's document/view architecture is that it simplifies development. Code to perform routine chores such as prompting the user to save unsaved data before a document is closed is provided for you by the framework. So is code to transform documents into OLE containers, to save documents to disk and read them back, to simplify printing, and to do much more.

MFC supports two types of document/view applications. *Single document interface* (SDI) applications support just one open document at a time. *Multiple document interface* (MDI) applications permit the user to have two or more documents open concurrently. The Windows 95 WordPad applet is an SDI application; Word for Windows and Excel are MDI applications. The framework hides many of the differences between the two programming models so that writing an MDI application is no more difficult than writing an SDI application, but developers are discouraged from using the multiple document interface in Windows 95 because the SDI model promotes a more document-centric user interface. If the user is to edit two documents simultaneously, Microsoft would prefer that each document be displayed in a separate instance of your application. This chapter therefore examines the document/view architecture with a decided emphasis on the single document interface. Most of what you'll learn here, however, applies to MDI applications, too, and for completeness we'll examine the multiple document interface as well as methods for supporting multiple views of documents in SDI applications in the next chapter.

DOCUMENT/VIEW FUNDAMENTALS

Let's begin our exploration of the document/view architecture with a conceptual look at the various objects involved and the relationships they share with one another. Figure 8-1 shows a schematic representation of an SDI document/view application. The frame window is the application's top-level window. The top-level window is normally a WS_OVERLAPPEDWINDOW-style window with a resizing border, a caption bar, a system menu, and minimize, maximize, and close buttons. The view is a

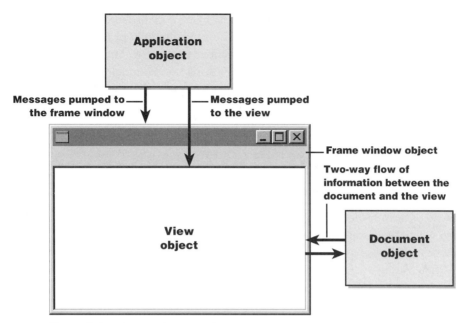

Figure 8-1 . *The SDI document/view architecture.*

child window sized to fit the frame window so that it becomes, for all practical purposes, the client area of its parent. When the frame window is resized, the view is resized automatically. The application's data is stored in the document object, a visible representation of which appears in the view. For an SDI application, the frame window class is derived from *CFrameWnd*, the document class is derived from *CDocument*, and the view class is derived from *CView* or a related class such as *CScrollView*.

The arrows in the diagram represent directions of data flow. The application object pumps messages to the frame window and to the view, and the frame window routes some of the messages it receives among the other objects in the application so that they, too, can have a crack at processing them. The view object translates mouse and keyboard input into commands that operate on the data in the document object, and the document object communicates information about the document's content to the view so that the view can render images of the data. The interaction among objects is complex, but you'll find the big picture easier to grasp after you've learned more about the role each object plays in a program's operation and have written a document/view application or two of your own.

The architecture depicted in Figure 8-1 has very real implications for the design and operation of an application program. In an MFC 1.0–style application, a program's data is often stored in member variables assigned to the frame window class. The program draws "views" of that data by accessing the member variables directly and using

GDI functions encapsulated in the *CDC* class to draw in the frame window's client area. The document/view architecture enforces a more modular program design by encapsulating data in a stand-alone document object and providing a view object for the program's screen output. A document/view application never grabs a client-area device context for its frame window and draws into it; instead, it draws into the view. It *looks* as if the drawing is being done in the frame window, but in reality all output goes to the view. You can have a program draw into the frame window if you want to, but you won't see the output because the drawable part of an SDI frame window is completely obscured by the view.

The *InitInstance* Function Revisited

One of the most interesting aspects of an SDI document/view application is the way in which the frame window, document, and view objects are created. If you look at the *InitInstance* function for an SDI application class generated by the Visual C++ AppWizard, you'll see something like this:

```
CSingleDocTemplate* pDocTemplate;
pDocTemplate = new CSingleDocTemplate (
    IDR_MAINFRAME,
    RUNTIME_CLASS (CMyDoc),
    RUNTIME_CLASS (CMainFrame),
    RUNTIME_CLASS (CMyView)
);
AddDocTemplate (pDocTemplate);

CCommandLineInfo cmdInfo;
ParseCommandLine (cmdInfo);

if (!ProcessShellCommand (cmdInfo))
    return FALSE;

return TRUE;
```

This code contains nothing even remotely similar to the startup code used in the sample programs in Part I of this book. Let's look more closely at the AppWizard version of *InitInstance* to see what it takes to get a document/view application up and running.

To begin with, the statements

```
CSingleDocTemplate* pDocTemplate;
pDocTemplate = new CSingleDocTemplate (
    IDR_MAINFRAME,
    RUNTIME_CLASS (CMyDoc),
    RUNTIME_CLASS (CMainFrame),
    RUNTIME_CLASS (CMyView)
);
```

create an SDI document template from MFC's *CSingleDocTemplate* class. The document template identifies the document class used to represent the application's documents, the frame window class that encloses views of the documents, and the view class used to draw visual representations of document data. The document template also stores a resource ID the framework uses to load menus, accelerators, and other resources that shape the user interface for a particular document type. IDR_MAIN-FRAME is the resource ID AppWizard uses, but you can use any nonzero integer ID you like. MFC's RUNTIME_CLASS macro returns a pointer to a *CRuntimeClass* structure for the specified class, which enables the framework to create objects of that class at run-time.

After the document template is created, the statement

```
AddDocTemplate (pDocTemplate);
```

adds it to the list of document templates maintained by the application object. Each template registered in this way defines one document type the application supports. SDI applications register just one document type, but MDI applications can register several types.

The statements

```
CCommandLineInfo cmdInfo;
ParseCommandLine (cmdInfo);
```

use *CWinApp::ParseCommandLine* to initialize a *CCommandLineInfo* object with values reflecting the parameters entered on the command line, which often include a document file name. The statements

```
if (!ProcessShellCommand (cmdInfo))
    return FALSE;
```

"process" the command line parameters. Among other things, *ProcessShellCommand* calls *CWinApp::OnFileNew* to start the application with an empty document if no file name was entered on the command line, or *CWinApp::OpenDocumentFile* to start the application and load a document if a document name was specified. It's during this phase of the program's execution that the framework creates the document, frame window, and view objects using the information stored in the document template. *ProcessShellCommand* returns TRUE if the initialization succeeded and FALSE if it did not. A FALSE return from *ProcessShellCommand* causes *InitInstance* to return FALSE also, which shuts down the application.

After the application is started and the document, frame window, and view objects are created, the message loop kicks in and the application begins to retrieve and process messages. Unlike MFC 1.0–type applications, which typically map all messages to member functions of the frame window class, document/view applications divide message processing among the application, document, view objects, and frame window. The framework does a lot of work in the background to make this division of labor possible. In Windows, only windows can receive messages, so the framework implements a sophisticated command-routing mechanism that sends command and update messages from menus and controls from one object to another in a predefined order until one of the objects processes the message or the message is passed to *::DefWindowProc* for default processing. When we look at command routing in action later in this chapter, it will become apparent to you why command routing is a powerful feature of the framework whose absence would severely inhibit the usefulness of the document/view architecture.

The Document Object

In a document/view application, data is stored in a document object of a class derived from *CDocument*. The term "document" is somewhat misleading because it stirs up visions of word processors and spreadsheet programs and other types of applications that deal with what we traditionally think of as documents. In reality, the "document" part of the document/view architecture is much more general than that. A document can be almost anything, from a deck of cards in a poker simulation to an online connection with a remote data source. The "document" in "document/view" refers to an abstract representation of a program's data that draws a clear boundary between how the data is stored and how it is presented to the user (the "view"). Typically, the document object provides public member functions that other objects (such as views connected to the document) can use to query and edit the document's data. All handling of the data is performed by the document object itself.

A document's data is usually stored in member variables belonging to the derived document class. The Scribble tutorial supplied with Visual C++ exposes its data directly to other objects by declaring it public, but stricter encapsulation is achieved by making document data private and providing public member functions for accessing it. The document object in a text editing program, for example, might store characters in a *CByteArray* object and provide *AddChar* and *RemoveChar* functions so that the view can convert the mouse and keyboard messages it receives into commands to add and remove characters. Other functions, such as *AddLine* and *DeleteLine*, could further enrich the interface between the document object and the views connected to it.

A derived document class inherits a number of important member functions from *CDocument*, a few of which are shown in the table on the facing page. *SetModifiedFlag* should be called whenever the document's data is modified. This function sets a flag inside the document object that tells the framework the document contains unsaved data. You can determine yourself whether a document contains unsaved data by calling the document's *IsModified* function. *GetTitle* and *GetPathName* retrieve the document's file name and the full path to the file. Both functions return a null *CString* object if the document has yet to be assigned a file name.

KEY *CDOCUMENT* MEMBER FUNCTIONS

Function	Description
GetFirstViewPosition	Returns a POSITION value that can be passed to *GetNextView* to enumerate the document's views.
GetNextView	Returns a *CView* pointer to the next view in the list of views associated with this document.
GetPathName	Retrieves the document's file name and path—for example, "C:\Documents\Personal\MyFile.doc." Returns a null string if the document has not been named.
GetTitle	Retrieves the document's title—for example, "MyFile." Returns a null string if the document has not been named.
IsModified	Returns a nonzero value if the document contains unsaved data, or 0 if it does not.
SetModifiedFlag	Sets or clears the document's modified flag, which indicates whether the document contains unsaved data.
UpdateAllViews	Updates all views associated with the document by calling each view's *OnUpdate* function.

Three of the *CDocument* functions shown in the table above allow the document object to interact with the view object (or objects) associated with it. *UpdateAllViews* commands all the views attached to the document to update themselves by calling each view's *OnUpdate* function. In an SDI application with just one view, *UpdateAllViews* frequently isn't used because the single view often updates itself in response to user input either before or after updating the document's data. But in a multiple view application, *UpdateAllViews* is called whenever the document is modified to keep all the different views in sync. A document object can enumerate its views and communicate with each view individually by using *GetFirstViewPosition* and *GetNextView* to walk the list of views. The following code fragment mimics the action of *UpdateAllViews* by calling each view's *OnUpdate* function:

```
POSITION pos = GetFirstViewPosition ();
while (pos != NULL)
    GetNextView (pos)->OnUpdate (NULL, 0, NULL);
```

Of course, it's easier just to call *UpdateAllViews* unless you want to vary the *OnUpdate* parameters passed to different views or skip certain views altogether.

The *CDocument* class also includes several virtual functions that can be overridden to customize a document's behavior. Some are almost always overridden in a derived document class. The four most commonly used overridables are shown in the table on the next page.

KEY *CDOCUMENT* OVERRIDABLES

Function	Description
OnNewDocument	Called by the framework when a new document is created. Override to initialize the document object before a new document is created.
OnOpenDocument	Called by the framework when a document is loaded from disk. Override to initialize the unserialized data members of the document object before a new document is loaded.
DeleteContents	Called by the framework to delete the document's contents. Override to free memory and other resources allocated to the document before it is closed.
Serialize	Called by the framework to serialize the document to or from a file. Override to provide document-specific serialization code so that your documents can be loaded and saved.

OnNewDocument is used to initialize each new document that is created, while *OnOpenDocument* is used to initialize the unserialized data members of the document object when a new document is loaded from disk. In an SDI application, the document object is constructed just once and reused each time a document is created or opened. Since the object's constructor is executed only one time no matter how many documents are opened and closed, an SDI application should perform one-time initializations in the document's constructor and put the initialization code for each new document in *OnNewDocument* and *OnOpenDocument*.

Before a new document is created or opened, the framework calls the document's virtual *DeleteContents* function to delete the document's existing data. Therefore, an SDI application should override *CDocument::DeleteContents* and take the opportunity to free any resources allocated to the document and perform other necessary cleanup chores in preparation for reusing the document object. MDI applications generally follow this model also, although MDI document objects differ from SDI document objects in that they are individually created and destroyed as documents are opened and closed by the user.

When you override *OnNewDocument* and *OnOpenDocument*, it's important to call the base class versions of those functions, too. Otherwise, *DeleteContents* won't be called when a new document is created or loaded and other important initialization tasks carried out by the framework won't be performed. In addition to calling *DeleteContents*, for example, the *CDocument* version of *OnOpenDocument* displays an Open dialog box to get a file name from the user and calls the document object's *Serialize* function to serialize the document from disk. *OnNewDocument* and *OnOpenDocument* overrides should call the base class implementations first and refrain from doing anything else if the base class returns FALSE, and they should return TRUE to indicate successful completion, as demonstrated here:

```
BOOL CMyDoc::OnNewDocument ()
{
    if (!CDocument::OnNewDocument ())
        return FALSE;
    // Initialize the document object as if it were new
    return TRUE;
}

BOOL CMyDoc::OnOpenDocument (LPCTSTR lpszPathName)
{
    if (!CDocument::OnOpenDocument (lpszPathName))
        return FALSE;
    // Initialize members of the document object that are not
    // initialized when the document is serialized from disk
    return TRUE;
}
```

When a document is opened or saved, the framework calls the document object's *Serialize* function to serialize the document's data. You write the *Serialize* function to stream the document data in and out; the framework does everything else, including opening the file for reading or writing and providing a *CArchive* object to insulate you from the vagaries of physical disk I/O. For a review of *CArchive* objects and their role in the serialization process, see Chapter 6.

Other *CDocument* overridables that aren't used as often but that can be useful under certain circumstances include *OnCloseDocument*, which is called when a document is closed; *OnSaveDocument*, which is called when a document is saved; *SaveModified*, which is called before a document containing unsaved data is closed to ask the user whether changes should be saved; and *ReportSaveLoadException*, which is called when an error occurs during serialization. There are others, but for the most part they constitute advanced overridables you'll rarely find occasion to use.

The View Object

While the sole purpose of a document object is to store an application's data, view objects exist for two purposes: to render visual representations of a document's data on the screen and to translate the user's input—particularly mouse and keyboard messages, which are not routed to document objects as command messages are—into commands that operate on the document's data. Thus, documents and views are tightly interrelated, and the information exchanged between the two flows in both directions.

A document object can have any number of views associated with it, but a view always belongs to just one document. The framework stores a pointer to the associated document object in a view's *m_pDocument* data member and exposes that pointer through the view's *GetDocument* member function. Just as a document object can identify its views using *CDocument::GetFirstViewPosition* and *CDocument::GetNextView*, a view can identify its document by calling *GetDocument*. When AppWizard generates the source code for a view class, it overrides the base class's *GetDocument* function with one that casts *m_pDocument* to the appropriate document type and returns the result. This override allows type-safe access of the document object and eliminates the need for an explicit cast each time *GetDocument* is called.

MFC's *CView* class defines the basic properties of a view, and derived view classes add functionality to the basic definition of a view. The derived view classes MFC provides are shown in the table below. Some, such as *CEditView*, are designed to be used directly. Others, such as *CScrollView*, are abstract base classes useful only for deriving view classes of your own.

MFC DERIVED VIEW CLASSES

View Class	Description
CCtrlView	Base class for *CEditView*, *CRichEditView*, *CListView*, and *CTreeView*. Can be used to derive other views that wrap Windows controls.
CEditView	Wraps the functionality of a Windows edit control and adds print, search, and search-and-replace capabilities.
CRichEditView	Wraps the functionality of a Windows rich edit control.
CListView	Wraps the functionality of a Windows list view control.
CTreeView	Wraps the functionality of a Windows tree view control.
CScrollView	Abstract base class derived from *CView* that adds scrolling capabilities to a view. Base class for *CFormView*, *CRecordView*, and *CDaoRecordView*.
CFormView	Implements scrollable views featuring controls created from a dialog template.
CRecordView	Combines a *CFormView* object and a *CRecordSet* object to provide views of a database.
CDaoRecordView	DAO version of *CRecordView*.

Like the *CDocument* class, *CView* and its derivatives include several virtual member functions you can override to customize a view's operation. The key overridables are shown in the table on the facing page. One of the most important overridables is a pure virtual function named *OnDraw*, which is called whenever the view receives a WM_PAINT message. In non-document/view applications, WM_PAINT messages are processed by an *OnPaint* handler that uses a *CPaintDC* object to do its drawing. In a document/view application, the framework fields the WM_PAINT message and calls the view's *OnDraw* function, passing it a generic *CDC* pointer for drawing. No message mapping is necessary because *OnDraw* is virtual. The following implementation of *OnDraw* displays "Hello, MFC" in the center of the view:

```
void CMyView::OnDraw (CDC* pDC)
{
    CRect rect;
    GetClientRect (&rect);
    pDC->DrawText ("Hello, MFC", -1, rect, DT_SINGLELINE |
        DT_CENTER | DT_VCENTER);
}
```

KEY *CVIEW* OVERRIDABLES

Function	*Description*
OnDraw	Called to draw the document's data. Override to paint views of a document.
OnInitialUpdate	Called when a view is first attached to a document. Override to initialize a view of a freshly loaded or created document.
OnUpdate	Called when the document's data has changed and the view needs to be updated. Override to implement "smart" update behavior that redraws only the part of the view that needs redrawing rather than the entire view.

The fact that the view doesn't have to construct its own device context object is a minor convenience. The real reason the framework uses *OnDraw* is that the same code can be used for output to a window, for printing, and for print previewing. When a WM_PAINT message arrives, the framework passes the view a pointer to a paint DC so that output will go to the window. When a document is printed, the framework calls the same *OnDraw* function and passes it a pointer to a printer DC. Because the GDI is a device-independent graphics system, the same code can produce identical (or nearly identical) output on two different devices if it is passed two different device contexts. The framework takes advantage of this fact to make printing—usually a chore in Windows—a less laborious undertaking. In fact, printing from a document/view application is *much* easier than printing from a conventional application. You'll learn about MFC's print architecture in Chapter 10.

Two other *CView* functions you'll frequently override in derived view classes are *OnInitialUpdate* and *OnUpdate*. Views, like documents, are constructed once and then reused over and over in SDI applications. An SDI view's *OnInitialUpdate* function gets called whenever a document is opened or created. The default implementation of *OnInitialUpdate* calls *OnUpdate*, and the default implementation of *OnUpdate* in turn invalidates the view's client area to force a repaint. Use *OnInitialUpdate* to initialize data members of the view class and perform other view-related initializations on a per-document basis. In a *CScrollView*-derived class, for example, it's common for *OnInitialUpdate* to call the view's *SetScrollSizes* function to initialize scrolling parameters. It's important to call the base class version of *OnInitialUpdate* from an overridden version, or the view will not be updated when a new document is opened or created.

A view's *OnUpdate* function is called when a document's data is modified and someone—usually either the document object or one of the document's views—calls *UpdateAllViews*. You never *have* to override *OnUpdate* because the default implementation repaints the view for you. But in practice, you'll often override *OnUpdate* to optimize performance by repainting just the part of the view that needs updating rather than repainting the entire view. This is especially helpful in multiple view applications because it eliminates the unpleasant flashing effect often seen in inactive views when a document is modified in the active view and the framework's default *OnUpdate* function is used. You'll see an example of an *OnUpdate* function that optimizes a derived view class's update performance in the next chapter.

In a multiple view application, a view can determine when it is activated and deactivated by overriding the base class's *OnActivateView* function. The first parameter to *OnActivateView* is nonzero if the view is being activated and 0 if it is being deactivated. The second and third parameters are *CView* pointers identifying the views that are being activated and deactivated, respectively. If the pointers are equal, the application's frame window was activated without causing a change in the active view. View objects sometimes use this feature of the *OnActivateView* function to realize a palette. A frame window can get and set the active view with the functions *CFrameWnd::GetActiveView* and *CFrameWnd::SetActiveView*.

The Frame Window Object

So far, we've looked at the roles of application objects, document objects, and view objects in document/view applications. The application object gets the ball rolling by creating document templates describing the types of documents the application supports and displaying a window on the screen; the document stores the application's data; and the view displays the data and translates user input into operations on the document.

The object we've yet to consider is the frame window object, which defines the application's physical workspace on the screen and serves as a container for a view. An SDI application uses just one frame window—a *CFrameWnd* that serves as the application's top-level window and frames the view of the document. As you'll see in the next chapter, an MDI application uses several frame windows—a *CMDIFrameWnd* that acts as a top-level window and *CMDIChildWnd* child windows that frame views of the application's documents.

Frame windows play an important and often misunderstood role in the operation of document/view applications. Beginning MFC programmers often think of a frame window as simply a window. In fact, a frame window is an intelligent object that orchestrates much of what goes on behind the scenes in a document/view application. For example, MFC's *CFrameWnd* class provides *OnClose* and *OnQueryEndSession* handlers that make sure the user gets a chance to save unsaved changes to a document before the application terminates or Windows shuts down. *CFrameWnd* also handles the all-important task of resizing a view when the frame window is resized or other aspects of the window layout change, and it includes member functions for manipulating toolbars and status bars, identifying active documents and views, and more.

Perhaps the best way to understand the contribution the *CFrameWnd* class makes is to compare it to the more generic *CWnd* class. The *CWnd* class is basically a C++ wrapper around an ordinary window. *CFrameWnd* is derived from *CWnd* and adds all the bells and whistles a frame window needs to assume a proactive role in the execution of a document/view application.

Dynamic Object Creation

If the framework is to create document, view, and frame window objects during the course of a program's execution, the classes from which those objects are constructed must support a feature known as *dynamic creation*. MFC makes it easy to write dynamically creatable classes with its DECLARE_DYNCREATE and IMPLEMENT_DYNCREATE macros. Here's all you have to do:

1. Include a call to the DECLARE_DYNCREATE macro in the class declaration. DECLARE_DYNCREATE accepts just one parameter—the name of the dynamically creatable class.

2. Call the IMPLEMENT_DYNCREATE macro from outside the class declaration. IMPLEMENT_DYNCREATE accepts two parameters—the name of the dynamically creatable class and the name of its base class.

An object of a class that uses these macros can be created at run-time with a statement like this one:

```
RUNTIME_CLASS (CMyClass)->CreateObject ();
```

This is basically no different from using the *new* operator to create a *CMyClass* object, but it circumvents a shortcoming of the C++ language that prevents statements like these from working:

```
CString strClassName = "CMyClass";
CMyClass* ptr = new strClassName;
```

The compiler, of course, will try to construct an object from a class named "strClassName" because it doesn't realize that *strClassName* is a variable name and not a literal class name. What MFC's dynamic object creation mechanism amounts to is a means for applications to register classes in such a way that the framework can create objects of those classes.

What happens when you write a class that's dynamically creatable? The DECLARE_DYNCREATE macro adds three members to the class declaration: a static data member whose type is *CRuntimeClass*, a virtual function named *GetRuntimeClass*, and a static function named *CreateObject*. When you write

```
DECLARE_DYNAMIC (CMyClass)
```

the compiler's preprocessor outputs this:

```
public:
    static AFX_DATA CRuntimeClass classCMyClass;
    virtual CRuntimeClass* GetRuntimeClass() const;
    static CObject* PASCAL CreateObject();
```

The IMPLEMENT_DYNCREATE macro initializes the *CRuntimeClass* structure with information such as the class name, the size of objects created from the class, and the base class's address. It also provides inline code for the *GetRuntimeClass* and *CreateObject* functions. If MFC 4's IMPLEMENT_DYNCREATE macro is called like this,

```
IMPLEMENT_DYNCREATE (CMyClass, CBaseClass)
```

CreateObject is implemented like this:

```
CObject* PASCAL CMyClass::CreateObject()
    { return new CMyClass; }
```

Previous versions of MFC used a different implementation of *CreateObject* that allocated memory using the size information stored in the class's *CRuntimeClass* structure and manually initialized an object in that memory space. MFC 4's implementation of *CreateObject* is truer to the C++ language because if a dynamically creatable class overloads the *new* operator, *CreateObject* will use the overloaded operator.

More on the SDI Document Template

Earlier in this chapter, we saw an example of how an SDI document template is created from the *CSingleDocTemplate* class. The template's constructor was passed four parameters: an integer value equal to IDR_MAINFRAME and three RUNTIME_CLASS pointers. The purpose of the three RUNTIME_CLASS macros should be clear by now, so let's look more closely at the integer passed in the first parameter, which is actually a multipurpose resource ID that identifies the following four resources:

- The application icon

- The menu associated with documents of this type

- The accelerator table that goes with the menu

- A "document string" specifying the default file name extension for documents of this type and other document properties

In an SDI document/view application, the framework creates an application's top-level window by first creating a frame window object using run-time class information stored in the document template and then calling that object's *LoadFrame* function. One of the parameters *LoadFrame* accepts is a resource ID identifying the four resources listed above. Not surprisingly, the resource ID that the framework passes to *LoadFrame* is the same one supplied to the document template. *LoadFrame* creates a frame window and loads the associated menu, accelerators, and icon all in one step, but if the process is to work, you must assign all these resources the same ID. That's why the .rc file AppWizard generates for a document/view application uses the same ID for a variety of different resources.

The document string is a string resource formed from a combination of as many as seven substrings separated by "\n" characters. Each substring describes one characteristic of the frame window or document type. In left-to-right order, the substrings specify the following:

- The title that appears in the frame window's title bar. For top-level frame windows, this is usually the name of the application—for example, "Microsoft Draw." For the child window document frames used in MDI applications, this substring is normally left blank.

- The name assigned to new documents. If this substring is omitted, the default is "Untitled."

- A descriptive name for the document type that appears along with other document types in a dialog box when the user selects New from the File menu—for example, "Spreadsheet" or "Drawing." This entry is needed only in MDI applications that register two or more document types.

- A descriptive name for the document type combined with a wildcard file specification that includes the default file name extension—for example, "Drawing Files (*.drw)." This string is used in the file-type field of the Open and Save As dialog boxes.

■ The default file name extension for documents of this type—for example, ".drw."

■ A name with no spaces that identifies the document type in the registry—for example, "Draw.Document." If your application calls *CWinApp-::RegisterShellFileTypes* to register its document types, this substring becomes the default value for the HKEY_CLASSES_ROOT subkey named after the document's file name extension.

■ A descriptive name for the document type—for example, "Microsoft Draw Document." Unlike the substring preceding it in the document string, this substring can include spaces. If your application uses *CWinApp-::RegisterShellFileTypes* to register its document types, this substring is the human-readable name the Windows 95 shell displays in property sheets for documents of this type.

You don't have to supply all seven substrings when you create a document string resource; you can omit individual substrings by following an \n separator character with another \n, and you can omit trailing null substrings altogether. If you build an application with AppWizard, AppWizard creates the document string for you using information entered in the Advanced Options property sheet. The resource statements for a typical SDI document string might look like this:

```
STRINGTABLE
BEGIN
    IDR_MAINFRAME "Microsoft Draw\n\n\nDraw Files(*.drw)\n.drw\n
        Draw.Document\nMicrosoft Draw Document"
END
```

(The SDI document string must be on a single line. This string has been broken to fit on the page.) STRINGTABLE creates a string table resource (a resource consisting of one or more text strings, each identifiable by a unique resource ID) just as DIALOG creates a dialog resource and MENU creates a menu resource. When this application is started with an empty document, its frame window will have the title "Untitled - Draw." The default file name extension for documents saved by this application is ".drw," and "Drawing Files (*.drw)" will be one of the choices listed in the Files Of Type combo box of the Open and Save As dialog boxes.

After a document template is created, substrings belonging to the document string can be retrieved with MFC's *CDocTemplate::GetDocString* function. For example, the statements

```
CString strDefExt;
pDocTemplate->GetDocString (strDefExt, CDocTemplate::filterExt);
```

copy the document's default file name extension to the *CString* variable named *strDefExt*.

Registering Document Types
with the Operating System Shell

In Windows 95, double-clicking a document icon or right-clicking it and selecting Open from the document's context menu opens the document along with the application that created it. In addition, a document can be printed by selecting Print from its context menu or dragging the document icon and dropping it over a printer icon.

For these operations to work, an application must register its document types with the operating system shell, which involves writing a series of entries to the HKEY-_CLASSES_ROOT branch of the registry identifying each document type's file name extension and the commands used to open and print files with that extension. In a conventional Windows application, registration is accomplished by supplying a .reg file the user can merge into the registry or by writing the necessary entries into the registry programmatically with *::RegCreateKey*, *::RegSetValue*, and other Win32 API functions. But an MFC application can make one simple function and register every document type it supports. Calling *CWinApp::RegisterShellFileTypes* and passing it a TRUE parameter after the final call to *AddDocTemplate* in *InitInstance* forges links among the application, the documents it creates, and the Windows 95 shell. The call to *RegisterShellFileTypes* also adds a DefaultIcon entry to the registry that registers the icon stored in the application's executable file to represent document objects displayed by the shell.

A related *CWinApp* function named *EnableShellOpen* adds a nifty feature to MDI document/view applications. If an MDI application registers its document type(s) with *RegisterShellFileTypes* and *EnableShellOpen* and the user double-clicks a document icon while the application is running, the shell doesn't start a second instance of the application; instead, it sends a DDE "open" command to the existing instance and passes along the document's file name. A DDE handler built into MFC's *CDocManager* class, which manages documents on behalf of *CWinApp*, fields the message and calls *OnOpenDocument* to open the document. Thus, the document appears in a new window inside the top-level MDI frame, just as if it had been opened with the application's File-Open command. Similar DDE commands allow running application instances to fulfill print requests placed through the operating system shell. Anyone who has written DDE code before will confirm that adding support for DDE commands on your own, without the framework's help, is no picnic.

You can add drag and drop document support to a document/view application by calling the frame window's *DragAcceptFiles* function. *DragAcceptFiles* registers a window to receive WM_DROPFILES messages when it is the target of drops involving document icons dragged from shell folders or other containers in the shell's namespace. The *CFrameWnd* class provides an *OnDropFiles* handler that responds to WM_DROPFILES messages by calling the application object's *OnOpenDocument* function with the names of the files that were dropped. *DragAcceptFiles* works equally well for SDI and MDI applications. It's usually called from *InitInstance* with a statement like this one:

```
m_pMainWnd->DragAcceptFiles ();
```

In an SDI application, it's important to call *DragAcceptFiles* after *ProcessShellCommand* because the frame window doesn't exist before *ProcessShellCommand* is called.

Command Routing

One of the most remarkable features of the document/view architecture is that an application can handle *command messages*—MFC's term for the WM_COMMAND and WM_NOTIFY messages generated when an item is selected from a menu, a keyboard accelerator is pressed, or a control sends a notification to its parent—almost anywhere. The frame window is the recipient of most command messages, but command messages can be handled in the view object, the document object, or even the application object if you simply include entries for the messages you want the class to handle in the class's message map. Command routing lets you handle command messages in the classes in which it makes sense to rather than handle them all in the frame window class. Update commands for menu items, toolbar buttons, and other UI objects are also subject to command routing, so you can put ON_UPDATE_COMMAND_UI handlers in nonframe window classes as well.

The mechanism that makes command routing work is hidden deep down in the bowels of the framework. When a frame window receives a WM_COMMAND or WM_NOTIFY message, it calls the virtual *OnCmdMsg* function featured in all *CCmdTarget*-derived classes to begin the routing process. The *CFrameWnd* implementation of *OnCmdMsg* looks like this:

```
BOOL CFrameWnd::OnCmdMsg(...)
{
    // Pump through current view FIRST.
    CView* pView = GetActiveView();
    if (pView != NULL && pView->OnCmdMsg(...))
        return TRUE;

    // Then pump through frame.
    if (CWnd::OnCmdMsg(...))
        return TRUE;

    // Last but not least, pump through application.
    CWinApp* pApp = AfxGetApp();
    if (pApp != NULL && pApp->OnCmdMsg(...))
        return TRUE;

    return FALSE;
}
```

CFrameWnd::OnCmdMsg first routes the message to the active view by calling the view's *OnCmdMsg* function. If *pView->OnCmdMsg* returns 0 indicating that the view did not process the message (that is, that the view's message map does not contain an entry for this particular message), the frame window tries to handle the message itself by calling *CWnd::OnCmdMsg*. If that, too, fails, the frame window then tries the application object. Ultimately, if none of the objects processes the message, *CFrameWnd::OnCmdMsg* returns FALSE and the framework passes the message to *::DefWindowProc* for default processing.

This explains how a command message received by a frame window gets routed to the active view and the application object, but what about the document object? When *CFrameWnd::OnCmdMsg* calls the active view's *OnCmdMsg* function, the view first tries to handle the message itself. If it doesn't have a handler for the message, the view then calls the document's *OnCmdMsg* function. If the document can't handle the message, it passes it up the ladder to the document template. Figure 8-2 illustrates the entire path a command message travels when it is delivered to an SDI frame window. The active view gets first crack at the message, followed by the document associated with that view, the document template, the frame window itself, and finally the application object. The routing stops if any object along the way processes the message, but it continues all the way up to *::DefWindowProc* if none of the objects' message maps contains an entry for the message. Routing is much the same for command messages delivered to MDI frame windows, with the framework making sure that all the relevant objects, including the child window frame that surrounds the active MDI view, get the opportunity to weigh in.

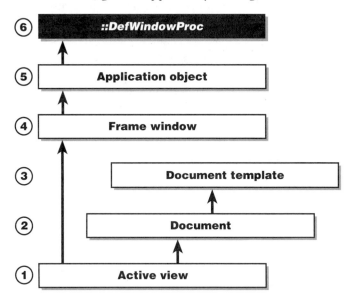

Figure 8-2. *Routing of command messages sent to an SDI frame window.*

The value of command routing becomes apparent when you look at how a typical document/view application handles commands from menus, accelerators, and toolbar buttons. By convention, the File-New, File-Open, and File-Exit commands are mapped to the application object, where *CWinApp* provides *OnFileNew*, *OnFileOpen*, and *OnAppExit* member functions for handling them. File-Save and File-Save As are normally mapped to the document object, which provides the default implementations *CDocument::OnFileSave* and *CDocument::OnFileSaveAs*. Commands to show and hide toolbars and status bars are handled by the frame window using *CFrameWnd* member functions, and most other commands are handled by either the document or the view.

An important point to keep in mind as you consider where to put your message handlers is that only command messages and UI updates are subject to routing. "Standard" Windows messages such as WM_CHAR, WM_LBUTTONDOWN, WM_CREATE, and WM_SIZE must be handled by the window that receives the message. Mouse and keyboard messages generally go to the view, and most other messages go to the frame window. Document objects and application objects never receive noncommand messages.

Predefined Command IDs and Default Command Implementations

When you write a document/view application, you typically don't write the handlers for all the menu commands yourself. *CWinApp*, *CDocument*, *CFrameWnd*, and other MFC classes provide default handlers for common menu commands such as File-Open and File-Save. In addition, the framework provides an assortment of standard menu item command IDs such as ID_FILE_OPEN and ID_FILE_SAVE, many of which are "prewired" into the message maps of classes that use them.

The table below lists the most commonly used predefined command IDs and their associated command handlers. The Prewired? column indicates whether the handler is called automatically (Yes) or called only if the programmer provides a corresponding entry in the class's message map (No). A prewired handler is enabled by your assigning the corresponding ID to a menu item; a handler that is not prewired is enabled only if you link the menu item ID to the function with a message map entry. For example, default implementations of the File-New and File-Open commands are found in *CWinApp*'s *OnFileNew* and *OnFileOpen* functions, but neither function is connected to the application unless you provide an ON_COMMAND message map entry for it. (If you allow AppWizard to create the skeleton of an SDI or MDI application, it will write ON_COMMAND entries for *OnFileNew*, *OnFileOpen*, and other default command handlers for you.) *CWinApp::OnAppExit*, on the other hand, works all by itself and requires no message map entry. All you have to do is assign the File-Exit menu item the ID ID_APP_EXIT, and *OnAppExit* will magically be called to end the application when the user selects Exit from the File menu. Why? Because *CWinApp*'s message map contains an

```
ON_COMMAND (ID_APP_EXIT, OnAppExit)
```

entry, and message maps, like other class members, are passed on by inheritance.

PREDEFINED COMMAND IDS AND COMMAND HANDLERS

Command ID	*Menu Item*	*Default Handler*	*Prewired?*
File menu			
ID_FILE_NEW	New	*CWinApp::OnFileNew*	No
ID_FILE_OPEN	Open	*CWinApp::OnFileOpen*	No
ID_FILE_SAVE	Save	*CDocument::OnFileSave*	Yes
ID_FILE_SAVE_AS	Save As	*CDocument::OnFileSaveAs*	Yes
ID_FILE_PAGE_SETUP	Page Setup	None	N/A
ID_FILE_PRINT_SETUP	Print Setup	*CWinApp::OnFilePrintSetup*	No
ID_FILE_PRINT	Print	*CView::OnFilePrint*	No
ID_FILE_PRINT_PREVIEW	Print Preview	*CView::OnFilePrintPreview*	No
ID_FILE_SEND_MAIL	Send Mail	*CDocument::OnFileSendMail*	
ID_FILE_MRU_FILE1– ID_FILE_MRU_FILE16	N/A	*CWinApp::OnOpenRecentFile*	Yes
ID_APP_EXIT	Exit	*CWinApp::OnAppExit*	Yes
Edit menu			
ID_EDIT_CLEAR	Clear	None	N/A
ID_EDIT_CLEAR_ALL	Clear All	None	N/A
ID_EDIT_CUT	Cut	None	N/A
ID_EDIT_COPY	Copy	None	N/A
ID_EDIT_PASTE	Paste	None	N/A
ID_EDIT_PASTE_LINK	Paste Link	None	N/A
ID_EDIT_PASTE_SPECIAL	Paste Special	None	N/A
ID_EDIT_FIND	Find	None	N/A
ID_EDIT_REPLACE	Replace	None	N/A
ID_EDIT_UNDO	Undo	None	N/A
ID_EDIT_REDO	Redo	None	N/A
ID_EDIT_REPEAT	Repeat	None	N/A
ID_EDIT_SELECT_ALL	Select All	None	N/A
View menu			
ID_VIEW_TOOLBAR	Toolbar	*CFrameWnd::OnBarCheck*	Yes
ID_VIEW_STATUS_BAR	Status Bar	*CFrameWnd::OnBarCheck*	Yes

(continued)

continued

Command ID	Menu Item	Default Handler	Prewired?
Window menu (MDI applications only)			
ID_WINDOW_NEW	New Window	*CMDIFrameWnd::OnWindowNew*	Yes
ID_WINDOW_ARRANGE	Arrange All	*CMDIFrameWnd::OnMDIWindowCmd*	Yes
ID_WINDOW_CASCADE	Cascade	*CMDIFrameWnd::OnMDIWindowCmd*	Yes
ID_WINDOW_TILE_HORZ	Tile Horizontal	*CMDIFrameWnd::OnMDIWindowCmd*	Yes
ID_WINDOW_TILE_VERT	Tile Vertical	*CMDIFrameWnd::OnMDIWindowCmd*	Yes
Help menu			
ID_APP_ABOUT	About *AppName*	None	N/A

The framework also provides ON_UPDATE_COMMAND_UI handlers for some commands, including:

- *CFrameWnd::OnUpdateControlBarMenu* for the ID_VIEW_TOOLBAR and ID_VIEW_STATUS_BAR commands

- *CMDIFrameWnd::OnUpdateMDIWindowCmd* for the ID_WINDOW-_ARRANGE, ID_WINDOW_CASCADE, ID_WINDOW_TILE_HORZ, ID-_WINDOW_TILE_VERT, and ID_WINDOW_NEW commands

- *CDocument::OnUpdateFileSendMail* for the ID_FILE_SEND_MAIL command

MFC's *CEditView* and *CRichEditView* classes include command handlers for some of the items in the Edit menu, but other views must provide their own.

You don't have to use the predefined command IDs or command handlers the framework provides. You can always strike out on your own and define your own command IDs, perhaps supplying message map entries to correlate your command IDs with default command handlers, or you can even replace the default command handlers with handlers of your own. In short, you can use as much or as little of the framework's support as you want to. But the more you can lean on the framework, the less code you'll have to write yourself.

YOUR FIRST DOCUMENT/VIEW APPLICATION

Now that you have an idea of what the document/view architecture is all about and a general feel for some of the implementation details, let's write a document/view application. If some of the concepts discussed in the first part of this chapter seem a little abstract, seeing the code for a working document/view application should help bring things into focus. Our application, Paint4, is an SDI document/view version of the paint program featured in Chapters 4 and 6. In Chapter 9, we'll add a splitter window that provides up to four different views of the same drawing, and then we'll modify the application again so that it supports multiple open documents. Happily, and thanks to power of the document/view architecture, neither modification will add substantially to the code's complexity. In fact, you'll probably be surprised at how easily Paint4 is converted into an MDI application and modified to include splitter windows like those seen in Visual C++ and other contemporary Windows applications.

The Paint4 Application

Figure 8-3 contains the source code for Paint4. One of the first things to notice about Paint4 is that it's broken into more files than our earlier applications have been—one .h file and one .cpp file for each class, plus the usual Resource.h file containing #*defines* and the .rc file containing resource statements. Up until now, we've used only one .h file and one .cpp file per application. From this point on, we'll follow the usual C++ convention of separating the classes into individual source code files. A class defined in its own .h and .cpp file stands on its own and can be reused in other applications without bringing other classes into the mix. And such source code modularity is a boon to productivity when you're working on large software projects: if you make a modification to one class, you can recompile the class and relink the application without having to recompile all the other classes, too.

Resource.h

```
//****************************************************************************
//
//  Resource.h
//
//****************************************************************************

#define IDR_MAINFRAME           100
#define IDR_CONTEXTMENU         101

#define IDD_ABOUTDLG            110
#define IDC_ICONRECT            111

#define ID_WIDTH_VTHIN          120
#define ID_WIDTH_THIN           121
#define ID_WIDTH_MEDIUM         122
#define ID_WIDTH_THICK          123
#define ID_WIDTH_VTHICK         124

#define ID_COLOR_BLACK          130
#define ID_COLOR_BLUE           131
```

Figure 8-3. *The Paint4 program.* *(continued)*

Resource.h *continued*

```
#define ID_COLOR_GREEN          132
#define ID_COLOR_CYAN           133
#define ID_COLOR_RED            134
#define ID_COLOR_MAGENTA        135
#define ID_COLOR_YELLOW         136
#define ID_COLOR_WHITE          137
```

Paint4.rc

```
//*****************************************************************************
//
//  Paint4.rc
//
//*****************************************************************************

#include <afxres.h>
#include "Resource.h"

IDR_MAINFRAME ICON Paint.ico

IDR_MAINFRAME MENU
BEGIN
    POPUP "&File" {
        MENUITEM "&New\tCtrl+N",            ID_FILE_NEW
        MENUITEM "&Open...\tCtrl+O",        ID_FILE_OPEN
        MENUITEM "&Save\tCtrl+S",           ID_FILE_SAVE
        MENUITEM "Save &As...\tCtrl+A",     ID_FILE_SAVE_AS
        MENUITEM SEPARATOR
        MENUITEM "Sen&d...",                ID_FILE_SEND_MAIL
        MENUITEM SEPARATOR
        MENUITEM "Recent File",             ID_FILE_MRU_FILE1
        MENUITEM SEPARATOR
        MENUITEM "E&xit",                   ID_APP_EXIT
    }
    POPUP "&Width" {
        MENUITEM "&Very Thin\tF5",          ID_WIDTH_VTHIN
        MENUITEM "Thi&n\tF6",               ID_WIDTH_THIN
        MENUITEM "&Medium\tF7",             ID_WIDTH_MEDIUM
        MENUITEM "Thic&k\tF8",              ID_WIDTH_THICK
        MENUITEM "Very &Thick\tF9",         ID_WIDTH_VTHICK
    }
    POPUP "&Color" {
        MENUITEM "",                        ID_COLOR_BLACK
        MENUITEM "",                        ID_COLOR_BLUE
```

```
        MENUITEM "",                        ID_COLOR_GREEN
        MENUITEM "",                        ID_COLOR_CYAN
        MENUITEM "",                        ID_COLOR_RED
        MENUITEM "",                        ID_COLOR_MAGENTA
        MENUITEM "",                        ID_COLOR_YELLOW
        MENUITEM "",                        ID_COLOR_WHITE
    }
    POPUP "&Help" {
        MENUITEM "&About Paint4...",        ID_APP_ABOUT
    }
END

IDR_MAINFRAME ACCELERATORS
BEGIN
    "N",    ID_FILE_NEW,        VIRTKEY,    CONTROL
    "O",    ID_FILE_OPEN,       VIRTKEY,    CONTROL
    "S",    ID_FILE_SAVE,       VIRTKEY,    CONTROL
    "A",    ID_FILE_SAVE_AS,    VIRTKEY,    CONTROL

    VK_F5,  ID_WIDTH_VTHIN,     VIRTKEY
    VK_F6,  ID_WIDTH_THIN,      VIRTKEY
    VK_F7,  ID_WIDTH_MEDIUM,    VIRTKEY
    VK_F8,  ID_WIDTH_THICK,     VIRTKEY
    VK_F9,  ID_WIDTH_VTHICK,    VIRTKEY

    "B",    ID_COLOR_BLACK,     VIRTKEY,    CONTROL
    "L",    ID_COLOR_BLUE,      VIRTKEY,    CONTROL
    "G",    ID_COLOR_GREEN,     VIRTKEY,    CONTROL
    "C",    ID_COLOR_CYAN,      VIRTKEY,    CONTROL
    "R",    ID_COLOR_RED,       VIRTKEY,    CONTROL
    "M",    ID_COLOR_MAGENTA,   VIRTKEY,    CONTROL
    "Y",    ID_COLOR_YELLOW,    VIRTKEY,    CONTROL
    "W",    ID_COLOR_WHITE,     VIRTKEY,    CONTROL
END

IDR_CONTEXTMENU MENU
BEGIN
    POPUP "" {
        POPUP "&Width" {
            MENUITEM "&Very Thin",          ID_WIDTH_VTHIN
            MENUITEM "&Thin",               ID_WIDTH_THIN
            MENUITEM "&Medium",             ID_WIDTH_MEDIUM
            MENUITEM "Thi&ck",              ID_WIDTH_THICK
            MENUITEM "Very Thic&k",         ID_WIDTH_VTHICK
        }
        POPUP "&Color" {
```

(continued)

Paint4.rc *continued*

```
            MENUITEM "",                    ID_COLOR_BLACK
            MENUITEM "",                    ID_COLOR_BLUE
            MENUITEM "",                    ID_COLOR_GREEN
            MENUITEM "",                    ID_COLOR_CYAN
            MENUITEM "",                    ID_COLOR_RED
            MENUITEM "",                    ID_COLOR_MAGENTA
            MENUITEM "",                    ID_COLOR_YELLOW
            MENUITEM "",                    ID_COLOR_WHITE
        }
    }
END


STRINGTABLE
BEGIN
    IDR_MAINFRAME "Paint4\n\n\nPaint Files (*.pnt)\n.pnt\nPaint.Document\nPaint Document"
END


IDD_ABOUTDLG DIALOG 0, 0, 256, 98
STYLE DS_MODALFRAME ¦ DS_CENTER ¦ WS_POPUP ¦ WS_VISIBLE ¦ WS_CAPTION ¦
    WS_SYSMENU
CAPTION "About Paint4"
FONT 8, "MS Sans Serif"
BEGIN
    LTEXT           "", IDC_ICONRECT, 14, 12, 80, 74
    LTEXT           "Paint4 Version 1.0", -1, 108, 12, 136, 8
    LTEXT           "From the book", -1, 108, 32, 136, 8
    LTEXT           """Programming Windows 95 with MFC""", -1,
                    108, 42, 136, 8
    LTEXT           "Copyright © 1996 by Jeff Prosise", -1,
                    108, 52, 136, 8
    DEFPUSHBUTTON   "OK", IDOK, 108, 72, 50, 14
END
```

Paint4.h

```
//*****************************************************************
//
// Paint4.h
//
//*****************************************************************

class CPaintApp : public CWinApp
{
public:
    virtual BOOL InitInstance ();
```

```
protected:
    afx_msg void OnAppAbout ();
    DECLARE_MESSAGE_MAP ()
};
```

Paint4.cpp

```
//*****************************************************************************
//
//  Paint4.cpp
//
//*****************************************************************************

#include <afxwin.h>
#include "Resource.h"
#include "CLine.h"
#include "Paint4.h"
#include "MainFrame.h"
#include "Paint4Doc.h"
#include "Paint4View.h"
#include "AboutDlg.h"

CPaintApp myApp;

BEGIN_MESSAGE_MAP (CPaintApp, CWinApp)
    ON_COMMAND (ID_FILE_NEW, CWinApp::OnFileNew)
    ON_COMMAND (ID_FILE_OPEN, CWinApp::OnFileOpen)
    ON_COMMAND (ID_APP_ABOUT, OnAppAbout)
END_MESSAGE_MAP ()

BOOL CPaintApp::InitInstance ()
{
    SetRegistryKey ("Programming Windows 95 with MFC");
    LoadStdProfileSettings ();

    CSingleDocTemplate* pDocTemplate;
    pDocTemplate = new CSingleDocTemplate (
        IDR_MAINFRAME,
        RUNTIME_CLASS (CPaintDoc),
        RUNTIME_CLASS (CMainFrame),
        RUNTIME_CLASS (CPaintView)
    );

    AddDocTemplate (pDocTemplate);
    RegisterShellFileTypes (TRUE);
```

(continued)

Paint4.cpp *continued*

```
    CCommandLineInfo cmdInfo;
    ParseCommandLine (cmdInfo);

    if (!ProcessShellCommand (cmdInfo))
        return FALSE;

    m_pMainWnd->DragAcceptFiles ();
    return TRUE;
}

void CPaintApp::OnAppAbout ()
{
    CAboutDialog dlg;
    dlg.DoModal ();
}
```

MainFrame.h

```
//***************************************************************************
//
//  MainFrame.h
//
//***************************************************************************

class CMainFrame : public CFrameWnd
{
    DECLARE_DYNCREATE (CMainFrame)

protected:
    afx_msg int OnCreate (LPCREATESTRUCT);
    afx_msg void OnMeasureItem (int, LPMEASUREITEMSTRUCT);
    afx_msg void OnDrawItem (int, LPDRAWITEMSTRUCT);

    DECLARE_MESSAGE_MAP ()
};
```

MainFrame.cpp

```
//***************************************************************************
//
//  MainFrame.cpp
//
//***************************************************************************
```

```
#define OEMRESOURCE

#include <afxwin.h>
#include "Resource.h"
#include "CLine.h"
#include "MainFrame.h"
#include "Paint4Doc.h"

IMPLEMENT_DYNCREATE (CMainFrame, CFrameWnd)

BEGIN_MESSAGE_MAP (CMainFrame, CFrameWnd)
    ON_WM_CREATE ()
    ON_WM_MEASUREITEM ()
    ON_WM_DRAWITEM ()
END_MESSAGE_MAP ()

int CMainFrame::OnCreate (LPCREATESTRUCT lpcs)
{
    if (CFrameWnd::OnCreate (lpcs) == -1)
        return -1;

    CMenu* pMenu = GetMenu ();
    for (int i=0; i<8; i++)
        pMenu->ModifyMenu (ID_COLOR_BLACK + i,
            MF_BYCOMMAND | MF_OWNERDRAW, ID_COLOR_BLACK + i);
    return 0;
}

void CMainFrame::OnMeasureItem (int nIDCtl, LPMEASUREITEMSTRUCT lpmis)
{
    lpmis->itemWidth = ::GetSystemMetrics (SM_CYMENU) * 4;
    lpmis->itemHeight = ::GetSystemMetrics (SM_CYMENU);
}

void CMainFrame::OnDrawItem (int nIDCtl, LPDRAWITEMSTRUCT lpdis)
{
    BITMAP bm;
    CBitmap bitmap;
    bitmap.LoadOEMBitmap (OBM_CHECK);
    bitmap.GetObject (sizeof (bm), &bm);

    CDC dc;
    dc.Attach (lpdis->hDC);

    CBrush* pBrush = new CBrush (::GetSysColor ((lpdis->itemState &
        ODS_SELECTED) ? COLOR_HIGHLIGHT : COLOR_MENU));
```

(continued)

MainFrame.cpp *continued*

```
        dc.FrameRect (&(lpdis->rcItem), pBrush);
        delete pBrush;

        if (lpdis->itemState & ODS_CHECKED) {
            CDC dcMem;
            dcMem.CreateCompatibleDC (&dc);
            CBitmap* pOldBitmap = dcMem.SelectObject (&bitmap);

            dc.BitBlt (lpdis->rcItem.left + 4, lpdis->rcItem.top +
                (((lpdis->rcItem.bottom - lpdis->rcItem.top) -
                bm.bmHeight) / 2), bm.bmWidth, bm.bmHeight, &dcMem,
                0, 0, SRCCOPY);

            dcMem.SelectObject (pOldBitmap);
        }

        pBrush = new CBrush (CPaintDoc::m_crColors[lpdis->itemID -
            ID_COLOR_BLACK]);
        CRect rect = lpdis->rcItem;
        rect.DeflateRect (6, 4);
        rect.left += bm.bmWidth;
        dc.FillRect (rect, pBrush);
        delete pBrush;

        dc.Detach ();
    }
```

Paint4Doc.h

```
//*****************************************************************************
//
//  Paint4Doc.h
//
//*****************************************************************************

class CPaintDoc : public CDocument
{
    DECLARE_DYNCREATE (CPaintDoc)

private:
    UINT m_nWidth;
    UINT m_nColor;
    CObArray m_lineArray;

    void InitWidthAndColor ();
```

```
public:
    static const COLORREF m_crColors[8];

    CPaintDoc ();
    virtual BOOL OnNewDocument ();
    virtual BOOL OnOpenDocument (LPCTSTR);
    virtual void DeleteContents ();
    virtual void Serialize (CArchive&);

    CLine* AddLine (CPoint, CPoint);
    CLine* GetLine (int);
    int GetLineCount ();

protected:
    afx_msg void OnWidth (UINT);
    afx_msg void OnColor (UINT);
    afx_msg void OnUpdateWidthUI (CCmdUI*);
    afx_msg void OnUpdateColorUI (CCmdUI*);

    DECLARE_MESSAGE_MAP ()
};
```

Paint4Doc.cpp

```
//*************************************************************************
//
// Paint4Doc.cpp
//
//*************************************************************************

#include <afxwin.h>
#include "Resource.h"
#include "CLine.h"
#include "Paint4Doc.h"

IMPLEMENT_DYNCREATE (CPaintDoc, CDocument)

BEGIN_MESSAGE_MAP (CPaintDoc, CDocument)
    ON_COMMAND (ID_FILE_SEND_MAIL, OnFileSendMail)
    ON_COMMAND_RANGE (ID_WIDTH_VTHIN, ID_WIDTH_VTHICK, OnWidth)
    ON_COMMAND_RANGE (ID_COLOR_BLACK, ID_COLOR_WHITE, OnColor)
    ON_UPDATE_COMMAND_UI (ID_FILE_SEND_MAIL, OnUpdateFileSendMail)
    ON_UPDATE_COMMAND_UI_RANGE (ID_WIDTH_VTHIN, ID_WIDTH_VTHICK,
        OnUpdateWidthUI)
```

(continued)

Paint4Doc.cpp *continued*

```
    ON_UPDATE_COMMAND_UI_RANGE (ID_COLOR_BLACK, ID_COLOR_WHITE,
        OnUpdateColorUI)
END_MESSAGE_MAP ()

const COLORREF CPaintDoc::m_crColors[8] = {
    RGB (  0,   0,   0),    // Black
    RGB (  0,   0, 255),    // Blue
    RGB (  0, 255,   0),    // Green
    RGB (  0, 255, 255),    // Cyan
    RGB (255,   0,   0),    // Red
    RGB (255,   0, 255),    // Magenta
    RGB (255, 255,   0),    // Yellow
    RGB (255, 255, 255)     // White
};

CPaintDoc::CPaintDoc ()
{
    m_lineArray.SetSize (0, 64);
}

BOOL CPaintDoc::OnNewDocument ()
{
    if (!CDocument::OnNewDocument ())
        return FALSE;

    InitWidthAndColor ();
    return TRUE;
}

BOOL CPaintDoc::OnOpenDocument (LPCTSTR lpszPathName)
{
    if (!CDocument::OnOpenDocument (lpszPathName))
        return FALSE;

    InitWidthAndColor ();
    return TRUE;
}

void CPaintDoc::InitWidthAndColor ()
{
    m_nColor = ID_COLOR_RED - ID_COLOR_BLACK;
    m_nWidth = ID_WIDTH_MEDIUM - ID_WIDTH_VTHIN;
}

void CPaintDoc::DeleteContents ()
{
```

```
    int nCount = m_lineArray.GetSize ();

    if (nCount) {
        for (int i=0; i<nCount; i++)
            delete m_lineArray[i];
        m_lineArray.RemoveAll ();
    }
}

void CPaintDoc::Serialize (CArchive& ar)
{
    m_lineArray.Serialize (ar);
}

CLine* CPaintDoc::AddLine (CPoint ptFrom, CPoint ptTo)
{
    static UINT nWidths[5] = { 1, 8, 16, 24, 32 };

    CLine* pLine;
    try {
        pLine = new CLine (ptFrom, ptTo, nWidths[m_nWidth],
            m_crColors[m_nColor]);
        m_lineArray.Add (pLine);
        SetModifiedFlag ();
    }
    catch (CMemoryException* e) {
        if (pLine != NULL) {
            delete pLine;
            pLine = NULL;
        }
        AfxMessageBox ("Out of memory", MB_ICONSTOP | MB_OK);
        e->Delete ();
    }
    return pLine;
}

CLine* CPaintDoc::GetLine (int nIndex)
{
    return (CLine*) m_lineArray[nIndex];
}

int CPaintDoc::GetLineCount ()
{
    return m_lineArray.GetSize ();
}
```

(continued)

Paint4Doc.cpp *continued*

```
void CPaintDoc::OnWidth (UINT nID)
{
    m_nWidth = nID - ID_WIDTH_VTHIN;
}

void CPaintDoc::OnColor (UINT nID)
{
    m_nColor = nID - ID_COLOR_BLACK;
}

void CPaintDoc::OnUpdateWidthUI (CCmdUI* pCmdUI)
{
    pCmdUI->SetCheck ((pCmdUI->m_nID - ID_WIDTH_VTHIN) == m_nWidth);
}

void CPaintDoc::OnUpdateColorUI (CCmdUI* pCmdUI)
{
    pCmdUI->SetCheck ((pCmdUI->m_nID - ID_COLOR_BLACK) == m_nColor);
}
```

Paint4View.h

```
//**********************************************************************
//
//  Paint4View.h
//
//**********************************************************************

class CPaintView : public CScrollView
{
    DECLARE_DYNCREATE (CPaintView)

private:
    CPoint m_ptFrom;
    CPoint m_ptTo;

    CPaintDoc* GetDocument () { return (CPaintDoc*) m_pDocument; }
    void InvertLine (CDC*, CPoint, CPoint);

public:
    virtual void OnInitialUpdate ();

protected:
    virtual void OnDraw (CDC*);

    afx_msg void OnLButtonDown (UINT, CPoint);
```

```
    afx_msg void OnMouseMove (UINT, CPoint);
    afx_msg void OnLButtonUp (UINT, CPoint);
    afx_msg void OnContextMenu (CWnd*, CPoint);

    DECLARE_MESSAGE_MAP1()
};
```

Paint4View.cpp

```
//***************************************************************************
//
//  Paint4View.cpp
//
//***************************************************************************

#include <afxwin.h>
#include "Resource.h"
#include "CLine.h"
#include "Paint4Doc.h"
#include "Paint4View.h"

IMPLEMENT_DYNCREATE (CPaintView, CScrollView)

BEGIN_MESSAGE_MAP (CPaintView, CScrollView)
    ON_WM_LBUTTONDOWN ()
    ON_WM_MOUSEMOVE ()
    ON_WM_LBUTTONUP ()
    ON_WM_CONTEXTMENU ()
END_MESSAGE_MAP ()

void CPaintView::OnInitialUpdate ()
{
    SetScrollSizes (MM_TEXT, CSize (2048, 2048));
    CScrollView::OnInitialUpdate ();
}

void CPaintView::OnDraw (CDC* pDC)
{
    CPaintDoc* pDoc = GetDocument ();
    int nCount = pDoc->GetLineCount ();

    if (nCount) {
        for (int i=0; i<nCount; i++)
            pDoc->GetLine (i)->Draw (pDC);
    }
}
```

(continued)

Paint4View.cpp *continued*

```
void CPaintView::OnLButtonDown (UINT nFlags, CPoint point)
{
    CClientDC dc (this);
    OnPrepareDC (&dc);
    dc.DPtoLP (&point);

    m_ptFrom = point;
    m_ptTo = point;
    SetCapture ();
}

void CPaintView::OnMouseMove (UINT nFlags, CPoint point)
{
    if (GetCapture () == this) {
        CClientDC dc (this);
        OnPrepareDC (&dc);
        dc.DPtoLP (&point);

        InvertLine (&dc, m_ptFrom, m_ptTo);
        InvertLine (&dc, m_ptFrom, point);
        m_ptTo = point;
    }
}

void CPaintView::OnLButtonUp (UINT nFlags, CPoint point)
{
    if (GetCapture () == this) {
        ReleaseCapture ();
        CClientDC dc (this);
        OnPrepareDC (&dc);
        dc.DPtoLP (&point);
        InvertLine (&dc, m_ptFrom, m_ptTo);

        CLine* pLine = GetDocument ()->AddLine (m_ptFrom, point);
        if (pLine != NULL)
            pLine->Draw (&dc);
    }
}

void CPaintView::InvertLine (CDC* pDC, CPoint ptFrom, CPoint ptTo)
{
    int nOldMode = pDC->SetROP2 (R2_NOT);

    pDC->MoveTo (ptFrom);
    pDC->LineTo (ptTo);
```

```
        pDC->SetROP2 (nOldMode);
}

void CPaintView::OnContextMenu (CWnd* pWnd, CPoint point)
{
        CMenu menu;
        menu.LoadMenu (IDR_CONTEXTMENU);
        CMenu* pContextMenu = menu.GetSubMenu (0);

        for (int i=0; i<8; i++)
                pContextMenu->ModifyMenu (ID_COLOR_BLACK + i,
                        MF_BYCOMMAND | MF_OWNERDRAW, ID_COLOR_BLACK + i);

        pContextMenu->TrackPopupMenu (TPM_LEFTALIGN | TPM_LEFTBUTTON |
                TPM_RIGHTBUTTON, point.x, point.y, AfxGetMainWnd ());
}
```

AboutDlg.h

```
//******************************************************************************
//
//  AboutDlg.h
//
//******************************************************************************

class CAboutDialog : public CDialog
{
private:
        CRect m_rect;

public:
        CAboutDialog (CWnd* pParentWnd = NULL) :
                CDialog (IDD_ABOUTDLG, pParentWnd) {}

        virtual BOOL OnInitDialog ();

protected:
        afx_msg void OnPaint ();
        DECLARE_MESSAGE_MAP ()
};
```

AboutDlg.cpp

```cpp
//******************************************************************************
//
//  AboutDlg.cpp
//
//******************************************************************************

#include <afxwin.h>
#include "Resource.h"
#include "AboutDlg.h"

BEGIN_MESSAGE_MAP (CAboutDialog, CDialog)
    ON_WM_PAINT ()
END_MESSAGE_MAP ()

BOOL CAboutDialog::OnInitDialog ()
{
    CDialog::OnInitDialog ();

    CStatic* pStatic = (CStatic*) GetDlgItem (IDC_ICONRECT);
    pStatic->GetWindowRect (&m_rect);
    pStatic->DestroyWindow ();
    ScreenToClient (&m_rect);

    return TRUE;
}

void CAboutDialog::OnPaint ()
{
    CPaintDC dc (this);
    HICON hIcon = (HICON) ::GetClassLong (AfxGetMainWnd ()->m_hWnd,
        GCL_HICON);

    if (hIcon != NULL) {
        CDC dcMem;
        dcMem.CreateCompatibleDC (&dc);

        CBitmap bitmap;
        bitmap.CreateCompatibleBitmap (&dc, 32, 32);
        CBitmap* pOldBitmap = dcMem.SelectObject (&bitmap);

        CBrush brush (::GetSysColor (COLOR_3DFACE));
        dcMem.FillRect (CRect (0, 0, 32, 32), &brush);
        dcMem.DrawIcon (0, 0, hIcon);
```

```
        dc.StretchBlt (m_rect.left, m_rect.top, m_rect.Width(),
            m_rect.Height (), &dcMem, 0, 0, 32, 32, SRCCOPY);

        dcMem.SelectObject (pOldBitmap);
    }
}
```

CLine.h

```
//*********************************************************************
//
//  CLine.h
//
//*********************************************************************

class CLine : public CObject
{
    DECLARE_SERIAL (CLine)

private:
    CPoint m_ptFrom;
    CPoint m_ptTo;
    UINT m_nWidth;
    COLORREF m_crColor;

public:
    CLine () {}
    CLine (CPoint, CPoint, UINT, COLORREF);
    virtual void Serialize (CArchive&);
    virtual void Draw (CDC*);
};
```

CLine.cpp

```
//*********************************************************************
//
//  CLine.cpp
//
//*********************************************************************

#include <afxwin.h>
#include "CLine.h"

IMPLEMENT_SERIAL (CLine, CObject, 1)
```

(continued)

CLine.cpp *continued*

```cpp
CLine::CLine (CPoint ptFrom, CPoint ptTo, UINT nWidth, COLORREF crColor)
{
    m_ptFrom = ptFrom;
    m_ptTo = ptTo;
    m_nWidth = nWidth;
    m_crColor = crColor;
}

void CLine::Serialize (CArchive& ar)
{
    CObject::Serialize (ar);

    if (ar.IsStoring ())
        ar << m_ptFrom << m_ptTo << m_nWidth << (DWORD) m_crColor;
    else
        ar >> m_ptFrom >> m_ptTo >> m_nWidth >> (DWORD) m_crColor;
}

void CLine::Draw (CDC* pDC)
{
    CPen pen (PS_SOLID, m_nWidth, m_crColor);

    CPen* pOldPen = pDC->SelectObject (&pen);
    pDC->MoveTo (m_ptFrom);
    pDC->LineTo (m_ptTo);

    pDC->SelectObject (pOldPen);
}
```

Paint4 uses six application-defined classes:

- The application class, *CPaintApp*, which is derived from *CWinApp* (Paint4.h and Paint4.cpp)

- The frame window class, *CMainFrame*, which is derived from *CFrameWnd* (MainFrame.h and MainFrame.cpp)

- The document class, *CPaintDoc*, which is derived from *CDocument* (Paint4Doc.h and Paint4Doc.cpp)

- The view class, *CPaintView*, which is derived from *CScrollView* (Paint4View.h and Paint4View.cpp)

- The dialog class, *CAboutDialog*, which is derived from *CDialog* (AboutDlg.h and AboutDlg.cpp)

- The class *CLine*, which is derived from *CObject* (CLine.h and CLine.cpp)

The *CAboutDialog* and *CLine* classes should look familiar to you because we used both classes in previous chapters. The other classes are new. Let's examine the application, frame window, document, and view classes more closely to see how they work and what roles they play in Paint4's operation.

The *CPaintApp* Class

CPaintApp is the application class. It includes just two member functions of its own: *InitInstance* and *OnAppAbout*. The latter displays the program's About dialog box when the user selects About Paint4 from the Help menu. An ON_COMMAND message map entry connects the menu item (ID=ID_APP_ABOUT) to *CPaintApp-::OnAppAbout*. *CPaintApp*'s message map also connects the File-New and File-Open menu items (ID_FILE_NEW and ID_FILE_OPEN) to the corresponding handlers in *CWinApp*. The application object handles the File-Exit command. The handler is *CWinApp::OnAppExit*, and no message map entry is required because ID_APP_EXIT is included in *CWinApp*'s message map.

CPaintApp's *InitInstance* function looks a lot like the *InitInstance* function examined earlier in this chapter. It creates a document template from MFC's *CSingleDocTemplate* class, registers the document template with *AddDocTemplate*, and gets a window up on the screen by calling *ProcessCommandLine*. Before doing any of that, however, it executes these statements:

```
SetRegistryKey ("Programming Windows 95 with MFC");
LoadStdProfileSettings ();
```

The call to *LoadStdProfileSettings*, combined with the ID_FILE_MRU_FILE1 item in the application's File menu, tells the framework to include a most recently used (MRU) file list in the File menu. The framework handles this completely on its own, caching the file names of the four most recently used documents and displaying them where ID_FILE_MRU_FILE1 appears in the menu. If four isn't enough (or if it's too many), you can set the number of file names displayed in the menu to any value from 0 through 16 when you call *LoadStdProfileSettings*. The following statement changes the MRU length from four file names to eight:

```
LoadStdProfileSettings (8);
```

The call to *SetRegistryKey* instructs the framework to store MRU file names in the registry rather than in a private .ini file, which is standard procedure for a Windows 95 application. You can view the stored MRU list by using RegEdit to examine the HKEY_CURRENT_USER\Software\Programming Windows 95 with MFC\PAINT4\Recent File List branch of the registry.

InitInstance also calls *RegisterShellFileTypes* to register Paint4's documents (files with the extension .pnt) with the operating system shell, and *DragAcceptFiles* to enable drag and drop document loading. The .pnt file name extension is specified in the document string defined in Paint4.rc.

The *CMainFrame* Class

CMainFrame is the frame window that serves as Paint4's main window. It includes three member functions that perform custom message processing: *OnCreate, OnMeasureItem,* and *OnDrawItem. OnCreate* converts the eight items in the program's Color menu to owner-drawn menu items, and *OnMeasureItem* and *OnDrawItem* draw the menu items. Note the use of the DECLARE_DYNCREATE and IMPLEMENT_DYNCREATE macros to make *CMainFrame* a dynamically creatable class:

```
// In MainFrame.h
DECLARE_DYNCREATE (CMainFrame)

// In MainFrame.cpp
IMPLEMENT_DYNCREATE (CMainFrame, CFrameWnd)
```

These statements are required so that the framework can create the application's window. Similar statements (with different class names, of course) are found in the source code files for *CPaintDoc* and *CPaintView*.

When the frame window paints an owner-drawn menu item in response to a WM_DRAWITEM message, it obtains a COLORREF value identifying the menu item's color from the document class's static *m_crColors* array. The brush that paints the color swatch in the menu is created like this:

```
pBrush = new CBrush (CPaintDoc::m_crColors[lpdis->itemID -
    ID_COLOR_BLACK]);
```

Because the colors that lines are drawn with are part of the document class, and because the frame window retrieves its color information from the document class, changing the colors in *CPaintDoc::m_crColors* will change not only the colors of lines drawn on the screen, but of the color samples in the application's Color menu, too.

The *CPaintDoc* Class

In Paint4, a "document" is a set of lines defined by *CLine* objects. Pointers to *CLine* objects are stored in *CPaintDoc::m_lineArray*, which is an array of type *CObArray*. *CPaintDoc* hides its data by declaring *m_lineArray* as a private data member and allows no direct access to it. All accesses are performed indirectly through the following public member functions:

- *CPaintDoc::AddLine*, which accepts two *CPoint* objects specifying the line's endpoints and combines that information with width and color information stored in the document object to create a *CLine* object and add it to *m_lineArray*

- *CPaintDoc::GetLine*, which, given a 0-based index, returns a pointer to the *CLine* object at that position in *m_lineArray*

■ *CPaintDoc::GetLineCount*, which returns the number of *CLine* objects currently recorded in *m_lineArray*

All three functions are called by the application's view object at appropriate times. *AddLine*, for example, is called by the view's *OnLButtonUp* handler to add a line to the document when the left mouse button is released to terminate a line-drawing operation. *GetLineCount* is called by the view's *OnDraw* function to determine how many lines must be drawn, and its return value is used in a *for* loop that calls *GetLine* repeatedly to invoke each line's *Draw* function. The view calls *CPaintDoc* functions through the pointer returned by *CPaintView::GetDocument*.

In addition to maintaining a record of *CLine* objects in *m_lineArray*, the document object also includes a pair of private member variables named *m_nWidth* and *m_nColor* that store indexes specifying the current line width and color. Why is this information stored in the document rather than in the view or perhaps in the frame window? Because the width and color that are currently selected are properties of the document, not of the view that depicts the document or of the frame window that encloses the view. If two views of the same document were shown and *m_nWidth* and *m_nColor* were part of the view class, width and color selections made in one view of the document would not update the width and color selected in the other view of the document. Conversely, if *m_nWidth* and *m_nColor* were members of the frame window class instead of the document class and Paint4 were an MDI application with two different documents open, selecting a width and color in document A would change the width and color selected in document B. Making *m_nWidth* and *m_nColor* members of the document class ensures that width and color selections made in one document won't affect other documents and ensures that width and color selections will be consistent across views no matter how many views of a document are displayed.

Since the document object keeps track of the current width and color, it also handles command and update messages for items in the Width and Color menus. *CPaintDoc*'s message map looks like this:

```
BEGIN_MESSAGE_MAP (CPaintDoc, CDocument)
    ON_COMMAND (ID_FILE_SEND_MAIL, OnFileSendMail)
    ON_COMMAND_RANGE (ID_WIDTH_VTHIN, ID_WIDTH_VTHICK, OnWidth)
    ON_COMMAND_RANGE (ID_COLOR_BLACK, ID_COLOR_WHITE, OnColor)
    ON_UPDATE_COMMAND_UI (ID_FILE_SEND_MAIL, OnUpdateFileSendMail)
    ON_UPDATE_COMMAND_UI_RANGE (ID_WIDTH_VTHIN, ID_WIDTH_VTHICK,
        OnUpdateWidthUI)
    ON_UPDATE_COMMAND_UI_RANGE (ID_COLOR_BLACK, ID_COLOR_WHITE,
        OnUpdateColorUI)
END_MESSAGE_MAP ()
```

MFC's *CDocument::OnFileSendMail* function makes it trivial to add a Send or Send Mail command to an application's File menu, which is just one of several "logo" requirements a product must meet before it can carry the Windows 95 logo. Paint4 demonstrates how the command is implemented by mapping ID_FILE_SEND_MAIL to *OnFileSend-Mail* in the document class. *OnFileSendMail* attaches the document file to an electronic mail message and sends the message via the resident MAPI (Messaging Application Programming Interface) mail host. If the document contains unsaved data, *OnFile-SendMail* serializes the document to a temporary file on your hard disk before transmitting it. The update handler *CDocument::OnUpdateFileSendMail* disables the menu item if MAPI support is not present.

When *CPaintDoc::AddLine* is called by the view to create a new *CLine*, *AddLine* consults *m_nWidth* and *m_nColor* for current width and color information. It then creates a new *CLine* object, adds it to *m_lineArray*, and returns a *CLine* pointer to the view:

```
CLine* pLine;
try {
    pLine = new CLine (pointFrom, pointTo, nWidths[m_nWidth],
        m_crColors[m_nColor]);
    m_lineArray.Add (pLine);
    SetModifiedFlag ();
}
catch (CMemoryException* e) {
    if (pLine != NULL) {
        delete pLine;
        pLine = NULL;
    }
    AfxMessageBox ("Out of memory", MB_ICONSTOP | MB_OK);
    e->Delete ();
}
return pLine;
```

Memory exceptions thrown by *new* or *CObArray::Add* are caught and handled cleanly so that *AddLine* can pop up a message box notifying the user of the error and return a NULL pointer indicating that the operation failed. If the line is successfully created and recorded, *AddLine* calls *SetModifiedFlag* to mark the document as "dirty." This flag is automatically cleared by the framework when a document is created, loaded, or saved, so *CPaintDoc* doesn't contain any explicit calls to clear the flag.

CPaintDoc overrides four virtual *CDocument* functions: two to initialize new documents, one to delete the contents of existing documents, and one to serialize a document to or from disk. It also includes a constructor that initializes *m_lineArray* when the document object is created:

```
CPaintDoc::CPaintDoc ()
{
    m_lineArray.SetSize (0, 64);
}
```

Remember that, in an SDI application, the document object is constructed just once and then reused when new documents are loaded and created. Therefore, the call to *SetSize* will be executed only once, but that's just what we want. Anytime a document is loaded with File-Open or created from scratch with File-New, the framework calls the document object's *DeleteContents* function. *CPaintDoc::DeleteContents* deletes all *CLine* objects referenced in *m_lineArray* and calls *RemoveAll* to deallocate array memory and reset the item count to 0:

```
void CPaintDoc::DeleteContents ()
{
    int nCount = m_lineArray.GetSize ();

    if (nCount) {
        for (int i=0; i<nCount; i++)
            delete m_lineArray[i];
        m_lineArray.RemoveAll ();
    }
}
```

The *OnNewDocument* and *OnOpenDocument* overrides initialize *m_nWidth* and *m_nColor* each time a document is created or loaded. Setting the values of *m_nWidth* and *m_nColor* in *CPaintDoc*'s constructor would accomplish nothing since SDI document objects are not created and destroyed as ordinary documents are created and destroyed. The private member function *InitWidthAndColor* does the resetting:

```
BOOL CPaintDoc::OnNewDocument ()
{
    if (!CDocument::OnNewDocument ())
        return FALSE;

    InitWidthAndColor ();
    return TRUE;
}

BOOL CPaintDoc::OnOpenDocument (LPCTSTR lpszPathName)
{
    if (!CDocument::OnOpenDocument (lpszPathName))
        return FALSE;

    InitWidthAndColor ();
    return TRUE;
}

void CPaintDoc::InitWidthAndColor ()
{
    m_nColor = ID_COLOR_RED - ID_COLOR_BLACK;
    m_nWidth = ID_WIDTH_MEDIUM - ID_WIDTH_VTHIN;
}
```

A neat modification you can make to Paint4 is to change *CPaintDoc::Serialize* to include *m_nWidth* and *m_nColor* in the serialization process. Then the override of *OnOpenDocument* would be unnecessary because both member variables would be initialized by the *Serialize* function and a loaded document would remember the last width and color settings that the user selected.

CPaintDoc::Serialize serializes the contents of *m_lineArray* to and from disk. Serialization is accomplished with a single statement because a *CObArray* is capable of serializing itself, as we noted in Chapter 6:

```
m_lineArray.Serialize (ar);
```

CPaintDoc::Serialize is called by the framework when a document is opened or saved. Selecting Open from the File menu activates *CWinApp::OnFileNew*, which ultimately calls the document object's *OnOpenDocument* function, which in turn opens the file, creates an archive object, and calls the document's *Serialize* function to load or "deserialize" the document. On the flip side, selecting Save or Save As from the File menu activates *CDocument::OnFileSave* or *CDocument::OnFileSaveAs*. These functions indirectly call the document object's *OnSaveDocument* function, which in turn opens the file, creates an archive object, and calls *Serialize* to save the document. This is a great example of how the framework works behind the scenes to reduce the amount of code you have to write. In Paint3, we wrote all the code to display dialog boxes, open files, create archives, and so on. In Paint4, it's all done for you by the framework.

The *CPaintView* Class

Paint4 supports just one view of an open document. The behavior of that view is modeled in the *CPaintView* class, which is derived from *CScrollView*. *CPaintView* has three primary responsibilities: to paint the document on the screen when *OnDraw* is called, to process mouse messages and convert them into lines added to the document, and to display a context menu when the right mouse button is clicked.

Paint3 painted its "document" by fetching *CLine* pointers from *m_lineArray* and calling the *CLines' Draw* functions. Paint4's *CPaintView* class works in much the same way, but rather than access *m_lineArray* directly, it works through the document object to obtain the *CLine* pointers it needs to paint the screen. The view's *OnDraw* function looks like this:

```
void CPaintView::OnDraw (CDC* pDC)
{
    CPaintDoc* pDoc = GetDocument ();
    int nCount = pDoc->GetLineCount ();

    if (nCount > 0) {
        for (int i=0; i<nCount; i++)
```

```
        pDoc->GetLine (i)->Draw (pDC);
    }
}
```

GetDocument is an inline *CPaintView* function that casts *m_pDocument* to a *CPaint-Doc* pointer and returns the result. Neither a *CLine* object nor the document object has any concept of windows and device contexts, so *OnDraw* supplies the device context *CLine::Draw* uses for screen output.

CPaintView::OnLButtonUp adds lines to the document by calling the document object's *AddLine* function. The *OnLButtonUp* code that creates a line and then draws it into the view looks like this:

```
CLine* pLine = GetDocument ()->AddLine (m_ptFrom, point);
if (pLine != NULL)
    pLine->Draw (&dc);
```

Before *OnLButtonUp* or any of the other mouse handling functions does anything with the cursor coordinates it receives, it calls a virtual *CView* function named *OnPrepareDC* and follows that with a call to *CDC::DPtoLP*. An example of this preliminary work can be seen in *CPaintView::OnLButtonDown*:

```
void CPaintView::OnLButtonDown (UINT nFlags, CPoint point)
{
    CClientDC dc (this);
    OnPrepareDC (&dc);
    dc.DPtoLP (&point);

    m_ptFrom = point;
    m_ptTo = point;
    SetCapture ();
}
```

CPaintView's implementation of *OnLButtonDown* demonstrates two basic principles you should always remember when using a *CScrollView*:

■ Points in a *CScrollView* are identified with logical coordinates, not device coordinates.

■ Before device coordinates are converted into logical coordinates outside *OnDraw*, the view's *OnPrepareDC* function must be called.

The reasons why have to do with the way a *CScrollView* works.

When a scroll event occurs, *CScrollView* captures the ensuing message with its *OnHScroll* or *OnVScroll* handler and calls *ScrollWindow* to scroll the window horizontally or vertically by the specified amount. Soon after, the view's *OnPaint* function is called to paint the area of the window that was invalidated by *ScrollWindow*. The code for *OnPaint*, which *CScrollView* inherits from *CView*, is shown on the next page.

```
CPaintDC dc(this);
OnPrepareDC(&dc);
OnDraw(&dc);
```

Before it calls *OnDraw*, *CView::OnPaint* calls *OnPrepareDC*. *CScrollView* overrides *OnPrepareDC* and calls *CDC::SetViewportOrg* to translate the viewport origin an amount that equals the horizontal and vertical scroll positions. Consequently, the scroll positions are automatically factored in when *OnDraw* repaints the view. Because of the work performed in *CScrollView::OnPrepareDC*, a generic *OnDraw* function ported from a *CView* to a *CScrollView* will automatically adapt to changes in the scroll position.

But now think about what happens if you instantiate a device context class on your own (outside *OnDraw*) and draw something in a *CScrollView* window. Unless you first call *OnPrepareDC* to prepare the device context as *OnPaint* does, *SetViewportOrg* won't get called and drawing will be performed relative to the upper left corner of the window rather than relative to the upper left corner of the view. Views of a document will get out of kilter pretty quickly if they're drawn using two different coordinate systems. Therefore, when you draw in a *CScrollView* window like this:

```
CClientDC dc (this);
// Draw something with dc...
```

make it a habit to pass the device context to *OnPrepareDC* first, like this:

```
CClientDC dc (this);
OnPrepareDC (&dc);
// Draw something with dc...
```

By the same token, if you have the coordinates of a point in a *CScrollView* in device coordinates and want to convert them to view coordinates, use the *CDC::DPtoLP* function. But call *OnPrepareDC* first so that the scroll position will be taken into account. *CPoint* objects passed to *OnLButtonDown* and other mouse handlers always use device coordinates, so conversion is essential if you want to know the coordinates of the corresponding point in view space.

A final aspect of *CPaintView* that deserves mentioning is its *OnContextMenu* handler. Before we displayed a context menu in Paint3, we had to do some checking to verify that the right-button click occurred in the window's client area. The equivalent checking is performed implicitly when the *OnContextMenu* handler is assigned to a view because, if the mouse button is clicked in the frame window's nonclient area, the view won't receive a WM_CONTEXTMENU message. Therefore, *CPaintView::OnContextMenu* loads the context menu, converts selected items to owner-drawn items, and displays the menu—nothing more. So that all messages generated by the menu (including owner-draw messages) will be directed to the frame window instead of to the view, *CPaintView::OnContextMenu* passes *TrackPopupMenu* an *AfxGetMainWnd* pointer to identify the menu's owner:

```
pContextMenu->TrackPopupMenu (TPM_LEFTALIGN | TPM_LEFTBUTTON |
    TPM_RIGHTBUTTON, point.x, point.y, AfxGetMainWnd ());
```

CPaintView isn't equipped to handle owner-draw messages as the frame window is, so passing a *this* pointer to *TrackPopupMenu* would produce one very ugly menu.

DOC + VIEW = LESS WORK FOR YOU

As you play around with Paint4, note how much more robust it is than Paint3. Paint3 would save documents to disk and load them back, but it wouldn't warn you when you were about to close a document that contained unsaved data. Nor would it accept dragged-and-dropped files, send documents as mail messages, list recently used documents in the File menu, or start up when a .pnt icon was double-clicked in a shell folder or an Explorer window. All of these features were added by the framework in Paint4 because we built the application using documents and views. We'll see other benefits of using the document/view architecture in chapters to come.

The first time I ever looked at a minimal MFC application generated by AppWizard, I was dumbfounded by how relatively little code there was. What I didn't realize at the time was that entire chunks of the application were provided by the framework as a result of innocent-looking message map entries like this one:

```
ON_COMMAND (ID_FILE_OPEN, CWinApp::OnFileNew)
```

Still other parts of the program (notably the File menu's Save and Save As commands) were also implemented by the framework but weren't even visible as message map entries because the message mapping was performed in the base class. All in all, it looked as if a lot of magic was going on and it was clear to me that I was going to have to do some digging before I would fully understand it.

As I soon found out, there's nothing magic about the document/view architecture—just some clever coding hidden in preprocessor macros and thousands of lines of code written to handle routine (and not-so-routine) chores such as resizing a view when a frame window is resized and carrying on DDE conversations with the shell. Many programmers fail to see the big picture because they don't take the time to look under the hood at the code AppWizard generates for them. Paint4 is a document/view application in existential form, unobscured by the nonessential extras AppWizard throws in. If you understand Paint4, you're well on your way to understanding the document/view architecture.

Chapter 9

Multiple Documents and Multiple Views

Document/view applications aren't limited to just one document and one view of a document's data. Using splitter windows whose functionality is provided entirely by the framework, a single document interface (SDI) application can present two or more views of the same document in resizeable "panes" that subdivide the frame window's client area. The document/view architecture also extends to multiple document interface (MDI) applications that support multiple views of the same document, multiple open documents, and even multiple document types. Although use of the multiple document interface is discouraged in Windows 95, applications that rely on the MDI model are still prevalent and probably will be for some time to come—as evidenced by the continued success of Word for Windows, Microsoft Excel, and other leading Windows 95 applications.

Now that we've seen what it takes to write an SDI document/view application, it's a simple matter to extend the paradigm to encompass multiple documents and multiple views. In this chapter, we'll see first how to use splitter windows to provide multiple views of a document open in an SDI application. Then we'll look into MFC's support for MDI applications and see how easy it is to convert an existing SDI application into MDI format.

SPLITTER WINDOWS

For SDI applications, the MFC application framework provides a convenient means of presenting two or more concurrent views of a document in the form of splitter windows based on MFC's *CSplitterWnd* class. A splitter window is a window that can be divided into two or more panes horizontally, vertically, or both horizontally and vertically by movable splitter bars. Each pane contains one view of a document's data. The views are children of the splitter window, and the splitter window itself is a child of a frame window. In an SDI application, the splitter window is a child of the top-level frame window. In an MDI application, the splitter window is a child of an MDI document frame that floats within the top-level frame window. A view positioned inside a splitter window can use *CView::GetParentFrame* to obtain a pointer to its parent frame window.

MFC supports two types of splitter windows: static and dynamic. The numbers of rows and columns in a static splitter window are set when the splitter is created and can't be changed by the user. The user is free to resize individual rows and columns, however. A static splitter window can contain a maximum of 16 rows and 16 columns. A dynamic splitter window is limited to at most two rows and two columns, but it can be split and unsplit interactively. The views displayed in a dynamic splitter window's panes aren't entirely independent of each other: when a dynamic splitter window is split horizontally, the two rows have independent vertical scroll bars but share a horizontal scroll bar. Similarly, the two columns of a dynamic splitter window split vertically contain horizontal scroll bars of their own but share a vertical scroll bar. The maximum number of rows and columns a dynamic splitter window can be divided into are specified when the splitter is created. Thus, it's a simple matter to create a dynamic splitter window that can be split horizontally or vertically but not both. Figure 9-1 shows examples of static and dynamic splitter windows and highlights some of their differences.

One criterion for choosing between static and dynamic splitter windows is whether you want the user to be able to change the splitter's row and column configuration interactively. Use a dynamic splitter window if you do. Another factor in the decision is what kinds of views you plan to use in the splitter's panes. It's easy to use two or more different classes of views in a static splitter window because you specify the type of view that goes in each pane. The views in a dynamic splitter window, however, are managed entirely by the framework, so a dynamic splitter uses the same view class for all of its views unless you derive a new class from *CSplitterWnd* and modify the splitter's default behavior.

Static splitter window

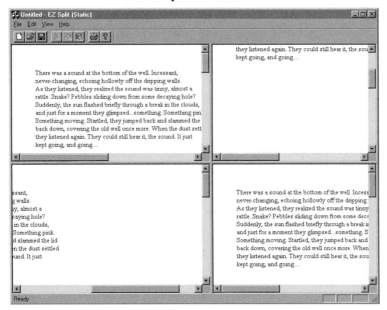

The maximum number of rows and columns equals 16 by 16. Rows and columns may be resized, but the total number of rows and columns is fixed.

Each pane has its own vertical and horizontal scroll bars.

Dynamic splitter window

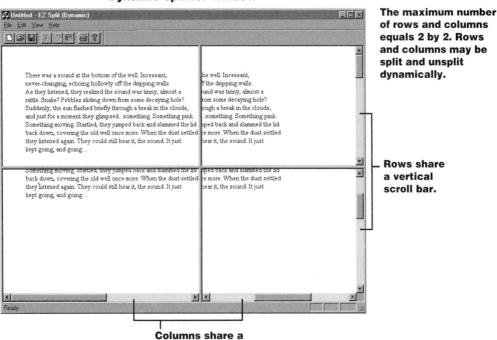

The maximum number of rows and columns equals 2 by 2. Rows and columns may be split and unsplit dynamically.

Rows share a vertical scroll bar.

Columns share a horizontal scroll bar.

Figure 9-1. *Static vs. dynamic splitter windows.*

Creating Dynamic Splitter Windows

Dynamic splitter windows are created with MFC's *CSplitterWnd::Create* function. Creating and initializing a dynamic splitter window is a simple two-step procedure:

1.   Add a *CSplitterWnd* data member to the frame window class.

2.   Override the frame window's virtual *OnCreateClient* function, and call *CSplitterWnd::Create* to create a dynamic splitter window in the frame window's client area.

The following *OnCreateClient* override creates a dynamic splitter window inside the frame window *CMyFrame*:

```
BOOL CMyFrame::OnCreateClient (LPCREATESTRUCT lpcs,
    CCreateContext* pContext)
{
    return m_wndSplitter.Create (this, 2, 2, CSize (1, 1), pContext);
}
```

In this example, *m_wndSplitter* is a *CSplitterWnd* object that's a member of the frame window class. The first parameter passed to *CSplitterWnd::Create* identifies the splitter window's parent. The second and third parameters specify the maximum number of rows and columns that the window can be split into. Since a dynamic splitter window supports a maximum of two rows and two columns, these parameter values will always be 1 or 2. The fourth parameter specifies each pane's minimum width and height in pixels. The framework uses these values to determine when panes should be created and destroyed as splitter bars are moved. *CSize* values equal to (1, 1) specify that panes can be as little as 1 pixel wide and 1 pixel tall. The fifth parameter is a pointer to a *CCreateContext* structure provided by the framework. The structure's *m_pNewViewClass* member identifies the view class that will be used in the splitter's panes. The framework creates the initial view for you and puts it into the first pane. Other views of the same class are created automatically as additional panes are created.

CSplitterWnd::Create supports optional sixth and seventh parameters specifying the splitter window's style and its child window ID. In most instances, the defaults are fine. The default child window ID of AFX_IDW_PANE_FIRST is a "magic number" that enables a frame window to identify the splitter window associated with it. The ID needs to be modified only if you create a second splitter window in a frame window that already contains a splitter.

Once a dynamic splitter window is created, the framework provides the logic to make it work. If the window is initially unsplit and the user drags a vertical splitter bar to the middle of the window, for example, the framework splits the window vertically and creates a view to go with the pane. Because the new view is created at run-time, the view class must support dynamic creation. If the user later drags the vertical splitter bar to the left or right edge of the window (or close enough to the edge that either pane's width is less than the minimum width specified when the splitter window was created), the framework destroys the secondary pane.

The *CSplitterWnd* class includes a number of useful member functions you can call on to query a splitter window for information. Among other things, you can ask for the number of rows or columns currently displayed, for the width or height of a row or column, or for a *CView* pointer to the view in a particular row and column. If you'd like to add a Split command to your application's menu, include a menu item whose ID is ID_WINDOW_SPLIT. This ID is prewired to the command handler *CView-::OnSplitCmd* and the update handler *CView::OnUpdateSplit* in *CView*'s message map. Internally, *CView::OnSplitCmd* calls *CSplitterWnd::DoKeyboardSplit* to begin a tracking process that allows phantom splitter bars to be moved with the up and down arrow keys. Tracking ends when Enter is pressed to accept the new splitter position or Esc is pressed to cancel the operation.

Linking the Views with *CDocument::UpdateAllViews* and *CView::OnUpdate*

When you add a splitter window to an SDI application, it's up to you to make sure that when the document is edited in one view, the other views get updated, too. The framework provides the mechanism to make this happen in the form of the *CDocument::UpdateAllViews* and *CView::OnUpdate* functions, which we looked at briefly in Chapter 8. It's time to examine these functions more closely.

Suppose you write a paint application that uses a dynamic splitter window to allow the user to display as many as four views of the document. If a change made in one of the views affects the images displayed in the others, all of the views should be updated to reflect the change. That's what *CDocument::UpdateAllViews* is for. A document object keeps a list of all the views that are associated with it, including the views displayed in the panes of a splitter window. When a document's data is modified in a multiple view application, either the object that made the modification (usually a view object) or the document object itself should call *UpdateAllViews* to update the views. *UpdateAllViews* iterates through the list of views, calling each view's virtual *OnUpdate* function. By calling *UpdateAllViews* whenever a document is modified, you can keep different views of the same document in sync with each other and ensure that changes made in one view of the document show up in all the other views of the document as well.

CView provides a trivial implementation of *OnUpdate* that invalidates the view and forces a call to *OnDraw*. However, this is an inefficient way to update a view because it forces the entire view to be redrawn. Frequently, only a small part of the view needs to be redrawn, so *UpdateAllViews* and *OnUpdate* support "hint" parameters you can use to optimize the repainting process. *UpdateAllViews* is prototyped as follows:

```
void UpdateAllViews (CView* pSender, LPARAM lHint = 0L,
    CObject* pHint = NULL)
```

The function prototype for *OnUpdate* looks very similar:

```
virtual void OnUpdate (CView* pSender, LPARAM lHint,
    CObject* pHint)
```

The first parameter, *pSender*, identifies the view that updated the document. If *pSender* is non-NULL, *UpdateAllViews* updates all views except the one identified by *pSender*. If *pSender* is NULL, *UpdateAllViews* updates all of the document's views. The usual practice is to let the view that changes the document update itself directly and then call *UpdateAllViews* with *pSender* equal to *this*. However, it's equally valid to let the view call *UpdateAllViews* with *pSender* equal to NULL and do its own updating in *On-Update*, just as if the document had been modified in another view. Sometimes the document object calls *UpdateAllViews* itself, in which case setting *pSender* to NULL ensures that all of the views get updated.

The *lHint* and *pHint* parameters contain hint information passed from *Update-AllViews* to *OnUpdate*. How you use these parameters is up to you and is highly application-specific. A simple use for hint information is to pass the address of a RECT structure or a *CRect* object in *lHint* specifying what part of the view needs updating. *OnUpdate* can then use that information to minimize the repainting it does. If the document's data consists of an array of *CObject*s and *UpdateAllViews* is called because a new *CObject* was added to the document, *pHint* could be used to pass the new *CObject*'s address. You shouldn't assume that *OnUpdate* won't be called with NULL *lHint* and *pHint* parameters just because your code passes non-NULL hint parameters to *UpdateAllViews*. The framework's default implementation of *OnInitialUpdate* calls *OnUpdate* with *lHint* and *pHint* equal to 0 and NULL, respectively, when a document is created or loaded. If *OnUpdate* is called and *lHint* and *pHint* hold values you didn't expect, forward the call to the base class and the framework will see that the view is redrawn.

UpdateAllViews and *OnUpdate* aren't just for splitter windows; they're useful for any application that supports multiple views of a document, including MDI applications that display different views of a document in separate MDI document frames. The sample program in the next section demonstrates how *UpdateAllViews* and *OnUpdate* are used in an SDI application with a splitter window. Later you'll see that once a view class is modified to use *UpdateAllViews* and *OnUpdate*, it will work perfectly well in MDI applications, too.

The Paint5 Application

Figure 9-2 contains the source code for Paint5, a modified version of Chapter 8's Paint4 program that uses a dynamic splitter window to provide multiple views of an SDI application's document. The Paint5 user interface is shown in Figure 9-3 on page 618, with the splitter window divided into two rows. By grabbing the splitter button in the lower left corner of the window and dragging it to the right, the user can split the window vertically and turn the two panes into four. The user can draw in any pane, and the changes will automatically show up in the other panes, too. Note that four of the source code files necessary to build Paint5—CLine.h, CLine.cpp, AboutDlg.h, and AboutDlg.cpp—are not reproduced here because they are identical to the files of the same name in Chapter 8.

Resource.h

```
//**********************************************************************
//
//   Resource.h
//
//**********************************************************************

#define IDR_MAINFRAME          100
#define IDR_CONTEXTMENU        101

#define IDD_ABOUTDLG           110
#define IDC_ICONRECT           111

#define ID_WIDTH_VTHIN         120
#define ID_WIDTH_THIN          121
#define ID_WIDTH_MEDIUM        122
#define ID_WIDTH_THICK         123
#define ID_WIDTH_VTHICK        124

#define ID_COLOR_BLACK         130
#define ID_COLOR_BLUE          131
#define ID_COLOR_GREEN         132
#define ID_COLOR_CYAN          133
#define ID_COLOR_RED           134
#define ID_COLOR_MAGENTA       135
#define ID_COLOR_YELLOW        136
#define ID_COLOR_WHITE         137
```

Figure 9-2. *The Paint5 program.*

Paint5.rc

```
//*********************************************************************
//
//   Paint5.rc
//
//*********************************************************************

#include <afxres.h>
#include "Resource.h"

IDR_MAINFRAME ICON Paint.ico

IDR_MAINFRAME MENU
BEGIN
    POPUP "&File" {
        MENUITEM "&New\tCtrl+N",            ID_FILE_NEW
        MENUITEM "&Open...\tCtrl+O",        ID_FILE_OPEN
        MENUITEM "&Save\tCtrl+S",           ID_FILE_SAVE
        MENUITEM "Save &As...\tCtrl+A",     ID_FILE_SAVE_AS
        MENUITEM SEPARATOR
        MENUITEM "Sen&d...",                ID_FILE_SEND_MAIL
        MENUITEM SEPARATOR
        MENUITEM "Recent File",             ID_FILE_MRU_FILE1
        MENUITEM SEPARATOR
        MENUITEM "E&xit",                   ID_APP_EXIT
    }
    POPUP "&Width" {
        MENUITEM "&Very Thin\tF5",          ID_WIDTH_VTHIN
        MENUITEM "Thi&n\tF6",               ID_WIDTH_THIN
        MENUITEM "&Medium\tF7",             ID_WIDTH_MEDIUM
        MENUITEM "Thic&k\tF8",              ID_WIDTH_THICK
        MENUITEM "Very &Thick\tF9",         ID_WIDTH_VTHICK
    }
    POPUP "&Color" {
        MENUITEM "",                        ID_COLOR_BLACK
        MENUITEM "",                        ID_COLOR_BLUE
        MENUITEM "",                        ID_COLOR_GREEN
        MENUITEM "",                        ID_COLOR_CYAN
        MENUITEM "",                        ID_COLOR_RED
        MENUITEM "",                        ID_COLOR_MAGENTA
        MENUITEM "",                        ID_COLOR_YELLOW
        MENUITEM "",                        ID_COLOR_WHITE
    }
```

```
    POPUP "&Help" {
        MENUITEM "&About Paint5...",          ID_APP_ABOUT
    }
END

IDR_MAINFRAME ACCELERATORS
BEGIN
    "N",      ID_FILE_NEW,          VIRTKEY,     CONTROL
    "O",      ID_FILE_OPEN,         VIRTKEY,     CONTROL
    "S",      ID_FILE_SAVE,         VIRTKEY,     CONTROL
    "A",      ID_FILE_SAVE_AS,      VIRTKEY,     CONTROL

    VK_F5,    ID_WIDTH_VTHIN,       VIRTKEY
    VK_F6,    ID_WIDTH_THIN,        VIRTKEY
    VK_F7,    ID_WIDTH_MEDIUM,      VIRTKEY
    VK_F8,    ID_WIDTH_THICK,       VIRTKEY
    VK_F9,    ID_WIDTH_VTHICK,      VIRTKEY

    "B",      ID_COLOR_BLACK,       VIRTKEY,     CONTROL
    "L",      ID_COLOR_BLUE,        VIRTKEY,     CONTROL
    "G",      ID_COLOR_GREEN,       VIRTKEY,     CONTROL
    "C",      ID_COLOR_CYAN,        VIRTKEY,     CONTROL
    "R",      ID_COLOR_RED,         VIRTKEY,     CONTROL
    "M",      ID_COLOR_MAGENTA,     VIRTKEY,     CONTROL
    "Y",      ID_COLOR_YELLOW,      VIRTKEY,     CONTROL
    "W",      ID_COLOR_WHITE,       VIRTKEY,     CONTROL
END

IDR_CONTEXTMENU MENU
BEGIN
    POPUP "" {
        POPUP "&Width" {
            MENUITEM "&Very Thin",            ID_WIDTH_VTHIN
            MENUITEM "&Thin",                 ID_WIDTH_THIN
            MENUITEM "&Medium",               ID_WIDTH_MEDIUM
            MENUITEM "Thi&ck",                ID_WIDTH_THICK
            MENUITEM "Very Thic&k",           ID_WIDTH_VTHICK
        }
        POPUP "&Color" {
            MENUITEM "",                      ID_COLOR_BLACK
            MENUITEM "",                      ID_COLOR_BLUE
            MENUITEM "",                      ID_COLOR_GREEN
            MENUITEM "",                      ID_COLOR_CYAN
            MENUITEM "",                      ID_COLOR_RED
            MENUITEM "",                      ID_COLOR_MAGENTA
```

(continued)

Paint5.rc *continued*

```
            MENUITEM "",                    ID_COLOR_YELLOW
            MENUITEM "",                    ID_COLOR_WHITE
        }
    }
END


STRINGTABLE
BEGIN
    IDR_MAINFRAME "Paint5\n\n\nPaint Files (*.pnt)\n.pnt\nPaint.Document\nPaint Document"
END


IDD_ABOUTDLG DIALOG 0, 0, 256, 98
STYLE DS_MODALFRAME | DS_CENTER | WS_POPUP | WS_VISIBLE | WS_CAPTION |
    WS_SYSMENU
CAPTION "About Paint5"
FONT 8, "MS Sans Serif"
BEGIN
    LTEXT           "", IDC_ICONRECT, 14, 12, 80, 74
    LTEXT           "Paint5 Version 1.0", -1, 108, 12, 136, 8
    LTEXT           "From the book", -1, 108, 32, 136, 8
    LTEXT           """Programming Windows 95 with MFC""", -1,
                    108, 42, 136, 8
    LTEXT           "Copyright © 1996 by Jeff Prosise", -1,
                    108, 52, 136, 8
    DEFPUSHBUTTON   "OK", IDOK, 108, 72, 50, 14
END
```

Paint5.h

```cpp
//*********************************************************************
//
// Paint5.h
//
//*********************************************************************

class CPaintApp : public CWinApp
{
public:
    virtual BOOL InitInstance ();

protected:
    afx_msg void OnAppAbout ();
    DECLARE_MESSAGE_MAP ()
};
```

Paint5.cpp

```
//******************************************************************************
//
//  Paint5.cpp
//
//******************************************************************************

#include <afxwin.h>
#include <afxext.h>
#include "Resource.h"
#include "CLine.h"
#include "Paint5.h"
#include "MainFrame.h"
#include "Paint5Doc.h"
#include "Paint5View.h"
#include "AboutDlg.h"

CPaintApp myApp;

BEGIN_MESSAGE_MAP (CPaintApp, CWinApp)
    ON_COMMAND (ID_FILE_NEW, CWinApp::OnFileNew)
    ON_COMMAND (ID_FILE_OPEN, CWinApp::OnFileOpen)
    ON_COMMAND (ID_APP_ABOUT, OnAppAbout)
END_MESSAGE_MAP ()

BOOL CPaintApp::InitInstance ()
{
    SetRegistryKey ("Programming Windows 95 with MFC");
    LoadStdProfileSettings ();

    CSingleDocTemplate* pDocTemplate;
    pDocTemplate = new CSingleDocTemplate (
        IDR_MAINFRAME,
        RUNTIME_CLASS (CPaintDoc),
        RUNTIME_CLASS (CMainFrame),
        RUNTIME_CLASS (CPaintView)
    );

    AddDocTemplate (pDocTemplate);
    RegisterShellFileTypes (TRUE);

    CCommandLineInfo cmdInfo;
    ParseCommandLine (cmdInfo);

    if (!ProcessShellCommand (cmdInfo))
        return FALSE;
```

(continued)

Paint5.cpp *continued*

```
    m_pMainWnd->DragAcceptFiles ();
    return TRUE;
}

void CPaintApp::OnAppAbout ()
{
    CAboutDialog dlg;
    dlg.DoModal ();
}
```

MainFrame.h

```
//*********************************************************************
//
//  MainFrame.h
//
//*********************************************************************

class CMainFrame : public CFrameWnd
{
    DECLARE_DYNCREATE (CMainFrame)

private:
    CSplitterWnd m_wndSplitter;

protected:
    virtual BOOL OnCreateClient (LPCREATESTRUCT, CCreateContext*);

    afx_msg int OnCreate (LPCREATESTRUCT);
    afx_msg void OnMeasureItem (int, LPMEASUREITEMSTRUCT);
    afx_msg void OnDrawItem (int, LPDRAWITEMSTRUCT);

    DECLARE_MESSAGE_MAP ()
};
```

MainFrame.cpp

```
//*********************************************************************
//
//  MainFrame.cpp
//
//*********************************************************************

#define OEMRESOURCE
```

```
#include <afxwin.h>
#include <afxext.h>
#include "Resource.h"
#include "CLine.h"
#include "MainFrame.h"
#include "Paint5Doc.h"


IMPLEMENT_DYNCREATE (CMainFrame, CFrameWnd)

BEGIN_MESSAGE_MAP (CMainFrame, CFrameWnd)
    ON_WM_CREATE ()
    ON_WM_MEASUREITEM ()
    ON_WM_DRAWITEM ()
END_MESSAGE_MAP ()

int CMainFrame::OnCreate (LPCREATESTRUCT lpcs)
{
    if (CFrameWnd::OnCreate (lpcs) == -1)
        return -1;

    CMenu* pMenu = GetMenu ();
    for (int i=0; i<8; i++)
        pMenu->ModifyMenu (ID_COLOR_BLACK + i,
            MF_BYCOMMAND | MF_OWNERDRAW, ID_COLOR_BLACK + i);
    return 0;
}


BOOL CMainFrame::OnCreateClient (LPCREATESTRUCT lpcs,
    CCreateContext* pContext)
{
    return m_wndSplitter.Create (this, 2, 2, CSize (1, 1), pContext);
}


void CMainFrame::OnMeasureItem (int nIDCtl, LPMEASUREITEMSTRUCT lpmis)
{
    lpmis->itemWidth = ::GetSystemMetrics (SM_CYMENU) * 4;
    lpmis->itemHeight = ::GetSystemMetrics (SM_CYMENU);
}


void CMainFrame::OnDrawItem (int nIDCtl, LPDRAWITEMSTRUCT lpdis)
{
    BITMAP bm;
    CBitmap bitmap;
    bitmap.LoadOEMBitmap (OBM_CHECK);
    bitmap.GetObject (sizeof (bm), &bm);
```

(continued)

MainFrame.cpp *continued*

```
        CDC dc;
        dc.Attach (lpdis->hDC);

        CBrush* pBrush = new CBrush (::GetSysColor ((lpdis->itemState &
            ODS_SELECTED) ? COLOR_HIGHLIGHT : COLOR_MENU));
        dc.FrameRect (&(lpdis->rcItem), pBrush);
        delete pBrush;

        if (lpdis->itemState & ODS_CHECKED) {
            CDC dcMem;
            dcMem.CreateCompatibleDC (&dc);
            CBitmap* pOldBitmap = dcMem.SelectObject (&bitmap);

            dc.BitBlt (lpdis->rcItem.left + 4, lpdis->rcItem.top +
                (((lpdis->rcItem.bottom - lpdis->rcItem.top) -
                bm.bmHeight) / 2), bm.bmWidth, bm.bmHeight, &dcMem,
                0, 0, SRCCOPY);

            dcMem.SelectObject (pOldBitmap);
        }

        pBrush = new CBrush (CPaintDoc::m_crColors[lpdis->itemID -
            ID_COLOR_BLACK]);
        CRect rect = lpdis->rcItem;
        rect.DeflateRect (6, 4);
        rect.left += bm.bmWidth;
        dc.FillRect (rect, pBrush);
        delete pBrush;

        dc.Detach ();
}
```

Paint5Doc.h

```
//*****************************************************************************
//
// Paint5Doc.h
//
//*****************************************************************************

class CPaintDoc : public CDocument
{
    DECLARE_DYNCREATE (CPaintDoc)

private:
```

```
        UINT m_nWidth;
        UINT m_nColor;
        CObArray m_lineArray;

        void InitWidthAndColor ();

public:
        static const COLORREF m_crColors[8];

        CPaintDoc ();
        virtual BOOL OnNewDocument ();
        virtual BOOL OnOpenDocument (LPCTSTR);
        virtual void DeleteContents ();
        virtual void Serialize (CArchive&);

        CLine* AddLine (CPoint, CPoint);
        CLine* GetLine (int);
        int GetLineCount ();

protected:
        afx_msg void OnWidth (UINT);
        afx_msg void OnColor (UINT);
        afx_msg void OnUpdateWidthUI (CCmdUI*);
        afx_msg void OnUpdateColorUI (CCmdUI*);

        DECLARE_MESSAGE_MAP ()
};
```

Paint5Doc.cpp

```
//************************************************************************
//
//  Paint5Doc.cpp
//
//************************************************************************

#include <afxwin.h>
#include "Resource.h"
#include "CLine.h"
#include "Paint5Doc.h"

IMPLEMENT_DYNCREATE (CPaintDoc, CDocument)

BEGIN_MESSAGE_MAP (CPaintDoc, CDocument)
    ON_COMMAND (ID_FILE_SEND_MAIL, OnFileSendMail)
```

(continued)

Paint5Doc.cpp *continued*

```
    ON_COMMAND_RANGE (ID_WIDTH_VTHIN, ID_WIDTH_VTHICK, OnWidth)
    ON_COMMAND_RANGE (ID_COLOR_BLACK, ID_COLOR_WHITE, OnColor)
    ON_UPDATE_COMMAND_UI (ID_FILE_SEND_MAIL, OnUpdateFileSendMail)
    ON_UPDATE_COMMAND_UI_RANGE (ID_WIDTH_VTHIN, ID_WIDTH_VTHICK,
        OnUpdateWidthUI)
    ON_UPDATE_COMMAND_UI_RANGE (ID_COLOR_BLACK, ID_COLOR_WHITE,
        OnUpdateColorUI)
END_MESSAGE_MAP ()

const COLORREF CPaintDoc::m_crColors[8] = {
    RGB (  0,   0,   0),    // Black
    RGB (  0,   0, 255),    // Blue
    RGB (  0, 255,   0),    // Green
    RGB (  0, 255, 255),    // Cyan
    RGB (255,   0,   0),    // Red
    RGB (255,   0, 255),    // Magenta
    RGB (255, 255,   0),    // Yellow
    RGB (255, 255, 255)     // White
};

CPaintDoc::CPaintDoc ()
{
    m_lineArray.SetSize (0, 64);
}

BOOL CPaintDoc::OnNewDocument ()
{
    if (!CDocument::OnNewDocument ())
        return FALSE;

    InitWidthAndColor ();
    return TRUE;
}

BOOL CPaintDoc::OnOpenDocument (LPCTSTR lpszPathName)
{
    if (!CDocument::OnOpenDocument (lpszPathName))
        return FALSE;

    InitWidthAndColor ();
    return TRUE;
}

void CPaintDoc::InitWidthAndColor ()
{
    m_nColor = ID_COLOR_RED - ID_COLOR_BLACK;
```

```
        m_nWidth = ID_WIDTH_MEDIUM - ID_WIDTH_VTHIN;
}

void CPaintDoc::DeleteContents ()
{
    int nCount = m_lineArray.GetSize ();

    if (nCount) {
        for (int i=0; i<nCount; i++)
            delete m_lineArray[i];
        m_lineArray.RemoveAll ();
    }
}

void CPaintDoc::Serialize (CArchive& ar)
{
    m_lineArray.Serialize (ar);
}

CLine* CPaintDoc::AddLine (CPoint ptFrom, CPoint ptTo)
{
    static UINT nWidths[5] = { 1, 8, 16, 24, 32 };

    CLine* pLine;
    try {
        pLine = new CLine (ptFrom, ptTo, nWidths[m_nWidth],
            m_crColors[m_nColor]);
        m_lineArray.Add (pLine);
        SetModifiedFlag ();
    }
    catch (CMemoryException* e) {
        if (pLine != NULL) {
            delete pLine;
            pLine = NULL;
        }
        AfxMessageBox ("Out of memory", MB_ICONSTOP | MB_OK);
        e->Delete ();
    }
    return pLine;
}

CLine* CPaintDoc::GetLine (int nIndex)
{
    return (CLine*) m_lineArray[nIndex];
}
```

(continued)

Paint5Doc.cpp *continued*

```
int CPaintDoc::GetLineCount ()
{
    return m_lineArray.GetSize ();
}

void CPaintDoc::OnWidth (UINT nID)
{
    m_nWidth = nID - ID_WIDTH_VTHIN;
}

void CPaintDoc::OnColor (UINT nID)
{
    m_nColor = nID - ID_COLOR_BLACK;
}

void CPaintDoc::OnUpdateWidthUI (CCmdUI* pCmdUI)
{
    pCmdUI->SetCheck ((pCmdUI->m_nID - ID_WIDTH_VTHIN) == m_nWidth);
}

void CPaintDoc::OnUpdateColorUI (CCmdUI* pCmdUI)
{
    pCmdUI->SetCheck ((pCmdUI->m_nID - ID_COLOR_BLACK) == m_nColor);
}
```

Paint5View.h

```
//*********************************************************************
//
//  Paint5View.h
//
//*********************************************************************

class CPaintView : public CScrollView
{
    DECLARE_DYNCREATE (CPaintView)

private:
    CPoint m_ptFrom;
    CPoint m_ptTo;

    CPaintDoc* GetDocument () { return (CPaintDoc*) m_pDocument; }
    void InvertLine (CDC*, CPoint, CPoint);
```

```
public:
    virtual void OnInitialUpdate ();

protected:
    virtual void OnDraw (CDC*);
    virtual void OnUpdate (CView*, LPARAM, CObject*);

    afx_msg void OnLButtonDown (UINT, CPoint);
    afx_msg void OnMouseMove (UINT, CPoint);
    afx_msg void OnLButtonUp (UINT, CPoint);
    afx_msg void OnContextMenu (CWnd*, CPoint);

    DECLARE_MESSAGE_MAP ()
};
```

Paint5View.cpp

```
//****************************************************************************
//
//  Paint5View.cpp
//
//****************************************************************************

#include <afxwin.h>
#include "Resource.h"
#include "CLine.h"
#include "Paint5Doc.h"
#include "Paint5View.h"

IMPLEMENT_DYNCREATE (CPaintView, CScrollView)

BEGIN_MESSAGE_MAP (CPaintView, CScrollView)
    ON_WM_LBUTTONDOWN ()
    ON_WM_MOUSEMOVE ()
    ON_WM_LBUTTONUP ()
    ON_WM_CONTEXTMENU ()
END_MESSAGE_MAP ()

void CPaintView::OnInitialUpdate ()
{
    SetScrollSizes (MM_TEXT, CSize (2048, 2048));
    CScrollView::OnInitialUpdate ();
}
```

(continued)

Paint5View.cpp *continued*

```
void CPaintView::OnUpdate (CView* pSender, LPARAM lHint, CObject* pHint)
{
    if (pHint != NULL) {
        CClientDC dc (this);
        OnPrepareDC (&dc);
        ((CLine*) pHint)->Draw (&dc);
        return;
    }
    CScrollView::OnUpdate (pSender, lHint, pHint);
}

void CPaintView::OnDraw (CDC* pDC)
{
    CPaintDoc* pDoc = GetDocument ();
    int nCount = pDoc->GetLineCount ();

    if (nCount) {
        for (int i=0; i<nCount; i++)
            pDoc->GetLine (i)->Draw (pDC);
    }
}

void CPaintView::OnLButtonDown (UINT nFlags, CPoint point)
{
    CClientDC dc (this);
    OnPrepareDC (&dc);
    dc.DPtoLP (&point);

    m_ptFrom = point;
    m_ptTo = point;
    SetCapture ();
}

void CPaintView::OnMouseMove (UINT nFlags, CPoint point)
{
    if (GetCapture () == this) {
        CClientDC dc (this);
        OnPrepareDC (&dc);
        dc.DPtoLP (&point);

        InvertLine (&dc, m_ptFrom, m_ptTo);
        InvertLine (&dc, m_ptFrom, point);
        m_ptTo = point;
    }
}
```

```
void CPaintView::OnLButtonUp (UINT nFlags, CPoint point)
{
    if (GetCapture () == this) {
        ReleaseCapture ();
        CClientDC dc (this);
        OnPrepareDC (&dc);
        dc.DPtoLP (&point);
        InvertLine (&dc, m_ptFrom, m_ptTo);

        CLine* pLine = GetDocument ()->AddLine (m_ptFrom, point);
        if (pLine != NULL) {
            pLine->Draw (&dc);
            GetDocument ()->UpdateAllViews (this, 0, pLine);
        }
    }
}

void CPaintView::InvertLine (CDC* pDC, CPoint ptFrom, CPoint ptTo)
{
    int nOldMode = pDC->SetROP2 (R2_NOT);

    pDC->MoveTo (ptFrom);
    pDC->LineTo (ptTo);

    pDC->SetROP2 (nOldMode);
}

void CPaintView::OnContextMenu (CWnd* pWnd, CPoint point)
{
    CMenu menu;
    menu.LoadMenu (IDR_CONTEXTMENU);
    CMenu* pContextMenu = menu.GetSubMenu (0);

    for (int i=0; i<8; i++)
        pContextMenu->ModifyMenu (ID_COLOR_BLACK + i,
            MF_BYCOMMAND | MF_OWNERDRAW, ID_COLOR_BLACK + i);

    pContextMenu->TrackPopupMenu (TPM_LEFTALIGN | TPM_LEFTBUTTON |
        TPM_RIGHTBUTTON, point.x, point.y, AfxGetMainWnd ());
}
```

Paint5 is identical to Paint4 except for a few lines of code. A private *CSplitterWnd* data member named *m_wndSplitter* has been added to the *CMainFrame* class, and *CFrameWnd::OnCreateClient* has been overridden to create a dynamic splitter window with *CSplitterWnd::Create*. The only other change is to the *CPaintView* class, which now features an *OnUpdate* function for updating the view when *UpdateAllViews*

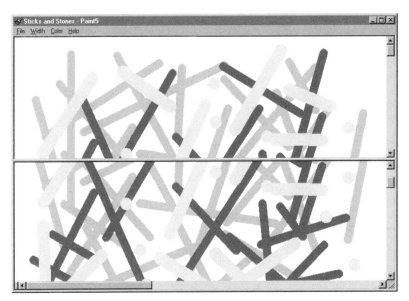

Figure 9-3. *The Paint5 window with a dynamic splitter window.*

is called. In addition, *CPaintView*'s *OnLButtonUp* handler now calls *UpdateAllViews* when a line is added to the document so that other views will be updated, too. The core *OnLButtonUp* code, which looked like this in Paint4:

```
CLine* pLine = GetDocument ()->AddLine (m_ptFrom, point);
if (pLine != NULL)
    pLine->Draw (&dc);
```

now looks like this:

```
CLine* pLine = GetDocument ()->AddLine (m_ptFrom, point);
if (pLine != NULL) {
    pLine->Draw (&dc);
    GetDocument ()->UpdateAllViews (this, 0, pLine);
}
```

After adding a line by calling the document's *AddLine* function and drawing the line in the current view, Paint5's view class calls *UpdateAllViews* through the document pointer with *pSender* equal to *this* so that all of the other views' *OnUpdate* functions will be called. *pHint* contains a pointer to the line that was added, making it a trivial matter for *OnUpdate* to update a view by drawing just one new line:

```
void CPaintView::OnUpdate (CView* pSender, LPARAM lHint,
    CObject* pHint)
{
    if (pHint != NULL) {
        CClientDC dc (this);
        OnPrepareDC (&dc);
```

```
        ((CLine*) pHint)->Draw (&dc);
        return;
    }
    CScrollView::OnUpdate (pSender, lHint, pHint);
}
```

This is much more efficient than redrawing the entire view with *OnDraw* because updating a view involves drawing just the one new line no matter how many lines are stored in the document. Note that if *pHint* equals NULL, the base class's *OnUpdate* function is called to redraw the entire view. That's important because, when *CPaint-View::OnInitialUpdate* calls *OnInitialUpdate* in the base class, the framework will call *OnUpdate* with a NULL *pHint* parameter. By handling both NULL and non-NULL *pHint* values properly, *OnUpdate* works hand in hand with the framework to ensure that all views are drawn properly at all times.

Creating Static Splitter Windows

Static splitter windows are handled very much as dynamic splitter windows are except that an extra step is involved in creating them. Static splitters are created with *CSplitterWnd::CreateStatic* rather than *CSplitterWnd::Create*, and after *CreateStatic* returns, it's up to you to add the views to the splitter's panes. *CSplitterWnd* provides a function named *CreateView* for this purpose. The procedure for adding a static splitter window to a frame window goes like this:

1. Add a *CSplitterWnd* data member to the frame window class.

2. Override the frame window's *OnCreateClient* function and call *CSplitter-Wnd::CreateStatic* to create a static splitter window.

3. Use *CSplitterWnd::CreateView* to create a view in each of the splitter window's panes.

One of the chief advantages of using a static splitter window is that since you put the views in the panes, you control what kinds of views are added. The following *OnCreateClient* override creates a static splitter window containing one row and two columns in a frame window and adds a *CTextView* to the left pane and a *CPictureView* to the right:

```
BOOL CMyFrame::OnCreateClient (LPCREATESTRUCT lpcs,
    CCreateContext* pContext)
{
    if (!m_wndSplitter.CreateStatic (this, 1, 2) ||
        !m_wndSplitter.CreateView (0, 0, RUNTIME_CLASS (CTextView),
            CSize (128, 0), pContext) ||
        !m_wndSplitter.CreateView (0, 1, RUNTIME_CLASS
            (CPictureView), CSize (0, 0), pContext))
```

(continued)

```
        return FALSE;

    return TRUE;
}
```

CreateStatic identifies the splitter window's parent as well as the number of rows and columns that the splitter contains. *CreateView* is called once for each pane. Panes are identified by 0-based row and column numbers. The first call to *CreateView* inserts a view of type *CTextView* into the left pane (row 0, column 0), and the second inserts a view of type *CPictureView* into the right pane (row 0, column 1). The views aren't instantiated directly but are created by the framework. Therefore, the application passes *CRuntimeClass* pointers to *CreateView* instead of pointers to real *CView* objects. As with a dynamic splitter window, the views used in a static splitter window must be dynamically creatable or the framework can't use them. The *CSize* objects passed to *CreateView* specify the panes' initial sizes. In this case, the *CTextView* pane will start out 128 pixels wide and the *CPictureView* pane will occupy the remaining width of the window. The width specified for the right pane and the heights specified for both the left and the right panes are 0 because these values are ignored by the framework. When a splitter window contains only one row, that row will occupy the full height of the parent's client area no matter what *CSize* values you specify. Similarly, if a splitter window contains *n* columns, the rightmost column will occupy all the space between the right edge of column *n*−1 and the edge of its parent.

Creating Three-Way Splitter Windows

You can create a three-way splitter window by nesting one static splitter window inside one of the panes of another static splitter window. The following *OnCreateClient* function creates a three-way static splitter that's divided into two panes vertically and whose right column is subdivided into two panes horizontally. The user can adjust the relative sizes of the panes by dragging the splitter bars, but the basic layout of the splitter can't be changed because the splitters are static rather than dynamic:

```
BOOL CMyFrame::OnCreateClient (LPCREATESTRUCT lpCreateStruct,
    CCreateContext* pContext)
{
    if (!m_wndSplitter1.CreateStatic (this, 1, 2) ||
        !m_wndSplitter1.CreateView (0, 0, RUNTIME_CLASS (CTextView),
            CSize (128, 0), pContext) ||
        !m_wndSplitter2.CreateStatic (&m_wndSplitter1, 2, 1, WS_CHILD
            | WS_VISIBLE, m_wndSplitter1.IdFromRowCol (0, 1)) ||
        !m_wndSplitter2.CreateView (0, 0, RUNTIME_CLASS (CPaintView),
            CSize (0, 128), pContext) ||
        !m_wndSplitter2.CreateView (1, 0, RUNTIME_CLASS (CPaintView),
            CSize (0, 0), pContext))
        return FALSE;
```

```
    return TRUE;
}
```

Here's a synopsis of what happens in the *if* statement that creates and initializes the three-way splitter:

1. The first splitter window (*m_wndSplitter1*) is created in the frame window with *CreateStatic*. *m_wndSplitter1* contains one row and two columns.

2. A *CTextView* is added to *m_wndSplitter1*'s first (left) pane with *CreateView*.

3. A second splitter window, *m_wndSplitter2*, is created in the right pane of *m_wndSplitter1*. *m_wndSplitter2* is parented to *m_wndSplitter1* rather than to the frame window and is assigned a child window ID that identifies it as the pane in row 0, column 1. The proper ID for *m_wndSplitter2* is obtained by calling *CSplitterWnd::IdFromRowCol*, which uses simple math to convert a row and column number into a numeric offset that's added to AFX_IDW_PANE_FIRST.

4. The *CreateView* function is called twice to add a *CPaintView* to each of the two *m_wndSplitter2* panes.

Using a dynamic splitter window for *m_wndSplitter2* would require a little more work because of some of the assumptions the framework makes when it creates new views to fill dynamically created splitter panes. If you try to nest a dynamic splitter window inside a static splitter window like this:

```
BOOL CMyFrame::OnCreateClient (LPCREATESTRUCT lpCreateStruct,
    CCreateContext* pContext)
{
    if (!m_wndSplitter1.CreateStatic (this, 1, 2) ||
        !m_wndSplitter1.CreateView (0, 0, RUNTIME_CLASS (CTextView),
            CSize (128, 0), pContext) ||
        !m_wndSplitter2.Create (&m_wndSplitter1, 2, 1, CSize (1, 1),
            pContext, WS_CHILD | WS_VISIBLE | WS_HSCROLL |
            WS_VSCROLL | SPLS_DYNAMIC_SPLIT,
            m_wndSplitter1.IdFromRowCol (0, 1)))
        return FALSE;

    return TRUE;
}
```

you'll sometimes generate access violations when splitting the dynamic splitter window. The reason why is rooted deep in the framework. When a dynamic splitter is split, the code in *CSplitterWnd* calls *CreateView* with a NULL *pContext* pointer to create a view for the new pane. Seeing that *pContext* is NULL, *CreateView* queries the frame window for a pointer to the active view (the view that has the input focus) and uses that view as a model for the new view. If the *CTextView* window happens to be the active view when a split occurs, the framework will see that the view is not a child of the dynamic splitter and create an "empty" view that isn't attached to a document object. The first time that view tries to access its document, an access violation will occur.

The Paint6 sample program in the next section demonstrates the proper way to nest a dynamic splitter inside a static splitter. The splitter windows are created exactly as shown in the example in the previous paragraph, but a little trick allows access violations to be avoided. Rather than instantiate the dynamic splitter window *m_wndSplitter2* directly from the class *CSplitterWnd*, Paint6 uses a *CSplitterWnd*-derived class named *CNestedSplitterWnd*. The only difference between *CSplitterWnd* and *CNestedSplitterWnd* is that the latter overrides the virtual *SplitRow* function called by the framework when a horizontal splitter bar is dragged to create a new pane. The override version of *SplitRow* makes the view in the dynamic splitter window's uppermost pane the active view before the split occurs, which neatly circumvents the dynamic view creation problems that result when the active view is a child of the static splitter window.

CNestedSplitterWnd::SplitRow contains just two lines of code:

```
BOOL CNestedSplitterWnd::SplitRow (int cyBefore)
{
    GetParentFrame ()->SetActiveView ((CView*) GetPane (0, 0));
    return CSplitterWnd::SplitRow (cyBefore);
}
```

The first statement retrieves a pointer to the splitter's parent frame and uses that pointer to set the active view with *SetActiveView*. The *CSplitterWnd::GetPane* function returns a *CWnd* pointer to the window that corresponds to the active view, so the return value must be cast to a *CView* pointer before being passed to *SetActiveView*. *GetParentFrame* is used instead of *GetParent* because the dynamic splitter window's parent is actually the static splitter window, not the frame window, and it is a frame window function (not a splitter window function) that sets the active view. The final statement calls the base class's *SplitRow* function to perform the split.

The Paint6 Application

The Paint6 application, listed in Figure 9-4, uses two splitter windows: a static splitter divided into one row and two columns, and a dynamic splitter nested inside the right column of the static splitter. The view in the static splitter window's left-hand column is a *CTextView*. The views in the right-hand column are *CPaintView*s just like the ones used in Paint5. The *CTextView* class draws a textual representation of the lines in the document. (See Figure 9-5.) The *CLine* class has been modified to include a new member function named *GetDescription*, which returns a *CString* with a textual description of a line. Drawing is done in the right pane(s), and each time a new line is drawn, a new line of text appears in the left pane. All three views are logically connected via their *OnUpdate* functions. AboutDlg.h and AboutDlg.cpp have been omitted from Figure 9-4 because they are identical to the AboutDlg files used in Paint4.

Resource.h

```
//****************************************************************
//
//  Resource.h
//
//****************************************************************

#define IDR_MAINFRAME          100
#define IDR_CONTEXTMENU        101

#define IDD_ABOUTDLG           110
#define IDC_ICONRECT           111

#define ID_WIDTH_VTHIN         120
#define ID_WIDTH_THIN          121
#define ID_WIDTH_MEDIUM        122
#define ID_WIDTH_THICK         123
#define ID_WIDTH_VTHICK        124

#define ID_COLOR_BLACK         130
#define ID_COLOR_BLUE          131
#define ID_COLOR_GREEN         132
#define ID_COLOR_CYAN          133
#define ID_COLOR_RED           134
#define ID_COLOR_MAGENTA       135
#define ID_COLOR_YELLOW        136
#define ID_COLOR_WHITE         137
```

Paint6.rc

```
//****************************************************************
//
//  Paint6.rc
//
//****************************************************************

#include <afxres.h>
#include "Resource.h"
```

Figure 9-4. *The Paint6 program.*

(continued)

Paint6.rc *continued*

```
IDR_MAINFRAME ICON Paint.ico

IDR_MAINFRAME MENU
BEGIN
    POPUP "&File" {
        MENUITEM "&New\tCtrl+N",            ID_FILE_NEW
        MENUITEM "&Open...\tCtrl+O",        ID_FILE_OPEN
        MENUITEM "&Save\tCtrl+S",           ID_FILE_SAVE
        MENUITEM "Save &As...\tCtrl+A",     ID_FILE_SAVE_AS
        MENUITEM SEPARATOR
        MENUITEM "Sen&d...",                ID_FILE_SEND_MAIL
        MENUITEM SEPARATOR
        MENUITEM "Recent File",             ID_FILE_MRU_FILE1
        MENUITEM SEPARATOR
        MENUITEM "E&xit",                   ID_APP_EXIT
    }
    POPUP "&Width" {
        MENUITEM "&Very Thin\tF5",          ID_WIDTH_VTHIN
        MENUITEM "Thi&n\tF6",               ID_WIDTH_THIN
        MENUITEM "&Medium\tF7",             ID_WIDTH_MEDIUM
        MENUITEM "Thic&k\tF8",              ID_WIDTH_THICK
        MENUITEM "Very &Thick\tF9",         ID_WIDTH_VTHICK
    }
    POPUP "&Color" {
        MENUITEM "",                        ID_COLOR_BLACK
        MENUITEM "",                        ID_COLOR_BLUE
        MENUITEM "",                        ID_COLOR_GREEN
        MENUITEM "",                        ID_COLOR_CYAN
        MENUITEM "",                        ID_COLOR_RED
        MENUITEM "",                        ID_COLOR_MAGENTA
        MENUITEM "",                        ID_COLOR_YELLOW
        MENUITEM "",                        ID_COLOR_WHITE
    }
    POPUP "&Help" {
        MENUITEM "&About Paint6...",        ID_APP_ABOUT
    }
END

IDR_MAINFRAME ACCELERATORS
BEGIN
    "N",    ID_FILE_NEW,        VIRTKEY,    CONTROL
    "O",    ID_FILE_OPEN,       VIRTKEY,    CONTROL
    "S",    ID_FILE_SAVE,       VIRTKEY,    CONTROL
    "A",    ID_FILE_SAVE_AS,    VIRTKEY,    CONTROL
```

```
    VK_F5,  ID_WIDTH_VTHIN,     VIRTKEY
    VK_F6,  ID_WIDTH_THIN,      VIRTKEY
    VK_F7,  ID_WIDTH_MEDIUM,    VIRTKEY
    VK_F8,  ID_WIDTH_THICK,     VIRTKEY
    VK_F9,  ID_WIDTH_VTHICK,    VIRTKEY

    "B",    ID_COLOR_BLACK,     VIRTKEY,    CONTROL
    "L",    ID_COLOR_BLUE,      VIRTKEY,    CONTROL
    "G",    ID_COLOR_GREEN,     VIRTKEY,    CONTROL
    "C",    ID_COLOR_CYAN,      VIRTKEY,    CONTROL
    "R",    ID_COLOR_RED,       VIRTKEY,    CONTROL
    "M",    ID_COLOR_MAGENTA,   VIRTKEY,    CONTROL
    "Y",    ID_COLOR_YELLOW,    VIRTKEY,    CONTROL
    "W",    ID_COLOR_WHITE,     VIRTKEY,    CONTROL
END

IDR_CONTEXTMENU MENU
BEGIN
    POPUP "" {
        POPUP "&Width" {
            MENUITEM "&Very Thin",          ID_WIDTH_VTHIN
            MENUITEM "&Thin",               ID_WIDTH_THIN
            MENUITEM "&Medium",             ID_WIDTH_MEDIUM
            MENUITEM "Thi&ck",              ID_WIDTH_THICK
            MENUITEM "Very Thic&k",         ID_WIDTH_VTHICK
        }
        POPUP "&Color" {
            MENUITEM "",                    ID_COLOR_BLACK
            MENUITEM "",                    ID_COLOR_BLUE
            MENUITEM "",                    ID_COLOR_GREEN
            MENUITEM "",                    ID_COLOR_CYAN
            MENUITEM "",                    ID_COLOR_RED
            MENUITEM "",                    ID_COLOR_MAGENTA
            MENUITEM "",                    ID_COLOR_YELLOW
            MENUITEM "",                    ID_COLOR_WHITE
        }
    }
END

STRINGTABLE
BEGIN
    IDR_MAINFRAME "Paint6\n\n\nPaint Files (*.pnt)\n.pnt\nPaint.Document\nPaint Document"
END
```

(continued)

Paint6.rc *continued*

```
IDD_ABOUTDLG DIALOG 0, 0, 256, 98
STYLE DS_MODALFRAME | DS_CENTER | WS_POPUP | WS_VISIBLE | WS_CAPTION |
    WS_SYSMENU
CAPTION "About Paint6"
FONT 8, "MS Sans Serif"
BEGIN
    LTEXT           "", IDC_ICONRECT, 14, 12, 80, 74
    LTEXT           "Paint6 Version 1.0", -1, 108, 12, 136, 8
    LTEXT           "From the book", -1, 108, 32, 136, 8
    LTEXT           """Programming Windows 95 with MFC""", -1,
                    108, 42, 136, 8
    LTEXT           "Copyright © 1996 by Jeff Prosise", -1,
                    108, 52, 136, 8
    DEFPUSHBUTTON   "OK", IDOK, 108, 72, 50, 14
END
```

Paint6.h

```
//*********************************************************************
//
// Paint6.h
//
//*********************************************************************

class CPaintApp : public CWinApp
{
public:
    virtual BOOL InitInstance ();

protected:
    afx_msg void OnAppAbout ();
    DECLARE_MESSAGE_MAP ()
};
```

Paint6.cpp

```
//*********************************************************************
/
// Paint6.cpp
//
//*********************************************************************

#include <afxwin.h>
#include <afxext.h>
#include "Resource.h"
```

```
#include "CLine.h"
#include "Paint6.h"
#include "Splitter.h"
#include "MainFrame.h"
#include "Paint6Doc.h"
#include "Paint6View.h"
#include "AboutDlg.h"

CPaintApp myApp;

BEGIN_MESSAGE_MAP (CPaintApp, CWinApp)
    ON_COMMAND (ID_FILE_NEW, CWinApp::OnFileNew)
    ON_COMMAND (ID_FILE_OPEN, CWinApp::OnFileOpen)
    ON_COMMAND (ID_APP_ABOUT, OnAppAbout)
END_MESSAGE_MAP ()

BOOL CPaintApp::InitInstance ()
{
    SetRegistryKey ("Programming Windows 95 with MFC");
    LoadStdProfileSettings ();

    CSingleDocTemplate* pDocTemplate;
    pDocTemplate = new CSingleDocTemplate (
        IDR_MAINFRAME,
        RUNTIME_CLASS (CPaintDoc),
        RUNTIME_CLASS (CMainFrame),
        RUNTIME_CLASS (CPaintView)
    );

    AddDocTemplate (pDocTemplate);
    RegisterShellFileTypes (TRUE);

    CCommandLineInfo cmdInfo;
    ParseCommandLine (cmdInfo);

    if (!ProcessShellCommand (cmdInfo))
        return FALSE;

    m_pMainWnd->DragAcceptFiles ();
    return TRUE;
}

void CPaintApp::OnAppAbout ()
{
    CAboutDialog dlg;
    dlg.DoModal ();
}
```

MainFrame.h

```
//*********************************************************************
//
//  MainFrame.h
//
//*********************************************************************

class CMainFrame : public CFrameWnd
{
    DECLARE_DYNCREATE (CMainFrame)

private:
    CSplitterWnd m_wndSplitter1;
    CNestedSplitterWnd m_wndSplitter2;

protected:
    virtual BOOL OnCreateClient (LPCREATESTRUCT, CCreateContext*);

    afx_msg int OnCreate (LPCREATESTRUCT);
    afx_msg void OnMeasureItem (int, LPMEASUREITEMSTRUCT);
    afx_msg void OnDrawItem (int, LPDRAWITEMSTRUCT);

    DECLARE_MESSAGE_MAP ()
};
```

MainFrame.cpp

```
//*********************************************************************
//
//  MainFrame.cpp
//
//*********************************************************************

#define OEMRESOURCE

#include <afxwin.h>
#include <afxext.h>
#include "Resource.h"
#include "CLine.h"
#include "Splitter.h"
#include "MainFrame.h"
#include "Paint6Doc.h"
#include "TextView.h"

IMPLEMENT_DYNCREATE (CMainFrame, CFrameWnd)
```

```
BEGIN_MESSAGE_MAP (CMainFrame, CFrameWnd)
    ON_WM_CREATE ()
    ON_WM_MEASUREITEM ()
    ON_WM_DRAWITEM ()
END_MESSAGE_MAP ()

int CMainFrame::OnCreate (LPCREATESTRUCT lpcs)
{
    if (CFrameWnd::OnCreate (lpcs) == -1)
        return -1;

    CMenu* pMenu = GetMenu ();
    for (int i=0; i<8; i++)
        pMenu->ModifyMenu (ID_COLOR_BLACK + i,
            MF_BYCOMMAND | MF_OWNERDRAW, ID_COLOR_BLACK + i);
    return 0;
}

BOOL CMainFrame::OnCreateClient (LPCREATESTRUCT lpcs,
    CCreateContext* pContext)
{
    if (!m_wndSplitter1.CreateStatic (this, 1, 2) ||
        !m_wndSplitter1.CreateView (0, 0, RUNTIME_CLASS (CTextView),
            CSize (160, 0), pContext) ||
        !m_wndSplitter2.Create (&m_wndSplitter1, 2, 1, CSize (1, 1),
            pContext, WS_CHILD | WS_VISIBLE | WS_HSCROLL | WS_VSCROLL |
            SPLS_DYNAMIC_SPLIT, m_wndSplitter1.IdFromRowCol (0, 1)))
        return FALSE;

    return TRUE;
}

void CMainFrame::OnMeasureItem (int nIDCtl, LPMEASUREITEMSTRUCT lpmis)
{
    lpmis->itemWidth = ::GetSystemMetrics (SM_CYMENU) * 4;
    lpmis->itemHeight = ::GetSystemMetrics (SM_CYMENU);
}

void CMainFrame::OnDrawItem (int nIDCtl, LPDRAWITEMSTRUCT lpdis)
{
    BITMAP bm;
    CBitmap bitmap;
    bitmap.LoadOEMBitmap (OBM_CHECK);
    bitmap.GetObject (sizeof (bm), &bm);
```

(continued)

MainFrame.cpp *continued*

```
    CDC dc;
    dc.Attach (lpdis->hDC);

    CBrush* pBrush = new CBrush (::GetSysColor ((lpdis->itemState &
        ODS_SELECTED) ? COLOR_HIGHLIGHT : COLOR_MENU));
    dc.FrameRect (&(lpdis->rcItem), pBrush);
    delete pBrush;

    if (lpdis->itemState & ODS_CHECKED) {
        CDC dcMem;
        dcMem.CreateCompatibleDC (&dc);
        CBitmap* pOldBitmap = dcMem.SelectObject (&bitmap);

        dc.BitBlt (lpdis->rcItem.left + 4, lpdis->rcItem.top +
            (((lpdis->rcItem.bottom - lpdis->rcItem.top) -
            bm.bmHeight) / 2), bm.bmWidth, bm.bmHeight, &dcMem,
            0, 0, SRCCOPY);

        dcMem.SelectObject (pOldBitmap);
    }

    pBrush = new CBrush (CPaintDoc::m_crColors[lpdis->itemID -
        ID_COLOR_BLACK]);
    CRect rect = lpdis->rcItem;
    rect.DeflateRect (6, 4);
    rect.left += bm.bmWidth;
    dc.FillRect (rect, pBrush);
    delete pBrush;

    dc.Detach ();
}
```

Paint6Doc.h

```
//****************************************************************************
//
// Paint6Doc.h
//
//****************************************************************************

class CPaintDoc : public CDocument
{
    DECLARE_DYNCREATE (CPaintDoc)
```

```
private:
    UINT m_nWidth;
    UINT m_nColor;
    CObArray m_lineArray;

    void InitWidthAndColor ();

public:
    static const COLORREF m_crColors[8];

    CPaintDoc ();
    virtual BOOL OnNewDocument ();
    virtual BOOL OnOpenDocument (LPCTSTR);
    virtual void DeleteContents ();
    virtual void Serialize (CArchive&);

    CLine* AddLine (CPoint, CPoint);
    CLine* GetLine (int);
    int GetLineCount ();

protected:
    afx_msg void OnWidth (UINT);
    afx_msg void OnColor (UINT);
    afx_msg void OnUpdateWidthUI (CCmdUI*);
    afx_msg void OnUpdateColorUI (CCmdUI*);

    DECLARE_MESSAGE_MAP ()
};
```

Paint6Doc.cpp

```
//****************************************************************************
//
// Paint6Doc.cpp
//
//****************************************************************************

#include <afxwin.h>
#include "Resource.h"
#include "CLine.h"
#include "Paint6Doc.h"

IMPLEMENT_DYNCREATE (CPaintDoc, CDocument)
```

(continued)

```
BEGIN_MESSAGE_MAP (CPaintDoc, CDocument)
    ON_COMMAND (ID_FILE_SEND_MAIL, OnFileSendMail)
    ON_COMMAND_RANGE (ID_WIDTH_VTHIN, ID_WIDTH_VTHICK, OnWidth)
    ON_COMMAND_RANGE (ID_COLOR_BLACK, ID_COLOR_WHITE, OnColor)
    ON_UPDATE_COMMAND_UI (ID_FILE_SEND_MAIL, OnUpdateFileSendMail)
    ON_UPDATE_COMMAND_UI_RANGE (ID_WIDTH_VTHIN, ID_WIDTH_VTHICK,
        OnUpdateWidthUI)
    ON_UPDATE_COMMAND_UI_RANGE (ID_COLOR_BLACK, ID_COLOR_WHITE,
        OnUpdateColorUI)
END_MESSAGE_MAP ()

const COLORREF CPaintDoc::m_crColors[8] = {
    RGB (  0,   0,   0),    // Black
    RGB (  0,   0, 255),    // Blue
    RGB (  0, 255,   0),    // Green
    RGB (  0, 255, 255),    // Cyan
    RGB (255,   0,   0),    // Red
    RGB (255,   0, 255),    // Magenta
    RGB (255, 255,   0),    // Yellow
    RGB (255, 255, 255)     // White
};

CPaintDoc::CPaintDoc ()
{
    m_lineArray.SetSize (0, 64);
}

BOOL CPaintDoc::OnNewDocument ()
{
    if (!CDocument::OnNewDocument ())
        return FALSE;

    InitWidthAndColor ();
    return TRUE;
}

BOOL CPaintDoc::OnOpenDocument (LPCTSTR lpszPathName)
{
    if (!CDocument::OnOpenDocument (lpszPathName))
        return FALSE;

    InitWidthAndColor ();
    return TRUE;
}

void CPaintDoc::InitWidthAndColor ()
{
```

```
    m_nColor = ID_COLOR_RED - ID_COLOR_BLACK;
    m_nWidth = ID_WIDTH_MEDIUM - ID_WIDTH_VTHIN;
}

void CPaintDoc::DeleteContents ()
{
    int nCount = m_lineArray.GetSize ();

    if (nCount) {
        for (int i=0; i<nCount; i++)
            delete m_lineArray[i];
        m_lineArray.RemoveAll ();
    }
}

void CPaintDoc::Serialize (CArchive& ar)
{
    m_lineArray.Serialize (ar);
}

CLine* CPaintDoc::AddLine (CPoint ptFrom, CPoint ptTo)
{
    static UINT nWidths[5] = { 1, 8, 16, 24, 32 };

    CLine* pLine;
    try {
        pLine = new CLine (ptFrom, ptTo, nWidths[m_nWidth],
            m_crColors[m_nColor]);
        m_lineArray.Add (pLine);
        SetModifiedFlag ();
    }
    catch (CMemoryException* e) {
        if (pLine != NULL) {
            delete pLine;
            pLine = NULL;
        }
        AfxMessageBox ("Out of memory", MB_ICONSTOP | MB_OK);
        e->Delete ();
    }
    return pLine;
}

CLine* CPaintDoc::GetLine (int nIndex)
{
    return (CLine*) m_lineArray[nIndex];
}
```

(continued)

Paint6Doc.cpp *continued*

```
int CPaintDoc::GetLineCount ()
{
    return m_lineArray.GetSize ();
}

void CPaintDoc::OnWidth (UINT nID)
{
    m_nWidth = nID - ID_WIDTH_VTHIN;
}

void CPaintDoc::OnColor (UINT nID)
{
    m_nColor = nID - ID_COLOR_BLACK;
}

void CPaintDoc::OnUpdateWidthUI (CCmdUI* pCmdUI)
{
    pCmdUI->SetCheck ((pCmdUI->m_nID - ID_WIDTH_VTHIN) == m_nWidth);
}

void CPaintDoc::OnUpdateColorUI (CCmdUI* pCmdUI)
{
    pCmdUI->SetCheck ((pCmdUI->m_nID - ID_COLOR_BLACK) == m_nColor);
}
```

Paint6View.h

```
//*********************************************************************
//
// Paint6View.h
//
//*********************************************************************

class CPaintView : public CScrollView
{
    DECLARE_DYNCREATE (CPaintView)

private:
    CPoint m_ptFrom;
    CPoint m_ptTo;

    CPaintDoc* GetDocument () { return (CPaintDoc*) m_pDocument; }
    void InvertLine (CDC*, CPoint, CPoint);
```

```
public:
    virtual void OnInitialUpdate ();

protected:
    virtual void OnDraw (CDC*);
    virtual void OnUpdate (CView*, LPARAM, CObject*);

    afx_msg void OnLButtonDown (UINT, CPoint);
    afx_msg void OnMouseMove (UINT, CPoint);
    afx_msg void OnLButtonUp (UINT, CPoint);
    afx_msg void OnContextMenu (CWnd*, CPoint);

    DECLARE_MESSAGE_MAP ()
};
```

Paint6View.cpp

```
//*********************************************************************
//
//  Paint6View.cpp
//
//*********************************************************************

#include <afxwin.h>
#include "Resource.h"
#include "CLine.h"
#include "Paint6Doc.h"
#include "Paint6View.h"

IMPLEMENT_DYNCREATE (CPaintView, CScrollView)

BEGIN_MESSAGE_MAP (CPaintView, CScrollView)
    ON_WM_LBUTTONDOWN ()
    ON_WM_MOUSEMOVE ()
    ON_WM_LBUTTONUP ()
    ON_WM_CONTEXTMENU ()
END_MESSAGE_MAP ()

void CPaintView::OnInitialUpdate ()
{
    SetScrollSizes (MM_TEXT, CSize (2048, 2048));
    CScrollView::OnInitialUpdate ();
}
```

(continued)

Paint6View.cpp *continued*

```
void CPaintView::OnUpdate (CView* pSender, LPARAM lHint, CObject* pHint)
{
    if (pHint != NULL) {
        CClientDC dc (this);
        OnPrepareDC (&dc);
        ((CLine*) pHint)->Draw (&dc);
        return;
    }
    CScrollView::OnUpdate (pSender, lHint, pHint);
}

void CPaintView::OnDraw (CDC* pDC)
{
    CPaintDoc* pDoc = GetDocument ();
    int nCount = pDoc->GetLineCount ();

    if (nCount) {
        for (int i=0; i<nCount; i++)
            pDoc->GetLine (i)->Draw (pDC);
    }
}

void CPaintView::OnLButtonDown (UINT nFlags, CPoint point)
{
    CClientDC dc (this);
    OnPrepareDC (&dc);
    dc.DPtoLP (&point);

    m_ptFrom = point;
    m_ptTo = point;
    SetCapture ();
}

void CPaintView::OnMouseMove (UINT nFlags, CPoint point)
{
    if (GetCapture () == this) {
        CClientDC dc (this);
        OnPrepareDC (&dc);
        dc.DPtoLP (&point);

        InvertLine (&dc, m_ptFrom, m_ptTo);
        InvertLine (&dc, m_ptFrom, point);
        m_ptTo = point;
    }
}
```

```
void CPaintView::OnLButtonUp (UINT nFlags, CPoint point)
{
    if (GetCapture () == this) {
        ReleaseCapture ();
        CClientDC dc (this);
        OnPrepareDC (&dc);
        dc.DPtoLP (&point);
        InvertLine (&dc, m_ptFrom, m_ptTo);

        CLine* pLine = GetDocument ()->AddLine (m_ptFrom, point);
        if (pLine != NULL) {
            pLine->Draw (&dc);
            GetDocument ()->UpdateAllViews (this, 0, pLine);
        }
    }
}

void CPaintView::InvertLine (CDC* pDC, CPoint ptFrom, CPoint ptTo)
{
    int nOldMode = pDC->SetROP2 (R2_NOT);

    pDC->MoveTo (ptFrom);
    pDC->LineTo (ptTo);

    pDC->SetROP2 (nOldMode);
}

void CPaintView::OnContextMenu (CWnd* pWnd, CPoint point)
{
    CMenu menu;
    menu.LoadMenu (IDR_CONTEXTMENU);
    CMenu* pContextMenu = menu.GetSubMenu (0);

    for (int i=0; i<8; i++)
        pContextMenu->ModifyMenu (ID_COLOR_BLACK + i,
            MF_BYCOMMAND | MF_OWNERDRAW, ID_COLOR_BLACK + i);

    pContextMenu->TrackPopupMenu (TPM_LEFTALIGN | TPM_LEFTBUTTON |
        TPM_RIGHTBUTTON, point.x, point.y, AfxGetMainWnd ());
}
```

TextView.h

```
//*********************************************************************
//
//  TextView.h
//
//*********************************************************************

class CTextView : public CEditView
{
    DECLARE_DYNCREATE (CTextView)

private:
    CFont m_font;

    inline CPaintDoc* GetDocument () { return (CPaintDoc*) m_pDocument; }
    void AddEntry (CLine*);

public:
    virtual BOOL PreCreateWindow (CREATESTRUCT&);
    virtual void OnInitialUpdate ();

protected:
    virtual void OnUpdate (CView*, LPARAM, CObject*);

    afx_msg int OnCreate (LPCREATESTRUCT);
    DECLARE_MESSAGE_MAP ()
};
```

TextView.cpp

```
//*********************************************************************
//
//  TextView.cpp
//
//*********************************************************************

#include <afxwin.h>
#include <afxext.h>

#include "Resource.h"
#include "CLine.h"
#include "Paint6Doc.h"
#include "TextView.h"

IMPLEMENT_DYNCREATE (CTextView, CEditView)
```

```
BEGIN_MESSAGE_MAP (CTextView, CEditView)
    ON_WM_CREATE ()
END_MESSAGE_MAP ()

BOOL CTextView::PreCreateWindow (CREATESTRUCT& cs)
{
    if (!CEditView::PreCreateWindow (cs))
        return FALSE;

    cs.style |= ES_MULTILINE | ES_AUTOHSCROLL | ES_AUTOVSCROLL |
        ES_READONLY | WS_VSCROLL;
    return TRUE;
}


int CTextView::OnCreate (LPCREATESTRUCT lpcs)
{
    if (CEditView::OnCreate (lpcs) == -1)
        return -1;

    CClientDC dc (this);
    int nHeight = -((dc.GetDeviceCaps (LOGPIXELSY) * 8) / 72);

    m_font.CreateFont (nHeight, 0, 0, 0, FW_NORMAL, 0, 0, 0,
        DEFAULT_CHARSET, OUT_CHARACTER_PRECIS, CLIP_CHARACTER_PRECIS,
        DEFAULT_QUALITY, DEFAULT_PITCH | FF_DONTCARE, "MS Sans Serif");

    SetFont (&m_font, FALSE);
    return 0;
}


void CTextView::OnInitialUpdate ()
{
    GetEditCtrl ().SetWindowText ("");

    CPaintDoc* pDoc = GetDocument ();
    int nCount = pDoc->GetLineCount ();

    if (nCount > 0) {
        for (int i=0; i<nCount; i++)
            AddEntry (pDoc->GetLine (i));
    }
}


void CTextView::OnUpdate (CView* pSender, LPARAM lHint, CObject* pHint)
```

(continued)

TextView.cpp *continued*

```
{
    if (pHint != NULL) {
        AddEntry ((CLine*) pHint);
        return;
    }
    CEditView::OnUpdate (pSender, lHint, pHint);
}

void CTextView::AddEntry (CLine* pLine)
{
    int nLine = GetEditCtrl ().GetLineCount () - 1;
    int nIndex = GetEditCtrl ().LineIndex (nLine);
    GetEditCtrl ().SetSel (nIndex, nIndex);

    BOOL bDocState = GetDocument ()->IsModified ();
    GetEditCtrl ().ReplaceSel (pLine->GetDescription ());
    GetDocument ()->SetModifiedFlag (bDocState);
}
```

Splitter.h

```
//*********************************************************************
//
//  Splitter.h
//
//*********************************************************************

class CNestedSplitterWnd : public CSplitterWnd
{
protected:
    virtual BOOL SplitRow (int);
};
```

Splitter.cpp

```
//*********************************************************************
//
//  Splitter.cpp
//
//*********************************************************************

#include <afxwin.h>
#include <afxext.h>
#include "Splitter.h"
```

```
BOOL CNestedSplitterWnd::SplitRow (int cyBefore)
{
    GetParentFrame ()->SetActiveView ((CView*) GetPane (0, 0));
    return CSplitterWnd::SplitRow (cyBefore);
}
```

CLine.h

```
//***************************************************************************
//
//  CLine.h
//
//***************************************************************************

class CLine : public CObject
{
    DECLARE_SERIAL (CLine)

private:
    CPoint m_ptFrom;
    CPoint m_ptTo;
    UINT m_nWidth;
    COLORREF m_crColor;

public:
    CLine () {}
    CLine (CPoint, CPoint, UINT, COLORREF);
    virtual void Serialize (CArchive&);
    virtual void Draw (CDC*);
    CString GetDescription ();
};
```

CLine.cpp

```
//***************************************************************************
//
//  CLine.cpp
//
//***************************************************************************

#include <afxwin.h>
#include "CLine.h"
```

(continued)

CLine.cpp *continued*

```
IMPLEMENT_SERIAL (CLine, CObject, 1)

CLine::CLine (CPoint ptFrom, CPoint ptTo, UINT nWidth, COLORREF crColor)
{
    m_ptFrom = ptFrom;
    m_ptTo = ptTo;
    m_nWidth = nWidth;
    m_crColor = crColor;
}

void CLine::Serialize (CArchive& ar)
{
    CObject::Serialize (ar);

    if (ar.IsStoring ())
        ar << m_ptFrom << m_ptTo << m_nWidth << (DWORD) m_crColor;
    else
        ar >> m_ptFrom >> m_ptTo >> m_nWidth >> (DWORD) m_crColor;
}

void CLine::Draw (CDC* pDC)
{
    CPen pen (PS_SOLID, m_nWidth, m_crColor);

    CPen* pOldPen = pDC->SelectObject (&pen);
    pDC->MoveTo (m_ptFrom);
    pDC->LineTo (m_ptTo);

    pDC->SelectObject (pOldPen);
}

CString CLine::GetDescription ()
{
    CString strDescription;
    strDescription.Format ("Line (%d,%d)-(%d,%d)\r\n",
        m_ptFrom.x, m_ptFrom.y, m_ptTo.x, m_ptTo.y);
    return strDescription;
}
```

The splitter windows are created using the technique described in the previous section. The derivation for the *CNestedSplitterWnd* class that represents the dynamic splitter window can be found in Splitter.h and Splitter.cpp.

The source code files TextView.h and TextView.cpp contain the derivation for the *CTextView* class. *CTextView* is derived from MFC's *CEditView* class, which is basically a *CEdit* edit control surrounded by a *CView* wrapper and fitted with some

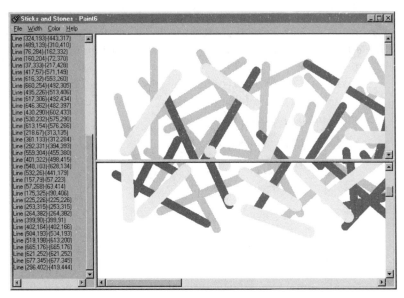

Figure 9-5. *The Paint6 window, with a dynamic splitter window nested inside the right column of a static splitter window.*

additional member functions. One of those functions, *GetEditCtrl*, permits a program to gain direct access to the edit control so that *CEdit* functions can be used on *CEdit-View* objects. *CTextView::AddEntry*, which is called by *CTextView::OnInitialUpdate* and *CTextView::OnUpdate* to add entries representing *CLine* objects to the *CTextView* window, uses *GetEditCtrl* to add a line of text to the view:

```
int nLine = GetEditCtrl ().GetLineCount () - 1;
int nIndex = GetEditCtrl ().LineIndex (nLine);
GetEditCtrl ().SetSel (nIndex, nIndex);

BOOL bDocState = GetDocument ()->IsModified ();
GetEditCtrl ().ReplaceSel (pLine->GetDescription ());
GetDocument ()->SetModifiedFlag (bDocState);
```

The first three statements move the caret (whose location defines the position at which new text will be inserted) to the last line of the edit control. The fifth statement adds the text. The fourth and sixth statements save and restore the document's modified flag so that adding an entry to the *CTextView* won't set the flag. By default, a *CEditView* sets its document's modified flag whenever the text of the edit control changes. (See the *CEditView::OnEditChange* function in Viewedit.cpp to see how.) That's not the behavior we want in Paint6, because the user can't edit the document by modifying the text of the *CTextView*. To prevent the user from modifying the text of the *CTextView* directly, *CTextView::PreCreateWindow* adds the style ES_READONLY to make the edit control read-only. That explains why the view's default background color is gray rather than white: read-only edit controls set their background colors to the system color COLOR_3DFACE as a visual reminder that the text inside them is for display only. *PreCreateWindow* also adds the other window styles to the *CTextView*, including styles to make the edit control a multiline edit control and to add a vertical scroll bar.

CTextView::OnInitialUpdate initializes the *CTextView* object by clearing the text of the edit control and then iterating through the lines contained in the document and passing *CLine* pointers to *AddEntry*:

```
GetEditCtrl ().SetWindowText ("");

CPaintDoc* pDoc = GetDocument ();
int nCount = pDoc->GetLineCount ();

if (nCount > 0) {
    for (int i=0; i<nCount; i++)
        AddEntry (pDoc->GetLine (i));
}
```

OnUpdate updates the *CTextView* object each time a line is added in a *CPaintView* by passing to *AddEntry* the *CLine* pointer contained in *pHint*:

```
if (pHint != NULL) {
    AddEntry ((CLine*) pHint);
    return;
}
CEditView::OnUpdate (pSender, lHint, pHint);
```

Like *CPaintView::OnUpdate*, *CTextView::OnUpdate* passes the call to the base class for default processing if *pHint* does not contain a *CLine* pointer.

Dynamic Splitter Windows with Multiple View Types

Paint6 demonstrates one way in which a splitter window can be customized by deriving from *CSplitterWnd* and overriding *CSplitterWnd::SplitRow*. The *CSplitterWnd* class includes other virtual functions you can override to customize a splitter window's behavior. One of those functions is *CreateView*, which is called by the framework to create a new view when a dynamic splitter window is split. You can create a dynamic splitter window that displays different types of views in different panes by deriving a class from *CSplitterWnd*, overriding *CreateView*, and calling *CSplitterWnd::CreateView* with a *CRuntimeClass* pointer to the view of your choice.

The following *CreateView* override forces a *CTextView* into the pane at row 1, column 0, regardless of the type of view contained in row 0, column 0:

```
BOOL CDynaSplitterWnd::CreateView (int row, int col,
    CRuntimeClass* pViewClass, sizeInit, pContext)
{
    if ((row == 1) && (col == 0))
```

```
        return CSplitterWnd::CreateView (row, col,
            RUNTIME_CLASS (CTextView), sizeInit, pContext);

    return CSplitterWnd::CreateView (row, col, pViewClass,
        sizeInit, pContext);
}
```

This code will probably have to be modified for every different splitter window you use because the view class is hardwired to the row and column number. However, you could build a generic (and reusable) dynamic splitter class that supports multiple view types by adding a *RegisterView* function that correlates view types identified by *CRuntimeClass* pointers to row and column numbers. Before *CSplitterWnd::Create* is called, the splitter window could be initialized with information about the type of view that goes in each pane, and *CreateView* could then use that information to generate the appropriate views.

Splitter Windows in MDI Applications

Although all of the examples presented in this chapter show splitter windows in SDI applications, splitters work equally well in MDI applications. All you have to do is make the splitter a child of the *CMDIChildWnd* window that frames a view of a document in an MDI application rather than a child of the top-level MDI frame; all other aspects of the splitter window are implemented exactly as they are in an SDI application.

I've mentioned before that top-level MDI frame windows are derived from *CMDIFrameWnd* rather than *CFrameWnd* and that MDI views are framed in MDI child windows whose functionality is encapsulated in MFC's *CMDIChildWnd* class. Now that we've examined the SDI document/view architecture in some detail, let's turn our attention to the multiple document interface and see how it compares. SDK-style applications require lots of extra code to implement the multiple document interface, but MFC handles most of the implementational details for you. In fact, an SDI application built to take advantage of the document/view architecture can be converted into an MDI application with just a few simple changes, as this chapter's final sample program will demonstrate.

MFC AND THE MULTIPLE DOCUMENT INTERFACE

The primary difference between the single and multiple document interfaces is that SDI applications allow just one document to be open at a time while MDI applications permit several documents to be open concurrently. To begin work on another document in an SDI application, the user must first close the currently open document. In an MDI application, the user can open as many documents as he or she wants—subject, of course, to limits on available memory and other resources. MDI applications can also support multiple document types. For example, an all-in-one software product might be implemented as an MDI application that supports three document types: word processing documents containing text, spreadsheet documents containing spreadsheets, and chart documents containing graphs.

Like their SDI counterparts, MDI document/view applications store data in document objects derived from *CDocument* and present views of that data in view objects derived from *CView* or one of its derivatives. Each open document can have any number of views associated with it. The framework creates the first view when the document is opened, and a simple function call can create additional views. Each view is displayed in a separate MDI child window clipped to the client area of the top-level frame window. The same update mechanism that keeps different views of a document in sync in an SDI application with a splitter window synchronizes multiple views of the same document in an MDI application, too. Creating an MDI application that supports multiple document types is as simple as registering a document template for each document type. When the user selects File-New to create a new document, the framework displays a dialog box with a list of document types the user can choose from.

Figure 9-6 shows a schematic representation of an MDI document/view application. (For reference, you might want to compare this diagram to the SDI document/view diagram in Figure 8-1 on page 549.) The application's main window is a frame window of a class derived from *CMDIFrameWnd*. The frame window's client area contains a special window known as an "MDI client" window that is created by the frame window from the predefined WNDCLASS named "MDICLIENT". View windows showing views of open documents are framed by MDI child windows, or "document frames," that float within the workspace defined by the MDI client. MFC encapsulates the functionality of document frame windows in the class *CMDIChildWnd*. Just as a view is a child of the top-level frame window in an SDI application, the MDI client window is a child of the top-level frame window in an MDI application. Further down in the hierarchy, document frame windows are children of the MDI client window, and views are children of the document frames. Document objects contain the data displayed in the views.

Hidden beneath the surface are literally dozens of details the framework handles for you, to simplify the development of MDI applications. MDI child windows, for example, can be minimized and maximized within the top-level MDI frame. When a child is maximized, its title bar disappears and a document icon appears in the top-level window's menu bar along with buttons to minimize, restore, and close the maximized document frame. When you base your MDI frame windows on *CMDIFrameWnd* and *CMDIChildWnd*, these and other aspects of the windows' behavior are implemented for you by the framework. The framework also provides command and update handlers for the following items in an MDI application's Window menu:

- A New Window command that creates a new view of an open document

- Cascade and Tile commands that organize open document frames

- An Arrange Icons command that organizes minimized document frames by lining them up at the bottom of the MDI client window

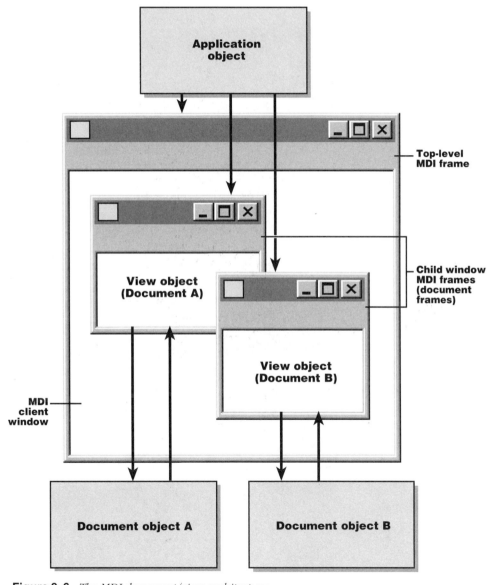

Figure 9-6. *The MDI document/view architecture.*

All you have to do to add a Window menu to an MDI application is include the requisite resource statements in the application's .rc file and assign the items in the menu the predefined IDs listed on page 568. The framework takes the additional step of appending a list of open documents to the Window menu so that the user can easily switch to a document whose frame is obscured behind other document frames.

In short, the framework manages almost every aspect of an MDI application's user interface to spare you the chore of having to write the code to do it yourself. That's why, in MFC, the differences between SDI and MDI applications boil down to a few relatively minor implementation details.

The Paint7 Application

The Paint7 application, which is listed in Figure 9-7 and shown with multiple documents open in Figure 9-8 on page 663, is a full-blown MDI version of our familiar Paint program. It uses the same view class, the same document class, the same *AboutDlg* class, and the same *CLine* class as Paint5. (Once more, the source code listings for CLine.h and CLine.cpp as well as AboutDlg.h and AboutDlg.cpp are not shown.) The only differences between Paint5 and Paint7 lie in the implementations of *CPaintApp::InitInstance*, in the derivations of the *CMainFrame* class, and in the .rc files defining the applications' resources. We'll look at these differences more closely to see what's involved in converting an SDI application into an MDI application.

Resource.h

```
//****************************************************************
//
//  Resource.h
//
//****************************************************************

#define IDR_MAINFRAME          100
#define IDR_CHILDFRAME         101
#define IDR_CONTEXTMENU        102

#define IDD_ABOUTDLG           110
#define IDC_ICONRECT           111

#define ID_WIDTH_VTHIN         120
#define ID_WIDTH_THIN          121
#define ID_WIDTH_MEDIUM        122
#define ID_WIDTH_THICK         123
#define ID_WIDTH_VTHICK        124

#define ID_COLOR_BLACK         130
```

Figure 9-7. *The Paint7 program.*

```
#define ID_COLOR_BLUE            131
#define ID_COLOR_GREEN           132
#define ID_COLOR_CYAN            133
#define ID_COLOR_RED             134
#define ID_COLOR_MAGENTA         135
#define ID_COLOR_YELLOW          136
#define ID_COLOR_WHITE           137
```

Paint7.rc

```
//***************************************************************************
//
//  Paint7.rc
//
//***************************************************************************

#include <afxres.h>
#include "Resource.h"

IDR_MAINFRAME    ICON Paint.ico
IDR_CHILDFRAME   ICON PaintDoc.ico

IDR_MAINFRAME MENU
BEGIN
    POPUP "&File" {
        MENUITEM "&New\tCtrl+N",              ID_FILE_NEW
        MENUITEM "&Open...\tCtrl+O",          ID_FILE_OPEN
        MENUITEM SEPARATOR
        MENUITEM "Recent File",               ID_FILE_MRU_FILE1
        MENUITEM SEPARATOR
        MENUITEM "E&xit",                     ID_APP_EXIT
    }
    POPUP "&Help" {
        MENUITEM "&About Paint7...",          ID_APP_ABOUT
    }
END

IDR_CHILDFRAME MENU
BEGIN
    POPUP "&File" {
        MENUITEM "&New\tCtrl+N",              ID_FILE_NEW
        MENUITEM "&Open...\tCtrl+O",          ID_FILE_OPEN
        MENUITEM "&Save\tCtrl+S",             ID_FILE_SAVE
        MENUITEM "Save &As...\tCtrl+A",       ID_FILE_SAVE_AS
        MENUITEM SEPARATOR
```

(continued)

Paint7.rc *continued*

```
        MENUITEM "Sen&d...",                ID_FILE_SEND_MAIL
        MENUITEM SEPARATOR
        MENUITEM "Recent File",             ID_FILE_MRU_FILE1
        MENUITEM SEPARATOR
        MENUITEM "E&xit",                   ID_APP_EXIT
    }
    POPUP "&Width" {
        MENUITEM "&Very Thin\tF5",          ID_WIDTH_VTHIN
        MENUITEM "Thi&n\tF6",               ID_WIDTH_THIN
        MENUITEM "&Medium\tF7",             ID_WIDTH_MEDIUM
        MENUITEM "Thic&k\tF8",              ID_WIDTH_THICK
        MENUITEM "Very &Thick\tF9",         ID_WIDTH_VTHICK
    }
    POPUP "&Color" {
        MENUITEM "",                        ID_COLOR_BLACK
        MENUITEM "",                        ID_COLOR_BLUE
        MENUITEM "",                        ID_COLOR_GREEN
        MENUITEM "",                        ID_COLOR_CYAN
        MENUITEM "",                        ID_COLOR_RED
        MENUITEM "",                        ID_COLOR_MAGENTA
        MENUITEM "",                        ID_COLOR_YELLOW
        MENUITEM "",                        ID_COLOR_WHITE

    }
    POPUP "&Window" {
        MENUITEM "&New Window",             ID_WINDOW_NEW
        MENUITEM "&Cascade",                ID_WINDOW_CASCADE
        MENUITEM "&Tile",                   ID_WINDOW_TILE_HORZ
        MENUITEM "&Arrange Icons",          ID_WINDOW_ARRANGE
    }
    POPUP "&Help" {
        MENUITEM "&About Paint7...",        ID_APP_ABOUT
    }
END

IDR_MAINFRAME ACCELERATORS
BEGIN
    "N",    ID_FILE_NEW,        VIRTKEY,    CONTROL
    "O",    ID_FILE_OPEN,       VIRTKEY,    CONTROL
    "S",    ID_FILE_SAVE,       VIRTKEY,    CONTROL
    "A",    ID_FILE_SAVE_AS,    VIRTKEY,    CONTROL

    VK_F5,  ID_WIDTH_VTHIN,     VIRTKEY
    VK_F6,  ID_WIDTH_THIN,      VIRTKEY
    VK_F7,  ID_WIDTH_MEDIUM,    VIRTKEY
    VK_F8,  ID_WIDTH_THICK,     VIRTKEY
    VK_F9,  ID_WIDTH_VTHICK,    VIRTKEY
```

```
        "B",     ID_COLOR_BLACK,       VIRTKEY,      CONTROL
        "L",     ID_COLOR_BLUE,        VIRTKEY,      CONTROL
        "G",     ID_COLOR_GREEN,       VIRTKEY,      CONTROL
        "C",     ID_COLOR_CYAN,        VIRTKEY,      CONTROL
        "R",     ID_COLOR_RED,         VIRTKEY,      CONTROL
        "M",     ID_COLOR_MAGENTA,     VIRTKEY,      CONTROL
        "Y",     ID_COLOR_YELLOW,      VIRTKEY,      CONTROL
        "W",     ID_COLOR_WHITE,       VIRTKEY,      CONTROL
END

IDR_CONTEXTMENU MENU
BEGIN
    POPUP "" {
        POPUP "&Width" {
            MENUITEM "&Very Thin",          ID_WIDTH_VTHIN
            MENUITEM "&Thin",               ID_WIDTH_THIN
            MENUITEM "&Medium",             ID_WIDTH_MEDIUM
            MENUITEM "Thi&ck",              ID_WIDTH_THICK
            MENUITEM "Very Thic&k",         ID_WIDTH_VTHICK
        }
        POPUP "&Color" {
            MENUITEM "",                    ID_COLOR_BLACK
            MENUITEM "",                    ID_COLOR_BLUE
            MENUITEM "",                    ID_COLOR_GREEN
            MENUITEM "",                    ID_COLOR_CYAN
            MENUITEM "",                    ID_COLOR_RED
            MENUITEM "",                    ID_COLOR_MAGENTA
            MENUITEM "",                    ID_COLOR_YELLOW
            MENUITEM "",                    ID_COLOR_WHITE
        }
    }
END


STRINGTABLE
BEGIN
    IDR_MAINFRAME     "Paint7"
    IDR_CHILDFRAME  "\n\n\nPaint Files (*.pnt)\n.pnt\nPaint.Document\nPaint Document"
END


IDD_ABOUTDLG DIALOG 0, 0, 256, 98
STYLE DS_MODALFRAME ¦ DS_CENTER ¦ WS_POPUP ¦ WS_VISIBLE ¦ WS_CAPTION ¦
    WS_SYSMENU
CAPTION "About Paint7"
FONT 8, "MS Sans Serif"
```

(continued)

Paint7.rc *continued*

```
BEGIN
    LTEXT           "", IDC_ICONRECT, 14, 12, 80, 74
    LTEXT           "Paint7 Version 1.0", -1, 108, 12, 136, 8
    LTEXT           "From the book", -1, 108, 32, 136, 8
    LTEXT           """Programming Windows 95 with MFC""", -1,
                    108, 42, 136, 8
    LTEXT           "Copyright © 1996 by Jeff Prosise", -1,
                    108, 52, 136, 8
    DEFPUSHBUTTON   "OK", IDOK, 108, 72, 50, 14
END
```

Paint7.h

```
//***************************************************************
//
// Paint7.h
//
//***************************************************************

class CPaintApp : public CWinApp
{
public:
    virtual BOOL InitInstance ();

protected:
    afx_msg void OnAppAbout ();
    DECLARE_MESSAGE_MAP ()
};
```

Paint7.cpp

```
//***************************************************************
//
// Paint7.cpp
//
//***************************************************************

#include <afxwin.h>
#include "Resource.h"
#include "CLine.h"
#include "Paint7.h"
#include "MainFrame.h"
#include "Paint7Doc.h"
```

```
#include "Paint7View.h"
#include "AboutDlg.h"

CPaintApp myApp;

BEGIN_MESSAGE_MAP (CPaintApp, CWinApp)
    ON_COMMAND (ID_FILE_NEW, CWinApp::OnFileNew)
    ON_COMMAND (ID_FILE_OPEN, CWinApp::OnFileOpen)
    ON_COMMAND (ID_APP_ABOUT, OnAppAbout)
END_MESSAGE_MAP ()

BOOL CPaintApp::InitInstance ()
{
    SetRegistryKey ("Programming Windows 95 with MFC");
    LoadStdProfileSettings ();

    CMultiDocTemplate* pDocTemplate;
    pDocTemplate = new CMultiDocTemplate (
        IDR_CHILDFRAME,
        RUNTIME_CLASS (CPaintDoc),
        RUNTIME_CLASS (CMDIChildWnd),
        RUNTIME_CLASS (CPaintView));

    // Convert items in the Color menu to MF_OWNERDRAW
    if (pDocTemplate->m_hMenuShared != NULL) {
        CMenu* pMenu = CMenu::FromHandle (pDocTemplate->m_hMenuShared);
        for (int i=0; i<8; i++)
            pMenu->ModifyMenu (ID_COLOR_BLACK + i,
                MF_BYCOMMAND | MF_OWNERDRAW, ID_COLOR_BLACK + i);
    }

    AddDocTemplate (pDocTemplate);

    CMainFrame* pMainFrame = new CMainFrame;
    if (!pMainFrame->LoadFrame (IDR_MAINFRAME))
        return FALSE;
    m_pMainWnd = pMainFrame;

    EnableShellOpen ();
    RegisterShellFileTypes (TRUE);
    m_pMainWnd->DragAcceptFiles ();

    CCommandLineInfo cmdInfo;
    ParseCommandLine (cmdInfo);

    if (!ProcessShellCommand (cmdInfo))
        return FALSE;
```

(continued)

Paint7.cpp *continued*

```
    pMainFrame->ShowWindow (m_nCmdShow);
    pMainFrame->UpdateWindow ();
    return TRUE;
}

void CPaintApp::OnAppAbout ()
{
    CAboutDialog dlg;
    dlg.DoModal ();
}
```

MainFrame.h

```
//*************************************************************************
//
//  MainFrame.h
//
//*************************************************************************

class CMainFrame : public CMDIFrameWnd
{
    DECLARE_DYNCREATE (CMainFrame)

protected:
    afx_msg void OnMeasureItem (int, LPMEASUREITEMSTRUCT);
    afx_msg void OnDrawItem (int, LPDRAWITEMSTRUCT);

    DECLARE_MESSAGE_MAP ()
};
```

MainFrame.cpp

```
//*************************************************************************
//
//  MainFrame.cpp
//
//*************************************************************************

#define OEMRESOURCE

#include <afxwin.h>
#include "Resource.h"
#include "CLine.h"
```

```
#include "MainFrame.h"
#include "Paint7Doc.h"

IMPLEMENT_DYNCREATE (CMainFrame, CMDIFrameWnd)

BEGIN_MESSAGE_MAP (CMainFrame, CMDIFrameWnd)
    ON_WM_CREATE ()
    ON_WM_MEASUREITEM ()
    ON_WM_DRAWITEM ()
END_MESSAGE_MAP ()

void CMainFrame::OnMeasureItem (int nIDCtl, LPMEASUREITEMSTRUCT lpmis)
{
    lpmis->itemWidth = ::GetSystemMetrics (SM_CYMENU) * 4;
    lpmis->itemHeight = ::GetSystemMetrics (SM_CYMENU);
}

void CMainFrame::OnDrawItem (int nIDCtl, LPDRAWITEMSTRUCT lpdis)
{
    BITMAP bm;
    CBitmap bitmap;
    bitmap.LoadOEMBitmap (OBM_CHECK);
    bitmap.GetObject (sizeof (bm), &bm);

    CDC dc;
    dc.Attach (lpdis->hDC);

    CBrush* pBrush = new CBrush (::GetSysColor ((lpdis->itemState &
        ODS_SELECTED) ? COLOR_HIGHLIGHT : COLOR_MENU));
    dc.FrameRect (&(lpdis->rcItem), pBrush);
    delete pBrush;

    if (lpdis->itemState & ODS_CHECKED) {
        CDC dcMem;
        dcMem.CreateCompatibleDC (&dc);
        CBitmap* pOldBitmap = dcMem.SelectObject (&bitmap);

        dc.BitBlt (lpdis->rcItem.left + 4, lpdis->rcItem.top +
            (((lpdis->rcItem.bottom - lpdis->rcItem.top) -
            bm.bmHeight) / 2), bm.bmWidth, bm.bmHeight, &dcMem,
            0, 0, SRCCOPY);

        dcMem.SelectObject (pOldBitmap);
    }

    pBrush = new CBrush (CPaintDoc::m_crColors[lpdis->itemID -
        ID_COLOR_BLACK]);
```

(continued)

MainFrame.cpp *continued*

```
    CRect rect = lpdis->rcItem;
    rect.DeflateRect (6, 4);
    rect.left += bm.bmWidth;
    dc.FillRect (rect, pBrush);
    delete pBrush;

    dc.Detach ();
}
```

Paint7Doc.h

```
//*********************************************************************
//
// Paint7Doc.h
//
//*********************************************************************

class CPaintDoc : public CDocument
{
    DECLARE_DYNCREATE (CPaintDoc)

private:
    UINT m_nWidth;
    UINT m_nColor;
    CObArray m_lineArray;

    void InitWidthAndColor ();

public:
    static const COLORREF m_crColors[8];

    CPaintDoc ();
    virtual BOOL OnNewDocument ();
    virtual BOOL OnOpenDocument (LPCTSTR);
    virtual void DeleteContents ();
    virtual void Serialize (CArchive&);

    CLine* AddLine (CPoint, CPoint);
    CLine* GetLine (int);
    int GetLineCount ();

protected:
    afx_msg void OnWidth (UINT);
    afx_msg void OnColor (UINT);
```

```
    afx_msg void OnUpdateWidthUI (CCmdUI*);
    afx_msg void OnUpdateColorUI (CCmdUI*);

    DECLARE_MESSAGE_MAP ()
};
```

Paint7Doc.cpp

```
//*********************************************************************
//
// Paint7Doc.cpp
//
//*********************************************************************

#include <afxwin.h>
#include "Resource.h"
#include "CLine.h"
#include "Paint7Doc.h"

IMPLEMENT_DYNCREATE (CPaintDoc, CDocument)

BEGIN_MESSAGE_MAP (CPaintDoc, CDocument)
    ON_COMMAND (ID_FILE_SEND_MAIL, OnFileSendMail)
    ON_COMMAND_RANGE (ID_WIDTH_VTHIN, ID_WIDTH_VTHICK, OnWidth)
    ON_COMMAND_RANGE (ID_COLOR_BLACK, ID_COLOR_WHITE, OnColor)
    ON_UPDATE_COMMAND_UI (ID_FILE_SEND_MAIL, OnUpdateFileSendMail)
    ON_UPDATE_COMMAND_UI_RANGE (ID_WIDTH_VTHIN, ID_WIDTH_VTHICK,
        OnUpdateWidthUI)
    ON_UPDATE_COMMAND_UI_RANGE (ID_COLOR_BLACK, ID_COLOR_WHITE,
        OnUpdateColorUI)
END_MESSAGE_MAP ()

const COLORREF CPaintDoc::m_crColors[8] = {
    RGB (  0,   0,   0),    // Black
    RGB (  0,   0, 255),    // Blue
    RGB (  0, 255,   0),    // Green
    RGB (  0, 255, 255),    // Cyan
    RGB (255,   0,   0),    // Red
    RGB (255,   0, 255),    // Magenta
    RGB (255, 255,   0),    // Yellow
    RGB (255, 255, 255)     // White
};
```

(continued)

Paint7Doc.cpp *continued*

```
CPaintDoc::CPaintDoc ()
{
    m_lineArray.SetSize (0, 64);
}

BOOL CPaintDoc::OnNewDocument ()
{
    if (!CDocument::OnNewDocument ())
        return FALSE;

    InitWidthAndColor ();
    return TRUE;
}

BOOL CPaintDoc::OnOpenDocument (LPCTSTR lpszPathName)
{
    if (!CDocument::OnOpenDocument (lpszPathName))
        return FALSE;

    InitWidthAndColor ();
    return TRUE;
}

void CPaintDoc::InitWidthAndColor ()
{
    m_nColor = ID_COLOR_RED - ID_COLOR_BLACK;
    m_nWidth = ID_WIDTH_MEDIUM - ID_WIDTH_VTHIN;
}

void CPaintDoc::DeleteContents ()
{
    int nCount = m_lineArray.GetSize ();

    if (nCount) {
        for (int i=0; i<nCount; i++)
            delete m_lineArray[i];
        m_lineArray.RemoveAll ();
    }
}

void CPaintDoc::Serialize (CArchive& ar)
{
    m_lineArray.Serialize (ar);
}
```

```
CLine* CPaintDoc::AddLine (CPoint ptFrom, CPoint ptTo)
{
    static UINT nWidths[5] = { 1, 8, 16, 24, 32 };

    CLine* pLine;
    try {
        pLine = new CLine (ptFrom, ptTo, nWidths[m_nWidth],
            m_crColors[m_nColor]);
        m_lineArray.Add (pLine);
        SetModifiedFlag ();
    }
    catch (CMemoryException* e) {
        if (pLine != NULL) {
            delete pLine;
            pLine = NULL;
        }
        AfxMessageBox ("Out of memory", MB_ICONSTOP | MB_OK);
        e->Delete ();
    }
    return pLine;
}

CLine* CPaintDoc::GetLine (int nIndex)
{
    return (CLine*) m_lineArray[nIndex];
}

int CPaintDoc::GetLineCount ()
{
    return m_lineArray.GetSize ();
}

void CPaintDoc::OnWidth (UINT nID)
{
    m_nWidth = nID - ID_WIDTH_VTHIN;
}

void CPaintDoc::OnColor (UINT nID)
{
    m_nColor = nID - ID_COLOR_BLACK;
}

void CPaintDoc::OnUpdateWidthUI (CCmdUI* pCmdUI)
{
    pCmdUI->SetCheck ((pCmdUI->m_nID - ID_WIDTH_VTHIN) == m_nWidth);
}
```

(continued)

Paint7Doc.cpp *continued*

```
void CPaintDoc::OnUpdateColorUI (CCmdUI* pCmdUI)
{
    pCmdUI->SetCheck ((pCmdUI->m_nID - ID_COLOR_BLACK) == m_nColor);
}
```

Paint7View.h

```
//*********************************************************************
//
// Paint7View.h
//
//*********************************************************************

class CPaintView : public CScrollView
{
    DECLARE_DYNCREATE (CPaintView)

private:
    CPoint m_ptFrom;
    CPoint m_ptTo;

    CPaintDoc* GetDocument () { return (CPaintDoc*) m_pDocument; }
    void InvertLine (CDC*, CPoint, CPoint);

public:
    virtual void OnInitialUpdate ();

protected:
    virtual void OnDraw (CDC*);
    virtual void OnUpdate (CView*, LPARAM, CObject*);

    afx_msg void OnLButtonDown (UINT, CPoint);
    afx_msg void OnMouseMove (UINT, CPoint);
    afx_msg void OnLButtonUp (UINT, CPoint);
    afx_msg void OnContextMenu (CWnd*, CPoint);

    DECLARE_MESSAGE_MAP ()
};
```

Paint7View.cpp

```
//*********************************************************************
//
//  Paint7View.cpp
//
//*********************************************************************

#include <afxwin.h>
#include "Resource.h"
#include "CLine.h"
#include "Paint7Doc.h"
#include "Paint7View.h"

IMPLEMENT_DYNCREATE (CPaintView, CScrollView)

BEGIN_MESSAGE_MAP (CPaintView, CScrollView)
    ON_WM_LBUTTONDOWN ()
    ON_WM_MOUSEMOVE ()
    ON_WM_LBUTTONUP ()
    ON_WM_CONTEXTMENU ()
END_MESSAGE_MAP ()

void CPaintView::OnInitialUpdate ()
{
    SetScrollSizes (MM_TEXT, CSize (2048, 2048));
    CScrollView::OnInitialUpdate ();
}

void CPaintView::OnUpdate (CView* pSender, LPARAM lHint, CObject* pHint)
{
    if (pHint != NULL) {
        CClientDC dc (this);
        OnPrepareDC (&dc);
        ((CLine*) pHint)->Draw (&dc);
        return;
    }
    CScrollView::OnUpdate (pSender, lHint, pHint);
}

void CPaintView::OnDraw (CDC* pDC)
{
    CPaintDoc* pDoc = GetDocument ();
    int nCount = pDoc->GetLineCount ();
```

(continued)

Paint7View.cpp *continued*

```
    if (nCount) {
        for (int i=0; i<nCount; i++)
            pDoc->GetLine (i)->Draw (pDC);
    }
}

void CPaintView::OnLButtonDown (UINT nFlags, CPoint point)
{
    CClientDC dc (this);
    OnPrepareDC (&dc);
    dc.DPtoLP (&point);

    m_ptFrom = point;
    m_ptTo = point;
    SetCapture ();
}

void CPaintView::OnMouseMove (UINT nFlags, CPoint point)
{
    if (GetCapture () == this) {
        CClientDC dc (this);
        OnPrepareDC (&dc);
        dc.DPtoLP (&point);

        InvertLine (&dc, m_ptFrom, m_ptTo);
        InvertLine (&dc, m_ptFrom, point);
        m_ptTo = point;
    }
}

void CPaintView::OnLButtonUp (UINT nFlags, CPoint point)
{
    if (GetCapture () == this) {
        ReleaseCapture ();
        CClientDC dc (this);
        OnPrepareDC (&dc);
        dc.DPtoLP (&point);
        InvertLine (&dc, m_ptFrom, m_ptTo);

        CLine* pLine = GetDocument ()->AddLine (m_ptFrom, point);
        if (pLine != NULL) {
            pLine->Draw (&dc);
            GetDocument ()->UpdateAllViews (this, 0, pLine);
        }
    }
}
```

```
void CPaintView::InvertLine (CDC* pDC, CPoint ptFrom, CPoint ptTo)
{
    int nOldMode = pDC->SetROP2 (R2_NOT);

    pDC->MoveTo (ptFrom);
    pDC->LineTo (ptTo);

    pDC->SetROP2 (nOldMode);
}

void CPaintView::OnContextMenu (CWnd* pWnd, CPoint point)
{
    CMenu menu;
    menu.LoadMenu (IDR_CONTEXTMENU);
    CMenu* pContextMenu = menu.GetSubMenu (0);

    for (int i=0; i<8; i++)
        pContextMenu->ModifyMenu (ID_COLOR_BLACK + i,
            MF_BYCOMMAND | MF_OWNERDRAW, ID_COLOR_BLACK + i);

    pContextMenu->TrackPopupMenu (TPM_LEFTALIGN | TPM_LEFTBUTTON |
        TPM_RIGHTBUTTON, point.x, point.y, AfxGetMainWnd ());
}
```

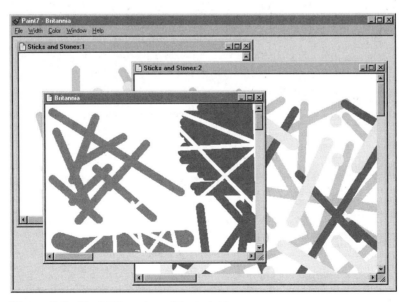

Figure 9-8. *The MDI version of the paint program.*

The Paint7 *InitInstance* Function

The MDI version of the application object's *InitInstance* function is similar to the SDI version, but it differs in several important respects. For starters, the class from which document templates are created is *CMultiDocTemplate* instead of *CSingleDocTemplate*. The code to create and register a document template now looks like this:

```
CMultiDocTemplate* pDocTemplate;
pDocTemplate = new CMultiDocTemplate (
    IDR_CHILDFRAME,
    RUNTIME_CLASS (CPaintDoc)
    RUNTIME_CLASS (CMDIChildWnd)
    RUNTIME_CLASS (CPaintView)
);
       .
       .
       .
AddDocTemplate (pDocTemplate);
```

Notice that the resource ID passed to the document template's constructor is IDR_CHILDFRAME instead of IDR_MAINFRAME and that the *CRuntimeClass* pointer for the frame window class references *CMDIChildWnd* instead of *CMainFrame*. In an MDI application, the resource ID and frame window parameters provided to the document template specify attributes of the document frame window rather than of the top-level frame window. If you look in Paint7.rc, you'll find that separate menus, icons, and document strings are defined for IDR_MAINFRAME and IDR_CHILDFRAME. Here's how these resources are used:

- The IDR_MAINFRAME icon is displayed in the title bar of the top-level MDI frame. The IDR_CHILDFRAME icon is displayed in the title bars of document frame windows. You can use the same icon for both if you like, but most MDI apps use a different icon for document windows.

- The IDR_MAINFRAME menu bar is displayed when there are no documents open. The IDR_CHILDFRAME menu bar is displayed when a document is open. Typically, IDR_MAINFRAME is a minimal menu bar that features a File menu with New, Open, and Exit commands and a recently used file list but little else. IDR_CHILDFRAME, on the other hand, is a full-blown menu bar with all the commands that pertain to a particular document type. The framework automatically updates the main window's menu bar as documents become active. If an MDI application supports multiple document types, the framework updates the menu each time a different document frame is activated so that the menu in the top-level MDI frame matches the type of document represented in the active view.

■   The IDR_MAINFRAME document string contains nothing more than the title for the top-level MDI frame's title bar. The IDR_CHILDFRAME document string contains all the relevant information about the document type.

A second difference in the Paint5 and Paint7 implementations of *InitInstance* arises from the fact that, in an SDI application, it's not necessary to create a top-level window explicitly because the *CFrameWnd* registered with the document template is created when *ProcessShellCommand* calls the application object's *OnFileNew* or *OpenDocumentFile* function to create and initialize a document object. In an MDI application, creating a new document creates a new MDI child window but not a top-level frame window. Therefore, you must create the top-level MDI frame yourself before calling *ProcessShellCommand*. In Paint7.cpp, the statements

```
CMainFrame* pMainFrame = new CMainFrame;
if (!pMainFrame->LoadFrame (IDR_MAINFRAME))
    return FALSE;
m_pMainWnd = pMainFrame;
```

create the frame window and load its icon, menu, accelerator, and document string all in one step. Later, after *ProcessShellCommand* is called, the statements

```
pMainFrame->ShowWindow (m_nCmdShow);
pMainFrame->UpdateWindow ();
```

display the frame window (and any MDI child windows that it contains) on the screen.

Paint7's *InitInstance* function calls *CWinApp::RegisterShellFileTypes* just as Paint5's does. But Paint7 also calls *CWinApp::EnableShellOpen* so that, if a .pnt icon is opened in an Explorer window or elsewhere in the shell's namespace while the application is running, the document will be opened in the existing instance of the application rather than cause another instance to be started. When *RegisterShellFileTypes* is called from an MDI application, it adds some entries to the registry that are unique to MDI applications. The extra entries specify DDE commands the shell can use to communicate with a running instance of the application. When the user opens a document through the shell, the shell broadcasts a WM_DDE_INITIATE message throughout the system to check whether an instance of Paint7 is currently running. If Paint7 is not running, the shell receives no response to the WM_DDE_INITIATE message and starts a new instance of the application, passing the document's file name on the command line. If the application *is* running, the shell strikes up a DDE conversation with it that ultimately results in a call being placed to the application object's *OpenDocumentFile* function with a pointer to the name of the file whose icon was clicked. Consequently, the document is opened just as if the user had picked it from the File menu. The application's end of the DDE conversation is performed by the framework. All you're responsible for is calling *EnableShellOpen* and *RegisterShellFileTypes*.

One other modification to Paint7's application class is the following code that was inserted just before the call to *AddDocTemplate*:

```
if (pDocTemplate->m_hMenuShared != NULL) {
    CMenu* pMenu = CMenu::FromHandle (pDocTemplate->m_hMenuShared);
    for (int i=0; i<8; i++)
        pMenu->ModifyMenu (ID_COLOR_BLACK + i,
            MF_BYCOMMAND | MF_OWNERDRAW, ID_COLOR_BLACK + i);
}
```

Paint5 used similar code to convert the items in the Color menu into owner-drawn menu items, but there the work was done in *CMainFrame::OnCreate* rather than in *CPaintApp::InitInstance*. Why the change? Because the IDR_MAINFRAME menu that's attached to the frame window by *LoadFrame* contains no Color submenu. Remember, the IDR_MAINFRAME menu is the "default" menu that's displayed when there are no documents open. The menu we need to modify is the IDR_CHILDFRAME menu that's displayed when at least one document is open. One way to get at that menu is to access it through the HMENU handle stored in the document template's *m_hMenu-Shared* data member. The code above creates a *CMenu* pointer from *m_hMenuShared* and then uses *CMenu::ModifyMenu* to add MF_OWNERDRAW flags to the items in the Color menu.

The Paint7 *CMainFrame* Class

In addition to modeling the behavior of top-level SDI frame windows, MFC's *CFrameWnd* class serves as the base class for the *CMDIFrameWnd* class that encapsulates top-level MDI frame windows. Since Paint7 is an MDI application, its *CMainFrame* class is derived from *CMDIFrameWnd* instead of *CFrameWnd*.

Alternatives to MDI

MDI isn't the only game in town if you'd like to give your users the ability to edit several documents at once in one instance of your application. *The Windows Interface Guidelines for Software Design* outlines three alternatives to the MDI programming model:

- A workspace-based model that groups related documents in objects called *workspaces* and allows documents contained in a workspace to be viewed and edited in MDI-like document frames that are children of a top-level frame window. Visual C++ 4 is one example of an application that uses the workspace containment model.

- A workbook model in which individual views successively occupy the full client area of a top-level frame window, with an appearance similar to maximized document frames in an MDI application. Each view is tabbed so that the user can switch from one view to another with a button click as if the views were pages in a property sheet.

■ A project model that groups related documents in projects but allows individual documents to be edited in SDI-like frame windows. The primary difference between the project model and the MDI and workspace models is that in the project model there is no top-level frame window providing containment for document frames.

MFC doesn't support any of the user interface alternatives to the MDI model directly, but you can always add the support yourself. Refer to *The Windows Interface Guidelines for Software Design* for more information about the visual and behavioral characteristics of workspace-, workbook-, and project-based applications.

Chapter 10

Printing and Print Previewing

Next to OLE, printing is probably the single most daunting aspect of Windows programming. Printing has never been easy in Windows because the same GDI that makes printing easier by providing a device-independent interface to every kind of printer imaginable makes your application jump through hoops to print a simple document. The GDI also gives you such precise control over the output that users expect a lot from Windows applications that produce printed documents. The good news is that the same GDI functions you use to draw on the screen can be used to draw on a sheet of paper. The bad news is that there are lots of extra details to take care of in printing, from paginating the output to giving the user the means to terminate an unfinished print job. And if you really want your product to be competitive, you should probably support print previewing so that the user can see exactly what the printed output will look like before he or she sends the first page to the printer.

In Chapters 8 and 9, we saw how the document/view architecture simplifies the development of SDI and MDI applications by letting the framework take over key aspects of a program's operation. In this chapter, we'll see how the same document/view architecture simplifies printing and print previewing. Even MFC-style printing isn't something to be taken lightly, but thanks to the support lent by the framework, the tedium of writing and testing code that renders documents on printers and other hardcopy devices is sharply reduced. And once you've given an application the ability to print, print previewing comes almost for free.

PRINTING WITH DOCUMENTS AND VIEWS

MFC's print architecture is built around a core formed by API print functions and protocols built into the Windows GDI. To understand what's on the outside, it helps to first understand what's on the inside. Our approach to learning about the code that enables an MFC application to print and preview documents will involve four steps:

- Look at the Windows printing model and examine the steps an SDK-style application goes through to print a document.

- Understand the relationship between the Windows print architecture and the MFC print architecture and the mechanics of printing from MFC applications, which revolve around a set of key virtual functions that are overridden in the view class.

- Develop a bare-bones printing program that demonstrates how the same code can be used to send output to either the screen or the printer.

- Develop a more ambitious printing program whose printing and previewing capabilities are on a par with those of commercial applications.

The Windows Print Architecture

Printing a document from a Windows application without benefit of the framework involves a number of steps. The application normally begins by obtaining a device context for the printer that output will go to. Just as an application needs a screen DC to send output to the screen, it needs a printer DC to send output to a printer. If you know the device name of the printer you want the application to print to, you can create a device context yourself with the Win32 *::CreateDC* function or MFC's *CDC-::CreateDC*:

```
CDC dc;
dc.CreateDC (NULL, "HP LaserJet IIP", NULL, NULL);
```

If you don't know the device name but would like the application to print to the default printer—the printer whose context menu has a check mark by the Set As Default menu item—you can let Windows create a device context for you by means of MFC's handy *CPrintDialog::GetDefaults* and *CPrintDialog::GetPrinterDC* functions:

```
CDC dc;
CPrintDialog dlg (FALSE);
dlg.GetDefaults ();
dc.Attach (dlg.GetPrinterDC ());
```

If you'd like to let the user select a printer and have the application get a handle to a printer DC in return, you can use *CPrintDialog::DoModal* to display a Print dialog (one of the common dialogs supplied for you by the operating system) on the screen and call *CPrintDialog::GetPrinterDC* after the user has dismissed the dialog:

```
CDC dc;
CPrintDialog dlg (FALSE);
if (dlg.DoModal () == IDOK)
    dc.Attach (dlg.GetPrinterDC ());
```

To prevent resource leakage, a printer DC obtained by any of these methods should be deleted when it's no longer needed. If you create a *CDC* object on the stack, of course, deletion is automatic.

Once you have a printer DC in hand, you're ready to begin printing. The next step is to call *::StartDoc* or its MFC equivalent, *CDC::StartDoc*, to mark the beginning of the print job. *CDC::StartDoc* accepts just one parameter: a pointer to a DOCINFO structure containing a descriptive name for the document that's about to be printed, the name of the file the output will go to if you're printing to a file rather than to a printer, and other information about the print job. The statements

```
DOCINFO di;
::ZeroMemory (&di, sizeof (DOCINFO));
di.cbSize = sizeof (DOCINFO);
di.lpszDocName = "Budget Figures for the Current Fiscal Year";
dc.StartDoc (&di);
```

start a print job on the printer associated with the *CDC* object *dc*. If the user opens a window to the printer while the document is printing, the string "Budget Figures for the Current Fiscal Year" will identify the print job in the window's Document Name column. If *StartDoc* fails, it returns a 0 or a less-than-0 value. If it succeeds, it returns a positive integer that equals the print job ID. The print job ID can be used in conjunction with Win32 print control functions such as *::GetJob* and *::SetJob*.

Next comes output to the page. Text and graphics are rendered on a printer with GDI functions. If *dc* refers to a screen device context, the statement

```
dc.Ellipse (0, 0, 100, 100);
```

draws an ellipse 100 logical units wide and 100 logical units high on the screen. If *dc* refers to a printer device context, the circle is drawn to the printer instead. Pages of output are framed between calls to *CDC::StartPage* and *CDC::EndPage* that mark the beginning and end of each page. A document that contains *nPageCount* pages of output could be printed as follows:

```
for (int i=1; i<=nPageCount; i++) {
    dc.StartPage ();
    // Print page i
    dc.EndPage ();
}
```

In a simplified sense, calling *EndPage* is analogous to outputting a form feed character to the printer. In between *StartPage* and *EndPage*, you print the page by calling *CDC* member functions. Your application should call *StartPage* and *EndPage* even if the document contains only one page.

One mistake programmers often make the first time they write printing code is failing to initialize the printer DC for each page. In Windows 95, the device context's default attributes are restored each time *StartPage* is called. You can't just select a font or set the mapping mode right after the DC is created and expect those attributes to remain in effect indefinitely as you can for a screen DC. Instead, you must reinitialize the printer DC for each page. (In Windows NT 3.5 and later, a printer DC retains its settings across calls to *StartPage* and *EndPage*, but even in a Windows NT application you should reinitialize the device context at the beginning of each page if you want your code to work under Windows 95, too.) If you print using the MM_LO-ENGLISH mapping mode, for example, *CDC::SetMapMode* should be called at the beginning of each new page like this:

```
for (int i=1; i<=nPageCount; i++) {
    dc.StartPage ();
    dc.SetMapMode (MM_LOENGLISH);
    // Print page i
    dc.EndPage ();
}
```

If you do it this way instead:

```
dc.SetMapMode (MM_LOENGLISH);
for (int i=1; i<=nPageCount; i++) {
    dc.StartPage ();
    // Print page i
    dc.EndPage ();
}
```

printing will be performed in the default MM_TEXT mapping mode.

After the final page is printed, an application terminates the print job by calling *CDC::EndDoc*. Printing is made slightly more complicated by the fact that *EndDoc* should not be called if a previous call to *EndPage* returned a code indicating that the print job had already been terminated by the GDI. *EndPage* returns a signed integer value greater than 0 if the page was successfully output to the printer. A 0 or negative return value indicates either that an error occurred or that the user canceled the print job while the page was being printed. In either of those two events, the return code will equal one of the values shown in the table on the facing page.

Return Code	*Description*
SP_ERROR	The print job was aborted for an unspecified reason.
SP_APPABORT	The print job was aborted because the user clicked the Cancel button in the dialog box that displays the status of the print job.
SP_USERABORT	The print job was aborted because the user canceled it through the operating system shell.
SP_OUTOFDISK	The system is out of disk space, so no further printer data can be spooled.
SP_OUTOFMEMORY	The system is out of memory, so no further printer data can be spooled.

The following loop prints each page of a document and calls *EndDoc* at the end of the print job if and only if each page was successfully printed:

```
if (dc.StartDoc (&di) > 0) {
    BOOL bContinue = TRUE;

    for (int i=1; i<=nPageCount && bContinue; i++) {
        dc.StartPage ();
        // Initialize the device context
        // Print page i
        if (dc.EndPage () <= 0)
            bContinue = FALSE;
    }

    if (bContinue)
        dc.EndDoc ();
    else
        dc.AbortDoc ();
}
```

CDC::AbortDoc signals the end of an uncompleted print job just as *EndDoc* signals the end of a successful print job. *AbortDoc* can also be called between calls to *StartPage* and *EndPage* to terminate a print job before the final page is printed.

The Abort Procedure and the Abort Dialog

If that's all there was to sending output to a printer under Windows, printing wouldn't be such a formidable task after all. But there's more. Because a large print job can take minutes or even hours to complete, the user should be able to terminate a print job before it's finished. Windows applications traditionally give the user the means to cancel a print job by displaying a print status dialog containing a Cancel button. Clicking the Cancel button cancels printing by forcing *EndPage* to return SP_APPABORT. The mechanism that links the Cancel button to the printing code in your application is a function that Windows calls an "abort procedure."

An abort procedure is an exported callback function that Windows calls repeatedly as it processes printed output. It's prototyped as follows:

```
BOOL CALLBACK AbortProc (HDC hDC, int nCode)
```

hDC holds the handle of the printer device context. *nCode* is 0 if printing is proceeding smoothly or SP_OUTOFDISK if the print spooler is temporarily out of disk space. *nCode* is usually ignored because the print spooler responds to an SP_OUTOFDISK condition by waiting around for more disk space to come free. The abort procedure's job is twofold:

- To check the message queue with *::PeekMessage* and retrieve and dispatch any messages waiting for the application

- To tell Windows whether printing should continue by returning TRUE (to continue printing) or FALSE (to abort)

You pass Windows the address of your abort procedure by calling *::SetAbortProc* or *CDC::SetAbortProc*. A very simple abort procedure looks like this:

```
BOOL CALLBACK AbortProc (HDC hDC, int nCode)
{
    MSG msg;
    while (::PeekMessage (&msg, NULL, 0, 0, PM_NOREMOVE))
        AfxGetThread ()->PumpMessage ();
    return TRUE;
}
```

The message loop inside *AbortProc* allows the WM_COMMAND message generated when the print status dialog's Cancel button is clicked to make it through to the window procedure even though the application is busy printing. In 16-bit Windows, the message loop plays an important role in multitasking by yielding so that the print spooler and other processes running in the system can get CPU time. In Windows 95, yielding in the abort procedure enhances multitasking performance when 32-bit applications print to 16-bit printer drivers by reducing contention for the Win16Mutex—the flag inside Windows that locks 32-bit applications out of the 16-bit kernel while a 16-bit application executes code in the kernel.

Before it begins printing (before calling *StartDoc*), the application calls *SetAbortProc* to set the abort procedure, disables its own window by calling *CWnd::EnableWindow* with a FALSE parameter, and displays the print status or "abort" dialog—a modeless dialog containing a Cancel button and usually one or more static controls listing the document's file name and the number of the page that's currently being printed. Disabling the main window ensures that no other input will interrupt the printing process. The window is reenabled when printing is finished and the dialog box is destroyed. The dialog, meanwhile, sets a flag—call it *bUserAbort*—from FALSE to TRUE if the Cancel button is clicked. And the abort procedure is modified so that it returns FALSE to shut down printing if *bUserAbort* is TRUE:

```
BOOL CALLBACK AbortProc (HDC hDC, int nCode)
{
    MSG msg;
    while (!bUserAbort &&
        ::PeekMessage (&msg, NULL, 0, 0, PM_NOREMOVE))
        AfxGetThread ()->PumpMessage ();
    return !bUserAbort;
}
```

Thus, printing proceeds unimpeded if the Cancel button isn't clicked because *Abort-Proc* always returns a nonzero value. But if Cancel is clicked, *bUserAbort* changes from FALSE to TRUE, the next call to *AbortProc* returns 0, and Windows terminates the printing process. *EndPage* returns SP_APPABORT, and the call to *EndDoc* is subsequently bypassed.

Print Spooling

Everything I've described up to this point constitutes the "front end" of the printing process—the part the application is responsible for. Windows handles the back end, which is a joint effort on the part of the GDI, the print spooler, the printer driver, and other components of the 32-bit print subsystem. Windows 95 supports two kinds of print spooling: EMF (enhanced metafile) print spooling and "raw" print spooling. If EMF print spooling is enabled, GDI calls executed through the printer DC are written to an enhanced metafile on the hard disk and stored there until the print spooler, which runs in a separate thread, unspools the commands and "plays" them into the printer driver. If raw print spooling (the only option available on PostScript printers) is selected instead, output is processed through the printer driver and spooled to disk in raw form. Spooling can also be disabled altogether. In that case, GDI commands are transmitted directly to the printer driver each time *EndPage* is called. Print spooling speeds the "return-to-application" time by preventing a program from having to wait for the printer to physically print each page of output. Spooling metafile commands instead of raw printer data further improves the return-to-application time by decoupling the performance of the application from the performance of the printer driver. That's one reason Windows 95 seems to print so much faster than Windows 3.1. In Windows 3.1, GDI commands were processed by the printer driver before they were spooled to disk. On most systems running Windows 95, output is spooled first and played through the printer driver later, so the translation of GDI commands into device-dependent printer data is performed entirely in the background.

Fortunately, applications can safely ignore what happens at the back end of the printing process and concentrate on the front end. Still, there are many details that must be attended to before an application can get down to the real business of printing—paginating the output and executing GDI calls between *StartPage* and *EndPage* to render each page on the printer, for example. With this background in mind, let's see what the MFC application framework does to help.

The MFC Print Architecture

MFC's simplified print architecture is just one more reason Windows programmers are migrating away from the SDK and toward object-oriented development environments. When you add print capabilities to a document/view application, you can forget about most of the code samples in the previous section. The framework creates a printer DC for you and deletes the DC when printing is finished. The framework also calls *StartDoc* and *EndDoc* to begin and end the print job and *StartPage* and *EndPage* to bracket GDI calls for individual pages. The framework even supplies the dialog that displays the status of the print job and the abort procedure that shuts down the print operation if the user clicks the dialog's Cancel button. And in some cases, the very same *OnDraw* function that renders a document on the screen can render it on the printer and in a print preview window, too.

The key to printing from a document/view application is a set of virtual *CView* functions the framework calls at various stages during the printing process. These functions are described in the table on the facing page. Which of the *CView* print functions you override and what you do in the overrides depend on the content of your printed output. At the very least, you'll always override *OnPreparePrinting* and call *DoPreparePrinting* from the override so that the framework will display a Print dialog and create a printer DC for you. A minimal *OnPreparePrinting* override looks like this:

```
BOOL CMyView::OnPreparePrinting (CPrintInfo* pInfo)
{
    return DoPreparePrinting (pInfo);
}
```

A nonzero return from *OnPreparePrinting* begins the printing process, while a 0 return cancels the print job before it begins. *DoPreparePrinting* returns 0 if the user cancels the print job by clicking the Cancel button in the Print dialog, if there are no printers installed, or if the framework is unable to create a printer DC.

KEY *CVIEW* PRINT OVERRIDABLES

Function	Description
OnPreparePrinting	Called at the very onset of a print job. Override to call *DoPreparePrinting* and to provide the framework with the page count (if known) and other information about the print job.
OnBeginPrinting	Called just before printing begins. Override to allocate fonts and other resources required for printing.
OnPrepareDC	Called before each page is printed. Override to set the viewport origin or the clipping region to print the current page if *OnDraw* will be used to produce the printed output.
OnPrint	Called to print one page of the document. A page number and a printer DC supplied by the framework. Override to print headers, footers, and other page elements that aren't drawn by the view's *OnDraw* function or to print each page without relying on *OnDraw*.
OnEndPrinting	Called when printing is finished. Override to deallocate resources allocated in *OnBeginPrinting*.

More on the *OnPreparePrinting* Function

The *CPrintInfo* object passed to *OnPreparePrinting* contains information describing the parameters of the print job, including the minimum and maximum page numbers. The minimum and maximum page numbers default to 1 and 0xFFFF, respectively, with 0xFFFF signaling the framework that the maximum page number is unknown. If your application knows how many pages the document contains when *OnPreparePrinting* is called, it should inform the framework by calling *CPrintInfo::SetMaxPage* before calling *DoPreparePrinting*:

```
BOOL CMyView::OnPreparePrinting (CPrintInfo* pInfo)
{
    pInfo->SetMaxPage (nMaxPage);
    return DoPreparePrinting (pInfo);
}
```

The framework, in turn, will display the maximum page number in the "to" box of the Print dialog.

SetMinPage and *SetMaxPage* are two of several *CPrintInfo* member functions you can call to specify print parameters or to query the framework about print options entered by the user. *GetFromPage* and *GetToPage* return the starting and ending page numbers the user has entered in the Print dialog's "from" and "to" boxes. *CPrintInfo* also includes several public data members, including an *m_pPD* variable that points to the initialized *CPrintDialog* object through which *DoPreparePrinting* displays the Print dialog. You can use this pointer to customize the Print dialog before it appears on the screen and to extract information from the dialog by calling *CPrintDialog* functions or accessing *CPrintDialog* data members directly. You'll see an example demonstrating how and why this is done later in the chapter.

The *OnBeginPrinting* and *OnEndPrinting* Functions

Often the maximum page number depends on the size of the printable area of each page output from the printer. Unfortunately, until the user has selected a printer and the framework has created a printer DC, you can only guess what that printable area will be. If you don't set the maximum page number in *OnPreparePrinting*, you should set it in *OnBeginPrinting* if at all possible. *OnBeginPrinting* receives a pointer to an initialized *CPrintInfo* structure and a pointer to a *CDC* object representing the printer DC the framework created when you called *DoPreparePrinting*. You can determine the dimensions of the printable page area in *OnBeginPrinting* by calling *CDC::GetDeviceCaps* twice—once with a HORZRES parameter and once with a VERTRES parameter. The following *OnBeginPrinting* override uses *GetDeviceCaps* to determine the height of the printable page area in pixels and uses that information to inform the framework how many pages the document contains:

```
void CMyView::OnBeginPrinting (CDC* pDC, CPrintInfo* pInfo)
{
    int m_nPageHeight = pDC->GetDeviceCaps (VERTRES);
    int nDocLength = GetDocument ()->GetDocLength ();
    int nMaxPage = max (1, (nDocLength + (m_nPageHeight - 1)) /
        m_nPageHeight);
    pInfo->SetMaxPage (nMaxPage);
}
```

In this example, *GetDocLength* is a document function that returns the length of the document in pixels. *CPrintInfo* contains a data member named *m_rectDraw* that describes the printable page area in logical coordinates, but don't try to use *m_rectDraw* in *OnBeginPrinting* because it isn't initialized until shortly before *OnPrint* is called.

Calling *SetMaxPage* in either *OnPreparePrinting* or *OnBeginPrinting* lets the framework know how many times it should call *OnPrint* to print a page. If it's impossible (or simply not convenient) to determine the document length before printing begins, you can perform "print-time pagination" by overriding *OnPrepareDC* and setting *CPrintInfo::m_bContinuePrinting* to TRUE or FALSE each time *OnPrepareDC* is called. An *m_bContinuePrinting* value equal to FALSE terminates the print job. If you don't call *SetMaxPage*, the framework assumes the document is only one page long. Therefore, you must override *OnPrepareDC* and set *m_bContinuePrinting* to print documents that are more than one page long if you don't set the maximum page number with *SetMaxPage*.

OnBeginPrinting is also the best place to create fonts and other GDI resources that will be used in the printing process. Suppose your view's *OnCreate* function creates a font that *OnDraw* uses to output text to the screen and that the font height is based on screen metrics returned by *GetDeviceCaps*. To print a WYSIWYG version of that font on the printer, you must create a separate font that's scaled to printer metrics rather than screen metrics. One solution is to let *OnDraw* create the font each time it's used so that the font will be scaled for the printer if output is going to the printer or for the screen if output is going to the screen. An alternative solution is to create the printer font in *OnBeginPrinting* and delete it in *OnEndPrinting*. That way, you avoid the overhead of creating and deleting a font each time *OnDraw* is called and increase the overall efficiency of the printing process.

 OnEndPrinting is the counterpart of *OnBeginPrinting*. It's a great place to free fonts and other resources allocated in *OnBeginPrinting*. If there are no resources to free, or if you didn't override *OnBeginPrinting* to begin with, you probably don't need to override *OnEndPrinting*, either.

The *OnPrepareDC* Function

OnPrepareDC is called once for each page of the printed document. One reason to override *OnPrepareDC* is to perform print-time pagination as described in the previous section. Another reason to override *OnPrepareDC* is to calculate a new viewport origin from the current page number so that *OnDraw* will render the current page on the printer. Like *OnBeginPrinting*, *OnPrepareDC* receives a pointer to a device context and a pointer to a *CPrintInfo* object. Unlike *OnBeginPrinting*, *OnPrepareDC* is called before screen repaints as well as in preparation for outputting a page to the printer. If the call to *OnPrepareDC* precedes a screen repaint, the *CDC* pointer refers to a screen DC and the *CPrintInfo* pointer is NULL. If *OnPrepareDC* is called as part of the printing process, the *CDC* pointer will reference a printer DC and the *CPrintInfo* pointer will be non-NULL. In the latter case, the number of the page that's about to be printed can be obtained from the *CPrintInfo* object's public *m_nCurPage* data member. You can determine whether *OnPrepareDC* was called for the screen or the printer by calling *CDC::IsPrinting* through the *CDC* pointer passed in the parameter list.

 The following implementation of *OnPrepareDC* moves the viewport origin in the *y* direction so that the device point (0, 0)—the pixel in the upper left corner of the printed page—corresponds to the logical point in the upper left corner of the document's current page. *m_nPageHeight* is a *CMyView* data member that holds the printable page height:

```
void CMyView::OnPrepareDC (CDC* pDC, CPrintInfo* pInfo)
{
    CView::OnPrepareDC (pDC, pInfo);
    if (pDC->IsPrinting ()) { // If printing...
        int y = (pInfo->m_nCurPage - 1) * m_nPageHeight;
        pDC->SetViewportOrg (0, -y);
    }
}
```

Setting the viewport origin this way ensures that an *OnDraw* function that tries to draw the entire document will actually draw only the part that corresponds to the current page. This simple example of *OnPrepareDC* assumes that you want to use the entire printable area of the page. Sometimes it's also necessary to set a clipping region to restrict the part of the document that's printed to something less than the page's full printable area. Rectangular regions are created with *CRgn::CreateRectRgn* and selected into DCs to serve as clipping regions with *CDC::SelectClipRgn*.

As a rule, you need to override *OnPrepareDC* only to print multipage documents for which *OnDraw* does the printing. If you do all of your printing from *OnPrint* as one of this chapter's sample programs does, then there's no need to override *OnPrepareDC*. When you do override *OnPrepareDC*, you should call the base class before doing anything else so that the default implementation will get a chance to do its thing. This is especially important when your view class is derived from *CScrollView* because *CScrollView::OnPrepareDC* sets the viewport origin for screen DCs to match the current scroll position. When a call to *CScrollView::OnPrepareDC* returns, the DC's mapping mode is set to the mapping mode specified in the call to *SetScrollSizes*. If your view class is not derived from *CScrollView*, *OnPrepareDC* is a good place to call *SetMapMode* to set the device context's mapping mode.

The *OnPrint* Function

After calling *OnPrepareDC* but before physically printing each page, the framework calls *CView::OnPrint*. Like many other *CView* printing functions, *OnPrint* receives a pointer to the printer DC and a pointer to a *CPrintInfo* object. The default implementation in Viewcore.cpp verifies the validity of *pDC* and calls *OnDraw*:

```
void CView::OnPrint(CDC* pDC, CPrintInfo*)
{
    ASSERT_VALID(pDC);

    // Override and set printing variables based on page number
    OnDraw(pDC);                      // Call Draw
}
```

If you prepared the printer DC for printing in *OnPrepareDC*, or if the document contains only one page, you don't have to override *OnPrint*; you can let the default implementation call *OnDraw* to do the printing.

In practice, *OnPrint* is frequently overridden to perform page-specific printing tasks. Probably the most common reason for overriding *OnPrint* is to print headers, footers, page numbers, and other visual elements that appear on the printed page but not in views of the document rendered on the screen (with the exception of print previews). The following *OnPrint* function calls a local member function named *PrintHeader* to print a header at the top of the page, another local member function named *PrintPageNumber* to print a page number at the bottom of the page, and *OnDraw* to print the body of the page:

```
void CMyView::OnPrint (CDC* pDC, CPrintInfo* pInfo)
{
    PrintHeader (pDC);
    PrintPageNumber (pDC, pInfo->m_nCurPage);
    // Set the viewport origin and/or clipping region before
    // calling OnDraw...
    OnDraw (pDC);
}
```

Note that any adjustments made to the printer DC with *SetViewportOrg* or *SelectClipRgn* so that *OnDraw* will draw just the part of the document that corresponds to the current page should now be made in *OnPrint* rather than *OnPrepareDC*. That way, headers and page numbers won't be affected. An alternative approach is to forgo the call to *OnDraw* and do all your printing in *OnPrint*. That's a perfectly legitimate way to architect an application. If your drawing and printing code are substantially different, doing all of your printing in *OnPrint* draws a clearer boundary between how you print a document and how you paint an onscreen view of it.

CView::OnFilePrint and Other Command Handlers

Printing usually begins when the user selects the Print command from the File menu, so MFC provides a *CView::OnFilePrint* function you can connect to the ID_FILE_PRINT menu item through the view's message map. Figure 10-1 on the next page shows what happens when *OnFilePrint* is called and when in the printing process each virtual *CView* printing function is called. It also shows how the MFC print architecture meshes with the Windows print architecture: if you take away the dark rectangles representing the virtual *CView* functions that the framework calls, you're left with a pretty good schematic of the Windows printing model. Note that *OnPrepareDC* is called twice per page when your code executes under Windows 95. The first call to *OnPrepareDC* is made to preserve compatibility with 16-bit versions of MFC, which called *On-PrepareDC* before *StartPage* and got away with it because in 16-bit Windows it's *EndPage*, not *StartPage*, that resets the device context. The second call to *OnPrepareDC* is made because in Windows 95 changes made to the device context in the first call to *OnPrepareDC* are nullified when *StartDoc* is called.

MFC also provides predefined command IDs and default command handlers for the File menu's Print Preview and Print Setup commands. The File-Print Preview command (ID=ID_FILE_PRINT_PREVIEW) is handled by *CView::OnFilePrintPreview*, and File-Print Setup (ID=ID_FILE_PRINT_SETUP) is handled by *CWinApp::OnFile-PrintSetup*. Like *OnFilePrint*, these command handlers are not prewired into the message maps of the classes to which they belong. To enable these handlers, you must do the message mapping yourself. Of course, if you use AppWizard to generate the skeleton of an application that prints, the message mapping is done for you. AppWizard also maps ID_FILE_PRINT_DIRECT to *CView::OnFilePrint* to enable "direct" printing—printing performed not by the user's selecting Print from the File menu, but by the user's selecting Print from a document's context menu or dropping a document icon onto a printer.

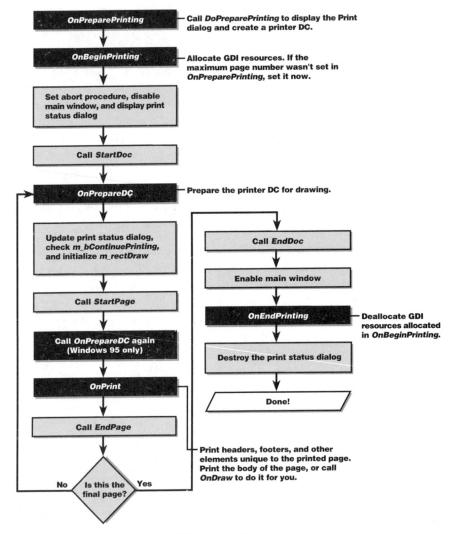

Figure 10-1. *Overview of the MFC print architecture.*

Print Previewing

Once a document/view application is given the ability to print, adding print preview is as simple as adding a Print Preview command to the File menu (ID=ID_FILE_PRINT-_PREVIEW) and adding an entry connecting the command ID to *CView::OnFilePrint-Preview* to the message map. There's a lot of code backing up *OnFilePrintPreview* (see the MFC source code file Viewprev.cpp for details), but what happens in

OnFilePrintPreview is pretty simple. *OnFilePrintPreview* takes over the frame window and fills it with a view created from a special *CScrollView*-derived class named *CPreviewView*. It also adds a toolbar with buttons for going to the next or the previous page, switching between one-page and two-page views, zooming in and out, and so on. *CPreviewView::OnDraw* draws a white rectangle representing a printed page (or two rectangles if two-page view is selected), sets some scaling parameters so that the "printable area" of the white rectangle matches the printable area of a real page, and calls *OnPrint* to draw in the rectangle. As far as your application is concerned, output is being sent to the printer; the same virtual functions that get called during printing also get called during print preview. But in reality, output goes to the print preview window instead.

Part of the magic that makes print preview work is that the device context referenced in the *pDC* parameter passed to *CView* printing functions is actually two device contexts in one. Every *CDC* object contains two device context handles: one for an "output" DC (*m_hDC*) and another for an "attribute" DC (*m_hAttribDC*). MFC uses the output DC for calls that produce physical output and the attribute DC for calls that ask for attribute information—for the current text color or current background mode, for example. Most of the time, *m_hDC* and *m_hAttribDC* hold the same device context handle. But during print preview, *m_hDC* references the screen DC where pages are previewed and *m_hAttribDC* references the printer DC. The result? If your application uses *GetDeviceCaps* or other *CDC* functions to query the GDI about the printer's capabilities or the properties of the printed page, the information it gets back is genuine because it comes from the printer DC. But all physical output is directed to the screen DC.

When the user closes the print preview window, the framework calls a virtual *CView* function named *OnEndPrintPreview* to notify the application that print preview is about to end. The default implementation of *OnEndPrintPreview* calls *OnEndPrinting*, reactivates the original view, and destroys the print preview window. Programmers sometimes override *OnEndPrintPreview* in order to scroll the view of the document to the last page displayed in print preview mode. (By default, the scroll position in the original view is preserved so that scrolling in print preview mode does not affect the original view.) The following *OnEndPrintPreview* override demonstrates how the scroll position in the original view can be linked to the scroll position in the print preview window for a *CScrollView*:

```
void CMyView::OnEndPrintPreview (CDC* pDC, CPrintInfo* pInfo,
    POINT point, CPreviewView* pView)
{
    UINT nPage = pInfo->m_nCurPage;
    POINT pt;
    // Convert nPage into a scroll position in pt
    ScrollToPosition (pt);
    CScrollView::OnEndPrintPreview (pDC, pInfo, point, pView);
}
```

You'll have to supply the code that converts the current page number into a scroll position yourself. Don't rely on the *point* parameter passed to *OnEndPrintPreview* to tell you anything; in current versions of MFC, *point* always equals (0, 0). The base class version of *OnEndPrintPreview* should be called from the overridden version so that the framework can exit print preview mode and restore the frame window to its original state.

If your printing code needs to discriminate between real printing and printing performed in print preview mode, it can check the *m_bPreview* data member of the *CPrintInfo* object referenced in calls to *OnBeginPrinting*, *OnPrint*, and other print overridables. *m_bPreview* is nonzero if the document is being previewed and 0 if it is not. In addition, *CPrintInfo::m_nNumPreviewPages* can be inspected to determine whether one or two pages are displayed.

A Bare-Bones Printing Application

The EZPrint application whose source code appears in Figure 10-2 demonstrates the minimum amount of work a document/view application must do to support printing and print previewing. An EZPrint "document" simply contains a blue circle whose diameter is 10 centimeters (1,000 units in the MM_LOMETRIC mapping mode) with a yellow interior. The application's File menu contains just four items: Print, Print Preview, Print Setup, and Exit. The Print and Print Preview commands are mapped to *CView::OnFilePrint* and *CView::OnFilePrintPreview* in *CPrintView*'s message map, and the Print Setup command is mapped to *CWinApp::OnFilePrintSetup* in *CPrintApp*'s message map. The Print command displays a Print dialog box in which the user can specify printing options such as the printer the output will go to, the print range, and the number of copies. Print Preview puts the application in print preview mode. (See Figure 10-3 on page 689.) Print Setup displays a Print Setup dialog box. The user can use the Print Setup dialog to choose a printer, select among the available paper sizes, and specify the page orientation—portrait or landscape.

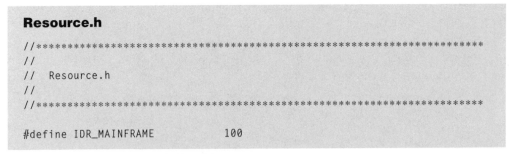

Figure 10-2. *The EZPrint program.*

EZPrint.rc

```
//***********************************************************************
//
//  EZPrint.rc
//
//***********************************************************************

#include <afxres.h>
#include "Resource.h"

IDR_MAINFRAME MENU
BEGIN
    POPUP "&File" {
        MENUITEM "&Print...\tCtrl+P",        ID_FILE_PRINT
        MENUITEM "Print Pre&view",           ID_FILE_PRINT_PREVIEW
        MENUITEM "P&rint Setup...",          ID_FILE_PRINT_SETUP
        MENUITEM SEPARATOR
        MENUITEM "E&xit",                    ID_APP_EXIT
    }
END

IDR_MAINFRAME ACCELERATORS
BEGIN
    "P", ID_FILE_PRINT, VIRTKEY, CONTROL
END

STRINGTABLE
BEGIN
    IDR_MAINFRAME "EZPrint"
END
```

EZPrint.h

```
//***********************************************************************
//
//  EZPrint.h
//
//***********************************************************************

class CPrintApp : public CWinApp
{
public:
    virtual BOOL InitInstance ();
```

(continued)

EZPrint.h *continued*

```
protected:
    DECLARE_MESSAGE_MAP ()
};
```

EZPrint.cpp

```
//***********************************************************************
//
//  EZPrint.cpp
//
//***********************************************************************

#include <afxwin.h>
#include "Resource.h"
#include "EZPrint.h"
#include "EZPrintDoc.h"
#include "EZPrintView.h"

CPrintApp myApp;

BEGIN_MESSAGE_MAP (CPrintApp, CWinApp)
    ON_COMMAND (ID_FILE_PRINT_SETUP, CWinApp::OnFilePrintSetup)
END_MESSAGE_MAP ()

BOOL CPrintApp::InitInstance ()
{
    CSingleDocTemplate* pDocTemplate;
    pDocTemplate = new CSingleDocTemplate (
        IDR_MAINFRAME,
        RUNTIME_CLASS (CPrintDoc),
        RUNTIME_CLASS (CFrameWnd),
        RUNTIME_CLASS (CPrintView)
    );

    AddDocTemplate (pDocTemplate);

    CCommandLineInfo cmdInfo;
    ParseCommandLine (cmdInfo);

    if (!ProcessShellCommand (cmdInfo))
        return FALSE;

    return TRUE;
}
```

EZPrintDoc.h

```
//*********************************************************************
//
//   EZPrintDoc.h
//
//*********************************************************************

class CPrintDoc : public CDocument
{
    DECLARE_DYNCREATE (CPrintDoc)
};
```

EZPrintDoc.cpp

```
//*********************************************************************
//
//   EZPrintDoc.cpp
//
//*********************************************************************

#include <afxwin.h>
#include "EZPrintDoc.h"

IMPLEMENT_DYNCREATE (CPrintDoc, CDocument)
```

EZPrintView.h

```
//*********************************************************************
//
//   EZPrintView.h
//
//*********************************************************************

class CPrintView : public CView
{
    DECLARE_DYNCREATE (CPrintView)

protected:
    virtual void OnDraw (CDC*);
    virtual BOOL OnPreparePrinting (CPrintInfo*);

    DECLARE_MESSAGE_MAP ()
};
```

EZPrintView.cpp

```
//********************************************************************
//
//  EZPrintView.cpp
//
//********************************************************************

#include <afxwin.h>
#include <afxext.h>
#include "EZPrintView.h"

IMPLEMENT_DYNCREATE (CPrintView, CView)

BEGIN_MESSAGE_MAP (CPrintView, CView)
    ON_COMMAND (ID_FILE_PRINT, CView::OnFilePrint)
    ON_COMMAND (ID_FILE_PRINT_PREVIEW, CView::OnFilePrintPreview)
END_MESSAGE_MAP ()

void CPrintView::OnDraw (CDC* pDC)
{
    CPen pen (PS_SOLID, 50, RGB (0, 0, 255));
    CBrush brush (RGB (255, 255, 0));

    pDC->SetMapMode (MM_LOMETRIC);
    CPen* pOldPen = pDC->SelectObject (&pen);
    CBrush* pOldBrush = pDC->SelectObject (&brush);

    pDC->Ellipse (100, -100, 1100, -1100);

    pDC->SelectObject (pOldBrush);
    pDC->SelectObject (pOldPen);
}

BOOL CPrintView::OnPreparePrinting (CPrintInfo* pInfo)
{
    pInfo->SetMaxPage (1);
    return DoPreparePrinting (pInfo);
}
```

There's not a lot to be said about EZPrint's printing and print previewing capabilities. What's important is that the framework does the bulk of the work. The view class *CPrintView* overrides just one *CView* printing function—*OnPreparePrinting*—and in the override calls *CPrintInfo::SetMaxPage* to set the page count to 1 and *DoPreparePrinting* to display the Print dialog and begin the printing process:

```
BOOL CPrintView::OnPreparePrinting (CPrintInfo* pInfo)
{
    pInfo->SetMaxPage (1);
    return DoPreparePrinting (pInfo);
}
```

CPrintView::OnDraw does all the drawing, regardless of whether the output is destined for the screen, a printer, or a print preview window. So that the circle will have the same proportions regardless of where it is drawn, *OnDraw* does all of its drawing using the MM_LOMETRIC mapping mode. That's important, because pixel-per-inch values for screens and printers are rarely the same. If you drew to the screen and the printer in the MM_TEXT mapping mode, the circle would be a lot smaller on a 600 dpi printer than it would be on the screen. To get WYSIWYG results, you'd have to scale the circle's height and width manually during printing and print previewing using ratios derived from pixel-per-inch counts for the screen and printer. Using a mapping mode in which logical units scale to physical distances rather than pixel counts allows the GDI to do the scaling and ensures that *OnDraw* can produce consistent results no matter where the output is rendered.

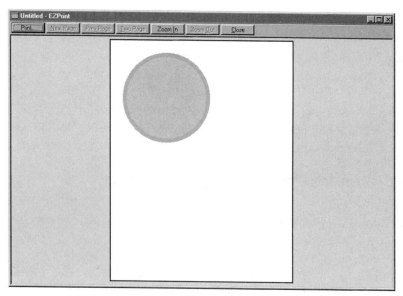

Figure 10-3. *Print preview mode.*

The framework's print preview support isn't perfect. EZPrint's preview page shows the circle in full-blown color even if the only printer attached to your PC is a black-and-white. (Naturally, the circle *will* be printed in color if you print it on a color printer.) You can add a nice touch to your print preview code by doing your rendering in shades of gray if both of the two conditions that follow are true.

- *CPrintInfo::m_bPreview* is nonzero.

- *pDC->GetDeviceCaps* (NUMCOLORS) returns 2, indicating that the printer is a monochrome device.

RGB color values can be converted into shades of gray with this formula:

```
r/g/b = (red * 0.30) + (green * 0.59) + (blue * 0.11)
```

The following statement creates a gray brush that simulates on the screen how yellow (RGB (255, 255, 0)) will look on a monochrome output device:

```
CBrush brush (RGB (227, 227, 227));
```

The value 227 was computed by plugging the color components 255, 255, and 0 into the color conversion formula.

To see a simple demonstration of black-and-white print preview, replace these lines in EZPrint's *CPrintView::OnDraw* function

```
CPen pen (PS_SOLID, 50, RGB (0, 0, 255));
CBrush brush (RGB (255, 255, 0));
```

with these:

```
BOOL bMono = (pDC->GetDeviceCaps (NUMCOLORS) == 2) &&
    (pDC->m_hDC != pDC->m_hAttribDC); // True only for preview mode
CPen pen (PS_SOLID, 50, bMono ? RGB (28, 28, 28) : RGB (0, 0, 255));
CBrush brush (bMono ? RGB (227, 227, 227) : RGB (255, 255, 0));
```

Print preview output will now be rendered in shades of gray when the default printer is a black-and-white model. Comparing *m_hDC* to *m_hAttribDC* is a sneaky way to detect print preview mode when *CPrintInfo* information isn't available.

A More Complex Printing Application

EZPrint is okay for a start, but it hardly represents the complexities of applications we find in the real world. It doesn't have to deal with the issue of pagination because its documents consist of one page each. It creates the GDI resources it needs each time *OnDraw* is called, so there's no reason to override *OnBeginPrinting* and *OnEndPrinting* to allocate printer-specific resources. Even *OnPrepareDC* and *OnPrint* don't need to be overridden because there's nothing in EZPrint that distinguishes a printed view from an onscreen view.

The HexDump application, listed in Figure 10-4, is more representative of the kinds of applications you're liable to write in the real world. As shown in Figure 10-5 on page 701, HexDump is a hexadecimal viewing program that displays the contents of any file in binary form. Printed documents have a header at the top that includes the file name (prefaced with a path name if there's room) and the page number. The header is underscored with a thin horizontal line. The line is drawn with *CDC::MoveTo* and *CDC::LineTo*; all other output is performed with *CDC::TextOut*. Figure 10-6 on page 701 shows one page of a document as seen in print preview mode. When a document is printed, HexDump queries the printer for the dimensions of the printable page area and adjusts its output accordingly. The page height is used to compute the number of lines printed per page, and the page width is used to center the output horizontally no matter what the page size.

Resource.h

```
//***********************************************************************
//
//  Resource.h
//
//***********************************************************************

#define IDR_MAINFRAME            100
```

HexDump.rc

```
//***********************************************************************
//
//  HexDump.rc
//
//***********************************************************************

#include <afxres.h>
#include "Resource.h"

IDR_MAINFRAME MENU
BEGIN
    POPUP "&File" {
        MENUITEM "&Open...\tCtrl+O",        ID_FILE_OPEN
        MENUITEM SEPARATOR
        MENUITEM "&Print...\tCtrl+P",       ID_FILE_PRINT
        MENUITEM "Print Pre&view",          ID_FILE_PRINT_PREVIEW
        MENUITEM "P&rint Setup...",         ID_FILE_PRINT_SETUP
        MENUITEM SEPARATOR
        MENUITEM "Recent File",             ID_FILE_MRU_FILE1
        MENUITEM SEPARATOR
        MENUITEM "E&xit",                   ID_APP_EXIT
    }
END

IDR_MAINFRAME ACCELERATORS
```

Figure 10-4. *The HexDump program.*

(continued)

HexDump.rc *continued*

```
BEGIN
    "O", ID_FILE_OPEN,  VIRTKEY, CONTROL
    "P", ID_FILE_PRINT, VIRTKEY, CONTROL
END

STRINGTABLE
BEGIN
    IDR_MAINFRAME "HexDump"
END
```

HexDump.h

```
//*********************************************************************
//
//  HexDump.h
//
//*********************************************************************

class CHexDumpApp : public CWinApp
{
public:
    virtual BOOL InitInstance ();

protected:
    DECLARE_MESSAGE_MAP ()
};
```

HexDump.cpp

```
//*********************************************************************
//
//  HexDump.cpp
//
//*********************************************************************

#include <afxwin.h>
#include "Resource.h"
#include "HexDump.h"
#include "HexDoc.h"
#include "HexView.h"

CHexDumpApp myApp;

BEGIN_MESSAGE_MAP (CHexDumpApp, CWinApp)
```

```
    ON_COMMAND (ID_FILE_OPEN, CWinApp::OnFileOpen)
    ON_COMMAND (ID_FILE_PRINT_SETUP, CWinApp::OnFilePrintSetup)
END_MESSAGE_MAP ()

BOOL CHexDumpApp::InitInstance ()
{
    SetRegistryKey ("Programming Windows 95 with MFC");
    LoadStdProfileSettings ();

    CSingleDocTemplate* pDocTemplate;
    pDocTemplate = new CSingleDocTemplate (
        IDR_MAINFRAME,
        RUNTIME_CLASS (CHexDoc),
        RUNTIME_CLASS (CFrameWnd),
        RUNTIME_CLASS (CHexView)
    );

    AddDocTemplate (pDocTemplate);

    CCommandLineInfo cmdInfo;
    ParseCommandLine (cmdInfo);

    if (!ProcessShellCommand (cmdInfo))
        return FALSE;

    m_pMainWnd->DragAcceptFiles ();
    return TRUE;
}
```

HexDoc.h

```
//***********************************************************************
//
// HexDoc.h
//
//***********************************************************************

class CHexDoc : public CDocument
{
    DECLARE_DYNCREATE (CHexDoc)

private:
    UINT m_nDocLength;
    BYTE* m_pFileData;

public:
```

(continued)

HexDoc.h *continued*

```
    CHexDoc ();
    virtual void DeleteContents ();
    virtual void Serialize (CArchive&);
    UINT GetBytes (UINT, UINT, PVOID);
    UINT GetDocumentLength ();
};
```

HexDoc.cpp

```
//****************************************************************************
//
// HexDoc.cpp
//
//****************************************************************************

#include <afxwin.h>
#include "HexDoc.h"

IMPLEMENT_DYNCREATE (CHexDoc, CDocument)

CHexDoc::CHexDoc ()
{
    m_nDocLength = 0;
    m_pFileData = NULL;
}

void CHexDoc::DeleteContents ()
{
    if (m_pFileData != NULL) {
        delete[] m_pFileData;
        m_pFileData = NULL;
        m_nDocLength = 0;
    }
}

void CHexDoc::Serialize (CArchive& ar)
{
    if (ar.IsLoading ()) {
        CFile* pFile = ar.GetFile ();
        m_nDocLength = (UINT) pFile->GetLength ();

        // Allocate a buffer for the file data
        try {
            m_pFileData = new BYTE[m_nDocLength];
        }
```

```
        catch (CMemoryException* e) {
            m_nDocLength = 0;
            throw e;
        }

        // Read the file data into the buffer
        try {
            pFile->Read (m_pFileData, m_nDocLength);
        }
        catch (CFileException* e) {
            delete[] m_pFileData;
            m_pFileData = NULL;
            m_nDocLength = 0;
            throw e;
        }
    }
}

UINT CHexDoc::GetBytes (UINT nIndex, UINT nCount, PVOID pBuffer)
{
    if (nIndex >= m_nDocLength)
        return 0;

    UINT nLength = nCount;
    if ((nIndex + nCount) > m_nDocLength)
        nLength = m_nDocLength - nIndex;

    ::CopyMemory (pBuffer, m_pFileData + nIndex, nLength);
    return nLength;
}

UINT CHexDoc::GetDocumentLength ()
{
    return m_nDocLength;
}
```

HexView.h

```
//****************************************************************************
//
// HexView.h
//
//****************************************************************************

class CHexView : public CScrollView
```

(continued)

```
{
    DECLARE_DYNCREATE (CHexView)

private:
    CFont m_screenFont;
    CFont m_printerFont;

    UINT m_cyScreen;
    UINT m_cyPrinter;
    UINT m_cxOffset;
    UINT m_cxWidth;

    UINT m_nLinesTotal;
    UINT m_nLinesPerPage;

    CHexDoc* GetDocument () { return (CHexDoc*) m_pDocument; }
    void FormatLine (UINT, CString&);
    void PrintPageHeader (CDC*, UINT);
    void PrintPage (CDC*, UINT);

public:
    virtual void OnInitialUpdate ();

protected:
    virtual void OnDraw (CDC*);
    virtual BOOL OnPreparePrinting (CPrintInfo*);
    virtual void OnBeginPrinting (CDC*, CPrintInfo*);
    virtual void OnPrint (CDC*, CPrintInfo*);
    virtual void OnEndPrinting (CDC*, CPrintInfo*);

    afx_msg int OnCreate (LPCREATESTRUCT);
    DECLARE_MESSAGE_MAP ()
};
```

HexView.cpp

```
//*************************************************************************
//
//  HexView.cpp
//
//*************************************************************************

#include <afxwin.h>
#include <afxext.h>
#include "HexDoc.h"
```

```
#include "HexView.h"

#define PRINTMARGIN 2

IMPLEMENT_DYNCREATE (CHexView, CScrollView)

BEGIN_MESSAGE_MAP (CHexView, CScrollView)
    ON_WM_CREATE ()
    ON_COMMAND (ID_FILE_PRINT, CScrollView::OnFilePrint)
    ON_COMMAND (ID_FILE_PRINT_DIRECT, CScrollView::OnFilePrint)
    ON_COMMAND (ID_FILE_PRINT_PREVIEW, CScrollView::OnFilePrintPreview)
END_MESSAGE_MAP ()

int CHexView::OnCreate (LPCREATESTRUCT lpcs)
{
    if (CScrollView::OnCreate (lpcs) == -1)
        return -1;

    CClientDC dc (this);
    int nHeight = -((dc.GetDeviceCaps (LOGPIXELSY) * 10) / 72);

    m_screenFont.CreateFont (nHeight, 0, 0, 0, FW_NORMAL, 0, 0, 0,
        DEFAULT_CHARSET, OUT_CHARACTER_PRECIS, CLIP_CHARACTER_PRECIS,
        DEFAULT_QUALITY, DEFAULT_PITCH | FF_DONTCARE, "Courier New");

    TEXTMETRIC tm;
    CFont* pOldFont = dc.SelectObject (&m_screenFont);
    dc.GetTextMetrics (&tm);
    m_cyScreen = tm.tmHeight + tm.tmExternalLeading;
    dc.SelectObject (pOldFont);
    return 0;
}

void CHexView::OnInitialUpdate ()
{
    UINT nDocLength = GetDocument ()->GetDocumentLength ();
    m_nLinesTotal = (nDocLength + 15) / 16;

    SetScrollSizes (MM_TEXT, CSize (0, m_nLinesTotal * m_cyScreen),
        CSize (0, m_cyScreen * 10), CSize (0, m_cyScreen));
    ScrollToPosition (CPoint (0, 0));

    CScrollView::OnInitialUpdate ();
}

void CHexView::OnDraw (CDC* pDC)
{
```

(continued)

HexView.cpp *continued*

```
    if (m_nLinesTotal != 0) {
        CRect rect;
        pDC->GetClipBox (&rect);

        UINT nStart = rect.top / m_cyScreen;
        UINT nEnd = min (m_nLinesTotal - 1,
            (rect.bottom + m_cyScreen - 1) / m_cyScreen);

        CString string;
        CFont* pOldFont = pDC->SelectObject (&m_screenFont);

        for (UINT i=nStart; i<=nEnd; i++) {
            FormatLine (i, string);
            pDC->TextOut (2, (i * m_cyScreen) + 2, string);
        }
        pDC->SelectObject (pOldFont);
    }
}

BOOL CHexView::OnPreparePrinting (CPrintInfo* pInfo)
{
    return DoPreparePrinting (pInfo);
}

void CHexView::OnBeginPrinting (CDC* pDC, CPrintInfo* pInfo)
{
    int nHeight = -((pDC->GetDeviceCaps (LOGPIXELSY) * 10) / 72);

    m_printerFont.CreateFont (nHeight, 0, 0, 0, FW_NORMAL, 0, 0, 0,
        DEFAULT_CHARSET, OUT_CHARACTER_PRECIS, CLIP_CHARACTER_PRECIS,
        DEFAULT_QUALITY, DEFAULT_PITCH | FF_DONTCARE, "Courier New");

    TEXTMETRIC tm;
    CFont* pOldFont = pDC->SelectObject (&m_printerFont);
    pDC->GetTextMetrics (&tm);
    m_cyPrinter = tm.tmHeight + tm.tmExternalLeading;
    CSize size = pDC->GetTextExtent ("---------1---------2---------" \
        "3---------4---------5---------6---------7---------8-", 81);
    pDC->SelectObject (pOldFont);

    m_nLinesPerPage = (pDC->GetDeviceCaps (VERTRES) -
        (m_cyPrinter * (3 + (2 * PRINTMARGIN)))) / m_cyPrinter;
    UINT nMaxPage = max (1, (m_nLinesTotal + (m_nLinesPerPage - 1)) /
        m_nLinesPerPage);
    pInfo->SetMaxPage (nMaxPage);

    m_cxOffset = (pDC->GetDeviceCaps (HORZRES) - size.cx) / 2;
```

```
    m_cxWidth = size.cx;
}

void CHexView::OnPrint (CDC* pDC, CPrintInfo* pInfo)
{
    PrintPageHeader (pDC, pInfo->m_nCurPage);
    PrintPage (pDC, pInfo->m_nCurPage);
}

void CHexView::OnEndPrinting (CDC* pDC, CPrintInfo* pInfo)
{
    m_printerFont.DeleteObject ();
}

void CHexView::FormatLine (UINT nLine, CString& string)
{
    BYTE b[17];
    ::FillMemory (b, 16, 32);
    UINT nCount = GetDocument ()->GetBytes (nLine * 16, 16, b);

    string.Format ("%0.8X    %0.2X %0.2X %0.2X %0.2X %0.2X %0.2X " \
        "%0.2X %0.2X - %0.2X %0.2X %0.2X %0.2X %0.2X %0.2X %0.2X " \
        "%0.2X    ", nLine * 16,
        b[0], b[1], b[2], b[3], b[4], b[5], b[6], b[7],
        b[8], b[9], b[10], b[11], b[12], b[13], b[14], b[15]);

    for (UINT i=0; i<nCount; i++) {
        if (!::IsCharAlphaNumeric (b[i]))
            b[i] = 0x2E;
    }

    b[nCount] = 0;
    string += b;

    if (nCount < 16) {
        UINT pos1 = 59;
        UINT pos2 = 60;
        UINT j = 16 - nCount;

        for (i=0; i<j; i++) {
            string.SetAt (pos1, ' ');
            string.SetAt (pos2, ' ');
            pos1 -= 3;
            pos2 -= 3;
            if (pos1 == 35) {
                string.SetAt (35, ' ');
                string.SetAt (36, ' ');
```

(continued)

HexView.cpp *continued*

```
                  pos1 = 33;
                  pos2 = 34;
              }
          }
      }
  }

void CHexView::PrintPageHeader (CDC* pDC, UINT nPageNumber)
{
    CString strHeader = GetDocument ()->GetPathName ();
    if (strHeader.GetLength () > 68)
        strHeader = GetDocument ()->GetTitle ();

    CString strPageNumber;
    strPageNumber.Format ("Page %d", nPageNumber);

    UINT nSpaces = 81 - strPageNumber.GetLength () -
        strHeader.GetLength ();
    for (UINT i=0; i<nSpaces; i++)
        strHeader += ' ';
    strHeader += strPageNumber;

    UINT y = m_cyPrinter * PRINTMARGIN;
    CFont* pOldFont = pDC->SelectObject (&m_printerFont);
    pDC->TextOut (m_cxOffset, y, strHeader);

    y += (m_cyPrinter * 3) / 2;
    pDC->MoveTo (m_cxOffset, y);
    pDC->LineTo (m_cxOffset + m_cxWidth, y);

    pDC->SelectObject (pOldFont);
}

void CHexView::PrintPage (CDC* pDC, UINT nPageNumber)
{
    if (m_nLinesTotal != 0) {
        UINT nStart = (nPageNumber - 1) * m_nLinesPerPage;
        UINT nEnd = min (m_nLinesTotal - 1, nStart + m_nLinesPerPage - 1);

        CString string;
        CFont* pOldFont = pDC->SelectObject (&m_printerFont);

        UINT y;
        for (UINT i=nStart; i<=nEnd; i++) {
            FormatLine (i, string);
            y = ((i - nStart) + PRINTMARGIN + 3) * m_cyPrinter;
            pDC->TextOut (m_cxOffset, y, string);
```

```
            }
        pDC->SelectObject (pOldFont);
    }
}
```

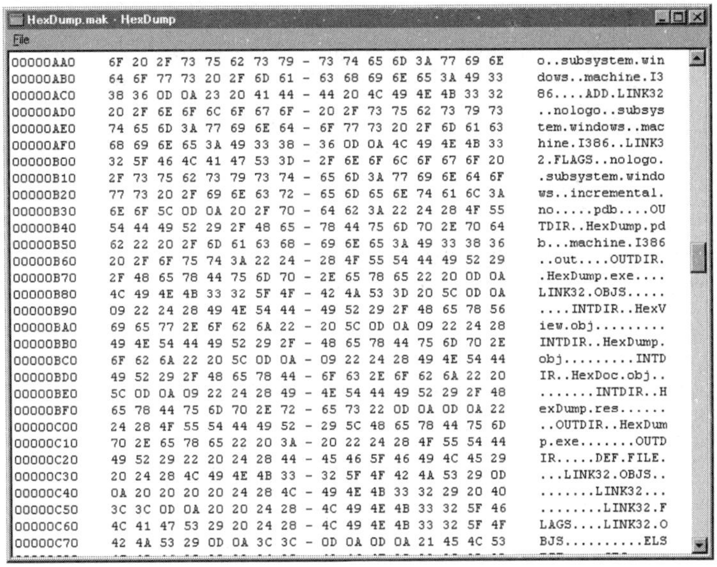

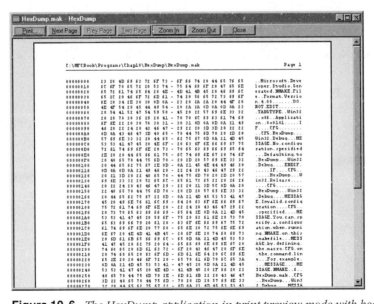

Figure 10-5. *The HexDump application showing a binary view of a file.*

Figure 10-6. *The HexDump application in print preview mode with header information.*

The heart of the HexDump application is the code in the view class *CHexView* that renders views of the document on the screen and on the printer. *CHexView* does all of its screen painting with *OnDraw*. *CHexView::OnCreate* initializes *CHexView-::m_screenFont* with a 10-point Courier New font sized for the screen, and *CHexView-::m_cyScreen* with the vertical distance (in pixels) separating consecutive lines of text on the screen. *CHexView::OnDraw* repaints the view by using *CDC::GetClipBox* to identify the rectangle that needs repainting, converting the *y* coordinates of the rectangle's top and bottom into starting and ending line numbers in the document, and drawing just those lines that need repainting. The scroll position is factored into the output automatically because *CHexView* is derived from *CScrollView*. Because *OnDraw* does the minimum amount of painting necessary, scrolling performance is acceptable even if the document is very large. To see how sluggish a *CScrollView* can become when a large document is loaded and *OnDraw* isn't optimized, try re-writing *CHexView::OnDraw* so that it tries to draw the entire document each time it's called, like this:

```
void CHexView::OnDraw (CDC* pDC)
{
    for (int i=0; i<m_nLinesTotal; i++) {
        FormatLine (i, string);
        pDC->TextOut (2, (i * m_cyScreen) + 2, string);
    }
}
```

Then load a file whose size is 10K or 20K and do some scrolling up and down. It will quickly become apparent why *CHexView::OnDraw* goes to the trouble of converting the clip box into a range of line numbers.

HexDump does all of its printing in *OnPrint*. *CHexView::OnPrint* calls *CHexView-::PrintPageHeader* to print the header at the top of the page and *CHexView::PrintPage* to print the body of the page. *OnBeginPrinting* sets the stage by initializing *CHexView-::m_printerFont* with a separate 10-point Courier New font sized for the printer, *CHexView::m_cyPrinter* with the interline spacing, *CHexView::m_nLinesPerPage* with the number of lines that will be printed per page based on the height of the printable page area, *CHexView::m_cxOffset* with the *x* indent required to center printed lines on the page, and *CHexView::m_cxWidth* with the width of each line of text. *CHexView-::PrintPage* calculates starting and ending line numbers from the current page number and the number of lines per page. The *for* loop that does the drawing is similar to the *for* loop in *OnDraw*, differing only in how it aligns the text on the page and in the fact that it uses *m_printerFont* for its output instead of *m_screenFont*. When printing (or print previewing) is complete, *OnEndPrinting* cleans up by deleting the printer font created by *OnBeginPrinting*.

Could *CHexView::OnDraw* have been written so that it handled output to both the screen and the printer? Sure. But the code is arguably simpler and more straightforward the way it's written now. MFC programmers sometimes make the mistake of feeling that they *have* to do their printing as well as their screen updating in *OnDraw*. HexDump not only demonstrates that it doesn't have to be that way but also provides a working example of an application that does its printing and screen updating separately.

A Unique Approach to Serialization

One other aspect of HexDump we should look at more closely is the unusual way in which it handles serialization. When *CHexDoc::Serialize* is called to read a document from disk, it doesn't read objects from the archive. Instead, it allocates a buffer whose size equals the file size and reads the file into the buffer with *CFile::Read*. With exception handling statements removed, here's how it looks in code:

```
if (ar.IsLoading ()) {
    CFile* pFile = ar.GetFile ();
    m_nDocLength = (UINT) pFile->GetLength ();
    m_pFileDate = new BYTE[m_nDocLength];
    pFile->Read (m_pFileDate, m_nDocLength);
}
```

CArchive::GetFile returns a *CFile* pointer for the file associated with the archive so that an application can call *CFile* functions on it directly. This is how serialization is typically handled when an MFC application reads and writes binary documents stored by someone else. When the document's *DeleteContents* function is called, HexDump frees the buffer containing the file data:

```
delete[] m_pFileData;
```

HexDump doesn't serialize the contents of a file back to disk because it's a hex viewer and not a hex editor, but if it did allow documents to be edited and saved, it would use *CFile::Write* to write modified documents back to disk the same way it uses *CFile::Read* to read them into memory.

Allocating a buffer whose size equals the file size isn't the most efficient approach to serializing and viewing large documents because it means that an entire document has to fit into memory at once. There are workarounds, but in HexDump's case it turns out to be a moot point because the limitations imposed by the *CScrollView* are typically more constricting than limitations imposed by available memory. To see what I mean, find a file that's a few hundred kilobytes and load it into HexDump. No matter how big the file is, HexDump won't display more than a couple thousand lines (and often not even that). How come?

The problem is related to Windows 95's 16-bit heritage—specifically, to the fact that scroll bar ranges are 16-bit values. When *CHexView::OnInitialUpdate* sets the limits of the scrolling view with *SetScrollSizes*, it computes the view's virtual height by multiplying the number of lines in the document by the number of pixels per line.

If the height of a line is 16 pixels and the document contains 1,000 lines, the view's virtual height is 16,000. For small documents, that's fine, but a *CScrollView* can't handle heights greater than 32,767 (the largest positive value that can be represented with a signed 16-bit integer) because that's the maximum upper limit of a scroll bar's range. The result? If you load a document that contains more than about 2,000 lines, the *CScrollView* will show only a part of the document even though printing and previewing will work just fine. To fix HexDump to handle large documents, you'll have to create a *CView* with a scroll bar and process scroll bar messages yourself. (The easiest way to add a scroll bar to a *CView* is to override *CView::PreCreateWindow* and add WS_VSCROLL or WS_HSCROLL to the window style.) In Chapter 2, I told you that the time we spent writing the scrolling logic for GdiDemo2 wouldn't be wasted. Now you see why. *CScrollView* is great for small and medium-sized documents, but for very large documents there is often no choice but to strike out on your own and implement the scrolling logic yourself.

PRINTING TIPS AND TRICKS

Here are a few tips, tricks, and answers to frequently asked questions to help you write better printing code and resolve problems that aren't addressed in this chapter's sample programs.

Enabling the Selection Button

The Print dialog the framework displays before printing begins includes a Selection radio button the user can click to print the current selection rather than the entire document or a range of pages. By default, the button is disabled. You can enable it by adding the following statement to your *OnPreparePrinting* override just before the call to *DoPreparePrinting*:

```
pInfo->m_pPD->m_pd.Flags &= ~PD_NOSELECTION;
```

To select the radio button after it's enabled, add this statement as well:

```
pInfo->m_pPD->m_pd.Flags != PD_SELECTION;
```

The *m_pPD* data member of the *CPrintInfo* structure passed to *OnPreparePrinting* points to the *CPrintDialog* object that *DoPreparePrinting* uses to display the Print dialog box. *CPrintDialog::m_pd* holds a reference to the PRINTDLG structure the dialog is based on, and PRINTDLG's *Flags* field holds bit flags that define the dialog box's properties. Removing the PD_NOSELECTION flag added by *CPrintInfo*'s constructor enables the Selection button, and adding a PD_SELECTION flag selects the button. If *DoPreparePrinting* returns a nonzero value indicating that the dialog was dismissed with the OK button, you can find out whether the Selection button was selected by calling *CPrintDialog::PrintSelection*. A nonzero return value means the button was selected; 0 means it was not:

```
if (pInfo->m_pPD->PrintSelection ()) {
    // Print the current selection
}
```

PrintSelection and other *CPrintDialog* functions that return information about settings entered in a Print or Print Setup dialog can be called through the *pInfo* parameter passed to *OnPreparePrinting* after *DoPreparePrinting* returns. They can also be called through the *pInfo* parameter passed to *OnBeginPrinting* and other *CView* print overridables.

You can use *CPrintInfo::m_pPD* in a number of ways to modify the default properties and behavior of the Print dialog the framework displays by modifying the values in the PRINTDLG structure. Refer to your compiler's documentation or the Win32 SDK for more information about PRINTDLG and its data members.

Assume Nothing—And Test Thoroughly!

When you send output to the printed page, it's generally a mistake to assume anything about the printable area of the pages you'll be printing. Even if you know you're printing to, say, an 8.5-by-11-inch page, the printable page area will differ for different printers. The printable page area can even differ for the same printer and the same paper size depending on which printer driver is being used, and the horizontal and vertical dimensions of the printable page area will be switched if the user opts to print in landscape rather than portrait mode. Rather than assume you have a given amount of space to work with, do as HexDump does and call *GetDeviceCaps* through the *CDC* pointer provided to *CView* print functions to determine the printable page area each time you print, or use *CPrintInfo::m_rectDraw* in your *OnPrint* function. This simple precaution will enable your printing code to work with any printer Windows can throw at it and will greatly reduce the number of problem reports you receive from users.

As you've already learned, calling *GetDeviceCaps* with HORZRES and VERTRES parameters returns the horizontal and vertical dimensions of the printable page area. The table on the next page lists the values you can pass to *GetDeviceCaps* to get more information about a printer or other hardcopy device.

You've already seen one use for the *GetDeviceCaps* NUMCOLORS parameter: to detect when a black-and-white printer is being used so that you draw print previews in shades of gray. The PHYSICALOFFSETX and PHYSICALOFFSETY parameters are useful for setting margin widths based on information the user enters in a Page Setup dialog. (MFC's *CWinApp::OnFilePrintSetup* function displays a Print Setup dialog instead of a Page Setup dialog, but you can display a Page Setup dialog yourself using MFC's *CPageSetupDialog* class.) If the user wants 1-inch margins on the left side of the page, for example, you can subtract the PHYSICALOFFSETX value returned by *GetDeviceCaps* from the number of pixels printed per inch (LOGPIXELSX) to compute the *x* offset from the left of the printable page area where printing should begin. If the printer driver returns accurate information, the resulting margin will fall within

Value	*Description*
HORZRES	Returns the width of the printable page area in pixels.
VERTRES	Returns the height of the printable page area in pixels.
HORSIZE	Returns the width of the printable page area in millimeters.
VERTSIZE	Returns the height of the printable page area in millimeters.
LOGPIXELSX	Returns the number of pixels per inch in the horizontal direction (300 for a 300 dpi printer).
LOGPIXELSY	Returns the number of pixels per inch in the vertical direction (300 for a 300 dpi printer).
PHYSICALWIDTH	Returns the page width in pixels (2,550 for an 8.5-by-11-inch page on a 300 dpi printer).
PHYSICALHEIGHT	Returns the page height in pixels (3,350 for an 8.5-by-11-inch page on a 300 dpi printer).
PHYSICALOFFSETX	Returns the distance in pixels from the left side of the page to the beginning of the page's printable area.
PHYSICALOFFSETY	Returns the distance in pixels from the top of the page to the beginning of the page's printable area.
TECHNOLOGY	Returns a value that identifies the type of output device the DC pertains to. The most common return values are DT_RASDISPLAY for screens, DT_RASPRINTER for printers, and DT_PLOTTER for plotters.
RASTERCAPS	Returns a series of bit flags identifying the level of GDI support provided by the printer driver. For example, an RC_BITBLT flag indicates that the printer supports *BitBlts*, and RC_STRETCHBLT indicates that the printer supports *StretchBlts*.
NUMCOLORS	Returns the number of colors the printer supports. The return value is 2 for black-and-white printers.

a few pixels of being exactly 1 inch. The HORZRES, VERTRES, LOGPIXELSX, LOG-PIXELSY, PHYSICALWIDTH, PHYSICALHEIGHT, PHYSICALOFFSETX, and PHYSICAL-OFFSETY values can be used to characterize the printable area of a page and pinpoint exactly where on the page the printable area lies.

If you're concerned about the occasional hardcopy device that won't draw bitmaps, you can find out whether *CDC::BitBlt* and *CDC::StretchBlt* are supported by calling *GetDeviceCaps* with a RASTERCAPS parameter and checking the return flags. For the most part, this is a concern only when output is directed to a vector device such as a plotter. If the driver for a raster device doesn't support blitting directly, the GDI will compensate by doing the blitting itself. You can determine outright whether printed output is destined for a plotter by calling *GetDeviceCaps* with a TECHNOL-OGY parameter and checking to see if the return value equals DT_PLOTTER.

When you use a number of different printers to test an application that prints, you'll find that printer drivers are maddeningly inconsistent in the information they report and the output they produce. For example, some printer drivers return the same values for PHYSICALWIDTH and PHYSICALHEIGHT that they return for HORZRES and VERTRES. And sometimes an ordinary GDI function such as *CDC::TextOut* will work fine on hundreds of printers but fail on one particular model because of a driver bug. Other times, a GDI function won't fail outright but will behave differently on different printers. I once ran across a printer driver that defaulted to the TRANSPAR-ENT background mode even though other drivers for the same family of printers correctly set the device context's default background mode to OPAQUE. Printer drivers are notoriously flaky, so it's important to anticipate problems and test as thoroughly as you can on as many printers as possible. The more ambitious your program's printing needs, the more likely that driver quirks will require you to write workarounds for problems that crop up only on certain printers.

Adding Default Pagination Support

HexDump calls *CPrintInfo::SetMaxPage* from *OnBeginPrinting* rather than from *OnPreparePrinting* because the pagination process relies on the printable page area and *OnBeginPrinting* is the first virtual *CView* function that's called with a pointer to a printer DC. Because the maximum page number isn't set until after *OnPrepare-Printing* returns, the "from" page number in the Print dialog is filled in (with a 1) but the "to" page number is not. To some users it may seem incongruous that an application can correctly paginate a document for print preview but can't fill in the maximum page number in a dialog box. In addition to displaying the maximum page number correctly, many commercial applications display page breaks outside print preview and "Page *mm* of *nn*" strings in status bars. How do these applications know how the document will be paginated when they don't know what printer the document will be printed on or what the page orientation will be?

The answer is that they don't know for sure, so they make their best guess based on the properties of the default printer. The following code snippet initializes a *CSize* object with the dimensions in pixels of the default printer's printable page area. It can be called from *OnPreparePrinting* or elsewhere to compute the maximum page number or get the information you need to provide other forms of default pagination support:

```
CSize size;
CPrintDialog dlg (FALSE);
if (dlg.GetDefaults ()) {
    CDC dc;
    dc.Attach (dlg.GetPrinterDC ());
    size.cx = dc.GetDeviceCaps (HORZRES);
    size.cy = dc.GetDeviceCaps (VERTRES);
}
```

CPrintDialog::GetDefaults initializes *CPrintDialog::m_pd* with values for the system's default printer without displaying a dialog box. A 0 return from *GetDefaults* means that the function failed, which usually indicates that no printers are installed or that a default printer has not been designated. *CPrintDialog::GetPrinterDC* returns the DC handle copied to *m_pd* by *GetDefaults*. Because it's up to the application to delete the device context even though Windows created it, the handle isn't detached before *dc* goes out of scope; it will be deleted by the object's destructor. It's important to pass the *CPrintDialog* constructor a FALSE parameter instead of TRUE, or *GetPrinterDC* will return a NULL device context handle.

Enumerating Printers

Sometimes it's useful to be able to build a list of all the printers available so that the user can select a printer outside a Print or Print Setup dialog box. The following routine uses the Win32 *::EnumPrinters* function to enumerate the local printers currently installed and adds an entry for each to the combo box pointed to by *pComboBox*. In Windows 95, network printers are included in the list because local and network printers are treated identically by *::EnumPrinters*:

```
#include <winspool.h>
    :
    :

DWORD dwSize, dwPrinters;
::EnumPrinters (PRINTER_ENUM_LOCAL, NULL, 5,
    NULL, 0, &dwSize, &dwPrinters);

BYTE* pBuffer = new BYTE[dwSize];

::EnumPrinters (PRINTER_ENUM_LOCAL, NULL, 5,
    pBuffer, dwSize, &dwSize, &dwPrinters);

if (dwPrinters != 0) {
    PRINTER_INFO_5* pPrnInfo = (PRINTER_INFO_5*) pBuffer;
    for (UINT i=0; i<dwPrinters; i++) {
        pComboBox->AddString (pPrnInfo->pPrinterName);
        pPrnInfo++;
    }
}

delete[] pBuffer;
```

The first call to *::EnumPrinters* retrieves the amount of buffer space needed to hold an array of PRINTER_INFO_5 structures describing individual printers. The second call to *::EnumPrinters* initializes the buffer pointed to by *pBuffer* with an array of PRINTER_INFO_5 structures. On return, *dwPrinters* holds a count of the printers enumerated (which equals the count of PRINTER_INFO_5 structures copied to the buffer), and each structure's *pPrinterName* field holds a pointer to an ASCIIZ string containing the device name of the associated printer. Enumerating printers with PRINTER_INFO_5 structures is fast because no remote calls are required; all information needed to fill the buffer is obtained from the registry. For fast printer enumerations in Windows NT, use PRINTER_INFO_4 structures instead.

If a printer is selected from the combo box and you want to create a device context for it, you can pass the device name copied from the PRINTER_INFO_5 structure to *CDC::CreateDC* as follows:

```
CString strPrinterName;
int nIndex = pComboBox->GetCurSel ();
pComboBox->GetLBText (nIndex, strPrinterName);

CDC dc;
dc.CreateDC (NULL, strPrinterName, NULL, NULL);
```

The resulting *CDC* object can be used in the same way a *CDC* object passed by address to *OnBeginPrinting* and other *CView* print functions can be used.

Chapter 11

Toolbars, Status Bars, and Versionable Schemas

This chapter concludes our look at the document/view architecture by introducing two new classes and one key programming technique you can use to enhance your applications. The new classes are *CToolBar* and *CStatusBar*. A toolbar is a child window with buttons and sometimes other types of controls that make frequently used commands more accessible. A status bar is a child window that displays context-sensitive help for menu items and toolbar buttons as well as other information that's helpful to the user. It's easy to add toolbars and status bars to document/view applications because *CToolBar* and *CStatusBar* provide such thorough encapsulations of toolbar and status bar controls. And the MFC 4 versions of *CToolBar* and *CStatusBar* automatically use the native toolbar and status bar implementations found in the Windows 95 common controls library rather than the private implementations carried over from previous versions of MFC.

The new programming technique you'll learn about in this chapter relies on *versionable schemas* to enable one version of an MFC application to deserialize (load) documents created by a previous version. Versionable schema support is important when an application's persistent storage format changes from one version to the next because it preserves compatibility with previous releases. The serialization examples presented thus far in this book use hardcoded schema numbers that cause the framework to throw an exception if an object whose schema number is 2 tries to deserialize an object whose schema number is 1. By using versionable schema numbers, you can create versionable classes that support a wide range of storage formats.

TOOLBARS

The primary reason for adding a toolbar to an application is to provide one-click access to commonly used commands. Toolbar buttons typically serve as shortcuts for items in the application's menus, but they can also operate as stand-alone UI objects. MFC's *CToolBar* class takes a bitmap resource containing images for the toolbar buttons and an array of button IDs and creates a toolbar object that docks to the side of a frame window or floats in its own mini–frame window. Clicking a toolbar button produces a WM_COMMAND message just as making a menu selection does, and when a menu item and a toolbar button are assigned matching command IDs, the command and update handlers that serve the menu item can serve the toolbar button, too. With a little work, you can add combo boxes, check boxes, and other non-push-button controls to a toolbar, or convert ordinary push buttons into check buttons that stay up or down when clicked or radio push buttons that work like radio button controls. The framework provides functions for hiding and displaying toolbars, saving and restoring toolbar states, and more.

If your application needs more than *CToolBar* can provide, you can access the underlying tool bar control directly and call member functions of the *CToolBarCtrl* class. *CToolBarCtrl::Customize*, for example, can be used to create toolbars that the user can reconfigure by adding, deleting, and moving buttons. Most of the time, however, *CToolBar* will do everything you need and then some. Let's see what it takes to get a *CToolBar* up and running.

Creating and Initializing a Toolbar

CToolBar and other *CControlBar*-derived classes are defined in the MFC header file Afxext.h, so an application that uses a toolbar should include Afxext.h in all relevant source code files. A toolbar is created by constructing a *CToolBar* object and calling *CToolBar::Create*. A toolbar is a child of the application's main frame window and is normally created when the frame window is created, so the usual practice is to add a *CToolBar* member to the frame window class and call *CToolBar::Create* from the frame window's *OnCreate* handler. If *m_wndToolBar* is a *CToolBar* data member, the statement

```
m_wndToolBar.Create (this);
```

creates a toolbar that is a child of *this*. Two parameters are implicit in the call: the toolbar's style and its child-window ID. The default style is WS_CHILD ¦ WS_VISIBLE ¦ CBRS_TOP. You can change the toolbar style by adding a second parameter to *Create* or calling the *SetBarStyle* function a toolbar inherits from *CControlBar* after the toolbar is created. For example, to replace CBRS_TOP with CBRS_BOTTOM so that the toolbar aligns itself along the bottom of its parent, you could create it like this:

```
m_wndToolBar.Create (this, WS_CHILD ¦ WS_VISIBLE ¦ CBRS_BOTTOM);
```

Or you could create it like this:

```
m_wndToolBar.Create (this);
m_wndToolBar.SetBarStyle ((m_wndToolBar.GetBarStyle () &
    ~CBRS_TOP) ¦ CBRS_BOTTOM);
```

CToolBar::Create also accepts an optional third parameter specifying the toolbar ID. The default is AFX_IDW_TOOLBAR. There's normally no need to change the toolbar ID unless a frame window contains multiple toolbars.

A freshly created toolbar is empty, so the next step is to add buttons to it. One way to add buttons is to call *CToolBar::LoadBitmap* to load a bitmap resource containing images for the button faces and *CToolBar::SetButtons* to tell the toolbar how many buttons it will have and what the buttons' command IDs are. The following statements create a toolbar and initialize it with the images stored in the bitmap resource IDR_TOOLBAR and the IDs in the array *nButtonIDs*. The special ID_SEPARATOR value places a small gap a few pixels wide between buttons.

```
// In the .rc file
IDR_TOOLBAR BITMAP Toolbar.bmp

// In the .cpp file
static UINT nButtons[] = {
    ID_FILE_NEW,
    ID_FILE_OPEN,
    ID_FILE_SAVE,
    ID_SEPARATOR,
    ID_EDIT_CUT,
    ID_EDIT_COPY,
    ID_EDIT_PASTE,
    ID_EDIT_UNDO,
    ID_SEPARATOR,
    ID_FILE_PRINT
};
```

(continued)

```
m_wndToolBar.Create (this);
m_wndToolBar.LoadBitmap (IDR_TOOLBAR);
m_wndToolBar.SetButtons (nButtons, 10);
```

The bitmap resource contains all of the toolbar button images, positioned end to end like frames in a filmstrip. (See Figure 11-1.) By default, each image is 16 pixels wide and 15 pixels high. *CToolBar* uses the images in the bitmap resource to draw the faces of the buttons, but it draws the background around the images and the button borders itself. After the borders are drawn, the resulting button measures 24 pixels wide and 22 pixels high. Both the image size and the button size can be changed with *CTool-Bar::SetSizes*. Drawing professional-looking toolbar buttons requires a little artistic flair, but for standard items such as New, Open, Save, Cut, Copy, Paste, and Print, you can borrow images from the Toolbar.bmp bitmap supplied with Visual C++.

Toolbar bitmap

The resulting toolbar

Figure 11-1. *Toolbar images.*

A second and somewhat easier way to create the toolbar buttons is to add a TOOLBAR resource describing the button IDs and image sizes to your application's .rc file and call *CToolBar::LoadToolBar* instead of *LoadBitmap* and *SetButtons*. The following statements create and initialize a toolbar just like the one in the previous paragraph:

```
// In the .rc file
IDR_TOOLBAR BITMAP Toolbar.bmp

IDR_TOOLBAR TOOLBAR 16, 15
BEGIN
    BUTTON ID_FILE_NEW
    BUTTON ID_FILE_OPEN
    BUTTON ID_FILE_SAVE
    SEPARATOR
    BUTTON ID_EDIT_CUT
    BUTTON ID_EDIT_COPY
    BUTTON ID_EDIT_PASTE
    BUTTON ID_EDIT_UNDO
    SEPARATOR
    BUTTON ID_FILE_PRINT
END
```

```
// In the .cpp file
m_wndToolBar.Create (this);
m_wndToolBar.LoadToolBar (IDR_TOOLBAR);
```

When you use a TOOLBAR resource, you can change the image size simply by changing the numbers in the resource statement. *LoadToolBar* loads the toolbar images, sets the button IDs, and sets the button sizes all in one step.

By default, toolbar buttons contain images but not text. You can add text strings to the faces of the buttons with *CToolBar::SetButtonText*. After you've specified the text of each button, use *CToolBar::SetSizes* to adjust the button sizes to accommodate the text strings. The following statements create a toolbar from IDR_TOOLBAR and add descriptive text to each button face:

```
m_wndToolBar.Create (this);
m_wndToolBar.LoadToolBar (IDR_TOOLBAR);

m_wndToolBar.SetButtonText (0, "New");
m_wndToolBar.SetButtonText (1, "Open");
m_wndToolBar.SetButtonText (2, "Save");
m_wndToolBar.SetButtonText (4, "Cut");
m_wndToolBar.SetButtonText (5, "Copy");
m_wndToolBar.SetButtonText (6, "Paste");
m_wndToolBar.SetButtonText (7, "Undo");
m_wndToolBar.SetButtonText (9, "Print");

m_wndToolBar.SetSizes (CSize (48, 40), CSize (16, 15));
```

The resulting toolbar is shown in Figure 11-2. The first parameter passed to *SetButtonText* specifies the button's index, with 0 representing the leftmost button on the toolbar, 1 representing the button to its right, and so on. *SetSizes* should be called *after* the button text is added, not before, or the button sizes won't stick.

Figure 11-2. *Toolbar buttons with text.*

Unless you take steps to have them do otherwise, toolbar buttons behave like standard push buttons: they go down when clicked and pop back up when released. You can use MFC's *CToolBar::SetButtonStyle* function to create check buttons that stay down when clicked and pop back up when clicked again, and radio push buttons that stay down until another button is clicked. The statements that follow create a text formatting toolbar that contains check buttons for selecting bold, italic, and underlined text and radio push buttons for selecting left aligned, centered, or right aligned text.

```
// In the .rc file
IDR_TOOLBAR BITMAP Toolbar.bmp

IDR_TOOLBAR TOOLBAR 16, 15
BEGIN
    BUTTON ID_CHAR_BOLD
    BUTTON ID_CHAR_ITALIC
    BUTTON ID_CHAR_UNDERLINE
    SEPARATOR
    BUTTON ID_PARA_LEFT
    BUTTON ID_PARA_CENTER
    BUTTON ID_PARA_RIGHT
END

// In the .cpp file
m_wndToolBar.Create (this);
m_wndToolBar.LoadToolBar (IDR_TOOLBAR);

m_wndToolBar.SetButtonStyle (0, TBBS_CHECKBOX);
m_wndToolBar.SetButtonStyle (1, TBBS_CHECKBOX);
m_wndToolBar.SetButtonStyle (2, TBBS_CHECKBOX);
m_wndToolBar.SetButtonStyle (4, TBBS_CHECKGROUP);
m_wndToolBar.SetButtonStyle (5, TBBS_CHECKGROUP);
m_wndToolBar.SetButtonStyle (6, TBBS_CHECKGROUP);
```

The TBBS_CHECKBOX style creates a check button. TBBS_CHECKGROUP, which is equivalent to TBBS_CHECKBOX ¦ TBBS_GROUP, creates a radio push button. Because buttons 4, 5, and 6 share the TBBS_CHECKGROUP style, clicking any one of them "checks" that button and unchecks the others. Buttons 0, 1, and 2, however, operate independently of each other and toggle up and down only when clicked directly. Other toolbar button styles that you can specify through *SetButtonStyle* include TBBS_BUTTON, which creates a standard push button, and TBBS_SEPARATOR, which creates a button separator. The complementary *CToolBar::GetButtonStyle* function retrieves button styles.

When you add radio push buttons to a toolbar, you should also check one member of each group to identify the default selection. The following code expands on the example in the previous paragraph by checking the ID_PARA_LEFT button:

```
int nState =
    m_wndToolBar.GetToolBarCtrl ().GetState (ID_PARA_LEFT);
m_wndToolBar.GetToolBarCtrl ().SetState (ID_PARA_LEFT, nState ¦
    TBSTATE_CHECKED);
```

CToolBar::GetToolBarCtrl returns a reference to the *CToolBarCtrl* that provides the basic functionality for a *CToolBar*. *CToolBarCtrl* is a wrapper around the toolbar control found in Comctl32.dll. *CToolBarCtrl::GetState* returns the state of a toolbar button, and *CToolBarCtrl::SetState* changes the button state. Setting the TBSTATE_CHECKED flag in the parameter passed to *SetState* checks the button.

In practice, you may never need *SetButtonStyle* because, in an MFC program, you can convert standard push buttons into check buttons and radio push buttons by providing update handlers that use *CCmdUI::SetCheck* to do the checking and unchecking. We'll discuss this aspect of button handling more in just a moment.

Docking and Floating

One feature that comes for free when you create a toolbar from MFC's *CToolBar* class is the ability for the user to grab the toolbar with the mouse, detach it from its frame window, and either dock it to another side of the window or allow it to float free in a mini–frame window of its own. You control which (if any) sides of the frame window a toolbar can be docked to and other parameters of the toolbar's operation. It's equally easy to create highly configurable toolbars that can be docked, floated, and resized at the user's behest, and static tool palettes that permanently float and retain rigid row and column configurations.

When a toolbar is first created, it's affixed to the side of its frame window and can't be detached. Floating and docking are enabled by calling the toolbar's *Enable-Docking* function (*CControlBar::EnableDocking*) with bit flags specifying which sides of the frame window the toolbar will allow itself to be docked to and the frame window's *EnableDocking* function (*CFrameWnd::EnableDocking*) with bit flags specifying which sides of the window are valid docking targets. The values shown in the table below can be ORed together and passed to either *EnableDocking* function.

Bit Flag	Description
CBRS_ALIGN_LEFT	Permit docking to the left side of the frame window.
CBRS_ALIGN_RIGHT	Permit docking to the right side of the frame window.
CBRS_ALIGN_TOP	Permit docking to the top of the frame window.
CBRS_ALIGN_BOTTOM	Permit docking to the bottom of the frame window.
CBRS_ALIGN_ANY	Permit docking to any side of the frame window.

Called from a member function of a frame window class, the statements

```
m_wndToolBar.EnableDocking (CBRS_ALIGN_ANY);
EnableDocking (CBRS_ALIGN_ANY);
```

enable the toolbar represented by *m_wndToolBar* to be docked to any side of its parent. The statements

```
m_wndToolBar.EnableDocking (CBRS_ALIGN_TOP | CBSR_ALIGN_BOTTOM);
EnableDocking (CBRS_ALIGN_ANY);
```

restrict docking to the inside top and bottom of the frame window. It might seem redundant for both the toolbar and the frame window to specify docking targets, but it comes in handy when a frame window contains more than one toolbar and each has different docking requirements. For example, if *m_wndToolBar1* and *m_wndTool-Bar2* belong to the same frame window, the statements

```
m_wndToolBar1.EnableDocking (CBRS_ALIGN_TOP | CBSR_ALIGN_BOTTOM);
m_wndToolBar2.EnableDocking (CBRS_ALIGN_LEFT | CBSR_ALIGN_RIGHT);
EnableDocking (CBRS_ALIGN_ANY);
```

enable *m_wndToolBar1* to be docked top and bottom and *m_wndToolBar2* to be docked left and right.

Toolbars are docked and undocked programmatically with the *CFrameWnd* member functions *DockControlBar* and *FloatControlBar*. *DockControlBar* docks a toolbar to its parent frame. The statement

```
DockControlBar (&m_wndToolBar);
```

docks *m_wndToolBar* in its default location—the inside top of the frame window if both the toolbar and its parent allow docking along the top edge and the toolbar style includes a CBRS_TOP flag. The statement

```
DockControlBar (&m_wndToolBar, AFX_IDW_DOCKBAR_RIGHT);
```

tries to dock the toolbar to the right edge of the frame window. To exercise even finer control over a toolbar's placement, you can pass *DockControlBar* a *CRect* object or a pointer to a RECT structure containing a docking position. Until *DockControl-Bar* is called, a toolbar can't be detached from its parent, even if docking has been enabled with *CControlBar::EnableDocking* and *CFrameWnd::EnableDocking*.

FloatControlBar is the opposite of *DockControlBar*. It's called to detach a toolbar from its frame window and tell it to begin floating. The framework calls this function when the user drags a docked toolbar and releases it in a nondocking position, but you can float a toolbar yourself by calling *FloatControlBar* and passing in a *CPoint* parameter specifying the position of the toolbar's upper left corner in screen coordinates:

```
FloatControlBar (&m_wndToolBar, CPoint (x, y));
```

You can also pass *FloatControlBar* a third parameter equal to CBRS_ALIGN_TOP to orient the toolbar vertically or CBRS_ALIGN_LEFT to orient it horizontally. Call *Float-ControlBar* instead of *DockControlBar* to create a toolbar that's initially floating instead of docked. If you call *EnableDocking* with a 0 and then call *FloatControlBar*, you get a floating toolbar that can't be docked to the side of a frame window. MFC programmers sometimes use this technique to create stand-alone tool palette windows. You can determine whether a toolbar is docked or floating at any given moment by calling *CControlBar::IsFloating*. You can also add a title to the mini–frame window that surrounds a floating toolbar by calling the toolbar's *SetWindowText* function.

By default, a floating toolbar aligns itself horizontally when docked to the top or bottom of a frame window and vertically when it's docked on the left or right, but it can't be realigned while it's floating. You can give the user the ability to resize a floating toolbar by adding a CBRS_SIZE_DYNAMIC flag to the toolbar style. Conversely, you can make sure that a toolbar's size and shape remain fixed (even when the toolbar is docked) by using CBRS_SIZE_FIXED. One use for CBRS_SIZE_FIXED is to create floating tool palette windows with permanent row and column configurations. You can create static tool palettes containing multiple rows of buttons by using the TBBS-_WRAPPED style to tell *CToolBar* where the line breaks are. A toolbar button with the style TBBS_WRAPPED is analogous to a carriage return/line feed pair in a text file: what comes after it begins on a new line. Assuming IDR_TOOLBAR represents a toolbar containing nine buttons, the following sample code creates a fixed tool palette window containing three rows of three buttons each:

```
m_wndToolBar.Create (this);
m_wndToolBar.LoadToolBar (IDR_TOOLBAR);
m_wndToolBar.SetBarStyle (m_wndToolBar.GetBarStyle () |
    CBRS_SIZE_FIXED);

m_wndToolBar.SetButtonStyle (2,
    m_wndToolBar.GetButtonStyle (0) | TBBS_WRAPPED);
m_wndToolBar.SetButtonStyle (5,
    m_wndToolBar.GetButtonStyle (0) | TBBS_WRAPPED);

m_wndToolBar.EnableDocking (CBRS_ALIGN_ANY);
FloatControlBar (&m_wndToolBar, CPoint (x, y));
```

Adding TBBS_WRAPPED bits to the buttons whose indexes are 2 and 5 creates a line break every third button. And because the tool palette's *EnableDocking* function was not called, the tool palette floats indefinitely and can't be docked to a frame window.

If an application uses two or more toolbars, you can include a CBRS_FLOAT-_MULTI flag in the toolbars' *EnableDocking* functions and allow the user to dock floating toolbars together to form composite toolbars that share a single mini–frame window. Unfortunately, the CBRS_FLOAT_MULTI and CBRS_SIZE_DYNAMIC styles are incompatible with each other, so you can't use both in the same toolbar.

Controlling a Toolbar's Visibility

Most applications that use toolbars feature a View menu that allows toolbars to be alternately hidden and displayed. MFC's *CFrameWnd* class makes it easy to control the visibility of a toolbar by providing a handy pair of functions named *OnBarCheck* and *OnUpdateControlBarMenu*. Called with a toolbar ID, *OnBarCheck* hides the toolbar if it is visible or displays it if it's hidden. *OnUpdateControlBarMenu* updates the View menu by checking or unchecking the menu item whose ID matches the toolbar ID. *OnBarCheck* and *OnUpdateControlBarMenu* work with status bars, too; all you have to do is pass a status bar ID instead of a toolbar ID.

If your application has only one toolbar and that toolbar is assigned the default ID AFX_IDW_TOOLBAR, you can create a menu item that lets the user hide and display the toolbar by assigning the menu item the special ID value ID_VIEW_TOOLBAR. For a status bar, use ID_VIEW_STATUS_BAR instead. No message mapping is necessary because *CFrameWnd*'s message map contains entries mapping these "magic" menu item IDs to the appropriate *CFrameWnd* member functions:

```
ON_UPDATE_COMMAND_UI (ID_VIEW_STATUS_BAR, OnUpdateControlBarMenu)
ON_COMMAND_EX (ID_VIEW_STATUS_BAR, OnBarCheck)
ON_UPDATE_COMMAND_UI (ID_VIEW_TOOLBAR, OnUpdateControlBarMenu)
ON_COMMAND_EX (ID_VIEW_TOOLBAR, OnBarCheck)
```

ON_COMMAND_EX is similar to ON_COMMAND, but an ON_COMMAND_EX handler, unlike an ON_COMMAND handler, receives a UINT parameter containing the ID of the UI object that generated the message. *OnBarCheck* assumes that the toolbar ID and the menu item ID are the same and uses that ID to hide or display the toolbar.

If your application uses a toolbar whose ID is not AFX_IDW_TOOLBAR, there are two ways to connect the toolbar to command and update handlers that control visibility. The simplest method is to assign the toolbar and the corresponding item in the View menu the same ID and to map that ID to *OnBarCheck* and *OnUpdateControlBarMenu* in the main frame window's message map. If the menu item ID is ID_VIEW_TOOLBAR2, here's what the message map entries will look like:

```
ON_UPDATE_COMMAND_UI (ID_VIEW_TOOLBAR2, OnUpdateControlBarMenu)
ON_COMMAND_EX (ID_VIEW_TOOLBAR2, OnBarCheck)
```

Don't forget that, for this method to work, the toolbar *must* be assigned the same ID as the menu item.

The second approach is to provide your own command and update handlers and use *CFrameWnd::ShowControlBar* to hide and display the toolbar. You can determine whether a toolbar is currently visible or invisible by checking the WS_VISIBLE bit of the value returned by *GetStyle*:

```
// In the message map
ON_COMMAND (ID_VIEW_TOOLBAR2, OnViewToolbar2)
ON_UPDATE_COMMAND_UI (ID_VIEW_TOOLBAR2, OnUpdateViewToolbar2UI)
    :
    :
void CMainFrame::OnViewToolbar2 ()
{
    ShowControlBar (&m_wndToolBar2, (m_wndToolBar2.GetStyle() &
        WS_VISIBLE) == 0, FALSE);
}
```

```
void CMainFrame::OnUpdateViewToolbar2UI (CCmdUI* pCmdUI)
{
    pCmdUI->SetCheck ((m_wndToolBar2.GetStyle () &
        WS_VISIBLE) ? 1 : 0);
}
```

Don't try to toggle a toolbar's visibility by turning the WS_VISIBLE flag on or off, because there's more to hiding and displaying a toolbar than flipping a style bit. When a toolbar is toggled on or off (or docked or undocked) in an SDI application, for example, the framework resizes the view to compensate for the change in the visible area of the frame window's client area. *ShowControlBar* takes these and other factors into account when it hides or displays a toolbar. For details, see the code for *CFrameWnd::ShowControlBar* in the MFC source code file Winfrm.cpp.

Keeping Toolbar Buttons in Sync with Your Application

Toolbar buttons are connected to command handlers in your source code the same way menu items are: through message maps. Toolbar buttons can also be assigned update handlers just as menu items can. That's one reason MFC passes an update handler a pointer to a *CCmdUI* object instead of a pointer to a *CMenu* or a *CButton*: the same *CCmdUI* functions that update menu items are equally capable of updating toolbar buttons. Calling *CCmdUI::SetCheck* during a menu update checks or unchecks the menu item. Calling the same function during a toolbar update checks or unchecks a toolbar button by pushing it down or popping it back up. Because *CCmdUI* abstracts the physical nature of UI objects, one update handler can do the updating for a toolbar button and a menu item as long as both objects share the same ID.

Suppose your application has an Edit menu with a Paste command that's enabled when there's text in the clipboard and disabled when there isn't. Suppose further that the application has a Paste toolbar button that performs the same action as Edit-Paste. Both the menu item and the toolbar button are assigned the predefined command ID ID_EDIT_PASTE, and ID_EDIT_PASTE is mapped to a handler named *OnEditPaste* with the following message map entry:

```
ON_COMMAND (ID_EDIT_PASTE, OnEditPaste)
```

To update the Paste menu item each time the Edit menu is displayed, you also map ID_EDIT_PASTE to an update handler named *OnUpdateEditPasteUI*:

```
ON_UPDATE_COMMAND_UI (ID_EDIT_PASTE, OnUpdateEditPasteUI)
```

OnUpdateEditPasteUI uses *CCmdUI::Enable* to enable or disable the Paste command based on the value returned by *::IsClipboardFormatAvailable*:

```
void CMyClass::OnUpdateEditPasteUI (CCmdUI* pCmdUI)
{
    pCmdUI->Enable (::IsClipboardFormatAvailable (CF_TEXT));
}
```

With this infrastructure in place, a paste operation can be performed by selecting Paste from the Edit menu or clicking the Paste button in the toolbar. In addition, the handler that keeps the menu item in sync with the clipboard state also updates the toolbar button. The only difference between menu item updates and toolbar updates is the timing of calls to the update handler. For a menu item, the framework calls the update handler in response to WM_INITMENUPOPUP messages. For a toolbar button, the framework calls the update handler during idle periods in which there are no messages for the application to process. Thus, although menu updates are deferred until just before a menu is displayed, toolbar buttons are updated almost immediately when a state change occurs. It's a good thing, too, because toolbar buttons, unlike menu items, are visible at all times. The physical calling mechanism is transparent to the application, which simply provides an update handler and then trusts the framework to call it as needed.

Earlier I mentioned that you can use update handlers to create check buttons and radio push buttons without changing the button styles. It's easy: You just provide an update handler for each button and use *CCmdUI::SetCheck* or *CCmdUI::SetRadio* to do the checking and unchecking. If a button's command handler toggles a Boolean variable between TRUE and FALSE and its update handler checks or unchecks the button based on the value of the variable, then the button acts like a check button. If the command handler sets the variable value to TRUE and sets the values of other buttons in the group to FALSE, then the button acts like a radio push button. The following message map entries, command handlers, and update handlers make a group of three toolbar buttons behave like radio push buttons:

```
// In the message map
ON_COMMAND (ID_BUTTON1, OnButton1)
ON_COMMAND (ID_BUTTON2, OnButton2)
ON_COMMAND (ID_BUTTON3, OnButton3)
ON_UPDATE_COMMAND_UI (ID_BUTTON1, OnUpdateButton1)
ON_UPDATE_COMMAND_UI (ID_BUTTON2, OnUpdateButton2)
ON_UPDATE_COMMAND_UI (ID_BUTTON3, OnUpdateButton3)
          :
          :

void CMyClass::OnButton1 ()
{
    m_bButton1Down = TRUE;
    m_bButton2Down = FALSE;
    m_bButton3Down = FALSE;
}

void CMyClass::OnButton2 ()
{
    m_bButton1Down = FALSE;
    m_bButton2Down = TRUE;
```

```
        m_bButton3Down = FALSE;
}

void CMyClass::OnButton3 ()
{
    m_bButton1Down = FALSE;
    m_bButton2Down = FALSE;
    m_bButton3Down = TRUE;
}

void CMyClass::OnUpdateButton1 ()
{
    pCmdUI->SetCheck (m_bButton1Down);
}

void CMyClass::OnUpdateButton2 ()
{
    pCmdUI->SetCheck (m_bButton2Down);
}

void CMyClass::OnUpdateButton3 ()
{
    pCmdUI->SetCheck (m_bButton3Down);
}
```

With these command and update handlers in place, it's irrelevant whether the toolbar buttons are TBBS_CHECKGROUP buttons or ordinary TBBS_BUTTON buttons. Clicking any one of the buttons sets the other button-state variables to FALSE, and the update handlers respond by drawing the buttons in their new states.

Adding Tooltips and Flyby Text

When toolbars first began appearing in Windows applications, they were sometimes more hindrance than help because the meanings of the buttons weren't always clear from the pictures on the buttons' faces. Some UI designers sought to alleviate this problem by adding text to the buttons. Others went one step further and invented *tooltips*—small windows with descriptive text such as "Open" and "Paste" that appear on the screen when the cursor pauses over a toolbar button for a half second or so. (See Figure 11-3 on the next page for an example.) Today tooltips are commonplace in Windows applications, and they offer a unique solution to the problem of button ambiguity because they make context-sensitive help for toolbar buttons readily available without requiring a commensurate increase in button size.

Figure 11-3. *A floating toolbar with a tooltip displayed.*

It's easy to add tooltips to an MFC toolbar. Simply add CBRS_TOOLTIPS to the toolbar style and create a string table resource containing tooltip text. The string IDs match the tooltips to the toolbar buttons. If you use standard MFC command IDs such as ID_FILE_OPEN and ID_EDIT_PASTE and include Afxres.h in your application's .rc file, the framework provides the tooltip text for you. For other command IDs, you provide the tooltip text by supplying string resources with IDs that match the toolbar button IDs. The following code sample creates a toolbar with buttons for performing common text formatting operations and tooltips to go with the buttons:

```
// In the .rc file
IDR_TOOLBAR BITMAP Toolbar.bmp

IDR_TOOLBAR TOOLBAR 16, 15
BEGIN
    BUTTON ID_CHAR_BOLD
    BUTTON ID_CHAR_ITALIC
    BUTTON ID_CHAR_UNDERLINE
    SEPARATOR
    BUTTON ID_PARA_LEFT
    BUTTON ID_PARA_CENTER
    BUTTON ID_PARA_RIGHT
END

STRINGTABLE
BEGIN
    ID_CHAR_BOLD        "\nBold"
    ID_CHAR_ITALIC      "\nItalic"
    ID_CHAR_UNDERLINE   "\nUnderline"
    ID_PARA_LEFT        "\nAlign Left"
    ID_PARA_CENTER      "\nAlign Center"
    ID_PARA_RIGHT       "\nAlign Right"
END

// In the .cpp file
m_wndToolBar.Create (this, WS_CHILD | WS_VISIBLE |
    CBRS_TOP | CBRS_TOOLTIPS);
m_wndToolBar.LoadToolBar (IDR_TOOLBAR);
```

When the cursor pauses over a toolbar button and there's a string resource whose ID matches the button ID, the framework displays the text following the newline character in a tooltip window. The tooltip disappears when the cursor moves. In the old days, you had to set timers, monitor mouse movements, and subclass windows to make tooltips work. Nowadays that functionality is provided for you.

If your application features a status bar as well as a toolbar, you can configure the toolbar to display "flyby" text in addition to (or in lieu of) tooltips by setting the CBRS_FLBY bit in the toolbar style. Flyby text is descriptive text displayed in the status bar when the cursor pauses over a toolbar button. Tooltip text should be short and to the point, but flyby text can be longer and richer. Did you wonder why the string resources in the previous paragraph began with "\n" characters? That's because the same string resource identifies flyby text and tooltip text. Flyby text comes before the newline character, and tooltip text comes after. Here's what the previous code sample would look like if it were modified to include flyby text as well as tooltips:

```
// In the .rc file
IDR_TOOLBAR BITMAP Toolbar.bmp

IDR_TOOLBAR TOOLBAR 16, 15
BEGIN
    BUTTON ID_CHAR_BOLD
    BUTTON ID_CHAR_ITALIC
    BUTTON ID_CHAR_UNDERLINE
    SEPARATOR
    BUTTON ID_PARA_LEFT
    BUTTON ID_PARA_CENTER
    BUTTON ID_PARA_RIGHT
END

STRINGTABLE
BEGIN
    ID_CHAR_BOLD        "Toggle boldface text on or off\nBold"
    ID_CHAR_ITALIC      "Toggle italics on or off\nItalic"
    ID_CHAR_UNDERLINE   "Toggle underline on or off\nUnderline"
    ID_PARA_LEFT        "Align text flush left\nAlign Left"
    ID_PARA_CENTER      "Center text between margins\nAlign Center"
    ID_PARA_RIGHT       "Align text flush right\nAlign Right"
END

// In the .cpp file
m_wndToolBar.Create (this, WS_CHILD | WS_VISIBLE |
    CBRS_TOP | CBRS_TOOLTIPS | CBRS_FLYBY);
m_wndToolBar.LoadToolBar (IDR_TOOLBAR);
```

If there are menu items that share the same IDs as the toolbar buttons, the text preceding the newline character in the corresponding string resource is also displayed when a menu item is highlighted. We'll discuss this and other features of status bars a few sections hence.

Adding Non-Push-Button Controls to a Toolbar

Push buttons far outnumber the other types of controls found on toolbars, but *CTool-Bar*s can also include non-push-button controls such as combo boxes and check boxes. Suppose that you'd like to add a combo box to a toolbar so that the user can select a typeface or a font size or something else from a drop-down list. Here's how to go about it.

The first step is to include a button separator in the TOOLBAR resource where you'd like the combo box to appear. The following TOOLBAR resource definition uses a separator as a placeholder for a combo box that will appear to the right of the final push button:

```
IDR_TOOLBAR TOOLBAR 16, 15
BEGIN
    BUTTON ID_CHAR_BOLD
    BUTTON ID_CHAR_ITALIC
    BUTTON ID_CHAR_UNDERLINE
    SEPARATOR
    BUTTON ID_PARA_LEFT
    BUTTON ID_PARA_CENTER
    BUTTON ID_PARA_RIGHT
    SEPARATOR,       // Space between button and combo box
    SEPARATOR        // Placeholder for combo box
END
```

The second step is to use *CToolBar::SetButtonInfo* to increase the width of the separator to make room for the combo box and then to create a combo box in that space. Assuming that the toolbar is represented by a custom toolbar class derived from *CToolBar*, that *m_ctlComboBox* is a *CComboBox* data member of the toolbar class, that IDC_COMBOBOX is the combo box's control ID, and that *nWidth* and *nHeight* hold the desired combo box dimensions, here's what the part of the toolbar class's *OnCreate* handler that creates the combo box might look like:

```
SetButtonInfo (8, IDC_COMBOBOX, TBBS_SEPARATOR, nWidth);

CRect rect;
GetItemRect (8, &rect);
rect.bottom = rect.top + nHeight;

m_ctlComboBox.Create (WS_CHILD | WS_VISIBLE | WS_VSCROLL |
    CBS_SORT | CBS_DROPDOWNLIST, rect, this, IDC_COMBOBOX);
```

The call to *CToolBar::SetButtonInfo* assigns the separator the same ID as the combo box and expands the separator horizontally so that its width equals the desired width of the combo box. Before *CComboBox::Create* is called to create the combo box, *CToolBar::GetItemRect* is called to retrieve the separator's control rectangle. That rectangle is then heightened to make room for the list box part of the combo box, and the combo box is created over the top of the button separator. The combo box is parented to the toolbar so that it will move when the toolbar moves. The toolbar also receives the combo box's WM_COMMAND messages, but thanks to command routing, the notifications that the combo box sends to its parent can be processed by the frame window, the view, and other standard command targets.

What about tooltips and flyby text for non-push-button controls? As far as the framework is concerned, the combo box is just another control on the toolbar and can include tooltips and flyby text just as push button controls can. All you have to do to add tooltip and flyby text to the combo box is define a string resource whose ID is IDC_COMBOBOX. A tooltip window will automatically appear when the cursor pauses over the combo box, and the flyby text will appear in the status bar.

Updating Non-Push-Button Controls

It wouldn't make sense to assign an update handler to a combo box in a toolbar because *CCmdUI* isn't designed to handle combo boxes. But MFC provides an alternative update mechanism that's ideal for non-push-button controls. *ControlBar::OnUpdateCmdUI* is a virtual function the framework calls as part of its idle-processing regimen. A derived toolbar class can override *OnUpdateCmdUI* and take the opportunity to update controls that don't have UI update handlers. It's the perfect solution for keeping custom toolbar controls in sync with other parts of the application, and for doing that in a passive way that closely mimics the update mechanism used for toolbar buttons and menu items.

Let's say you've derived a toolbar class named *CStyleBar* from *CToolBar* that includes a combo box with a list of all the fonts installed in the system. As the user moves the caret through a document, you want to update the combo box so that the item selected in it is the name of the typeface at the current caret position. Rather than respond to each change in the caret position by updating the combo box selection directly, you could override *OnUpdateCmdUI* as shown here:

```
void CStyleBar::OnUpdateCmdUI (CFrameWnd* pTarget,
    BOOL bDisableIfNoHndler)
{
    CToolbar::OnUpdateCmdUI (pTarget, bDisableIfNoHndler);
    CString string = GetTypefaceAtCaret ();
    if (m_ctlComboBox.SelectString (-1, string) == CB_ERR)
        m_ctlComboBox.SetCurSel (-1);
}
```

GetTypefaceAtCaret is another *CStyleBar* function that retrieves font information from the document or view and returns a *CString* with the typeface name. After *GetTypeface-Name* returns, *CComboBox::SelectString* is called to select the corresponding combo box item, and *CComboBox::SetCurSel* is called with a −1 to blank the visible portion of the combo box if *SelectString* fails. With this simple update handler in place, the combo box selection will stay in sync with the caret as the user cursors through the document. The MyWord application presented later in this chapter uses a similar *OnUpdateCmdUI* handler to keep a pair of combo boxes—one for typefaces and one for font sizes—in sync with the caret position.

Generally speaking, you can ignore the *pTarget* and *bDisableIfNoHndler* parameters passed to *OnUpdateCmdUI*. But be sure to call *CToolBar::OnUpdateCmdUI* from the derived class's *OnUpdateCmdUI* function to avoid short-circuiting the update handlers for conventional toolbar buttons.

Making Toolbar Settings Persistent

MFC provides two convenient functions you can use to preserve toolbar settings across sessions: *CFrameWnd::SaveBarState* and *CFrameWnd::LoadBarState*. *SaveBarState* writes information about each toolbar's docked or floating state, position, orientation, and visibility to the registry or a private .ini file. (In Windows 95, you should call *CWinApp::SetRegistryKey* from your application object's *InitInstance* function so that *SaveBarState* will use the registry.) If your application includes a status bar, *Save-BarState* records information about the status bar, too. Calling *LoadBarState* when the application restarts reads the settings back from the registry and restores each toolbar and status bar to its previous state. Normally, *LoadBarState* is called from the main frame window's *OnCreate* handler after the toolbars and status bars are created, and *SaveBarState* is called from the frame window's *OnClose* handler. If you'd also like to save control bar settings if Windows is shut down while your application is running, call *SaveBarState* from an *OnEndSession* handler, too.

SaveBarState should not be called from the frame window's *OnDestroy* handler if you want to preserve the states of floating toolbars as well as docked toolbars. A docked toolbar is a child of the frame window it's docked to, but a floating toolbar is a child of the mini–frame window that surrounds it. The mini–frame window is a popup window owned by the frame window, but it's not a child of the frame window. (A popup window is a window with the style WS_POPUP; a child window has the WS_CHILD style instead.) The distinction is important because popup windows owned by a frame window are destroyed before the frame window is destroyed. Child windows, on the other hand, are destroyed *after* their parents are destroyed. A floating toolbar no longer exists when the frame window's *OnDestroy* function is called. Consequently, if it's called from *OnDestroy*, *SaveBarState* will fail to save state information for toolbars that aren't docked to the frame window.

STATUS BARS

It has becoming increasingly common, even expected, for Windows applications to include status bars that display context-sensitive help for toolbar buttons and menu items. Windows applications written in C customarily display descriptive help text for menu items by trapping WM_MENUSELECT messages identifying the currently selected menu item and updating the status bar accordingly. In MFC, there's an easier way. When a *CStatusBar* is connected to a frame window, it automatically displays a string of help text when a menu item is highlighted. If the application includes a toolbar and if the toolbar style includes a CBRS_FLYBY flag, the status bar also displays flyby text for toolbar buttons. The best part is that all you're responsible for besides creating and initializing the status bar (something that requires just a few lines of code) is providing the help text in the form of string resources in your application's .rc file. The framework does the rest.

Status bars can do much more than just display help text, of course. A status bar can be divided into one or more areas variously referred to as panes, panels, or indicators. The text of each pane can be set individually, so one pane can display the current line number or page number in a document while another displays menu and toolbar help and still others display the current Caps Lock and Num Lock states. Some status bars even contain progress controls that report percent-complete figures for common operations such as document saving and loading.

Creating and Initializing a Status Bar

A status bar is an object instantiated from MFC's *CStatusBar* class. An application that uses a status bar typically declares a *CStatusBar* object as a member of the frame window class. Then the frame window's *OnCreate* handler creates the status bar:

```
m_wndStatusBar.Create (this);
```

The lone argument passed to *Create* identifies the status bar's parent window. Passing a *this* pointer referring to a frame window makes the status bar a child of the frame window. A status bar created in this way doesn't need to be destroyed before the application terminates because it's destroyed automatically when its parent is destroyed. *CStatusBar::Create* also accepts parameters specifying the status bar's style and child window ID, but the default values MFC provides for these parameters do quite nicely for most applications.

After a status bar is created, it's initialized by calling *CStatusBar::SetIndicators*. *SetIndicators* specifies the number of panes the status bar will contain and optionally assigns string resources to individual panes. The statements

```
UINT nIndicator = ID_SEPARATOR;
m_wndStatusBar.Create (this);
m_wndStatusBar.SetIndicators (&nIndicator, 1);
```

create a simple status bar with just one pane. ID_SEPARATOR is a generic ID value that says there is no string resource associated with this pane. You can create a simple "binary" pane that indicates whether a particular feature of your application is on or off by specifying a string resource ID instead of ID_SEPARATOR and connecting the pane to an update handler that uses *CCmdUI::Enable* to enable and disable the pane. An enabled pane displays the string resource assigned to it, but a disabled pane is blank. The status bar created by the following code sample includes a pane that displays the text string "INS" when the application is in insert mode and nothing when it's in overstrike mode. For the purposes of this example, assume that insert mode is on when *m_bInsert* is TRUE and off when *m_bInsert* is FALSE:

```
// In the .rc file
STRINGTABLE
BEGIN
    ID_INDICATOR_INS "INS"
END

// In the frame window's message map
ON_UPDATE_COMMAND_UI (ID_INDICATOR_INS, OnUpdateIndicator)

// In the frame window's OnCreate function
static UINT nIndicators[] = {
    ID_SEPARATOR,
    ID_INDICATOR_INS
};

m_wndStatusBar.Create (this);
m_wndStatusBar.SetIndicators (nIndicators, 2);

// Elsewhere in the frame window implementation
void CMainFrame::OnUpdateIndicator (CCmdUI* pCmdUI)
{
    pCmdUI->Enable (m_bInsert);
}
```

In this example, the frame window handles the UI update commands. In a real application, it might be more appropriate to make *OnUpdateIndicator* a member of the document or the view class. ID_INDICATOR_INS is a symbolic constant defined elsewhere in the application; it is not defined for you by MFC.

MFC defines four special indicator IDs for status bar panes that display keyboard states and maps them to a common update handler in the *CFrameWnd* class. The IDs are

- ID_INDICATOR_CAPS, which corresponds to the Caps Lock key

- ID_INDICATOR_NUM, which corresponds to the Num Lock key

- ID_INDICATOR_SCRL, which corresponds to the Scroll Lock key

- ID_INDICATOR_KANA, which corresponds to the Kana key on Japanese keyboards

A status bar pane assigned the ID value ID_INDICATOR_CAPS displays the word "CAP" when Caps Lock is on. Similarly, an ID_INDICATOR_NUM pane displays "NUM" when Num Lock is on, an ID_INDICATOR_SCRL pane displays "SCRL" when Scroll Lock is on, and an ID_INDICATOR_KANA pane displays "KANA" when Kana mode is enabled on Japanese keyboards. The framework (in reality, *CFrameWnd::OnUpdate-KeyIndicator*) keeps these indicators in sync with the keyboard. As a result, you can create a status bar with Caps Lock, Num Lock, and Scroll Lock indicators simply by adding the magic ID values to the array passed to *SetIndicators*:

```
static UINT nIndicators[] = {
    ID_SEPARATOR,
    ID_INDICATOR_CAPS,
    ID_INDICATOR_NUM,
    ID_INDICATOR_SCRL
};

m_wndStatusBar.Create (this);
m_wndStatusBar.SetIndicators (nIndicators, 4);
```

The resulting status bar is shown in Figure 11-4. The blank pane indicates that the corresponding keyboard state is inactive. *CStatusBar* automatically positions all panes after the first at the far right end of the status bar and stretches the leftmost pane to fill the remaining space. It sizes the other panes so that they're just wide enough to display the text strings assigned to them. Panes other than the first are also drawn "indented" so that they're visible even when they're blank.

Figure 11-4. *Status bar with Caps Lock, Num Lock, and Scroll Lock indicators.*

Providing Context-Sensitive Help for Menu Items

When you assign the first (leftmost) pane in a status bar the value ID_SEPARATOR, you enable a special feature of the framework that is elegant in both design and simplicity. When the user highlights a menu item, the framework checks to see if the application's .exe file contains a string resource whose ID equals the menu item ID. If the search turns up a match, the string resource is loaded and displayed in the status bar pane. As a result, you can provide context-sensitive help for your application's menus by providing string resources whose IDs match the menu item IDs. If a menu item and a toolbar button share the same ID, the same string resource doubles as help text for the menu item and as flyby text for the toolbar.

As it does for toolbar buttons, the framework provides default help strings for ID_FILE_NEW, ID_FILE_OPEN, and other common command IDs. It also provides default help strings for commands found in the system menu. (For a complete list of predefined IDs and the help text and tooltip text associated with them, look in the MFC source code file Prompts.rc.) Simply include the header file Afxres.h in your application's .rc file, and the framework's predefined string resources will be included, too. You can override the help text for predefined menu item IDs by defining your own string resources with identical ID values. For a nice touch, include an

```
AFX_IDS_IDLEMESSAGE "Ready"
```

statement in your application's string table, and the framework will display the word "Ready" in the status bar when no menu is pulled down or no item is selected.

Creating Custom Status Bar Panes

Now you know how to display help text in a status bar, add Caps Lock, Num Lock, and Scroll Lock indicators, and create simple on/off indicators by combining string resources and update handlers. But what about more complex status bars like the ones featured in Microsoft Word, Microsoft Excel, Microsoft PowerPoint, and other Windows 95 applications? How, for example, would you create a status bar pane that displays the time of day or the current page number?

For starters, you can add panes to a status bar and size them any way you want them using *CStatusBar*'s *SetPaneInfo* function. *SetPaneInfo* accepts four parameters: the 0-based index of the pane whose attributes you want to modify and the pane's ID, style, and width, in that order. The pane style specifies whether the pane will be drawn indented, protruding, or flush with the face of the status bar. It also determines whether the pane is currently enabled or disabled and identifies variable-width panes that expand and contract with the status bar. The style is a combination of one or more of the values shown in the table below.

Style	*Description*
SBPS_NOBORDERS	Draw the pane flush with the surface of the status bar.
SBPS_POPOUT	Draw the pane so that it protrudes from the status bar.
SBPS_NORMAL	Draw the pane so that it is indented into the status bar.
SBPS_DISABLED	Disable the pane. Disabled panes don't display text.
SBPS_STRETCH	Stretch the pane to fill unused space when the status bar is resized. Only one pane per status bar can have this style.
SBPS_OWNERDRAW	Create an owner-drawn pane.

The following code creates a status bar with three custom panes. The first pane is 64 pixels wide and is drawn flush with the surface of the status bar. The second is also 64 pixels wide, but it protrudes from the status bar. The third is a variable-width pane whose right edge follows the right edge of the status bar. It's drawn with an indented border:

```
static UINT nIndicators[] = {
    ID_SEPARATOR,
    ID_SEPARATOR,
    ID_SEPARATOR
};

m_wndStatusBar.Create (this);
m_wndStatusBar.SetIndicators (nIndicators, 3);

m_wndStatusBar.SetPaneInfo (0, ID_SEPARATOR, SBPS_NOBORDERS, 64);
m_wndStatusBar.SetPaneInfo (1, ID_SEPARATOR, SBPS_POPOUT, 64);
m_wndStatusBar.SetPaneInfo (2, ID_SEPARATOR, SBPS_NORMAL |
    SBPS_STRETCH, 0);
```

In a real application, you'll probably want to avoid hard pixel counts and base pane widths on a scalable screen metric such as the average width of a character in the status bar font. You can get a *CFont* pointer for the default status bar font by calling the *GetFont* function a *CStatusBar* inherits from *CWnd*.

Once a custom pane is created, it's your job to tell the status bar what to display inside the pane. There are two ways to add text to a pane. You can call *CStatusBar::SetPaneText* to set the text directly, or you can assign the pane an update handler and let the update handler set the text with *CCmdUI::SetText*. Which method you use depends on how you want the pane to be updated. The following code fragment sets a timer to fire every 200 milliseconds and uses *SetPaneText* to update an hours:minutes:seconds display in pane 2. In this case, the ID assigned to the pane in the call to *SetIndicators* or *SetPaneInfo* is irrelevant because *SetPaneText* identifies panes by index:

```
// In CMainFrame::OnCreate
SetTimer (ID_TIMER, 200, NULL);
    .
    .
    .
void CMainFrame::OnTimer (UINT nTimerID)
{
    CTime time = CTime::GetCurrentTime ();
    int nSecond = time.GetSecond ();
    int nMinute = time.GetMinute ();
    int nHour = time.GetHour () % 12;
```

(continued)

```
        CString string;
        string.Format ("%0.2d:%0.2d:%0.2d", nHour, nMinute, nSecond);
        m_wndStatusBar.SetPaneText (2, string);
    }
```

An alternative approach is to assign the pane a unique ID such as ID_INDICATOR_TIME and connect it to an update handler with a message map entry. Now the time-of-day display in the status bar will be continually updated by the framework:

```
// In the message map
ON_UPDATE_COMMAND_UI (ID_INDICATOR_TIME, OnUpdateTime)
    :
    :
void CMainFrame::OnUpdateTime (CCmdUI* pCmdUI)
{
    CTime time = CTime::GetCurrentTime ();
    int nSecond = time.GetSecond ();
    int nMinute = time.GetMinute ();
    int nHour = time.GetHour () % 12;

    CString string;
    string.Format ("%0.2d:%0.2d:%0.2d", nHour, nMinute, nSecond);
    pCmdUI->SetText (string);
}
```

CStatusBar prevents a pane from flashing when it's updated too frequently by comparing the current text in the pane to the text specified in a call to *SetPaneText* or *SetText* and doing nothing if the two are equal.

Putting It All Together: The MyWord Application

The sample program depicted in Figure 11-5 demonstrates many of the principles we've looked at in the preceding sections. MyWord is a miniature word processor built from a frame window and a *CRichEditView*. MFC's *CRichEditView* class is like a *CEditView* on steroids; based on the rich text edit control supplied in the common controls library, it features superior text formatting capabilities and can read and write rich text format (.rtf) files with a simple function call. MyWord doesn't use all the features of a *CRichEditView*; in fact, it barely scratches the surface. (For a more in-depth look at *CRichEditView*, see the Wordpad sample program provided with MFC. The Wordpad files are the actual source code for the Wordpad applet that ships with Windows 95.) But MyWord packs a lot of punch for a program that's only a few hundred lines long, and it's a good starting point for writing *CRichEditView*-based applications of your own.

MyWord uses two toolbars and one status bar. The main toolbar includes buttons that serve as shortcuts for the New, Open, and Save items in the File menu and

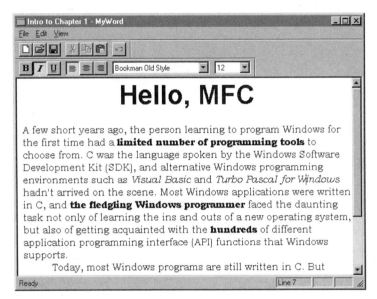

Figure 11-5. *The MyWord application.*

the Cut, Copy, Paste, and Undo items in the Edit menu. The other toolbar, which I'll refer to as the *style bar,* includes check buttons for setting the character format (bold, italic, and underline), radio push buttons for setting the paragraph alignment (left aligned, centered, and right aligned), and combo boxes for selecting typefaces and font sizes. Both toolbars can be detached from the frame window, floated, and docked at other locations; and both can be resized while they're floating. Try it: Drag the main toolbar to the right side of the window, and dock it in a vertical position. Grab the style bar and release it in the center of the window so that it becomes a floating palette. Use the View menu to hide and display the toolbars and the status bar. You can also hide a toolbar by clicking the close button in the mini–frame window it floats in when it's detached from the main frame window. To redisplay the toolbar, simply select the Toolbar or Style Bar command in the View menu.

The status bar at the bottom of MyWord's frame window displays help text for menu items and toolbar controls. It also includes Caps Lock and Num Lock indicators and a line number display that's continually updated as the caret moves through the document. The Caps Lock and Num Lock indicators were added using MFC's predefined ID_INDICATOR_CAPS and ID_INDICATOR_NUM IDs. The line number indicator is updated by an ON_UPDATE_COMMAND_UI handler that, when called, retrieves the current line number from the *CRichEditView*, formulates a text string containing the line number, and updates the status bar display with *CCmdUI::SetText*. The line number pane is sized by initially assigning it the dummy string "Line 00000," whose resource ID is ID_INDICATOR_LINE. The dummy string is never seen because the pane is updated with a real line number before the status bar appears on the screen.

The source code for MyWord is listed in Figure 11-6. Take a moment to look it over to see how the toolbars and status bar are handled. Then flip forward a few pages to read about pertinent parts of the source code in greater detail.

Resource.h

```
//****************************************************************
//
//   Resource.h
//
//****************************************************************

#define IDR_MAINFRAME            100
#define IDR_TOOLBAR              101
#define IDR_STYLE_BAR            102

#define IDW_STYLE_BAR            200
#define ID_VIEW_STYLE_BAR        200

#define ID_INDICATOR_LINE        300

#define ID_CHAR_BOLD             400
#define ID_CHAR_ITALIC           401
#define ID_CHAR_UNDERLINE        402
#define ID_PARA_LEFT             403
#define ID_PARA_CENTER           404
#define ID_PARA_RIGHT            405

#define IDC_FONTNAMES            500
#define IDC_FONTSIZES            501
```

MyWord.rc

```
//****************************************************************
//
//   MyWord.rc
//
//****************************************************************

#include <afxres.h>
#include "Resource.h"

IDR_TOOLBAR BITMAP Toolbar.bmp
IDR_STYLE_BAR BITMAP StyleBar.bmp
```

Figure 11-6. *The MyWord program.*

```
IDR_TOOLBAR TOOLBAR 16, 15
BEGIN
    BUTTON       ID_FILE_NEW
    BUTTON       ID_FILE_OPEN
    BUTTON       ID_FILE_SAVE
    SEPARATOR
    BUTTON       ID_EDIT_CUT
    BUTTON       ID_EDIT_COPY
    BUTTON       ID_EDIT_PASTE
    SEPARATOR
    BUTTON       ID_EDIT_UNDO
END

IDR_STYLE_BAR TOOLBAR 16, 15
BEGIN
    BUTTON       ID_CHAR_BOLD
    BUTTON       ID_CHAR_ITALIC
    BUTTON       ID_CHAR_UNDERLINE
    SEPARATOR
    BUTTON       ID_PARA_LEFT
    BUTTON       ID_PARA_CENTER
    BUTTON       ID_PARA_RIGHT
    SEPARATOR
    SEPARATOR    // Placeholder for font name combo box
    SEPARATOR
    SEPARATOR    // Placeholder for font size combo box
END

IDR_MAINFRAME MENU
BEGIN
    POPUP "&File" {
        MENUITEM "&New\tCtrl+N",          ID_FILE_NEW
        MENUITEM "&Open...\tCtrl+O",       ID_FILE_OPEN
        MENUITEM "&Save\tCtrl+S",          ID_FILE_SAVE
        MENUITEM "Save &As...\tCtrl+A",    ID_FILE_SAVE_AS
        MENUITEM SEPARATOR
        MENUITEM "Sen&d...",               ID_FILE_SEND_MAIL
        MENUITEM SEPARATOR
        MENUITEM "Recent File",            ID_FILE_MRU_FILE1
        MENUITEM SEPARATOR
        MENUITEM "E&xit",                  ID_APP_EXIT
    }
    POPUP "&Edit" {
        MENUITEM "&Undo\tCtrl+Z",          ID_EDIT_UNDO
        MENUITEM SEPARATOR
```

(continued)

MyWord.rc *continued*

```
        MENUITEM "Cu&t\tCtrl+X",            ID_EDIT_CUT
        MENUITEM "&Copy\tCtrl+C",           ID_EDIT_COPY
        MENUITEM "&Paste\tCtrl+V",          ID_EDIT_PASTE
        MENUITEM "Paste &Special...",       ID_EDIT_PASTE_SPECIAL
        MENUITEM "C&lear\tDel",             ID_EDIT_CLEAR
        MENUITEM "Select A&ll\tCtrl+A",     ID_EDIT_SELECT_ALL
        MENUITEM SEPARATOR
        MENUITEM "&Find...\tCtrl+F",        ID_EDIT_FIND
        MENUITEM "F&ind Next\tF3",          ID_EDIT_REPEAT
        MENUITEM "R&eplace...\tCtrl+H",     ID_EDIT_REPLACE
    }
    POPUP "&View" {
        MENUITEM "&Toolbar",                ID_VIEW_TOOLBAR
        MENUITEM "Style &Bar",              ID_VIEW_STYLE_BAR
        MENUITEM "&Status Bar",             ID_VIEW_STATUS_BAR
    }
END


IDR_MAINFRAME ACCELERATORS
BEGIN
    "N",    ID_FILE_NEW,         VIRTKEY,    CONTROL
    "O",    ID_FILE_OPEN,        VIRTKEY,    CONTROL
    "S",    ID_FILE_SAVE,        VIRTKEY,    CONTROL
    "A",    ID_FILE_SAVE_AS,     VIRTKEY,    CONTROL

    "Z",    ID_EDIT_UNDO,        VIRTKEY,    CONTROL
    "X",    ID_EDIT_CUT,         VIRTKEY,    CONTROL
    "C",    ID_EDIT_COPY,        VIRTKEY,    CONTROL
    "V",    ID_EDIT_PASTE,       VIRTKEY,    CONTROL
    "A",    ID_EDIT_SELECT_ALL,  VIRTKEY,    CONTROL
    "F",    ID_EDIT_FIND,        VIRTKEY,    CONTROL
    VK_F3,  ID_EDIT_REPEAT,      VIRTKEY
    "H",    ID_EDIT_REPLACE,     VIRTKEY,    CONTROL

    "B",    ID_CHAR_BOLD,        VIRTKEY,    CONTROL
    "I",    ID_CHAR_ITALIC,      VIRTKEY,    CONTROL
    "U",    ID_CHAR_UNDERLINE,   VIRTKEY,    CONTROL
END


STRINGTABLE
BEGIN
    IDR_MAINFRAME "MyWord\n\n\nMyWord Files
        (*.mwd)\n.mwd\nMyWord.Document\nMyWord Document"
END
```

```
STRINGTABLE
BEGIN
    AFX_IDS_IDLEMESSAGE      "Ready"

    ID_VIEW_TOOLBAR          "Show or hide the main toolbar"
    ID_VIEW_STYLE_BAR        "Show or hide the style bar"

    ID_CHAR_BOLD             "Toggle boldface on or off\nBold"
    ID_CHAR_ITALIC           "Toggle italics on or off\nItalic"
    ID_CHAR_UNDERLINE        "Toggle underline on or off\nUnderline"

    ID_PARA_LEFT             "Align text flush left\nAlign Left"
    ID_PARA_CENTER           "Center text between margins\nAlign Center"
    ID_PARA_RIGHT            "Align text flush right\nAlign Right"

    IDC_FONTNAMES            "Select a typeface\nTypeface"
    IDC_FONTSIZES            "Select a point size\nFont Size"

    ID_INDICATOR_LINE        "Line 00000"
    ID_INDICATOR_CAPS        "CAPS"
END
```

MyWord.h

```
//*********************************************************************
//
//  MyWord.h
//
//*********************************************************************

class CWordApp : public CWinApp
{
public:
    virtual BOOL InitInstance ();

protected:
    DECLARE_MESSAGE_MAP ()
};
```

MyWord.cpp

```
//***********************************************************************
//
//  MyWord.cpp
//
//***********************************************************************

#include <afxwin.h>
#include <afxext.h>
#include <afxcmn.h>
#include <afxrich.h>
#include "Resource.h"
#include "MyWord.h"
#include "StyleBar.h"
#include "MainFrame.h"
#include "MyWordDoc.h"
#include "MyWordView.h"

CWordApp myApp;

BEGIN_MESSAGE_MAP (CWordApp, CWinApp)
    ON_COMMAND (ID_FILE_NEW, CWinApp::OnFileNew)
    ON_COMMAND (ID_FILE_OPEN, CWinApp::OnFileOpen)
END_MESSAGE_MAP ()

BOOL CWordApp::InitInstance ()
{
    SetRegistryKey ("Programming Windows 95 with MFC");
    LoadStdProfileSettings ();

    CSingleDocTemplate* pDocTemplate;
    pDocTemplate = new CSingleDocTemplate (
        IDR_MAINFRAME,
        RUNTIME_CLASS (CWordDoc),
        RUNTIME_CLASS (CMainFrame),
        RUNTIME_CLASS (CWordView)
    );

    AddDocTemplate (pDocTemplate);
    RegisterShellFileTypes (TRUE);

    CCommandLineInfo cmdInfo;
    ParseCommandLine (cmdInfo);

    if (!ProcessShellCommand (cmdInfo))
        return FALSE;
```

```
    m_pMainWnd->DragAcceptFiles ();
    return TRUE;
}
```

MainFrame.h

```
//*********************************************************************
//
//  MainFrame.h
//
//*********************************************************************

class CMainFrame : public CFrameWnd
{
    DECLARE_DYNCREATE (CMainFrame)

private:
    CToolBar m_wndToolBar;
    CStyleBar m_wndStyleBar;
    CStatusBar m_wndStatusBar;

    BOOL CreateToolBar ();
    BOOL CreateStyleBar ();
    BOOL CreateStatusBar ();

protected:
    afx_msg int OnCreate (LPCREATESTRUCT);
    afx_msg void OnClose ();

    DECLARE_MESSAGE_MAP ()
};
```

MainFrame.cpp

```
//*********************************************************************
//
//  MainFrame.cpp
//
//*********************************************************************

#include <afxwin.h>
#include <afxext.h>
#include "Resource.h"
```

(continued)

MainFrame.cpp *continued*

```cpp
#include "StyleBar.h"
#include "MainFrame.h"

IMPLEMENT_DYNCREATE (CMainFrame, CFrameWnd)

BEGIN_MESSAGE_MAP (CMainFrame, CFrameWnd)
    ON_WM_CREATE ()
    ON_COMMAND_EX (ID_VIEW_STYLE_BAR, OnBarCheck)
    ON_UPDATE_COMMAND_UI (ID_VIEW_STYLE_BAR, OnUpdateControlBarMenu)
    ON_WM_CLOSE ()
END_MESSAGE_MAP ()

int CMainFrame::OnCreate (LPCREATESTRUCT lpcs)
{
    if (CFrameWnd::OnCreate (lpcs) == -1)
        return -1;

    EnableDocking (CBRS_ALIGN_ANY);

    if (!CreateToolBar () ||
        !CreateStyleBar () ||
        !CreateStatusBar ())
        return -1;

    LoadBarState ("BarSettings");
    return 0;
}

void CMainFrame::OnClose ()
{
    SaveBarState ("BarSettings");
    CFrameWnd::OnClose ();
}

BOOL CMainFrame::CreateToolBar ()
{
    if (!m_wndToolBar.Create (this) ||
        !m_wndToolBar.LoadToolBar (IDR_TOOLBAR))
        return FALSE;

    m_wndToolBar.SetBarStyle (m_wndToolBar.GetBarStyle () |
        CBRS_TOOLTIPS | CBRS_FLYBY | CBRS_SIZE_DYNAMIC);

    m_wndToolBar.SetWindowText ("Main");
    m_wndToolBar.EnableDocking (CBRS_ALIGN_ANY);
```

```
        DockControlBar (&m_wndToolBar);
        return TRUE;
}

BOOL CMainFrame::CreateStyleBar ()
{
        if (!m_wndStyleBar.Create (this, WS_CHILD | WS_VISIBLE | CBRS_TOP |
            CBRS_TOOLTIPS | CBRS_FLYBY | CBRS_SIZE_DYNAMIC, IDW_STYLE_BAR))
            return FALSE;

        m_wndStyleBar.SetWindowText ("Styles");
        m_wndStyleBar.EnableDocking (CBRS_ALIGN_TOP | CBRS_ALIGN_BOTTOM);
        DockControlBar (&m_wndStyleBar);
        return TRUE;
}

BOOL CMainFrame::CreateStatusBar ()
{
        static UINT nIndicators[] = {
            ID_SEPARATOR,
            ID_INDICATOR_LINE,
            ID_INDICATOR_CAPS,
            ID_INDICATOR_NUM
        };

        if (!m_wndStatusBar.Create (this))
            return FALSE;

        m_wndStatusBar.SetIndicators (nIndicators, 4);
        return TRUE;
}
```

MyWordDoc.h

```
//*********************************************************************
//
//  MyWordDoc.h
//
//*********************************************************************

class CWordDoc : public CRichEditDoc
{
        DECLARE_DYNCREATE (CWordDoc)
```

(continued)

MyWordDoc.h *continued*

```
public:
    virtual BOOL OnNewDocument ();
    virtual CRichEditCntrItem* CreateClientItem (REOBJECT*) const;

protected:
    DECLARE_MESSAGE_MAP ()
};
```

MyWordDoc.cpp

```
//*************************************************************************
//
//  MyWordDoc.cpp
//
//*************************************************************************

#include <afxwin.h>
#include <afxcmn.h>
#include <afxrich.h>
#include "Resource.h"
#include "MyWordDoc.h"

IMPLEMENT_DYNCREATE (CWordDoc, CRichEditDoc)

BEGIN_MESSAGE_MAP (CWordDoc, CRichEditDoc)
    ON_COMMAND (ID_FILE_SEND_MAIL, OnFileSendMail)
    ON_UPDATE_COMMAND_UI (ID_FILE_SEND_MAIL, OnUpdateFileSendMail)
END_MESSAGE_MAP ()

BOOL CWordDoc::OnNewDocument ()
{
    if (!CRichEditDoc::OnNewDocument ())
        return FALSE;

    CHARFORMAT cf;
    cf.cbSize = sizeof (CHARFORMAT);
    cf.dwMask = CFM_BOLD | CFM_ITALIC | CFM_UNDERLINE |
        CFM_PROTECTED | CFM_STRIKEOUT | CFM_FACE | CFM_SIZE;
    cf.dwEffects = 0;
    cf.yHeight = 240; // 240 twips == 12 points
    ::lstrcpy (cf.szFaceName, "Times New Roman");
    GetView ()->SetCharFormat (cf);
```

```
    return TRUE;
}

CRichEditCntrItem* CWordDoc::CreateClientItem (REOBJECT* preo) const
{
    return new CRichEditCntrItem (preo, (CWordDoc*) this);
}
```

MyWordView.h

```
//**********************************************************************
//
//  MyWordView.h
//
//**********************************************************************

class CWordView : public CRichEditView
{
    DECLARE_DYNCREATE (CWordView)

public:
    void GetFontInfo (LPSTR, int&);
    void ChangeFont (LPCSTR);
    void ChangeFontSize (int);

protected:
    afx_msg void OnCharBold ();
    afx_msg void OnCharItalic ();
    afx_msg void OnCharUnderline ();
    afx_msg void OnParaLeft ();
    afx_msg void OnParaCenter ();
    afx_msg void OnParaRight ();
    afx_msg void OnUpdateCharBoldUI (CCmdUI*);
    afx_msg void OnUpdateCharItalicUI (CCmdUI*);
    afx_msg void OnUpdateCharUnderlineUI (CCmdUI*);
    afx_msg void OnUpdateParaLeftUI (CCmdUI*);
    afx_msg void OnUpdateParaCenterUI (CCmdUI*);
    afx_msg void OnUpdateParaRightUI (CCmdUI*);
    afx_msg void OnUpdateLineNumber (CCmdUI*);

    DECLARE_MESSAGE_MAP ()
};
```

MyWordView.cpp

```cpp
//*************************************************************************
//
// MyWordView.cpp
//
//*************************************************************************

#include <afxwin.h>
#include <afxcmn.h>
#include <afxrich.h>
#include "Resource.h"
#include "StyleBar.h"
#include "MainFrame.h"
#include "MyWordView.h"

IMPLEMENT_DYNCREATE (CWordView, CRichEditView)

BEGIN_MESSAGE_MAP (CWordView, CRichEditView)
    ON_COMMAND (ID_CHAR_BOLD, OnCharBold)
    ON_COMMAND (ID_CHAR_ITALIC, OnCharItalic)
    ON_COMMAND (ID_CHAR_UNDERLINE, OnCharUnderline)
    ON_COMMAND (ID_PARA_LEFT, OnParaLeft)
    ON_COMMAND (ID_PARA_CENTER, OnParaCenter)
    ON_COMMAND (ID_PARA_RIGHT, OnParaRight)
    ON_UPDATE_COMMAND_UI (ID_CHAR_BOLD, OnUpdateCharBoldUI)
    ON_UPDATE_COMMAND_UI (ID_CHAR_ITALIC, OnUpdateCharItalicUI)
    ON_UPDATE_COMMAND_UI (ID_CHAR_UNDERLINE, OnUpdateCharUnderlineUI)
    ON_UPDATE_COMMAND_UI (ID_PARA_LEFT, OnUpdateParaLeftUI)
    ON_UPDATE_COMMAND_UI (ID_PARA_CENTER, OnUpdateParaCenterUI)
    ON_UPDATE_COMMAND_UI (ID_PARA_RIGHT, OnUpdateParaRightUI)
    ON_UPDATE_COMMAND_UI (ID_INDICATOR_LINE, OnUpdateLineNumber)
END_MESSAGE_MAP ()

void CWordView::OnCharBold ()
{
    CHARFORMAT cf;
    cf = GetCharFormatSelection ();

    if (!(cf.dwMask & CFM_BOLD) || !(cf.dwEffects & CFE_BOLD))
        cf.dwEffects = CFE_BOLD;
    else
        cf.dwEffects = 0;

    cf.dwMask = CFM_BOLD;
    SetCharFormat (cf);
}
```

```
void CWordView::OnCharItalic ()
{
    CHARFORMAT cf;
    cf = GetCharFormatSelection ();

    if (!(cf.dwMask & CFM_ITALIC) || !(cf.dwEffects & CFE_ITALIC))
        cf.dwEffects = CFE_ITALIC;
    else
        cf.dwEffects = 0;

    cf.dwMask = CFM_ITALIC;
    SetCharFormat (cf);
}

void CWordView::OnCharUnderline ()
{
    CHARFORMAT cf;
    cf = GetCharFormatSelection ();

    if (!(cf.dwMask & CFM_UNDERLINE) || !(cf.dwEffects & CFE_UNDERLINE))
        cf.dwEffects = CFE_UNDERLINE;
    else
        cf.dwEffects = 0;

    cf.dwMask = CFM_UNDERLINE;
    SetCharFormat (cf);
}

void CWordView::OnParaLeft ()
{
    OnParaAlign (PFA_LEFT);
}

void CWordView::OnParaCenter ()
{
    OnParaAlign (PFA_CENTER);
}

void CWordView::OnParaRight ()
{
    OnParaAlign (PFA_RIGHT);
}

void CWordView::OnUpdateCharBoldUI (CCmdUI* pCmdUI)
{
    OnUpdateCharEffect (pCmdUI, CFM_BOLD, CFE_BOLD);
}
```

(continued)

MyWordView.cpp *continued*

```
void CWordView::OnUpdateCharItalicUI (CCmdUI* pCmdUI)
{
    OnUpdateCharEffect (pCmdUI, CFM_ITALIC, CFE_ITALIC);
}

void CWordView::OnUpdateCharUnderlineUI (CCmdUI* pCmdUI)
{
    OnUpdateCharEffect (pCmdUI, CFM_UNDERLINE, CFE_UNDERLINE);
}

void CWordView::OnUpdateParaLeftUI (CCmdUI* pCmdUI)
{
    OnUpdateParaAlign (pCmdUI, PFA_LEFT);
}

void CWordView::OnUpdateParaCenterUI (CCmdUI* pCmdUI)
{
    OnUpdateParaAlign (pCmdUI, PFA_CENTER);
}

void CWordView::OnUpdateParaRightUI (CCmdUI* pCmdUI)
{
    OnUpdateParaAlign (pCmdUI, PFA_RIGHT);
}

void CWordView::OnUpdateLineNumber (CCmdUI* pCmdUI)
{
    int nLine = GetRichEditCtrl ().LineFromChar (-1) + 1;

    CString string;
    string.Format ("Line %d", nLine);
    pCmdUI->Enable (TRUE);
    pCmdUI->SetText (string);
}

void CWordView::ChangeFont (LPCSTR pszFaceName)
{
    CHARFORMAT cf;
    cf.cbSize = sizeof (CHARFORMAT);
    cf.dwMask = CFM_FACE;
    ::lstrcpy (cf.szFaceName, pszFaceName);
    SetCharFormat (cf);
}

void CWordView::ChangeFontSize (int nSize)
{
```

```
        CHARFORMAT cf;
        cf.cbSize = sizeof (CHARFORMAT);
        cf.dwMask = CFM_SIZE;
        cf.yHeight = nSize;
        SetCharFormat (cf);
}

void CWordView::GetFontInfo (LPSTR pszFaceName, int& nSize)
{
        CHARFORMAT cf = GetCharFormatSelection ();
        ::lstrcpy (pszFaceName, cf.dwMask & CFM_FACE ? cf.szFaceName : "");
        nSize = cf.dwMask & CFM_SIZE ? cf.yHeight : -1;
}
```

StyleBar.h

```
//**********************************************************************
//
//  StyleBar.h
//
//**********************************************************************

class CStyleBar : public CToolBar
{
private:
        CFont m_font;
        CComboBox m_ctlNameComboBox;
        CComboBox m_ctlSizeComboBox;

        void FillNameComboBox (CDC*);

public:
        virtual void OnUpdateCmdUI (CFrameWnd*, BOOL);

        static int CALLBACK EnumFontNameProc (ENUMLOGFONT*,
            NEWTEXTMETRIC*, int, LPARAM);

protected:
        afx_msg int OnCreate (LPCREATESTRUCT);
        afx_msg void OnSelectFont ();
        afx_msg void OnSelectSize ();
        afx_msg void OnCloseUp ();

        DECLARE_MESSAGE_MAP ()
};
```

StyleBar.cpp

```
//****************************************************************************
//
//  StyleBar.cpp
//
//****************************************************************************

#include <afxwin.h>
#include <afxext.h>
#include <afxcmn.h>
#include <afxrich.h>
#include <stdlib.h>
#include "Resource.h"
#include "MyWordView.h"
#include "StyleBar.h"

BEGIN_MESSAGE_MAP (CStyleBar, CToolBar)
    ON_WM_CREATE ()
    ON_CBN_SELENDOK (IDC_FONTNAMES, OnSelectFont)
    ON_CBN_SELENDOK (IDC_FONTSIZES, OnSelectSize)
    ON_CBN_CLOSEUP (IDC_FONTNAMES, OnCloseUp)
    ON_CBN_CLOSEUP (IDC_FONTSIZES, OnCloseUp)
END_MESSAGE_MAP ()

int CStyleBar::OnCreate (LPCREATESTRUCT lpcs)
{
    static int nFontSizes[] = {
        8, 9, 10, 11, 12, 14, 16, 18, 20, 22, 24, 26, 28, 32, 36, 48, 72
    };

    if (CToolBar::OnCreate (lpcs) == -1)
        return -1;

    // Load the toolbar
    if (!LoadToolBar (IDR_STYLE_BAR))
        return -1;

    // Create an 8-point MS Sans Serif font for the combo boxes
    CClientDC dc (this);
    int nHeight = -((dc.GetDeviceCaps (LOGPIXELSY) * 8) / 72);

    m_font.CreateFont (nHeight, 0, 0, 0, FW_NORMAL, 0, 0, 0,
        DEFAULT_CHARSET, OUT_CHARACTER_PRECIS, CLIP_CHARACTER_PRECIS,
        DEFAULT_QUALITY, DEFAULT_PITCH | FF_DONTCARE, "MS Sans Serif");

    CFont* pOldFont = dc.SelectObject (&m_font);
```

```
    TEXTMETRIC tm;
    dc.GetTextMetrics (&tm);
    int cxChar = tm.tmAveCharWidth;
    int cyChar = tm.tmHeight + tm.tmExternalLeading;

    dc.SelectObject (pOldFont);

    // Add the font name combo box to the toolbar
    SetButtonInfo (8, IDC_FONTNAMES, TBBS_SEPARATOR, cxChar * 32);

    CRect rect;
    GetItemRect (8, &rect);
    rect.bottom = rect.top + (cyChar * 16);

    if (!m_ctlNameComboBox.Create (WS_CHILD | WS_VISIBLE | WS_VSCROLL |
        CBS_DROPDOWNLIST | CBS_SORT, rect, this, IDC_FONTNAMES))
        return -1;

    m_ctlNameComboBox.SetFont (&m_font);
    FillNameComboBox (&dc);

    // Add the font size combo box to the toolbar
    SetButtonInfo (10, IDC_FONTSIZES, TBBS_SEPARATOR, cxChar * 12);

    GetItemRect (10, &rect);
    rect.bottom = rect.top + (cyChar * 14);

    if (!m_ctlSizeComboBox.Create (WS_CHILD | WS_VISIBLE | WS_VSCROLL |
        CBS_DROPDOWNLIST, rect, this, IDC_FONTSIZES))
        return -1;

    m_ctlSizeComboBox.SetFont (&m_font);

    CString string;
    for (int i=0; i<17; i++) {
        string.Format ("%d", nFontSizes[i]);
        m_ctlSizeComboBox.AddString (string);
    }
    return 0;
}

void CStyleBar::OnSelectFont ()
{
    char szFaceName[LF_FACESIZE];
    int nIndex = m_ctlNameComboBox.GetCurSel ();
    m_ctlNameComboBox.GetLBText (nIndex, szFaceName);
```

(continued)

751

StyleBar.cpp *continued*

```
    CWordView* pView =
        (CWordView*) ((CFrameWnd*) AfxGetMainWnd ())->GetActiveView ();
    pView->ChangeFont (szFaceName);
}

void CStyleBar::OnSelectSize ()
{
    char szSize[8];
    int nIndex = m_ctlSizeComboBox.GetCurSel ();
    m_ctlSizeComboBox.GetLBText (nIndex, szSize);

    int nSize = atoi (szSize) * 20; // Need twips

    CWordView* pView =
        (CWordView*) ((CFrameWnd*) AfxGetMainWnd ())->GetActiveView ();
    pView->ChangeFontSize (nSize);
}

void CStyleBar::OnCloseUp ()
{
    ((CFrameWnd*) AfxGetMainWnd ())->GetActiveView ()->SetFocus ();
}

void CStyleBar::FillNameComboBox (CDC* pDC)
{
    ::EnumFontFamilies (pDC->m_hDC, NULL,
        (FONTENUMPROC) EnumFontNameProc, (LPARAM) this);
}

int CALLBACK CStyleBar::EnumFontNameProc (ENUMLOGFONT* lpelf,
    NEWTEXTMETRIC* lpntm, int nFontType, LPARAM lParam)
{
    CStyleBar* pWnd = (CStyleBar*) lParam;
    if (nFontType & TRUETYPE_FONTTYPE)
        pWnd->m_ctlNameComboBox.AddString (lpelf->elfLogFont.lfFaceName);
    return 1;
}

void CStyleBar::OnUpdateCmdUI (CFrameWnd* pTarget,
    BOOL bDisableIfNoHndler)
{
    CToolBar::OnUpdateCmdUI (pTarget, bDisableIfNoHndler);

    CWnd* pWnd = GetFocus ();
    if ((pWnd == &m_ctlNameComboBox) || (pWnd == &m_ctlSizeComboBox))
        return;
```

```
// Get the font name and size
int nTwips;
char szFaceName[LF_FACESIZE];

CWordView* pView =
    (CWordView*) ((CFrameWnd*) AfxGetMainWnd ())->GetActiveView ();
pView->GetFontInfo (szFaceName, nTwips);

// Update the font name combo box
char szSelection[LF_FACESIZE];
m_ctlNameComboBox.GetWindowText (szSelection, sizeof (szSelection));

if (::lstrcmp (szFaceName, szSelection) != 0) {
    if (szFaceName[0] == 0)
        m_ctlNameComboBox.SetCurSel (-1);
    else {
        if (m_ctlNameComboBox.SelectString (-1, szFaceName) == CB_ERR)
            m_ctlNameComboBox.SetCurSel (-1);
    }
}

// Update the font size combo box
char szSize[4];
m_ctlSizeComboBox.GetWindowText (szSize, sizeof (szSize));
int nSizeFromComboBox = atoi (szSize);
int nSizeFromView = nTwips / 20;

if (nSizeFromComboBox != nSizeFromView) {
    if (nTwips == -1)
        m_ctlSizeComboBox.SetCurSel (-1);
    else {
        CString string;
        string.Format ("%d", nSizeFromView);
        if (m_ctlSizeComboBox.SelectString (-1, string) == CB_ERR)
            m_ctlSizeComboBox.SetCurSel (-1);
    }
}
}
```

The Main Toolbar

MyWord's main toolbar is a standard *CToolBar* that's created along with the style bar and status bar in *CMainFrame::OnCreate*. After the main toolbar is created, the styles CBRS_TOOLTIPS, CBRS_FLYBY, and CBRS_SIZE_DYNAMIC are added and *CToolBar::EnableDocking* is called with a CBRS_ALIGN_ANY parameter so that the toolbar can be docked to any side of the frame window. *DockControlBar* is called to dock the toolbar in its default location at the top of the window so that it can be detached and floated. The call to *LoadBarState* in *CMainFrame::OnCreate* after the toolbars and status bar are created restores the toolbar to its previous location if the application has been run before.

Handlers for all of the buttons on the main toolbar—and for all of the items in MyWord's menus, for that matter—are provided by the framework. As usual, *CWinApp* provides handlers for the New, Open, and Exit commands in the File menu, and *CDocument* handles the Save, Save As, and Send commands. *CRichEditView* provides handlers for the items in the Edit menu (all prewired into the message map, of course), and *CFrameWnd* handles the commands in the View menu. *CRichEditView* also provides update handlers for Edit commands, which explains why the Cut, Copy, Paste, and Undo buttons in the toolbar are automatically enabled and disabled in response to actions performed by the user. To see what I mean, type a line or two of text and highlight a few characters to form a selection. The Cut and Copy buttons will light up when the first character is selected and blink out again when the selection is canceled. Updates are automatic because of the following entries in *CRichEditView*'s message map:

```
ON_UPDATE_COMMAND_UI (ID_EDIT_CUT, OnUpdateNeedSel)
ON_UPDATE_COMMAND_UI (ID_EDIT_COPY, OnUpdateNeedSel)
```

Scan the *CRichEditView* message map in the MFC source code file Viewrich.cpp to see the full range of commands for which *CRichEditView* provides default command and update handlers.

The Style Bar

MyWord's style bar is created from the *CToolBar*-derived class *CStyleBar*. The style bar is constructed when the frame window is constructed and created in *CMainFrame::OnCreate*, but it also contains its own *OnCreate* handler that creates (and initializes) the font name and font size combo boxes. Other *CStyleBar* member functions include *OnSelectFont*, which applies typefaces selected from the font name combo box; *OnSelectSize*, which applies sizes selected from the font size combo box; *OnCloseUp*, which restores the input focus to the view when either combo box's drop-down list box is closed; *FillNameComboBox* and *EnumFontNameProc*, which work together to enumerate fonts and add their names to the font name combo box; and *OnUpdateCmdUI*, which updates the combo boxes so that the font name and the font size shown in the style bar are consistent with the character at the caret or the characters in a selection.

MyWord's view class provides command and update handlers for the buttons in the style bar. Clicking the Bold button activates *CWordView::OnCharBold*, which is implemented as follows:

```
void CWordView::OnCharBold ()
```

```
{
    CHARFORMAT cf;
    cf = GetCharFormatSelection ();

    if (!(cf.dwMask & CFM_BOLD) || !(cf.dwEffects & CFE_BOLD))
        cf.dwEffects = CFE_BOLD;
    else
        cf.dwEffects = 0;

    cf.dwMask = CFM_BOLD;
    SetCharFormat (cf);
}
```

GetCharFormatSelection is a *CRichEditView* function that returns a CHARFORMAT structure containing information about the text that is currently selected in the view or, if there is no selection, about the default character format. *SetCharFormat* is another *CRichEditView* function that applies the text attributes described in a CHARFORMAT structure to the selected text. If no text is currently selected, *SetCharFormat* sets the view's default character format.

Boldface text is toggled on or off by setting the CFM_BOLD bit in the *dwMask* field of the CHARFORMAT structure passed to *SetCharFormat* and either setting or clearing the CFE_BOLD bit in the structure's *dwEffects* field. To determine the proper setting for the CFE_BOLD flag, *OnCharBold* inspects both the CFM_BOLD and CFE_BOLD flags in the CHARFORMAT structure returned by *GetCharFormatSelection*. The CFM_BOLD flag is clear if the current selection includes a mix of bold and nonbold text. If CFM_BOLD is set, then either the selection consists entirely of bold or nonbold text or there is currently no text selected. In either case, the CFE_BOLD flag indicates whether the selected (or default) text is bold or nonbold. There are five possible scenarios in which *OnCharBold* can be called. The table on the next page describes each set of circumstances and documents the result. The view's *OnCharItalic* and *OnCharUnderline* handlers use similar logic to toggle italics and underlines on and off.

The handlers for the paragraph alignment buttons are simpler because their actions don't depend on the current paragraph alignment. *CRichEditView* provides a convenient *OnParaAlign* function for setting the paragraph alignment to left, right, or centered. (Unfortunately, neither a *CRichEditView* nor the rich edit control that is the foundation for a *CRichEditView* supports fully justified text that extends the width between both margins.) The statement

```
OnParaAlign (PFA_LEFT);
```

in *OnParaLeft* selects left aligned text. If no text is selected in the view, *OnParaAlign* reformats the paragraph that contains the caret. If text is selected, all paragraphs touched by the selection are transformed so that the text in them is left aligned.

Circumstances Under Which OnCharBold *Is Called*	dwMask & CFM_BOLD	dwEffects & CFE_BOLD	Action Taken by OnCharBold
One or more characters are selected; the selection contains a mix of bold and nonbold text.	0	Undefined	Makes all characters in the selection bold.
One or more characters are selected; the selection consists entirely of bold text.	Nonzero	Nonzero	Makes all characters in the selection nonbold.
One or more characters are selected; the selection consists entirely of nonbold text.	Nonzero	0	Makes all characters in the selection bold.
No text is selected; the default character format is bold.	Nonzero	Nonzero	Sets the default character format to nonbold.
No text is selected; the default character format is nonbold.	Nonzero	0	Sets the default character format to bold.

Each of the buttons in the style bar is mapped to an update handler that calls either *CRichEditView::OnUpdateCharEffect* or *CRichEditView::OnUpdateParaAlign*. In addition to checking and unchecking the buttons as appropriate, these *CRichEdit-View* functions also set a button to the indeterminate state when a selection includes a mix of character formats or paragraph alignments. For a simple demonstration, try this test: First enter some text if you haven't already. Then highlight some characters, click the Italic button to italicize the selection, and select a range of characters that includes both italicized and nonitalicized text. Because *OnUpdateCharItalicUI* calls *OnUpdateCharEffect*, the Italic button will assume a half-grayed visage, indicating that the selection contains a mix of character formats. And because each style bar button is assigned an update handler, the buttons will behave like check buttons and radio push buttons even though none is assigned the TBBS_CHECKBOX or TBBS_CHECK-GROUP style.

When a font name or a font size is selected from the combo boxes, the style bar retrieves the font name or font size and calls a public member function of the view class to implement the change. Selecting a font name activates *CStyleBar::OnSelectFont*, which passes the new typeface name to the view through *CWordView::ChangeFont*. *ChangeFont*, in turn, changes the font in the view by setting the CFM_FACE flag in a CHARFORMAT structure's *dwMask* field, copying the typeface name to the structure's *szFaceName* field and calling *SetCharFormat*:

```
void CWordView::ChangeFont (LPCSTR pszFaceName)
{
    CHARFORMAT cf;
    cf.cbSize = sizeof (CHARFORMAT);
    cf.dwMask = CFM_FACE;
```

```
        ::lstrcpy (cf.szFaceName, pszFaceName);
        SetCharFormat (cf);
    }
```

CStyleBar::OnSelectSize uses a similar procedure to change the font size through the view's *ChangeFontSize* member function. Font sizes passed to *CRichEditView*s are expressed in twips, and 1 twip equals $\frac{1}{20}$ of a point. Therefore, *OnSelectSize* multiplies the point size retrieved from the combo box by 20 to convert points to twips before calling *ChangeFontSize*.

Which brings up a question: since the command message generated when an item is selected from a combo box is subject to command routing, why doesn't MyWord let the view handle combo box notifications directly? Actually, that *would* be ideal. But it would also pose a problem. Since the combo boxes are private members of the style bar class, the view would have no way of retrieving the selected item from the combo box. We could fix that by making the combo boxes public members of the style bar and the style bar a public member of the frame window class, but private data members provide stricter encapsulation. Letting the style bar handle combo box notifications and pass the information to the view through public member functions allows the style bar to hide its data yet still communicate style changes to the view.

So that the items selected in the combo boxes will match the character format in the view as the caret is moved through the document and selections are made, *CStyleBar* overrides the *OnUpdateCmdUI* function it inherits from *CToolBar* and updates the combo boxes based on information obtained from the view. After verifying that neither of the combo boxes has the input focus so that the combo boxes won't flicker if *OnUpdateCmdUI* is called while a drop-down list box is displayed, *OnUpdateCmdUI* calls *CWordView::GetFontInfo* to get the current font name and size. If the font name obtained from the view doesn't match the font name selected in the font name combo box, *OnUpdateCmdUI* changes the combo box selection. Similarly, the selection is updated in the font size combo box if the size shown in the combo box doesn't match the size reported by *GetFontInfo*. Leaving the current selection intact if it hasn't changed prevents the combo boxes from flickering as a result of repeated (and unnecessary) updates. The update handler is also smart enough to blank the combo box selection if the font name or font size obtained from *GetFontInfo* doesn't match any of the items in the combo box, or if the text selected in the view contains a mixture of typefaces or font sizes.

One thing *CStyleBar* doesn't do is update the list of typefaces in the font name combo box if the pool of installed fonts changes while MyWord is running. When fonts are added or deleted, Windows sends all top-level windows a WM_FONT-CHANGE message notifying them of the change. To respond to changes in font availability while an application is running, include an ON_WM_FONTCHANGE entry in the frame window's message map and an *OnFontChange* handler to go with it. The message map entry and handler must be members of the frame window class because

WM_FONTCHANGE messages are not routed in the same way that WM_COMMAND and WM_NOTIFY messages are.

To simplify the logic for updating the selection in the font size combo box, MyWord's style bar lists TrueType fonts only. If the font name combo box included raster fonts as well, the font size combo box would need to be reinitialized each time the selection changed in the font name combo box because raster fonts come in a limited number of sizes. Limiting the user's choice of fonts to TrueType only makes the point sizes listed in the font size combo box independent of the typeface selected in the font name combo box because TrueType fonts can be accurately rendered in any point size from 1 through 999.

More About *CRichEditView*

Most of MyWord's functionality comes from *CRichEditView*, which is built around the powerful rich text edit control provided in the Windows 95 common controls library. MFC's *CRichEditView* class doesn't act alone in encapsulating the features of a rich text edit control; help comes from *CRichEditDoc* and *CRichEditCntrItem*. *CRichEditDoc* represents the data stored in a *CRichTextView*, which can include embedded OLE objects, and *CRichEditCntrItem* represents OLE objects embedded in a *CRichEditView*. When you derive a view class from *CRichEditView*, you must also derive a document class from *CRichEditDoc* and override *CRichEditDoc::CreateClientItem*, which is pure virtual. MyWord's *CWordDoc* document class implements *CreateClientItem* by creating a *CRichEditCntrItem* object and returning a pointer:

```
CRichEditCntrItem* CWordDoc::CreateClientItem (REOBJECT* preo) const
{
    return new CRichEditCntrItem (preo, (CWordDoc*) this);
}
```

This simple override enables the Paste and Paste Special commands in the Edit menu to paste OLE items into the document. For a demonstration, copy a picture created with the Windows 95 Paint applet to the clipboard and paste it into a MyWord document. Then double-click the embedded image in MyWord, and Paint will merge its menus and toolbars with MyWord's menus and toolbars so that you can edit the picture in place. If the document is saved, the embedded Paint object is saved, too, so that it will come back up just as you left it when you reload the document.

CWordDoc overrides one other *CRichEditDoc* function—*OnNewDocument*—and in the override calls *CRichEditView::SetCharFormat* to set the default font to 12-point Times New Roman. The pointer through which *SetCharFormat* is called is obtained from *CRichEditDoc::GetView*. Normally, a document class can have any number of views associated with it, so view pointers are obtained with *CDocument::GetFirstViewPosition* and *CDocument::GetNextView*. The *CRichEditDoc* class, however, is designed to handle just one *CRichEditView* at a time. The *GetView* function provides quick and direct access to the associated *CRichEditView*.

In case you hadn't noticed, MyWord is fully capable of saving the documents you create and loading them back in. It can even read .rtf files created by other word processors and serialize embedded OLE objects. Yet you won't find any serialization code in *CWordDoc* because *CRichEditDoc* can handle serialization on its own. *CRichEditDoc::Serialize* streams data to and from a *CRichEditView* by calling the view's *Serialize* function, which in turn relies on the streaming capabilities built into a rich text edit control. (For more information, see the documentation for the EM_STREAMIN and EM_STREAMOUT messages that can be sent to a rich text edit control and the equivalent *StreamIn* and *StreamOut* function members of MFC's *CRichEditCtrl* class.) It's relatively easy to write an SDK application that saves and loads documents in a rich text edit control, but it's downright simple to do it in MFC because *CRichEditDoc* and *CRichEditView* work together with other components of the framework to handle all phases of the serialization process for you.

By default, *CRichEditDoc* serializes documents in rich text format. You can instruct a *CRichEditDoc* to write text files that lack formatting information and embedded OLE items by setting the *CRichEditDoc* data member *m_bRTF* equal to FALSE before storing a document. By the same token, you can read files in plain text format by setting *m_bRTF* to FALSE before dearchiving a document. It wouldn't be hard to give MyWord the ability to read and write text files as well as rich text format files, but you'd have to add some fancy logic to the front end of the deserialization process to identify the type of file that's about to be read. *CRichEditDoc* won't load a text file if *m_bRTF* is TRUE, and if it reads a rich text format document with *m_bRTF* equal to TRUE, it converts .rtf formatting commands to ordinary text. A full treatment of *CRichEditDoc* serialization options is beyond the scope of this book, but if you're interested in learning more, a good place to start is the Wordpad source code provided with MFC.

VERSIONABLE SCHEMAS

One of the keystones of a Windows application that uses MFC's document/view architecture is the unique way in which it loads and saves documents. When the user selects the Open or Save command from the application's File menu, the framework opens the file for reading or writing, attaches a *CArchive* object to abstract the physical storage medium, and calls the document's *Serialize* function with a reference to the *CArchive*. You write the *Serialize* function that streams the document's data in or out, and the framework provides the context in which *Serialize* executes.

Often an entire document can be serialized with just a few lines of code because the document's data is stored in objects that are themselves serializable. When you write a serializable class in MFC, you assign the class an integer ID called a schema number that MFC uses to enact a crude form of version control. MFC tags objects of the class with the schema number when it archives them to disk, and when it reads them back, it compares the schema number recorded in the file to the schema number of the objects in memory. If the two don't match, the application framework throws a *CArchiveException* with a cause code equal to *CArchiveException::badSchema*. An unhandled exception of this type displays a message box with the warning "Unexpected file format." By incrementing the schema number each time you revise an object's storage format, you provide an effective safeguard against inadvertent attempts to read an old version of an object stored on disk into a new version that resides in memory.

One problem you're forced to contend with when writing serializable classes is handling objects that were created with older versions of your application. If an object's persistent storage format changes from one version of the application to the next, you'll probably want the new version to be able to read both formats. But as soon as MFC sees the mismatched schema numbers, it will throw an exception. Because of the way MFC is architected, there's no good way to handle the exception other than to do as MFC does and abort the serialization process.

That's where versionable schemas come in. A versionable schema is simply a schema number that includes a VERSIONABLE_SCHEMA flag. The flag tells MFC that the application can handle multiple document formats. It suppresses the *CArchive-Exception* and allows an application to respond intelligently to different schema numbers. An application that uses versionable schemas can provide the backward compatibility for its documents that users expect.

For two very good reasons, versionable schemas have a reputation for being difficult to implement and unreliable. First, 16-bit versions of MFC didn't support versionable schemas. Second, a bug in early 32-bit versions of MFC prevented versionable schemas from working consistently. It wasn't until MFC 4 was introduced that you could use versionable schemas and be confident that your code would work. Now it's easy to write a version 2.0 of your application that will read documents created by version 1.0, even if the serialized document formats differ. The remainder of this chapter describes MFC's versionable schema mechanism and how to take advantage of it. As you're about to discover, versionable schemas aren't exactly the rocket science their reputation makes them out to be.

Under the Hood: How Serialization Works

To understand how versionable schemas work, it helps to understand first how MFC reads and writes serializable classes. Let's use Chapter 9's Paint6 program as an example and look inside a document containing a few *CLine* objects to see what gets written to disk and what the framework does when it reads the serialized objects back into memory.

Recall that a document in our Paint6 program is serialized by calling the *Serialize* function of the *CObArray* object in which *CLine* pointers are stored. The document class's *Serialize* function contains just one line of code:

```
    m_lineArray.Serialize (ar);
```

A *CObArray* serializes itself to disk by writing the number of elements in the array to the archive and then serializing each object whose pointer is stored in the array. The pertinent code in *CObArray::Serialize* looks like this:

```
if (ar.IsStoring())
{
    ar.WriteCount(m_nSize);
    for (int i = 0; i < m_nSize; i++)
        ar << m_pData[i];
}
```

Adding a *CLine* object to an archive with a << operator calls *CArchive::WriteObject* with a pointer to the object, and *CArchive::WriteObject*, in turn, serializes the *CLine* to disk. *WriteObject* ultimately calls the *CLine*'s *Serialize* function to archive the object's data members, but before it does it writes some additional information to the archive that identifies the class the object was created from.

The very first time it serializes a *CLine* to disk, *WriteObject* inserts a *new class tag*—a 16-bit integer whose value is −1, or 0xFFFF—into the archive, followed by the object's 16-bit schema number, then a 16-bit value denoting the number of characters in the object's class name, and finally the class name itself, in ASCII format. *WriteObject* then calls the *CLine*'s *Serialize* function so that the *CLine* can serialize itself. *WriteObject* builds an in-memory database of the classes whose names and schema numbers it records in the archive and assigns each class a unique identifier that is actually an index into the database. Since Paint6 documents contain just one class type (*CLine*), the first *CLine* written to disk is assigned an index of 1. When *WriteObject* writes a second *CLine* to the archive, it knows that information regarding the *CLine* class is already in the archive, so instead of writing out the class information again, it writes a 16-bit value that consists of the class index ORed with an *old class tag* (0x8000). It then calls the *CLine*'s *Serialize* function just as before. Thus, the first instance of a class written to the archive is tagged with a new class tag, a schema number, and an ASCII class name; subsequent instances are tagged with 16-bit values whose lower 15 bits are indexes referencing classes already recorded in the archive.

Figure 11-7 on the next page shows a hex dump of a Paint6 document that contains two *CLine*s. The hex dump is broken down so that each line in the listing represents one component of the serialized document. I've numbered the lines in the listing for reference purposes. Line 1 contains the object count (2) that *CObArray::Serialize* wrote to the archive. Line 2 contains information written by *WriteObject* that defines the *CLine* class. The first 16-bit word is the new class tag; the second word is the class's schema number (1); the third word holds the length of the class name (5); and the final five bytes hold the text of the class name ("CLine"). Immediately following the class information, in lines 3 through 8, is the serialized *CLine*: six 32-bit

Schema number   **Length of "CLine"**

New class tag   **Class name ("CLine")**

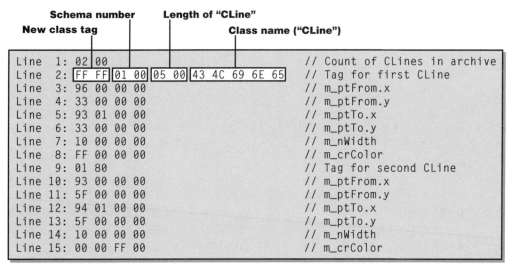

```
Line  1: 02 00                        // Count of CLines in archive
Line  2: FF FF 01 00 05 00 43 4C 69 6E 65   // Tag for first CLine
Line  3: 96 00 00 00                  // m_ptFrom.x
Line  4: 33 00 00 00                  // m_ptFrom.y
Line  5: 93 01 00 00                  // m_ptTo.x
Line  6: 33 00 00 00                  // m_ptTo.y
Line  7: 10 00 00 00                  // m_nWidth
Line  8: FF 00 00 00                  // m_crColor
Line  9: 01 80                        // Tag for second CLine
Line 10: 93 00 00 00                  // m_ptFrom.x
Line 11: 5F 00 00 00                  // m_ptFrom.y
Line 12: 94 01 00 00                  // m_ptTo.x
Line 13: 5F 00 00 00                  // m_ptTo.y
Line 14: 10 00 00 00                  // m_nWidth
Line 15: 00 00 FF 00                  // m_crColor
```

Figure 11-7. *Hex dump of a Paint6 document.*

values that specify, in order, the *x* component of the *CLine*'s *m_ptFrom* data member; the *y* component of *m_ptFrom*; the *x* component of *m_ptTo*; the *y* component of *m_ptTo*; the line's width (*m_nWidth*); and the line's color (*m_crColor*). Similar information for the second *CLine* appears on lines 10 through 15, but in between—on line 9—is a 16-bit tag that identifies the following data as a *CLine*. *CLine*'s class index is 1 because it was the first class added to the archive. The 16-bit value 0x8001 is the class index ORed with an old class tag.

So far, so good. It's not too difficult to understand what goes into an archived Paint6 document. Now let's see what happens when the framework reads the *CLine*s back from the archive.

When Paint6's document class calls *CObArray::Serialize* to deserialize the document, the *CObArray* reads the object count from the archive, sets the array size so that it equals the number of *CLine*s stored in the archive, and dearchives the *CLine*s one by one:

```
DWORD nOldSize = ar.ReadCount();
SetSize(nOldSize);
for (int i = 0; i < m_nSize; i++)
    ar >> m_pData[i];
```

The >> operator invokes *CArchive::ReadObject* and passes it a NULL pointer. *ReadObject*, in turn, calls another *CArchive* function named *ReadClass* to determine what kind of object it's about to read. *ReadClass* reads a word from the archive, sees that it's a new class tag, reads the schema number and the class name from the archive, and uses the class name to locate the *CRuntimeClass* object for the class named "CLine."

(Remember the DECLARE_SERIAL and IMPLEMENT_SERIAL macros discussed in Chapter 6? One of the things these macros do is declare a static *CRuntimeClass* object containing the class name and other information about the class that the framework can use during the deserialization process. *CRuntimeClass* objects are stored in a linked list maintained by the framework.) *ReadClass* then compares the schema number read from the archive to the schema number stored in the *CRuntimeClass*. If the schemas are the same, *ReadClass* returns the *CRuntimeClass* pointer to *ReadObject*. *ReadObject*, in turn, calls *CreateObject* through the *CRuntimeClass* pointer to create a new instance of the class in memory and then calls the *CLine*'s *Serialize* function to load the data from the archive into the object's data members.

As class information is read from the archive, *ReadObject* builds a class database in memory just as *WriteObject* does. When the second *CLine* is read from the archive, the 0x8001 tag preceding it tells *ReadClass* that it can get the *CRuntimeClass* pointer requested by *ReadObject* from the database.

That's basically what happens during the serialization process if all goes well. I've skipped many of the details, including the numerous error checks the framework performs and the special treatment given to NULL object pointers and multiple references to the same object. But now let's consider what happens if the schema number of the first *CLine* read from the archive doesn't match the schema number stored in *CLine*'s *CRuntimeClass*. The framework first checks to see if the class supports versionable schemas. If the VERSIONABLE_SCHEMA flag is absent from the schema number stored in the *CRuntimeClass*, the framework throws a *CArchiveException*. At that point, the serialization process is over, done, finis. There's very little you can do about it other than display an error message, which the framework will do for you if you don't catch the exception. If the VERSIONABLE_SCHEMA flag is set, however, then the framework skips the call to *AfxThrowArchiveException* and stores the schema number where the application can retrieve it later by calling *CArchive::GetObjectSchema*. *GetObjectSchema* is the key that opens the door to versionable schemas that work.

Writing a Versionable Class

The process the framework goes through to serialize an object to or from disk may be complex, but writing a serializable class that takes advantage of MFC 4's versionable schema mechanism requires just two simple steps:

1. OR the value VERSIONABLE_SCHEMA into the schema number assigned to the class in the IMPLEMENT_SERIAL macro.

2. Write the class's *Serialize* function so that it calls *CArchive::GetObjectSchema* when loading an object from an archive and adapts its deserialization method accordingly.

GetObjectSchema returns the schema number of the object that's about to be read from the archive, or −1 if the schema is unknown. There are a few rules to be aware of when using *GetObjectSchema*. First, it should be called only when an object is being loaded. Second, it should be called before any of the object's data members are streamed in. And third, it should be called only once. If called a second time in the context of the same call to *Serialize*, *GetObjectSchema* returns −1.

Rather than create two versions of the same sample program that demonstrate how versionable schemas work, let's see what it would take to modify Paint6 so that version 2.0 could read version 1.0 documents if the *CLine* class were modified to include an extra data member. *CLine* currently includes four data members, which are declared as follows:

```
class CLine : public CObject
{
    DECLARE_SERIAL (CLine)

private:
    CPoint m_ptFrom;
    CPoint m_ptTo;
    UINT m_nWidth;
    COLORREF m_crColor;
        .
        .
};
```

Let's say that in version 2.0 you decide to add a data member that specifies the line's style (solid, dotted, dashed, and so on) as an integer from 0 through 7. The revised class *CLine* declaration would look like this:

```
class CLine : public CObject
{
    DECLARE_SERIAL (CLine)

private:
    CPoint m_ptFrom;
    CPoint m_ptTo;
    UINT m_nWidth;
    UINT m_nStyle;
    COLORREF m_crColor;
        .
        .
};
```

Because the class's persistent data format would now have to be modified, you'd increase the schema number from 1 to 2. The original class implementation invoked MFC's IMPLEMENT_SERIAL macro like this:

```
IMPLEMENT_SERIAL (CLine, CObject, 1)
```

In the new class implementation, however, IMPLEMENT_SERIAL should be called like this:

```
IMPLEMENT_SERIAL (CLine, CObject, 2 | VERSIONABLE_SCHEMA)
```

When the revised paint program reads a *CLine* object whose schema number is 1, the framework won't throw a *CArchive* exception because of the VERSIONABLE-_SCHEMA flag in the new class's schema number. But it will know that the two schemas are different because the base schema number was increased from 1 to 2.

You're halfway there. The next step is to modify *CLine::Serialize* so that it deserializes a *CLine* differently depending on the value returned by *GetObjectSchema*. The original *Serialize* function looked like this:

```
void CLine::Serialize (CArchive& ar)
{
    if (ar.IsStoring ())
        ar << m_ptFrom << m_ptTo << m_nWidth << (DWORD) m_crColor;
    else
        ar >> m_ptFrom >> m_ptTo >> m_nWidth >> (DWORD) m_crColor;
}
```

The new one should be implemented like this:

```
void CLine::Serialize (CArchive& ar)
{
    if (ar.IsStoring ())
        ar << m_ptFrom << m_ptTo << m_nWidth <<
            m_nStyle << (DWORD) m_crColor;
    else {
        UINT nSchema = ar.GetObjectSchema ();

        switch (nSchema) {
        case 1: // Version 1
            ar >> m_ptFrom >> m_ptTo >> m_nWidth >> (DWORD) m_crColor;
            m_nStyle = 0; // Default style
            break;

        case 2: // Version 2
            ar >> m_ptFrom >> m_ptTo >> m_nWidth >>
                m_nStyle >> (DWORD) m_crColor;
            break;

        default: // Unknown version
            AfxThrowArchiveException (CArchiveException::badSchema);
            break;
        }
    }
}
```

See how it works? When a *CLine* object is written *to* the archive, it's always formatted as a version 2.0 *CLine*. But when a *CLine* is read *from* the archive, the schema number returned by *GetObjectSchema* determines how the object is deserialized. If the schema number is 1, the object is read the old way and *m_nStyle* is set to 0, which presumably specifies a solid line. If the schema number is 2, all of the object's data members, including *m_nStyle*, are serialized from the archive. Any other schema number, and a *CArchive* exception is thrown because we're unable to handle the format. If, in the future, you revise *CLine* again, you can bump the schema number up to 3 and add a *case* statement for the new schema.

Part III

Advanced Topics

Chapter 12

Bitmaps, Palettes, and Regions

Getting a firm grasp of the Windows GDI is an important milestone on the road to becoming a Windows programmer because all graphical output to screens, printers, and other devices is performed through the GDI. So far in this book, we've used three of the six MFC classes that represent GDI objects: *CPen*, *CBrush*, and *CFont*. In this chapter, we'll get to the remaining three: *CPalette*, *CBitmap*, and *CRgn*.

CPalette represents palettes—tables of color that allow Windows to balance the sometimes conflicting needs of applications that demand more colors than the video adapter can provide. If every video adapter displayed 24-bits-per-pixel color (8 bits each for red, green, and blue), palettes would be unnecessary. But 256-color video adapters are a fact of life and probably will be for some time to come. By default, a Windows application that executes in a 256-color environment has access to only 20 colors. If you're careful about how you pick your colors and make those colors part of a palette, you can expand the selection to 256 colors and write Windows applications whose color output is almost as good on a 256-color screen as it is on one that displays millions of colors. This chapter will show you how to use palettes in your applications to generate color output as rich as the hardware will allow.

MFC's *CBitmap* class represents GDI bitmaps. *CBitmap* is a primitive class that does very little on its own. But combined with MFC's *CDC* class, *CBitmap* makes it relatively easy to draw on virtual display surfaces in memory, load bitmap resources, and display simple bitmap images on the screen. *CBitmap* can also be used to build more capable bitmap classes that exploit the capabilities of the 32-bit Windows 95

DIB engine. One technique you'll see demonstrated in this chapter is a method for creating DIB sections from .bmp files and attaching them to ordinary *CBitmap* objects—all in just three lines of code.

CRgn is one of MFC's more obscure classes, but it can be used for some exotic graphics effects. Rather than spoil the fun, I'll leave the details for the end of the chapter.

PALETTES

Have you ever written a Windows application that makes generous use of color only to find that the output looks crummy on 16- and 256-color video adapters? There's not a whole lot you can do about it when the adapter itself supports only 16 colors, but there's plenty you can do to improve output on 256-color devices. The key to better color output is MFC's *CPalette* class. Before we get into the specifics of *CPalette*, let's briefly review how colors are specified in Windows and what Windows does with the color information you provide.

How Windows Uses Color

One of the benefits of a device-independent output model is that the colors an application uses can be specified without regard for the physical characteristics or capabilities of the output device. When you pass a color to the Windows GDI, you pass a COLORREF value containing 8 bits each for red, green, and blue. The RGB macro makes it easy to combine individual red, green, and blue values into a single COLORREF. The statement

```
COLORREF cr = RGB (255, 0, 255);
```

creates a COLORREF value named *cr* that represents magenta—the color you get when you mix equal parts red and blue. Correspondingly, you can extract 8-bit red, green, and blue values from a COLORREF value with the GetRValue, GetGValue, and GetBValue macros. A number of GDI functions accept COLORREF values, including those that create pens and brushes.

What the GDI does with the COLORREF values you pass it depends on several factors, including the color resolution of the video hardware and the context in which the colors are used. In the simplest and most ideal scenario, the video adapter is a 24-bits-per-pixel device and COLORREF values are translated directly into colors on the screen. Video adapters that support 24-bit color, or *true color,* are becoming increasingly common, but Windows still runs on millions of PCs whose video adapters are limited to 4 or 8 bits per pixel. Typically, these devices are *palettized devices,* meaning that they support a wide range of colors but can display only a limited number of colors at one time. A standard VGA, for example, can display 262,144 different colors—6 bits each for red, green, and blue. However, a VGA running at a resolution of

640 by 480 pixels can display only 16 different colors at a time because each pixel is limited to 4 bits of color information in the video buffer. The more common case is a video adapter that can display more than 16.7 million colors but can display only 256 colors at once. The 256 colors that can be displayed are determined from RGB values that are programmed into the adapter's hardware palette. On a palettized device, individual pixel values specify indexes into the hardware palette rather than physical RGB color values.

Windows handles palettized devices by preprogramming a standard selection of colors into the adapter's hardware palette. A 256-color adapter is preprogrammed with the 20 colors shown in the table below, which are also known as the *static colors*. The four colors marked with asterisks are "default" colors that may be changed by the operating system, so you shouldn't write code that depends on their being there.

Color	R	G	B	Color	R	G	B
Black	0	0	0	Cream*	255	251	240
Dark red	128	0	0	Intermediate gray*	160	160	164
Dark green	0	128	0	Medium gray	128	128	128
Dark yellow	128	128	0	Red	255	0	0
Dark blue	0	0	128	Green	0	255	0
Dark magenta	128	0	128	Yellow	255	255	0
Dark cyan	0	128	128	Blue	0	0	255
Light gray	192	192	192	Magenta	255	0	255
Money green*	192	220	192	Cyan	0	255	255
Sky blue*	166	202	240	White	255	255	255

* Denotes default colors that are subject to change.

When you draw on a palettized device, the GDI maps each COLORREF value to the nearest static color using a simple color-matching algorithm. If you pass a COLORREF value to a function that creates a pen, Windows assigns the pen the nearest static color. If you pass a COLOREF value to a function that creates a brush and there isn't a matching static color, Windows dithers the brush color using static colors. Because the static colors include a diverse (if limited) assortment of hues, Windows can do a reasonable job of simulating any COLORREF value you throw at it. A picture painted with 100 different shades of red won't come out very well because Windows has to simulate all 100 shades with just two reds. On the other hand, you're guaranteed that red won't undergo a wholesale transformation to blue, green, or some other color because except under certain rare circumstances the static colors are always there and are always available.

For many applications, the primitive form of color mapping that Windows performs using static colors is good enough. But for others, accurate color output is a foremost concern and 20 colors just won't get the job done. In a single-tasking environment such as MS-DOS, a program running on a 256-color adapter can program the hardware palette itself and use any 256 colors it wants. In Windows, applications can't be allowed to program the hardware palette directly because the video adapter is a shared resource. So how do you take advantage of the 236 colors left unused in a 256-color adapter after Windows adds the 20 static colors? The answer lies in a GDI object known as a logical palette.

Logical Palettes and the *CPalette* Class

A *logical palette* is a table of RGB color values that tells Windows what colors an application would like to display. The term *system palette* refers to the hardware color palette. At an application's request, the palette manager built into Windows will transfer the colors in a logical palette to unused entries in the system palette—a process known as *realizing a palette*—so that the application can take full advantage of the video adapter's color capabilities. With the help of a logical palette, an application running on a 256-color video adapter can use the 20 static colors plus an additional 236 colors of its own. And because all requests to realize a palette go through the GDI, the palette manager can serve as an arbitrator between programs with conflicting color needs and thus ensure that the system palette is used cooperatively.

What happens if two or more applications realize logical palettes and the sum total of the colors they request is more than the 236 additional colors a 256-color video adapter can handle? The palette manager assigns color priorities based on each window's position in the z-order. The window at the top of the z-order (the foreground window) receives top priority, the window that's second gets the next highest priority, and so on. If the foreground window realizes a palette of 200 colors, all 200 get mapped to the system palette. If a background window then realizes a palette of, say, 100 colors, 36 get programmed into the system palette entries left over after the foreground application has realized its palette, and the remaining 64 get mapped to the nearest matching colors. That's the worst case. Unless directed to do otherwise, the palette manager avoids duplicating entries in the system palette. Therefore, if four of the foreground application's colors and ten of the background application's colors match static colors, and if another ten of the background application's colors match nonstatic colors in the foreground application, the background application ends up getting 60 exact matches in the system palette.

You can see the palette manager at work by switching Windows to 256-color mode, launching two instances of the Windows 95 Paint applet, loading a different 256-color bitmap in each, and clicking back and forth between the two a few times. The bitmap in the foreground will always look the best because it gets first crack at the system palette. The bitmap in the background gets what's left over. If both bitmaps use similar colors, the background image won't look too bad. But if the colors are vastly different—for example, if bitmap A contains lots of bright, vibrant colors while bitmap B uses primarily earth tones—the image in the background may be so color-corrupted that it's hardly recognizable. The palette manager's role in the process is to try to satisfy the needs of both programs. But when those needs conflict, the foreground window receives priority over all others so that the application the user is working with looks the best.

Creating a Logical Palette

It's not difficult to write an application that uses a logical palette. In MFC, logical palettes are created with *CPalette* member functions. Once a logical palette is created, it can be selected into a device context and realized with *CDC* member functions.

CPalette provides two member functions for palette creation: *CreatePalette* creates a custom palette from RGB values you specify; *CreateHalftonePalette* creates a "halftone" palette containing a generic and fairly uniform distribution of colors. Custom palettes give better results when an image contains few distinctly different colors but many subtle variations in tone. Halftone palettes are ideal for images containing a wide range of colors. The statements

```
CPalette palette;
palette.CreateHalftonePalette (pDC);
```

create a halftone palette tailored to the device context pointed to by *pDC*. If the device context corresponds to a 256-color device, the halftone palette will also contain 256 colors. Twenty of the colors will match the static colors; the other 236 will expand the selection of colors available by adding subtler shades of red, green, and blue and mixtures of primary colors. Specifically, a 256-color halftone palette includes all the colors in a 6-by-6-by-6-color cube (colors composed of six shades each of red, green, and blue), plus an array of grays for gray-scale imaging and other colors hand-picked by the GDI. Passing a NULL DC handle to *CreateHalftonePalette* creates a 256-color halftone palette independent of the characteristics of the output device. However, because *CPalette::CreateHalftonePalette* mistakenly asserts in debug builds if it's passed a NULL DC handle, you must go around MFC to exercise this feature of the GDI:

```
CPalette palette;
palette.Attach (::CreateHalftonePalette (NULL));
```

::CreateHalftonePalette is the API equivalent of *CPalette::CreateHalftonePalette*.

Creating a custom palette is a little more work because, before you call *CreatePalette*, you first have to fill in a LOGPALETTE structure with information describing the palette colors. LOGPALETTE is defined in Wingdi.h as shown on the next page.

```
typedef struct tagLOGPALETTE {
    WORD            palVersion;
    WORD            palNumEntries;
    PALETTEENTRY    palPalEntry[1];
} LOGPALETTE;
```

palVersion specifies the LOGPALETTE version number; in all current releases of Windows, it should be set to 0x300. *PalNumEntries* specifies the number of colors in the logical palette. *palPalEntry* is an array of PALETTEENTRY structures defining the colors themselves. The number of elements in the array should equal the value of *palNumEntries*. PALETTEENTRY is defined as follows:

```
typedef struct tagPALETTEENTRY {
    BYTE peRed;
    BYTE peGreen;
    BYTE peBlue;
    BYTE peFlags;
} PALETTEENTRY;
```

peRed, *peGreen*, and *peBlue* specify a color's 8-bit RGB components. *peFlags* contains zero or more bit flags describing the *type* of palette entry. It can be set to any of the values shown in the table below or to 0 to create a "normal" palette entry:

Flag	*Description*
PC_EXPLICIT	Creates a palette entry that specifies an index into the system palette rather than an RGB color. Used by programs that display the contents of the system palette.
PC_NOCOLLAPSE	Creates a palette entry that's mapped to an unused entry in the system palette even if there is already an entry for that color. Used to ensure the uniqueness of palette colors when two entries map to the same color.
PC_RESERVED	Creates a palette entry that's private to this application. When a PC_RESERVED entry is added to the system palette, it isn't mapped to colors in other logical palettes even if the colors match. Used by programs that perform palette animation.

Most of the time, *peFlags* is simply set to 0. We'll discuss one use for the PC_RESERVED flag later on in the section on palette animation.

The PALETTEENTRY array in the LOGPALETTE structure is declared with just one array element because Windows has no way of anticipating how many colors a logical palette will contain. As a result, you can't just declare an instance of LOGPALETTE on the stack and fill it in; instead, you have to allocate memory for it based on the number of PALETTEENTRY structures it contains. The following code allocates a "full" LOGPALETTE structure on the stack and then creates a logical palette containing 32 shades of red:

```
struct {
    LOGPALETTE lp;
    PALETTEENTRY ape[31];
} pal;

LOGPALETTE* pLP = (LOGPALETTE*) &pal;
pLP->palVersion = 0x300;
pLP->palNumEntries = 32;

for (int i=0; i<32; i++) {
    pLP->palPalEntry[i].peRed = i * 8;
    pLP->palPalEntry[i].peGreen = 0;
    pLP->palPalEntry[i].peBlue = 0;
    pLP->palPalEntry[i].peFlags = 0;
}

m_palette.CreatePalette (pLP);
```

m_palette is a *CPalette* data member. Like other GDI objects, logical palettes should be deleted when they're no longer needed. A logical palette created this way will be deleted automatically when the object it belongs to is deleted or goes out of scope.

How many entries can a logical palette contain? As many as you want it to. Of course, the number of colors that can be mapped directly to the system palette is limited by the capabilities of the video adapter. If you realize a palette containing 1,024 colors on a 256-color output device, only the first 236 will be mapped directly; the remaining colors will be matched as closely as possible to colors already in the system palette. When you use logical palettes (especially large ones), it's helpful to arrange the colors in order of importance, where *palPalEntry*[0] defines the most important color, *palPalEntry*[1] defines the next most important color, and so on. The palette manager maps palette colors in array order, so by putting important colors first, you increase the chances that those colors will be displayed in their native form. In general, you shouldn't make a logical palette any larger than it has to be. Large palettes take longer to realize, and the more palette colors a foreground application uses, the fewer colors the palette manager can make available to palette-aware applications running in the background.

After a palette is created, you can retrieve the values of individual palette entries with *CPalette::GetPaletteEntries* or change them with *CPalette::SetPaletteEntries*. You can also resize a palette with *CPalette::ResizePalette*. If the palette is enlarged, the new palette entries initially contain all 0s.

Realizing a Logical Palette

For a logical palette to be effective, it must be selected into a device context and realized before any drawing takes place. The current logical palette is a device context attribute just as the current pen and brush are device context attributes. (In case you're wondering, a device context's default logical palette is a trivial one whose entries correspond to the static colors.) The following *OnPaint* handler selects the logical palette *m_palette* into a paint device context and realizes the palette before repaint-ing the screen:

```
void CMainWindow::OnPaint ()
{
    CPaintDC dc (this);
    CPalette* pOldPalette = dc.SelectPalette (&m_palette, FALSE);
    dc.RealizePalette ();
    // Do some drawing
    dc.SelectPalette (pOldPalette);
}
```

In this example, the pointer to the default palette is saved and used later to select *m_palette* out of the device context. Note that palettes are selected with *CDC-::SelectPalette* instead of *CDC::SelectObject*. The second parameter is a BOOL value that, when TRUE, forces the palette to behave as if it were in the background even when the window that created it is in the foreground. Background palettes can be handy in applications that use multiple palettes, but normally you'll specify FALSE in calls to *SelectPalette. CDC::RealizePalette* realizes the palette that's currently selected into the device context by asking the palette manager to map colors from the logical palette to the system palette.

Drawing with a Logical Palette

Once you create a palette, select it into a device context, and realize it, you're ready to start drawing. If you use *CDC::BitBlt* to display a bitmap, the realized colors are used automatically. But if you're drawing images with brushes or pens or using func-tions such as *CDC::FloodFill* that use neither a brush nor a pen directly but do accept COLORREF values, there's something else to consider.

The RBG macro is one of three macros that create COLORREF values. The oth-ers are PALETTEINDEX and PALETTERGB. Which of the three macros you use deter-mines how the GDI treats the resultant COLORREF. When you draw with a COLORREF value created with the RGB macro, the GDI ignores the colors that were added to the system palette when the logical palette was realized and uses only the static colors. If you want the GDI to use *all* the palette colors, use the PALETTERGB macro. PALETTE-RGB creates a *palette-relative* color value by setting bit 25 of the resultant COLORREF. The PALETTEINDEX macro creates a COLORREF value that specifies an index into the logical palette rather than an RGB color value. A color specifier of this type is identified by a 1 in bit 24. It's also the fastest kind of color to draw with because it prevents the GDI from having to match RGB color values to colors in the logical palette.

The following code sample demonstrates how all three macros are used:

```
void CMainWindow::OnPaint ()
{
    CPaintDC dc (this);

    // Select and realize a logical palette
    CPalette* pOldPalette = dc.SelectPalette (&m_palette, FALSE);
    dc.RealizePalette ();

    // Create three pens
    CPen pen1 (PS_SOLID, 16, RGB (242, 36, 204));
    CPen pen2 (PS_SOLID, 16, PALETTERGB (242, 36, 204));
    CPen pen3 (PS_SOLID, 16, PALETTEINDEX (3));

    // Do some drawing
    dc.MoveTo (0, 0);
    CPen pOldPen* pOldPen = dc.SelectObject (&pen1);
    dc.LineTo (300, 0);          // Nearest static color
    dc.SelectObject (&pen2);
    dc.LineTo (150, 200);        // Nearest static or palette color
    dc.SelectObject (&pen3);
    dc.LineTo (0, 0);            // Exact palette color
    dc.SelectObject (pOldPen);

    // Select the palette out of the device context
    dc.SelectPalette (pOldPalette, FALSE);
}
```

Since pens use solid, undithered colors and because its COLORREF value is specified with an RGB macro, *pen1* will use the static color that most closely approximates the RGB value (242, 36, 204). *pen2*, on the other hand, will be assigned the nearest matching color from the static colors or *m_palette*. *pen3* will use the color in the system palette that corresponds to the fourth color (index=3) in the logical palette, regardless of what that color might be.

WM_QUERYNEWPALETTE and WM_PALETTECHANGED

When you write an application that uses a logical palette, you should include handlers for a pair of messages named WM_QUERYNEWPALETTE and WM_PALETTE-CHANGED. The former is sent to a top-level window when it or one one of its children receives the input focus. The latter is sent to all top-level windows in the system when a palette realization causes a change in the system palette. An application's normal response to either message is to realize its palette and repaint itself. Realizing a palette and repainting in response to a WM_QUERYNEWPALETTE message enables a window brought to the foreground to put on its best face by taking advantage of the fact that it now has priority in realizing its palette. Realizing a palette and repainting in response to a WM_PALETTECHANGED message enables background windows to adapt to changes in the system palette and take advantage of any unused entries that remain after windows higher in the z-order have realized their palettes.

The following message handler demonstrates a typical response to a WM_QUERY-NEWPALETTE message:

```
// In the message map
ON_WM_QUERYNEWPALETTE ()

    .
    .
    .

BOOL CMainWindow::OnQueryNewPalette ()
{
    CClientDC dc (this);
    CPalette* pOldPalette = dc.SelectPalette (&m_palette, FALSE);

    UINT nCount;
    if (nCount = dc.RealizePalette ())
        Invalidate ();

    dc.SelectPalette (pOldPalette, FALSE);
    return nCount;
}
```

The strategy is to grab a screen DC, select and realize a palette, and force a repaint by invalidating the window's client area. The value returned by *RealizePalette* is a count of the number of palette entries whose mappings to entries in the system palette have changed. A 0 return value means that realizing the palette had no effect, which should be extremely rare for a foreground window. If *RealizePalette* returns 0, the call to *Invalidate* is skipped. *OnQueryNewPalette* should return a nonzero value if a logical palette was realized and 0 if it was not. It should also return 0 if it tried to realize a palette but *RealizePalette* returned 0. The return value is not used in current versions of Windows.

WM_PALETTECHANGED messages are handled in a similar way. Here's what a typical *OnPaletteChanged* handler looks like:

```
// In the message map
ON_WM_PALETTECHANGED ()

    .
    .
    .

void CMainWindow::OnPaletteChanged (CWnd* pFocusWnd)
{
    if (pFocusWnd != this) {
        CClientDC dc (this);
        CPalette* pOldPalette = dc.SelectPalette (&m_palette,
            FALSE);
```

```
        if (dc.RealizePalette ())
            Invalidate ();
        dc.SelectPalette (pOldPalette, FALSE);
    }
}
```

The *CWnd* pointer passed to *OnPaletteChanged* identifies the window that realized a palette and caused the message to be sent. To avoid unnecessary recursion and possible infinite loops, *OnPaletteChanged* should do nothing with the message if *pFocusWnd* points to the application's own window.

The *OnQueryNewPalette* and *OnPaletteChanged* handlers shown above assume that the part of the screen to be updated is the client area of the frame window represented by *CMainWindow*. In a document/view application, that won't be the case; it's the frame window's views that will need updating, not the frame window itself. The ideal solution would be to put the *OnQueryNewPalette* and *OnPaletteChanged* handlers in the view class instead of in the frame window class, but that wouldn't work because views don't receive palette messages—only top-level windows do. What document/view applications do instead is have their main frame windows update the various views in response to palette messages. The following *OnQueryNewPalette* and *OnPaletteChanged* handlers work well for most SDI applications that display just one view of a document:

```
BOOL CMainFrame::OnQueryNewPalette ()
{
    GetActiveView ()->Invalidate ();
    return TRUE;
}

void CMainFrame::OnPaletteChanged (CWnd* pFocusWnd)
{
    if (pFocusWnd != this)
        GetActiveView ()->Invalidate ();
}
```

Very often document/view applications make the logical palette part of the document object. As such, the view's *OnDraw* function can retrieve the palette from the document before selecting it into the device context and calling *RealizePalette* to realize it.

Palettes are a little trickier in MDI applications and in SDI applications that display multiple views of their documents because all of the views need to be updated. The simplest approach is to call *CFrameWnd::GetActiveDocument* and then either have the document invalidate its views or let the frame window call *UpdateAllViews* through the document pointer. In an MDI application, you'll probably want to update the views associated with inactive documents as well. Assuming each document has its own palette, when a view associated with an inactive document selects the document's palette into a device context, it should force the palette to the background by passing

TRUE rather than FALSE in *SelectPalette*'s second parameter. Otherwise, inactive documents will be accorded the same priority in the system palette as the active document and the active document's views could be corrupted.

Another problem you'll run into with MDI applications that use multiple palettes is how to update the views' colors as the user clicks among the various views. One solution is to override *CView::OnActivateView* in each view class so that a view knows when it's activated or deactivated. In an MDI application, you basically end up writing your own palette manager to share the system palette among open documents and make sure the views associated with the active document get priority among all the others. For one example of how this is done, see the DIBLOOK sample program provided with MFC.

Rather than do full repaints in response to WM_PALETTECHANGED messages, background applications can call *CDC::UpdateColors* instead. *UpdateColors* updates a window by matching the color of each pixel to the colors in the system palette. It's usually faster than a full repaint, but the results typically aren't as good because the color matching is done based on the contents of the system palette *before* it changed. If you use *UpdateColors*, maintain a variable that counts the number of times *UpdateColors* has been called. Then, every third or fourth time, do a full repaint and reset the counter to 0. This will prevent the colors in a background window from becoming too out of sync with the colors in the system palette.

Deciding Whether a Logical Palette Is Needed

Now that you understand the mechanics of using a logical palette, ask yourself this question: how do I know if I need a logical palette in the first place? If color accuracy is of paramount concern, you'll probably want to use a logical palette when your application runs on a palettized 256-color video adapter. But the same application doesn't need a logical palette when the hardware color depth is 24 bits because in that environment perfect color output comes for free. And if the application runs on a standard 16-color VGA, palettes are superfluous because the system palette is initialized with 16 static colors that leave no room for colors in logical palettes.

You can determine at run-time whether a logical palette will improve color output by calling *CDC::GetDeviceCaps* with a RASTERCAPS parameter and checking the RC_PALETTE bit in the return value, as demonstrated here:

```
CClientDC dc (this);
BOOL bUsePalette = FALSE;
if (dc.GetDeviceCaps (RASTERCAPS) & RC_PALETTE)
    bUsePalette = TRUE;
```

RC_PALETTE is set in palettized color modes and clear in nonpalettized modes. Generally speaking, the RC_PALETTE bit will be set in 8-bit color modes and will be clear in 4-bit and 24-bit color modes. The RC_PALETTE bit will also be clear if the adapter is running in 16-bit color ("high color") mode, which for most applications produces color output every bit as good as true color. Don't make the mistake many programmers do and rely on bit counts to tell you whether to use a palette. As sure as you do, you'll run across an oddball video adapter that defies the normal conventions and fools your application into using a palette when a palette isn't needed or not using a palette when a palette would help.

What will happen if you ignore the RC_PALETTE setting and use a logical palette regardless of the video hardware's color depth? The application will still work because the palette manager works even on nonpalettized devices. If RC_PALETTE is 0, palettes can still be created and selected into device contexts, but calls to *RealizePalette* will do nothing. PALETTEINDEX values are dereferenced and converted into RGB colors in the logical palette, and PALETTERGB values are simply treated as if they were standard RGB color values. *OnQueryNewPalette* and *OnPaletteChanged* are not called because no WM_QUERYNEWPALETTE and WM_PALETTECHANGED messages are sent. As Ron Gery puts it in an excellent article entitled "The Palette Manager: How and Why" available on the Microsoft Developer Network (MSDN) CD, "The goal is to allow applications to use palettes in a device-independent fashion and to not worry about the actual palette capabilities of the device driver."

Still, you can avoid wasted CPU cycles by checking the RC_PALETTE flag and skipping palette-related function calls if the flag is clear. And if your application *relies* on the presence of hardware palette support and won't work without it—for example, if it uses palette animation, a subject we'll get to in a moment—you can use RC_PALETTE to determine whether your application is even capable of running in the current hardware environment.

An equally important question to ask yourself when considering whether to use logical palettes is, "How accurate does my program's color output need to be?" The Paint applications developed in this book don't need palette support because they draw lines in just eight different colors and all eight correspond to static colors in the system palette. You could add palette support, but you'd see no difference in the output. On the other hand, a .bmp file viewer almost certainly needs palette support because without it all but the simplest bitmaps would look terrible on 256-color video adapters. Assess your program's color needs, and do as little work as you have to. You'll write better applications as a result.

The PaletteDemo Application

The PaletteDemo application, listed in Figure 12-1 on the next page, demonstrates how a logical palette can benefit an application. Like the DlgDemo programs in Chapter 6, PaletteDemo uses a series of blue brushes to draw a window background that fades smoothly from blue to black behind a text string drawn in white. But unlike the DlgDemo programs, PaletteDemo produces a beautiful gradient fill even on 256-color video adapters. The key to the quality of PaletteDemo's output is the use of a logical palette containing 64 shades of blue ranging from almost pure black (R=0, G=0, B=3) to high-intensity blue (R=0, G=0, B=255). Brush colors are specified using palette-relative COLORREF values so that the GDI will match the brush colors to colors in the system palette after the logical palette is realized. You can judge the results for yourself by running PaletteDemo in both 8-bit and 24-bit color modes and seeing that the output is identical. Only when it is run in 16-color VGA mode does PaletteDemo fail to produce a smooth gradient fill. But even then the results aren't bad because the GDI dithers the brush colors.

PaletteDemo.h

```
//*********************************************************************
//
//  PaletteDemo.h
//
//*********************************************************************

class CMyApp : public CWinApp
{
public:
    virtual BOOL InitInstance ();
};

class CMainWindow : public CFrameWnd
{
private:
    CPalette m_palette;

    void DoGradientFill (CDC*, CRect*);
    void DoDrawText (CDC*, CRect*);

public:
    CMainWindow ();

protected:
    afx_msg int OnCreate (LPCREATESTRUCT);
    afx_msg BOOL OnEraseBkgnd (CDC*);
    afx_msg void OnPaint ();
    afx_msg BOOL OnQueryNewPalette ();
    afx_msg void OnPaletteChanged (CWnd*);

    DECLARE_MESSAGE_MAP ()
};
```

Figure 12-1. *The PaletteDemo program.*

PaletteDemo.cpp

```
//***********************************************************************
//
//  PaletteDemo.cpp
//
//***********************************************************************

#include <afxwin.h>
#include "PaletteDemo.h"

#define FONTHEIGHT 72

CMyApp myApp;

///////////////////////////////////////////////////////////////////////
// CMyApp member functions

BOOL CMyApp::InitInstance ()
{
    m_pMainWnd = new CMainWindow;
    m_pMainWnd->ShowWindow (m_nCmdShow);
    m_pMainWnd->UpdateWindow ();
    return TRUE;
}

///////////////////////////////////////////////////////////////////////
// CMainWindow message map and member functions

BEGIN_MESSAGE_MAP (CMainWindow, CFrameWnd)
    ON_WM_CREATE ()
    ON_WM_ERASEBKGND ()
    ON_WM_PAINT ()
    ON_WM_QUERYNEWPALETTE ()
    ON_WM_PALETTECHANGED ()
END_MESSAGE_MAP ()

CMainWindow::CMainWindow ()
{
    Create (NULL, "Palette Demo");
}

int CMainWindow::OnCreate (LPCREATESTRUCT lpcs)
{
    if (CFrameWnd::OnCreate (lpcs) == -1)
        return -1;
```

(continued)

PaletteDemo.cpp *continued*

```
    CClientDC dc (this);
    if (dc.GetDeviceCaps (RASTERCAPS) & RC_PALETTE) {
        struct {
            LOGPALETTE lp;
            PALETTEENTRY ape[63];
        } pal;

        LOGPALETTE* pLP = (LOGPALETTE*) &pal;
        pLP->palVersion = 0x300;
        pLP->palNumEntries = 64;

        for (int i=0; i<64; i++) {
            pLP->palPalEntry[i].peRed = 0;
            pLP->palPalEntry[i].peGreen = 0;
            pLP->palPalEntry[i].peBlue = 255 - (i * 4);
            pLP->palPalEntry[i].peFlags = 0;
        }
        m_palette.CreatePalette (pLP);
    }
    return 0;
}

BOOL CMainWindow::OnEraseBkgnd (CDC* pDC)
{
    CRect rect;
    GetClientRect (&rect);

    CPalette* pOldPalette;
    if ((HPALETTE) m_palette != NULL) {
        pOldPalette = pDC->SelectPalette (&m_palette, FALSE);
        pDC->RealizePalette ();
    }

    DoGradientFill (pDC, &rect);

    if ((HPALETTE) m_palette != NULL)
        pDC->SelectPalette (pOldPalette, FALSE);
    return TRUE;
}

void CMainWindow::OnPaint ()
{
    CRect rect;
    GetClientRect (&rect);

    CPaintDC dc (this);
```

```
        DoDrawText (&dc, &rect);
}

BOOL CMainWindow::OnQueryNewPalette ()
{
    if ((HPALETTE) m_palette == NULL)    // Shouldn't happen, but
        return 0;                        // let's be sure

    CClientDC dc (this);
    CPalette* pOldPalette = dc.SelectPalette (&m_palette, FALSE);

    UINT nCount;
    if (nCount = dc.RealizePalette ())
        Invalidate ();

    dc.SelectPalette (pOldPalette, FALSE);
    return nCount;
}

void CMainWindow::OnPaletteChanged (CWnd* pFocusWnd)
{
    if ((HPALETTE) m_palette == NULL)    // Shouldn't happen, but
        return;                          // let's be sure

    if (pFocusWnd != this) {
        CClientDC dc (this);
        CPalette* pOldPalette = dc.SelectPalette (&m_palette, FALSE);
        if (dc.RealizePalette ())
            Invalidate ();
        dc.SelectPalette (pOldPalette, FALSE);
    }
}

void CMainWindow::DoGradientFill (CDC* pDC, CRect* pRect)
{
    CBrush* pBrush[64];
    for (int i=0; i<64; i++)
        pBrush[i] = new CBrush (PALETTERGB (0, 0, 255 - (i * 4)));

    int nWidth = pRect->Width ();
    int nHeight = pRect->Height ();
    CRect rect;

    for (i=0; i<nHeight; i++) {
        rect.SetRect (0, i, nWidth, i + 1);
        pDC->FillRect (&rect, pBrush[(i * 63) / nHeight]);
    }
```

(continued)

PaletteDemo.cpp *continued*

```
    for (i=0; i<64; i++)
        delete pBrush[i];
}

void CMainWindow::DoDrawText (CDC* pDC, CRect* pRect)
{
    CFont font;
    int nHeight = -((pDC->GetDeviceCaps (LOGPIXELSY) * FONTHEIGHT) / 72);

    font.CreateFont (nHeight, 0, 0, 0, FW_BOLD, TRUE, 0, 0,
        DEFAULT_CHARSET, OUT_CHARACTER_PRECIS, CLIP_CHARACTER_PRECIS,
        DEFAULT_QUALITY, DEFAULT_PITCH | FF_DONTCARE, "Times New Roman");

    pDC->SetBkMode (TRANSPARENT);
    pDC->SetTextColor (RGB (255, 255, 255));

    CFont* pOldFont = pDC->SelectObject (&font);
    pDC->DrawText ("Hello, MFC", -1, pRect, DT_SINGLELINE | DT_CENTER |
        DT_VCENTER);

    pDC->SelectObject (pOldFont);
}
```

Here are a few points of interest in PaletteDemo's source code. First, the logical palette is created by the frame window's *OnCreate* handler and stored in *CMainWindow::m_palette*. Before it creates the palette, *OnCreate* instantiates a *CClientDC* object, calls *GetDeviceCaps*, and checks the return value. If the RC_PALETTE bit isn't set, *OnCreate* leaves *m_palette* uninitialized. *CMainWindow::OnEraseBkgnd* checks the palette handle associated with *m_palette* and selects the palette into the device context and realizes it only if the handle is not NULL. Here's the relevant code:

```
if ((HPALETTE) m_palette != NULL) {
    pOldPalette = dc.SelectPalette (&m_palette, FALSE);
    dc.RealizePalette ();
}
```

CPalette's HPALETTE operator returns the GDI handle of the palette attached to a *CPalette* object. *OnEraseBkgnd* adapts itself to the environment it's run in by selecting and realizing a logical palette if a palette exists but skipping the code that selects and realizes the palette if a logical palette doesn't exist. The *DoGradientFill* function that draws the window background will work either way because brush colors are specified with PALETTERGB macros.

One consideration that PaletteDemo doesn't address is what happens if the system's color settings change while the application is running. This can't happen in

16-bit Windows, but it's a distinct possibility in Windows 95. You can account for such occurrences by processing WM_DISPLAYCHANGE messages, which are sent when the user changes the screen's resolution or color depth, and reinitializing the palette based on the new settings. There is no ON_WM_DISPLAYCHANGE macro, so you have to do the message mapping manually with ON_MESSAGE. The *wParam* parameter encapsulated in a WM_DISPLAYCHANGE message contains the new color depth expressed as the number of bits per pixel, and the low and high words of *lParam* contain the latest horizontal and vertical screen resolution in pixels.

WM_DISPLAYCHANGE isn't only for applications that use palettes. You should also use it if, for example, you initialize variables with the average width and height of a character in the system font when the application starts and later use those variables to space the application's output. If the variables aren't reinitialized when the screen resolution changes, subsequent output may be distorted.

Palette Animation

One of the more novel uses for a logical palette is for performing palette animation. Conventional computer animation is performed by repeatedly drawing, erasing, and redrawing images on the screen. Palette animation involves no drawing and erasing (just reprogramming of the system palette), but it can make images appear to move just the same. A classic example of palette animation is a simulated lava flow that cycles shades of red, orange, and yellow to produce an image that resembles lava flowing down a hill. What's interesting is that the image is drawn only one time. The illusion of motion is created by repeatedly reprogramming the system palette so that red becomes orange, orange becomes yellow, yellow becomes red, and so on. Palette animation is fast because it doesn't involve moving any pixels. A simple value written to a palette register on a video adapter can change the color of an entire screenful of pixels in the blink of an eye—to be precise, in the $1/60$ of a second or so it takes for a monitor's electron guns to complete one screen refresh cycle.

What does it take to do palette animation in Windows? Just these three steps:

1. Call *GetDeviceCaps*, and check RC_PALETTE to verify that palettes are supported. Palette animation won't work if the RC_PALETTE bit isn't set.

2. Create a logical palette containing the colors you want to animate, and mark each palette entry with a PC_RESERVED flag. Only palette entries marked PC_RESERVED can be used for palette animation.

3. Draw an image using colors in the logical palette, and then call *CPalette::AnimatePalette* repeatedly to change the palette colors. Each time you change the palette with *AnimatePalette*, the colors in the image will change accordingly.

The LivePalette application, listed in Figure 12-2, demonstrates how palette animation works. The window background is painted with bands of color (eight different colors in all) from PC_RESERVED entries in a logical palette. Brush colors are specified with PALETTEINDEX values. PALETTERGB values would work, too, but ordinary RGB values wouldn't because it's essential that pixels whose colors will be animated be painted with PC_RESERVED colors in the logical palette, not static colors. A timer is set to fire every 500 milliseconds, and the timer procedure *OnTimer* animates the palette as follows:

```
PALETTEENTRY pe[8];
m_palette.GetPaletteEntries (7, 1, pe);
m_palette.GetPaletteEntries (0, 7, &pe[1]);
m_palette.AnimatePalette (0, 8, pe);
```

The calls to *CPalette::GetPaletteEntries* initialize an array of PALETTEENTRY structures with values from the logical palette and simultaneously rotate every color up one position so that color 7 becomes color 0, color 0 becomes color 1, and so on. *AnimatePalette* then updates the colors on the screen by copying the values from the array directly to the corresponding entries in the system palette. It isn't necessary to call *RealizePalette* because the equivalent of a palette realization has already been performed. The remainder of the program is very similar to the previous section's PaletteDemo program, with one notable exception: if RC_PALETTE is NULL, *OnCreate* displays a message box informing the user that "palette animation is not supported on this device" and shuts down the application by returning −1.

LivePalette.h

```
//***************************************************************************
//
// LivePalette.h
//
//***************************************************************************

class CMyApp : public CWinApp
{
public:
    virtual BOOL InitInstance ();
};


class CMainWindow : public CFrameWnd
{
private:
    CPalette m_palette;
```

Figure 12-2. *The LivePalette program.*

```
        void DoBkgndFill (CDC*, CRect*);
        void DoDrawText (CDC*, CRect*);

public:
        CMainWindow ();

protected:
        afx_msg int OnCreate (LPCREATESTRUCT);
        afx_msg BOOL OnEraseBkgnd (CDC*);
        afx_msg void OnPaint ();
        afx_msg void OnTimer (UINT);
        afx_msg BOOL OnQueryNewPalette ();
        afx_msg void OnPaletteChanged (CWnd*);
        afx_msg void OnDestroy ();

        DECLARE_MESSAGE_MAP ()
};
```

LivePalette.cpp

```
//***********************************************************************
//
//  LivePalette.cpp
//
//***********************************************************************

#include <afxwin.h>
#include "LivePalette.h"

#define FONTHEIGHT 72

CMyApp myApp;

///////////////////////////////////////////////////////////////////////
// CMyApp member functions

BOOL CMyApp::InitInstance ()
{
    m_pMainWnd = new CMainWindow;
    m_pMainWnd->ShowWindow (m_nCmdShow);
    m_pMainWnd->UpdateWindow ();
    return TRUE;
}
```

(continued)

LivePalette.cpp *continued*

```
/////////////////////////////////////////////////////////////////////////
// CMainWindow message map and member functions

BEGIN_MESSAGE_MAP (CMainWindow, CFrameWnd)
    ON_WM_CREATE ()
    ON_WM_ERASEBKGND ()
    ON_WM_PAINT ()
    ON_WM_TIMER ()
    ON_WM_QUERYNEWPALETTE ()
    ON_WM_PALETTECHANGED ()
    ON_WM_DESTROY ()
END_MESSAGE_MAP ()

CMainWindow::CMainWindow ()
{
    Create (NULL, "Palette Animation Demo");
}

int CMainWindow::OnCreate (LPCREATESTRUCT lpcs)
{
    static BYTE bColorVals[8][3] = {
        128, 128, 128,  // Dark gray
          0,   0, 255,  // Blue
          0, 255,   0,  // Green
          0, 255, 255,  // Cyan
        255,   0,   0,  // Red
        255,   0, 255,  // Magenta
        255, 255,   0,  // Yellow
        192, 192, 192   // Light gray
    };

    if (CFrameWnd::OnCreate (lpcs) == -1)
        return -1;

    CClientDC dc (this);
    if ((dc.GetDeviceCaps (RASTERCAPS) & RC_PALETTE) == 0) {
        MessageBox ("Palette animation is not supported on this device",
            "Sorry!", MB_ICONINFORMATION | MB_OK);
        return -1;
    }

    struct {
        LOGPALETTE lp;
        PALETTEENTRY ape[7];
    } pal;
```

```
    LOGPALETTE* pLP = (LOGPALETTE*) &pal;
    pLP->palVersion = 0x300;
    pLP->palNumEntries = 8;

    for (int i=0; i<8; i++) {
        pLP->palPalEntry[i].peRed = bColorVals[i][0];
        pLP->palPalEntry[i].peGreen = bColorVals[i][1];
        pLP->palPalEntry[i].peBlue = bColorVals[i][2];
        pLP->palPalEntry[i].peFlags = PC_RESERVED;
    }

    m_palette.CreatePalette (pLP);

    SetTimer (1, 500, NULL);
    return 0;
}

void CMainWindow::OnTimer (UINT nTimerID)
{
    PALETTEENTRY pe[8];
    m_palette.GetPaletteEntries (7, 1, pe);
    m_palette.GetPaletteEntries (0, 7, &pe[1]);
    m_palette.AnimatePalette (0, 8, pe);
}

BOOL CMainWindow::OnEraseBkgnd (CDC* pDC)
{
    CRect rect;
    GetClientRect (&rect);

    CPalette* pOldPalette;
    pOldPalette = pDC->SelectPalette (&m_palette, FALSE);
    pDC->RealizePalette ();

    DoBkgndFill (pDC, &rect);

    pDC->SelectPalette (pOldPalette, FALSE);
    return TRUE;
}

void CMainWindow::OnPaint ()
{
    CRect rect;
    GetClientRect (&rect);

    CPaintDC dc (this);
    DoDrawText (&dc, &rect);
```

(continued)

LivePalette.cpp *continued*

```
}

BOOL CMainWindow::OnQueryNewPalette ()
{
    CClientDC dc (this);
    dc.SelectPalette (&m_palette, FALSE);

    UINT nCount;
    if (nCount = dc.RealizePalette ())
        Invalidate ();

    return nCount;
}

void CMainWindow::OnPaletteChanged (CWnd* pFocusWnd)
{
    if (pFocusWnd != this) {
        CClientDC dc (this);
        dc.SelectPalette (&m_palette, FALSE);
        if (dc.RealizePalette ())
            Invalidate ();
    }
}

void CMainWindow::OnDestroy ()
{
    KillTimer (1);
}

void CMainWindow::DoBkgndFill (CDC* pDC, CRect* pRect)
{
    CBrush* pBrush[8];
    for (int i=0; i<8; i++)
        pBrush[i] = new CBrush (PALETTEINDEX (i));

    int nWidth = pRect->Width ();
    int nHeight = pRect->Height () / 8;

    CRect rect;
    int y1, y2;

    for (i=0; i<8; i++) {
        y1 = i * nHeight;
        y2 = (i == 7) ? pRect->Height () : y1 + nHeight;
```

```
            rect.SetRect (0, y1, nWidth, y2);
            pDC->FillRect (&rect, pBrush[i]);
    }
    for (i=0; i<8; i++)
        delete pBrush[i];
}

void CMainWindow::DoDrawText (CDC* pDC, CRect* pRect)
{
    CFont font;
    int nHeight = -((pDC->GetDeviceCaps (LOGPIXELSY) * FONTHEIGHT) / 72);

    font.CreateFont (nHeight, 0, 0, 0, FW_BOLD, TRUE, 0, 0,
        DEFAULT_CHARSET, OUT_CHARACTER_PRECIS, CLIP_CHARACTER_PRECIS,
        DEFAULT_QUALITY, DEFAULT_PITCH | FF_DONTCARE, "Times New Roman");

    pDC->SetBkMode (TRANSPARENT);
    pDC->SetTextColor (RGB (255, 255, 255));

    CFont* pOldFont = pDC->SelectObject (&font);
    pDC->DrawText ("Hello, MFC", -1, pRect, DT_SINGLELINE | DT_CENTER |
        DT_VCENTER);

    pDC->SelectObject (pOldFont);
}
```

The *::SetSystemPaletteUse* Function

A final word on palette usage: if your application absolutely, unequivocally has to have access to the entire system palette and not just the unused color entries that remain after the static colors are added, it can call *::SetSystemPaletteUse* with a device context handle and a SYSPAL_NOSTATIC parameter to reduce the number of static colors from 20 to 2—black and white. On a 256-color video adapter, this means that 254 colors can be copied from a logical palette to the system palette instead of just 236. The Win32 API documentation makes it pretty clear how *::SetSystemPaletteUse* and its companion function *::GetSystemPaletteUse* are used, so I'll say no more about them here. However, realize that replacing the static colors with colors of your own is an extremely unfriendly thing to do because it could corrupt the colors of title bars, push buttons, and other window elements throughout the entire system. Don't do it unless you have to.

BITMAPS

The bitmapped image, or simply *bitmap,* is a staple of modern computer graphics because it allows us to store complex images in the form of 1s and 0s that a computer can understand. In Windows, bitmaps are GDI objects that are handled at a fairly high level just as fonts, brushes, pens, and other GDI objects are. You can create bitmaps with a paint program, store them in an application's .exe file, and load them with a simple function call, or you can create bitmaps on the fly by using GDI functions to draw to virtual display surfaces in memory. Once initialized, a bitmap can be displayed on the screen or reproduced on the printer with a simple function call.

Windows 95 supports two types of bitmaps: *device-dependent bitmaps* (DDBs) and *device-independent bitmaps* (DIBs). It also supports a variation on the device-independent bitmap that was first introduced in Windows NT—something programmers refer to as a *DIB section.* DDBs are the simplest of the lot as well as the most limiting. They also happen to be the only type of bitmap that MFC thoroughly encapsulates. We'll get the fundamentals out of the way first by covering *CBitmap*s and DDBs, and later we'll move on to the more powerful DIBs and DIB sections. As you read, be aware that I'll often use the term "bitmap" interchangeably with the more specific terms DDB, DIB, and DIB section. Which type of bitmap I'm referring to (or whether I'm using the term generically) should be clear from the context of the discussion.

Device-Dependent Bitmaps and the *CBitmap* Class

It goes without saying that before you can do anything with a bitmap, you must first create it. One way to create a bitmap is to construct a *CBitmap* object and call *CBitmap::CreateCompatibleBitmap*:

```
CBitmap bitmap;
bitmap.CreateCompatibleBitmap (&dc, nWidth, nHeight);
```

In this example, *dc* represents a screen device context and *nWidth* and *nHeight* specify the bitmap's dimensions in pixels. The reason *CreateCompatibleBitmap* requires a device context pointer is that the format of the resulting DDB is closely tied to the architecture of the output device. Providing a pointer to a device context enables Windows to structure the DDB so that it's compatible with the device you'll be displaying it on. The alternative is to call *CBitmap::CreateBitmap* or *CBitmap::CreateBitmapIndirect* and specify the number of color planes and number of bits per pixel per color plane, both of which are device-dependent values. These days, about the only practical use for *CreateBitmap* and *CreateBitmapIndirect* is for creating monochrome bitmaps. But monochrome bitmaps are sometimes useful even in color environments, as one of this chapter's sample programs will demonstrate.

A DDB created with *CreateCompatibleBitmap* initially contains random data. If you want to do something with the DDB—say, display it in a window—you'll probably want to draw something into the bitmap first. You can use GDI functions to draw into a bitmap by first creating a special type of device context known as a *memory device context* and then selecting the bitmap into the memory device context. In essence, a bitmap selected into a memory DC becomes the DC's display surface, just as the display surface that corresponds to a screen DC is the screen itself. The following code creates an uninitialized DDB that measures 100 pixels square. It then creates a memory DC, selects the bitmap into it, and initializes all the pixels in the bitmap to blue:

```
CClientDC dcScreen (this);

CBitmap bitmap;
bitmap.CreateCompatibleBitmap (&dcScreen, 100, 100);

CDC dcMem;
dcMem.CreateCompatibleDC (&dcScreen);

CBrush brush (RGB (0, 0, 255));
CBitmap* pOldBitmap = dcMem.SelectObject (&bitmap);
dcMem.FillRect (CRect (0, 0, 100, 100), &brush);
dcMem.SelectObject (pOldBitmap);
```

CDC::CreateCompatibleDC creates a memory DC compatible with the specified device DC. The device context whose address you pass in is usually a screen DC, but it could just as easily be a printer DC if the image you're preparing is destined for a printer instead of for the screen. Once a bitmap is selected into a memory DC, you can draw into the DC (and hence into the bitmap) using the same *CDC* member functions you'd use to draw to a device DC.

The big difference between drawing to a memory DC and drawing to a screen DC is that pixels drawn to a memory DC aren't displayed. To display them, you have to copy them from the memory DC to a screen DC. Drawing to a memory DC first and then transferring pixels to a screen DC can be useful for replicating the same image on the screen several times. Rather than draw the image anew each time, you can draw it once in a memory DC and then transfer the image to a screen DC as many times as you want. (The architecture of many display adapters means that you can often get better performance by copying the image to the screen DC one time and then copying additional images from the screen DC rather than from the memory DC.) Bitmaps play an important role in the process because when a memory DC is first created it contains just one pixel you can draw to, and that pixel is a monochrome pixel. Selecting a bitmap into a memory DC gives you a larger display surface to draw on and also more colors to work with if the bitmap isn't monochrome.

Blitting Bitmaps to Screens and Other Devices

How do you draw a bitmap on the screen once it's ready to be displayed? Bitmaps can't be selected into nonmemory DCs; if you try, *SelectObject* will return NULL. But you can use *CDC::BitBlt* or *CDC::StretchBlt* to "blit" pixels from a memory DC to a screen DC. *BitBlt* transfers a block of pixels from one DC to another and preserves the block's dimensions; *StretchBlt* transfers a block of pixels between DCs and scales the block to the dimensions you specify. If *dcMem* is a memory DC that contains a 100-pixel by 100-pixel bitmap image and *dcScreen* is a screen DC, the statement

```
dcScreen.BitBlt (0, 0, 100, 100, &dcMem, 0, 0, SRCCOPY);
```

copies the image to the screen DC and consequently displays it on the screen. The first two parameters passed to *BitBlt* specify the coordinates of the image's upper left corner in the destination (screen) DC, the next two specify the width and height of the block to be transferred, the fifth is a pointer to the source (memory) DC, the sixth and seventh specify the coordinates of the upper left corner of the block of pixels in the source DC, and the eighth and final parameter specifies the type of raster operation to be used in the transfer. SRCCOPY copies the pixels unchanged from the memory DC to the screen DC.

If you'd like to shrink or expand the bitmap as it's blitted, use *StretchBlt* instead of *BitBlt*. *StretchBlt*'s argument list looks a lot like *BitBlt*'s, but it includes an additional pair of parameters specifying the width and height of the image at the destination. The following statement blits a 100-by-100 image from a memory DC to a screen DC and stretches the image to fit a 50-by-200 rectangle at the destination:

```
dcScreen.StretchBlt (0, 0, 50, 200, &dcMem, 0, 0, 100, 100,
    SRCCOPY);
```

By default, rows and columns of pixels are simply removed from the resultant image when the width or height in the destination DC is less than the width or height in the source DC. You can call *CDC::SetStretchBltMode* before calling *StretchBlt* to specify other stretching modes that use various methods to preserve discarded color information. Refer to the MFC documentation on *SetStretchBltMode* for further details, but be advised that the most potentially useful alternative stretching mode—HALFTONE— works in Windows NT but not in Windows 95.

You can get information about a bitmap by calling the *GetObject* function it inherits from *CGdiObject* and passing a pointer to a BITMAP structure. BITMAP is defined as follows:

```
typedef struct tagBITMAP {
    LONG    bmType;
    LONG    bmWidth;
    LONG    bmHeight;
    LONG    bmWidthBytes;
    WORD    bmPlanes;
```

```
    WORD     bmBitsPixel;
    LPVOID   bmBits;
} BITMAP;
```

The *bmType* field always contains 0. *bmWidth* and *bmHeight* specify the bitmap's dimensions in pixels. *bmWidthBytes* specifies the length (in bytes) of each line in the bitmap and is always a multiple of 2 because rows of bits are padded to 16-bit boundaries. *bmPlanes* and *bmBitsPixel* specify the number of color planes and the number of pixels per bit in each color plane. The maximum number of colors the bitmap may contain can be determined from the following equation:

```
int nColors = 1 << (bmPlanes * bmBitsPixel);
```

Finally, *bmBits* contains a NULL pointer following a call to *GetObject* if the bitmap is a DDB. If *bitmap* represents a *CBitmap* object, the statements

```
BITMAP bm;
bitmap.GetObject (sizeof (BITMAP), &bm);
```

initialize *bm* with information about the bitmap.

The bitmap dimensions returned by *GetObject* are expressed in device units (pixels), but both *BitBlt* and *StretchBlt* use logical units. If you want to write a generic *DrawBitmap* function that blits a bitmap to a DC, you need to anticipate the possibility that the DC passed to the function will use a mapping mode other than MM_TEXT. The following *DrawBitmap* function, which is designed to be included in a class derived from *CBitmap*, works in all mapping modes. *pDC* points to the device context the bitmap will be blitted to; *x* and *y* specify the location of the image's upper left corner in the destination DC:

```
CMyBitmap::DrawBitmap (CDC* pDC, int x, int y)
{
    BITMAP bm;
    GetObject (sizeof (BITMAP), &bm);
    CPoint size (bm.bmWidth, bm.bmHeight);
    pDC->DPtoLP (&size);

    CPoint org (0, 0);
    pDC->DPtoLP (&org);

    CDC dcMem;
    dcMem.CreateCompatibleDC (pDC);
    CBitmap* pOldBitmap = dcMem.SelectObject (this);
    dcMem.SetMapMode (pDC->GetMapMode ());
    pDC->BitBlt (x, y, size.x, size.y, &dcMem, org.x, org.y,
        SRCCOPY);
    dcMem.SelectObject (pOldBitmap);
}
```

Because of some inadvertent skullduggery that MFC's *CDC::DPtoLP* function performs on *CSize* objects, the *size* variable that holds the bitmap's dimensions is a *CPoint* object, not a *CSize* object. When you pass *CDC::DPtoLP* the address of a *CPoint* object, the call goes straight through to the *::DPtoLP* API function and the conversion is performed properly, even if one or more of the coordinates comes back negative. But when you pass *CDC::DPtoLP* the address of a *CSize* object, MFC performs the conversion itself and converts any negatives to positives. It might make intuitive sense that sizes shouldn't be negative, but that's exactly what *BitBlt* expects in mapping modes in which the *y* axis points upward.

Loading Bitmap Resources

If all you want to do is display a predefined bitmap image—one created with the SDK's Image Editor, Visual C++'s resource editor, or a paint program that generates .bmp files—you don't have to call *CreateBitmap*. Instead, you can declare a bitmap resource in your application's .rc file like this.

```
IDR_LOGOIMAGE BITMAP Logo.bmp
```

Then you can create a bitmap from it like this:

```
CBitmap bitmap;
bitmap.LoadBitmap (IDR_LOGOIMAGE);
```

In this example, IDR_LOGOIMAGE is the bitmap's integer resource ID and Logo.bmp is the name of the file that contains the bitmap image. You can also assign a bitmap resource a string ID and load it like this:

```
bitmap.LoadBitmap ("LogoImage");
```

LoadBitmap will accept resource IDs of either type. Once a bitmap is loaded in this way, it is displayed just as any other bitmap is—by selecting it into a memory DC and blitting it to a screen DC. Splash screens like the one you see when Visual C++ starts up are typically stored as bitmap resources and loaded with *LoadBitmap* (or its API equivalent, *::LoadBitmap*) just before they're displayed.

CBitmap also includes a related function named *LoadMappedBitmap* that loads a bitmap resource and transforms one or more colors in the bitmap to the colors you specify. *LoadMappedBitmap* is a wrapper around *::CreateMappedBitmap*, which was added to the Win32 API so that colors in bitmaps used to paint owner-drawn buttons, toolbar buttons, and other controls could be transformed into system colors upon loading. The statement

```
bitmap.LoadMappedBitmap (IDR_BITMAP);
```

loads a bitmap resource whose ID is IDR_BITMAP and automatically transforms black pixels to the system color COLOR_BTNTEXT, dark gray (R=128, G=128, B=128) pixels to COLOR_BTNSHADOW, light gray (R=192, G=192, B=192) pixels to COLOR-

_BTNFACE, white pixels to COLOR_BTNHIGHLIGHT, dark blue (R=0, G=0, B=128) pixels to COLOR_HIGHLIGHT, and magenta (R=255, G=0, B=255) pixels to COLOR-_WINDOW. The idea behind mapping magenta to COLOR_WINDOW is that you can add "transparent" pixels to a bitmap by coloring them magenta. If *LoadMappedBitmap* transforms magenta pixels into COLOR_WINDOW pixels and the bitmap is displayed against a COLOR_WINDOW background, the remapped pixels will be invisible against the background.

You can perform custom color conversions by passing *LoadMappedBitmap* a pointer to an array of COLORMAP structures specifying the colors you want to have changed and the colors you want them to be changed to. One use for custom color mapping is for simulating transparent pixels by transforming an arbitrary background color in the image you're loading to the background color of your choice. Later we'll examine a technique for drawing bitmaps with transparent pixels that works with any kind of background (even those that aren't solid) and requires no color mapping.

DIBs and DIB Sections

The problem with device-dependent bitmaps is—well, that they're device-dependent. You can manipulate the bits in a DDB directly using *CBitmap::GetBitmapBits* and *CBitmap::SetBitmapBits*, but because pixel color data is stored in a device-dependent format, it's difficult to know what to do with the data returned by *GetBitmapBits* (or what to pass to *SetBitmapBits*) unless the bitmap is monochrome. Worse, the color information encoded in a DDB is meaningful only to the device driver that displays it. If you write a DDB to disk on one PC and read it back on another, there's a very good chance that the colors won't come out the same. DDBs are fine for loading and displaying bitmap resources (although you'll get poor results if a bitmap resource contains more colors than your hardware is capable of displaying) and for drawing images in memory DCs before rendering them on an output device. But their lack of portability makes DDBs unsuitable for just about anything else.

That's why Windows 3.0 introduced the device-independent bitmap, or DIB. The term "DIB" describes a device-independent format for storing bitmap data, a format that's meaningful outside the context of a display driver and even outside the framework of Windows itself. When you call *::CreateBitmap* (the API equivalent of *CBitmap::CreateBitmap*) to create a bitmap, you get back an HBITMAP handle referencing a DDB. When you call *::CreateDIBitmap* to create a bitmap, you also get back an HBITMAP handle to a DDB. The difference is what goes into the bitmaps. Pixel data passed to *::CreateBitmap* is stored in device driver format, but pixel data passed to *::CreateDIBitmap* is stored in DIB format. Moreover, the DIB format includes color information so that colors can be interpreted consistently by different device drivers. The API includes a pair of functions named *::GetDIBits* and *::SetDIBits* for reading and writing DIB-formatted bits. It also includes functions for rendering raw DIB data stored in a buffer owned by the application to an output device. Windows .bmp files store bitmaps in DIB format, so it's relatively easy to write a function that uses *::Create-DIBitmap* to convert the contents of a .bmp file into a GDI bitmap object.

DIB sections are similar to DIBs and were created to solve a performance problem involving the *::StretchDIBits* function in Windows NT. Some graphics programs allocate a buffer to hold DIB bits and then render those bits directly to the screen with *::StretchDIBits*. By not passing the bits to *::CreateDIBitmap* and creating an HBITMAP, the programs enjoy direct access to the bitmap data but can still display the bitmap on the screen. Unfortunately, the client/server architecture of Windows NT dictates that bits blitted from a buffer on the client side be copied to a buffer on the server side before they're transferred to the frame buffer, and the extra overhead causes *::StretchDIBits* to perform sluggishly.

Rather than compromise the system architecture, the Windows NT team came up with DIB sections. A DIB section is the Windows NT equivalent of having your cake and eating it, too: you can select a DIB section into a DC and blit it to the screen (thus avoiding the undesirable memory-to-memory moves), but you can also access the bitmap bits directly. Speed isn't as much of an issue with the *::StretchDIBits* function in Windows 95 because the operating system is architected differently, but Windows 95 supports DIB sections just as Windows NT does and offers some handy new API functions for dealing with DIB sections. Win32 programmers are encouraged to use DIB sections in lieu of ordinary DIBs and DDBs whenever possible to give the operating system the greatest amount of flexibility in handling bitmap data.

The bad news about DIBs and DIB sections is that current versions of MFC don't encapsulate them. To use DIBs and DIB sections in your MFC applications, you'll either have to resort to the API or write your own classes to encapsulate the relevant API functions. It's not difficult to write a basic *CDib* class or to extend *CBitmap* to include functions for DIBs and DIB sections, but I'm not going to do it here because the next major release of MFC will include a comprehensive set of classes for DIBs and DIB sections. What I'll do instead is show you how to get the most out of MFC's *CBitmap* class and how to combine *CBitmap* with new Windows 95 API functions to get some very DIB-like behavior out of ordinary *CBitmap*s.

Blits, Raster Operations, and Color Mapping

The most common use for *CDC::BitBlt* is to blit bitmap images to the screen. But *BitBlt* does more than just transfer raw bits. In reality, it's a complex function that computes the color of each pixel it outputs by using Boolean operations to combine pixels from the source DC, the destination DC, and the brush currently selected in the destination DC. The SRCCOPY raster-op code is simple; it merely copies pixels from the source to the destination. Other raster-op codes aren't so simple. MERGEPAINT, for example, inverts the colors of the source pixels with a Boolean NOT operation and ORs the result with the pixel colors at the destination. *BitBlt* supports 256 raster-op codes in all, of which the 15 shown in the table below are given names with *#define* statements in Wingdi.h.

BitBlt RASTER-OP CODES

Name	Binary Equivalent	Operation(s) Performed
SRCCOPY	0xCC0020	dest = source
SRCPAINT	0xEE0086	dest = source OR dest
SRCAND	0x8800C6	dest = source AND dest
SRCINVERT	0x660046	dest = source XOR dest
SRCERASE	0x440328	dest = source AND (NOT dest)
NOTSRCCOPY	0x330008	dest = (NOT source)
NOTSRCERASE	0x1100A6	dest = (NOT src) AND (NOT dest)
MERGECOPY	0xC000CA	dest = (source AND pattern)
MERGEPAINT	0xBB0226	dest = (NOT source) OR dest
PATCOPY	0xF00021	dest = pattern
PATPAINT	0xFB0A09	dest = pattern OR (NOT src) OR dest
PATINVERT	0x5A0049	dest = pattern XOR dest
DSTINVERT	0x550009	dest = (NOT dest)
BLACKNESS	0x000042	dest = BLACK
WHITENESS	0xFF0062	dest = WHITE

Custom raster-op codes can be derived by applying the logical operations you want to the bit values in the following table and using the result to look up a DWORD-sized raster-op code in the "Ternary Raster Operations" appendix of the Win32 SDK *Programmer's Reference:*

Pat	1	1	1	1	0	0	0	0
Src	1	1	0	0	1	1	0	0
Dest	1	0	1	0	1	0	1	0

Pat (for "pattern") represents the color of the brush selected into the destination DC; *Src* represents the pixel color in the source DC; and *Dest* represents the pixel color in the destination DC. Let's say you want to find a raster-op code that inverts a source bitmap, ANDs it with the pixels at the destination, and ORs the result with the brush color. First apply these same operations to each column of bits in the table. The result is shown at the top of the next page.

Pat	1 1 1 1 0 0 0 0	
Src	1 1 0 0 1 1 0 0	
Dest	1 0 1 0 1 0 1 0	
	1 1 1 1 0 0 1 0	= 0xF2

Look up 0xF2 in the ternary raster operations table, and you'll find that the full raster-op code is 0xF20B05. Consequently, you can pass *BitBlt* the hex value 0xF20B05 instead of SRCCOPY or some other raster-op code and it will perform the raster operation described on the preceding page.

So what can you *do* with all those raster-op codes? The truth is that in color environments you probably won't use many of them. After SRCCOPY, the next most useful raster operations are SRCAND, SRCINVERT, and SRCPAINT. But as the sample program in the next section will demonstrate, sometimes using an unnamed raster-op code can reduce the number of steps required to achieve a desired result.

BitBlt is part of a larger family of *CDC* blitting functions that includes *StretchBlt* (which we've already discussed), *PatBlt*, *MaskBlt*, and *PlgBlt*. *PatBlt* combines pixels in a rectangle in the destination DC with the brush selected into the device context, basically duplicating the subset of *BitBlt* raster operations that don't use a source DC. *MaskBlt* combines pixels in source and destination DCs and uses a monochrome bitmap as a mask. One raster operation (the "foreground" raster operation) is performed on pixels that correspond to 1s in the mask, and another raster operation (the "background" raster operation) is performed on pixels that correspond to 0s in the mask. *PlgBlt* blits a rectangular block of pixels in a source DC to a parallelogram in the destination DC and optionally uses a monochrome bitmap as a mask during the transfer. Pixels that correspond to 1s in the mask are blitted to the parallelogram; pixels that correspond to 0s in the mask are not. Unfortunately, *MaskBlt* and *PlgBlt* are supported in Windows NT but not in Windows 95. If you call either of them in Windows 95, you'll get a 0 return indicating that the function failed.

Some output devices (notably plotters) don't support *BitBlt* and other blitting functions. To determine whether or not *BitBlt*s are supported on a given device, get a device context and call *GetDeviceCaps* with a RASTERCAPS parameter. If the RC_BITBLT bit is set in the return value, then the device supports *BitBlt*s; if the RC_STRETCHBLT bit is set, then the device also supports *StretchBlt*s. There are no specific RASTERCAPS bits for other blit functions, but if you're writing for Windows NT and *BitBlt* isn't supported, you should assume that *PatBlt*, *MaskBlt*, and *PlgBlt* aren't supported, either. Generally, plotters and other vector-type devices that don't support blits will set the RC_NONE bit in the value returned by *GetDeviceCaps* to indicate that they don't support raster operations of any type.

BitBlt and other blitting functions produce the best results (and also perform the best) when the color characteristics of the source and destination DCs match. If you blit a 256-color bitmap to a 16-color destination DC, Windows must map the colors in the source DC to the colors in the destination DC. There are occasions, however, when you can use color mapping to your advantage. When *BitBlt* blits a monochrome bitmap to a color DC, it converts 0 bits to the destination DC's current foreground color (*CDC::SetTextColor*) and 1 bits to the destination DC's current background color (*CDC::SetBkColor*). Conversely, when it blits a color bitmap to a monochrome DC, *BitBlt* converts pixels that match the destination DC's background color to 1 and all other pixels to 0. You can use the latter form of color mapping to create a monochrome mask from a color bitmap and use that mask in a routine that blits all pixels except those of a certain color from a bitmap to a screen DC, in effect creating transparent pixels in the bitmap.

Sound interesting? Icons implement transparent pixels by storing two bitmaps for every icon image: a monochrome AND mask and a color XOR mask. You can draw bitmaps with transparent pixels by writing an output routine that uses *BitBlt*s and raster ops to build the AND and XOR masks on the fly. The BitmapDemo sample program in the next section shows you how.

The BitmapDemo Application

The BitmapDemo application, listed in Figure 12-3, demonstrates how to load a bitmap resource and *BitBlt* it to the screen. BitmapDemo also demonstrates how to make clever use of *BitBlt*s to blit irregularly shaped images by designating one color in the bitmap as the transparency color. The program's output consists of a rectangular array of bitmap images drawn against a background that fades from blue to black. When the Draw Opaque command is checked in BitmapDemo's Options menu, the bitmaps are blitted to the screen unchanged, producing the result shown in Figure 12-4 on page 812. If Draw Transparent is checked instead, red pixels are removed from the bitmaps blitted to the screen. The result is pictured in Figure 12-5.

Resource.h

```
//**********************************************************************
//
//  Resource.h
//
//**********************************************************************

#define IDM_OPTIONS_DRAW_OPAQUE        100
#define IDM_OPTIONS_DRAW_TRANSPARENT   101
#define IDM_OPTIONS_EXIT               102

#define IDR_MAINFRAME                  200
#define IDR_BITMAP                     201
```

Figure 12-3. *The BitmapDemo program.*

BitmapDemo.rc

```
//***********************************************************************
//
//  BitmapDemo.rc
//
//***********************************************************************

#include <afxres.h>
#include "Resource.h"

IDR_BITMAP BITMAP Drive.bmp

IDR_MAINFRAME MENU
BEGIN
    POPUP "&Options" {
        MENUITEM "Draw &Opaque",            IDM_OPTIONS_DRAW_OPAQUE
        MENUITEM "Draw &Transparent",       IDM_OPTIONS_DRAW_TRANSPARENT
        MENUITEM SEPARATOR
        MENUITEM "E&xit",                   IDM_OPTIONS_EXIT
    }
END
```

BitmapDemo.h

```
//***********************************************************************
//
//  BitmapDemo.h
//
//***********************************************************************

class CMyApp : public CWinApp
{
public:
    virtual BOOL InitInstance ();
};

class CMaskedBitmap : public CBitmap
{
public:
    virtual void Draw (CDC*, int, int);
    virtual void DrawTransparent (CDC*, int, int, COLORREF);
};

class CMainWindow : public CFrameWnd
{
```

```
private:
    BOOL m_bDrawOpaque;
    CPalette m_palette;
    CMaskedBitmap m_bitmap;

    void DoGradientFill (CDC*, CRect*);

public:
    CMainWindow ();

protected:
    afx_msg int OnCreate (LPCREATESTRUCT);
    afx_msg BOOL OnEraseBkgnd (CDC*);
    afx_msg void OnPaint ();
    afx_msg BOOL OnQueryNewPalette ();
    afx_msg void OnPaletteChanged (CWnd*);
    afx_msg void OnOptionsDrawOpaque ();
    afx_msg void OnOptionsDrawTransparent ();
    afx_msg void OnOptionsExit ();
    afx_msg void OnUpdateDrawOpaqueUI (CCmdUI*);
    afx_msg void OnUpdateDrawTransparentUI (CCmdUI*);

    DECLARE_MESSAGE_MAP ()
};
```

BitmapDemo.cpp

```
//****************************************************************************
//
//  BitmapDemo.cpp
//
//****************************************************************************

#include <afxwin.h>
#include "Resource.h"
#include "BitmapDemo.h"

CMyApp myApp;

///////////////////////////////////////////////////////////////////////////
// CMyApp member functions

BOOL CMyApp::InitInstance ()
{
    m_pMainWnd = new CMainWindow;
    m_pMainWnd->ShowWindow (m_nCmdShow);
```

(continued)

BitmapDemo.cpp *continued*

```
    m_pMainWnd->UpdateWindow ();
    return TRUE;
}


/////////////////////////////////////////////////////////////////////////
// CMainWindow message map and member functions

BEGIN_MESSAGE_MAP (CMainWindow, CFrameWnd)
    ON_WM_CREATE ()
    ON_WM_ERASEBKGND ()
    ON_WM_PAINT ()
    ON_WM_QUERYNEWPALETTE ()
    ON_WM_PALETTECHANGED ()
    ON_COMMAND (IDM_OPTIONS_DRAW_OPAQUE, OnOptionsDrawOpaque)
    ON_COMMAND (IDM_OPTIONS_DRAW_TRANSPARENT, OnOptionsDrawTransparent)
    ON_COMMAND (IDM_OPTIONS_EXIT, OnOptionsExit)
    ON_UPDATE_COMMAND_UI (IDM_OPTIONS_DRAW_OPAQUE, OnUpdateDrawOpaqueUI)
    ON_UPDATE_COMMAND_UI (IDM_OPTIONS_DRAW_TRANSPARENT,
        OnUpdateDrawTransparentUI)
END_MESSAGE_MAP ()

CMainWindow::CMainWindow ()
{
    m_bDrawOpaque = TRUE;
    Create (NULL, "Bitmap Demo", WS_OVERLAPPEDWINDOW, rectDefault,
        NULL, MAKEINTRESOURCE (IDR_MAINFRAME));
}

int CMainWindow::OnCreate (LPCREATESTRUCT lpcs)
{
    if (CFrameWnd::OnCreate (lpcs) == -1)
        return -1;

    m_bitmap.LoadBitmap (IDR_BITMAP);

    CClientDC dc (this);
    if (dc.GetDeviceCaps (RASTERCAPS) & RC_PALETTE) {
        struct {
            LOGPALETTE lp;
            PALETTEENTRY ape[63];
        } pal;

        LOGPALETTE* pLP = (LOGPALETTE*) &pal;
        pLP->palVersion = 0x300;
        pLP->palNumEntries = 64;
```

```
        for (int i=0; i<64; i++) {
            pLP->palPalEntry[i].peRed = 0;
            pLP->palPalEntry[i].peGreen = 0;
            pLP->palPalEntry[i].peBlue = 255 - (i * 4);
            pLP->palPalEntry[i].peFlags = 0;
        }
        m_palette.CreatePalette (pLP);
    }
    return 0;
}

BOOL CMainWindow::OnEraseBkgnd (CDC* pDC)
{
    CRect rect;
    GetClientRect (&rect);

    CPalette* pOldPalette;
    if ((HPALETTE) m_palette != NULL) {
        pOldPalette = pDC->SelectPalette (&m_palette, FALSE);
        pDC->RealizePalette ();
    }

    DoGradientFill (pDC, &rect);

    if ((HPALETTE) m_palette != NULL)
        pDC->SelectPalette (pOldPalette, FALSE);
    return TRUE;
}

void CMainWindow::OnPaint ()
{
    CRect rect;
    GetClientRect (&rect);
    CPaintDC dc (this);

    BITMAP bm;
    m_bitmap.GetObject (sizeof (BITMAP), &bm);
    int cx = (rect.Width () / (bm.bmWidth + 8)) + 1;
    int cy = (rect.Height () / (bm.bmHeight + 8)) + 1;

    int i, j, x, y;
    for (i=0; i<cx; i++) {
        for (j=0; j<cy; j++) {
            x = 8 + (i * (bm.bmWidth + 8));
            y = 8 + (j * (bm.bmHeight + 8));
            if (m_bDrawOpaque)
                m_bitmap.Draw (&dc, x, y);
```

(continued)

BitmapDemo.cpp *continued*

```
            else
                m_bitmap.DrawTransparent (&dc, x, y, RGB (255, 0, 0));
        }
    }
}

BOOL CMainWindow::OnQueryNewPalette ()
{
    if ((HPALETTE) m_palette == NULL)    // Shouldn't happen, but
        return 0;                        // let's be sure

    CClientDC dc (this);
    CPalette* pOldPalette = dc.SelectPalette (&m_palette, FALSE);

    UINT nCount;
    if (nCount = dc.RealizePalette ())
        Invalidate ();

    dc.SelectPalette (pOldPalette, FALSE);
    return nCount;
}

void CMainWindow::OnPaletteChanged (CWnd* pFocusWnd)
{
    if ((HPALETTE) m_palette == NULL)    // Shouldn't happen, but
        return;                          // let's be sure

    if (pFocusWnd != this) {
        CClientDC dc (this);
        CPalette* pOldPalette = dc.SelectPalette (&m_palette, FALSE);
        if (dc.RealizePalette ())
            Invalidate ();
        dc.SelectPalette (pOldPalette, FALSE);
    }
}

void CMainWindow::DoGradientFill (CDC* pDC, CRect* pRect)
{
    CBrush* pBrush[64];
    for (int i=0; i<64; i++)
        pBrush[i] = new CBrush (PALETTERGB (0, 0, 255 - (i * 4)));

    int nWidth = pRect->Width ();
    int nHeight = pRect->Height ();
    CRect rect;
```

```
    for (i=0; i<nHeight; i++) {
        rect.SetRect (0, i, nWidth, i + 1);
        pDC->FillRect (&rect, pBrush[(i * 63) / nHeight]);
    }

    for (i=0; i<64; i++)
        delete pBrush[i];
}

void CMainWindow::OnOptionsDrawOpaque ()
{
    m_bDrawOpaque = TRUE;
    Invalidate ();
}

void CMainWindow::OnOptionsDrawTransparent ()
{
    m_bDrawOpaque = FALSE;
    Invalidate ();
}

void CMainWindow::OnOptionsExit ()
{
    SendMessage (WM_CLOSE, 0, 0);
}

void CMainWindow::OnUpdateDrawOpaqueUI (CCmdUI* pCmdUI)
{
    pCmdUI->SetCheck (m_bDrawOpaque ? 1 : 0);
}

void CMainWindow::OnUpdateDrawTransparentUI (CCmdUI* pCmdUI)
{
    pCmdUI->SetCheck (m_bDrawOpaque ? 0 : 1);
}

/////////////////////////////////////////////////////////////////////
// CMaskedBitmap member functions

void CMaskedBitmap::Draw (CDC* pDC, int x, int y)
{
    BITMAP bm;
    GetObject (sizeof (BITMAP), &bm);
    CPoint size (bm.bmWidth, bm.bmHeight);
    pDC->DPtoLP (&size);

    CPoint org (0, 0);
```

(continued)

BitmapDemo.cpp *continued*

```
    pDC->DPtoLP (&org);

    CDC dcMem;
    dcMem.CreateCompatibleDC (pDC);
    CBitmap* pOldBitmap = dcMem.SelectObject (this);
    dcMem.SetMapMode (pDC->GetMapMode ());

    pDC->BitBlt (x, y, size.x, size.y, &dcMem, org.x, org.y, SRCCOPY);

    dcMem.SelectObject (pOldBitmap);
}

void CMaskedBitmap::DrawTransparent (CDC* pDC, int x, int y,
    COLORREF crColor)
{
    BITMAP bm;
    GetObject (sizeof (BITMAP), &bm);
    CPoint size (bm.bmWidth, bm.bmHeight);
    pDC->DPtoLP (&size);

    CPoint org (0, 0);
    pDC->DPtoLP (&org);

    // Create a memory DC (dcImage) and select the bitmap into it
    CDC dcImage;
    dcImage.CreateCompatibleDC (pDC);
    CBitmap* pOldBitmapImage = dcImage.SelectObject (this);
    dcImage.SetMapMode (pDC->GetMapMode ());

    // Create a second memory DC (dcAnd) and in it create an AND mask
    CDC dcAnd;
    dcAnd.CreateCompatibleDC (pDC);
    dcAnd.SetMapMode (pDC->GetMapMode ());

    CBitmap bitmapAnd;
    bitmapAnd.CreateBitmap (bm.bmWidth, bm.bmHeight, 1, 1, NULL);
    CBitmap* pOldBitmapAnd = dcAnd.SelectObject (&bitmapAnd);

    dcImage.SetBkColor (crColor);
    dcAnd.BitBlt (org.x, org.y, size.x, size.y, &dcImage, org.x, org.y,
        SRCCOPY);

    // Create a third memory DC (dcXor) and in it create an XOR mask
    CDC dcXor;
    dcXor.CreateCompatibleDC (pDC);
    dcXor.SetMapMode (pDC->GetMapMode ());
```

```
CBitmap bitmapXor;
bitmapXor.CreateCompatibleBitmap (&dcImage, bm.bmWidth, bm.bmHeight);
CBitmap* pOldBitmapXor = dcXor.SelectObject (&bitmapXor);

dcXor.BitBlt (org.x, org.y, size.x, size.y, &dcImage, org.x, org.y,
    SRCCOPY);

dcXor.BitBlt (org.x, org.y, size.x, size.y, &dcAnd, org.x, org.y,
    0x220326);

// Copy the pixels in the destination rectangle to a temporary
// memory DC (dcTemp)
CDC dcTemp;
dcTemp.CreateCompatibleDC (pDC);
dcTemp.SetMapMode (pDC->GetMapMode ());

CBitmap bitmapTemp;
bitmapTemp.CreateCompatibleBitmap (&dcImage, bm.bmWidth, bm.bmHeight);
CBitmap* pOldBitmapTemp = dcTemp.SelectObject (&bitmapTemp);

dcTemp.BitBlt (org.x, org.y, size.x, size.y, pDC, x, y, SRCCOPY);

// Generate the final image by applying the AND and XOR masks to
// the image in the temporary memory DC
dcTemp.BitBlt (org.x, org.y, size.x, size.y, &dcAnd, org.x, org.y,
    SRCAND);

dcTemp.BitBlt (org.x, org.y, size.x, size.y, &dcXor, org.x, org.y,
    SRCINVERT);

// Blit the resulting image to the screen
pDC->BitBlt (x, y, size.x, size.y, &dcTemp, org.x, org.y, SRCCOPY);

// Restore the default bitmaps
dcTemp.SelectObject (pOldBitmapTemp);
dcXor.SelectObject (pOldBitmapXor);
dcAnd.SelectObject (pOldBitmapAnd);
dcImage.SelectObject (pOldBitmapImage);
}
```

Figure 12-4. *The BitmapDemo screen with transparency disabled.*

Figure 12-5. *The BitmapDemo screen with transparency enabled.*

BitmapDemo derives a new class from *CBitmap* named *CMaskedBitmap*. *CMaskedBitmap* contains two member functions that *CBitmap* doesn't: a *Draw* function for blitting a bitmap to a DC, and a *DrawTransparent* function for blitting a bitmap to a DC and simultaneously filtering out all pixels that match a specified color. With *CMaskedBitmap* to lend a hand, the statements

```
CMaskedBitmap bitmap;
bitmap.LoadBitmap (IDR_BITMAP);
bitmap.Draw (pDC, x, y);
```

are all that's needed to create a bitmap object, load a bitmap resource into it, and draw that bitmap on the device represented by *pDC*. The *x* and *y* parameters specify where the upper left corner of the bitmap will be placed. The statements

```
CMaskedBitmap bitmap;
bitmap.LoadBitmap (IDR_BITMAP);
bitmap.DrawTransparent (pDC, x, y, RGB (255, 0, 255));
```

do the same but don't blit any pixels in the bitmap whose color is bright magenta—RGB (255, 0, 255). Creating a bitmap with "holes" or a nonrectangular profile is easy: just assign all the transparent pixels in the bitmap a common color and pass that color to *DrawTransparent* when you display the bitmap. *DrawTransparent* will make sure that the transparent pixels don't get blitted along with the others.

The source code for *CMaskedBitmap::Draw* should look familiar to you: it's identical to the *DrawBitmap* function on page 797. *CMaskedBitmap::DrawTransparent* is a little more complicated. The comments in the source code should help you understand what's going on. If the comments don't make things clear enough, here's a summary of the steps involved in blitting a bitmap to the screen but omitting pixels of a certain color:

1. Create a memory DC, and select the bitmap into it.

2. Create a second memory DC, and select in a monochrome bitmap the same size as the original bitmap. Create an AND mask by setting the background color of the memory DC created in step 1 to the transparency color and blitting the bitmap to the DC. The resultant AND mask will have 1s everywhere the original bitmap has pixels whose color equals the transparency color and 0s everywhere else.

3. Create a third memory DC, and select in a bitmap whose size and color characteristics match those of the original bitmap. Create an XOR mask in this DC by first blitting the image from the memory DC created in step 1 to this DC with a SRCCOPY raster-op code and then blitting the AND mask to this DC with the raster-op code 0x220326.

4. Create a fourth memory DC, and select in a bitmap whose size and color characteristics match those of the original bitmap. Blit the pixels from the rectangle in which the bitmap will go in the output DC to the newly created memory DC.

5. Create the final image in the memory DC created in step 4 by first blitting in the AND mask with a SRCAND raster-op code and then blitting in the XOR mask with a SRCINVERT raster-op code.

6. Copy the image from the memory DC to the output DC.

Note how we let *BitBlt* generate the AND mask for us in step 2. Because the destination DC is monochrome, the GDI translates pixels whose color equals the background color to 1s and all other pixels to 0s at the destination. It's important to set the source DC's background color equal to the bitmap's transparency color first so that the transformation will be performed properly. If you look at the code in *CMaskedBitmap::DrawTransparent* that corresponds to step 2, you'll see that the destination DC's size and color characteristics are set by using *CBitmap::CreateBitmap* to create a monochrome bitmap whose dimensions equal the dimensions of the original bitmap and then selecting the monochrome bitmap into the DC. This underscores an important point: you control the size of a memory DC's display surface and the number of colors that it supports by selecting a bitmap into it. That's why you see so many calls to *CreateBitmap* and *CreateCompatibleBitmap* in *DrawTransparent*.

One other point of interest in *DrawTransparent* is the raster-op code 0x220326 used in step 3, which performs the following raster operation involving pixels at the source and destination:

```
dest = (NOT src) AND dest
```

You can accomplish the same thing using "standard" raster-op codes by calling *BitBlt* twice: once with the raster-op code NOTSRCCOPY to invert the image in the source DC and again with SRCAND to AND the inverted image with the pixels in the destination DC. It's obviously more efficient to perform one *BitBlt* instead of two, but don't be surprised if the 0x220326 code doesn't perform any faster than the NOTSRCCOPY/SRCAND combination on some PCs. Most display drivers are optimized to perform certain raster operations faster than others, and it's always possible that a NOTSRCCOPY or SRCAND will execute very quickly but a 0x220326 won't.

As you experiment with the BitmapDemo program, notice that the screen takes longer to repaint when BitmapDemo draws transparent pixels. That's because *DrawTransparent* has to do a lot more work than *Draw* to get a single image to the screen. The worst performance hit occurs when *DrawTransparent* generates the same AND and XOR masks over and over again. If you want the functionality of *DrawTransparent* in an application in which output performance is critical (for example, if you use transparent bitmaps to create spritelike objects that move about the screen), you should modify the *CMaskedBitmap* class so that the masks can be generated just once and then reused as many times as they're needed. Performance could also be improved by applying the AND and XOR masks directly to the destination DC rather than to a memory DC containing a copy of the pixels at the destination, but the small amount of flickering produced by the short delay between the application of the masks could be too much if you're using the bitmap for animation.

Writing a .bmp File Viewer

The disk-and-drive image drawn by BitmapDemo looks pretty good because it's a simple 16-color bitmap whose colors match the static colors in the system palette. As long as you draw the bitmaps yourself and stick to the primary colors in the default palette, bitmaps will display just fine without custom *CPalette*s. But if you write an application that reads bitmaps from .bmp files created by other programs and rely on the default palette for color mapping, bitmaps containing 256 or more colors will be posterized—some rather severely. You can dramatically improve the quality of the output by creating a *CPalette* whose colors match the colors in the bitmap. The sample program in this section demonstrates how. It also shows one way MFC 4 program-mers can combine *CBitmap*s with DIB sections to get more functional bitmaps.

The sample program, which I'll call Vista, is listed in Figure 12-6. It's a .bmp file viewer that will read virtually any .bmp file containing any number of colors and draw a reasonable representation of it on a screen that's capable of displaying 256 or more colors. (Vista works with 16-color screens, too, but don't expect a lot from the output if the bitmap contains more than 16 colors.) The source code is surprisingly simple. Other than the code that creates a logical palette after a .bmp file is read from disk, there's very little there other than the standard stuff that forms the core of every docu-ment/view application.

Figure 12-7 on page 825 shows what Vista looks like on a 256-color screen with a 256-color bitmap displayed. The indented status bar pane in the window's lower right corner tells you the image's dimensions in pixels and its color depth in bits per pixel (bpp).

Resource.h
```
//*********************************************************************
//
//  Resource.h
//
//*********************************************************************

#define IDR_MAINFRAME           100
```

Figure 12-6. *The Vista program.*

Vista.rc

```
//****************************************************************************
//
//  Vista.rc
//
//****************************************************************************

#include <afxres.h>
#include "Resource.h"

IDR_MAINFRAME MENU
BEGIN
    POPUP "&File" {
        MENUITEM "&Open...\tCtrl+O",        ID_FILE_OPEN
        MENUITEM SEPARATOR
        MENUITEM "Recent File",             ID_FILE_MRU_FILE1
        MENUITEM SEPARATOR
        MENUITEM "E&xit",                   ID_APP_EXIT
    }
    POPUP "&View" {
        MENUITEM "&Status Bar",             ID_VIEW_STATUS_BAR
    }
END

IDR_MAINFRAME ACCELERATORS
BEGIN
    "O", ID_FILE_OPEN,  VIRTKEY, CONTROL
END

STRINGTABLE
BEGIN
    IDR_MAINFRAME        "Vista\n\n\nBMP Files (*.bmp)\n.bmp"
    AFX_IDS_IDLEMESSAGE "Ready"
    ID_APP_EXIT         "Quit the application"
    AFX_IDS_SCCLOSE     "Quit the application"
END
```

Vista.h

```
//****************************************************************************
//
//  Vista.h
//
//****************************************************************************
```

```
class CVistaApp : public CWinApp
{
public:
    virtual BOOL InitInstance ();

protected:
    DECLARE_MESSAGE_MAP ()
};
```

Vista.cpp

```
//*********************************************************************
//
//  Vista.cpp
//
//*********************************************************************

#include <afxwin.h>
#include <afxext.h>
#include "Resource.h"
#include "Vista.h"
#include "MainFrame.h"
#include "VistaDoc.h"
#include "VistaView.h"

CVistaApp myApp;

BEGIN_MESSAGE_MAP (CVistaApp, CWinApp)
    ON_COMMAND (ID_FILE_OPEN, CWinApp::OnFileOpen)
END_MESSAGE_MAP ()

BOOL CVistaApp::InitInstance ()
{
    SetRegistryKey ("Programming Windows 95 with MFC");
    LoadStdProfileSettings ();

    CSingleDocTemplate* pDocTemplate;
    pDocTemplate = new CSingleDocTemplate (
        IDR_MAINFRAME,
        RUNTIME_CLASS (CVistaDoc),
        RUNTIME_CLASS (CMainFrame),
        RUNTIME_CLASS (CVistaView)
    );

    AddDocTemplate (pDocTemplate);
```

(continued)

Vista.cpp *continued*

```
        CCommandLineInfo cmdInfo;
        ParseCommandLine (cmdInfo);

        if (!ProcessShellCommand (cmdInfo))
            return FALSE;

        m_pMainWnd->DragAcceptFiles ();
        return TRUE;
    }
```

MainFrame.h

```
//***************************************************************************
//
//  MainFrame.h
//
//***************************************************************************

class CMainFrame : public CFrameWnd
{
    DECLARE_DYNCREATE (CMainFrame)

private:
    CStatusBar m_wndStatusBar;

protected:
    afx_msg int OnCreate (LPCREATESTRUCT);
    afx_msg LONG OnUpdateImageStats (UINT, LONG);
    afx_msg BOOL OnQueryNewPalette ();
    afx_msg void OnPaletteChanged (CWnd*);

    DECLARE_MESSAGE_MAP ()
};
```

MainFrame.cpp

```
//***************************************************************************
//
//  MainFrame.cpp
//
//***************************************************************************

#include <afxwin.h>
#include <afxext.h>
```

```
#include "MainFrame.h"

IMPLEMENT_DYNCREATE (CMainFrame, CFrameWnd)

BEGIN_MESSAGE_MAP (CMainFrame, CFrameWnd)
    ON_WM_CREATE ()
    ON_MESSAGE (WM_USER, OnUpdateImageStats)
    ON_WM_QUERYNEWPALETTE ()
    ON_WM_PALETTECHANGED ()
END_MESSAGE_MAP ()

int CMainFrame::OnCreate (LPCREATESTRUCT lpcs)
{
    static UINT nIndicators[] = {
        ID_SEPARATOR,
        ID_SEPARATOR,
    };

    if (CFrameWnd::OnCreate (lpcs) == -1)
        return -1;

    if (!m_wndStatusBar.Create (this))
        return -1;

    m_wndStatusBar.SetIndicators (nIndicators, 2);

    TEXTMETRIC tm;
    CClientDC dc (this);
    CFont* pFont = m_wndStatusBar.GetFont ();
    CFont* pOldFont = dc.SelectObject (pFont);
    dc.GetTextMetrics (&tm);
    dc.SelectObject (pOldFont);

    int cxWidth;
    UINT nID, nStyle;
    m_wndStatusBar.GetPaneInfo (1, nID, nStyle, cxWidth);
    cxWidth = tm.tmAveCharWidth * 24;
    m_wndStatusBar.SetPaneInfo (1, nID, nStyle, cxWidth);
    return 0;
}

LONG CMainFrame::OnUpdateImageStats (UINT wParam, LONG lParam)
{
    m_wndStatusBar.SetPaneText (1, (LPCTSTR) lParam, TRUE);
    return 0;
}
```

(continued)

MainFrame.cpp *continued*

```
BOOL CMainFrame::OnQueryNewPalette ()
{
    GetActiveView ()->Invalidate (FALSE);
    return TRUE;
}

void CMainFrame::OnPaletteChanged (CWnd* pFocusWnd)
{
    if (pFocusWnd != this)
        GetActiveView ()->Invalidate (FALSE);
}
```

VistaDoc.h

```
//**************************************************************************
//
//  VistaDoc.h
//
//**************************************************************************

class CVistaDoc : public CDocument
{
    DECLARE_DYNCREATE (CVistaDoc)

private:
    CBitmap m_bitmap;
    CPalette m_palette;

public:
    virtual BOOL OnOpenDocument (LPCTSTR);
    virtual void DeleteContents ();
    virtual void Serialize (CArchive&);

    CBitmap* GetBitmap ();
    CPalette* GetPalette ();
};
```

VistaDoc.cpp

```
//**************************************************************************
//
//  VistaDoc.cpp
//
//**************************************************************************
```

```
#include <afxwin.h>
#include "VistaDoc.h"

IMPLEMENT_DYNCREATE (CVistaDoc, CDocument)

BOOL CVistaDoc::OnOpenDocument (LPCTSTR lpszPathName)
{
    if (!CDocument::OnOpenDocument (lpszPathName)) {
        POSITION pos = GetFirstViewPosition ();
        CView* pView = GetNextView (pos);
        pView->OnInitialUpdate ();
        return FALSE;
    }

    // Return now if this device doesn't support palettes
    CClientDC dc (AfxGetMainWnd ());
    if ((dc.GetDeviceCaps (RASTERCAPS) & RC_PALETTE) == 0)
        return TRUE;

    // Create a palette to go with the DIB section
    if ((HBITMAP) m_bitmap != NULL) {
        DIBSECTION ds;
        m_bitmap.GetObject (sizeof (DIBSECTION), &ds);

        int nColors;
        if (ds.dsBmih.biClrUsed != 0)
            nColors = ds.dsBmih.biClrUsed;
        else
            nColors = 1 << ds.dsBmih.biBitCount;

        // Create a halftone palette if the DIB section contains more
        // than 256 colors
        if (nColors > 256)
            m_palette.CreateHalftonePalette (&dc);

        // Create a custom palette from the DIB section's color table
        // if the number of colors is 256 or less
        else {
            RGBQUAD* pRGB = new RGBQUAD[nColors];

            CDC memDC;
            memDC.CreateCompatibleDC (&dc);
            CBitmap* pOldBitmap = memDC.SelectObject (&m_bitmap);
            ::GetDIBColorTable ((HDC) memDC, 0, nColors, pRGB);
            memDC.SelectObject (pOldBitmap);
```

(continued)

VistaDoc.cpp *continued*

```
            UINT nSize = sizeof (LOGPALETTE) +
                (sizeof (PALETTEENTRY) * (nColors - 1));
            LOGPALETTE* pLP = (LOGPALETTE*) new BYTE[nSize];

            pLP->palVersion = 0x300;
            pLP->palNumEntries = nColors;

            for (int i=0; i<nColors; i++) {
                pLP->palPalEntry[i].peRed = pRGB[i].rgbRed;
                pLP->palPalEntry[i].peGreen = pRGB[i].rgbGreen;
                pLP->palPalEntry[i].peBlue = pRGB[i].rgbBlue;
                pLP->palPalEntry[i].peFlags = 0;
            }

            m_palette.CreatePalette (pLP);
            delete[] pLP;
            delete[] pRGB;
        }
    }
    return TRUE;
}

void CVistaDoc::DeleteContents ()
{
    if ((HBITMAP) m_bitmap != NULL)
        m_bitmap.DeleteObject ();

    if ((HPALETTE) m_palette != NULL)
        m_palette.DeleteObject ();

    CDocument::DeleteContents();
}

void CVistaDoc::Serialize (CArchive& ar)
{
    if (ar.IsLoading ()) {
        CString strFileName = ar.GetFile ()->GetFilePath ();

        HBITMAP hBitmap = (HBITMAP) ::LoadImage (AfxGetInstanceHandle (),
            (LPCTSTR) strFileName, IMAGE_BITMAP, 0, 0, LR_LOADFROMFILE |
            LR_CREATEDIBSECTION);

        if (hBitmap == NULL)
            AfxThrowArchiveException (CArchiveException::badIndex);

        m_bitmap.Attach (hBitmap);
```

```
    }
}

CBitmap* CVistaDoc::GetBitmap ()
{
    return ((HBITMAP) m_bitmap == NULL) ? NULL : &m_bitmap;
}

CPalette* CVistaDoc::GetPalette ()
{
    return ((HPALETTE) m_palette == NULL) ? NULL : &m_palette;
}
```

VistaView.h

```
//*********************************************************************
//
// VistaView.h
//
//*********************************************************************

class CVistaView : public CScrollView
{
    DECLARE_DYNCREATE (CVistaView)

private:
    CVistaDoc* GetDocument () { return (CVistaDoc*) m_pDocument; }

public:
    virtual void OnInitialUpdate ();

protected:
    virtual void OnDraw (CDC*);
};
```

VistaView.cpp

```
//*********************************************************************
//
// VistaView.cpp
//
//*********************************************************************

#include <afxwin.h>
#include "VistaDoc.h"
```

(continued)

VistaView.cpp *continued*

```cpp
#include "VistaView.h"

IMPLEMENT_DYNCREATE (CVistaView, CScrollView)

void CVistaView::OnInitialUpdate ()
{
    CScrollView::OnInitialUpdate ();

    CString string;
    CSize sizeTotal;

    CBitmap* pBitmap = GetDocument ()->GetBitmap ();
    if (pBitmap != NULL) {
        DIBSECTION ds;
        pBitmap->GetObject (sizeof (DIBSECTION), &ds);
        sizeTotal.cx = ds.dsBm.bmWidth;
        sizeTotal.cy = ds.dsBm.bmHeight;
        string.Format ("%d x %d, %d bpp", ds.dsBm.bmWidth,
            ds.dsBm.bmHeight, ds.dsBmih.biBitCount);
    }
    else {
        sizeTotal.cx = sizeTotal.cy = 0;
        string.Empty ();
    }

    AfxGetMainWnd ()->SendMessage (WM_USER, 0,
        (LPARAM) (LPCTSTR) string);
    SetScrollSizes (MM_TEXT, sizeTotal);
}

void CVistaView::OnDraw (CDC* pDC)
{
    CVistaDoc* pDoc = GetDocument ();
    CBitmap* pBitmap = pDoc->GetBitmap ();

    if (pBitmap != NULL) {
        CPalette* pOldPalette;
        CPalette* pPalette = pDoc->GetPalette ();

        if (pPalette != NULL) {
            pOldPalette = pDC->SelectPalette (pPalette, FALSE);
            pDC->RealizePalette ();
        }

        DIBSECTION ds;
        pBitmap->GetObject (sizeof (DIBSECTION), &ds);
```

```
CDC memDC;
memDC.CreateCompatibleDC (pDC);
CBitmap* pOldBitmap = memDC.SelectObject (pBitmap);

pDC->BitBlt (0, 0, ds.dsBm.bmWidth, ds.dsBm.bmHeight, &memDC,
    0, 0, SRCCOPY);

memDC.SelectObject (pOldBitmap);

if (pPalette != NULL)
    pDC->SelectPalette (pPalette, FALSE);
}
}
```

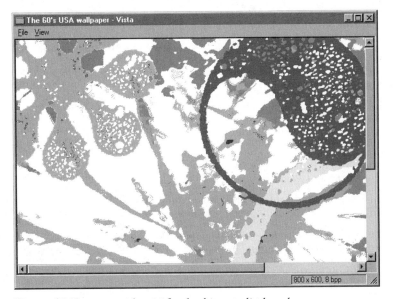

Figure 12-7. *Vista with a 256-color bitmap displayed.*

The view class does the work of displaying bitmaps on the screen by selecting the logical palette associated with the bitmap into the device context (provided such a palette exists) and *BitBlt*ing the bitmap to a *CScrollView*. The view class retrieves the logical palette by calling the document's *GetPalette* function, and it retrieves the bitmap by calling the document's *GetBitmap* function. *GetPalette* returns a *CPalette* pointer to the palette the document object created when the bitmap was loaded. A NULL return means that no palette is associated with the bitmap, which in turn means that Vista is being run on a nonpalettized video adapter. *GetBitmap* returns a pointer to the bitmap that constitutes the document itself. Vista's document class *CVistaDoc* stores the bitmap in a *CBitmap* data member named *m_bitmap* and the palette (if any) that goes with the bitmap in a *CPalette* member named *m_palette*. The bitmap and palette objects are initialized when Open is selected from the File menu and destroyed when the document's *DeleteContents* function is called.

The job of reading a .bmp file from disk and creating a bitmap—actually, a DIB section—from the file's contents is handled by *CVistaDoc::Serialize*. *Serialize* first obtains the file's path name by calling *CFile::GetFilePath* through the pointer returned by *CArchive::GetFile*. Then it passes the path name to the versatile Windows 95 *::Load-Image* function to create a DIB section from the file's contents:

```
CString strFileName = ar.GetFile ()->GetFilePath ();

HBITMAP hBitmap = (HBITMAP) ::LoadImage (AfxGetInstanceHandle (),
    (LPCTSTR) strFileName, IMAGE_BITMAP, 0, 0, LR_LOADFROMFILE |
    LR_CREATEDIBSECTION);
```

The value returned by *::LoadImage* is a valid HBITMAP if a DIB section was success-fully created and NULL if it was not. The most likely cause of failure is that the file didn't contain a valid DIB image. If *::LoadImage* returns NULL, *Serialize* throws a *CArchive* exception with the cause code *CArchiveException::badIndex*, which causes the framework to display an "Unexpected file format" message:

```
if (hBitmap == NULL)
    AfxThrowArchiveException (CArchiveException::badIndex);
```

If the HBITMAP is not NULL, *Serialize* attaches it to *m_bitmap*. The document (bitmap) is now loaded and ready to be displayed—almost.

If Vista is running on a palettized display device, the bitmap isn't going to look very good unless there's a logical palette to go with it. The code to create the palette appears in *CVistaDoc::OnOpenDocument*. After calling the base class version of *OnOpenDocument* to serialize the bitmap, *CVistaDoc::OnOpenDocument* grabs a device context for the frame window and calls *GetDeviceCaps* to determine whether a logical palette is needed. If the return value doesn't contain an RC_PALETTE flag, *OnOpenDocument* returns immediately and leaves *m_palette* uninitialized. Otherwise, *OnOpenDocument* initializes *m_palette* with a logical palette.

To determine how best to create the palette, *OnOpenDocument* first finds out how many colors the bitmap contains by calling *GetObject* with a pointer to a DIBSECTION structure. One of the members of a DIBSECTION structure is a BITMAPINFOHEADER structure, and the BITMAPINFOHEADER structure's *biClrUsed* and *biBitCount* fields reveal the number of colors in the bitmap. If *biClrUsed* is non-zero, it specifies the color count. If *biClrUsed* is 0, then the number of colors equals

```
1 << biBitCount
```

The following code in *OnOpenDocument* sets *nColors* equal to the number of colors in the bitmap:

```
DIBSECTION ds;
m_bitmap.GetObject (sizeof (DIBSECTION), &ds);

int nColors;
if (ds.dsBmih.biClrUsed != 0)
    nColors = ds.dsBmih.biClrUsed;
else
    nColors = 1 << ds.dsBmih.biBitCount;
```

What *OnOpenDocument* does next depends on the value of *nColors*. If *nColors* is greater than 256, indicating that the bitmap has a color depth of 16, 24, or 32 bits (images stored in .bmp files always use 1-, 4-, 8-, 16-, 24-, or 32-bit color), *OnOpenDocument* creates a halftone palette by calling *CPalette::CreateHalftonePalette* with a pointer to the screen DC it obtained earlier:

```
if (nColors > 256)
    m_palette.CreateHalftonePalette (&dc);
```

In return, the system creates a generic palette with a rainbow of colors that's suited to the device context. In most cases, a logical palette created by *CreateHalftonePalette* will contain 256 colors. This won't allow a bitmap that contains thousands or perhaps millions of colors to be displayed with 100 percent accuracy, but it will produce much better results than you'd get if you used the device context's default palette.

If *nColors* is less than or equal to 256, *CVistaDoc::OnOpenDocument* will use *CPalette::CreatePalette* to initialize *m_palette* with a logical palette whose colors match the colors in the bitmap. The key to matching the bitmap's colors is a call to the API function *::GetDIBColorTable*, which copies the color table associated with a 1-, 4-, or 8-bit DIB section to an array of RGBQUAD structures. That array, in turn, is used to initialize an array of PALETTEENTRY structures in preparation for creating a logical palette:

```
RGBQUAD* pRGB = new RGBQUAD[nColors];

CDC memDC;
memDC.CreateCompatibleDC (&dc);
CBitmap* pOldBitmap = memDC.SelectObject (&m_bitmap);
::GetDIBColorTable ((HDC) memDC, 0, nColors, pRGB);
memDC.SelectObject (pOldBitmap);

UINT nSize = sizeof (LOGPALETTE) +
    (sizeof (PALETTEENTRY) * (nColors - 1));
LOGPALETTE* pLP = (LOGPALETTE*) new BYTE[nSize];
```

(continued)

```
pLP->palVersion = 0x300;
pLP->palNumEntries = nColors;

for (int i=0; i<nColors; i++) {
    pLP->palPalEntry[i].peRed = pRGB[i].rgbRed;
    pLP->palPalEntry[i].peGreen = pRGB[i].rgbGreen;
    pLP->palPalEntry[i].peBlue = pRGB[i].rgbBlue;
    pLP->palPalEntry[i].peFlags = 0;
}

m_palette.CreatePalette (pLP);
```

::GetDIBColorTable works only if the DIB section is selected into a device context, so *OnOpenDocument* creates a memory DC and selects *m_bitmap* into it before making the call. The rest is just detail: allocating memory for a LOGPALETTE structure, transferring the RGBQUAD values from the color table to the corresponding PALETTEENTRY entries, and calling *CreatePalette*. Once it has a palette to work with, Vista will display most 256-color bitmaps with stunning accuracy on 256-color screens.

More on the *::LoadImage* Function

One reason Vista can do so much with so little code is that the Windows 95 *::LoadImage* function allows a DIB section to be built from a .bmp file with just one statement. Here's that statement again:

```
HBITMAP hBitmap = (HBITMAP) ::LoadImage (AfxGetInstanceHandle (),
    (LPCTSTR) strFileName, IMAGE_BITMAP, 0, 0, LR_LOADFROMFILE |
    LR_CREATEDIBSECTION);
```

::LoadImage is to DIB sections as *::LoadBitmap* and *CDC::LoadBitmap* are to DDBs. But it's also much more. I won't rehash all the input values it accepts because you can get that from the documentation, but here's a short summary of some of the things you can do with *::LoadImage*:

■ Load bitmap resources and create DDBs and DIB sections from them

■ Load bitmaps stored in .bmp files and create DDBs and DIB sections from them

■ Automatically convert three shades of gray (RGB (128, 128, 128), RGB (192, 192, 192), and RGB (223, 223, 223)) to the system colors COLOR_SHADOW, COLOR_3DFACE, and COLOR_3DLIGHT as an image is loaded

■ Automatically convert the color of the pixel in the upper left corner of the bitmap to the system color COLOR_WINDOW or COLOR_3DFACE so that the pixel and others like it will be invisible against a COLOR_WINDOW or COLOR_3DFACE background

■   Convert a color image to monochrome

Note that *::LoadImage*'s color mapping capabilities work only with images that contain 256 or fewer colors. DIBs with 256 or fewer colors contain built-in color tables that make color mapping fast and efficient. Rather than examine every pixel in the image to perform a color conversion, *::LoadImage* can simply modify the color table.

Vista demonstrates how *::LoadImage* can be used to create a DIB section from a .bmp file and attach it to a *CBitmap* object. One advantage of loading a bitmap as a DIB section instead of as an ordinary DDB is that you can call functions such as *::GetDIBColorTable* on it. Had the LR_CREATEDIBSECTION flag been omitted from the call to *::LoadImage*, we would have been unable to access the bitmap's color table and create a logical palette from it. In general, your applications will port more easily to future versions of Windows (and probably perform better, too) if you start using DIB sections instead of DDBs whenever possible now.

REGIONS

MFC's *CRect* class represents rectangles—simple regions of space enclosed by four boundaries aligned at right angles. More complex regions of space can be represented with the *CRgn* class, which encapsulates GDI objects called, appropriately enough, *regions*. The most common use for regions is to create complex patterns that serve as clipping boundaries for GDI drawing functions. But *CRgn* can be used in other ways, too. Here's a brief look at regions and some interesting things you can do with them.

Regions and the *CRgn* Class

CRgn provides functions for creating geometrically shaped regions, combining existing regions to create more complex regions, and performing operations on regions. The *CDC* class provides the tools for doing something with a region once it's created, such as filling it with a brush pattern or using it as a clipping boundary for other drawing operations. Let's see first how regions are created. Then we'll look at the *CDC* functions that act on regions and finish up by building a sample program that uses regions to generate some rather unusual output.

Creating a Region

After a *CRgn* object is constructed, a region is created and attached to the object by calling any one of several member functions the *CRgn* class provides for region creation. The pertinent *CRgn* functions are summarized in the table on the next page.

CRgn FUNCTIONS FOR CREATING REGIONS

Function	Description
CreateRectRgn	Creates a rectangular region from a set of coordinates.
CreateRectRgnIndirect	Creates a rectangular region from a RECT structure or a CRect object.
CreateEllipticRgn	Creates an elliptical region from a set of coordinates.
CreateEllipticRgnIndirect	Creates an elliptical region from a RECT structure or a CRect object.
CreateRoundRectRgn	Creates a rectangular region with rounded corners.
CreatePolygonRegion	Creates a polygonal region from a set of points.
CreatePolyPolygonRegion	Creates a region composed of multiple polygons from a set of points.
CreateFromPath	Creates a region from the device context's current path.
CreateFromData	Creates a region by applying 2D coordinate transformations to an existing region.
CopyRgn	Creates a region that is a copy of an existing region.

The use of most of these functions is straightforward. For example, to create an elliptical region from a *CRect* object named *rect* that defines a bounding box, you would write

```
CRgn rgn;
rgn.CreateEllipticalRgnIndirect (&rect);
```

To create a rectangular region with rounded corners, you'd do it this way instead:

```
CRgn rgn;
rgn.CreateRoundRectRgn (rect.left, rect.top, rect.right,
    rect.bottom, nCornerWidth, nCornerHeight);
```

The variables *nCornerWidth* and *nCornerHeight* represent the horizontal and vertical dimensions, respectively, of the ellipses used to round the corners. All coordinates passed to functions that create regions are logical coordinates. Like other GDI objects, a region must be deleted when it's no longer needed. Creating a *CRgn* on the stack makes destruction automatic because when a *CRgn* goes out of scope it destroys the GDI region it's attached to.

One of the most powerful region-creation functions is *CRgn::CreateFromPath*, which converts the device context's current path into a region. A *path* is an outline generated by bracketing calls to other GDI drawing functions between calls to *CDC::BeginPath* and *CDC::EndPath*. The following statements generate a simple elliptical path and convert it into a region:

```
dc.BeginPath ();          // Define a path in the device
dc.Ellipse (0, 0, 400, 200);    // context dc
dc.EndPath ();
```

```
CRgn rgn;                          // Convert the path into a region
rgn.CreateFromPath (&dc);
```

There's nothing very remarkable about this code because you could do the same thing by simply calling *CRgn::CreateEllipticRgn*. But what's cool about *CreateFromPath* is that paths can be created from more complex objects such as Bézier curves and text outlines. The following statements create a region from the characters in the text string "Hello, MFC":

```
dc.BeginPath ();
dc.TextOut (0, 0, CString ("Hello, MFC"));
dc.EndPath ();
```

And once created, the path can be converted into a region with *CRgn::CreateFromPath*. *Ellipse* and *TextOut* are but two of several *CDC* drawing functions that work with *BeginPath* and *EndPath*; for a complete list, refer to the MFC documentation for *BeginPath*. (The subset of GDI drawing functions that can be used to generate paths varies slightly between Windows 95 and Windows NT, so watch out.) Paths can also be used in ways unrelated to regions. To learn about the drawing operations you can perform with paths, see the MFC documentation for the *CDC* functions *FillPath*, *StrokePath*, *StrokeAndFillPath*, and *WidenPath*.

Another way to create complex regions is to combine existing regions with *CRgn::CombineRgn*. *CombineRgn* accepts three parameters: *CRgn* pointers to the two regions to be combined (region 1 and region 2) and an integer value specifying the combine mode. The combine mode can be any one of the five values shown below.

Mode	*Description*
RGN_COPY	Sets the region equal to region 1.
RGN_AND	Sets the region equal to the intersection of regions 1 and 2.
RGN_OR	Sets the region equal to the union of regions 1 and 2.
RGN_DIFF	Sets the region equal to the area bounded by region 1 minus the area bounded by region 2.
RGN_XOR	Sets the region equal to the nonoverlapping areas of regions 1 and 2.

What the combine mode amounts to is a value that tells the GDI what Boolean operations to use to combine the regions. The statements

```
CRgn rgn1, rgn2, rgn3;
rgn1.CreateEllipticRgn (0, 0, 100, 100);
rgn2.CreateEllipticRgn (40, 40, 60, 60);
rgn3.CreateRectRgn (0, 0, 1, 1);
rgn3.CombineRgn (&rgn1, &rgn2, RGN_DIFF);
```

create a donut-shaped region consisting of a circle with a hole in the middle. Note that *CombineRgn* can't be called until the region it's called for is created by some other means (that is, until there's an HRGN to go with the *CRgn*). That's why *CreateRectRgn* is called to create a trivial rectangular region for *rgn3* before *CombineRgn* is called.

Using a Region

Just what can you do with a region after it's created? To start with, there are four *CDC* drawing functions that use regions:

- *CDC::FillRgn*, which fills a region using a specified brush

- *CDC::PaintRgn*, which fills a region using the current brush

- *CDC::InvertRgn*, which inverts the colors in a region

- *CDC::FrameRgn*, which borders a region with a specified brush

You can also invalidate a region with *CWnd::InvalidateRgn*. Internally, Windows uses regions rather than rectangles to track the invalid areas of a window. When you call *CDC::GetClipBox*, what you get back is a rectangle that bounds the window's invalid region. That region could be a simple rectangle, or it could be something much more complex.

You can perform hit-testing in regions with *CRgn::PtInRegion*. Let's say you create an elliptical region that's centered in a window's client area. You used *PaintRgn* or *FillRgn* to paint the region a different color from the window background color, and now you want to know when the user clicks the left mouse button inside the ellipse. If *m_rgn* is the *CRgn* object, here's what the *OnLButtonDown* handler might look like:

```
void CMyWindow::OnLButtonDown (UINT nFlags, CPoint point)
{
    CClientDC dc (this);
    dc.DPtoLP (&point); // Convert to logical coordinates
    if (m_rgn.PtInRegion (point))
        // The point falls within the region
}
```

MFC's *CRect* class provides an analogous function for rectangles: *PtInRect*. In fact, there are many parallels in the API (and in MFC member functions) between regions and rectangles: *InvalidateRect* and *InvalidateRgn*, *FillRect* and *FillRgn*, and so on. Rectangle functions are faster, so when possible you should avoid using region functions to operate on simple rectangles and use the equivalent rectangle functions instead.

Using regions really pays when you use them as clipping boundaries for complex graphic images. A region can be selected into a device context with *CDC::SelectObject* or *CDC::SelectClipRgn*. Once selected, the region serves as a clipping boundary for all subsequent output to the device context. The RegionDemo application in the next section uses a clipping region to create an image that would be murderously difficult to draw by other means. (Look ahead at Figure 12-9 on page 836.) But with a region acting as a virtual stencil for graphics output, the image is relatively easy to render. The drawback to complex clipping regions is that they're slow. But sometimes using a clipping region is the only practical way to get the output you're looking for. Note that if you want to use a path as a clipping region you don't have to convert it into a region and then select it into a device context. You can do the same thing in one step by calling *CDC::SelectClipPath* instead.

One of the more imaginative uses for a region is to pass it to the *::SetWindowRgn* API function so that it becomes a *window region*. A window region is a clipping region for an entire window. Windows doesn't allow anything outside the window region to be painted, including title bars and other nonclient-area window elements. Create an elliptical region and pass its handle to *::SetWindowRgn*, and you'll get an elliptical window. If the window is a top-level window and its title bar is hidden from view, use an *OnNcHitTest* handler like the one described in Chapter 3 to convert HTCLIENT hit-test codes into HTCAPTION codes so that the window can be dragged by its client area. A more practical use for nonrectangular window regions is to create stylized text bubbles that are actually windows and that receive messages just as other windows do. With *::SetWindowRgn* to help out, it wouldn't be too difficult to create a popup window class that displays help text in a window shaped like a thought balloon and that automatically destroys itself when it's clicked.

The RegionDemo Application

The RegionDemo application, listed in Figure 12-8, uses a clipping region to draw a radial array of lines forming the words "Hello, MFC." Its output is shown in Figure 12-9 on page 836. The clipping region is generated from a path, and the path, in turn, is generated by calling *CDC::TextOut* between calls to *CDC::BeginPath* and *CDC::EndPath*. All the work is done in *OnPaint*. Look over the source code; it should be pretty apparent what's going on in each phase of the painting operation, with the possible exception of the code that uses two different *CRgn* objects and various calls to *CRgn* member functions to generate the final clipping region (*rgn1*) that is selected into the device context with *CDC::SelectClipRgn*.

RegionDemo.h

```
//*************************************************************************
//
//   RegionDemo.h
//
//*************************************************************************
```

Figure 12-8. *The RegionDemo program.*   *(continued)*

RegionDemo.h *continued*

```
class CMyApp : public CWinApp
{
public:
    virtual BOOL InitInstance ();
};

class CMainWindow : public CFrameWnd
{
public:
    CMainWindow ();

protected:
    afx_msg void OnPaint ();
    DECLARE_MESSAGE_MAP ()
};
```

RegionDemo.cpp

```
//*************************************************************************
//
//  RegionDemo.cpp
//
//*************************************************************************

#include <afxwin.h>
#include <math.h>
#include "RegionDemo.h"

#define FONTHEIGHT 72

CMyApp myApp;

/////////////////////////////////////////////////////////////////////////
// CMyApp member functions

BOOL CMyApp::InitInstance ()
{
    m_pMainWnd = new CMainWindow;
    m_pMainWnd->ShowWindow (m_nCmdShow);
    m_pMainWnd->UpdateWindow ();
    return TRUE;
}
```

```
/////////////////////////////////////////////////////////////////////////
// CMainWindow message map and member functions

BEGIN_MESSAGE_MAP (CMainWindow, CFrameWnd)
    ON_WM_PAINT ()
END_MESSAGE_MAP ()

CMainWindow::CMainWindow ()
{
    Create (NULL, "Region Demo");
}

void CMainWindow::OnPaint ()
{
    CPaintDC dc (this);

    // Create a 72-point Times New Roman font
    CFont font;
    int nHeight = -((dc.GetDeviceCaps (LOGPIXELSY) * FONTHEIGHT) / 72);

    font.CreateFont (nHeight, 0, 0, 0, FW_BOLD, TRUE, 0, 0,
        DEFAULT_CHARSET, OUT_CHARACTER_PRECIS, CLIP_CHARACTER_PRECIS,
        DEFAULT_QUALITY, DEFAULT_PITCH | FF_DONTCARE, "Times New Roman");

    // Create a clipping region from the text string "Hello, MFC"
    CRect rect;
    GetClientRect (&rect);
    CString string ("Hello, MFC");

    CFont* pOldFont = dc.SelectObject (&font);
    CSize size = dc.GetTextExtent (string);
    int x = (rect.Width () - size.cx) / 2;
    int y = (rect.Height () + nHeight) / 2;

    dc.BeginPath ();
    dc.TextOut (x, y, string);
    dc.EndPath ();
    dc.SelectObject (pOldFont);

    CRect rcText;
    CRgn rgn1, rgn2;
    rgn1.CreateFromPath (&dc);
    rgn1.GetRgnBox (&rcText);
    rgn2.CreateRectRgnIndirect (&rcText);
    rgn1.CombineRgn (&rgn2, &rgn1, RGN_DIFF);

    dc.SelectClipRgn (&rgn1);
```

(continued)

RegionDemo.cpp *continued*

```
    // Draw a radial array of lines
    dc.SetViewportOrg (rect.Width () / 2, rect.Height () / 2);
    double fRadius = hypot (rect.Width () / 2, rect.Height () / 2);

    for (double fAngle = 0.0; fAngle < 6.283; fAngle += 0.01745) {
        dc.MoveTo (0, 0);
        dc.LineTo ((int) ((fRadius * cos (fAngle)) + 0.5),
            (int) ((fRadius * sin (fAngle)) + 0.5));
    }
}
```

Figure 12-9. *The output from RegionDemo.*

Here's a blow-by-blow analysis of the code that creates the clipping region after the path outlining the characters in the text string is generated. The statement

```
    rgn1.CreateFromPath (&dc);
```

initializes *rgn1* with a region that matches the path. Figure 12-10 shows what region 1 looks like. The interior of the region is a rectangle with the outline of the letters "Hello, MFC" stamped out in the middle. (Some graphics systems—notably PostScript—handle paths generated from character outlines differently by making the interiors of the regions the interiors of the characters themselves. GDI does essentially the opposite, creating a region from the characters' bounding box and then subtracting the areas enclosed by the character outlines.) Next the statements

```
    rgn1.GetRgnBox (&rcText);
    rgn2.CreateRectRgnIndirect (&rcText);
```

copy *rgn1*'s bounding box to a *CRect* object named *rcText* and create a region (*rgn2*) from it. The final statement effectively inverts *rgn1* by subtracting *rgn1* from *rgn2*:

```
rgn1.CombineRgn (&rgn2, &rgn1, RGN_DIFF);
```

The resulting region is one whose interior exactly matches the insides of the characters drawn by *TextOut*. After the region is selected into the device context, a radial array of lines is drawn outward at 1-degree increments from the center of the window's client area. And because the lines are clipped to the boundaries of the clipping region, nothing is drawn outside the outlines of the characters formed from the text string "Hello, MFC."

Figure 12-10. *The path generated from the text string "Hello, MFC."*

You could make RegionDemo slightly more efficient by moving the code that generates the region out of *OnPaint* and into *OnCreate*. Then the region wouldn't have to be generated anew each time the window was repainted, but it would need to be repositioned with *CRgn::OffsetRgn* each time *OnPaint* was called to keep it aligned in the center of the window. Eliminating redundant calls to *CRgn* functions will improve the speed of RegionDemo's output somewhat, but the biggest speed hit still comes when the lines are drawn on the screen and clipped to the region's boundaries. That complex clipping regions exact a price in performance is a fact of life in computer graphics, so it's wise to avoid using nonrectangular clipping regions except in cases in which there's no reasonable alternative.

Chapter 13

The Common Controls

Since version 1.0, Windows has provided a core set of controls such as push buttons, radio buttons, list boxes, and other common UI objects that developers can use in their applications. Windows 95 expands the selection of controls available with a set of 15 new controls implemented in Comctl32.dll. Collectively known as the *common controls,* these new controls run the gamut from simple progress controls, which provide graphical feedback on the status of ongoing operations, to richer and more complex tree view controls, which present hierarchical views of data in treelike structures whose branches expand and collapse in response to mouse clicks.

Common controls are used throughout Windows 95 and are an important part of the operating system's look and feel. Figure 13-1 on the next page shows some of the common controls as they appear in the Windows 95 user interface. The header control in the Explorer window is a part of the list view control, but header controls can also be created apart from list views. The magnifying glass that moves in a circle while Find performs a search is an animation control. So are the pieces of paper that fly across the screen when groups of files are moved, copied, or deleted. Animation controls make displaying simple animations such as these easy by playing back scenes recorded in Windows Audio Video Interleaved (AVI) format.

In this chapter, we'll look at the common controls and their MFC interfaces. We'll begin with an overview of what the common controls are, how they're created, and the unique way in which they send notifications to their parents. Then we'll look at several of the controls in more detail and write some code to demonstrate their use.

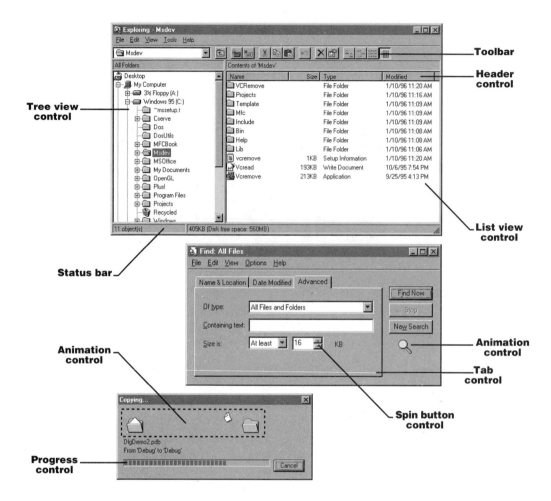

Figure 13-1. *Common controls and the Windows 95 user interface.*

COMMON CONTROL FUNDAMENTALS

MFC provides classes to wrap the common controls just as it provides classes to wrap the core control types implemented in User.exe. The table on the facing page shows the 15 types of common controls, the WNDCLASSes upon which they're based, and the corresponding MFC classes. The table also shows aliases for the WNDCLASSes defined in the header file Commctrl.h. Image lists and property sheets don't have WNDCLASSes because they're not controls in the strict sense of the word, but they're nearly always counted among the common controls because their code resides in Comctl32.dll. You'll sometimes see drag list boxes shown with the common controls. I didn't include them here because drag list boxes aren't stand-alone controls; they're conventional list boxes that are converted into "drag" list boxes by calling a function in Comctl32.dll. MFC provides a convenient implementation of drag list boxes in *CDragListBox*, so for more information, see the documentation for *CDragListBox*.

THE COMMON CONTROLS

Control	*WNDCLASS*	*WNDCLASS Alias*	*MFC Class*
Animation	"SysAnimate32"	ANIMATE_CLASS	*CAnimateCtrl*
Header	"SysHeader32"	WC_HEADER	*CHeaderCtrl*
Hotkey	"msctls_hotkey32"	HOTKEY_CLASS	*CHotKeyCtrl*
Image list	N/A	N/A	*CImageList*
List view	"SysListView32"	WC_LISTVIEW	*CListCtrl*
Progress	"msctls_progress32"	PROGRESS_CLASS	*CProgressCtrl*
Property sheet	N/A	N/A	*CPropertySheet*
Rich edit	"RICHEDIT"	N/A	*CRichEditCtrl*
Slider	"msctls_trackbar32"	TRACKBAR_CLASS	*CSliderCtrl*
Spin button	"msctls_updown32"	UPDOWN_CLASS	*CSpinButtonCtrl*
Status bar	"msctls_statusbar32"	STATUSCLASSNAME	*CStatusBarCtrl*
Tab	"SysTabControl32"	WC_TABCONTROL	*CTabCtrl*
Toolbar	"ToolbarWindow32"	TOOLBARCLASSNAME	*CToolBarCtrl*
Tooltip	"tooltips_class32"	TOOLTIPS_CLASS	*CToolTipCtrl*
Tree view	"SysTreeView32"	WC_TREEVIEW	*CTreeCtrl*

Creating a Common Control

There are two ways to create a common control without resorting to API functions. You can instantiate the corresponding MFC control class and call the resulting object's *Create* function, or you can add a CONTROL statement to a dialog template and then create a dialog. The following statements create a progress control using the first of the two methods:

```
#include <afxcmn.h>
    .
    .
    .
CProgressCtrl ctlProgress;
ctlProgress.Create (WS_CHILD | WS_VISIBLE | WS_BORDER,
    CRect (x1, y1, x2, y2), this, IDC_PROGRESS);
```

The header file Afxcmn.h contains the declarations for *CProgressCtrl* and other common control classes.

The next statement adds a progress control to a dialog template. When you create a common control this way, you can specify either the literal WNDCLASS name or its alias, whichever you prefer:

```
CONTROL "", IDC_PROGRESS, PROGRESS_CLASS, WS_BORDER, 32, 32, 80, 16
```

The Visual C++ dialog editor writes CONTROL statements for you when you use it to add common controls to a dialog box.

Most of the common controls support their own window styles, which you can combine with WS_CHILD, WS_VISIBLE, and other standard window styles. The table below shows the "generic" common control styles that, at least in theory, aren't specific to any particular control type. CCS_ADJUSTABLE and CCS_NODIVIDER apply only to toolbar controls, although they could conceivably be extended to other control types one day. The other styles can be applied to toolbars, status bars, and header controls. These are by no means all the styles you can use with common controls. We'll take up control-specific styles when we look at individual control types.

COMMON CONTROL STYLES

Style	Description
CCS_TOP	Positions the control at the top of its parent's client area and matches the control's width to the width of its parent. Toolbars have this style by default.
CCS_BOTTOM	Positions the control at the bottom of its parent's client area and matches the control's width to the width of its parent. Status bars have this style by default.
CCS_NORESIZE	Prevents the control from resizing itself when the size of its parent changes. If this style is specified, the control assumes the width and height specified in the control rectangle.
CCS_NOMOVEY	Causes the control to resize and move itself horizontally but not vertically when its parent is resized. Header controls have this style by default.
CCS_NOPARENTALIGN	Prevents the control from sticking to the top or bottom of its parent's client area. A control with this style retains its position relative to the upper left corner of its parent's client area. If this style is combined with CCS_TOP or CCS_BOTTOM, the control assumes a default height but its width and position don't change when its parent is resized.
CCS_NODIVIDER	Eliminates the divider drawn at the top of a toolbar control.
CCS_ADJUSTABLE	Enables a toolbar control's built-in customization features. Double-clicking a toolbar of this type displays a Customize Toolbar dialog. Toolbar buttons can be deleted and rearranged using drag and drop.

Toolbars, status bars, and header controls don't take full responsibility for sizing and positioning themselves as the preceding descriptions might lead you to believe. The parent of a toolbar or status bar must forward WM_SIZE messages to the control if the control is to maintain its alignment at the top or bottom of its parent's client area. The parent of a header control must manually size and position the control when its own size changes. *CHeaderCtrl* provides a *Layout* function the parent can call to compute the header's size and position, but the fact remains that CCS_TOP, CCS_BOTTOM, and other alignment styles do nothing unless the parent does its part, too. If you create a toolbar or status bar from *CToolBar* or *CStatusBar* instead of *CToolBarCtrl* or *CStatusBarCtrl*, you don't have to worry about alignment styles and WM_SIZE messages because the class library handles them for you.

Once a common control is created, you manipulate it using member functions of the corresponding control class. For controls created from dialog templates, you can use any of the techniques discussed in Chapter 5 to manufacture type-specific pointers for accessing a control's function and data members. The following statement creates a *CProgressCtrl* pointer that references a progress control created from a dialog template:

```
CProgressCtrl* pProgress =
    (CProgressCtrl*) GetDlgItem (IDC_PROGRESS);
```

CProgressCtrl functions called through *pProgress* will act on the progress control whose control ID is IDC_PROGRESS.

When you program the common controls in an SDK-style application, it's up to you to call an API function named *::InitCommonControls* to load Comctl32.dll and register the controls' WNDCLASSes. In an MFC application, the framework calls *::InitCommonControls* for you. It's called automatically each time a dialog box is created and when a common control's *Create* function is called. If for some reason you decide to create a common control or a dialog that contains a common control using an API function instead of an MFC function (or if you create a common control with *CreateEx* instead of *Create*), call *::InitCommonControls* first. A good place to do this is in the main window's constructor or *OnCreate* handler, although you can defer the call until just before the control or dialog is created if you'd prefer. It's not harmful to call *::InitCommonControls* multiple times during an application's lifetime, but the control or dialog creation process will fail if *::InitCommonControls* has not been called.

Processing Notifications: The WM_NOTIFY Message

Unlike the controls introduced in Chapter 5, which send notifications to their parents using WM_COMMAND messages, most common controls package their notifications in WM_NOTIFY messages. A WM_NOTIFY message's *wParam* holds the child window ID of the control that sent the message, and *lParam* holds a pointer to either an

NMHDR structure or a structure that's a superset of NMHDR. NMHDR is defined as follows:

```
typedef struct tagNMHDR {
    HWND hwndFrom;
    UINT idFrom;
    UINT code;
} NMHDR;
```

hwndFrom holds the control's window handle, *idFrom* holds the control ID (the same value that's passed in *wParam*), and *code* specifies the notification code. The following notifications are not specific to any particular control type:

Notification	Sent When
NM_CLICK	The control is clicked with the left mouse button.
NM_DBLCLICK	The control is double-clicked with the left mouse button.
NM_RCLICK	The control is clicked with the right mouse button.
NM_RDBLCLICK	The control is double-clicked with the right mouse button.
NM_RETURN	The Enter key is pressed while the control has the input focus.
NM_KILLFOCUS	The control loses the input focus.
NM_SETFOCUS	The control gains the input focus.
NM_OUTOFMEMORY	An operation on the control has failed due to insufficient memory.

Many common controls define additional notification codes to signify control-specific events. For example, a tree view control notifies its parent when a subtree is expanded by sending it a WM_NOTIFY message with *code* equal to TVN_ITEMEX-PANDED. *lParam* points to an NM_TREEVIEW structure, which contains the following data members:

```
typedef struct _NM_TREEVIEW {
    NMHDR     hdr;
    UINT      action;
    TV_ITEM   itemOld;
    TV_ITEM   itemNew;
    POINT     ptDrag;
} NM_TREEVIEW;
```

Note that the structure's first member is an NMHDR structure, making NM_TREEVIEW a functional superset of NMHDR. The type of structure *lParam* points to depends on the type of control the notification came from. It sometimes even depends on the notification code. For instance, the *lParam* accompanying a TVN_GETDISPINFO notification from a tree view control points to a TV_DISPINFO structure, which is defined differently than NM_TREEVIEW is:

```
typedef struct _TV_DISPINFO {
    NMHDR   hdr;
    TV_ITEM item;
} TV_DISPINFO;
```

How do you know what kind of pointer to cast *lParam* to? You start by casting to an NMHDR pointer and examining the notification code. Then, if necessary, you can recast to a more specific pointer type, as demonstrated here:

```
NMHDR* pnmh = (NMHDR*) lParam;
switch (pnmh->code) {

case TVN_ITEMEXPANDED:
    NM_TREEVIEW* pnmtv = (NM_TREEVIEW*) pnmh;
    // Process the notification
    break;

case TVN_GETDISPINFO:
    NM_DISPINFO* pnmdi = (NM_DISPINFO*) pnmh;
    // Process the notification
    break;
}
```

If the window that processes these notifications contains two or more tree view controls, it can examine the *hwndFrom* or *idFrom* field of the NMHDR structure to determine which control sent the notification.

switch statements like the one above are usually unnecessary in MFC applications because notifications encapsulated in WM_NOTIFY messages are mapped to class member functions with ON_NOTIFY and ON_NOTIFY_RANGE message map macros. In addition, WM_NOTIFY notifications can be reflected to derived control classes by means of ON_NOTIFY_REFLECT. (MFC also supports extended forms of these macros named ON_NOTIFY_EX, ON_NOTIFY_EX_RANGE, and ON_NOTIFY_RE-FLECT_EX.) The following message map entries map TVN_ITEMEXPANDED and TVN_GETDISPINFO notifications from a tree view control whose ID is IDC_TREEVIEW to a pair of handling functions named *OnItemExpanded* and *OnGetDispInfo*:

```
ON_NOTIFY (TVN_ITEMEXPANDED, IDC_TREEVIEW, OnItemExpanded)
ON_NOTIFY (TVN_GETDISPINFO, IDC_TREEVIEW, OnGetDispInfo)
```

Casting to specific pointer types is performed inside the notification handlers:

```
void OnItemExpanded (NMHDR* pnmh, LRESULT* pResult)
{
    NM_TREEVIEW* pnmtv = (NM_TREEVIEW*) pnmh;
    // Process the notification
}

void OnGetDispInfo (NMHDR* pnmh, LRESULT* pResult)
```

(continued)

845

```
    {
        NM_DISPINFO* pnmdi = (NM_DISPINFO*) pnmh;
        // Process the notification
    }
```

The *pnmh* parameter passed to an ON_NOTIFY handler is identical to the WM-_NOTIFY message's *lParam*. The *pResult* parameter points to a 32-bit LRESULT variable that receives the handler's return value. Many notifications attach no meaning to the return value, in which case the handler can safely ignore *pResult*. But often what happens after the handler returns depends on the value of *pResult*. For example, you can prevent branches of a tree view control from being expanded by processing TVN_ITEMEXPANDING notifications and setting *pResult* to a nonzero value. A 0 return value, on the other hand, allows the expansion to occur:

```
// In the message map
ON_NOTIFY (TVN_ITEMEXPANDING, IDC_TREEVIEW, OnItemExpanding)
     .
     .
     .
void OnItemExpanding (NMHDR* pnmh, LRESULT* pResult)
{
    NM_TREEVIEW* pnmtv = (NM_TREEVIEW*) pnmh;
    if (...) {
        *pResult = TRUE; // Under certain conditions, prevent
        return;          // the expansion from taking place
    }
    *pResult = FALSE;    // Allow the expansion to proceed
}
```

A TVN_ITEMEXPANDING notification differs from a TVN_ITEMEXPANDED notification in that it is sent *before* an item in a tree view control is expanded, not after. As with the standard control types, you can ignore notifications you're not interested in and process only those that are meaningful to your application. Windows provides appropriate default responses for unhandled messages.

SLIDER, SPIN BUTTON, AND TOOLTIP CONTROLS

Now that you're familiar with the general characteristics of the common controls, let's look at specifics for a few of the control types. We'll start with sliders, spin buttons, and tooltip controls, which are all relatively simple to program and which are also generic enough that they can be put to use in a variety of applications. After we've looked at these controls and the corresponding MFC control classes, we'll write a sample program that creates a slider and a pair of spin buttons in a dialog box and uses a tooltip control to provide context-sensitive help. We'll also use *CToolTipCtrl* as a base class for a class of our own in which we'll add a pair of handy member functions that correct a rather severe deficiency in MFC's default implementation.

Slider Controls

Slider controls, also known as *trackbar controls,* are similar to the sliding volume controls found on many radios and stereo systems. A slider on the screen has a thumb that moves like the thumb in a scroll bar. After you create a slider, you set the minimum and maximum values representing the extremes of the thumb's travel and optionally set the initial thumb position. The user can then reposition the thumb by dragging it with the left mouse button or clicking the channel in which the thumb slides. When a slider has the input focus, its thumb can also be moved with the arrow keys, the Page Up and Page Down keys, and the Home and End keys. A simple function call returns an integer representing the thumb position. If you'd like to, you can respond to positional changes as the thumb is moved by processing control notifications. Figure 13-2 shows what a simple slider control looks like. Tick marks denote the positions the thumb can assume.

Figure 13-2. *A horizontal slider with tick marks denoting thumb stops.*

MFC represents sliders with the *CSliderCtrl* class. The table below shows slider-specific control styles. A slider can be oriented horizontally or vertically. The default orientation, if neither TBS_HORZ nor TBS_VERT is specified, is horizontal. The TBS-_AUTOTICKS style marks thumb stops with tick marks. If the slider's range is 0 through

SLIDER CONTROL STYLES

Style	Description
TBS_HORZ	Orients the slider horizontally.
TBS_VERT	Orients the slider vertically.
TBS_LEFT	Draws tick marks to the left of a vertical slider.
TBS_RIGHT	Draws tick marks to the right of a vertical slider.
TBS_TOP	Draws tick marks above a vertical slider.
TBS_BOTTOM	Draws tick marks below a vertical slider.
TBS_BOTH	Draws tick marks both above and below a horizontal slider or to the left and the right of a vertical slider.
TBS_NOTICKS	Removes tick marks from the slider.
TBS_AUTOTICKS	Positions a tick mark at each stop in the slider's range.
TBS_NOTHUMB	Removes the thumb from the slider.
TBS_ENABLESELRANGE	Widens the slider's channel so that a selection range can be displayed.

8, TBS_AUTOTICKS creates nine tick marks—one at each end of the slider and seven in between. TBS_NOTICKS removes the tick marks altogether, and TBS_NOTHUMB creates a slider that has no thumb. If you specify neither TBS_AUTOTICKS nor TBS-_NOTICKS, the slider will have a tick mark at each end but none in between. By default, tick marks are drawn below a horizontal slider and to the right of a vertical slider. You can move the tick marks to the top or the left by specifying TBS_TOP or TBS_LEFT, or you can use TBS_BOTH to create a slider that has tick marks both above and below or to its right and left.

A slider's range and thumb position are set with *CSliderCtrl::SetRange* and *CSliderCtrl::SetPos*. The related *CSliderCtrl::GetRange* and *CSliderCtrl::GetPos* functions retrieve range and position information. If *pSlider* is a pointer to a *CSliderCtrl*, the statements

```
pSlider->SetRange (0, 8);
pSlider->SetPos (2);
```

set the slider's range to 0 through 8 and its thumb's position to 2. By default, the thumb can come to rest at any incremental position in the slider's range—0, 1, 2, and so on. However, you can use *CSliderCtrl::SetLineSize* to impose a coarser granularity on thumb travel. The statements

```
pSlider->SetRange (0, 8);
pSlider->SetLineSize (2);
```

position the thumb stops two units apart instead of one. If the slider is of the TBS-_AUTOTICKS variety, tick marks will still be drawn one unit apart. You can adjust the distance between tick marks with *CSliderCtrl::SetTicFreq*:

```
pSlider->SetRange (0, 8);
pSlider->SetLineSize (2);
pSlider->SetTicFreq (2);
```

In this example, tick marks are drawn two units apart to match the thumb stop intervals.

SetTicFreq is meaningful only when it's used with the TBS_AUTOTICKS style. To create a slider with tick marks at irregular intervals, omit the TBS_AUTOTICKS style and use *CSliderCtrl::SetTic* to put tick marks where you want them. The statements

```
pSlider->SetRange (0, 8);
pSlider->SetTic (2);
pSlider->SetTic (3);
pSlider->SetTic (6);
pSlider->SetPos (2);
```

place tick marks at 2, 3, and 6 in addition to the ones drawn at 0 and 8. Note that there is no physical correlation between thumb stops and tick marks. You can put tick marks wherever you want them, but thumb stops are still governed by the slider's range and line size.

The TBS_ENABLESELRANGE style creates a slider with a wide channel for displaying a selection range. The selection range is set with *CSliderCtrl::SetSelection* and is represented by a bar drawn in the system color COLOR_HIGHLIGHT. The statements

```
pSlider->SetRange (0, 8);
pSlider->SetSelection (43, 7);
```

set the range to 0 through 8 and the selection to 3 through 7, producing the slider seen in Figure 13-3. Setting a selection does not limit the thumb's travel; the thumb can still be positioned anywhere in the slider range. If you'd like to limit the thumb's travel to the selection range or allow the user to alter the selection, you must implement a custom slider control UI. The most practical approach to customizing the UI is to derive a class from *CSliderCtrl* and add message handlers that change the way the control responds to presses of the Home, End, Page Up, Page Down, and arrow keys, and clicks of the left mouse button. To perform default processing on selected messages, simply pass those messages to the base class.

Figure 13-3. *A slider with a selection range.*

As its thumb is moved, a slider sends its parent WM_HSCROLL or WM_VSCROLL messages just as a scroll bar does when its thumb is moved. An *OnHScroll* or *OnVScroll* handler for a slider receives three parameters: a notification code, an integer specifying the latest thumb position, and a *CScrollBar* pointer that can be cast to a *CSliderCtrl* pointer. The table on the next page shows the nine possible notification codes and the actions that generate them. The thumb position passed to *OnHScroll* or *OnVScroll* is valid only when the notification code is TB_THUMBPOSITION or TB_THUMB-TRACK. Use *CSliderCtrl::GetPos* to retrieve the thumb position in response to other types of notifications.

One use for slider notifications is for dynamically updating an image on the screen in response to positional changes. The Settings page of the Windows 95 Display Properties property sheet, which is displayed when you right-click the desktop and select Properties from the ensuing context menu, processes TB_THUMBTRACK notifications from the slider in the "Desktop area" box and redraws an image of the computer screen each time the thumb moves, to preview the effect the new setting will have on the desktop.

CSliderCtl provides more than two dozen functions you can use to operate on slider controls. Other useful member functions include *SetPageSize*, which sets the number of units the thumb moves when the channel is clicked with the mouse or when Page Up or Page Down is pressed; *GetTic*, *GetTicPos*, *GetTicArray*, and *Get-NumTicks*, which return information about tick marks; and *ClearSel*, which removes a selection range. See the MFC documentation for information regarding these and other *CSliderCtrl* function members.

SLIDER NOTIFICATION CODES

Notification	*Sent When*
TB_TOP	The Home key is pressed while the slider has the input focus.
TB_BOTTOM	The End key is pressed while the slider has the input focus.
TB_LINEDOWN	The down or right arrow key is pressed while the slider has the input focus.
TB_LINEUP	The up or left arrow key is pressed while the slider has the input focus.
TB_PAGEDOWN	The Page Down key is pressed while the slider has the input focus, or the channel is clicked right of the thumb in a horizontal slider or below the thumb in a vertical slider.
TB_PAGEUP	The Page Up key is pressed while the slider has the input focus, or the channel is clicked left of the thumb in a horizontal slider or above the thumb in a vertical slider.
TB_THUMBTRACK	The thumb is dragged to a new position with the mouse.
TB_THUMBPOSITION	The left mouse button is released after the thumb is dragged.
TB_ENDTRACK	The key or mouse button used to move the thumb to a new position is released.

Spin Button Controls

Spin button controls, which are also known as *up-down controls,* are small windows containing arrows that point up and down or left and right. Like scroll bars and sliders, spin buttons maintain their own ranges and positions. Clicking the up- or right-arrow increments the current position, and clicking the down- or left-arrow decrements it. Spin button controls send their parents notification messages before and after each positional change, but often those notifications are ignored because spin buttons are capable of doing some extraordinarily useful things on their own.

You can choose from the styles shown in the table on the facing page when you're creating a spin button control. UDS_SETBUDDYINT creates a spin button control that automatically updates an integer value displayed in a "buddy" control, which is typically an edit control or a static text control. When a UDS_SETBUDDYINT-style spin button control undergoes a positional change, it converts the integer describing the new position into a text string (think *_itoa*) and uses *::SetWindowText* to display the string in its buddy. UDS_SETBUDDYINT makes it trivial to add a set of arrows to an edit control so that the user can enter a number by either typing it at the keyboard or dialing it in with the mouse.

SPIN BUTTON CONTROL STYLES

Style	Description
UDS_HORZ	Orients the arrows horizontally rather than vertically.
UDS_WRAP	Causes the position to wrap around if it's decremented or incremented beyond the minimum or maximum.
UDS_ARROWKEYS	Adds a keyboard interface. If a spin button control with this style has the input focus, the up and down arrow keys increment and decrement its position.
UDS_NOTHOUSANDS	Removes thousands separators so that 1,234,567 is displayed as 1234567.
UDS_SETBUDDYINT	Creates a spin button control that updates the text of a designated "buddy" control when the position is incremented or decremented.
UDS_AUTOBUDDY	Selects the previous control in the z-order as the spin button's buddy.
UDS_ALIGNRIGHT	Attaches the spin button control to the right inside border of its buddy.
UDS_ALIGNLEFT	Attaches the spin button control to the left inside border of its buddy.

There are two ways to connect a spin button control to its buddy. You can explicitly link the two by calling *CSpinButton::SetBuddy* with a *CWnd* pointer identifying the buddy control. Or you can specify UDS_AUTOBUDDY when creating the spin button control, which automatically selects the previous control in the z-order as the spin button's buddy. In a dialog template, the statements

```
EDITTEXT    IDC_EDIT, 60, 80, 40, 14, ES_AUTOHSCROLL
CONTROL     "", IDC_SPIN, "MSCTLS_UPDOWN32", UDS_SETBUDDYINT |
            UDS_AUTOBUDDY | UDS_ALIGNRIGHT, 0, 0, 0, 0
```

create a single-line edit control and attach a spin button control to its right inside border, as shown in Figure 13-4 on the next page. The edit control is shrunk by the width of the spin button control, and the spin button's height is adjusted to match the height of its buddy. Consequently, the edit control and the spin button control together occupy the same amount of space as the original edit control. Information regarding a spin button control's size and position is ignored when UDS_ALIGNLEFT or UDS-_ALIGNRIGHT is specified.

Figure 13-4. *A spin button control attached to an edit control.*

By default, a UDS_SETBUDDYINT spin button control displays numbers in decimal format and inserts a thousands separator every third digit. You can configure the control to display hexadecimal numbers instead with *CSpinButtonCtrl::SetBase*:

```
pSpinButton->SetBase (16);
```

Hex numbers are preceded by 0x characters so that it's obvious they're hexadecimal. Calling *SetBase* with a 10 switches output back to decimal format. You can remove separators from decimal numbers by specifying UDS_NOTHOUSANDS when you create the control; thousands separators are omitted from hex numbers by default.

A spin button control's range and position are set with *CSpinButtonCtrl::SetRange* and *CSpinButtonCtrl::SetPos*. Valid minimums and maximums range from −32,767 through 32,767, but the difference between the low and high ends of the range can't exceed 32,767. It's legal to specify a maximum that's less than the minimum. When you do, the actions of the arrows are reversed.

Each discrete click of an arrow in a spin button control (or press of an arrow key if the control's style includes UDS_ARROWKEYS) increments or decrements the position by 1. If you press and hold a button, the increments change to ±5 after two seconds and ±20 after five seconds. You can alter the number of seconds that elapse before the incremental value changes and also control the magnitude of the changes with *CSpinButtonCtrl::SetAccel*. *SetAccel* accepts two parameters: a pointer to an array of UDACCEL structures and the number of structures in the array. The following statements configure a spin button control to increment or decrement the position by 1 for the first two seconds, 2 for the next two seconds, 10 for the next two seconds, and 100 for the remainder of the time a button is held down:

```
UDACCEL uda[4];
uda[0].nSec = 0;
uda[0].nInc = 1;
uda[1].nSec = 2;
uda[1].nInc = 2;
uda[2].nSec = 4;
uda[2].nInc = 10;
uda[3].nSec = 8;
uda[3].nInc = 100;
pSpinButton->SetAccel (4, uda);
```

Another use for *SetAccel* is to specify incremental values other than 1. If you'd like each button click to increment or decrement the position by 5, call *SetAccel* like this:

```
UDACCEL uda;
uda.nSec = 0;
```

```
uda.nInc = 5;
pSpinButton->SetAccel (1, &uda);
```

You can retrieve accelerator values by passing the address of an array of UDACCEL structures to *CSpinButton::GetAccel*. But there's a trick: How do you know how many structures to allocate space for? This fact doesn't appear to be documented anywhere, but calling *GetAccel* as shown below returns the number of UDACCEL structures in the accelerator array:

```
UINT nCount = pSpinButton->GetAccel (0, NULL);
```

Once the count is known, you can allocate a buffer for the array and retrieve it like this:

```
UDACCEL* puda = new UDACCEL[nCount];
pSpinButton->GetAccel (nCount, puda);
// Do something with the array
delete[] puda;
```

See? Nothing to it when you know the secret.

Before its position is incremented or decremented, a spin button control sends its parent a WM_NOTIFY message with a notification code equal to UDN_DELTAPOS and an *lParam* pointing to an NM_UPDOWN structure. Inside the structure are integers specifying the current position (*iPos*) and the amount by which the position is about to change (*iDelta*). A UDN_DELTAPOS handler can set *pResult* to FALSE to allow the change to occur or TRUE to prevent it from occurring. UDN_DELTAPOS notifications are followed by WM_HSCROLL or WM_VSCROLL messages (depending on whether the spin button is oriented horizontally or vertically) reporting the new position. Clicking the down-arrow when the control's current position is 8 produces the sequence of messages shown in the table below:

Message	*Notification Code*	*Parameters*
WM_NOTIFY	UDN_DELTAPOS	*iPos*=8, *iDelta*=−1
WM_VSCROLL	SB_THUMBPOSITION	*nPos*=7
WM_VSCROLL	SB_ENDTRACK	*nPos*=7

If the button is held down for more than a half second or so, several UDN_DELTAPOS and SB_THUMBPOSITION notifications will be sent in sequence.

Tooltip Controls

A tooltip is a miniature help-text window that appears when the cursor pauses over a "tool" such as a button on a toolbar or a control in a dialog. A tooltip control is a control that monitors mouse movements and automatically displays a tooltip for you when the cursor remains motionless over a tool for a predetermined period of time. MFC provides a convenient C++ interface to Windows 95 tooltip controls through the *CToolTipCtrl* class. With *CToolTipCtrl* to help out, it's relatively easy to add tooltips to controls in dialog boxes and implement other forms of interactive "cursor help." You simply create a tooltip control and register the tools you'd like to have tooltips displayed for and the text to go with them. Then the control does the rest.

CToolTipCtrl::Create creates a tooltip control. (Tooltip controls can also be created from dialog templates, but the more common approach is to add a *CToolTipCtrl* data member to the dialog class and call *Create* from *OnInitDialog* instead.) If *m_ctlTT* is a *CToolTipCtrl* data member of a window class, the statement

```
m_ctlTT.Create (this);
```

creates a tooltip control. *CToolTipCtrl::Create* accepts an optional second parameter specifying the control's style. The only two styles supported are TTS_ALWAYSTIP and TTS_NOPREFIX. By default, tooltips appear over only active windows. A TTS_ALWAYSTIP-style tooltip control displays tooltips over both active and inactive windows. TTS_NOPREFIX tells the control not to strip ampersands from tooltip text. The default behavior is to ignore ampersands so that you can use the same text strings for menus and tooltips.

After a tooltip control is created, the next step is to add tools to it. A tool is either another window—usually a child window control that belongs to the tooltip control's parent—or a rectangular area of a window. *CToolTipCtrl::AddTool* registers a tool and the tooltip text that goes with it. One tooltip control can have any number of tools associated with it. The statement

```
m_ctlTT.AddTool (pWnd, "This is a window", NULL, 0);
```

assigns the tooltip text "This is a window" to the window identified by *pWnd*. The second parameter passed to *AddTool* can be a pointer to a text string or the ID of a string resource, whichever you prefer. Similarly, the statement

```
m_ctlTT.AddTool (pWnd, "This is a rectangle",
    CRect (32, 32, 64, 64), IDT_RECTANGLE);
```

creates a tool from the specified rectangle in *pWnd*'s client area. IDT_RECTANGLE is a nonzero integer that identifies the rectangle and is analogous to a child window ID identifying a control.

So far, so good. There's just one problem. A tooltip control has to be able to see the mouse messages a tool receives so that it can monitor mouse events and know when to display a tooltip, but Windows sends mouse messages to the window underneath the cursor. In the examples above, it's still up to our application to forward mouse messages going to *pWnd* to the tooltip control. If *pWnd* corresponds to a top-level window or a dialog box, forwarding mouse messages is no big deal because we can map the relevant mouse messages to handlers in the window or dialog class and relay them to the tooltip control with *CToolTipCtrl::RelayEvent*. But if *pWnd* points to a child window control or any window other than our own, we have to resort to window subclassing or other devices in order to see mouse messages going to the window and relay them to the tooltip control. Late in the beta cycle, the Windows 95 designers recognized this problem and added some intelligence to tooltip controls so that the designers could do their own subclassing. Unfortunately, this feature was added too late to be incorporated into *CToolTipCtrl*. So to make tooltips truly easy to use, we must customize the *CToolTipCtrl* class by adding some smarts of our own.

Whenever I use a tooltip control in an MFC application, I first derive a class from *CToolTipCtrl* named *CMyToolTipCtrl* and add a pair of member functions that take advantage of the fact that a tooltip control can do its own subclassing. Here's what the derived class looks like:

```
class CMyToolTipCtrl : public CToolTipCtrl
{
public:
    BOOL AddWindowTool (CWnd*, LPCTSTR);
    BOOL AddRectTool (CWnd*, LPCTSTR, LPCRECT, UINT);
};

BOOL CMyToolTipCtrl::AddWindowTool (CWnd* pWnd, LPCTSTR pszText)
{
    TOOLINFO ti;
    ti.cbSize = sizeof (TOOLINFO);
    ti.uFlags = TTF_IDISHWND | TTF_SUBCLASS;
    ti.hwnd = pWnd->GetParent ()->GetSafeHwnd ();
    ti.uId = (UINT) pWnd->GetSafeHwnd ();
    ti.hinst = AfxGetInstanceHandle ();
    ti.lpszText = (LPTSTR) pszText;

    return (BOOL) SendMessage (TTM_ADDTOOL, 0, (LPARAM) &ti);
}

BOOL CMyToolTipCtrl::AddRectTool (CWnd* pWnd, LPCTSTR pszText,
    LPCRECT lpRect, UINT nIDTool)
{
    TOOLINFO ti;
    ti.cbSize = sizeof (TOOLINFO);
    ti.uFlags = TTF_SUBCLASS;
    ti.hwnd = pWnd->GetSafeHwnd ();
    ti.uId = nIDTool;
    ti.hinst = AfxGetInstanceHandle ();
    ti.lpszText = (LPTSTR) pszText;
    ::CopyRect (&ti.rect, lpRect);

    return (BOOL) SendMessage (TTM_ADDTOOL, 0, (LPARAM) &ti);
}
```

With this infrastructure in place, creating a tool from a child window control—subclassing and all—requires just one simple statement:

```
m_ctlTT.AddWindowTool (pWnd, "This is a window");
```

Creating a tool from a rectangle in a window is equally simple:

```
m_ctlTT.AddRectTool (pWnd, "This is a rectangle",
    CRect (32, 32, 64, 64), IDT_RECTANGLE);
```

The *pWnd* parameter passed to *AddWindowTool* identifies the window the tooltip will be applied to. The *pWnd* parameter passed to *AddRectTool* references the window whose client area contains the rectangle referenced in the third parameter. Because of the TTF_SUBCLASS flag passed in the *uFlags* field of the TOOLINFO structure, the tooltip control will do its own window subclassing and mouse messages don't have to be relayed manually.

When you call *AddTool*, *AddWindowTool*, or *AddRectTool*, you can specify LPSTR_TEXTCALLBACK for the LPCTSTR parameter specifying the tooltip text, and the tooltip control will send a notification to its parent asking for a text string before it displays a tooltip. You can use LPSTR_TEXTCALLBACK to create dynamic tooltips whose text varies from one invocation to the next. Text callbacks come in the form of WM_NOTIFY messages with a notification code equal to TTN_NEEDTEXT and *lParam* pointing to a structure of type TOOLTIPTEXT. TOOLTIPTEXT is defined as follows:

```
typedef struct {
    NMHDR     hdr;
    LPTSTR    lpszText;
    char      szText[80];
    HINSTANCE hinst;
    UINT      uFlags;
} TOOLTIPTEXT;
```

A tooltip control's parent responds to TTN_NEEDTEXT notifications in one of three ways: by copying the address of a text string to the TOOLTIPTEXT structure's *lpszText* field; by copying the text (as many as 80 characters, including the zero terminator) directly to the structure's *szText* field; or by copying a string resource ID to *lpszText* and copying the application's instance handle, which an MFC application can obtain with *AfxGetInstanceHandle*, to *hinst*. The *idFrom* field of the NMHDR structure that's nested inside the TOOLTIPTEXT structure contains either a window handle or an application-defined tool ID identifying the tool for which text is needed.

The following code fragment supplies tooltip text on the fly for a rectangle in a dialog box. The rectangle's application-defined tool ID is IDT_RECTANGLE, and the text displayed in the tooltip window is the current time:

```
// In the message map
ON_NOTIFY (TTN_NEEDTEXT, NULL, OnNeedText)
    .
    .
    .

BOOL CMyDialog::OnInitDialog ()
{
    m_ctlTT.Create (this);
    m_ctlTT.AddRectTool (this, LPSTR_TEXTCALLBACK,
        CRect (0, 0, 32, 32), IDT_RECTANGLE);
    return TRUE;
}


void CMyDialog::OnNeedText (NMHDR* pnmh, LRESULT* pResult)
{
    TOOLTIPTEXT* pttt = (TOOLTIPTEXT*) pnmh;
    if (pttt->hdr.idFrom == IDT_RECTANGLE) {
        CString string;
        CTime time = CTime::GetCurrentTime ();
        string.Format ("%0.2d:%0.2d:%0.2d", time.GetHour () % 12,
            time.GetMinute (), time.GetSecond ());
        ::lstrcpy (pttt->szText, (LPCTSTR) string);
    }
}
```

Note the NULL child window ID specified in the second parameter to the ON_NOTIFY macro in *CMyDialog*'s message map. This parameter has to be NULL because *CTool-TipCtrl::Create* registers a NULL child window ID for tooltip controls.

MFC's *CToolTipCtrl* class includes an assortment of member functions you can use to operate on tooltip controls. For example, you can use *GetText* to retrieve the text assigned to a tool, *UpdateTipText* to change tooltip text, *Activate* to activate and deactivate a tooltip control, and *SetDelayTime* to change the delay time—the number of milliseconds the cursor must remain motionless before a tooltip is displayed. The default delay time is 500 milliseconds.

The GridDemo Application

The GridDemo application, listed in Figure 13-5 beginning on the next page, provides a practical demonstration of how slider controls, spin button controls, and tooltip controls can be put to work in a dialog box. GridDemo divides a frame window's client area into a grid by drawing intersecting horizontal and vertical lines. By default, the grid contains 8 rows and 8 columns and grid lines are drawn in a medium shade of gray. The user can vary the number of rows and columns as well as the darkness of the grid lines by choosing Settings from the Options menu and entering the new settings in the dialog box shown in Figure 13-6 on page 865. The slider control selects the line weight, and the values in the edit controls specify the numbers of rows and columns. Valid values range from 2 through 64; the user can type in the numbers or use the arrow buttons to increment and decrement the row and column counts. When the cursor pauses over the slider or either of the edit controls, a tooltip window appears with a short description of the tool underneath.

The tooltip control is an object created from the *CMyToolTipCtrl* class presented in the previous section. The slider and spin button controls are part of the dialog template and are programmed using *CSliderCtrl* and *CSpinButtonCtrtl* member functions. The slider's range and initial position are set in *OnInitDialog*, and the final thumb position is retrieved in *OnOK*. The spin buttons' ranges are also initialized in *OnInitDialog*, but their positions don't have to be explicitly set or retrieved because the edit controls that the spin buttons are buddied to are served by DDX and DDV routines.

Because GridDemo doesn't create a logical palette with shades of gray representing the different line weight settings, the full range of line weights won't be displayed on 16- and 256-color video adapters. As an exercise, you might try adding palette support by adding a *CPalette* data member to the frame window and using PALETTE-RGB or PALETTEINDEX colors to draw the grid lines. Refer to Chapter 12 for more information on GDI palettes and MFC's *CPalette* class.

Resource.h

```
//*******************************************************************
//
//   Resource.h
//
//*******************************************************************

#define IDR_MAINFRAME              100

#define IDM_OPTIONS_SETTINGS       110
#define IDM_OPTIONS_EXIT           111

#define IDD_SETTINGSDLG            120
#define IDC_SLIDER                 121
#define IDC_EDITHORZ               122
#define IDC_SPINHORZ               123
#define IDC_EDITVERT               124
#define IDC_SPINVERT               125

#define IDS_SLIDER                 130
#define IDS_EDITHORZ               131
#define IDS_EDITVERT               132
```

Figure 13-5. *The GridDemo program.*

GridDemo.rc

```
//*********************************************************************
//
//  GridDemo.rc
//
//*********************************************************************

#include <afxres.h>
#include "Resource.h"

IDR_MAINFRAME MENU
BEGIN
    POPUP "&Options" {
        MENUITEM "Grid &Settings...",           IDM_OPTIONS_SETTINGS
        MENUITEM SEPARATOR
        MENUITEM "E&xit",                       IDM_OPTIONS_EXIT
    }
END

IDD_SETTINGSDLG DIALOG 0, 0, 196, 130
STYLE DS_MODALFRAME | DS_CENTER | WS_POPUP | WS_VISIBLE |
    WS_CAPTION | WS_SYSMENU
CAPTION "Settings"
FONT 8, "MS Sans Serif"
BEGIN
    GROUPBOX        "Line Weight", -1, 8, 8, 124, 52, WS_GROUP
    CONTROL         "", IDC_SLIDER, "MSCTLS_TRACKBAR32",
                    TBS_AUTOTICKS | WS_TABSTOP, 20, 24, 100, 20
    LTEXT           "Darkest", -1, 16, 44, 30, 8
    LTEXT           "Lightest", -1, 100, 44, 30, 8
    GROUPBOX        "Grid Spacing", -1, 8, 68, 124, 52
    LTEXT           "&Horizontal", -1, 20, 84, 32, 8
    EDITTEXT        IDC_EDITHORZ, 60, 80, 40, 14, ES_AUTOHSCROLL
    CONTROL         "", IDC_SPINHORZ, "MSCTLS_UPDOWN32", UDS_ARROWKEYS |
                    UDS_AUTOBUDDY | UDS_SETBUDDYINT | UDS_ALIGNRIGHT,
                    0, 0, 0, 0
    LTEXT           "&Vertical", -1, 20, 104, 36, 8
    EDITTEXT        IDC_EDITVERT, 60, 100, 40, 14, ES_AUTOHSCROLL
    CONTROL         "", IDC_SPINVERT, "MSCTLS_UPDOWN32", UDS_ARROWKEYS |
                    UDS_AUTOBUDDY | UDS_SETBUDDYINT | UDS_ALIGNRIGHT,
                    0, 0, 0, 0
    DEFPUSHBUTTON   "OK", IDOK, 140, 12, 50, 14, WS_GROUP
    PUSHBUTTON      "Cancel", IDCANCEL, 140, 30, 50, 14, WS_GROUP
END
```

(continued)

GridDemo.rc *continued*

```
STRINGTABLE
BEGIN
    IDS_SLIDER      "Controls grid line visibility"
    IDS_EDITHORZ    "Sets the number of columns in the grid"
    IDS_EDITVERT    "Sets the number of rows in the grid"
END
```

GridDemo.h

```
//****************************************************************************
//
//  GridDemo.h
//
//****************************************************************************

class CMyApp : public CWinApp
{
public:
    virtual BOOL InitInstance ();
};

class CMainWindow : public CFrameWnd
{
private:
    int m_cx;
    int m_cy;
    int m_nWeight;

public:
    CMainWindow ();

protected:
    afx_msg void OnPaint ();
    afx_msg void OnOptionsSettings ();
    afx_msg void OnOptionsExit ();

    DECLARE_MESSAGE_MAP ()
};

class CMyToolTipCtrl : public CToolTipCtrl
{
public:
    BOOL AddWindowTool (CWnd*, LPCTSTR);
    BOOL AddRectTool (CWnd*, LPCTSTR, LPCRECT, UINT);
};
```

```
class CSettingsDialog : public CDialog
{
private:
    CMyToolTipCtrl m_ctlTT;

public:
    int m_cx;
    int m_cy;
    int m_nWeight;

    CSettingsDialog (CWnd* pParentWnd = NULL) :
        CDialog (IDD_SETTINGSDLG, pParentWnd) {}

    virtual BOOL OnInitDialog ();

protected:
    virtual void DoDataExchange (CDataExchange*);
    virtual void OnOK ();
};
```

GridDemo.cpp

```
//****************************************************************************
//
//  GridDemo.cpp
//
//****************************************************************************

#include <afxwin.h>
#include <afxcmn.h>
#include "Resource.h"
#include "GridDemo.h"

CMyApp myApp;

///////////////////////////////////////////////////////////////////////////
// CMyApp member functions

BOOL CMyApp::InitInstance ()
{
    m_pMainWnd = new CMainWindow;
    m_pMainWnd->ShowWindow (m_nCmdShow);
    m_pMainWnd->UpdateWindow ();
    return TRUE;
```

(continued)

GridDemo.cpp *continued*

```
}

///////////////////////////////////////////////////////////////////////////
// CMainWindow message map and member functions

BEGIN_MESSAGE_MAP (CMainWindow, CFrameWnd)
    ON_WM_PAINT ()
    ON_COMMAND (IDM_OPTIONS_SETTINGS, OnOptionsSettings)
    ON_COMMAND (IDM_OPTIONS_EXIT, OnOptionsExit)
END_MESSAGE_MAP ()

CMainWindow::CMainWindow ()
{
    m_cx = m_cy = 8;
    m_nWeight = 4;

    Create (NULL, "Grid Demo", WS_OVERLAPPEDWINDOW, rectDefault,
        NULL, MAKEINTRESOURCE (IDR_MAINFRAME));
}

void CMainWindow::OnPaint ()
{
    CRect rect;
    GetClientRect (&rect);

    int nShade = m_nWeight * 32;
    if (nShade != 0)
        nShade--;

    CPaintDC dc (this);
    CPen pen (PS_SOLID, 1, RGB (nShade, nShade, nShade));
    CPen* pOldPen = dc.SelectObject (&pen);

    int x;
    for (int i=1; i<m_cx; i++) {
        x = (rect.Width () * i) / m_cx;
        dc.MoveTo (x, 0);
        dc.LineTo (x, rect.Height ());
    }

    int y;
    for (i=1; i<m_cy; i++) {
        y = (rect.Height () * i) / m_cy;
        dc.MoveTo (0, y);
        dc.LineTo (rect.Width (), y);
    }
```

```
    dc.SelectObject (pOldPen);
}

void CMainWindow::OnOptionsSettings ()
{
    CSettingsDialog dlg (this);

    dlg.m_cx = m_cx;
    dlg.m_cy = m_cy;
    dlg.m_nWeight = m_nWeight;

    if (dlg.DoModal () == IDOK) {
        m_cx = dlg.m_cx;
        m_cy = dlg.m_cy;
        m_nWeight = dlg.m_nWeight;

        Invalidate ();
    }
}

void CMainWindow::OnOptionsExit ()
{
    SendMessage (WM_CLOSE, 0, 0);
}

///////////////////////////////////////////////////////////////////////
// CSettingsDialog message map and member functions

BOOL CSettingsDialog::OnInitDialog ()
{
    CDialog::OnInitDialog ();

    // Initialize the slider
    CSliderCtrl* pSlider = (CSliderCtrl*) GetDlgItem (IDC_SLIDER);
    pSlider->SetRange (0, 8);
    pSlider->SetPos (m_nWeight);

    // Initialize the first spin button
    CSpinButtonCtrl* pSpin = (CSpinButtonCtrl*) GetDlgItem (IDC_SPINHORZ);
    pSpin->SetRange (2, 64);

    // Initialize the second spin button
    pSpin = (CSpinButtonCtrl*) GetDlgItem (IDC_SPINVERT);
    pSpin->SetRange (2, 64);
```

(continued)

GridDemo.cpp *continued*

```
    // Create and initialize a tooltip control
    m_ctlTT.Create (this);
    m_ctlTT.AddWindowTool (GetDlgItem (IDC_SLIDER),
        MAKEINTRESOURCE (IDS_SLIDER));
    m_ctlTT.AddWindowTool (GetDlgItem (IDC_EDITHORZ),
        MAKEINTRESOURCE (IDS_EDITHORZ));
    m_ctlTT.AddWindowTool (GetDlgItem (IDC_EDITVERT),
        MAKEINTRESOURCE (IDS_EDITVERT));

    return TRUE;
}

void CSettingsDialog::OnOK ()
{
    CSliderCtrl* pSlider = (CSliderCtrl*) GetDlgItem (IDC_SLIDER);
    m_nWeight = pSlider->GetPos ();
    CDialog::OnOK ();
}

void CSettingsDialog::DoDataExchange (CDataExchange* pDX)
{
    CDialog::DoDataExchange (pDX);

    DDX_Text (pDX, IDC_EDITHORZ, m_cx);
    DDV_MinMaxInt (pDX, m_cx, 2, 64);
    DDX_Text (pDX, IDC_EDITVERT, m_cy);
    DDV_MinMaxInt (pDX, m_cy, 2, 64);
}

///////////////////////////////////////////////////////////////////////////
// CMyToolTipCtrl member functions

BOOL CMyToolTipCtrl::AddWindowTool (CWnd* pWnd, LPCTSTR pszText)
{
    TOOLINFO ti;
    ti.cbSize = sizeof (TOOLINFO);
    ti.uFlags = TTF_IDISHWND | TTF_SUBCLASS;
    ti.hwnd = pWnd->GetParent ()->GetSafeHwnd ();
    ti.uId = (UINT) pWnd->GetSafeHwnd ();
    ti.hinst = AfxGetInstanceHandle ();
    ti.lpszText = (LPTSTR) pszText;

    return (BOOL) SendMessage (TTM_ADDTOOL, 0, (LPARAM) &ti);
}

BOOL CMyToolTipCtrl::AddRectTool (CWnd* pWnd, LPCTSTR pszText,
    LPCRECT lpRect, UINT nIDTool)
```

```
{
    TOOLINFO ti;
    ti.cbSize = sizeof (TOOLINFO);
    ti.uFlags = TTF_SUBCLASS;
    ti.hwnd = pWnd->GetSafeHwnd ();
    ti.uId = nIDTool;
    ti.hinst = AfxGetInstanceHandle ();
    ti.lpszText = (LPSTR) pszText;
    ::CopyRect (&ti.rect, lpRect);

    return (BOOL) SendMessage (TTM_ADDTOOL, 0, (LPARAM) &ti);
}
```

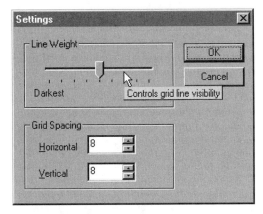

Figure 13-6. *GridDemo's Settings dialog with a tooltip displayed.*

IMAGE LIST, TREE VIEW, AND LIST VIEW CONTROLS

Image lists, tree view controls, and list view controls are three of the most powerful common controls. They're also three of the most complex. The classes that encapsulate them include more than 120 member functions, and tree view and list view controls together support more than 20 control styles and send out more than 30 different types of notifications.

But don't let statistics intimidate you. These controls are well worth the effort it takes to learn them, and you can get a basic image list, tree view control, or list view control up and running in no time. After that, adding more advanced features such as drag and drop support for tree view items and in-place label editing for list view items is simply a matter of adding notification handlers. I'll use a broad brush to paint a picture of all three control types and introduce you to the fundamental principles involved in programming them. Then we'll see just how powerful these controls can be by developing an Explorer knockoff in just a few hundred lines of code.

Image Lists

An image list is a collection of identically sized bitmap images joined into one object. MFC's *CImageList* class provides functions for creating image lists, adding and deleting images, drawing images on the screen, writing image lists to an archive and reading them back, and more. Image lists are useful in and of themselves because many of the functions that operate on them have no direct counterparts elsewhere in Windows. But image lists were added to the operating system in the first place so that bitmaps could be grouped and passed as a unit to other common controls. When you supply images to a tree view control, for example, you don't pass it an array of *CBitmap*s; you pass it a handle to an image list (an HIMAGELIST) or a pointer to a *CImageList* object. Individual images are then referenced with 0-based indexes.

The best way to picture an image list is to think of a film strip with images laid horizontally from end to end. The leftmost image is image number 0, the one to its right is image number 1, and so on. The images can be any height and width, but they must all be the same height and width.

There are three ways to create an image list. You can create an empty image list and add images to it with *CImageList::Add*. You can create an initialized image list from an existing bitmap containing an array of images. And you can create an initialized image list by merging images from existing image lists. *CImageList::Create* is overloaded to support all three creation methods. The second (and probably the most common) of these methods is illustrated below. Suppose IDR_BITMAP is the resource ID of a bitmap that contains five images, each measuring 18 pixels wide and 16 pixels high. The bitmap itself is 90 pixels wide (5 times 18) and 16 pixels high. The following statements create an image list from the bitmap:

```
CImageList imageList;
imageList.Create (IDR_BITMAP, 18, 1, CLR_NONE);
```

The first parameter passed to *Create* is the bitmap's resource ID. You can also pass a string resource ID for this parameter. The second parameter is the width, in pixels, of the individual images. Windows determines how many images to add to the list by dividing the bitmap width by the image width. The third parameter is the *grow size*. Image lists are sized dynamically just as arrays created from MFC collection classes are, and the grow size tells the image list how many additional images to make room for when more memory must be allocated to accommodate new images. The final parameter—CLR_NONE—creates an *unmasked* image list. Unmasked images are ordinary bitmaps that are blitted directly to the output DC when they're drawn on the screen.

Passing *CImageList::Create* a COLORREF value instead of CLR_NONE creates a *masked* image list. In addition to storing color information for a masked image, Windows also stores a monochrome bit mask that allows the system to distinguish between foreground and background pixels. The COLORREF value passed to *CImageList::Create* specifies the background color, and any pixel set to that color is assumed to be a background pixel. What's cool about masked images is the fact that you can call *CImageList::SetBkColor* before drawing from an image list and set the background color to any color you like. The background color in the original bitmap might have been magenta, but if you set the background color to red and draw the image, all the magenta pixels will come out red. What's *really* cool is that you can pass *CImageList::SetBkColor* a CLR_NONE parameter and background pixels won't be drawn at all. Consequently, image lists provide a simple means of drawing bitmaps with transparent pixels. Remember the *DrawTransparent* function we added to *CBitmap* in Chapter 12 so that we could draw nonrectangular bitmaps? An image list lets you do the same thing with less code. The image list method is faster, too, because the masks don't have to be generated anew each time the image is blitted to the screen.

CImageList::Draw draws images on the screen. The following statement draws the third image in the list (image number 2) to the screen DC referenced by the *CDC* pointer *pDC*:

```
imageList.Draw (pDC, 2, pt, ILD_NORMAL);
```

pt is a POINT structure containing the *x* and *y* coordinates of the point in the destination DC where the upper left corner of the image will be drawn. ILD_NORMAL is a flag that tells the *Draw* function to draw a masked image using the current background color. (This flag has no effect on unmasked images.) If you'd like background pixels to be transparent regardless of what the current background color happens to be, you can use an ILD_TRANSPARENT flag instead:

```
imageList.Draw (pDC, 2, pt, ILD_TRANSPARENT);
```

For some truly interesting effects, try drawing a masked image with an ILD_BLEND25 or ILD_BLEND50 flag to blend in the system highlight color (COLOR_HIGHLIGHT), or with an ILD_OVERLAYMASK flag to overlay one image with another. *CImageList::Draw* will also accept ILD_SELECTED and ILD_FOCUS flags, but they're nothing more than ILD_BLEND50 and ILD_BLEND25 in disguise. To see blending at work, click an icon on the Windows 95 desktop to put it in a selected state. The system dithers the icon image with the system highlight color by redrawing the image with an ILD_BLEND50 flag.

An aside: Note that drawing with an ILD_TRANSPARENT flag or with the background color set to CLR_NONE is always a little slower than drawing an unmasked image. If an image contains transparent pixels but is being blitted to a solid background, use *CImageList::SetBkColor* to set the image list's background color to the color of the solid background and then call *CImageList::Draw* with an ILD_NORMAL flag. You'll improve performance and still get those transparent pixels you wanted.

Scan the list of *CImageList* member functions, and you'll get a pretty good idea of what else you can do with image lists. Eight of the functions have "Drag" in their names—they're for animating dragging operations. *CImageList::Write* and *CImage-List::Read* serialize image lists to and from an archive. Image lists are also useful for adding bitmaps to tree views, list views, and other common controls that display graphical images.

Tree View Controls

The tree view control is the long-awaited Windows answer to the question of how to present hierarchical information to the user in an interactive format that makes all the data equally—and easily—accessible. Tree view controls make it a snap to create tree-like structures containing items composed of text and images. Items can have subitems; and lists of subitems, or *subtrees,* can be expanded and collapsed to display and hide the information contained therein. Tree view controls, whose functionality is encapsulated in MFC's *CTreeCtrl* class, are ideal for depicting data that's inherently hierarchical in nature such as the directory structure of a hard disk. The Windows 95 Explorer uses a tree view control to represent items in the shell's namespace. If you do even a moderate amount of Windows programming, you'll probably find uses for tree view controls, too.

Creating a Tree View Control

Creating and initializing a tree view control is a three-step process. First you create the control, with either *CTreeCtrl::Create* or a CONTROL statement in a dialog template. Next, if tree view items will include images, you call *CTreeCtrl::SetImageList* and pass a pointer to a *CImageList* containing the images. Finally, you use *CTreeCtrl-::InsertItem* to add items to the control.

When you create a tree view control, you can specify any of the styles shown in the table on the facing page in addition to WS_CHILD, WS_VISIBLE, WS_BORDER, and other standard window styles. Figure 13-7 shows the different looks you can get from a tree view control by applying different styles. The control on the right combines the styles TVS_HASLINES, TVS_LINESATROOT, and TVS_HASBUTTONS. The control on the left has none of these styles, but the user can still expand or collapse a subtree in the tree view control by double-clicking the subtree's parent. However, the buttons make it obvious which items have subitems and which ones don't.

TREE VIEW CONTROL STYLES

Style	Description
TVS_HASLINES	Adds lines connecting subitems to their parents.
TVS_LINESATROOT	Adds lines connecting items at the top level, or root, of the hierarchy. Valid only if TVS_HASLINES is also specified.
TVS_HASBUTTONS	Adds buttons containing plus or minus signs to items that have subitems. Clicking a button expands or collapses the associated subtree.
TVS_EDITLABELS	Enables in-place label editing notifications.
TVS_DISABLEDRAGDROP	Disables drag-drop notifications.
TVS_SHOWSELALWAYS	Specifies that the item that's currently selected should always be highlighted. By default, the highlight is removed when the control loses the input focus.

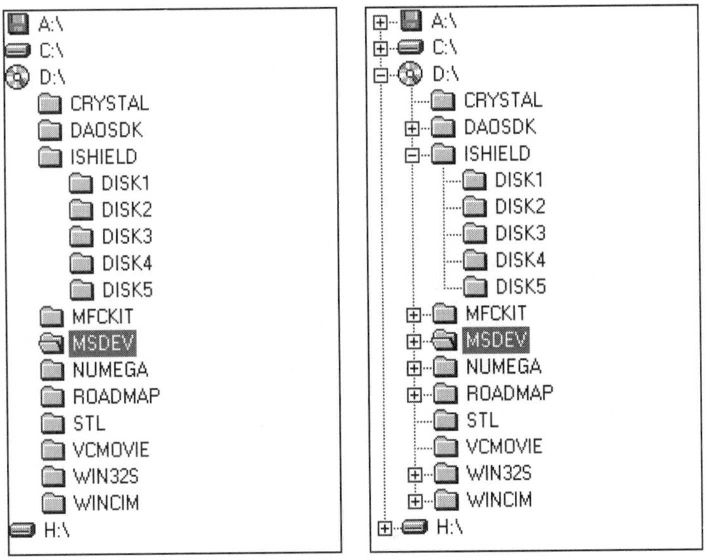

Figure 13-7. *Tree view controls with and without lines and buttons.*

Each item in a tree view control consists of a text string (also known as a *label*) and optionally an image from an image list. If you plan to include images as well as text in a tree view, the next step after creating the control is to add an image list. If *pTree* points to a *CTreeCtrl* control object and *pImageList* points to a valid *CImageList* object, the statement

```
pTree->SetImageList (pImageList, TVSIL_NORMAL);
```

associates the image list with the control. The TVSIL_NORMAL flag tells the tree view control that the images in the image list will be used to represent selected and unselected items. A separate TVSIL_STATE image list can be added to represent items that are in application-defined states. The image lists associated with a tree view control are not automatically deleted when the control is deleted—unless, of course, they are data members of a derived tree view class.

Adding Items to a Tree View Control

CTreeCtrl::InsertItem adds an item to a tree view control. Items are identified by HTREEITEM handles, and one of the parameters input to *InsertItem* is the HTREEITEM handle of the item's parent. A subitem is created by specifying an existing item as the new item's parent. Root items—items in the uppermost level of the tree—are created by specifying TVI_ROOT as the parent. The following code fragment initializes a tree view control with the names of two of my favorite '70s rock groups along with subtrees listing the names of some of their albums:

```
// Root items first, with automatic sorting
HTREEITEM hEagles = pTree->InsertItem ("Eagles",
    TVI_ROOT, TVI_SORT);
HTREEITEM hDoobies = pTree->InsertItem ("Doobie Brothers",
    TVI_ROOT, TVI_SORT);

// Eagles subitems second (no sorting)
pTree->InsertItem ("Eagles", hEagles);
pTree->InsertItem ("On the Border", hEagles);
pTree->InsertItem ("Hotel California", hEagles);
pTree->InsertItem ("The Long Run", hEagles);

// Doobie subitems third (no sorting)
pTree->InsertItem ("Toulouse Street", hDoobies);
pTree->InsertItem ("The Captain and Me", hDoobies);
pTree->InsertItem ("Stampede", hDoobies);
```

Passing a TVI_SORT flag to *InsertItem* automatically sorts items added to the tree with respect to other items in the same subtree. The default is TVI_LAST, which simply adds the item to the end of the list. You can also specify TVI_FIRST to add an item to the head of the list.

That's one way to add items to a tree view control. There are several ways you can go about it because *CTreeCtrl* provides four different versions of *InsertItem*. Let's take the example in the previous paragraph a little further and assume that you'd like to include images as well as text in the tree view items. Suppose you've created an image list that contains two images. Image 0 depicts a manila folder, and image 1 depicts an album cover. You'd like folders to appear alongside the names of the rock groups and album images to appear next to album titles. Here's what the code to initialize the control would look like:

```
// Add the image list to the control
pTree->SetImageList (pImageList, TVSIL_NORMAL);

// Root items first, with automatic sorting
HTREEITEM hEagles = pTree->InsertItem ("Eagles", 0, 0,
    TVI_ROOT, TVI_SORT);
HTREEITEM hDoobies = pTree->InsertItem ("Doobie Brothers", 0, 0,
    TVI_ROOT, TVI_SORT);

// Eagles subitems second (no sorting)
pTree->InsertItem ("Eagles", 1, 1, hEagles);
pTree->InsertItem ("On the Border", 1, 1, hEagles);
pTree->InsertItem ("Hotel California", 1, 1, hEagles);
pTree->InsertItem ("The Long Run", 1, 1, hEagles);

// Doobie subitems third (no sorting)
pTree->InsertItem ("Toulouse Street", 1, 1, hDoobies);
pTree->InsertItem ("The Captain and Me", 1, 1, hDoobies);
pTree->InsertItem ("Stampede", 1, 1, hDoobies);
```

The second and third parameters passed to this form of *InsertItem* are image indexes. The first specifies the image the tree view control will display when the item is not selected, and the second specifies the image the control will display when the item is selected. Specifying the same index for an item's selected and nonselected states means that the same image will be used for both. The tree view control in the left pane of the Windows 95 Explorer uses a closed folder for nonselected folder items and an open folder for selected folder items. Thus, if you move the highlight up and down with the arrow keys, a folder "opens" when it becomes highlighted and closes when the highlight passes to another item.

Tree View Member Functions and Notifications

CTreeCtrl provides a wide range of member functions for operating on tree view controls and manipulating individual items. *DeleteItem*, for example, deletes an item from the control, and *DeleteAllItems* deletes all the items; *Expand* expands or collapses a subtree; *SetItemText* changes an item's label, and *GetItemText* retrieves it; and *Sort-Children* sorts the items in a subtree. You name it, and there's probably a way to do it. The key to nearly every function is an HTREEITEM handle identifying the item that's the target of the operation. If you'd like, you can save the handles returned by *InsertItem* in an array or a linked list or some other structure so that you can reference them again later. You can retrieve the handle of the selected item with *CTreeCtrl::GetSelected-Item*. And if necessary, you can start with the very first item in a tree view control and walk the list item by item using *GetParentItem*, *GetChildItem*, *GetNextItem*, *GetNext-SiblingItem*, and other *CTreeCtrl* functions.

TREE VIEW CONTROL NOTIFICATIONS

Notification	Sent When
TVN_BEGINDRAG	A drag and drop operation is begun using the left mouse button. Not sent if the control has the style TVS_DISABLEDRAGDROP.
TVN_BEGINRDRAG	A drag and drop operation is begun using the right mouse button. Not sent if the control has the style TVS_DISABLEDRAGDROP.
TVN_BEGINLABELEDIT	A label editing operation is begun. Sent only if the control has the style TVS_EDITLABELS.
TVN_ENDLABELEDIT	A label editing operation is completed. Sent only if the control has the style TVS_EDITLABELS.
TVN_GETDISPINFO	A tree view control needs additional information to display an item. Sent if the item text is LPSTR_TEXTCALLBACK or the image index is I_IMAGECALLBACK.
TVN_DELETEITEM	An item is deleted.
TVN_ITEMEXPANDED	A subtree has been expanded or collapsed.
TVN_ITEMEXPANDING	A subtree will be expanded or collapsed.
TVN_KEYDOWN	A key is pressed while the control has the input focus.
TVN_SELCHANGED	The selection has been changed.
TVN_SELCHANGING	The selection is about to change.
TVN_SETDISPINFO	The information in a TV_DISPINFO structure needs to be updated.

Once items are added to a tree view control, the control is capable of processing most user input on its own. The user can browse the items in the tree by selectively expanding and collapsing branches and can make selections by clicking items or using keyboard input to move the highlight. You can add even more capabilities to a tree view control (or customize its default response to conventional input) by processing the notifications shown in the table above. Notifications come in the form of WM_NOTIFY messages, and in most cases *lParam* points to an NM_TREEVIEW structure containing additional information about the event that prompted the message. Here are some of the useful things you can do with tree view notifications:

■ Enable in-place label editing so that the user can edit text in a tree view control.

■ Update item text and images dynamically by passing LPSTR_TEXTCALLBACK and I_IMAGECALLBACK parameters to *InsertItem* and processing TVN_GETDISPINFO notifications.

■ Customize the control's response to keyboard input by processing TVN-_KEYDOWN notifications.

■ Support drag and drop operations.

There's more (of course!), but this short list should give you an idea of a tree view control's wide-ranging flexibility. Later in this chapter, we'll develop an application that uses a tree view control and makes gainful use of TVN_ITEMEXPANDING and TVN_SELCHANGED notifications.

List View Controls

List view controls are similar to tree view controls in that they provide a powerful and relatively painless way to present complex collections of data to the user. But whereas tree view controls are ideal for depicting hierarchical relationships, list view controls are best suited for presenting "flat" collections of data, such as lists of file names. Like items in a tree view control, items in a list view control may include both text and images. In addition, items can have text-only *subitems* containing additional information about the associated items. The subitems are visible when the control is in "report" view, which is one of the four types of views a list view control supports. The other types of views are large icon view, small icon view, and list view. You can see examples of all four view types by starting the Windows 95 Explorer and using the View menu to change the view in Explorer's right pane. The Large Icons command in the View menu corresponds to large icon view, Small Icons corresponds to small icon view, List corresponds to list view, and Details corresponds to report view.

Creating and Initializing a List View Control

MFC wraps list view controls in the class *CListCtrl*. The table on the next page summarizes the styles you can specify when you create a list view control.

Like a tree view control, a list view control is empty when it's first created. Initialization is a five-step process:

1. Create a pair of image lists containing images for the list view items. One image list contains "large" images, and the other contains "small" images. *CImageList::Add* allows you to add icons as well as bitmaps to an image list, so you can use large and small icons if you like.

2. Use *CListCtrl::SetImageList* to associate the image lists with the list view control. Pass *SetImageList* an LVSIL_NORMAL flag for the image list containing large images and an LVSIL_SMALL flag for the image list containing small images.

3. Add columns to the list view control with *CListCtrl::InsertColumn*. The leftmost column displays the items added to the control. The columns to the right display subitems and are visible only in report view.

LIST VIEW CONTROL STYLES

Style	Description
LVS_ICON	Selects large icon view.
LVS_SMALLICON	Selects small icon view.
LVS_LIST	Selects list view.
LVS_REPORT	Selects report view.
LVS_NOCOLUMNHEADER	Removes the header control that's normally displayed in report view.
LVS_NOSORTHEADER	Disables the LVN_COLUMNCLICK notifications that are sent by default when a column header is clicked in report view.
LVS_ALIGNLEFT	Left-aligns items in large and small icon view.
LVS_ALIGNTOP	Aligns items with the top of the control in large and small icon view.
LVS_AUTOARRANGE	Specifies that the control should automatically arrange items in rows and columns in large and small icon views.
LVS_EDITLABELS	Enables in-place label editing notifications.
LVS_NOLABELWRAP	Restricts labels to single lines in large icon view.
LVS_NOSCROLL	Disables scrolling. Scrolling is enabled by default.
LVS_OWNERDRAWFIXED	Specifies that the control's owner will draw the items in response to WM_DRAWITEM messages.
LVS_SHAREIMAGELISTS	Prevents a list view control from automatically deleting the image lists associated with it when the control itself is deleted.
LVS_SINGLESEL	Specifies that the list view control does not permit multiple selections.
LVS_SHOWSELALWAYS	Specifies that the selected items should always be highlighted. By default, the highlight is removed when the control loses the input focus.
LVS_SORTASCENDING	Specifies that items should be sorted in ascending order (for example, A through Z).
LVS_SORTDESCENDING	Specifies that items should be sorted in descending order (for example, Z through A) .

4. Add items to the control with *CListCtrl::InsertItem*.

5. Assign text strings to the item's subitems with *CListCtrl::SetItemText*.

It's really not as hard as it sounds. The following code fragment initializes a list view control with items representing eight of the states in the United States of America. Each item consists of a label and an image. The label is the name of a state, and the image presumably shows a thumbnail rendition of the state's outline. Each item also contains a pair of subitems: a text string naming the state capital and a text string describing the state's land area. In report view, the subitems appear in columns under headers labeled *Capital* and *Area (sq. miles)*. Assuming that the list view control is created from a dialog template and that its control ID is IDC_LISTVIEW, here's what the *OnInitDialog* code to initialize the control would look like:

```
static CString text[8][3] = {
    "Tennessee",       "Nashville",     "41,154",
    "Alabama",         "Montgomery",    "50,766",
    "Mississippi",     "Jackson",       "47,234",
    "Florida",         "Tallahassee",   "54,157",
    "Georgia",         "Atlanta",       "58,060",
    "Kentucky",        "Frankfort",     "39,674",
    "North Carolina",  "Raleigh",       "48,843",
    "South Carolina",  "Columbia",      "30,207"
};

// Get a pointer to the control
CListCtrl* pList = (CListCtrl*) GetDlgItem (IDC_LISTVIEW);

// Add the image lists
pList->SetImageList (&imageLarge, LVSIL_NORMAL);
pList->SetImageList (&imageSmall, LVSIL_SMALL);

// Add the columns
pList->InsertColumn (0, "State", LVCFMT_LEFT, 96);
pList->InsertColumn (1, "Capital", LVCFMT_LEFT, 96);
pList->InsertColumn (2, "Area (sq. miles)", LVCFMT_RIGHT, 96);

// Add the items and subitems
for (int i=0; i<8; i++) {
    pList->InsertItem (i, (LPCTSTR) text[i][0], i);
    pList->SetItemText (i, 1, (LPCTSTR) text[i][1]);
    pList->SetItemText (i, 2, (LPCTSTR) text[i][2]);
}
```

The parameters passed to *InsertColumn* specify, in order, the column's 0-based index, the label that appears at the top of the column, the column alignment (whether data displayed in the column is left justified, right justified, or centered), and the column width in pixels. You can base column widths on the actual widths of characters in the control font by using *CListCtrl::GetStringWidth* to convert text strings into pixel counts. The parameters passed to *InsertItem* specify the item's 0-based index, the item label, and the index of the corresponding images in the image lists. The parameters passed to *SetItemText* specify the item number, the subitem number, and the subitem text, in that order.

Changing the View

When a list view control is created, its style—LVS_ICON, LVS_SMALLICON, LVS_LIST, or LVS_REPORT—determines whether it starts up in large icon view, small icon view, list view, or report view. You can switch views on the fly by changing the control's style. The following statement switches the list view control referenced by *pList* to small icon view:

```
pList->ModifyStyle (LVS_TYPEMASK, LVS_SMALLICON);
```

Similarly, this statement switches the control to report view:

```
pList->ModifyStyle (LVS_TYPEMASK, LVS_REPORT);
```

ModifyStyle is a *CWnd* function that's handed down through inheritance to *CListCtrl*. The first parameter passed to *ModifyStyle* specifies the style bits to turn off, and the second parameter specifies the style bits to turn on. LVS_TYPEMASK is a mask for all the LVS view styles that's defined for you in Commctrl.h.

LVS_ICON, LVS_SMALLICON, LVS_LIST, and LVS_REPORT aren't true bit flags, so LVS_TYPEMASK comes in handy when you query a list view control to determine the view type. The following code won't work:

```
// Wrong!
DWORD dwStyle = pList->GetStyle ();
if (dwStyle & LVS_ICON)
    // Large icon view
else if (dwStyle & LVS_SMALLICON)
    // Small icon view
else if (dwStyle & LVS_LIST)
    // List view
else
    // Report view
```

But the code shown here will:

```
DWORD dwStyle = pList->GetStyle () & LVS_TYPEMASK;
if (dwStyle == LVS_ICON)
    // Large icon view
else if (dwStyle == LVS_SMALLICON)
    // Small icon view
else if (dwStyle == LVS_LIST)
    // List view
else
    // Report view
```

This is the proper technique for determining the view type before updating menu items or other UI objects that depend on the list view style.

Sorting by Column

When a list view control that lacks the LVS_NOCOLUMNHEADER style switches to report view, it automatically displays a header control with buttonlike "header items" captioning the columns of information. The user can change the column widths by dragging the vertical dividers separating the header items. (For a nice touch, you can retrieve the column widths with *CListCtrl::GetColumnWidth* before destroying a list view control and save the widths in the registry. Restore the column widths the next time the list view control is created, and the user's column width preferences will be persistent.) Unless a list view control has the style LVS_NOSORTHEADER, clicking a header item sends an LVN_COLUMNCLICK notification to the control's parent. The message's *lParam* points to an NM_LISTVIEW structure, and the structure's *iSubItem* field contains a 0-based index identifying the column that was clicked.

An application's usual response to an LVN_COLUMNCLICK notification is to call *CListCtrl::SortItems* to sort the list view items. Great, you say. Now I can create a list view that sorts, and I won't have to write the code to do the sorting. You do have to provide a callback function that the control's built-in sorting routine can call to compare a pair of arbitrarily selected items, but writing a comparison function is substantially less work than writing a full-blown bubble sort or quick sort routine. And the fact that the comparison function is application-defined means that you enjoy complete control over how the items in a list view control are lexically ordered.

The bad news is that the comparison function receives just three parameters: the 32-bit *lParam* values of the two items being compared and an application-defined *lParam* value that equals the second parameter passed to *SortItems*. An item can be assigned an *lParam* value in the call to *InsertItem* or in a separate call to *CListCtrl::SetItemData*. Unless an application maintains a private copy of each item's data and stores a value in *lParam* that allows the item's data to be retrieved, the comparison function can't possibly do its job. It's not difficult for an application to allocate its own per-item memory and stuff pointers into the items' *lParam*s, but it does complicate matters a bit because the memory must be deallocated, too. And an application that stores its own item data uses memory inefficiently if it assigns text strings to the list view's items and subitems because then the data ends up being stored in memory twice. You can avoid such wastefulness by specifying LPSTR_TEXTCALLBACK for the item and subitem text and providing text to the list view control in response to LVN-_GETDISPINFO notifications. But this, too, complicates the program logic and means that the infrastructure required to support *CListCtrl::SortItems* isn't as simple as it first appears. In just a moment, we'll develop a sample application that implements sortable columns in a list view control so that you can see firsthand how it's done.

Hit Testing

You can respond to mouse clicks in a list view control by processing NM_CLICK, NM_DBLCLK, NM_RCLICK, and NM_RDBLCLK notifications. Very often the way you respond to these events will depend on what, if anything, was under the cursor when the click (or double-click) occurred. You can use *CListCtrl::HitTest* to perform hit testing on the items in a list view control. Given the coordinates of a point, *HitTest* returns the index of the item at that point or −1 if the point doesn't correspond to an item.

The following NM_DBLCLICK handler echoes the names of items double-clicked with the left mouse button to the debug terminal using MFC's TRACE1 macro. *m_ctlList* represents the list view control:

```
// In the message map
ON_NOTIFY (NM_DBLCLK, IDC_LISTVIEW, OnDoubleClick)
    :
    :
void CMyWindow::OnDoubleClick (NMHDR* pnmh, LRESULT* pResult)
{
    DWORD dwPos = ::GetMessagePos ();
    CPoint point ((int) LOWORD (dwPos), (int) HIWORD (dwPos));
    m_ctlList.ScreenToClient (&point);

    int nIndex;
    if ((nIndex = m_ctlList.HitTest (point)) != -1) {
        CString string = m_ctlList.GetItemText (nIndex, 0);
        TRACE1 ("%s was double-clicked\n", string);
    }
}
```

NM_DBLCLK notifications don't include cursor coordinates, so the cursor position is retrieved with *::GetMessagePos*. The screen coordinates returned by *::GetMessagePos* are converted into client coordinates local to the list view control and passed to *CListCtrl::HitTest*. If *HitTest* returns an item index, the index is used to retrieve the item's text.

The *CTreeView* and *CListView* Classes

CTreeCtrl and *CListCtrl* aren't the only classes that wrap tree view and list view controls. There's also *CTreeView* and *CListView*, which transform tree view and list view controls into full-fledged views suitable for use in document/view applications. A *CTreeView* or *CListView* occupies the full extent of a frame window or splitter pane and receives routed command messages just as *CScrollView*s and other views do. Moreover, you can call *CTreeCtrl* and *CListCtrl* member functions on *CTreeView* and *CListView* objects by first calling *CTreeView::GetTreeCtrl* or *CListView::GetListCtrl* to get a reference to the underlying control.

CTreeView and *CListView* are derived from *CCtrlView*, which provides the core functionality for making child window controls behave as views behave. MFC provides control view wrappers for the control types shown in the following table.

Control View Class	Corresponding Control Type
CEditView	Edit control (*CEdit*)
CRichEditView	Rich edit control (*CRichEdit*)
CListView	List view control (*CListCtrl*)
CTreeView	Tree view control (*CTreeCtrl*)

It's relatively simple to derive your own view classes from *CCtrlView* to create *CView* equivalents for other types of controls. Refer to the source code for *CTreeView* and other *CCtrlView*-derived classes for guidance.

Putting It All Together: The Windows Wanderer

The application shown in Figure 13-8 is a scaled-down version of the Windows Explorer that I named the Windows Wanderer. The frame window is divided into two panes by a static *CSplitterWnd*. The splitter's left pane contains a *CDriveView*, which is a *CTreeView* customized to display the directory structure of the host PC, and the right pane contains a *CFileView*, which is a *CListView* that lists the files in the directory selected in the *CDriveView*. The images displayed next to the items in the tree view and the list view come from image lists. The *CFileView* window defaults to report view, but the user can switch to large icon, small icon, or list view using the commands in the Options menu.

In addition to providing a hands-on demonstration of MFC's *CTreeView* and *CListView* classes and showing how to implement sortable columns in a list view,

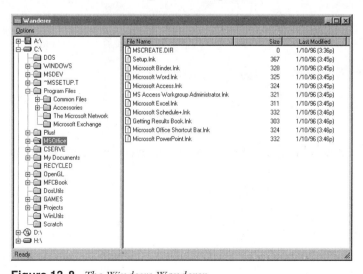

Figure 13-8. *The Windows Wanderer.*

Wanderer introduces some useful new functions and programming techniques that aren't control-related. Among them:

- Win32 functions for enumerating drives, identifying drive types, walking directory structures, and enumerating the files in a directory

- A technique for modifying MFC's command routing mechanism so that inactive views see command and UI update messages, too

- A technique for removing the document title from the title bar of a frame window in a document/view application

Wanderer's source code appears in Figure 13-9.

There's a fundamental difference between Explorer and Wanderer that goes well beyond their feature lists. Wanderer is a file browser that displays drive, directory, and file names. Explorer is a *namespace browser* that serves as a virtual window into the Windows 95 shell's namespace. You can see how the shell's namespace is structured and what kinds of objects it includes by studying the left pane of an Explorer window. The desktop object sits at the uppermost level of the hierarchy, followed by My Computer, Network Neighborhood, and Recycle Bin at the next level, drives at the level beneath that, and so on. Drives, directories, and files are merely a subset of the shell's namespace. The namespace also includes printers, printer folders, and other objects for which there are no direct analogues in the file system. The Windows 95 shell supports a set of API functions all its own that applications can use to access its namespace. Some are conventional API functions with names such as *::SHGet-DesktopFolder*, and others are OLE functions accessed through *IShellFolder* interfaces. For more information, see Article 11 ("Shell's Namespace") in the book *Programmer's Guide to Microsoft Windows 95* (Microsoft Press, 1995).

Resource.h

```
//**********************************************************************
//
//   Resource.h
//
//**********************************************************************

#define IDR_MAINFRAME        100
#define IDR_DRIVEIMAGES      101
#define IDR_LARGEDOC         102
#define IDR_SMALLDOC         103


#define ID_VIEW_LARGE_ICON   110
```

Figure 13-9. *The Wanderer program.*

```
#define ID_VIEW_SMALL_ICON   111
#define ID_VIEW_LIST         112
#define ID_VIEW_REPORT       113
```

Wanderer.rc

```
//***********************************************************************
//
// Wanderer.rc
//
//***********************************************************************

#include <afxres.h>
#include "Resource.h"

IDR_DRIVEIMAGES BITMAP Drives.bmp
IDR_LARGEDOC    BITMAP Large.bmp
IDR_SMALLDOC    BITMAP Small.bmp

IDR_MAINFRAME MENU
BEGIN
    POPUP "&Options" {
        MENUITEM "Large &Icon View",    ID_VIEW_LARGE_ICON
        MENUITEM "&Small Icon View",    ID_VIEW_SMALL_ICON
        MENUITEM "&List View",          ID_VIEW_LIST
        MENUITEM "&Report View",        ID_VIEW_REPORT
        MENUITEM SEPARATOR
        MENUITEM "E&xit",               ID_APP_EXIT
    }
END

STRINGTABLE
BEGIN
    IDR_MAINFRAME         "Wanderer"

    AFX_IDS_IDLEMESSAGE "Ready"
    AFX_IDS_SCCLOSE     "Terminate the application"

    ID_VIEW_LARGE_ICON  "Switch to large icon view"
    ID_VIEW_SMALL_ICON  "Switch to small icon view"
    ID_VIEW_LIST        "Switch to list view"
    ID_VIEW_REPORT      "Switch to report view"
    ID_APP_EXIT         "Terminate the application"
END
```

Wanderer.h

```
//***************************************************************************
//
//  Wanderer.h
//
//***************************************************************************

class CMyApp : public CWinApp
{
public:
    virtual BOOL InitInstance ();
};
```

Wanderer.cpp

```
//***************************************************************************
//
//  Wanderer.cpp
//
//***************************************************************************

#include <afxwin.h>
#include <afxext.h>
#include <afxcview.h>
#include "Resource.h"
#include "Wanderer.h"
#include "MainFrame.h"
#include "WandDoc.h"
#include "DriveView.h"

CMyApp myApp;

BOOL CMyApp::InitInstance ()
{
    SetRegistryKey ("Programming Windows 95 with MFC");
    LoadStdProfileSettings ();

    CSingleDocTemplate* pDocTemplate;
    pDocTemplate = new CSingleDocTemplate (
        IDR_MAINFRAME,
        RUNTIME_CLASS (CWandDoc),
        RUNTIME_CLASS (CMainFrame),
        RUNTIME_CLASS (CDriveView)
    );

    AddDocTemplate (pDocTemplate);
```

```
    CCommandLineInfo cmdInfo;
    ParseCommandLine (cmdInfo);

    if (!ProcessShellCommand (cmdInfo))
        return FALSE;

    return TRUE;
}
```

MainFrame.h

```
//*************************************************************************
//
//  MainFrame.h
//
//*************************************************************************

class CMainFrame : public CFrameWnd
{
    DECLARE_DYNCREATE (CMainFrame)

private:
    CStatusBar m_wndStatusBar;
    CSplitterWnd m_wndSplitter;

protected:
    virtual BOOL PreCreateWindow (CREATESTRUCT&);
    virtual BOOL OnCreateClient (LPCREATESTRUCT, CCreateContext*);
    virtual BOOL OnCmdMsg (UINT, int, void*, AFX_CMDHANDLERINFO*);

    afx_msg int OnCreate (LPCREATESTRUCT);
    DECLARE_MESSAGE_MAP ()
};
```

MainFrame.cpp

```
//*************************************************************************
//
//  MainFrame.cpp
//
//*************************************************************************

#include <afxwin.h>
#include <afxext.h>
```

(continued)

MainFrame.cpp *continued*

```cpp
#include <afxcview.h>
#include "Resource.h"
#include "MainFrame.h"
#include "WandDoc.h"
#include "DriveView.h"
#include "FileView.h"

IMPLEMENT_DYNCREATE (CMainFrame, CFrameWnd)

BEGIN_MESSAGE_MAP (CMainFrame, CFrameWnd)
    ON_WM_CREATE ()
END_MESSAGE_MAP ()

BOOL CMainFrame::PreCreateWindow (CREATESTRUCT& cs)
{
    if (!CFrameWnd::PreCreateWindow (cs))
        return FALSE;

    cs.style &= ~FWS_ADDTOTITLE;
    return TRUE;
}

int CMainFrame::OnCreate (LPCREATESTRUCT lpcs)
{
    if (CFrameWnd::OnCreate (lpcs) == -1)
        return -1;

    m_wndStatusBar.Create (this);
    UINT nIndicator = ID_SEPARATOR;
    m_wndStatusBar.SetIndicators (&nIndicator, 1);
    return 0;
}

BOOL CMainFrame::OnCreateClient (LPCREATESTRUCT lpcs,
    CCreateContext* pContext)
{
    if (!m_wndSplitter.CreateStatic (this, 1, 2) ||
        !m_wndSplitter.CreateView (0, 1, RUNTIME_CLASS (CFileView),
            CSize (0, 0), pContext) ||
        !m_wndSplitter.CreateView (0, 0, RUNTIME_CLASS (CDriveView),
            CSize (192, 0), pContext))
        return FALSE;

    return TRUE;
}

BOOL CMainFrame::OnCmdMsg (UINT nID, int nCode, void* pExtra,
```

```
        AFX_CMDHANDLERINFO* pHandlerInfo)
{
    // Route to standard command targets first
    if (CFrameWnd::OnCmdMsg (nID, nCode, pExtra, pHandlerInfo))
        return TRUE;

    // Route to inactive views second
    CWandDoc* pDoc = (CWandDoc*) GetActiveDocument ();
    if (pDoc != NULL) {
        if (pDoc->RouteCmdToAllViews (GetActiveView (), nID, nCode,
            pExtra, pHandlerInfo))
            return TRUE;
    }

    return FALSE;
}
```

WandDoc.h

```
//*************************************************************************
//
//  WandDoc.h
//
//*************************************************************************

class CWandDoc : public CDocument
{
    DECLARE_DYNCREATE (CWandDoc)

public:
    virtual BOOL RouteCmdToAllViews (CView*, UINT, int, void*,
        AFX_CMDHANDLERINFO*);
};
```

WandDoc.cpp

```
//*************************************************************************
//
//  WandDoc.cpp
//
//*************************************************************************

#include <afxwin.h>
#include "WandDoc.h"
```

(continued)

WandDoc.cpp *continued*

```
IMPLEMENT_DYNCREATE (CWandDoc, CDocument)

BOOL CWandDoc::RouteCmdToAllViews (CView* pView, UINT nID, int nCode,
    void* pExtra, AFX_CMDHANDLERINFO* pHandlerInfo)
{
    POSITION pos = GetFirstViewPosition ();

    while (pos != NULL) {
        CView* pNextView = GetNextView (pos);
        if (pNextView != pView) {
            // Cast CView upward to CCmdTarget because OnCmdMsg is
            // erroneously declared protected in CView
            if ((((CCmdTarget*) pNextView)->OnCmdMsg (nID, nCode,
                pExtra, pHandlerInfo))
                return TRUE;
        }
    }
    return FALSE;
}
```

DriveView.h

```
//********************************************************************
//
//  DriveView.h
//
//********************************************************************

class CDriveView : public CTreeView
{
    DECLARE_DYNCREATE (CDriveView)

protected:
    CImageList m_imglDrives;

    int InitTree ();
    BOOL AddDriveNode (CString&);
    BOOL SetButtonState (HTREEITEM, CString&);
    CString GetPathFromNode (HTREEITEM);
    int AddDirectories (HTREEITEM, CString&);
    void DeleteFirstChild (HTREEITEM);
    void DeleteAllChildren (HTREEITEM);

    virtual BOOL PreCreateWindow (CREATESTRUCT&);
    virtual void OnSelectionChanged (CString&);
```

```
    afx_msg int OnCreate (LPCREATESTRUCT);
    afx_msg void OnItemExpanding (NMHDR*, LRESULT*);
    afx_msg void OnSelChanged (NMHDR*, LRESULT*);

    DECLARE_MESSAGE_MAP ();
};
```

DriveView.cpp

```
//***************************************************************************
//
//  DriveView.cpp
//
//***************************************************************************

#include <afxwin.h>
#include <afxcview.h>
#include "Resource.h"
#include "DriveView.h"


// Image indexes
#define ILI_HARD_DISK        0
#define ILI_FLOPPY           1
#define ILI_CD_ROM           2
#define ILI_NET_DRIVE        0
#define ILI_RAM_DRIVE        0
#define ILI_CLOSED_FOLDER    3
#define ILI_OPEN_FOLDER      4


IMPLEMENT_DYNCREATE (CDriveView, CTreeView)

BEGIN_MESSAGE_MAP (CDriveView, CTreeView)
    ON_WM_CREATE ()
    ON_NOTIFY_REFLECT (TVN_ITEMEXPANDING, OnItemExpanding)
    ON_NOTIFY_REFLECT (TVN_SELCHANGED, OnSelChanged)
END_MESSAGE_MAP ()

BOOL CDriveView::PreCreateWindow (CREATESTRUCT& cs)
{
    if (!CTreeView::PreCreateWindow (cs))
        return FALSE;

    cs.style != TVS_HASLINES | TVS_LINESATROOT | TVS_HASBUTTONS |
        TVS_SHOWSELALWAYS;
    return TRUE;
}
```

(continued)

DriveView.cpp *continued*

```
int CDriveView::OnCreate (LPCREATESTRUCT lpcs)
{
    if (CTreeView::OnCreate (lpcs) == -1)
        return -1;

    m_imglDrives.Create (IDR_DRIVEIMAGES, 16, 1, RGB (255, 0, 255));
    GetTreeCtrl ().SetImageList (&m_imglDrives, TVSIL_NORMAL);

    InitTree ();
    return 0;
}

void CDriveView::OnItemExpanding (NMHDR* pnmh, LRESULT* pResult)
{
    NM_TREEVIEW* pnmtv = (NM_TREEVIEW*) pnmh;
    HTREEITEM hItem = pnmtv->itemNew.hItem;
    CString string = GetPathFromNode (hItem);

    *pResult = FALSE;

    if (pnmtv->action == TVE_EXPAND) {
        DeleteFirstChild (hItem);
        if (AddDirectories (hItem, string) == 0)
            *pResult = TRUE;
    }
    else { // pnmtv->action == TVE_COLLAPSE
        DeleteAllChildren (hItem);
        if (GetTreeCtrl ().GetParentItem (hItem) == NULL)
            GetTreeCtrl ().InsertItem ("", ILI_CLOSED_FOLDER,
                ILI_CLOSED_FOLDER, hItem);
        else
            SetButtonState (hItem, string);
    }
}

void CDriveView::OnSelChanged (NMHDR* pnmh, LRESULT* pResult)
{
    NM_TREEVIEW* pnmtv = (NM_TREEVIEW*) pnmh;
    CString strPath = GetPathFromNode (pnmtv->itemNew.hItem);
    OnSelectionChanged (strPath);
}

void CDriveView::OnSelectionChanged (CString& strPath)
{
    //
    // Override this function in a derived class to respond to
```

```
        // selection changes differently. Here UpdateAllViews is used
        // as a conduit for updating the companion CFileView.
        //
        GetDocument ()->UpdateAllViews (this, (LPARAM) (LPCTSTR) strPath);
}

int CDriveView::InitTree ()
{
        int nPos = 0;
        int nDrivesAdded = 0;
        CString strDrive = "?:\\";

        DWORD dwDriveList = ::GetLogicalDrives ();

        while (dwDriveList) {
                if (dwDriveList & 1) {
                        strDrive.SetAt (0, 0x41 + nPos);
                        if (AddDriveNode (strDrive))
                                nDrivesAdded++;
                }
                dwDriveList >>= 1;
                nPos++;
        }
        return nDrivesAdded;
}

BOOL CDriveView::AddDriveNode (CString& strDrive)
{
        CString string;
        HTREEITEM hItem;
        static BOOL bFirst = TRUE;

        UINT nType = ::GetDriveType ((LPCTSTR) strDrive);

        switch (nType) {

        case DRIVE_REMOVABLE:
                hItem = GetTreeCtrl ().InsertItem (strDrive, ILI_FLOPPY,
                        ILI_FLOPPY);
                GetTreeCtrl ().InsertItem ("", ILI_CLOSED_FOLDER,
                        ILI_CLOSED_FOLDER, hItem);
                break;

        case DRIVE_FIXED:
                hItem = GetTreeCtrl ().InsertItem (strDrive, ILI_HARD_DISK,
                        ILI_HARD_DISK);
                SetButtonState (hItem, strDrive);
```

(continued)

DriveView.cpp *continued*

```
        // If this is the first fixed disk, select and expand it
        if (bFirst) {
            GetTreeCtrl ().SelectItem (hItem);
            GetTreeCtrl ().Expand (hItem, TVE_EXPAND);
            bFirst = FALSE;
        }
        break;

    case DRIVE_REMOTE:
        hItem = GetTreeCtrl ().InsertItem (strDrive, ILI_NET_DRIVE,
            ILI_NET_DRIVE);
        SetButtonState (hItem, strDrive);
        break;

    case DRIVE_CDROM:
        hItem = GetTreeCtrl ().InsertItem (strDrive, ILI_CD_ROM,
            ILI_CD_ROM);
        GetTreeCtrl ().InsertItem ("", ILI_CLOSED_FOLDER,
            ILI_CLOSED_FOLDER, hItem);
        break;

    case DRIVE_RAMDISK:
        hItem = GetTreeCtrl ().InsertItem (strDrive, ILI_RAM_DRIVE,
            ILI_RAM_DRIVE);
        SetButtonState (hItem, strDrive);
        break;

    default:
        return FALSE;
    }

    return TRUE;
}

BOOL CDriveView::SetButtonState (HTREEITEM hItem, CString& strPath)
{
    HANDLE hFind;
    WIN32_FIND_DATA fd;
    BOOL bResult = FALSE;

    CString string = strPath;
    if (string.Right (1) != "\\")
        string += "\\";
    string += "*.*";
```

```
    if ((hFind = ::FindFirstFile ((LPCTSTR) string, &fd)) ==
        INVALID_HANDLE_VALUE)
        return bResult;

    do {
        if (fd.dwFileAttributes & FILE_ATTRIBUTE_DIRECTORY) {
            CString strCmp = (LPCTSTR) &fd.cFileName;
            if ((strCmp != ".") && (strCmp != "..")) {
                GetTreeCtrl ().InsertItem ("", ILI_CLOSED_FOLDER,
                    ILI_CLOSED_FOLDER, hItem);
                bResult = TRUE;
                break;
            }
        }
    } while (::FindNextFile (hFind, &fd));

    ::CloseHandle (hFind);
    return bResult;
}

CString CDriveView::GetPathFromNode (HTREEITEM hItem)
{
    CString strResult = GetTreeCtrl ().GetItemText (hItem);

    HTREEITEM hParent;
    while ((hParent = GetTreeCtrl ().GetParentItem (hItem)) != NULL) {
        CString string = GetTreeCtrl ().GetItemText (hParent);
        if (string.Right (1) != "\\")
            string += "\\";
        strResult = string + strResult;
        hItem = hParent;
    }
    return strResult;
}

int CDriveView::AddDirectories (HTREEITEM hItem, CString& strPath)
{
    HANDLE hFind;
    WIN32_FIND_DATA fd;
    HTREEITEM hNewItem;

    int nCount = 0;

    CString string = strPath;
    if (string.Right (1) != "\\")
        string += "\\";
    string += "*.*";
```

(continued)

DriveView.cpp *continued*

```
        if ((hFind = ::FindFirstFile ((LPCTSTR) string, &fd)) ==
            INVALID_HANDLE_VALUE) {
            if (GetTreeCtrl ().GetParentItem (hItem) == NULL)
                GetTreeCtrl ().InsertItem ("", ILI_CLOSED_FOLDER,
                    ILI_CLOSED_FOLDER, hItem);
            return 0;
        }

        do {
            if (fd.dwFileAttributes & FILE_ATTRIBUTE_DIRECTORY) {
                CString strCmp = (LPCTSTR) &fd.cFileName;
                if ((strCmp != ".") && (strCmp != "..")) {
                    hNewItem =
                        GetTreeCtrl ().InsertItem ((LPCTSTR) &fd.cFileName,
                            ILI_CLOSED_FOLDER, ILI_OPEN_FOLDER, hItem);

                    CString strNewPath = strPath;
                    if (strNewPath.Right (1) != "\\")
                        strNewPath += "\\";

                    strNewPath += (LPCTSTR) &fd.cFileName;
                    SetButtonState (hNewItem, strNewPath);
                    nCount++;
                }
            }
        } while (::FindNextFile (hFind, &fd));

        ::CloseHandle (hFind);
        return nCount;
    }

    void CDriveView::DeleteFirstChild (HTREEITEM hParent)
    {
        HTREEITEM hItem;
        if ((hItem = GetTreeCtrl ().GetChildItem (hParent)) != NULL)
            GetTreeCtrl ().DeleteItem (hItem);
    }

    void CDriveView::DeleteAllChildren (HTREEITEM hParent)
    {
        HTREEITEM hItem;
        if ((hItem = GetTreeCtrl ().GetChildItem (hParent)) == NULL)
            return;

        do {
            HTREEITEM hNextItem = GetTreeCtrl ().GetNextSiblingItem (hItem);
```

```
            GetTreeCtrl ().DeleteItem (hItem);
            hItem = hNextItem;
    } while (hItem != NULL);
}
```

FileView.h

```
//*************************************************************************
//
//  FileView.h
//
//*************************************************************************

class CFileView : public CListView
{
    DECLARE_DYNCREATE (CFileView)

protected:
    CImageList m_imglLarge;
    CImageList m_imglSmall;

    static const DWORD m_dwStyleList[4];

    int InitList (LPCTSTR);
    BOOL AddItem (int, WIN32_FIND_DATA*);
    void FreeItemMemory ();

    static int CALLBACK CompareFunc (LPARAM, LPARAM, LPARAM);

    virtual void OnUpdate (CView*, LPARAM, CObject*);
    virtual BOOL PreCreateWindow (CREATESTRUCT&);

    afx_msg int OnCreate (LPCREATESTRUCT);
    afx_msg void OnDestroy ();
    afx_msg void OnGetDispInfo (NMHDR*, LRESULT*);
    afx_msg void OnColumnClick (NMHDR*, LRESULT*);
    afx_msg void OnChangeView (UINT);
    afx_msg void OnUpdateViewUI (CCmdUI*);

    DECLARE_MESSAGE_MAP ();
};

typedef struct tagITEMINFO {
    CString     strFileName;
    DWORD       nFileSizeLow;
    FILETIME    ftLastWriteTime;
} ITEMINFO;
```

FileView.cpp

```
//*************************************************************************
//
// FileView.cpp
//
//*************************************************************************

#include <afxwin.h>
#include <afxcview.h>
#include "Resource.h"
#include "FileView.h"

IMPLEMENT_DYNCREATE (CFileView, CListView)

BEGIN_MESSAGE_MAP (CFileView, CListView)
    ON_WM_CREATE ()
    ON_WM_DESTROY ()
    ON_COMMAND_RANGE (ID_VIEW_LARGE_ICON, ID_VIEW_REPORT, OnChangeView)
    ON_UPDATE_COMMAND_UI_RANGE (ID_VIEW_LARGE_ICON, ID_VIEW_REPORT,
        OnUpdateViewUI)
    ON_NOTIFY_REFLECT (LVN_GETDISPINFO, OnGetDispInfo)
    ON_NOTIFY_REFLECT (LVN_COLUMNCLICK, OnColumnClick)
END_MESSAGE_MAP ()

const DWORD CFileView::m_dwStyleList[4] = {
    LVS_ICON,
    LVS_SMALLICON,
    LVS_LIST,
    LVS_REPORT
};

BOOL CFileView::PreCreateWindow (CREATESTRUCT& cs)
{
    if (!CListView::PreCreateWindow (cs))
        return FALSE;

    cs.style &= ~LVS_TYPEMASK;
    cs.style |= LVS_REPORT;
    return TRUE;
}

int CFileView::OnCreate (LPCREATESTRUCT lpcs)
{
    if (!CListView::OnCreate (lpcs) == -1)
        return -1;
```

```
    m_imglLarge.Create (IDR_LARGEDOC, 32, 1, RGB (255, 0, 255));
    m_imglSmall.Create (IDR_SMALLDOC, 16, 1, RGB (255, 0, 255));

    GetListCtrl ().SetImageList (&m_imglLarge, LVSIL_NORMAL);
    GetListCtrl ().SetImageList (&m_imglSmall, LVSIL_SMALL);

    GetListCtrl ().InsertColumn (0, "File Name", LVCFMT_LEFT, 192);
    GetListCtrl ().InsertColumn (1, "Size", LVCFMT_RIGHT, 96);
    GetListCtrl ().InsertColumn (2, "Last Modified", LVCFMT_CENTER, 128);
    return 0;
}

void CFileView::OnDestroy ()
{
    FreeItemMemory ();
    CListView::OnDestroy ();
}

void CFileView::OnUpdate (CView* pView, LPARAM lHint, CObject* pHint)
{
    if (lHint != NULL) {
        FreeItemMemory ();
        GetListCtrl ().DeleteAllItems ();
        InitList ((LPCTSTR) lHint);
        return;
    }
    CListView::OnUpdate (pView, lHint, pHint);
}

void CFileView::OnChangeView (UINT nID)
{
    ModifyStyle (LVS_TYPEMASK,
        m_dwStyleList[nID - ID_VIEW_LARGE_ICON]);
}

void CFileView::OnUpdateViewUI (CCmdUI* pCmdUI)
{
    DWORD dwCurrentStyle = GetStyle () & LVS_TYPEMASK;
    pCmdUI->SetCheck (dwCurrentStyle ==
        m_dwStyleList[pCmdUI->m_nID - ID_VIEW_LARGE_ICON]);
}

void CFileView::OnGetDispInfo (NMHDR* pnmh, LRESULT* pResult)
{
    CString string;
    LV_DISPINFO* plvdi = (LV_DISPINFO*) pnmh;
```

(continued)

FileView.cpp *continued*

```
        if (plvdi->item.mask & LVIF_TEXT) {
            ITEMINFO* pItem = (ITEMINFO*) plvdi->item.lParam;

            switch (plvdi->item.iSubItem) {

            case 0: // File name
                ::lstrcpy (plvdi->item.pszText, (LPCTSTR) pItem->strFileName);
                break;

            case 1: // File size
                string.Format ("%u", pItem->nFileSizeLow);
                ::lstrcpy (plvdi->item.pszText, (LPCTSTR) string);
                break;

            case 2: // Date and time
                CTime time (pItem->ftLastWriteTime);

                BOOL pm = FALSE;
                int nHour = time.GetHour ();
                if (nHour == 0)
                    nHour = 12;
                else if (nHour == 12)
                    pm = TRUE;
                else if (nHour > 12) {
                    nHour -= 12;
                    pm = TRUE;
                }

                string.Format ("%d/%0.2d/%0.2d (%d:%0.2d%c)",
                    time.GetMonth (), time.GetDay (), time.GetYear () % 100,
                    nHour, time.GetMinute (), pm ? 'p' : 'a');
                ::lstrcpy (plvdi->item.pszText, (LPCTSTR) string);
                break;
            }
        }
}

void CFileView::OnColumnClick (NMHDR* pnmh, LRESULT* pResult)
{
    NM_LISTVIEW* pnmlv = (NM_LISTVIEW*) pnmh;
    GetListCtrl ().SortItems (CompareFunc, pnmlv->iSubItem);
}

int CALLBACK CFileView::CompareFunc (LPARAM lParam1, LPARAM lParam2,
    LPARAM lParamSort)
{
    ITEMINFO* pItem1 = (ITEMINFO*) lParam1;
```

```
        ITEMINFO* pItem2 = (ITEMINFO*) lParam2;
        int nResult;

        switch (lParamSort) {

        case 0: // File name
            nResult = pItem1->strFileName.CompareNoCase (pItem2->strFileName);
            break;

        case 1: // File size
            nResult = pItem1->nFileSizeLow - pItem2->nFileSizeLow;
            break;

        case 2: // Date and time
            nResult = ::CompareFileTime (&pItem1->ftLastWriteTime,
                &pItem2->ftLastWriteTime);
            break;
        }
        return nResult;
    }

    int CFileView::InitList (LPCTSTR pszPath)
    {
        CString strPath = pszPath;
        if (strPath.Right (1) != "\\")
            strPath += "\\";
        strPath += "*.*";

        HANDLE hFind;
        WIN32_FIND_DATA fd;
        int nCount = 0;

        if ((hFind = ::FindFirstFile ((LPCTSTR) strPath, &fd)) !=
            INVALID_HANDLE_VALUE) {

            if (!(fd.dwFileAttributes & FILE_ATTRIBUTE_DIRECTORY)) {
                AddItem (nCount, &fd);
                nCount++;
            }

            while (::FindNextFile (hFind, &fd)) {
                if (!(fd.dwFileAttributes & FILE_ATTRIBUTE_DIRECTORY))
                    if (!AddItem (nCount, &fd))
                        break;
                    nCount++;
            }
            CloseHandle (hFind);
```

(continued)

FileView.cpp *continued*

```
        }
    return nCount;
}

BOOL CFileView::AddItem (int nIndex, WIN32_FIND_DATA* pfd)
{
    ITEMINFO* pItem;
    try {
        pItem = new ITEMINFO;
    }
    catch (CMemoryException* e) {
        e->Delete ();
        return FALSE;
    }

    pItem->strFileName = pfd->cFileName;
    pItem->nFileSizeLow = pfd->nFileSizeLow;
    pItem->ftLastWriteTime = pfd->ftLastWriteTime;

    LV_ITEM lvi;
    lvi.mask = LVIF_TEXT | LVIF_IMAGE | LVIF_PARAM;
    lvi.iItem = nIndex;
    lvi.iSubItem = 0;
    lvi.iImage = 0;
    lvi.pszText = LPSTR_TEXTCALLBACK;
    lvi.lParam = (LPARAM) pItem;

    if (GetListCtrl ().InsertItem (&lvi) == -1)
        return FALSE;

    return TRUE;
}

void CFileView::FreeItemMemory ()
{
    int nCount = GetListCtrl ().GetItemCount ();
    if (nCount) {
        for (int i=0; i<nCount; i++)
            delete (ITEMINFO*) GetListCtrl ().GetItemData (i);
    }
}
```

Most of Wanderer's functionality comes from the classes *CDriveView* and *CFileView*. Both are self-contained classes you can remove from Wanderer and plug into other applications. You can even derive classes of your own from them to further customize their behavior.

The *CDriveView* Class

CDriveView is basically a *CTreeView* with an *OnCreate* function that enumerates all the drives on the host PC. *OnCreate* uses *SetImageList* to import an image list containing bitmaps for different drive types (floppy disk, hard disk, and CD-ROM) and then calls a protected member function named *InitTree* to initialize the drive list. *InitTree* uses Windows 95's *::GetLogicalDrives* function to identify the logical drives in the system. For each drive, it then calls *CDriveView::AddDriveNode* to add a "drive node"—a tree view item representing a drive—to the tree's uppermost level. *::GetLogicalDrives* returns a DWORD value with "on" bits identifying the valid logical drives, where bit 0 corresponds to drive A:, bit 1 to drive B:, and so on. *InitTree* needs just a few lines of code to enumerate the drives present in the system and call *AddDriveNode* for each:

```
int nPos = 0;
int nDrivesAdded = 0;
CString strDrive = "?:\\";

DWORD dwDriveList = ::GetLogicalDrives ();

while (dwDriveList) {
    if (dwDriveList & 1) {
        strDrive.SetAt (0, 0x41 + nPos);
        if (AddDriveNode (strDrive))
            nDrivesAdded++;
    }
    dwDriveList >>= 1;
    nPos++;
}
```

The *CString* passed to *AddDriveNode* is a string describing the path to a drive's root directory—"A:\" for drive A:, "B:\" for drive B:, and so on.

AddDriveNode calls *CTreeCtrl::InsertItem* to add a drive item to the tree and adds a "dummy" child item so that the drive will have a button with a plus sign next to it. *AddDriveNode* also has to determine the type of drive it's dealing with so that it can decide which image to use to represent the drive. Given a character string specifying the path to a drive's root directory, *::GetDriveType* returns a UINT value identifying the drive type. The possible return values are shown in the table on the next page.

AddDriveNode uses a *switch-case* structure to handle each of the possible return values. DRIVE_REMOVABLE drives are assigned an image that looks like a floppy disk, DRIVE_CDROM drives are assigned an image that resembles a compact disc, and all other types of drives are assigned an image that depicts a hard disk. The images themselves are stored in Drives.bmp. A series of ILI_ values defined near the top of DriveView.cpp correlates drive types and image indexes.

Return Value	Meaning
0	Unknown drive type.
1	The root directory does not exist.
DRIVE_REMOVABLE	The drive is removable (returned for floppy drives).
DRIVE_FIXED	The drive is fixed (returned for hard disks).
DRIVE_REMOTE	The drive is remote (returned for network drives).
DRIVE_CDROM	The drive is a CD-ROM drive.
DRIVE_RAMDISK	The drive is a RAM disk.

Much of the remaining code in DriveView.cpp is devoted to processing TVN_ITEMEXPANDING notifications. For performance reasons, *CDriveView* doesn't initialize itself with items representing every directory on every drive. Instead, it adds items representing directories to a subtree just before the subtree is displayed and removes them when the subtree is collapsed. If a collapsed subtree contains at least one directory, a single child item is inserted, so a plus sign will appear next to the subtree. That child item is never seen because it's deleted before the subtree is expanded and replaced with items representing actual directories. An ON_NOTIFY-_REFLECT entry in the message map reflects TVN_ITEMEXPANDING notifications so that *CDriveView* can handle them itself. The notification handler *OnItemExpanding* either adds items to the subtree or removes them, depending on whether the *action* field of the NM_TREEVIEW structure indicates that the subtree is about to expand or collapse.

CDriveView also includes an *OnSelChanged* function that processes reflected TVN_SELCHANGED messages. *OnSelChanged* converts the HTREEITEM handle of the item that's currently selected into a path name using *CDriveView::GetPathFromNode* and then calls a virtual function named *OnSelectionChanged* and passes it the path name. The *CDriveView* implementation of *OnSelectionChanged* calls the document object's *UpdateAllViews* function to inform other views (in Wanderer's case, the companion *CFileView*) of the selection change. The *lHint* parameter passed to *UpdateAll-Views* contains a pointer to the path name. The result? If you derive a class from *CDriveView*, all you have to do to respond to selection changes is override *OnSelection-Changed*. Call the base class's implementation if you'd like other views to know about the selection change, too.

The Win32 *::FindFirstFile* and *::FindNextFile* functions

CDriveView::OnItemExpanding uses a helper function named *AddDirectories* to initialize an expanding subtree with a list of directory names. *AddDirectories* uses the Win32 *::FindFirstFile* and *::FindNextFile* functions to enumerate a directory's contents. The following routine enumerates all the files and directories in the root directory of drive C: and adds their names to a list box pointed to by *pListBox*:

```
HANDLE hFind;
WIN32_FIND_DATA fd;

if ((hFind = ::FindFirstFile ("C:\\*.*", &fd)) !=
    INVALID_HANDLE_VALUE) {
    pListBox->AddString (fd.cFileName);
    while (::FindNextFile (hFind, &fd))
        pListBox->AddString (fd.cFileName);
    ::CloseHandle (hFind);
}
```

Path names passed to *::FindFirstFile* can be absolute or relative. Substituting "*.*" for "C:*.*" in the example above would enumerate the contents of the current directory.

If *::FindFirstFile* returns a value other than INVALID_HANDLE_VALUE or *::Find-NextFile* returns non-NULL, the WIN32_FIND_DATA structure referenced in the functions' argument lists contains information about the file or directory that was found. WIN32_FIND_DATA is defined as follows:

```
typedef struct _WIN32_FIND_DATA {
    DWORD       dwFileAttributes;
    FILETIME    ftCreationTime;
    FILETIME    ftLastAccessTime;
    FILETIME    ftLastWriteTime;
    DWORD       nFileSizeHigh;
    DWORD       nFileSizeLow;
    DWORD       dwReserved0;
    DWORD       dwReserved1;
    CHAR        cFileName[MAX_PATH];
    CHAR        cAlternateFileName[14];
} WIN32_FIND_DATA;
```

dwFileAttributes contains a series of bit flags defining the attributes of the file or directory described in the WIN32_FIND_DATA structure. The possible values are shown in the table on the next page.

ftCreationTime, *ftLastAccessTime*, and *ftLastWriteTime* specify the date and time of creation, the date and time of the most recent access, and the date and time of the most recent modification. In current versions of Windows 95 (versions that use the VFAT file system), only *ftLastWriteTime* is supported. You can convert FILETIME values into calendar dates and wall-clock times with the *::FileTimeToSystemTime* API function. You can also construct an MFC *CTime* object from a FILETIME value and use *CTime* member functions to extract date and time information. A WIN32_FIND-_DATA structure's *nFileSizeHigh* and *nFileSizeHigh* fields specify the file size in bytes. *cFileName* and *cAlternateFileName* hold the long and short versions of the file or directory name.

Attribute	Meaning
FILE_ATTRIBUTE_ARCHIVE	The file has been modified since it was last backed up.
FILE_ATTRIBUTE_COMPRESSED	The file is compressed.
FILE_ATTRIBUTE_DIRECTORY	This data structure describes a directory, not a file.
FILE_ATTRIBUTE_HIDDEN	The file or directory is hidden.
FILE_ATTRIBUTE_NORMAL	The file is "normal"—that is, it possesses none of the other attributes.
FILE_ATTRIBUTE_READONLY	The file is marked read-only and therefore can't be written to.
FILE_ATTRIBUTE_SYSTEM	The file is a system file.
FILE_ATTRIBUTE_TEMPORARY	The file is a temporary file (not used in Windows 95).

Knowing this, you should be able to look at the code for *CDriveView::OnItem-Expanding* and understand exactly what's going on. *OnItemExpanding* distinguishes between file and directory names by checking *dwFileAttributes* for a FILE_ATTRI-BUTE_DIRECTORY flag. It also weeds out the "." and ".." directory entries present in every subdirectory by performing string comparisons on directory names returned in *cFileName*. Wanderer's *CFileView* class also uses *::FindFirstFile* and *::FindNextFile* to examine a directory's contents, but it builds lists of files by discarding directory names rather than file names. See *CFileView::InitList* for details.

The *CFileView* Class

Wanderer's *CFileView* class displays the names of all the files in the directory selected in the companion *CDriveView*. *CFileView* knows when the selection changes in the *CDriveView* window because its *OnUpdate* function gets called with a string describing the path to the selected directory when *CDriveView::OnSelectionChanged* calls *UpdateAllViews*. Just as *CDriveView* modifies *CTreeView* by initializing a tree view control with items representing the drives and directories on the host PC, *CFileView* modifies *CListView* by automatically enumerating the contents of directories whose path names are passed to *OnUpdate*.

CFileView::InitList builds the list of enumerated file names each time *OnUpdate* is called. For each file that it identifies with *::FindFirstFile* and *::FindNextFile*, *InitList* adds an item to the list view by calling *CFileView::AddItem*. *AddItem*, in turn, allocates memory for an ITEMINFO data structure, initializes the structure with the file's name, size, and date-time stamp, and adds an item to the list view whose *lParam* is actually the address of the corresponding data structure. Here's how it looks with error-checking code removed:

```
ITEMINFO* pItem;
pItem = new ITEMINFO;

pItem->strFileName = pfd->cFileName;
pItem->nFileSizeLow = pfd->nFileSizeLow;
pItem->ftLastWriteTime = pfd->ftLastWriteTime;

LV_ITEM lvi;
lvi.mask = LVIF_TEXT | LVIF_IMAGE | LVIF_PARAM;
lvi.iItem = nIndex;
lvi.iSubItem = 0;
lvi.iImage = 0;
lvi.pszText = LPSTR_TEXTCALLBACK;
lvi.lParam = (LPARAM) pItem;

GetListCtrl ().InsertItem (&lvi);
```

Note the LPSTR_TEXTCALLBACK value specified in the LV_ITEM structure's *pszText* field. Rather than assign the item a text string, *AddItem* tells the list view, "Call me back when you need a label for the item." It's not necessary to initialize the subitems because LPSTR_TEXTCALLBACK is the default for subitems.

CFileView uses callbacks for item and subitem text so that it can maintain its own item data without forcing the control to maintain copies of the data, too. Callbacks come in the form of LVN_GETDISPINFO notifications, which *CFileView* reflects to its own *OnGetDispInfo* handler with an ON_NOTIFY_REFLECT message map entry. When *OnGetDispInfo* is called, *pnmh* points to an LV_DISPINFO structure. The structure's *item.lParam* field contains the address of the ITEMINFO structure for the item in question, and the *item.iSubItem* field contains the index of the requested subitem. *CFileView::OnGetDispInfo* formulates a text string from the data stored in the ITEMINFO structure's *strFileName*, *nFileSizeLow*, or *ftLastWriteTime* field and copies the result to the address contained in the LV_DISPINFO structure's *item.pszText* field. The list view control then displays the text on the screen.

CFileView maintains its own item data so that *CListCtrl::SortItems* can be called and *CFileView::CompareFunc* can retrieve any or all of an item's data by using the pointer stored in the item's *lParam*. If the user clicks a column header while the list view is in report view, an ON_NOTIFY_REFLECT entry in the message map activates *CFileView::OnColumnClick*, and *OnColumnClick*, in turn, calls the list view's *SortItems* function, passing in the index of the column that was clicked:

```
void CFileView::OnColumnClick (NMHDR* pnmh, LRESULT* pResult)
{
    NM_LISTVIEW* pnmlv = (NM_LISTVIEW*) pnmh;
    GetListCtrl ().SortItems (CompareFunc, pnmlv->iSubItem);
}
```

CompareFunc is the application-defined sorting routine the list view calls to compare pairs of items. It's declared static in FileView.h because it's a true callback function. *CompareFunc* uses the ITEMINFO pointers passed in *lParam1* and *lParam2* to retrieve the data for the items it's asked to compare and uses the column index in *lParamSort* to determine which of the items' subitems to use as the basis for the comparison. The entire function requires fewer than 20 lines of code:

```
int CALLBACK CFileView::CompareFunc (LPARAM lParam1, LPARAM lParam2,
    LPARAM lParamSort)
{
    ITEMINFO* pItem1 = (ITEMINFO*) lParam1;
    ITEMINFO* pItem2 = (ITEMINFO*) lParam2;
    int nResult;

    switch (lParamSort) {

    case 0: // File name
        nResult = pItem1->strFileName.CompareNoCase
            (pItem2->strFileName);
        break;

    case 1: // File size
        nResult = pItem1->nFileSizeLow - pItem2->nFileSizeLow;
        break;

    case 2: // Date and time
        nResult = ::CompareFileTime (&pItem1->ftLastWriteTime,
            &pItem2->ftLastWriteTime);
        break;
    }
    return nResult;
}
```

A negative return value from *CompareFunc* indicates that item 1 is less than (should come before) item 2, 0 means that they're equal, and a positive return value means that item 1 is greater than item 2. The *::CompareFileTime* API function makes it easy to compare dates and times encapsulated in FILETIME values. You can also create *CTime* objects from FILETIME values and use <, >, and other operators to compare dates and times.

It may not be obvious to you yet, but you just saw why a list view class with sortable columns has to store its own data. The only information *CompareFunc* receives about the items it's asked to compare is the items' *lParam* values. Therefore, *lParam* has to provide full access to all of an item's data. One way to make sure that it does is to store item data in memory allocated by the application (in Wanderer's case, in ITEMINFO structures allocated with *new*) and to store a pointer to the data in each item's own *lParam*. Storing item data yourself rather than converting it to text and handing it over to the list view control provides greater flexibility in sorting because the data can be stored in binary. How else could you sort the information that appears in *CFileView*'s Last Modified column? A string sort wouldn't work very well because "1/1/96" comes before "9/30/85" even though the former represents a later calendar date. But since *CFileView* stores dates and times in their native FILETIME format, sorting is a piece of cake.

A final note concerning *CFileView* has to do with the method it uses to delete the ITEMINFO structures allocated by *AddItem*. *CFileView::FreeItemMemory* deallocates the memory set aside for each item by iterating through the list of items registered with the list view control and calling *delete* on the pointers stored in the items' *lParam*s:

```
int nCount = GetListCtrl ().GetItemCount ();
if (nCount) {
    for (int i=0; i<nCount; i++)
        delete (ITEMINFO*) GetListCtrl ().GetItemData (i);
}
```

FreeItemMemory is called by *CFileView::OnUpdate* just before the list view is initialized with a new set of file names, and by *CFileView::OnDestroy* so that item memory will be freed when the list view control is destroyed.

Removing the Document Name from the Window Title

Wanderer doesn't include a document name in its frame window title because it doesn't make sense to display a document name when an application doesn't support the loading and saving of documents. But since the document name is added and updated by the framework, Wanderer has to include some special code to prevent "Untitled" from being added to the window title.

The *PreCreateWindow* override in MainFrame.cpp contains the statement

```
cs.style &= ~FWS_ADDTOTITLE;
```

FWS_ADDTOTITLE is a special window style defined by the framework that's included in frame windows by default. Windows that have this style have document names automatically added to their window titles; windows that lack this style don't. By stripping the FWS_ADDTOTITLE bit from the window style in *PreCreateWindow*, *CMainFrame* prevents the framework from modifying its window title.

Custom Command Routing

As you already know, MFC's *CFrameWnd* class routes the command messages and UI update messages it receives to other objects so that commands from menu items and other UI objects don't have to be processed by the frame window. Thanks to command routing, events involving menu items and toolbar buttons can be handled just as easily in the application class or the document class as they can in the frame window class. Chapter 8 described the command routing mechanism, and Figure 8-2 documented the path a command or a UI update message follows after it's received by a frame window. The active view sees the message first, followed by the view's document, the document template, the frame window itself, and finally the application object. For most document/view applications, the command routing sequence shown in Figure 8-2 is fine because it gives each object that's likely to want to see a command or an update message a crack at processing it.

Every now and then you'll run into an application for which default command routing is not sufficient. Wanderer is one of them, and here's why. Commands and UI updates for the view items in Wanderer's Options menu are processed in the *CFileView* class. When *CFileView* is the active view, its command and update handlers work just fine because the active view is included in the framework's routing list. But when *CDriveView* is the active view, *CFileView* is not notified of events involving View commands because it's not the active view. Consequently, the commands in the Options menu are grayed out and can't be selected when the *CDriveView* in the left pane has the input focus.

To circumvent this problem, Wanderer modifies the command routing so that command and update messages that aren't handled by any of the standard command targets are routed to inactive views. The work is done in *CMainFrame::OnCmdMsg*, which first forwards command and update messages to the standard command targets by calling *CFrameWnd::OnCmdMsg*:

```
if (CFrameWnd::OnCmdMsg (nID, nCode, pExtra, pHandlerInfo))
    return TRUE;
```

If *CFrameWnd::OnCmdMsg* returns 0, indicating that none of the standard command targets handled the message, *CMainFrame::OnCmdMsg* calls a function in the document class to route the message to all the inactive views:

```
CWandDoc* pDoc = (CWandDoc*) GetActiveDocument ();
if (pDoc != NULL) {
    if (pDoc->RouteCmdToAllViews (GetActiveView (), nID, nCode,
        pExtra, pHandlerInfo))
        return TRUE;
}
```

CWandDoc::RouteCmdToAllViews iterates through the views associated with the document and calls each view's *OnCmdMsg* function:

```
POSITION pos = GetFirstViewPosition ();

while (pos != NULL) {
    CView* pNextView = GetNextView (pos);
    if (pNextView != pView) {
        if ((((CCmdTarget*) pNextView)->OnCmdMsg (nID, nCode,
            pExtra, pHandlerInfo))
```

```
                return TRUE;
        }
    }
    return FALSE;
```

The *CView* pointers returned by *GetNextView* are cast upward to *CCmdTarget* pointers because *OnCmdMsg* is erroneously declared a protected member function in *CView*. It's meant to be public and is declared as such in *CCmdTarget*. *CMainFrame* passes *RouteCmdToAllViews* a pointer to the active view so that the document can avoid calling the active view's *OnCmdMsg* function. The active view has already been called as part of the standard command routing sequence, so it's wasteful to call it again. The frame window provides the pointer to the active view because the document class has no concept of active and inactive views. By the same token, a frame window knows which view is active but doesn't how many views there are. That's why *CMainFrame* calls a function in the document class to iterate through all the views rather than enumerate the views itself.

Custom routing is a powerful tool for routing commands and UI update messages to nonstandard command targets. You can tap into the command routing sequence just about anywhere you want to by overriding the right *OnCmdMsg* function. In general, you should call the base class version of *OnCmdMsg* from an override to keep default command routing intact. And be careful about whose *OnCmdMsg* functions you call because it's possible to fall into a recursive loop in which object A calls object B and object B calls object A. You wouldn't, for example, want to call a view's *OnCmdMsg* function from a document's *OnCmdMsg* function because the view calls the document as part of the standard command routing sequence.

A WORD ON THE OTHER COMMON CONTROLS

Now that you've seen how sliders, spin buttons, tooltips, image lists, tree views, and list views work, it shouldn't be too difficult to get a handle on the other common controls. As an MFC programmer, you may never need to create a *CToolBarCtrl* or *CStatusBarCtrl* directly because the *CToolBar* and *CStatusBar* classes provide much better abstractions of the toolbar and status bar controls found in Comctl32.dll. You already know how to program property sheets using MFC's *CPropertySheet* class (for a review, turn to Chapter 6), and you got a pretty good look at rich edit controls in Chapter 11 when we built an application around a *CRichEditView*. There are only five common controls we haven't covered in one form or another: progress controls, animation controls, hotkey controls, header controls, and tab controls. I'll close out the chapter with a quick (and I do mean quick!) look at progress controls and animation controls because, of the five, these are the ones you're most likely to need.

Progress controls are trivial to implement. Once a progress control is created, you set its range with *CProgressCtrl::SetRange* and its position with *CProgressCtrl-::SetPos*. Often you don't even have to do that because the default range is 0 through 100 and the default position is 0—perfect for displaying the progress of an operation as a percentage of work completed. The bar in a progress control is "stepped" by calling *CProgressCtrl::SetPos* or *CProgressCtrl::OffsetPos* to change the position. You can also establish a step size with *CProgressCtrl::SetStep* and step the control with *CProgressCtrl::StepIt*. A neat trick you can perform with a progress control is to put it inside an indented pane in a status bar. (Be sure you omit WS_BORDER from the progress control's style so that it won't have a border of its own.) Set the progress control's position to 0 when it's not being used, and it will look like an ordinary status bar pane. But start stepping it when a lengthy operation is begun, and the progress bar will appear to be part of the status bar itself.

Animation controls are equally simple to program. *CAnimateCtrl::Open* loads an AVI clip from a resource or an external file. *CAnimateCtrl::Play* plays the clip, and *CAnimateCtrl::Stop* stops it. The clip is played in a separate thread of execution, so the *Play* command returns almost as soon as you call it and the clip runs all by itself. One mistake programmers often make the first time they hear about animation controls is to assume that they can use *CAnimateCtrl* to build a quick and dirty AVI file viewer. Unfortunately, an animation control is choosy about the AVI clips it will play and will ignore audio information altogether. And while the control responds ably to commands such as *Play* and *Stop*, it won't divulge frame numbers, frame counts, and other useful information about the clips it loads. *CAnimateCtrl* is the perfect tool for displaying canned animations such as the circling magnifying glass in the operating system's Find window, but it's not generically useful as a multimedia AVI viewer.

Chapter 14

Threads and Thread Synchronization

In the Win32 environment, each running application constitutes a *process* and each process consists of one or more threads of execution. A *thread* is a path of execution through a process's code. One fundamental difference between 16- and 32-bit Windows is that 32-bit Windows doesn't limit its applications to just one thread each. A process in a 32-bit Windows application begins its life as a single thread, but that thread can spawn additional threads. A preemptive scheduler inside the operating system divides CPU time among active threads so that they appear to run simultaneously. Secondary threads are ideal for performing background tasks such as paginating documents and performing garbage collection. They can also play more visible roles by creating windows and processing messages to those windows, just as the primary thread processes messages sent to an application's main window.

Multithreading is not for everyone. Multithreaded applications are difficult to write and debug because the parallelism of the concurrently running threads adds an extra layer of complexity to the code. But used properly, multiple threads can dramatically improve an application's responsiveness. A word processor that does its spell checking in a dedicated thread, for example, can continue to process input in the primary thread so that the user doesn't have to wait for the spell checker to finish. What makes writing a threaded spell checker difficult is that the spell checking thread will invariably have to synchronize its actions with other threads in the application. Most programmers have been conditioned to think about their code in synchronous terms—function A calls function B, function B initializes variable *foo* and returns to A, and so on. But threads are asynchronous by nature. In a multithreaded application you have to think about what happens if, say, two threads call function B at the same time or one thread reads a variable while another writes it. If function A launches function B in a separate thread, you also must anticipate what problems could occur if function A continues to run while function B executes. For example, it's common to pass the address of a variable created on the stack in function A to function B for processing. But if function B is in another thread, the variable may no longer exist when function B gets around to accessing it. Even the most innocent-looking code can be fatally flawed when it involves the use of multiple threads.

MFC encapsulates threads of execution in the *CWinThread* class. It also includes synchronization classes encapsulating events, mutexes, and other thread synchronization objects found in the Windows 95 kernel. Does MFC make multithreading easier? Not exactly. Developers who have written multithreaded Windows applications in C are often surprised to learn that MFC adds complexities all its own. The key to writing multithreaded programs in MFC is having a keen understanding of what you're doing and knowing where the trouble spots are. This chapter is designed to help you do both.

THREADS

As far as Windows is concerned, all threads are alike. MFC, however, distinguishes between two types of threads: *user interface* (UI) *threads* and *worker threads*. The difference between the two is that UI threads have message loops and worker threads do not. UI threads can create windows and process messages sent to those windows. Worker threads perform background tasks that receive no direct input from the user and therefore don't need windows and message loops.

When you open a folder in the Windows 95 shell, the shell launches a UI thread that creates a window showing the folder's contents. If you drag-copy a group of files to the newly opened folder, that folder's thread performs the file transfers. (Sometimes the UI thread creates yet another thread—this time a worker thread—to copy the files.) The benefit of this multithreaded architecture is that, once the copy operation has begun, you can switch to windows opened onto other folders and continue working while the files are copied in the background. Launching a UI thread that creates a window is conceptually similar to launching an application within an application. The most common use for UI threads is to create multiple windows serviced by separate threads of execution.

Worker threads are ideal for performing isolated tasks that can be broken off from the rest of the application and performed in the background while other processing takes place in the foreground. A classic example of a worker thread is the thread an animation control uses to play AVI clips. Basically all the thread does is draw a frame, put itself to sleep for a fraction of a second, and wake up and start again. It adds little to the processor's workload because it spends most of its life suspended between frames, and yet it also provides a valuable service. This is a great example of multithreaded design because the background thread is given a specific task to do and then allowed to perform that task over and over until the primary thread signals that it's time to end.

Creating a Worker Thread

There are two ways to create a thread in an MFC application. You can construct a *CWinThread* object and call that object's *CreateThread* function to create the thread, or you can use *AfxBeginThread* to construct a *CWinThread* object and create a thread in one step. MFC defines two different versions of *AfxBeginThread*: one for UI threads and another for worker threads. The source code for both is found in Thrdcore.cpp. Don't use the Win32 *::CreateThread* function to create a thread in an MFC program unless the thread doesn't use MFC. *AfxBeginThread* and *CWinThread::CreateThread* aren't merely wrappers around *::CreateThread*; in addition to launching threads of execution, they also initialize internal variables used by the framework, perform sanity checks at various points during the thread creation process, and take steps to ensure that functions in the C run-time library are accessed in a thread-safe way.

AfxBeginThread makes it simple—almost trivial, in fact—to create a worker thread. The statement

```
CWinThread* pThread = AfxBeginThread (ThreadFunc, &threadInfo);
```

starts a worker thread and passes it the address of an application-defined data structure named *threadInfo* that contains input to the thread. *ThreadFunc* is the *thread function*—the function that gets executed when the thread itself begins to execute. A very simple thread function that spins in a loop, eating CPU cycles, and then terminates looks like this:

```
UINT ThreadFunc (LPVOID pParam)
{
    UINT nIterations = pParam;
    for (UINT i=0; i<nIterations; i++);
    return 0;
}
```

We'll look at thread functions in more detail in the next section.

The worker thread form of *AfxBeginThread* accepts as many as four additional parameters that specify the thread's priority, stack size, creation flags, and security attributes. The complete function prototype is shown on the next page.

```
CWinThread* AfxBeginThread (AFX_THREADPROC pfnThreadProc,
    LPVOID pParam, int nPriority = THREAD_PRIORITY_NORMAL,
    UINT nStackSize = 0, DWORD dwCreateFlags = 0,
    LPSECURITY_ATTRIBUTES lpSecurityAttrs = NULL)
```

nPriority specifies the thread's execution priority. High-priority threads are always scheduled for CPU time before low-priority threads, but in practice even threads with extremely low priorities usually get all the processor time they need. *nPriority* doesn't specify an absolute priority level. It specifies a priority level relative to the priority level of the process to which the thread belongs. The default is THREAD_PRIORITY-_NORMAL, which assigns the thread the same priority as the process that owns it. A thread's priority level can be changed at any time with *CWinThread::SetThreadPriority*.

The *nStackSize* parameter passed to *AfxBeginThread* specifies the thread's maximum stack size. In the Win32 environment, each thread receives its own stack. The 0 default *nStackSize* value allows the stack to grow as large as 1 MB. This doesn't mean that every thread requires a minimum of 1 MB of memory; it means that each thread is assigned 1 MB of address space in the larger 4-GB address space in which 32-bit Windows applications execute. Memory isn't committed (assigned) to the stack's address space until it's needed, so most thread stacks never use more than a few kilobytes of physical memory. Placing a limit on the stack size allows the operating system to trap runaway functions that recurse endlessly and eventually consume the stack. The default limit of 1 MB is fine for almost all applications.

dwCreateFlags can be one of two values. The default value 0 tells the system to start executing the thread immediately. If CREATE_SUSPENDED is specified instead, the thread starts out in a suspended state and doesn't begin running until another thread (usually the thread that created it) calls *CWinThread::ResumeThread* on the suspended thread, as demonstrated here:

```
CWinThread* pThread = AfxBeginThread (ThreadFunc, &threadInfo,
    THREAD_PRIORITY_NORMAL, 0, CREATE_SUSPENDED);
        :
        :
pThread->ResumeThread (); // Start the thread
```

Sometimes it's useful to create a thread but defer its execution until later. As you'll see later, it's also possible to create a thread that suspends itself until a specified event occurs.

The final parameter in *AfxBeginThread*'s argument list, *lpSecurityAttrs*, is a pointer to a SECURITY_ATTRIBUTES structure that specifies the new thread's security attributes and also tells the system whether child processes should inherit the thread handle. The NULL default value assigns the new thread the same properties the thread that created it has.

The Thread Function

A worker thread's thread function can be a static class member function or a function declared outside a class. It is prototyped this way:

```
UINT ThreadFunc (LPVOID pParam)
```

pParam is a 32-bit value whose value equals the *pParam* passed to *AfxBeginThread*. Very often *pParam* is the address of an application-defined data structure containing information passed to the worker thread by the thread that created it. It can also be a scalar value, a handle, or even a pointer to an MFC object. It's perfectly legal to use the same thread function for two or more threads, but you should be sensitive to reentrancy problems caused by global and static variables. As long as the variables (and objects) a thread uses are created on the stack, there are no reentrancy problems since each thread gets its own stack.

Creating a User Interface Thread

Creating a UI thread is an altogether different process than creating a worker thread. A worker thread is defined by its thread function, but a UI thread's behavior is governed by a dynamically creatable class derived from *CWinThread* that very much resembles an application class derived from *CWinApp*. The UI thread class shown below creates a top-level frame window that closes itself when clicked with the left mouse button. Closing the window terminates the thread, too, because *CWnd::OnNcDestroy* posts a WM_QUIT message to the thread's message queue. Posting a WM_QUIT message to a secondary thread ends the thread. Posting a WM_QUIT message to a primary thread ends the thread and ends the application, too.

```
// The CUIThread class
class CUIThread : public CWinThread
{
    DECLARE_DYNCREATE (CUIThread)

public:
    virtual BOOL InitInstance ();
};

IMPLEMENT_DYNCREATE (CUIThread, CWinThread)

BOOL CUIThread::InitInstance ()
{
    m_pMainWnd = new CMainWindow;
    m_pMainWnd->ShowWindow (SW_SHOW);
    m_pMainWnd->UpdateWindow ();
    return TRUE;
}
```

(continued)

```
// The CMainWindow class
class CMainWindow : public CFrameWnd
{
public:
    CMainWindow ();

protected:
    afx_msg void OnLButtonDown (UINT, CPoint);
    DECLARE_MESSAGE_MAP ()
};

BEGIN_MESSAGE_MAP (CMainWindow, CFrameWnd)
    ON_WM_LBUTTONDOWN ()
END_MESSAGE_MAP ()

CMainWindow::CMainWindow ()
{
    Create (NULL, "UI Thread Window");
}

void CMainWindow::OnLButtonDown (UINT nFlags, CPoint point)
{
    PostMessage (WM_CLOSE, 0, 0);
}
```

Note the SW_SHOW parameter passed to *ShowWindow* in place of the normal *m_nCmdShow* parameter. *m_nCmdShow* is a *CWinApp* data member, so when you create a top-level window from a UI thread, it's up to you to specify the window's initial show state.

A *CUIThread* is launched by calling the form of *AfxBeginThread* that accepts a *CRuntimeClass* pointer to the thread class:

```
CWinThread* pThread = AfxBeginThread (RUNTIME_CLASS (CUIThread));
```

The UI-thread version of *AfxBeginThread* accepts the same four optional parameters as the worker-thread version, but it doesn't accept a *pParam* value. Once started, a UI thread runs asynchronously with respect to the thread that created it, almost as if it belonged to another application.

Suspending and Resuming Threads

A running thread can be suspended with *CWinThread::SuspendThread* and started again with *CWinThread::ResumeThread*. A thread can call *SuspendThread* on itself, or another thread can call *SuspendThread* for it. However, a suspended thread can't call *ResumeThread* to wake itself up; someone else must call *ResumeThread* on its behalf. A suspended thread consumes next to no processor time and imposes essentially zero overhead on the system.

For each thread, Windows maintains a *suspend count* that's incremented by *SuspendThread* and decremented by *ResumeThread*. A thread is scheduled for processor time only when its suspend count is 0. If *SuspendThread* is called twice in succession, *ResumeThread* must be called twice also. A thread created without a CREATE_SUSPENDED flag is assigned an initial suspend count of 0. A thread created with a CREATE_SUSPENDED flag begins with a suspend count of 1. Both *Suspend-Thread* and *ResumeThread* return the thread's previous suspend count, so you can make sure a thread gets resumed no matter how high its suspend count is by calling *ResumeThread* repeatedly until it returns 1. *ResumeThread* returns 0 if the thread it's called on is not currently suspended.

Putting Threads to Sleep

A thread can put itself to sleep by calling the API function *::Sleep*. A sleeping thread uses no processor time and is automatically awakened after a specified number of milliseconds. The statement

```
::Sleep (10000);
```

suspends the current thread for 10 seconds. One use for *::Sleep* is for implementing threads whose actions are inherently time-based, such as the background thread in an animation control or a thread that moves the hands of a clock. Another use for *::Sleep* is for relinquishing the remainder of a thread's timeslice to other threads waiting to execute. The statement

```
::Sleep (0);
```

suspends the current thread and allows the scheduler to run other threads of equal priority. If there are no other equal priority threads awaiting execution time, the function call returns immediately and the scheduler resumes executing the current thread. If you write an application that uses multiple threads to draw to a display surface, a few strategically placed *::Sleep (0)* statements can do wonders for the quality of the output. You'll see what I mean in a few moments.

Terminating a Thread

Once a thread begins, it can terminate in two ways. A worker thread ends when the thread function executes a *return* statement or calls *AfxEndThread*. A UI thread terminates when a WM_QUIT message is posted to its message queue or a function within the thread calls *AfxEndThread*. A thread can post a WM_QUIT message to itself with the API function *::PostQuitMessage*. *AfxEndThread*, *::PostQuitMessage*, and *return* all accept a 32-bit exit code that can be retrieved with *::GetExitCodeThread* after the thread has terminated. The statement at the top of the next page copies the exit code of the thread referenced by *pThread* to the DWORD variable *dwExitCode*.

```
DWORD dwExitCode;
::GetExitCodeThread (pThread->m_hThread, &dwExitCode);
```

If called for a thread that's still executing, *::GetExitCodeThread* sets *dwExitCode* equal to STILL_ACTIVE (0x103).

One complication in calling *::GetExitCode* in an MFC application is that by default a *CWinThread* object automatically deletes itself when the corresponding thread terminates. Therefore, a *::GetExitCodeThread* statement like the one above will probably generate an access violation if the thread has terminated because *pThread* will no longer be valid. You can avoid such problems by setting the thread object's *m_bAutoDelete* data member to FALSE so that the *CWinThread* object won't be deleted automatically upon thread termination. (Don't forget to delete the *CWinThread* object yourself to avoid memory leaks.) An alternative approach is to save the thread handle stored in the *CWinThread* object's *m_hThread* data member and pass it to *::GetExitCodeThread* directly. Thread handles passed to *::GetExitCodeThread* can identify existing threads or threads that once existed but have since terminated.

Terminating a Thread from Another Thread

Generally speaking, threads can terminate only themselves. If you want thread A to terminate thread B, you need to set up a signaling mechanism that allows thread A to tell thread B to terminate itself. In most cases, a simple variable can serve as a flag that signals a thread to terminate, as demonstrated here:

```
// Thread A
static BOOL bContinue = TRUE;
CWinThread* pThread = AfxBeginThread (ThreadFunc, &bContinue);
// Do some work
bContinue = FALSE; // Tell thread B to terminate
    :
    :

// Thread B
UINT ThreadFunc (LPVOID pParam)
{
    BOOL* pContinue = (BOOL*) pParam;
    while (*pContinue) {
        // Do some work
    }
    return 0;
}
```

Conventional wisdom says that this is a poor way for threads to communicate, but in fact it's just as effective as using a thread synchronization object. Of course, to prevent access violations, you need to ensure that *bContinue* doesn't go out of scope while thread B is running. That's why *bContinue* is declared static in the example.

Even if the function that sets *bContinue* to FALSE in thread A returns before thread B terminates, the variable will still be valid because it's located in the application's data segment, not on the stack.

Now suppose that you'd like to modify this example so that, once it sets *bContinue* to FALSE, thread A stops what it's doing until thread B is no longer running. Here's the proper way to do it:

```
// Thread A
static BOOL bContinue = TRUE;
CWinThread* pThread = AfxBeginThread (ThreadFunc, &bContinue);
// Do some work
HANDLE hThread = pThread->m_hThread; // Save the thread handle
bContinue = FALSE; // Tell thread B to terminate
::WaitForSingleObject (hThread, INFINITE);
    :
    :

// Thread B
UINT ThreadFunc (LPVOID pParam)
{
    BOOL* pContinue = (BOOL*) pParam;
    while (*pContinue) {
        // Do some work
    }
    return 0;
}
```

::WaitForSingleObject waits until the specified object—in this case, another thread—enters a "signaled" state. A thread object goes from nonsignaled to signaled when the thread terminates. The first parameter passed to *::WaitForSingleObject* is the handle of the object you want to wait on. (It can also be a process handle, the handle of a synchronization object, or a file-change notification handle, among other things.) The handle is retrieved from the *CWinThread* object before *bContinue* is set to FALSE because the *CWinThread* object may no longer exist when the call to *::WaitForSingle-Object* is executed. The second parameter is the length of time the thread that calls *::WaitForSingleObject* is willing to wait. INFINITE means wait as long as it takes. When you specify INFINITE, you take the chance that the calling thread could lock up if the object it's waiting on never becomes signaled. If you specify a number of milliseconds instead, as in

```
::WaitForSingleObject (hThread, 5000);
```

::WaitForSingleObject will return after the specified time—here 5 seconds—has elapsed even if the object still hasn't become signaled. You can check the return value to determine why the function returned. WAIT_OBJECT_0 means that the object became signaled, and WAIT_TIMEOUT means that it did not.

Given a thread handle or a *CWinThread* object wrapping a thread handle, you can quickly determine whether the thread is still running by calling *::WaitForSingle-Object* and specifying 0 for the time-out period, as shown here:

```
if (::WaitForSingleObject (hThread, 0) == WAIT_OBJECT_0)
    // The thread no longer exists
else
    // The thread still exists
```

Called this way, *::WaitForSingleObject* doesn't wait; it returns immediately. A return value equal to WAIT_OBJECT_0 means that the thread is signaled (no longer exists), and a return value equal to WAIT_TIMEOUT means that the thread is nonsignaled (still exists). Remember: because a *CWinThread* object is automatically deleted when a thread terminates, it doesn't make sense to call *::WaitForSingleObject* to find out whether a *CWinThread* is signaled or nonsignaled unless the *CWinThread* object's *m_bAutoDelete* data member is set to FALSE.

Don't make the mistake of waiting for a thread to terminate by writing code like this:

```
// Thread A (don't do this!)
static BOOL bContinue = TRUE;
CWinThread* pThread = AfxBeginThread (ThreadFunc, &bContinue);
// Do some work
HANDLE hThread = pThread->m_hThread; // Save the thread handle
bContinue = FALSE; // Tell thread B to terminate
DWORD dwExitCode;
do {
    ::GetExitCodeThread (hThread, &dwExitCode);
} while (dwExitCode == STILL_ACTIVE);
    .
    .
    .
// Thread B
UINT ThreadFunc (LPVOID pParam)
{
    BOOL* pContinue = (BOOL*) pParam;
    while (*pContinue) {
        // Do some work
    }
    return 0;
}
```

In addition to spending CPU time needlessly by forcing the primary thread to spin in a *do-while* loop, this code will probably cause the application to lock up. When a thread calls *::WaitForSingleObject*, it waits very efficiently because it is effectively suspended until the function call returns. The thread is said "to be blocked" or "to block" until *::WaitForSingleObject* returns.

There is one way a thread can kill another directly, but you should use it only as a last resort. The statement

```
::TerminateThread (pThread->m_hThread, 0);
```

terminates *pThread* and assigns it an exit code of 0. The Win32 API reference documents some of the many problems *::TerminateThread* can cause, which range from orphaned thread synchronization objects to DLLs that don't get a chance to execute normal thread-shutdown code.

Threads, Processes, and Priorities

The scheduler is the component of the operating system that decides which threads run when and for how long. Thread scheduling is a complex task whose goal is to divide CPU time among multiple threads of execution as efficiently as possible to create the illusion that all of them are running at once. On machines with multiple CPUs, Windows NT really does run two or more threads at the same time by assigning different threads to different processors. This feature is known as *symmetric multiprocessing,* or SMP. Windows 95 is not an SMP system, so it schedules all of its threads on the same CPU even if several CPUs are present.

The Windows 95 scheduler uses a variety of techniques to improve multitasking performance and to try to ensure that each thread in the system gets an ample amount of CPU time, but ultimately the decision about which thread should execute next boils down to the thread with the highest priority. At any given moment, each thread is assigned a priority level from 0 through 31, with higher numbers indicating higher priorities. If a priority-16 thread is waiting to execute and all of the other threads vying for CPU time have priority levels of 15 or less, the priority-16 thread gets scheduled next. If two priority-16 threads are waiting to execute, the scheduler executes the one that has executed the least recently. When that thread's timeslice is up, the other priority-16 thread gets executed if all of the other threads still have lower priorities. As a rule, the scheduler *always* gives the next timeslice to the thread waiting to execute that has the highest priority.

Does this mean that lower-priority threads will never get executed? Not at all. First, remember that Windows is a message-based operating system. If a thread's message queue is empty when the thread calls *::GetMessage* to retrieve a message, the thread blocks until a message becomes available. This gives lower priority threads a chance to execute because blocked threads receive no timeslices. Most UI threads spend the major part of their time blocked on the message queue waiting for input, so as long as a high-priority worker thread doesn't monopolize the CPU, even very low priority threads typically get all the CPU time they need. (A worker thread never blocks on the message queue because it doesn't process messages.)

The scheduler also plays a lot of tricks with threads' priority levels to enhance the overall responsiveness of the system and reduce the chance that any thread will be starved for CPU time. A thread may have a priority level of 7, but if that thread goes for too long without receiving a timeslice, the scheduler may temporarily boost the thread's priority level to 8 or 9 or even higher to give it a chance to execute. Windows 95 boosts the priorities of all threads that belong to the foreground process to improve the responsiveness of the application in which the user is working, and it boosts a thread's priority even further when the thread has an input message to process. The system also uses a technique called *priority inheritance* to prevent high-priority threads from blocking for too long on synchronization objects owned by low-priority threads. For example, if a priority-16 thread tries to access a critical section owned by a priority-10 thread, the scheduler will treat the priority-10 thread as if it had priority 16 until the thread releases the critical section. This way, the critical section will come free faster and the priority-16 thread won't get stuck waiting on a lower-priority thread.

How do thread priorities get assigned in the first place? When you call *AfxBeginThread* or *CWinThread::SetThreadPriority*, you specify the *relative thread priority* value. (An aside: The *::CreateThread* API function that starts a thread doesn't accept a relative thread priority value. When *AfxBeginThread* starts a thread for you, it calls *SetThreadPriority* after it creates the thread to set the thread's relative priority.) The operating system combines the relative priority level with the priority class of the process that owns the thread (more about that in a moment) to compute a *base priority level* for the thread. The thread's actual priority level—a number from 0 through 31—varies from moment to moment depending on whether the process that owns it is running in the foreground or the background. The actual priority level is also subject to change from the system's dynamic boosting, but most of the time it stays within 2 or 3 digits of the base priority level. You can't control boosting (and you wouldn't want to even if you could), but you can control the base priority level by setting the process priority class and the relative thread priority level.

Process Priority Classes

Most processes begin life with the priority class NORMAL_PRIORITY_CLASS. Once started, however, a process can change its priority class by calling *::SetPriorityClass*, which accepts a process handle (obtainable with *::GetCurrentProcess*) and one of the specifiers shown in the table on the facing page.

Most applications don't need to change their priority classes. HIGH_PRIORITY-_CLASS and REALTIME_PRIORITY_CLASS processes can severely inhibit the responsiveness of the system and even delay critical system activities such as flushing of the disk cache. One legitimate use for HIGH_PRIORITY_CLASS is for system applications that remain hidden most of the time but pop up a window when a certain input event occurs. These applications impose very little overhead on the system while they're blocked waiting for input, but once the input appears, they receive priority over normal applications. REALTIME_PRIORITY_CLASS is provided primarily for the benefit of real-time data acquisition programs that must have the lion's share of the CPU time in order to work properly. IDLE_PRIORITY_CLASS is ideal for screen savers, system monitors, and other low priority applications that operate unobtrusively in the background.

PROCESS PRIORITY CLASSES

Priority Class	Description
IDLE_PRIORITY_CLASS	The process runs only when the system is idle— for example, when other threads are blocked on the message queue waiting for input.
NORMAL_PRIORITY_CLASS	The default process priority class. The process has no special scheduling needs.
HIGH_PRIORITY_CLASS	The process should receive priority over IDLE_PRIORITY_CLASS and NORMAL_PRIORITY_CLASS processes.
REALTIME_PRIORITY_CLASS	The process must have the highest possible priority, and its threads should preempt even threads belonging to HIGH_PRIORITY_CLASS processes.

Relative Thread Priorities

The table on the next page shows the relative thread priority values you can pass to *AfxBeginThread* and *CWinThread::SetThreadPriority*. The default is THREAD_PRIORITY_NORMAL, which *AfxBeginThread* automatically assigns to a thread unless you specify otherwise. In Windows 95, a THREAD_PRIORITY_NORMAL thread that belongs to a NORMAL_PRIORITY_CLASS process has a base priority level of 7 if the process is in the background and of 8 if the process is in the foreground. At various times, the thread priority may be boosted for any of the reasons mentioned earlier, but it will eventually return to 7 or 8. A THREAD_PRIORITY_LOWEST thread running in a HIGH_PRIORITY_CLASS background or foreground process has a base priority of 11. The actual numbers aren't as important as realizing that you can fine-tune the relative priorities of the threads within a process to achieve the best responsiveness and performance—and if necessary, you can adjust the priority of the process itself.

Now that you understand where thread priorities come from and how they affect the scheduling process, how do you know when to adjust thread priorities and what to adjust them to? As a rule, if a thread needs a high priority, it's usually obvious that the thread needs a high priority. If it's not obvious that a thread requires a high priority, a normal thread priority will probably do. For most threads, the default THREAD_PRIORITY_NORMAL is just fine. But if you're writing a communications program that uses a dedicated thread to read and buffer data from a serial port, you might miss bytes here and there unless the thread that does the reading and buffering has a relative priority value of THREAD_PRIORITY_HIGHEST or THREAD_PRIORITY_CRITICAL.

RELATIVE THREAD PRIORITIES

Priority Value	Description
THREAD_PRIORITY_IDLE	The thread's base priority level is equal to 1 if the process's priority class is HIGH_PRIORITY-_CLASS or lower; the thread's base priority level is equal to 16 if the process's priority class is REALTIME_PRIORITY_CLASS.
THREAD_PRIORITY_LOWEST	The thread's base priority level is equal to the process's priority class minus 2.
THREAD_PRIORITY_BELOW_NORMAL	The thread's base priority level is equal to the process's priority class minus 1.
THREAD_PRIORITY_NORMAL	The default thread priority value. The thread's base priority level is equal to the process's priority class.
THREAD_PRIORITY_ABOVE_NORMAL	The thread's base priority level is equal to the process's priority class plus 1.
THREAD_PRIORITY_HIGHEST	The thread's base priority level is equal to the process's priority class plus 2.
THREAD_PRIORITY_CRITICAL	The thread's base priority level is equal to 15 if the process's priority class is HIGH_PRIORITY-_CLASS or lower; the thread's base priority level is equal to 31 if the process's priority class is REALTIME_PRIORITY_CLASS.

One thing's for sure: if an application is a CPU hog and it's not designed to fulfill a specific purpose such as performing real-time data acquisition on a PC dedicated to that task, the market will look upon it unfavorably. CPU time is a computer's most precious resource. Use it judiciously, and don't get caught in the trap of bumping up priority levels to make your own application execute 5 percent faster when that will subtract 50 percent from the speed and responsiveness of other applications.

Sharing MFC Objects Among Threads

Now for the bad news about writing multithreaded MFC applications. As long as threads are written so that they don't call member functions belonging to objects created by other threads, there are few restrictions on what they can do. However, if thread A passes a *CWnd* pointer to thread B and thread B calls a member function of that *CWnd* object, MFC is likely to halt a debug build of the application with an assertion error. A release build might work fine—but then again, it might not. There's also a possibility in this situation that a debug build won't assert but that it won't work properly, either. It all depends on what goes on inside the framework when that particular *CWnd* member function is called. You can avoid a potential minefield of problems by compartmentalizing your threads and having each thread create the objects it uses rather than rely on objects created by other threads. But for cases in which that's simply not practical, here are a few rules to go by.

First, there are many MFC member functions that *can* be safely called on objects in other threads. Most of the inline functions defined in the .inl files in MFC's Include directory can be called through object pointers passed in from other threads because they are little more than wrappers around API functions. But calling a noninline member function is asking for trouble. For example, the following code, which passes a *CWnd* pointer named *pWnd* from thread A to thread B and has B call *CWnd::GetParent* through the pointer, works without problems:

```
CWinThread* pThread = AfxBeginThread (ThreadFunc, pWnd);
    :
    :

UINT ThreadFunc (LPVOID pParam)
{
    CWnd* pWnd = (CWnd*) pParam;
    CWnd* pParent = pWnd->GetParent ();
    return 0;
}
```

Simply changing *GetParent* to *GetParentFrame*, however, causes an assertion error the moment thread B is started:

```
CWinThread* pThread = AfxBeginThread (ThreadFunc, pWnd);
    :
    :

UINT ThreadFunc (LPVOID pParam)
{
    CWnd* pWnd = (CWnd*) pParam;
    // Get ready for an assertion error!
    CWnd* pParent = pWnd->GetParentFrame ();
    return 0;
}
```

Why does *GetParent* work when *GetParentFrame* doesn't? Because *GetParent* calls through almost directly to the *::GetParent* function in the API. Here's how *CWnd::GetParent* is defined in Afxwin2.inl, with a little reformatting thrown in to enhance readability:

```
_AFXWIN_INLINE CWnd* CWnd::GetParent () const
{
    ASSERT (::IsWindow (m_hWnd));
    return CWnd::FromHandle (::GetParent (m_hWnd));
}
```

No problem there; *m_hWnd* is valid because it's part of the *CWnd* object that *pWnd* points to, and *FromHandle* converts the HWND returned by *::GetParent* into a *CWnd* pointer.

But now consider what happens when you call *GetParentFrame*, whose source code is found in Wincore.cpp. The line that causes the assertion error is

```
ASSERT_VALID (this);
```

ASSERT_VALID calls *CWnd::AssertValid*, which performs a sanity check by making sure that the HWND associated with *this* appears in the permanent or temporary handle map the framework uses to convert HWNDs into *CWnd*s. Going from a *CWnd* to an HWND is easy because the HWND is a data member of the *CWnd*, but going from an HWND to a *CWnd* can be done only through the handle maps. And here's the problem: Handle maps are local to each thread and are not visible to other threads. If the *CWnd* whose address is passed to ASSERT_VALID was created by another thread, the corresponding HWND won't appear in the current thread's permanent or temporary handle map and MFC will assert. Many of MFC's noninline member functions call ASSERT_VALID, but inline functions do not—at least not in current releases.

Frequently MFC's assertions protect you from calling functions that wouldn't work anyway. In a release build, *GetParentFrame* returns NULL when called from a thread other than the one in which the parent frame was created. But in cases in which assertion errors are spurious—that is, in cases in which the function would work okay despite the per-thread handle tables—you can avoid assertions by passing real handles instead of object pointers. For example, it's safe to call *CWnd::GetTopLevelParent* in a secondary thread if *FromHandle* is called first to create an entry in the thread's temporary handle map, as shown here:

```
CWinThread* pThread = AfxBeginThread (ThreadFunc, pWnd->m_hWnd);
    :
    :
UINT ThreadFunc (LPVOID pParam)
{
    CWnd* pWnd = CWnd::FromHandle ((HWND) pParam);
    CWnd* pParent = pWnd->GetTopLevelParent ();
    return 0;
}
```

That's why the MFC documentation warns that windows, GDI objects, and other objects should be passed between threads by means of handles instead of by means of pointers to MFC objects. In general, you'll have fewer problems if you pass handles instead of object pointers and then use *FromHandle* to "re-create" objects in the temporary handle map of the current thread. But don't take that to mean that just any function will work. It won't.

What about calling member functions belonging to objects created from "pure" MFC classes such as *CDocument* and *CRect*—classes that don't wrap HWNDs, HDCs, or other handle types and therefore don't rely on handle maps? Just what you wanted to hear: some work and some don't. There's no problem with this code:

```
CWinThread* pThread = AfxBeginThread (ThreadFunc, pRect);

    .
    .
    .

UINT ThreadFunc (LPVOID pParam)
{
    CRect* pRect = (CRect*) pParam;
    int nArea = pRect->Width () * pRect->Height ();
    return 0;
}
```

But the following code will assert on you:

```
CWinThread* pThread = AfxBeginThread (ThreadFunc, pDoc);

    .
    .
    .

UINT ThreadFunc (LPVOID pParam)
{
    CMyDocument* pDoc = (CMyDocument*) pParam;
    pDoc->UpdateAllViews (NULL);
    return 0;
}
```

Even seemingly innocuous functions such as *AfxGetMainWnd* frequently don't work when they're called from secondary threads.

The bottom line is that before you go calling member functions of MFC objects created in other threads, you *must understand the implications*. And the only way to understand the implications is to study the MFC source code to see how a particular member function behaves. Also keep in mind that MFC isn't thread safe, a subject we'll explore further later in this chapter. So even if a member function appears to be safe, ask yourself what might happen if an object created by thread A were accessed by thread B and thread A preempted thread B in the middle of the access. This is incredibly difficult stuff to sort out and only adds to the complexity of writing multi-threaded applications. Avoid crossing thread boundaries with calls to MFC member functions, and you'll avoid a lot of problems, too.

Using C Run-Time Functions in Multithreaded Applications

Certain functions in the standard C run-time library pose problems for multithreaded applications. *strtok*, *asctime*, and many other C run-time functions use global variables to store intermediate data. If thread A calls one of these functions and thread B preempts thread A and calls the same function, global data stored by thread A could be overwritten by global data stored by thread B. One solution to this problem is to use thread synchronization objects to serialize access to C run-time functions. But even simple synchronization objects can be expensive in terms of processor time. Therefore, most modern C and C++ compilers come with two versions of the C run-time library: one that's thread safe (can be called into by multiple concurrent threads) and one that isn't. The thread-safe versions of the run-time library typically don't rely on thread synchronization objects. Instead, they store intermediate values in per-thread data structures.

Visual C++ comes with six versions of the C run-time library. Which one you should choose depends on whether you're compiling a debug build or a release build, whether you want to link with the C run-time library statically or dynamically, and, of course, whether your application is single threaded or multithreaded. The table below shows the library names and the corresponding compiler switches:

Library Name	*Application Type*	*Switch*
Libc.lib	Single-threaded; static linking; release builds	/ML
Libcd.lib	Single-threaded; static linking; debug builds	/MLd
Libcmt.lib	Multithreaded; static linking; release builds	/MT
Libcmtd.lib	Multithreaded; static linking; debug builds	/MTd
Msvcrt.lib	Single-threaded or multithreaded; dynamic linking; release builds	/MD
Msvcrtd.lib	Single-threaded or multithreaded; dynamic linking; debug builds	/MDd

Libc.lib, Libcd.lib, Libcmt.lib, and Libcmtd.lib are static link libraries containing C run-time code; Msvcrt.lib and Msvcrtd.lib are import libraries that enable an application to dynamically link to functions in the Visual C++ C run-time DLL. Of course, you don't have to fuss with compiler switches unless you build your own make files. If you're using Visual C++, just select the appropriate entry in the "Use run-time library" field of the Project Settings dialog and the IDE will add the switches for you. Even if you write a multithreaded application that doesn't use C run-time functions, you should link with one of the multithreaded libraries anyway because MFC calls certain C run-time functions itself.

In an MFC application, that's all you have to do to make calls to C run-time functions thread safe: Simply set the compiler switches, and trust the class library to do the rest. In an SDK application, you must also replace calls to *::CreateThread* with calls to *_beginthreadex*. *AfxBeginThread* and *CWinThread::CreateThread* call *_beginthreadex* for you.

Your First Multithreaded Application

The Threads demo, shown in Figure 14-1, demonstrates some of the basic principles involved in writing a multithreaded application. Initially, Threads displays a blank frame window. The Options menu contains commands for starting as many as four additional threads of execution, which we'll refer to as threads 1 through 4. Thread 1 repeatedly draws and redraws a colorful design in the window's upper left corner.

Threads 2, 3, and 4 draw the same design in the upper right, lower left, and lower right corners, respectively. You can alternately start and stop individual threads by selecting the same commands from the menu again or pressing the F1, F2, F3, and F4 accelerator keys. The application's source code is shown in Figure 14-2.

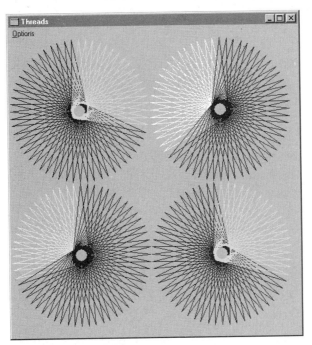

Figure 14-1. *The Threads window.*

Resource.h

```
//*****************************************************************************
//
//  Resource.h
//
//*****************************************************************************

#define IDR_MAINFRAME            100

#define IDM_THREAD_1             110
#define IDM_THREAD_2             111
#define IDM_THREAD_3             112
#define IDM_THREAD_4             113
#define IDM_FRIENDLY_THREADS     114
#define IDM_EXIT                 115
```

Figure 14-2. *The Threads program.*

Threads.rc

```
//****************************************************************************
//
//  Threads.rc
//
//****************************************************************************

#include <afxres.h>
#include "Resource.h"

IDR_MAINFRAME MENU
BEGIN
    POPUP "&Options" {
        MENUITEM "Start Thread &1\tF1",   IDM_THREAD_1
        MENUITEM "Start Thread &2\tF2",   IDM_THREAD_2
        MENUITEM "Start Thread &3\tF3",   IDM_THREAD_3
        MENUITEM "Start Thread &4\tF4",   IDM_THREAD_4
        MENUITEM SEPARATOR
        MENUITEM "&Friendly Threads",     IDM_FRIENDLY_THREADS
        MENUITEM SEPARATOR
        MENUITEM "E&xit",                 IDM_EXIT
    }
END

IDR_MAINFRAME ACCELERATORS
BEGIN
    VK_F1,  IDM_THREAD_1,   VIRTKEY
    VK_F2,  IDM_THREAD_2,   VIRTKEY
    VK_F3,  IDM_THREAD_3,   VIRTKEY
    VK_F4,  IDM_THREAD_4,   VIRTKEY
END
```

Threads.h

```
//****************************************************************************
//
//  Threads.h
//
//****************************************************************************

class CMyApp : public CWinApp
{
public:
    virtual BOOL InitInstance ();
};
```

```
class CMainWindow : public CFrameWnd
{
private:
    CWinThread* m_pThread[4];
    BOOL m_bContinue[4];
    BOOL m_bFriendlyThreads;

    void DrawHand (CDC*, int, int, int, COLORREF);
    static UINT ThreadFunc (LPVOID);

public:
    CMainWindow ();

protected:
    virtual BOOL PreCreateWindow (CREATESTRUCT&);

    afx_msg void OnClose ();
    afx_msg void OnToggleThread (UINT);
    afx_msg void OnFriendlyThreads ();
    afx_msg void OnUpdateThreadUI (CCmdUI*);
    afx_msg void OnUpdateFriendlyThreadsUI (CCmdUI*);
    afx_msg void OnExit ();

    DECLARE_MESSAGE_MAP ()
};

typedef struct tagTHREADPARMS {
    CPoint point;
    BOOL* pContFlag;
    BOOL* pFriendFlag;
    LPARAM lParam;
} THREADPARMS;
```

Threads.cpp

```
//*********************************************************************
//
//  Threads.cpp
//
//*********************************************************************

#include <afxwin.h>
#include <math.h>
```

(continued)

Threads.cpp *continued*

```
#include "Resource.h"
#include "Threads.h"

#define RADIUS 120

CMyApp myApp;

///////////////////////////////////////////////////////////////////////////
// CMyApp member functions

BOOL CMyApp::InitInstance ()
{
    m_pMainWnd = new CMainWindow;
    m_pMainWnd->ShowWindow (m_nCmdShow);
    m_pMainWnd->UpdateWindow ();
    return TRUE;
}


///////////////////////////////////////////////////////////////////////////
// CMainWindow message map and member functions

BEGIN_MESSAGE_MAP (CMainWindow, CFrameWnd)
    ON_WM_CLOSE ()
    ON_COMMAND_RANGE (IDM_THREAD_1, IDM_THREAD_4, OnToggleThread)
    ON_COMMAND (IDM_FRIENDLY_THREADS, OnFriendlyThreads)
    ON_UPDATE_COMMAND_UI_RANGE (IDM_THREAD_1, IDM_THREAD_4,
        OnUpdateThreadUI)
    ON_UPDATE_COMMAND_UI (IDM_FRIENDLY_THREADS,
        OnUpdateFriendlyThreadsUI)
    ON_COMMAND (IDM_EXIT, OnExit)
END_MESSAGE_MAP ()

CMainWindow::CMainWindow ()
{
    m_bFriendlyThreads = FALSE;
    for (int i=0; i<4; i++) {
        m_pThread[i] = NULL;
        m_bContinue[i] = FALSE;
    }

    CString strWndClass = AfxRegisterWndClass (
        0,
        myApp.LoadStandardCursor (IDC_ARROW),
        (HBRUSH) (COLOR_3DFACE + 1),
        myApp.LoadStandardIcon (IDI_APPLICATION)
    );
```

```
        Create (strWndClass, "Threads", WS_OVERLAPPEDWINDOW, rectDefault,
            NULL, MAKEINTRESOURCE (IDR_MAINFRAME)));

        LoadAccelTable (MAKEINTRESOURCE (IDR_MAINFRAME));
    }

    BOOL CMainWindow::PreCreateWindow (CREATESTRUCT& cs)
    {
        if (!CFrameWnd::PreCreateWindow (cs))
            return FALSE;

        cs.dwExStyle &= ~WS_EX_CLIENTEDGE;
        return TRUE;
    }

    void CMainWindow::OnClose ()
    {
        for (int i=0; i<4; i++) {
            if (m_pThread[i] != NULL)
                delete m_pThread[i];
        }
        CFrameWnd::OnClose ();
    }

    void CMainWindow::OnToggleThread (UINT nID)
    {
        static int nCoords[4][2] = {
            RADIUS,     -RADIUS,        // Thread 1
            RADIUS * 3, -RADIUS,        // Thread 2
            RADIUS,     -RADIUS * 3,    // Thread 3
            RADIUS * 3, -RADIUS * 3     // Thread 4
        };

        UINT i = nID - IDM_THREAD_1;

        if (m_pThread[i] == NULL) { // Create a thread
            THREADPARMS* pThreadParms = new THREADPARMS;
            pThreadParms->point.x = nCoords[i][0];
            pThreadParms->point.y = nCoords[i][1];
            pThreadParms->pContFlag = &m_bContinue[i];
            pThreadParms->pFriendFlag = &m_bFriendlyThreads;
            pThreadParms->lParam = (LPARAM) this;

            m_bContinue[i] = TRUE;
            m_pThread[i] = AfxBeginThread (ThreadFunc, pThreadParms);
        }
```

(continued)

Threads.cpp *continued*

```
        else { // Terminate a thread
            HANDLE hThread = m_pThread[i]->m_hThread;
            m_bContinue[i] = FALSE;
            ::WaitForSingleObject (hThread, INFINITE);
            m_pThread[i] = NULL;
        }
    }
}

void CMainWindow::OnFriendlyThreads ()
{
    m_bFriendlyThreads = m_bFriendlyThreads ? FALSE : TRUE;
}

void CMainWindow::OnUpdateFriendlyThreadsUI (CCmdUI* pCmdUI)
{
    pCmdUI->SetCheck (m_bFriendlyThreads);
}

void CMainWindow::OnExit ()
{
    SendMessage (WM_CLOSE, 0, 0);
}

void CMainWindow::OnUpdateThreadUI (CCmdUI* pCmdUI)
{
    UINT i = pCmdUI->m_nID - IDM_THREAD_1;

    CString string;
    if (m_pThread[i] == NULL)
        string.Format ("Start Thread &%d\tF%d", i + 1, i + 1);
    else
        string.Format ("Terminate Thread &%d\tF%d", i + 1, i + 1);

    pCmdUI->SetText (string);
}

void CMainWindow::DrawHand (CDC* pDC, int nLength, int nScale,
    int nDegrees, COLORREF crColor)
{
    CPoint point[4];
    double nRadians = (double) nDegrees * 0.017453292;

    point[0].x = (int) (nLength * sin (nRadians));
    point[0].y = (int) (nLength * cos (nRadians));

    point[2].x = -point[0].x / nScale;
    point[2].y = -point[0].y / nScale;
```

```
    point[1].x = -point[2].y;
    point[1].y = point[2].x;

    point[3].x = -point[1].x;
    point[3].y = -point[1].y;

    CPen pen (PS_SOLID, 0, crColor);
    CPen* pOldPen = pDC->SelectObject (&pen);

    pDC->MoveTo (point[0]);
    pDC->LineTo (point[1]);
    pDC->LineTo (point[2]);
    pDC->LineTo (point[3]);
    pDC->LineTo (point[0]);

    pDC->SelectObject (pOldPen);
}

UINT CMainWindow::ThreadFunc (LPVOID pParam)
{
    static COLORREF crColors[8] = {
        RGB (  0,   0,   0),    // Black
        RGB (  0,   0, 255),    // Blue
        RGB (  0, 255,   0),    // Green
        RGB (  0, 255, 255),    // Cyan
        RGB (255,   0,   0),    // Red
        RGB (255,   0, 255),    // Magenta
        RGB (255, 255,   0),    // Yellow
        RGB (255, 255, 255)     // White
    };

    THREADPARMS* pThreadParms = (THREADPARMS*) pParam;
    CPoint point = pThreadParms->point;
    BOOL* pContFlag = pThreadParms->pContFlag;
    BOOL* pFriendFlag = pThreadParms->pFriendFlag;
    CMainWindow* pWnd = (CMainWindow*) pThreadParms->lParam;
    delete pThreadParms;

    int nMinute = 0;
    int nIndex = 0;

    while (*pContFlag) {
        CDC* pDC = pWnd->GetDC ();
        pDC->SetMapMode (MM_LOENGLISH);
```

(continued)

Threads.cpp *continued*

```
        CPoint org = point;
        pDC->LPtoDP (&org);
        pDC->SetViewportOrg (org.x, org.y);

        pWnd->DrawHand (pDC, RADIUS, 8, nMinute * 6, crColors[nIndex]);
        pWnd->ReleaseDC (pDC);

        if (++nMinute == 60) {
            nMinute = 0;
            if (++nIndex == 8)
                nIndex = 0;
        }

        if (*pFriendFlag)
            ::Sleep (0);
    }
    return 0;
}
```

One of the things you can learn from Threads is that there's no such thing as a free lunch. When all four threads are running, the designs are drawn at about one-fourth the speed at which they're drawn when there's just one thread running and the drawing motions are more irregular. But watch what happens when all four threads are going and you check Friendly Threads in the Options menu. Friendly Threads sets a flag that causes the threads to execute a

```
::Sleep (0);
```

statement after each call to *CMainWindow::DrawHand*. Rather than run until it is preempted again, a "friendly thread" does a small amount of work and then gives up the remainder of its timeslice. This has a rather dramatic effect on the program's output, which instantly goes from jerky to smooth. When multiple threads draw into a window, it's advantageous to have each thread do its drawing in small increments and delegate leftover time to other threads.

When it creates a new worker thread, *CMainWindow::ToggleThread* passes data to the worker thread function in an application-defined data structure of type THREAD-PARMS. One of the items included in the data structure is a pointer to the *CMain-Window* object. Threads is a simple enough program that it can get away with passing an object pointer rather than an HWND and suffer no ill effects. Note that storage for the THREADPARMS structure is allocated in the primary thread and deallocated in the secondary thread, as shown below:

```
// In the primary thread
THREADPARAMS* pThreadParms = new THREADPARMS;
```

```
        ⋮
        ⋮
m_pThread[i] = AfxBeginThread (ThreadFunc, pThreadParms);

// In the secondary thread
THREADPARMS* pThreadParms = (THREADPARMS*) pParam;
        ⋮
        ⋮
delete pThreadParms;
```

Why create the structure in one thread and delete it in another? Because if the structure is created on the stack in the primary thread, it's very possible that it will go out of scope before the secondary thread gets a chance to copy the data out of it. This is one of those annoying little details that can cause seemingly random errors if it isn't handled properly. Allocating the structure with *new* ensures that there won't be any scoping problems, and it isn't harmful to allocate memory in one thread and delete it in another. Making the structure a class data member or declaring it globally is an equally effective method of ensuring that it won't go away too soon.

When an application's primary thread terminates, the process terminates and any other threads that belong to the process terminate, too. Multithreaded SDK applications frequently don't bother to kill background threads before a process terminates, but MFC applications that end without terminating background threads often suffer memory leaks because of *CWinThread* objects that don't get autodeleted. Such leaks aren't a big deal because the operating system cleans them up almost immediately. However, an application can avert memory leaks by killing worker threads just before it shuts down or by simply deleting the *CWinThread* objects it created. That's why the Threads frame window includes an *OnClose* handler that calls *delete* on the pointers in the *m_pThread* array. It's not harmful to delete a running *CWinThread*, but of course you can't call *CWinThread* functions on a deleted *CWinThread* object, either.

THREAD SYNCHRONIZATION

The Threads demo isn't a very realistic example of a multithreaded application program because it's unusual to have the luxury of starting a thread and just letting it run. More often than not, a means of communication must be established so that one thread can tell another that an operation is complete. If a primary thread launches a secondary thread to process data in a buffer, for example, the primary thread probably needs to know when processing is finished so that it can use the data. Another example of an instance in which threads must communicate is when two threads require access to the same resource. If two threads use the same linked list, for example, accesses must be coordinated so that both threads don't try to modify the linked list at the same time or so that one thread doesn't write to the list while the other reads it. Simply letting a thread go off and do its own thing can lead to all sorts of synchronization problems that show up only randomly in testing and that are often fatal to the application.

Windows 95 supports four types of thread synchronization objects that can be used to synchronize the actions of concurrently running threads:

- Events

- Critical sections

- Mutexes

- Semaphores

MFC encapsulates these objects in the classes *CEvent*, *CCriticalSection*, *CMutex*, and *CSemaphore*. It also includes a pair of classes named *CSingleLock* and *CMultiLock* that further abstract the interfaces to thread synchronization objects. The sections that follow describe how to use these classes to synchronize the actions of concurrently executing threads.

Events

The first type of thread synchronization object that we'll examine is the *event*. Encapsulated in MFC's *CEvent* class, an event is basically just a flag in the operating system kernel that's either raised (set) or lowered (reset). A set event object is said to be in a signaled state, while a reset event object is said to be nonsignaled.

Events are most often used to serialize the actions of two or more concurrently running threads. For example, suppose thread A copies data to a buffer and thread B does something with that data. Thread B can't be turned loose on the buffer until thread A has finished copying the data. To synchronize itself with thread B, thread A could create an event object that's initially nonsignaled. Meanwhile, thread B blocks until the event becomes signaled. When thread A is finished filling the buffer, it sets the event to the signaled state and the operating system wakes up thread B so that it can process the data. This way, there's no chance that thread B will begin accessing the buffer too early. And while it waits for the event to become signaled, thread B consumes no processor time.

An event object is created by constructing a *CEvent* object. *CEvent::CEvent* accepts four parameters, all of them optional. It's prototyped as follows:

```
CEvent (BOOL bInitiallyOwn = FALSE,
    BOOL bManualReset = FALSE, LPCTSTR lpszName = NULL,
    LPSECURITY_ATTRIBUTES lpsaAttribute = NULL)
```

The first parameter, *bInitiallyOwn*, specifies whether the event object is initially signaled (TRUE) or nonsignaled (FALSE). The default is fine in most cases because you normally want an event to start out in the nonsignaled state. *bManualReset* specifies whether the event should be set back to the nonsignaled state manually or automatically after it becomes signaled and the operating system wakes up a thread that's waiting on the event. Specifying TRUE for this parameter creates a manual-reset event object that must be reset manually with *CEvent::ResetEvent*. FALSE creates an auto-reset event object that's automatically reset to the nonsignaled state. For reasons that will be explained shortly, auto-reset events are normally used when there's just one thread waiting for the event to become signaled and manual-reset events are used when there are multiple threads waiting. The third parameter to *CEvent::CEvent*, *lpszName*, assigns a name to the event object. A name isn't normally used for the event unless the threads synchronizing on the event belong to different processes. The final parameter, *lpsaAttribute*, is a pointer to a SECURITY_ATTRIBUTES structure describing the object's security attributes. NULL accepts the default security attributes, which are fine for most applications.

CEvent provides three member functions for setting events to signaled and nonsignaled states. *CEvent::SetEvent* sets an event to the signaled state, and *CEvent::ResetEvent* sets it to the nonsignaled state. *CEvent::PulseEvent* sets a nonsignaled event to the signaled state and then resets the event to the nonsignaled state, all in one step. *PulseEvent* is handy when there are multiple threads waiting for a manual-reset event to become signaled. Rather than write

```
event.SetEvent ();   // Release waiting threads
event.ResetEvent (); // Reset the event to the nonsignaled state
```

you can write

```
event.PulseEvent ();
```

instead.

So how do you use events to synchronize threads? Let's go back to the example of a thread A that fills a buffer and a thread B that does something with the data in the buffer. If *g_event* is a globally declared *CEvent* object (we'll use global synchronization objects in our examples to ensure that a synchronization object is equally visible to all the threads in a process), thread B "locks" the event by calling the *Lock* function a *CEvent* object inherits from its base class, *CSyncObject*. Once *Lock* is called, thread B blocks until the event becomes signaled. Here's how it looks in code:

```
// Global data
CEvent g_event; // Auto-reset, initially nonsignaled
   :
   :
// Somewhere in thread A
AfxBeginThread (ThreadFunc, &buffer); // Start thread B
   :
   :
```

(continued)

```
// Somewhere else in thread A
InitBuffer (&buffer); // Initialize the buffer
g_event.SetEvent (); // Release thread B
    .
    .
    .
// Thread B
UINT ThreadFunc (LPVOID pParam)
{
    while (TRUE) {
        g_event.Lock (); // Go to sleep
        // Wake up and do something with the buffer
    }
    return 0;
}
```

Because *g_event* is an auto-reset event object, it is automatically reset to the nonsignaled state after *SetEvent* is called and thread B is released. If *g_event* were a manual-reset event, thread A would need to call *ResetEvent* after calling *SetEvent* to reset the event. Once started, thread B loops continually and locks on the event at the beginning of each loop. It's always lurking in the background, waiting to be executed the moment thread A calls *SetEvent*. Therefore, thread A can initialize the buffer and set thread B to work on it whenever it wants to. If thread B is called numerous times throughout the life of the application, this is more efficient than starting thread B anew each time and allowing it to terminate when it's through.

The lone parameter passed to *Lock* specifies how long the caller is willing to wait, in milliseconds. The default is INFINITE, which means wait as long as necessary. A nonzero return value means that *Lock* returned because the object became signaled or the time-out period expired; 0 means that an error occurred. A 0 return should be extremely rare. It generally means that the handle encapsulated in the event object whose *Lock* function was called is invalid, possibly because it has been corrupted. If you peek inside Mtcore.cpp, you'll find that all *CSyncObject::Lock* does is call *::WaitForSingleObject* on the event handle and return TRUE if *::WaitForSingleObject* returns anything but WAIT_ERROR. MFC isn't doing anything fancy here. It's simply recasting the kernel's thread synchronization objects and the API functions that operate on them in a more object-oriented mold.

Auto-reset events are fine for awakening single threads, but what if there's a thread C that runs in parallel with thread B and does something entirely different with the buffered data? Now we need a manual-reset event because, if the event is reset automatically after thread B is awakened, thread C won't be awakened. We can fix this by making *g_event* a manual-reset event and having thread A perform a manual reset after awakening the other threads:

```
// Global data
CEvent g_event (FALSE, TRUE); // Manual-reset, nonsignaled
```

```
        .
        .
        .
// Somewhere in thread A
AfxBeginThread (ThreadFuncB, &buffer); // Start thread B
AfxBeginThread (ThreadFuncC, &buffer); // Start thread C
    .
    .
    .
// Somewhere else in thread A
InitBuffer (&buffer);  // Initialize the buffer
g_event.SetEvent ();    // Release threads B and C
g_event.ResetEvent (); // Manual reset
    .
    .
    .
// Thread B
UINT ThreadFuncB (LPVOID pParam)
{
    while (TRUE) {
        g_event.Lock ();
        // Wake up and do something with the buffer
    }
    return 0;
}

// Thread C
UINT ThreadFuncC (LPVOID pParam)
{
    while (TRUE) {
        g_event.Lock ();
        // Wake up and do something else with the buffer
    }
    return 0;
}
```

This code could be simplified by substituting one call to *PulseEvent* for the separate
calls to *SetEvent* and *ResetEvent*. I used *SetEvent* and *ResetEvent* to emphasize the point
that it's up to the thread that sets a manual-reset event to reset it.

Critical Sections

MFC's *CCriticalSection* class encapsulates critical section synchronization objects,
which are ideal for serializing access to a shared resource in a process such as a linked
list, a variable, or a data structure. The idea behind critical sections is that each thread
that requires exclusive access to a resource can lock a critical section before accessing that resource and unlock it when the access is complete. If another thread running in the process comes along and tries to lock the same critical section while it's
locked by the first thread, the second thread blocks until the critical section is unlocked.

Let's say that a document class includes a linked-list data member created from MFC's *CObList* class and that two separate threads use the linked list. Thread A adds entries to the list, and thread B retrieves entries from the list. To prevent either thread from accessing the linked list at the same time that the other thread is accessing it, which could be disastrous if one thread preempted the other at precisely the wrong moment, you could protect the list with a critical section, as shown here:

```
// Global data
CCriticalSection g_criticalSection;
    .
    .
    .
// Thread A
g_criticalSection.Lock ();
// Add an entry to the linked list
g_criticalSection.Unlock ();
    .
    .
    .
// Thread B
g_criticalSection.Lock ();
// Read an entry from the linked list
g_criticalSection.Unlock ();
```

Now it's virtually impossible for threads A and B to access the linked list at the same time because both lock the same critical section before an access occurs.

The documentation for *CCriticalSection::Lock* states that you can pass it a time-out value and *Lock* will return if the time-out period expires before the critical section becomes locked. The documentation is wrong. You can specify a time-out value all right, but *Lock* will still not return until it succeeds in claiming the critical section.

It's obvious why a linked list should be protected from simultaneous thread accesses, but what about simple variables? For example, suppose thread A increments a variable with an

```
nVar++;
```

statement and thread B does something else that sets the value of the variable. Should *nVar* be protected with a critical section? In general, yes. What looks to be an atomic operation in a C++ program—even the application of a simple ++ operator—might compile into a sequence of several machine instructions. And one thread can pre-empt another between any two machine instructions. As a rule, it's a good idea to protect any data subject to simultaneous write accesses. And a critical section is the perfect tool to do the job.

The Win32 API includes a trio of functions named *::InterlockedIncrement*, *::InterlockedDecrement*, and *::InterlockedExchange* that you can use to increment, decrement, and exchange 32-bit variable values in a thread-safe way without resorting to synchronization objects. If *nVar* is a UINT, DWORD, or other 32-bit data type, you can increment it with the statement

```
::InterlockedIncrement (&nVar);
```

and the system will ensure that other accesses to *nVar* performed by means of *Interlocked* functions will not interfere. *nVar* should be aligned on a 32-bit boundary, or *::InterlockedIncrement*, *::InterlockedDecrement*, and *::InterlockedExchange* will fail on multiprocessor Windows NT systems.

Mutexes

"Mutex" is a contraction of the words "mutually" and "exclusive." Like critical sections, mutexes are used to ensure exclusive access to a resource that's available to multiple threads. However, mutexes can be used to synchronize threads running in different processes while critical sections are available only to threads running in the same process. Mutexes can also be used to synchronize threads running within a process, but critical sections are slightly faster and therefore generally preferred for intraprocess thread synchronization.

Suppose two instances of an application are running and you want to serialize access to a file or some other resource used by both instances. A critical section won't work since it can't be used across process boundaries, but a mutex will do the job nicely. Here's all you have to do:

```
// Global data
CMutex g_mutex (FALSE, "MyMutex");
    :
    :

g_mutex.Lock ();
// Access the file
g_mutex.Unlock ();
```

The first parameter passed to the *CMutex* constructor specifies whether the mutex is initially locked (TRUE) or unlocked (FALSE). The second specifies the mutex's name, which is essential if the mutex is to be used to synchronize threads in two different processes. *CMutex::CMutex* also accepts an optional third parameter that holds a pointer to a SECURITY_ATTRIBUTES structure. Naturally, *Lock* blocks on a mutex locked by someone else, and *Unlock* frees the mutex so that others can lock it.

By default, *Lock* will wait forever for a mutex to become unlocked. You can build in a fail-safe mechanism by specifying a maximum waiting time in milliseconds. In the following example, the thread waits for a maximum of one minute before proceeding with the buffer access.

```
// Global data
CMutex g_mutex (FALSE, "MyMutex");
    :
    :

g_mutex.Lock (60000);
```

(continued)

941

```
// Access the file
g_mutex.Unlock ();
```

Unfortunately, MFC makes it impossible to determine whether *Lock* returned because the mutex was successfully locked or because the time-out period expired, even though that information *is* available from *::WaitForSingleObject*. Sometimes the reason *Lock* returned is valuable information to have because an expired time-out period may mean that a deadlock has occurred—a condition in which two threads are irreversibly hung because each is suspended, waiting for the other to perform some action. The following code fragment calls *::WaitForSingleObject* directly on a mutex object and bypasses the code that accesses the shared resource if the time-out period expires before the mutex is locked:

```
if (::WaitForSingleObject (g_mutex.m_hObject, 60000) ==
    WAIT_TIMEOUT)
    TRACE ("Unable to lock the mutex; possible deadlock\n");
else {
    // Access the file
    mutex.Unlock ();
}
```

Too bad you have to go around MFC to find out why *Lock* returned. But those are the breaks.

There is one other difference between mutexes and critical sections. If a thread locks a critical section and then terminates without unlocking the critical section, other threads waiting for the critical section to come free will remain blocked indefinitely. However, if a thread that locks a mutex fails to unlock it before terminating, threads blocked on that mutex are resumed. *::WaitForSingleObject* returns WAIT_ABANDONED to let the threads know what happened, but once again MFC's insistence on returning TRUE or FALSE from its *Lock* functions instead of the value returned by *::WaitForSingleObject* makes the information impossible to get at unless you call *::WaitForSingleObject* directly.

Semaphores

The fourth and final type of synchronization object is the *semaphore*. Events, critical sections, and mutexes are "all or nothing" objects in the sense that *Lock* blocks on them if any other thread has them locked. Semaphores are different. Semaphores maintain resource counts representing the number of resources available. Locking a semaphore decrements its resource count, and unlocking a semaphore increments the resource count. A thread blocks only if it tries to lock a semaphore and the count is 0. In that case, the thread blocks until another thread unlocks the semaphore and thereby raises the resource count, or until a specified time-out period has elapsed. Semaphores can be used to synchronize threads within a process or threads that belong to different processes.

MFC encapsulates semaphores with the class *CSemaphore*. The statement

```
CSemaphore g_semaphore (2, 2);
```

constructs a semaphore object that has an initial resource count of 2 (parameter 1) and a maximum resource count of 2 (parameter 2). If the semaphore will be used to synchronize threads in two different processes, you should include a third parameter specifying the semaphore's name. An optional fourth parameter points to a SECURITY_ATTRIBUTES structure (default=NULL). Each thread that accesses a resource controlled by a semaphore can do so, as shown here:

```
g_semaphore.Lock ();
// Access the resource
g_semaphore.Unlock ();
```

As long as no more than two threads try to access the resource at the same time, *Lock* won't suspend the thread. But if the semaphore is locked by two threads and a third thread calls *g_semaphore.Lock*, that thread will block until one of the other threads calls *g_semaphore.Unlock*. To limit the time that *Lock* will wait for the semaphore's resource count to become nonzero, pass the maximum wait time (in milliseconds, as always) to the *Lock* function.

A second form of the *CSemaphore::Unlock* function may be used to increment the resource count by more than 1 and also to find out what the resource count was before *Unlock* was called. For example, suppose the same thread calls *Lock* twice in succession to lay claim to two resources guarded by a semaphore. Rather than call *Unlock* twice, the thread can do its unlocking like this:

```
LONG lPrevCount;
g_semaphore.Unlock (2, &lPrevCount);
```

There are no functions in either MFC or the API that return a semaphore's resource count outside a call to *CSemaphore::Unlock*.

The *CSingleLock* and *CMultiLock* Classes

Calling a synchronization object's *Lock* or *Unlock* function directly isn't the only way to lock or unlock the object. MFC also provides a pair of classes named *CSingleLock* and *CMultiLock* that include *Lock* and *Unlock* functions of their own. Using a *CSingleLock* to do your locking and unlocking isn't all that different from calling *Lock* and *Unlock* directly because *CSingleLock::Lock* and *CSingleLock::UnLock* call the *Lock* and *Unlock* functions of the associated synchronization object. But *CMultiLock* is an altogether different animal. Rather than pass the buck to the synchronization object or call *::WaitForSingleObject*, *CMultiLock* calls *::WaitForMultipleObjects*. A thread that uses *CMultiLock* can block on as many as 64 synchronization objects simultaneously. And depending on how it calls *CMultiLock::Lock*, the thread can either wake up when any one of the synchronization objects comes free or remain blocked until all of them come free.

The following code fragment initializes an array of four *CEvent* objects and demonstrates how other threads can lock on one or all of the events:

```
// Global data
CEvent g_event[4]; // Construct four auto-reset events
    :
    :

// In another thread: sleep until all four events are signaled
CMultiLock multiLock (g_event, 4);
multiLock.Lock ();
    :
    :

// In another thread: wake up when any event becomes signaled
CMultiLock multiLock (g_event, 4);
multiLock.Lock (INFINITE, FALSE);
```

CMultiLock::Lock accepts three parameters, all of which are optional. The first specifies a time-out value (default=INFINITE). The second is a BOOL value that specifies whether the thread should be awakened when one of the synchronization objects becomes unlocked (FALSE) or when all of them become unlocked (TRUE, the default). The third is a *wakeup mask* that specifies other conditions that will wake up the thread—for example, WM_PAINT messages or mouse-button messages. The default wakeup mask value of 0 prevents the thread from being awakened for any reason other than that the synchronization object (or objects) came free or the time-out period expired. A thread can determine whether a particular synchronization object is currently locked with *CMultiLock::IsLocked*.

Here's one example of a situation in which *CMultiLock* could be useful. Suppose three separate threads—threads A, B, and C—are working together to prepare data in a buffer. Once the data is ready, thread D transmits the data to a serial port or writes it to a file. However, thread D can't be called until threads A, B, and C have completed their work. The solution? Create separate event objects to represent threads A, B, and C, and let thread D use a *CMultiLock* object to block until all three events become signaled. As each thread completes its work, it sets the corresponding event object to the signaled state. Thread D therefore blocks until the last of the three threads signals that it's done.

Writing Thread-Safe Classes

MFC classes are thread safe at the class level but not at the object level. Translated, this means that it's safe for two threads to access two separate objects of the same class but that allowing two threads to access the same object at the same time could cause problems. MFC's designers chose not to make it thread safe at the object level for performance reasons. The simple act of locking an unlocked critical section can consume hundreds of clock cycles on a Pentium processor. If every access to an object of an MFC class locked a critical section, the performance of single-threaded applications would suffer needlessly.

To illustrate what it means for a class to be thread safe, think about what might happen if two threads using the same *CString* object made no attempt to synchronize their accesses. Let's say that thread A decides to set the string, whose name is *g_strFileName*, equal to the text string referenced by *pszFile*:

```
g_strFileName = pszFile;
```

At about the same time, thread B decides to display *g_strFileName* on the screen by passing it to *CDC::TextOut*:

```
pDC->TextOut (x, y, g_strFileName);
```

What gets displayed on the screen? The old value of *g_strFileName* or the new value? Maybe neither. Copying text to a *CString* object is a multistep operation that involves allocating buffer space to hold the text, performing a *memcpy* to copy the characters, setting the *CString* data member that stores the string length equal to the number of characters that were copied, adding a terminating 0 to the end, and so on. If thread B interrupts this process at the wrong moment, there's no telling what the *CString* will look like when it's passed to *TextOut*. The output might be improperly truncated. Or *TextOut* might display garbage on the screen or cause an access violation.

One way to synchronize access to *g_strFileName* is to protect it with a critical section, as shown here:

```
// Global data
CCriticalSection g_criticalSection;
    :
    :

// Thread A
g_criticalSection.Lock ();
g_strFileName = pszFile;
g_criticalSection.Unlock ();
    :
    :

// Thread B
g_criticalSection.Lock ();
pDC->TextOut (x, y, g_strFileName);
g_criticalSection.Unlock ();
```

An alternative approach is to derive a class from *CString* and make the derived class thread safe by building in a critical section that automatically gets locked anytime an access occurs. Then the object itself ensures that accesses are performed in a thread-safe way, and it's no longer incumbent upon the application that *uses* the object to synchronize the actions of its threads. Deriving a class and making it thread safe is basically a matter of overriding every member function that reads or writes an object's data and wrapping calls to member functions in the base class with calls to lock and unlock a synchronization object that's a member of the derived class. Ditto for thread-safe classes that aren't derived from other classes but are designed from the ground up: add a *CCriticalSection* or *CMutex* data member to the class, and lock and unlock the synchronization object before and after every access.

It's not always possible to make a class entirely thread safe. If a thread uses *GetBuffer* or an LPCTSTR operator to get a pointer to the text of a *CString*, for example, the *CString* itself has no control over what the caller does with that pointer. In that case, it's still the responsibility of the thread that uses the *CString* object to coordinate its accesses with those of other threads.

The point to take home from all of this is that objects are not thread-safe by default. You can use synchronization objects to access other objects in a thread-safe way, and you can develop classes that are inherently thread safe by controlling access to objects created from those classes. But allowing one thread to read data from an object while another thread modifies the object's data—or vice versa—is a recipe for disaster. To make matters worse, errors of this nature often show up randomly in testing. You may run the application 1,000 times and never experience the debilitating effects of an overlapping access. But as sure as the possibility exists, someone using your application will experience a dual access that occurs at the worst possible moment and brings the entire application (and possibly the operating system, too) crashing to the ground.

The MTDemo Application

The MTDemo program, listed in Figure 14-3, is an enhanced version of Chapter 12's Vista application, one that uses a separate thread to perform a complex image processing task in the background. When you select Convert To Gray Scale from the Effects menu, MTDemo scans the current bitmap pixel by pixel, converts each pixel's color to a shade of gray, and adjusts the color palette if necessary to display an accurate gray-scale rendition of the original color image. The conversion function is an ideal candidate for a worker thread because it can take anywhere from a few seconds to several minutes to run, depending on the size of the bitmap, the workload on the CPU, and other factors. The code that performs the conversion is far from optimal; in fact, its speed could easily be improved by a factor of 10 or more if it were rewritten to work on bitmap bits directly rather than call *CDC::GetPixel* and *CDC::SetPixel* on every pixel. But for demonstration purposes, it's fine. And using *CDC* pixel functions to get and set pixel colors allows us to do in about 20 lines of code what could easily require 500 or more if MTDemo had to process raw bitmap data.

Resource.h

```
//***********************************************************************
//
//   Resource.h
//
//***********************************************************************

#define IDR_MAINFRAME               100

#define ID_EFFECTS_GRAY_SCALE       110

#define WM_USER_UPDATE_STATS        WM_USER
#define WM_USER_THREAD_UPDATE       WM_USER + 1
#define WM_USER_THREAD_FINISHED     WM_USER + 2
#define WM_USER_THREAD_ABORTED      WM_USER + 3
```

MTDemo.rc

```
/***********************************************************************
//
//   MTDemo.rc
//
//***********************************************************************

#include <afxres.h>
#include "Resource.h"

IDR_MAINFRAME MENU
BEGIN
    POPUP "&File" {
        MENUITEM "&Open...\tCtrl+O",        ID_FILE_OPEN
        MENUITEM SEPARATOR
        MENUITEM "Recent File",             ID_FILE_MRU_FILE1
        MENUITEM SEPARATOR
        MENUITEM "E&xit",                   ID_APP_EXIT
    }
    POPUP "&Effects" {
        MENUITEM "Convert to &Gray-scale",  ID_EFFECTS_GRAY_SCALE
    }
    POPUP "&View" {
        MENUITEM "&Status Bar",             ID_VIEW_STATUS_BAR
    }
END
```

Figure 14-3. *The MTDemo program.*

(continued)

MTDemo.rc *continued*

```
IDR_MAINFRAME ACCELERATORS
BEGIN
    "O", ID_FILE_OPEN,  VIRTKEY, CONTROL
END

STRINGTABLE
BEGIN
    AFX_IDS_IDLEMESSAGE       "Ready"
    ID_EFFECTS_GRAY_SCALE     "Convert colors to shades of gray"
    IDR_MAINFRAME             "MTDemo\n\n\nBMP Files (*.bmp)\n.bmp"
    ID_APP_EXIT               "Quit the application"
    AFX_IDS_SCCLOSE           "Quit the application"
END
```

MTDemo.h

```
//*********************************************************************
//
// MTDemo.h
//
//*********************************************************************

class CMTApp : public CWinApp
{
public:
    virtual BOOL InitInstance ();

protected:
    DECLARE_MESSAGE_MAP ()
};
```

MTDemo.cpp

```
//*********************************************************************
//
// MTDemo.cpp
//
//*********************************************************************

#include <afxwin.h>
#include <afxext.h>
#include <afxmt.h>
#include "Resource.h"
#include "MTDemo.h"
#include "MainFrame.h"
```

```
#include "MTDoc.h"
#include "MTView.h"

CMTApp myApp;

BEGIN_MESSAGE_MAP (CMTApp, CWinApp)
    ON_COMMAND (ID_FILE_OPEN, CWinApp::OnFileOpen)
END_MESSAGE_MAP ()

BOOL CMTApp::InitInstance ()
{
    SetRegistryKey ("Programming Windows 95 with MFC");
    LoadStdProfileSettings ();

    CSingleDocTemplate* pDocTemplate;
    pDocTemplate = new CSingleDocTemplate (
        IDR_MAINFRAME,
        RUNTIME_CLASS (CMTDoc),
        RUNTIME_CLASS (CMainFrame),
        RUNTIME_CLASS (CMTView)
    );

    AddDocTemplate (pDocTemplate);

    CCommandLineInfo cmdInfo;
    ParseCommandLine (cmdInfo);

    if (!ProcessShellCommand (cmdInfo))
        return FALSE;

    m_pMainWnd->DragAcceptFiles ();
    return TRUE;
}
```

MainFrame.h

```
//********************************************************************
//
//  MainFrame.h
//
//********************************************************************

class CMainFrame : public CFrameWnd
{
    DECLARE_DYNCREATE (CMainFrame)
```

(continued)

MainFrame.h *continued*

```
private:
    CStatusBar m_wndStatusBar;
    int m_nPercentDone;

public:
    CMainFrame ();

protected:
    afx_msg int OnCreate (LPCREATESTRUCT);
    afx_msg LONG OnUpdateImageStats (UINT, LONG);
    afx_msg LONG OnThreadUpdate (UINT, LONG);
    afx_msg LONG OnThreadFinished (UINT, LONG);
    afx_msg LONG OnThreadAborted (UINT, LONG);
    afx_msg BOOL OnQueryNewPalette ();
    afx_msg void OnPaletteChanged (CWnd*);

    DECLARE_MESSAGE_MAP ()
};
```

MainFrame.cpp

```
//*********************************************************************
//
//   MainFrame.cpp
//
//*********************************************************************

#include <afxwin.h>
#include <afxext.h>
#include <afxmt.h>
#include "Resource.h"
#include "MainFrame.h"
#include "MTDoc.h"

IMPLEMENT_DYNCREATE (CMainFrame, CFrameWnd)

BEGIN_MESSAGE_MAP (CMainFrame, CFrameWnd)
    ON_WM_CREATE ()
    ON_MESSAGE (WM_USER_UPDATE_STATS, OnUpdateImageStats)
    ON_MESSAGE (WM_USER_THREAD_UPDATE, OnThreadUpdate)
    ON_MESSAGE (WM_USER_THREAD_FINISHED, OnThreadFinished)
    ON_MESSAGE (WM_USER_THREAD_ABORTED, OnThreadAborted)
    ON_WM_QUERYNEWPALETTE ()
    ON_WM_PALETTECHANGED ()
END_MESSAGE_MAP ()
```

```
CMainFrame::CMainFrame ()
{
    m_nPercentDone = -1;
}

int CMainFrame::OnCreate (LPCREATESTRUCT lpcs)
{
    static UINT nIndicators[] = {
        ID_SEPARATOR,
        ID_SEPARATOR,
    };

    if (CFrameWnd::OnCreate (lpcs) == -1)
        return -1;

    if (!m_wndStatusBar.Create (this))
        return -1;

    m_wndStatusBar.SetIndicators (nIndicators, 3);

    TEXTMETRIC tm;
    CClientDC dc (this);
    CFont* pFont = m_wndStatusBar.GetFont ();
    CFont* pOldFont = dc.SelectObject (pFont);
    dc.GetTextMetrics (&tm);
    dc.SelectObject (pOldFont);

    int cxWidth;
    UINT nID, nStyle;
    m_wndStatusBar.GetPaneInfo (1, nID, nStyle, cxWidth);
    m_wndStatusBar.SetPaneInfo (1, nID, nStyle, tm.tmAveCharWidth * 24);
    m_wndStatusBar.SetPaneInfo (2, nID, nStyle, tm.tmAveCharWidth * 8);
    return 0;
}

LONG CMainFrame::OnUpdateImageStats (UINT wParam, LONG lParam)
{
    m_wndStatusBar.SetPaneText (1, (LPCTSTR) lParam, TRUE);
    return 0;
}

LONG CMainFrame::OnThreadUpdate (UINT wParam, LONG lParam)
{
    int nPercentDone = ((int) wParam * 100) / (int) lParam;
    if (nPercentDone != m_nPercentDone) {
        m_nPercentDone = nPercentDone;
        CString string;
```

(continued)

MainFrame.cpp *continued*

```
            string.Format ("%d%%", m_nPercentDone);
            m_wndStatusBar.SetPaneText (2, (LPCTSTR) string, TRUE);
        }
        return 0;
    }

    LONG CMainFrame::OnThreadFinished (UINT wParam, LONG lParam)
    {
        ((CMTDoc*) GetActiveDocument ())->ThreadFinished ();
        m_wndStatusBar.SetPaneText (2, "", TRUE);
        m_nPercentDone = -1;
        return 0;
    }

    LONG CMainFrame::OnThreadAborted (UINT wParam, LONG lParam)
    {
        ((CMTDoc*) GetActiveDocument ())->ThreadAborted ();
        m_wndStatusBar.SetPaneText (2, "", TRUE);
        m_nPercentDone = -1;
        return 0;
    }

    BOOL CMainFrame::OnQueryNewPalette ()
    {
        GetActiveView ()->Invalidate (FALSE);
        return TRUE;
    }

    void CMainFrame::OnPaletteChanged (CWnd* pFocusWnd)
    {
        if (pFocusWnd != this)
            GetActiveView ()->Invalidate (FALSE);
    }
```

MTDoc.h

```
//*********************************************************************
//
//  MTDoc.h
//
//*********************************************************************

typedef struct tagTHREADPARMS {
    CWnd* pWnd;
    CBitmap* pBitmap;
    CPalette* pPalette;
```

```
        CCriticalSection* pCriticalSection;
        CEvent* pEvent;
} THREADPARMS;

class CMTDoc : public CDocument
{
        DECLARE_DYNCREATE (CMTDoc)

private:
        BOOL m_bWorking;
        HANDLE m_hThread;

public:
        CBitmap m_bitmap;
        CPalette m_palette;
        THREADPARMS m_threadParms;
        CCriticalSection m_criticalSection;
        CEvent m_event;

        CMTDoc ();
        virtual BOOL OnOpenDocument (LPCTSTR);
        virtual void DeleteContents ();
        virtual void Serialize (CArchive&);

        CBitmap* GetBitmap ();
        CPalette* GetPalette ();
        void ThreadFinished ();
        void ThreadAborted ();

protected:
        afx_msg void OnGrayScale ();
        afx_msg void OnUpdateGrayScaleUI (CCmdUI*);

        DECLARE_MESSAGE_MAP ()
};
```

MTDoc.cpp

```
//****************************************************************
//
//  MTDoc.cpp
//
//****************************************************************

#include <afxwin.h>
#include <afxmt.h>
```

(continued)

MTDoc.cpp *continued*

```cpp
#include "Resource.h"
#include "MTDoc.h"

UINT ThreadFunc (LPVOID);
LOGPALETTE* CreateGrayScale ();

IMPLEMENT_DYNCREATE (CMTDoc, CDocument)

BEGIN_MESSAGE_MAP (CMTDoc, CDocument)
    ON_COMMAND (ID_EFFECTS_GRAY_SCALE, OnGrayScale)
    ON_UPDATE_COMMAND_UI (ID_EFFECTS_GRAY_SCALE, OnUpdateGrayScaleUI)
END_MESSAGE_MAP ()

CMTDoc::CMTDoc ()
{
    m_hThread = NULL;
    m_bWorking = FALSE;
}

void CMTDoc::OnGrayScale ()
{
    if (!m_bWorking) {
        m_threadParms.pWnd = AfxGetMainWnd ();
        m_threadParms.pBitmap = &m_bitmap;
        m_threadParms.pPalette = &m_palette;
        m_threadParms.pCriticalSection = &m_criticalSection;
        m_threadParms.pEvent = &m_event;

        m_bWorking = TRUE;
        m_event.ResetEvent (); // Just to be sure
        CWinThread* pThread = AfxBeginThread (ThreadFunc, &m_threadParms);
        m_hThread = pThread->m_hThread;
    }
    else // Kill the thread
        m_event.SetEvent ();
}

void CMTDoc::ThreadFinished ()
{
    ::WaitForSingleObject (m_hThread, INFINITE);
    m_bWorking = FALSE;

    if ((HPALETTE) m_palette != NULL) {
        m_palette.DeleteObject ();
        LOGPALETTE* pLP = CreateGrayScale ();
        m_palette.CreatePalette (pLP);
```

```
        delete[] pLP;
    }
    UpdateAllViews (NULL, 0, NULL);
}

void CMTDoc::ThreadAborted ()
{
    ::WaitForSingleObject (m_hThread, INFINITE);
    m_bWorking = FALSE;
}

void CMTDoc::OnUpdateGrayScaleUI (CCmdUI* pCmdUI)
{
    if (m_bWorking) {
        pCmdUI->SetText ("Stop &Gray-scale Conversion");
        pCmdUI->Enable ();
    }
    else {
        pCmdUI->SetText ("Convert to &Gray-scale");
        pCmdUI->Enable ((HBITMAP) m_bitmap != NULL);
    }
}

BOOL CMTDoc::OnOpenDocument (LPCTSTR lpszPathName)
{
    if (m_bWorking) {
        AfxMessageBox ("You must stop the gray-scale conversion " \
            "before opening another document", MB_ICONSTOP | MB_OK);
        return FALSE;
    }

    if (!CDocument::OnOpenDocument (lpszPathName)) {
        POSITION pos = GetFirstViewPosition ();
        CView* pView = GetNextView (pos);
        pView->OnInitialUpdate ();
        return FALSE;
    }

    // Return now if this device doesn't support palettes
    CClientDC dc (AfxGetMainWnd ());
    if ((dc.GetDeviceCaps (RASTERCAPS) & RC_PALETTE) == 0)
        return TRUE;

    // Create a palette to go with the DIB section
    if ((HBITMAP) m_bitmap != NULL) {
        DIBSECTION ds;
        m_bitmap.GetObject (sizeof (DIBSECTION), &ds);
```

(continued)

955

MTDoc.cpp *continued*

```
        int nColors;
        if (ds.dsBmih.biClrUsed != 0)
            nColors = ds.dsBmih.biClrUsed;
        else
            nColors = 1 << ds.dsBmih.biBitCount;

        // Create a halftone palette if the DIB section contains more
        // than 256 colors
        if (nColors > 256)
            m_palette.CreateHalftonePalette (&dc);

        // Create a custom palette from the DIB section's color table
        // if the number of colors is 256 or less
        else {
            RGBQUAD* pRGB = new RGBQUAD[nColors];

            CDC memDC;
            memDC.CreateCompatibleDC (&dc);
            m_criticalSection.Lock ();
            CBitmap* pOldBitmap = memDC.SelectObject (&m_bitmap);
            ::GetDIBColorTable ((HDC) memDC, 0, nColors, pRGB);
            memDC.SelectObject (pOldBitmap);
            m_criticalSection.Unlock ();

            UINT nSize = sizeof (LOGPALETTE) +
                (sizeof (PALETTEENTRY) * (nColors - 1));
            LOGPALETTE* pLP = (LOGPALETTE*) new BYTE[nSize];

            pLP->palVersion = 0x300;
            pLP->palNumEntries = nColors;

            for (int i=0; i<nColors; i++) {
                pLP->palPalEntry[i].peRed = pRGB[i].rgbRed;
                pLP->palPalEntry[i].peGreen = pRGB[i].rgbGreen;
                pLP->palPalEntry[i].peBlue = pRGB[i].rgbBlue;
                pLP->palPalEntry[i].peFlags = 0;
            }

            m_palette.CreatePalette (pLP);
            delete[] pLP;
            delete[] pRGB;
        }
    }
    return TRUE;
}
```

```
void CMTDoc::DeleteContents ()
{
    if ((HBITMAP) m_bitmap != NULL)
        m_bitmap.DeleteObject ();

    if ((HPALETTE) m_palette != NULL)
        m_palette.DeleteObject ();

    CDocument::DeleteContents();
}

void CMTDoc::Serialize (CArchive& ar)
{
    if (ar.IsLoading ()) {
        CString strFileName = ar.GetFile ()->GetFilePath ();

        HBITMAP hBitmap = (HBITMAP) ::LoadImage (AfxGetInstanceHandle (),
            (LPCTSTR) strFileName, IMAGE_BITMAP, 0, 0, LR_LOADFROMFILE |
            LR_CREATEDIBSECTION);

        if (hBitmap == NULL)
            AfxThrowArchiveException (CArchiveException::badIndex);

        m_bitmap.Attach (hBitmap);
    }
}

CBitmap* CMTDoc::GetBitmap ()
{
    return ((HBITMAP) m_bitmap == NULL) ? NULL : &m_bitmap;
}

CPalette* CMTDoc::GetPalette ()
{
    return ((HPALETTE) m_palette == NULL) ? NULL : &m_palette;
}

//////////////////////////////////////////////////////////////////////
// Thread function and other globals

UINT ThreadFunc (LPVOID pParam)
{
    THREADPARMS* pThreadParms = (THREADPARMS*) pParam;
    CWnd* pWnd = pThreadParms->pWnd;
    CBitmap* pBitmap = pThreadParms->pBitmap;
```

(continued)

```
    CPalette* pPalette = pThreadParms->pPalette;
    CCriticalSection* pCriticalSection = pThreadParms->pCriticalSection;
    CEvent* pKillThread = pThreadParms->pEvent;

    DIBSECTION ds;
    pBitmap->GetObject (sizeof (DIBSECTION), &ds);
    int nWidth = ds.dsBm.bmWidth;
    int nHeight = ds.dsBm.bmHeight;

    // Initialize one memory DC (memDC2) to hold a color copy of the
    // image and another memory DC (memDC1) to hold a gray-scale copy
    CClientDC dc (pWnd);
    CBitmap bitmap1, bitmap2;
    bitmap1.CreateCompatibleBitmap (&dc, nWidth, nHeight);
    bitmap2.CreateCompatibleBitmap (&dc, nWidth, nHeight);

    CDC memDC1, memDC2;
    memDC1.CreateCompatibleDC (&dc);
    memDC2.CreateCompatibleDC (&dc);
    CBitmap* pOldBitmap1 = memDC1.SelectObject (&bitmap1);
    CBitmap* pOldBitmap2 = memDC2.SelectObject (&bitmap2);

    CPalette* pOldPalette1 = NULL;
    CPalette* pOldPalette2 = NULL;
    CPalette grayPalette;

    if (pPalette->m_hObject != NULL) {
        LOGPALETTE* pLP = CreateGrayScale ();
        grayPalette.CreatePalette (pLP);
        delete[] pLP;

        pOldPalette1 = memDC1.SelectPalette (&grayPalette, FALSE);
        pOldPalette2 = memDC2.SelectPalette (pPalette, FALSE);
        memDC1.RealizePalette ();
        memDC2.RealizePalette ();
    }

    // Copy the bitmap to memDC2
    CDC memDC3;
    memDC3.CreateCompatibleDC (&dc);
    pCriticalSection->Lock ();
    CBitmap* pOldBitmap3 = memDC3.SelectObject (pBitmap);
    memDC2.BitBlt (0, 0, nWidth, nHeight, &memDC3, 0, 0, SRCCOPY);
    memDC3.SelectObject (pOldBitmap3);
    pCriticalSection->Unlock ();
```

```
// Convert the colors in memDC2 to shades of gray in memDC1
int x, y;
COLORREF crColor;
BYTE grayLevel;

for (y=0; y<nHeight; y++) {
    for (x=0; x<nWidth; x++) {
        crColor = memDC2.GetPixel (x, y);
        grayLevel = (BYTE)
            (((((UINT) GetRValue (crColor)) * 30) +
            (((UINT) GetGValue (crColor)) * 59) +
            (((UINT) GetBValue (crColor)) * 11)) / 100);
        memDC1.SetPixel (x, y,
            PALETTERGB (grayLevel, grayLevel, grayLevel));
    }

    // Kill the thread if the pKillThread event is signaled
    if (::WaitForSingleObject (pKillThread->m_hObject, 0) ==
        WAIT_OBJECT_0) {

        memDC1.SelectObject (pOldBitmap1);
        memDC2.SelectObject (pOldBitmap2);

        if (pPalette->m_hObject != NULL) {
            memDC1.SelectPalette (pOldPalette1, FALSE);
            memDC2.SelectPalette (pOldPalette2, FALSE);
        }
        pWnd->PostMessage (WM_USER_THREAD_ABORTED, y + 1, 0);
        return (UINT) -1;
    }
    pWnd->PostMessage (WM_USER_THREAD_UPDATE, y + 1, nHeight);
}

// Copy the gray-scale image over the original bitmap
CPalette* pOldPalette3 = NULL;
if (pPalette->m_hObject != NULL) {
    pOldPalette3 = memDC3.SelectPalette (&grayPalette, FALSE);
    memDC3.RealizePalette ();
}
pCriticalSection->Lock ();
pOldBitmap3 = memDC3.SelectObject (pBitmap);
memDC3.BitBlt (0, 0, nWidth, nHeight, &memDC1, 0, 0, SRCCOPY);
memDC3.SelectObject (pOldBitmap3);
pCriticalSection->Unlock ();
```

(continued)

MTDoc.cpp *continued*

```cpp
    // Clean up the memory DCs
    memDC1.SelectObject (pOldBitmap1);
    memDC2.SelectObject (pOldBitmap2);

    if (pPalette->m_hObject != NULL) {
        memDC1.SelectPalette (pOldPalette1, FALSE);
        memDC2.SelectPalette (pOldPalette2, FALSE);
        memDC3.SelectPalette (pOldPalette3, FALSE);
    }

    // Tell the frame window we're done
    pWnd->PostMessage (WM_USER_THREAD_FINISHED, 0, 0);
    return 0;
}

LOGPALETTE* CreateGrayScale ()
{
    UINT nSize = sizeof (LOGPALETTE) + (sizeof (PALETTEENTRY) * 63);
    LOGPALETTE* pLP = (LOGPALETTE*) new BYTE[nSize];

    pLP->palVersion = 0x300;
    pLP->palNumEntries = 64;

    for (int i=0; i<64; i++) {
        pLP->palPalEntry[i].peRed = i * 4;
        pLP->palPalEntry[i].peGreen = i * 4;
        pLP->palPalEntry[i].peBlue = i * 4;
        pLP->palPalEntry[i].peFlags = 0;
    }
    return pLP;
}
```

MTView.h

```cpp
//******************************************************************************
//
// MTView.h
//
//******************************************************************************

class CMTView : public CScrollView
{
    DECLARE_DYNCREATE (CMTView)

private:
    CMTDoc* GetDocument () { return (CMTDoc*) m_pDocument; }
```

```
public:
    virtual void OnInitialUpdate ();

protected:
    virtual void OnDraw (CDC*);
};
```

MTView.cpp

```
//*********************************************************************
//
//  MTView.cpp
//
//*********************************************************************

#include <afxwin.h>
#include <afxmt.h>
#include "Resource.h"
#include "MTDoc.h"
#include "MTView.h"

IMPLEMENT_DYNCREATE (CMTView, CScrollView)

void CMTView::OnInitialUpdate ()
{
    CScrollView::OnInitialUpdate ();

    CString string;
    CSize sizeTotal;

    CBitmap* pBitmap = GetDocument ()->GetBitmap ();
    if (pBitmap != NULL) {
        DIBSECTION ds;
        pBitmap->GetObject (sizeof (DIBSECTION), &ds);
        sizeTotal.cx = ds.dsBm.bmWidth;
        sizeTotal.cy = ds.dsBm.bmHeight;
        string.Format ("%d x %d, %d bpp", ds.dsBm.bmWidth,
            ds.dsBm.bmHeight, ds.dsBmih.biBitCount);
    }
    else {
        sizeTotal.cx = sizeTotal.cy = 0;
        string.Empty ();
    }
```

(continued)

MTView.cpp *continued*

```
        AfxGetMainWnd ()->SendMessage (WM_USER_UPDATE_STATS, 0,
            (LPARAM) (LPCTSTR) string);
        SetScrollSizes (MM_TEXT, sizeTotal);
}

void CMTView::OnDraw (CDC* pDC)
{
    CMTDoc* pDoc = GetDocument ();
    CBitmap* pBitmap = pDoc->GetBitmap ();

    if (pBitmap != NULL) {
        CPalette* pOldPalette;
        CPalette* pPalette = pDoc->GetPalette ();

        if (pPalette != NULL) {
            pOldPalette = pDC->SelectPalette (pPalette, FALSE);
            pDC->RealizePalette ();
        }

        DIBSECTION ds;
        pBitmap->GetObject (sizeof (DIBSECTION), &ds);

        CDC memDC;
        memDC.CreateCompatibleDC (pDC);
        GetDocument ()->m_criticalSection.Lock ();
        CBitmap* pOldBitmap = memDC.SelectObject (pBitmap);

        pDC->BitBlt (0, 0, ds.dsBm.bmWidth, ds.dsBm.bmHeight, &memDC,
            0, 0, SRCCOPY);

        memDC.SelectObject (pOldBitmap);
        GetDocument ()->m_criticalSection.Unlock ();

        if (pPalette != NULL)
            pDC->SelectPalette (pPalette, FALSE);
    }
}
```

I wanted to show a multithreaded document/view application in this chapter because there are certain issues unique to writing multithreaded document/view programs that don't come up in multithreaded SDK applications or even in multi-threaded MFC applications that don't use documents and views. For example, it's not unusual for the document object to launch a thread because threads are frequently used to process data in the document. But how can a background thread let the document object know that processing is complete? It can't post a message to the document because a document isn't a window. It's not a good idea for the document to call *::WaitForSingleObject* on the thread handle because then the application's primary thread will block and input will be suspended until the thread terminates. Yet the document usually needs to know when the thread is finished so that it can update its views. The question is, "How?"

MTDemo demonstrates a very practical solution to the problem of how a worker thread can let a document object know when it's finished. When Convert To Gray Scale is selected from the Effects menu, the document's *OnGrayScale* function launches a background thread that executes the *ThreadFunc* function. *ThreadFunc* processes the bits in the bitmap and posts a WM_USER_THREAD_FINISHED message to the application's frame window just before it terminates. The frame window, in turn, calls the document's *ThreadFinished* function to notify the document that the image has been converted, and *ThreadFinished* calls *UpdateAllViews*.

Posting a message to the frame window and having it call the document object is *not* the same as having the thread function call a function in the document object directly because the *PostMessage* call ensures that *UpdateAllViews* is called in the context of the primary thread. If *ThreadFunc* called the document object itself, *UpdateAllViews* would be called in the context of the background thread and it would fail. *PostMessage* is an effective tool for performing a virtual transfer of control from one thread to another. And with a window object serving as an intermediary, *PostMessage* can be used to communicate with nonwindow objects, too.

For good measure, *ThreadFunc* posts a WM_USER_THREAD_UPDATE message to the frame window each time it completes another line in the bitmap. The frame window responds by updating a percent-complete figure in the status bar, so the user is never left wondering when the gray-scale image will appear.

MTDemo uses two thread synchronization objects: a *CEvent* object named *m_event* and a *CCriticalSection* object named *m_criticalSection*. Both are members of the document class, and both are passed by address to the thread function in a THREADPARMS structure. The event object is used to terminate the worker thread if a gray-scale conversion is terminated midstream. To kill the thread, the document sets the event to the signaled state:

```
m_event.SetEvent ();
```

Upon completion of each scan line, the conversion routine inside *ThreadFunc* checks the event object and terminates if the event is signaled:

```
if (::WaitForSingleObject (pKillThread->m_hObject, 0) ==
    WAIT_OBJECT_0) {
        .
        .
        .
    pWnd->PostMessage (WM_USER_THREAD_ABORTED, y + 1, 0);
    return (UINT) -1;
}
```

The WM_USER_THREAD_ABORTED message alerts the frame window that the thread has been aborted. The frame window notifies the document by calling *CMTDoc-::ThreadAborted*, and *ThreadAborted* blocks on the thread handle just in case the thread hasn't quite terminated and resets an internal flag that indicates the thread is no longer running.

The critical section prevents the application's two threads from trying to select the bitmap into a device context at the same time. The primary thread selects the bitmap into a device context when the view needs updating; the background thread momentarily selects the bitmap into a memory DC once when a gray-scale conversion begins and again when it ends. A bitmap can be selected into only one device context at a time, so if either thread tries to select the bitmap into a DC while the other has it selected into a DC, one of the threads will fail. (Palettes, on the other hand, can be selected into several device contexts concurrently, and *ThreadFunc* takes advantage of that fact when it performs a gray-scale conversion on a palettized device.) The odds that the two threads will try to select the bitmap at the same time are small, but the use of a critical section ensures that the code executed between calls to *SelectObject* won't be interrupted by a call to *SelectObject* from another thread. The bitmap doesn't stay selected into a device context for any length of time, so neither thread should have to wait long if the critical section is locked.

ODDS AND ENDS

Here are a few odds and ends related to multitasking and multithreading that might be useful to you.

Message Pumps

One common misconception programmers have about multithreading is that it makes applications run faster. It doesn't; it makes applications more *responsive*. One way to demonstrate the difference in responsiveness multithreading can make is to write an application that draws a few thousand ellipses in response to a menu command. If the drawing is done by the primary thread and the thread doesn't occasionally take time out to check its message queue and dispatch any waiting messages, input will be frozen until the drawing loop has run its course. If the same application is written so that drawing is done in a separate thread, it will continue to respond to user input while the drawing loop executes.

In a scenario as simple as this, however, multithreading may be overkill. An alternative solution is to use a *message pump* to keep the messages flowing while the primary thread draws ellipses. Suppose the message handler that does the drawing looks like this:

```
void CMainWindow::OnStartDrawing ()
{
    for (int i=0; i<NUMELLIPSES; i++)
        DrawRandomEllipse ();
}
```

If NUMELLIPSES is a large number, the program could be stuck for a long time once the *for* loop is started. You could try adding another menu command that sets a flag and interrupts the *for* loop, as shown here:

```
void CMainWindow::OnStartDrawing ()
{
    m_bQuit = FALSE;
    for (int i=0; i<NUMELLIPSES && !m_bQuit; i++)
        DrawRandomEllipse ();
}

void CMainWindow::OnStopDrawing ()
{
    m_bQuit = TRUE;
}
```

But that wouldn't work. Why? Because the WM_COMMAND message that activates *OnStopDrawing* can't get through as long as the *for* loop in *OnStartDrawing* executes without pumping messages. In fact, a menu can't even be pulled down while the *for* loop is running.

This problem is easily solved with a message pump. Here's the proper way to execute a lengthy procedure in a single-threaded MFC program:

```
void CMainWindow::OnStartDrawing ()
{
    m_bQuit = FALSE;
    for (int i=0; i<NUMELLIPSES && !m_bQuit; i++) {
        DrawRandomEllipse ();
        if (!PeekAndPump ())
            break;
    }
}

void CMainWindow::OnStopDrawing ()
{
    m_bQuit = TRUE;
}

BOOL CMainWindow::PeekAndPump ()
{
    MSG msg;
    while (::PeekMessage (&msg, NULL, 0, 0, PM_NOREMOVE)) {
```

(continued)

```
        if (!AfxGetApp ()->PumpMessage ()) {
            ::PostQuitMessage (0);
            return FALSE;
        }
    }
    LONG lIdle = 0;
    while (AfxGetApp ()->OnIdle (lIdle++));
    return TRUE;
}
```

The *PeekAndPump* function creates a message loop within a message loop. Called at the conclusion of each iteration through *OnStartDrawing*'s *for* loop, *PeekAndPump* first calls *CWinThread::PumpMessage* to retrieve and dispatch messages if *::Peek-Message* indicates that there are messages waiting in the queue. A 0 return from *PumpMessage* indicates that the last message retrieved and dispatched was a WM_QUIT message, which calls for special handling because the application won't terminate unless the WM_QUIT message is retrieved by the *main* message loop. That's why *PeekAndPump* posts another WM_QUIT message to the queue if *PumpMessage* returns 0, and that's why the *for* loop in *OnStartDrawing* falls through if *PeekAndPump* returns 0. If a WM_QUIT message doesn't prompt an early exit, *PeekAndPump* simulates the framework's idle mechanism by calling the application object's *OnIdle* function before returning.

With *PeekAndPump* inserted into the drawing loop, the WM_COMMAND message that activates *OnStopDrawing* is retrieved and dispatched normally. Because *OnStopDrawing* sets *m_bQuit* to TRUE, the drawing loop will fall through before the next ellipse is drawn.

Child Processes

Win32 processes can launch other processes with the same ease with which they launch additional threads. The following statements launch Notepad.exe from the \Windows directory of drive C:

```
STARTUPINFO si;
::ZeroMemory (&si, sizeof (STARTUPINFO));
si.cb = sizeof (STARTUPINFO);
PROCESS_INFORMATION pi;

if (::CreateProcess (NULL, "C:\\Windows\\Notepad", NULL, NULL,
    FALSE, NORMAL_PRIORITY_CLASS, NULL, NULL, &si, &pi)) {
    ::CloseHandle (pi.hThread);
    ::CloseHandle (pi.hProcess);
}
```

::CreateProcess is a versatile function that takes the name of (and optionally the path to) an executable file and then loads and executes it. If the drive and directory name

are omitted from the executable file name, the system automatically searches for the file in the Windows directory, the Windows system directory, all directories in the current path, and elsewhere. The file name can also include command line parameters, as in

```
"C:\\Windows\\Notepad C:\\Windows\\Desktop\\Ideas.txt"
```

::CreateProcess fills a PROCESS_INFORMATION structure with pertinent information about the process, including the process handle (*hProcess*) and the handle of the process's primary thread (*hThread*). These handles should be closed with *::Close-Handle* sometime after the process is started. If you have no further use for the handles, you can close them as soon as *::CreateProcess* returns.

A nonzero return from *::CreateProcess* means that the process was successfully launched. Win32 processes are launched and executed asynchronously, so *::Create-Process* does *not* wait until the process has ended to return. If you'd like to launch a child process and suspend the current process until the child process terminates, call *::WaitForSingleObject* on the process handle, as shown here:

```
STARTUPINFO si;
::ZeroMemory (&si, sizeof (STARTUPINFO));
si.cb = sizeof (STARTUPINFO);
PROCESS_INFORMATION pi;

if (::CreateProcess (NULL, "C:\\Windows\\Notepad", NULL, NULL,
    FALSE, NORMAL_PRIORITY_CLASS, NULL, NULL, &si, &pi)) {
    ::CloseHandle (pi.hThread);
    ::WaitForSingleObject (pi.hProcess, INFINITE);
    ::CloseHandle (pi.hProcess);
}
```

If *::WaitForSingleObject* returns anything but WAIT_FAILED, you can call *::GetExitCode-Process* to retrieve the child process's exit code.

Sometimes the need arises to launch a child process and delay just long enough to make sure the process is started and ready to receive input. If the child creates a window, for example, and the parent process wants to send that window a message, the parent might have to wait for a moment after *::CreateProcess* returns to call *Send-Message* or *PostMessage*. Right after *::CreateProcess* returns, the window might not exist yet. This problem is easily solved with the Win32 *::WaitForInputIdle* function:

```
STARTUPINFO si;
::ZeroMemory (&si, sizeof (STARTUPINFO));
si.cb = sizeof (STARTUPINFO);
PROCESS_INFORMATION pi;

if (::CreateProcess (NULL, "C:\\Windows\\Notepad", NULL, NULL,
```

(continued)

```
                   FALSE, NORMAL_PRIORITY_CLASS, NULL, NULL, &si, &pi)) {
               ::CloseHandle (pi.hThread);
               ::WaitForInputIdle (pi.hProcess, INFINITE);
               // Get the child's window handle and send or post a message
               ::CloseHandle (pi.hProcess);
           }
```

::WaitForInputIdle suspends the current process until the specified process begins processing messages. I don't show the code to find the child's window handle because there isn't a simple MFC or API function you can call to convert a process handle into a window handle. Instead, you must use *::EnumWindows*, *::FindWindow*, or a related function to search for the window based on some known characteristic of the child process.

File Change Notifications

Earlier in this chapter, I mentioned that the HANDLE parameter passed to *::WaitFor-SingleObject* can be a "file change notification handle." Windows 95 includes an API function named *::FindFirstChangeNotification* that returns a handle you can use to wake a blocked thread whenever a change occurs involving a specified directory or its subdirectories—for example, when a file is renamed or deleted or a new directory is created.

Let's say you want to enhance Chapter 13's Wanderer application so that changes to the file system are instantly reflected in the left or right pane. The most efficient way to do it is to start one background thread for each drive and put each thread to sleep until the system wakes it with a file change notification. Here's what the thread function for the thread that monitors drive C: might look like:

```
UINT ThreadFunc (LPVOID pParam)
{
    HWND hwnd = (HWND) pParam; // Window to notify
    HANDLE hChange = ::FindFirstChangeNotification ("C:\\",
        TRUE, FILE_NOTIFY_FILE_NAME | FILE_NOTIFY_DIR_NAME);

    if (hChange == INVALID_HANDLE_VALUE) {
        TRACE ("Error: FindFirstChangeNotification failed\n");
        return (UINT) -1;
    }

    while (TRUE) {
        ::WaitForSingleObject (hChange, INFINITE);
        ::PostMessage (hwnd, WM_USER, 0, 2);
        ::FindNextChangeNotification (hChange);
    }
    return 0;
}
```

The first parameter passed to *::FindFirstChangeNotification* identifies the directory you want to monitor, the second specifies whether you want to monitor just that directory (FALSE) or that directory and all of its subdirectories (TRUE), and the third specifies the kinds of changes the thread should be notified of. In this example, the thread will be awakened when a file is created, renamed, or deleted anywhere on the C: drive (FILE_NOTIFY_FILE_NAME) or when a directory is created, renamed, or deleted (FILE_NOTIFY_DIR_NAME). When the thread is awakened, it posts a WM-_USER message to the window whose handle was passed in *pParam*. The message's *lParam* holds a drive number (2 for drive C:). The window that receives the message—presumably the application's top-level frame window—can respond to the message by updating its views. Note that a thread awakened by a file change notification doesn't receive any information about the nature of the change or about where in the directory tree the change occurred.

After a thread is awakened with a file change notification, it should call *::FindNextChangeNotification* before calling *::WaitForSingleObject* again to set the file change notification object to the nonsignaled state. When you're through with a file change notification handle, close it with *::FindCloseChangeNotification*. The handle isn't closed in the example on the previous page because the thread that obtains the handle runs continuously until the application is shut down.

Index

Note: An italic page-number reference indicates a figure or a table.

O

JEFF PROSISE

Jeff Prosise graduated from the University of Tennessee in 1982 with a B.S. in mechanical engineering and practiced engineering until 1990. In 1983, he bought his first computer and began a hobby that would eventually become his livelihood.

Today Jeff divides his working hours among writing articles for *PC Magazine* and *Microsoft Systems Journal,* writing books about programming, developing software, and trying to keep up with the day-to-day developments in Windows programming. In the off hours, he enjoys skiing, scuba diving, playing the guitar, and spending time with his family. Jeff and his wife, Lori, have two children: Adam, born in 1990, and Amy, born in 1993.

The manuscript for this book was prepared and submitted to Microsoft Press in electronic form. Text files were prepared using Microsoft Word 6.0 for Windows. Pages were composed by Microsoft Press using Adobe PageMaker 6.0 for Windows, with text in Garamond and display type in Helvetica Black. Composed pages were delivered to the printer as electronic prepress files.

Cover Graphic Designer

Gregory J. Erickson

Cover Illustrator

Glenn Mitsui

Interior Graphic Designer

Kim Eggleston

Interior Graphic Artist

Michael Victor

Compositors

Peggy Herman
Sandra Haynes

Principal Proofreader/Copy Editor

Shawn Peck

Indexer

Julie Kawabata

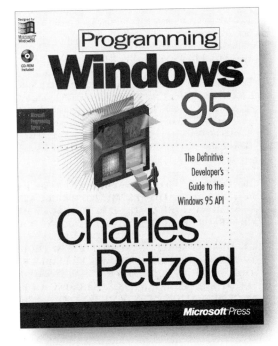

IMPORTANT—READ CAREFULLY BEFORE OPENING SOFTWARE PACKET(S). By opening the sealed packet(s) containing the software, you indicate your acceptance of the following Microsoft License Agreement.

MICROSOFT LICENSE AGREEMENT
(Book Companion CD)

This is a legal agreement between you (either an individual or an entity) and Microsoft Corporation. By opening the sealed software packet(s) you are agreeing to be bound by the terms of this agreement. If you do not agree to the terms of this agreement, promptly return the unopened software packet(s) and any accompanying written materials to the place you obtained them for a full refund.

MICROSOFT SOFTWARE LICENSE

1. GRANT OF LICENSE. Microsoft grants to you the right to use one copy of the Microsoft software program included with this book (the "SOFTWARE") on a single terminal connected to a single computer. The SOFTWARE is in "use" on a computer when it is loaded into the temporary memory (i.e., RAM) or installed into the permanent memory (e.g., hard disk, CD-ROM, or other storage device) of that computer. You may not network the SOFTWARE or otherwise use it on more than one computer or computer terminal at the same time.

2. COPYRIGHT. The SOFTWARE is owned by Microsoft or its suppliers and is protected by United States copyright laws and international treaty provisions. Therefore, you must treat the SOFTWARE like any other copyrighted material (e.g., a book or musical recording) except that you may either (a) make one copy of the SOFTWARE solely for backup or archival purposes, or (b) transfer the SOFTWARE to a single hard disk provided you keep the original solely for backup or archival purposes. You may not copy the written materials accompanying the SOFTWARE.

3. OTHER RESTRICTIONS. You may not rent or lease the SOFTWARE, but you may transfer the SOFTWARE and accompanying written materials on a permanent basis provided you retain no copies and the recipient agrees to the terms of this Agreement. You may not reverse engineer, decompile, or disassemble the SOFTWARE. If the SOFTWARE is an update or has been updated, any transfer must include the most recent update and all prior versions.

4. DUAL MEDIA SOFTWARE. If the SOFTWARE package contains more than one kind of disk (3.5", 5.25", and CD-ROM), then you may use only the disks appropriate for your single-user computer. You may not use the other disks on another computer or loan, rent, lease, or transfer them to another user except as part of the permanent transfer (as provided above) of all SOFTWARE and written materials.

5. SAMPLE CODE. If the SOFTWARE includes Sample Code, then Microsoft grants you a royalty-free right to reproduce and distribute the sample code of the SOFTWARE provided that you: (a) distribute the sample code only in conjunction with and as a part of your software product; (b) do not use Microsoft's or its authors' names, logos, or trademarks to market your software product; (c) include the copyright notice that appears on the SOFTWARE on your product label and as a part of the sign-on message for your software product; and (d) agree to indemnify, hold harmless, and defend Microsoft and its authors from and against any claims or lawsuits, including attorneys' fees, that arise or result from the use or distribution of your software product.

DISCLAIMER OF WARRANTY

The SOFTWARE (including instructions for its use) is provided "AS IS" WITHOUT WARRANTY OF ANY KIND. MICROSOFT FURTHER DISCLAIMS ALL IMPLIED WARRANTIES INCLUDING WITHOUT LIMITATION ANY IMPLIED WARRANTIES OF MERCHANTABILITY OR OF FITNESS FOR A PARTICULAR PURPOSE. THE ENTIRE RISK ARISING OUT OF THE USE OR PERFORMANCE OF THE SOFTWARE AND DOCUMENTATION REMAINS WITH YOU.

IN NO EVENT SHALL MICROSOFT, ITS AUTHORS, OR ANYONE ELSE INVOLVED IN THE CREATION, PRODUCTION, OR DELIVERY OF THE SOFTWARE BE LIABLE FOR ANY DAMAGES WHATSOEVER (INCLUDING, WITHOUT LIMITA-TION, DAMAGES FOR LOSS OF BUSINESS PROFITS, BUSINESS INTERRUPTION, LOSS OF BUSINESS INFORMATION, OR OTHER PECUNIARY LOSS) ARISING OUT OF THE USE OF OR INABILITY TO USE THE SOFTWARE OR DOCUMENTATION, EVEN IF MICROSOFT HAS BEEN ADVISED OF THE POSSIBILITY OF SUCH DAMAGES. BECAUSE SOME STATES/COUNTRIES DO NOT ALLOW THE EXCLUSION OR LIMITATION OF LIABILITY FOR CONSEQUENTIAL OR INCIDENTAL DAMAGES, THE ABOVE LIMITATION MAY NOT APPLY TO YOU.

U.S. GOVERNMENT RESTRICTED RIGHTS

The SOFTWARE and documentation are provided with RESTRICTED RIGHTS. Use, duplication, or disclosure by the Government is subject to restrictions as set forth in subparagraph (c)(1)(ii) of The Rights in Technical Data and Computer Software clause at DFARS 252.227-7013 or subparagraphs (c)(1) and (2) of the Commercial Computer Software — Restricted Rights 48 CFR 52.227-19, as applicable. Manufacturer is Microsoft Corporation, One Microsoft Way, Redmond, WA 98052-6399.

If you acquired this product in the United States, this Agreement is governed by the laws of the State of Washington.

Should you have any questions concerning this Agreement, or if you desire to contact Microsoft Press for any reason, please write: Microsoft Press, One Microsoft Way, Redmond, WA 98052-6399.

Register Today!

Return this
Programming Windows® 95 with MFC
registration card for a Microsoft Press® catalog

U.S. and Canada addresses only. Fill in information below and mail postage-free. Please mail only the bottom half of this page.

1-55615-902-1A   *PROGRAMMING WINDOWS® 95 WITH MFC*   *Owner Registration Card*

NAME

INSTITUTION OR COMPANY NAME

ADDRESS

CITY   STATE   ZIP

Microsoft®*Press*
Quality Computer Books

For a free catalog of
Microsoft Press® products, call
1-800-MSPRESS